Frommer's®

Here's what the critics say about Frommer's:

"Amazingly easy to use. Very portable, very complete."
—*Booklist*

♦

"The only mainstream guide to list specific prices. The Walter Cronkite of guidebooks—with all that implies."
—*Travel & Leisure*

♦

"Complete, concise, and filled with useful information."
—*New York Daily News*

♦

"Hotel information is close to encyclopedic."
—*Des Moines Sunday Register*

♦

"The best series for travelers who want one easy-to-use guidebook."
—*U.S. Air Magazine*

Other Great Guides for Your Trip:

Frommer's England

Frommer's London

Frommer's France

Frommer's Paris

Frommer's Provence & the Riviera

Frommer's Italy

Frommer's Rome

Frommer's Tuscany & Umbria

Frommer's Greece

Frommer's Greek Islands

Frommer's Germany

Frommer's Spain

Frommer's Barcelona, Madrid & Seville

Frommer's Portugal

Frommer's Prague & the Best of the Czech Republic

Frommer's Belgium, Holland & Luxembourg

Frommer's Amsterdam

Frommer's Europe

Frommer's Europe from $60 a Day

Frommer's Europe's Greatest Driving Tours

The Complete Idiot's Guide to Planning Your Trip to Europe

Frommer's®

1st Edition

GAY & LESBIAN EUROPE

by David Andrusia, Haas Mroue,
D0nald Olson & Todd Savage

MACMILLAN • USA

MACMILLAN TRAVEL USA
A Pearson Education Macmillan Company
1633 Broadway
New York, NY 10019

Find us online at **www.frommers.com.**

ISBN 0-02-862640-0
ISSN 1521-8082

Editor: Ron Boudreau
Production Editor: Kristi Hart
Photo Editor: Richard Fox
Design by Michele Laseau
Staff Cartographers : John Decamillas and Roberta Stockwell
Page Creation by John Bitter, Ellen Considine, Laura Goetz, Melissa Auciello-Brogan and Sean Monkhouse

Front cover photo: *Invention* by Haig Patigian (1915)
Back cover photo: Three lesbians in a fountain, Trafalgar Square

Manufactured in the United States of America

Contents

Part 4 Germany: Berlin Stories 278

by Donald Olson

Part 5 Greece: Where It All Began 320

by Haas Mroue

Part 6 Italy: In the Gay Footsteps of Michelangelo & Leonardo 385

by Donald Olson

18 Sitges: A Eurobeach for Euroboys & You 651

19 Ibiza: Madness, Money & Music 659

Appendix: European Tourist Offices 670

Index 673

List of Maps

About the Authors

Sexy, sassy, sissy scribe **David Andrusia** divides his time between the East Village and East Hollywood while updating his books *New York Hot & Hip* and *L.A. Hot & Hip,* part of the travel series *Vogue* called "the hippest." David's *Gay Europe* (Penguin Putnam/Perigee, 1995) was the first gay travel tome from a major American publisher and a Barnes & Noble Readers' Catalog Selection. He's also the author of the celebrated career guide *The Perfect Pitch* (Warner Books) and the upcoming *Branding Yourself* (Ballantine); his book *Natural Healing for Your Baby and Child* (with Andrea Candee) came out from Pocket Books in summer 1999. This GWM stands 5′11$^{1}/_{8}$″, weighs 160 lbs., and has flaxen hair and aquamarine eyes. Please respond only if your name is Sergio or Yves.

Hot and handsome **Haas Mroue** (5′10″, 150 lbs., 33, brown eyes and hair) has published his poems, short stories, and travel articles in magazines and journals in the United States and Europe; his work has been broadcast on the BBC World Service, New York's WBAI radio, and Starz! cable network, among others. A graduate of UCLA Film School, this GWM has lived in Paris and London and is currently at work on a screenplay and a novel. His first book, *Beirut Seizures,* was published in 1993. He divides his time between San Diego (where he plays) and the Olympic Peninsula (where he writes). He can be reached at haasmro@aol.com.

Donald Olson is a novelist, playwright, and travel writer. A busybody both home and abroad, this GWM (6′, 160 lbs., blue eyes, full head of blond hair, gym-trained body) has contributed travel stories to the *New York Times* and many non–sexually explicit national publications. He's the author of guidebooks to Oregon and Berlin, as well as *The Complete Idiot's Travel Guide to London* for Macmillan Travel. His gay novels include *The Secrets of Mabel Eastlake, Paradise Gardens,* and *A Movie.* Bantam London published his last novel, *The Confessions of Aubrey Beardsley;* his play *Beardsley* has been produced in Amsterdam, Rotterdam, and London. *Queer Corners,* his new novel inspired by the anti-gay-rights battles in Oregon, was published by BridgeCity Books in June 1999.

With his name, **Todd Savage** figured that a lucrative career as a stripper, porn star, or sex-advice columnist awaited, but to save his family some grief he settled on the life of an itinerant writer. This blue-eyed, salt-and-pepper-haired, boyish 33-year-old Chicago GWM has played tourist in his own town as the author of and/or contributor to *Frommer's Chicago '99* and *Frommer's Irreverent Guide to Chicago.* He also contributes to *Chicago Reader,* the *Chicago Tribune, Chicago* magazine, *The Advocate,* and *Town & Country.*

ACKNOWLEDGMENTS

David Andrusia extends hearty thanks to Alberto Veloso, Odette Maia, and Gloria Melo of TAP Air Portugal—always the best way to get to Lisbon and beyond!—and to Mariao João Ramires of the Portuguese Tourist Office for their kind and invaluable assistance. He also wishes to thank Pilar Vico and all her colleagues at the Spanish National Tourist Office as well as Iberia Airlines, the official Spanish airline sponsor for this book.

Haas Mroue would like to thank David Gregg and Elfie Trann at the French Government Tourist Office, AOM Airlines, and RailEurope. He'd also like to thank Katherine Tierce, Gilbert Marty, Valerie Pelligrini-Couvreur, Michelle Lee, and Tony Ajlaz; Gilbert Gayparme, Bill Shipley, and Patricia Stott in Nice; Esther Vitalis at the Greek National Tourist Office; Thomas Doustaly for editing *Têtu* (the best gay magazine in Europe); and Marlene Bennett and all the Centrum staff. He'd like to extend special thanks to David Masello.

Donald Olson would like to thank BritRail and RailEurope for their assistance with train travel in England, Germany, and Italy.

Todd Savage would like to thank Delta Airlines, DER Travel Services, Renaissance Hotel Prague, Kateřina Pavlivtová of the Czech Tourist Authority, Oldřich Bureš, Peter Alfano, Felicia Morton, Radek Chalupa, and Nadine Ekrek. He'd also like to thank the Netherlands Tourist Board, the Amsterdam Tourist Office, Nobu Yamanouchi, Kurt Schmidt, COC-Amsterdam, Martijn Bakker, Sasha Engels, J. A. Schwaanhuyser, and Heinz-Gerd Roes aka "Miss Mopsy."

An Invitation to the Reader

In researching this book, we discovered many wonderful places—hotels, restaurants, shops, and more. We're sure you'll find others. Please tell us about them, so we can share the information with your fellow travelers in upcoming editions. If you were disappointed with a recommendation, we'd love to know that too. Please write to:

Frommer's Gay & Lesbian Europe, 1st Edition
Macmillan Travel
1633 Broadway
New York, NY 10019

An Additional Note

Please be advised that travel information is subject to change at any time—and this is especially true of prices. We therefore suggest that you write or call ahead for confirmation when making your travel plans. The authors, editors, and publisher cannot be held responsible for the experiences of readers while traveling. Your safety is important to us, however, so we encourage you to stay alert and be aware of your surroundings. Keep a close eye on cameras, purses, and wallets, all favorite targets of thieves and pickpockets.

What the Symbols Mean

✪ Frommer's Favorites

Our favorite places and experiences—outstanding for quality, value, or both.

The following abbreviations are used for credit cards:

AE	American Express	EU	EuroCard
CB	Carte Blanche	JCB	Japan Credit Bureau
DC	Diners Club	MC	MasterCard
DISC	Discover	V	Visa

Find Frommer's Online

Arthur Frommer's Budget Travel Online (www.frommers.com) offers more than 6,000 pages of up-to-the-minute travel information—including the latest bargains and candid, personal articles updated daily by Arthur Frommer himself. No other Web site offers such comprehensive and timely coverage of the world of travel.

Introduction

Having a Gay Old Time in Europe

by Donald Olson

Gays and lesbians have always been great explorers. I'm sure we've trailblazed our way through every continent—it's just that until recently nobody has bothered to address themselves to our travel experiences. We've forged ahead anyway, finding our way around by reading our internal maps as well as those in the standard straight-oriented guidebooks.

When we look for truly useful and comprehensive travel guides to aid us on our European journeys, what do we find? Not much. At least, not much of *real* value. Yet gays and lesbians represent a large share of the travel market and boast what envious economists sometimes call "a disproportionate share of disposable income." If that's the case, why have we been ignored for so long?

As gay travelers, we often have different needs and different sensibilities. And that's why ***Frommer's Gay & Lesbian Europe*** is so valuable. It's an attempt to break new ground—*our* ground—the ground covered by the tens of thousands of gays and lesbians who travel to Europe every year and want a European experience incorporating gay interests instead of ignoring them or just hinting at them.

When it comes to the basics, we have the same needs as other travelers. We want to find good comfortable hotels, special restaurants, wonderful little shops, and "stimulating" nightlife. And we want to see the major sights. But what about those sights that might be of specific interest to gays? And what about specifically gay and lesbian sights and sites? This guidebook answers those questions.

1 Traveling Gay: What You'll Find Between the Covers

THE HOTTEST DESTINATIONS

Europe is a gay adventure just waiting to happen. Whether we're out or in, we're all over the place. In this guide, we take you to the great European cities and capitals: London, Paris, Berlin, Amsterdam, Athens, Rome, Prague, Lisbon, Barcelona, and Madrid. These are cities of legendary stature and highly polished sophistication. In them, gay visitors from around the world can enjoy an astonishing array of queer diversions. And at the end of each city chapter you'll find an easy day trip to nearby towns or sights of special interest.

Europe

Norwegian Sea
North Atlantic Ocean
Bergen
NORWAY
GRAMPIAN
Aberdeen
TAYSIDE
Perth
Edinburgh
North Sea
Belfast
DENMARK
IRELAND
Dublin
DINGLE PENINSULA
KERRY COUNTY
Manchester
Liverpool
U. K.
THE NETHERLANDS
Hamburg
COTSWOLDS
Bath
Oxford
STONEHENGE
London
Salisbury
Amsterdam
Brighton
Bruges
GERMANY
BELGIUM
English Channel
Brussels
Bonn
Liege
Le Havre
Frankfurt
LUX.
Paris
Strasbourg
Augsburg
LOIRE VALLEY
Munich
BAVARIAN ALP
Bern
Innsbruck
FRANCE
SWITZERLAND
Bay of Biscay
Geneva
Bordeaux
Milan
Bilbao
Toulouse
Arles
PROVENCE
MONACO
Marseille
Nice
Florence
Porto
ANDORRA
Côte d'Azur
TUSCAN
PORTUGAL
Madrid
Barcelona
Lisbon
Sitges
CORSICA
SPAIN
Córdoba
MAJORCA
Valencia
ALGARVE
Seville
ANDALUSIA
IBIZA
SARDINIA
Cagliari
Granada
Malaga
Costa del Sol
Mediterranean Sea
0
250 km
155 mi
N

SWEDEN
Trondheim
Sundsvall
Gulf of Bothnia
FINLAND
Tampere
Helsinki
St. Petersburg
Gavle
Oslo
Stockholm
Tallinn
ESTONIA
RUSSIA
Moscow
Riga
LATVIA
Göteborg
Baltic Sea
Copenhagen
LITHUANIA
Vilnius
Tver
Minsk
Gdansk
BELARUS
Berlin
Poznan
Warsaw
POLAND
Kiev
Karlovy Vary (Carlsbad)
Prague
Krakow
Lvov
UKRAINE
CZECH REPUBLIC
SLOVAKIA
Danube River
Vienna
Bratislava
KITZBUHEL ALPS
DANUBE VALLEY
Salzburg
Budapest
MOLDOVA
Chisinau
Odessa
AUSTRIA
HUNGARY
Lake Balaton
Cluj-Napoca
Ljubljana
SLOVENIA
Zagreb
CROATIA
ROMANIA
Venice
Constanta
Black Sea
Bucharest
BOSNIA
Sarajevo
Belgrade
SERBIA
Varna
BULGARIA
Adriatic Sea
ITALY
MONTENEGRO
Sofiya
Titograd
Skopje
MACEDONIA
Istanbul
Rome
Tirana
Naples
POMPEII
ALBANIA
TURKEY
Tyrrhenian Sea
GREECE
Aegean Sea
Delphi
Ionian Sea
Athens
CYCLADES
Palermo
PELOPONNESE
CYPRUS
SICILY
MALTA
CRETE

A Word from the Editor

When I came up with the idea for ***Frommer's Gay & Lesbian Europe,*** my goal was to get into one guide *all* the info queer travelers would want to know about the top destinations—from how to plan your trip to how to enjoy every minute while you're there to how to return home with great memories and even a few chic souvenirs.

You'll find everything our regular Frommer's guides are best known for: exact prices, so you can plan the perfect trip no matter what your budget; dozens of easy-to-read maps plotting hotels, restaurants, and sights; a wide selection of hotels and restaurants, with candid reviews; the practical details you need to make the most of your time and money; and a new take on the top attractions, plus undiscovered gems.

And in *Frommer's Gay & Lesbian Europe* you'll get even more, written from a totally gay perspective by four travel writers who know all the ins and outs and want to share them with you. I hope this guide will help you put together the European vacation you've always dreamed of, whether you've been to Europe many times or are still a virgin. If you have any comments, both positive and negative, I'd love to hear them.

—*Ron Boudreau*

From the major cities we branch out to smaller but culturally and historically important destinations, like Florence, Venice, and Milan in Italy. We also show off our pecs in popular gay resort meccas like Nice and the Côte d'Azur in France; Sitges and Ibiza in Spain; Brighton in southern England; and the Greek islands of Mykonos, Santorini, and Folegandros. We've put in Manchester, England, because of its throbbing gay club scene and have included the top draws of Bohemia in the Czech Republic because more and more gays are curious to explore Eastern Europe (and those Eastern Europeans!).

We've tried to make all these destinations fun and exciting and easy for you to navigate. Our only regret is that space limitations forced us to leave out other equally wonderful cities. In future editions, we hope to give you the gay lowdown on Copenhagen, Toulouse, Vienna, Salzburg, Hamburg, Budapest, Edinburgh, Glasgow, Dublin, and perhaps a few other places as well.

GETTING THERE & GETTING AROUND

Some of you are seasoned travelers, but others will be earning a Gay Scout badge for their first trip to Europe. Either way, there's plenty of advance planning involved, and once you arrive there's lots of navigating to do. Foreign parts bring out the best and the worst in travelers, gay and otherwise. So we help you with the ABCs.

First, we list the major airports and/or train stations where you'll make your entrance, with information on airport-to-city travel options. To help you get your bearings, we sketch in the layout of the city, telling you where the main gay drags are. We'll cue you in to the currency and where you can change all that disposable income. And once you're in the city, we'll tell you how to get around by subway, bus, tram, vaporetto, taxi, or on foot. You can obtain additional on-site information—maps, current events listings, and so on—at the national or city tourist offices listed under every destination.

Under the "Fast Facts" section in every chapter we list the addresses and/or phone numbers of whatever gay resources are available: community centers, information bureaus, hot lines to call if you require information on AIDS or HIV, and more. Don't be afraid to visit or call them. If there's one thing that traveling in Europe has taught me, it's that we are family, no matter what language we speak. We help one another. That's part of traveling gay.

BEDDING DOWN

If you're planning a trip to Europe, finding the right hotel is essential. You'll be sleeping in strange beds, so they'd better be comfortable. We provide you with a selection of lodging choices in all price ranges—running the gamut from top-of-the-line four-star havens of luxury to small, inexpensive B&Bs and pensiones. *All rates quoted are rack rates.* That means the standard price, with no discounts. When you're making your reservations, be sure to ask if there are any special weekend, off-season, senior, or longer-stay rates. In some cases, the price drops dramatically if you can be flexible about when you're traveling.

You know as well as we do that most hotels are "straight." That doesn't mean they're gay-unfriendly, though; it just means that most of their clientele is presumed hetero. We include the best of these for each city, then include the best "gay-friendly" and "gay" choices.

But listen: Just because a hotel advertises in a local gay paper doesn't mean it's the sort of place you'd want to stay. Two such hotels I visited in Milan might've been gay-friendly, but they also turned out to be tacky rent-by-the-hour whorehouses (heterosexual at that). Too many gay guides simply list the addresses of supposedly gay-friendly hotels without really checking into them. Don't you want to know what the hotel and its rooms (especially the bathrooms) look like? In this guide, we describe each hotel—gay and straight—so you'll know what you can expect.

We've also tried to anticipate special problems you may encounter as a gay or lesbian traveler checking singly or as a couple into a "straight" hotel. In Italy, for instance, if you book a double room, you'll inevitably be given two single beds. You must request a quaintly named *matrimoniale* (double bed) if you want to sleep together. And if you're going to violate local customs by bringing someone back to your hotel, we'll let you know.

SATISFYING YOUR HUNGER

A trip to Europe is wonderful if for no other reason than it forces you to eat out all the time. A mouth-watering array of new culinary experiences lies just across the Atlantic, and we want you to make the most of it. At our recommended restaurants you'll be wrapping your lips around the real thing, not a version of it: sublime Italian pastas, yummy Greek gyros loaded with hot-off-the-spit lamb, hearty French bouillabaise, tangy Spanish tapas, fresh seafood, an assortment of unique meat dishes, exotic salad greens, and—of course—huge German sausages. And then there are all those cream-filled desserts to look forward to. And the wine and beer. And the coffee . . .

Our eating choices range from deluxe Michelin-starred temples of gastronomy with haughty waiters to rustic ma 'n' pa holes-in-the-wall, vegetarian restaurants, the hottest in-spots of the moment, take-away joints, and cafes where the cruising is as important as the cuisine. We guide you to the best places for nouvelle cuisine, nuova cucina, New British Cuisine, neue Deutsche Küche, international fare, vegetarian food, and local favorites.

Of course, navigating foreign menus can be stressful. I once exceeded my personal comfort level when I was in a country whose language I didn't speak and thought I was ordering something quite different from the revolting plate of cooked beef intestines that

Keeping Your Money Pink

Nowadays, throughout the world, many of us feel a gaytriotic duty to support gay businesses. I'm not talking about just erotica shops selling nipple clamps and Falcon videos. I'm talking about gay-owned and/or gay-friendly hotels, restaurants, cafes, bookstores, card shops, clothing and antiques stores, theaters, bars, cabarets, and services of all kinds. Gay businesses, in one form or another, are found in nearly every major European city. If you want to keep your pounds, francs, lire, or whatever pink, we'll tell you where to go and what you'll find when you get there.

Of course, we all have a choice when it comes to how we want to spend our money. Our goal with this guide has been to provide you with as much up-to-date information on gay and gay-friendly businesses as possible. It may be that the "gay equation" just doesn't equate for you and you simply want the best (as we all do), whatever it may be. And the best, both gay and straight, is what we've tried to give you. If a hotel, restaurant, shop, or sight is particularly worthwhile, we give it a star.

You may have heard that a single European currency, called the **euro,** is slowly going into effect in Europe. The European Union has finally settled on which 5

was set before me. (And remember poor Lucy Ricardo and her escargots in Paris.) In some countries you too will be reading incomprehensible menus, and we don't want you ordering bull's testicles in sweet-and-sour sauce by mistake. So we clue you in to the regional cuisine and tell you about local specialties you may want to look for (or avoid).

Under every restaurant listing you'll find a low-to-high price range for main courses. This doesn't always mean your meal will cost that amount. A dinner in Italy or France is typically three or four courses, and in much of Europe a "service charge" as well as VAT (value-added tax) is tacked onto your bill.

Just as there are now gay hotels in Europe, so there are gay and gay-friendly restaurants. Again, we've been discerning in our gay choices. The restaurants that advertise in local gay media aren't always the best. But sometimes they're truly wonderful. Finding a suitable restaurant for a romantic tête-à-tête with your sweetie is one of the most challenging aspects of traveling anywhere. If there's a place serving good food where you can hold hands in public, we'll tell you about it. When you're traveling alone, it's not always fun to sit in a straight restaurant (at the table they've given you by the restroom door). So whenever possible we've also included a large selection of gay or gay-friendly pubs and cafes where you can eat in more casual and congenial surroundings (by the restroom door if you wish).

GAY PAST, PRESENT & ALWAYS

As a gay or lesbian traveling through history-soaked Europe, you're bound to wonder at times what life was like for your forebrothers and foresisters. We do, after all, have a history that extends back beyond bars and discos. Where did we hang out—or where, for that matter, were we hanged? Where did we cruise or meet one another? Who were our leaders? What happened to those of us who were "found out"? And where do we stand today?

The writers of this guide have ferreted out this information for you. Uncovering the history and current political status of gays in every European city, region, or island we cover has been part of our task. We've included the top sights for every destination—but from a gay perspective.

countries will adopt the euro: Austria, Belgium, Finland, France, Germany, Ireland, Italy, Luxembourg, the Netherlands, Portugal, and Spain. Several countries—Britain, Denmark, and Sweden—have opted out from switching over (they may do so in 2002); Greece hasn't yet made the economic requirements to join.

As a visitor, you don't have to worry about dealing with euro coins and notes until 2002. Although the changeover took effect on paper on January 1, 1999, it basically applies only to financial transactions between businesses in Europe. You'll likely see prices in shops, hotels, and restaurants quoted in both the local currency and euros. The euro itself won't be issued as banknotes and coins until January 1, 2002, and it won't fully replace national currencies until July 1, 2002. Since you'll still be dealing with marks, lire, francs, and pesetas until then, prices in this book are quoted in the local national currencies.

One thing to keep in mind: About 10 months elapse from the time manuscript copy is submitted to the time a travel book of any kind actually hits the bookstores. The prices we quoted in this book were correct in 1998, but they may be higher by 4% to 5% in 1999, and that much again in 2000.

The trouble is that our unique gay and lesbian history is such a silent one, with large gaps in it. Too often all we know is what was done to us instead of what we have done. Our amazing contributions to European culture are never mentioned, at least in mainstream guidebooks. People are always "setting the record straight." Isn't it time we set *our* record gay? That's what we've done in this book.

FINDING OUR GAY ROOTS

Today, as more and more of us come out of the closet to claim our places in the sun, we have the luxury of looking on our lives as an open celebration—despite the invidious endeavors of those who'd like to shove us back in the closet . . . or worse. Earlier generations of gays and lesbians weren't anywhere near as lucky. Either they were afraid to admit to themselves they might be gay (much less write openly about their gay lives and loves) or assumed their experiences had no validity. As we all know, keeping mum is easier than being persecuted for who you are. In England, up until 1967, being frank and open about one's sexuality could lead to a prison sentence (remember Oscar Wilde?) or fag-bashing of the sort Quentin Crisp endured for much of his life. Consequently, our lives and our communal history have been swept under the rug.

In Europe there are two monuments to homos—one by a canal in Amsterdam (called the Homomonument), the other on a wall in Berlin (called the Homo Memorial). Both commemorate the tens of thousands of gays who were arrested by the Nazis and sent to almost certain death in the work camps. The memorials aren't happy celebrations of who we are today but solemn reminders of what we've endured in the past. As we move toward our gay future as citizens of the world, it's important for us to know our struggles and triumphs have been shared by countless others. When we discover our roots, we discover something of ourselves and the universality of the "gay experience."

But it's not only grim monuments to homophobia—important as those are—that you'll find in this guide. We've tried to include everything of potential gay interest, however serious, trivial, camp, or celebrity driven.

An Event Alert: World Pride 2000

We're interested in the gay past, but we're not living in it. So if there are major gay events to look forward to, we tell you. Perhaps the best news is that in 2000, Rome will host the first-ever gay and lesbian **World Pride** event. See the Rome chapter for more details.

In the Berlin chapter, for example, you'll find out about the world's only gay museum, the plaque honoring early gay-rights pioneer Magnus Hirschfeld, and the cemetery where Marlene Dietrich is buried and how you can tour the film studio where she made *The Blue Angel.* In the London chapter, you'll find out what part of Kensington Palace Princess Diana lived in, as well as how to tour her childhood home and visit her grave site. In the Paris chapter, you'll be led to Oscar Wilde's grave in Père-Lachaise cemetery, a place of gay pilgrimage for almost a century—here you'll also find the graves of Gertrude Stein and Alice B. Toklas and of Marcel Proust and Maurice Ravel (the friends/lovers wanted to be buried together but their families wouldn't permit it). And in the Florence chapter, you'll find out that Leonardo da Vinci, Sandro Botticelli, and Benevenuto Cellini were all arrested and fined for . . . but I mustn't give that away.

SHOP 'TIL YOU DROP

Everyone says shopping is fun. I hate it—until I get to Europe. Suddenly there are all sorts of things I just can't live without. Wandering down a foreign street, I'm constantly on the prowl for what I can't find at home. I look for things that'll give me a pleasant memory jolt later on, that I can give to friends, or that I know can be found only in a particular city. Shopping in Europe is a pleasure—perhaps because it's less mall-oriented. Poking around in curious old shops, checking out the latest rags in ultra-chic fashion boutiques, scanning the merchandise in foreign department stores, sniffing the soaps in a 200-year-old perfumerie, and pawing through the goods in a flea market are all part of the day's sensory overload.

Our shopping sections are selective and eclectic but never dull, paying particular attention to gay shops. More and more of these are popping up in European cities. Gay bookstores are high on the list, but if you want a kinky leather "ouch-fit," shoulder-length rubber gloves, retro disco togs, a gold nipple ring, or size 13 ladies' pumps, we'll tell you where to find them (assuming they're available). Ditto piercing and tattoo salons. But shopping generally transcends sexuality, so we also tell you where to look for top-name designer clothing and local specialty goods.

HOT SPOTS & COOL CULTURE

Europe is loaded with gay neighborhoods, community centers, sports clubs, theaters, bars, pubs, cafes, cabarets, drag shows, and discos. In some cities, like London, Berlin, and Paris, the choices are amazing. We present you with whatever gay life is out there: quiet gay bars, kinky clubs with a leather scene and a backroom, women-only clubs, camp cabarets with gender-bending shows, gay gyms, gay sports teams, and more. The only thing we ask you to remember is that gay bars, clubs, and discos sometimes disappear overnight. Check with each city's gay (or even mainstream) mags to find out what exactly is open and what has opened since our research was done. We give you a list of all local gay publications and other magazines with listings.

For many gay travelers, no trip would be complete without hearing a performance by a great orchestra in one of Europe's fabulous concert halls, seeing an opera, attending the ballet, or going to the theater. We provide you with information on all the major performing arts venues a city has to offer. (Some of these places are as cruisy as any bar.)

Getting Your VAT Refund

All European countries charge a **value-added tax (VAT)** of 15% to 33% on goods and services. Rates vary from country to country, though the goal in European Union countries is to arrive at a uniform rate of about 15%.

Don't let the VAT keep you from indulging your shopping whims, though. If you're a non-EU citizen, you can get some or all the VAT refunded. The actual refund amount depends on how much you spend in a particular store; it's as low as $80 in England—though some stores, like Harrods, require as much as $150—up to $200 in France or Italy.

When you make your purchase, request a VAT refund invoice from the cashier. Bring this invoice and your receipts to the Customs office at the airport of the last EU country you'll be in and have it stamped (allow at least half an hour for this process). In other words, if you're flying home from England, bring all your slips from Italy, France, Germany, and so on to the airport in London. Once you're back home, mail all the Customs-stamped invoices back to the original stores within 90 days of the purchase. They'll send you a refund check in a few weeks or months or will credit your account if you paid with plastic.

As for libido-enhancing saunas and cruising grounds—well, guys, those are here too, if you want them.

2 Talk to My Agent: Using a Travel Agent or Tour Operator

You've got your passport (haven't you?), saved up your "disposable income," and decided where you want to go. Now you have to get there. If you want to plan things yourself, see "No Fear of Flying: Getting to Europe" below. But if you want someone else to handle the logistics of your trip, you can seek out a gay travel agent or a gay tour operator.

If you decide to use a travel agent, make sure he or she is a member in good standing with the **American Society of Travel Agents (ASTA)**, 1101 King St., Alexandria, VA 22314 (☎ **703/739-8739;** www.astanet.com).

GAY TRAVEL AGENTS

If you want to keep your hard-earned travel money pink, you can use a gay travel service. The **International Gay and Lesbian Travel Association** (**IGLTA**) maintains a worldwide network of gay and lesbian travel-agent professionals who can help you plan your trip. For information on the nearest IGLTA travel agent, contact **IGLTA,** 4331 N. Federal Hwy., Suite 304, Fort Lauderdale, FL 33308 (☎ **800/448-8550;** e-mail: IGLTA@aol.com; www.IGLTA.org).

GAY TOUR OPERATORS

In addition to individual travel agents, there are gay tour operators and travel agencies that have special gay or gay-friendly travel packages. Options vary from business to business: Some offer customized (and/or escorted) tours on a specific subject or theme; others deal with specific gay events; still others specialize in certain countries at different times of the year. Here are tour operators who deal in one way or another with gay European travel packages:

IN THE UNITED STATES **Above and Beyond Tours,** 230 N. Via Las Palmas, Palm Springs, CA 92262 (☎ 800/397-2681; fax 760/325-1702; e-mail info@abovebeyondtours.com; www.abovebeyondtours.com. **Alyson Adventures,** P.O. Box 180179, Boston, MA 02118 (☎ 800/825-9766; e-mail info@alysonadventures.com). **Cruise World,** 901 Fairview Ave., no. #A-150, Seattle, WA 98109 (☎ 800/340-0221; fax 206/343-0771; e-mail cruiseworld@juno.com). **David's Trips and Tours,** 310 Dahlia Place, Suite A, Corona del Mar, CA 92625-2821 (☎ 888/723-0699; fax 949/723-0666; e-mail info@davidtours.com; www.davidtours.com). **Family Abroad,** 40 W. 57th St., Suite 430, New York, NY 10019-4001 (☎ 800/999-5500 or 212/459-1800; fax 212/581-3756; www.familyabroad.com). **Hanns Ebensten Travel,** 513 Fleming St., Key West, FL 33040 (☎ 305/294-8174; fax 305/292-9665). **IMTC Inc.,** 3025 Maple Drive, Suite 5, Atlanta, GA 30305 (☎ 800/790-4682; fax 404/240-0948; e-mail imtc@mindspring.com). **Progressive Travels,** 224 W. Galer, #C, Seattle, WA 98119 (☎ 800/245-2229; fax 206/285-1988; e-mail progtrav@aol.com; www.progressivetravel.com). **Zeus Tours,** 209 W. 40th St., New York, NY 10018 (☎ 800/447-5667; fax 212/764-7912; www.zeustours.com).

IN CANADA **Stonewall Connection Travel & Tours,** 3545 32nd Ave. NE, #320, Calgary, AB T1Y 6M6 Canada (☎ 888/228-7477; fax 403/250-1041; e-mail stonewall@canuck.com; www.canuck.com/stonewall).

IN THE UNITED KINGDOM Alternative Holidays, P.O. Box 16393, London SE1 4NU England (☎ **020/7701-7040;** fax 020/7708-5668; e-mail info@alternativeholidays.com; www.alternativeholidays.com). **Best of Both Worlds Travel Ltd.,** 117 Phyllis Ave., New Malden, Surrey KT3 6LB England (☎ and fax 020/8942-0533; e-mail WorldCroll@aol.com). **In Touch Holidays Ltd.,** 24 Chiswick High Rd., London W4 1TE England (☎ 020/8742-7749; fax 020/8742-7407; www.bogo.co.uk/alternatives). **London Handling Ltd.,** 12 Kendrick Mews, London SW7 3HG England (☎ 020/7589-2212; fax 020/7225-1033). **Sensations,** 22 Blenheim Terrace, St. John's Wood, London NW8 0EB (☎ 020/7625-6969; fax 020/7624-0167). **Uranian Travel,** Infocus House, 111 Kew Rd., Richmond, Surrey TW9 2PN England (☎ 020/8332-1022; fax 020/8332-1619; e-mail info@uranian.co.uk; www.uranian.co.uk). **Zone One,** 140 Buckingham Palace Rd., London SW1 W9SA, England (☎ 020/7730-2347; fax 020/7730-9756).

IN AUSTRALIA **Jornada,** Level 1, 53 Cross St., Double Bay, NSW 2028 Australia (☎ 02/9362-0900; fax 02/9362-0788; e-mail justask@jornada.com.au).

IN FRANCE **French Touch,** 13 rue Stephenson, Paris 75018, France (☎ 01-41-10-38-37; fax 01-41-10-39-55). **Mistral Tours,** Île de la Barthelasse, Avignon 84000, France (☎ and fax 04-90-85-861; e-mail drbusiness@avignon-pacwan.net). **Promenades de Style,** 52 rue de Faubourg Poissonière, Paris 75010, France (☎ 01-46-71-73-35; fax 01-46-71-61-70; e-mail 100442.423@compuserve.com).

IN GERMANY **Gaygantic Tours,** Neptun Reisen & Touristik, Dom-Pedro-Strasse 16, Munich 80637, Germany (☎ 089/1591-9086; fax 089/157-5834; e-mail Neptun.Reisen@T-Online.de). **Hellkamp Reisen,** Hellkamp 17, Hamburg 20255, Germany (☎ 040/491-9054; fax 040/491-9100; e-mail hellkamp@aol.com; www.gaytravel.de). **Wolff + Zink Travel Services,** Hans-Sachs-Strasse 22, Munich 80469 Germany (☎ 089/260-5962; fax 089/260-5962). **Teddy Travel,** Mathiasstrasse 4–6, Cologne 50676, Germany (☎ 0221/219-886; fax 0221/242-774; e-mail teddy-travel@t-online.du).

IN GREECE **Windmills Travel & Tourism,** P.O. Box 154, Mykonos 84600, Greece (☎ 0289/23877; [Apr–Oct only]; fax 0289/22066; e-mail windmills@travelling.gr).

IN ITALY **Zipper Travel Association,** Via Francesco Carletti 8, Rome 00154, Italy (☎ 06-578-3170 or 06-488-2730; fax 06-488-2729; e-mail tptravel@aconet.it).

IN THE NETHERLANDS **De Gay Krant Reisservice,** Kloveniersburgwal 40, Amsterdam 1012 CW, The Netherlands (☎ 020/421-0000; fax 020/620-6217; e-mail reis@gayworld.nl; www.gayworld.nl/reis/index.html). **Vaarschool Grietje,** Prinsengracht T/O 187, Amsterdam 1015 AZ, The Netherlands (☎ and fax 020/625-9105); women only.

3 No Fear of Flying: Getting to Europe

Out & About, 8 W. 19th St., Suite 401, New York, NY 10011 (☎ **800/929-2268** or 212/645-6922; www.outandabout.com), is a monthly newsletter packed with good information on the global gay and lesbian scene. A year's subscription is $49. ***Our World,*** 1104 North Nova Rd., Suite 251, Daytona Beach, FL 32117 (☎ **904/441-5367**; www.ourworldmag.com), is a slicker monthly magazine promoting and highlighting travel bargains and opportunities. Annual subscription rates are $35 in the United States and $45 outside the States. You might also want to check out ***Circuit Noize*** (www.circuitnoize.com) to find out about circuit party events worldwide.

FROM THE UNITED STATES

BY NORTH AMERICAN AIRLINE North American carriers with frequent service and flights to Europe are **Air Canada** (☎ 800/776-3000 in the U.S., 800/555-1212 in Canada; www.aircanada.ca), **American Airlines** (☎ 800/433-7300; www.americanair.com), **Canadian Airlines** (☎ 800/426-7000 in the U.S., 800/665-1177 in Canada; www.cdnair.ca), **Continental Airlines** (☎ 800/231-0856; www.flycontinental.com), **Delta Airlines** (☎ 800/241-4141; www.delta-air.com), **Northwest Airlines** (☎ 800/447-4747; www.nwa.com), **Tower Air** (☎ 800/221-2500; www.towerair.com), **TWA** (☎ 800/892-4141; www.twa.com), and **U.S. Airways** (☎ 800/622-1015; www.usairways.com).

For the latest on airline Web sites, check **airlines-online.com** or **www.itn.com.**

BY EUROPEAN NATIONAL AIRLINE Major national and country-affiliated European airlines include the following:

- **Czech Republic:** CSA Czech Airlines. *In the U.S. & Canada:* 800/223-2365. *In the U.K.:* 020/7255-1898. *In Australia:* 02/9247-6196. *Web site:* www.csa.cz.
- **France:** Air France. *In the U.S.:* 800/237-2747. *In Canada:* 514/847-1106. *In the U.K.:* 020/8742-6600. *In Australia:* 02/9321-1000. *In New Zealand:* 068/725-8800. *Web site:* www.airfrance.com.
- **Germany:** Lufthansa. *In the U.S.:* 800/645-3880. *In Canada:* 800/563-5954. *In the U.K.:* 0345/737-747. *In Australia:* 02/9367-3888. *In New Zealand:* 09/303-1529. *Web site:* www.lufthansa.com.
- **Greece:** Olympic Airways. *In the U.S.:* 800/223-1226, or 212/735-0200 in New York State. *In Canada:* 514/878-3891 (Montréal) or 416/920-2452 (Toronto). *In the U.K.:* 020/7409-2400. *In Australia:* 02/9251-2044. *Web site:* agn.hol.gr/info/olympic1.htm.
- **Italy:** Alitalia. *In the U.S.:* 800/223-5730. *In Canada:* 514/842-8241 (Montréal) or 416/363-1348 (Toronto). *In the U.K.:* 020/8745-8200. *In Australia:* 02/9247-1307. *In New Zealand:* 09/379-4457. *Web site:* www.alitalia.com.
- **The Netherlands:** KLM Royal Dutch Airlines. *In the U.S.:* 800/374-7747. *In Canada:* 514/939-4040 (Montréal) or 416/204-5100 (Toronto). *In the U.K.:* 0990/750-9900. *In Australia:* 02/9231-6333. *In New Zealand:* 09/309-1782. *Web site:* www.klm.nl.

Cruising the Internet

You can obtain lots of specific travel information by cruising the Net. **Yahoo** (www.yahoo.com), **Excite** (www.excite.com), **Lycos** (www.lycos.com), **Infoseek** (www.infoseek.com), and the other major indexing sites have subcategories for travel, country/regional information, and culture—click on all three for links to travel-related sites. One of the best hot lists is Excite's **City.Net** (www.city.net).

Other good clearinghouse sites are Microsoft's **Expedia** (expedia.msn.com), **Travelocity** (www.travelocity.com), **Internet Travel Network** (www.itn.com), **TravelWeb** (www.travelweb.com), **European Travel Commission** (www.visiteurope.com), **TheTrip.Com** (www.thetrip.com), and **Discount Tickets** (www.discount-tickets.com).

The Web sites listed above can also point you to many on-line travel magazines. Two of the best are **Condé Nast's Epicurious** (www.epicurious.com), based on articles from the company's glossy magazines *Condé Nast Traveler* and *Bon Appétit*; and **Arthur Frommer's Outspoken Encyclopedia of Travel** (www.frommers.com), written and updated by the guru of budget travel himself.

General gay-travel Web sites include **www.planetout.com** and **www.gaytravel.com.**

- **Portugal:** TAP Air Portugal. *In the U.S.:* 800/221-7370. *In the U.K.:* 020/7828-0262. *Web site:* www.tap-airportugal.pt.
- **Spain:** Iberia. *In the U.S.:* 800/772-4642. *In Canada:* 800/363-4534. *In the U.K.:* 020/7830-0011. *In Australia:* 02/9283-3660. *In New Zealand:* 09/379-3076. *Web site:* www.iberia.com.
- **United Kingdom:** (1) British Airways. *In the U.S. & Canada:* 800/247-9297. *In the U.K.:* 020/8897-4000 or 034/522-2111. *In Australia:* 02/9258-3300. *Web site:* www.british-airways.com. (2) Virgin Atlantic Airways. *In the U.S. & Canada:* 800/862-8621. *In the U.K.:* 01293/747-747. *In Australia:* 02/9352-6199. *Web site:* www.fly.virgin.com.

FROM THE UNITED KINGDOM

BY CHUNNEL You've probably heard about the extraordinary ***Eurostar,*** connecting Paris (or Brussels) to London (and vice versa) via the underground Chunnel in just 3 hours (instead of the 10 hours required for the traditional train-ferry-train route). Claustrophobes take note: Twenty minutes of that time is spent beneath the English Channel. The Eurail pass doesn't cover this service, though Eurail and BritRail passholders receive a considerable discount. One-way *Eurostar* fares in 1998 were $299 for First Premium class (with meal), $199 Full Fare (without meal), and $139 for those with a Eurail or BritRail pass.

Eurostar trains arrive and depart from Waterloo Station in London, Gare du Nord in Paris, and Central Station in Brussels. You can phone for reservations (☎ **0990/300-003** in London, **01-44-51-06-02** in Paris, and in the U.S. RailEurope at **800/EUROSTAR** or **800/94-CHUNNEL;** www.eurostar.com or www.raileurope,com).

BY TRAIN You can also travel to the Continent by "regular" trains, which include a ferry or Hovercraft crossing on top of, not beneath, the English Channel. If you're in London, stop in at the **International Rail Centre,** Victoria Station, London SW1V 1JY (☎ **0990/848-848**), or **Wasteels,** opposite Platform 2 in Victoria Station

(☎ **020/7834-7066**), for information on the various rail passes and discounts available in the United Kingdom for travel in continental Europe.

If you're under 26 (proof of age required, I'm afraid), **Inter-Rail** or **EuroYouth passes** allows you unlimited second-class travel in 26 European countries. **Eurotrain "Explorer" tickets** allow passengers to move leisurely from London to Rome, for example, with as many stopovers as desired, and return by a different route for £195 ($322) round-trip (£160/$265 without stopovers). All travel must be completed within 2 months of the departure date.

Wasteels also sells a £5 ($8) **Rail Europe Senior Pass** entitling the holder to discounted tickets on many European rail lines. Purchasers must be U.K. residents over 60 and hold a British Senior Citizen rail card, available for £16 at any BritRail office.

BY FERRY OR HOVERCRAFT **Brittany Ferries** (☎ **01705/892-200**) is the largest British ferry/drive outfit, sailing from the southern coast of England to Spain and France. From Portsmouth, sailings reach St-Malo and Caen; from Poole, Cherbourg; from Plymouth, Santander in Spain.

P&O Channel Lines (☎ **0990/980-980**) operates car and passenger ferries between Portsmouth and Cherbourg (3 departures a day; 5 to 7 hours); Portsmouth to Le Havre (3 a day; $5^1/_2$ hours); and Dover to Calais (25 a day; 75 minutes).

P&O's major competitor is **Stena Sealink** (☎ **01233/615-455**), which carries both passengers and vehicles and is represented in North America by **BritRail** (☎ **800/677-8585,** or 212/575-2667 in New York). Stena offers ferryboat service between Newhaven and Dieppe (four departures daily; 4 hours), but the car ferries between Dover and Calais are more popular (20 a day; 90 minutes). One-way fares for a car with driver and one passenger are $134 to $255, depending on the season; passengers without cars cost $40 in any season.

Unless you're interested in a leisurely sea voyage, foot passengers might be better off using the quicker, slightly cheaper **Hoverspeed** (☎ **01304/240-241**). Within North America, contact BritRail (see above). Hoverspeeds make the 35-minute crossings 12 times daily for only $39.

BY CAR Many rental companies won't let you rent a car in Britain and take it to the Continent, so always check ahead. There are many drive-on/drive-off car-ferry services across the Channel (see above). There are also Chunnel trains that run a drive-on/drive-off service every 15 minutes (once an hour at night) for the 35-minute ride between Ashford and Calais.

BY COACH Though considerably slower than the trains, on a budget you may opt for one of **Eurolines'** regular departures from London's Victoria Coach Station to destinations throughout Europe. Contact them at 52 Grosvenor Gardens, Victoria, London SW1W OAU (☎ **020/7730-8235** or 01582/404511). A one-way ticket from London to Rome, for example, is £89 to £95 ($147 to $157), depending on the season, for the 34-hour trip (departures twice weekly).

4 "Doing" the Continent: Getting Around Europe

BY TRAIN

In the air and on the ground, saving money is part of the game. If you're going to be traveling around in Europe, do yourself a favor and take the train. There's a European network of sleek high-speed trains that'll whisk you from one foreign capital to the next in style and comfort, without the hassles of driving, parking, and getting to/from airports. It's enormous fun and scenically superb, and train travel generally costs way less than flying.

For city-to-city rail travel on the Continent, your best bet is the time-honored **Eurail pass,** allowing for first-class travel in and between 17 European countries (excluding England and Eastern Europe). There are any number of variations: You can get them for 15 days ($538), 21 days ($698), 1 month ($864), 2 months ($1224), and 3 months ($1,512). A **Eurail Flexipass** allows for unlimited 10- ($634) or 15-day ($836) first-class travel within a 2-month period. If your travel will be limited exclusively to France, Germany, Italy, Spain, and Switzerland, a **Europass** will be even cheaper.

And here's the really good news: Couples or friends traveling together can save even more with a **Eurail Saver Flexipass,** available for 10 days ($540) or 15 days ($710) within a 2-month period. If you go for the five-country Europass, your companion saves an additional 40% (split the difference and have a few good meals). The only restriction with these "companion passes" is that you must travel together at all times—so be sure you're with someone whose company doesn't drive you crazy. Reserving a seat (a small extra charge) for peak travel times is a wise idea. Your travel agent can help you obtain a Eurail pass, or you can contact **Rail Europe,** 500 Mamaroneck Ave., Harrison, NY 10528 (☎ **800/438-7245** in the U.S., or 800/361-7245 in Canada). You can also do your booking through the Internet by using their Web site at **www.raileurope.com.**

Great Britain, ever the odd man out when it comes to the European Community, doesn't recognize Eurail passes. If you're going to travel around England by train, consider getting a BritRail pass. You can order them from Rail Europe (see above), just like the Eurail passes. There's a slew of options: a choice of either first- or second-class, time periods from 8 consecutive days to 1 month, and Flexipasses allowing you to a certain number of days within 1 month. In 1998, an 8-consecutive-day pass was $375 first class and $259 second; a 4-day Flexipass was $315 first class and $219 second.

BY CAR

European rental-car rates aren't as cheap as those in the States. And gasoline costs as much as three times more. The price may look lower, but you're buying it in liters, not gallons: There are 3.8 liters in 1 U.S. gallon; in Britain, the Imperial gallon is the equivalent of 1.2 U.S. gallons. Tootling around the continent in a car will be exorbitant—if there are only one or two of you. But a ménage à trois traveling together can usually go cheaper by car than by train (even with rail passes). Many rental companies grant discounts if you reserve in advance (usually 48 hours), and it's always cheaper to reserve from your home country. Weekly rentals are usually less expensive than day rentals.

If you're going to explore the rural areas of Europe—France's Riviera, Italy's Tuscany, southern Spain's Andalusia—driving is the best way to do it. But if you're going from city to city, trains are far easier. You might want to take a train between cities and use an occasional rental car to explore a region or two. *Never* rent a car just to drive around a European city. Parking is difficult and expensive, and the public transportation is usually excellent.

TAXES & INSURANCE When you reserve a car, ask if the price includes the value-added tax (VAT), personal accident insurance (PAI), collision-damage waiver (CDW), and any other insurance options. If not, ask what they'll cost, because at the end of your rental they can make a big difference in your bottom line. Some rental companies may require you to purchase a theft-protection policy in Italy.

CDW costs around $10 per day. It can add up but can also allow you to hobble away from a totaled rental car without owing a cent. CDW and other insurance may be covered by your credit card if you use it to pay for the rental; check with the card issuer. **Travel Guard International,** 1145 Clark St., Stevens Point, WI 54481-9970 (☎ **800/826-1300;** www.travel-guard.com), offers CDW for $5 per day.

CAR-RENTAL AGENCIES The main car-rental companies are **Avis** (☎ 800/331-1212; www.avis.com); **Budget** (☎ 800/527-0700; www.budgetrentacar.com); **Dollar** (known as Europcar in Europe; ☎ 800/800-6000; www.dollarcar.com); **Hertz** (☎ 800/654-3131; www.hertz.com); and **National** (☎ 800/227-7368; www.nationalcar.com).

U.S.-based companies that specialize in European car rentals are **Auto-Europe** (☎ 800/223-5555; www.autoeurope.com); **Europe by Car** (☎ 800/223-1516, 800/252-9401 in California, or 212/581-3040 in New York; www.europebycar.com); and **Kemwel** (☎ 800/678-0678; www.kemwel.com).

SOME ROAD RULES Driving on the right is standard, except in Great Britain and Ireland. Roads are marked in kilometers (km), one of which equals 0.6 miles. Except for the German autobahn, most highways do indeed have speed limits of around 60 to 80 m.p.h. (100 to 135 k.p.h.). Self-service gas stations are readily available, and prices tend to be lower off the freeway. Never leave anything of value in the car overnight and nothing visible any time you leave the car (this goes doubly in Italy).

PERMITS & HIGHWAY STICKERS Though a valid U.S. state driver's license usually suffices, it's wise to carry an **International Driving Permit,** which costs $10 from any AAA branch. Some countries, like Austria and Switzerland, require that cars riding the national highways have special stickers. If you rent within the country, the car will already have one, but if you're crossing a border, check at the crossing station to see whether you need to purchase a sticker on the spot for a nominal fee.

BY BUS

Bus transportation is generally less expensive than train travel and covers a more extensive area, but it's slower and much less comfortable. On the other hand, European buses, like the trains, outshine their American counterparts.

BY PLANE

Though the train remains the cheapest and easiest way to get around Europe, air transport options have greatly improved in the last few years. Competition with rail and ferry companies has forced some airfares into the bargain basement. British Airways and other scheduled airlines now fly regularly to Paris for only £60 to £75 ($96 to $136) round-trip, depending on the season. Lower fares usually apply to midweek flights.

Another recent development in European air travel is the **no-frills airline.** They keep their overhead (and prices) low by using electronic ticketing, forgoing meal service, and flying from less popular airports. Look out for: in England, **Debonair** (☎ 44-541/500-300) and **EasyJet** (☎ 44-1582/700-004; www.easyjet.com); in Spain, **Air Europa** (☎ 071/178-191); in Italy, **Air One** (☎ 39-1478/48-880 or 39-6/488-800; www.air-one.com); and in Belgium, **Virgin Express** (☎ 32-2/752-0505; www.virgin-express.com).

Lower airfares are also available throughout Europe on **charter flights** rather than on regularly scheduled ones. Look in local newspapers to find out about them. **Consolidators** cluster in cities like London and Athens.

The Czech Republic

Coming Out of the Past

by Todd Savage

What a difference a decade makes: It has been 10 years since the collapse of Soviet communism, and nowhere was its disappearance swifter and more peaceful than in Czechoslovakia, which later split into the **Czech Republic** and the Slovak Republic. When the Iron Curtain was pulled down, curiosity seekers were thrilled by the wonders of **Prague.** They quickly made into a hot new destination this ancient city that was seemingly mothballed during half a century of totalitarian rule. Hundreds of years of history are still on display, from fairy-tale castles dotting the Bohemian countryside to fanciful baroque buildings enlivening the most mundane streets to the coarse communist-era manners of waiters. Millions of tourists and tens of thousands of expats later, this country continues to fascinate as it evolves and fashions a new identity in the heart of an integrated Europe.

The memory of masses protesting in Wenceslas Square is still fresh, but the changes have been dramatic, especially in the pulsing capital. The sound and dust of construction are constant elements of Prague life. Centuries-old buildings have been given bright coats of paint and carefully restored to their grandeur. (Avoid comparisons to Disneyland if you want to score points with the locals.) The

Czech-ing the Internet

Before hitting the cobblestone streets, you may want to investigate a few Web sites for the latest on the gay scene in Prague and the Czech Republic and on general tourism. Start with **www.gay.cz,** with gay tourist information in Czech and English and links to other gay and lesbian Czech organizations and services.

Both of the major Czech gay magazines offer on-line companions to their print versions, provided in both Czech and English: ***SOHO Revue*** (**http://jidas.pm. cesnet.cz/~bobrik/soho**), published by SOHO (Association of Organizations of Homosexual Citizens), and ***Amigo*** (**www.amigo.cz**). The English-language ***Prague Post*** (**www.praguepost.cz**) has a good site with not only articles from its print version but also a special guide for visitors.

You might also want to check the general sites maintained by the **Czech Tourist Authority** (**www.czech-tourinfo.cz**), the **Czech Republic's Ministry of Foreign Affairs** (**www.czech.cz**), and **Radio Prague** (**www.radio.cz**).

As a crossroads for so many backpackers, expats, and international thrill-seekers, Prague has cultivated several Internet cafes where you can drink a cold Pilsner or strong Turkish coffee and send an electronic postcard to the girls and boys back home (see the box on cybercafes later in this chapter).

The Czech Crown

The Czech currency is the **crown** or **koruna** (plural, **kuruny**), abbreviated **Kč.** Each crown is divided into 100 **haléřů** (**hellers**), but chances are you won't encounter many of them. Crown bank notes come in denominations of 20Kč, 50Kč, 100Kč, 500Kč, 1,000Kč, 2,000Kč, and 5,000Kč. There are also 1Kč, 2Kč, 5Kč, 10Kč, and 50Kč coins.

At this writing, the U.S. dollar was equivalent to 32.35Kč, and this was the exchange rate I used throughout. Prices over U.S. $5 have been rounded to the nearest dollar.

Czech Republic is a country where legendary figures like Holy Roman Emperor Charles IV, Franz Kafka, and adopted son Wolfgang Amadeus Mozart still loom large and where locals and guidebooks wax pseudo-spiritual with talk of ghosts and magic—but hokey as it may sound, when you see the haunting silhouette of Prague Castle at dusk, you'll know what they're talking about.

Homosexual relations have been legal here since 1961, but under communism they were officially ignored as perversion and an example of bourgeois indulgence and served as a convenient threat for the secret police to use to investigate opponents. Many gays and especially lesbians were closeted and socially isolated. Several bars and a gay-rights group operated prior to the Revolution, but since then, gays have quickly taken bolder steps toward societal visibility and acceptance, pushing the Czech Republic to the fore of the former Warsaw Pact nations in advancing equal rights for gays and lesbians.

Nevertheless, the lingering effects of 5 decades of communism seem to be still at work, even extending to the streets and subway, where, try as you might, you rarely seem to catch another person's eye. (Okay, maybe I'm just justifying my rotten luck at cruising.) Many gay people have been slow to come out and prefer to guard the details of their private lives. Even the most committed young activists seem not to understand the Western impulse to draw attention to yourself; they prefer to pursue their goals with quiet seriousness. Formed in 1991, Sdružení Organizací Homosexuáních Občanů or SOHO (Association of Organizations of Homosexual Citizens) coordinates the efforts of nearly 2 dozen gay-rights groups operating in just about every major city. But after being forced to parade for years to celebrate the glories of the socialist cause, the Czechs are leery of demonstrations. As Heather Faulkner, a lesbian expat at the English-language *Prague Post,* observed, "It's kind of pre- and post-Stonewall at the same time."

Czechs seem willing to acknowledge the presence of gays and lesbians in their new democratic society. Though the Czech Republic is traditionally a Catholic country, there's little organized religious opposition, and the people are too busy with economic worries to bother. (It doesn't hurt that they all know at least *one* queer: The country gave us one of the most famous lesbians in the world, tennis legend Martina Navrátilová, who was born in a small town outside Prague and defected in 1975 at age 18.)

In 1990, the Czech parliament lowered the age of consent to 15 for same-gender couples, putting them on par with their straight counterparts. There's also no restriction on travel for tourists with HIV. In 1998, SOHO pushed for a bill in the legislature that would've created a domestic partnership registration. While the measure was eventually defeated by only three votes, the publicity surrounding it got Czechs talking, and it even showed up as the theme of a billboard campaign for a soft drink (depicting two sweet-faced guys exchanging wedding rings). Activists plan to try again. You'd expect any country with an artist as its leader to be pretty cool with homos. President Václav Havel comes by his compassion honestly—a favorite uncle, Miloš Havel, who left much of his estate to his nephew, was gay. He may have bequeathed some of his aesthetics as well: On taking office, President Havel ordered smart new uniforms for the guards at Prague Castle, who had suffered through decades of communism in drab khaki duds.

Yes, there have been reported gay-bashings, but there hasn't been a single galvanizing incident to activate gays. The country's first-ever gay-and-lesbian event was held in May 1998 in the Bohemian spa town of Karlovy Vary. During the weekend-long festival, 150 supporters held a series of discussions and workshops and awkwardly yet proudly marched together. The event was cosponsored by the town and drew mild curiosity from Czechs in Prague. Later that week, a group of smiling Czechs appeared on the cover of the *Prague Post,* with one of the supporters waving a pride flag over his head.

There's much to explore in the Czech Republic, but I devote most of my coverage to Prague, the capital and one of the oldest and most important centers of history and culture in Europe. Yet every visitor will want to venture outside the city for a day trip or an overnight, so I've included sections on **Karlštejn Castle,** the ancient towns of **Český Krumlov,** and the spa town of **Karlovy Vary (Carlsbad).** Though Praguers can be fairly cosmopolitan in their attitudes, outside the city you may encounter less enlightened views, just as you might in many small towns in the States.

1 Prague: The Art of Eastern European Seduction

How else to put it? **Prague** has sex appeal. Just the name—*Praha* in Czech—has a certain exotic allure. Over the half century it was closed to all but communism, this great city of domes and spires (it's known as the City of a Thousand Spires) built up an air of mystery . . . like a tall, dark, handsome stranger. In the post-revolutionary era, Prague immediately set to work seducing the curious visitors who made their way to the city. Today you may feel a wistful "wish I'd seen it then," but the city's essential character still has the power to romance.

Turn-ons: The Czech language with its lusty Slovak edge; the great shadows and light playing off the beauty of centuries-old baroque, Gothic, and art-nouveau buildings and churches; and, atop buildings and framing doorways, the statuary posed in heroic fashion, clothed and often not, staring out with knowing eyes. And who can miss the flesh-and-blood humans: all those amazing cheekbones, those super-fem women who'd be the envy of every dyke and drag queen on the block, and those aloof, brooding guys who look like they threw on whatever clothes were lying on the floor when they awoke after an active night.

You can understand immediately what brought the Bel Ami producers to Prague (come on, tell me you've never heard of Lukas, Dano, or Johan). In fact, Prague guys are used to foreigners arriving looking for their Bel Ami fantasy come true. Says Olda Bureš, a young gay activist, "Sometimes they know Milan Kundera, but they *always* know Bel Ami."

A sense of openness about sex, drugs, and alcohol is giving Prague a reputation as a kind of Eastern Bloc Amsterdam. Being added to Prague's storied past is a new chapter marked by a free-wheeling spirit. It's like a frontier town where everybody is out to make his or her mark. Prepare for Prague to put the moves on you.

1 Prague Essentials

ARRIVING & DEPARTING

BY PLANE About 12 miles from the center of Prague, **Ruzyně Airport** (☎ **02/36 77 60**) is surprisingly small and simple but has most of the conveniences you'd expect. Free luggage carts are available at the entrance to the baggage claim area. You can also stow your luggage if you like for 30Kč (less than $1) per bag per day. The main terminal also has a Czech Airlines (ČSA) tourism office with airport shuttle bus tickets and a hotel accommodation service, a branch of Čedok (the Czech travel agency) with its own hotel booking service, a hotel call-board with more than 50 lodging options (and where you may be approached with offers for private housing), ATMs, a newspaper stand, and several restaurants. All the major car-rental agencies are represented here.

At the cabstand outside the terminal, the going rate for **taxis** is about 600Kč ($19), but you can save yourself some money by taking one of the **hotel shuttle vans** for 360Kč ($11). Operating every half an hour, the van drops off riders next door to the Renaissance Prague Hotel, which is convenient to downtown and the Náměstí Republiky Metro station. An even cheaper option (12Kč/35¢) is taking **city bus no. 119,** which will take you to the Metro's A (or green) line at the Dejvická station, putting you only three stops from Staroměstské (Old Town Square).

You can buy bus tickets in the airport at the newspaper stand near the restaurant area. This is also a good place to pick up a copy of the English-language *Prague Post* for a preview of what's going on in town in the coming week.

BY TRAIN International visitors arrive at the **Hlavní Nádraží (Main Station),** Wilsonova 80, Praha 2 (☎ **02/2422 3887** or 02/2422 4200 for rail schedules), easily one of the least lovely European train stations. The exterior is rendered in grand art nouveau style, but inside it's a dim multilevel maze of ticket counters and food vendors. There's also a Prague Tourist Information Center counter, luggage storage, and showers. The station is a 10-minute walk to Václavské náměstí (Wenceslas Square) and adjacent to the Hlavní Nádraží Metro station on the C line. At night, the train station is a pickup spot for male prostitutes.

A second major station is **Nádraží Holešovice (Holesovice Station),** Partyzănskă at Vrbenského, Praha 7 (☎ **02/2422 4200**), also on the C line.

BY CAR If you're motoring into Prague, it's a good idea to drop that thing off at the rental agency. You don't need or want a car. You're going to get lost and frustrated, and there's no place to park anyway. On the other hand, a car is certainly a good option if you plan to explore towns outside Prague and will often get you there faster and more directly than a train or bus.

VISITOR INFORMATION

The city operates four **Prague Tourist Information Centers,** where you can load up on brochures, maps, and schedules of tours and cultural attractions. The main phone number is ☎ **02/54 44 44** (Mon–Fri 8am–7pm). The tourist offices can assist with booking hotel rooms and sell tickets to concerts, theater, and other events. You can also check out their Web site at **http://pis.eunet.cz.**

Offices are in the Staré Město Town Hall, Staroměstské nam. 1, Praha 1 (Metro: Staroměstská; open Apr–Oct Mon–Fri 9am–7pm, Sat–Sun to 6pm, and Nov–Mar Mon–Fri 9am–6pm, Sat–Sun to 5pm); at Na příkopě 20, Praha 1 (Metro: Můstek; open Apr–Oct Mon–Fri 9am–7pm, Sat–Sun to 5pm, and Nov–Mar Mon–Fri 9am–6pm, Sat–Sun to 3pm); in the lobby of Hlavní Nadraží (Main Rail Station),

The Prague Card

A **Prague Card** allows 3 days of free unlimited travel on city transport, as well as admission to 40 museums, galleries, and other places of interest. It's sold at the American Express Travel Office on Wenceslas Square, the Čedok travel offices, the Czech Airlines (ČSA) office at the airport, and several Metro and train stations. The cost is 480Kč ($15). For information, call ☎ **02/996 1067.**

Wilsonova 80, Praha 2 (Metro: Hlavní Nadraží; open Apr–Oct Mon–Fri 9am–7pm, Sat–Sun to 4pm, and Nov–Mar Mon–Fri 9am–6pm, Sat–Sun to 3pm); and in the Malá Strana Bridge Tower, immediately on the other side of Charles Bridge (Metro: Malostranská; open summer daily 10am–6pm).

The city's **Cultural and Information Center,** on the ground floor of the remodeled Municipal House (Obecní dům), náměstí Republiky 5, Praha 1 (☎ **02/2200 2100;** fax 02/2200 2636; open daily 10am–6pm), is a new attempt at visitor-friendly relations, offering advice, tickets, souvenirs, refreshments, and rest rooms.

CITY LAYOUT

Prague's 1.2 million residents inhabit an area spread over 300 square miles. The city is divided into 10 **postal districts,** from Praha 1 (Prague 1) to Praha 10 (Prague 10). You'll often hear locals use these numerical designations to describe the location of a particular place.

As a visitor, most of your travels will keep you well within the boundaries of Praha 1, which embraces the ancient parts of the city on both sides of the **river Vltava** (the neighborhoods of Staré Město and Malá Strana), and Praha 2, a newer, more commercial area south and east of Old Town. All this area can easily be covered on foot, but reaching some of the gay bars, concentrated in Praha 2 and Praha 3, is easier by taking public transport or a cab.

Dating to the early 13th century, **Staré Město (Old Town)** is the historic heart of Prague, with **Staroměstská náměstí (Old Town Square)** its busy pulse point of activity. Even a map doesn't seem to help navigating the twisting, turning cobblestone paths of Old Town, with its many delightful shops and restaurants and intimate squares and churches. It's often best to go with your gut and follow a road that looks interesting. This area is served by the Staroměstská and Můstek Metro stops.

As it name suggests, **Nove Město (New Town)** was laid out later, but much of the older 14th-century buildings were destroyed and replaced in the 19th century. The area is now a busy construction site, with new hotels and other office complexes going up. In addition to the National Theater, the area is famed for **Václavské náměstí (Wenceslas Square),** not a square at all but a wide avenue with some of the city's grand 19th-century architecture and the oft-photographed statue of King Wenceslas on horseback; it now serves as a backdrop for late 20th-century capitalism with Times Square–style neon and good old-fashioned seediness. You can reach this area by the Náměstí Republiky, Můstek, or Muzeum Metro stop.

The most charming area is **Malá Strana (Lesser Town),** the hilly area across Charles Bridge, spilling down from Prague Castle. Here you'll find winding streets, hidden gardens, and the beautifully weathered look of the red-roofed buildings with their earthy golds, greens, and browns that'll no doubt send you rushing home with lots of ideas for color washes for your walls. The steep main road, **Nerudova,** leads up to the castle and is lined with touristy shops, but you can easily spend a day wandering on side streets among the variety of cute interesting shops and spend the night hopping among the hip bars and restaurants. The neighborhood, home to many of the country's foreign embassies, leads up to **Hradčany,** the area immediately surrounding the castle.

A Tip on Czech Terms

You should know that *město* means "town," *ulice* (abbreviated ul.) "street," *třída* "avenue," *náměstí* (abbreviated nám.) "square" or "plaza," *most* "bridge," and *nábřeží* "quay." In Czech, none of these is capitalized. In addresses street numbers follow the street name (like Václavské nám. 25).

Other areas worth noting are **Vinohrady,** a 19th-century area of grand apartment buildings up the hill from the National Museum; it gets its name from the days when it was home to the king's vineyards. This part of Prague is increasingly becoming a fashionable area to live, and several gay bars and cafes have opened here. Farther east is the working-class area of **Žižkov,** a kind of East Village of Prague, with hip rock clubs and several gay and lesbian nightspots. While Prague has no concentrated gay area, many gay bars and clubs are scattered throughout these neighborhoods.

GETTING AROUND

Of course, walking is the best way to see Prague, so make sure you pack those comfortable shoes—however, be aware that you'll get a major workout negotiating the hills, steep staircases, and uneven cobblestone streets. When you want to speed things along or reach outlying parts of town, the public transit system is efficient and easy to use, if you don't mind getting shoved out of the way by grannies rushing to board.

Prague Public Transit (www.dp-praha.cz, with information provided only in Czech at the moment), which operates the subway, tram, and bus system, staffs in four stations information centers where you can pick up brochures and maps: Muzeum, Můstek, Nádraží Holešovice, and Karlovo náměstí. Tickets are sold from yellow wall-mounted machines near the entrance to Metro stations, as well as at tobacco shops, newsstands, and other shops. Transit agents in the Metro stations often can help you with the ticket machine or even sell tickets directly if you get stuck.

Before you buy a ticket, think through your itinerary. Transit riders must get their tickets, which are valid for varying lengths of time, stamped in the validation machine as they board the train, tram, or bus. **Nontransfer tickets** (8Kč/25¢) are good for 15 minutes after marking on trams and buses (no transfers or rides on night trams or buses) and are valid for half an hour on the Metro and up to four stations (excluding the station of origin). **Transfers** (12Kč/37¢) are valid on the Metro, trams, and buses for 1 hour from the time the ticket is stamped during the work day and 90 minutes 8pm to 5am and on weekends and holidays. There are additional charges for large pieces of luggage.

A **24-hour pass** is 70Kč ($2.15), a **3-day pass** 180Kč ($6), a **7-day pass** 250Kč ($8), and a **15-day pass** 280Kč ($9). In addition, there's the **Prague Card** allowing 3 days of free unlimited travel on city transport and much more (see above).

Public transit in Prague operates on the honor system, so you risk getting busted if you skip onto a train or tram without a ticket. Plain-clothes inspectors regularly stop transit riders and ask to see their ticket (they'll identify themselves with a small yellow-and-red badge). If you can't produce the goods, be prepared to pay a 200Kč ($6) fine on the spot.

BY METRO The Soviet-built subway is sleek and cool, its futuristic stations appointed with aluminum walls in red, gold, blue, or silver. Seductive prerecorded voices call out the stops (you can just imagine some beauty breathlessly leaning over her microphone, purring "Nam-esssss-tee Meeee-rooo"). Women who love women will find it especially fun taking the trains: Czech women with legs that go on for days are setting records for the shortest skirts on the planet, and this becomes quite obvious when one of them is floating down toward you as you're riding up one of the subway's long tunnel escalators.

The Metro runs along three lines with transfer stations connecting them: A (green), B (yellow), and C (red). Trains run roughly every 2 minutes during weekday rush hours and 4 to 10 minutes during off-peak times. The subway operates daily 5am to midnight. If you're out late (and you will be) and see people dashing through the stations, you'd best chase after them, because they know by their watches that the night's

Prague Metro

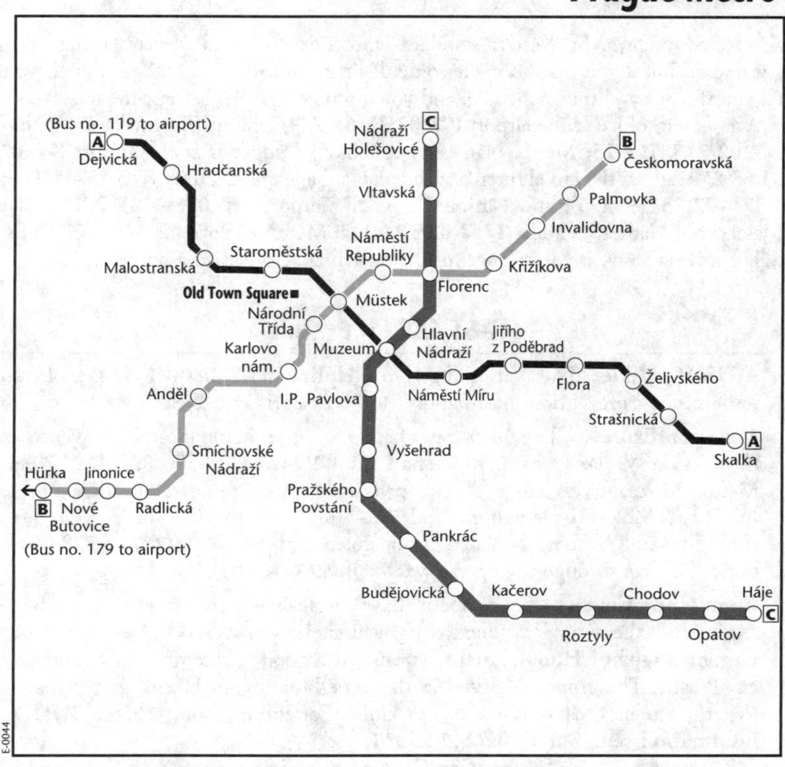

last train is about to leave. To keep yourself walking or running in the right direction, remember that *výstup* means exit and *přestup* is a connection (to another line).

BY TRAM Prague has a network of red trams (they even go clang-clang-clang, like the trolley) that give the city some of its character, and they often get you closer to your destination and afford a view along the way. But it's probably going to take a little study on your part to figure out which lines will suit your needs. A particularly convenient and popular route is the **no. 22 tram,** which goes from Národni Třída, by the National Theater, across the Vltava River, past the Malostranská Metro station, and to within steps of the castle. Thieves also know this tram is filled each day with tourists who are ripe for the picking, so guard your possessions closely. Trams run 4:30am to 12:15am each day, with several night trams (nos. 51 to 58) taking everybody home after hours.

BY TAXI Every Praguer has a favorite nightmare taxi story: huge fares, wildly spinning meters, rude drivers, and other assorted atrocities. Fares start at a maximum 25Kč (77¢) boarding fare, then go up 17Kč (about 50¢) per kilometer. These rates should be posted on the taxi door in the cab, and all customers should be able to request a receipt before paying. A lot of locals swear by **Taxi AAA** (☎ **02/10 80**) and **Profitaxi** (☎ **02/10 35**), which have English-speaking drivers who'll treat you right. It's also best to avoid cabstands in tourist zones and rely on dispatched taxis.

BY CAR There's no point in renting a car in the city, unless you feel like exploring a maze of narrow one-way medieval streets that are confusing enough on foot. Parking is also scarce and, even by Western standards, rather expensive. However, renting a car is a viable option if you plan to make some day trips outside Prague. You don't have to rely on the bus and train schedule, and you'll probably make better time too.

Avis has an office at the airport (☎ **02/31 66 739**) and at Klimentská 46, Praha 1 (☎ **02/218 512 25;** Metro: Náměstí Republiky); **Budget** is at the airport (☎ **02/31 65 214**) and at the Hotel Inter-Continental Praha, namĕstí Curieových 43–45, Praha 1 (☎ **02/23 19 595**); and **National** is at the airport (☎ **02/31 65 277**) and at Masarykovo Nábřeží 4, Praha 2 (☎ **02/297 263;** Metro: Karlovo Náměstí). Of course, it'll be less expensive if you arrange for the car rental before leaving home.

FAST FACTS: Prague

AIDS Hot Line The **National AIDS Helpline** at ☎ **0800/1 44444** offers resources and prevention information Monday to Friday 1 to 6pm.

American Express The main travel center is conveniently located on Wenceslas Square at Václavské nám. 56, Praha 1 (☎ **02/2422 7786;** fax 02/2422 7708; Metro: Muzeum; exchange office open daily 9am–7pm; travel office open July–Sept Mon–Fri 9am–6pm and Sat–Sun to 2pm, Oct–June Mon–Fri 9am–5pm and Sat to noon). For a lost or stolen card, call ☎ **02/2421 9978** (you can call collect through the operator at ☎ **0042 004 401**).

Community Center Prague doesn't have a walk-in gay community center, but the office of the nation's leading gay rights organization, **SOHO (Association of Organizations of Homosexual Citizens),** is a good source of information on gay Prague. The group is housed in the same building, at Husitská 7, Praha 3 (Metro: Florenc), as a couple of gay clubs. For information, call the **SOHO information center** at ☎ **02/2422 3811.**

There's also a **"Gay Information Center,"** but it isn't as impressive as it sounds: It's actually a small porn shop at Krakovská 2, at Žitná, Praha 2 (☎ **02/126 4408;** Metro: Muzeum), but they may be able to answer your questions too.

Currency Exchange One of the city's most ubiquitous currency-exchange outlets, Cheque Point, is also one of the most expensive, charging 9Kč per 100Kč, so you're better off looking around for a better deal. American Express assesses no commission, and anyone is welcome to change money there whether or not they're cardholders (see above). Beware of freelance operators making offers.

Embassies & Consulates The **U.S. Embassy** is at Tržiště 15, a block or so up from Karmelitská, Praha 1 (☎ **02/5732 0663** or 02/531 200 after hours; www.usis.cz; Metro: Malostranská; Tram: 22; open Mon–Fri 9am–noon and 1–4:30pm). The **Canadian Embassy** is at Mickiewiczova 6, Praha 6 (☎ **02/243 11108;** Metro: Hradčanská; Tram: 22; open Mon–Fri 8am–noon and 2–4pm). The **U.K. Embassy** is at Thunovská 14, Praha 1 (☎ **02/5732 0355;**

Country & City Codes

The **country code** for the Czech Republic is **420.** The **city code** for Prague is **2;** use this code if you're calling from outside the Czech Republic. If you're within the Czech Republic but not in Prague, use **02.** If you're calling within Prague, simply leave off the code and dial the regular phone number.

Metro: Malostranská; Tram: 22; open Mon–Fri 9am–noon). The **Irish Embassy** is at Tržiště 13, Praha 1 (☎ **02/575 300 61;** Metro: Malostranská; Tram: 22; open Mon–Fri 9:30am–12:30pm and 2:30–4:30pm). The **Australian Consulate** is at Na Ořechovce 38, Praha 6 (☎ **02/243 107 43;** Metro: Dejvicka; open Mon–Thurs 8:30am–5pm, Fri 8:30am–2pm). The **New Zealand Consulate** is at Dykova 19, Praha 3 (☎ **02/254 198;** Metro: Jiřího z Poděbrad; open by appointment only; contact the British Embassy for lost passports).

Emergencies For an emergency in Prague, dial ☎ **158** for police, ☎ **150** for fire services, and ☎ **155** for ambulance from any phone. (When you get a look at the Prague police in their baby-blue shirts, black combat boots, and billy clubs stashed at their waists, you may be tempted to commit some minor offense just to get their attention.)

Hospitals There's a foreigner's clinic in Prague providing 24-hour emergency services with an English-speaking staff at **Na Homolce Hospital,** Roentgenova 2, Praha 5 (☎ **02/5292 2146,** or 02/5292 2191 after hours, weekends, and holidays; Tram: 2, 4, or 9). The U.S. Embassy also can provide a complete list of medical services.

Newspapers & Magazines The gay rights organization SOHO (Association of Organizations of Homosexual Citizens) publishes a glossy monthly magazine, ***SOHO Revue,*** with articles primarily in Czech, but there's also a helpful map, bar listings, and lots of interesting pictures. It's sold at most bars for 40Kč ($1.25). The monthly ***Amigo*** (30Kč/93¢) is primarily a vehicle for personal ads and escort services but also carries a map and listings. Both publications also contain some info for towns outside the capital.

A particularly handy guide to Prague is the English-language ***Prague Post*** (45Kč/$1.40), a weekly newspaper founded in 1991. The *Post* is published on Wednesdays and sold at most newsstands and many hotels. The "Night and Day" pullout section contains reviews, articles, and listings of restaurants and cultural happenings and often includes items of interest to gays and lesbians. The weekly calendar is a good way to find an opera, a concert, or a film to attend.

Look for ***Do Města/Downtown,*** a free weekly foldable broadsheet that has a comprehensive listings in Czech and English of films, theater, concerts, and nightclubs. If you can't find it, call ☎ **02/5731 4626** or plan your days in Prague in advance by checking it on the web at **www.downtown.cz.** Other local English-language publications worth perusing are the ***Prague Business Journal*** and ***Think,*** an English-language expat magazine.

Telephone Public phones are usually found in Metro stations and on the street in bright yellow kiosks. Unless you understand or feel like deciphering a little Czech, it's also useful to know you can select English (or French or German) on the public phone, so you'll understand what the recorded voice is saying when you're doing something wrong. Some phones operate exclusively with coins, while others take only phone cards, which are a whole lot more convenient. Phone cards, with stored value that's automatically deducted while you use the phone, are sold in amounts from 150Kč to 450Kč ($4.65 to $14) at newsstands, tobacco shops, post offices, hotels, and department stores.

Be aware that the Czech Republic is going through a massive overhaul of its telephone network, and phone numbers can change overnight without notice.

2 Pillow Talk

While you can eat and drink on the cheap in Prague, lodging tends to be surprisingly steep. And, for the most part, hotels are still striving to meet our fussy Western expectations for quality and service. With a big demand for rooms, a little fresh competition is helping, as older hotels are updated and refurbished and new hotels introduced by chains like Radisson/SAS and Marriott.

Where you stay depends on what you're looking for: Will you be content with a plain room that screams late-1970s communist chic? Or do you want a quaint hotel experience that oozes late Middle Ages? Or do you want to go deluxe all the way? Location is something else to consider. Maybe you want to be in the center of the action, with a constant stream of tourists outside your door, or maybe you want to escape the crush. Embarrassingly romantic couples will want to bed down in Malá Strana, easily the most atmospheric part of the city. Here there are a number of small inn-like hotels, some on the main drag with views of Charles Bridge and others tucked away on back streets. A close second for ambience is Old Town, where there are still more small hotels offering rooms with beamed ceilings and antiquish furnishings. Many of the city's larger hotels are lined up along Wenceslas Square, a convenient site for reaching most of the city's attractions but a rather seedy strip after hours. Some of the newer hotels, including some of larger convention-style places, are in other parts of New Town, especially near náměstí Republiky.

A popular and inexpensive alternative is taking a room in a private residence. Many Praguers open their homes to earn some extra money, and you'll often get a rather spacious and private room or even your own apartment not far from the town center. Grandmothers and other residents go to the main train station to find guests to rent their rooms, but always use good judgment in deciding whether to take up an offer. (Be sure to inquire about the proximity of public transit stops.) One reputable housing service is the guy who calls himself the **Private Accommodation Association** (☎ **0602/267663**). Rooms generally run 330Kč to 540Kč ($10 to $17) per night, with discounts for longer stays. English-speaking coordinators will meet you and take you to the apartment, answer questions about local attractions, and even sell you a map.

You can book hotels through any of the **Prague Tourist Information Centers** (see above) or the travel agency **Čedok,** with offices at the airport and at Na příkopě 18 (☎ **02/2419 7111;** fax 02/232 1656). Prague attracts a heavy volume of visitors nearly year-round, so it's essential to reserve your room as early as possible.

STARÉ MĚSTO (OLD TOWN)

Hotel Inter-Continental Praha. Nám. Curieových 43–45, Praha 1. ☎ **02/2488 1111.** Fax 02/2481 1216. 364 units. A/C MINIBAR TV TEL. 11,322Kč ($350) double; from 12,616Kč ($390) suite. Rates include buffet breakfast. AE, DC, MC, V. Metro: Staroměstská.

The choice of celebs and other style hounds, the Inter-Continental has a fashionable location at the end of Pařížská, perched on the riverbank. In stark contrast to the centuries-old buildings around it, it's done in International Style on a wide plaza (the kind of cold architecture you either love or hate). With city or river views, the rooms are nicely proportioned, done in tasteful muted colors, and furnished with a sofa, sitting chair, and desk. The marble baths with a tub/shower are on the anemic side but stocked with goodies, like terry-cloth robes, hair dryers, scales, and fancy toiletries. The junior suites are more spacious, and the few "family" suites offer a pair of king-size beds. The fitness-inclined will love Prague's best health club, a glass-topped complex with weights, cardio equipment, a golf putting green, a lap pool, and a sauna.

Hey, Big Spender

If you've finally come into your trust fund and want to blow a wad on a Prague hotel, there are many deluxe places that'll be more than glad to bend over backward for you. Be prepared to drop a minimum of $200 a night for a double at any of them.

The **Hotel Inter-Continental Praha, Hotel Hoffmeister, Hotel Palace,** and **Prague Hilton Atrium,** four of the toniest, are listed in full below. Here are some others where you'll feel like a princess, no matter what sex you are:

Grandhotel Bohemia, Králodvorská 4, Praha 1 (☎ **02/2480 4111;** fax 02/ 232 9545; Metro: Náměstí Republiky).

Hotel Esplanade, Washingtonova 19, Praha 1 (☎ **800/444-7462** in the U.S., 800/181-535 in the U.K., or 02/2421 3696; fax 02/2422 9306; Metro: Muzeum).

Hotel Savoy, Keplerova 6, Praha 1 (☎ **02/2430 2430;** fax 02/2430 2128; Tram: 22).

✪ **Hotel Paříž.** U Obecního domu 1, Praha 1. ☎ **800/888-4747** or 02/2422 2151. Fax 02/2422 5475. www.hotel-pariz.cz. E-mail booking@hotel-pariz.cz. 93 units. A/C MINIBAR TV TEL. 5,823–8,411Kč ($180–260) double; 10,880Kč ($340) suite. Rates include breakfast. AE, DC, EU, JCB, MC, V. Self-park 600Kč ($19) in nearby garage. Metro: Náměstí Republiky.

The gorgeous art-nouveau Paříž was restored in 1997 to its turn-of-the-century glory. The high-ceilinged lobby has a decadent jazz-age feel and opens onto a restaurant, the Sarah Bernhardt, and the Cafe de Paris, both among the grandest spaces in Prague. Connected by a handsome cast-iron stairway, the rooms get lots of light and have been furnished in keeping with the vintage feel of the rest of the hotel (though in these old hotels rooms never seem to match the magnificence of the lobby). The baths are clean and bright, equipped with tubs and showerhead attachments, robes, and hair dryers. A short walk from Old Town Square, the Paříž neighbors the Obecní dům (Municipal House), another architectural treasure, and several high-end boutiques.

Hotel Ungelt. Malá Štupartská 1, Praha 1. ☎ **02/2481 1330.** Fax 02/231 9505. 9 units. MINIBAR TV TEL. 5,120–6,330Kč ($158–$196) double. Rates include breakfast. AE, DC, MC, V. Metro: Staroměstská.

Attached to a complex of buildings from the 10th century, the Ungelt (named for the custom duties foreign merchants once had to pay in this vicinity) has the feeling of an old inn, with its inviting lobby walls decorated with sepia-toned photos of old Prague and some very butch medieval weaponry on the walls. The hotel provides a measure of privacy since all the rooms are apartment-style suites with 20-foot-high ceilings (some with painted wooden beams) and separate bedrooms and living areas. The management plans to update the baths, some of which look a bit outdated. A few of the rooms have French doors opening onto terraces, and all have kitchenettes with minibars.

Hotel U Staré Paní. Michalská 9, Praha 1. ☎ **02/267 267.** Fax 02/26 79 841. 17 units. MINIBAR TV TEL. 3,060–3,830Kč ($95–$118) double; 3,950–4,860Kč ($122–$150) suite. Rates include breakfast. AE, EU, MC, V. Metro: Staroměstská.

Simple, clean, and friendly, U Staré Paní (At the Old Lady) is 3-year-old hotel with a great location on a narrow gallery-filled street and an easygoing staff that speaks English well. There are a dozen doubles and five apartments, all furnished with an armoire, a table, and a wicker chair; the loft ceilings and big windows lend them a spacious feel. The tiny baths come with pedestal sinks, showers, and separate toilet areas. Some rooms face the noisy street. Downstairs is a small jazz club with live music nightly.

✪ **U Zlaté Studny.** Karlova 3, Praha 1. ☎ **02/9000 4741.** Fax 02/2421 0539. 6 units. MINIBAR TV TEL. 3,500–3,900Kč ($108–$121) double; 3,990–4,600Kč ($123–$142) suite. Rates include breakfast. AE, MC, V. Metro: Staroměstská.

A small hotel in the thick of Old Town, U Zlaté Studny (At the Golden Well) offers charming rooms at a winning price. While a stay in this 16th-century building puts you in the center of the historic heart of the city and offers some lovely views, be prepared to share the setting with everybody else hoofing their way along the Royal Road. Located on three floors connected by an elevator, the rooms are cozy and quaint with hardwood floors covered by Oriental rugs, painted wooden ceilings, chandeliers, lace-draped windows (double-paned to muffle street sounds), and some great antique pieces. One of the larger rooms has a separate sitting area with a stereo boom box. The staff is engaging and speaks excellent English. Breakfast pastries and coffee are offered in the dining room, and there's a restaurant in the basement vault.

NOVÉ MĚSTO (NEW TOWN) & VÁCLAVSKÉ NÁMĚSTÍ (WENCESLAS SQUARE)

Hotel Atlantic. Na Poříčí 9, Praha 1. ☎ **02/2481 1084.** Fax 02/2481 2378. 60 units. A/C TV TEL. 3,200–4,100Kč ($99–$127) double; 4,750Kč ($147) suite. Rates include breakfast. AE, DC, JCB, MC, V. Free limited parking. Metro: Náměstí Republiky.

Spartan and utilitarian, the Atlantic is pretty standard for Prague. The rooms are modern and efficient, with tons of closet space and a sort of Scandinavianish feel to the furnishings that give them a timeless quality; some are pretty big. But the thin mattresses and rotary-dial phones are quaint echoes of days gone by. The tile baths have stall showers and hair dryers. The hotel is convenient to the tram line, on the street out front, so you might consider a room at the back for more restful sleeping. A Chinese restaurant is off the lobby.

Hotel Axa. Na Poříčí 40, Praha 1. ☎ **02/232 0603.** Fax 02/2421 4489. www.vol.cz/AXA. E-mail axapraha@mbox.vol.cz. 131 units. TV TEL. 2,420–2,850Kč ($74–$88) double. Rates include breakfast. AE, DC, MC, V. Metro: Náměstí Republiky.

The rooms at the Axa, packaged in a bland 1970s building, aren't romantic by any stretch of the imagination—unless you want to relive (or invent) some college-dorm fantasy. But they do have cheery yellow drapes, small-screen TVs, cherry/maple furniture (a sleigh bed, a couple of embroidered sitting chairs, and a desk), and slightly angst-ridden art (moody mermaids grace the walls of one room). The baths are a bit teeny, as are the elevators, so luggage queens consider yourself warned. There aren't views to speak of (except the funky Prague TV Tower visible from rooms in back). Besides proximity to tram and Metro stops, a perk is the convenience of the ground-floor health club and pool; however, it's independently owned, so there's a modest entrance fee.

Fun Fact: The Ambassador

You probably won't get far asking for the specific room, but Allen Ginsberg slept at the Ambassador on his European travels in 1965. Try to be a little better behaved than he was. After being crowned King of Majales (a kind of May Fair), the beat poet drank too much, fooled around with countless young Czech guys, and incited large masses of reveling students in the streets. The government was not amused: Ginsberg was finally expelled from the country after police found some rather explicit descriptions of orgies and favorite masturbatory techniques. (If you want the graphic details, check out his memoirs.)

Hotel Evropa. Václavské nám. 25, Praha 1. ☎ **02/2422 8117.** Fax 02/2422 4544. 125 units, 90 with bathroom. 2,160Kč ($67) double without bathroom, 3,400Kč ($105) double with bathroom; from 4,350Kč ($134) suite. Rates include breakfast. AE, DC, EU, MC, V. Metro: Muzeum or Můstek.

The Evropa gets lots of good press for its history (built in 1889) and the "faded elegance" of its art-nouveau trappings (added around the turn of the century), but the hotel is definitely a bit more faded than elegant these days. The facade is one of the most remarkable on Wenceslas Square, but, hey, you don't plan on sleeping outside, right? The service can be cranky and the rooms are a bit of a gamble (some are quite large, with fireplaces and Louis XVI–style antiques; some are tiny and charmless), but if you've got a highly developed sense of camp, this just might be the place for you. Many rooms wrap around a lovely skylit three-story courtyard. There's a couple of restaurants and the fabled Cafe Evropa (see "Cafe Culture" under "Whet Your Appetite" below).

Hotel Palace. Panská 12, Praha 1. ☎ **800/457-4000** or 02/2409 3111. Fax 02/2422 1240. E-mail palhoprg@mbox.vol.cz. 134 units. MINIBAR TV TEL. 6,000–8,000Kč ($185–$247) double; 12,000Kč ($371) suite. Rates include breakfast. AE, DC, EU, V. Parking 300Kč ($9). Metro: Můstek.

Imagine being welcomed back to your hotel each day by two loincloth-clad statuesque studs. Emphasis on *statue*, mind you, but the 10-foot-tall duo guarding the entrance to the Palace aren't bad. Across from the Mucha Museum, the pistachio-colored Palace dates from 1913 and boasts a fussy lobby of marble, mirrors, and mahogany that's popular with business types, tourists, and the occasional American movie star. (In the old days, it saw the likes of Josephine Baker and opera stars Emma Destinova and Enrico Caruso.) The standard doubles have two twin beds (apart or together), and these are some of the nicer rooms in Prague, even though they haven't renovated in years. The juniors suites are more deluxe, with three phones (including one in the marble bath), a free minibar, a pullout bed, and terry robes. A couple of luxury restaurants, a piano bar, and a sauna add to the appeal.

Interhotel Ambassador–Zlatá Husa. Václavské nám. 5–7, Praha 1. ☎ **02/2419 3122.** Fax 02/2422 6167. E-mail ambassad@mbox.vol.cz. 172 units. MINIBAR TV TEL. 6,211–7,764Kč ($192–$240) double; from 7,279Kč ($225) suite. Rates include breakfast. AE, DC, JCB, MC, V. Parking 480Kč ($15). Metro: Můstek.

Two hotels in one, the Ambassador and Zlatá Husa have been combined to form one of the larger hotels on Wenceslas Square. The result is a very busy place. The front rooms have large windows that let in lots of light, high ceilings, sizable closets, and somewhat dated furniture. The ample marble baths contain a nice whirlpool tub and small shower stall, plus a hair dryer. The rooms in back have a old-world feel updated for the 1990s with painted white furniture and watercolors of Prague on the walls. All rooms are furnished with robes. There are several restaurants and bars and a sidewalk cafe.

Prague Hilton Atrium. Pobřeží 1, Praha 8. ☎ **02/2484 1111.** Fax 02/2484 2378. 788 units. A/C MINIBAR TV TEL. 9,762Kč ($302) double; from 12,455Kč ($385) suite. AE, DC, JCB, MC, V. Self-parking 500–850Kč ($15–$26). Metro: Florenc.

A big mirrored-glass block of a building that would be at home in Houston or Los Angeles, the Atrium is a mega-convention hotel (the largest in the Czech Republic), its soaring lobby filled with glass elevators whizzing up and down, potted palms, and bubbling fountains. It has a very international flavor, with business types from all over Europe and the world milling about. The rooms are typically Hilton, as up-to-date as you'd expect. There are five restaurants (including a bistro open "nonstop," as they say) and a casino, plus a well-equipped health club with a pool, sauna, and indoor tennis courts. The Hilton, which has a good reputation among gay Czechs for its helpful

Prague Accommodations & Dining

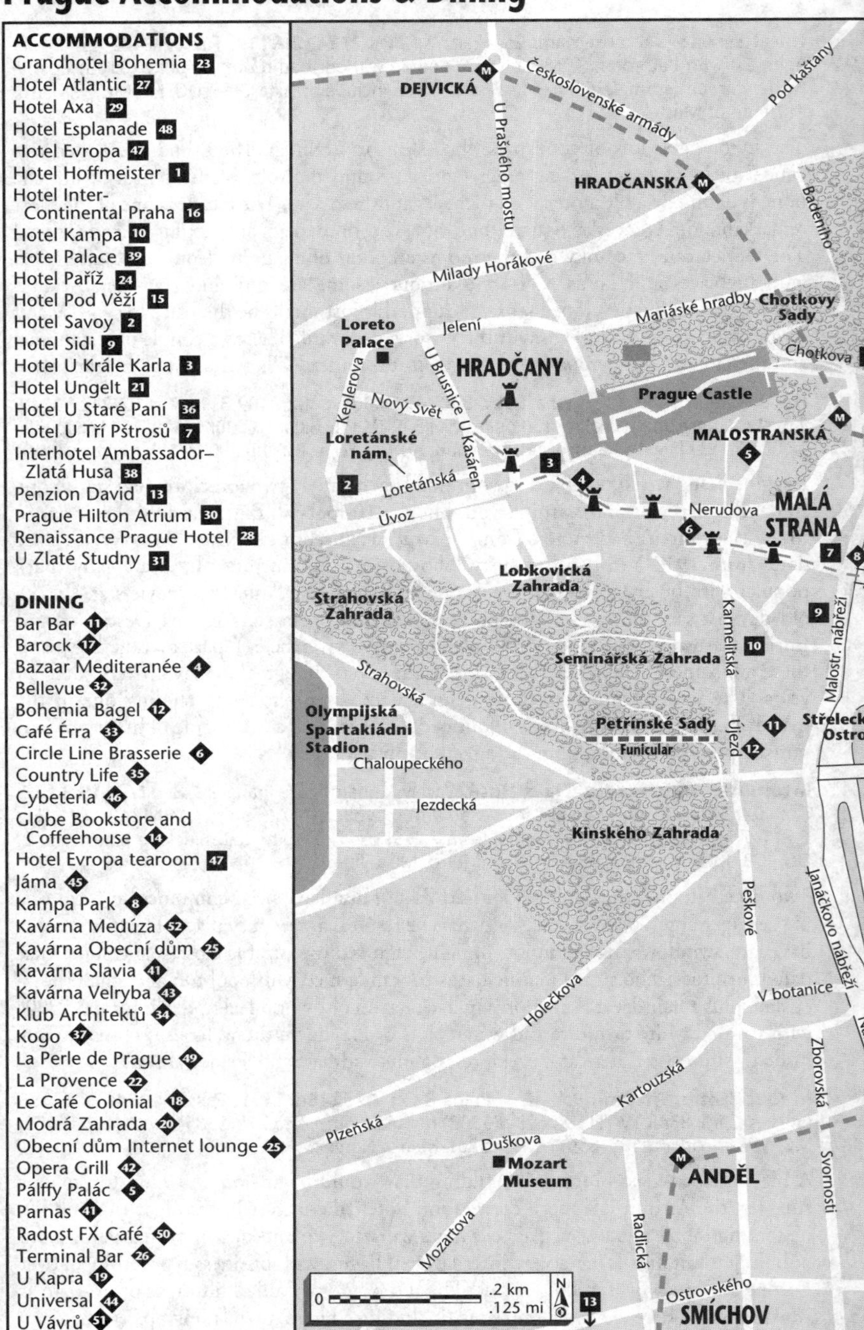

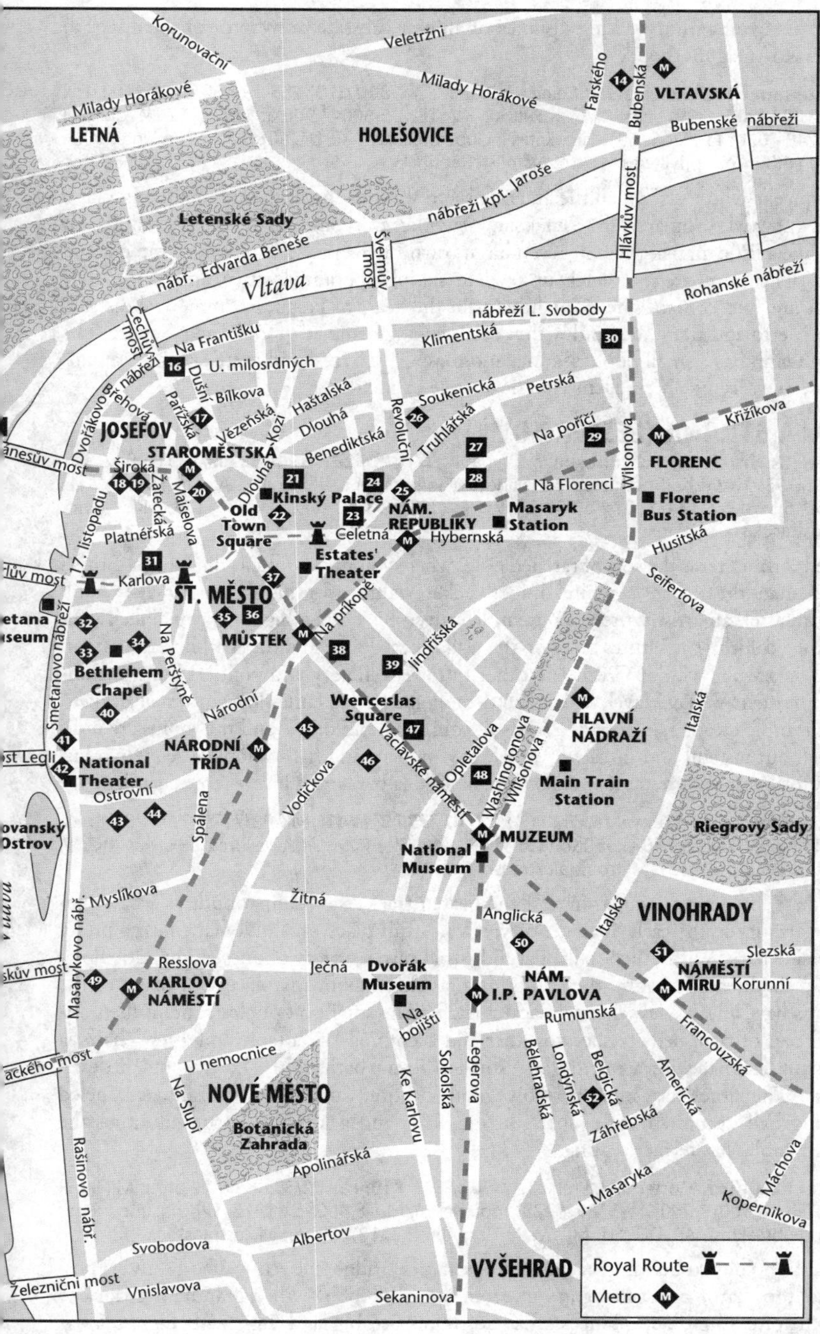
LETNÁ
HOLEŠOVICE
Letenské Sady
Vltava
JOSEFOV
STAROMĚSTSKÁ
Kinský Palace
Old Town Square
NÁM. REPUBLIKY
Masaryk Station
FLORENC
Florenc Bus Station
Estates' Theater
ST. MĚSTO
MŮSTEK
Bethlehem Chapel
National Theater
NÁRODNÍ TŘÍDA
Wenceslas Square
HLAVNÍ NÁDRAŽÍ
Main Train Station
MUZEUM
National Museum
Riegrovy Sady
VINOHRADY
NÁMĚSTÍ MÍRU
NÁM. I.P. PAVLOVA
Dvořák Museum
KARLOVO NÁMĚSTÍ
NOVÉ MĚSTO
Botanická Zahrada
VYŠEHRAD
VLTAVSKÁ
Royal Route
Metro

staff, puts you within walking distance or an easy cab ride from some of the discos in the žižkov neighborhood.

Renaissance Prague Hotel. V Celnici 7, Praha 1. ☎ **800/HOTELS-1** or 02/2182 2100. Fax 02/2182 2200. 309 units. A/C MINIBAR TV TEL. 5,600–7,900Kč ($173–$244) double; 7,667–8,702Kč ($237–$269) suite. Rates include breakfast. AE, DC, JCB, MC, V. Parking 500Kč ($15) with in/out privileges. Metro: Náměstí Republiky.

For queens who insist on all the amenities and want to forget they're in a foreign land (you know who you are), the Renaissance supplies the comforts of a Western hotel. (If you like a little drama, the hotel even has its own English-style doorman in top hat and cape.) The rooms are completely up-to-date, sharply appointed with Scandinavian-style furniture, and contain safes. The hotel is in the heart of Prague's commercial district, near Metro and tram lines and within easy walking distance of Old Town Square. The health club has a small pool, a sauna, and massage services, and there are three restaurants, one serving an excellent American-style brunch.

MALÁ STRANA (LESSER TOWN)

Hotel Hoffmeister. Pod Bruskou 7, Praha 1. ☎ **800/207-6900** or 02/5731 0942. Fax 02/530 959. www.hoffmeister.cz. E-mail hotel@hoffmeister.cz. 42 units. A/C MINIBAR TV TEL. 4,350–6,513Kč ($134–$201); 6,988–11,537Kč ($216–$357) suite. AE, DC, JCB, MC. Metro: Malostranská.

The Hoffmeister is the sort of rarefied hotel where you might find in the lobby a British gentleman dressed in a white dinner jacket waiting for his driver. Owner Adolf Hoffmeister, an artist/writer/raconteur, has given his hotel a highly personal feel, with his own colorful caricatures hung on the walls of the lobby and the sparkling restaurant. They're a who's who of Czech and other European literary and political lions, including President Václav Havel, Milan Kundera, Franz Kafka, James Joyce, Samuel Beckett, and Jean Cocteau. The hotel is a series of connected buildings, and the rooms are individual but tasteful and updated, with heavy drapery and half-canopied beds. In addition to the upscale restaurant Ada, there's a cafe, a bar, and a lovely terrace garden.

Hotel Kampa. Všehrdova 16, Praha 1. ☎ **02/7175 1941.** Fax 02/7175 0274. 83 units. MINIBAR TV TEL. 3,150–3,550Kč ($97–$110) double. Rates include breakfast. AE, MC, V. Parking 150Kč ($4.65). Metro: Malostranská.

If you're looking for something off the beaten track, the Kampa, built as a baroque-style armory in the early 17th century, is a no-frills place on a quiet lane near a pretty riverside park. With touches like flat industrial carpet, rotary phones, and plastic flowers in the breakfast room, there's nothing fabulous about the place, but many of the rooms have a leafy view through lacy curtains. The smallish doubles contain the standard pair of twin beds pushed together and accommodate a table and a few chairs, a dressing cabinet with a mirror, and small efficient baths with showers and pedestal sinks. The hotel has an unbeatably good location, and the restaurant, a paneled dining hall decorated with sabers on the walls and a kitschy cherub adorning the buffet table, has terrace seating.

Hotel Pod Věží. Mostecká 2, Praha 1. ☎ **02/533 710.** Fax 02/531 859. 12 units. MINIBAR TV TEL. 6,100–7,200Kč ($189–$223) double; 6,900–8,400Kč ($213–$260) suite. Rates include breakfast. AE, DC, EU, MC, V. Parking 400Kč ($12). Metro: Malostranská.

A salmon-colored building at the foot of Charles Bridge, the red-roofed Pod Věží possesses the charm and scale of an inn, from the small lobby with a grandfather clock to the helpful English-speaking staff. The rooms are big and airy, with high ceilings (some with decorative painting) and lots of light, and they've been decorated with brass fixtures and contemporary furnishings (a pair of chairs and table, a bureau), arty prints, and velvety drapes. The baths are clean and equipped with hair dryers, two robes, and a tub with massager. Some rooms have postcard-perfect views of Charles Bridge, but you may want to avoid the sound from the crowds by opting for a quieter room in back. There's also a nice white-tablecloth restaurant with outdoor seating, and it's possible to arrange an in-room massage.

Hotel Sidi. Na Kampě 10, Praha 1. ☎ **02/536 135.** Fax 02/531 444. 4 units. MINIBAR TV TEL. 3,900–4,400Kč ($121–$136) double. Rates include breakfast. No credit cards. Metro: Malostranská.

The gay-friendly Sidi is in a quaint red-tile-roofed building above a restaurant of the same name on a pretty cobblestone courtyard steps below Charles Bridge. The furnishings are functionally pleasant (white lacquer in one of the larger rooms). One generously sized room with a small bath looks onto the square, while a smaller room offers a remarkable river view. The beds are the typical Euro-twin, which you can push together for a larger bed; the mattresses are a bit thin. There's no elevator, so the walk up to the rooms is a winding set of stairs. The restaurant serves Czech cuisine.

✪ **Hotel U Krále Karla.** Úvoz 4 (at Nerudova), Praha 1. ☎ **02/538 805.** Fax 02/538 811. 19 units. MINIBAR TV TEL. 5,800Kč ($164) double; 6,400Kč ($198) suite. Rates include breakfast. AE, MC, V. Limited free parking. Tram: 22.

The super-romantic U Krále Karla (At the King Charles), in a 16th-century baroque house at the top of the steep road leading to the castle, never lets you forget you're visiting an old medieval city. It has been gorgeously appointed with hardwood floors, antiques, and stained glass, and the rooms are arranged around an atrium connecting two old buildings and decorated with old oil paintings and busts. Easily some of the coziest in Prague, the rooms boast Oriental rugs, large carved-wood beds with peach silk-type coverings, Gothic ceilings, and spacious closets. Historical prints of various Bohemian royals line the walls. (Recovering Catholics may not find the stained-glass saints peering down in their room especially welcoming.) The baths are finished with marblelike floors and big sinks and tubs, brass fixtures, hair dryers, and bidets. With fireplaces and both tubs and showers, the suites are worth the extra crowns. There's a cozy restaurant, a bar, and a cafe.

Hotel U Tří Pštrosů. Dražického nám. 12, Praha 1. ☎ **02/5732 0565.** Fax 02/5732 0611. 14 units. MINIBAR TV TEL. 5,400–6,200Kč ($167–$192) double; 6,800–9,900Kč ($210–$306) suite. Rates include breakfast. AE, DC, EU, MC, V. Limited free parking. Metro: Malostranská.

At the centuries-old U Tří Pštrosů (At the Three Ostriches), you'll find yourself practically staying on Charles Bridge. Some rooms offer views of the bridge's statues, as well as Renaissance-painted ceilings, Oriental rugs, and antique furnishings. The baths can be small but come with hair dryers. Stories abound about how the house became associated with the ostrich (the eponymous trio are featured on an exterior mural): Perhaps a supplier of ostrich feathers lived in the building or the birds themselves once bedded down in the company of a foreign delegation en route to see the emperor. Today the hotel's historical ambience and unbeatable location set it apart (though you may prefer a less busy area of town). There's a cafe and a restaurant.

OUTSIDE THE CITY CENTER

Penzion David. Holubova 5, Praha 5. ☎ **02/549 820** or 02/9001 1293. E-mail pension@login.cz. 7 units. AC MINIBAR TV TEL. 2,040Kč ($63) double; 510Kč ($16) extra bed. Rates include breakfast. AE, V. Street parking. Metro: Radlická or tram no. 14 from Anděl.

If you want to go gay all the way, Penzion David is the most extensive gay housing option in Prague. The owners prominently display their rainbow flag in front of the handsome three-story house, with a lushly landscaped front yard. The rooms are clean and fresh, with lilac coloring and black lacquer furniture. Each average-size bath has a shower and tub. But for the comforts of a homo home away from home (the place attracts mostly gay men), it's not especially convenient, located in a suburbanish area. It's a 10-minute walk from the Radlická Metro station, but when the Metro closes after midnight, you're going to need to take a taxi. The David has a bar and restaurant with terrace seating and a sauna, and it's near a public sports facility with clay tennis courts and an indoor pool.

3 Whet Your Appetite

Prague restaurateurs have learned well the real-estate axiom "location, location, location." One of the pleasures of eating out here is enjoying a dining room with a view (say a lush rooftop terrace featuring a sunset over Prague Castle) or a dining room with romance (maybe a candlelit Gothic vaulted cellar). And, surprise, surprise, a couple of gay restaurant owners have proved skilled at fashioning some of the more style-savvy places in town.

There's always the danger that all this theater will overwhelm the food, and sometimes it does in Prague, a city with a bad rep for its culinary offerings. When it comes to food, Prague clearly isn't Paris, but that's not necessarily a bad thing: One big up side is that a favorable exchange means you can eat a feast for a pittance. The restaurant "scene" grows more varied and interesting all the time, and a new generation of chefs seems determined to expand the diversity and quality of the local kitchens.

Word spreads quickly among the small number of serious foodies when something new or offbeat appears, whether it's a promising French bistro or an interesting Yugoslav kitchen or the latest place to sample great pizza. Since Czechs generally haven't had the means to eat out a lot, restaurateurs haven't had the incentive to get adventurous . . . until now. You'll definitely want to go native and sample some Czech goulash, potato soup, and other pub staples. Czech restaurants are especially known for their wild game and freshwater fish.

Czech service is an oxymoron: Many old-school waiters haven't yet caught on to the concept of taking care of their customers, so you may feel inclined to file a missing-persons report after an initial brush with your server. (But try not to condescend: I actually saw a couple of expats insist a rather blasé waitress smile for them. She wasn't having it.) It's always a good idea to make reservations, especially in the busy summer. If you're dining alone or with a small group, don't be surprised if strangers ask, as is Czech custom, if they can occupy the vacant chairs at your table.

Note: For the locations of the restaurants below, see the "Prague Accommodations & Dining" map on pp. 30–31.

STARÉ MĚSTO (OLD TOWN)

✪ **Bellevue (formerly Parnas).** Smetanovo nábřeží 2 or 18, Praha 1. ☎ **02/2422 7614** or 02/2422 9248. Reservations recommended. Main courses 360–690Kč ($11–$21); fixed-price menu 790–990Kč ($24–$31). AE, DC, MC, V. Daily noon–3pm and 5:30–11pm; brunch Sun 11am–3pm. Metro: Staroměstská. INTERNATIONAL.

In 1997, Parnas restaurant moved to the Bellevue from its location on the same riverfront street while its home was being renovated. However, the Parnas regulars soon realized the view of the castle was far better here, near Charles Bridge, so Parnas became Bellevue for good. New owners have since opened the old Parnas (see below).

The Blue Moon Group (which runs other restaurants here, like the Circle Line Brasserie) has put lots of energy into Bellevue's menus of choice beef, nouvelle sauces, well-dressed fish, delicate pastas, and fabulous desserts. Several wild game choices are

A Dining Warning

Be sure to check restaurant bills and credit-card slips carefully, as there are some shifty waiters who'll add an extra charge or an extra digit here or there. If you pay with plastic, perhaps write out the total in words on the credit-card bill, as you would on a check. Also be aware that the taxi driver afterward could really take you for a ride—monetarily speaking.

---

always available, like Fallow deer with oysters and mushrooms. For a tamer treat, try the poached Norwegian salmon in a light herb sauce or the New Zealand lamb. The desserts feature crème brûlée, rich tiramisu, or wild berries in port or cognac. The service is pleasant and perfectly timed.

Country Life. Melantrichova 15 (at Havelská), Praha 1. ☎ **02/2421 3366.** Main courses 30–70Kč (93¢–$2.15). No credit cards. Sun–Thurs 11am–9:30pm, Fri to 4pm. Metro: Můstek. VEGETARIAN.

Crunchy queers will want to belly up to the bar at Country Life, a vegetarian cafeteria off Old Town Square. With a forest-green facade and rustic carved wood tables and benches, the place has an earthy decor that complements the fresh items sold by the kilogram. You can create your own salad and then select a prepared sandwich, warm and cold dishes like whole-wheat veggie pizza and lentils, fresh bread and rolls, and juices and soy milk. Next door is a Country Life grocery store selling natural bath and skincare products as well as food items.

✪ **Klub Architektů.** Betlémské nám. 5A, Praha 1. ☎ **02/2440 1214.** Reservations recommended. Main courses 90–130Kč ($2.70–$4). AE, V. Daily 11:30am–midnight. Metro: Národní třída. CZECH.

The architect-owners of this restaurant on Bethelem Square knew a cool space when they saw it. Off a pretty little courtyard, the candlelit restaurant is in a medieval cellar with a few architectural touches throughout, from the drawings lining the staircase to the exposed ductwork. The food doesn't involve anything structurally complicated, just basic inexpensive Czech food like Chinese cabbage soup or ham roll with horseradish and main courses like chicken in cream sauce with peaches, pork steak with garlic and leeks, and fried celery root steak. For dessert, you can indulge with pancakes and lots of ice cream and whipped cream. During busy times, service can be harried but pleasant. On a nice day you may want to pass on the windowless dining rooms and stay aboveground in the courtyard, with its separate menu of salads, burritos, and other eats.

Kogo. Havelská 27 (at Melantrichova), Praha 1. ☎ **02/2421 4543.** Pizza 90–130Kč ($2.80–$4); main courses 150–250Kč ($4.65–$8). V. Daily 11am–11pm. Metro: Můstek. ITALIAN.

A good refueling spot in Old Town, this pizzeria/Italian restaurant is blocks from the Estates' Theater. A skylit courtyard bridges two sides of the restaurant, on one side a casual cafe and on the other a more fashionable room with orangy Tuscan coloring and pretty faux star lights on the ceiling. Kogo has an exhaustive menu of pastas (the lasagna and tortellini are excellent) and pizzas, as well as a variety of salads and some heartier meat and fish entrees. The desserts come from an Italian bakery.

La Provence. Štupartská 9, Praha 1. ☎ **02/232 4801.** Reservations recommended. Main courses 140–590Kč ($4.35–$18). AE, EU, V. Daily noon–1am. Metro: Náměstí Republiky. FRENCH/TAPAS.

La Provence is a schizophrenic place for sure: In the cellar it's a romantic candlelit room decorated in French rustic style; upstairs is a tapas bar and the Banana Cafe, where go-go dancers and drag queens (travesties in local parlance) entertain. For all these reasons (and the cuteish waiters), gay-owned La Provence attracts big crowds looking for fun. Appetizers include salmon crêpes with crème fraîche, spinach, and basil; fried calamari; and garlic soup. There's a nice mix of fish, game, and meat main courses, like bouillabaisse Marseille style with vegetables, roasted rack of lamb with gratinéed potatoes and vegetables, and duck breast with lavender honey, potatoes, and vegetables. The chef's special themed menu is a variety of salads, appetizers, and entrees prepared around a common ingredient, such as asparagus (asparagus soup to grilled salmon with asparagus and hollandaise). The service is so-so, and the mood definitely changes gears when the disco party starts upstairs.

Le Café Colonial. Široká 6, Praha 1. ☎ **02/2481 8322.** Reservations recommended for dinner. Main courses 230–290Kč ($7–$9). AE, MC, V (minimum order of 1,000Kč/$31). Mon–Sat 8:30am–1am, Sun 8:30am–5pm. Metro: Staroměstská. FRENCH/VIETNAMESE.

Newcomer Le Café Colonial brings the whole French-Vietnamese colonial thing to Prague. The designers have really gone to town, with wrought-iron furniture and black-painted wooden floors and bursts of blues and reds on the walls, which are appointed with torchières and illuminated picture boxes of Asian scenes. The French chef has fashioned a menu of salads and main courses like minced chicken with curry sauce and rice, spare ribs caramelized with honey and lemongrass, and cod fillet with preserved lemon, shallots, parsley, and boiled potatoes. The desserts are appealing, with such selections as a fruit tart of the day, flan with coconut and cardamom, and ice cream sundaes. The restaurant's lounge is a nice spot to wake up in the morning with a flaky croissant (also sold takeout in the adjacent boulangerie) and café au lait or to linger into the night for over cocktails. There's also a Sunday brunch.

✪ **Modrá Zahrada.** Pařížská 14, Praha 1. ☎ **02/232 7171.** Pizza 76–139Kč ($2.35–$4.30). No credit cards. Daily 11am–midnight. Metro: Staroměstská. PIZZA.

The wood oven at the "Blue Garden" is the source of some of the best pizza in Prague. Made with fresh ingredients and a thin crispy crust, the choices include *katka* (onions, garlic, peppers), *quattro stagione* (ham, mushrooms, oysters), *el capo* (ham, mushrooms, artichokes), *el pokero* (mozzarella, smoked cheese, edam, camembert), and *vegetariana* (sliced tomatoes, cucumbers, peppers). The menu also features a number of salads, and wine is sold by the glass and bottle. If it looks crowded, you'll find additional seating in the attractive brick cellar.

Opera Grill. Karolíny Světlé 35, Praha 1. ☎ **02/265508.** Reservations recommended. Main courses 280–680Kč ($9–$21). AE, MC, V. Daily 7pm–2am. Metro: Staroměstská. CONTINENTAL.

Dining at the Opera Grill is an intimate affair. First there's the matter of arriving: You ring a buzzer to gain admittance and then are led back through a courtyard entrance to the restaurant. It isn't a place to go if you're shy about dining with a companion: The dining room is supercozy, with only about seven candlelit tables and diners resting on overstuffed armchairs. The menu at the Opera Grill, which got its name from

A Dining Warning

Some Czech restaurants are notorious for placing seemingly harmless nuts or olives on the table or offering platters of appetizers or aperitifs that appear to be compliments of the house. *They're not.* If you partake, when the bill comes you may find you've paid about $5 for a bowl of stale cashews. Always ask first.

its former location near the National Theater, features appetizers like artichoke hearts with French dressing, escargots on puff pastry with garlic-and-herb butter, and traditional Czech potato soup. For the main course, choose from fish; meat items like lamb on a bed of spinach, fillet of venison, and T-bone steak; potato pancakes and dumplings; and turkey steak with curry sauce. There are sides of potatoes, Brussels sprouts, rices, and dumplings. Save room for dessert: Your choices may include crêpes Suzette, apple strudel, and peach-and-banana flambée.

✪ **Parnas.** Smetanovo nábřeží 2, Praha 1. ☎ **02/2421 1901.** Reservations recommended. Main courses 280–1,120Kč ($9–$35). AE, MC, V. Daily 11:30am–3pm and 6pm–midnight. Metro: Národní třída. CZECH/INTERNATIONAL.

If you packed a smart outfit and are looking for a special night out, Parnas fits the bill. (Refer to the Bellevue entry above for the history of Parnas.) Along the river in a building where the composer Smetana once lived, this elegant white-tablecloth restaurant has a wall of windows affording a front-row view of Prague Castle and the rooftops of Malá Strana. The vintage 1930s interior glows—from the tables set with too much silverware and wine glasses and elaborately folded napkins (has Martha Stewart made it to Prague?) to the Asian-motif murals inlaid with mother-of-pearl and mosaic above the bar entitled *The Absinthe Drinkers.* Tuxedoed waiters take your orders from the menu, which features appetizers like turkey terrine with avocado-and-kiwi sauce and chive pancake stuffed with chicken breast and mushroom ragout. The large assortment of fish and seafood includes sage-roasted eel, butter-roasted trout with steamed mushrooms and potato croquettes, and sole stuffed with smoked salmon and served on a bed of noodles. House specialties are the veal, beef steak, and pork fillet, but there are also a few vegetarian options. There's live music nightly on the grand piano.

U Kapra. Žatecká 7 (at Siroká), Praha 1. ☎ **02/2481 3635.** Reservations recommended. Main courses 58–88Kč ($1.80–$2.70). No credit cards. Mon–Thurs 11am–1am, Fri to 2am, Sat 4pm–2am, Sun 1pm–2am. Metro: Staroměstská. CZECH/SEAFOOD.

A cozy little cafe, "At the Carp" is close enough to the old Jewish Quarter and the river to siphon some of the stream of tourists, but it's also a gay hangout since much of the staff is that way. The restaurant, named for the fish that's a traditional Czech Christmas dish, has two small rooms, with a pretty patio out back. The menu offers a mix of Czech and Central European cuisine. Among the specialties are preparations of carp, both fried and accompanied by ham and cheese; pork with almonds and garlic; and spicy beef goulash. The restaurant's proximity to the river and Charles Bridge makes for a pleasant way to walk off your meal.

✪ **Universal.** V Jirchářich 6, Praha 1. ☎ **02/2491 8182.** Main courses 73–155Kč ($2.30–$4.80). No credit cards. Daily 11:30am–1am. Metro: Národní třída. CZECH/FRENCH.

Opened in 1998 on a corner near the National Theater, Universal has an inviting minimalist decor with subdued lighting and handsome green wainscoting, plus funky touches like a plaster elephant head and a traffic light. The restaurant, attracting a mix of ages and types, is a place you go to read the paper and comfortably while away an afternoon or evening. For Prague, the service is attentive and friendly, and the artsy staff features goateed boys and at least one Jodie Foster–ish chick (all of whom may or not be gay but are cute enough to be and you really wish they were). The menu is derived from the chef's French background with a few Czech influences. Look for nightly specials (I enjoyed the gazpacho and Indian chicken). There are a few appetizers, like rabbit terrine and cauliflower cream soup, and salads either as a starter or a full meal, including everything from tabouli with couscous and fresh mint to a Thai salad with wild rice. For the main course, there's beef entrecote with bleu-cheese sauce; a mixed brochette of beef, pork, and liver; and fish items like Basque-style tuna with

Cafe Culture

Gay Prague is out in the open at **Café Érra,** Konviktská 11, Praha 1 (☎ **02/2423 3427;** Metro: Národní třída; open daily 9am–11pm), an intimate gay-owned spot with a lot of sex appeal—it's a place to make your little hangout while in Prague (it takes some perseverance to find, but don't give up). The walls and furnishings are bold shades of blue, yellow, and orange; the patrons are clearly gay or curiously ambiguous (advertising types in pinstripes to People in Black); and the food is substantial enough to make a solid meal. On a quiet brick lane off Betlemské náměstí, Érra also has a darker downstairs lounge. The salads are generously sized (try the mango with chicken) and tasty and the desserts delish. There's also a weekend brunch.

Look for sidewalk tables (some piled high with mobile phones) and you'll know you've found **Barock,** Pařížská 24, Praha 1 (☎ **02/232 9221;** Metro: Staroměstská; open Mon–Fri 8:30am–1am, Sat 8:30am–2am, Sun 10am–1am), a Eurotrash watering hole on fashionable Pařížská, just off Old Town Square. Here you'll find cafe creatures modeling their. hip shades, soaking up some sun and glasses of afternoon bubbly. Inside, the cafe is done up with mirrors, glitzy chandeliers, and big supermodel photos. Besides an array of coffee and booze, Barock serves breakfast items, sandwiches, salads, and homemade croissants. There's also a dinner menu of sushi and other Asian dishes.

A focal point for Czech intellectual life for more than a century, **Kavárna Slavia,** Smetanovo nábřeží 2, at Národni, Praha 1 (☎ **02/2422 0957;** Metro: Národní třída; open Mon–Fri 8am–midnight, Sat–Sun 9am–midnight), reopened in 1997 after an eagerly awaited overhaul that returned the grand cafe to top form. With an unbeatable location along the Vltava across from the National Theater, the Slavia is ideal for a pre- or posttheater snack or a rest stop at day's end to take in the sun setting over Prague Castle. Inside, the cafe is large and airy, with handsome mahogany paneling and green leather booths. The often beautiful, always blasé waiters are outfitted in crisp white shirts, black ties, and white aprons—don't you just love a man in uniform? The beverage list has all the coffee drinks you'd expect, plus a simple menu of cold and warm dishes, like salami with pickled peppers and gherkins, veal paprika with sour cream, toasted sandwiches, and fresh salads. Look for a tempting array of desserts.

An antidote to the trendy new cafes appearing in Prague, the tearoom at the landmark **Hotel Evropa,** Václavské nám. 25, Praha 1 (☎ **02/2422 8117;** Metro: Můstek; open daily 7am–midnight,) is a frozen-in-time spot that reassures with its old-world ways, most especially the faded art nouveau decor of double-high

ratatouille and cod steak with shallot sauce. For dessert, go for the delicious brick of tiramisu. There's also a full bar and a wine list.

NOVE MĚSTO (NEW TOWN)

Jáma. V Jámě 7, Praha 1. ☎ **02/264127.** Main courses 98–229Kč ($3.05–$7). AE, MC, V. Daily 11am–1am. Metro: Muzeum. CZECH/AMERICAN/BREAKFAST.

Outfitted with pinball machines and rock posters of Bruce and Jimi, Jáma is an American-owned pub that would easily fit into any college town. You probably don't want to hang out nights with the straight crowd, but Jáma is especially recommendable the morning after for its hearty breakfasts (pancakes, homemade sausage, Belgian ceilings, chandeliers, and marble-top tables. (Equally faded are the stern communist-era servers.) On a lazy Sunday afternoon, you can watch the transactions of the sidewalk crystal merchants through the windows as their wares reflect in the afternoon sun. Gays have traditionally lingered here on Sundays, so don't be surprised if you see some guy with his grandmother eyeing you over his cappuccino. There's often a small admission fee in late afternoon.

Another historic setting is **Kavárna Obecní dům,** in the Municipal House, Republiky náměstí 5, Praha 1 (☎ **02/2200 2101;** Metro: Náměstí Republiky), a splendid cafe in Prague's magnificently restored concert and cultural hall. It features waiters in black tie and 1920s jazz playing, transporting you to another time. You can order a variety of open-face sandwiches, fish specialties, salads, and cheeses.

The **Globe Bookstore and Coffeehouse,** Janovského 14, Praha 7 (☎ **02/6671 2610;** Metro: Vltaksá; open daily 10am–midnight), is the kind of place where you might observe a cute 20-something backpacker writing in his journal, growing his first beard, and smoking a pipe. (Really, I actually saw this guy.) If that's not too much for you, you may even be able to strike up a conversation with him. After all, this English-language bookstore is one of the city's major hangs for American, Canadian, and British expats. The cafe has fine coffee and smoothies and a lunch and dinner menu, plus a few choice outdoor seats on the wooden deck.

If you want to get away from the English-speaking world, **Kavárna Velryba,** Opatovická 24, Praha 1 (☎ **02/2491 2391;** Metro: Národní třída; open daily 11am–2am), is a safe haven. "The Whale" has been a popular hangout for students, actors, and other intense types since the Velvet Revolution. With a large round mirror hanging over the bar and graffiti on some of the walls, this garden-level space is a mellow spot with a few queers thrown into a mix. The beer is cheap, and there's a large menu (available in English) of pork cutlets, fried chicken steak, pasta, lentils with sausage, and some vegetarian dishes and salads. Pass through the hall (where the bathrooms are located) and you'll find a back room that's spiffier and trendier; downstairs is an art gallery.

In the Vinohrady neighborhood not far from gay bars like U Dubu and Stella, the lesbian-owned **Kavárna Meduza,** Belgicka 19 (no phone; Metro: Náměstí Míru; open daily 11am–2am), is a homey space with a nostalgic decor of old paintings and sturdy wooden tables and chairs. Run by a couple of red-haired Czech chicks, the cafe has a warm vibe that makes it popular with gays and straights alike (one Brit expat even goes so far to call it a "poofter parlor").

waffles, and such) served 11am to 5pm. For lunch and dinner, there are Czech items like onion soup, fried mushrooms, potatoes, smoked meat with lentils, and Czech renditions of tacos, burritos, and chicken kebab with rice. Most everything is served with sides of croquettes or fries.

La Perle de Prague. Rašínovo nábřeží 80, Praha 2. ☎ **02/2198 4160.** Reservations recommended. Main courses 500–750Kč ($15–$23); lunch business special 490Kč ($15). AE, JCB, MC, V. Mon 7:30–10:30pm, Tues–Sat noon–2pm and 7:30–10:30pm. Metro: Karlovo náměstí. FRENCH.

La Perle de Prague has the distinction of being ensconced on the top floor of the "Fred and Ginger Building," the postmodern Frank Gehry/Vladimir Milunic–designed apartment structure so named because it appears like two separate forms dancing together (for more on the building, see "Exploring Prague"). The restaurant has a small number of tables, offering stunning views over the river. Specialties include Dover sole, venison, and foie gras. The three-course lunch special is a great deal. The astute service is the height of luxury for some, a bit off-putting for others.

MALÁ STRANA (LESSER TOWN)

Bar Bar. Všehrdova 17, Praha 1. ☎ **02/532941.** Main courses 16–169Kč (50¢–$5); crêpes 54–92Kč ($1.70–$2.85). EU, V. Mon–Fri 11am–midnight, Sat–Sun noon–midnight. Tram: 12 or 22. CZECH/CRÊPES.

You know there's a gay sensibility at work in this low-key spot with flea-market finds as decor and the house specialty crêpes named Mykonos (feta, tomato, onion, chiles) and Paris (a three-cheese affair with apple, sour cream, cranberries) and even Nancy (Amaretto, plum jam, whipped cream), plus several fruit-filled dessert crêpes. They're fairly filling themselves, but open-face sandwiches, toasts, and grilled items are also on the menu. There's a bar up front, and in European fashion, you may be asked to share a table with other diners if the room is busy. Keep your eyes wide open when trying to find the place—it's below street level on a quiet lane near Kampa Park.

✪ **Bazaar Mediteranée.** Nerudova 40, Praha 1. ☎ **02/900 54 510.** Reservations recommended. Main courses 99–329Kč ($3–$10). AE, EU, MC, V. Daily noon–1am (cafe 10am–9pm). Metro: Malostranská. MEDITERRANEAN/INTERNATIONAL.

One of the most talked about places since its 1998 opening, Bazaar is a hypertrendy restaurant/nightclub (from the gay owner of La Provence, above). It sprawls from a fabulously theatrical dining room—arched brick ceilings, big mirrors over pillow-strewn banquettes, gaudy chandeliers, and wax-dripping candelabras—to stairways lined with photos of supermodels leading to a rooftop terrace and assorted genielike dens and other hideouts. (It's easy to get lost looking for the bathroom or your way back to your table.) Menu reading is a challenge under the glow of votive candles, but that seems fitting since the atmosphere upstages the food. So do the people who work and hang out here, the kind who are so beautiful you can't help wondering if they might be alien beings. The menu embraces Mediterranean cuisine from France to Morocco, from octopus with cayenne pepper and olive oil to risotto with seafood to couscous à la Marrakech with lamb and vegetables. The dessert menu arrives with a bang: A waiter slips a piece of paper in front of you and presses on it an ink stamp of the dessert specials, which may be baked apples with vanilla rice, tiramisu, or chocolate mousse. After dinner, wander over to the bar area to find the source of the throbbing disco music, which pumps up each night as go-go boys and girls go to work.

Bohemia Bagel. Újezd 16, Praha 1. ☎ **02/530921.** Bagels and sandwiches 80–125Kč ($2.50–$3.90). No credit cards. Mon–Fri 7am–2am, Sat–Sun 9am–2am. Tram: 12 or 22. DELI.

You shouldn't be surprised to see that McDonald's and Dunkin' Donuts have made it to Prague, but so has that other invasive staple of American life: bagels. This cleverly named restaurant, started by an American and set for expansion in Eastern Europe, is notable as a place to pick up lunch and then take the funicular to the mini–Eiffel Tower on Petřín Hill. Choose from more than a dozen varieties of fresh bagels, and specialty sandwiches include turkey club, Reuben, and roasted veggie salad.

Circle Line Brasserie. Malostranské nám. 12, Praha 1. ☎ **02/530 308.** Reservations recommended. Main courses 495–795Kč ($15–$25); prix-fixe menu 890–1,190Kč ($28–$37). AE, MC, V. Mon–Sat 6–11pm. Metro: Malostranská. Tram: 11 or 22. SEAFOOD/CONTINENTAL.

Tucked away off Malostranské náměstí, Circle Line is below ground in cheerfully colored room with a sophisticated crowd dining to the quiet sound of a live pianist. You can order à la carte from a menu strong on seafood: Appetizers include house-smoked salmon with buckwheat pancakes, caper mousseline and fresh tomato compote, and a crispy tartlet with fresh artichoke hearts. Main courses may be pink sea bream spiked with wild asparagus tips; beef tenderloin with hot foie gras, truffles, and porto sauce; veal liver pan-fried with shallots. Your other option is to create your own meal from the prix-fixe menu. For dessert, there's crêpes Suzette, a decadent chocolate dish, and a selection of the day.

✪ **Kampa Park.** Na Kampě 8B, Praha 1. ☎ **02/573 134 93.** Reservations recommended. Main courses 495–595Kč ($15–$18). AE, DC, MC, V. Daily 11:30am–1am. Metro: Malostranská. CONTINENTAL.

In a city blessed with so many sublime restaurant settings, Kampa Park boasts one of the best: After dark, you approach it along a torch-lit path south of Charles Bridge. But daylight is just as good a time to visit, with brunch views from the patio of the city's towers and spires. The restaurant is casual chic, with about a dozen blond-wood tables and contemporary furnishings that are a giveaway to the owners' Scandinavian heritage. Though Czech, the waiters are tall and blond and handsome and attend you with sober seriousness. The meals are given an inviting presentation. All the appetizers are tempting, from the chili-marinated grilled tiger prawns with couscous salad to the smoked duck breast with a watercress and white radish salad to the spicy lobster bisque with five types of Atlantic fish. The entree selection may include grilled Norwegian salmon, poached roulade of plaice with coconut-ginger sauce, the restaurant's signature pepper steak, and New Zealand leg of lamb. For dessert, try the chocolate terrine with almond and caramel or the apricot parfait and sorbet.

✪ **Pálffy Palác.** Valdštejnská 14, Praha 1. ☎ **02/5732 0570.** www.czechreality.cz/palffy. Reservations recommended. Main courses 220–480Kč ($7–$15). AE, DC, JCB, MC, V. Mon–Fri noon–11pm, Sat–Sun 10:30am–11pm. Metro: Malostranská. CONTINENTAL.

Pálffy Palác is hidden on a picturesque lane with old street lanterns, up the crumbling stairs of a music conservatory and through a couple of giant doors. Inside you'll find the candlelit ballroom of an early 18th-century mansion with 15-foot ceilings, a marble fireplace, old family portraits, gilt-framed mirrors, and about a dozen tables. You'll expect some powder-wigged ghosts to come waltzing in. The fragrance of orchids and lilies, abundantly displayed in tabletop vases, and bowls of fruit add to the decadence. Yes, the owner is gay, a 20-something restaurant mogul who also owns Cafe Érra and Mecca, and you'll find same-sex couples mixed in with the gray-headed tourists, film crews, and big families out for a celebration.

The menu lists an eclectic mix, starting with excellent salads (shrimp, avocado, and grapefruit and endive, pear, and goat cheese), cream of broccoli soup, smoked eel with apples and horseradish, and white asparagus baked with Brie. Entrees include cod rolled with smoked salmon and cheese, grilled duck breast with curry and orange sauce, vegetarian lasagna with eggplant and tomatoes, and venison medallions with vegetable cream sauce. The food and the service are well intended though uneven, but the ambience is so special you'll be willing to forgive anything. Top your meal with the caramel ice cream with apricot pith, the trio of mousses, or the profiteroles with ice cream and chocolate sauce. There's a nice list of Bohemian, French, and Italian wines. Equally beautiful is the lush terrace overlooking the red-tile roofs of Malá Strana.

VINOHRADY

✪ **Radost FX Cafe.** Bělehradská 120, Praha 2. ☎ **02/2425 4776.** www.techno.cz/radostfx. Main courses 90–160Kč ($2.80–$4.95). No credit cards. Sun–Tues 11am–2am, Wed–Sat to 5am. Metro: I.P. Pavlova. VEGETARIAN.

Cybercafes

Techno-chic **Terminal Bar,** Soukenická 6, half a block east of Revoluční, Praha 1 (☎ **02/2187 1115;** www.terminal.cz; Metro: Náměstí Republiky; open daily 11am–1am), is a place to do some cruising, cyber and otherwise. They certainly got the name right: This nexus of Prague youth/expat culture is terminally hip, with all sorts of attractive locals and globe-trotting trust-fund babies. Designed by Bořek Šipek, the official architect of Prague Castle, Terminal has a couple of computer rooms, including hookups for laptops, and computer help is friendly if a little frazzled. There's a variety of other distractions for anyone who needs to idle away some time: a cool bar with an imported Italian espresso maker said to be the only one in Prague, a bright solarium cafe (with a happy-hour sushi special), a bookstore, and a video screening room. Computer time runs 100Kč ($3.10) per hour, and you can also set up a free e-mail account if you don't have one.

When you want your cyberfix without the scene, try **Cybeteria,** Štěpánská 18, off Václavské náměstí, Praha 1 (☎ **02/2423 3024;** www.cybeteria.cz; Metro: Můstek; open Mon–Fri 10am–8pm, Sat noon–6pm). It's a bit sterile, but there's still a bar (where you sign up for computer time as well as order a cuppa joe) and a quiet low-lit computer room with 10 monitors. Computer time is 50Kč ($1.50) per half hour.

Just off the cafe at the **Obecni dům (Municipal House),** Republiky náměstí 5, is a small Internet lounge with half a dozen computers and two comfortable booths (open daily 8am–11pm). The cost is 40Kč ($1.25) for the first minute and 3Kč (10¢) for each additional minute.

Radost provides one-stop shopping for the hip-oisie of Prague. They can start the day with the popular "American brunch," gaze at art in the gallery, browse CDs in the record shop, eat dinner in the vegetarian cafe, dance in the basement nightclub, and then snack on a late-night bite. One of the city's first fashion-forward spots, Radost has become a social center for the expat community and at the same time draws a cool Czech crowd—and no doubt your gaydar will active. The menu is stocked with everything from pizzas to a pesto potato (topped with spinach pesto, mushrooms, and cheese), salads, and tempting desserts. There's also a full bar. Sunday night features a special Italian menu. American films are screened free on Sunday nights.

✪ **U Vávrů.** Šuperova 4, Praha 2. ☎ **02/2423 7239.** Main courses 30–120Kč (93¢–$3.70). No credit cards. Mon–Fri 11:30am–11pm, Sat 4pm–midnight. Metro: Náměstí Míru. CZECH.

More polished than a typical Czech pub, U Vávrů is a congenial place in residential Vinohrady (it's a good prebar destination since it's not far from Stella and a few other gay bars). Most nights the restaurant, named for a famous Czech theater family, gets a theater-going crowd since it's next door to one of the city's big theaters, but it's also a popular with neighborhood folks and younger people as the nights wears on. The staff is friendly, and the meals are nicely presented. Meat is the star attraction, with beef soup as a starter and entrees like pepper steak, filet mignon, and Wiener schnitzel, plus chicken fillet curry and fruit and a couple of vegetarian options.

4 Exploring Prague

The smartest way to see Prague is to start walking and let yourself get lost. (And whether or not that's your intention, believe me, you will.) But if you prefer a little orientation and don't mind traveling in a herd, there are a plenty of tour operators that'll lead you around and can supply interesting commentary.

In a walking city, it makes sense to go on foot: **Prague Walks,** Václavské nám. 60 (☎ **02/6121 4603;** Metro: Muzeum), conducts thematic tours, like "Old Town Through the Centuries," "Sites of the Velvet Revolution," and "Ghost Tour." Costing 230Kč to 250Kč ($7 to $8), they last 1½ to 2 hours and are led primarily in English; no reservations are necessary.

There are plenty of sightseeing options by bus and boat. Tours are offered by **Martin Tour** (☎ **02/2421 2473** for reservations; www.martintour.cz), which has sightseeing tours by bus and boat of historic sections of Prague, as well as outlying areas like the former concentration camp of Terezín, the spa town of Karlovy Vary, Karlštejn Castle, Konopiště Chateau, and Brewery Benešov. It operates kiosks at Václavské náměstí, Melantrichova, Parížska, Na Příkopě, and Republiky náměstí. Times range from about 1 hour to 10 hours, and the cost ranges from 370Kč to 1,100Kč ($11 to $34). **Premiant City Tour,** Na Příkopě 23 and Národní 40 (☎ **0601/212 625;** www.sos.cz), offers more than a dozen tours of Prague and outlying attractions, including historic towns like Kutná Hora and Český Krumlov and a tour by boat and bus of Prague by night. Tours runs 350Kč to 1,590Kč ($11 to $49).

THE HITS YOU SHOULDN'T MISS

✪ **Charles Bridge (Karlův most).** Connecting Staré Město (Old Town) to Malá Strana (Lesser Town) and Prague Castle, Praha 1. Metro: Staroměstská or Malostranská.

Built in the 14th century by the Czech king and Holy Roman Emperor Charles IV, Prague's celebrated 1,700-foot-long pedestrian bridge, with its colonnade of 30 saints (see the map), takes on a carnival atmosphere with artists and buskers taking their places along the stream of tourists (see map on p. 45). The human traffic never seems to stop. (Only Barbra Streisand managed to shut it off, to the displeasure of some Czechs, when she reportedly closed the bridge in the early 1980s during the filming of *Yentl.*) The more you walk it, the greater the feeling you'll have for it when you leave Prague: Hit the bridge as soon as you get your luggage stowed. Then return daily for laps—early morning, dusk, in the middle of the night. The mood, the energy, and the shadows are always different on the most famous of the 15 bridges crossing the Vltava. Think of it as the world's longest catwalk. Now work it, girl.

Prague Castle (Pražský Hrad). Hradčandské nám. ☎ **02/2437 3368.** Grounds free. Main castle attractions (St. Vitus Cathedral, Royal Palace, St. George's Basilica) 100Kč ($3.10). Buildings Apr–Oct daily 9am–5pm; Nov–Mar daily to 4pm. Grounds Apr–Oct daily 5am–midnight; Nov–Mar daily 6am–11pm. Metro: Hradčanská. Tram: 22.

Beware the Hand in Your Pocket

Prague has developed a reputation, but not necessarily one it wants: The city is thick with stories of thieves who'll do their best to separate you from your possessions. So follow common sense and keep your valuables guarded, especially in tourist-heavy districts. Be especially careful on tram no. 22, a popular line with tourists and the bands of pickpockets who prey on them.

Looming on the horizon like some movie backdrop, Prague Castle has been the seat of Czech power for 10 centuries (sse map on p. 47). You can imagine peasants casting their eyes toward it and shivering at what mysteries it held. The "castle" is actually an architecturally rich complex of dozens of palaces, churches, galleries, monuments, and gardens. The signature Gothic towers are part of **St. Vitus Cathedral (Chrám sv. Víta).** The spectacular cathedral was begun in 1344, and work ended in 1929, when its builders finally decided enough already! It was named for a wealthy 4th-century Sicilian martyr. In 1997, the pope visited Prague to honor the 1,000th anniversary of the death of 10th-century Slavic evangelist St. Vojtěch and conferred the saint's name on the cathedral along with St. Vitus's, but officially the Czech state calls it just St. Vitus. There's much to explore, from the basement crypt containing the tombs of Bohemian kings and archbishops (including Charles IV) to the south tower with its sweeping views. Don't miss the finest of the 21 chapels, the **Chapel of St. Wenceslas,** encrusted with hundreds of pieces of jasper and amethyst and decorated with paintings from the 14th to the 16th century.

The **Royal Palace (Královský palác),** in the third courtyard of the castle grounds, served as the residence of kings between the 10th and the 17th century. Vaulted Vladislav Hall, the interior's centerpiece, was used for coronations and special occasions. Here Václav Havel was inaugurated president. The adjacent Diet was where the king met with advisers and where the supreme court was held. **St. George's Basilica (Kostel sv. Jiří),** adjacent to the Royal Palace, is Prague's oldest Romanesque structure, from the 10th century. It was also Bohemia's first convent. No longer serving a religious function, the building now houses a museum of historic Czech art.

End your visit to the castle with a stroll down **Golden Lane (Zlatá ulička),** a row of miniature 16th-century cottages built into the castle walls. They were said to have housed alchemists and astrologers under Rudolph II; later, Franz Kafka is said to have lived in house no. 22.

Jewish Museum of Prague. Ticket office at U Starého hřbitova 3a, Praha 1. ☎ **02/2481 0099.** Admission 450Kč ($14) for all seven parts. Sun–Fri 9am–6pm; closed all Jewish holidays. Metro: Staroměstská. Two to three tours in English are given daily; call for the schedule.

While most of Prague's architectural legacies survived World War II, many of its human inhabitants didn't. The city was home to one of the oldest Jewish communities in Europe, and the Nazi Holocaust devastated the old Jewish ghetto, which had lost much of its history to urban renewal early in the century. Today the remaining Jewish neighborhood of **Josefov,** north of Old Town Square, preserves the story of these people in the cluster of seven historic synagogues that together form the Jewish Museum of Prague.

Among them are one the oldest synagogues in Europe, the **Old-New Synagogue,** a 13th-century Gothic building where services are still held, and the **Pinkas Synagogue,** which was built in the 1530s and today is a Holocaust memorial bearing the names of the 80,000 people and 153 communities that were wiped out by the Nazis. The **Maisel Synagogue** is dedicated as an exhibition space to the history of the Jewish people in Moravia and Bohemia; it contains numerous artifacts, especially silverware used in religious services. Newly refurbished is the Spanish Synagogue. To deepen your sense of the community's history, walk through the **Old Jewish Cemetery,** an eerily calm place crammed with tilting Hebrew-inscribed gravestones stretching back to the 15th century. At the ticket office, you can buy tickets to individual synagogues or a combination pass to all of them, including the cemetery.

Šternberk Palace Art Museum (Šternberský palác). Hradčanské nám. 15, Praha 1. ☎ **02/2051 4599.** Admission 70Kč ($2.15). Tues–Sun 10am–6pm. Metro: Malostranská or Hradčanská.

Charles Bridge

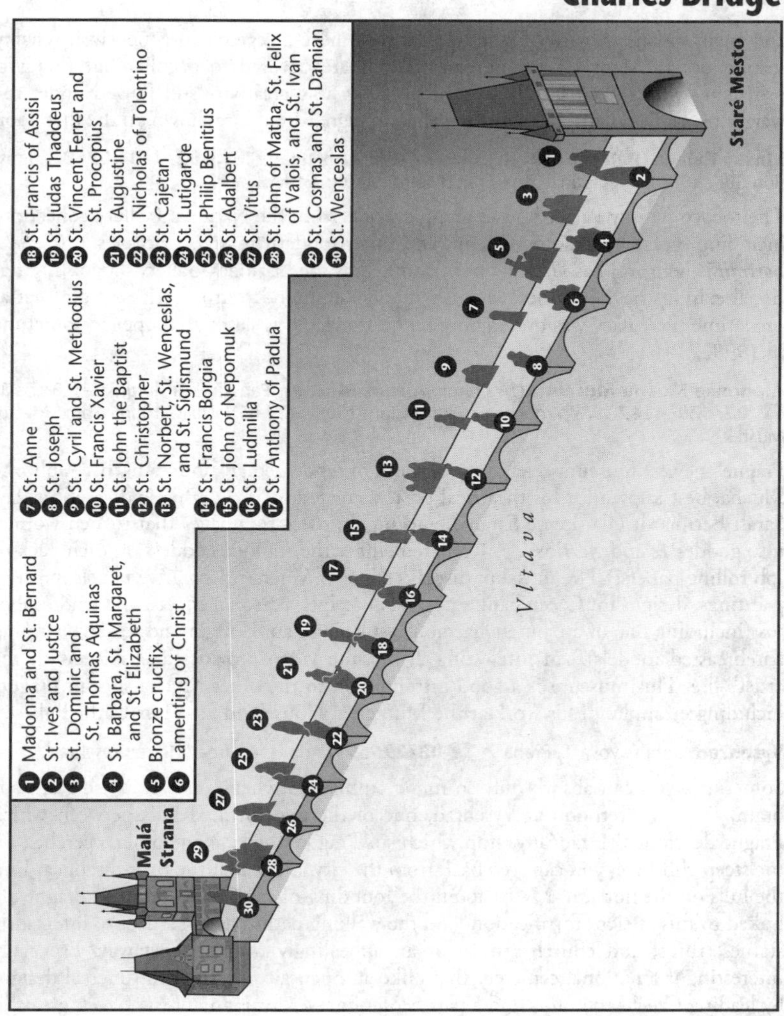

The jewel in the National Gallery crown, the gallery at Šternberk Palace, adjacent to the main gate of Prague Castle, displays a wide menu of European art throughout the ages. It features 6 centuries of everything from oils to sculptures. The permanent collection is divided chronologically into pre–19th-century art, 19th- and 20th-century art, and 20th-century French painting and sculpture. There's also a good selection of cubist works by Braque and Picasso. Temporary exhibits, like Italian Renaissance bronzes, are always on show.

Veletržní Palace. Veletržní at Dukelských hrdinů 47, Praha 7. ☎ **02/2430 1111.** Admission 80Kč ($2.50). Tues–Sun 10am–6pm, Thurs to 9pm. Metro: Vltavská. Tram: 17.

This remodeled 1925 palace now holds the bulk of the National Gallery's collection of 20th-century works by Czech and other European artists. Three atrium-lit concourses provide a comfortable setting for some catchy and kitschy Czech sculpture and multimedia works. Alas, the best cubist works by Braque and Picasso, Rodin bronzes, and many other primarily French pieces have been relegated to a poorly lit chalky section on the second floor. Several sections are devoted to peculiar but thought-provoking works from Czech artists that show how creativity still flowed under the weight of the Iron Curtain. Many traveling foreign exhibits are shown on the first floor.

Kinský Palace (Palác Kinských). Staroměstské nám., Praha 1. ☎ **02/2481 0758.** Admission 30Kč (95¢). Tues–Sun 10am–6pm. Metro: Staroměstská.

The rococo Kinský Palace houses graphic works from the National Gallery collection, including pieces by Braque, Derain, and other modern masters. Picasso's 1907 *Self-portrait* is here and has virtually been adopted as the National Gallery's logo. International exhibits have included Max Ernst and Rembrandt retrospectives. Note that at press time the palace was undergoing renovations and is slated to reopened sometime in 1999.

Alphonse Mucha Museum (Muzeum Alfons Muchy). Panská 7 (at Jindřišská), Praha 1. ☎ **02/628 4162.** www.mucha.cz. Admission 150Kč ($4.65). Daily 10am–6pm. Metro: Můstek.

Prague's newest museum celebrates the work of renowned art nouveau artist Alphonse Mucha, best known for his theatrical posters created for the dramatic diva of his day, Sarah Bernhardt ("la divine Sarah"), and highly patriotic images that turned women into goddesses and warriors. (Anyone remember the sinuous goddess on each pack of Job rolling papers?) The museum displays some of Mucha's decorative panels, posters, paintings, designs for Czech banknotes, manuscripts, personal effects, and studio photos (including one of a pantless harmonica-playing Paul Gaugin and several vamping barebreasted models). An interesting 27-minute video provides an overview of the artist's life. This museum is a good introduction to the other Mucha sites in Prague, including examples of his work at the Municipal House and St. Vitus Cathedral.

Vyšehrad. Soběslavova 1, Praha 2. ☎ **02/296651.** Admission free. Metro: Vyšehrad.

Sometimes you can absorb only so much culture, so when you're ready to rest your brain, take an afternoon at Vyšehrad, one of the two fortified hills between which Prague developed (Hradčany, atop which sits Prague Castle, is the other). Perched on the steep cliff here, you can step back from the city and watch the river disappear into the hills on the horizon. Myths about the founding of the Czech state and Prague are linked to this ancient fortification, and the walking paths passing a host of interesting statues, ruins, and churches make it an appealingly romantic getaway. Especially interesting is a national cemetery that's like an open-air gallery, with funereal designs by leading Czechs sculptors and a pantheon of graves for many of the Czech greats in art, music, and science (Dvořák, Smetana, Mucha). To reach the site, walk south from the tram stop, past the railway bridge, to the second traffic light. Cross a small parking lot and you'll see the church spires.

Municipal House (Obecní dům). Republiky nám. 5. ☎ **02/2200 2100.** Daily 10am–6pm (call for tour schedule). Tours 150Kč ($4.65) per person. Metro: Náměstí Republiky.

One of the most eagerly awaited restoration projects in post-revolutionary Prague was this cupola-topped art-nouveau showplace. The greatest Czech artists of the turn of

Take a Tram

For a good orientation to the city, take **tram no. 22** from Prague Castle down through Malá Strana and past the National Theater to Wenceslas Square. However, beware pickpockets!

Prague Castle

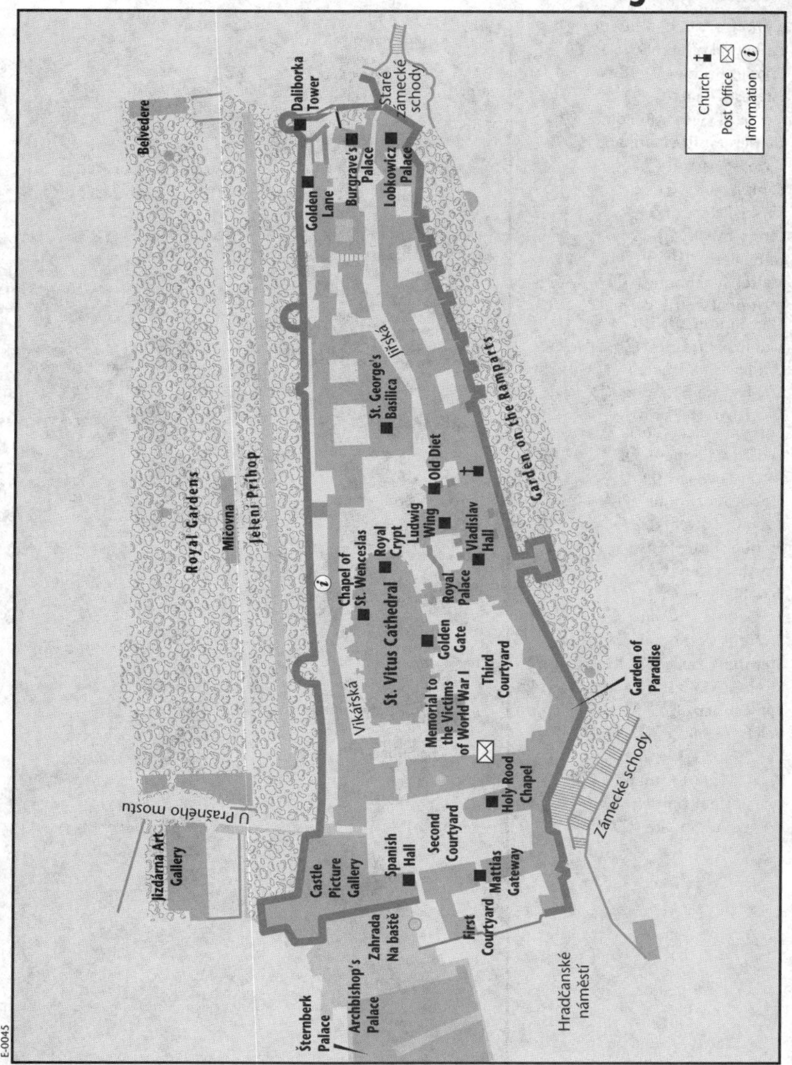

the century contributed to the resplendent building, which when it opened in 1912 was to be a great social center to rival those of the German institutions; it definitely shows in all the details, luxurious materials, colors, and imagery.

The sublime complex contains several grand **restaurants** and **cafes** on the ground floor and the lower level, as well as the **Cultural and Information Center** (see "Visitor Information"); **Smetana Hall,** the home of the Prague Symphony Orchestra with its lovely murals depicting music, dance, poetry, and drama; a series of smaller jewelbox **salons, lecture halls,** and **meeting rooms,** each more exquisite than the last; and a basement **gift shop.** You can wander the ground and first floors for free but must take a guided tour to view the rest of the building. Even if you have to suffer through

Prague Attractions

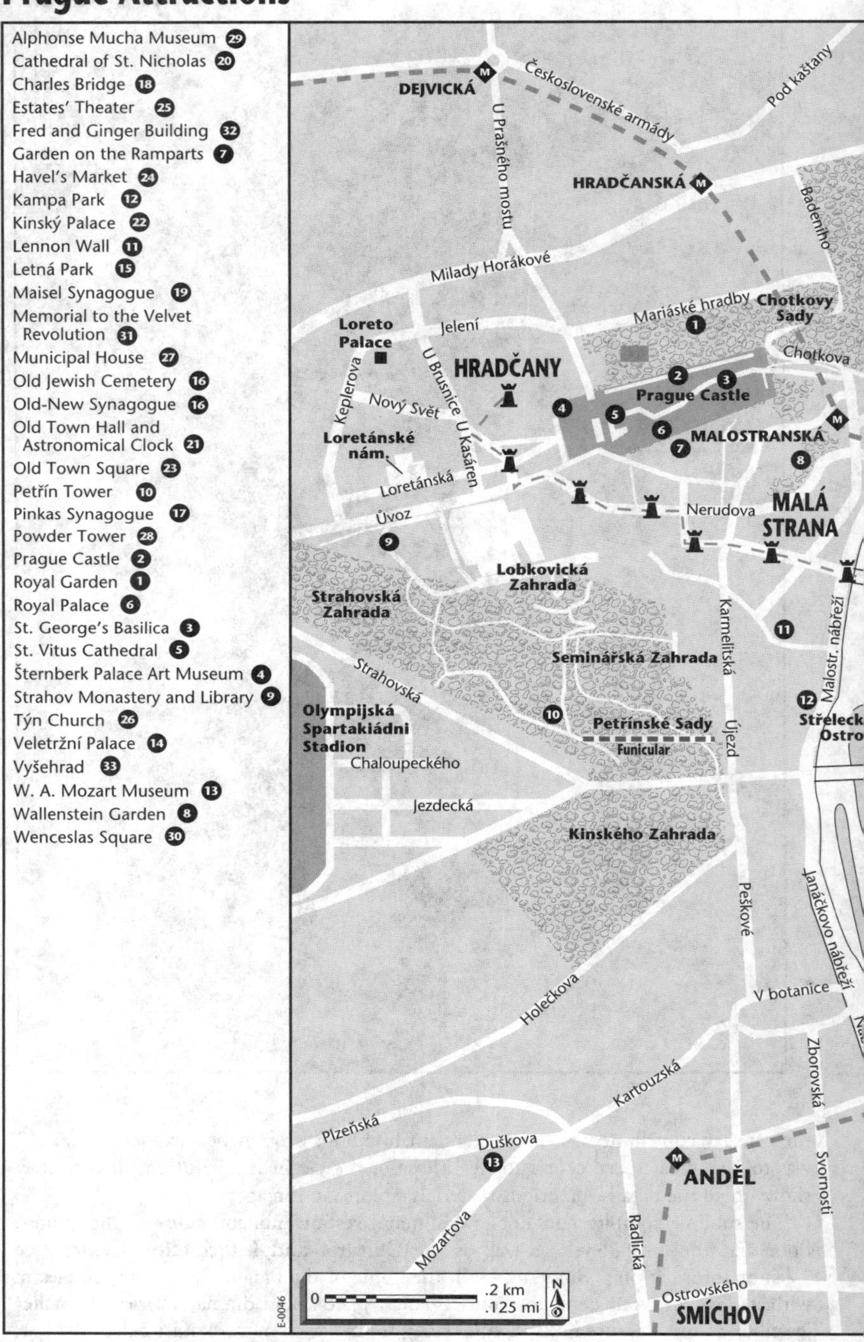

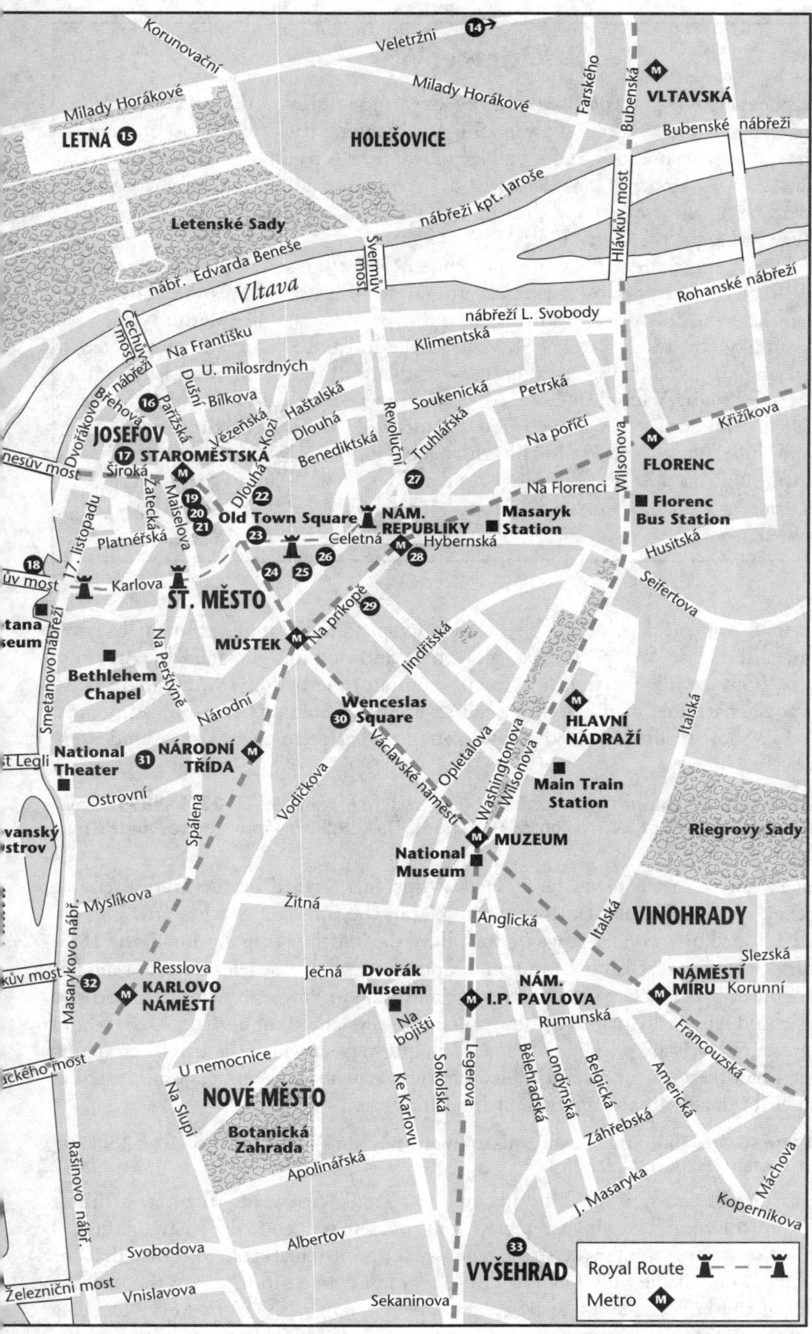
LETNÁ
HOLEŠOVICE
Letenské Sady
Vltava
VLTAVSKÁ
JOSEFOV
STAROMĚSTSKÁ
Old Town Square
NÁM. REPUBLIKY
Masaryk Station
FLORENC
Florenc Bus Station
ST. MĚSTO
MŮSTEK
Bethlehem Chapel
Wenceslas Square
HLAVNÍ NÁDRAŽÍ
Main Train Station
National Theater
NÁRODNÍ TŘÍDA
MUZEUM
National Museum
Riegrovy Sady
VINOHRADY
KARLOVO NÁMĚSTÍ
Dvořák Museum
NÁM. I.P. PAVLOVA
NÁMĚSTÍ MÍRU
NOVÉ MĚSTO
Botanická Zahrada
VYŠEHRAD
Royal Route
Metro

Points of View

Prague demands that you do a lot of looking (and not just at the guys and gals). You can spend days aimlessly wandering and looking back on the city from an array of vantage points. Hoof it up **Nerudova,** the steep climbing path to Prague Castle, at twilight and look across to the greensward of Petřín Hill and down below to the city, so still and drifting into darkness, and you'll understand why they call Prague the Golden City.

Take your pick of all the spires and domes: The best observation points are the 140-foot-tall **Powder Tower (Prašná brána),** the 500-year-old Gothic fortification that's the only preserved tower from the former city walls (Metro: Náměstí Republiky); the south tower of **St. Vitus Cathedral** at the castle, with a 287-step dizzying ascent to the breathtaking view at the top (Metro: Hradčanská; Tram: 22); the **Prague Television Tower,** the rocketlike ueber-phallis blasting off in the žižkov neighborhood (Metro: Jiřího z Poděbrad); and the **Petřín Tower,** the mini–Eiffel Tower atop Petřín Hill with a fabulous panoramic view (Tram: 22 to Petřín funicular). Admissions range from 25Kč to 30Kč (80¢ to $1).

Another great spot for views is atop **Vyšehrad** hill (see "Working Up a Sweat" below).

a less-than-wonderful guide, it's all worth it to spend a few minutes in the **Mayor's Salon,** a showcase for the murals, glasswork, and curtains designed by Alphonse Mucha. (Guys, while you're in the room, look onto the balcony for an appreciative peek at the backsides of the beefcake statues atop the building's entrance. And, girls, don't feel short-shrifted: Gilded nubile young thangs seem to cavort around every corner elsewhere.)

W. A. Mozart Museum (Bertramka). Mozartova 169, Praha 5. ☎ **02/543893.** E-mail bertramka@comenius.cz. Admission 50Kč ($1.55). Daily 9:30am–5pm. Metro: Anděl; then tram 4, 6, 9, 12, or 14.

When Wolfie came to town, he crashed at this villa, owned by the musical couple František and Josefína Dušek. It was here he put the finishing touches on *Don Giovanni.* Located in a woodsy grove in the hills of the Smíchov neighborhood, the 18th-century classical house is now a museum. Spread over half a dozen rooms is a modest collection of papers related to Mozart's life and time in Prague, a hammer piano and harpsichord reportedly played by him, and even a few strands of his hair. Alas, most of the museum labels are printed only in Czech, but make it worth the trip by arranging a tour when there's a concert scheduled on the pretty outdoor terrace. Call the above number for details about concert schedules and tickets.

Fred and Ginger Building (Rašín Embankment Building). Rašínovo nábřeží (at Resslova), Praha 2. Metro: Karlovo Náměstí.

The cartoonish creation of California architect Frank Gehry and Yugoslav architect Vladimir Milunic, all curving steel, glass, and concrete set beside the Vltava, has taken its place so well on the Prague streetscape you'll find it remarkable to realize that the building is one of the only modern things around. Named for the way the two elements of the building seem to be caught up in a tango, the eight-story "Dancing Building" houses a bar at its base and a much-lauded French restaurant at its crown (see La Perle de Prague under "Whet Your Appetite"). The staggered design of the windows gives the structure motion when seen from afar—check it out from the other side

Cruising the River

Skip the big tour boats and go on your own self-powered float on the Vltava. A couple of boat rental companies have docks on **Slovanksý Ostrov (Slavic Island),** 2 blocks south of the National Theater, with paddlewheelers and row boats seating two to four people available. (Take a good look at how hard those folks are working the sticklike oars on the row boats before you decide which type of boat to take.) Hourly rates for both companies are comparable—50Kč ($1.55) for row boats and 120Kč ($3.70) for paddlewheelers. The best way to appreciate the water and the romantic city lights is take a lantern-lit ride at night. Weather permitting, the boats operate daily 10am to 10pm.

of the river. It was built in 1996 for a Dutch insurance company amid a row of art nouveau–style apartments and presents a sophisticated forward-looking post-revolution Prague. President Havel owns the building next door and lived in a flat there during the early years of his presidency.

Memorial to the Velvet Revolution. Near Nárdoní třída 20 (at Mikulandská). Metro: Nárdoní třída.

Small and easily overlooked is this simple memorial to the popular uprising that began in Prague and led to the dissolution of the Communist system in what was then Czechoslovakia. Look for a group of bronze hands on the south side of the street commemorating the place where student protesters first clashed with police on November 17, 1989, setting off 3 weeks of dramatic events that led to free elections and dissident Václav Havel's big promotion.

Cathedral of St. Nicholas (Chrám sv. Mikuláše). Malostranské nám., Praha 1. ☎ **02/536 983.** Admission 30Kč (93¢). Daily 9am–5pm. Metro: Malostranská.

This church is critically regarded as one of the best examples of the high baroque north of the Alps. K. I. Dienzenhofer's 1711 design was augmented by his son Krystof's 260-foot-high dome, which dominates the Malá Strana skyline and was completed in 1752. While Prague's smog has played havoc with the building's exterior, its gilded interior is stunning. Gold-capped marble-veneered columns frame altars packed with statuary and frescoes.

Strahov Monastery and Library (Strahovský klášter). Strahovské nádvoří, Praha 1. ☎ **02/2051 6671.** Admission 35Kč ($1.10). Tues–Sun 9am–noon and 1–5pm. Tram: 22.

The second oldest monastery in Prague, Strahov was founded high above Malá Strana in 1143 by Vladislav II. It's still home to Premonstratensian monks, a scholarly order closely related to the Jesuits, and their dormitories and refectory are off-limits. What draws visitors are the monastery's ornate libraries, holding more than 125,000 volumes.

Lennon Wall. Velkopřevorské náměstí, Praha 1. Tram: 12 or 22.

Perhaps it was the Beatles after all who helped the West win the Cold War. After singer John Lennon's 1980 assassination in New York, Prague mourners spray-painted a huge image of the peacenik poster child on a Malá Strana garden wall, and it became a rallying place for visual anti-government sloganeering. Over the years, the wall has been decorated with pro-democracy and other slogans, despite the government's attempts to keep it whitewashed. Look for Lennon's image (which was slowly being chipped away by the weather and souvenir hounds but was restored in late 1998) near Charles Bridge, across from the French Embassy on the path leading to Kampa Park.

GAY PRAGUE

Being gay surely has its Kafkaesque moments (for Kafka's grave, go to the New Jewish Cemetery), but Prague doesn't yet boast any especially gay street or neighborhood or any gay monuments. If you don't want to hit the bars looking for local gay life, there's always the opera. And Prague has more opera houses than plenty of cities have decent bars. Productions run in repertory, so you can see some of the greatest hits or fill in some gaps in your own opera repertoire by choosing from more than a dozen productions over a week's time, from *Aïda* to *The Magic Flute*. You can pick up tickets, often at the last minute, for as little as $5. (For more information on the opera, see "All the World's a Stage.")

PARKS, GARDENS & SQUARES

Prague is blessed with many fine public spaces. The old heart of the city is **Old Town Square (Staroměstské náměstí),** an expansive pedestrian space that overstimulates with all its activity, both human and architectural. It's like inhabiting a large outdoor room walled by an awe-inspiring collection of monuments, from the Gothic witchiness of **Týn Church** to the high baroque of the **Cathedral of St. Nicholas** to the haunting sculpture honoring religious martyr **Jan Hus.** The square is a giant stage for tourists, and at one time or another you'll join them in standing before **Old Town Hall (Staroměstská radnice)** and looking up at its **Astronomical Clock,** the 15th-century timepiece that does a little animated number on the hour (8am–8pm) as figures of saints and skeletons dance about; the clock is meant not to tell time but to mark the phases of the moon, the equinoxes, the seasons and day, and innumerable Christian holidays. (According to legend, after the timepiece was remodeled at the end of the 15th century, clock artist Master Hanuš was blinded by the Municipal Council so he couldn't repeat his fine work elsewhere. In retribution, Hanuš threw himself into the clock mechanism and promptly died. The clock remained out of kilter for almost a century.) If you want to go for a little spin of your own, horse-drawn carriages line up in the square until 10pm nightly (about 500Kč/$15 for a 20-minute ride). Walking south from here to Wenceslas Square is like leaping ahead several centuries in time.

Wenceslas Square (Václavské náměstí) is one of Prague's most famed squares, and the broad avenue leading up to the equestrian statue of the square's namesake, King Wenceslas, and the National Museum has been the site for many major political upheavals over the years (most recently, the massive gatherings during the 1989 Velvet Revolution). Today it has a thoroughly big-city capitalist bustle, with tall buildings on each side dating to the turn of the century, cars and cabs zooming about, and people parading up and down among the hotels, shops, and restaurants. At night the activity doesn't slow, from the flashy neon signs to the prostitutes to the vendors selling food that tastes good only after 2am.

Many of Prague's subtler charms are more hidden away, especially the gardens and courtyards so prevalent across the river in **Malá Strana,** home of many old palaces and churches. Hidden behind 30-foot walls is the **Wallenstein Garden (Valdštejnská zahrada),** a lovely green space in the baroque style connected to Wallenstein Palace, Prague's largest. The quiet oasis contains a series of leafy paths and classical bronze statues and is a site of summer concerts.

It's always good to be a king (or a queen), and the **Royal Garden (Královská zahrada),** on the north side of Prague Castle, is one of the most beautifully tended in the city, full of lemon trees, shrubbery, and fountains. The **Garden on the Ramparts (Zahrada Na Valech),** on the city-side ramparts below the castle, offers groomed lawns and shrubbery as well as views of the castle above and the city below.

A couple of other nice parks in the city center are **Kampa Park,** the sliver of an island at Charles Bridge affording picturesque views of boats on the river and a grass lawn for picnicking and lazing about, and **Letná,** a rather overgrown area with nice views of the bridges, a giant metronome (atop the pedestal that once held the world's largest Stalin monument), and several cafes. Letná is also a popular gay cruising spot (see "In the Heat of the Night" below).

BOYS ON THE BEACH

The unofficial gay "beach" in Prague is a rooftop terrace at the city's largest public watering hole, **Stadion Podoli,** Podolská 74, Praha 4 (☎ **02/6121 4343**), an enormous indoor/outdoor complex along the river about half an hour from the city center. Look for a three-story building that vaguely resembles a motel, directly south of the main pavilion. While children and families frolic below on the water slides and in the Olympic-size outdoor pool, gay Czech men, young and old and in varying stages of undress, soak up the sun from a private perch with a nice westward-facing vista of the river valley. Queue up to buy a 1-hour pass for 40Kč ($1.25) and keep a 100Kč bill handy as a deposit on a lock. Take tram no. 3, 17, or 21 south along the river from Karlovo naměsti.

WORKING UP A SWEAT

Gym devotees can work out in style at Prague's poshest facility, the **Fitness Club** at the Hotel Inter-Continental Praha, Curieových náměstí 43–45, Praha 1 (☎ **02/2488 1525;** Metro: Staroměstská; open Mon–Fri 6am–11pm, Sat–Sun 9am–10pm). A one-time pass costs 150Kč ($4.65) for the gym only or 400Kč ($12) for the pool, sauna, and gym; there are extra charges for aerobics and use of a putting green. You enter the club from a separate entrance on the hotel's river side.

You're likely to see bigger arms than anywhere in Prague at the muscle-head gym in the **Hotel Axa,** Na Poříčí 40 (☎ **02/232 9359;** Metro: Náměstí Republiky; open Mon–Fri 7am–10pm, Sat–Sun 9am–6pm). One central room holds fixed and free weights, half a dozen exercise bikes, and other cardio equipment, plus a handful of gym bunnies in leotards. The club operates independently of the hotel. The cost is 70Kč ($2.16) for one visit or 600Kč ($19) for 10 days. A 1-hour massage is impossible to resist at 200Kč ($6). Also at the Axa is the best pool for lap swimming (open Mon–Fri 6am–7am and 5pm–10pm, Sat–Sun 9am–8pm). It'll run you 1Kč (3¢) per minute with a deposit of 100Kč ($3.10). For information, call ☎ **02/232 3967.**

Running and biking outdoors can be rough in a city of cobblestone streets. A place with smooth leafy paths and a dramatic setting overlooking the city is the ancient fortification at **Vyšehrad.** Closer to the center of town is **Letná Park,** across the river from the Hotel Inter-Continental.

5 Hitting the Stores

Prague is still catching up to the consumer culture we in the West have perfected. And because its ancient streets and storefronts weren't laid out according to some developer's master plan, ferreting out the special places takes some legwork. But you'll be rewarded for your curiosity, especially when you take your shopping adventure off-road in Staré Město and Malá Strana and descend a steep stairway, pass into a courtyard, or turn down some narrow path and stumble across a fab little shop.

The major tourist-trodden ways—especially **Karlova** from Old Town Square to Charles Bridge and along **Nerudova,** the steep path leading up to the castle—are naturally lined with shops selling souvenir trinkets. Most conspicuous of all the shopping streets, **Wenceslas Square** is a bustling boulevard where capitalism is splashily on display, from the gigantic neon signs atop the buildings to the Euro-mallrats patrolling the stores (mostly middlebrow, with a few high-end boutiques, such as DKNY, thrown in).

Here and throughout Prague, look for other stores tucked away in ***pasáž* (passages),** basically off-the-street minimalls sheltering from a handful to several dozen stores (one of the most historic passages, **Lucerna,** was designed by the grandfather of Czech president Václav Havel). Wenceslas Square runs perpendicular into the brick pedestrian path of **Na příkopě,** another congested shopping street (heads up, gym boys: bilevel Adidas shop ahead!). A third major shopping street, once one of Prague's most fashionable, is pedestrian **Celetná,** connecting Old Town Square to náměstí Republiky.

Funny how a street lives up to its name: One of the toniest in Prague is ✪ **Parížska (Paris Street),** lined with a splendid collection of neo-baroque and art nouveau buildings running northwest from Old Town Square toward the river. Some of the biggest names in French fashion are represented here, including **Hermès, Vuitton,** and **Dior,** as well as **Ricci** and **Leica.** Other big-name fashionistas are setting up shop in other parts of Old Town: **Versace** and **Ungaro** around the corner from the Obecni dům (Municipal House); **Escada** in Malé Náměstí (literally a "small square" off Old Town Square); **Kookaï** at Viva Diva, Karoliny Světlé 12; and **Hugo Boss** at Jungmannovo nám. 18.

Aside from a porn shop, Prague doesn't have any shops with obvious interest to gays and lesbians. Yes, times are still hard for people shopping for rainbow-pride mouse pads and "I'm Not Gay But My Boyfriend Is" T-shirts. As one local says, "Gay hasn't hit yet." But there are a few areas with a queerish counterculture sensibility where hipster homos will find some kinship, starting with ✪ **Saská** (Metro: Malostranská; Tram: 22), known locally as the "small street" because it's really small (size doesn't matter, remember). Over the last few years, a string of trendy shops has set up on this lane south of Charles Bridge in Malá Strana. And on the other side of the river, near Old Town Square, is a **passage** at Jilská 22 (Metro: Národní třída) that meets all your Gen-X needs, including vintage, skater, and clubwear; alternative records (trance to techno); shoes; and a tattooing/piercing salon.

If you're looking for other edgy stuff, keep your eyes peeled for ***Streetwise,*** a slick bilingual booklet of "underground" shops, complete with a map. It's distributed through some of the hipper boutiques and record shops. For info about where to pick up a copy, call ☎ **02/0603 46 5135.**

SHOPS A TO Z

Shops generally open weekdays 9am to 6pm and close at 1 or 2pm on Saturday, but many businesses, especially around Old Town Square, keep longer hours.

ART & ANTIQUES Antiques shops are plentiful. Just look for signs of BAZAR, ANTIK, or ANTIKVARIA'T (the latter for rare books, maps, and prints).

Junkers will appreciate a couple of places where you can find something that fits into your suitcase: **Vetešnictví,** Saská 3, Praha 1 (☎ **02/9004 1985;** Metro: Malostranská), a small Malá Strana shop crammed with wonderful old things like watches, clocks, figurines, keys, coins, costume jewelry, toys, glassware, porcelain decorative objets, and paintings; and ✪ **Art Deco Galerie,** Michalská 21, Praha 1 (☎ **02/261 367;** Metro: Můstek), a creaky-floored Old Town shop that feels like the attic of your pack-ratting great aunt, with most items from that stylish era between the wars, such as furniture, lamps, clothing, hats, shoes, and perfume bottles, including many items adorned with the images of women.

✪ **B&F Keramika,** Nosticova 8/740, Praha 1 (☎ **02/9004 1744;** Tram: 12 or 22), is an out-of-the-way shop in Malá Strana, near Kampa Park, that specializes in beautiful ceramics made on the premises. Another unique ceramics dealer is ✪ **Broc and Brole,** Lazenská 7, Praha 1 (☎ **02/534 570;** Metro: Malostranská), on a charming square near Charles Bridge; it represents the colorful contemporary works of Czech artist Sylvia Choisullova, who has produced everything from tableware to pitchers and jugs to tea cups. Owners Annemarie and Nicolas Aver, married architects (she's Dutch, he's French), have filled the two-room shop with beautiful antique furniture and collectibles. They're also a great source on the latest area restaurants.

BOOKS The best-stocked foreign-language bookstore is **U Knihomola,** Mánesova 79, Praha 2 (☎ **02/627 7767;** Metro: Jiřího z Poděbrad), with a range of fiction and nonfiction, some of it rather brainy, and a good selection of art and coffee-table books. Most of the stock is in English, but there are sections in Czech, French, and German. Downstairs is a relaxing cafe where you can sit with a new purchase and order everything from a continental breakfast to sandwiches to a tasty carrot cake.

Equal parts coffeehouse and bookstore, the ✪ **Globe,** Janovského 14, at Heřmanova, Praha 7 (☎ **02/6671 2610;** Metro: Vltavská), is the city's biggest English-language bookstore. It's cozied up with sitting chairs and Oriental rugs, and you can pick up the "essential" English-language reading matter *(Details, Vogue)* and browse the tall shelves of 10,000 new and used books, including paperback mysteries, Czech literature, and a few gay and lesbian titles (in the "Erotica and Sexuality" section, where else?).

The only English-language shop near the center of town is the tiny **Big Ben Bookshop,** Malá Štupartská 5, Praha 1 (☎ **02/231 8021;** Metro: Náměstí Republiky), a good place to pick up some gifts among the volumes of Kafka and Kundera, coffee-table books, and nice sections on travel, children's books, and history. The shop also carries the *New York Review of Books,* the *Wall Street Journal, USA Today,* and the *International Herald Tribune.*

CONDOMS The first condom shop in the Czech Republic, **Kondomerie,** Karolíny Světlé 9, at Národní, Praha 1 (☎ **02/9000 1526;** www.kondomerie.cz; Metro: Národní třída), debuted in 1997 not far from the National Theater. The inviting boutique cleverly displays 250 kinds of jimmies from half a dozen countries, as well as women's condoms, lube, and other novelties. Gift wrapping is available.

CRYSTAL You can't help but stumble over Bohemian crystal everywhere you look in Prague, but you'll have to do some comparative shopping to get the best quality and best prices. Even if you have no intention of buying, it's worth wandering into world-famous ✪ **Moser,** Na Příkopě 12, Praha 1 (☎ **02/2421 1293;** Metro: Můstek), the country's leading crystal manufacturer. The second-floor showroom is a museumlike space with stained glass, inlaid paneling, Oriental rugs, and chandeliers. Another big showroom (but with less of an intimidation factor) is **Celetná Crystal,** Celetná 15, Praha 1 (☎ **02/232 4022;** Metro: Náměstí Republiky), with three floors of crystal, garnets, porcelain, jewelry, and traditional arts and crafts.

FASHION The best source for body-conscious women's and men's clubwear, produced by about half a dozen Prague designers, is **Faux Pas,** Újezd 26, at Řični, Praha 1 (☎ **02/5731 5261;** Tram: 12 or 22). You'll find racks of rubber skirts, latex corsets, metal bras, and teeny miniskirts and tops. Gay fashion designer Josev Čechota has developed a collection of men's clingy shirts, including some practical T-shirts with pockets sized especially for condoms.

A couple of shops on Saská (Metro: Malostranská), a tiny street in Malá Strana below Charles Bridge, are colorful **Devátá Vlna** (☎ **02/781 2972**), carrying original work from young designers, with club and street wear for men and women, as well as handbags, outerwear, and more. **Mýrnyx Týrnyx** (☎ **02/297 938**) brings a little bit of Melrose Avenue to Prague. That's because this small vintage clothing shop, one of the first in Prague, was set up by an expat from Los Angeles. Owner Maya, who's made Prague home for the last few years, was happy to proclaim her bisexuality on my visit to her shop, named for the German expression meaning "to each his own." Some of her garments, collected on buying trips to the States and increasingly from Czechs cleaning out their closets, have appeared in fashion spreads in the Czech versions of *Cosmo* and *Elle;* she also puts on fashion shows at clubs (often putting men in skirts and other genderbending mischief) and runs an alternative modeling agency.

British clothier **Red or Dead,** Myslíkova 31, Praha 1 (☎ **02/2491 9219;** Metro: Karlovo Náměstí), recently brought an outlet to Prague selling its sporty youthful (if pricey) fashion with a retro flair, featuring cool men's shirts and pants, women's separates, shoes, and backpacks. When you want to look good underneath it all, **Anima Tua,** Na přikopě 23, Praha 1 (☎ **02/2163 7166;** Metro: Můstek), in the Rathova Passage, specializes in sexy designer underwear and swimwear for women and men, as well as women's tiny party dresses and some men's shirts.

JEWELRY A few blocks off Staré Město, the factory store of **Granát Turnov,** Dlouhá 30, Praha 1 (☎ **02/231 56 12;** Metro: Staroměstská), has two large showrooms of ruby-colored Bohemian garnets, the Czech national gem, which can be set in an array of gold and silver jewelry.

MARKETS With an array of artists hawking their endeavors, **Charles Bridge** is always a veritable open-air market. The biggest market in the city center is **Havel's Market (Havelské Tržiště),** Havelská at Melantrichova, Praha 1 (Metro: Staroměstká), a short street completely taken over by nearly 100 covered stalls of fruit and vegetables, fresh flowers, and plenty of random tchotchkes. The vendors are open daily 8am to 6pm.

Nearby on a parallel street, **V Kotcích,** are a bunch of junky souvenir stands, but isn't it always nice to know where you can get a "The KGB Is Still Watching You" T-shirt? A small **produce market** is held daily behind the Tesco department store near the Národní třída Metro station.

SHOES Serious shoe fetishists should pay their respects at the temple of footwear that is ✪ **Bat'a,** Václavské nám. 6, Praha 1 (☎ **02/2421 8133;** Metro: Můstek). At the head of Wenceslas Square, it boasts one of Prague's most extensive selections of shoes under one roof, both men's and women's and everything from gym shoes to comfy walking wear, plus belts, socks, hose, belts, and other accessories. For shoes with a hipper edge, make tracks to **Tunel,** Jilská 22, Praha 1 (☎ **02/2423 2708;** Metro: Staroměstská), a compact Old Town boutique that carries mostly English-made leather boots and sandals, snazzy Italian shoes, and some club fashion.

TOYS & PUPPETS Some of the finest Czech hand-carved wooden toys are sold in Old Town at **Dřevěné Hrăky,** Karlova 26, Praha 1 (☎ **02/496 873 87;** Metro: Staroměstská). You'll find all sorts of unpainted animals, mobiles, trains, mice on wheels, helicopters, skiers, weightlifters, and hand-decorated Easter eggs. You probably wouldn't want to let kids get their hands on some of the stuff at Malá Strana's ✪ **Obchod loutkami,** Nerudova 47, Praha 1 (☎ **02/53 00 65;** Metro: Malostranksá), carrying some creepy puppets in the form of ghosts of old Prague (hookers with exposed breasts, bug-eyed chaplains, four-armed thieves), as well as G-rated marionettes of musicians, royalty, clowns, storybook characters, and so on.

6 All the World's a Stage

Even before you ever set foot in one of Prague's magnificent concert halls or theaters, you'll see that the arts are deeply rooted here. Sure, the locals may be playing up to outsiders' expectations, but it's still an unexpected pleasure to stumble across a trio of young violinists performing an impromptu concert or a solitary middle-aged soprano singing "Ave Maria" on a side street off Old Town Square.

This is all for free, but for a few crowns more you can sample some of the rich cultural offerings in a city known for its devotion to opera and music. Sometimes it's worth the price of admission just to see the richly ornamented theaters the Czechs have so proudly established.

And while high culture has long enjoyed widespread support, the collapse of communism has been music to the ears of young Praguers, who now flock to the city's burgeoning club scene.

GETTING TICKETS Stick out your hand as you walk down the street and it'll soon be flush with handbills advertising Mozart arias and church concerts. Concerts are held nearly every day in venues all over the city, so it's easy to find one to attend at the last minute if you're feeling spontaneous.

If you're one of those planning kinds of people and want to ensure your seat, you can pick up tickets to cultural events at many hotels in town or at one of the **Prague Tourist Information Centers** (see "Visitor Information"). Of the several ticket services (which naturally charge an extra fee), **Ticketpro,** Salvátorská 10, near Old Town Square, Praha 1 (☎ **02/2481 4020;** www.ticketpro.cz; open Mon–Fri 9am–5pm), sells tickets to nearly everything in town, from operas to rock concerts to theatrical performances. Tickets to the State Opera are sold exclusively through **Bohemia Ticket International,** Malé nám. 13, Praha 1 (☎ **02/2422 7832;** www.ticketsBTI.csad.cz; open Mon–Fri 9am–6pm, Sat to 2pm), or Na příkopě 16, Praha 1 (open Mon–Fri 9am–6pm, Sat to 4pm, Sun 10am–3pm), which also sells passes to classical music and theater.

Pick up monthly listings of concerts and performances through the Prague Tourist Center, browsing the weekly listings in the English-language ***Prague Post,*** or skimming the freebie newsletter ***Do Město/Downtown.***

THE PERFORMING ARTS

OPERA & CLASSICAL MUSIC The **National Opera,** the country's leading company, isn't among the world's best, but its productions are solid and international stars occasionally join the cast. Performances are staged at the **National Theater (Národní divaldo),** Národní 2, Praha 1 (☎ **02/2491 3437;** Metro: Národní třída), on the banks of the Vltava River. The theater was founded in the mid-19th century to nurture Czech language and culture during a time of German dominance. The current golden-topped building, designed in an opulent late Renaissance style, was built in 1883 with funds contributed by the Czech people (an earlier theater burned). It's the setting for ballet and opera of both classical Czech and world repertoires, as well as dramatic theatrical performances.

A 1992 split led to the creation of the **Prague State Opera,** which has found a home in a beautiful 1887 German opera hall, the **State Opera House (Státní opera),** Wilsonova 4, Praha 2 (☎ **02/265 353;** Metro: Muzeum). The company tends to stick to classics in the original language by Verdi, Puccini, and Wagner, with the fabulous sets and costumes you'd expect. Mozart operas are also regularly performed at the lovely ✪ **Estates' Theater (Stavovské divaldo),** Ovocný třída 1, Praha 1 (☎ **02/2421 5001;** Metro: Můstek). The pale green classically inspired theater, built in 1783, had the distinction of staging the 1787 world premiere of *Don Giovanni* and retains its appearance from the time when Mozart held the baton on opening night. (Czech filmmaker Miloš Forman used the theater in his *Amadeus.*) Today the Estates' has no resident company but usually plays host to Mozart operas, as well as theater and ballet.

Prague's leading classical music group, the **Czech Philharmonic Orchestra,** was established late in the 19th century, with its first concert led by the celebrated Czech composer Antonín Dvořák. It favors Czech composers like Dvořák, Smetana, and Janáček and performs in Dvořák Hall at the stately **Rudolfinum,** Alšovo nábřezi 12, Praha 1 (☎ **02/2489 3111;** Metro: Staroměstká), which cuts an impressive neo-Renaissance profile on the river's edge with its pantheon of statuary of beloved artists and composers. The building (the "House of Artists") is home to both the Czech Philharmonic and the renowned ✪ **Prague Spring International Music Festival,** held for more than half a century. With performances held at concert halls and churches around Prague, the festival traditionally begins May 12 on the anniversary of Smetana's death with a performance of his "My Country" and closes on June 4 with Beethoven's "9th Symphony." (For ticket information, contact ☎ **02/530 293** or www.festival.cz.)

A second orchestra in town is the **Prague Symphony Orchestra,** which leans toward more adventurous works from the 20th century. It performs in the sublimely restored Smetana Hall (Smetanova sín), the centerpiece of the **Municipal House (Obecní dům),** náměstí Republiky 5 (☎ **02/2200 2336;** Metro: Náměstí Republiky). Beside the Prague Symphony, the concert hall is busy with a variety of chamber and performing groups.

The garden at **Bertramka,** Mozartova 169, Praha 5 (☎ **02/543 893;** Metro: Anděl, then tram 4, 6, 9, 12, or 14), the villa where Mozart often stayed when he visited Prague and now a Mozart museum, is the setting for summer concerts, operas, and chamber music festivals.

Concerts are regularly scheduled at the **Týn** and **St. Nicholas** churches in Staré Město (Old Town Square), **St. Nicholas Church** in Malostranské náměstí in Malá Strana, and **St. Vitus Cathedral** at Prague Castle.

THEATER Theater has long played a leading role in Czech life, most recently as a staging ground for the 1989 Velvet Revolution; today some of the country's appeal is inspired by its playwright-president Václav Havel.

Dramatic works are staged nightly in more than a dozen professional theaters, including the **National Theater** (see above), though most shows are performed in Czech. One of the few English-language theaters, **Misery Loves Company,** in the Celetná Theater, Celetná 17, Praha 1 (☎ **02/232 68 43;** Metro: Náměstí Republiky), performs a repertoire drawn from original plays written by all those starry-eyed young writers who've flooded Prague over the last decade.

There's no language barrier in two theatrical forms indigenous to the Czech Republic. Puppet theater has a long history in the country, and several companies stage shows in Prague. The best of the bunch, the **National Marionette Theater (Národní divadlo marionet),** Žatecká 1, Praha 1 (☎ **02/232 2536;** Metro: Staroměstká), has made a name for itself with its long-running spirited adaptation of Mozart's *Don Giovanni.*

Another popular theatrical genre is black-light theater, a kind of pantomime performed in the dark with performers and props coated in a luminescent stage paint, and half a dozen theaters produce this kind of unusual work. Along the same lines, **Laterna Magika (Magic Lantern),** Národní 4, Praha 1 (☎ **02/2491 4129;** Metro: Národní třída), a multimedia theater in a new wing of the National Theater, employs optical tricks with lighting, projections, film, song, dance, and performance. While the theater was considered avant-garde a while ago, today some would say it has lost its, er, magic.

DANCE Prague's dance scene takes a backseat to opera and classical music, but the **National Ballet Theater** (☎ **02/2491 2673**) fills the house at the National Theater (see above) with a repertoire of traditional ballet as well as a few unusually inspired modern storylines.

LIVE-MUSIC CLUBS

Prague's most established jazz club is **Reduta Jazz Club,** Národní 20, Praha 1 (☎ **02/2491 2246;** Metro: Národní třída; open daily 9pm–midnight; cover 120Kč/$3.70 some nights), an intimate room where no one is more than 50 feet from the stage. The musical bill spans Dixieland to modern, and the club books a mix of ensembles and soloists, both Czech and touring foreign acts like Wynton Marsalis. The club dates to 1958, making it one of the oldest in Europe, but it has achieved acclaim for a couple of nonprofessional jazzmen who performed in 1994: President Bill Clinton and Czech President Václav Havel.

Another key venue is **AghaRTA Jazz Centrum,** Krakovská 5, Praha 1 (☎ **02/2221 1275;** e-mail: artarec@vol.cz; Metro: Muzeum; open Mon–Fri 5pm–midnight, Sat–Sun 7pm–midnight; cover 80Kč/$2.50). Nightly shows kick off at 9pm, and it hosts a popular jazz festival in June. And for a place with unbeatable atmosphere, find your way to ✪ **Jazz Club Železná,** Železná 16, Praha 1 (☎ **02/2423 9697;** Metro: Staroměstská; open daily 3pm–1am; cover 80–120Kč/$2.50–$3.70). It's off Old Town Square through a *pasáž* (passage) and deep underground in a Gothic cellar, where all the architectural stonework is aglow with lighting. Music begins each night at 9pm, and the club brings in everything from Latin fusion to Hungarian avant-garde jazz. Sharing the space is a small CD shop and even a resident white rat (caged in a lofted lounge area).

For alternative rock, electronic, and whatever else the kids are listening to, head to the **Roxy,** Dlouhá 33, Praha 1 (☎ **02/2481 0951;** Metro: Náměstí Republiky; open daily 9pm–6am; cover 100–160Kč/$3.10–$5), a converted theater run by a Czech cultural organization. In the edgy Zižkov neighborhood, **Palác Akropolis,** Kubelíkova 27, Praha 3 (☎ **02/697 6411;** www.spinet.cz/akropolis; Metro: Jiřího z Poděbrad; open daily 7pm–5am; cover 90–300Kč/$2.80–$9), is a kind of avant-garde cultural center presenting everything from jazz and world music to alternative rock to theater. And in the tiny basement of the Malá Strana pub **U Malého Glena,** Karmelitská 23, Praha 1 (☎ **02/535 8115;** Metro: Malostranská; open daily 10am–1am; cover 50–80Kč/$1.55–$2.50), look for live blues and jazz nightly, beginning around 9pm.

7 In the Heat of the Night

While some ambitious new bars and quasi-restaurant/clubs have generated fresh energy, Prague's nightlife hasn't yet made a claim to fabulousness. But if only because the narrow streets and alleys of areas like Old Town and Malá Strana are cast after dark in a spooky romantic glow, this is a city worthy of nocturnal exploration. The Czech pub tradition seems to keep the scene firmly grounded. Most bars put the focus on conversation and beer consumption, not video parades and swizzle-stick cocktails. However, if you're bent on partying toward a sunrise stroll on Charles Bridge, you'll find a diverse array of distractions—from cozy drinking dens to cheesy straight discos to suitably sleazy gay pickup joints to the occasional techno-rave. The crowd swirling through these places is a curious mix of local scenesters, precocious expats, and adventure-seeking tourists. You're bound to engage in some interesting liaisons during your after-hours exploits.

The gay scene is rather limited, and the serious party boy or girl may want to rest up for a trip to London or Berlin. Prague has no "gay area" with a cluster of clubs or shops, but a handful of bars are scattered throughout the Vinohrady and Zižkov neighborhoods, so with a good map and a sense of direction, you can hit a few spots in one evening. Bartenders are often friendly, but you may feel a bit awkward in some of the more intimate bars and pubs. Of course, it's a different story in the dark, where no one knows you're from out of town: Prague has several bars and discos with backrooms, offering ample opportunities to get up close and personal with the natives.

The gay bars here are perfectly legit, though stepping into one may give you the sensation of time travel back to the 1950s. Depending on your view, many bars are either refreshingly unslick or depressingly drab. They're identified with minimal signage, and in most cases you have to ring a bell to notify the door minders of your arrival. (Once inside, you'll become accustomed to the quaint ring of what sounds like a rotary phone.) Exiting often requires the assistance of the door staff too. As you enter, expect to be handed a bar tab in the form of a narrow slip of paper—bartenders use it to track your drinks (it's also a handy way to remind yourself how many *pivo* you've poured back). Before you leave the bar, you'll need to settle your bill with the bartender or door staff.

For the latest on the ever-changing scene, scan the listings in ***SOHO Revue*** and ***Amigo*** (both primary in Czech but with helpful maps of bars) and the gay-friendly weekly ***Prague Post.***

MAINSTREAM BARS & PUBS

When you see the hordes of foreigners arriving by the busload at **U Fleků,** Křemencova 11, Praha 2 (☎ **02/2491 5118;** Metro: Národní třída; open daily 9am–11pm), you'll know it has to be "something." What it is is a 500-year-old German-style beerhall/restaurant that has become a major tourist trap (read: overpriced), with mugs of its own dark beer, oompah bands, and drunks dancing on the tables (and room for 1,200 of them). It's that kind of scary place. But if you can manage to get there in the late afternoon, it's quite pleasant to sit under the beer garden's shade trees.

Another local legend, **Jo's Bar,** Malostranské nám. 7, Praha 1 (☎ **02/530 942;** Metro: Malostranská; open daily 11am–2am), has served as a pickup spot since it opened in 1991 for the precocious expat backpackers and 20-something postcollegiate types who've colonized post-revolutionary Prague. In Malá Strana up the hill from Malostranské náměstí and about 100 meters from the Charles Bridge, the centuries-old space housing the bar has plenty of candle wattage and comfortably worn furnishings in the bar and lounge areas, nice streetfront seating, and a cavelike lower level with a dance floor known as Jo's Garáž. Though it's a pretty hetero spot, everyone passes through here at one time or another, and I've heard of at least one M2M groping incident on the stairway.

While you're in the neighborhood, there are a few other places worth adding to a pub crawl: **St. Nicholas Café,** Tržiště 10, at Karmelitská, Praha 1 (☎ **02/0603 460 570;** Metro: Malostranská; open Mon–Fri noon–1am, Sat–Sun 4pm–1am), is a loungy bar with catacombs, arched ceilings, mismatched cafe chairs, a dozen lamps, and decorative murals, all tucked below street level and entered through a short passage off the main street. **U Malého Glena,** Karmelitská 23, Praha 1 (☎ **02/535 8115;** Metro: Malostranská; open daily 10am–1am), is an American-owned bar (the name translates as Little Glen's) with live blues and jazz every night; it serves sandwiches and other bar food all day. And **Blue Light,** Josefská 1 (☎ **02/531 675;** Metro: Malostranská; open Mon–Fri 6pm–2am, Sat–Sun 4pm–3am; occasional cover), is a romantically decrepit jazz bar with occasional live music and weathered posters of Lionel Hampton, Wynton Marsalis, and even Blind James Brewer from Maxwell Street in Chicago on the walls; this good-vibe place gets an eclectic crowd of people chatting on old wooden stools along the bar or seated close around tables.

A couple of bars popular with the bold and the beautiful create some synergy with their proximity to each other in Old Town: Not a leather bat at all, the **Marquis de Sade,** Templová 8, at Jakobská, Praha 1 (☎ **02/0602 855 937;** Metro: Můstek; open

Mon–Sat noon–2am, Sun 3pm–2am), is a bit of a tease of a name—and its slogan is even worse ("Come Feel the Pain"). This grungy bar is an enormous deep-red room where a rock or alternative band is always playing; there's a shot bar and a casual jeans kind of crowd. Nearby is **Chapeau Rouge,** Jakubská 2, Praha 1 (☎ **02/231 63 28;** Metro: Náměstí Republiky; open daily 4pm–5am), an attitude-filled bar with lighting that casts a sinister glow on its partying crowd pumped up by the DJ's groovy house beats. It's ragingly straight but still feels queer and ambiguous, with lots of guys sporting bleached-out blond hair and piercings. The bar has something of a reputation as a place where it's easy to score drugs (you might even find people lighting up outside) and where slimy guys are prone to paw over the women. Happy hour is 4 to 7pm, when you can get 15Kč (50¢) beers.

Another late-night hangout is the **Banana Cafe,** Štupartská 9, Praha 1 (☎ **02/232 4801;** Metro: Náměstí Republiky; open daily 7pm–1am), on the first floor of La Provence restaurant (see "Whet Your Appetite"). As the night wears on, the bar gets silly with all sorts of go-go dancers and drag queens strutting on stage to the delight of the gawking crowd—it's just odd enough to be interesting.

For something more traditional, try Prague's own Irish pub, **James Joyce,** down the passage at Liliová 10, Praha 1 (☎ **02/2424 8793;** Metro: Staroměstská; open daily 10:30am–1am), where they have the usual Irish brews on tap served up by barkeeps with sexy Irish accents, pretty good Irish food, and strapping rugby players grabbing one another with Guinness-induced straight-guy friskiness. A legend hangs on the wall, "There are no strangers, only friends who have not yet met"—and you can't help wondering how long you need to stick around to meet the team.

GAY CAFES & BARS

Tucked away on a back street in Old Town, ✪ **Cafe Érra.** Konviktská 11, Praha 1 (☎ **02/2423 3427;** Metro: Národní Třída; open daily 9am–11pm), draws all kinds of customers, gay and straight, professional and punk to its colorful cool space. It's a fun spot for a cocktail or a light dinner, and there are two levels of seating, including a cozy basement with a fireplace.

A newish addition not far from Charles Bridge also proving popular with gay Czech professionals is **Friends,** Náprstkova 1, Praha 1 (☎ **02/2163 5408;** www.friends-prague.cz; Metro: Národní Třída; open Sun–Thurs 2pm–2am, Fri–Sat to 5am). This video bar occupies a nicely designed cellar with a scattering of tables and chairs.

Unpretentious **Kafírna U Českého Pána,** Kozí 13, Praha 1 (☎ **02/232 8283;** Metro: Staroměstská; open Mon–Fri 11am–10pm, Sat–Sun 2–10pm), is a cafe/bar near Old Town Square that's a friendly hangout day and night. It's outfitted with a handful of linen-covered cocktail tables and wicker cafe chairs, an overflowing bookshelf of magazines, and lace curtains filtering the natural light streaming in during the day. There are occasional "travesty" (drag) shows. The crowd is skewed older, but cheap beer is cheap beer, so the bar attracts a mix of ages.

If you had a Czech grandmother, her parlor might've looked like ✪ **Klub Stella,** Lužická 10, at šumavaská, Praha 2 (☎ **02/2425 7869;** Metro: Náměstí Míru; open daily 8pm–5am). This laid-back bar, found on a quiet residential street in Vinohrady, boasts loads of atmosphere, with gilt-framed paintings of somebody's dead ancestors, Oriental rugs, and heavy drapes. It's a good launching pad for a night out, but if you're single and feeling blue it doesn't help to watch cute couples pouring cream into each other's coffee or even make-out sessions on the cushy couches and armchairs (my presence on the sprawling corner sofa didn't seem to inhibit my new friend Petra and her pickup). The moody red lighting from the flea-market lamps provides a suitable backdrop for your first (and probably last) taste of the flaming blue elixir known as absinthe—the potent potion made from wormwood and banned nearly everywhere but the Czech Republic. Stella, with a friendly staff and mixed crowd of men and women, has several other rooms, from an intimate nook of a bar to a leafy backyard patio.

Walking into **U Dubu,** Záhřebská 14, Praha 2 (no phone; Metro: Náměstí Míru; open daily 10am–3pm and 6pm–midnight), you might have a tough time realizing you've entered a gay bar. As in many neighborhood Czech pubs, you'll find harsh lighting, storm clouds of smoke (cigarettes are even on the menu, as well as standard pub fare), and a bunch of guys sitting shoulder to shoulder at tables ringing the room. These guys, mostly in their 30s to 50s, give newcomers the same probing stares you'd get walking into any local pub . . . but, of course, the stares here linger just a bit longer.

A local pub in Vinohrady across from the Pavilion Mall, **Hostinec U Hrocha,** Slezská 26, Praha 2 (☎ **02/259 351;** Metro: Náměstí Míru; open Mon–Thurs 9:30am–11pm, Fri to midnight, Sat 10am–midnight, Sun 11am–9pm), isn't immediately obvious as a gay hangout, but watch the body language of some of the ambiguous young patrons and you'll see who's who and what's what. What's more obvious is the trés gay decor (sponge-painted walls, kitchen bric-a-brac) and the campy double-entendre-packed menu headings ("something sweet for your mouth," "how about something small and hot"), but the place is basically open to anyone in search of a heavy mug of beer and a round of darts.

Look for the image of a pink gramophone and you'll be at **U Starého Songu ("By the Old Song"),** Štítného 27, at Miličova, Praha 3 (☎ **02/2278 2047;** Metro: Jiřího z Poděbrad; open Sun–Thurs 6pm–midnight, Fri–Sat to 2am), a romantic kind of place with a musical theme. Once you descend into the cellar and buzz at the rainbow-colored door, three brick-walled rooms unfold festooned with old mandolins, trumpets, zithers, and old 45s. This sit-down place, which serves a Czech/international menu in addition to beer, wine, and champagne, attracts lots of guys on dates, some expats in their 20s and 30s, and Czech guys with fag hags in tow. The music is subdued and tends toward Czech "show tunes" (you might get to hear a rendition of "The Beat Goes On" by Helenou Vondráčkorou). Wednesday is singles night.

The clearly marked **Piano Bar,** Milešovska 10, Praha 3 (☎ **02/627-54-67;** Metro: Jiřího z Poděbrad; Tram: 11; open daily 5–10pm or so), has an antiquey feel and a typical pub layout, with lots of guys sitting around tables chatting. The music is mostly bland pop, the mood low-key, and the beer some of the cheapest you'll find in a gay bar in Prague (15Kč/40¢ for a large draft). A pool table is in front, and the namesake upright piano and local artwork are displayed in back. Look for a younger crowd on Thursdays, when a gay student group congregates here. The bar is near the Prague TV Tower and a pleasant walk from Jiřího z Poděbrad square, which is anchored by an unusual church designed by architect Jože Plěnik (known for his work on Prague Castle).

DRAG BARS

Attention, out-of-work drag queens: Point your pumps toward Prague! After being cruelly deprived of drag shows for half a century under communism, liberated Czechs are relishing their new freedoms. And Praguers, mostly straight, can't seem to get enough of drag (or "travesty" shows, as they're often known in Europe).

Only blocks from the National Theater, **U Střelce,** Karolíny Světlé 12, Praha 1 (☎ **02/2423 8278;** Metro: Národní třída; open Sun–Thurs 6pm–4am, Fri–Sat to 6am), is a dingy basement spot where drag queens lip-synch their hearts out. Expect lots of Czech folk and pop songs and plenty of costume changes. Get there early to guarantee your sight lines in the two cramped rooms. The club is a big hit with straight college types, so guys shouldn't be surprised if inebriated (and oblivious) Czech chicks start hitting on them.

Another travesty venue on the circuit is **Aqua Club 2000,** Husitská 7, Praha 3 (☎ **02/627 8971;** Metro: Florenc, then transfer to bus 133 or 207; shows Wed, Fri, and Sat 10pm–4am), in Žižkov. Make a reservation to get a spot among the mostly young straight women (and their reluctant boyfriends) toting video cameras; they get worked up into a religious fever over the drag artists, including a pretty fierce Tina Turner. The emcee keeps the girls coming one after another, and the appreciative crowd guarantees that every performer gets an encore. (There's also a sauna on site open in late afternoon.)

If you're visiting Prague in summer, you may want to board one of the **drag boat cruises** on the Vltava River, where the queens blow air kisses to tourists strolling along Charles Bridge. Look for details about dates and prices at most of the gay bars around Prague.

A LEATHER BAR

With the usual spooky exterior (a red light and the words PRIVATA KLUB), ✪ **SAM,** Čajkovského 34, Praha 3 (no phone; Metro: Jiřího z Poděbrad; open daily 9pm–4am; cover 50Kč/$1.50, including one drink), is the only serious leather bar in town. The tiny bar is done up with camouflage netting, rubber army boots, and even a helpful hanky chart (it might be a good idea to learn your Czech colors lest you wear a červeny-colored hanky and inadvertently indicate you're into "faust," whatever that is). It gets progressively darker as you venture back, from the small candlelit table up front, to the narrow bar in between, to the sort of anteroom with porn playing, and finally to the dark room. You'll find it easy to "make friends" while squeezing by the small bar. The place gets its share of guys in leather, but otherwise insists on no dress code (there is a small leather shop). Check the schedule for SAM's rotating parties—from underwear nights to "absolutely naked" events.

A LESBIAN BAR

The Czech Republic's first lesbian bar is appropriately called ✪ **A Club,** Milíčova 25, Praha 3 (☎ **02/9004 4303;** Tram: 5, 9 or 26; open Mon–Sat 6pm–midnight, Sun 3pm–midnight; cover 50Kč/$1.50). Located down a spiral staircase, the bar attracts a big sports dyke crowd (ice and floor hockey, basketball) but draws everybody at one time or another. It feels like someone's modern apartment, with high ceilings, comfortable furnishings, and pinkish walls decorated with Mucha prints. There's a pool table, a short menu, and a compact dance floor. The club is welcoming to gay men, but Fridays are exclusively for women.

While A Club is the only lesbian spot in Prague, women can be found in numbers at **U Petra Voka** (below) and **Klub Stella** (above).

DANCE CLUBS

GAY CLUBS Like most cities, the Prague gay dance club scene is mercurial. At press time, the owners of the city's leading gay nightclub, Connection, moved the place nearby to a bigger space and changed the name to **Connection After Dark,** Rokycanova 29, Praha 3 (☎ 02/627 8971; Metro: Florenc or Flora; open Sun–Thurs 10pm–3am, Fri–Sat 9pm–5am; cover 70Kč/$2.20). The club has two bars, a disco, plenty of space to sit and chat, and a de rigueur darkroom.

A reliable dance club that has persisted while others have come and gone, **Tom's Bar,** Pernerova 48, Praha 8 (☎ **02/2481 3802;** Metro: Florenc; open Tues–Sun 9pm–2am, Fri–Sat to 4am; cover 20Kč/62¢), is popular with a fairly young and clean-cut crowd of guys, plus a few butch tattoo boys with shaved heads and tank tops (a practical consideration besides a fashion statement since the club seems about 15° hotter than outside). Everyone seems pretty focused on dancing in this low-ceilinged basement space, with smoke floating over the small dance floor, separated from the bar area by a fence, and the music is happy bubblegum pop that encourages vigorous vogueing and miming. There's also another room with porn and a dark area (watch for pickpockets, as you should in all backrooms).

U Petra Voka, Na Bělidle 40, Praha 5 (☎ **02/530-694;** Metro: Anděl; open daily 8pm–2am; cover 80Kč/$2.50), isn't conveniently located but is worth checking out if you want to visit Prague's oldest gay bar, predating the Velvet Revolution. With a cocktail lounge vibe and a small dance floor, the club won't win any prizes with its black walls crudely decorated with images of erect musclemen and its stuck-in-time DJ play list (Bonnie Tyler, Rick Astley, Tina Turner), but the bar has its partisans, both gays and lesbians, who come to dance and hang out. The doorman is congenial and will call you a taxi.

Discriminating Prague gays have pretty much abandoned the once-popular **L Club,** Lublaňská 48, Praha 2 (☎ **02/9000 1189 536;** Metro: I.P. Pavlova; open daily 8pm–4am; cover 50Kč/$1.50), after rent boys colonized it. You'll find some women here, but they're straight: Believe or not, they're the girlfriends of the (straight) male prostitutes. Still, the music is fun, with a compact dance floor and smoke machine, and you can order pub food too.

MIXED CLUBS The downstairs disco at the hipster expat compound ✪ **Radost FX,** Bělehradská 120, Praha 2 (☎ **02/251 210;** www.techno.cz/radostfx; Metro: I.P. Pavlova; Tram: 4, 6, 11, 16 or 22; open daily 9pm–5am; 50–200Kč/$1.55–$6), is so hyper-trendy that being gay is as fashionable as platform shoes. While any night of the week is worth showing up to groove to some of the best DJs in town (techno to jungle) and enjoy the stylized sci-fi decor, look for gay nights when bouncy go-go boys take the stage and cute youngish crowd turns out. When you're ready to cool down or want a few quiet moments with a new friend, you can move upstairs for late-night munchies in Radost's vegetarian cafe or laid-back lounge.

There's always something interesting—a fashion show, a cool DJ, a concert—on the docket at the dance palace **Roxy,** Dlouha 33, Praha 1 (☎ **02/2481 0951;** Metro: Náměstí Republiky; open daily 9pm–6am; cover 100–160Kč/$3.10–$5), a raw old theater with an underground vibe. The DJ is god up on stage, often with video loops of old Speed Racer cartoons or some Japanese animation projected behind him or her; below, legions of groovy, kinda bratty youngsters (basic raver kids and a few baby dykes) dance alone (lots of spinning and jumping, little balletic moves, and even an Irish jiglike move now and then).

A little out of the way is the mostly straight **Klub Letná,** Veletržní 7, Praha 7 (☎ **02/379 278;** Metro: Vltaská; Tram: 1, 8, 25, or 26; open daily 4pm–6am; cover 50–80Kč/$1.55–$2.50), a happening two-story-high disco featuring some of Prague's young and beautiful, all maddeningly sexually ambiguous. The women are dressed to slay, while the butch guys stick to jeans as their fashion statement. Some patrons are a lesbian's (and a straight guy's) fantasy. Are those two skinny minnies in matching black-and-white-striped tops, black hip-huggers, and stacked heels dancing real close just friends? Are those butch dykes here celebrating a birthday or just straight girls with no-nonsense haircuts? It's all so confusing, and I haven't even mentioned the wildly popular travesty shows. The club is your basic black shell, but the dance floor is equipped with big sound and lights. It's clearly the center of activity, with a raised bar at one end and tiered seating wrapping around. There are also pool tables and video games.

The expat outpost **Jo's Bar** (see "Mainstream Bars & Pubs" above) has a cavelike basement dance floor where a DJ puts on some familiar fun tunes.

A scene in the making is **Mecca,** U Průhonu 3, Praha 7 (☎ **02/5731 2243;** Metro: Haksa; open daily 11pm–3am; cover 120–380Kč/$3.70–$12), a dance club/restaurant/gallery hosting weekend house parties that's been carved out of an old factory and owned by 20-something Roman Řezniček, who owns trendy gayish spots Pálffy Palác and Cafe Érra (see "Whet Your Appetite" above).

DOWN & DIRTY: CINEMAS, SAUNAS & MORE

Male prostitutes, or **rent boys** as they're charmingly called (how about rent Czechs?), are about as ubiquitous in Prague as Bohemian crystal shops. They're often very young emigrants from other Eastern European countries and usually straight. They can spot a foreigner in no time but can be a little tricky to detect themselves. So don't put your vanity too far ahead of your common sense if you find yourself flattered by some guy with awkward subject-verb agreement. He may well be a prostitute. OK, this may be your best offer of the night, but be prepared—in the least he may expect you to pay his bar tab and at the worst he may steal you blind in the night. Rent boys congregate at many of the clubs and often at the main train station, which is a bit of a creepy place late at night.

If you don't want to pay for it, several of Prague's bars and clubs are furnished with backrooms where guests are welcome to get to know one another a little better (wink, wink). The most active outdoor rendezvous is **Letná Park,** across the river from the Intercontinental Hotel at the end of Pařížská. Look for the giant metronome on the hill.

There also are other alternatives for those who prefer a little more privacy when they're dancing in the dark.

Originally opened by an American expat and now part of the William Higgins chain, the we-never-close **Drake's,** Petřínská 5, at Zborovská, Praha 5 (☎ **02/53 4909;** Metro: Andrel; open 24 hours; admission 500Kč/$15), has a small bar up front connected to a corridor of booths for film screenings and private cabins (or "relax rooms"). There are also live strip shows and an erotic shop. The biggest porn venue of its kind in Prague, **Heaven,** Gordazdova 11, Praha 2 (☎ **02/2492 1282;** Metro: Karlovo Náměstí; open Mon–Sat 11am–midnight, Sun 2pm–midnight; cinema admission 100Kč ($3.10) for the day, 50Kč ($1.55) for men 25 and younger), is a branch of a German business that came to town in late 1998. Look for mags, videos, and a cinema. Another place to find gay porn mags, videos, and sex toys is the small **Lambda City Man,** Krakovská 2, Praha 1 (☎ **02/9623 0015;** Metro: Muzeum; open daily 2–8pm), which also sells Czech gay magazines like *Soho Revue* and *Amigo.*

Praguers love their saunas. The newest, biggest, and spiffiest goes by the inspired name of **Babylonia,** Martinská 6, Praha 1 (☎ **02/24 23 23 04;** Metro: Národní třída; open daily noon–3am; admission 190Kč/$6), a clean and pleasant place that opened in 1998 in the center of town near the Tesco department store. At the front bar you might have a friendly chat with a towel-clad Brit expat and his Slovak boyfriend, or you might enjoy a friendlier encounter with one of the other patrons in the steam room, dry sauna, whirlpool, or downstairs cabins.

Other saunas are **Sauna Chaos Klub,** Dusni 13 B, Praha 1 (☎ **02/2423 8510;** Metro: Staroměstská; open daily 5pm–2am; admission 140Kč/$4.30), near Old Town Square, and **Sauna David,** Sokolovská 77, Praha 8 (☎ **02/231 7869;** Metro: Křižíkova; open daily 2pm–2am; admission 150Kč/$4.65), a bit outside the center of town.

8 Side Trips from Prague: Český Krumlov, Karlštejn Castle & Karlovy Vary

The rush of visitors into the new Czech Republic has been concentrated in Prague, but there are several worthy (though not especially gay) destinations in the outlying regions. You can book train tickets and check schedules in Prague at **Čedok,** Na příkopě 18, Praha 1 (☎ **02/2419 7111**). Čedok also arranges tours with guides in several languages. Several other operators also offer day trips (see "Exploring Prague").

ČESKÝ KRUMLOV

If you have time for only one excursion, make it ✪ **Český Krumlov,** 12 miles southwest of české Budějovice (below) and 104 miles south of Prague. It's a living gallery of elegant Renaissance-era buildings housing cafes, pubs, restaurants, shops, and galleries. In 1992, UNESCO named it a World Heritage Site.

The only way to reach Český Krumlov by **train** from Prague is via České Budějovice, a slow ride that'll deposit you at a station far from the town center. It takes 3½ hours; the fare is 136Kč ($4.20) first class or 96Kč ($3) second. From České Budějovice, it's about a 45-minute **drive** to Krumlov, depending on traffic. Take Hwy. 3 leading from the south of České Budějovice and turn onto Hwy. 159. The roads are clearly marked, with several signs directing traffic to the town. From Prague, it's a 2-hour drive.

SEEING THE SIGHTS The town is split into the **Inner town** and **Latrán,** which houses the castle. Begin at the **Okresní Muzeum (Regional Museum)** (☎ **0337/711 674**) at the top of Horní ulice, containing artifacts and displays relating to Český Krumlov's 1,000-year history. The highlight is a giant model of the town. Admission is 20Kč (60¢), and it's open Tuesday to Sunday 10am to 12:30pm and 1 to 6pm.

Across the street is the **Hotel Růže (Rose),** once a Jesuit student house. Built in the late 16th century, the hotel and the prelature next door show Gothic, Renaissance, and rococo influences. Don't be afraid to walk around and even ask questions at the reception desk. Continue down the street to the impressive Late Gothic **St. Vitus Cathedral.** Be sure to climb the tower for its spectacular view.

Continue down the street to **náměstí Svorností.** Few buildings show any character, making the main square of such an impressive town a bit disappointing. The **Radnice** (Town Hall), at Svorností náměstí 1, is one of the few exceptions. Its Gothic arcades and Renaissance vault inside are beautiful. From the square, streets fan out in all directions. Take some time just to wander through them. As you cross the bridge and head toward the castle, you'll see to your right the former **hospital and church of St. Jošt.** Founded at the beginning of the 14th century, it has since been turned into apartments.

The second-largest castle in Bohemia (after Prague Castle), the ✪ **Český Krumlov Chateau** was built in the 13th century. There's a long climb up. First greeting you will be a round 12th-century **tower,** with a Renaissance balcony, and then you'll pass over the moat, now occupied by two brown bears. Next is the **Dolní Hrad** (Lower Castle) and then the **Horní Hrad** (Upper Castle). The château is open April to October, exclusively by 1-hour guided tour. Most tours are in Czech or German. If you want an English-language tour, arrange it ahead by calling ☎ **0337/711 465.** Past the main castle building, you can see one of the more stunning views of Český Krumlov from **most Na Plášti,** a walkway that doubles as a belvedere.

The castle hours are Tuesday to Sunday: May to August 7:45am to noon and 12:45 to 4pm, September 8:45am to noon and 12:45 to 4pm, and April and October 8:45am to noon and 12:45 to 3pm. The last entrance is 1 hour before closing. The tour is 100Kč ($3.10).

WHET YOUR APPETITE Open daily 7am to 11pm, **Rybařská Bašta Jakuba Krčína,** Kájovská 54 (☎ **0337/712 692**), specializes in freshwater fish, with main courses at 120Kč to 300Kč ($3.70 to $10). Trout, perch, pike, and eel are sautéed, grilled, baked, and fried in a variety of herbs and spices. Venison, rabbit, and other game are also available, along with roast beef and pork cutlet. Reservations are recommended.

KARLŠTEJN CASTLE

On the most popular day trip from Prague, people come by the busload 18 miles west of Prague to see the spectacular Romanesque **Karlštejn Castle,** founded in 1348 by Charles IV. However, it's more spectacular outside than inside since vandalism has forced the closure of several of its finest rooms.

Trains leave from Prague's Smíchov Station (at the Smichovské nádraží Metro stop) hourly and take about 45 minutes. One-way second-class fare is 22Kč (68¢). You can also **drive:** Leave Prague from the southwest along Highway 4 in the direction of Strakonice and take the Karlštejn cutoff, following the signs. It'll take 30 minutes.

SEEING THE CASTLE The walk up the hill to Karlštejn, along with the view, makes the trip worthwhile. When you do reach the top, take some time to look out over the town and down the Well Tower. You then need to decide if the 100Kč ($3.10) tour is worth it. Be prepared: The **Holy Rood Chapel,** famous for the more than 2,000 precious and semiprecious inlaid gems adorning its walls, and the **Chapel of St. Catherine** were closed recently—check ahead to see if they'll be open at the time of your visit. What definitely are open are several rooms, most in the south palace. But the tour isn't a total waste of time. The **Audience Hall** and the **Imperial Bedroom** are impressive, despite being stripped of the original furnishings. The castle is open daily: May, June, and September 9am to noon and 12:30 to 6pm; July and August 9am to noon and 12:30 to 7pm; and November and December 9am to noon and 1 to 4pm.

WHET YOUR APPETITE The ✪ **Restaurace Blanky z Valois,** on the main street, tries for a Provençal feel. While this cozy place doesn't exactly take you to France, the covered patio (where all but two of the eight or so tables are located) can be romantic. The food is a cut above the standard, with wild game like rabbit, boar, and venison the specialty. Main courses are 150Kč to 320Kč ($4.65 to $10). The restaurant is open daily 11am to 10pm.

KARLOVY VARY (CARLSBAD)

Charles IV's discovery of **Karlovy Vary,** 75 miles west of Prague, reads like a 14th-century episode of *The Beverly Hillbillies.* According to local lore, the king was out huntin' for some food when up from the ground came abubblin' water. Charles set to work building a small castle in the area, naming the town that evolved around it Karlovy Vary (Charles's Boiling Place). The first spa buildings were built in 1522, and before long notables like Peter the Great, Bach, Beethoven, Freud, and Marx were showing up.

There's definitely something in the water. In May 1998 this western Bohemian town hosted the first-ever Czech gay pride event, a conference and rally that drew about 150 supporters. Perhaps it's no coincidence that the Czech word for fag—*teplouš*—is a shade off the river—the Tepla—that runs through town. (The word means "warm," which the river definitely is not.)

Avoid the ***train*** *from Prague,* which takes over 4 hours. If you're arriving from another direction, Karlovy Vary's main train station is connected to the town center by bus no. 13. Frequent **express buses** arrive from Prague's Florenc station to Karlovy Vary's náměstí Dr. M. Horákové in about 2½ hours. They leave from platform 21 or 22 daily at 7, 9, and 9:40am, noon, and 4pm. Take a 10-minute walk or local bus no. 4 into the town center. You must have a ticket (6Kč/19¢) to board local transportation; buy these tickets at the main station stop or, if you have no change, at the kiosk across the street during regular business hours.

The nearly 2-hour **drive** from Prague to Karlovy Vary is easy. Take Hwy. E48 from the western end of Prague and follow it straight through to Karlovy Vary.

SEEING THE SIGHTS The pedestrian promenades, lined with turn-of-the-century art nouveau buildings, turn strolling into an art form. Nighttime walks take on an even more mystical feel as the sewers, the river, and the many major cracks in the roads emit steam from the hot springs running underneath.

A good place to start is the **Hotel Thermal** at the north end of the old town's center. The 1960s glass, steel, and concrete Thermal sticks out like a sore communist thumb amid the rest of the town's 19th-century architecture (check out the groovy chairs in the lobby). Nonetheless, a good place for sunning is the large outdoor public pool and the hotel's upper terrace, boasting a truly spectacular view. In the same complex are a gym, a sauna, and massage services.

As you enter the heart of the town on the river's west side, you'll see a white wrought-iron gazebo, the **Sadová Kolonáda,** adorning a beautiful park, the **Dvořakový Sady.** Continue on and you'll come to the **Mlýnská Kolonáda,** a long covered walkway housing several springs, which you can sample free 24 hours. Bring your own cup or buy one just about anywhere to sip the waters. When you hit the river bend, you'll see the majestic church of **St. Mary Magdalene** up overlooking the **Vřídlo,** the hottest spring. Housing Vřídlo, which blasts some 50 feet into the air, is the glass building where the statue of Soviet cosmonaut Yuri Gagarin once stood. (Gagarin's statue has since made a safe landing at the Karlovy Vary airport.) Now called the **Vřídelní Kolonáda,** the structure, built in 1974, houses several hot springs you can sample free daily 7am to 8pm. The building also holds the Kuri-Info information center.

Heading away from the Vřídelní Kolonáda are Stará and Nova Louka streets, which line either side of the river. Along **Stará (Old) Louka** are several fine cafes and glass and crystal shops. **Nova (New) Louka** is lined with hotels and the historic town's main theater, built in 1886. Both streets lead to the **Grandhotel Pupp.** Once catering to nobility from all over central Europe, the Pupp still houses one of the town's finest restaurants, the Grand.

Atop the hill behind the Pupp is the **Diana Lookout Tower.** Footpaths lead to the tower through the forests and eventually spit you out at the base, as if to say, "Ha, the trip is only half over." The five-story climb up the tower tests your stamina, but the view of the town is more than worth it. For those who aren't up to the climb just to get to the tower, a cable car runs up every 15 minutes daily 7am to 7pm.

WHET YOUR APPETITE A new addition to the pub scene in town, **Hospoda U Šejka,** Stará Louka 10 (no phone; open daily 11am–11pm), plays on the tried-and-true touristy Good Soldier Svejk theme. Luckily, the tourist trap goes no further—once inside, you'll find a refreshingly unsmoky though thoroughly Czech atmosphere. Locals and tourists alike rub elbows while throwing back some fine lager and pub favorites like goulash and beef tenderloin in cream sauce.

After dinner, bliss out at **Dobrá Čajovna,** Varšarska 13 (☎ **017/323-0623;** open Mon–Fri 11am–11pm, Sat 3–11pm, Sun 3–10pm), a mellow temple of a tearoom that continues Karlovy Vary's tradition as a healing place. Ambient music washes over "The Good Tearoom," a bilevel salon with a pillow-strewn lair on the lower level. Choose from more than 80 varieties of tea from all over the world and notify one of the bald sandal-shoed waiters you're ready to order by ringing a tiny tabletop brass bell. The tearoom's menu also lists a range of simple Mediterranean dishes.

2 England

Cool Britannia

by Donald Olson

Ask anyone who's been to England recently, especially to London, and he or she will tell you it's a "happening" place once again. Now that the conservative Tories led by Margaret Thatcher and her successor, John Major, are finally out and Labourite Tony Blair is in, Rule Britannia has given way to Cool Britannia. The legendary stiff upper lip and impeccably polite manners are still there, but now you'll find a fresh energy and openness and an urge to party.

For gays and lesbians, there's never been a better time to visit England. The queer scene is growing larger, more visible, and more vibrant by the day.

Of course, English gay history (like gay history everywhere) is full of cautionary tales and violent reversals. Just over 100 years ago, a burgeoning gay scene came to an abrupt end with the arrest and imprisonment of Oscar Wilde. Anyone who had been associated with him in even a tenuous way (such as artist Aubrey Beardsley) was ostracized. It's said that on the day of Wilde's 1895 sentencing, the boat trains were packed with frightened men fleeing to the Continent. Under the Sexual Offences Act, which wasn't repealed until 1967, British homosexuals caught in the act could be and often were sentenced to prison (remember the Merchant/Ivory film *Maurice?*). As a result, British gays were forced underground and subject to blackmail and intimidation. *The Naked Civil Servant* by Quentin Crisp (also made into a TV movie) will give you a harrowing picture of English gay-bashing in this century.

It all sounds impossibly archaic to those of us lucky enough to be out today. But official homophobia and prudery reared its ugly head again not too long ago, under Maggie Thatcher. Her government crafted and passed Section 28, legislation forbidding public monies to any program "promoting" homosexuality. And up until a few years ago, British customs officers confiscated works by gay authors, as these were automatically considered "obscene."

On the other hand, when the AIDS epidemic hit, every U.K. household received an informative brochure outlining the dangers of unprotected sex and telling people how to take precautions. It was certainly more than Americans ever got.

But there are still laws on the books, and so there are some things you, as a gay traveler, should know. The U.K.'s legal age of consent is 18 for men and 16 for women. (In mid-1998 the House of Commons voted to lower the age for males from 18 to 16, but the conservative House of Lords squashed it, pulling out every tired old homophobic argument they could think of. At press time, it was still uncertain whether the Commons could break the deadlock.) What you do in private is now your own affair, so long as it's consensual and the legal-age limit is observed. But any form of "public sex" is liable to prosecution. Discretion is the watchword. If you go to the sauna, restrict your activities to your private cubicle. Hard-core porn remains illegal. And gay-bashing isn't unknown—in fact, one out of four gay men polled in London had experienced some form of it.

The British Pound

The British currency is the **pound sterling (£),** divided into 100 **pence (p).** The pound used to be a note, but now it's a heavy coin that makes your pocket bulge. There are also 50p, 20p, 10p, 2p, and 1p coins as well as a £2 coin. Notes come in £5, £10, £20 and £50 denominations.

At this writing, the pound was equivalent to $1.72 U.S., and that was the rate of exchange I used throughout. Prices over $5 U.S. have been rounded to the nearest dollar.

What will happen when the United Kingdom becomes part of the European Union remains to be seen. A recent test case, in which a lesbian British Rail worker sued to get for her partner the same benefits given to heterosexual spouses, failed in the European Labor Court. We can only hope the enlightened antidiscriminatory policy currently in place in the Netherlands will eventually help protect gays and lesbians throughout England and the entire European Union. (Being an American, I have nothing to brag about when it comes to equal rights for gays.)

Politics aside, there are countless pleasures for you to find in what Shakespeare called "this green and sceptre'd isle." England hasn't escaped the fast-moving homogenizing currents of modern life and is in many ways actively shedding its "quaint" image, wanting to promote itself as a player in the modern world. But enough of "old England" remains to charm and beguile the millions who regularly descend on London and spread out through the rest of the country. The country's visible history—seen in ancient monuments like Stonehenge, massive castles, stately homes, magnificent cathedrals, and bucolic villages—easily stirs the imagination. Many of us feel we "know" England already: The works of so many great writers have imprinted indelible images on the mind, in print and in film versions.

Most of my England coverage is devoted to **London,** because that's where everyone goes. And with good reason: The city is a cosmopolitan feast, an inexhaustible treasure trove of art and culture, both high and low, straight and gay and everything in between. London right now is fizzing with homo energy, and you don't want to miss it. While in London, you might want to take a side trip to Henry VIII's **Hampton Court,** Elizabeth II's **Windsor Castle,** or the Regency spa town of **Bath.** I also cover **Brighton,** that charming poofter's paradise by the sea, and **Manchester.** Why Manchester? This Victorian city has taken on a remarkable new life as a gay destination, and I think it's good to explore the untried and new. Alas, space limitations didn't allow me to cover other U.K. cities you might enjoy, such as Edinburgh, Glasgow, and Dublin. I hope to be able to introduce you to gay life in Scotland and Ireland in the next edition.

2

London: The Queen's at Home

London is one of those cities everyone wants to visit. It's "in Europe," sort of, giving it a dash of foreign glamour, but it's linguistically accessible because, as I once heard someone say, "they talk real good English over there." Even my mother, who rarely traveled, had an itch to go to London. When she finally got there and saw Buckingham Palace with her own eyes, she reverently whispered, "Who washes all those windows?"

No matter how you view it, London *is* one of the great cities of the world. It balances the weight of its old traditions with a jumpy, trend-setting, contemporary energy. It loves pomp and ceremony as much as it loves lurid sex scandals. London is the politest city you'll ever visit and also one of the rudest, a hybrid cross between *As You Like It* and *Absolutely Fabulous.*

1 London Essentials

ARRIVING & DEPARTING

BY PLANE Five airports serve the London metropolitan area. **Heathrow** (☎ **020/8759-4321**), the main international airport, is west of the city, on the **Piccadilly Line** of the Underground, so for £3.30 ($6) you can travel by Tube to central London in about 50 minutes. The new **FastTrain** service (☎ **0845/600-1515**) runs between Heathrow and Paddington Station every 15 minutes 5:10am to 10:40pm; it costs £5 ($9) and requires a simple bus transfer between your terminal and the train. The **Airbus** (☎ **020/7222-1234**), which stops at all Heathrow terminals, offers bus service to Victoria and Euston stations for £6 ($10). Buses depart from all four Heathrow terminals at about 30-minute intervals; times vary from terminal to terminal, but generally service is 6:30am to 10:30pm. The A1 route runs from Heathrow to Victoria station; the A2 route to Kings Cross station.

Gatwick (☎ **01293/535-353**), 25 miles south of London, is a smaller airport. **Gatwick Express** trains leave for Victoria Station in Central London every 15 minutes 5am to 11pm and every hour 11pm to 4:30am; the trip takes about half an hour and costs £8.90 ($15).

Stansted (☎ **01279/680-500**), about 50 miles northeast, is used for national and European flights. **Stansted Express** trains leave for Liverpool Street Station every 30 minutes 6am to 11:59pm and to

A Queen's English

Back in the criminally homophobic 1940s and 1950s, British gays developed a secret language, *parlare,* a clever defense stratagem allowing them to carry on queer conversations in public. This camp and extremely complicated mix of pig Latin, rhyming slang, word reversals, and foreign embellishments is, alas, no longer in use. But those who think American English is the same as British English may still find themselves struggling to understand certain gay slang and general expressions.

The words *gay* and *queer* are perfectly acceptable, but you may also hear gays referred to as *poofs* or *poofters, shirt lifters,* or *fudge packers.* (A *fag* to a Brit is either a cigarette or a junior university student assigned to slave for a senior.) In England, you don't go to the bathroom unless you're going to take a bath; you go to the *loo* or the *toilet.* A *cottage* is what Americans call a tearoom (just ask George Michael). A *tearoom* is where you actually drink tea. Your butt becomes a *bum* or an *arse* (also *cupcakes, back porch,* and *love buns*).

Bold guys are *cheeky.* Club queens are *disco dollies*; those who like to clean and iron are *domestic dollies.* Masturbation is *wanking, flogging, tossing off,* and *banging the bishop. Shagging* is what you do with a partner. A label queen is a *tag hag.* A swish is a *ponce.* A male prostitute is a *rent boy.* A rubber is an *eraser* and a condom is a *rubber.* If you "open your purse" you're passing gas. And if you ever say, "I fell on my fanny," the Brits will look at you with astonishment: A fanny in England is a woman's vagina.

Victoria Station every hour 8am to 6pm (then one at 8pm and another at 10pm); the trip takes 40 minutes and costs £11 ($19).

Luton (☎ **01582/405-100**) services mostly charter flights, and trains from the airport will take you to King's Cross Station for £8.10 ($14). And **London City Airport** (☎ **020/7474-5555**), 6 miles east of The City, services European destinations. A blue-and-white bus charges £3 ($5) to take you from the airport to Liverpool Street Station; service is every 10 minutes 6:40am to 10:30pm; travel time is 25 minutes.

BY TRAIN London has several train stations. Trains from Amsterdam arrive at **Liverpool Street Station** and those from Edinburgh at **King's Cross Station.** The fabulous 3-hour *Eurostar* service between Paris and London via the Chunnel arrives at **Waterloo International Station.** If you're traveling to London from elsewhere in the United Kingdom, you may arrive at **Victoria, Paddington,** or **Euston station.** Every train station has an Underground link.

The trains in Great Britain are separate from those in the rest of Europe, so a Eurail pass isn't valid in England. If you're going to be traveling within the United Kingdom, check out the various **BritRail** passes available by calling ☎ **800/677-8585.**

BY FERRY & HOVERCRAFT If you're coming from the Continent, **P&O European Ferries** (☎ **01304/212121**) offers daily ferry/car service between Cherbourg and Portsmouth (3–4 ferries a day; crossing time 5 hours; fare £20/$33 one-way), Le Havre and Portsmouth (1–3 ferries a day; crossing time 5½ hours; fare £20/$33 one-way), and Calais and Dover (24 crossings a day; travel time 75 minutes; fare £24/$41 one-way). **Stena Sealink,** represented by BritRail (☎ **800/677-8585** in U.S. or 01233/615455) runs ferries between Dieppe and Newhaven (2 crossings a day; travel time 90 minutes; fare £24/$41 one-way) and Dover and Calais (15–20 crossing a day; travel time 90 minutes; fare £24/$41 one-way).

The hovercrafts operated by **Hoverspeed** (☎ **01304/340241**) zip across the Channel between Calais and Dover in 35 minutes (6–12 per day; fare £25/$43 one-way); their SeaCats (jet-propelled catamarans) run between Boulogne and Folkestone in 55 minutes (4–5 a day; fare £25/$43 one-way). Once you're on British soil, frequent train or bus service will shuttle you into London.

BY CAR One word of advice for travelers who want to drive into London: Don't. But if you must . . . just follow the signs marked LONDON. From the Channel Tunnel terminal you'll head in on the **M20.** The **M25** and the inner ring of the London **North Circular** and **South Circular** roads connect with most highways from the coast.

Parking spots are at a premium. Your options are a strategically placed expensive garage, valet service at an expensive hotel, or metered parking, in which case you face substantial fines if the meter runs out. The time limit and the cost of metered parking are posted on the meter; they take £1 and smaller coins. Never park in a "Permit Holders Only" zone; these are for locals, and violators are likely to be towed. A yellow line along the curb indicates "No Parking"; a double yellow line signifies "No Waiting." However, at night (meters indicate exact times) and on Sunday, you're allowed to park along a curb with a single yellow line.

VISITOR INFORMATION

The **Britain Visitor Centre,** Rex House, 1 Lower Regent St., SW1 (Tube: Piccadilly Circus; open Mon–Fri 9am–6:30pm, Sat–Sun 10am–4pm), offers information on London and all parts of the United Kingdom. So does the **Tourist Information Centre** in the forecourt of Victoria Station, SW1 (Tube: Victoria; open Easter–Oct daily 8am–7pm and Nov–Easter Mon–Sat 8am–6pm, Sun 9am–4pm). Neither has phone service, but both provide hotel-booking services, theater-ticket agencies, and useful bookshops. The London Tourist Board has smaller offices in the Underground Concourse at Heathrow's Terminals 1, 2, and 3 and at Liverpool Street Station.

Visitorcall at ☎ **01839/123-456** provides 24-hour recorded info on major attractions for 49p (84¢) per minute.

LONDON GAY & LESBIAN EVENTS

For more information on current events, call the **London Lesbian and Gay Switchboard** at ☎ **020/7837-7324** or check out their Web site at **www.lgs.org.uk.**

MARCH The **London Lesbian & Gay Film Festival** marked its twelfth year in 1998 with an impressive roster of films. Screenings are at the National Film Theatre, South Bank, Waterloo (☎ **020/7928-3232**). Held in mid-March at the Business Design Centre in Islington, the **Freedom Fair** is a gay and lesbian consumer exhibition featuring lots of gay and gay-friendly businesses, seminars, workshops, and demonstrations. For details, contact ☎ **020/7793-7450** (www.freedom.co.uk/gaytoz/).

MAY The **Royal Vauxhall Tavern Sports Day** is an annual daylong charity event held behind the Royal Vauxhall Tavern with teams from pubs and clubs around London competing in various events; there's dancing and entertainment. Contact 372 Kennington Lane, Vauxhall SE11 (☎ **020/7562-0833**). The bars and cafes along Old Compton Street (London's gay Village) sponsor **Soho Pink Weekend,** a charity weekend that includes a campy parade through Soho, stage acts, and a costume competition. Thirty guys from around the United Kingdom flex their pecs for the title of **Mr. Gay UK.** You'll need to check local gay listings or call the hot line to find out where the event will be held.

JUNE For the **Gay and Lesbian Tennis Tournament** (☎ **020/7286-1896,** ask for Tony), international contestants of all ages and abilities participate; all proceeds go to the Lesbian and Gay Switchboard and London Lighthouse.

JUNE–JULY London's biggest gay event, **Pride,** began in 1971 to commemorate the Stonewall Riots (in New York); a huge parade winds through central London to the festival ground (location changes every year), where the celebrations begin in earnest. Contact the Pride Trust, Suite 28, Eurolink Business Centre, 49 Effra Rd., Brixton SW2 1BZ (☎ **020/7738-7644**). The **Pride Arts Festival** honors the cultural contributions of gays and lesbians and features a full range of performance art and film screenings.

OCTOBER The annual **Stonewall Equality Show** is a concert headlined by gay and/or gay-friendly celebrity performers, with proceeds going to the lobbying group Stonewall. It's the largest ticketed gay event in Europe. Contact Stonewall, 16 Clerkenwell Close, Clerkenwell EC1R 0DY (☎ **020/7336-8860**).

DECEMBER London participates in **World AIDS Day** to raise awareness of a global epidemic with exhibitions, charity nights, church services, and a concert at Wembley Stadium (☎ **020/7972-2845;** www.wad.hea.org.uk).

CITY LAYOUT

London is an enormous place that has been growing for 2,000 years. In general terms, **Central London** is the area covered by the Circle Line Underground route. Within Central London, the city center is divided into two areas: **The City** and the **West End.** The City is the original 1 square mile the Romans called Londinium; today it's the Wall Street of London. The West End, less clearly defined, is divided into a bewildering plethora of neighborhoods: Soho, Kensington, Mayfair, and so on. Both The City and the West End are girdled by **Inner London,** and Inner London is encircled by the dreary sprawl of **Outer London.** The **river Thames** runs through the city and is another dividing line; if something is on the **South Bank,** it's on the "other side" of the river (nobody calls the rest of London the North Bank, however).

GETTING AROUND

It's simple, so long as you walk, take the Tube, or hail a taxi. **London Travel Information** at ☎ **020/7222-1234** provides 24-hour details about buses and the Underground.

BY UNDERGROUND London's subway, called the Underground or the Tube, is fast and convenient. It's also a great place to cruise and people-watch. You'll find everything in London is cued to the nearest Tube stop. For fare purposes, the city is divided into zones. Zone 1 covers all Central London.

A **single-fare ticket** in one zone is £1.30 ($2.25). You can save lots of money by purchasing a 1-day, weekend, or 1-week ✪ **Travelcard,** allowing unlimited travel by Underground and bus. A 1-day Travelcard for Zones 1 and 2 (everything in Central London) is £3.50 ($6), the weekender £5.20 ($9), and the 1-weeker £13 ($22). You can buy Travelcards at Heathrow Airport and many Underground stations, but you'll need a picture ID.

Most of the Underground system operates with automated entry and exit gates. You feed your ticket into the slot, it disappears and pops up again like a piece of toast, the turnstile bangs open, then you remove your ticket and pass through. At the other end you do the same to get out—but the machine keeps the ticket (unless it's a Travelcard).

The only drawback to the Underground is that service generally stops at 11:30pm. Keep this in mind when you're out partying.

Note: See the front cover of this guide for a London Underground map.

London by Association

Here's an exclusive *Frommer's Gay & Lesbian Europe* trick to help you remember London in simple associative terms.

Knightsbridge = Harrods and shopping

Mayfair = Poshly exclusive

Kensington = Museums and the garden

St. James's = Buckingham Palace

Westminster = The abbey and the Houses of Parliament

Earl's Court = Gay

Soho = Very gay

Leicester Square & the West End = Major theaters and entertainment

Bloomsbury = Russell Square and the British Museum

Piccadilly = Trafalgar Square, Regent Street, and the National and National Portrait Gallery

South Bank = Waterloo Station (*Eurostar*), the Royal Festival Hall, and the Royal National Theatre

BY BUS Yes, they're very picturesque, but unless you have plenty of time or a claustrophobic aversion to the Underground, you're better off on the Tube or walking, since the pace is about the same as the bus. Unless you have a Travelcard, you buy your ticket on board. A **one-zone fare** is 90p ($1.55). Buses run about 6am to midnight; after that, night buses (marked with an "N") run on selected routes only.

BY TAXI Oh, didn't we all love the old-fashioned London taxis. They're still there, but so are many smaller and newer models, all far better than the springless rattletraps careening through New York. Hail a cab from the street. (Its yellow FOR HIRE sign will be lit.) The **fare** starts at £1.40 ($2.40), with 40p (70¢) for each extra passenger. There's an additional 40p (70¢) on Saturday and 60p ($1) on Sunday. But that's not all. After 8pm, another 40p (70¢) is tacked on—except for Saturdays, when it's 60p ($1). After all this, the meter leaps 20p (35¢) every 111 yards. **Minicabs** also cruise the streets, but they don't have meters so you must negotiate the price with the driver before you set off.

Freedom Cab Company at ☎ **020/7734-1313** is the city's first gay and lesbian round-the-clock cab service; **Q Cars** at ☎ **020/8671-0011** is another radio-cab service with gay and lesbian drivers. For a "regular" cab, call ☎ **020/7272-0272** or 020/7253-5000. The meter starts ticking from the time the driver receives the dispatch, of course.

BY CAR London streets are confusing, the traffic is awful, the parking is impossible, and petrol (gas) is incredibly expensive. To make matters worse, the steering wheel on British cars is on the right (but remember you drive in the *left* lane). Any form of transportation is preferable to driving. If you're in London and decide to rent a car to drive out on an excursion, try one of the following: **Avis** (☎ **020/8848-8733**), **Budget** (☎ **0800/181-181**), or **Hertz** (☎ **020/8679-1799**). Of course, you'll get the best deal if you reserve a car before leaving home.

FAST FACTS: London

AIDS Organizations The **National AIDS Helpline** at ☎ **0800/567-123** operates 24 hours. The **Terrence Higgins Trust,** 52–54 Gray's Inn Rd., London WC1X 8JU (☎ **020/7831-0330;** helpline 020/7242-1010 noon–10pm) is London's main AIDS/HIV resource center.

American Express The main office is at 6 Haymarket, SW1 (☎ **020/7930-4411;** Tube: Piccadilly; open Mon–Fri 9am–5:30pm, Sat 9am–4pm). The foreign-exchange bureau is open the same hours as above but Saturday to 6pm and also Sunday 10am to 5pm.

Community Center London doesn't have one all-purpose lesbian and gay community center. Instead, it has dozens of social groups and special-interest clubs that meet weekly or monthly at various places. There's something for everyone: classical music lovers, bears, cross-dressers, gay artists, over 40s—even a gay dog-walking group. Call the **Lesbian and Gay Switchboard** (below) or check the listings in ***Gay Times*** (£2.50/$4.30), London's gay monthly magazine sold at newsagents, or ***Boyz,*** a free weekly available in most gay bars and cafes, for meeting times and places.

Consulates & High Commissions The **U.S. Embassy** is at 24 Grosvenor Sq., W1 (☎ **020/7499-9000;** Tube: Bond St.; open Mon and Wed–Fri 8:30am–noon and 2–4pm, Tues 8:30am–noon). For passport and visa information, go to the **U.S. Passport and Citizenship Unit,** 55–56 Upper Brook St., W1 (☎ **020/7499-9000**, ext. 2563 or 2564; Tube: Bond St. or Marble Arch; open Mon and Wed–Fri 8:30am–noon and 2–4pm, Tues to noon).

The **Canadian High Commission** is in MacDonald House, 38 Grosvenor Sq., W1 (☎ **020/7258-6600;** Tube: Bond St.; open Mon–Fri 8–11am). The **Irish Embassy** is at 17 Grosvenor Place, SW1 (☎ **020/7235-2171;** Tube: Hyde Park Corner; open Mon–Fri 9:30am–1pm and 2:15–5pm). The **Australian High Commission** is in Australia House, on the Strand, WC2 (☎ **020/7379-4334;** Tube: Charing Cross; open Mon–Fri 9am–1pm). The **New Zealand High Commission** is in New Zealand House, 80 Haymarket at Pall Mall, SW1 (☎ **020/7930-8422;** Tube: Charing Cross or Aldwych; open Mon–Fri 9am–5pm).

Currency Exchange There are currency exchange services at all the major airports and train stations. American Express, Thomas Cook, and the post office also provide currency exchange. Major banks, generally open 9:30am to 3pm (sometimes to 5pm) will cash traveler's checks and sterling. You'll pay a commission at all these places (except American Express if you're cashing their traveler's checks) and you'll need to show your passport. Avoid the bureaux de changes on major tourist streets; though they may not charge a commission, their rates aren't as good.

Cybercafe You can check your e-mail or send messages at **Cafe Internet,** 22–24 Buckingham Palace Rd., SW1 (☎ **020/7233-5786;** Tube: Victoria; open daily 9am–9pm).

Directory Assistance For directory assistance, dial ☎ **142** (London), ☎ **192** (within the United Kingdom), or ☎ **153** (international). To reach an operator, dial ☎ **100** (within the United Kingdom) or ☎ **155** (international).

Emergencies Dial ☎ **999** for police, ambulance, or fire.

Country & City Codes

The **country code** for the United Kingdom is **44.** The two London **city codes** (171 and 181) changed in 1999, and now only one code, **20,** is used when calling from outside the United Kingdom. This code is then followed by an eight-digit number beginning with either 7 (for old 171 numbers) or 8 (for old 181 numbers). If you're within the United Kingdom but not in London, use **020** followed by the new eight-digit number. If you're calling within London, simply leave off the code and dial only the eight-digit number.

Hospitals Emergency care is available 24 hours at the **Royal Free Hospital,** Pond Street (☎ **020/7794-0500;** Tube: Belsize Park), and the **University College Hospital,** Glower Street (☎ **020/7387-9300;** Tube: Warren St.).

Hot Lines The **London Lesbian and Gay Switchboard** at ☎ **020/7837-7324** provides information, general support, and tourist advice 24 hours. The **London Lesbian Line** at ☎ **020/7251-6911** (Mon and Fri 2–10pm, Tues–Thurs 7–10pm) offers advice, information, and support for lesbians.

Magazines & Newspapers The most popular freebies, available in gay pubs, clubs, bars, and cafes and useful for their listings, are ***Boyz, Pink Paper,*** and ***QX*** **(*Queer Xtra*).** ***Gay Times*** (£2.50/$4.30) is a high-quality monthly news-oriented mag available at most newsagents. ***Time Out,*** indispensable for its city-wide listings (including gay listings), appears at newsagents on Wednesday.

Radio **GLR Radio** (94.9 FM) has a gay and lesbian London talk show on Thursdays 9 to 10pm. **Radio 5 Live** (909/693 MW) runs a lesbian and gay news and current affairs program on Sundays 10:35 to 11pm.

Telephone British TeleCom (BT) has phone boxes throughout the city. One kind accepts coins, another accepts only phonecards, and the third accepts credit cards (American Express, Diners Club, MasterCard, and Visa), phonecards, and coins. Instead of dealing with coins, it's easier to purchase a **phonecard** from a newsagent or post office. They're priced according to the number of "units" on the card and cost £1 to £20 ($1.70 to $34).

The minimum cost of a **local call** is 10p (16¢) for the first 2 minutes (peak hours). You can deposit up to four coins at a time, but phones don't make change, so unless you're calling long distance, use 10p coins only. Phonecard phones automatically deduct the price of your call from the card, and these cards are especially handy if you want to call abroad. Some large hotels and touristy street corners also have phones that accept major credit cards. Lift the handle and follow the instructions on the screen.

To reach the **local operator,** dial ☎ **100.** London **information** ("directory enquiries") can be reached by dialing ☎ **192,** and there' no charge if you call from a phone box. To make an **international call,** dial ☎ **155** to reach the international operator. To dial direct, dial **00,** then your country code (Australia, 61; New Zealand, 64; South Africa 27; United States, 1), then the local number. You can phone home by dialing a local toll-free number in London and paying with your calling card. To phone Australia, dial ☎ 0800/89-0061; for New Zealand, ☎ 0800/89-0064; for South Africa, ☎ 0800/89-0027; and for the United States, ☎ 0800/89-0011 (AT&T), 0800/89-0222 (MCI), or 0800/89-0877 (Sprint).

Television **Gaytime TV** on BBC2 is a gay and lesbian chat show. **Gay TV,** Britain's first gay erotic channel, is available by subscription (U.K. only) by calling ☎ **0990/160-160**—it airs every night/morning at 4am.

2 Pillow Talk

London can be terrible when it comes to finding a decent hotel. The task is much simpler, of course, if money is no object. Then you can choose among some of the greatest hotels in the world. The rest of us must compete for what's available, and in high season that may not be much. The city does contain an abundance of moderately priced B&Bs, but many of them are pretty gruesome.

Luckily, this is one area where gay travelers actually have an edge over straights. Along with a few high-end choices, I've listed several B&Bs and small hotels that cater exclusively to the gay community. All of them offer comfort and cleanliness at very reasonable prices. They're right in the heart of the city, you don't have to put up with snoopy, suspicious desk clerks, and by staying in them you're keeping your pounds pink.

Do yourself a big favor and book your hotel room before you arrive. You'll save yourself endless wear and tear and frustration. If you do arrive hotelless, there are two places where you can book rooms, but you have to do it in person because neither has a phone number: the **British Travel Centre** and the **Tourist Information Centre** near Victoria Station (see "Visitor Information" for addresses and hours). **Outlet** (☎ **020/7287-4244**), a new gay accommodations agency, is useful for both long- and short-term rentals of a month or more, but not for overnights.

Unless otherwise noted, the 17.5% VAT (value-added tax) will be added to the room rates below.

WEST END & SOHO

Clone Zone Luxury Apartments. 64 Old Compton St., London W1. ☎ **020/7287-3530.** Fax 020/7287-3531. 2 units, 1 studio apt. A/C TV TEL. £70 ($120) double; £80 ($137) studio apt. AE, DC, MC, V. Tube: Leicester Sq. or Tottenham Court Rd.

Don't be put off by the name, suggesting a gay sci-fi flick set in 1970s San Francisco. Clone Zone is a U.K.-based gay retail chain with stores in several cities (see "Hitting the Stores"). Two floors above their shop in London's gay village, they rent out self-contained doubles and a studio apartment that can sleep four. The surprise is how clean and pleasant the accommodations are and (given the location—you literally look out on Old Compton Street, Soho's main gay drag) how inexpensive. *Luxury* is a misleading word: The decor is sparse and somewhat dormlike but still a cut above most London hotels and B&Bs in this range. The rooms have better-than-average baths, fridges, and tea- and coffee-making facilities, and the studio has a separate lounge area and full kitchen. You're on the doorstep of the Soho clubs, pubs, cafes, and West End theaters and have all the privacy you want. It's used mostly by gay men, but women are equally welcome.

Covent Garden Hotel. 10 Monmouth St., London WC2H 9HB. ☎ **800/553-6674** or 020/7806-1000. Fax 020/7806-1100. 50 units. A/C MINIBAR TV TEL. £200–£255 ($344–$438) double; from £295 ($507) suite. AE, MC, V. Tube: Covent Garden or Leicester Sq.

Finicky attention to detail makes this stylish boutique hotel near Covent Garden a decorator's dream come true. Tim and Kit Kemp, darlings of British interior design, have turned an old French hospital/dispensary into a luxurious haven of dramatic elegance. No two rooms are alike—except for the somewhat weird tailor's mannequin that presides as a design trademark in all of them but somehow comes across as a

Hey, Big Spender

If you've finally come into your trust fund and want to blow a wad on a London hotel, there are several world-famous places that'll be more than glad to bend over backward for you. Oozing with class and style, they're the crème de la crème when it comes to service and amenities, known for their posh interiors and astronomical prices. Be prepared to drop a minimum of $375 a night for a double (and not even get breakfast) at any of them.

The **Park Lane,** one of the toniest, is listed in full below. Here are some others where you'll feel like a princess, no matter what sex you are:

Brown's Hotel, 29–34 Albemarle St., London W1X 4BP (☎ **800/225-5843** in the U.S. or 020/7493-6020; fax 020/7493-9381; E-mail: brownshotel@ukbusiness.com; www.brownshotel.com; Tube: Green Park).

Claridge's, Brook St., London W1A 2JQ (☎ **800/223-6800** in the U.S. or 020/7629-8860; fax 020/7499-2210; E-mail: info@claridges.co.uk; Tube: Bond St.).

The Dorchester, 53 Park Lane, London W1A 2HJ (☎ **800/727-9820** in the U.S. or 020/7629-8888; fax 020/7409-0114; Tube: Hyde Park Corner or Marble Arch).

Halcyon Hotel, 81 Holland Park Ave., London W11 3RZ (☎ **800/595-5416** or 800/457-4000 in the U.S. or 020/7727-7288; www.halcyon-hotel.co.uk; Tube: Holland Park).

headless nanny. Many rooms have large windows looking out over the rooftops. The decor is a lush mix of superb antiques and fine contemporary furniture, and the granite-tiled baths with spacious glass-walled showers and heated towel racks are among the best in London. This is a smart choice for business travelers since all the rooms have modems and you can have a fax machine on request and even rent a mobile phone. The wood-paneled public rooms are equally luxe. Brasserie Max, off the lobby, has a stunning pewter bar and features an eclectic selection of dishes.

Fielding Hotel. 4 Broad Court, Bow St., London WC2B 5QZ. ☎ **020/7836-8305.** Fax 020/7497-0064. 25 units. TV TEL. £88–£98 ($151–$168) double; £113 ($194) suite. AE, DC, MC, V. Tube: Covent Garden.

The gay-friendly Fielding is on a beautiful old London street lit by 19th-century gas lamps, across from the Bow Street Magistrates Court (where Oscar Wilde was taken for arrest in 1895) and steps from the Royal Opera. There's no elevator, the stairs are steep and narrow, and the rather cramped rooms (filled with white wicker furniture) show no sign of decor perception. Those quibbles aside, this quirky hotel is an excellent value and attracts a regular gay contingent from Los Angeles and New York. Every room has a small shower and a toilet. Breakfast, for a modest £2.50 to £4 ($4.30 to $7), is cooked up by Paco, who's been on duty for 20 years and is something of a character. Smokey, the parrot presiding over the tiny residents' bar, has been around even longer.

✪ **Hazlitt's.** 6 Frith St., Soho Sq., London W1V 5TZ. ☎ **020/7434-1771.** Fax 020/7439-1524. 23 units. TV TEL. £163 ($280) double. AE, DC, MC, V. Tube: Leicester Sq. or Tottenham Court Rd.

The personable staff at Hazlitt's won't blink an eye if you and your partner request a room with a double bed, and if you get a craving for Thai food they'll send someone out to get it for you. Staying in this intimate gem, built in 1718, is a delight, in part because of its old-fashioned atmosphere. The hotel has installed lovely baths, many with clawfoot tubs and all with hair dryers, but there's no elevator. The Georgian-era guest rooms are charming and elegant, with mahogany and pine furnishings and antiques. It's quieter in the back; the front rooms are lighter, but restrictions on historic properties don't allow for double glazing. The location couldn't be better: Step out the door and you're in the heart of hip gay Soho. There's a small sitting room downstairs, and you can order a continental breakfast for £7.25 ($13).

The Savoy. The Strand, London WC2R 0EU. ☎ **800/62-SAVOY** or 020/7420-2300. Fax 020/7872-8901. E-mail info@the-savoy.co.uk. 202 units. A/C MINIBAR TV TEL. £280–£305 ($483–$524) double; from £365 ($627) suite. AE, DC, MC, V. Tube: Embankment or Charing Cross.

The Savoy, opened in 1889, is synonymous with luxury, meaning ripped blue jeans and dirty sneakers will be frowned on as aberrations of taste. The opulent landmark hotel has 15 types of rooms, including some famous art-deco ones with their original features. They're all spacious, and the decor throughout is splendid. The baths, as large as some hotel rooms, have red-and-white marble tiles, large chrome fittings, enormous glass-walled showers, heated towel racks, and Floris toiletries. Beside every bed is an old-fashioned call panel to summon a waiter, maid, or valet. Artfully concealed behind closed doors are state-of-the-art entertainment systems. The most expensive rooms have river views; others look out over the hotel courtyard. Special amenities include an ISDN system for fast Internet use and in-room fax machines on request. The Savoy Grill is one of London's most famous restaurants (see "Whet Your Appetite" below), and in the Thames Foyer you can get a superlative English tea for £18.75 ($32).

MAYFAIR

Park Lane Hotel. Piccadilly, London W1Y 8BX. ☎ **800/223-5652** or 020/7499-6321. Fax 020/7499-1965. 308 units. MINIBAR TV TEL. £230–£305 ($395–$524) double; from £325 ($559) suite. Ask about weekend/seasonal rates. AE, DC, MC, V. Tube: Hyde Park Corner or Green Park.

This prestigious landmark opened in 1927 and is sometimes called the "Iron Lady of Piccadilly"—not because it's a torture to stay here, but because the place is so well built. The Park Lane has been used as a tony backdrop in many films, including *Brideshead Revisited.* The art-deco ballroom is truly fabulous, and the Palm Court Lounge is a swank place for a cocktail. The cheapest rooms (not yet remodeled) are quiet and fairly spacious but lack air-conditioning and are disappointingly drab. Far more enticing are the renovated executive rooms and suites, with beautiful marble baths and a warm mix of classic English furnishings. No two rooms are alike, and the price goes up according to location (particularly for a suite overlooking Green Park), size, and decor. The service is smooth and discreet. Buckingham Palace, Bond Street, Knightsbridge, and the West End theaters are all close by.

BLOOMSBURY

Hotel Russell. Russell Sq., London WC1B 5BE. ☎ **020/7837-6470.** Fax 020/7837-2857. www.forte-hotels.com. E-mail hotelrussell@ukbusiness.com. 329 units. A/C TV TEL. £160 ($275) double. AE, MC, V. Tube: Russell Square.

Though video surveillance cameras have been installed and all the shrubbery has been hacked away to prevent shadowy liaisons, Russell Square remains one of London's age-old cruising grounds. And for 100 years the massive redbrick Hotel Russell has been looking down on the action. This is a grand hotel in the Victorian style, with an imposing marble staircase, gleaming wood paneling, and crystal chandeliers. It's so big that guests become anonymous, which for some people is a plus. The rooms are furnished in an uninspired traditional style but come with tea- and coffee-making facilities, trouser presses, and hair dryers. It's rather like being in an enormous castle in the city center. Virginia Woolf would turn over in her grave if she knew the hotel had a restaurant named after her serving burgers and grills.

Russell Lodge. 20 Little Russell St., London WC1A 2HN. ☎ **020/7430-2489.** Fax 020/7681-7604. E-mail 100256.563@compuserve.com. 11 units, 2 with bathroom. TV. £55 ($95) double without bathroom, £65 ($112) double with bathroom. MC, V. Tube: Holborn or Tottenham Court Rd.

Near the British Museum on a quiet narrow street behind St. George's Church, this B&B caters exclusively to the gay community. The rooms are in two adjoining late-18th-century small buildings with no name on the doors, giving the hotel a pleasant air of secrecy. You'll get your own keys so you can come and go as you please, and the vegetarian breakfast is served until noon, an added boon to club-crawlers. There's no elevator, so you have to maneuver your bags up and down narrow curving stairs (the buildings are considered historically important so can't be altered very much). The inset beams in some rooms have been painted an odd orangy-yellow, and the overall decor certainly won't win any design awards. You'll find a washbasin in every room but will otherwise have to share baths (some with tubs, others with showers only). But given the fact that you're centrally located and within walking distance of Soho and Russell Square, it's a good place to know about.

MARYLEBONE

Bryanston Court Hotel. 56–60 Great Cumberland Place, London W1H 7FD. ☎ **020/7262-3141.** Fax 020/7262-7248. 54 units. TV TEL. £110 ($176) double. Rates include continental breakfast. AE, DC, MC, V. Tube: Marble Arch.

Three individual houses were joined to form this 200-year-old hotel, one of the finest moderately priced hotels in central London, in a neighborhood with lots of pretty squares. Family owned and operated, the Bryanston Court offers small rooms (and equally small baths) that are comfortably furnished and well maintained. Just *don't* let them send you down to the basement room or you'll feel like Cinderella before she met Prince Charming. There's a comfy bar with fireplace in the back of the lounge.

Dorset Square Hotel. 39 Dorset Sq., London NW1 6QN. ☎ **800/553-6674** or 020/7723-7874. Fax 020/7724-3328. www.firmdale.com. E-mail dorset@firmdale.com. 38 units. A/C MINIBAR TV TEL. £125–£195 ($215–$335) double. AE, MC, V. Tube: Baker St.

This sophisticated hotel occupies a beautifully restored Regency town house overlooking Dorset Square, a leafy private garden surrounded by graceful buildings. Aggressively gorgeous inside and out, the hotel is the epitome of traditional English style. The owners and decorators are the same Kemps who did the more eclectic Covent Garden Hotel. All the rooms are unique, filled with a superlative mix of antiques, original oils, fine furniture, fresh flowers, and richly textured fabrics. These folks really know how to give good bathrooms: the ones here are marble and mahogany. Room service is available around the clock. In short, it's a place that makes you feel like purring and so comfortable you can't wait to get back in the evening.

SOUTH KENSINGTON & KNIGHTSBRIDGE

Aston's Budget Studios. 39 Rosary Gardens, London SW7 4NQ. ☎ **800/525-2810** or 020/7370-0737. Fax 020/7835-1419. 60 units. A/C TV TEL. £68 ($117) double; £105 ($180) designer studio. MC, V. Tube: Gloucester Rd.

For price, location, decor, and privacy, you won't find a better deal in London. Housed in carefully restored Victorian town houses, the rooms here are self-contained apartments. Each has a compact kitchenette, a small bath, and bright functional furnishings. The more expensive designer studios feature marble baths with showers, hair dryers, and robes and have better-quality contemporary furnishings enhanced by rich fabrics. The electricity is metered, so you need to allow a few extra pounds a week to stay warm. Aston's is on a quiet street in the heart of South Kensington, close to the Gloucester Road Tube station, so you're close to virtually everything in the city and can come and go as you please.

✪ **Cadogan Hotel.** 75 Sloane St., London SW1X 9SG. ☎ **800/260-8338** or 020/7235-7141. Fax 020/7245-0994. E-mail info@thecadogan.u-net.com. 69 units. MINIBAR TV TEL. £185–£230 ($318–$395) double; £295–£350 ($507–$602) suite. AE, MC, V. Tube: Knightsbridge.

The Cadogan (Ca-*dug*-en) is where Oscar Wilde was staying when he was arrested, and so it occupies a special place in gay history. Wildeophiles can book room no. 118, the Oscar Wilde Suite, for £290 ($499). Memories of the Victorian era haunt this extremely atmospheric hotel close to Harrods and the exclusive Knightsbridge shops. Parts of it were once the home of actress Lillie Langtry, Wilde's great friend and the mistress of Edward VII. With its small wood-paneled lobby, open elevator, and sumptuously furnished Drawing Room, it truly is like stepping into another era. (To give you some idea of how old-fashioned it is, the use of laptops and cell phones isn't permitted in the public areas.) The large rooms, many overlooking the gardens in Cadogan Place, are tasteful and splendidly comfortable, with large baths, modem lines, and trouser presses. The service is impeccable. The Drawing Room is a time-honored spot for afternoon tea, and the sedate Edwardian restaurant is known for its excellent cuisine.

Claverley Hotel. 13–14 Beaufort Gardens, London SW3 1PS. ☎ **800/747-0398** or 020/7589-8541. Fax 020/7584-3410. 32 units. MINIBAR TV TEL. £120–£160 ($192–$256) double. Rates include English breakfast. AE, DC, MC, V. Tube: Knightsbridge.

If you want to stay in tony Knightsbridge, this is a good place to know about, set on a quiet cul-de-sac within walking distance of Harrods. Small and cozy, it was recently renovated in a Georgian-era style on the ground floor; most guest rooms have Victorian-inspired wallpaper, wall-to-wall carpeting, and upholstered armchairs, plus marble baths with power showers and hair dryers. The Claverley serves one of the best English breakfasts in London: bacon, tomato, eggs, Cumberland sausage, homemade waffles, and fresh salmon *kedgeree* (a casserole dish made with cream).

✪ **The Cranley.** 10–12 Bina Gardens, London SW5 OLA. ☎ **800/448-8355** or 020/7373-0123. Fax 020/7373-9497. www.thecranley.co.uk. 37 units. A/C MINIBAR TV TEL. £120–£160 ($206–$275) double; £180–£220 ($309–$378) suite. Rates include continental breakfast. AE, DC, MC, V. Tube: Gloucester Rd.

On a quiet street near South Kensington's museums, the Cranley is housed in a trio of recently restored 1875 town houses. It's a real find for this price category: luxuriously appointed with fine furnishings, period detailing and antiques, and regal artwork. The high-ceilinged rooms have large windows, original plasterwork, and (rather surprisingly) concealed kitchens. There's a trouser press in each. The white-tiled baths are large and nicely finished with a tub and shower. The overall tone is handsome and extremely comfortable. Suites on the ground (first) floor open onto a charming private garden and have Jacuzzis. Breakfast is served in a pleasant dining room.

✪ **The Gore.** 189 Queen's Gate, London SW7 5EX. ☎ **800/637-7200** or 020/7584-6601. Fax 020/7589-8127. E-mail reservations@gorehotel.co.uk. 54 units. MINIBAR TV TEL. £165–£264 ($283–$454) double. AE, DC, MC, V. Tube: Gloucester Rd.

Lovers of Victoriana will adore the Gore, on a busy road near Kensington Gardens and the Royal Albert Hall. Once owned by the family of the Marquess of Queensberry (the homophobic jerk who instituted the libel action that brought about Oscar Wilde's downfall), the hotel has been in more or less continuous operation since 1892 and today is gay-friendly. Like Hazlitt's, its sibling, this place is loaded with historic charm: walnut and mahogany paneling, potted palms, Oriental rugs, and prints covering every inch of wall space. In addition, you'll find some of the campiest and most unusual rooms in London: The Venus Room has an ornate bed used by Judy Garland in one of her movies; the Tudor Room has its own minstrel gallery, a 16th-century four-poster bed, and stained-glass windows; and the Dame Nellie Room has an enormous recessed sleeping alcove and a mirrored bath presided over by coy statues. Even the potties, concealed within old commodes, are noteworthy. Definitely a place to write home about. Bistrot 190, just off the lobby, is hip and popular (see "Whet Your Appetite"). The restaurant Downstairs at 190 is noted for its seafood.

Hotel 167. 167 Old Brompton Rd., London SW5 OAN. ☎ **020/7373-0672** or 020/7373-3221. Fax 020/7373-3360. 18 units. MINIBAR TV TEL. £82–90 ($141–$155) double. Rates include continental breakfast. AE, DC, MC, V. Tube: South Kensington or Gloucester Rd.

If you want to stay in fashionable "South Ken," the 167 is another good choice, though without an elevator. I'd call it gay-neutral rather than gay-friendly: You won't feel uncomfortable here, but don't expect to meet up with a lot of other traveling gays. The pluses are that every room has a decent-sized bath, and the overall ambience is clean, bright, and attractive. The rooms are furnished with a mix of fabrics and styles, all tending to the beigey-brown end of the palette, and there's even artwork that's worth looking at. The two nearby Tube stations make access to the rest of London a snap, and the neighborhood itself is charming and fun to explore.

Swiss House. 171 Old Brompton Rd., London SW5 A11. ☎ **020/7373-2769.** Fax 020/7373-4983. E-mail recep@swiss-hh.demon.co.uk. 16 units. TV TEL. £75–£82 ($128–141) double. Rates include continental breakfast. AE, MC, V. Tube: South Kensington or Gloucester Rd.

That's Swiss, not swish. Like the 167 next door (above), Swiss House isn't known for its gay crowd, but you can be assured of a comfortable stay. Hotel 167 is the more stylish, but both places lack elevators, so you have to schlep your bags up to your room. The rooms in Swiss House are clean and perfectly adequate if not particularly noteworthy. They have pale walls, floral print bedspreads, and serviceable furniture. The singles are small and narrow, with knotty-pine chests and armoires and a wicker chair. The doubles in back are your best choice, with views of a garden. The continental breakfast buffet, served in the basement dining room, includes croissants, cereals, cheeses, toast, and fresh coffee. The hotel is known as a good place for budget travelers, so it's wise to book early.

EARL'S COURT—THREE GAY HOTELS

New York Hotel. 32 Philbeach Gardens, London SW5 9EB. ☎ **020/7244-6884.** Fax 020/7370-4961. 14 units, 12 with bathroom. TV TEL. £70–£90 ($120–$154) double with bathroom. Rates include continental breakfast. AE, MC, V. Tube: Earl's Court (Warwick Rd. exit).

In 1990, the gay New York opened next door to the gay Philbeach. It's slightly more expensive, and the difference between them is primarily one of size, style, and in-room amenities. The New York (unlike the city it's named after) is less crowded, more upscale, and more sedate, without the partylike atmosphere you'll often find next door. It has a touch of hauteur, but that's part of its character (though there's no elevator). I doubt you'd ever see a middle-aged man wearing a white minidress, as you might at the Philbeach. In the public areas, architectural prints are hung on mauve walls offset by patterned carpets. All but the two single rooms have small but nicely tiled baths with showers, hair dryers, and itty-bitty sinks. All have trouser presses,

Central London Accommodations & Dining

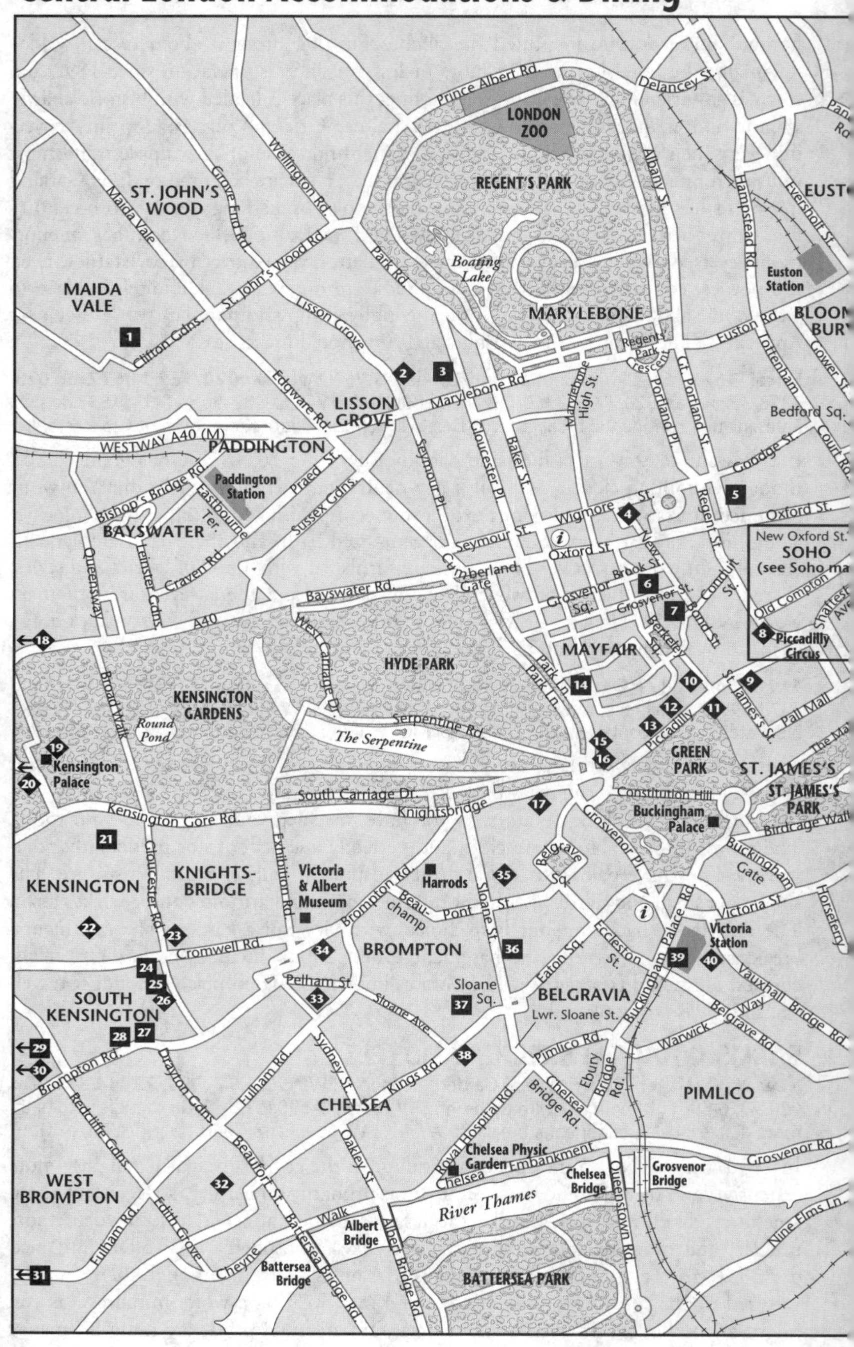

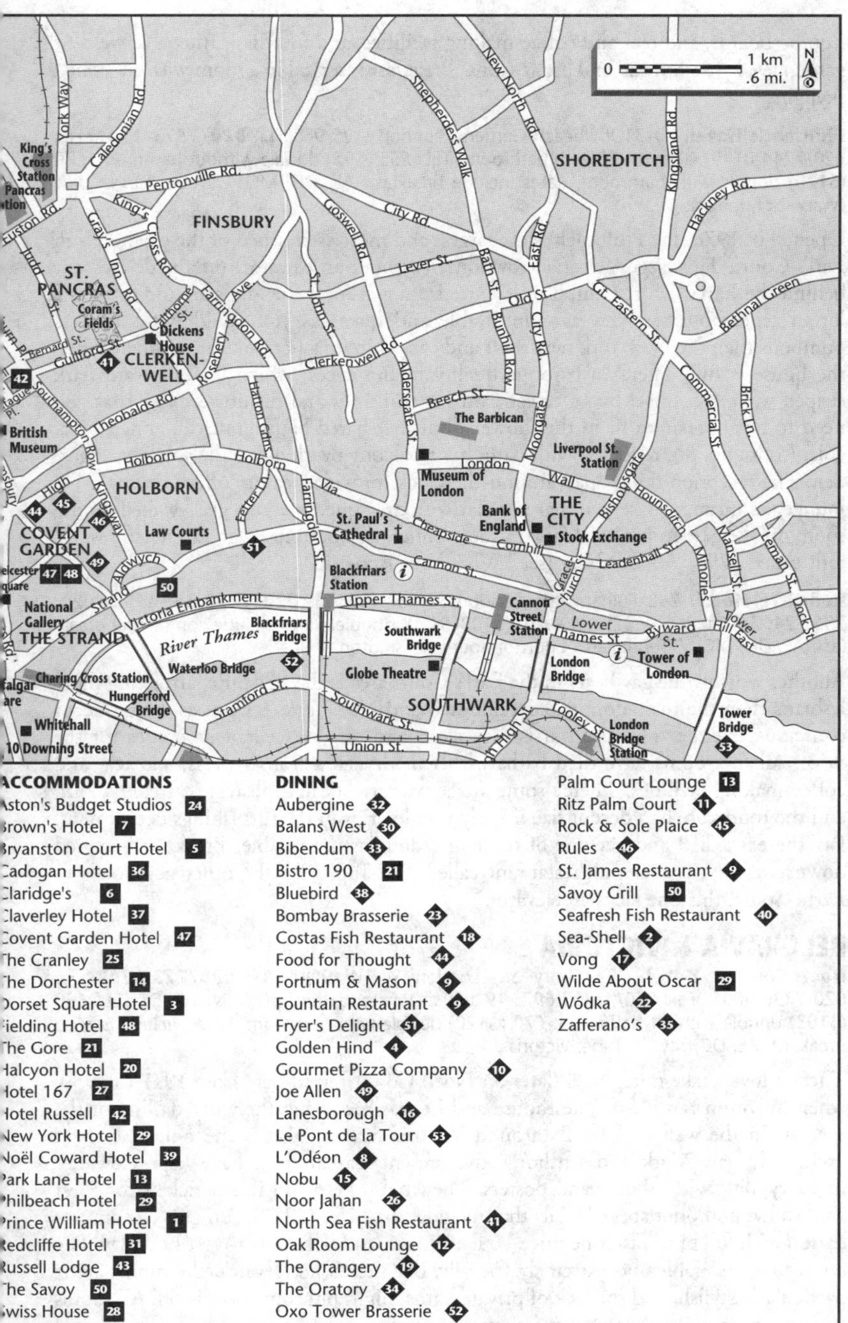

0
1 km
.6 mi.
N
King's Cross Station
Pancras
York Way
Caledonian Rd.
Pentonville Rd.
Euston Rd.
Judd St.
ST. PANCRAS
Coram's Fields
Gray's Inn Rd.
King's Cross Rd.
FINSBURY
Calthorpe St.
Dickens House
Bernard St.
Guilford St.
41
CLERKEN-WELL
42
Southampton Row
Theobalds Rd.
British Museum
Rosebery Ave
Farringdon Rd.
Hatton Gdns.
Holborn
HOLBORN
High
44
45
46
Kingsway
COVENT GARDEN
47
48
49
Law Courts
Aldwych
51
Fetter Ln.
Farringdon St.
50
Strand
National Gallery
THE STRAND
Victoria Embankment
River Thames
Waterloo Bridge
Blackfriars Bridge
52
Charing Cross Station
Hungerford Bridge
Whitehall
10 Downing Street
Stamford St.
Shepherdess Walk
New North Rd.
Goswell Rd.
St. John St.
City Rd.
Lever St.
Bath St.
East Rd.
Clerkenwell Rd.
Old St.
Aldersgate St.
Bunhill Row
City Rd.
Beech St.
The Barbican
Moorgate
Museum of London
London Wall
Via
St. Paul's Cathedral
Cheapside
Cannon St.
Blackfriars Station
Upper Thames St.
Southwark Bridge
Globe Theatre
Southwark St.
SOUTHWARK
Union St.
Bank of England
THE CITY
Stock Exchange
Cornhill
Cannon Street Station
Gracechurch St.
Lower Thames St.
London Bridge
Tooley St.
London Bridge Station
SHOREDITCH
Kingsland Rd.
Hackney Rd.
Gt. Eastern St.
Bethnal Green
Commercial St.
Brick Ln.
Liverpool St. Station
Bishopsgate
Houndsditch
Leadenhall St.
Minories
Mansell St.
Leman St.
Dock St.
Byward St.
Tower Hill
Tower of London
Tower Bridge
53
ACCOMMODATIONS
ston's Budget Studios 24
rown's Hotel 7
ryanston Court Hotel 5
adogan Hotel 36
laridge's 6
laverley Hotel 37
ovent Garden Hotel 47
he Cranley 25
he Dorchester 14
orset Square Hotel 3
ielding Hotel 48
he Gore 21
alcyon Hotel 20
otel 167 27
otel Russell 42
ew York Hotel 29
oël Coward Hotel 39
ark Lane Hotel 13
hilbeach Hotel 29
rince William Hotel 1
edcliffe Hotel 31
ussell Lodge 43
he Savoy 50
wiss House 28
DINING
Aubergine 32
Balans West 30
Bibendum 33
Bistro 190 21
Bluebird 38
Bombay Brasserie 23
Costas Fish Restaurant 18
Food for Thought 44
Fortnum & Mason 9
Fountain Restaurant 9
Fryer's Delight 51
Golden Hind 4
Gourmet Pizza Company 10
Joe Allen 49
Lanesborough 16
Le Pont de la Tour 53
L'Odéon 8
Nobu 15
Noor Jahan 26
North Sea Fish Restaurant 41
Oak Room Lounge 12
The Orangery 19
The Oratory 34
Oxo Tower Brasserie 52
Palm Court Lounge 13
Ritz Palm Court 11
Rock & Sole Plaice 45
Rules 46
St. James Restaurant 9
Savoy Grill 50
Seafresh Fish Restaurant 40
Sea-Shell 2
Vong 17
Wilde About Oscar 29
Wódka 22
Zafferano's 35

ironing boards, and tea- and coffee-making facilities, and four have fridges as well. At garden level are a hot tub and cedar sauna. Breakfast is served in a room with an arched skylight.

Philbeach Hotel. 30–31 Philbeach Gardens, London SW5 9EB. ☎ **020/7373-1244.** Fax 020/7244-0149. 40 units, 20 with bathroom. TEL. £55 ($95) double without bathroom, £70 ($120) double with bathroom. Rates include breakfast. AE, DC, MC, V. Tube: Earl's Court (Warwick Rd. exit).

Opened in 1978, the Philbeach is the largest and most established of the gay hotels in Earl's Court. This large Victorian rowhouse (without an elevator) on a wide crescent behind the Earl's Court Exhibition Centre is known for a friendly staff and attracts a lot of repeat business. It's as comfortable and queer as you could wish. It's less pompous than the New York next door and can whip up a partylike atmosphere when the house is full. There's a baroque quality to the decor, which tends toward dark striped wallpaper offset by an eclectic mix of paintings and furniture. Note that you need to be anorexic to fit in the showers, but the shared baths are clean and serviceable. Room no. 8A, a double with bath, has a balcony overlooking the small back garden. The reception desk, open around-the-clock, provides tea or coffee. There's a TV lounge, an intimate basement bar popular with drag queens, and a glass-walled dining room off the garden for breakfast. In the evening, this becomes a good French restaurant called Wilde About Oscar (see "Whet Your Appetite").

Redcliffe Hotel. 268 Fulham Rd., London SW10 9EW. ☎ **020/7823-3494.** Fax 020/7351-2467. 15 units. TV TEL. £60–£70 ($103–$120) double. Rates include continental breakfast. AE, DC, MC, V. Tube: Earl's Court or South Kensington.

Another worthwhile gay hotel in the Earl's Court area is the Redcliffe, attracting more lesbians than the male-dominated Philbeach and New York. It's not as design-decor conscious as either of those but is very clean and offers excellent amenities for the price. All the rooms have tiled baths with hair dryers, a trouser press, and tea- and coffee-making facilities. There's some attractive artwork and posters scattered about, and the rooms are of a decent size if fairly nondescript in the furnishings department. Pay the extra £10 and get one of the larger doubles if available. Breakfast is served downstairs in a corner pub/restaurant called The Tup. Like the other gay hotels in Earl's Court, this one lacks an elevator.

BELGRAVIA & VICTORIA

Noël Coward Hotel. 111 Ebury St., London SW1W 9QU. ☎ **020/7730-2094** or 020/7730-9005. Fax 020/7730-8697. 19 units, 4 with bathroom. MINIBAR TV TEL. £60 ($103) double without bathroom, £70 ($120) double with bathroom. Rates include English breakfast. AE, DC, MC, V. Tube: Victoria.

Theater lovers take note: Noël (later Sir Noël) Coward lived here from 1917 to 1930, when his mum ran it as a guesthouse and he was becoming the witty darling of the theater. In the welter of B&Bs around Victoria Station, this is the only one that's exclusively gay. Mark and Anthony, the present leaseholders, have kept Coward's memory alive with photos and posters. They'll also help you to get tickets for West End shows and offer special deals that include, for £150 ($258), 3 nights' accommodation with full breakfast, one three-course dinner, and tickets to a West End play. The service is personable and extremely friendly, but there's no elevator, the rooms aren't particularly stylish, and the lack of private baths might put some people off. All rooms have washbasins, and some have showers you can barely squeeze into. The shared baths are kept immaculate, however, so there's no need to feel squeamish. A full English breakfast is served in the cheery dining room downstairs. Victoria's first gay pub, The Nile, is a block away (see "In the Heat of the Night").

PADDINGTON

Prince William Hotel. 42–44 Gloucester Terrace, London W2 3DA. ☎ **020/7724-7414.** Fax 020/7706-2411. 43 units, 35 with bathroom. TV TEL. £45 ($78) double without bathroom, £55–£75 ($91–$129) double with bathroom. Rates include continental breakfast. AE, MC, V. Tube: Paddington.

This gay-friendly hotel might seem a bit out-of-the-way for some, but you can easily hop on a Tube at nearby Paddington and get anywhere in Central London in a few minutes. For budget travelers it's one of the best bargains going—and believe it or not, there's an elevator. But don't expect anything fancy or high on the glam. The rooms are small, and so are the baths, but they're clean and comfortable and have tea- and coffee-making facilities. There's a special promotional rate for a 2-night-minimum stay that'll knock a few more pounds off your tab.

BRIXTON

No. 7 Guesthouse. 7 Josephine Ave., London SW2 2JU. ☎ **020/8674-1880.** Fax 020/8671-6032. www.no7.com. 8 units. A/C MINIBAR TV TEL. £69–£79 ($118–$135) double. 2-night minimum weekends and holidays. MC, V. Tube: Brixton.

This friendly and exclusively gay/lesbian guesthouse is on a leafy avenue 10 minutes from the Brixton Tube station in the south London borough of Lambeth. More important for some guests, it's 5 minutes from The Fridge, one of London's largest gay dance clubs, and Substation South, a popular new gay club. The rooms aren't large by American standards, but they're bright and nicely furnished with contemporary pine furniture and have hair dryers. Largest and most luxurious is the Honeymoon Suite, which has a larger bath (including a bidet). The renovated Victorian house retains some of its original features. The continental breakfast, served in a conservatory overlooking a walled garden, is £4.50 ($8).

3 Whet Your Appetite

London used to be one of the worst cities in the world for food, but that's all changed and the city is now in the grip of a gastronomic revolution. You can still get greasy fish and chips, gluey steak-and-kidney pie, bangers and mash (sausage and mashed potatoes) with a side of cold peas and carrots, and spotted dick, which sounds like a venereal disease but is actually a dessert. But you can also dine well on what's now called "Modern British" cuisine, taking old standards and jazzing them up with foreign influences. The city has a huge assortment of restaurants serving Indian, French, Italian, Japanese, vegetarian, and every other kind of cuisine you can imagine. In Earl's Court and Soho, lots of restaurants and cafes cater almost exclusively to gays and lesbians.

The annoying 17.5% VAT (value-added tax) will automatically be added to your bill and a moderate "cover charge" for bread may be tacked on as well. But look at the menu to see if a "service charge" will be added. If it is, you're not expected to leave any further gratuity. If the menu says "service not included," then you leave an additional tip (15% to 20% if the service has been good or the waiter particularly cute). Be aware that some places may be tacky enough to tack on a service charge and also have a space for "gratuity" on your credit-card receipt. Don't be conned into double-tipping.

You'll be comfortable as a couple eating in all my recommended restaurants, so long as you remember that British decorum and good manners frown on ostentatious displays of any kind. Sexuality really doesn't enter into the picture when you're dining out in London unless you come in wearing leather chaps or an Edwardian ball gown. If a restaurant is gay-oriented, I've mentioned it in the description, but you'll be treated with civil respect at all my suggestions.

Hot & Pricey

To become a culinary hot spot in London, a restaurant must have one or more of the following: a celebrity owner, a celebrity chef, memorable food, a long-standing reputation, a fabulous view, a chic location, some kind of special ambience. One of the newer trends is the mega-eatery, which may hold up to several hundred diners at one time. The prices at a hot London restaurant are high—expect to pay upward (way upward) of $50 for an appetizer, a main course, a dessert, and maybe mineral water. Order drinks and/or wine and expect the bill to soar. You can cut your tab considerably by ordering a set menu or going for lunch instead of dinner. Of course, you'll need to dress up for these places (get out those tiaras)—and be sure to book *way* ahead of time.

Sir Terence Conran is the big name behind two big-view French restaurants: **Oxo Tower Brasserie** (see below), perched above the Thames on the South Bank, and the equally stunning **Le Pont de la Tour,** Butlers Wharf Building, 36D Shad Thames, Butlers Wharf, SE1 (☎ **020/7403-8403;** Tube: London Bridge), overlooking Tower Bridge. He also started Chelsea's phenomenally successful **Bluebird,** 350 King's Rd., SW3 (☎ **020/7559-1000;** Tube: Sloane Square, then bus 19, 22 or 49), serving Modern European cuisine, as well as South Kensington's ever-popular and (g)astronomically priced French **Bibendum,** Michelin House, 81 Fulham Rd., SW3 (☎ **020/7581-5817;** Tube: South Kensington).

The classic French cooking at Chelsea's **Aubergine,** 11 Park Walk, SW10 (☎ **020/7352-3449;** Tube: Sloane Square, then bus 11, 19, or 22), has earned it two Michelin stars. **Wódka,** 12 St. Alban's Grove, W8 (☎ **020/7937-6513;** Tube: Gloucester Rd. or High Street Kensington), is a smart and pretend-simple Kensington eatery where you wash down Eastern European food with vodka. And **Nobu,** in the Metropolitan Hotel, 19 Old Park Lane, W1 (☎ **020/7447-4747;** Tube: Hyde Park or Green Park), is the London branch of the New York hit owned by Robert DeNiro, chef Nobu Matsuhisa, and restaurateur Drew Nieporent. If you're into superbly innovative Japanese cuisine, Nobu is the place for you.

All the following have entries below: The **Savoy Grill** in the Savoy hotel continues to be a downplayed power-player hangout, while **Zafferano's** is a superlative Italian restaurant in tony Knightsbridge. The windowside tables at stylish **L'Odéon** provide a bird's-eye view of Piccadilly Circus. And star chef Jean-Georges Vongerichten's **Vong** in Knightsbridge offers superb French/Thai cooking in an artily minimalist atmosphere.

Note: For the locations of the restaurants below, see the "Central London Accommodations & Dining" map on pp. 84–85.

PICCADILLY

Fortnum & Mason. 181 Piccadilly, W1. ☎ **020/7734-8040.** À la carte £7.50–£115.95 ($13–$27). AE, DC, MC, V. St. James's and The Patio, Mon–Sat 9:30am–5:30pm; Fountain, Mon–Sat 9am–8pm. Tube: Piccadilly Circus. BRITISH.

Fortnum & Mason is a legendary posh store famous for its food section, where jars of marmalade, canisters of tea, and tins of soup are displayed on old-fashioned mahogany shelves. But it also has three restaurants: the mezzanine-level **Patio** (lunch, tea), the lower-level **Fountain** (breakfast, lunch, tea, dinner), and the fourth-floor **St. James's** (lunch, afternoon tea). Though crowded with tourists, these remain pleasant places where you can get a good meal and a glimpse of the fading Empire. The Patio's lunch menu offers an assortment of pricey sandwiches (from a toasted club to Scotch smoked salmon) and main courses like warm scallops and crispy bacon salad and tea-smoked duck with orange relish. The Patio specializes in hot and cold pies (steak and kidney, curried fish and banana, chicken, game) and Welsh rarebit, prepared with Guinness stout. The more well-heeled dine at the St. James's, where the menu is even more traditionally British. For starters, try the kipper mousse or potato-and-Stilton brûlée; main courses include pies and roast rib of Scottish beef.

Gourmet Pizza Company. 7–9 Swallow Walk, W1. ☎ **020/7734-5182.** Pizzas £4.80–£8.45 ($8–$15); pastas £6.60–£8.45 ($11–$15). AE, DC, MC, V. Mon–Sat noon–11pm, Sun noon–10:30pm. Tube: Piccadilly Circus. PIZZA/PASTA.

You've blown a wad shopping on Piccadilly and now you're starving but want to economize. The answer, of course, is pizza. If you arrive at noon, you can sit at any table you want; half an hour later and the place is packed with shop and office workers. It's large, bright, clean, and pleasant, and there are 15 pizzas to choose from. This is pizza as in pie, not slice. Everything from a B.L.T. version to one with Cajun chicken and prawns is available. The crusts are light and crispy, the toppings fresh and flavorful. Instead of pizza you might want to try the yummy wild mushroom tortelloni with chopped basil, tomato, and olive oil.

✪ **L'Odéon.** 65 Regent St. (entrance on Air St.), W1. ☎ **020/7287-1400.** Main courses £14.50–£22.50 ($25–$39); lunch and pretheater menus £14.50–£18 ($25–$31). AE, DC, MC, V. Mon–Sat noon–2:45pm and 5:30–11:30pm, Sun noon–3:30pm, 7–10:30pm. Reservations essential. Tube: Piccadilly Circus. FRENCH.

L'Odéon created quite a stir when it opened, as much for its size and super-sophisticated interior as for its food. Some of its trendiness has dissipated, however, which means getting a table is easier, but it remains a wonderfully chic place for a dress-up lunch or dinner. Located in Nash Terrace, the huge room is broken up into smaller areas by partitions and has large semicircular windows overlooking the bustle of Regent Street and Piccadilly Circus. The cuisine is Gallic with international overtones, always fresh and beautifully presented. For starters, try the foie gras on a toasted brioche or the tuna carpaccio with seaweed salad. Main courses worth ordering are pot au feu with sauce vert, vegetable stew with foie gras and prosciutto, and whole roast young bass with grilled fennel. You can cut your bill in half by ordering from the set menu. There's an ample wine list. The service can be a bit dodgy, but chances are you'll be more than satisfied.

SOHO

✪ **Andrew Edmunds.** 46 Lexington St., W1. ☎ **020/7437-5708.** Reservations essential well in advance. Main courses £7.50–£10 ($13–$17). AE, MC. Daily 12:30–3pm and 6–10:45pm. Tube: Oxford Circus or Piccadilly Circus. MODERN BRITISH.

You'll need to book well in advance to get a seat at this tiny bistro. It's not gay per se but attracts a large gay following. Avoid it if you're claustrophobic or have emphysema because it's cramped, loud, and filled with cigarette smoke. But the food is remarkably good, the service is personable, and it's the sort of special "find" you'll tell your friends about when you get back home. The menu is limited to five or six entrees and changes often. It'll always include fish (like poached skate or cod fillet) and meat (maybe calf's liver or beef fillet) with potatoes or a vegetable. You'll also find dishes like potato-and-artichoke torta served with gazpacho salsa. The wine list is reasonably priced.

Fishin' for Chippies

In England, a fish-and-chips place is a "chippie." At some chippies the food is wonderful, at others it's hideous. At the best places, the fish (usually cod, haddock, or plaice) is fresh, the batter is crisp, and the fries (chips) are hand-cut. Malt vinegar (as opposed to ketchup) is the standard condiment. Usually a plate of fish and chips costs around $7, but it'll be more in heavily touristed areas. The following chippies aren't "smart" places, but the food is good.

North Sea Fish Restaurant, 7–8 Leigh St., WC1 (☎ **020/7387-5892;** Tube: Russell Square; open Mon–Sat noon–11:30pm). **Rock & Sole Plaice,** 47 Endell St., WC2 (☎ **020/7836-3785;** Tube: Covent Garden; open Mon–Sat 11:30am–10pm, Sun 11:30am–9pm). **Fryer's Delight,** 19 Theobald Rd., WC1, across from the Holborn Police Station (☎ **020/7405-4114;** Tube: Chancery Lane or Holborn; open Mon–Sat noon–10pm). **Golden Hind,** 73 Marylebone Lane, W1 (☎ **020/7486-3644;** Tube: Baker St. or Bond St.; open Mon–Sat noon–3pm and 6–10pm). **Sea-Shell,** 49–51 Lisson Grove, NW1 (☎ **020/7723-8703;** Tube: Marylebone; open Mon–Fri noon–2pm and 5:15–10:30pm, Sat noon–10:30pm). **Seafresh Fish Restaurant,** 80–81 Wilton Rd., SW1, near Victoria Station (☎ **020/7828-0747;** Tube: Victoria; open Mon–Sat noon–10:30pm). **Costas Fish Restaurant,** 18 Hillgate St., W8 (☎ **020/7727-4310;** Tube: Notting Hill Gate; open Tues–Sat noon–2:30pm and 5:30–10:30pm).

Balans. 60 Old Compton St., W1. ☎ **020/7437-5212.** Main courses £5.50–£13 ($10–$22). AE, MC, V. Sun–Thurs 8am–4am, Fri–Sat 8am–6am. Tube: Piccadilly Circus or Leicester Sq. ECLECTIC BRITISH.

Probably the best-known gay restaurant in London, Balans opened in 1993 and is still packed. This, in part, is because it's open almost around-the-clock, so you can drop in for breakfast, lunch, brunch, or dinner. The menu is an all-purpose affair, with fresh salads, pastas, grills, and roasts. It's good without being particularly brilliant, and you'll probably be so busy cruising you may not know what's on your plate anyway. The best of the grills are the charred roast chicken and tuna teriyaki with a sinus-opening sauce of pickled ginger, Chinese mustard, and garlicky soy. The pastas—penne with tomato, basil, and wild mushrooms and scallop and black ink tortelloni—are tasty but not terribly authentic. If you want a good old-fashioned breakfast after your night in disco Heaven, try the "American pancakes" with maple syrup. Balans has recently opened a new branch in Earl's Court (see below).

Ed's Easy Diner. 12 Moor St., W1. ☎ **020/7439-1955.** Main courses £4.50–£5.50 ($8–$9). MC, V. Mon–Thurs 11:30am–midnight, Fri 11:30am–1am, Sat 9am–1am, Sun 9am–11pm. Tube: Leicester Sq. NORTH AMERICAN.

At London's version of an old American diner, you perch on stools around a wraparound counter and snap your gum as "Don't Be Cruel" blares from the jukebox. It's more authentic than a "theme restaurant" but still attracts a fair share of teens-on-the-town and a lot of gays like it. Go here if you're lonely for all the comforting, cholesterol-laden chow no one's supposed to eat anymore. I'm talking about big hamburgers served with fries or onion rings, giant Kosher weenies slathered with cheddar cheese, chili, tuna melts, and grilled cheese sandwiches. You'll need a thick chocolate malt to go with it, of course. The Lumberjack breakfast served on Saturdays and Sundays will set you up the rest of the day.

The Gay Hussar. 2 Greek St., W1. ☎ **020/7437-0973.** Reservations recommended. Main courses £20–£25 ($33–$41); fixed-price lunch £16 ($28). Mon–Sat 12:15–2:30pm and 5:30–10:45pm. AE, DC, MC, V. Tube: Tottenham Court Rd. HUNGARIAN.

The Gay Hussar isn't. But we still eat there. Why? Because it's the world's best Hungarian restaurant with undeniably authentic cuisine. Maybe begin with the chilled wild-cherry soup or smoked Hungarian sausage (a specialty of the Gay Hussar). Gigantic main courses include cabbage stuffed with minced veal and rice (you'll be windy afterward); perfectly done chicken served in mild paprika sauce with cucumber salad and noodles; mouthwatering roast duck with red cabbage and Hungarian-style caraway potatoes; and, of course, veal goulash with egg dumplings. If you have room for dessert, try the poppy-seed strudel or walnut pancakes. Then stroll around Soho and see the other meaning of the word *gay.*

Old Compton Cafe. 34 Old Compton St., W1. ☎ **020/7439-3309.** Main courses £1.55–£3.95 ($2.65–$7). No credit cards. Daily 24 hours. Tube: Leicester Sq. BRITISH.

A perennial Soho favorite, in part because it's so friendly and downmarket, the Old Comp has the ambience of a greasy spoon and a mostly denim-clad gay crowd. It's completely packed on weekends but busy all week long, day and night. Breakfast is big and wisely adheres to no set hour. They serve baked potatoes (generally called "jacket potatoes" in England) filled with a variety of unusual toppings (sun-dried tomato pesto chicken and Thai chicken curry) but are best known for their generous and tasty "baps." These are sandwiches oozing with chicken and roasted vegetables or egg mayonnaise and bacon. It's fun and frantic at peak times.

Soho Soho. 11–13 Frith St., W1. ☎ **020/7494-3491.** Main courses £8.25–£13.25 ($14–$23). AE, MC, V. Mon–Sat noon–11pm, Sun noon–10:30pm. Tube: Leicester Sq. or Tottenham Court Rd. FRENCH.

This is one of the most popular and upscale gay-friendly restaurants in Soho, and it's a shame the food isn't always what it should be and the service can be painfully slow. The cafe/bar/rotisserie on the ground floor tends to become chaotic after 8pm, but you might be better off getting a meal there. It's a bright open room with large windows, a tiled floor, wooden tables, and blue walls covered with nervous white squiggles that look as if they're about to coalesce into a Keith Haring drawing. The omelet with ham and button mushrooms and the grilled chicken flavored with thyme are good. The restaurant on the upper floor is more sedate and serves Provençal cuisine. Your best bet is grilled fish, like the tuna steak with sage and sun-dried tomato salsa. The specialty, wild boar, is couriered in from France. Best of all are the desserts, like lemon tart with crème fraîche and warm bread-and-butter pudding with raspberry coulis.

Steph's. 39 Dean St., W1. ☎ **020/7734-5976.** Main courses £6.95–£14.95 ($12–$26). AE, DC, MC, V. Mon–Fri noon–3pm and 5:30–11:30pm, Sat 5:30pm–midnight. Tube: Leicester Sq. MODERN BRITISH.

Oh, look: flaming pink flamingoes on the dark green walls. Could it mean Steph's is gay? Well, yes and no. It prefers the term *eclectic,* which means lots of straights eat here too. The food is basically Brit fare with some foreign accents; it's good, filling, and generally reliable. The best thing on the menu is Snuffy's Chicken, diced breast of chicken in a sauce of white wine and cream, sprinkled with prawns and red and green peppers. The homemade pie (I don't mean the dessert kind) changes daily. They make a good hamburger, which comes with fries and a salad, and you can get good old bangers and mash with onion gravy. The wonderful bread-and-butter pudding takes 30 minutes to prepare and is worth the wait.

✪ **Wagamama Noodle Bar.** 10A Lexington St., W1. ☎ **020/7292-0990.** Reservations not accepted. Main courses £3.50–7.60 ($6–$13). MC, V. Mon–Sat noon–11pm, Sun 12:30–10:00pm. Tube: Oxford Circus or Piccadilly Circus. JAPANESE.

If you're exploring Soho and want a good nutritious meal in a smoke-free environment, this gay-friendly noodle bar will fit the bill. A trendsetting masterpiece of Zen design, it's modeled after the ramen shops popular in Japan. You enter at street level and pass along a stark corridor with the busy open kitchen to one side. If the lines are long, as they often are, you can order sake, beer, or raw juice from a mobile drinks cart. Descending to the lower level, you enter a large open room and are seated at long communal tables. The specialties are ramen, Chinese-style thread noodles served in soups with various toppings, and the fat white noodles called udon. The ramen can't be eaten without slurping, but the slurping supposedly creates extra oxygen that adds to the flavor. Rice dishes, vegetarian dishes, dumplings, vegetable and chicken skewers, and tempura are also on the menu. Your order is sent via radio signal to the kitchen and arrives the moment it's ready, which means not everyone in a group will be served at the same time.

COVENT GARDEN & THE STRAND

Food for Thought. 31 Neal St., WC2. ☎ **020/7836-0239.** Main courses £3–£5.50 ($5–$10). Mon–Sat noon–3:30pm and 5:30–8:15pm, Sun noon–4pm. No credit cards. Tube: Covent Garden. VEGETARIAN.

Okay, we're not talking glamour. We're not talking decor. We're talking cheap, we're talking good, and we're talking vegetarian. This basement hole-in-the-wall is a pleasant respite from the hubbub of Covent Garden with all its expensive restaurants geared to carnivores. The menu changes constantly, but there's always a daily soup (like carrot and fresh coriander) and a couple of good main courses. You might find sweet and tangy Jamaican curry with aubergine (eggplant), okra, red pepper, spinach and sweet potatoes, or a pasta with a not-very-spicy sauce made of roasted red peppers and tomatoes. There are daily quiche and salad specials. The sweets (desserts) generally include apple-and-rhubarb crumble and fruit with yogurt. Service is cafeteria-style.

Joe Allen. 13 Exeter St., WC2. ☎ **020/7836-0651.** Reservations advised. Main courses £6.50–£13.50 ($11–$23); special lunch menu (Mon–Fri noon–4pm) £11–£13 ($19–$22); pretheater menu (Mon–Sat 5pm–6:45pm) £12–£14 ($21–$24). AE, MC, V. Mon–Fri noon–12:45am, Sat 11:30am–12:45am, Sun 11:30am–11:30pm. Tube: Covent Garden. NORTH AMERICAN.

Come before the show for the best prices, come after for the best stargazing. Joe Allen's is the sort of place where famous actors often come after a performance to wolf down a bowl of chili con carne or gnaw on a plate of barbecued ribs. The likes of Maggie Smith, of course, always eat with a knife and fork. Joe Allen keeps a low profile on a backstreet in Covent Garden. With its checkered tablecloths and crowded tables, it looks like the Joe Allen in New York, but the accents are different. The food, American classics with some international twists thrown in, is sturdy and dependable. The set menu is a real value. After your starter (maybe smoked haddock vichyssoise), you can choose main courses like pan-fried Parmesan-crusted lemon sole, Cajun chicken breast, or grilled spicy Italian sausages. If you're feeling homesick, console yourself with a burger, a brownie, and a Coke.

Rules. 35 Maiden Lane, WC2. ☎ **020/7836-5314.** Reservations essential. Main courses £12–£17 ($21–$29); pre- and posttheater meals (Mon–Fri 3–6pm and 10:30–11:30pm) £15.95 ($27); Sat–Sun lunch £17.95 ($31). AE, DC, MC, V. Daily noon–midnight. Tube: Covent Garden or Charing Cross. BRITISH.

London's oldest restaurant, Rules was founded in 1798 and is decorated with two centuries' worth of prints, cartoons, and paintings. It's not as exclusive as it once was, but it's still not the sort of place for jeans and running shoes. If you want to eat classic British cuisine in a memorable (nay, venerable) setting, dig some decent duds out of your suitcase and head for Maiden Lane. If you're game for game, go for it because that's what Rules is famous for. Ptarmigan, widgeon, and snipe—weirdly named game birds shot at the restaurant's hunting seat—are roasted to order September to February. In recent years, they've added a few vegetarian dishes, like wild mushroom lasagna in basil cream sauce, and fish is also available. But where else will you have the opportunity to try jugged hare, confit of wild duck with apple and five-spice chutney, stuffed teal, or breast of partridge with port, cream and juniper sauce? If it's feathered, furred, scaled, and edible, you'll find it at Rules.

Savoy Grill. In the Savoy Hotel, the Strand, WC2. ☎ **020/7240-6040.** Reservations essential. Main courses £15–£37 ($26–$64). Mon–Fri 12:30–2:30pm; Mon–Sat 6–11:15pm. AE, DC, MC, V. Tube: Embankment or Charing Cross. BRITISH.

Like the hotel housing it, the Savoy Grill caters to the rich, the powerful, the prestigious, and anyone else who can dress up and pay for a meal. It's favored by professionals in the arts, the media, the law, and finance, though all the power-players tend to keep their voices down. The dining room is spacious but not as luxurious as you might suppose: The yew-paneled walls give it a warm woody blush, but it's otherwise so low-key as to be boring. If you like old-fashioned meat dishes, choose the daily special "from the trolley": saddle of lamb, roasted sirloin, beef Wellington, pot-roasted guinea hen with a horseradish crust. For other dishes, the chef tarts up traditional British cooking with some interesting mixes, like roast duck with caramelized oranges, asparagus and pancetta, pan-fried salmon with mushroom risotto, and fish cakes with roasted tomato and fennel compote. The service is impeccable and the food good, but you may leave with the impression that money and power have made Jack a rather dull boy.

SOUTH KENSINGTON & KNIGHTSBRIDGE

Bistro 190. In the Gore Hotel, 190 Queens Gate, SW7. ☎ **020/7581-5666.** Main courses £9–£13 ($16–$22). AE, DC, MC, V. Mon–Sat 7am–12:30am, Sun 7am–11:30pm. Tube: Gloucester Rd. or South Kensington. MODERN BRITISH.

There have been complaints of lackluster meals here, accompanied by even more lackluster service, so did I just luck out or does it all depend on phases of the moon? Bistro 190 is a hip, lively place, rather unadorned and woody. If you like soup—and the Brits can come up with some very unusual ones, like parsnip and chili with sweet potato crisps—they can generally be relied on. The specialty is a salmon-and-cod cake with spinach-and-sorrel sauce. The roast loin of pork with baked apple and Jerusalem artichoke puree is worth trying, and if you're into entrails, try the pan-fried calves' liver and lamb kidney with roasted red onions and lentils. The place isn't particularly gay, but it's in South Ken, which means you'll feel quite comfortable.

Bombay Brasserie. Courtfield Close, Courtfield Rd., SW7. ☎ **020/7370-4040.** Reservations advised. Main courses £13.75–£16.95 ($24–$29); buffet lunch £15.95 (27); set dinner £34.10 ($59). AE, DC, MC, V. Daily 12:30–3pm and 7:30–11:30pm. Tube: Gloucester Rd. INDIAN.

On the giant glossy menu you'll see photos of countless grinning celebs, Tom Cruise and Nicole Kidman, Goldie Hawn, Mel Gibson, and Mick Jagger among them. But it's more likely you'll see businesspeople on expense accounts. British colonialism sets the stage in the ornate dining room, but ask for a table in the pleasanter conservatory. The menu covers the Indian subcontinent, offering up Tandoori, Goan, Moghlai, and Parsi specialties. All main courses are served with potatoes, veg of the day, and a lentil dish. I can recommend the mixed grill, lamb dhansak (cooked with spicy lentils and pureed vegetables), chicken biryani, and chicken korma rizala with cashew-nut paste and puree of fresh coriander. Alas, success has brought with it some culinary disappointments, so you can't always be guaranteed warm food or properly prepared breads. But when it's good, it's very good. The lunch buffet is the best deal for noncelebs.

Noor Jahan. 2A Bina Gardens (off Old Brompton Rd.), SW5. ☎ **020/7373-6522.** Main courses £7.50–£15 ($13–$26); set menu £18.50 ($32). AE, DC, MC, V. Daily noon–2:45pm and 6–11:45pm. Tube: Gloucester Rd. or South Kensington. INDIAN.

Small, unpretentious, and always reliable for good Indian food, Noor Jahan has become a neighborhood favorite in South Ken. The marinated chicken and lamb dishes cooked Tandoori style in a clay oven are moist and flavorful. Chicken tikka, a staple of northern India, is one specialty worth trying. So are the biryani dishes—in these, chicken, lamb or prawns are mixed with basmati rice, fried in ghee (clarified butter), and served with a mixed vegetable curry. If you're unfamiliar with Indian food, the waiters will gladly explain the various dishes.

✪ **The Oratory.** 232 Brompton Rd., SW3. ☎ **020/7584-3493.** Main courses £4.50–£9 ($8–$16); set-menu lunch £7.95 ($14). MC, V. Mon–Sat 11:30am–11pm, Sun 11:30am–5pm. Tube: Knightsbridge or South Kensington. MODERN BRITISH.

Close to Kensington Palace and the shopping on Kings Road and Brompton Road, this funky bistro serves up some of the best and least expensive food in tony South Ken. The high-ceilinged room is decorated in what might be called Modern Rococo, with enormous glass chandeliers, patterned walls and ceiling, and wooden tables with wrought-iron chairs. It's a great spot for a light meal and a glass of their good inexpensive house wine. Take note of the daily specials on the chalkboard, especially any pasta dishes, which are always well prepared. The homemade fish cakes, stir-fried prawns with noodles, and breast of chicken stuffed with Parma ham and fontina cheese are all noteworthy. For dessert, the sticky toffee pudding with ice cream is a melt-in-the-mouth delight. To reach the "loos" you have to make one of the most complicated and surreal trips in London—upstairs, downstairs, around corners, and into a separate building.

✪ **Vong.** In the Berkeley Hotel, Wilton Place, SW1. ☎ **020/7235-1010.** Reservations required 7 days in advance. Main courses £9–£26.75 ($14–$45); tasting menu £45 ($77); 2-course fixed-price dinner £27 ($45); 3-course fixed-price dinner £36.50 ($63); pre- and posttheater dinner £17.50 ($30). Mon–Sat noon–2:30pm and 6–11:30pm. AE, DC, MC, V. Tube: Knightsbridge. FRENCH/THAI.

Just 600 yards from Harrods, this artily minimalist restaurant on three levels is a chic hangout. It's a "famous chef" place: Jean-Georges Vongerichten was the darling of New York (he has three restaurants there) before he brought his award-winning French/Thai menu here. The food is more than noteworthy: It's subtle, innovative, and inspired. The "black plate" provides samples of six starters. You can dine on perfectly roasted halibut or a sublime lobster-and-daikon roll with rosemary-and-ginger sauce. Other temptations: the crab spring roll with vinegary tamarind dipping sauce and the sautéed foie gras with ginger and mango, which literally melts in your mouth. The exotic desserts include a salad of banana and passion fruit with white-pepper ice cream.

✪ **Zafferano's.** 15 Lowndes St., SW1. ☎ **020/7235-5800.** Reservations essential far in advance. Set lunch £16.50–£19.50 ($28–$34); set dinner £24.50–£28.50 ($42–$49). AE, MC, V. Mon–Sat noon–2:30pm and 7pm–11pm. Tube: Knightsbridge. ITALIAN.

If you want what's perhaps the best Italian food in London, you'll have to reserve a table as far in advance as you can. Upscale Zafferano's is very popular but not pretentious, and you'll be guaranteed a truly memorable meal. The decor is quietly elegant, with tiled floors and linen-draped tables. Giorgio Locatelli is a hands-on kind of chef who takes his kitchen very seriously. The semolina pastas are perfectly cooked and come with various additions, such as sausage and fennel seeds, pheasant parcels with rosemary, sweet chili garlic and crab, or meat and black truffle. Main courses like roast rabbit with Parma ham and polenta, charcoal-grilled chicken, and tuna with rocket (arugula) and tomato salad are deliciously simple and tender. If you order octopus, the taste and texture will be right on pitch. And finally, the desserts. Or dessert, really, since there's one you must try: the lemon-and-marscapone tart.

EARL'S COURT

Balans West. 239 Old Brompton Rd. ☎ **020/7244-8838.** Main courses £5.50–£11.50 ($10–$20). AE, DC, MC, V. Daily 8am–1am. Tube: Earl's Court. BRITISH/ECLECTIC.

This Balans opened in 1996 and isn't quite as glossy and packed as the Soho branch, but the menu is basically the same (see above). It's a large, bright corner room with big windows and the look of an upscale diner. Filled with gays and lesbians, who begin trickling in at breakfast time and keep arriving throughout the day and into the night, it's a relaxed place to get a good meal with a minimum of fuss. Unlike its Soho counterpart, this Balans remains open only until 1am.

Wilde About Oscar. In the Philbeach Hotel, 30–31 Philbeach Gardens, SW5. ☎ **020/7373-1244.** Reservations required. Main courses £8.60–£12.70 ($15–$22). AE, DC, MC, V. Daily 7–10:30pm. Tube: Earl's Court (Warwick Rd. exit). FRENCH.

This gay restaurant in the gay Philbeach serves surprisingly good French cuisine in a tiny dining room overlooking the back garden (and in the garden during summer). It's a place where you can be as outré or romantic as your mood swings dictate. The candlelit room is decidedly intimate, with only a few linen-covered tables. The menu is small and selective, the service effective and refreshingly unfussy. Among the starters are a creamy salmon mousse, delicious mussels in white-wine herb sauce, and a salad of sautéed chicken liver with raspberry vinegar. The meat and fish dishes are tender and classically sauced. The roast duckling has a cherry sauce; the lamb comes with a rich ginger, rosemary, and honey sauce; the pork fillet is served with onion, French mustard, and gherkin sauce; and the grilled red snapper is enhanced by a cream sauce with white shallots, saffron, and julienned leeks. For dessert, choose the achingly rich chocolate mousse or the banofie pie served with cream.

SOUTH BANK

✪ **Oxo Tower Brasserie.** Oxo Tower Wharf, Barge House St., SE1. ☎ **020/7803-3888.** Reservations essential. Main courses £12.50–£14.50 ($22–$25). AE, DC, MC, V. Daily noon–3pm and 5:30–11pm. Tube: Waterloo or Blackfriars. FRENCH.

Even if the food were lousy (which it certainly isn't), this place would rate a star for its breathtaking view. Perched atop the Oxo Tower on the South Bank, it provides a sweeping panorama of the entire city. The Oxo Tower Restaurant is the name this place generally goes by, but I recommend the adjacent brasserie. It's not as chi-chi, the food is marvelous, and it costs about half of what you pay to dine on tablecloths on the other side. Book well in advance and plead for a window table (easier if you come early). This is one of Terence Conran's dreamchilds, with a sleek and stylish decor. The starter of chicken liver and mixed-leaf salad with roasted peppers, pancetta, and new potatoes was sublime. The main courses were excellent: The roast poussin (French for rabbit) with rocket (English for arugula), French beans, and lemon and green olive butter was tender and tart; the seared salmon with a spring onion mash and Meaux mustard beurre blanc was equally fine. The Oxo Tower may be a little hard to find if you don't know London, so hop into a taxi once you get out of the Tube station.

Tea for Two, Please

Yes, they drink coffee, but mostly the Brits drink tea. In fact they swill down some 171 million cups a day. But there's tea (drunk all day long) and then there's "tea," a more elaborate and dressy afternoon affair. Afternoon tea (with cakes, sandwiches, scones, and clotted cream) "taken" in a high-toned hotel or restaurant isn't something many Brits "do." (Maybe because of the cost.) But tourists love it. If you're part of a male-male couple, there's no need to feel self-conscious or like you're doing something outrageously prissy. It's just part of being civilized. Same-sex female couples don't have to worry; female tête-à-têtes over tea are a long-established custom. Afternoon teas are expensive, but that's part of the ritual too. Try one the following if you want a memorable experience.

At the **Palm Court Lounge** in the Park Lane Hotel, Piccadilly, W1 (☎ **020/7499-6321;** Tube: Hyde Park Corner or Green Park; open daily 3:30–6:30pm), afternoon tea costs £14 ($22) and reservations are required. In Le Méridien's **Oak Room Lounge,** 21 Piccadilly, W1 (☎ **020/7734-8000;** Tube: Piccadilly Circus or Green Park; open daily 3:30–6pm), afternoon tea runs £13.50 to £19.50 ($22 to $31), and reservations aren't accepted.

Reservations are required at least 8 weeks in advance for tea at the **Ritz Palm Court** in the Ritz Hotel, Piccadilly, W1 (☎ **020/7493-8181;** Tube: Green Park; open daily 2–6pm). Afternoon tea costs £23.50 ($38), and a jacket and tie are required for men. At the **St. James Restaurant** in Fortnum & Mason, 181 Piccadilly, W1 (☎ **020/7734-8040;** Tube: Piccadilly Circus; open Mon–Sat 3–5:30pm), a full tea costs £10.50 to £12.25 ($17 to $20); in the same store is also the **Fountain Restaurant** (open Mon–Sat 3–6pm), where a full tea is £7 to £10 ($11 to $16). Reservations aren't required for either.

At the **Lanesborough,** Hyde Park Corner, SW1 (☎ **020/7259-5599;** Tube: Hyde Park Corner; open daily 3:30–5:30pm), reservations are required. High tea (more of a meal than afternoon tea) costs £18.50 ($30), and high tea with strawberries and champagne goes for £22.50 ($36); a simple pot of tea is £3.50 ($5.60). And in the gardens of Kensington Palace you'll find **The Orangery,** W8 (☎ **020/7376-0239**)—see the Kensington Palace entry under "Exploring London" for more details.

GAY CAFE/BARS

You'll probably be hanging out at least part of the time in Soho, where the Central London gay scene is a nonstop affair. In addition to the gay-friendly restaurants above, Soho has some very hip gay cafe/bars where you can order a coffee, a drink, or a light meal. Unlike the bars, pubs, and clubs, these places have trendsetting decor and big windows that look out onto the street.

Blue Room. 3 Bateman St., W1. ☎ **020/7437-4827.** Sandwiches £2.40–£3.50 ($4.10–$6). No credit cards. Mon–Sat 8am–midnight, Sun noon–11pm. Tube: Leicester Sq. or Charing Cross.

No booze, but great fruit smoothies. This tiny cafe attracts a younger mixed crowd less interested in drinking and cruising than in sitting around to yak over a double espresso. There's no pressure to rush you out. The food is light, lean, and greaseless, with fresh sandwiches the mainstay. The cruelly rich desserts offset any health benefits derived from the rest of the menu.

The Box. 32–34 Monmouth St., WC2. ☎ **020/7240-5828.** Main courses £5.50–6.20 ($9–$11). MC, V. Mon–Sat 11am–11pm, Sun noon–10:30pm. Meals Mon–Sat 11am–5:30pm, Sun 11am–7pm. Tube: Leicester Sq.

The Box is small and chipper, with yellow walls, bright-colored tables, and pale wood accessories. And it's very popular, which means it's generally packed. The menu includes an all-day breakfast, good snacks and starters, and a small array of main courses. Salmon fish cakes and artichoke and mushroom lasagna are worthwhile choices, but also check out the daily specials. The crowd is mixed but definitely gay-heavy. The bar downstairs serves dozens of specialty cocktails and becomes a disco on Friday and Saturday. Sundays from 7pm the bar is for women only.

Freedom. 60–66 Wardour St., W1. ☎ **020/7734-0071.** Bar food £3.25–£6.50 ($6–$11). MC, V. Mon–Sat noon–3am, Sun noon–midnight. Tube: Piccadilly Circus.

Freedom is a cafe/restaurant/bar/club that attracts a hip artsy crowd. Breakfast and lunch are pretty leisurely, and you can hang out all day if you like, eating the soups, salads, and sandwiches or just nursing a coffee. The scene heats up in the evening and late night. The downstairs bar/club is open Wednesday to Saturday 9:30pm to 3am; cover is £5 ($8) after 10pm.

✪ **Kudos.** 10 Adelaide St., WC2. ☎ **020/7379-4573.** Main courses £3.50–£4.95 ($6–$9). MC, V. Mon–Sat 11am–11pm, Sun 11am–10:30pm. Tube: Charing Cross.

The bar crowd is mostly gay men, including well-dressed "suits." The cafe in the back serves snacks: baked potatoes with toppings, small pizzas, and smoked salmon on a bagel. You can also get main courses, like grilled chicken with a Dijon mustard and cream sauce, tagliatelle with smoked salmon, burgers, and Thai chicken salad. There are daily specials as well. Kudos offers customers free or reduced-price entry tickets to nearby clubs like G.A.Y. and Heaven.

Rupert Street. 50 Rupert St., W1. ☎ **020/7734-5614.** Main courses £6.95–£12.95 ($12–$22). AE, DC, MC, V. Mon–Sat 11am–11pm, Sun noon–10:30pm. Tube: Piccadilly Circus.

The newest, chicest, and most ambitious (culinarily speaking) of the gay Soho cafe/bars is Rupert Street. You can start your gay day with a toasted bagel heaped with scrambled eggs and smoked ham or get a full English breakfast. For lunch, try a ciabatta roll filled with spicy chicken breast or mozzarella, avocado, and tomato drizzled with olive oil. Small plates include tangy Welsh rarebit prepared with cheddar, Guinness stout, and mustard and sweet, steaming mussels in white wine sauce. This is one of the few places to offer that old favorite called Bubble and Squeak: sausages served on creamy potatoes with shredded cabbage and spring onions topped with a hot, thick gravy. Always lively, with a youngish crowd.

✪ **The Yard.** 57 Rupert St., W1. ☎ **020/7437-2652.** Snacks £2.45–5.95 ($4.20–$10). AE, DC, MC, V. Mon–Sat noon–11pm, Sun noon–10:30pm. Food served noon–5pm. Tube: Leicester Sq. or Piccadilly Circus.

This is more of a bar than a cafe, and a very attractive one at that. You enter through a secretive arch and enter a paved courtyard set back from the teeming Soho streets. In warm weather, as darkness falls over London, the courtyard becomes one of the favorite gay gathering spots in Soho. The bar/cafe faces the courtyard and has an upstairs lounge that allows double-decker cruising. No food is served at night, but you can get a light, simple meal during the afternoon. They serve soup, one pasta dish, and good baguette sandwiches.

4 Exploring London

London boasts an inexhaustible array of museums, historic buildings, famous streets, intriguing neighborhoods, beautiful parks, cruising areas, and attractive men. It's a great walking city (compulsively so), but distances can be daunting and you'll need a detailed map. **London A to Z,** available at newsagents and bookstores, is best—don't leave home without it.

The **Original London Sightseeing Tour** (☎ **020/8877-1722**) and **London Pride Sightseeing** (☎ **01708/631-122**) (no relation to Gay Pride) provide excellent short tours on a fleet of double-decker buses. You don't have to book in advance, you pay on the bus, and you can hop on and off at major sightseeing stops along the way. Tours covering various sections of London run all day every day, about every 30 minutes. London Pride departs from Cockspur Street on Trafalgar Square or outside the Trocadero at Piccadilly Circus; Original London Sightseeing has pickup points at Victoria Coach Station, Marble Arch, Haymarket, and Baker Street. For both outfits, a ticket good for 24 hours on all routes costs £12 ($20); you can take shorter hops for less money.

✪ **Catamaran Cruisers** (☎ **020/7839-1034**) runs a fleet of boats on the Thames from Charing Cross Pier to the Tower of London and Greenwich; the majestic views of London from the water make this a special experience. Round-trip fares between Charing Cross and the Tower (Apr–Oct every 30 minutes 10:30am–4pm; Nov–Mar every 45 minutes 10:30am–3pm) are £5.80 ($10); round-trips between Charing Cross and Greenwich (same departure times) are £7 ($12).

London Walks (☎ **020/7624-1932;** http://london.walks.com) provides a terrific array of walking tours, including "Jack the Ripper's London," "Christopher Wren's London," "The Beatles' Magical Mystery Tour," and "Where the Other Half Lives." Tickets are £4.50 ($8); departures are daily from various Tube stops around the city, all at different times, so you need to call. There's also an independently operated weekly ✪ **Gay Walk** costing £5 ($9) and lasting 1½ to 2 hours; check the gay listings in *Time Out* for times and departure points. The walks cover gay literary life and history.

If you want to take walking tours on your own, including strolls of Dickens's London, Clerkenwell, and Hampstead, check out ***Frommer's Memorable Walks in London.***

THE HITS YOU SHOULDN'T MISS

British Museum. Great Russell St., WC1. ☎ **020/7323-8599** or 020/7636-1555 (recording). Admission free. Guided tours £6 ($10). Mon–Sat 10am–5pm, Sun 2:30–6pm. Closed Jan 1, Good Friday, Dec 24–26. Tube: Holborn, Tottenham Court Rd., or Russell Sq.

One of the world's greatest repositories of art and artifacts, the British Museum is so huge you'd need a year just to scratch the surface. If you have only a couple of hours to cover the highlights (and not get lost in the 2½ miles of galleries), consider taking one of the £6 ($10) guided tours offered Monday to Saturday at 10:45 and 11:15am and 1:45 and 2:15pm and Sunday at 3, 3:20, and 3:45pm.

The most famous of the museum's countless treasures are the **Elgin Marbles,** housed in the Duveen Gallery on the ground (first) floor. These are the sculptures that once adorned the Parthenon and that Melina Mercouri, the smoky-voiced actress who later became the Secretary of Culture for Greece, tried unsuccessfully to get back. In the **Greek and Roman rooms** (nos. 1–15) you can cast your eyes on several painted vases and kraters showing "sporting scenes" from ancient times. The athletes back then didn't worry about lucrative endorsements because they rarely wore clothes. You'll find some buff male figures in the classical sculpture galleries as well. Most of them are marble, but some may be ambulatory.

The British Museum

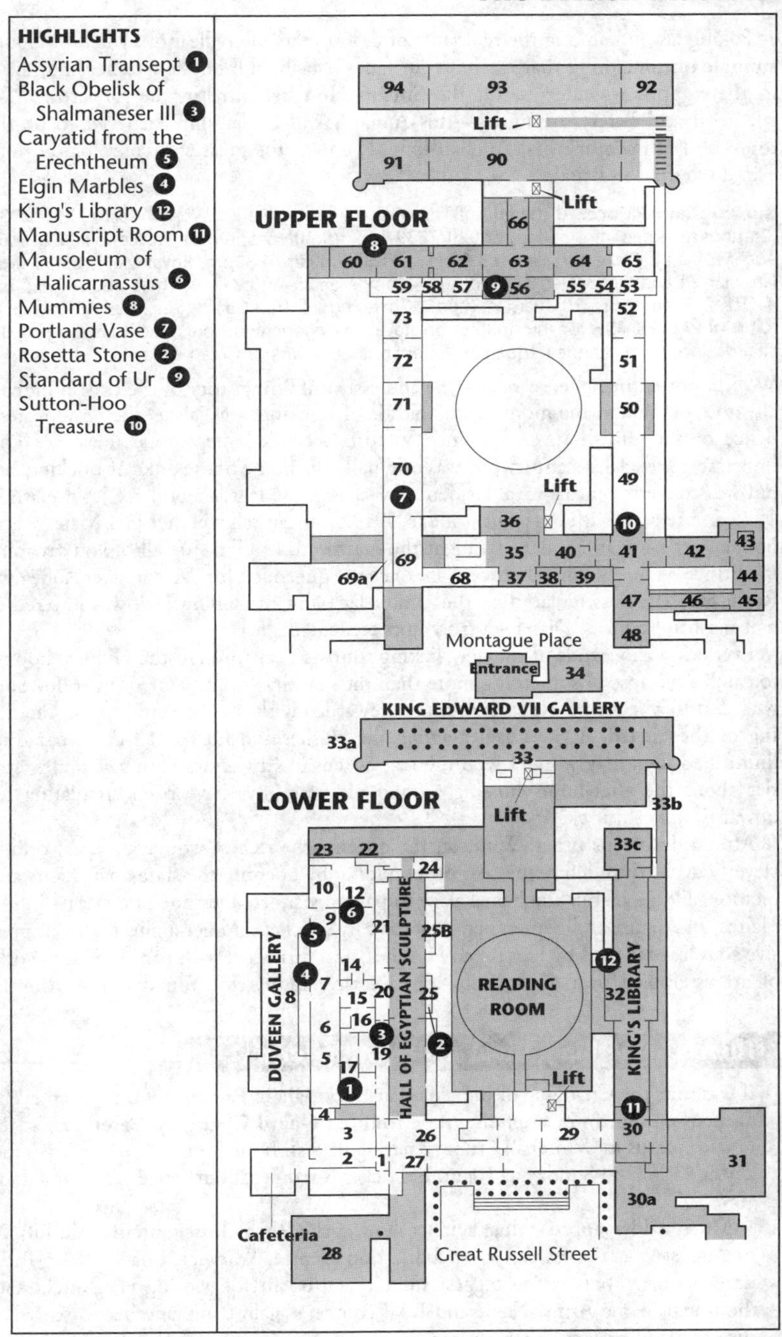

HIGHLIGHTS
Assyrian Transept 1
Black Obelisk of Shalmaneser III 3
Caryatid from the Erechtheum 5
Elgin Marbles 4
King's Library 12
Manuscript Room 11
Mausoleum of Halicarnassus 6
Mummies 8
Portland Vase 7
Rosetta Stone 2
Standard of Ur 9
Sutton-Hoo Treasure 10
UPPER FLOOR
Lift
Montague Place
Entrance
KING EDWARD VII GALLERY
LOWER FLOOR
DUVEEN GALLERY
HALL OF EGYPTIAN SCULPTURE
READING ROOM
KING'S LIBRARY
Cafeteria
Great Russell Street

Poking around among the remnants of 4,500 years of civilization, you'll no doubt stumble on something that catches your fancy. Maybe it'll be the wizened mummies in the **Egyptian Galleries.** Or the **Sutton Hoo Treasure** in the Department of Medieval and Later Antiquities—this Anglo-Saxon burial ship, believed to be the tomb of a 7th-century East Anglian king, is one of the greatest archaeological finds ever discovered in Britain.

Buckingham Palace. At the end of The Mall, St. James's Park, SW1. ☎ **020/7799-2331** (24-hour recorded information) or 020/7839-1377 (9:30am–5:30pm). Palace tours £9 ($16), Aug–Sept only. Queen's Gallery £3.50 ($6), daily 9:30am–4:30pm. Royal Mews £3.50 ($6), Jan–Mar 24 and Oct 3–Dec 31 Wed noon–4pm; Mar 25–Aug 3 Tues–Thurs noon–4pm; Aug 4–Oct 2 Mon–Thurs 10:30am–4:30pm. Changing of the Guard free. Call Visitorcall at ☎ **01839/123-456** for information on Royal Mews opening hours and Changing of the Guard, since both change frequently. Tube: St. James's Park or Green Park.

Wealth, power, intrigue, scandal—the endlessly unfolding story of the British monarchy goes on behind the monumental facade of Buckingham Palace, the London residence of the British sovereign since Victoria ascended the throne in 1837. This impressive early 18th-century pile was originally the home of the duke of Buckingham but was converted into a royal residence by George IV. It was rebuilt by John Nash in 1825 and refaced with Portland stone in 1913. You can tell whether Her Majesty is at home by the Royal Standard flying at the masthead. (As I'm sure all of you saw during Princess Diana's funeral procession, once the queen left for Westminster Abbey the Royal Standard was replaced by the Union Jack and the Union Jack was lowered to half mast in honor of Diana—a truly unprecedented act.)

Every day, thousands of camera-clicking tourists peer through the railings, hoping to catch a glimpse of something more than the gravelly "front yard" of the 600-room palace. If they're lucky, at 11:30am they're rewarded with the pageantry of the **Changing of the Guard.** A gay traveler ogling the plumes and furs on all those parading uniformed men may wonder who the real queens of England are; in gay circles, stories about the after-hours horsing around of these guys have been circulating for upwards of a century.

After a disastrous fire at Windsor, the queen—the richest woman in the world—cleverly decided to defray the cost of rebuilding by opening the state apartments and picture galleries in Buckingham Palace to paying visitors when the family isn't in residence. In August and September, you can buy a ticket and get a glimpse of impressive **state rooms** used by Her Royal Highness and furnished with paintings and works of art assembled over 4 centuries by successive monarchs. You can also visit the

There's Something About a Man in Uniform . . .

If you miss the Changing of the Guard at Buckingham Palace, you can get an eyeful of men in uniform by attending the **Mounted Guard Changing Ceremony** at the Horse Guards in Whitehall (Tube: Charing Cross). It takes place Monday to Saturday at 11am and Sunday at 10am. No ticket is required, but arrive early for a good view.

Much wilder, approaching a circus show, is the **Royal Tournament,** held July 21 to August 2 at the Earl's Court Exhibition Centre, Warwick Road, SW5 (Tube: Earl's Court). This is the biggest military tattoo in the world: The butchest of the butch in the Army, Navy, and RAF compete against one another to see who's strongest and bravest. It takes place Tuesday to Saturday at 2 and 7:30pm, Monday at 7:30pm, and Sunday at 2pm. For tickets, call ☎ **020/7244-0244** or e-mail boxoffice@eco.co.uk.

Queen's Gallery, which features changing exhibits of works from the Royal Collection. At the **Royal Mews,** one of the finest working stables in existence, you can view the magnificent Gold State Coach and other royal conveyances.

The area around St. James's Park is "Royal Land," since the Queen Mum—reputed to be fond of her gay courtiers—lives in **Clarence House,** next door to **St. James's Palace,** the abode of Prince Charles and the boys (when they're not in school).

Note: You can charge tickets for palace tours by phone at ☎ **020/7321-2233,** guaranteeing you entry at a specific time and saving you the bother of queuing for tickets outside the palace. All other ticket holders should be prepared to spend upward of an hour in line before getting inside the palace and sometimes that long at the ticket office beforehand.

✪ **Tower of London.** Tower Hill, EC3. ☎ **020/7709-0765.** Admission £8.50 ($15). Mar–Oct Mon–Sat 9am–6pm, Sun 10am–6pm; Nov–Feb Tues–Sat 9am–5pm, Sun 10am–5pm. Closed Jan 1 and Dec 24–26. Tube: Tower Hill.

"Take him [her] to the Tower!" How many times, in how many costume epics, have you heard that unforgettable line? The blood has been cleaned up, but the Tower can still grip the imagination. To make the most of your visit, arrive early and hook up with one of the 1-hour tours led by the beefy Beefeaters in their cute black-and-red costumes. These tours of the entire compound take place every half an hour, starting at 9:25am, from the Middle Tower near the main entrance. The last guided walk starts about 3:30pm in summer and 2:30pm in winter.

The city's best-known and oldest historic site, the Tower was built by William the Conqueror in 1066 and served as his fortress. Later it was used as a prison, with the **White Tower** and subsequent keeps holding such famous prisoners as Sir Walter Raleigh and Princess Elizabeth I. It was a place where queens were forced to give head: Anne Boleyn and Catherine Howard were wedded, bedded, and beheaded by Henry VIII. Lady Jane Grey also got the chop. Make a point to see Henry VIII's anatomically exaggerated armor (you'll know it when you see it) in the White Tower.

There's enough here to keep you occupied for several hours, but make sure you save time for the **Crown Jewels,** which include the Imperial State Crown worn by the queen at the opening of Parliament (it's encrusted with more than 2,800 diamonds), the exquisite Koh-i-noor diamond, in the crown of the Queen Mother; and the Star of Africa, the largest cut diamond in the world, set in the cross of the Queen Mother's Orb and Scepter. Your tiara back home will never look quite the same after seeing these baubles. As you wander around visiting the various sites, you'll notice huge black ravens hopping around and squawking. There's an old legend that says the world will end when the ravens leave the Tower. Their wings have been clipped as a precaution.

✪ **Westminster Abbey.** Broad Sanctuary, SW1. ☎ **020/7222-5152.** Admission to abbey free (donation invited); Royal Chapels and Poets' Corner £4 ($7). Mon–Fri 9am–3:45pm, Sat 9:15am–1:45pm and 4–4:45pm. Tube: Westminster.

A Tower Tip

If you've planned ahead, at 9:30pm you can attend the free **Ceremony of the Keys,** during which the Tower is secured for the night and attendees find themselves locked in this imposing fortress. (Don't worry: The Tower has long since ceased to be a prison and you're politely ushered out through a small side door.) You must book tickets at least 6 weeks in advance by writing to Ceremony of the Keys, HM Tower of London, London EC3N 4AB.

Central London Attractions

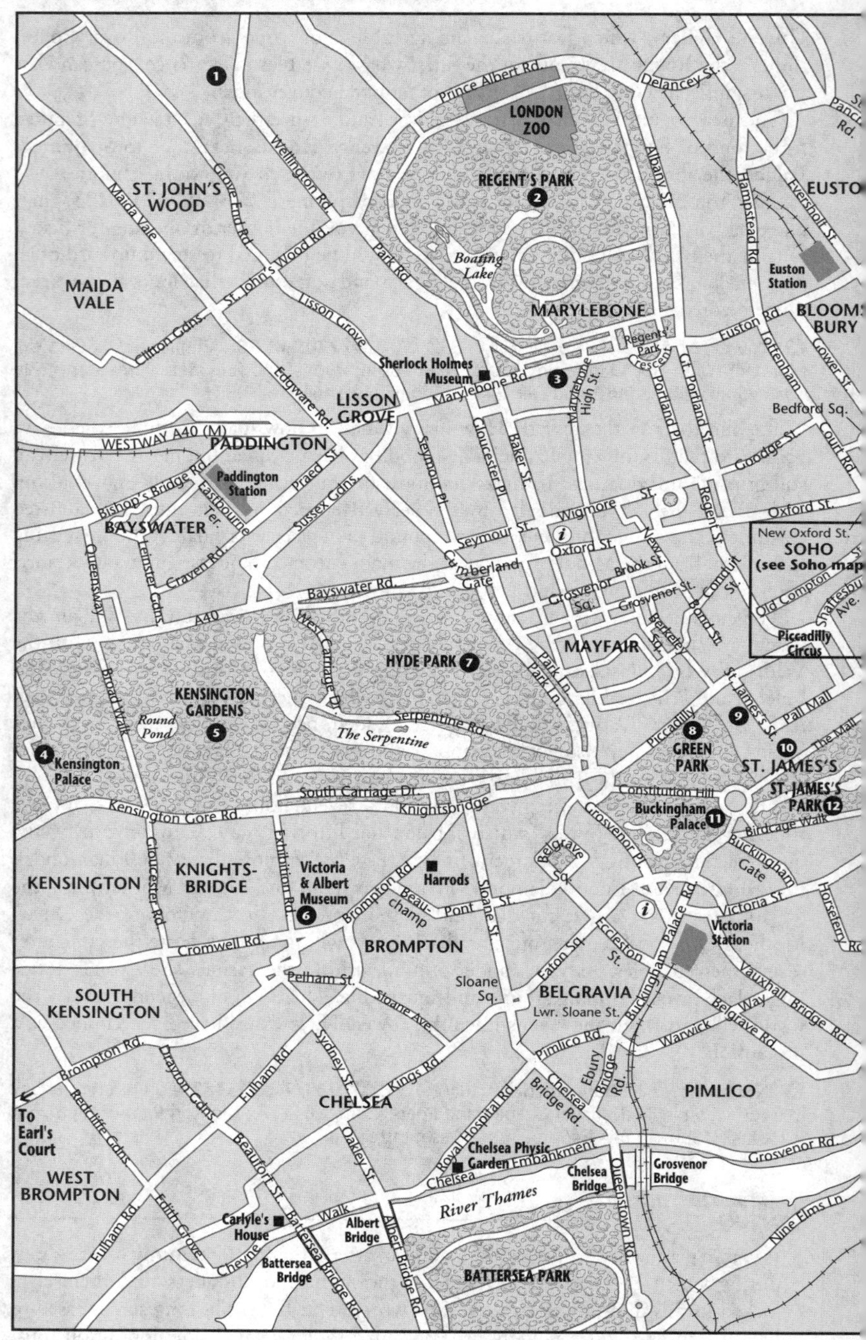

LONDON ZOO
REGENT'S PARK
Boating Lake
MARYLEBONE
ST. JOHN'S WOOD
MAIDA VALE
LISSON GROVE
PADDINGTON
Paddington Station
BAYSWATER
Sherlock Holmes Museum
HYDE PARK
KENSINGTON GARDENS
Round Pond
The Serpentine
Kensington Palace
MAYFAIR
GREEN PARK
ST. JAMES'S
ST. JAMES'S PARK
Buckingham Palace
Victoria & Albert Museum
Harrods
KENSINGTON
KNIGHTS-BRIDGE
BROMPTON
SOUTH KENSINGTON
BELGRAVIA
Victoria Station
PIMLICO
CHELSEA
Chelsea Physic Garden
Carlyle's House
River Thames
Albert Bridge
Battersea Bridge
Chelsea Bridge
Grosvenor Bridge
BATTERSEA PARK
WEST BROMPTON
To Earl's Court
Euston Station
EUSTO
BLOOMS BURY
New Oxford St.
SOHO (see Soho map
Piccadilly Circus

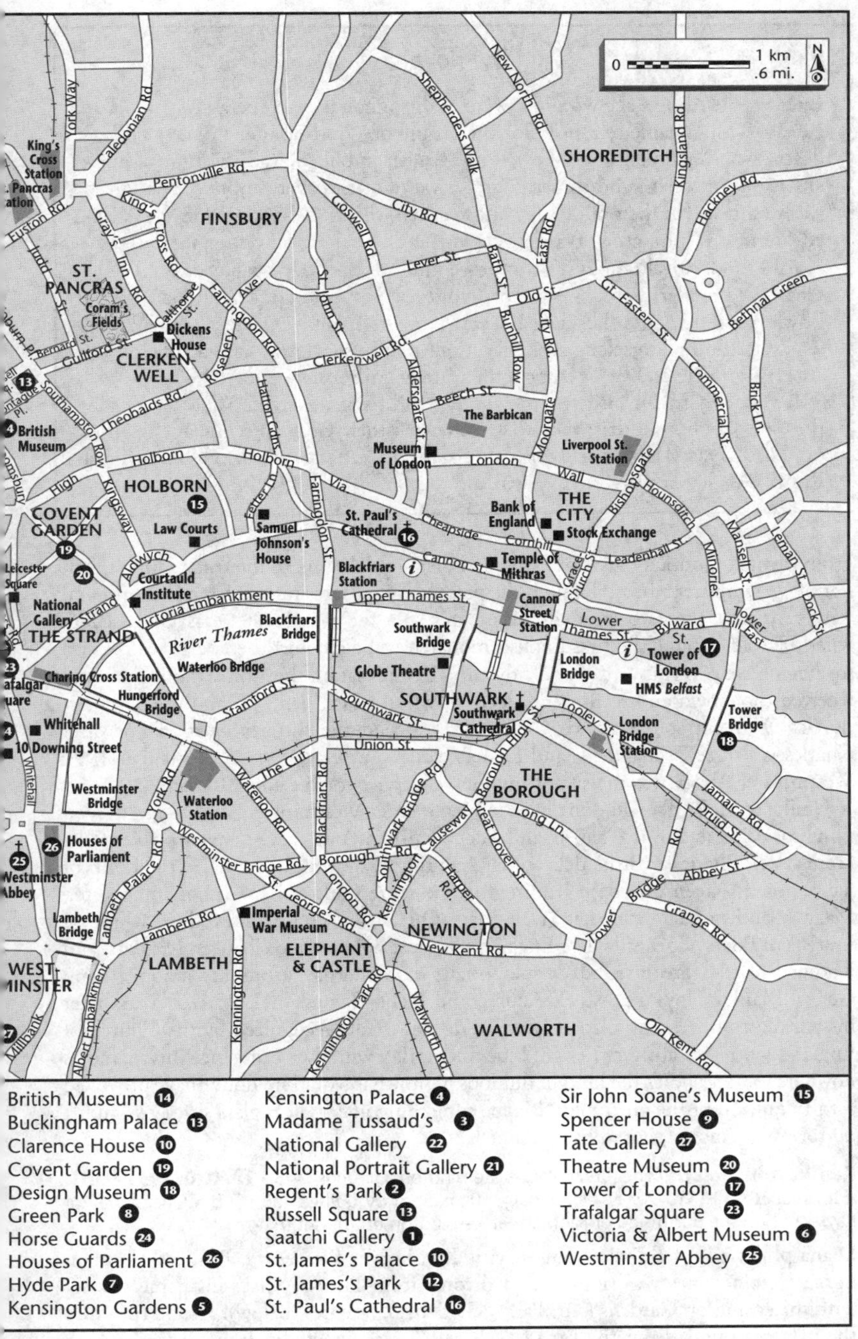
0
1 km
.6 mi.
N
SHOREDITCH
FINSBURY
ST. PANCRAS
CLERKENWELL
HOLBORN
COVENT GARDEN
THE STRAND
THE CITY
SOUTHWARK
THE BOROUGH
NEWINGTON
ELEPHANT & CASTLE
LAMBETH
WALWORTH
King's Cross Station
York Way
Caledonian Rd.
Pentonville Rd.
King's Cross Rd.
Euston Rd.
Judd St.
Gray's Inn Rd.
Coram's Fields
Calthorpe St.
Dickens House
Bernard St.
Guilford St.
Farringdon Rd.
Rosebery Ave.
Goswell Rd.
City Rd.
Shepherdess Walk
New North Rd.
Kingsland Rd.
Hackney Rd.
East Rd.
Bath St.
Lever St.
St. John St.
Old St.
Bunhill Row
City Rd.
Gt. Eastern St.
Bethnal Green
Commercial St.
Brick Ln.
Clerkenwell Rd.
Aldersgate St.
Beech St.
The Barbican
Moorgate
Theobalds Rd.
Southampton Row
Hatton Gdns.
British Museum
Museum of London
London Wall
Liverpool St. Station
Bishopsgate
Houndsditch
Holborn
Holborn Via
High
Kingsway
Fetter Ln.
Farringdon St.
Law Courts
Samuel Johnson's House
St. Paul's Cathedral
Cheapside
Bank of England
Stock Exchange
Cornhill
Leadenhall St.
Minories
Mansell St.
Leman St.
Dock St.
Aldwych
Courtauld Institute
Blackfriars Station
Cannon St.
Temple of Mithras
Gracechurch St.
Leicester Square
National Gallery
Strand
Victoria Embankment
Upper Thames St.
Cannon Street Station
Lower Thames St.
Byward St.
Tower Hill East
River Thames
Blackfriars Bridge
Southwark Bridge
Tower of London
London Bridge
HMS Belfast
Waterloo Bridge
Globe Theatre
Charing Cross Station
Hungerford Bridge
Stamford St.
Southwark St.
Southwark Cathedral
Tooley St.
London Bridge Station
Tower Bridge
Whitehall
10 Downing Street
Union St.
Borough High St.
The Cut
Jamaica Rd.
Druid St.
Westminster Bridge
York Rd.
Waterloo Station
Waterloo Rd.
Blackfriars Rd.
Southwark Bridge Rd.
Great Dover St.
Long Ln.
Houses of Parliament
Westminster Abbey
Lambeth Palace Rd.
Westminster Bridge Rd.
Borough Rd.
Causeway
Harper Rd.
Abbey St.
Tower Bridge Rd.
Grange Rd.
Lambeth Bridge
Lambeth Rd.
Imperial War Museum
St. George's Rd.
London Rd.
Kennington Rd.
New Kent Rd.
WESTMINSTER
Kennington Park Rd.
Walworth Rd.
Old Kent Rd.
Albert Embankment
Millbank
British Museum 14
Buckingham Palace 13
Clarence House 10
Covent Garden 19
Design Museum 18
Green Park 8
Horse Guards 24
Houses of Parliament 26
Hyde Park 7
Kensington Gardens 5
Kensington Palace 4
Madame Tussaud's 3
National Gallery 22
National Portrait Gallery 21
Regent's Park 2
Russell Square 13
Saatchi Gallery 1
St. James's Palace 10
St. James's Park 12
St. Paul's Cathedral 16
Sir John Soane's Museum 15
Spencer House 9
Tate Gallery 27
Theatre Museum 20
Tower of London 17
Trafalgar Square 23
Victoria & Albert Museum 6
Westminster Abbey 25

The Royals

By now everyone in the world is aware of the ongoing soap opera known as The Royals. Things came to a head for the House of Windsor after Princess Diana's death, when national polls showed the British public viewed the monarchy as aloof, out of touch, and something of a waste of taxpayers' money. The queen was so shocked at the findings (so out of touch) that in February 1998 she decided to hire a Washington-style spin doctor to boost the family's sagging ratings.

And those Royal ratings have improved in the year since Diana's death. Prince Charles's popularity has gone up, and even his paramour, Camilla Parker-Bowles, is receiving a flicker of respect. Now it's Diana's brother, Earl Spencer, who's defending himself against allegations that he's callously capitalizing on his sister's untimely end by opening a museum at Althorp.

If you're dying for history, information, and trivia about the Windsors (really the Saxe-Coburg-Gothas; they wisely changed their German name at the onset of World War I) and the British monarchy in general, check out the official Royal Web site at **www.royal.gov.uk.**

From the neo-Gothic Houses of Parliament, it's a quick walk to the true Gothic splendor of Westminster Abbey. Though the present abbey dates mostly from the 13th and 14th centuries, there's been a church on this spot for over 1,000 years. Since 1066, when Harold became the first English monarch to be crowned here, every successive sovereign save two (Edward V and Edward VIII) has sat on the Coronation Chair and received the crown and scepter. Elizabeth II was the last, in 1953, and the big question is: Will unpopular Prince Charles ever ascend the throne? Next in line after Charles is Prince William, his and Diana's elder son. Of course, in September 1997 Westminster Abbey was the site of the funeral service for the adored Diana.

Unlike at St. Paul's, you don't have to pay to enter Westminster Abbey—unless you want to visit the Royal Chapels and Poets' Corner. And they're well worth it. The **Henry VII Chapel** with its delicate fan vaulting is beautiful. You'll see the tomb of hawk-nosed Queen Elizabeth I, buried in the same vault as her Catholic half sister, Mary I, and not far from her rival, Mary Queen of Scots. Follow the ant-line of tourists to **Poets' Corner,** where England's greatest writers (like Chaucer, Dickens, and Thomas Hardy) are interred or memorialized. Some gay greats are among them: Gerard Manley Hopkins, W. H. Auden, and Henry James. In 1995, 100 years after his release from Reading Gaol, Oscar Wilde was finally recognized by the Church of England with an abstract-design blue memorial window. But since his name is nowhere to be seen, it's the kind of dubious honor that would no doubt have provoked a witty quip from the great man. Maybe something like: "Clear glass simply wouldn't do for my memorial, it had to be stained."

Kensington Palace. The Broad Walk, Kensington Gardens, W8. ☎ **020/7937-9561.** Admission £7.50 ($13). May–Oct 5 daily 10am–5pm by guided tour. Tube: Queensway or Bayswater on the north side or High Street Kensington on the south.

Diana-philes will definitely want to visit Kensington Palace, the Princess's London home after her messy separation and divorce from Prince What's-his-name. It's set within Kensington Gardens (see "Parks, Gardens & Squares" below). As you turn into the palace grounds from the Broad Walk you'll see, directly in front of you, a high brick wall. A building wing barely visible behind the wall was where Diana lived. After her death, tens of thousands of mourners gathered in front of the palace and left a sea

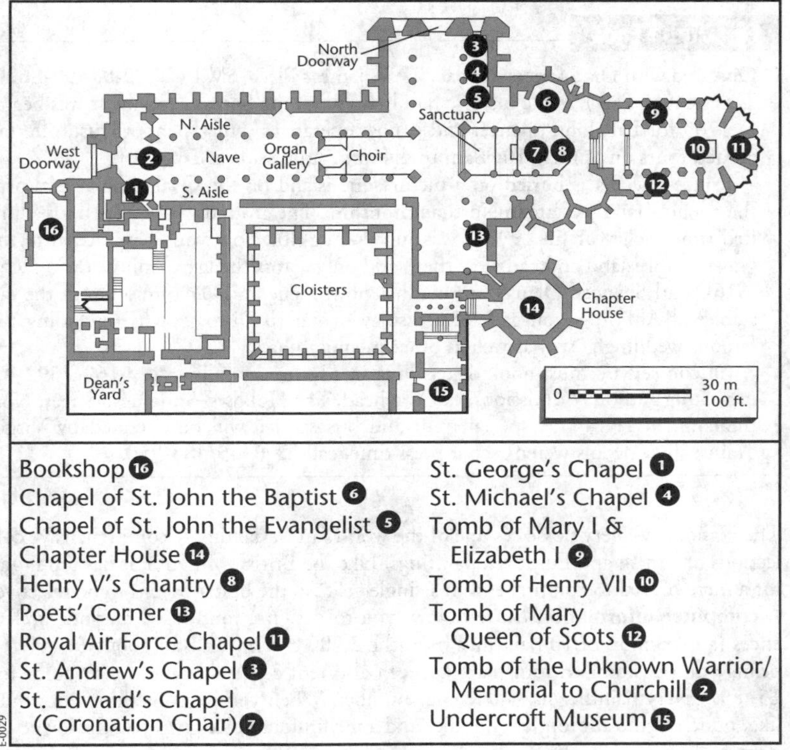

of floral tributes. In fact, there was talk of building here some sort of monument or garden dedicated to Diana, but local residents have objected and the project's fate is uncertain. However, on the first anniversary of her death it was announced that a 16-acre memorial garden is planned here.

Acquired by William III in 1689 and remodeled by Sir Christopher Wren, the palace was used as a royal residence until 1760. Victoria, who was born here, would no doubt be aghast at the number of strangers who now tramp through the bedroom where in 1837 she was informed she was the new Queen of England. The palace is still the home of Princess Margaret and other lesser royals (like the duke and duchess of Kent), so much of it's closed off to prying eyes. But the state apartments you can visit are filled with fine art and *objets* (check out the porcelain) from the Royal Collection and also contain the Royal Ceremonial Dress Collection (lots of useful nonsense on the sartorial and financial agony of being "presented" at Court).

If you're in the mood for a cuppa (tea) or a sweetie after visiting Kensington Palace, head over to **The Orangery** (☎ **020/7376-0239;** open Oct–Mar daily 10am–4pm, Apr–Sept daily 10am–6pm), the brick building about 50 yards north. Queen Anne had this garden conservatory built in 1704 and used it for royal tea parties. Potted orange trees were (and still are) grown inside amid a collection of urns and statuary. It's teddibly quaint, the sort of place where visiting queens feel right at home.

✪ **National Gallery.** Trafalgar Sq., WC2. ☎ **020/7839-3321.** Admission free. Mon–Tues and Thurs–Sat 10am–6pm, Wed 10am–8pm, Sun noon–6pm. Closed Jan 1, Good Friday, Dec 24–26. Tube: Leicester Sq.

For Diana Fans

Obsessed with Di? **Spencer House.** 27 St. James's Place, SW1 (☎ **020/7499-8620;** Tube: Green Park), is the historic family home of the Spencer family. It was begun in 1765 for Earl John Spencer and is now operated by the Spencer Trust, offering guided tours on Sunday 10:30am to 4:45pm. Admission is £6 ($10).

Princess Diana is buried on a picturesque island on the Oval Lake at **Althorp,** the Spencer family estate in Northamptonshire. The grounds will be open for a limited time each year (in 1998 it was July 1–Aug 30). You won't have access to the grave site or island and can view the island only across the lake. Admission is £9.50 ($16). Earl Spencer, Diana's brother, has now opened a Diana museum in the old stables at Althorp—you can see a display of her to-Di-for gowns (including the famous wedding gown) as well as other memorabilia.

Of course, you must book tickets long in advance by calling ☎ **01604/592-020** or writing Althorp Admissions, c/o Wayhead, The Hollows, St. James's Street, Nottingham, NG1 6FJ. A special train and bus service will be operated by Virgin Trains; since details weren't set at press time, call ☎ **0345/484-950.**

The National Gallery possesses one of the world's most dazzlingly comprehensive collections of British and European paintings. Like the British Museum, it has too much for a mere mortal to comprehend in a single visit, so the best advice is to be selective. A **computer information center** allows you to design a tour based on your preferences (a maximum of 10 paintings from the 2,200 entries) and for about £1 ($1.70) prints out a customized tour map. You can also rent a portable audio tour guide for £5 ($9). Every painting has a reference number. When you see something you really like, punch in the appropriate number and a mellifluous voice gives you the lowdown on it.

All the major schools from the 13th to the 20th century are represented, but the Italians get the lion's share of wall space. As well they should, with artists like Leonardo, Botticelli, Raphael, Masaccio, and Mantegna on the roster. The Italian works are housed in the newer **Sainsbury Wing.** Among the endless "Adorations" and Madonnas (the original one) and biblical scenes, it's refreshing to come across paintings like Titian's *Bacchus and Ariadne,* a 16th-century version of heterosexual revelry, and Tintoretto's fanciful *The Origin of the Milky Way,* showing a comely goddess squirting milky stars from her Jane Russell–sized orbs.

The French Impressionist and post-Impressionist works by Monet, Manet, Seurat, Cézanne, Degas, and van Gogh are shimmering and sublime. And since you're on English soil, you'd be well advised to check out at least a few of the stunning seascapes by Turner, landscapes by Constable, and society portraits by Sir Joshua Reynolds. And don't forget the Rembrandts.

✪ **National Portrait Gallery.** St. Martin's Place, WC2. ☎ **020/7306-0055.** Admission free. Mon–Sat 10am–6pm, Sun noon–6pm. Tube: Leicester Sq.

The National Portrait Gallery is right behind the National Gallery. Here you'll find a truly fabulous pictorial Who's Who of famous Brits—gay, straight, and in-between.

If Nicholas Hilliard's miniature of dishy Sir Walter Raleigh is accurate—he's wearing white tights and a pair of those puffy 16th-century pantaloons—no wonder Elizabeth I had the hots for him. She was only human after all, though Hilliard's full-length portrait turns her into a power icon so encumbered by jewels and brocade she looks like one of those saints carried aloft in Spanish religious festivals. And who ever thought a genius like "Bill" Shakespeare could be so darkly handsome? The gold earring he's wearing in this portrait might lead one to suppose he liked to swing both ways, as some scholars and directors have long surmised.

Cruising through the various galleries, especially the redesigned first floor devoted to Victorian and early-20th-century portraits, you'll come across photographs of Oscar Wilde; Cecil Beaton's arty snaps of Vita Sackville-West, Siegfried Sassoon, and E. M. Forster; Roger Fry's canvas of Edward Carpenter; Augustus John's drawing of Ronald Firbank; Vanessa Bell's portrait of her sister, Virginia Woolf; Simon Bussy's pastel of Lytton Strachey; a self-portrait by Denton Welch; portraits and photographs of Noël Coward; a watercolor of Benjamin Britten; and Don Bachardy's pen-and-ink drawing of W. H. Auden. You'll also run across homophobic termagants like Baroness Thatcher and gay-friendly idols like Princess Diana, whose portrait is on the Royal Landing.

Houses of Parliament. Parliament Sq., SW1. House of Commons ☎ **020/7219-4272;** House of Lords ☎ **020/7219-3107.** Admission free. House of Lords open Mon–Wed from 2:30pm, Thurs from 3pm, and some Fri (check by phone). House of Commons open Mon–Tues and Thurs from 3:30pm, Wed and Fri from 9:30am. Entrance at St. Stephen's. Tube: Westminster.

For movie nuts, the Houses of Parliament and their phallic clocktower, containing **Big Ben** (the name of the largest bell in the chime, not the tower itself), will probably conjure up old British flicks in which the famous buildings are used for "you're in bustling London" shots, and Big Ben strikes the midnight hour as the fogs rise, hounds howl, and caped fiends stalk their pretty victims.

This undeniably impressive example of Victorian architecture doing its neo-Gothic thing is officially known as the Royal Palace of St. Stephen at Westminster. The buildings, designed by Sir Charles Barry and Augustus Pugin, were completed in 1857. Covering some 8 acres, they occupy the site of an 11th-century Thames-side palace of Edward the Confessor. At one end (Old Palace Yard) is the **Jewel Tower,** built in 1366 and once the treasury house of Edward III (reigned 1327–1377).

No one I know has ever stepped foot in this place, but if you want to sit in the **Strangers' Gallery** to hear the fights and childish squabbling that passes for debate in the House of Commons, you can line up (pardon me, *queue*) for tickets at the St. Stephen's entrance. The latest parliamentary hot-button topic of interest to gays concerns lowering the legal age of consent for males from 18 to 16 (as it is for women). In his election campaign, PM Tony Blair promised to do just that, and in mid-1998 the Commons voted for it with an overwhelming majority. Everyone thought it was a go until the ultraconservative aristos in the House of Lords smashed it down by using every nonsensical and homophobic scare story on the books. The bill's outcome was unclear at this writing, but generally the Commons wins out. From the Houses of Parliament it's a short walk to Westminster Abbey.

St. Paul's Cathedral. St. Paul's Churchyard, Ludgate Hill, EC4. ☎ **020/7236-4128.** Cathedral £4 ($7); galleries £3.50 ($6). Church Mon–Sat 8:30am–4:15pm; galleries 9:30am–4pm; no sightseeing on Sun (services only). Guided tours £3.50 ($5.60) Mon–Sat at 11am, 11:30am, 1:30pm, and 2pm; recorded tours £3 ($4.80). Tube: St. Paul's.

It still seems a bit sacrilegious to have to pay to enter a church, but given the enormous cost of upkeep it's evidently the only way St. Paul's can keep its doors open. Many will want to see the place simply because it was here that 20-year-old Diana Spencer wed 32-year-old Prince Charles in what was prematurely billed as "the fairy-tale wedding of the century."

After the catastrophic Great Fire of 1666 destroyed most of medieval London, including the city's Gothic cathedral, it was decided that a new cathedral should rise on the same spot. The great architect Christopher Wren, who designed dozens of

The Dish on the Dome & Another Millennium Site

With 14 themed zones around a central performance area, the £700-million Millennium Dome, Greenwich, SE10 (Tube: North Greenwich), opens on January 1, 2000. At the dome's center, a thrice-daily show (created by Mark Fisher and Peter Gabriel) with 200 performers and stunning visual effects will "propel visitors through the story of humanity." Among the zones are "Body," a walk through the world's largest representation of the human form (sounds like fun to me). Admission and hours weren't set at press time, so check with the Britain Visitor Centre (see "Visitor Information") or on the Web at www.LondonMillenniumCity.com.

Opening in December 1999, the British Airways London Eye, Jubilee Gardens, SE1 (☎ 020/7487-0294; Tube: Embankment or Waterloo), is an extraordinary Ferris wheel that'll be the world's highest observation wheel. Protected from the elements inside 32 high-tech capsules, you rise slowly to a height of 450 feet and receive a 30-minute slow-moving "flight" over the heart of the capital, complete with commentary and bird's-eye views. Admission will be £6.95 ($11). Exact hours weren't set at press time.

London's smaller post-fire churches, was called on to design this huge Renaissance-leaning-toward-Baroque edifice. Construction began in 1675 and wasn't completed until 35 years later. St. Paul's miraculously escaped destruction in the Nazi bombing raids, but the surrounding area was wiped out. Today Wren's masterpiece, capped by the most famous dome in London, rises majestically above a crowded sea of disconcertingly banal office buildings.

Huge and harmonious, the cathedral is laid out in the form of a Greek cross, with the splendid soufflé of its dome marking the center. You can climb up to the Whispering Gallery that girdles it and have a bit of acoustical fun. Or gasp your way up to the very top for a breathtaking (literally) view of London. There's not much in the way or art except for the exceptionally beautiful choir stalls carved by Grinling Gibbons. Christopher Wren lies in the crypt, his tomb bearing the Latin inscription "Lector, si monumentum requiris, circumspice" ("Reader, if you seek his monument, look around you). Also in the crypt are those famous national heroes the Duke of Wellington and Lord Nelson. Guided tours last 1½ hours and include parts of the cathedral not open to the general public. Recorded tours lasting 45 minutes are available throughout the day.

✪ **Victoria & Albert Museum.** Cromwell Rd., SW7. ☎ **020/7938-8500,** or 020/7938-8441 for a recording. Admission £5 ($8); free 4:30–5:50pm. Mon noon–5:50pm, Tues–Sun 10am–5:50pm. Tube: South Kensington.

The V&A is the world's greatest repository of the decorative arts: If it's aesthetic and useful—and has been crafted in the last 15 centuries—you'll find it here. Look for porcelain figurines, costume jewelry, enamel washing bowls, silver forks and spoons, musical instruments, gilded mirrors, ceramic bowls and plates, stained-glass lamps, lace doilies—you name it. The famous Dress Collection covers fashion from the 16th century to the present—no, you can't try anything on.

Tate Gallery. Millbank, Pimlico, SW1. ☎ **020/7887-8000,** or 020/7420-0055 for advance ticket sales. Admission free; varying admission fees for special exhibits. Audio tours £3 ($5). Daily 10am–5:40pm. Tube: Pimlico, then a 10-minute walk south on Vauxhall Bridge Rd. to the river and north on Millbank to museum entrance.

If you like the dreamy works of the British Pre-Raphaelite school, the celestial visions of William Blake, the satirical works of William Hogarth, the genteel portraits by Sir Joshua Reynolds, the bucolic landscapes of John Constable, the shimmering seascapes of J. M. W. Turner, the sculptures of Henry Moore, or the disturbing canvases of Francis Bacon, make a point to visit the Tate, a major repository for British art. Equally grand is the collection of international modern art, with important works by Matisse, Dalí, Modigliani, Munch, Bonnard, Picasso, and Rothko. In 2,000, the modern art collection will move to the **Tate Gallery of Modern Art,** Bankside, SE1 (☎ 020/7887-8729; Tube: Mansion House or London Bridge). Admission and hours weren't set at press time. The completion of the **Millenium Bridge** will provide a pedestrian walkway from the steps of St. Paul's over the Thames to the new gallery.

Covent Garden. Bounded by Long Acre to the north, Kingsway to the east, Strand to the south, and Charing Cross to the west. Tube: Covent Garden.

Covent Garden used to be London's public market, a teeming, raucous place where loud-mouthed vendors hawked everything from fish to fruit (and sometimes themselves). It's where Cockney Eliza Doolittle in George Bernard Shaw's *Pygmalion* (played by Wendy Hiller in the old black-and-white film version and by Audrey Hepburn in the Technicolor *My Fair Lady* version) sold flowers and dropped her 'aitches before being linguistically rehabilitated by Professor 'enry 'iggins. Covent Garden is also the home of the Royal Opera House (currently closed for reconstruction).

In 1970, the odiferous market that gave Covent Garden so much of its character moved out, and the area became the site of one of London's earliest and most successful "urban recycling" schemes. On weekends it's positively "heaving," as the Brits say, as tourists from around the globe congregate to cruise, schmooze, eat, and check out the retail. The clothing shops tend toward the trendy and expensive, but the wrought-iron stalls from the old flower market are loaded with more downmarket vendors selling the good, the bad, and the ugly.

Drama queens may want to check out the **Theatre Museum** on Russell Street (☎ **020/7836-7891;** open Tues–Sun 11am–7pm); admission £3.50/$6). All the world's a stage at this branch of the Victoria & Albert Museum, where you can enjoy an hour or so perusing the National Collections of the Performing Arts. British theater, ballet, opera, music-hall pantomime, puppets, circus, and rock and pop music—both past and present—are all represented. The exhibits focus on the development of the British stage and its performers from Shakespeare to Stoppard—and the daily makeup demonstrations can be very useful.

Madame Tussaud's. Marylebone Rd., NW1/ ☎ **020/7935-6861.** Admission £9.25 ($16). Daily 9am–5:30pm. Tube: Baker St.

Eerily lifelike figures have made this century-old museum world famous. But do you really want to spend $16 to look at a bunch of boring wax dummies? (Cybill Shepherd, of all people, was the latest addition.) The line to get in takes forever, and once inside you aren't even allowed to pose for photos beside Princess Di or any of the Royals. The original moldings of members of the French court, to whom Mme Tussaud had direct access (quite literally, since she made molds of their heads once they were guillotined during the French Revolution), are undeniably fascinating. But the modern superstars and the Chamber of Horrors are the stuff tourist traps are made of. If you *must* go, go early to beat the crowds; better still, reserve tickets 1 day in advance, then go straight to the head of the line.

Design Museum. Butler's Wharf, SE1. ☎ **020/7378-6055.** Admission £5.25 ($9). Daily 11:30am–6pm. Tube: Tower Hill, then a half-hour walk across Tower Bridge to Butler's Wharf east of the bridge on the South Bank.

It's a bit difficult to get to this South Bank museum, but if you've got a Design for Living or simply live for design, it's worth it. We all know the tremendous impact commercial design plays in our everyday lives, but who would've guessed that an old toaster would end up in a museum? Classical, kitsch, modern, surreal, and innovative, from Corbusier chairs to the Coke bottle, it's all chronicled here. It's the sort of place that makes you say, "We had one of those when I was a kid." Plus, there are great river views.

Saatchi Gallery. 98A Boundary Rd., NW8. ☎ **020/7624-8299.** Admission £4 ($6); free Thurs. Thurs–Sun noon–6pm. Tube: Swiss Cottage, then a 10-minute walk south on Finchley Rd. to Boundary Rd.

Advertising and media mogul Charles Saatchi has assembled a brilliant collection of contemporary cutting-edge, and it's all beautifully displayed in this white-on-white space in northwest London. You enter through the unmarked metal gateway of a former paint warehouse. The main focus is on works by young British artists, though Americans are represented as well. Some of the work, like Damien Hirst's 14-foot tiger shark preserved in a formaldehyde-filled tank, are controversial and repugnant. If you've ever wondered what many Brits think of American tourists (not you, of course), catch Duane Hanson's *Tourists II.*

Sir John Soane's Museum. 13 Lincoln's Inn Fields, WC2. ☎ **020/7430-0175.** Admission free (donations invited). Tues–Sat 10am–5pm. Tours given Sat at 2:30pm for £3 ($5). Tube: Holborn.

Everyone seems to call this museum-house "eccentric," but that's probably because they're not gay and don't appreciate witty architectural interiors. The house of Sir John Soane (1753–1837), architect of the Bank of England, is a treasure trove of ancient sculpture, artifacts, and art mixed with fun-house architectural perspectives, fool-the-eye mirrors, flying arches, and domes. The oldest piece in the house is the 3,300-year-old sarcophagus of Pharaoh Seti I. Top prize in the picture gallery goes to William Hogarth's satirical and sometimes bawdy series from *The Rake's Progress.* The museum is rarely crowded, which makes it even more of a treat.

Royal Botanic Gardens (Kew Gardens). Kew Rd., Richmond Surrey. ☎ **020/8940-1171.** Admission £5 ($8). One-hour garden tours Mar–Nov daily at 11am and 2pm for £1 ($2) per person per hour (call ☎ 020/8332-5623 for information). Gardens daily 9:30am–dusk; Kew Palace and Queen Charlotte's Cottage Apr–Oct daily 11am–5:30pm. Tube: Kew Gardens, then a 10-minute walk west on Broomfield St. to Victoria Gate entrance on Kew Rd.

The Royal Botanic Gardens in Kew, 7 miles west of Central London, are a feast for the eyes (and nose) of garden lovers. This trip, with travel time and garden browsing, will take the better part of a day but is well worth it. On display in the 300-acre gardens is a marvelous array of specimens first planted in the 17th and 18th centuries. Orchids and palms are nurtured in the Victorian "glass pavilion" hothouse. There's also a lake, aquatic gardens, and a Chinese pagoda. **Kew Palace,** the smallest and most picturesque of the former royal compounds, is where George III went off his rocker. **Queen Charlotte's Cottage** was the kew-kew king's summer retreat.

GAY LONDON

London was a mecca for gay travelers long before the city decided to invest several million pounds to promote gay tourism. But now it's gayer than ever and pride is bursting out all over.

There's quite literally something for everyone in this teeming metropolis—and I don't just mean the gay bars, pubs, and clubs scattered far and wide. Central London boasts two gay neighborhoods worth exploring: Earl's Court and Soho.

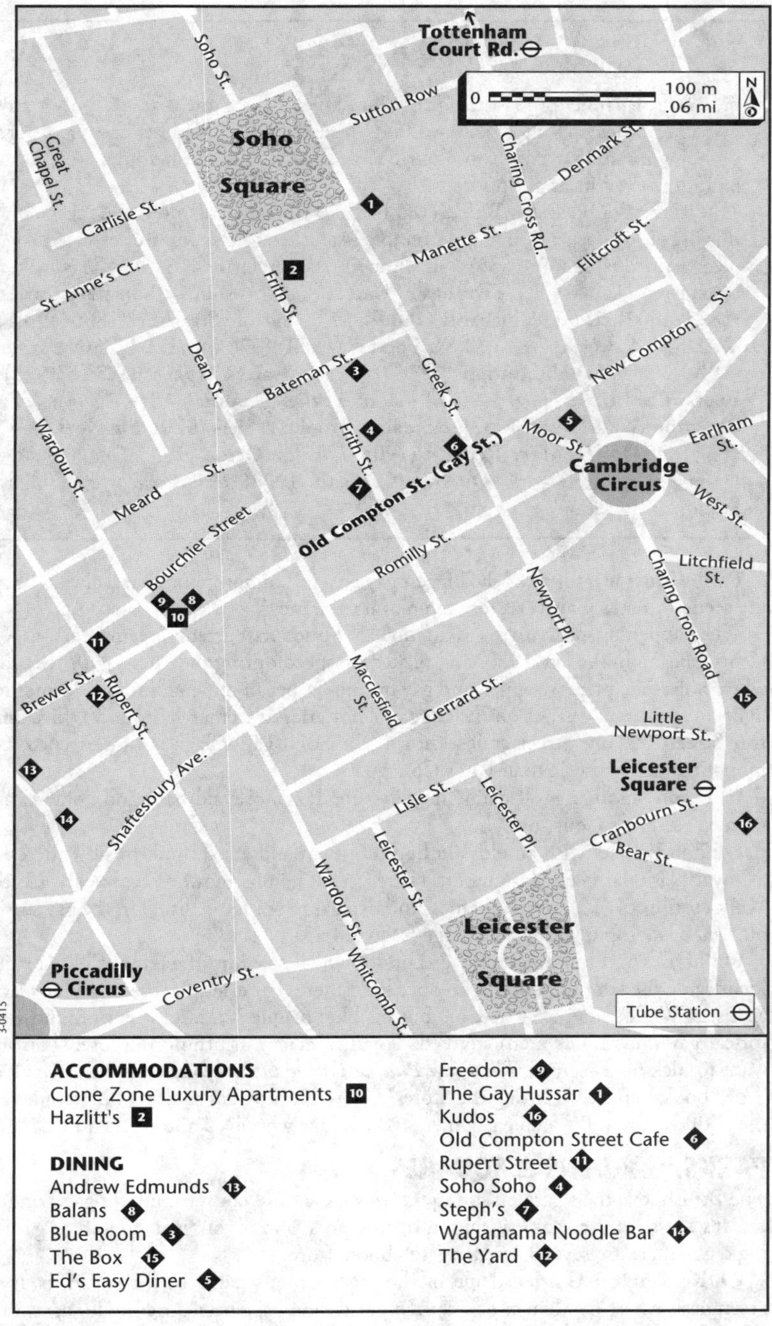
Tottenham
Court Rd.
100 m
.06 mi
0
N
Soho St.
Sutton Row
Soho
Square
Great
Chapel St.
Carlisle St.
St. Anne's Ct.
Charing Cross Rd.
Denmark St.
Manette St.
Flitcroft St.
Frith St.
Dean St.
Bateman St.
Greek St.
New Compton
St.
Wardour St.
Moor St.
Earlham
St.
Cambridge
Circus
West St.
Meard
St.
Old Compton St. (Gay St.)
Bourchier Street
Romilly St.
Litchfield
St.
Newport Pl.
Charing Cross Road
Brewer St.
Rupert St.
Macclesfield
St.
Gerrard St.
Little
Newport St.
Leicester
Square
Shaftesbury Ave.
Lisle St.
Leicester Pl.
Cranbourn St.
Bear St.
Leicester St.
Wardour St.
Leicester
Square
Piccadilly
Circus
Coventry St.
Whitcomb St.
Tube Station
3-0415
ACCOMMODATIONS
Clone Zone Luxury Apartments 10
Hazlitt's 2
DINING
Andrew Edmunds 13
Balans 8
Blue Room 3
The Box 15
Ed's Easy Diner 5
Freedom 9
The Gay Hussar 1
Kudos 16
Old Compton Street Cafe 6
Rupert Street 11
Soho Soho 4
Steph's 7
Wagamama Noodle Bar 14
The Yard 12

The Queer Quiz

Hey, kids, it's time for . . . the Queer Quiz, an exciting game that asks how many London homos you know about. Literature, theater, art, and history majors are probably aware that dozens of their favorite gay heroes and heroines were born in and/or lived in London.

Without doubt, **Oscar Wilde** (1854–1900) is the most famous. But check out this list of full- or part-time gay Londoners and see how many names you recognize: **Erasmus** (1469–1536), **Sir Francis Bacon** (1561–1626), **Christopher Marlowe** (1564–93), **Elizabeth Carter** (1717–1806), **Samuel Butler** (1835–1902), **Ronald Firbank** (1886–1926), **Lytton Strachey** (1880–1932), **W. H. Auden** (1907–73), **E. M. Forster** (1879–1970), **Dame Lillian Barker** (1874–1955), **Natalie Barney** (1876–1972), **Edward Carpenter** (1844–1929), **Benjamin Britten** (1913–1976), **Dame Ethel Smythe** (1858–1944), **Vita Sackville–West** (1892–1962), **Romaine Brooks** (1874–1970), **Sir Noël Coward** (1899–1973), **Mary Renault** (1905–83), **Joe Orton** (1933–67), and still-living (but in New York) **Quentin Crisp** (b. 1908), one of the great "stately homos of England."

Earl's Court was for years the biggest gay area in London; though it'll always be gay, the scene in Earl's Court has lost some of its vibrancy.

The happening place to be right now is **Soho;** its current preeminence as Gay Central began in the late 1980s and picked up speed during the early 1990s recession, when real-estate prices dropped and gay businesses began moving into this former red-light 'n' restaurant district on the edge of Theaterland. Centered around **Old Compton Street,** or **Gay Street** as it's known, the Soho gay village is more trendy, cosmopolitan, and upscale than Earl's Court.

Islington, another gay-friendly neighborhood, is more laid-back and domesticated than either Earl's Court or Soho.

London is a city with an old, old homo history, and you'd think by now there'd be a Royal National Gay Monument. There isn't. There is, however, a weekly ✪ **Gay Walk** costing £5 ($9); times, themes, and departure points are listed in the gay section of *Time Out.* Topics and walk charge frequently.

On houses and buildings all over London you'll run into the famous blue plaques identifying the famous people who once lived there. For example, there's a blue plaque at Oscar Wilde's house, 34 Tite St. But his blue plaque is a rare exception; most historical gay households aren't marked. For further gay sleuthing purposes, you may want to pick up a copy of ***The Pink Plaque Guide to London,*** available at Gay's the Word bookshop (see "Hitting the Stores" below). It provides succinct biographies and the addresses of 100 notable gay men and lesbians who lived and worked in London.

PARKS, GARDENS & SQUARES

The British love their gardens, but *gardening* has a different meaning for gay Londoners. It's the term used for cruising in open spaces, and if you want to join a "gardening club" there are several "gardens" to choose from.

✪ **Kensington Gardens,** one of the most famous parks in the world, is a vast green oasis where gentlemen of a certain persuasion have been strolling for ages. Here you'll find a well-known statue of Peter Pan, J. M. Barrie's famous flying boy (the one who refused to grow up and later became a syndrome). "Pete," you may recall, lived under a tree in Kensington Gardens with his band of Lost Boys. Late Princess Diana's

Kensington Palace is here, and so is the freshly restored **Albert Memorial.** Anyone familiar with a "Prince Albert" will understand why Queen Victoria was so miserable when he died—she'd lost the most valuable member of her household.

Kensington Gardens abuts **Hyde Park,** famous for the ranting orators who try to incite the crowds at **Speakers' Corner.** Anyone can stand up and put in their 2 pence worth, but you can't blaspheme, be obscene, or incite a riot. Every Sunday at 3pm a speaker from Hyde Park Sapphics and Gays attempts to raise the consciousness of the crowds.

East of Hyde Park stretch **Green Park** and **St. James's Park,** both lovely and much perambulated. **Regent's Park,** north of Baker Street and Marylebone Road, was designed by John Nash in the 18th century. London's most classically beautiful park, it's the home of the London Zoo and has a famous rose garden. For the **Royal Botanic Gardens (Kew Gardens),** see above.

Trafalgar Square is for tourists and pigeons (or for cavorting lesbians—see the back cover of this guide). Far more interesting, in terms of gay history, is **Russell Square** in Bloomsbury, where London's gay "gardening club" has been meeting for at least 100 years. A few years ago, following a gay bashing and a murder, the police stepped in with tea, sympathy, and even free condoms. The city then installed surveillance cameras and hacked down all the shrubbery. But the "gardening club" still meets there on a discretionary basis. They also congregate among the gravestones in **Brompton Cemetery,** in Earl's Court. A bit macabre unless you're into memento mori.

BOYS & GIRLS ON THE BEACH

About 4 miles north of the city center (20 minutes by Tube) is one of London's greatest and busiest parks, 800-acre ✪ **Hampstead Heath** (Tube: Hampstead Heath). The "gardening club" meets at the western end. Others may strip down to their skimpies to soak up the rays and frolic in the ✪ **Highgate Men's Pond,** the closest thing London has to a beach; there's an enclosed sundeck for sunbathing au naturel (swimmers share the water with lots of quacking ducks and algae). Daughters of Sappho, no matter how butch, must use the nearby **Kenwood Ladies' Pond,** which is prettier and for women only. These outdoor ponds are open year-round from dawn to dusk with no admission.

There are other reasons to visit the Heath too. **Kenwood House,** Hampstead Lane, NW3 (☎ **020/8348-1286;** Tube: Archway, then bus 210 west; open Apr–Oct daily 10am–6pm, Nov–Mar to 4pm; admission free), in the northern section of the Heath, is a lovely neoclassical villa designed by Robert Adam. Inside is a small but impressive collection of paintings and jewelry. The Kenwood Lakeside concert bowl beside the house is the sublime setting for outdoor symphony concerts in summer (see below).

If you're going to the Heath, you might want to combine it with a visit to **Hampstead Village** (Tube: Hampstead), just south of the park. It remains a village of charm and character, filled with Regency and Georgian houses favored by artists, writers, and queers with taste. Along **Flask Walk,** the village's pedestrian mall, you'll find a mix of historic pubs, chic boutiques, and occasional cruising, The village itself boasts lots of old alleys, steps, courts, and groves to be explored.

WORKING UP A SWEAT

SPORTS If you're an athletic supporter or just like guys who wear them, you may want to check out a gay game or two. The **Stonewall Football Club** (☎ **020/7281-9430**) plays straight teams in regularly held matches. The **King's Cross Steelers** (☎ **020/7928-0668**), a gay rugby team, plays on Sundays. **Gay London Swimmers** (☎ **020/8800-8880**) practice nude swimming techniques at various pools and baths.

You can get information on gay sporting events by calling **Out For Sport** at ☎ **020/ 8534-6681;** there's a £2 ($3.45) charge.

GYMS Need a workout? **Paris Gymnasium,** Arch 73, Goding Street, SE11 (☎ **020/7735-8989;** Tube: Vauxhall), is a gay gym with weights, machines, and a sauna. There's also a decent gym at the huge gay sauna **Pleasuredrome,** 125 Alaska St., SE1 (☎ **020/7633-9194;** Tube: Waterloo), where you can work out for £4 ($7) without entering the sauna itself. Other London gyms that cater to both gays and straights are **Earl's Court Gym,** 254 Earl's Court Rd., SW5 (☎ **020/7370-1402;** Tube: Earl's Court), and the popular **London Central YMCA,** 112 Great Russell St., WC1 (☎ **020/7637-8131;** Tube: Tottenham Court Rd.), which also has a pool and a sauna. Prices and opening times vary from place to place, so call before going.

5 Hitting the Stores

It's a shopper's paradise, dear old London, with many, many stores you'll never find back in Dubuque or Auckland. You could take your mother to most of them, but there are some she definitely wouldn't approve of.

The sweeping curve of **Regent Street** is one place to go for traditional upscale togs. **Knightsbridge** has the famed Harrods, owned by Dodi's father, and hundreds of expensive boutiques. Trendy tag hags will adore **Covent Garden.** Bibliophiles head for the great bookstores on **Charing Cross Road** (as in *84 Charing Cross Road* by Helene Hanff, the movie version starring Ann Bancroft). Scroungers looking for second-hand bargains paw through the goods in **Camden Markets** (forget Portobello Road, which has become too well-known for its own good). **Soho** has its fair share of gay shops, but you'll find gay goods in Earl's Court and other places as well.

Hours for London shops are generally Monday to Saturday 10am to 5:30pm, with a late closing (7 or 8pm) on Wednesday or Thursday. Stores may legally be open for 6 hours on Sunday, usually 11am to 5pm.

SHOPS A TO Z

The gay version of the pound sterling is the pound pink, or the pink pound as it's more generally called. In London, there are an increasing number of places where you might want to shed a few of your pink pounds.

ART & ANTIQUES ✪ **Adonis Art and Antiques,** Antiquarius Antique Centre, 135 King's Rd., SW3 (☎ **020/7349-0399;** Tube: Sloane Sq.), specializes in art treasures depicting the male nude; the store is upscale, unusual, and the only one like it in the United Kingdom, perhaps in the world. **The Mall at Camden Passage,** Islington, N1 (☎ **020/7351-5353;** Tube: Angel), houses some 35 antiques dealers.

BOOKS ✪ **Gay's the Word,** 66 Marchmont St., WC1 (☎ **020/7278-7654;** Tube: Russell Sq.), is the city's only all-round gay and lesbian bookstore; it stocks a fine selection of new and used books and current periodicals. ✪ **Hatchards,** 187 Piccadilly, W1 (☎ **020/7439-9921;** Tube: Piccadilly Circus), established in 1797, is London's most historic and atmospheric bookstore; it was where Oscar Wilde came to stock up on reading material after being released from prison (his wife, Constance, reputedly had an affair with the owner).

The following bookstores, all along Charing Cross Road, also invite prowling among their selection of gay titles: **Blackwells,** 100 Charing Cross Rd. (☎ **020/ 7292-5100**); **Books Etc.,** 120 Charing Cross Rd. (☎ **020/7379-6836**); and **Waterstone's,** 121 Charing Cross Rd. (☎ **020/7434-4291**). Lesbians, there's something on Charing Cross for you too: **Silver Moon Women's Bookshop,** 64–68 Charing Cross Rd. (☎ **020/7836-7906**).

DEPARTMENT STORES **Harrods,** 87–135 Brompton Rd., SW1 (☎ **020/7730-1234;** Tube: Knightsbridge), has more surveillance equipment than the White House; it's overrated, if you ask me, but carrying around the famous green plastic Harrods bag they give you with every purchase does convey a certain sense of accomplishment. Fans of *Absolutely Fabulous* may want to check out Edina's fave, Harvey Nicks, officially known as **Harvey Nichols,** 109–125 Knightsbridge, SW1 (☎ **020/7235-5000;** Tube: Knightsbridge); once a favorite of the late Princess Di, the store is large and crammed with the designer home furnishings, gifts, and fashions. **Fortnum & Mason,** 181 Piccadilly, W1 (☎ **020/7734-8040;** Tube: Green Park or Piccadilly Circus), is an incredibly old-fashioned London department store, famed for its regal food department; pop into for a look and maybe lunch or tea (see "Whet Your Appetite" above).

✪ **Prowler Soho,** 3–7 Brewer St., W1 (no phone; Tube: Leicester Sq.), is a gay version of a "superstore," with 1,200 square feet of merchandise, including books, clothing, erotica, CDs, and gifts; there's even a gay travel agency and a very pleasant coffee bar.

FASHION **Aquascutum,** 100 Regent St., W1 (☎ **020/7734-6090;** Tube: Piccadilly Circus), is a popular stop for American tourists wanting to look more British than the Brits. **Austin Reed,** 103–113 Regent St., W1 (☎ **020/7734-6789;** Tube: Piccadilly Circus), has long stood for superior-quality clothing and excellent tailoring for men and women. **Berk,** 46 Burlington Arcade, Piccadilly, W1 (☎ **020/7493-0028;** Tube: Piccadilly Circus), boasts one of London's largest collections of cashmere sweaters, as well as capes, stoles, scarves, and camel-hair sweaters.

Burberry, 18–22 Haymarket, SW1 (☎ **020/7930-3343;** Tube: Piccadilly Circus), sells the famous raincoats, plus excellent men's shirts, sportswear, knitwear, and accessories. **Gieves & Hawkes,** 1 Savile Row, W1 (☎ **020/7434-2001;** Tube: Piccadilly Circus), has a list of clients that includes the Prince of Wales; you'll find good-quality cotton shirts, silk ties, Shetland sweaters, and ready-to-wear and tailor-made suits. **Hilditch & Key,** 37 and 73 Jermyn St., SW1 (☎ **020/7734-4707;** Tube: Piccadilly Circus or Green Park), sells tailor-made men's shirts and women's ready-made shirts.

Hennes, 261 Regent St., W1 (☎ **020/7493-4004;** Tube: Oxford Circus), is good for hot-off-the-catwalk women's knockoffs that won't last more than a season. **Hype DF,** 48–52 Kensington High St., W8 (☎ **020/7937-3100;** Tube: High St. Kensington), showcases young designers for men's and women's sports and evening wear. **Katharine Hamnett,** 20 Sloane St., SW1 (☎ **020/7823-1002;** Tube: Knightsbridge), earned a title for her "slut dresses"; this bad girl of Brit fashion stocks a complete line of men's and women's day and eveningwear using "nature friendly" fabrics. **Vivienne Westwood,** 6 Davies St., W1 (☎ **020/7629-3757;** Tube: Bond St.), is one of the hottest British designers for women; this flagship store carries a full range of jackets, skirts, trousers, blouses, dresses, and eveningwear.

LEATHER, RUBBER & FETISH GEAR Call me old-fashioned, but when I see a leather harness I think of *My Friend Flicka,* and when I see rubber shirts I think of Lloyd Bridges in *Sea Hunt.*

But if you're so inclined . . . the two branches of **Clone Zone,** 266 Old Brompton Rd., SW5 (☎ **020/7373-0598;** Tube: Earl's Court), and 64 Old Compton St., W1 (☎ **020/7287-3530;** Tube: Leicester Sq.), offer both leather and rubberwear as well as "regular" clothes, cards, magazines, condoms, and piercing services. The more discriminating aficionado of fetish couture should check out **Expectations,** 75 Great Eastern St., EC2 (☎ **020/7739-0292**), for the latest in clamps, harnesses, firemen's outfits, and handmade leather and rubber outfits; there's an alteration service if you need the cuff on your chaps turned up.

Just about any kind of fetishistical fantasy outfit can be found at **Regulation,** 17a St. Alban's Place, Islington, N1 (☎ **020/7226-0665;** Tube: Angel), which sells new and abused leather, rubber, plastic goods, and items for your military, medical, and industrial complexes. Men and women who take their rubber seriously will find elbow-length black gloves, catsuits, leggings, and what-have-you at **Invincible Rubber,** 19e, 2nd floor, Tower Workshops, Riley Road, Southwark, SE1 (☎ **020/7237-4017;** Tube: London Bridge).

SHOES At **Church's,** 13 New Bond St., W1 (☎ **020/7493-1474;** Tube: Bond St.), you'll find classy shoes said to be recognizable to all the snobby maîtres-d'hôtel in London. **Dr. Marten's Department Store,** 1–4 King St., WC2 (☎ **020/7497-1460;** Tube: Covent Garden), is the flagship for internationally famous "Doc Marts," with prices are far better than those in the States. **Lilley & Skinners,** 360 Oxford St., W1 (☎ **020/7560-2000;** Tube: Bond St.), is the largest shoe store in Europe, displaying many different brands.

TOILETRIES There are two shops you should know about. Both sell shaving items, soaps, and scents that'll keep the boys and girls back home sniffing. ✪ **Floris,** 89 Jermyn St., SW1 (☎ **020/7930-2885;** Tube: Piccadilly Circus), is a small mahogany-clad store that's been selling its own line since 1851. And **Penhaligon's,** 41 Wellington St., WC2 (☎ **020/7836-2150;** Tube: Covent Garden), another Victorian perfumery dedicated to good grooming, makes good scents.

T-SHIRTS & CARDS **Rainbows,** 20 Brewer St. (☎ **020/7287-5373;** Tube: Leicester Sq.), sells gay T-shirts with inscriptions that really make you laugh and stocks an assortment of rainbow cards and goods.

VINTAGE & SECONDHAND **Annie's Vintage Costume and Textiles,** 10 Camden Passage, N1 (☎ **020/7359-0796;** Tube: Angel), concentrates on carefully preserved dresses from the 1920s and 1930s but has a range of clothing and textiles from the 1880s through the 1960s. For secondhand menswear, try **Old Hat,** 62 and 66 Fulham High St., SW6 (☎ **020/7736-5446;** Tube: Putney Bridge); this is the place to find used Savile Row suits, Jermyn Street silk ties, and Burberry's raincoats.

Pandora, 16–22 Cheval Place, SW7 (☎ **020/7589-5289;** Tube: Knightsbridge), sells the cast-offs of England's gentry. **Pop Boutique,** 6 Monmouth St., WC2 (☎ **020/7497-5262;** Tube: Covent Garden), has the best original streetwear from the 1950s, 1960s, and 1970s. And London's leading dealer in vintage costume jewelry and clothing is **Steinberg & Tolkien,** 193 King's Rd., SW3 (☎ **020/7376-3660;** Tube: Sloane Square).

6 All the World's a Stage

London, for some of us, is synonymous with invigorating theater, grand opera, and world-class symphony orchestras. Plays routinely star the likes of Dames Judi Dench and Maggie Smith, Vanessa Redgrave (still considered too radical to be a Dame), Sir Ian McKellan (one of the few openly gay stars), and all those great British actors you see on *Masterpiece Theatre.* The National Theatre produced *Angels in America* before it ever came to Broadway. And let's not forget it was here in London that a major ballet company had enough balls to mount an all-male *Swan Lake.*

For the best local listings of everything that's going on, check the weekly magazine ***Time Out.***

GETTING TICKETS The **Society of London Theatres** (☎ **020/7836-0971**) operates a half-price booth in Leicester Square. Tickets are sold only on the day of performance, daily 12:30 to 6:30pm, and no credit cards are accepted. The hottest shows

A Ticket Warning

Beware of unlicensed ticket agencies in London that charge far more than the face value of the ticket. And wave away those pesky scalpers who hang out in front of hit shows. Even if the tickets scalpers are selling may look valid, there are many reports of forged tickets.

---

won't be available, but you might luck out, and tickets for the English National Opera are occasionally available as well.

Many theaters accept phone bookings at regular prices with a credit card. They'll hold your tickets at the box office, where you pick them up at show time with a credit card. If you've got your heart set on seeing a specific show, particularly one of the big hits, you may have to reserve in advance through a London ticket agency. For tickets and information before you go, on just about any show and entertainment option in London, try **Edwards & Edwards,** 1270 Ave. of the Americas, Suite 2414, New York, NY 10020 (☎ **800/223-6108** or 914/328-2150; fax 914/328-2752). They also have offices in London at the **Palace Theatre,** Shaftesbury Avenue, W1 (☎ **020/7734-4555;** Tube: Leicester Square), or at the **Harrods** ticket desk, 87–135 Brompton Rd. (☎ **020/7589-9109;** Tube: Knightsbridge). They'll mail tickets to your home, fax you a confirmation, or leave your tickets at the box office; a booking and handling fee of up to 20% is added.

You might also try calling **Keith Prowse/First Call** (☎ **020/7836-9001;** fax 212/302-4251). This agency also has an office in the United States that allows you to reserve months in advance for hit shows: Suite 1000, 234 W. 44th St., New York, NY 10036 (☎ **800/669-8687** or 212/398-1430). Various locations exist in London; the fee for booking a ticket is 25% in London and 35% in the United States.

Another option is **Theatre Direct International (TDI)** (☎ **800/334-8457,** U.S. only). TDI specializes in providing London theater and fringe production tickets but also has tickets to most London productions, including the Royal National Theatre and the Barbican.

THE PERFORMING ARTS

Theater and music happens all over London. The "big" shows (musicals and commercial hits) are concentrated mostly in the West End, and there are major performing-arts centers at the Barbican and on the South Bank.

The **Barbican Centre,** Silk Street, EC2 (Tube: Barbican) is a multiarts center in the city of London. The major venue here is the **Barbican Concert Hall** (☎ **020/7638-8891**), home of the London Symphony Orchestra. The prestigious ✪ **Royal Shakespeare Company** (☎ **020/7638-8891**) performs at the Barbican Centre's two theaters.

The **Royal Opera** and **Royal Ballet** (☎ **020/7240-1066** or 020/7240-1911) usually perform at the **Royal Opera House,** Covent Garden (Tube: Covent Garden), but the house is currently being renovated and scheduled to reopen until sometime in 1999. Both companies still perform, but they're gypsies traveling around to various venues, so call to find out where they are. The **English National Opera** presents a full season of grand operas in English at the **London Coliseum,** St. Martin's Lane (☎ **020/7632-8300;** Tube: Leicester Square). One of London's most eagerly awaited summer musical events is the July-August series of classical and pops concerts known as the Proms. All Proms concerts are held at **Royal Albert Hall,** Kensington Gore (☎ **020/7589-8212;** Tube: Gloucester Rd. or Knightsbridge), a South Kensington landmark since it opened in 1871.

The **South Bank Arts Centre,** South Bank, SE1 (Tube: Waterloo) is another music/theater/art complex. The ✪ **Royal National Theatre** (☎ **020/7928-2252**) performs at its complex of three theaters beside the Thames. Over 1,200 performances a year take place in the three concert halls in the ✪ **Royal Festival Hall** (☎ **020/7960-4242**). The newest addition to the South Bank theater scene is ✪ **Shakespeare's Globe Theatre,** New Globe Walk, Bankside, SE1 (☎ **020/7401-9919;** Tube: Cannon St. or London Bridge), which presents a May-to-September season of Shakespeare plays in a reconstructed Elizabethan theater.

Some of the city's most interesting work is performed in "fringe" theaters away from the bright lights of the West End. One of the best-known venues is the **Almeida,** Almeida St., N1 (☎ **020/7359-4404;** Tube: Angel). ✪ **Gay Sweatshop,** Holborn Centre, Three Cups Yard, Sandland Street, WC1 (☎ **020/7242-1168;** Tube: Holborn), is the country's leading gay theater troupe. London's gay repertory theater, the ✪ **Drill Hall,** 16 Chenies St., Bloomsbury, WC1 (☎ **020/7637-8270;** Tube: Goodge St.) is another place to check out.

International performers light up the stage of the **London Palladium,** Argyll Street, W1 (☎ **020/7494-5020;** Tube: Oxford Circus); you may know the name from your scratchy old recording of "Judy Garland at the Palladium." The **Sadler's Wells Theatre,** Rosebery Avenue, Islington, EC1 (☎ **020/7314-8800;** Tube: Angel), is London's premier venue for dance. **Kenwood Lakeside Concerts,** Hampstead Lane, Hampstead Heath (☎ **020/8348-1286;** Tube: East Finchley, then a free shuttle bus), presents outdoor summer concerts at a marvelous lakeside estate.

JAZZ & ROCK CLUBS

London isn't New York when it comes to numbers of jazz clubs, but the late-night hours and smoky atmosphere is the same (actually, London's jazz clubs are smokier). The action usually begins around 10pm, but this varies from club to club, so call to see who's playing when and if there's a cover. The jazz clubs aren't really gay, but the rock clubs I've listed are or at least have gay nights.

The **Blue Note,** 1 Hoxton Square, N1 (☎ **020/7729-8440;** Tube: Old St.), is a two-tiered club considered a cool hangout. The **Jazz Cafe,** 5 Parkway, NW1 (☎ **020/7916-6000;** Tube: Camden Town), occupies a converted bank and gets great combos from all over. The **100 Club,** 100 Oxford St., W1 (☎ **020/7636-0933;** Tube: Tottenham Court Rd.), is a time-honored jazz and blues dive. And **Ronnie Scott's,** 47 Frith St., W1 (☎ **020/7439-0747;** Tube: Leicester Sq.), is the Soho granddaddy of London jazz clubs and always has hot lineups (you usually have to book).

For live rock, not as plentiful as you'd suppose, try the following. ✪ **London Astoria,** 157 Charing Cross Rd., Soho, WC2 (☎ **020/7434-9592;** Tube: Charing Cross), is known mostly for its Wednesday-night G.A.Y. bash, the largest queer disco party in London, but it occasionally has live performers. **Back Bar,** 10 Brewer St., Soho, WC2 (☎ **020/7734-2626;** Tube: Leicester Square), beneath Madame Jo-Jo's gay drag cabaret, has live music Wednesday to Saturday at 10:30pm.

Camden Palace, Camden High St., NW1 (☎ **020/7387-0428;** Tube: Camden Town), used to be looked down on, but thanks to its recent refurbishment clubbers can now look down on the action from tiers. Small and grungy, **The Garage,** 22 Highbury Corner, Islington, N5 (☎ **020/7607-1818;** Tube: Islington), hosts Club V, a gay night with live music, every other Saturday.

CABARETS

Some cabarets are in pubs, some in clubs, and all have different hours for their shows. If it's a professional club show, there'll be an admission; if it's amateur (usually in a pub), there may or may not be a cover. I know it all sounds confusing, so call these places first if you have any questions.

The **Black Cap,** 171 Camden High St., Camden Town (☎ **020/7485-1742;** Tube: Camden Town; open Mon–Thurs 9pm–2am, Fri–Sat to 3am, Sun to 10:30pm), is where London's most famous men in frocks perform. Voted Pub of the Year in 1998, **Central Station,** 37 Wharfdale Rd., King's Cross (☎ **020/7278-3294;** Tube: King's Cross; open Mon–Thurs 5pm–2am, Sat noon–5am, Sun noon–midnight), has more social activities going on than a cruise liner but hosts cabaret and male stripper acts nearly every night. The **Cock & Comfort,** 359 Bethnal Green Rd. (☎ **020/7729-1090;** Tube: Bethnal Green; open Sun–Thurs to 11pm, Fri–Sat to 1am), besides having a wonderful name, offers drag cabaret on weekends. **Screamers Comedy Club,** upstairs at The Yard, Rupert Street, Soho, W1 (☎ **020/7724-5577;** Tube: Leicester Sq.), presents Queer Comedy every Wednesday at 8:30pm; tickets are £4.50 ($8), and both lesbians and gay men perform.

Madame Jo-Jo's, 8–10 Brewer St., Soho, W1 (☎ **020/7734-2473;** Tube: Leicester Sq.; open daily 10pm–4am), has been a fixture of the drag/cabaret scene for years; the shows produced in its plush theater-bar can be campy and fun but are mostly of the "Old Drag School" variety and attract a lot of straights; tickets are £8 to £10 ($14 to $17) but £5 ($9) on Wednesday. The **Royal Vauxhall Tavern,** 372 Kennington Lane, Vauxhall, SE11 (☎ **020/7582-0833;** Tube: Vauxhall; open Mon–Thurs 9pm–1am, Fri–Sat to 2am, Sun noon–10:30pm), a big barnlike pub with a large stage, has nightly drag cabaret and a dance floor. And **Ruby's Champagne Cabaret,** 13 Gerrard St., Soho, W1 (☎ **020/7494-1060;** Tube: Leicester Sq.; open Mon–Sat 5pm–3am), is an intimate old-fashioned venue presided over by drag queen Ruby Venezuela, who introduces the artistes and sometimes takes the stage herself; nonmembers pay £10 ($17).

7 In the Heat of the Night

The most popular freebies, available in gay pubs, clubs, bars, and cafes and useful for their listings, are ***Boyz, Pink Paper,*** and ***QX (Queer Xtra). Gay Times*** is a high-quality monthly news-oriented mag available at most newsagents. ***Time Out,*** indispensable for its city-wide listings (including gay listings), appears at newsagents on Wednesday.

GAY PUBS & BARS

Americans visiting London have a hard time distinguishing between bars and pubs. In the crudest terms, a bar is where you go after the pubs close or before the clubs open. Bars tend to be darker than pubs (though the new cafe/bars are turning darkness into light) and sometimes have dance floors. Pubs are more quintessentially English, traditional gathering places where conversation may actually take precedence over posing. We tend to think of pubs as cozier than bars and more intimate, but they can be just as loud and smoky.

Though you can get a "hard" drink at both bars and pubs, when you're in a pub you're better off confining yourself to beer. Pubs are affiliated with one particular brewery and sell only that company's ales (you order either a pint or a half-pint). But they'll also have bitter, stout, lager, and bottled beers.

Most pubs, gay and straight, adhere to **strict hours** governed by Parliament: Monday to Saturday 11am to 11pm and Sunday noon to 10:30pm (listed as "pub hours" below). Americans take note: There's no service charged or expected in a pub and you never tip the bartender; the best you can do is offer to buy him or her a drink. Ten minutes before closing a bell rings, signaling that it's time to make your next move.

SOHO & VICINITY The first gay pub in Soho, ✪ **Comptons,** 53 Old Compton St., Soho, W1 (☎ **020/7437-4445;** Tube: Leicester Sq.; open pub hours), remains a loud, popular, and unpretentious cruise 'n' schmooze joint with lots of denim.

✪ **Brief Encounter,** 42 St. Martin's Lane, Covent Garden (☎ **020/7240-2221;** Tube: Charing Cross Rd.; open pub hours), like the English National Opera next door, is loud and cruisy, but the music is disco and the crowd lots dishier; it's at its best postwork and preclub.

Ku Bar, 75 Charing Cross Rd., Soho, W1 (☎ **020/7437-4303;** Tube: Leicester Sq.; open pub hours), is an attitude-zone for parading snoot-suits; it's packed before the clubs open. So is ✪ **79CXR,** next door at 79 Charing Cross Rd., W1 (☎ **020/7734-0769;** Tube: Leicester Sq.; open Mon–Sat 1pm–2am, Sun to 10:30pm), but this one is more American in style and less pompous.

✪ **The Edge,** 11 Soho Sq., Soho, W1 (☎ **020/7439-1313;** Tube: Tottenham Court Rd.; open Mon–Wed 10am–3am, Thurs–Sat to 6am, Sun to 10:30pm), has three bars on three floors and doesn't care if the Tube stops running at midnight.

✪ **Halfway to Heaven,** 7 Duncannon St., Charing Cross, WC2 (☎ **020/7930-8312;** Tube: Charing Cross; open pub hours), one of the more pleasant and traditional gay pubs, attracts a friendly, fun-loving crowd from all walks of life.

Iron Bar, 4 Carlisle St., Soho, W1 (☎ **020/7734-0551;** Tube: Tottenham Court Rd.; open Mon–Thurs noon–1am, Fri–Sat to 2am, Sun to 11:30pm), is another trileveler for smart, upscale poofters (its name comes from Cockney rhyming slang in which "iron hoof" means "poof") and turns its basement bar into a disco on the weekends.

The ✪ **King's Arms,** 23 Poland St., Soho, W1 (☎ **020/7734-5907;** Tube: Oxford Circus; open pub hours), is a relaxed, fairly cruisy, leaning-toward-cloney pub for regular guys; as you ascend to the upstairs bar, you'll glimpse through the window an assortment of gay garden gnomes doing naughty things on the roof.

The **Admiral Duncan,** 54 Old Compton St., W1 (☎ **020/7437-5300;** Tube: Piccadilly Circus; open pub hours), also for "regular guys," is a smallish new pub with a dark, secretive ambience.

Back Bar, 10 Brewer St., Soho, W1 (☎ **020/7734-2626;** Tube: Leicester Sq.; open Mon–Sat 11am–3am, Sun noon–midnight), draws a mixed gay/straight crowd interested in designer clothes and funky music.

BarCode, 3–4 Archer St., Soho, W1 (☎ **020/7734-3342;** Tube: Piccadilly Circus; open pub hours), is a stylish hangout for 30-somethings on the lookout for mirror images.

The **City of Quebec,** 12 Old Quebec St., Marble Arch, W1 (☎ **020/7629-6159;** Tube: Marble Arch; open pub hours), a venerable pub that's been gay since 1945, is for an older crowd that prefers old-fashioned conversation to blaring music.

Jonathan's, 16 Irving St., W1 (☎ **020/7930-4770;** Tube: Leicester Sq.; open pub hours), a private theater bar for the quaint and queenly at heart, charges a £10 ($17) yearly membership fee.

The **Locomotion,** 18 Bear St., WC2 (☎ **020/7839-3552;** Tube: Leicester Sq.; open pub hours), an upstairs bar behind the Leicester Square cinemas, is for post-teenyboppers who like loud music and firm buns.

Play It Safe

Packs of condoms and lube are available free in some London gay pubs and clubs. Ask the bartender if they have Rubberstuffers.

Village Soho, 81 Wardour St., Soho, W1 (☎ **020/7434-2124;** Tube: Leicester Sq.; open Mon–Sat noon–11pm, Sun 4–10:30pm), set the stage for all the trendy "I don't think we're in quaint olde England anymore, Toto" cafe/bars that are now such a regular feature of Soho life; there's a cafe on the ground floor.

EARL'S COURT & WEST LONDON **Brompton's,** 294 Old Brompton Rd. at Warwick Street, SW5 (☎ **020/7370-1344;** Tube: Earl's Court, Warwick Rd. exit; open Mon–Sat 4pm–2am, Sun 1pm–midnight), is a huge and popular gay men's cruise/dance bar, but there's absolutely no action before 11pm, when the pubbers pour in.

✪ **The Champion,** 1 Wellington Terrace, Bayswater Road, W2 (☎ **020/7229-5056;** Tube: Notting Hill Gate; open pub hours), is a large Victorian-era pub with a courtyard and a low-key but definitely cruisy crowd of men in their prime.

The **Coleherne,** 261 Old Brompton Rd., SW5 (☎ **020/7373-9859;** Tube: Earl's Court; open Mon–Thurs noon–11pm, Fri–Sat to midnight, Sun to 11:30pm), one of London's landmark gay pubs, was for years and years the hangout for clones and leathermen; by the time this book hits the shelves, the Coleherne will have reopened with a redesigned interior more in keeping with the millennium.

Queen's Head, 27 Tryon St., Chelsea, SW3 (☎ **020/7589-0262;** Tube: Sloane Sq.; open pub hours), is a small pub where local Chelsea queens have been heading for years; you'll find a friendly, quiet, more mature crowd.

✪ **The Nile,** 152 Ebury St., SW1 (☎ **020/7834-1001**); Tube: Victoria; open pub hours), the Victoria area's first gay pub, is relaxed-leaning-toward-upscale; one of the best things about it is that between 11am and 8pm you can get a good meal; Sundays, the owner's mum steps into the kitchen and cooks up lunch ("good Scottish grub") noon to 6pm. Food prices are £3.25 to £5.95 ($6 to $10).

LESBIAN BARS

Lipstick lesbians head for the comfy couches and candlelight at the **Glass Bar,** West Lodge, Euston Square Gardens, 190 Euston Rd., NW1 (☎ **020/7387-6184;** Tube: Euston; open Tues–Fri from 6pm, Sat from 7pm, Sun noon–6pm); there's no entry after 11:30pm, and the club closes when the management gets tired.

The ✪ **Candy Bar,** 4 Carlisle St., W1 (☎ **020/7494-4041;** Tube: Tottenham Court Rd.; open Mon–Fri 5–11pm, Sat pub hours, Sun 5–10:30pm), is the country's newest (and only) triple-decker lesbian bar; men are welcome as guests. This is *the* hot scene for women.

The Box, 32–34 Monmouth St., WC2 (☎ **020/7240-5828;** Tube: Leicester Sq.), has a women-only night on Sundays beginning at 7pm in its downstairs bar.

The **Artful Dodger,** 139 Southgate Rd., Islington, N1 (☎ **020/7226-0841;** Tube: Angel; open Mon–Sat 5–11pm, Sun 1–10:30pm), is a mixed gay/lesbian bar with more lesbians before 9:30pm, when the boys start arriving.

The **Duke of Wellington,** 119 Balls Pond Rd., Islington, N1 (☎ **020/7503-9672;** Tube: Islington or Highbury; open Mon–Sat 11:30am–1am, Sun to 11pm), despite its street address, draws as many lesbians as gays; it's neighborhoody.

The **Royal Vauxhall Tavern** (see "Cabarets") has a Friday women-only night 9pm to 2am.

DRAG BARS

Funny, given the continuing allure of drag acts in London cabaret bars, that you don't see more lads cum lassies in the other bars and pubs. **Black Cap, Central Station, Royal Vauxhall Tavern,** and **Ruby's Champagne Cabaret** (see "Cabarets") are all drag-friendly.

The **Royal Oak,** 73 Columbia Rd., Bethnal Green, E2 (☎ **020/7739-8204;** Tube: Old St. or Shoreditch; open Mon–Fri 4pm–midnight, Sat 1pm–2am, Sun noon–midnight), is an old-fashioned East End pub that becomes gay in the evenings and welcomes men in tasteful frocks.

The tiny bar in the basement of the **Philbeach Hotel,** 30–31 Philbeach Gardens, SW5 (☎ **020/7373-1244;** Tube: Earl's Court), is an intimate and relaxing setting for dragsters; on Mondays 7 to 10:30pm, the hotel's restaurant (Wilde About Oscar, see "Whet Your Appetite" above), hosts a transvestite buffet (you can change on the premises; the bar itself is generally open 8pm–2am).

LEATHER & FETISH BARS

If you're into leather, uniforms, and dress codes, these raunchy on-the-edge bars will take care of all your needs—not for the faint-hearted. Many London bars have various dress-code nights as well, so check the bar and pub listings in *Boyz* and *Time Out.*

The **Anvil,** 88 Tooley St., Southwark, SE1 (☎ **020/7407-0371;** Tube: London Bridge; open Mon–Wed 8:30pm–1am, Thurs–Sat to 2am, Sun noon–11pm), is painted black to match all the leather and rubber; other uniforms add a splash of color.

Hoist, Arch 47C, South Lambeth Road, Vauxhall, SW8 (☎ **020/7735-9972;** Tube: Vauxhall; open Mon–Thurs 8pm–midnight, Fri–Sat 10pm–3am), is for hard-core gay, bisexual, and lesbian S&Mers; a lot of controlled pain.

The **Mildmay,** 130 Balls Pond Rd., at the corner of Mildmay Park, Islington, N1 (☎ **020/7354-0611;** Tube: Islington or Highbury; open Mon–Thurs 7pm–1am, Fri–Sat to 2am, Sun 4pm–midnight), has so many dress codes for different nights you should call first to find out what to wear when; for men who like it rough.

The **Service Station,** The Crown, 144 Whiston Rd., Shoreditch, E2 (☎ **020/7613-2672;** Tube: Bethnal Green; open Mon–Fri 7pm–11pm, Sat noon–11pm, Sun 2–10:30pm), is another dress-code delight for leather, rubber, and denim boys; there's a £10 ($17) yearly membership fee.

DANCE CLUBS

London boasts some of the largest dance clubs in the world. In some cases, these venues are gay and lesbian on only certain nights of the week, so check local listings. You'll pay a cover at all of them, and since the Tube won't be running when you get out, bring cab fare. Besides the clubs below, there's **Brompton's** (see "Gay Bars & Pubs").

✪ **G.A.Y.,** London Astoria, 157 Charing Cross Rd., Soho, WC2 (☎ **020/7434-9592;** Tube: Tottenham Court Rd.; open Sat 10:30pm–5am), is the biggest gay dance venue in Europe—you simply must go.

✪ **Heaven,** Under the Arches, Villiers Street, WC2 (☎ **020/7839-5210;** Tube: Charing Cross or Embankment; open different hours nightly), is nearly 20 years old and shows no sign of stopping; it continues to be London's prime must-visit gay dance club; packed butt to butt, which everyone likes, and attitude-free fun.

✪ **The Fridge,** Town Hall Parade, Brixton Hill, SW2 (☎ **020/7326-5100;** Tube: Brixton; open Thurs 9pm–3am, Sat 10pm–6am), famous for its frenetic Saturday Love Muscle dance night, is one of London's hunkiest and most popular gay clubs.

The **Gardening Club,** 4 The Piazza, Covent Garden, WC2 (☎ **020/7836-4052;** Tube: Covent Garden; open Thurs 9pm–3am), in the hiply renovated cellars beneath Covet Garden, hosts a Queer Nation night that attracts lots of foreign visitors to its two bars and groovy music.

Club 180, 180 Earl's Court Rd., SW5 (☎ **020/7835-1826;** Tube: Earl's Court; open Mon–Thurs 10pm–2am, Fri–Sat 9pm–2am), a large dance club under Earl's pub, has lots of theme nights; it's fun after midnight and not what you'd call upscale.

The **Albany Empire,** Douglas Way, Deptford, SE8 (☎ **020/8692-4446;** Tube: New Cross), a theater-cum-disco, has a mixed gay/lesbian dancefest one night a month.

The Eclipse, 17 Greek St., Soho, W1 (no phone; Tube: Leicester Sq.; open Sat 11pm–5am), attracts a cool mixed crowd to an atmosphere that verges on posh.

The **Chunnel Club,** 101 Tinworth St., SE11 (☎ **020/7498-6040;** Tube: Vauxhall; open Fri 10:30pm–5am), is a double-barreled entertainment complex with cabaret on one side and hard-edged disco on the other.

The **End Club,** 16A W. Central St., Bloomsbury, WC1 (☎ **020/7287-2715;** Tube: Tottenham Court Rd.; open Sun 6pm–late), is heavy on techno and has a state-of-the-art sound system; you can rest on chic seating designed by Philippe Starck.

The **Flamingo Bar,** 9 Hanover St., Mayfair, W1 (☎ **020/7491-1558;** open Tues 10pm–3am; Tube: Oxford Circus), is high on the glam factor and plays a mix of trash, easy listening, and indie pop.

Substation South, 9 Brighton Terrace, Brixton, SW9 (☎ **020/7737-2095;** Tube: Brixton; open different hours nightly), is cruisiest on Friday and has various dress-code nights, including a monthly underwear party; it's small and poorly lit and not really worth the schlep out to Brixton.

Turnmills, 63B Clerkenwell Rd., EC1 (☎ **020/7250-3409;** Tube: Farringdon; open different hours nightly), boasts a sunken dance floor crammed to capacity with gyrating hunks; Saturday is the popular Trade night. You have to arrive late and won't feel comfortable without perfect pecs and washboard abs you can show off when you rip off your shirt.

DOWN & DIRTY: CINEMAS, SAUNAS & MORE

CINEMAS The **London Lesbian & Gay Film Festival,** held every March, marked its 12th year in 1998 with an incredibly impressive roster. Screenings are at the **National Film Theatre,** South Bank, Waterloo, SE1 (☎ **020/7928-3232;** Tube: Waterloo). Another venue worth checking out is the **Gay Film Night** held every Monday at the **Prince Charles Cinema,** Leicester Place, WC2 (☎ **020/7437-8181;** Tube: Leicester Square); pick up a reduced-price ticket at Ku Bar on Charing Cross Road (above) and after the movie you can dance at G.A.Y. (above).

SAUNAS The days of dingy, smelly saunas aren't gone for good, but why would you want to go to one when these three spiffy-clean places are on the scene? They're beating out (but not off) most of the competition.

London's newest and largest sauna is **Chariots Roman Spa,** Chariots House, Fairchild Street, EC2 (☎ **020/7247-5333;** Tube: Liverpool St.; open Mon–Thurs noon–midnight, Fri–Sat to 9am; admission £12/$21), a huge Roman-themed sex 'n hygiene emporium, offers sunbeds, saunas, steamrooms, Jacuzzis, a large pool, a snack bar, and professional masseurs on duty 2 to 10pm.

Equally large but not quite so faux posh is **Pleasuredrome,** 125 Alaska St., SE1 (☎ **020/7633-9194;** Tube: Waterloo; open Mon–Sat 24 hours, Sun noon–2am; admission £10/$17); it has saunas, steamrooms, sunbeds, and a real gym, and it's so close to Waterloo International that gay Parisians sometimes pop over on the *Eurostar* just to "steam."

The **Covent Garden Health Spa,** 29 Endell St., WC2 (☎ **020/7836-2236;** Tube: Covent Garden; open daily 11am–11pm; admission £13.50/$23), offers, in addition to the sweaty stuff, a panoply of pampering services like aromatherapy, massage, reflexology, a barber shop, and a fully licensed bar.

And finally, yes, London does have phone-sex lines; you'll find the various numbers in *Boyz.*

8 Side Trips from London: Hampton Court Windsor & Bath

The Brits do love to complain about how "far" everything is, but to Americans and others accustomed to vast distances, practically every place in England could be a side trip from London. Especially with the fast trains.

I'm covering Manchester and Brighton separately and with more detail, because they're gay destinations where you may want to spend a night or two. Hampton Court and Windsor Castle are two wonderful side trips close to London. Bath is farther away but still easily accessible as a day trip.

HAMPTON COURT PALACE

In 1514, Cardinal Wolsey began building the superb Tudor **Hampton Court** in East Moseley, Surrey, 13 miles west of London on the north side of the Thames. But that greedy monarch Henry VIII (of six wives fame) desired a pretty home in the country. In 1525, he grabbed Hampton Court for himself and made it a royal residence, which it remained until 1760. One of his wives, Anne Boleyn (mother of Elizabeth I), supposedly haunts the place to this day, though you'd think the hordes of tourists would've scared her away by now. The Anne Boleyn Gate, with its 16th-century astronomical clock, and the Great Hall, with its hammer-beam ceiling, are remnants from Hampton Court's Tudor days. Later it was much altered by Sir Christopher Wren for William and Mary; Wren also designed the famous Maze, where you can wander in dizzy confusion. Inside you'll see various state apartments, including the King's Dressing Room, wooden carvings by Grinling Gibbons, and Italian paintings. The gardens alone are worth the trip.

Mid-March to mid-October, Hampton Court is open daily 9:30am to 6pm; the rest of the year, hours are Monday 10:15am to 6pm and Tuesday to Sunday 9:30am to 6pm. Admission is £8.50 ($15). For information, call ☎ **020/8781-9500.** The simplest way to get there is by train from London's Waterloo Station to Hampton Court Station; it takes half an hour and costs about £4 ($7) round-trip. The best way is by boat from Westminster Pier; the ferry takes about 3½ hours, costs £8 ($14) round-trip, and stops at Kew Gardens on the way.

WINDSOR CASTLE

Located in Windsor, Berkshire, 20 miles from the center of London, **Windsor Castle** is one of the queen's official residences. The castle, its imposing skyline of towers and battlements rising from the center of the 4,800-acre Great Park, was constructed by William the Conqueror some 900 years ago and has been used as a royal residence ever since. The State Apartments open to visitors range from the intimate chambers of Charles II to the enormous Waterloo Chamber, built to commemorate the victory over Napoléon in 1815. All are superbly furnished with important works of art from the Royal Collection. There are masterpieces by Rembrandt and Rubens, portraits by Holbein and Van Dyck, and a mouthwatering collection of French and English furniture. Even Queen Mary's royal dollhouse is worth a gander. St. George's Chapel, one of the finest examples of late Gothic architecture in Great Britain, dates from the 15th and 16th centuries. From the ramparts of Windsor you can look down on the playing fields of Eton College, where countless aristocratic boys have been whipped into shape. You can explore the famous school (all the Royals go there) by strolling across the Thames Bridge.

The castle is open daily (except March 28, June 16, December 25–26, and January 1): November to February 10am to 4pm (last admission 3pm) and March to

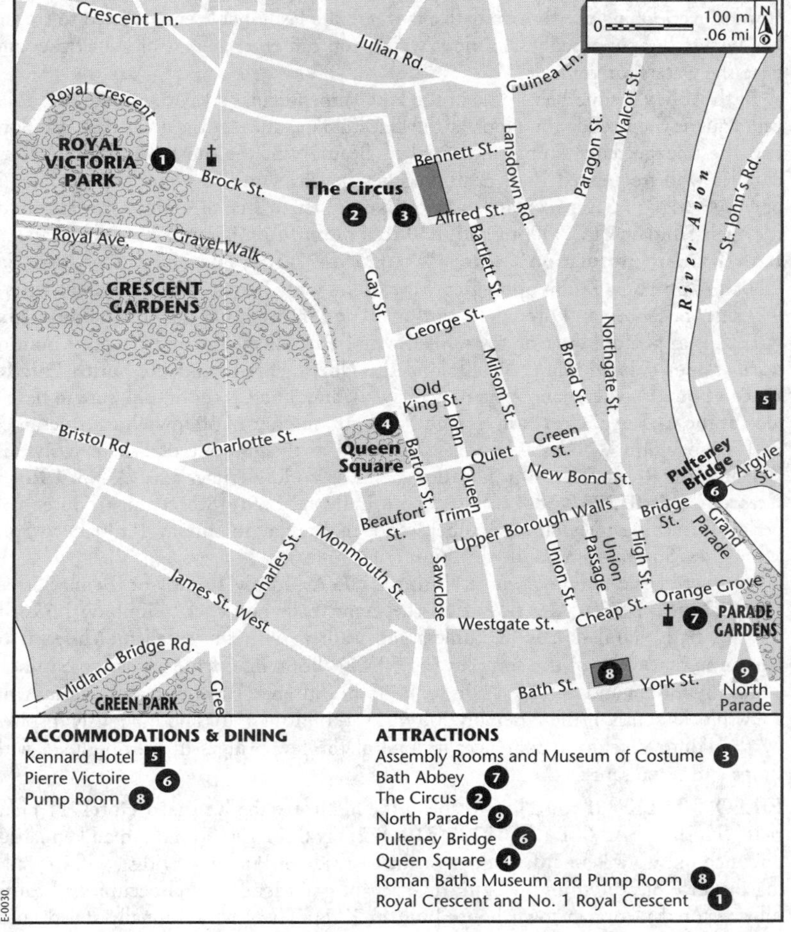

October 10am to 5:30pm (last admission 4pm). Admission is £9.80 ($17). For information, call ☎ **01753/868-286.** The trip by train from Waterloo or Paddington Station takes 50 minutes and involves a transfer at Slough to the Slough–Windsor shuttle train. There are more than a dozen trains per day, with fares starting at £6.20 ($10) round-trip.

BATH

A splendid Regency spa town on the Avon River, **Bath** is 115 miles west of London but only 90 minutes away by train from Paddington Station.

SEEING THE SIGHTS The hot, healing waters of its mineral springs were considered sacred by ancient British tribes, but in A.D. 75 it was the Romans who built the enormous bath complex that forms the nucleus of the ✪ **Roman Baths Museum** (☎ **01225/477-785**), located beside Bath Abbey; it's open daily 9:30am to 5:30pm, and admission is £6.30 ($11). On entering. you're given a portable self-guided audio tour that's keyed to everything on display, including the original Roman baths and heating system; it's fun, informative and very well done. The late-18th-century **Pump**

Room, overlooking the Roman baths, is where the fashionable congregated to sip the vile-tasting but supposedly salubrious water; you can enter as part of your ticket and taste the waters for yourself).

Bath Abbey, a superb example of the Late Perpendicular style, dominates the adjacent square. Step inside for a look at the graceful fan vaulting, the great East Window, and the unexpectedly simple memorial to Beau Nash, the most flamboyant of the dandies who frequented Bath in its Regency heyday. April to October, the abbey is open Monday to Saturday 9am to 6pm (November to March 4:30pm); year-round, it's open Sunday 1 to 2:30pm and 4:30 to 5:30pm. Admission is by donation. The **Bath Tourist Information Centre** (☎ **01225/477-101;** open June–Sept Mon–Sat 9:30am–7pm, Sun 10am–6pm; Oct–May Mon–Sat 9:30am–5pm, Sun 10am–4pm), is beside the Abbey and provides useful maps and information on all the local sights.

Bath is a splendid walking town filled with beautiful squares and crescents built of warm honey-colored stone. Stroll along the **North Parade** and the **South Parade, Queen Square** (where Jane Austen once lived), and **The Circus** and be sure to have a look at the ✪ **Royal Crescent,** a magnificent curving row of 30 town houses designed in 1767 by John Wood the Younger. Regarded as the epitome of Palladian style in England, the Royal Crescent is now designated a World Heritage site. ✪ **No. 1 Royal Crescent** (☎ **01225/428-126**) is a beautifully restored 18th-century house with period furnishings; March to October, it's open Tuesday to Sunday 10:30am to 5pm (Nov Tues–Sun to 4pm), and admission is £3.50 ($6).

Another classic building worth visiting is the **Assembly Rooms** on Bennet Street (☎ **01225/477-789**), the site of all the grand balls and social climbing in 18th-century Bath; admission is free unless you want to visit the excellent **Museum of Costume** that's part of the complex (£3.50/$6). Both are open Monday to Saturday 11am to 4:30pm and Sunday 11am to 4:30pm. **Pulteney Bridge,** spanning the Avon a few blocks south of the Assembly Rooms, was built in 1770 and obviously inspired by the Ponte Vecchio in Florence; it's one of the few bridges in Europe lined with shops and restaurants.

PILLOW TALK If you'd like to spend the night, try the **Kennard Hotel,** 11 Henrietta St., Bath BA2 6LL (☎ **01225/310-472;** fax 01225/460-054; e-mail kennard@dirconco.uk; www.kennard.co.uk). On the east side of Pulteney Bridge, within walking distance of everything in Bath, this elegant gay-friendly hotel occupies a beautifully restored Georgian town house built in 1794. The 13 traditionally-styled guest rooms are furnished with top-grade antiques, contain TVs and phones, and have a comfortably high-toned charm. The bathrooms are on the small side but come with hair dryers. A full English or continental breakfast is served in a poshly pleasant dining room. The use of tobacco is taboo on the premises. Rates are £78 to £88 ($140 to $158) double, breakfast included.

WHET YOUR APPETITE There are several good places to dine. One of the most picturesque (and popular) is on Pulteney Bridge: At **Pierre Victoire,** 16 Argyle St. (☎ **01225/334-334;** open daily noon–3pm and 6–10pm;), the menu changes daily and you'll find three-course fixed-price lunches and dinners; you need to book in advance on weekends. The historic **Pump Room,** Stall Street (☎ **01225/444-477;** open Mon–Sat 9:30am–4:40pm, Sun 10:30am–4:30pm), is an amusingly old-fashioned place for lunch or afternoon tea, often with musical accompaniment. The cooking is Modern British, and they have fixed-price lunches.

GAY BARS & PUBS The **Bath Tap,** St. James's Parade (☎ **01225/429-197**), is a new gay pub I wasn't able to visit. The **Green Room,** Garrick's Head, St. John's Place (no phone; open pub hours), is a long-established gay pub mostly used by locals; students and visiting performers sometimes drop in for a pint.

3

Brighton: Poofter's Paradise by the Sea

"Oh, I do like to be beside the seaside. . . ." This lyric, from an old British music-hall song, might've been written with **Brighton** in mind. On the Sussex coast, a mere 50 miles south of London, Brighton is England's most famous, and probably most popular, seaside town. It's also a homo heaven and has been for years. Unofficial statistics claim that one out of every four Brightonians is gay. For gay travelers, Brighton is the place that puts the sex in Sussex.

It's no mystery why Brighton is so appealing: It's heavy on quaint. It was a small fishing village until the Prince Regent, who would become George IV, became enamored of the place and had the fabulous Royal Pavilion built. Where royalty moves, fashion follows, and Brighton eventually became one of the most fashionable towns in Europe. The lovely Georgian terraces you see everywhere date from this period. The Royal Pavilion, interestingly enough, wasn't built with a view of the sea, which was still considered rather "vulgar"—too wild and uncontrollable for refined tastes. Later in the 19th century, when breathing the ozone-laden sea air was considered healthy, the Victorians descended in hordes. Today, Brighton is something of a commuter suburb of London and a popular place for conventions. The presence of Brighton University and the University of Sussex gives it an added vitality.

Brighton is a place of many charms, an irresistibly attractive and easy-to-reach seaside resort for both gays and straights. The pink pound adds so much to the economy, in fact, that the tourist office provides a Gay Information Sheet for visitors. It's a great place to spend a weekend, strolling on the beach, exploring the winding streets, clubbing and pubbing, and listening to the sound of gulls as they wheel and turn in the sea air.

1 Brighton Essentials

ARRIVING & DEPARTING

BY TRAIN The easiest and fastest way to reach Brighton is by train. **Connex South Central** has over 40 trains a day from London's **Victoria Station.** The trip takes about an hour. If you travel off-peak (after 9:30am), a cheap round-trip ticket is £13.30 ($23); full fare is £26.80 ($46).

Country & City Codes

The **country code** for the United Kingdom is **44.** The **city code** for Brighton is **1273;** use this code if you're calling from outside the United Kingdom. If you're within the United Kingdom but not in Brighton, use **01273.** If you're calling within Brighton, simply leave off the code and dial only the regular phone number.

BY CAR The M23 motorway from central London leads to Brighton. The drive should take about an hour, but if roads are clogged it'll take twice that.

VISITOR INFORMATION

Opposite the town hall, about a 10-minute walk south from the train station, is Brighton's **Tourist Information Centre,** 10 Bartholomew Sq. (☎ **01273/292-599;** open June to mid-July Mon–Fri 9am–6pm, Sat 10am–5pm, Sun 10am–4pm; mid-July to Aug Mon–Fri 9am–6pm, Sat–Sun 10am–6pm; Sept–May Mon–Fri 9am–5pm, Sat 10am–5pm, Sun 10am–4pm; closed Sun Dec–Feb). It's a good place to pick up details on current events and actually distributes a **Gay Information Sheet** listing gay guesthouses and pubs. You can reserve a room from the information center if you haven't already done so.

CITY LAYOUT & GETTING AROUND

Brighton's southern boundary is the English Channel. **Hove,** a separate town that has basically become part of Brighton, adjoins Brighton to the west. The train station is at the north end of town, within walking distance of the sea and the Royal Pavilion, the town's main sightseeing attraction. **Kemptown,** the gay village, lies to the east of the Royal Pavilion.

Brighton is a compact town, and the easiest way to get around is by foot. Walking to Kemptown, the gay village, from the train station takes about 15 minutes. The **Brighton and Hove Bus and Coach Company** at ☎ **01273/886-200** offers frequent and efficient service; local fares are 70p ($1.20). Taxis are usually available at the train station, or you can call **Streamline** at ☎ **01273/327-282.** A trip by taxi from the station to Kemptown will cost about £4 ($7).

FAST FACTS: Brighton

AIDS Organization The **Sussex AIDS Centre** is located in Graham Wilkinson House, P.O. Box 17, Brighton (☎ **01273/552-255,** 24-hour helpline).

Community Center The **Lesbian & Gay Resource Center,** 4th Floor, Community Base, 113–117 Queen's Rd., Brighton BN12 3XG (☎ **01273/234-005;** open daily 10am–1pm), provides helpful advice on all aspects of the gay scene in Brighton.

Hot Lines The **Brighton Lesbian & Gay Switchboard** is at ☎ **01273/690-825** (Mon–Sat 6–10pm, Sun 8–10pm). The **Bright Lesbian Line** is at ☎ **01273/603-298** (Tues and Fri 8–10pm); ask about monthly lesbian bar nights.

Telephone See "Fast Facts: London" in chapter 2.

2 Pillow Talk

Brighton has several small gay B&Bs, a gay hotel, and five-star luxury places. If my preferred choices below are full, the Visitor Information Center has a list of other gay B&Bs.

Note: For the locations of the hotels below, see the "Brighton" map on p. 130–131.

Bannings Guesthouse. 14 Upper Rock Gardens, Brighton, Sussex BN2 1QE. ☎ **01273/ 681-403.** 6 units, 4 with shower only, 2 with bathroom. TV TEL. AE, DC, MC, V. £36–£42 ($62–$72) double. Rates include breakfast. Parking free on adjacent streets. Closed Dec.

Bannings is a dream come true for lesbians who want to stay in a charming guesthouse and be waited on by attentive men. Part of a Georgian terrace, the small house is immaculately kept. It's close to everything, but once you're inside you feel snug and cozy. The rooms, painted in pastels and with twin or double beds, are calmly feminine without being overly sweet. All have tea- and coffee-making facilities. Vegetarian, vegan, and full breakfasts are served in a lovely dining room.

Brighton Thistle. King's Rd., Brighton, Sussex BN1 2GS. ☎ **01273/206-700.** Fax 01273/820-692. 204 units. A/C MINIBAR TV TEL. £164–£192 ($282–$330) double; £120 ($206) weekend B&B. AE, DC, MC, V.

Like its neighbor, the Grand (below), the Thistle is a five-star place, but it was built over 100 years later (in the 1980s). The central feature is an enormous atrium filled with plants and restaurants and sitting areas. It's well done, but you may feel like you're in a shopping mall. The rooms are quite glamorous, done up in a stylish clash of eclectic contemporary pieces. All have large tiled baths, trouser presses, irons, and hair dryers. Sea views are more expensive; other rooms look into the atrium.

Coward's Guest House. 12 Upper Rock Gardens, Brighton, Sussex BN2 1QE. ☎ **01273/ 692-677.** 10 units, 6 with shower only, 4 with bathroom. TV TEL. £42–55 (72–$95) double. Rates include breakfast. Ask about winter rates. MC, V.

This smart charmer, part of the same Georgian terrace as Banning's (above), is really with it when it comes to understanding gay men's personal needs: Besides tea- and coffee-making facilities, every room contains complimentary condoms and lubes, and the managers provide cards for temporary membership rates at gay clubs. Coward's is perhaps the most stylishly decorated of the Brighton B&Bs (men only), with lemony yellow walls in the halls and pale green guest rooms. The door may be opened by Cyril Coward, Noël's nephew, or his partner, Gerry Breen.

The Grand. King's Rd., Brighton, Sussex BN1 2FW. ☎ **01273/321-188.** Fax 01273/ 202-694. E-mail grandbrighton.co.uk. 200 units. A/C MINIBAR TV TEL. £180–£270 ($310–$464) double. Rates include full English breakfast. Special rates often available. AE, DC, MC. V.

Grand it is, gay it ain't. Well, except for those of us who simply insist on five-star luxury wherever we travel. If that's you, this huge 1864 seaside resort hotel, dazzlingly white, will fit the bill. A few years ago, the front of it was blown off by an IRA bomb during Margaret Thatcher's visit, but that's all been repaired and the brass is gleaming again. The rooms are spacious and predictably gorgeous, done mostly in blues and yellows, with big tile baths and floor-to-ceiling double-glazed windows. The most expensive have balconies (but King's Road is cursed with as much traffic as Marine Parade), and all come with a trouser press and a hair dryer. The ornate Victorian wrought-iron stairway just off the lobby is quite a sight.

✪ **Hudson's Guest House.** 22 Devonshire Place, Brighton, Sussex BN2 1QA. ☎ **01273/683-642.** Fax 10273/696-088. 9 units, 5 with shower only, 4 with bathroom. TV TEL. £38–£50 ($65–$86) double. Rates include full English breakfast. 2-night minimum on weekends.

Hudson's, on a side street in the heart of Brighton's gay village, is a place where both men and women will feel right at home (a 5-minute walk from the Royal Pavilion and all the gay venues). You're welcomed with a drink and given your keys and a handy

Brighton

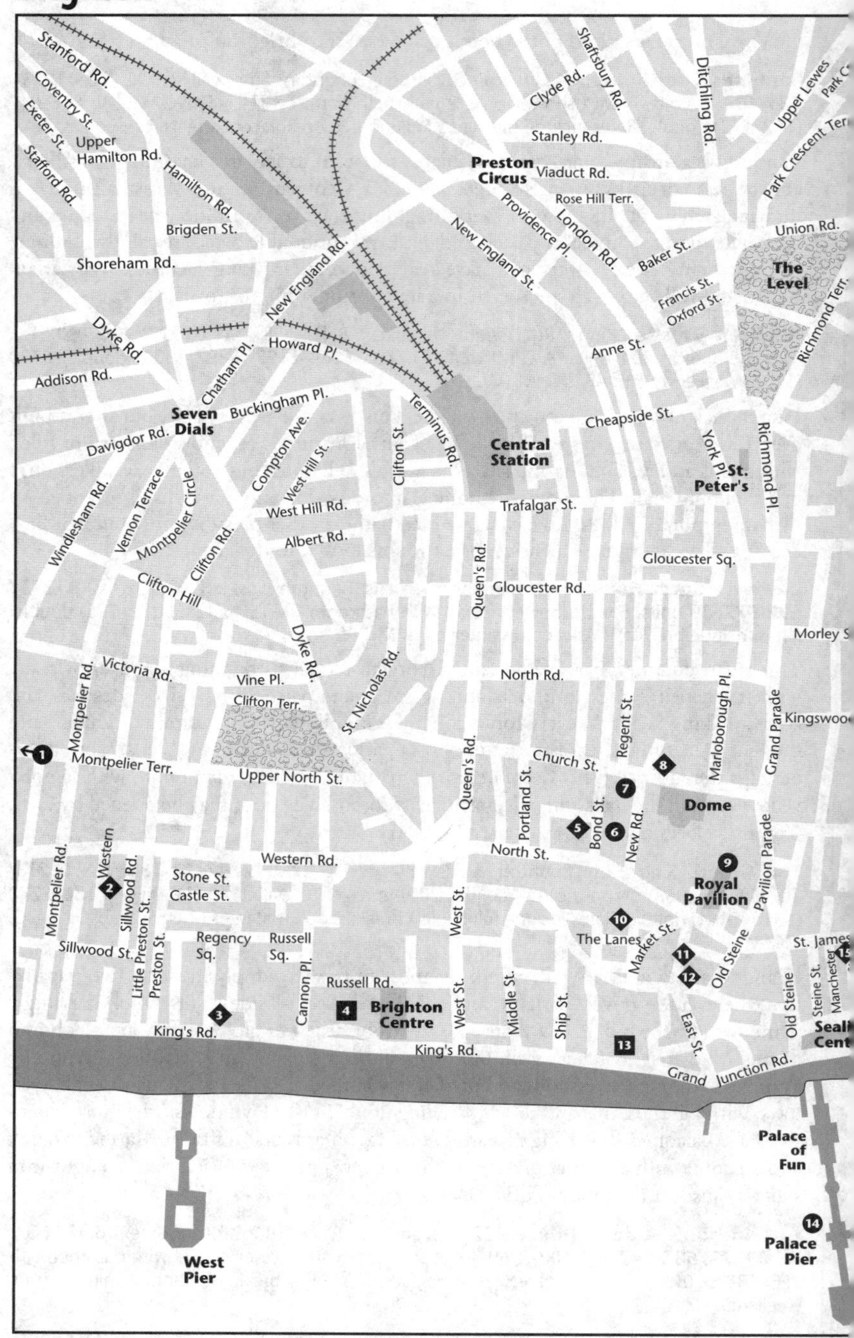

Stanford Rd.
Coventry St.
Exeter St.
Stafford Rd.
Upper Hamilton Rd.
Hamilton Rd.
Brigden St.
Shoreham Rd.
Dyke Rd.
Addison Rd.
New England Rd.
Howard Pl.
Chatham Pl.
Seven Dials
Buckingham Pl.
Davigdor Rd.
Clyde Rd.
Shaftsbury Rd.
Stanley Rd.
Preston Circus
Viaduct Rd.
Rose Hill Terr.
Providence Pl.
London Rd.
New England St.
Ditchling Rd.
Upper Lewes
Park Crescent Terr.
Union Rd.
The Level
Baker St.
Francis St.
Oxford St.
Richmond Terr.
Anne St.
Cheapside St.
Terminus Rd.
Central Station
Clifton St.
Compton Ave.
West Hill St.
West Hill Rd.
Albert Rd.
Windlesham Rd.
Vernon Terrace
Montpelier Circle
Clifton Rd.
Clifton Hill
York Pl.
St. Peter's
Richmond Pl.
Trafalgar St.
Gloucester Sq.
Gloucester Rd.
Queen's Rd.
Morley St.
Victoria Rd.
Vine Pl.
Dyke Rd.
St. Nicholas Rd.
North Rd.
Clifton Terr.
Montpelier Rd.
Montpelier Terr.
Upper North St.
Regent St.
Marlborough Pl.
Grand Parade
Kingswood
Church St.
Portland St.
Bond St.
New Rd.
Dome
Western Rd.
North St.
Pavilion Parade
Royal Pavilion
Western
Sillwood Rd.
Stone St.
Castle St.
West St.
Sillwood St.
Little Preston St.
Preston St.
Regency Sq.
Russell Sq.
Cannon Pl.
Russell Rd.
Brighton Centre
Middle St.
Ship St.
The Lanes
Market St.
Old Steine
East St.
St. James
Steine St.
Manchester
King's Rd.
Grand Junction Rd.
Sea Life Cent
Palace of Fun
Palace Pier
West Pier
1
2
3
4
5
6
7
8
9
10
11
12
13
14

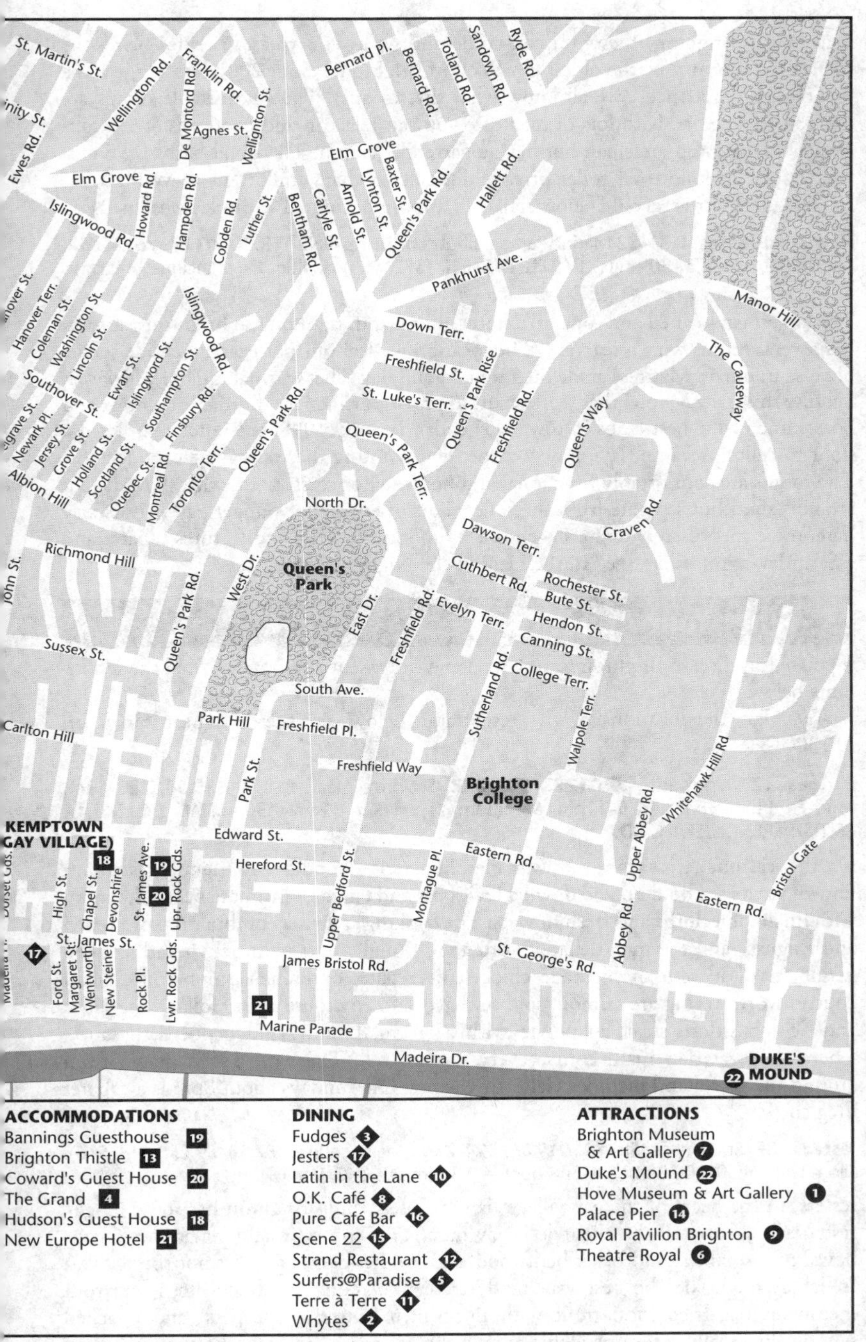
St. Martin's St.
Wellington Rd.
Franklin Rd.
De Montord Rd.
Agnes St.
Wellington St.
Bernard Pl.
Bernard Rd.
Totland Rd.
Sandown Rd.
Ryde Rd.
Ewes Rd.
Elm Grove
Elm Grove
Howard Rd.
Hampden Rd.
Cobden Rd.
Luther St.
Bentham Rd.
Carlyle St.
Arnold St.
Lynton St.
Baxter St.
Queen's Park Rd.
Hallett Rd.
Islingwood Rd.
Pankhurst Ave.
Manor Hill
Hanover Terr.
Coleman St.
Washington St.
Lincoln St.
Islingwood Rd.
Down Terr.
Freshfield St.
St. Luke's Terr.
Queen's Park Rise
Freshfield Rd.
Queens Way
The Causeway
Southover St.
Ewart St.
Islingword St.
Southampton St.
Finsbury Rd.
Queen's Park Rd.
Queen's Park Terr.
Newark Pl.
Jersey St.
Grove St.
Holland St.
Scotland St.
Quebec St.
Montreal Rd.
Toronto Terr.
Albion Hill
North Dr.
Dawson Terr.
Craven Rd.
Richmond Hill
John St.
Queen's Park
West Dr.
East Dr.
Cuthbert Rd.
Rochester St.
Bute St.
Freshfield Rd.
Evelyn Terr.
Hendon St.
Canning St.
Queen's Park Rd.
Sussex St.
College Terr.
Sutherland Rd.
South Ave.
Walpole Terr.
Carlton Hill
Park Hill
Freshfield Pl.
Whitehawk Hill Rd
Freshfield Way
Park St.
Brighton College
Upper Abbey Rd.
KEMPTOWN
GAY VILLAGE)
Edward St.
Eastern Rd.
Bristol Gate
18
19
20
Hereford St.
St. James Ave.
Upr. Rock Gds.
High St.
Chapel St.
Devonshire
Upper Bedford St.
Montague Pl.
Eastern Rd.
Abbey Rd.
St. James St.
17
St. George's Rd.
James Bristol Rd.
Ford St.
Margaret St.
Wentworth
New Steine
Rock Pl.
Lwr. Rock Gds.
21
Marine Parade
Madeira Dr.
DUKE'S
MOUND
22
ACCOMMODATIONS
Bannings Guesthouse 19
Brighton Thistle 13
Coward's Guest House 20
The Grand 4
Hudson's Guest House 18
New Europe Hotel 21
DINING
Fudges 3
Jesters 17
Latin in the Lane 10
O.K. Café 8
Pure Café Bar 16
Scene 22 15
Strand Restaurant 12
Surfers@Paradise 5
Terre à Terre 11
Whytes 2
ATTRACTIONS
Brighton Museum & Art Gallery 7
Duke's Mound 22
Hove Museum & Art Gallery 1
Palace Pier 14
Royal Pavilion Brighton 9
Theatre Royal 6

map of gay Brighton, then you can come and go as you please. Besides being the friendliest, this may be the oldest gay B&B in Brighton: About 200 years ago it was a "gentlemen's residence" (we all know what that means). The comfortable rooms are done in pale colors, with lots of furniture you can relax on and good poster art. Singles at the very top are small but have a garretlike charm. The small baths have louvred doors, making total toilet privacy difficult (if that's important to you). A big English breakfast is served "below stairs" in a room decorated with play posters.

New Europe Hotel. 31–32 Marine Parade, Brighton, Sussex BN2 1TR. ☎ **01273/624-462.** Fax 01273/624-575. 30 units. TV TEL. £45–£50 ($77–$86) double. Rates include breakfast. MC, V.

The largest gay-owned and -operated hotel in England, right on the Brighton seafront, has several rooms with a sea view. The location is ideal but not exactly seaside serene because traffic on Marine Parade buzzes night and day. That's a small quibble, however, because this is a gay hotel that works hard to provide attractive, affordable comfort and boasts one of the best clubs in town (Legends). In early 1998, the hotel completed a floor-to-ceiling revamp, laying new carpet and painting the walls "pale cappuccino." The rooms are comfortably functional and not heavily accessorized, with showers that are pint-sized but separate from the toilet. Lots of energetic younger gay visitors stay here, more men than women. Legends is a hip local favorite and features cabaret and a Saturday-night disco (see "In the Heat of the Night" below).

3 Whet Your Appetite

If you're traveling to Brighton for the weekend, it's essential to reserve at all the restaurants below.

Note: For the locations of the restaurants below, see the "Brighton" map on p. 130–131.

Fudges. 127 King's Rd. ☎ **01273/205-852.** Set-price meals £13.50–£19.50 ($23–$34). Mon–Fri 11am–3pm and 5–11pm, Sat 11am–11pm, Sun 11am–9:30pm. AE, DC, MC, V. BRITISH/FRENCH/SEAFOOD.

On the seafront across from the West Pier, Fudges is a popular gay-friendly restaurant known for its seafood. You go down a few stairs and enter an intimate bistrolike room with linen tablecloths and fresh flowers. The cooking style is a combination of French and English, and the menu changes often. You might start with prawn and smoked haddock vol-au-vent, homemade chicken liver pâté, or French onion soup. Main courses worth trying are salmon, sole, and avocado en croute with Hollandaise sauce and Scotch sirloin steak au poivre with a cream, brandy, and peppercorn sauce. There's a vegetarian main course every day as well. The wine list is drawn from around the world and includes California wines. On Sundays about 8pm is a cabaret drag show.

Jesters. 87 St. James's St. ☎ **01723/624-233.** Main courses £7.50–£9.25 ($13–$16). Mon–Thurs 5:30–10:30pm, Sat–Sun noon–10:30pm. AE, MC, V. BRITISH.

Jesters, in the heart of the gay village, is the closest thing Brighton has to an all-gay restaurant. Nearly all the clientele is gay men. This corner restaurant has large windows, round tables, and black bentwood chairs. The food is good if not spectacular; "reliable" might be the best way to describe it. Among the best things are trout meunière (pan-fried local trout with nut-brown butter and capers) and poached salmon. Especially recommendable among the pastas is spaghetti asparago (asparagus in a creamy Parmesan-and-wine sauce). If you have a sweet tooth, finish up with Death by Chocolate or lemon cheesecake. The wine list is limited.

Gay-Friendly Cafes

The **O.K. Cafe,** 110 Church St. (☎ **01273/606-424;** open Mon–Sat 9am–5pm, Sun 10am–3pm), is a small unpretentious cafe that won't win any glamour awards but serves hearty breakfasts all day and has daily lunch specials. It caters mainly to women. MasterCard and Visa are accepted. The **Pure Cafe Bar,** 50 George St. (☎ **01273/692-457;** open Mon–Tues 11am–6pm, Wed–Sat to 11pm, Sun noon–10:30pm), is a newly opened smart little cafe/bar in Kemptown. It accepts American Express, MasterCard, and Visa.

Scene 22, 129 St. James's St. (☎ **01273/626-682;** open daily 10:30am–6pm), is a funky, friendly little gay store that dispenses gay tourist information and sells magazines and leather and rubber items; it also has a small cafe serving what's reputedly the worst coffee in Brighton. No credit cards are accepted.

Latin in the Lane. 10–11 King's Rd. ☎ **01273/321-600.** Main courses £6–£14 ($10–$24). Daily noon–2:15pm and 6:30–11pm (Fri–Sat to 11:30pm). AE, DC, MC, V. ITALIAN/ SEAFOOD.

This Italianate restaurant specializes in fresh local and exotic seafood, beautifully displayed Italian style in a refrigerated case. The crowd is pretty straight, but not entirely so, and there are usually lots of tourists. The tables and floor are marble, and the posters and prints on the pale walls add to the quasi-Italian ambience. You can sample Italian antipasti, like melon with Parma ham or mixed salami with fresh figs, and then go on to pastas or fish, which comes fresh from the market every day. The seafood risotto with wild mushrooms, cream, and white wine is very good, as is the casserole of fresh seasonal seafood and the mussels in white wine, parsley, and garlic. Classic Italian and French wines are available.

✪ **Strand Restaurant.** 6 East St. ☎ **01273/747-096.** Main courses £8–£15 ($14–$26); 3-course set meal £9.95 ($17). Daily 12:30–10pm (to 10:30pm weekends). AE, DC. MC, V. MODERN BRITISH.

This bow-fronted restaurant, just behind Dr. Brighton's gay pub, has become one of Brighton's socioculinary hot spots. Very gay-friendly, it's packed by 8:30pm. With a subdued nautical theme (the toilets are marked "Mermen" and "Mermaids"), it's cool without being pretentious. And the food is very good. The ever-changing fixed-price dinner menu is an extremely good value. You start with something like herby homemade vegetable soup, pâté, or mussels cooked with fresh cream, wine, and garlic. Then go on to chicken breast with leeks and blue cheese sauce, artichoke-and-pesto lasagna, or lamb chops with gravy. Dessert might be a tart and sweet lemon sponge pudding or a toothachingly sweet chocolate cheesecake on a fudge-cake base. Very friendly service too.

Surfers@Paradise. 18A Bond St. ☎ **01273/684-184.** Main courses £4.95–£14.95 ($9–$26). Sun–Mon 10am–7pm, Tues–Fri 10am–11pm, Sat 9am–11pm. AE, DC, MC, V. MODERN BRITISH.

If you're into dining on computer chips, this trendy Internet cafe allows you to rent a computer and get to work sending e-mail messages back home. It operates on two levels, with the computers in between. It's probably best to confine yourself to coffee or one of the lighter meals offered, such as leek-and-basil croquettes with salad and mango salsa, vegetarian sausages with mashed potatoes, or the S@P burger that comes with salad and chips (not the micro kind). There's a cocktail menu and wines from

Australia, California, and Washington State. Renting a computer costs £1.50 ($2.60) for 15 minutes, £3 ($5) for half an hour, and £5 ($9) for an hour; you can set up your own Internet account. The staff is young and friendly but a bit disorganized.

✪ **Terre a Terre.** 71 East St. ☎ **01273/729-051.** Main courses £7.50–£9.75 ($13– $17). AE, MC, V. Tues–Sun noon–10:30pm, Mon 6–10:30pm. DC, MC, V. VEGETARIAN.

Don't stick up your nose: This is the best vegetarian restaurant in England, perhaps in all Europe. It elevates meatless cuisine into the art it should be but rarely is. The atmosphere has an upscale Zen simplicity, with soft burnt-orange walls, sanded wood floors, and sleek wooden tables and chairs. The food is impeccably fresh and beautifully presented. For starters, try a saffron goatee—not a beard but poached goat's cheese surrounded by saffron butter sauce and finished with a black olive tapinade. Or skip the starters and eat your way through the menu with the Terre a Tapas, a superb selection of all their best dishes; served with toasted garlic focaccia, it's big enough for two. When you've finished, I promise you'll have an entirely new outlook on vegetarian food.

✪ **Whytes.** 33 Western St. ☎ **01273/776-618.** Table d'hôte dinners £16.45–£20.50 ($28–$35). Tues–Sat 7–9:30pm. MC, V. MODERN BRITISH.

Housed in a tiny bow-fronted cottage just off the seafront, Whytes has won a few awards in its time. The cooking at this dressy place is considered by many to be the best in Brighton. The two- and three-course set menu wisely limits your choices for ordering. Starters might be loin of pork with tomato-and-apple confit, wild smoked salmon strips, or a warm salad with Thai-spiced local cod. The superb mains can include succulent roast fillet of lamb with shallot compote, medallions of fillet steak on a horseradish rosti with wild mushroom sauce, or crispy roast duckling with raspberry-vinegar sauce. The custardy desserts are meltingly rich. The restaurant isn't really gay, but this is Brighton, after all, so you never know who might be sitting next to you.

4 Exploring Brighton

Forget about that frantic need for sightseeing and relax. That's what Brighton is all about. It's a place for leisurely strolling, either in the town or along the seaside promenades. The town is small enough so you won't get lost and large enough to offer some good cultural diversions.

Note: For the locations of the sights below, see the "Brighton" map on p. 130–131.

THE HITS YOU SHOULDN'T MISS

✪ **Royal Pavilion Brighton.** Bounded by North St., Church St., Olde Steine, and New Rd. ☎ **01273/290-900.** Admission £4.10 ($7). Oct–Mar daily 10am–5pm (Apr–Sept to 6pm). Closed Dec 25–26.

The Royal Pavilion is Brighton's one "must-see" attraction. It's been called the most extraordinary palace in Europe and also the campiest. Take the tour and judge for yourself. If you've seen Barbra Streisand in *On a Clear Day You Can See Forever,* you'll recognize the pavilion as where her former self meets the love of her former life.

Between 1815 and 1822, John Nash redesigned the original farmhouse and villa on this site for George IV (when the king was still Prince Regent), who lived here with his mistress, Lady Conyngham, until 1827. The exterior, as crazily wonderful as anything King Ludwig of Bavaria could've dreamed up, is an Indian fantasy of turrets and minarets. The interior, decorated in the "Chinese" style, is sumptuous and fantastically extravagant. The **Long Gallery** has a color scheme of bright blues and pinks, the **Music Room** has a domed ceiling of gilded scallop-shaped shells, and the **King's**

private apartments on the upper floors epitomize the Regency lifestyle of the rich and infamous. The pavilion was also used by the king's brother, William IV, and their niece, Queen Victoria. Finding it too cramped and lacking a sea view, Victoria closed it down, put the furnishings into storage, and moved to Osborne House on the Isle of Wight. The city of Brighton eventually got the furnishings back and opened the pavilion to the public.

Before you leave the pavilion, consider having lunch or a cream tea in the superbly restored **Queen Adelaide Tea Room** (☎ **01723/292-736;** open daily 10:30am–4:30pm, to 5pm in summer). Queen Adelaide, who used this suite in 1830, didn't appreciate the epicurean tastes of her husband, George IV. Dismissing his renowned French chefs, she reverted back to British cuisine so dreary that Lord Dudley complained "you now get cold pâté and hot champagne." The lunch selections range from £2 to £5 ($3.45 to $8.60) and cream teas from £4 to £6 ($7 to $10).

Brighton Museum & Art Gallery. Church St. (just behind The Dome, adjacent to the Royal Pavilion). ☎ **01273/290-900.** Admission free. Mon–Tues and Thurs–Sat 10am–5pm, Sun 2–5pm.

This is a small museum with some interesting art-nouveau and art-deco collections of furniture, glass, and ceramics, plus a Fashion Gallery. It's good for an hour or two on a rainy day when you can't go to the beach.

Hove Museum & Art Gallery. 19 New Church Rd. ☎ **01273/290-200.** Admission free. Tues–Fri 10am–5pm, Sat–Sun 10am–4:30pm.

Housed in an impressive Victorian villa, the museum contains a good collection of 20th-century paintings and drawings, 18th-century furniture and decorative art, and the "Hove to Hollywood" film collection featuring film of the town in 1900 by local moviemakers (the British film industry started in Hove). I'm told that in their film archives are some of the earliest hetero porn movies ever made.

Palace Pier. On the seafront.

The town's famous amusement area, the pier juts out into the sea and no doubt had some real charm when it was built in the late 19th century. Today it's garish and tacky, a haven for bored teens and tourists with kiddies in tow. At night, all lit up with twinkling lights, it's almost cheerily irresistible. Spend half an hour but don't expect much to find more than junk food and arcade games.

There's one super free **photo op,** though: a wooden Queen Victoria with an empty space where your face could be. Queen for a day?

GAY BRIGHTON

There's a large gay presence in Brighton and has been for some time. Maybe it's the relaxed resort-town atmosphere or the preponderance of charming Georgian houses just waiting to be decorated. The town boasts the largest **Gay Pride** parade in England after London's—in 1998, 75,000 to 80,000 queers showed up for this August event.

Kemptown, Brighton's gay village, is just east of the Royal Pavilion. The area is bounded by Marine Parade to the south, Edward Street to the north, Old Steine to the west and Rock Garden to the east, but gay venues are scattered all over town (none more than a 15-minute walk). **St. James's Street,** Kemptown's main thoroughfare, is lined with an assortment of shops, restaurants, and stores—a few of them gay, more of them not. It's low-key and unpretentious. The area, abutting the seafront, does boast some lovely Georgian town-house terraces, but it's mostly cozy and well maintained rather than glitzy or glam. Brighton is an extremely popular summer weekend getaway for gays from all over England and, increasingly, the rest of Europe.

For more information on gay Brighton, you can check out the gay site on **Virtual Brighton & Hove,** the town's Web page at **www.brighton.co.uk.**

G Scene, Brighton's free gay monthly magazine, is your best bet for current listings on gay places and events in the area; it's available in gay bars and businesses.

PARKS, GARDENS & SQUARES

Brighton's seafront is where the action is, but strolling through the town is fun too. The innumerable Georgian terraces, some of them fronting onto open grassy parks, will be of interest to anyone who likes architecture.

The **Royal Pavilion Gardens** surrounding the Royal Pavilion have been restored to their original Regency splendor; following John Nash's plans of the 1820s, which were an attempt to imitate forest scenery, the gardens have serpentine paths weaving through lawns and shrubbery. **Duke's Mound,** the major gay cruising area, is about a mile west of Palace Pier; it's a shrubby, litter-strewn area that rises up the hillside behind the gay nude beach.

BOYS & GIRLS ON THE BEACH

The gay boys and girls are definitely on the beach in Brighton. Braving chill winds, sullen gray skies, and a gravelly beach that goes far behind the Princess-and-the-pea discomfort level, they bare their pasty torsos all summer long.

And yes, there's a **nude gay beach**—the only one in England. It's about a mile west of Brighton Pier, and if you're lazy you can take (during summer) a little electric train from the pier directly to the beach. If you're into nude sunbathing, be aware that foreign families sometimes walk through the area to gawk at the exposed bodies. This beach is accessible to anyone. **Duke's Mound,** the not-very-large gay cruising area, is on the other side of the road. It has paths running up the slope of a hill, and the abundance of shrubbery makes it popular for evening trysts; discretion is advised.

5 Hitting the Stores

The Lanes, Brighton's original fishing village, is now a warren of narrow streets filled with small shops selling upmarket trinkets, mostly to tourists. It's fun to stroll through, but with London so close at hand why would you want to buy anything here? **North Laines** has more interesting shops, including some trendy outfitters. **Duke's Lane** is a good place to look for men's clothing, and **Duke Street** is good for antiques.

SHOPS A TO Z

Shops in Brighton basically adhere to the same hours as London: Monday to Saturday 10am to 6pm, with a later closing on Thursday or Friday. During the summer tourist season, some shops are open on Sunday and closed on Monday.

ART **Clairmonte Galleries,** 56 Gardner St. (☎ **01273/622-027**), features a good selection of oils, watercolors, photographs, pottery, and cards.

BOOKS & CARDS **Out!,** 4–7 Dorset St. (☎ **01273/623-356**), Brighton's gay and lesbian bookstore, stocks books, magazines, and nonliterary items like videos, toys, and rubber and leather gear. **Cardome,** 47A St. James's St. (☎ **01273/692-916**), has a small selection of gay cards and novelty items.

FASHION **Retro Men,** 82 St. James's St. (☎ **01273/673-102**), is a trendy new men's store. And **Papillon,** 52 St. James's St. (☎ **01273/686-307**), is a nifty shop for all you lads who want to slip into something more comfortable—like stiletto heels (large sizes), leopard-print miniskirts, wigs, jewelry, nylons, corsets, makeup, and breast forms. There's even a made-to-measure service for men's frocks.

6 All the World's a Stage

The **Brighton Festival** (☎ **01273/292-950**), one of England's best-known arts festivals, is held in May and features a wide array of drama, literature, visual art, dance, and concert programs ranging from classical to hard rock. England's best actors regularly trod the boards at the **Theatre Royal,** New Road (☎ **01273/328-488**), which presents a full season of dramatic works.

The **Gardner Arts Center** (☎ **01273/685-861**), on the campus of Sussex University a few miles northeast of town in Falmer, produces a full season of plays in a modern theater-in-the-round. Music and dance programs are regularly held in the University of Brighton's **Sallis Benney Theatre,** Grand Parade (☎ **01273/643-010**).

The highly regarded **Brighton Philharmonic Orchestra** (☎ **01273/622-900**) performs a season of classical music concerts at **The Dome,** 29 New Rd. (adjacent to the Royal Pavilion). Built in 1803 as the stables for George IV's horses and remodeled into a concert hall in 1935, The Dome is a venue for concerts of all kinds. When internationally known performers (such as Shirley Bassey) come to town, they perform at the 5,000-seat **Brighton Centre,** Russell Road (☎ **01273/202-881**).

7 In the Heat of the Night

Brighton fills up on the weekends, especially summer weekends, with gays and lesbians looking for a good time. During winter, the town's bars and pubs are geared more to the locals. In general, you'll find less attitude here than in London. Many of the bars and pubs feature weekly cabaret performances. Usual pub hours are Monday to Saturday 11am to 11pm and Sunday noon to 10:30pm.

Maybe it's the holiday atmosphere, but Brighton is a town that just loves drag and cabaret shows. The cabarets are amateur affairs on small stages in the bars and pubs. Gays and lesbians mix more in Brighton than in London, so women will feel welcome at all the places listed below.

GAY BARS, PUBS & CABARETS

All the Brighton pubs and bars are a hop and a skip from one another. On weekends, the scene picks up with the infiltration of visitors, and on weekdays the local pubbers hang out until the 11pm closing.

✪ **Legends,** the smartly redecorated residents' bar in the New Europe Hotel, 31–32 Marine Parade (☎ **01273/624-462;** open pub hours), is green, glam, and gorgeous and has a cabaret area for weekly entertainment; the **Schwarz Bar,** in the hotel basement, is cruisy and has a dress code on weekends (Fri–Sat 10pm–2am).

✪ **Aquarium,** 6 Steine St. (☎ **01273/605-525;** open pub hours), a small pub with a dark green facade and a rosy-orange interior, is popular with locals and hosts weekend drag acts and cabaret; the crowd is friendly, and the atmosphere gets cruisy toward closing.

✪ **Dr. Brighton's,** 16 King's Rd. (☎ **01273/328-765;** open pub hours), is a large laid-back pub on the seafront close to Palace Pier.

The **Black Horse,** 112 Church St. (☎ **01273/606-864**), is a small pub close to the Theatre Royal (attracts a theater crowd) and next door to the O.K. Cafe; it's best on Saturday Party Night and has a fun Sunday lunch cabaret at 2:15pm.

The **Bulldog Tavern,** 31 St. James's St. (☎ **01273/684-097**), a pub with a weekend piano bar, is on the main street in the gay village and boasts a cozy "locals" ambience and friendly staff.

Marilyn's, 43 Providence Place (☎ **01273/620-630;** open pub hours), is a cabaret bar with weekly drag shows, karaoke, and a Divas Camp Quiz on Monday nights.

The **Oriental Cabaret Bar,** 5 Montpelier Rd. (☎ **01273/728-808;** open pub hours), an intimate pub with a tiny stage, is famed for its cabaret shows held Wednesday, Friday, and Saturday evenings and Sunday at lunch.

LESBIAN BARS

Queen's Head, 10 Steine St. (☎ **01273/602-939;** open pub hours), a wraparound corner pub with lace curtains, is a traditional watering hole frequented by more and more girlz.

Marlborough, 4 Princes St. (☎ **01273/570-028;** open pub hours), a traditional pub in the heart of the town, has become popular with lesbians.

Just Sisters, a women-only club night disco, is held every Saturday 8:30pm to 1am at the **Basement Bar,** in the Excelsior Hotel, 205–209 Kingsway, Hove (☎ **01273/723-807**).

DANCE CLUBS

✪ **Club Revenge,** 32 Old Steine St., opposite the Palace pier (☎ **01273/606-064;** open Mon–Thurs 10:30pm–2am, Fri–Sat 10pm–2am; admission £5–£6/$9–$10), is the hottest dance club in Brighton and the one you'll probably want to hit. Spread out over two floors, it holds about 700 people, has lasers and smoke machines and views of the seafront, and is always packed with a sociable young crowd. There are various theme nights when dress codes are in effect.

Wild Fruit, 78 West St., at the Paradox Club (☎ **01273/321-628**), is a party (popular with men and women) held on the first Monday of every month 10pm to 2am; with varying themes, it's a regular "event" in Brighton's gay social calendar; call for details and dates.

Village, 74 St. James's St. (☎ **01273/622-260;** open Mon-Sat 2pm–2am, Sun pub hours), has a cheap drink night on Wednesday, a Student Night on Friday, and really backs them in on Saturday . . . but late.

Zanzibar, 129 St. James's St. (☎ **01273/622-100**), is a slightly scruffy late-night cellar bar with bottled drinks, video screens, disco, and a youngish crowd.

The **Zap Club,** 191 Kings Rd., Under the Arches on the seafront (☎ **01273/775-987**), isn't really gay but is certainly gay-friendly; the trendy club attracts lots of out-of-towners, both gay and straight.

SAUNAS

The best is the **Denmark Sauna,** 86 Denmark Villas, Hove (☎ **01273/723-733;** open daily noon–10pm), with a sauna, a Jacuzzi, a steam room, massage facilities, and a coffee shop. **Bright 'n Beautiful,** 9 St. Margaret's Place, just behind the Metropole Hotel (no phone), is clean and draws all types. There's also **Fitness Camp,** 19c Camelford St. (☎ **01273/674-455**)

4

Manchester: The Hottest Club Scene in England

When friends give you a bewildered look and ask why you want to go to **Manchester,** of all places, you can answer in five simple words: "hottest club scene in England." OK, in provincial England. Don't ask me why, just take my word for it: Manchester has become a "destination spot" for gays from all over England and the rest of Europe. In the heart of the industrial northwest (202 miles northwest of London, 86 miles north of Birmingham, and 35 miles east of Liverpool), it's a perfect weekend city because you can go and have fun but leave again and not have to live there.

Not that it's awful or anything. In fact, Manchester has never looked better. It used to be horrible, though: the kind of soot-choked industrial nightmare Charles Dickens wrote about in *Hard Times.* And it's almost entirely recovered from the massive IRA bomb attack that devastated the central section of the city in 1996. The fabric of Manchester remains pompously Victorian, but there's some interesting new architecture around, and gentrification, which we all love (and usually instigate), is everywhere.

More to the point, there's a hopping gay village filled with all manner of bars, pubs, clubs, and very groovy cafes and restaurants. The Mancunians, as the residents are called, are free of London attitude and more down-to-earth than Brightonians, and they seem to live for the weekend.

1 Manchester Essentials

ARRIVING & DEPARTING

BY PLANE There are now many direct flights from the United States and the Continent to **Manchester Airport,** 15 miles south of town. **Airport Link,** an above-ground train, runs from the airport terminal to Piccadilly Railway Station in downtown Manchester every 15 minutes 5:15am to 10:10pm, less often through the night; the trip takes about 20 minutes. Bus nos. 44 and 105 travel between the airport and Piccadilly Gardens Bus Station every 15 minutes during the day and hourly during evenings and on Sunday; the ride takes about 55 minutes.

BY TRAIN **Virgin,** a privatized arm (or crotch) of BritRail, offers frequent daily service from London's Euston Station to Manchester's Piccadilly Station. The trip takes about 2½ hours. Call **Virgin TrainLine** at ☎ **0345/484-950** for inquiries on departure times and special advance-purchase discounts.

Country & City Codes

The **country code** for the United Kingdom is **44.** The **city code** for Manchester is **161;** use this code if you're calling from outside the United Kingdom. If you're within the United Kingdom but not in Brighton, use **0161.** If you're calling within Brighton, simply leave off the code and dial only the regular phone number.

BY CAR From London, drive north on the M1 and M6 motorways to junction 21A, where you head east on the M62. The M62 becomes the M602 as you enter Manchester. By car, the trip generally takes between 3 and 4 hours, but be prepared for traffic and construction tie-ups.

VISITOR INFORMATION

The **Manchester Visitor Information Centre,** Town Hall Extension, Lloyd Street (☎ **0161/234-3157;** open Mon–Sat 10am–5:30pm, Sun 11am–4pm; Metrolink: St. Peter's Square), is well-stocked with brochures on local sites and can answer any questions you may have.

CITY LAYOUT & GETTING AROUND

Trains from London stop at **Piccadilly Station** on the eastern end of Manchester. Nearby **Piccadilly Gardens,** which has a bus station, is a busy inner-city transportation hub. From there, **Mosley Street** and **Portland Street** are the two principal north-south arteries. **Whitworth Street** loops around the city's south side, following parts of the old Bridgewater and Rochdale canals. The **Irwell River** forms the western boundary of the inner city.

Central Manchester, where you'll want to be, is compact and easily walkable. **Metrolink Trams** (☎ **0161/228-2000**), connects the Piccadilly bus and train stations to central Manchester. Self-service ticket machines dispense zone-based fares. **Buses** operate 6am to 11pm, with limited route service until 3am; tickets are available from the driver. The £5.60 ($10) **Wayfarer** (☎ **0161/228-7811**), good for one day of unlimited bus travel, is available from the **Travel Shop** at the Piccadilly Gardens Bus Station, Market Street (open Mon–Fri 7am–8pm, Sat 8am–8pm). Two taxi companies patronized by the gay community are **Village Cars,** 41 Bloom St. (☎ **0161/237-3383**), and **Yellow Cars,** 4A Whitworth St. (☎ **0161/228-3355**).

FAST FACTS: Manchester

AIDS Organization & Hot Line Call the **Body Positive NW Helpine** at ☎ **0161/237-9717** or visit **Lawrence House,** City Road, Hulme (☎ **0161/873-8100;** open Mon–Fri noon–5pm).

Community Center The **Lesbian and Gay Centre,** 49–51 Sidney St., off Oxford Road (☎ **0161/274-3999;** open daily 7pm–10pm), is a helpful drop-in place for information on gay Manchester.

Hot Line The **Lesbian and Gay Switchboard** (☎ **0161/274-3999**) is open daily 4 to 10pm.

Telephone See "Fast Facts: London" in chapter 2.

2 Pillow Talk

This isn't a city where you probably want to drop a lot of cash on accommodations, so I've listed three inexpensive gay or gay-friendly B&Bs and one larger, centrally located hotel.

Note: For the locations of the hotels below, see the "Manchester" map on p. 143.

Clone Zone Manchester Holiday Apartment. 36 Sackville St., Manchester M1 3LZ. ☎ and fax **0161/236-1398;** 2 units, neither with bathroom. TV. £25 ($43) double. AE, MC, V. Metrolink: St. Peter's Sq.

Clone Zone, one of the U.K.'s largest gay retail chains, rents out two second-floor rooms in a small building on Bloom Street, around the corner from its Manchester shop. These aren't glamorous but are clean and perfectly adequate. Both units have a king-size bed and are simply furnished, sharing one bathroom with a shower.

✪ **Holiday Inn Crowne Plaza Midland Hotel.** Peter St., St. Peter's Square, Manchester M60 2DS. ☎ **800/897-121** or 0161/236-3333. Fax 0161/932-4100. 303 units. A/C MINIBAR TV TEL. Mon–Thurs £150 ($258) double, Fri–Sun £125 ($215) double including breakfast. AE, DC, MC, V. Metrolink: St. Peter's Sq.

Primarily a business hotel, the Holiday Inn is busy during the week, less so on weekends. The hotel is ideally located, right off St. Peter's Square, around the corner from Bridgewater Hall and a 10-minute walk from the gay action on Canal Street. And it's pleasantly grand, occupying an enormous Edwardian railroad hotel built in 1903 and now a city landmark. As far as Holiday Inns go, this is top of the line, with beautifully appointed public spaces, two good restaurants, and excellent service. The guest rooms contain a full array of amenities: remote-control radio and TV, in-house movies, trouser press, ironing board, hair dryer, complimentary evening newspaper, and 24-hour room service. The fitness center is one of the best around, with a pool, a Jacuzzi, a sauna, sunbeds, and a full array of workout equipment.

Rembrandt Hotel. 33 Sackville St., Manchester M1 3LZ ☎ **0161/236-1311.** Fax 0161/236-4257. 6 units, none with bathroom; annex 12 units, all with bathroom. TV. £35 ($60) double without bathroom, £45 ($77) double with bathroom. Rates include full breakfast. AE, MC, V. Metrolink: St. Peter's Sq.

"The Rem," Manchester's oldest gay pub and hotel, has been around since the 1960s. The six rooms in their main building, above the pub and a second-floor restaurant, are clean and simply furnished. They tend to be booked solid on weekends, sometimes for months in advance, so call ahead. In 1998, the Rembrandt added 12 rooms with bath in their annex across the street. The rooms here look out on Canal Street, the main thoroughfare of the gay village, so they can be noisy on weekends. They too are clean, modestly but adequately furnished, and a very good value. A full English breakfast is served in the pleasant Bistro (see "Whet Your Appetite" below).

Smithfield Hotel & Bar. 37 Swan St., Manchester M4 5PF. ☎ **0161/839-4424.** 9 units, none with bathroom. TV. £35 ($60) double. Rates include full breakfast. No credit cards. Metrolink: Piccadilly Gardens.

The hotel, north of Piccadilly Gardens in a run-down area full of peep shows and hetero sex shops, is far from glamorous. But the owner, Jennifer Poole, makes up for any environmental inadequacies. A warm, funny, friendly Mancunian, she loves Yanks and has a regular gay crowd on weekends. You'll probably end up wanting to adopt her. The building is an old one but, unlike Jennifer, doesn't have a great deal of character. She has spruced up the rooms, all of which have washbasins and tea- and coffeemaking facilities, she'll let you do your laundry and serves a real English breakfast in the dining room to one side of the bar. The hotel is about a 10-minute walk from the gay village.

3 Whet Your Appetite

Along gentrified **Canal Street** are several trendy and very attractive gay and gay-friendly restaurants and cafe/bars that serve good food.

Note: For the locations of the restaurants below, see the "Manchester" map on p. 143. The closest Metrolink for all of them is St. Peter's Square.

The Bistro. In the Rembrandt Hotel, 33 Sackville St. ☎ **0161/236-1311.** Main courses £6 ($10). AE, DC, MC, V. Daily noon–8pm. BRITISH/VEGETARIAN.

Located above the gay Rembrandt pub, the Bistro is that rarity of rarities on ultra-hip Canal Street: a casual unpretentious place where you can get a good homecooked British meal for not very much money. How about Lancashire hot pot, a bubbling mix of meat and veg, or a gammon steak with a pineapple slice or an egg? If you're longing for a simple ploughman's lunch, bread and cheese, or smoked mackerel salad, this is your place.

Manto. 46 Canal St. ☎ **0161/236-2667.** Main courses £4.50–£5 ($8–$9). AE, MC, V. Mon–Sat 10am–midnight, Sun 11am–midnight, Sat–Sun 2–6am. BRITISH/SNACKS.

This slick, spare cafe/bar gallery is a preclub hangout popular with young disco dollies, but you can get a decent inexpensive meal here. The menu is fairly limited: various salads, omelets, jacket potatoes with toppings, and hot and cold sandwiches. Heartier main courses include chili con carne, Cajun chicken breast, and spaghetti tossed in red pesto. The Friday and Saturday Breakfast Club is a hit with clubbers—it starts when the bars close and runs until 6am.

Metz. 3 Brazil St. ☎ **0161/237-9852.** Main courses £7–£12 ($12–$21). AE, MC, V. Mon–Thurs noon–11pm (Fri–Sat to midnight, Sun to 10:30pm). EASTERN EUROPEAN.

Another stylish cafe/bar on Canal Street, Metz bills itself as a place "where queens are treated like kings." Needless to say, it's very gay. To get to it, you cross a little bridge over to the other side of the Rochdale canal. They've spent a fortune on the decor, and the food is good, if not outstanding. The menu concentrates on various exotic-sounding dishes from Eastern Europe. The Krusevo stroganoff is one of the better offerings: prime fillet steak strongly flavored with paprika, sour cream, and red wine and served on egg noodles. The kebabs, chicken and vegetable, are tasty. You might want just a dessert—like the homemade crème caramel of the sticky toffee pudding topped with hot-fudge and walnut sauce. In warm weather the crowd, many of them "professionals" (they work instead of just going to clubs), moves out canalside and onto a floating barge.

Pure Lush. 27 Sackville St. ☎ **0161/288-7800.** Main courses £6–£10 ($10–$17). AE, DC, MC, V. Mon–Sat noon–11pm (Sun to midnight). CALIFORNIAN/VEGETARIAN.

Another recent debutante at the Trendy Restaurant Ball, Pure Lush is cool and spare with a minimalist design, good music, and an open kitchen. It's in a cavernous space on the second floor of an old building in the gay village. The menu is more health-conscious than at some of the other restaurants and takes its cue from California (which means eclectic). The pizzas are yummy, with light crispy crusts, and the grilled fish is fresh and unsauced. There are several vegetarian choices for those who eschew meat.

✪ **Velvet.** 2 Canal St. ☎ **0161/230-9003.** Main courses £7–£10 ($11–$17). AE, DC, MC, V. Mon–Wed noon–11pm (Thurs–Sat to 1am, Sun to 10:30pm). INTERNATIONAL.

On gay-trendy Canal Street, Velvet out-trends the trendiest. There's a fish tank set into the staircase floor (the former resident, a lizard, understandably became vicious), the women's loo (I'm told) is carpeted in fake leopard skin, and the men's john (as I saw with my own eyes) allows you to relieve yourself while watching the QVC shopping channel. The overall atmosphere in the dining room, accented with velvet drapes and pink and blue chairs and sofas, is surprisingly relaxed and friendly. And what about the food? Happily, it's good enough to make for a memorable gay evening out. You might want just a sandwich or a light meal, in which case spring for the spring rolls or the crab-and-coriander fish cakes. For mains, try the creamy chicken-and-bacon carbonara, curried lamb passanda, or salmon poached and served with lemongrass butter sauce. The desserts are blissfully rich.

Manchester

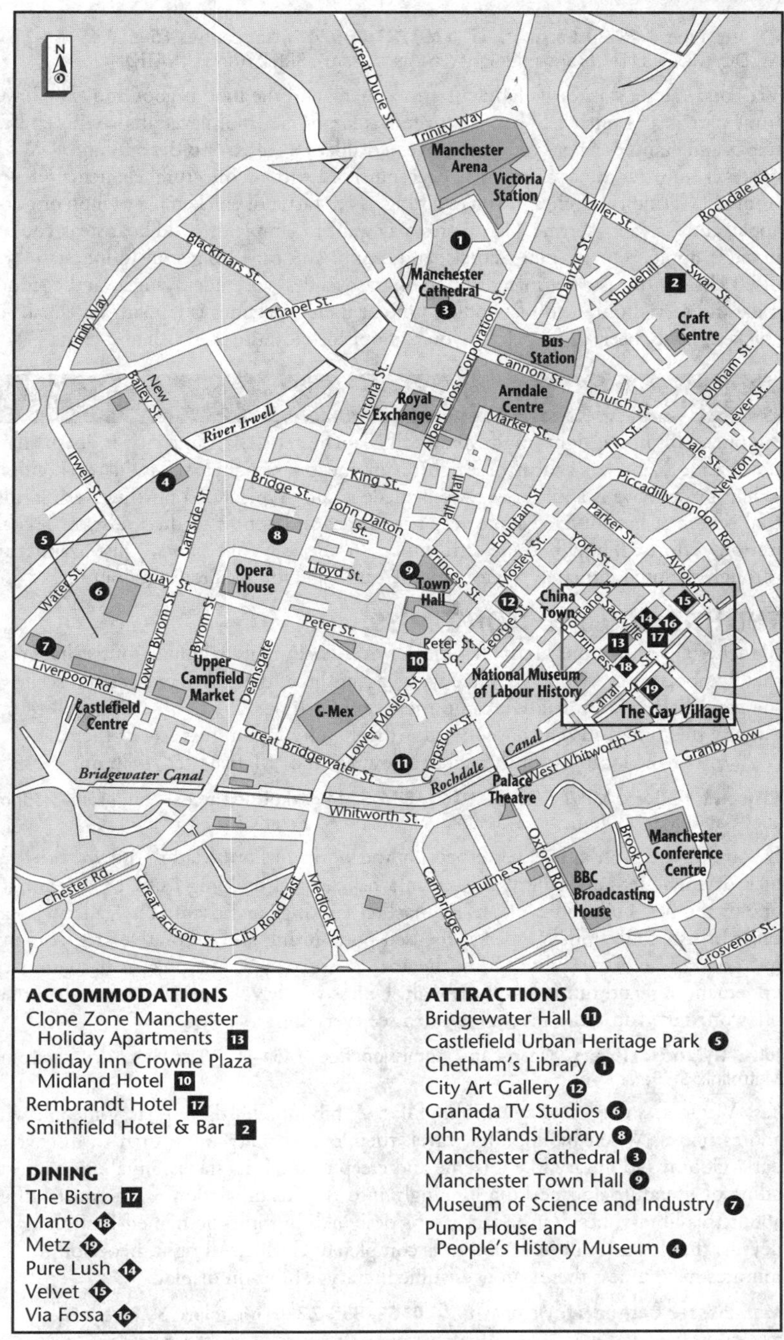
N
Great Ducie St.
Trinity Way
Manchester Arena
Victoria Station
Miller St.
Rochdale Rd.
Blackfriars St.
Manchester Cathedral
Dantzic St.
Shudehill
Swan St.
Chapel St.
Corporation St.
Craft Centre
Trinity Way
Bus Station
New Bailey St.
Cannon St.
Oldham St.
Victoria St.
Royal Exchange
Albert Cross
Arndale Centre
Church St.
Lever St.
River Irwell
Market St.
Tib St.
Dale St.
Newton St.
Irwell St.
King St.
Bridge St.
Pall Mall
Piccadilly London Rd.
Gartside St.
John Dalton St.
Fountain St.
Parker St.
York St.
Mosley St.
Aytoun St.
Quay St.
Opera House
Lloyd St.
Princess St.
Town Hall
Water St.
China Town
Portland St.
Sackville St.
Byrom St.
Peter St.
George St.
Princess St.
Lower Byrom St.
Peter St. Sq.
Upper Campfield Market
Deansgate
National Museum of Labour History
Liverpool Rd.
Canal St.
Castlefield Centre
G-Mex
Lower Mosley St.
The Gay Village
Great Bridgewater St.
Chepstow St.
Canal
West Whitworth St.
Granby Row
Bridgewater Canal
Rochdale
Palace Theatre
Whitworth St.
Oxford Rd.
Brook St.
Manchester Conference Centre
Chester Rd.
Hulme St.
BBC Broadcasting House
Great Jackson St.
City Road East
Medlock St.
Cambridge St.
Grosvenor St.
ACCOMMODATIONS
Clone Zone Manchester Holiday Apartments 13
Holiday Inn Crowne Plaza Midland Hotel 10
Rembrandt Hotel 17
Smithfield Hotel & Bar 2
DINING
The Bistro 17
Manto 18
Metz 19
Pure Lush 14
Velvet 15
Via Fossa 16
ATTRACTIONS
Bridgewater Hall 11
Castlefield Urban Heritage Park 5
Chetham's Library 1
City Art Gallery 12
Granada TV Studios 6
John Rylands Library 8
Manchester Cathedral 3
Manchester Town Hall 9
Museum of Science and Industry 7
Pump House and People's History Museum 4

✪ **Via Fossa.** 28–30 Canal St. ☎ **0161/236-0074.** Main courses £5–£10.45 ($9–$18). AE, DC, MC, V. Daily 11am–midnight (Fri–Sat to 2am). BRITISH/INTERNATIONAL.

Via Fossa rates a star for its fabulous atmosphere, and the food is good too. The lower front part is a popular gay bar. The cafe/restaurant is a multilevel affair with endless nooks and crannies where you can sit over a drink or a coffee or order a full meal. What makes it so extraordinary is that it's been outfitted with architectural elements rescued from old German churches. If you're dining, try a starter of chicken liver Dijon or pork, apple, and Calvados terrine. Carnivores may want to sample the wild boar steak cooked in cider, apple, tomato, pine kernels, and cream. You can also get an Indonesian-style diced chicken breast, marinated in lemongrass, chiles, coriander, ginger, and coconut milk and served on a bed of noodles. One of their specialties is teppanyaki kebabs of chicken, lamb, beef, or fennel. Or you can opt for old-fashioned fish and chips.

4 Exploring Manchester

No one in his or her right mind would call Manchester a charming city. It doesn't have the seaside Georgian charm of Brighton or the cosmopolitan glamour of London. What it does have is a kind of raw, self-made vitality typical of a northwestern industrial center. It has survived some very hard times and is now in the midst of "revitalization" efforts. Though there isn't much in the way of "sights," just wandering through the predominately Victorian core can make for an interesting outing.

THE HITS YOU SHOULDN'T MISS

Manchester's attractions aren't the kind of overwhelmingly fabulous tourist hangouts that'll appeal to everyone. If you're weekending here, the clubs and general scene in the gay village will probably take up most of your time. The sights below will round out any free time you may have, but don't feel guilty if you miss any of them.

Note: For the locations of the sights below, see the "Manchester" map on p. 143.

City Art Gallery. Mosley St. ☎ **0161/236-5244.** Admission free. Mon 11am–5:30pm, Tues–Sat 10am–5:30pm, Sun 2–5:30pm. Metrolink: St. Peter's Sq.

If you like the pre-Raphaelites, especially the works of Ford Madox Brown, you're in luck. Manchester's art gallery, housed in a neoclassical building from 1834, contains one of the best collections of pre-Raphaelite paintings in Britain. The gallery's small Euro-British collection, most of it focused on painting and decorative arts, contains one good piece of everything from the 13th century up to the present. It's compact, undemanding, and fun to stroll through. Unless you have a special interest, it probably won't take you more than an hour to see everything.

John Rylands Library. Deansgate. Admission free. Mon–Fri 10am–5pm (Sat to 1pm). Metrolink: St. Peter's Sq.

Yes, Virginia, some of us are bibliophiles. A bibliophile, darling, is someone who adores books. When bibliophiles travel, they love nothing more than to discover a dark, gloomy old library like this one and creep through its stacks, inhaling the dusty odors of literature and peeking longingly into the "reading room." The queer thing about this library, besides the fact it was designed by someone named Basil Champneys, is that it was built in 1900 but is completely Gothic. All right, neo-Gothic. Ten minutes max, unless there's an irresistible literary exhibit on display.

Manchester Cathedral. Victoria St. ☎ **0161/833-2220.** Metrolink: St. Peter's Sq.

The city's cathedral dates from the 15th century but somehow feels Victorian. Its exterior is more notable than the interior, which isn't particularly inspiring or inviting. It does, however, have the widest nave in the country and some good medieval wood carving.

✪ **Chetham's Library.** Long Millgate. ☎ **0161/834-7961.** Admission free. Mon–Fri 9:30am–12:30pm and 1:30–4:30pm. Metrolink: St. Peter's Sq.

This is the oldest public library in the English-speaking world. It was founded in 1653 and is housed in a building from 1421. In a city as relentlessly Victorian as Manchester, that alone makes this little gem noteworthy. There's not a whole lot to see, unless you like to stare at rare leather-bound books behind locked doors; it's the biblio history that makes it so unique. The library is part of a music school, so you may hear strains of Debussy as you take a peek (or a leak—there's a toilet on the premises).

Castlefield Urban Heritage Park. Visitor Centre, 101 Liverpool Rd. ☎ **0161/839-8747.** Individual attractions and facilities have varying opening times and admission charges. Metrolink: GMEX. Bus: 33 from Piccadilly Gardens Bus Station.

Sometimes a city's past is like an outmoded garment: It no longer fits, it'll never come back into fashion, but it's too historically important to throw away. When that's the case, the past can be recycled into something like the Castlefield. Manchester, the Victorian industrial city par excellence, once was a hellhole of factory smoke and brutalized workers, but that's all been cleaned up and turned into a kind of industrial-historical theme park. The **Pump House** on Bridge Street contains the **People's History Museum** (☎ **0161/839-6061;** admission £1/$2), chronicling the lives of ordinary people (gays not included) in Britain over the last 200 years. On Liverpool Road, the world's oldest passenger rail station, from 1830, is now the home of the **Museum of Science and Industry** (☎ **0161/832-1830;** admission £5/$9), devoted to the city's machine-driven past. Excursion boats ply the old canals. The biggest draw is the tour of **Granada TV Studios** (☎ **0161/832-4999;** admission £14.99/$26) on Water Street, a "television theme park" best avoided unless you're a small child or familiar with the British soap opera *Coronation Street,* which is filmed here.

Manchester Town Hall. Albert Sq.

Since the 1996 IRA bombing of central Manchester, security has been tightened at the Town Hall. You wouldn't want to go in, in any case, but this is one of those enormous buildings you might pass as you wander through town and wonder what the hell it is. It's neo-Gothic, so you know it's Victorian. The architect was Alfred Waterhouse. It opened in 1877. Its tower is 300 feet high. That's all you need to know.

GAY MANCHESTER

Over the last 10 or so years, Manchester has turned into the gay mecca of the northwest. There's even a 3-day gay **Mardi Gras** with a big parade, floats, and performers. About 100,000 lads and lezzies showed up for the last one, which also features a fun fair and raises money for HIV/AIDS. Europe's largest lesbian and **gay arts festival**—called "It's Queer Up North" in 1998—is an annual spring event. And in the summer of 1999, gay and lesbian Manchester will put itself on the European map when it hosts the gay sport **Euro-Games Sporting Festival.** You find out more about upcoming events and festivals by calling the Lesbian and Gay Switchboard (see "Fast Facts: Manchester" above) or by checking the Gay Village Web site at **www.gayvillage.co.uk.**

The reasons Manchester has become such a hot gay weekend destination are something of a mystery. What came first, the clubs or the queers? Certainly it was a city ripe for rediscovery. It's in the heart of a densely populated region. And maybe the international flights that started arriving here helped in some way.

Whatever the reason, there's plenty of gay nightlife, nearly all of it centered around the **Gay Village** that has **Canal Street** as its main drag (it's Manchester's open-air cruising ground; sometimes the "C" is crossed out to make it "anal Street"). Many have complained of the increased police presence, which is, in part, a response to the gang and drug wars that've plagued the city. Be aware that it's possible to be jailed for "loitering with intent." The Gay Village encompasses a very small area, just a few city blocks. Its old shops, industrial buildings, and warehouses are tarted up into sleek restaurants and clubs.

Note that I'm calling it the Gay Village even though the city council (shades of Manchester's Puritan past), trying to downplay the gay scene, had "Gay" dropped from the area's official designation.

5 Hitting the Stores

There's a lot of upscale retail happening in upwardly mobile Manchester, but I recommend you save your time for other pursuits and do your shopping in London. For trendy Manchester boutiques, check out **St. Ann Square** and the **Royal Arcade,** which has an entrance on the square. The **Corn Exchange,** badly damaged in the 1996 bomb attack, will probably be reopened by the time this book hits the shelves; it'll probably again become known for its antiques and specialty shops.

Manchester has the United Kingdom's only gay shopping arcade, **Phoenix Centre,** 105 Princess St., but at this point it's more useful for services (flowers, men's beauty clinic) than hard-core retail. Stores basically keep the same hours as in London and Brighton, but few are open on Sunday.

SHOPS A TO Z

ART & ANTIQUES **Design Goes Pop,** in the basement of Café Pop, 34–36 Oldham St. (☎ **0161/237-9688;** Metrolink: Piccadilly Gardens), has original decorations and "artifacts" from the 1950s to the 1970s. The **Gallery Manchester's Art House,** 131 Portland St. (☎ **0161/237-3551;** Metrolink: St. Peter's Sq.), sells original artists' work, mostly things classified as the Northern School.

ARTS & CRAFTS The **Manchester Craft Centre,** 17 Oak St. (☎ **0161/832-4274;** Metrolink: Piccadilly Gardens), is a good place to look for handcrafted ceramics, glass, and textiles.

BOOKS **Frontline Books,** 1 Newton St. (☎ **0161/236-1101**), in the City Centre, is a very gay- and lesbian-friendly bookstore with magazines, postcards, T-shirts, and a headshop with a useful community bulletin board. **Village Books,** 8 Canal St. (☎ **0161/237-3500;** Metrolink: St. Peter's Sq.), stocks gay and lesbian books, magazines, and videos. The **Cornerhouse,** 70 Oxford St. (Metrolink: St. Peter's sq.), a regional arts center, has two art and cinema bookshops (see "All the World's a Stage" below).

EROTICA & WHATNOT **Clone Zone,** 36–38 Sackville St. (☎ **0161/236-1398;** Metrolink: St. Peter's Sq.), sells gay magazines and cards, leather and rubber clothing and accessories, and toys (you may recognize the best part of Jeff Stryker on the shelf).

PIERCING **L'Homme Piercing Studio,** 1 Central Buildings, Oldham Street (☎ **0161/236-9759;** Metrolink: St. Peter's Sq.), is a registered and professional body-piercing studio.

6 All the World's a Stage

Manchester is the home of the acclaimed **Halle Orchestra,** the **BBC Philharmonic,** and the **Manchester Camerata** chamber music group. They perform at **Bridgewater Hall** (☎ **0161/907-9000;** Metrolink: St. Peter's Sq.), a marvelous new concert hall with outstanding acoustics, situated just off St. Peter's Square. The **Royal Exchange Theatre Company,** Upper Canfield Market (☎ **0161/833-9833;** Metrolink: Piccadilly Gardens), is one of England's most venerable companies. The **Library Theatre,** Central Library, St. Peter's Square (☎ **0161/236-7110;** Metrolink: St. Peter's Sq.), presents an intriguing season of new and classic stage works. The **Palace Theatre,** Oxford Street, and the **Opera House,** Quay Street (☎ **0161/242-2525** for both; Metrolink: St. Peter's Sq. for both), are major venues for traveling shows, musicals, and dance programs.

The **Cornerhouse,** 70 Oxford St. (☎ **0161/228-2463;** Metrolink: St. Peter's Sq.), is Britain's major regional center for cinema and the visual arts. It's hip and always has an intriguing array of films and contemporary art exhibits. Its slick **Cinema Cafe** is open Monday to Saturday 9am to 8:30pm and Sunday 1:30 to 8:30pm.

7 In the Heat of the Night

The restaurants and cafe/bars above are all gathering places where you can order a pint or a gin and tonic. Below are more pub and bar options, many of which have cabaret evenings. Keep in mind that Manchester's restless club and bar scene seems to reinvent itself every couple of years. Some of the places listed may have vanished by the time you arrive, but another gay venue will undoubtedly have taken its place. Pub hours (Mon–Sat 11am–11pm, Sun noon–10:30pm) apply unless otherwise noted.

GAY BARS & PUBS

The Mancunians live for weekends and love to drink—at least those Mancunians who hang out in the pubs and bars. Some are into drugs too (shock!), and one of the biggest discos, Danceteria, was recently closed because of suspected drug dealing. The Manchester scene isn't as sleek as London's—it's more rawly down home. Club hours (and clubs) change all the time and often host different theme nights, so I can't always provide exact opening hours. Pub hours (Mon–Sat 11am–11pm, Sun noon–10:30pm) apply. You can assume the others will be open by 9pm and probably close at 2am, though some run all right. Call first if you have any questions. Unless otherwise noted, the closest Metrolink stop for all the venues below is St. Peter's Square.

The ✪ **Rembrandt,** 33 Sackville St., (☎ **0161/236-2435;** open pub hours), Manchester's oldest and friendliest gay pub, occupies a central position in the Gay Village and packs in a casual, mostly denim-clad crowd; on Fridays the upstairs bar is women-only.

The **Castro,** 34 Canal St. (☎ **0161/237-9117;** open pub hours), is a hidden gem (inasmuch as anything can be hidden on Canal Street) where you can get imported wines and beers.

✪ **Central Park,** 24 Sackville St. (☎ **0161/237-5919;** open pub hours, late on weekends), is a perennial pub favorite with both lesbians and gays; it has pool tables, live DJs, and a good selection of freebie gay lit; weekends it hosts the Danceteria club nights for all-nighters.

Recently given a facelift, **Churchill's,** 37 Chorlton St. (☎ **0161/236-5529;** open pub hours), is mostly a pub for village locals.

Dotz, Richmond St. (☎ **0161/236-4412;** open pub hours), a recently opened piano and cocktail bar, is a sophisticated little place to relax before hitting the streets.

Bar Icarus, Bloom St. (☎ **0161/236-3995**), is very sleek, with a fab minimalist interior and a younger hard-to-classify crowd.

Mash, Chorlton St. (☎ **0161/661-1111**), is a gay-friendly cafe/bar with its own microbrews.

New Union, 111 Princess St. (☎ **0161/228-1492;** open Mon–Wed to 1am, Thurs–Sat to 2am, Sun to 10:30pm), has a certain "scream appeal," with a high-spirited stage show, Camp Karaoke, and disco all rolled into one.

New York, New York, 98 Main St. (☎ **0161/236-6556);** open Mon–Sat to 2am, Sun to 11pm), boasts a neon sign of a limp-wristed Statue of Liberty (is that an insult,

New Yorkers?) out front and a wild party sense of camp within; when it really gets going it almost has a feeling of crazy old Berlin.

THEME & DRESS-CODE BARS

Chains, 4–6 Whitworth St. (☎ **0161/236-0335;** open Mon–Sat 11pm–2am), is a small and cruisy men-only leather, uniform, and fetish club that has special pervy theme nights; Bulk, their hugely popular bar night for big men and bears, is every other Friday.

The **Cellar Bar** at Napoleons, 35 Bloom St. (☎ **0161/366-8800;** open nightly from 10:30pm), is a men-only bar with a strict (of course) leather and fetish dress code.

Cybercafe, 12 Oxford St. (☎ **0161/236-6300;** open Mon–Wed 11am–11pm, Thurs to 1am, Fri–Sat to 2am, Sun 2–9pm), is a fully licensed cafe/bar with computer workstations; you can rent a computer and use the e-mail service for £5 ($9) an hour; it's not gay.

LESBIAN VENUES

Climax, held at **Club Code,** 11–13 New Wakefield St. (☎ **0161/236-4899**), on Bank Holiday Sundays, was recently voted the "Best Women-Only Night in the U.K."; it draws gals, girls, ladies, and women from all over the North.

Follies, 6 Whitworth St. (☎ **0161/236-8149;** open pub hours), is a long-standing club for dykes of all stripes. The Vegas Suite at **Paradise Factory,** 112 Princess St. (☎ **0161/273-5422**), is women-only on Friday from 8pm.

DANCE CLUBS

✪ **Cruz 101,** 101 Princess St. (☎ **0161/237-1554**), is Manchester's biggest, with five bars on two floors and a host of special disco theme nights and promotions (like cheap beer) to keep the boys hoppin'; you'll need a membership but you can buy it at the door.

✪ **Danceteria at Central Park,** 24 Sackville St. (☎ **0161/237-5919**), begins at midnight on Saturday and goes nonstop until 2am on Monday—testosterone-challenged AYOR.

Dickens, 74A Fulham St. (☎ **0161/236-5196;** Metrolink: Piccadilly Gardens), not part of the mainstream gay Canal Street scene, draws a mixed crowd of hets, homos (male and female), and transvestites.

Napoleons, 35 Bloom St. (☎ **0161/366-8800;** open Sun–Sat 9:30pm–2am), has survived the changing disco scene and come out the wiser: It welcomes everyone.

Club Odyssey, Bloom St. (☎ **0161/236-3995;** open nightly 10pm–2am), beneath Bar Icarus, hosts various music nights for a mixed queer-clubbing lesbian and gay guy crowd. The club has a popular "shag tag" cruising system that lets you leave notes for anyone who's caught your fancy.

✪ **Paradise Factory,** 112 Princess St. (☎ **0161/273-5422**), is a huge four-story dance/nightclub that draws queer clubbers from all over the United Kingdom; there's a good cabaret lounge (Vegas Suite), a disco, and a mixed crowd except on Fridays, when it's almost entirely gay and the top level is women-only from 8pm.

SAUNAS

Eurosauna, 202 Hill Lane, Blackley (☎ **0161/740-5152;** open daily 1–10pm), is the Manchester area's most popular sauna. **Stallions,** under the Carlton Hotel, 153 Upper Chorlton Rd. (☎ **0161/881-4653**), is another option, but maybe the name should be changed to "Stables."

3 France

Oooh La La!

by Haas Mroue

France is lucky in geography, rich in history, and drenched in art. From the crashing waves of the Atlantic to the gentle lap of the Mediterranean, from the flat plains of Normandy to the jagged cliffs of the Alps, from 13th-century cathedrals to the world's largest museum, from delicate cheeses to earthy wines, from delicious *hommes* to luscious *femmes*, France can satisfy (almost) all your desires.

It's one of the world's gay-friendliest countries (at least in the larger cities), where a live-and-let-live attitude prevails and everybody is just *un peu gai* (at least in spirit). This is where American and British (gay and not-so-gay) artists and writers came for freedom, to live without censorship, judgment, or rules. This is where openly queer writer André Gide was publishing gay novels before such a genre was even thought possible and Jean Cocteau led an openly gay life back when such a life usually meant total alienation. And they weren't shunned or ridiculed (at least not in a debilitating way)—both were highly respected, as was Marcel Proust and countless others who lived here freely without social persecution.

Paris is the queen of all cities, the eternal City of Light, and it never disappoints whether you're a first-timer or a native. **Nice** and the magnificent towns along the **Côte d'Azur** provide the perfect setting for a sun-drenched vacation whether you spend it tanning on the beach, lounging by the pool of a fabulous belle-époque mansion, or hiking in the hills. The nude gay beaches attract queers from around the world.

Toulouse is Europe's most up-and-coming gay destination, a charming pink city filled with beautiful mansions and the second-largest student population in France, after Paris (look for a chapter on Toulouse in the second edition of this guide). Other worthy destinations not covered here are **Bordeaux** and **Marseille,** both welcoming cities with a sizable gay community and both gateways from which to discover the southwest of France. Smaller towns like **Avignon** in the heart of Provence, **Deauville** on the shores of Normandy, and **Courchevel** at

France on the Net

A good place to start your on-line explorations is the site of **La France Gaie et Lesbienne,** the France Queer Resource Directory at **www.france.gd.org.** You'll find lots of info, from gay associations to travel advice to lists of gay homepages. **Www.gaymania.com** covers all France—from restaurants to saunas and clubs; you'll find just listings though, with no explanations or reviews, but it might help you with out-of-the-way places or cities not covered here.

A couple of interesting general sites are the **Paris Pages** at **www.paris.org** and **FranceScape** at **http://198.147.102.107/francescape/top.html.**

The French Franc

The French **franc (F)** is divided into 100 **centimes.** There are coins of 5, 10, and 20 centimes and ½ F, 1F, 2F, 5F, 10F, and 20F. Sometimes you'll find two types of coin for one denomination (new commemorative coins were minted for the 1989 bicentennial of the Revolution). Bills come in denominations of 20F, 50F, 100F, and 500F.

At this writing, the franc was equivalent to 18¢ U.S. (or $1 = 5.50F), and that was the rate of exchange I used throughout. Prices over $5 U.S. have been rounded to the nearest dollar.

the top of the Alps (where you can ski for days and not once go down the same slope) are all worthy of discovery if you have time (and all have at least one gay bar). Train service is exceptionally good; you can get practically anywhere in the country in less than 8 hours. Domestic air travel has also become affordable after the recent EEC deregulation. If you're truly pressed for time, you could certainly, say, fly from Paris to Toulouse for a full day of sightseeing and return the same evening. Or take the high-speed train (TGV) connecting Paris to Brussels and London in less than 3 hours and Geneva in less than 5.

From Nice, you can jump on the ferry to **Corsica,** fast becoming a leading destination for adventure-bike tours and hiking trips (it has great beaches and mountains and few tourists). Some visitors prefer to make a circuit beginning in Paris, going on to Nice, and then trekking through northern Italy, ending in Salzurg or Vienna before flying home. Another popular itinerary is from Paris to Toulouse and on to Barcelona, to Andalusia, and then across Gibraltar to Tangiers in Morocco. Or start in Paris and head north to Brussels, Amsterdam, Copenhagen, and Stockholm. The possibilities are endless.

While planning your trip, don't hesitate to contact the French Government Tourist Offices in your home country (see the appendix). They're one of the few government offices in the world that publish specific information for gay and lesbian travelers and are prepared to answer any queries, even those pertaining to homo issues. *Bon voyage!*

5

Paris: They Don't Call It Gay Paree for Nothing

At the turn of the 21st century, **Paris** is as beautiful, vibrant, and bright as ever. The City of Light continues to delight not only with the magnificence of its venerable monuments and breathtaking bridges and churches and squares but also with the sleek new designs being added constantly to keep this city aesthetically ahead of the rest. Just consider I. M. Pei's glass pyramid at the Louvre, the Grande Arche de La Défense, the Opéra Bastille, the Cité de la Musique, the Bibliothèque Nationale de France, the sparkling (post 21st century?) terminals at Charles de Gaulle airport, the reopening of the Centre Pompidou (in 2000), and the almost-completed task of cleaning Notre-Dame, returning it to its original color and splendor. Paris is now more than ever a tourist-friendly and gay-friendly destination.

Gay life has come a long way in the past 15 or so years, when in the mid-1980s a whole new neighborhood was established in the **Marais**—new restaurants, bars, and clubs continue to open every week. Gays and lesbians have always come to Paris for freedom and the good life, but times haven't always been easy. After the bohemian days of St-Germain-des-Prés and the Latin Quarter ended in the late 1960s (due to the May 1968 student riots), gay life experienced a long period of stagnation, when there was no real community or any "gay" area. By the mid-1970s, though, rue St-Anne began to take shape as more gay bars, clubs, and bathhouses opened in the area between the Palais Royal and the Opéra Garnier, gathering around Le Vagabond, the oldest gay bar in France (opened in 1956).

Then came AIDS. By 1985, all the bathhouses were closed and death had wreaked havoc on the lives of so many; the area was abandoned and businesses and lifetimes were dismantled. Across town close to Les Halles (where the Centre Pompidou opened in the 1970s), the Marais was a rundown neighborhood with cheap real estate—it provided the perfect "community" for a new generation of gays and lesbians. But the Marais is too young to hold much queer history (though it is the oldest part of Paris and the heart of the Jewish quarter). That history is spread all over Paris.

As you stroll around the city, the streets echo with the lives of gays and lesbians who made Paris their home over the years. Imagine Oscar Wilde strutting around St-Germain-des-Prés ("The way to get rid of temptation is to yield to it") or Marcel Proust writing away in his cork-lined bedroom at 102 bd. Haussmann in the 8th arrondissement (you can see a replica at the Musée Carnavalet in the Marais). Imagine

Gertrude Stein and Alice B. Toklas (who called each other Pussy and Lovey) driving Godiva (their car) on a Sunday afternoon in the Bois de Boulogne or Sylvia Beach hurrying to print copies of James Joyce's *Ulysses* for her bookstore Shakespeare and Company in the Latin Quarter. Imagine Rudolf Nureyev in tights twirling and captivating audiences at the Opéra Garnier or James Baldwin writing the day away at a cafe in Montparnasse. Even now, writers are still flocking here—Edmund White lived on Ile St-Louis for many years, researching the life of Genet and Proust and writing his Farewell Symphony; and in 1998 Mathew Stadler lived in Paris, writing a fictional account of Allan Stein, Gertrude's nephew.

But Paris is especially about little things that make the best memories. The mouth-watering smell of fresh croissants wafting from bakeries and elegant old ladies dragging their shopping caddies and poodles after a spin at the open-air market. A warm baguette and a wedge of ripe brie. A shared bottle of wine and a few French kisses on the banks of the Seine. A macaroon dipped in café au lait at a sidewalk table on the Champs-Elysées. Smiling at strangers in Parc Monceau. Reading in the shade of a chestnut tree on place des Vosges. Taking an early jog from Ile St-Louis to the Hôtel des Invalides. Dressing up for the opera and dressing down for the clubs. Ditching Mona and Venus at the Louvre for a stroll in the Tuileries. Dancing until dawn and watching the sunrise from the hills of Montmartre.

Paris is leaving your heart and knowing you'll come back. Paris is all this and much, much more.

1 Paris Essentials

ARRIVING & DEPARTING

BY PLANE Paris is served by two major airports: Charles de Gaulle and Orly.

Charles de Gaulle The largest and newest is **Aéroport Charles-de-Gaulle** or **CDG** (☎ **01-48-62-22-80**), frequently referred to simply as Roissy after the area it's in, 14 miles northeast of the city. Terminal 1 (Aérogare 1) is served by foreign airlines like Aer Lingus, British Airways, Lufthansa, United, and Qantas; Terminal 2 is reserved for Air France and several of its partner airlines, like Air Canada and Sabena (always check with your airline since alliances are constantly changing). Air France now has six sub-terminals at Terminal 2 (Aérogare 2A, 2B, 2C, 2D, 2E, 2F), with two more under construction; ask when you confirm your flight which terminal you're arriving at and departing from.

The two terminals, about 3 miles apart, are connected by a **free shuttle** (*navette*) service. A **taxi** into the city is 200F to 300F ($36 to $55), depending on where you're going (northern points of the city will be less expensive); taxis are 40% more expensive between 7pm and 7am when the night rate is in effect (which also occurs all day Sunday and on public holidays). The busiest time for taxis is 7 to 10am, when an hour's wait isn't uncommon.

The most convenient and comfortable way to travel into Paris is on a luxurious **Air France coach** operating every 12 minutes from both terminals to the Arc de Triomphe off the Champs-Elysées (with a stop in Porte Maillot). From there you can catch the Métro or a cab to your hotel. Buses operate daily 5:40am to 11pm; the one-way fare is 55F ($10). Follow the signs for Cars Air France at the terminal to get to the pickup points. The trip takes 40 to 50 minutes, depending on traffic. Air France buses are also available every 30 minutes 7am to 9pm to the Gare de Lyon and Gare Montparnasse (if you're heading straight to the train stations). The fare is 65F ($12) each way; and to Orly for the 1-hour ride, the fare is 70F ($13).

Getting from the Airports: By New Shuttle or Luxury Limo

The brand-new **Airport Shuttle** at ☎ **01-45-38-55-72** runs from both airports and is the first door-to-door service in Paris. The charge is 120F ($22) for one person or 89F ($16) per person for two or three people, with no added baggage cost (discounts on groups of four or more). Call the number above, e-mail ashuttle@club-internet.fr, or fax 01-43-21-35-67 at least 24 hours before your arrival and they'll be waiting for you. This service is by reservation only, available daily 6am to 6pm.

If you want to arrive at your hotel in style in your own limo (or minivan if you're a group), call **First Class Service** at ☎ and fax **01-45-18-00-00** at least 24 hours before your arrival. Using Mercedes and other luxury cars, they pick up and drop off at either airport, with rates starting at 800F ($145).

The least expensive way to get into the city is by the **Roissybus** operating every 15 minutes (6am–11pm) to rue Scribe, by the Opéra Garnier; the one-way fare is 45F ($8), and the trip takes about 50 minutes.

There's now a train station at Terminal 2 serving Avignon, Brussels, Lille, London, and Nice with high-speed TGVs, eliminating the need to go through Paris; other cities are being added constantly, so check with **Rail Europe** in the U.S. at ☎ **800-4EURAIL** (www.raileurope.com), or call the **Société Nationale des Chemins de Fer (SNCF)** in France at ☎ **08-36-35-35-35** (daily 8am–7pm; www.sncf.fr); reservations are required. When you arrive at Terminal 2, follow the signs for the TGV or hop on the free shuttle (*navette*) from Terminal 1 to the TGV/RER station.

If you don't have heavy bags and want to avoid rush hour on the airport roads, you can catch the **RER B** (suburban train) into Paris from Terminal 2 (a free shuttle operates every 15 minutes from Terminal 1). Trains operate every 10 to 20 minutes (4:55am–11:55pm) for the 30- to 40-minute ride; the fare is 47F ($9), and the stops are Gare du Nord, Châtelet–Les Halles (close to the Marais), St-Michel, Luxembourg, Port-Royal, and Denfert-Rochereau.

Orly **Aéroport d'Orly** (☎ **01-49-75-15-15**), 8½ miles south of Paris, is the older airport (but still very busy), and it also has two terminals, South and West. Orly South (Sud) receives mostly the non-European flights, like American; flights to most domestic and European cities leave from Orly West (Ouest). This is changing constantly due to the new EU laws, so double-check with your carrier as to which terminal you're arriving at/departing from. AOM now operates all its flights (including those to Nice and Los Angeles) from Orly South.

Taxis from Orly cost 150F to 250F ($27 to $45) into the city. Comfortable air-conditioned **Air France coaches** operate every 12 minutes from both terminals (5:50am–11pm) to the Gares des Invalides in the 7th arrondissement, with stops in Porte d'Orléans, Montparnasse, and Duroc; the fare is 40F ($7).

Orlybus operates every 15 minutes (6:30am–11:30pm) from both terminals to Denfert-Rochereau (where you can catch the Métro or RER); the fare is 30F ($5), and the trip takes half an hour.

You can also catch the **RER C** (suburban train) by hopping on the shuttle operating every 15 minutes (5:45am–10:50pm) from both terminals to the station; from there trains operate every 12 to 20 minutes to Gare d'Austerlitz, St-Michel, Invalides, and Porte-Maillot; the fare is 30F ($5). The **Orlyval service** uses RER Line B (going to Luxembourg, St-Michel, and Châtelet near the Marais); the shuttle leaves every

12 minutes (6am–10:30pm, Sun 7am–11:55pm) from both terminals for the Antony station, where you jump on the RER; the fare is 57F ($10).

BY TRAIN There are six major train stations around the city. Each serves a specific area: From the south (Nice, Milan, Geneva), trains pull into the **Gare de Lyon,** 20 bd. Diderot; from the southwest (Barcelona, Lisbon, Toulouse), at the **Gare d'Austerlitz,** 55 quai d'Austerlitz; from the northwest (Normandy), at the **Gare St-Lazare,** 13 rue d'Amsterdam; from the east (Budapest, Prague, Vienna, Zurich), at the **Gare de l'Est,** place du 11-Novembre 1918; from the north (Amsterdam, Brussels, Copenhagen, London by *Eurostar*), at the **Gare du Nord,** 18 rue de Dunkerque; and from western France (Brittany), at the **Gare du Montparnasse,** 17 bd. Vaugirard, 15e.

For all train information, call the **Société Nationale des Chemins de Fer (SNCF)** at ☎ **08-36-35-35-35** (daily 8am–7pm); operators speak English and can give you both schedule and fare details. Information is also available on-line at **www.sncf.fr** or for *Eurostar* at **www.eurostar.com.** Buying your tickets and making reservations before leaving home gets you better deals and eliminates having to wait in line. Rail Europe has rail passes valid for travel in France (and most of Europe) at highly reduced rates; it also has rates that include car rentals picked up and dropped off at train stations so you can combine a train and car holiday (ask for the France Rail and Drive Pass). Contact **Rail Europe** in the U.S. at ☎ **800/4EURAIL** or on the Internet at **www.raileurope.com.**

BY BUS International coaches arrive at the **Gare Routière Internationale du Paris-Gallieni** (International Bus Terminal), 28 av. du Général-de-Gaulle, Bagnolet (☎ **01-49-72-51-51;** Métro: Gallieni).

BY CAR Driving in Paris is unpleasant and unnecessary, so if you happen to arrive by car, find a garage quick. Several autoroutes serve the city: A1 from the north if you're coming from Great Britain, A10 from Toulouse and the southwest, A6 from Lyon if you're driving in from Nice or Italy, A4 from the east if you're driving in from Germany, and A13 from the northwest. Paris is encircled by a ring road called the *périphérique.* You'll need the exact name of the exit in order not to get lost. Always get detailed directions before hitting the autoroute.

Details are available on-line at **www.autoroutes.fr** or by calling ☎ **01-47-05-90-01.**

VISITOR INFORMATION

The main **Office de Tourisme de Paris** is at 127 av. des Champs-Elysées, 8e (☎ **01-49-52-53-54;** www.francetourism.com; Métro: Charles-de-Gaulle–Etoiles or George-V; open May–Oct daily 9am–8pm, Nov–Apr Mon–Sat 9am–8pm and Sun 11am–6pm). In summer, this office is very busy; expect to wait in line. Fees for hotel reservations are 20F to 50F ($3.65 to $9), depending on the room rate.

There are several satellite offices, including one at the **Louvre** (open Wed–Mon 10am–7pm), at the **Gare de Lyon** and the **Gare du Nord** (both open Mon–Sat 8am–8pm), and at the **Eiffel Tower** (open May–Sept daily 11am–6pm).

La Carte Musées et Monuments

La Carte Musées et Monuments (Museum and Monuments Pass) is sold at any of the museums that honor it, at any branch of the Paris tourist office, or in Métro and RER stations. It offers free entrance to the permanent collections of 65 monuments and museums in Paris and the Ile de France. The cost of a 1-day pass is 80F ($15), a 3-day pass 160F ($29), and a 5-day pass 240F ($44). In addition to the substantial savings offered, the pass allows you to bypass long waiting lines to get into the Louvre.

The Office de Tourisme also operates a phone information service called **Paris: User's Guide** to help with any questions, addresses, or phone numbers you may need. Call ☎ **01-44-29-12-12** (9am–6pm) or check online at **www.paris.org** or **www.paris-anglo.com.**

PARIS GAY & LESBIAN EVENTS

All Paris gay events are listed in the gay press, most notably in ***e.m@le magazine,*** available free at all gay clubs and cafes (e-mail requests to emalemagazine@wanadoo. fr).

JANUARY During the last week of January, many of the bars and clubs offer discounts (or free cover) during **La Folle Semaine de la St-Sebastien.** For more information, contact the **Centre Gai et Lesbien,** 3 rue Keller, 11e (☎ **01-43-57-21-47;** fax 01-43-57-27-93; Métro: Bastille).

JUNE The ✪ **Pride Parade** in Paris is usually held the third weekend in June. Debates, meetings, talks, and lectures are held throughout the city the week preceding the big event (including special evening concerts and parties featuring well-known gay rock stars, gay DJs, and a lot of techno music). On the day of the event (usually Saturday), the carnival parade is held during the day, followed by the final evening of dancing in the streets and open-air concerts. Call **Lesbian and Gay Pride,** 27 rue du Faubourg-Montmartre at ☎ **01-47-70-01-50** (fax 01-45-23-10-66) or the **Centre Gai et Lesbien** at ☎ **01-43-57-21-47** for schedules.

JULY On July 13 (the eve of French Independence Day), the **Bastille Ball** is held usually at place de la Bastille, with dancing and partying late into the night. There has been a problem with financing and organizing recently, and the ball is in jeopardy of falling apart; call the **Centre Gai et Lesbian** at ☎ **01-43-57-21-47** a few months before to find out if and where it'll be held.

DECEMBER The **Paris Gay and Lesbian Film Festival (Festival des Films Gais et Lesbiens)** is usually held in mid-December and lasts 1 week. Gay and lesbian films from around the world are shown; location and dates vary from year to year. The best place to get information is the Centre Gai et Lesbien (above).

CITY LAYOUT

The **river Seine** divides Paris into the **Right Bank (Rive Droite)** and the **Left Bank (Rive Gauche).** In the middle of the river are two islands, **Ile de la Cité** and **Ile St-Louis.** The heart of Paris and the place from which all distances in France are measured is Notre-Dame cathedral on Ile de la Cité. Directly north across the river, the sprawling palace of the Louvre is the starting point for the city's system of ***arrondissements*** **(districts).** They're numbered from 1 to 20 progressing in a clockwise spiral from the Louvre's courtyard. The key to finding any address in Paris is looking for the number of the arrondissement, rendered either as a number followed by "e" or "er" (1er, 2e, 3e, and so on) or, more formally, as part of the postal code (the last two digits indicate the arrondissement—75007 indicates the 7th arrondissement, 75017 the 17th). Each arrondissement has a unique feel and is known by a major landmark (the Louvre in 1er, the Eiffel Tower in 7e, the Champs-Elysées in 8e, and so on).

THE RIGHT BANK The **1er** is where much of monumental Paris is found: the Louvre, rue de Rivoli, rue St-Honoré with its fabulous boutiques, and place Vendôme with its infamous Hôtel Ritz. The **2e** is the **Bourse** (stock market), the city's financial center; the **3e** and **4e** form the **Marais,** the old Jewish quarter that was home to the aristocracy in the 17th century and is now the heart of gay and lesbian Paris; also here is Ile St-Louis, home to Notre-Dame and one of Paris's most elegant residential neighborhoods. The **8e** is considered the heart and soul of the Right Bank, as it covers the Arc de Triomphe, the Champs-Elysées (and all the streets around it, such as avenue Montaigne, with its legendary Hôtel Plaza Athénée and designer boutiques, and rue du faubourg St-Honoré, where the presidential palace is located). The **8e** extends all the way to place de la Concorde, where the U.S. Embassy and the Hôtel de Crillon majestically preside over one of Paris's most beautiful squares.

The **9e** is home to major department stores (Galeries Lafayette, Le Printemps), as well as the Opéra Garnier, and the **10e, 11e,** and **12e** include many residential areas, government offices, and museums; the 11e features the bustling Bastille neighborhood around the Opéra Bastille. The **16e** is where upper-crust Parisians live; curiously, there are few hotels here, and tourists rarely venture to the really French (and terribly chic) shopping areas around avenues Passy and Victor-Hugo (the 16e is large and also borders the Bois de Boulogne in places). The **17e** is home to the lovely Parc Monceau and to the commercial boulevards around Porte Maillot, with its business hotels and excellent restaurants; the **18e** and **19e** are mainly residential areas known for having the least expensive rents in Paris; part of the 18e, known as **Montmartre,** is where Sacré-Coeur and the sex-shop-filled Pigalle are located. The **20e** is also very residential, but in the eternal sense—many of the city's most famous are buried here at the Père-Lachaise Cemetery, including Oscar Wilde, Jim Morrison, and Gertrude Stein and Alice B. Toklas.

THE LEFT BANK The Left Bank is generally more laid-back and less touristy than the right. The huge Sorbonne University is in the **5e,** known as the **Latin Quarter,** and consequently the area is home to a huge number of students and teachers and intellectuals who frequent the hundreds of cafes around place St-Michel. The **6e** is home to the elegant shopping district of St-Germain-des-Prés and one of Paris's most famous cafes, Deux-Magots, where writers and artists have been flocking for over a century. The **7e** is where you'll find the most visible of Paris's erections: the Eiffel Tower. The **13e, 14e** (known as **Montparnasse**), and **15e** are largely residential and sprawling with new and old apartment buildings, huge grocery stores, shopping streets, schools, government offices, and everything a city needs to function.

Beyond the arrondissements are the ***banlieu*** (suburbs) areas like Neuilly and Boulogne, where many Parisians live.

GETTING AROUND

BY MÉTRO (SUBWAY) There's a Métro station every 2 or 3 blocks in Paris. The Métro is everything here—it's how Parisians get their bearings and find addresses, and frequently a Métro station defines a whole neighborhood. It's a safe, reliable, and quick way to get around Paris. Some Parisians avoid the train late at night if they're alone (mostly women), but for the most part only pickpockets have been known to disrupt a visitor's Métro ride, so keep a close watch on your belongings. The Métro is operated by the Régie Autonome des Transports Parisiens (RATP), which also operates all city buses. Trains run from 5:30am to 12:30am, with all stations closing by 1am.

The key to finding your way underground is to know the final destination of the Métro you need to hop on. For example, if you're heading to the Louvre from the Arc de Triomphe (Métro: Charles-de-Gaulle–Etoile), you follow the signs for the Château de Vincennes to find the correct platform and the correct train. There are 13 Métro lines, most connecting with one another and with the fast Réseau Express Régional (RER) trains operating to the outlying suburbs (Versailles, St-Germain-en-Laye) and the airports.

Note: See the back cover of this guide for a Paris Métro map.

A **single ticket** costs 8F ($1.50), but you can buy a **carnet of 10 tickets** for 46F ($8), saving you money and time waiting in ticket lines. Special rates apply for RER routes depending on your destination; you'll have to buy a special ticket at the counter. (Métro tickets can also be used on all buses.) The **Paris Visite** is a pass valid for 1, 2, 3, or 5 consecutive days on all Métro, bus, RER, and SNCF lines within the Ile de France (the area around Paris, including Versailles, Fontainebleau, and the airports). The pass begins at 150F ($27) for 1 day and goes to 350F ($64) for 5 days. Inquire at the RATP offices (below) or at the Office de Tourisme (see "Visitor Information" above). You could also buy weekly or monthly **Carte Orange** passes, but you'll need a passport-sized photo; inquire at the ticket counter for these rates.

Always hold on to your ticket until you exit the station; an inspector may request to see it at any time.

Métros are marked by a large M or MÉTROPOLITAIN sign (a few are beautiful old art-nouveau gateways). At every stop you'll find a large map and signs pointing out the *direction* (line) and stops the train makes. To change trains, look for the orange CORRESPONDANCE signs; blue signs reading SORTIE mark the exits. Changing trains is sometimes an involved affair where you climb stairs and escalators and walk for what seems like miles in underground tunnels. Always follow the signs of the direction you're going and you'll eventually find your platform. The worst stations for long underground walks are Châtelet, Montparnasse, Franklin-Roosevelt, and Charles-de-Gaulle–Etoile.

Close to every exit is a *plan du quartier* (neighborhood map). Large stations have several exits marked with the different street names (especially for large intersections); always try to find out what exit you need.

For more info on the city's public transportation, visit or call the **Services Touristiques de la RATP** at 53 bis quai des Grands-Augustins, 6e (☎ **01-53-46-44-50;** Métro: St-Michel), or at place de la Madeleine, 1er (☎ **01-40-06-71-45;** Métro: Madeleine). Information is also available from English-speaking operators at ☎ **08-36-68-41-14.**

BY BUS Buses are reliable if slow. They're also wonderful for getting to know the city and its streets and monuments; Métro and bus tickets are interchangeable. Every bus stop has a map and schedule for the specific route it serves. When you get on the bus, you must validate your ticket in the little machine behind the driver; then hold onto it as an inspector may ask to see it at any time. Buses operate on a zone system, and you may need more than one ticket if you're heading outside central Paris.

BY TAXI There are only 14,900 taxis in this densely populated city, so don't expect to find one easily, especially during rush hours (weekdays 8–10am and especially 5–7pm) and Fridays and Saturdays 11pm to 3am, when it might be close to impossible to find a cab (since the Métro stops running at 12:30am, all late-night transportation is by taxi). When it rains taxis are hardest to come by, no matter what time of day.

There are taxi stands where cabs park, or you can hail them on the street if their light is on, though you might wait for a long time. Calling a radio taxi service sometimes is a good way to guarantee a cab (it beats standing around), but frequently the wait can be long and you have to pay for the radio taxi from its point of dispatch (an extra 20–35F/$3.60–$6). The fare 7am to 7pm is 3.45F (60¢) per kilometer; 7pm to 7am and all day Sunday and holidays, it goes up to 5.70F ($1.05) per kilometer. Rates to/from the suburban areas are higher at all times. There's a charge of 8 to 12F ($1.45 to $2.20) per suitcase. Tipping is generally 10% to 15% of the fare.

Always make sure the meter is running; most drivers are honest, but some will try to trick foreigners. For radio taxis, the meter shouldn't read more than 35F ($6) when you get in; meters read 14F ($2.50) for taxis hailed on the street. And remember taxis are obligated to carry only three passengers; a fourth may be subject to a supplement (it's at the discretion of the driver whether to accept a fourth passenger or not).

If you have any problems, call the **Police-Service des Taxi** at ☎ **01-55-76-20-00.** For **radio taxis,** call ☎ **01-45-85-85-85,** 01-47-39-47-39, or 01-49-36-10-10.

BY BOAT April to late September, you can get around Paris by **ferryboats** operating on the Seine between the Eiffel Tower (Port de la Bourdonnais) and the Louvre (quai du Louvre), with stops at the Musée d'Orsay (quai de Solferino), St-Germain-des-Prés (quai Malaquais), Notre-Dame (quai de Montebello), and Hôtel de Ville (quai de l'Hôtel-de-Ville) closest to the Marais. The fare is 12F ($2) per stop or 60F ($11) for unlimited travel in one day; you can hop on or off at any of the stops. Boats operate daily 9:30am to 5:30pm; frequency depends on the day and time, but most often there's a boat every 30 minutes. For more, contact **Bateaux Parisiens,** port de la Bourdonnais (☎ **01-44-11-33-44;** Métro: Bir-Hakeim or Trocadéro).

BY BICYCLE More bike lanes are appearing in the city, but it's still dangerous and noisy and chaotic on the streets. A day in the park is what most Parisians use bikes for. **Paris-Velos,** 2 rue du Fer-à-Moulin, 5e (☎ **01-43-37-59-22;** Métro: Censier-Daubenton; open Mon–Sat 10am–12:30pm and 2–7pm), rents by the day, weekend, or week. Rates range from 90F ($16) to 130F ($24) per day, with a 2,000F ($364) deposit (credit cards accepted).

BY CAR A car in Paris is a major headache. Rent one only if you're planning on hitting the countryside. You can get some great deals on car rentals if you book before leaving home. The least expensive rates are those booked (and paid for) in North America 14 days in advance. Always ask for rates that include the French VAT (value-added tax) of 20.6% and collision damage and theft insurance (theft is a problem in France's large cities). If you're renting a car for 17 days or more, you qualify for a tax-free rental on new cars. Rates including full insurance and tax for 17 days begin at $499 for a small manual car and go up to $899 for a compact automatic with air-conditioning. Pick up and drop off is available at most French and many European airports. The best company offering these rates is **Europe By Car** (☎ **800/223-1516** in the U.S. or 212/581-3040 or 213/272-0424). Their weekly rates are excellent, starting at $149 for 7 days with insurance and tax for a tiny Ford Fiesta. If booked in France, the average rate is 400F ($73) per day for a small car.

Budget has over 30 locations in Paris; the main branch is at 81 av. Kléber, 16e (☎ **01-46-86-65-65;** Métro: Trocadéro). **Hertz** has about 15 branches, including the main office at 27 rue St-Ferdinand, 17e (☎ **01-39-38-38-38;** Métro: Argentine). The main office for **Avis** (which also has several branches) is at 5 rue Bixio, 7e (☎ **01-46-10-60-60;** Métro: Ecole-Militaire). All these companies also have offices at Charles-de-Gaulle and Orly, but remember that cars picked up at the airport are subject to the airport surcharge, from 68 to 96F ($12 to $17).

The **National Road Travel Information Center** at ☎ **01-48-99-33-33** can give you information about road conditions and weather in the Paris area (they can also answer questions about best routes to take and so on). For road information throughout France, call ☎ **08-36-68-20-00.**

An Autoroute Warning

If you're planning to drive say from Paris to Nice, remember that not only is fuel exorbitantly expensive but also the autoroutes in this country aren't free. Fees from Paris to Nice may add up to more than 250F ($45) just for the highway tolls. To put things in perspective: A one-way fare by plane or train for that route is currently 240F ($44), with a 14-day advance purchase.

FAST FACTS: Paris

AIDS Organizations & Hot Lines For the **SIDA Info Service** (AIDS Information Service), call ☎ **0-800-840-800** 24 hours; they answer any questions related to HIV prevention and treatment. The English-language **Anonymous AIDS/HIV Information and Support** is available by calling ☎ **01-44-93-16-69** (Mon–Wed and Fri 6–10pm).

American Express The huge **American Express** office is at 11 rue Scribe, 9e (☎ **01-47-77-70-07;** Métro: Opéra, Chaussée-d'Antin, or Havre-Caumartin; open Mon–Fri 9am–6:30pm, bank also open Sat same hours). There's a full travel agency and mail pick-up window.

Community Centers The **Centre Gai et Lesbien,** 3 rue Keller, 11e (☎ **01-43-57-21-47;** Métro: Bastille; open Mon–Sat noon–8pm, Sun 2–7pm), is a good source of info for such things as dates of gay pride and other general questions, but the staff isn't as knowledgeable as you might expect; their main event is the Sunday Café Positif, an informal collection of readings, talks, and performances related to AIDS and HIV prevention and treatment. The **Gay Association of Paris Professionals (GAPP),** 14 rue Houdon, 18e (☎ **01-45-72-56-09;** e-mail: gapp98@club-internet.fr; Métro: Pigalle), hosts occasional events that might be worth checking out; many of its members are English-speaking professionals.

Consulates & Embassies Embassies are usually open 9am to 1 or 2pm for consular business; they keep bizarre hours, so call ahead. The **U.S. Embassy** is at 2 av. Gabriel, 8e (☎ **01-43-12-22-22;** Métro: Concorde); the **Consulate** for passport replacement is close by at 2 rue Florentin (☎ **01-42-96-12-02**). The **Canadian Embassy/Consulate** are at 35 av. Montaigne, 8e (☎ **01-44-43-29-00;** Métro: Franklin-Roosevelt). The **U.K. Embassy** is at 35 rue du faubourg St-Honoré, 8e (☎ **01-44-51-31-00;** Métro: Concorde or Madeleine); the **Consulate** is at 16 rue d'Anjou, 8e (☎ **01-44-51-31-00;** Métro: Concorde or Madeleine). The **Australian Embassy** is at 4 rue Jean-Rey, 15e (☎ **01-40-59-33-00;** Métro: Bir-Hakeim). The **Irish Embassy/Consulate** are at 12 av. Foch, 16e (☎ **01-45-00-20-87;** Métro: Argentine). The **New Zealand Embassy/Consulate** are at 7 rue Léonard-de-Vinci, 16e (☎ **01-45-00-24-11;** Métro: Victor-Hugo).

Currency Exchange Every day except Sunday in the *International Herald Tribune* you'll find the official franc exchange rates. The rates at banks or exchange bureaus are very rarely close to this official rate, though. Most credit-card companies, however, are bound to do business at official rates, so paying by credit card is always a good idea. You can withdraw money at the hundreds of ATMs throughout the city; the main bank names to look for are BNP (Banque Nationale de Paris), Société Générale, and Crédit Lyonnais. If you need immediate cash, banks are better than the *bureaux de change* (exchange offices), as they're less likely to charge exorbitant fees. Some fees on the Champs-Elysées are as high as 30F ($6) per transaction, but they remain open until late into the night; you're paying for convenience. One exception is the Office de Tourisme's **official exchange office** at 127 av. des Champs-Elysées (☎ **01-49-52-53-47;** Métro: Charles-de-Gaulle–Etoile or George-V; open daily 9am–7:30pm); they have favorable exchange rates. Regular banking hours are Monday to Friday 9am to 4:30pm.

Country & City Codes

The **country code** for France is **33.** The **city code** for Paris is **1;** use this code if you're calling from outside France. If you're calling Paris within Paris or from anywhere else in France, use **01,** which is now built into all phone numbers, making them 10 digits long.

Cybercafes If you're aching to check e-mail and still feel like you're on vacation, the **Web Bar,** 32 rue de Picardie, 3e (☎ **01-42-72-57-47;** Métro: République), has over 20 computers and a trendy bar in what used to be a silversmith's workshop. Computer rates are 40F ($7) per hour; there's an attached restaurant, art gallery, and theater, and the mixed crowd is young and friendly. **Café Orbital,** 13 rue de Médicis, 6e (☎ **01-43-25-76-77;** Métro: Cluny–La-Sorbonne), is the city's oldest cybercafe, where a mainly young student crowd taps onto the Web while sipping café au lait. Rates are 55F ($10) per hour.

Emergencies For **police** dial ☎ **17;** for an **ambulance** dial ☎ **15;** to report a **fire** dial ☎ **18.**

If you need a doctor, call **SOS Médécins** at ☎ **01-47-07-77-77** and they'll dispatch a doctor to wherever you are 24 hours a day. They usually arrive within 2 hours and are mostly young English-speaking doctors. The most convenient 24-hour pharmacy is **Pharmacie Dhery,** 84 av. des Champs-Elysées, in the Galerie des Champs-Elysées shopping center, 8e (☎ **01-45-62-02-41;** Métro: Charles-de-Gaulle–Etoile). **SOS Help** is an English-language hot line at ☎ **01-47-23-80-80** (daily 3–11pm).

Gay Media Radio FG **98.2 FM** (51 rue de Rivoli, 1e; ☎ **01-40-13-88-00**) is Paris's gay radio station, with gay DJs playing the latest hits.

Hospitals The **American Hospital** is the best for English-speaking doctors and is in Neuilly (just west of the city) at 63 bd. Victor-Hugo (☎ **01-46-41-25-25;** Métro: Port-Maillot, then bus no. 82). The **Franco-British Hospital** is at 3 rue Barbes in Levallois-Perret (☎ **01-46-39-22-22;** Métro: Anatole-France).

To find a gay doctor near you, call the **Association Médécins Gais** (Association of Gay Doctors) at ☎ **01-48-05-81-71** (Wed 6–8pm and Sat 2–4pm).

Hot Lines **Ecoute Gais** at ☎ **01-44-93-01-02** (Mon–Fri 6–10pm) offers advice on gay issues. **SOS Homophobie** at ☎ **01-48-06-42-41** (Mon–Fri 8–10pm) is dedicated to helping/advising victims of homophobia or gay-related discrimination. It's about a 50/50 chance you'll get a person who speaks English, though most speak at least broken *anglais.*

Magazines & Newspapers ***Têtu*** is France's most lively gay and lesbian publication. A large-format magazine (like *Interview*), it runs regular features on many of the country's famous and not-so-famous gays and lesbians. ***Trixx, Idol, Men,*** and ***Fresh*** are the top nudie gay rags.

Telephone Public phone booths are in cafes, restaurants, Métro stations, post offices, airports, and train stations and sometimes on the streets. Finding a coin-operated phone in France may be an arduous task. Simpler and more widely accepted is the **télécarte,** a prepaid calling card. These debit cards are priced at 40F ($7) and 96F ($17) for 50 and 120 *unités,* respectively. Télécartes are available at most post offices and Métro stations. Even more widely accepted and more convenient is your **credit card;** most phones now accept them.

If possible, avoid making calls from your hotel, which might double or triple the charges. Also note that numbers beginning with 08 carry a special surcharge that runs about 50¢ a minute. To make **international calls,** dial ☎ **00** (double zero) to access international lines. For **information,** dial ☎ **12.**

2 Pillow Talk

There's such a dizzying variety of hotels in Paris—from amazingly luxurious palaces to inexecrably dismal dumps. Choose your location carefully, as it'll determine what you get out of your stay. If you plan to stay out late at night, remember the Métro stops running at 12:30am and hailing a cab is no easy task at that hour. Getting a hotel within walking distance of your primary points of nocturnal interest would be most important to ensuring a stress-free vacation. I've listed many hotels in and around the gay Marais; hotels in St-Germain-des-Prés and the Latin Quarter are a 20- to 30-minute walk from the Marais.

Rates quoted for the less expensive hotels rarely vary, but the larger hotels frequently offer promotional rates (even the Ritz and Crillon), especially if you call ahead. Discounts are easiest to be had in November, January, and February. July and August also drive certain hotel prices down because there's absolutely no business travel in Europe then. Most of commercial Paris shuts down from late July to late August, leaving the city for the tourists (hotels remain open, but many restaurants close down).

Same-sex couples will never have any problems checking into a Paris hotel, but I've noted the more gay-friendly ones. Other guides list a few exclusively gay hotels that I haven't because I found them seedy, and most don't have private baths. ("Gay" doesn't mean "sleazy" in *my* dictionary.)

It used to be that breakfast was included in most hotel rates in Paris. Not anymore. Breakfast is an extra 35F to 230F ($6 to $42), though if you score a promotional rate you might find it includes both tax and breakfast. Always ask. (You can probably get a cheaper breakfast at a nearby cafe anyway.)

And remember that a twin-bedded room is more expensive than a room with one double bed. If you're looking for the least expensive room, always ask for the lowest category. Showers are pretty lame at the less expensive hotels in Paris. They don't come with showerheads but with a hand-held contraption (so you never have two hands free). If that's a big issue, always ask to see the bath before you accept the room, or stick to luxury hotels if expense isn't an issue.

The most knowledgeable gay travel agency in Paris is **Eurogays,** 23 rue du Bourg-Tibourg, 4e (☎ **01-48-87-37-77;** fax 01-48-87-39-99; Metro: Hôtel-de-Ville). Ask for Jean-Marie or Basilio. Not only can they help with hotel reservations in Paris, but they can plan and advise on gay travel all over Europe. If you arrive without a reservation and have trouble finding a room, your best bet is the **Office du Tourisme** (see "Visitor Information" above).

BETWEEN PLACE DE LA MADELEINE & THE LOUVRE

Astor Westin Demeure Hôtel. 11 rue d'Astorg, 75008 Paris. ☎ **01-53-05-05-05.** Fax 01-53-05-05-03. 134 units. A/C MINIBAR TV TEL. 2,000–2,900F ($364–$527) double; from 3,000F ($545) suite. Métro: St-Augustin.

Echoes of Proust permeate this wonderfully chic hotel on a quiet street between place de la Concorde and place de la Madeleine. The 1907 art-nouveau building was once an apartment complex across from the mansion of the comtesse Greffulhe, who inspired Proust's princesse de Guermantes (she threw some wicked parties back then). In 1996, the hotel was renovated by celebrated designer Frédéric Mechiche into 1930s

Hey, Big Spender

If you've finally come into your trust fund and want to blow a wad on a Paris hotel, there are many deluxe places that'll be more than glad to bend over backward for you. Be prepared to drop a minimum of $200 a night for a double at any of them, though expect the deluxe doubles to cost at least $400.

The **Ritz, Hôtel Costes, Relais Christine,** and **Pavillon de la Reine,** some of the toniest, are listed in full below. Here are some others where you'll feel like a princess, no matter what sex you are:

Hôtel Balzac, 6 rue Balzac, 75008 Paris (☎ **800/457-4000** in the U.S. and Canada, or 01-44-35-18-00; fax 01-44-35-18-05; E-mail: liz.tabet@wanadoo.fr; Métro: George-V).

Hôtel de Crillon, 10 place de la Concorde, 75008 Paris (☎ **800/241-3333** in the U.S. and Canada, or 01-44-71-15-00; fax 01-44-71-15-02; E-mail: crillon@crillon-paris.com; Métro: Concorde).

Hôtel du Louvre, place André-Malraux, 75001 Paris (☎ **800/777-4182** in the U.S., 800/673-1286 in Canada, or 01-44-58-38-38; fax 01-44-58-38-01; Métro: Louvre).

Hôtel Meurice, 228 rue de Rivoli, 75001 Paris (☎ **01-44-58-10-10;** fax 01-44-58-10-15; Métro: Concorde).

Hôtel Montalembert, 3 rue de Montalembert, 75007 Paris (☎ **800/447-7462** in the U.S. and Canada, or 01-45-49-68-68; fax 01-45-49-69-49; www. montalembert.com; E-mail: welcome@hotel-montalembert.fr; Métro: Rue-du-Bac).

Hôtel Plaza Athénée, 27 av. Montaigne, 75008 Paris (☎ **800/448-8355** in the U.S. and Canada, or 01-53-67-66-65; fax 01-53-67-64-66; Métro: F.-D.-Roosevelt or Alma-Marceau).

Hôtel Regina, 2 place des Pyramides, 75001 Paris (☎ **01-42-60-31-10;** fax 01-40-15-95-16; www.reginotel.com; E-mail: helene@reginotel.com; Métro: Pyramides or Tuileries).

Relais St-Germain, 9 carrefour de l'Odéon, 75006 Paris (☎ **01-43-29-12-05;** fax 01-46-33-45-30; Métro: Odéon).

"sumptuous Proustian ambiance." Perhaps Marcel wouldn't have approved of the big-screen TVs or the Stairmaster in the small fitness room, but he'd have surely adored the magnifying mirrors in the marble baths, the white-marble fireplaces in some of the larger units (those come with CD players), the magnificent views from the top-floor suites, the cozy salon/library where afternoon tea is served, and the lobby bar with its Aubusson leopard carpet and mahogany gondola armchairs. Be sure to ask about promotional rates and try to stay away from the small least expensive "standard" and "superior" rooms on the lower floors (they're a bit dark) and opt for the spacious deluxe or executive rooms. The restaurant L'Astor (see "Whet Your Appetite" below), with Joël Robuchon as principal advisor, is getting raves.

✪ **Hôtel Costes.** 239 rue St-Honoré, 75001 Paris. ☎ **01-42-44-50-00.** Fax 01-42-44-50-01. 83 units. A/C MINIBAR TV TEL. 2,250–3,500F ($409–$636) double; from 4,500F ($818) suite. AE, DC, MC, V. Métro: Tuileries or Concorde.

This is the hottest and most absolutely fabulous hotel in town. Since opening in 1996 on elegant boutique-lined rue St-Honoré a block from place Vendôme, it has become the most coveted address for visiting models, designers, and hip movie stars. Good luck getting a room, though: They boast the city's highest occupancy rates. The main focus is the interior courtyard restaurant splashed with natural light—it has become all the rage for Parisian Cafe Society (see "Whet Your Appetite" below). The most sought after designer, Jacques Garcia, and owner Jean-Louis Costes (who created Café Marly at the Louvre) teamed up to create this Italian-style palace with its heavy somber colors (mostly red and gold) and "a few touches of Moroccan and Indo-Portuguese to give it a sense of romantic mystery." The rooms are of varying sizes, but more than half are very small, the most spacious being the duplex suites; all boast silk-covered walls, heavy drapes, antiques, and baroque paintings. The baths have mosaic tile, some with porcelain claw-footed tubs. Candles and incense flicker in the dark halls, giving the hotel the look and smell of an old church. Even the decadently elegant indoor pool and fitness center are dimly lit. The staff is young, quite gay, and good-looking, and the guests are even better looking, mostly under 45 and oh-so hip, wealthy, and beautiful.

Hôtel Ritz. 15 place Vendôme, 75001 Paris. ☎ **01-43-16-30-30.** Fax 01-43-16-31-78. E-mail resa@ritzparis.com. 187 units. A/C MINIBAR TV TEL. 3,600–4,000F ($655–$727) double; from 6,200F ($1,127) suite. AE, DC, MC, V. Métro: Concorde, Tuileries, or Opéra.

"When you're in Paris, the only good reason for not staying at the Ritz is lack of money," Hemingway once said, and many people still consider it the best in the world. César Ritz founded the hotel in 1898 and, with the help of culinary master Escoffier, immediately attracted world royalty that hasn't stopped coming. Mohammed Al Fayed, Dodi's father, bought the Ritz in 1979 and spent 9 years renovating it before it ultimately become known as the place where Princess Diana and Dodi had their last supper. Paparazzi with long-necked cameras still loiter around the entrance, and security guards watch the doors closely and keep day tourists out. When you step into the Ritz you feel like you're setting sail on a luxury liner to a place where time has stood still. A world of discreet service awaits—butlers unpack your suitcases and press and hang your clothes (at extra cost, of course); the service is impeccable yet impersonal, efficient yet aloof. (The hotel can arrange for a private escort to meet you at the airport so you won't have to chip your nails lifting your bags; they'll see you through Customs, too). Rooms vary greatly in size and price but are opulent, mostly in Louis XV, with plush rugs and tapestries, luxurious mattresses, antique clocks, and fireplaces; the marble baths are large and still have the original fixtures. The magnificent fitness center includes an indoor pool, a sauna, and massage. The Ritz's Escoffier cooking school offers cooking lessons to guests and the public. There are two bars and two wonderful restaurants forever linked with the tragic end of a young couple in love, but as Hemingway said, "When I dream of afterlife in heaven, the action always takes place at the Paris Ritz." Let's hope they're all having a ball.

✪ **Hyatt Regency Paris-Madeleine.** 24 bd. Malesherbes, 75008 Paris. ☎ **01-55-27-12-34.** Fax 01-55-27-12-35. www.paris.hyatt.com. 86 units. A/C MINIBAR TV TEL. 2,100–2,600F ($382–$473) double; from 3,100F ($564) suite. AE, DC, MC, V. Métro: Madeleine.

On lively boulevard Malesherbes, steps from the trendy shops around place de la Madeleine and the Opéra, this new luxury hotel offers personalized service and a casual elegance. Hyatt has done an excellent job of un-"chain"-ing this location by making it a truly boutique hotel, with a distinct Parisian flavor (ask about promotional rates). The smiling professional staff is very gay-friendly, and their average age is 25 (the general manager is just 36). Each of the fabulous rooms is unique, but all have cherrywood desks and plush mattresses. The interior architect, Aldo Riva, gave the rooms "a chic masculine feel with warm woods enlivened with chrome" (whatever happened to the female business traveler?). If you're tired of luxury always meaning Louis XV chairs and somber colors, this hotel is for you: It's strictly contemporary. Special touches like feather-filled duvets instead of blankets and large baths with two-person showers (perfect for frolicking) make the Hyatt truly stand out. There's a fitness center with a sauna, a steam room, and massage. Café M is gaining popularity for its delectable dishes created by 29-year-old chef Christophe David.

IN & AROUND ST-GERMAIN-DES-PRES

Hôtel d'Angleterre. 44 rue Jacob, 75006 Paris. ☎ **01-42-60-34-72.** Fax 01-42-60-16-93. 26 units. MINIBAR TV TEL. 680–1,200F ($124–$218) double; from 1,500F ($273) suite. AE, DC, MC, V. Métro: St-Germain-des-Prés.

This beautiful minipalace was the British Embassy in the 19th century; Hemingway lived here for a while in the 1920s. If you want charm and character on a typical Paris street, then this is it. Guests are a healthy mix of Europeans and North Americans, with a few gays and lesbians, mostly art dealers and interior designers who appreciate the location steps from the trendiest art galleries. The staff is professional and reserved but will do their best to make your stay enjoyable and help with dinner reservations. The most fabulous rooms are the top-floor large doubles and suites with their own terraces and spacious baths. But even if you're staying in a small basic room (all with 18th-century furniture and slightly fading bedspreads and carpet), you have access to the lovely patio, overflowing with flowers in summer. Breakfast is served here when the weather is fine, and you can have drinks here or in the lobby bar.

Hôtel La Villa. 29 rue Jacob, 75006 Paris. ☎ **01-43-26-60-00.** Fax 01-46-34-63-63. 32 units. A/C MINIBAR TV TEL. 900–1,800F ($164–$327) double; from 2,000F ($364) suite. AE, DC, MC, V. Métro: Mabillon or St-Germain-des-Prés.

You must be open to postmodern art deco to stay here, for this is a place you'll either love or love to hate. It can only be described as 1970s meets Gen-X, conceived by 20-something decorator Christine Dorner. From the moment you step into the minimalist lobby with its sleek leather chairs and screaming blue rugs, you'll feel as if you've stepped into a modern art museum's work-in-progress. The 32 rooms are each unique, but all promise more bold colors (orange and violet leather chairs, gray walls, and bathrooms done with sanded glass, chrome, and green marble). The staff is young and slightly standoffish; the guests are trendy, including many musicians who hail from all over the world, mostly straight. The basement Jazz Club Le Villa attracts big names for a nightly 10:15pm concert.

Hôtel Lenox. 9 rue de l'Université, 75007 Paris. ☎ **01-42-96-10-95.** Fax 01-42-61-52-83. 34 units. TV TEL. 740–1,500F ($135–$273) double. AE, DC, MC, V. Métro: Mabillon.

This is the best bargain in the pricey neighborhood between St-Germain-des-Prés and the Musée Rodin. The Lenox is a meticulously maintained small hotel most recently renovated in the mid-1990s, and you can be sure of a good night's sleep (note there's

Hey . . . Wanna Know a Secret?

The best-kept secret in Paris is **Le Relais Carré d'Or,** 46 av. George V, 75008 Paris (☎ **01-40-70-05-05;** fax 01-47-23-30-30-90; Métro: George V), just off the Champs-Elysées. Here privacy and space are the key to your own fabulous apartment in this boutique hotel—units come with fully equipped kitchens, 24-hour room service, and daily maid service. Rates begin at 3,480F ($632).

no air-conditioning). The rooms are small, with just enough space for one or two beds, but the large windows make the units seem larger. The marble baths are sparkling clean, and the showerheads have good pressure (a refreshing change for Paris). There's a good mix of Europeans and North Americans, all ages, but very few gays and lesbians. The **Hôtel Montparnasse Lenox** is a sibling property offering comparable rooms and rates close to the Jardin du Luxembourg at 15 rue Délambre, 14e (☎ **01-43-35-34-50;** fax 01-43-20-46-64; Métro: Vavin).

Hôtel Lutétia. 45 bd. Raspail, 75006 Paris. ☎ **01-49-54-46-46.** Fax 01-49-54-46-00. 250 units. A/C TV TEL. 1,700–2,050F ($309–$373); from 3,200F ($582) suite. AE, DC, MC, V. Métro: Sèvres-Babylone.

Long a favorite of writers, musicians, and artists (Cocteau and Gide both stayed here), the Lutétia is a marvel of belle époque and art deco (it first opened in 1910). Its location is perfect if you want to be steps from the best Left Bank shopping. The soundproofed rooms are decorated in art deco (some people find them drab if not downright ugly) and were renovated recently by celebrated designer Sonia Rykiel (who also designed parts of Le Crillon). The most beautiful unit is the two-bedroom Arman suite designed for the sculptor who stays here on a regular basis. When he's away it's up for grabs, starting at 11,000F ($2,000) per night. It features two baths and a wonderful terrace with magnificent views; the master bedroom has a blond maple violin-shaped headboard and a bedspread designed like sheet music. The Brasserie Lutétia is a very hip and trendy place for models and artists (see listing below).

✪ **Hôtel Millésime.** 15 rue Jacob, 75006 Paris. ☎ **01-44-07-97-97.** Fax 01-46-34-55-97. 22 units. A/C MINIBAR TV TEL. 950–1,100F ($173–$200) double. AE, MC, V. Métro: Mabillon or St-Germain-des-Prés.

The newest hotel to open in this neighborhood in many years, the Millésime (which means "exceptional vintage," as in good wine) opened in 1997 after a complete renovation of its 16th-century building. The friendly young staff tries hard to make everybody feel welcome. It's an airy quiet hotel with a 3-centuries-old staircase (there's also a newer glass elevator) leading to the five floors of rooms. Provençal colors, wrought-iron lamps, bright bedspreads, and marble baths make this a very pleasant contemporary place to call home. The windows are double-glazed to block out the minimal street noise, and the air-conditioning works well. The best unit is the most expensive Millésime Room, with exposed wood beams and a view of the St-Germain-des-Prés church. The guests tend to be young and trendy, mostly straight and mostly European (Americans haven't discovered this little gem yet). Breakfast is served in the little garden or the vaulted stone breakfast room.

Hôtel Rive Gauche. 25 rue des Sts-Pères, 75006 Paris. ☎ **01-42-60-34-68.** Fax 01-42-61-29-78. 21 units. TV TEL. 395–530F ($72–$96) double. MC, V. Métro: St-Germain-des-Prés.

If you're looking for the least expensive clean accommodations in a good area of Paris, look no further. This isn't a fleabag but isn't a hotbed of charm either. The location couldn't be better—2 blocks from the Seine between St-Germain-des-Prés and the quai du Louvre. You're well placed to walk practically anywhere in less than 45 minutes. The rooms are very simple but sparkling, all with small baths. There's a small breakfast room with exposed stone that's actually the most interesting area of the hotel. The guests tend to be a younger bunch, a mix of Americans and Europeans and a scattering of gays and lesbians. The French staff try hard to understand and help out, but don't expect concierge service.

L'Hôtel. 13 rue des Beaux-Arts, 75006 Paris. ☎ **01-44-41-99-00.** Fax 01-43-25-64-81. 26 units. A/C MINIBAR TV TEL. 600–2,500F ($109–$455) double; from 1,700F($309) suite. AE, DC, MC, V. Métro: St-Germain-des-Prés.

Oscar's Last Wilde Words

"Alas, I am dying beyond my means. . . . Ah, well, then I suppose I shall have to die beyond my means."

In 1900, when this was the Hôtel d'Alsace, Oscar Wilde died in room no. 16 (see his last words above), many years before the place was fully renovated and turned from a dump into a four-star in the mid-1980s. The staff now is impoverished in spirit, and their rudeness deserves at least censure if not a boycott of this elegant location on a street lined with Paris's hottest art galleries. Grit your teeth and check in and you'll be pleasantly surprised at the lovely indoor fountain as you head up to your room. Like everywhere else in this area, the rooms vary greatly in size. The least expensive doubles are tiny and have equally tiny baths. Get a double with a full bath and you won't be disappointed; it's not exactly spacious, but at least you won't hurt your elbows. The individually decorated rooms (some art deco, some Louis XV, many with antiques) are quite grand, as are the Italian-marble baths. The mattresses are changed on a regular basis, so you can expect a firm and plush place to sleep or frolic. Breakfast is served in the winter garden.

Relais Christine. 3 rue Christine, 75006 Paris. ☎ **01-43-26-71-80.** Fax 01-43-26-89-38. 51 units. A/C MINIBAR TV TEL. 1,650–2,000F ($300–$364) double; from 2,400F ($436) duplex or suite. AE, DC, MC, V. Métro: Odéon.

A sibling property to the Pavillon de la Reine (both owned by the same French family), this former 16th-century cloister sits in the heart of the bustling Odéon district, between St-Germain-des-Prés and the Latin Quarter. It's the most exclusive hotel on the Left Bank and attracts an eclectic mix (some hip, some gay, many straight, most under 50). The rooms would please Louis XIII, though they have touches of contemporary elegance like wrought-iron lamps; many come with king-sized beds and very firm mattresses. The baths, like the rooms, vary greatly in size, but all are done in pink marble and include the amenities you'd expect. The best rooms are the duplexes with huge French doors opening onto the lush garden and courtyard—definitely worth a splurge. The breakfast room with its thick exposed stone used to be part of the cloister's kitchen.

IN THE LATIN QUARTER

Hôtel des Grands Hommes. 17 place du Panthéon, 75005 Paris. ☎ **01-46-34-19-60.** Fax 01-43-26-67-32. 32 units. A/C MINIBAR TV TEL. 800F ($145) double; from 900F ($164) suite. AE, DC, MC, V. Métro: Cardinal-Lemoine.

No, the "Hotel of the Big Men" isn't just for the well hung or for size queens (it refers to the famous Frenchmen buried in the Panthéon across the street), but it's a good place to consider if you want to be in this area crawling with students, a block from the Jardins du Luxembourg and close to the Sorbonne. The very friendly staff cater mostly to a French and North American clientele (straight) who come on business or pleasure. The rooms are nicely decorated with flowery faux Laura Ashley wallpaper in some and aging but clean baths in all. Renovations are planned for late 1999 (when the hotel will be closed for several weeks). The rooms in back are much quieter than those facing the Panthéon.

Libertel Quartier Latin. 9 rue des Ecoles, 75005 Paris. ☎ **01-44-27-06-45.** Fax 01-43-25-36-70. 29 units. A/C TV TEL. 1025F ($186) double; from 1,250F ($227) suite. AE, DC, MC, V. Métro: Cardinal-Lemoine.

Opened in 1997, this is the Latin Quarter's most gay-friendly (and visitor-friendly) hotel. Proust and Gide live on in the most bizarre spots of this whimsical hotel (the footmats on the top floor bear Proust quotes, and photos of Gide at work are hung over some beds). The rooms vary greatly in size but are carefully decorated in a contemporary IKEA art deco style; duvets, plump pillows, and checkered carpeting lend a unique and light feel. The baths are small but have unique wood-pedestal sinks and extra-large mirrors. The most charming units are the top-floor rooms—they may not be spacious but do offer lovely views over the rooftops and Notre-Dame. The staff is young, and the management doesn't shy away from acknowledging its gay and lesbian clientele. A fabulous breakfast buffet is served in the basement, where the walls are painted with Baudelaire quotes.

IN & AROUND THE MARAIS

Hôtel Beaumarchais. 3 rue Oberkampf, 75011 Paris. ☎ **01-53-36-86-86.** Fax 01-43-38-32-86. TV TEL. 33 units. 460F ($84) double. AE, MC, V. Métro: Filles-du-Calvaire.

This sleek multicolored hotel, within a 15-minute walk from the Marais and place de la Bastille, may have the best rates in town. Newly renovated and decorated with Keith Haring prints, this artsy place is run by a very gay-friendly English-speaking staff. The postmodern rooms are small but bursting with color, like lipstick red. The baths are small but sparkling clean and new. The number of gay guests here continues to multiply, with young northern European men (British and German) leading the way.

Hôtel Caron de Beaumarchais. 12 rue Vieille-du-Temple, 75004 Paris. ☎ **01-42-72-34-12.** Fax 01-42-72-34-63. 19 units. A/C MINIBAR TV TEL. 730–850F ($133–$155) double. AE, MC, V. Métro: Hôtel-de-Ville.

Named after the author who wrote the *Marriage of Figaro* in 1778 (he lived down the street at 47 rue Vieille-du-Temple), this hotel is well situated and managed with care by the efficient Bigeard family (father and son). Curiously (take your guesses) it's not as gay-friendly as you'd think, considering it's half a block from the heart of the Marais. It does get its share of gays by default, but the Bigeards don't pursue the market or actively acknowledge their gay guests ("Stay But Don't Tell"). But you just can't beat these rates for the amenities offered: new carpeting, elegant silk wall fabric, and king-size beds (especially rare in Paris) on request. The baths have just been renovated, with tubs and robes added. Many rooms have a view (of the street and rooftops) and are larger than those in most other hotels in this category. Breakfast is served until noon.

Hôtel de la Bretonnerie. 22 rue St-Croix-de-la-Bretonnerie, 75004 Paris. ☎ **01-48-87-77-63.** Fax 01-42-77-26-78. 30 units. MINIBAR TV TEL. 650–795F ($118–$145) double; from 990F ($180) suite. Closed Aug. MC, V. Métro: Hôtel-de-Ville or St-Paul.

The street this 17th-century hotel sits on is crawling day and night with same-sex couples who live in the area or come to the bars (or the best gay bookstore a few doors down—see "Hitting the Stores" below). Inside, though, there's nothing at all gay, almost as if the older crowd and staff try hard to be oblivious to the newer crowd that has transformed the area into a hopping neighborhood. That isn't to say they're homophobic, they're just not using anything gay to promote their hotel. All this said, every room is charming, many with exposed beams and four-poster beds with heavy drapes, antique chairs, and lamps (you'll feel like the world has stopped if you stay here; there's nothing modern about it yet it fits well in the Marais). Room no. 20 has red walls, a four-poster bed, and three large windows making it the brightest room they have; no. 33 has exposed wood beams. The baths in the upper-floor rooms are larger (request the slightly more expensive "charming rooms" when you make your reservation and you'll get more space). The staff is efficient and runs the place like a B&B with a lot of love and care.

Paris Accommodations & Dining

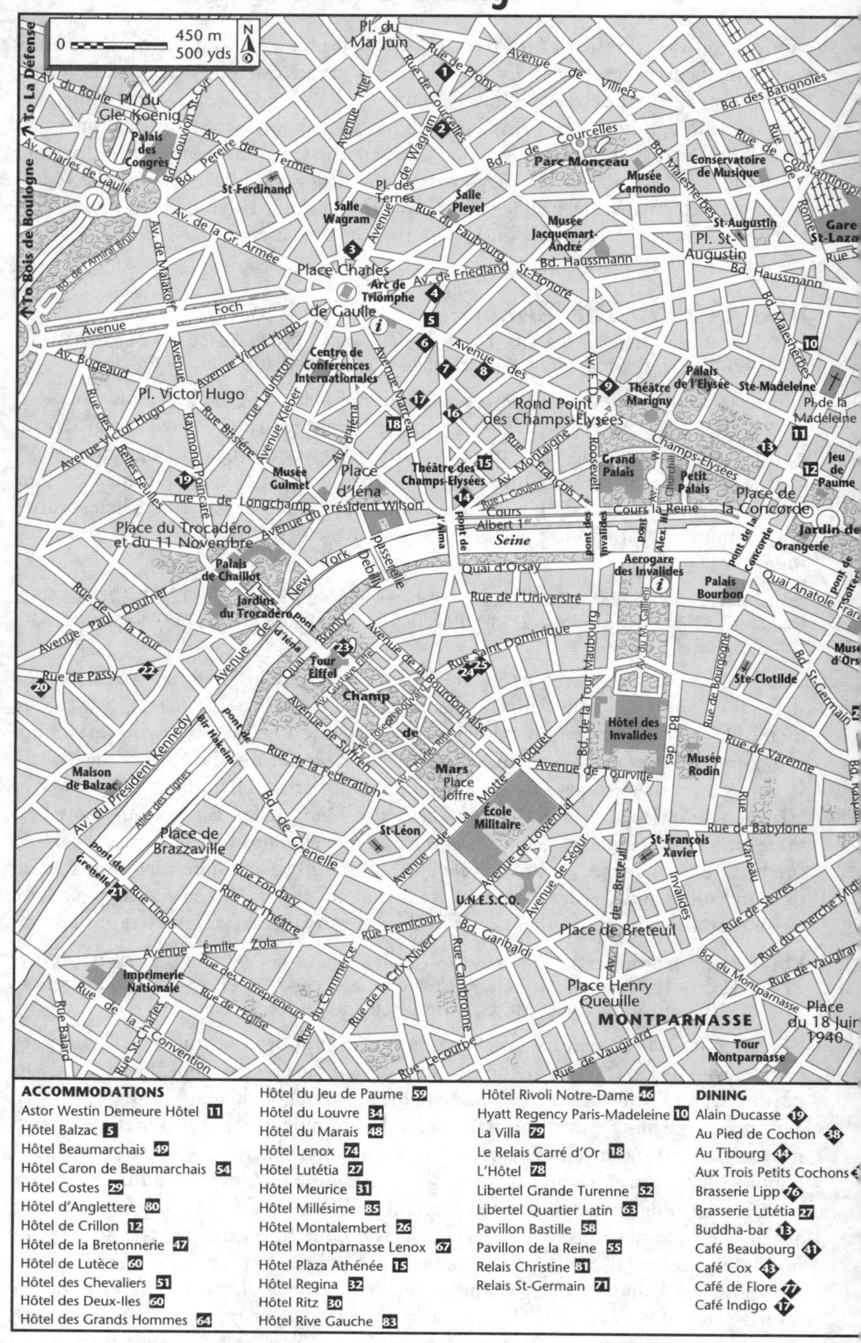

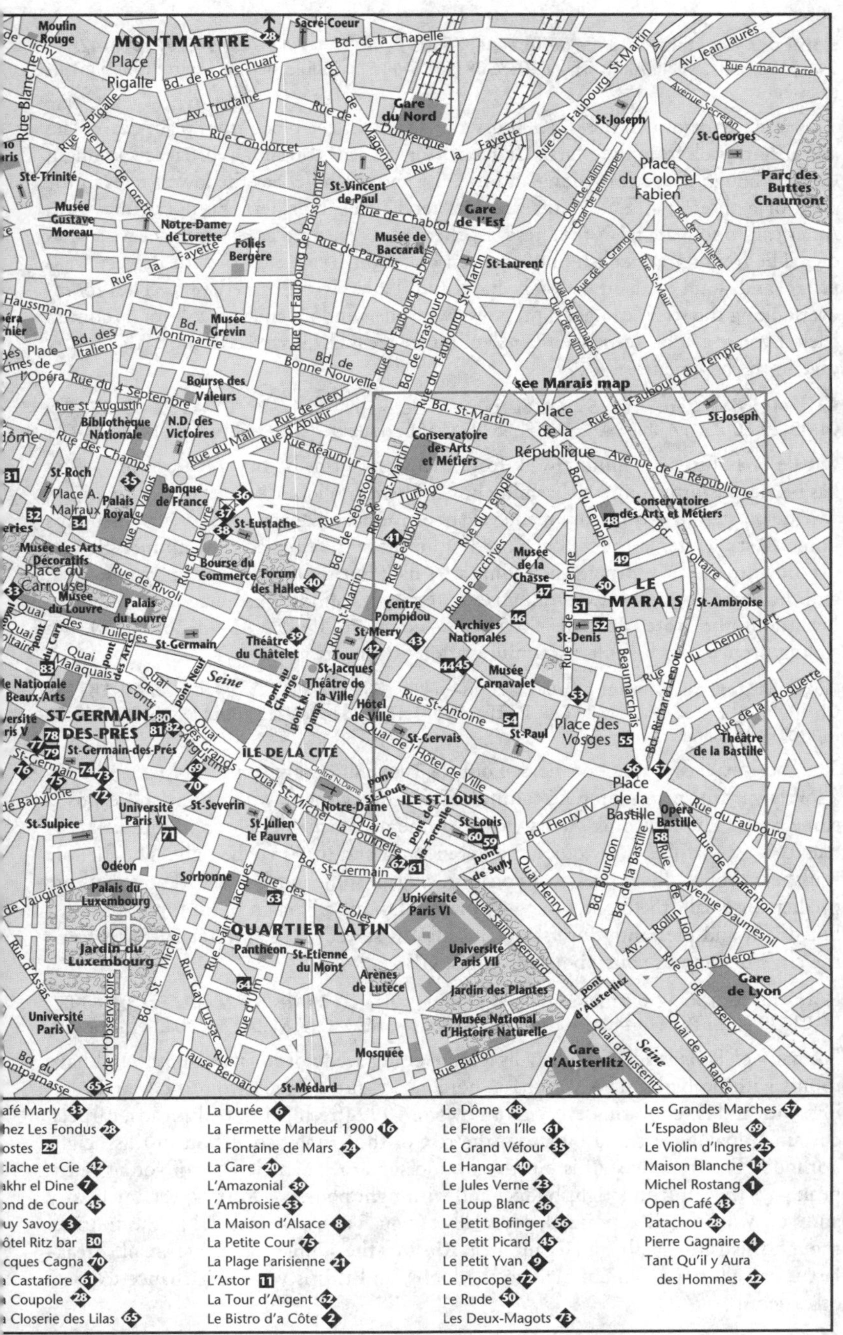
MONTMARTRE
Moulin Rouge
Place Pigalle
Sacré-Coeur
Bd. de la Chapelle
Bd. de Rochechuart
Av. Trudaine
Rue Condorcet
Gare du Nord
Rue de Dunkerque
Rue la Fayette
Ste-Trinité
Musée Gustave Moreau
Notre-Dame de Lorette
Folies Bergère
St-Vincent de Paul
Rue de Chabrol
Gare de l'Est
Musée de Baccarat
Rue de Paradis
St-Laurent
St-Joseph
St-Georges
Place du Colonel Fabien
Parc des Buttes Chaumont
Av. Jean Jaurès
Rue Armand Carrel
Avenue Secrétan
Bd. de la Villette
Rue St-Maur
Quai de Valmy
Quai de Jemmapes
Rue du Faubourg St-Martin
Rue du Faubourg St-Denis
Bd. de Strasbourg
Rue du Faubourg Poissonnière
Haussmann
Musée Grevin
Bd. Montmartre
Bd. des Italiens
Bd. de Bonne Nouvelle
Rue du 4 Septembre
Rue St Augustin
Bourse des Valeurs
Bibliothèque Nationale
N.D. des Victoires
Rue des Champs
Rue du Mail
Rue d'Abukir
Rue de Cléry
Rue Réaumur
see Marais map
Rue du Faubourg du Temple
Bd. St-Martin
Place de la République
Avenue de la République
Conservatoire des Arts et Métiers
St-Roch
Place A. Malraux
Palais Royal
Banque de France
St-Eustache
Bourse du Commerce
Forum des Halles
Musée des Arts Décoratifs
Place du Carrousel
Musée du Louvre
Palais du Louvre
Rue de Rivoli
Quai des Tuileries
Quai Voltaire
Quai Malaquais
St-Germain
Théâtre du Châtelet
Tour St-Jacques
Théâtre de la Ville
Hôtel de Ville
Seine
Rue Beaubourg
Rue de Turbigo
Bd. de Sébastopol
Rue St-Martin
Rue du Temple
Rue des Archives
Centre Pompidou
St-Merry
Archives Nationales
Musée de la Chasse
Musée Carnavalet
Rue de Turenne
Bd. du Temple
LE MARAIS
St-Denis
St-Ambroise
Rue du Chemin Vert
Bd. Voltaire
Bd. Beaumarchais
Bd. Richard Lenoir
Rue St-Antoine
St-Gervais
St-Paul
Place des Vosges
Théâtre de la Bastille
Rue de la Roquette
Place de la Bastille
Opéra Bastille
Rue du Faubourg
Rue de Charenton
Avenue Daumesnil
ST-GERMAIN-DES-PRÉS
St-Germain-des-Prés
ÎLE DE LA CITÉ
Notre-Dame
ÎLE ST-LOUIS
St-Louis
Quai de l'Hôtel de Ville
Bd. Henry IV
Quai Henry IV
Bd. Bourdon
Bd. de la Bastille
Quai de la Tournelle
Quai St-Michel
Université Paris VI
St-Severin
St-Julien le Pauvre
St-Sulpice
Odéon
Sorbonne
Palais du Luxembourg
Rue de Vaugirard
Rue des Ecoles
Bd. St-Germain
QUARTIER LATIN
Jardin du Luxembourg
Panthéon
St-Etienne du Mont
Arènes de Lutèce
Université Paris VII
Jardin des Plantes
Musée National d'Histoire Naturelle
Quai Saint Bernard
Gare d'Austerlitz
Quai d'Austerlitz
Gare de Lyon
Bd. Diderot
Rue de Lyon
Rue de Bercy
Quai de la Rapée
Université Paris V
Bd. St. Michel
Rue Saint Jacques
Rue Gay Lussac
Rue d'Ulm
Rue Clause Bernard
Rue Buffon
Mosquée
St-Médard
Rue d'Assas
Av. de l'Observatoire
Bd. du Montparnasse

afé Marly 33
hez Les Fondus 28
ostes 29
:lache et Cie 42
akhr el Dine 7
ond de Cour 45
uy Savoy 3
ôtel Ritz bar 30
cques Cagna 70
a Castafiore 61
a Coupole 28
a Closerie des Lilas 65
La Durée 6
La Fermette Marbeuf 1900 16
La Fontaine de Mars 24
La Gare 20
L'Amazonial 39
L'Ambroisie 53
La Maison d'Alsace 8
La Petite Cour 75
La Plage Parisienne 21
L'Astor 11
La Tour d'Argent 62
Le Bistro d'a Côte 2
Le Dôme 68
Le Flore en l'Ile 61
Le Grand Véfour 35
Le Hangar 40
Le Jules Verne 23
Le Loup Blanc 36
Le Petit Bofinger 56
Le Petit Picard 45
Le Petit Yvan 9
Le Procope 72
Le Rude 50
Les Deux-Magots 73
Les Grandes Marches 57
L'Espadon Bleu 69
Le Violin d'Ingres 25
Maison Blanche 14
Michel Rostang 1
Open Café 43
Patachou 28
Pierre Gagnaire 4
Tant Qu'il y Aura des Hommes 22

Hôtel des Chevaliers. 30 rue de Turenne, 75003 Paris. ☎ **01-42-72-73-47.** Fax 01-42-72-54-10. 24 units. MINIBAR TV TEL. 640–830F ($116–$151) double. MC, V. Métro: Chemin-Vert or St-Paul.

This recently renovated hotel is on busy rue de Turenne, a block from place des Vosges and a short walk from the Marais. It gets its share of gays but not as often as you might expect, though the staff is young and friendly and the hotel has the lowest rates in the area for a three star. The younger guests tend to be Northern European or North American, but apart from the breakfast there really isn't a place to interact with anyone. The rooms are smallish but bright and pleasant (if a bit tacky with flowery wallpaper and loud bedspreads); all have full baths with hair dryers. The rooms overlooking the street can get quite noisy with the window open, so ask for a room in back if you're a light sleeper. An excellent buffet breakfast is served in the 17th-century cave in the basement.

✪ **Hôtel des Deux-Iles.** 59 rue St-Louis-en-l'Ile, 75004 Paris. ☎ **01-43-26-13-35.** Fax 01-43-29-60-25. 17 units. A/C TV TEL. 870F ($158) double. AE, V. Métro: Pont-Marie.

On Ile St-Louis, a 10-minute walk from the Marais, this homey 17th-century house has been transformed into a charming hotel. There's no lobby but rather a living room where you step in off the tiny medieval street and feel like you've entered somebody's home. If it's winter, a fire will be crackling in the stone fireplace; in summer, flowers overflow from every corner. The rooms are small, but they've been recently renovated and the baths upgraded. Everything is so pretty—it's almost like being in a dollhouse. Next door, the **Hôtel de Lutèce,** 65 rue St-Louis-en-l'Ile (☎ **01-43-26-23-52**), is a sibling property with similar accommodations at similar rates.

Hôtel du Jeu de Paume. 54 rue St-Louis-en-l'Ile, 75004 Paris. ☎ **01-43-26-14-18.** Fax 01-40-46-02-76. 32 units. MINIBAR TV TEL. 895–1,185F ($163–$215) double. AE, DC, MC, V. Métro: Pont-Marie.

The most expensive hotel on Ile St-Louis (a 10-minute walk from the Marais) boasts a lovely garden surrounding a beautiful 17th-century house with salons and exposed stone walls. The returning guests (many of them French, straight, and middle-aged) like to boast that this is the quietest hotel in Paris, and they may be right. The friendly staff helps you'll almost feel as if you're staying in somebody's home. The rooms are predictably small (the highest category of doubles isn't a bargain but is more spacious) but bright and pleasantly furnished. Breakfast is served in the lovely gallery that was the city's first tennis court, built for Louis XIII.

Hôtel du Marais. 2 bis rue Commines, 75003 Paris. ☎ **01-48-87-78-27.** Fax 01-48-87-09-01. 39 units. TV TEL. 440–540F ($80–$98) double. AE, MC, V. Métro: St-Sébastien-Froissart.

So many of Paris's exclusively gay hotels are either seedy or noisy (or both) and have rooms with no baths. This very basic hotel, a 15-minute walk from the Marais, has low rates and is renovating every room by late 1999 (fresh paint, bedspreads, carpets, curtains), making it stand out from the rest of the grungy collection in this neighborhood. The friendly staff is mostly gay and so is the clientele (lots of young European gays traveling on a tight budget and with tight bodies). Don't expect any luxury and you won't be disappointed, especially if you like being away from the tourists, though this isn't exactly an elegant area. Most of the simple rooms are small. Breakfast is served in a room adjacent to the lobby, and this is your best chance to meet other guys.

✪ **Hôtel Rivoli Notre-Dame.** 19 rue du Bourg-Tibourg, 75004 Paris. ☎ **01-42-78-47-39.** Fax 01-40-29-07-00. E-mail rivoli.notre.dame@wanadoo.fr. 31 units. MINIBAR TV TEL. 680–740F ($124–$135) double. AE, DC, MC, V. Métro: Hôtel-de-Ville.

Not only is this the best bargain in the Marais, but also it's on a quiet street a block from the most popular gay bars, cafes, and restaurants. There's nothing gay about the hotel, however, and the guests tend to be older regulars and mostly French. The charming rooms are warmly decorated with yellow wallpaper; many have large windows overlooking the street. Bathrooms are small but most have windows too, and they're bright and clean. Perhaps the only drawback to this hotel is the lack of air-conditioning; don't stay here in the summer unless you don't mind sleeping with the window open. The thick 17th-century walls help keep things cool on the lower floors even on the warmest of Parisian summer days. There's a lovely vaulted breakfast room with exposed stone walls in the basement.

Libertel Grande Turenne. 6 rue de Turenne, 75004 Paris. ☎ **01-42-78-43-25.** Fax 01-42-74-10-72. 41 units. MINIBAR TV TEL. 860–920F ($156–$167) double. AE, DC, MC, V. Métro: St-Paul.

Steps from place des Vosges and the Marais, this small elegant hotel is part of a chain that maintains excellence without the high rates. The staff is very professional and helpful and the eclectic guests young and trendy. The rooms are modern and bright (no-smoking units on request), and the baths sparkle. As at most hotels in this neighborhood, the rooms aren't air-conditioned and might be stuffy in summer. You can have the continental breakfast delivered to your room (a nice perk if you got lucky the night before).

Pavillon Bastille. 65 rue de Lyon, 75012 Paris. ☎ **01-43-43-65-65.** Fax 01-43-43-96-52. E-mail hotel-pavillon@akaMail.com. 25 units. A/C MINIBAR TV TEL. 815–955F ($148–$173) double; from 1,375F ($250) suite. AE, DC, MC, V. Métro: Bastille.

You'll find this quirky hotel on a busy street a block from trendy place de la Bastille with its excellent Opéra (a 20-minute walk from the Marais gay bars). The friendly young staff will arrange for your opera tickets if you request them when booking your room. The drawback is noisy rue de Lyon, which means you'll have to keep the windows closed and the curtains drawn to block out the noise (windows are double-glazed, so it helps a bit). Every room is unique, but all are modern and comfortable, with immaculate white baths (however, the bathroom doors are thin accordion-style, so don't stay here unless you're really close with your roommate). The hotel has recently won awards for its innovative interior design, and if you like contemporary art deco, you'll love it. An excellent breakfast is served in the yellow basement done with faux-marble walls. Thursday to Saturday nights, the manager hosts a tasting of French wines in the leather-and-chrome-filled lobby.

✪ **Pavillon de la Reine.** 28 place des Vosges, 75003 Paris. ☎ **01-42-77-96-40.** Fax 01-42-77-63-06. 55 units. A/C MINIBAR TV TEL. 1,650–2,100F ($300–$382) double; from 2,650F ($482) suite. AE, DC, MC, V. Métro: Bastille or Chemin-Vert.

This is the most charming, romantic hotel close to the Marais, on beautiful place des Vosges. A 17th-century building and a new addition blend to create a country château feel in the city. The hotel's name literally translates as "Queen's Pavillion," and it's discreetly run by a dedicated team of queen-friendly young staff who tend to your needs without getting too chummy. A good number of gays stay here, but most of the guests are French or North American straight couples and many low-key celebs like Tina Turner and Sheryl Crow. The meticulously decorated rooms are done individually—some have exposed wood beams, four-poster beds, and antiques; others are more modern, with Ethan Allen–ish loveseats, striped wallpaper, and hand-painted wood headboards. The duplexes have lovely sleeping lofts above spacious living areas. All the marble baths come with hair dryers and designer toiletries. A breakfast buffet is served in the 17th-century basement with its coved ceiling and Persian carpets.

3 Whet Your Appetite

Dining in Paris can be a very grand elaborate affair but can also be a quick bite on the street, standing up at a bar, or sitting at a cafe table either inside or out. Most Parisians go out for meals several times a week, and stopping at a cafe is a daily ritual for many. Cafes generally serve three-course meals at lunch (noon–2:30pm) and dinner (8–11pm). Some set aside a small area where you can order just a coffee anytime during the day, but others allow this only between meals. Always specify your desire before being seated—it's customary to tell the maître d' you're there for just *un café* or for *déjeuner* (lunch) or *diner* (dinner). Most cafes serve a simple breakfast (*petit déjeuner*) of coffee and croissants too.

The trendiest restaurants in Paris right now are **Buddha-bar, Costes,** and **Café Marly** (see below). The most expensive and all-around best choice for a meal of classic cuisine is **L'Ambroisie** (below). Venerable **Alain Ducasse** of the six Michelin stars, 59 av. Raymond-Poincaré, 16e (☎ **01-47-27-12-27;** Métro: Trocadéro), is the ultimate innovator and still has the most sought after tables for his light southern cuisine at exorbitant prices (if you're heading to the Côte d'Azur after Paris, check out his restaurant in Monaco's Hôtel de Paris). The bevy of outstanding chefs working in Paris now is dizzying (most have eponymous restaurants), including **Guy Savoy,** 18 rue Troyon, 17e (☎ **01-43-80-40-61;** Métro: Charles-de-Gaulle–Etoile); **Michel Rostang,** 20 rue Rennequin, 17e (☎ **01-47-63-40-77;** Métro: Ternes); **Jacques Cagna,** 14 rue des Grands-Augustins, 6e (☎ **01-43-26-49-39;** Métro: St-Michel); **Pierre Gagnaire,** 6 rue Balzac, 8e (☎ **01-44-35-18-25;** Métro: George V); and **Christian Constant** with his Le Violin d'Ingres, 135 rue St-Dominique, 7e (☎ **01-45-55-15-05;** Métro: Ecole-Militaire).

To choose among these top chefs requires some research if you're not on the inside track of Paris gastronomy; some are traditionalists following the rules of classic French cuisine and others innovators who follow only their instincts. A good way to try the creations of these great chefs is by going to one of their **"baby bistros,"** usually close (and sometimes attached) to the main restaurant. Here you can get a feel for the chef's talents before you decide where to go all out; baby bistros keep their rates down to below 200F ($36) for three-course meals. A stand-out example is Michel Rostang's **Le Bistro d'a Côte** (see below). And in summer 1998, celebrated chef Jacques Cagna opened **L'Espadon Bleu,** 25 rue des Grands-Augustins, 6e (☎ **01-46-33-00-85;** Métro: St-Michel), across from his formal dining room. It's fast becoming the hottest baby bistro for fresh seafood at affordable prices.

Reservations at the top restaurants are necessary far in advance (about 2 months); always confirm your reservations a few days before and have your concierge call a few hours before to reconfirm. And of course you know that looking sharp is part of the French culture, particularly at the fancier places; in Paris the level of service you receive is still based on what you're wearing (and ultimately what you'll order and how you'll tip).

The staff won't look kindly if in a good restaurant you order only a little appetizer "to experience the place"; in Paris *ça ne fait pas.* Alain Ducasse is one of the first to establish a bar area where you can drop in for a drink and an appetizer, but this is still not encouraged (yet). Blasphemy is ordering a good meal without wine (or ordering the wrong color, say red with fish! *Mon Dieu!*). Dinner without wine is like sex without orgasm. Let the sommelier guide you or look him straight in the eye and tell him you don't drink.

Prix-fixe menus usually come with two courses at lunch and three at dinner, and that's the most economical way to dine. At some places you have a wide choice of

A Parisian *Pique-Nique*

One of the best ways to save money and also to participate in Parisian life is to picnic. Go to a *fromagerie* and purchase some cheese; to a *boulangerie* for a baguette or two; to a *charcuterie* for some pâté, sausage, or salad; and to a *pâtisserie* for some luscious pastries. Add a friendly bottle of Côtes du Rhone—it usually goes well with picnics—and you'll have the makings of a delightful and typically French meal you can take to the nearest park. Pretend you're in Manet's *Le Déjeuner sur l'herbe* and enjoy! (Hey, don't forget that corkscrew.)

appetizers and main courses; at others you have to settle for only one choice (usually the least expensive). The *plat du jour* (dish of the day) is also an inexpensive way to have a decent meal; most casual restaurants serve at least one. (The law requires that a 10% service charge be added to each bill, but it's customary to add a further 5% or 10% depending on how you feel toward the servers.)

As for gay restaurants in Paris, they're not known for haute cuisine, especially good service, or outstanding decor. They're fun and lively, with generally more attitude and panache and a more *laissez-faire* atmosphere. Gay Parisians don't go to gay restaurants to have an exquisite meal but to be with fellow queers. Most of these restaurants are in and around the Marais.

Note: For the locations of the restaurants below, see the "Paris Accommodations & Dining" map on pp. 168–169.

BETWEEN THE LOUVRE & PLACE DE LA MADELEINE

✪ **Buddha-bar.** 8 rue Boissy d'Anglais, 8e. ☎ **01-53-05-90-00.** Reservations required. Main courses 115–260F ($21–$47). AE, MC, V. Mon–Fri noon–3pm and 7:30pm–2am, Sat–Sun 7:30pm–2am. Métro: Concorde. ASIAN.

Don't let the name fool you—this is much more than a bar. It's the city's trendiest restaurant, and the young and terribly cool of all persuasions claw at one another for reservations on weekends. The location couldn't be more glamorous: facing the U.S. Embassy just behind the Hôtel de Crillon, off place de la Concorde. Entering the darkened basement, you'll feel as if you've stepped onto a Hollywood set (once you get past the hostess with attitude): a vast dining room with a huge Buddha presiding over the choreographed prancing of the waiters, some of whom seem stricken with an extreme case of megalomania. The food is original, a fusion of east and west (Thai-Californian), with delicious appetizers like fried spicy crayfish with black bean aïoli and cilantro-marinated salmon. Main courses include delectable seared sesame tuna with shiitake vinaigrette served extremely rare, grilled chicken breast with tamarind glaze, and crispy quail with orange sauce. Reservations are taken for two dining shifts: first or second (8 or 11pm).

✪ **Café Marly.** At the Louvre, 93 rue de Rivoli, 1e (enter on Cour Napoléon). ☎ **01-49-26-06-60.** Main courses 90–180F ($16–$33). Daily 8am–2am. AE, DC, MC, V. Métro: Palais-Royale. FRENCH.

One of the hippest restaurant/cafes in town commands a prime spot under the arcades of the Louvre facing the glass pyramid (beautifully lit at night). The outdoor tables in summer are the most coveted, though the slutty-red Napoléon III dining room is also great. Another of Paris's innovative young chefs, Frédéric Vives has revolutionized cafe food, raising it almost to haute cuisine levels. The tuna burger with coriander and herbs melts in your mouth and has only the slightest hint of the sea (served with rice, no bun). The *brique de chevre* is a thin pastry filled with goat cheese and deep fried, served with fresh spinach salad. The house wines are especially good; the Brouilly is served chilled as it should be (one of the few red wines not served at room temperature). Here you pour your own milk into the *café au lait* (in response to the many stick-figured models who raise a stink about too much milk in their coffee). They do serve Diet Coke (with a twist of lemon), referred to as Coca Light.

✪ **Costes.** In the Hôtel Costes, 239 rue St-Honoré, 1e. ☎ **01-42-44-50-00.** Reservations required. Main courses 120–180F ($22–$33). AE, DC, MC, V. Daily 7am–1am. Métro: Tuileries. FRENCH.

Jean-Louis Costes, creator of Café Beaubourg and Café Marly, has hit the jackpot with this restaurant occupying the courtyard of his fabulous Napoléon III–style hotel. You'll feel as if you're dining in a petit palace, surrounded by baroque furniture, Persian carpets, and crystal chandeliers. The crowd couldn't be more mixed, eclectic, or fabulous. *Le tout* Paris wants a bite of this place—and whether for breakfast, lunch, afternoon tea, or dinner, the waiting list is long and you need to keep calling back to make sure your name hasn't mysteriously been removed to make room for Julia Roberts or Kevin Costner (have your concierge confirm the reservation). The food is light and the menu short, continuing the latest Parisian fad of combining cafe food with haute cuisine to create a typical Costes meal: arugula salad with shaved parmesan or Norwegian smoked salmon followed by chicken breast with curried spinach or a thick slab of Nebraska steak served as red as you can handle it. Save room for the delicate desserts: The stewed figs with cinnamon are superb and the tiny mango tarts heavenly.

L'Astor. In the Hôtel Astor. 11 rue d'Astorg, 8e. ☎ **01-53-05-05-20.** Reservations recommended. Main courses 110–240F ($19–$41); fixed-price lunch menu 290F ($53). AE, DC, MC, V. Mon–Fri noon–2pm and 7:30–10pm. Métro: St-Augustin. FRENCH.

L'Astor opened in 1996 and garnered immediate respect for its innovative cuisine based on traditional cooking (not surprising, since celebrated retired chef Joël Robuchon oversees the operation). The dining room is intimate and elegant, done in 1930s art deco with black-and-gray floors, black-lacquered chairs with sculpted lion heads, and a trompe-l'oeil glass ceiling that splashes the room with seemingly natural light. Expect to see many businesspeople at lunch; in dinner crowd is international, middle-aged, and mostly straight. Appetizers include a wonderful carpaccio of Breton lobster with olive oil and candied tomatoes and delicate eggplant canneloni with fresh tuna fillet. Main courses are on the heavier side, like *suprême de pigeon au chou et au foie gras* (pigeon baked with cabbage and foie gras) and *rougets aux aubergines et oignons frites* (tender red mullet with eggplant and fried onions). For dessert, the little napoléon with vanilla bourbon will blow you away.

Le Grand Véfour. 17 rue de Beaujolais, 1er. ☎ **01-42-96-56-27.** Reservations required. Main courses 290–340F ($53–$62); fixed-price menus 345–750F ($63–$137) at lunch, 780F ($142) at dinner. AE, DC, MC, V. Mon–Fri 12:30–2:15pm and 7:30–10:15pm. Métro: Louvre. FRENCH.

This grand restaurant (opened during the reign of Louis XV!) is one of Paris's best. Cocteau dined here, as did Colette and Joséphine and Bonaparte (engraved wall plaques bear the names of the famous who've passed through). The dining room is bursting with 18th-century pieces—gilt-edged mirrors, crystal chandeliers, and Directoire chairs. The young (and hunky) chef, Guy Martin, is carrying the restaurant's outstanding reputation into the 21st century. Feast on his creations based on classic French cuisine (served on Limoges china): artichoke tart with candied vegetables accompanied by a bitter-almond sorbet, veal sweetbreads with mushrooms and truffles, and an excellent selection of fresh seafood that changes daily (there's usually Breton lobster). The service is crisp, but the guests are a staid group of businesspeople and older couples.

IN & AROUND THE MARAIS

Au Tibourg. 29 rue du Bourg-Tibourg, 4e. ☎ **01-42-74-45-25.** Reservations recommended on weekends. Main courses 50–125F ($9–$23); fixed-price menu 115F ($21). MC, V. Daily noon–2pm and 7–11:30pm. Métro: Hôtel-de-Ville. SOUTHWEST FRENCH.

This gay restaurant is owned by a charming couple, Frédéric and Gérard, who cook, manage, and wait tables while their dog naps in a corner of the rustic dining room. It resembles the kitchen of a French farmhouse: exposed wood beams, checkered tablecloths, and wood tables and chairs (there's a no-smoking section). Most of the crowd is made up of gay men, half tourists and half locals. They come for the excellent cuisine, with recipes passed down from the chef's grandfather, like *cassoulet de Carcassone* (beans simmered with duck and foie gras in tomato sauce). The food is hearty and the portions large, and many of the dishes revolve around duck, such as delicious foie gras cooked with Rivesaltes sweet wine and figs. There's usually a fish special too. For dessert, try the puréed candied chestnuts with bits of chocolate.

✪ **La Castafiore.** 51 rue St-Louis-en-l'Ile, 4e. ☎ **01-43-54-78-62.** Reservations recommended. Main courses 70–130F ($13–$24); fixed-price menus 59F ($11) at lunch, 158F ($29) at dinner. AE, DC, MC, V. Daily noon–2:30pm and 7–11pm. Métro: Pont-Marie. FRENCH/ITALIAN.

This tiny restaurant on one of Ile St-Louis's quaintest streets is owned by two young men: Ed from Chicago and Gerard from England. The dining room barely seats 16 people (usually an equal number of straight tourists and locals), and the food is fresh and very well prepared. You may start with *caviar d'aubergine* (pulverized eggplant with garlic, lemon, and olive oil) or spaghetti with pimentos. Move on to the pan-fried veal with mushroom Marsala wine sauce or creamy gnocchi with gorgonzola. The specialty is ravioli: your choice of spinach, asparagus, or artichoke, all delicately made with Italian pecorino cheese. If you're in the mood for fish, the *pavé de thon à la Castafiore* (tuna fillet in a spicy tomato, black olive, and caper sauce) is delicious. There are a few excellent wines under 130F ($24). For dessert, the warm pear with Barolo wine is awesome.

L'Amazonial. 3 rue Ste-Opportune, 1er. ☎ **01-42-33-53-13.** Main courses 65–120F ($12–$22); fixed-price menus 85–129F ($15–$23). AE, MC, V. Daily noon–3pm and 7pm–1am. Métro: Châtelet. SOUTH AMERICAN/FRENCH.

Gay boys (and a few girls) just arriving in town meander in here clutching their guidebooks looking for good food and friendship. Friendship they might find, but good food is a stretch. One of Paris's most popular gay restaurants, it's large and bustling and the atmosphere is festive and flamboyant. The tacky decor is nothing more than plastic plants and colorful cardboard figures (snowmen in winter, Easter bunnies in spring). The food is inexpensive and very unpredictable, a mix of French and South American and whatever. Stick to simple dishes like smoked salmon, green salad with walnuts, foie gras, *steak au poivre* (pepper steak), or grilled chicken. The exotic (but not bursting with flavor) choices include a gratin of crayfish tails with Antillean spices and sautéed ostrich steak with balsamic vinegar. The standoffish waiters can get to you (bring your sense of humor). Don't expect a quiet romantic meal, but if you have a beau (or belle) you can hold hands and feel completely at ease (you can even kiss!).

✪ **L'Ambroisie.** 9 place des Vosges, 4e. ☎ **01-42-78-51-45.** Reservations required. Main courses 280–530F ($50–$96). AE, MC, V. Tues–Sat noon–1:30pm and 8–10:15pm. Métro: St-Paul. FRENCH.

Alain Ducasse may be known as the guru of creation, but it's Bernard Pacaud who's the most talented chef in Paris when it comes to classic French cuisine. If you're planning to spend a fortune on a fabulous dinner, this terribly romantic restaurant in a 17th-century town house right on place des Vosges should be your first choice. There's no

Romancing with a View

There's nowhere like Paris for romance, exquisite views, and incredible food. Combining all three is the perfect vacation treat.

What better place than **Le Jules Verne,** on the second level of the Eiffel Tower, 7e (☎ **01-45-55-61-44;** Métro: Trocadéro; open daily noon–2:30pm and 7:30–10:30pm), for a sumptuous dinner with a to-die-for view over the whole city? Though it fills with tourists most days, it serves very good French cuisine focusing on fresh seafood. The service is surprisingly attitude-free. Main courses run 230 to 360F ($42 to $65), with fixed-price menus 310F ($56) at lunch and 695F ($126) at dinner. Reserve 2 months in advance.

If a grand view of Notre-Dame is more what you're after, book a table at the infamous **La Tour d'Argent,** 15–17 quai de la Tournelle, 5e (☎ **01-43-54-23-31;** Métro: Pont-Marie; open Tues–Sun noon–2:30pm and 8–10:30pm); it has been around in some form since 1582. This penthouse restaurant serves traditional French cuisine on Limoges china in a formal setting. The house specialty is duck, and the service and wine list are exquisite. Main courses are 220 to 400F ($40 to $73), with a fixed-price lunch at 395F ($72). Reserve at least 2 weeks in advance.

If you'd rather be in a livelier location and still have views, then head to the White House, the ✪ **Maison Blanche,** 15 av. Montaigne, 8e (☎ **01-47-23-55-99;** Métro: Alma-Marceau; open Mon and Sat 8–11pm, Tues–Fri noon–3pm and 8–11pm), where a trendier crowd takes in the heavenly views of the Seine on the top floor of the Théâtre des Champs-Elysées. It's popular with models and designers (avenue Montaigne is lined with boutiques like Valentino, Dolce & Gabbana, and Prada). The food is exquisite, but it's the desserts that are out of this world, like rhubarb ravioli swimming in decadently sweet almond milk. Main courses run 160 to 295F ($29 to $54). Reserve a week in advance.

Not high in the sky but in a thick forest, ✪ **Le Pré Catelan,** rte. de Suresnes in the Bois de Boulogne, 16e (☎ **01-44-14-41-14;** Métro: Porte-Dauphine; open

fixed-price menu (the place is too fancy even for that); a three-course meal with a decent wine will cost around 1,600F ($290) per person. When Bill and Hillary Clinton came to Paris, this is where Jacques Chirac took them. There's garden seating in summer. Let the headwaiter explain the usually short menu (the sommelier will follow with his advice on wine). The fillet of turbot braised with celery and served with a julienne of black truffles is exquisite, or you might try the Bresse chicken roasted with black truffles and truffled vegetables. There's usually a foie gras special and a fresh fish like grilled sea bass with rosemary-scented artichokes. The wine list is superb, and the desserts are divine.

Le Flore en l'Ile. 42 quai d'Orléans, 4e. ☎ **01-43-29-88-27.** Reservations recommended. Main courses 60–98F ($11–$18). MC, V. Daily 9am–2am. Métro: Pont-Marie. FRENCH/CAFE.

Though it's on Ile St-Louis, right on the bank overlooking the Seine and part of Notre-Dame, this place is surprisingly laid-back and not expensive. In fact, you can have a good meal here quite cheaply. You'll have to put up with grumpy waiters, but if you score a table by the window you'll feel as if you own the city. It can get pretty touristy, but there's always something yummy to look at—besides, the Marais is only a 10-minute walk away. There's always a *plat du jour,* usually a traditional French offering like coq au vin. Appetizers include escargots in buttery parsley sauce; for a main course, the salmon fillet with fresh berries is deliciously unique. There's also a good

Tues–Sat noon–2:30pm and 8–10:30pm, Sun noon–3pm), is as scenic as you can get without leaving the city. It's one of the most romantic restaurants for a leisurely Sunday lunch or dinner on a warm summer's eve. The specialties revolve around fresh truffles and the award-winning pastry chef's mouth-watering array of desserts. Main courses are 280 to 390F ($51 to $71), with fixed-price menus 310F ($56) at weekday lunch and 570 and 750F ($104 and $136) at dinner. Reserve a month in advance.

Dining on a terrace jutting into the middle of the river is as romantic as you can get without the exorbitant prices of the places above. **La Plage Parisienne,** port de Javel Haut (enter off pont de Grenelle), 15e (☎ **01-40-59-41-00;** Métro: Javel; open summer daily noon–midnight, in cooler months Mon–Fri 8:30–11:30pm, Sat–Sun noon–3pm and 8:30–11:30pm), has a glorious summer terrace and a cozy winter dining room with floor-to-ceiling windows. The food doesn't rise to gastronomic levels, but neither do the prices. Main courses are 160 to 220F ($29 to $40), with fixed-price menus at 300 to 350F ($55 to $64). Reserve several days in advance, especially for midsummer evenings.

One of the least expensive meals you can have with Paris spread at your feet is in Montmartre, not far from Sacré-Coeur on the plant-filled terrace of **Patachou,** 9 place du Tertre, 18e (☎ **01-42-51-06-06;** Métro: Anvers; open daily 8:30am–midnight). You'll dine on fresh seafood, pastas, and traditional French favorites while sitting on purple plastic chairs and tables with purple cloths. Despite the very touristy atmosphere of place du Tertre, the views are truly incredible. Come for a simple breakfast of fresh croissants and cups of *café au lait*—a perfect way to start the day. Main courses run 140 to 195F ($25 to $35), with fixed-price menus 165F ($30) at lunch and 220F ($40) at dinner. Reservations are required for dinner only.

selection of omelets and club sandwiches. Whatever you do, save room for the best ice creams in Paris (made by Berthillon down the street)—try the lemon sorbet with Grand Marnier. In winter, they serve the best *tarte tatin* (warm apple pie) in the city.

✪ **Le Hangar.** 12 impasse Berthaud, 3e. ☎ **01-42-74-55-44.** Reservations recommended. Main courses 68–118F ($12–$21). No credit cards. Daily noon–2:30pm and 7:30pm–midnight. Closed Aug. Métro: Rambuteau. FRENCH.

This is one of those rare restaurants where there's usually an equal number of gays, lesbians, and straights. The food is not only good but outstanding—and very reasonably priced. Perhaps the only drawback is it's somewhat hard to find, hidden in a nondescript alley close to Les Halles, not far from the Centre Pompidou (call ahead for directions or take a taxi; it's worth the effort). There's a small terrace for warm days and a rustic dining room for cooler ones. The same owners have lovingly kept up the high standards and low prices since it opened in 1982, and they've built a loyal clientele. You might start with the delicious lamb carpaccio with truffles or the tangy fish soup with five spices; main courses include excellent seafood dishes like pink scampi served with lemon fettuccine or the *tartare de saumon au basilic* (fresh raw salmon with basil) or the tasty beef stroganoff. There are interesting specials for vegetarians, such as baked fennel with mozzarella. The chocolate soufflé is to die for and the wine list wonderfully affordable, with many excellent selections below 130F ($24).

Other Gay Spots to Graze

In addition to Au Tibourg and L'Amazonial (above), here are some of the most popular gay restaurants, where the priority is frequently not the food or service but the convivial atmosphere. Most of the gay eateries are in either the Marais or Les Halles, and those below (with the exception of Fond de Cour) offer main courses averaging a reasonable 50 to 70F ($9 to $13). Reservations are recommended on weekends.

One of the most popular is **Aux Trois Petits Cochons** (Three Little Pigs), 31 rue Tiquetonne, 2e (☎ **01-42-33-39-69;** Métro: Etienne-Marcel; open Tues–Sun 8:30pm–midnight), owned by three (small) French guys. The patrons are almost exclusively gay (a youngish party crowd mostly), and it's inevitable that you talk to your neighbors as you dine (the tables are pushed together real close). The food is okay, with the usual French offerings like pan-fried salmon fillet and steak and fries. Not far down the street is **Le Loup Blanc,** 42 rue Tiquetonne, 2e (☎ **01-40-13-08-35;** Métro: Etienne-Marcel; open Mon–Sat 8pm–midnight, Sun noon–5pm), another popular place for gay boys; the light French food is inexpensive and consistently fresh.

The trendy **Le Rude,** 23 rue du Temple, 4e (☎ **01-42-74-05-15;** Métro: Hôtel-de-Ville; open daily noon–2am), pulls in a lot of hot men for light lunches and dinners. Good sandwiches, salads, and omelets keep the boys happy as they watch the action on the street from tiny sidewalk tables. For consistently decent brasserie fare, drop by **Le Petit Picard,** 42 St-Croix-de-la-Bretonnerie, 4e (☎ **01-42-78-54-03;** Métro: Hôtel-de-Ville; open Mon–Fri noon–2pm and 7:30–11:30pm, Sat 7:30–11:30pm), which has been popular for many years with gays and lesbians, though straights come here too.

In the heart of the Marais, the most expensive gay restaurant is **Fond de Cour,** 3 rue St-Croix-de-la-Bretonnerie, 4e (☎ **01-48-04-91-12;** Métro: Hôtel-de-Ville; open daily noon–2pm and 7:30–11:30pm), very popular for special occasions with gay couples for its pleasant garden seating and traditional French cuisine. In the fall of 1998, the restaurant changed ownership and got an embarrassingly bad review in *Figaroscope* (a mainstream French weekly). Let's hope they get their act together. Expect to pay no less than 250F ($45) per person.

Perhaps the best all-around gay restaurant that's slowly making a name for itself is ✪ **Eclache et Cie,** 10 rue St-Merri, 4e (☎ **01-42-74-62-62:** Métro: Hôtel-de-Ville; open daily 8:30am–1am). The indoor dining room shines with a hundred little lights on the thick slabs of exposed stone walls; the nice terrace occupies the site of a historic cul-de-sac. Expect country French cuisine (andouillette sausages, roasted chicken), friendly service, and an elegant, slightly older crowd. The 100F ($18) weekend brunch is popular.

Le Petit Bofinger. 6 rue de la Bastille, 4e. ☎ **01-42-72-05-23.** Reservations recommended. Main courses 78–81F ($14–$15); fixed-price menus 95F ($17) at lunch, 138F ($25) at dinner. Daily noon–3pm and 7pm–midnight. Métro: Bastille. FRENCH.

Across from the beautiful (and expensive) Bofinger, this baby bistro is just steps from bustling place de la Bastille. You may have to wait for a table even if you call ahead, and once you're seated you'll probably be rubbing elbows with your fellow diners. This place draws gays, straights, whatever, and everybody puts up with the cramped quarters in exchange for excellent food at unbeatable prices. The menu changes daily depending on what's found at the market, but for appetizers, there's usually a salmon carpaccio with a delicious fennel salad or six escargots in a yummy garlic-parsley sauce. Main courses include at least three fresh fish choices, like tasty cod roasted with olives. The chicken ravioli with fresh basil is excellent, as is the duck breast glazed with honey and fresh ginger. End with ripe camembert or the apple sorbet with Calvados (a Normandy liqueur made from apples).

Les Grandes Marches. 6 place de la Bastille, 12e. ☎ **01-43-42-90-32.** Reservations recommended. Main courses 120–190F ($22–$35); fixed-price menus 148–175F ($27–$32). AE, MC, V. Daily 10am–1am. Métro: Bastille. FRENCH.

Next to the Opéra Bastille, this large turn-of-the-century brasserie has a nice terrace surrounded by large verdant bushes; the ground-floor area is bright, while the upper-floor dining room is oak-trimmed and dimly lit. This would be an excellent choice for a pre-opera dinner or late-night supper. Seafood reigns supreme: platters of shellfish, plump oysters, pan-fried scallops, lobster au gratin, and salt-crusted grilled daurade (sea bream) bursting with flavor. The crowd is mixed, with a healthy dose of gays and lesbians, but the most visible group is dressed up middle-aged Parisians; during the day there are many "suits." If you order carefully, you could have a reasonably priced meal, though you might have to skip the lobster.

ST-GERMAIN-DES-PRES & THE LATIN QUARTER

Brasserie Lutétia. 45 bd. Raspail, 6e. ☎ **01-49-54-46-46.** Reservations recommended. Main courses 95–180F ($17–$33); fixed-price menus 155–195F ($28–$35). AE, DC, MC, V. Daily 7am–midnight. Métro: Sèvres-Babylone. FRENCH.

This 200-seat art-deco brasserie has become all the rage for those in the fashion world (designers, photographers, gorgeous models). There are a lot of mirrors (surprise, surprise), chrome, and artificial light in the bustling room. The youngish servers work very hard and try to stay friendly, but when it gets real busy you'll need some patience. This is one of the few places in Paris that has a set menu for vegetarians: figs and goat cheese for an appetizer followed by spiced rice with several kinds of vegetables sautéed or puréed with herbs, and poached peaches for dessert (this waif food for models on strict diets is actually delicious). But the real treat is the sumptuous seafood platters on ice (including raw shellfish) and other specials from the water, like the fine smoked salmon and cold lobster with lemony avocado. The specialty is roasted chicken with thyme and garlic served with yummy mashed potatoes (not for anorexic models). Save room for the desserts: apple crumble, roasted pears, coffee éclairs, and a delectable fig-and-almond sorbet. (If you're modeling after lunch, you might want to stick to the plain yogurt with fresh fruit.)

La Petite Cour. 8 rue Mabillon, 6e. ☎ **01-43-26-52-26.** Reservations recommended. Main courses 140–220F ($25–$40); fixed-price menus 170F ($30) at lunch, 210F ($38) at dinner. AE, MC, V. Daily noon–2:30pm and 7:30–11pm. Métro: Mabillon. FRENCH.

This must be the most charming garden restaurant in St-Germain-des-Prés. You'll dine in a little paved courtyard (*petite cour*) overflowing with bougainvillea and ivy, seated at elegant tables with white cloths. If it's winter, you'll be in the Napoléon III dining room. This place draws an elegant crowd of mostly straight French diners; tourists don't seem to come here much since it doesn't sit right on a busy road. Expect to dine on excellent French dishes with a Provençal touch, like *ravioli de langoustine à l'estragon* (prawn ravioli with tarragon), roasted leg of lamb with black olives and eggplant, seafood casserole with asparagus, and tender duck breast with nutmeg and honey. Try the awesome strawberry-and-raspberry soup with sweet red wine for dessert.

✪ **Le Bistro d'a Côte.** 16 bd. St-Germain, 5e. ☎ **01-43-54-59-10.** Reservations recommended. Main courses 110–180F ($20–$33); fixed-price menu 189F ($34). AE, MC, V. Mon–Fri noon–2:30pm and 7:30–11:30pm, Sat 7:30–11:30pm. Métro: Maubert-Mutualité. FRENCH.

Michel Rostang's baby bistro is still one of the area's best eateries. It's a small dining room with tables set very close together, making it difficult to have an intimate conversation (the diners are mostly French and middle-aged), but the food is exquisite and the prices are unbelievably reasonable. Start with what may well be Paris's best appetizer under 70F ($13): tender baked lamb with Acacia honey and spices in a thin crispy filo dough. (You may have to resist the urge to moan.) For the main course, go for the wonderful tuna with white beans (it almost tastes like osso bucco) or guinea fowl baked with wine and spices. Save room for the fabulous selection of goat cheeses—the best is the fresh chevre marinated in olive oil and thyme. Excellent half bottles of wine are 59F ($11).

Les Deux-Magots. 6 place St-Germain-des-Prés, 6e. ☎ **01-45-88-55-25.** Reservations recommended. Light meals 70–195F ($13–$35). MC, V. Daily 7:30am–1:30am. Métro: St-Germain-des-Prés. CAFE/FRENCH.

It used to be that locals and tourists flocked here just to sip coffee and people-watch, but ever since the cafes began claiming their right to serve decent meals, Deux-Magots has become a favorite for the hip crowd who prefer to eat and look at the same time. Grab a table on the terrace or in the brightly lit plush dining room with crystal chandeliers. This is where the intellectuals and writers used to come during the Roaring '20s and still come to this day. There's always a few gays and lesbians owing to the large number of modeling agencies in the area. Don't expect elaborate meals, just very French light fare like warm goat cheese on toast with a green salad. The club sandwiches are excellent, or try a delicious *croque monsieur* (toasted ham and cheese). If it's real busy, you'll need a lot of patience; the waiters become rude and pushy.

ON OR NEAR THE CHAMPS-ELYSEES

Café Indigo. 40 av. George-V, 8e. ☎ **01-47-20-89-56.** Main courses 95–145F ($17–$26). Daily noon–11pm. AE, DC, MC, V. Métro: George-V or Alma-Marceau. FRENCH.

Opened in summer 1998 just off the Champs-Elysées, this elegant place takes the laid-back ambience of a cafe (large armchairs in which you can lounge) and combines it with the light, simple menu of a good restaurant. Though you can come between meals and order just coffee, most of the young mixed crowd comes at mealtimes and orders three courses. The *salade niçoise* is excellent, as are the gazpacho and tasty salmon tartare. Main courses include a *faux fillet* (sirloin with homemade fries and béarnaise sauce on the side) and salmon rubbed with coarse salt and pan-fried, usually served rare unless you specify otherwise. The portions are small, leaving room for one of the desserts, which outdo the entrees: *le fondant de chocolat amer* has the delicate taste of a chocolate soufflé and the *millefeuille aux fraises* (napoleon with strawberries) is so carefully layered you won't want to upset the fabulous creation. The servers, young and attractive, are friendly and speak fluent English; the manager watches over everything with a smile (so rare in Paris).

Fakhr el Dine. 3 rue Quentin-Bauchart, 8e. ☎ **01-47-23-44-42.** Reservations recommended. Main courses 120–200F ($22–$36); fixed-price menus 170–360F ($30–$65). AE, MC, V. Daily noon–3pm and 7:30–11:30pm. Métro: George-V. LEBANESE.

There's no better place outside Beirut to try Lebanese food, in a slightly formal setting just off the Champs-Elysées. Come here for a leisurely meal, ask for a glass of *arak* (an aniseed drink similar to pastis or ouzo) or Lebanese wine, and order 8 to 20 little plates of *mezzes* (appetizers): delicate spinach pie, marinated eggplant, tangy dandelion salad, tabouli, creamy *hummus* (chick peas puréed with sesame butter and garlic), and the best little sausages stuffed with pine nuts, herbs, and spices. If you still have room for a main course, the grilled meat and chicken dishes are excellent, but be brave and go for something more exotic, like the *kibbe bi labban* (fragrant lamb and cracked wheat balls swimming in garlicky yogurt sauce). The desserts are wonderful, especially the *nammoura* (moist semolina cake with orange-blossom syrup) and the pastries filled with dates. The service is extremely courteous, and the international crowd means most of the somewhat older waiters speak passable English.

La Durée. 75 av. des Champs-Elysées, 8e. ☎ **01-40-75-08-75.** Reservations recommended. Main courses 110–150F ($20–$27); fixed-price menu 195F ($35). AE, DC, MC, V. Daily 8am–1am. Métro: George-V. FRENCH.

La Durée has been making the best macaroons in Paris since 1862, but its location on the Champs-Elysées was opened only a few years ago and instantly became a hit. The service is gracious if slightly rushed, and the endless stream of trendy Parisians make it an excellent spot for people-watching. In addition to the most amazing selection of macaroons (like the isphahan, with rose water and rose petal cream), you can have breakfast, lunch, afternoon tea, and dinner in the grand beaux arts dining room or on a lovely stretch of sidewalk. The small menu focuses on *les tartes salées chaudes* (warm salty pastry) like the melt-in-your-mouth *bouchée à la Reine* (puff pastry filled with veal, mushrooms, and spices) or an exquisite selection of quiches. Excellent choices are also the baked cod with candied lemons and green olives and the orgasmic homemade foie gras simply served with a green salad. The knockout desserts include the decadent *coupe La Durée* (chestnut ice cream with candied chestnut pieces and crème chantilly). You can buy sandwiches and goodies from the gourmet shop attached to the dining room.

La Fermette Marbeuf 1900. 5 rue Marbeuf, 8e. ☎ **01-53-23-08-00.** Reservations recommended. Main courses 140–200F ($25–$36); fixed-price menu 178F ($32). AE, DC, MC, V. Daily noon–3pm and 7–11:30pm. Métro: Alma-Marceau or George-V. FRENCH.

This belle-époque beauty was designated a national monument in 1983. Breathtaking etched glass lines the walls; don't forget to look up at the richly decorated ceiling. You'll dine on plush red velvety chairs among businesspeople and tourists. The service isn't a priority, though most of the waiters do speak good English. Gilbert Isaac has been consistently turning out classic French dishes for 15 years, and everything is tasty if not exactly haute cuisine. Try the braised veal sweetbreads (his specialty) served with mushrooms simmered in a separate casserole or the fillet of sole with basil and homemade pasta. The list of Bordeaux wines is impressive (prices vary widely, but there are a few reasonable selections). This is the place to go all out and try a Grand Marnier soufflé.

✪ **Le Petit Yvan.** 1 bis rue Jean-Mermoz, 8e. ☎ **01-42-89-49-65.** Reservations recommended. Fixed-price menu 168F ($31). AE, MC, V. Mon–Fri noon–2pm and 8–11:30pm, Sat 8pm–midnight. Métro: Franklin-Roosevelt. FRENCH.

This is one of the best values on the Right Bank, especially at such an excellent location steps from the Champs-Elysées. Next to the much more expensive Yvan, this baby bistro serves all the good food but without extra service or fancy presentations. It's frequently very busy, and the tables are crammed together in the homey dining room on two levels; try to arrive by 8pm for dinner and you might score a corner (and more private) table. The giant ravioli stuffed with crab is the best appetizer. For a main course, the tuna is magnificent, served with sautéed spinach and light pepper sauce. The three-course fixed-price menu is the only way to go, but you can opt for a salad with walnuts and a slice of cheese instead of dessert. If you have a sweet tooth, indulge it with the crème brûlée that comes with dried fruit.

Cafe Society

Before gay bars and clubs became the popular places to meet, greet, and contemplate lustful acts, Parisians headed to their cafes. Cafes are where the most passionate meetings of writers, artists, philosophers, and thinkers took place. It's a daily ritual now for Parisians to drop by their favorite cafe to meet an old friend or make a new one or even to sit in solitary seclusion with a coffee and a newspaper.

It all started at **Le Procope,** 13 rue de l'Ancienne-Comédie, 6e (☎ **01-40-46-79-00;** Métro: Odéon), opened in 1686, making it Paris's oldest cafe. Here you could find the likes of Voltaire, Verlaine, Robespierre, and Balzac. Oscar Wilde came here often too. Nowadays it's more of an upscale restaurant where you come for full meals. In the 1920s, the neo–art deco **Le Dôme,** 108 bd. du Montparnasse, 14e (☎ **01-43-35-25-81;** Métro: Vavin), became the focus of the English and American expat writers. Hemingway, Fitzgerald, Sylvia Beach, and Gertrude Stein frequently drank, talked, and argued here. André Gide's favorite cafe was the **Brasserie Lipp,** 151 bd. St-Germain-des-Prés, 6e (☎ **01-45-48-53-91;** Métro: St-Germain-des-Prés), known for its beer and *choucroute garni* (the best sauerkraut in Paris).

Across the street, **Café de Flore,** 172 bd. St-Germain, 6e (☎ **01-45-48-55-26;** Métro: St-Germain-des-Prés), will always be known for Simone de Beauvoir and Jean-Paul Sartre (they used it as if it were their living room, spending hours daily working and meeting friends). Djuna Barnes would come often and sit alone. In the 1950s, James Baldwin sat indoors and wrote all day, drinking cup after cup of coffee, then switching to alcohol in the evening. It's still a prime spot for people-watching and gets its share of gays and lesbians. When James Baldwin arrived in Paris in 1948, his first stop was **Les Deux-Magots** (see above), where he met James Wright. Later, in Giovanni's room, he wrote "I felt elated yet, as I walked down Raspail toward the Cafes of Montparnasse . . . Giovanni and I had walked there." He was referring to both La Coupole and La Closerie des Lilas. The immense art deco marvel **La Coupole,** 102 bd. du Montparnasse, 14e (☎ **01-43-20-14-20;** Métro: Vavin), was also a hot spot for Gertrude Stein and Alice B. Toklas, among countless others who came to dine on seafood and sip champagne. It's still a good place to spend a boisterous evening, though many of the patrons now are straight and not too colorful.

NEAR THE EIFFEL TOWER

La Fontaine de Mars. 129 rue St-Dominique, 7e. ☎ **01-47-05-46-44.** Reservations recommended. Main courses 70–140F ($13–$25). AE, MC, V. Mon–Sat noon–2:30pm and 7:30–11pm. Métro: Alma-Marceau or Ecole-Militaire. FRENCH.

In a quiet residential neighborhood, this down-to-earth place overlooks a charming fountain not far from the Eiffel Tower. It's great for alfresco dining on a warm summer's eve—grab a table on the large terrace, order a carafe of chilled rosé, and sit back and relax. Some of the professors and students from the nearby American University come here, but mostly it's a straight French crowd. Expect simple country-style food like grilled salmon steaks, pork chops, and *entrecôte* with frites (steak with french fries). The desserts are excellent, especially the cold fruit tarts served in summer; in winter, try the yummy warm apple pie with whipped cream.

La Gare. 19 chaussée de la Muette, 16e. ☎ **01-42-15-15-31.** Reservations recommended. Main courses 95–140F ($16–$25). AE, MC, V. Daily noon–3pm and 7pm–midnight. Métro: La Muette. INTERNATIONAL.

The most important literary cafe in Paris is **La Closerie des Lilas,** 171 bd. du Montparnasse, 6e (☎ **01-40-51-34-50;** Métro: Vavin). Hemingway describes it in *A Moveable Feast* as "one of the best cafes in Paris." He wrote a large part of *The Sun Also Rises* while standing at the bar. Oscar Wilde had come here many years before when it was a simpler place. Stein and Picasso often met here too. The "Pleasure Garden of the Lilies," as its name suggests, is still charming, and every day it fills with writers and artists on its lovely plant-studded terrace or in the wood-trimmed bar and elegant dining room.

Marcel Proust, ill and weak to the end, stayed on the Right Bank, preferring the quiet elegance of the bar at the **Hôtel Ritz,** 15 place Vendôme, 1e (☎ **01-43-16-30-30;** Métro: Concorde or Opéra). When he didn't want to be seen in public, he'd retreat upstairs to the suite named after him. There, wrapped in his fur coat, he entertained princesses and princes (most likely serving tea and madeleines). Even on his deathbed, Proust had the Ritz on his mind. On the morning of November 18, 1922, Proust sent his driver, Odilon, to get cold beer, predicting gloomily that "like everything else, it will come too late." But Odilon returned to hear Proust murmur some of his last words: "Thank you, my dear Odilon, for fetching the beer at the Ritz." Place Vendôme, facing the hotel, is still a prime spot for spotting the rich and celebrated; the paparazzi loiter here at all hours.

Nowadays, most of the gay writers and artists frequent the cafes around Les Halles and the Marais. **Café Beaubourg,** 100 rue St-Martin, 4e (☎ **01-48-87-63-96;** Métro: Rambuteau), is one of the trendiest spots, where a mix of gays, lesbians, and straights meet and chat the night away while watching the beautiful people go by. In the heart of the Marais, **Open Café,** 17 rue des Archives, 4e (☎ **01-42-72-26-18;** Métro: Hôtel-de-Ville), occupies a lovely corner that elevates boy-watching to an art. Small tables are crammed together (perfect for an impromptu conversation with your neighbor) on the sidewalk, and all the men's attention is focused on the street and the *assortiments* of goodies walking on it. Even while standing at the bar inside, you can watch the street through the huge open windows. This is where many gay writers, artists, and their lovers will congregate well into the 21st century.

This airy restaurant, a 20-minute walk from the Eiffel Tower, used to be the Muette train station and has been redone with its history in mind. The vast dining room used to be the platform where passengers boarded trains, the bar used to be the station buffet, and in the huge garden a few cargo train cars are home to lush plants and bushes (there's terrace seating in summer). The neighborhood is very upscale, and you'll find many local wealthy boys (most straight) bellied up to the bar or having dinner with their girlfriends. It's a younger crowd and very French; few tourists venture here. Don't expect fine dining but rather an eclectic mix of dishes well prepared if not awesome. The gazpacho is nice on a summer day, or try the hearty cassoulet (white beans simmered in tomato sauce) with wild mushrooms instead of duck. The Nebraska steak is succulent and the roast chicken garlicky and good. A must-try dessert is the *baba au rhum* (sponge cake doused with rum and crowned with a slice of pineapple).

Tant Qu'il y Aura des Hommes. 1 rue Jean-Bologne, 16e. ☎ **01-45-27-76-64.** Main courses 89–160F ($16–$29). MC, V. Tues–Sat noon–2pm and 7:45–10:15pm. Métro: Passy or La Muette. FRENCH.

The name of this restaurant is the most intriguing aspect of it—literally translated, it means "As Long As There Will Be Men." It's not a gay place, but the name refers to the heavy (and manly) food served, much different from the usual delicate French dishes found in most restaurants. This is country-farmhouse cuisine with big flavors and hearty portions. If you've been hankering to try one of the many kinds of French sausages (you know what I mean), this would be the place. The *saucisse du Buron* (a thick sausage) is chewy but good, served with *cornichons* (little pickles). Try the half-chicken rubbed with spices, herbs, and garlic or a thick slab of Aubrac beef. There's usually at least two fish specials (cod, salmon, or sole) and a good selection of market vegetables and interesting side dishes like *farsou* (little pancakes with fresh herbs). You'll dine among locals; to get here, walk down rue de l'Exposition, where the neighborhood *marché* (open-air market) happens daily except Monday.

IN MONTMARTRE

Chez Les Fondus. 17 rue des Trois-Frères, 18e. ☎ **01-42-55-22-65.** Reservations recommended. Fixed-price menu 89F ($16). No credit cards. Tues–Sat 7pm–midnight. Métro: Abbesses or Anvers. FONDUE.

If you're looking for a fun, unusual, and cheap place, look no further. This hilly neighborhood close to Sacré-Coeur is home to many inexpensive eateries, but this is the most original. There are only two long wooden tables in this hole-in-the-wall, and you'll have to jump over the table to get into the inside seats (such acrobatics are encouraged by the boisterous waiters). Chatting with your neighbors is an inevitable part of the experience. As soon as you're seated, you'll be served red wine in little baby bottles. The waiters won't accept you drinking from a glass (those are the rules and are strictly followed), so if you come here you're destined to suck on a nipple (!). Dinner is your choice of *fondue bourguigonne* (meat) or *savoyarde* (cheese), with a little plate of dried sausage as an appetizer. Most of the diners are under 30, cute, seemingly straight, and intent on having a good time. The cheese fondue is tasty but too heavy for some; the meat is tender and comes with several sauces. For dessert, you'll get a whole frozen orange filled with sorbet.

4 Exploring Paris

The best way to explore Paris is on foot. You can walk from monument to monument and museum to museum, keeping each walk to less than 45 minutes. For example, you can stroll from the Arc de Triomphe to the Louvre (passing through the Champs-Elysées, place de la Concorde, and rue de Rivoli), from place de la Bastille to Notre-Dame (passing through place des Vosges and the Marais), from Les Halles to St-Germain-des-Prés (passing through the Latin Quarter), and so on. Stop at a cafe to recharge or take the Métro if you get tired. Hopping on a bus or a boat on the Seine will give your legs, but not your eyes, a rest.

Everybody wants to see the Louvre, the world's largest and most magnificent museum. But while you're there don't try to see more than is humanly possible—it'll only get you frustrated and exhausted. And be aware that if you just can't leave Paris without seeing the big draws—*Mona Lisa, Venus de Milo, Winged Victory*—you're going to face unbelievable crowds. I tell my friends who are visiting Paris for the first time to hit a smaller museum first, such as the Musée Rodin: Not only are the sculptures exquisite, but the mansion and museum gardens are themselves testimony to a bygone era of grandness and you get to stroll around in relative serenity not possible in the larger museums. Instead of cramming in several sights per day, try to incorporate a visit with something leisurely and fun; there's so much to see in Paris and you don't want to burn out. Take a picnic lunch and sit with the hundreds of backpackers on the steps of Sacré-Coeur (with its breathtaking city view) instead of just rushing in and out of the church. Or stretch out on the grass on Champs-de-Mars under the Eiffel Tower and marvel at its height. If it's a nice day, you can sit on the riverbank not far from Notre-Dame and hold hands with your sweetheart or rent a bike and meander around the Bois de Boulogne (better yet, rent a little rowboat and open a bottle of wine in the middle of the lake, creating your very own impressionist moment).

Another way to get oriented is by guided tour. The most reputable companies are **ParisVision,** 214 rue de Rivoli, 1e (☎ **01-42-60-30-01;** www.parisvision.com; Métro: Palais-Royal), and **Cityrama,** 4 place des Pyramides, 1e (☎ **01-44-55-61-00;** www.cityrama.com; Métro: Pyramides). Both offer 2-hour (150F/$27), 4-hour (240F/$44), and full-day (505F/$92) tours on air-conditioned double-decker coaches. Pickup can be arranged from major hotels. These companies also offer excellent tours to Versailles, Giverny, Chartres, the Champagne and Loire regions, and other popular day trips. If a more personalized service appeals to you, try **TouringScope,** 11 bis bd. Haussmann, 9e (☎ **01-53-34-11-91;** www.touringscope.com; Métro: Chausée d'Antin). It offers many itineraries using small white vans with large windows. Prices range from 150F ($27) for a 3-hour tour to 520F ($95) for a full tour of Paris, including the Louvre and lunch (with wine).

To see Paris from the water, you can take a 1-hour cruise on the boats called **Bateaux-Mouches** (☎ **01-42-25-96-10**), departing from the pont de l'Alma (Métro: Alma-Marceau). If it's warm, you can sit out on the deck as the slow boat meanders up and down the Seine, passing under beautiful bridges and alongside Notre-Dame and the Eiffel Tower. The loud commentary in six languages is rather irritating; you might want to bring headphones and your favorite music. Boats depart every 30 minutes 10am to 11pm, costing 40F ($7). Call ahead during foul weather, as tours might be canceled.

If you want to follow a prescribed walking tour of the city—of, say, the Latin Quarter or Père-Lachaise Cemetery—check out the 11 strolls in *Frommer's Memorable Walks in Paris.*

THE HITS YOU SHOULDN'T MISS

✪ **Musée du Louvre.** 34–36 quai du Louvre, 1er. ☎ **01-40-20-53-17,** or 01-40-20-51-51 for recorded information; advance credit card sales 01-49-87-54-54. www.louvre.fr. Admission 45F ($8) before 3pm, 26F ($4.75) after 3pm and all day Sun. Free first Sun of every month. Mon and Wed 9am–9:45pm (Mon, short tour only), Thurs–Sun to 6pm. 90-minute English-language tours leave Mon and Wed–Sat at various times for 17F ($3). Métro: Palais-Royal–Musée-du-Louvre.

This is the world's largest museum, housing over 30,000 works of art. It's also the world's largest palace—built as a fortress in 1200, it became the royal residence three centuries later (half Gothic, half Renaissance) and finally opened as a museum in 1793. Most of the works were purchased by or were willed to the kings of France, most notably Louis XVIII, Charles X, and Louis-Philippe (the works Napoléon pillaged from every country he conquered were returned to their owners in 1815).

The latest (and very controversial) addition to the Louvre, I. M. Pei's **glass pyramid,** was completed in 1989 and is the main entrance (it looks fabulous all lit up at night). Escalators carry you down through the pyramid to the giant marble lobby where you buy tickets, check bags, and disperse to the various wings. Pick up a detailed map here. The three wings are **Richelieu, Sully,** and **Denon.** As I said above, don't even try to see everything. Pick a "department" (Paintings; Greek, Etruscan and Roman Antiquities; Art Objects; and so on) that interests you most and go there.

For virgins, a leisurely stroll will give you an idea of the vastness and complexity of this place. The 90-minute guided tour will give you a first taste. Or you can just relax, bring your Walkman (to block out other people's conversations), and let your eyes marvel. The most famous works are the *Mona Lisa,* where people gather 10 deep to catch a glimpse (it's not worth the pushing and shoving); the armless *Venus de Milo,* discovered in 1820 and bought by the French government for 6,000 francs; and the *Winged Victory of Samothrace.* The newest department (opened in 1998) chronicles the art of ancient Egypt from the earliest times to Cleopatra. The Napoléon III apartments with their priceless objets d'art are worth a day's visit alone. Whatever you do, don't miss the divine sculptures (many of rippled Greek gods) by Donatello and Bellini and the achingly beautiful *Psyche and Cupid* by Canova. The most moving work, however, is Michelangelo's *The Slaves,* exuding centuries of anger, fierceness, and virility. This giant sculpture (carved between 1513 and 1520) of men shackled and weighed down with the immense burden of history could very well be the most heart-wrenching work of art in the world.

While you're here, be sure to stop in at **Café Marly** (see "Whet Your Appetite" above).

Musée d'Orsay. 1 rue de Bellechasse or 62 rue de Lille, 7e. ☎ **01-40-49-48-48.** www.musee-orsay.fr. Admission 40F ($7); 30F ($6) on Sun. Tues–Wed and Fri–Sat 10am–6pm, Thurs to 9:45pm, Sun 9am–6pm. June 20–Sept 20 opens 9am. Métro: Solférino.

This magnificent museum opened in the mid-1980s after years of construction that transformed the early 1900s Gare d'Orsay (a rail station) into the neoclassical home for a significant number of impressionist and post-impressionist works (Toulouse-Lautrec, Manet, Renoir). Many of these works were on display at the Louvre until 1947, when they were moved to a lovely little Jeu de Paume in the Tuileries (now open for temporary exhibits only). There Manet's 1863 *Le Déjeuner sur l'herbe* was displayed in a room by itself (as if it were too salacious to be with the others) and you could spend hours in quiet contemplation. When the Musée d'Orsay, a bright open space (you'll love the arching glass roof), opened, the works were moved here. Lovers of impressionist art might find the setting too distracting to truly appreciate the work; others claim this is the most successful new museum in the world.

In addition to Manet's paintings, don't miss Paul Cézanne's *Les Baigneurs* (The Swimmers) with its quiet eroticism, the many dancers of Degas, van Gogh's infamous self-portrait, and Renoir's *Moulin de la Galette.* And of course there's *Whistler's Mother.* A special section is dedicated to Gaugin's Tahitian period, and decorative arts rooms contain fabulous art-nouveau and belle-époque furniture, ceramics, and glassware. Lesser-known works are worth a glimpse too: Gustave Caillebotte's 1875 painting the *Raboteurs des parquets* (3 shirtless guys waxing hardwood floors) is sublimely erotic, and John Delville's 1898 *L'Ecole de Platon* (12 naked men and Jesus) is stunning. The museum's Café des Hauters is a great place to refuel.

Arc de Triomphe. Place Charles-de-Gaulle–Etoile, 16e. ☎ **01-55-37-73-77.** Admission 35F ($6). Apr–Sept daily 9:30am–11pm, Oct–Mar daily 10am–10:30pm. Métro: Charles-de-Gaulle–Etoile.

One of Paris's most famous landmarks, the Arc de Triomphe was commissioned by Napoléon to commemorate his many victories and is the world's biggest triumphal arch (163 feet high and 147 feet wide). It sits on the busiest intersection in Paris—12 avenues (the Champs-Elysées being the most famous) emanate from here, and the traffic at best can be described as insane (to get here, take the underground passageways from the Métro station—don't try to cross the square). The monument was completed in 1836 under the reign of Louis-Philippe, and four years later Napoléon's remains passed beneath on the way to his tomb at the Hôtel des Invalides (below). The Arc de Triomphe has since become the main focus of state funerals. (In 1885, Victor Hugo's body was placed under the arch, and throngs of Parisians came to pay tribute to the

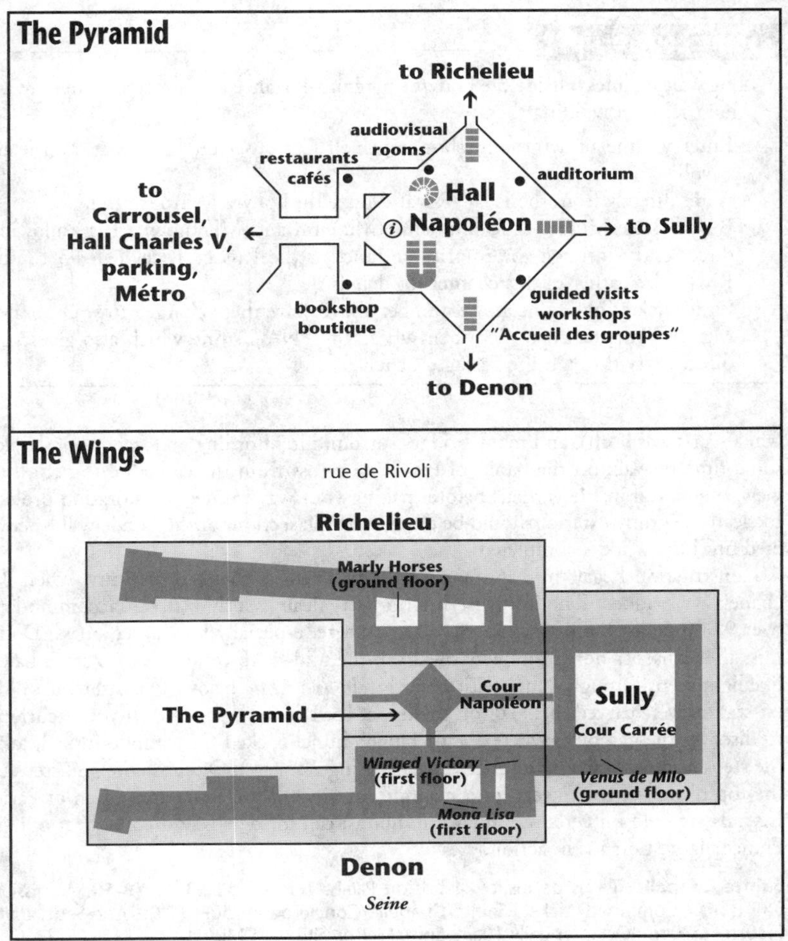

great writer.) In 1940, the Nazis marched underneath when they occupied the city, and in 1944 a happier parade (the Liberation of Paris) passed through. Several 19th-century sculptures cover the arch, most notably Rude's *La Marseillaise* on the Champs-Elysées side. Climb up or take an elevator to the top (162 feet and 284 steps high) where you have a panoramic view stretching all the way to the obelisk in place de la Concorde in one direction and all the way to the Grande Arche de La Défense in the other.

✪ **Cathédrale Notre-Dame.** 6 place du Parvis Notre-Dame, 4e. ☎ **01-42-34-56-10.** Cathedral, free; towers and crypt 32F ($6); museum and treasury 15F ($2.75). Cathedral daily 8am–6:45pm year-round; towers and crypt Apr–Sept daily 9:30am–6pm, Oct–Mar daily 10am–4:15pm; museum Wed and Sat–Sun 2:30–6pm; treasury Mon–Sat 9:30–11:30am and 12:30–5:30pm. Métro: Cité or St-Michel.

This Gothic masterpiece of the Middle Ages is France's most famous structure, and over 12 million people come each year to marvel at the beauty of its facade and its interior. It's located on the tiny Ile de la Cité in the middle of the Seine (the island

Some Louvre Tips

Long waiting lines outside the Louvre's pyramid entrance are notorious, but here are some tricks for avoiding them:

- Enter via the underground shopping mall Carrousel du Louvre at 99 rue de Rivoli.
- Enter directly from the Palais-Royal–Musée du Louvre Métro station.
- Buy a Carte Musées et Monuments (Museum and Monuments Pass) allowing direct entry through the priority entrance at the Passage Richelieu, 93 rue de Rivoli. See earlier in this chapter for details.
- Order tickets by phone at the number above, have them charged to your Visa or MasterCard, and then pick them up at any FNAC store, which also gives you direct entry through the Passage Richelieu.

---

where Paris was born), and many bridges surround it, affording good photo ops. Take some time to walk on the banks of the Seine across from the cathedral to get a full view, then stroll in the gardens before making your way inside. A restoration project to clean the grimy exterior should be done by 2000; sections of the facade will be covered until the work is completed.

Construction began in 1163 and was completed in the 14th century, when 37 chapels were added. The immense interior is typically Gothic (it can accommodate over 9,000 people) and worshipers still flock here, especially for Sunday mass. Don't miss the transept's north rose window, from the mid–13th century; at sunset, a halo-like light seeps through, illuminating the *Virgin and Child* below. The cathedral's oldest statues were carved in 1170 (on the upper level of the typanum). If you're curious to discover the gargoyles where Victor Hugo's hunchbacked Quasimodo lurked, take the steps leading to the twin square towers (rising 225 feet). Or climb the 387 steps to the top of one of the towers for a magnificent view of the Seine and much of Paris. Recitals are held on certain Sunday afternoons; call for details and come hear one of France's largest organs in action.

Sainte-Chapelle. Palais de Justice, 4 bd. du Palais, 1er. ☎ **01-53-73-78-50.** Admission 35F ($6). Combined ticket Sainte-Chapelle/Conciergerie 50F ($9). Apr–Sept daily 9:30am–6:30pm; Oct–Mar daily 10am–5pm. Métro: Cité or St-Michel.

After Notre-Dame, Sainte-Chapelle on Ile de la Cité is the most important monument in Paris. Proust called it "the pearl among them all," referring to Gothic cathedrals. Built in a record three years (completed in 1248), the chapel has two levels. You enter through the lower chapel, which was used by the servants of the palace. To ascend to the upper chapel, where the king and his courtiers sat, take the narrow spiral stairs. Here you can best appreciate the stars of Sainte-Chapelle: 15 magnificent stained-glass windows (the oldest in Paris). They illustrate scenes from both the Old and the New Testament and boast incredibly full-bodied and vivid colors. The over 1,000 scenes create a visual multicolored bible: Genesis (Adam and Eve), Exodus (Moses on Mt. Sinai) and the Apocalypse (a flamboyant rose window divided into 86 panels), and so on. They haven't faded with time (though they were removed during the Revolution and the two world wars) and the whole structure hasn't suffered a crack in seven centuries. Of course, try to visit on a sunny day so you can fully appreciate those windows. Concerts are frequently held in the evenings.

Conciergerie. 1 quai de l'Horloge, 1er. ☎ **01-53-73-78-50.** Admission 35F ($6). Combined ticket Sainte-Chapelle/Conciergerie 50F ($9). Apr–Sept daily 9:30am–6:30pm; Oct–Mar daily 10am–5pm. Métro: Cité or St-Michel.

Most of this building dates from the 14th century, when Philippe le Bel decided to extend the ancient Capetian palace that once stood here. Later, this building's prisons were used as holding cells for the Revolution's tribunals. Marie Antoinette was held here before her execution; others imprisoned prior to execution included Robespierre and Danton. You can visit the renovated cells where these unfortunates spent their last days and hours and marvel at the vagaries of fate.

Eiffel Tower (Tour Eiffel). Champ-de-Mars, 7e. ☎ **01-44-11-23-23.** www.tour-eiffel.fr. First landing 20F ($3.65); second landing 42F ($8); third landing 59F ($11); stairs to second landing 14F ($3). Sept–May daily 9:30am–11pm; June–Aug daily 9am–midnight (fall and winter, stairs close at 6:30pm). Métro: Trocadéro or Bir-Hakeim.

This is the first image of Paris most of us know as kids (before puberty kicks in and such large pointy erections take on a whole new meaning—at least for us boys). Once you see this landmark up close you won't be disappointed. The Eiffel Tower is truly visible from every part of the city and often a good way to get your bearings. Built for the 1889 Universal Exhibition by Gustave-Alexandre Eiffel, the tower wasn't meant to be permanent, and many Parisians wanted it destroyed (among them writer Guy de Mauspassant and architect Charles Garnier, creator of the Paris Opéra). Three hundred luminaries signed a petition in protest, but slowly they succumbed to its charm as poets and artists began celebrating it. The tower (with the added length of a 55-foot TV antenna) is 1,056 feet high. Over 5 million visitors per year stand in line waiting for the elevators to whisk them up (the stairs are an option too) for the most panoramic vista of all Paris and the Ile de France. There are three levels (the first is where the Jules Verne restaurant is located). To get the best views, you have to climb to the second or third level (where you can see as far as 40 miles away on a clear day). Try to get here early in the morning to avoid long lines or come in the evening, when it's beautifully lit and the crowds are thinner (after 8pm). Throughout 1999, the tower will display huge lit numbers you can see from all over the city: a countdown to 2000.

Hôtel des Invalides (Napoléon's Tomb). Place des Invalides, 7e. ☎ **01-44-42-37-77.** Admission to Musée de l'Armée, Napoléon's Tomb, and Musée des Plans-Reliefs 37F ($7). Oct–Mar daily 10am–5pm; Apr–May and Sept daily to 6pm; June–Aug daily to 7pm. Closed Jan 1, May 1, Nov 1, and Dec 25. Métro: Latour-Maubourg, Varenne, or Invalides.

The immense "hotel" housing Napoléon's tomb was built in 1670 by the Sun King as a kind gesture to the thousands of crippled men who fought his wars (thus the name). The sprawling structure has an air of somberness; as you enter its cobblestone courtyard, you'll see several ominous-looking cannons lined as if ready to blow you away.

The New Millennium & the New Pompidou

In the cruisy, slightly seedy area of Les Halles, the main attraction is the immense **Centre Pompidou,** place Georges-Pompidou or plateau Beaubourg, 1er (☎ **01-44-78-12-33;** www.cnac-gp.fr; Métro: Châtelet–Les Halles), most of which has been closed for major renovations since 1997. It plans to reopen fully on January 1, 2000. You can still stroll around and admire what has been called the most avant-garde building in the world (others call it hideously impersonal, with shiny glass and colorful exposed pipes). It's very much a 1970s creation (only Charles de Gaulle airport rivals it in its eccentric modernity). Within its sharp-edged walls you'll find the **National Modern Art Museum (Musée National d'Art Moderne)** and the **Public Information Library (Bibliothèque Publique d'Informations),** both of which attract a sizable number of gays and lesbians. Wild celebrations are expected here on December 31, 1999, to welcome the new millennium and the new Pompidou.

Paris Attractions

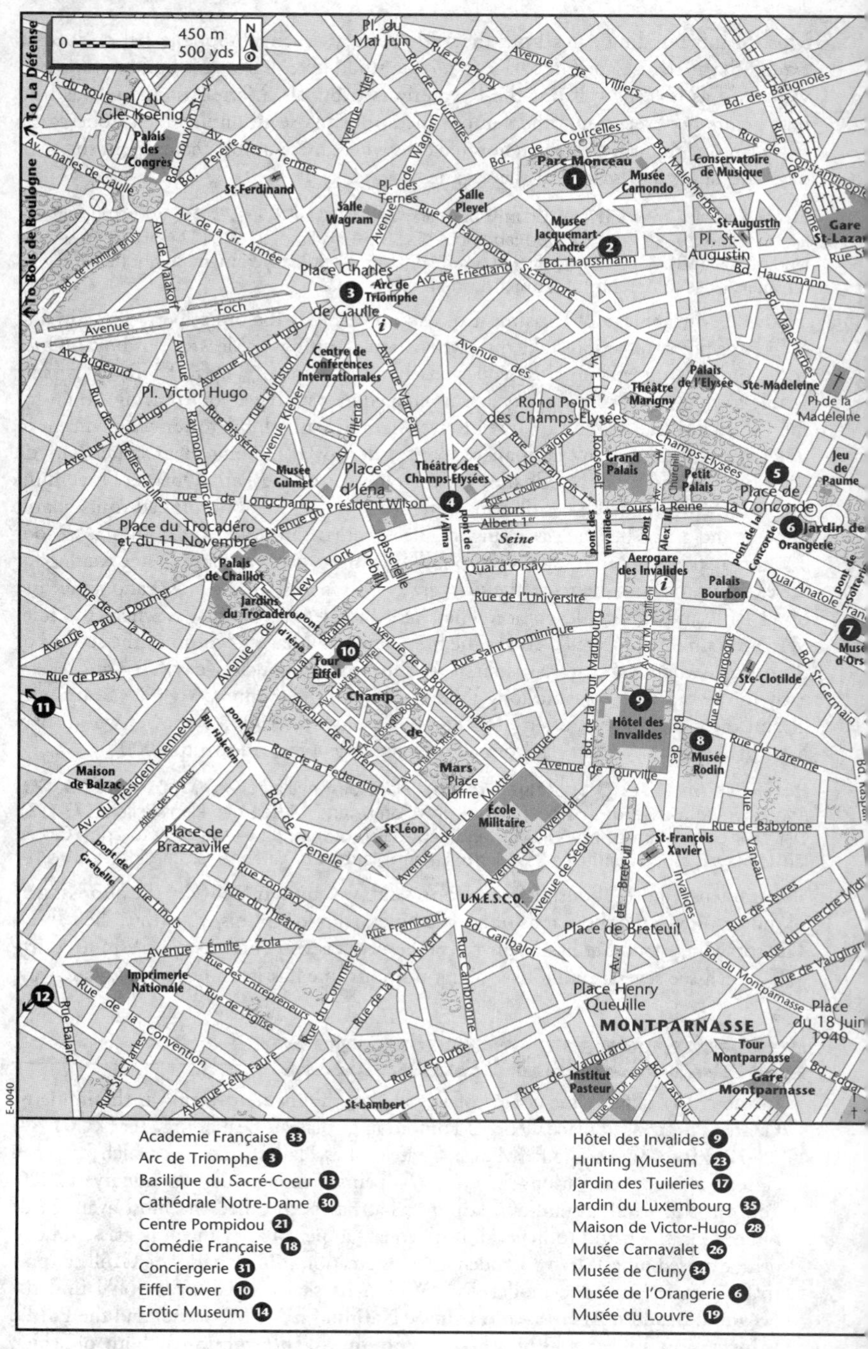

Academie Française 33
Arc de Triomphe 3
Basilique du Sacré-Coeur 13
Cathédrale Notre-Dame 30
Centre Pompidou 21
Comédie Française 18
Conciergerie 31
Eiffel Tower 10
Erotic Museum 14
Hôtel des Invalides 9
Hunting Museum 23
Jardin des Tuileries 17
Jardin du Luxembourg 35
Maison de Victor-Hugo 28
Musée Carnavalet 26
Musée de Cluny 34
Musée de l'Orangerie 6
Musée du Louvre 19

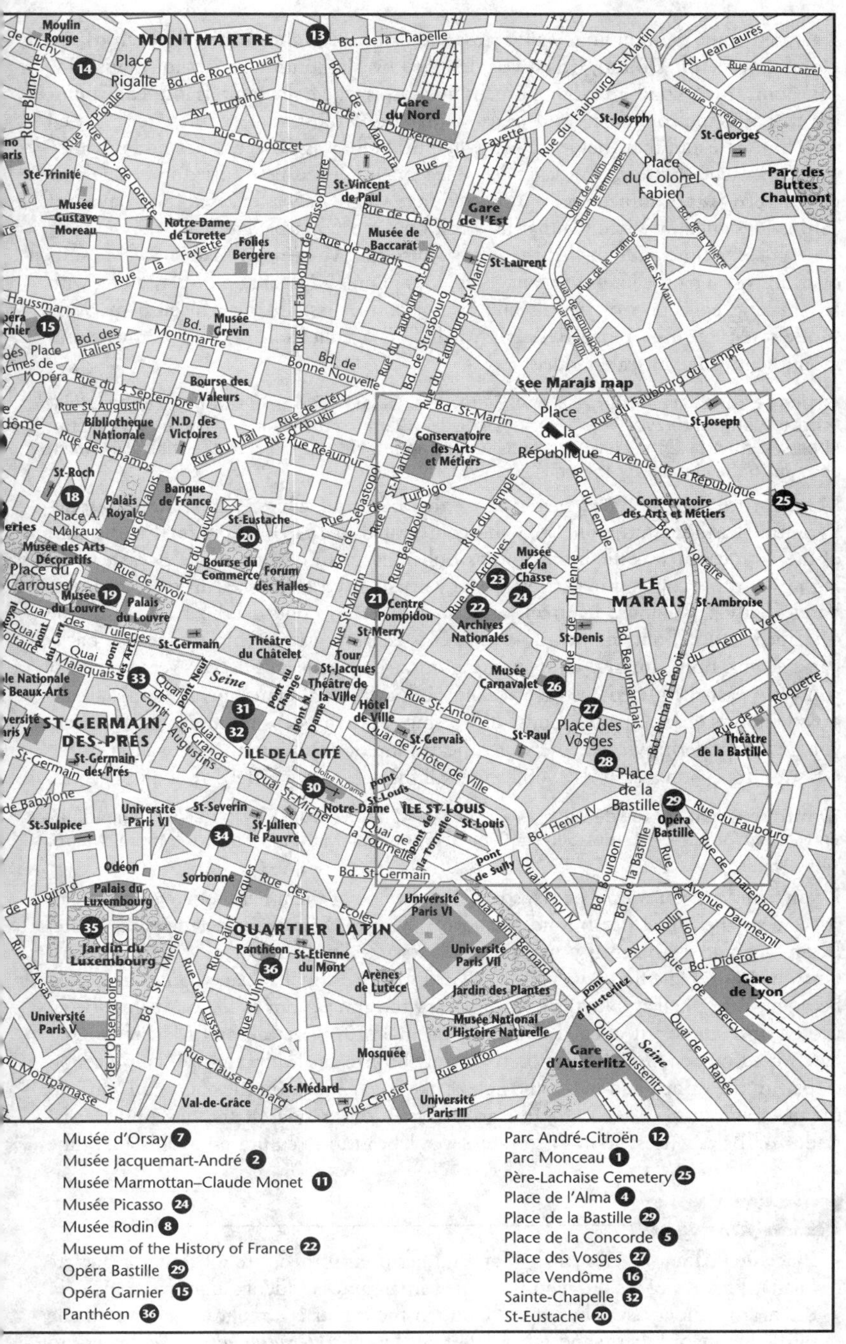

Moulin Rouge
MONTMARTRE
Place Pigalle
Bd. de Rochechouart
Bd. de la Chapelle
Rue Blanche
Rue Pigalle
Av. Trudaine
Rue de Dunkerque
Gare du Nord
Rue Condorcet
Rue N.D. de Lorette
Ste-Trinité
Musée Gustave Moreau
Notre-Dame de Lorette
Folies Bergère
Rue la Fayette
Rue du Faubourg Poissonnière
St-Vincent de Paul
Rue de Chabrol
Gare de l'Est
Musée de Baccarat
Rue de Paradis
St-Laurent
Bd. de Magenta
Rue du Faubourg St-Martin
Av. Jean Jaurès
Rue Armand Carrel
Avenue Secrétan
St-Joseph
St-Georges
Place du Colonel Fabien
Parc des Buttes Chaumont
Quai de Valmy
Quai de Jemmapes
Bd. de la Villette
Rue de la Grange
Rue St-Maur
Haussmann
Opéra Garnier
Bd. des Italiens
Place de l'Opéra
Bd. Montmartre
Musée Grevin
Bd. de Bonne Nouvelle
Rue du 4 Septembre
Bourse des Valeurs
Rue St. Augustin
Bibliothèque Nationale
N.D. des Victoires
Rue du Mail
Rue de Cléry
Rue d'Abukir
Rue Réaumur
Rue des Champs
St-Roch
Palais Royal
Banque de France
Place A. Malraux
St-Eustache
Rue de Valois
Rue du Louvre
Musée des Arts Décoratifs
Place du Carrousel
Bourse du Commerce
Forum des Halles
Rue de Rivoli
Musée du Louvre
Palais du Louvre
Quai des Tuileries
Quai Voltaire
Quai Malaquais
St-Germain
Théâtre du Châtelet
Seine
pont Neuf
pont des Arts
pont du Carr.
pont au Change
pont N. Dame
Quai de Conti
Quai des Grands Augustins
Tour St-Jacques
Théâtre de la Ville
Hôtel de Ville
ST-GERMAIN-DES-PRÉS
St-Germain-des-Prés
ÎLE DE LA CITÉ
Notre-Dame
Cloître N. Dame
Quai St-Michel
St-Severin
St-Julien le Pauvre
Université Paris VI
St-Sulpice
Odéon
Palais du Luxembourg
Jardin du Luxembourg
Sorbonne
Rue des Écoles
Rue St. Jacques
QUARTIER LATIN
Panthéon
St-Etienne du Mont
Arènes de Lutèce
Rue Gay Lussac
Rue d'Ulm
Bd. St. Michel
Rue d'Assas
Université Paris V
Av. de l'Observatoire
Rue Clause Bernard
Val-de-Grâce
St-Médard
Mosquée
Rue Censier
Université Paris III
Rue Buffon
Jardin des Plantes
Musée National d'Histoire Naturelle
Université Paris VII
Gare d'Austerlitz
Quai d'Austerlitz
pont d'Austerlitz
Quai Saint Bernard
Quai Henry IV
Bd. St-Germain
Quai de la Tournelle
pont de la Tournelle
pont de Sully
ÎLE ST-LOUIS
St-Louis
pont St-Louis
Quai de l'Hôtel de Ville
St-Gervais
Rue St-Antoine
St-Paul
Bd. Henry IV
Bd. Bourdon
Bd. de la Bastille
Centre Pompidou
St-Merry
Rue Beaubourg
Rue de Turbigo
Bd. de Sebastopol
Rue St-Martin
Conservatoire des Arts et Métiers
Rue du Temple
Rue des Archives
Archives Nationales
Musée de la Chasse
Musée Carnavalet
Rue de Turenne
St-Denis
Place des Vosges
Place de la Bastille
Opéra Bastille
see Marais map
Bd. St-Martin
Place de la République
Bd. du Temple
Avenue de la République
Rue du Faubourg du Temple
LE MARAIS
Bd. Beaumarchais
Bd. Richard Lenoir
Bd. Voltaire
St-Ambroise
Rue du Chemin Vert
Rue de la Roquette
Théâtre de la Bastille
Rue du Faubourg
Rue de Charenton
Avenue Daumesnil
Rue de Lyon
Av. L. Rollin
Bd. Diderot
Gare de Lyon
Rue de Bercy
Quai de la Rapée
Musée d'Orsay 7
Musée Jacquemart-André 2
Musée Marmottan–Claude Monet 11
Musée Picasso 24
Musée Rodin 8
Museum of the History of France 22
Opéra Bastille 29
Opéra Garnier 15
Panthéon 36
Parc André-Citroën 12
Parc Monceau 1
Père-Lachaise Cemetery 25
Place de l'Alma 4
Place de la Bastille 29
Place de la Concorde 5
Place des Vosges 27
Place Vendôme 16
Sainte-Chapelle 32
St-Eustache 20

After you enter the building, walk across the Court of Honor to the **Church of the Dome (Eglise du Dôme),** which was designed by Hardouin-Mansart for Louis XIV. The dome, the second-tallest monument in Paris, is where the tomb is located. Rumor has it that Napoléon's penis and heart (a man's two most vital organs) aren't buried with him here and that they were lost when his body was dissected (it's not as if they were misplacing car keys, but legends are legends). He was first buried in St. Helena, but in 1861 was exhumed and transported here where he was encased in six layers of coffins (designed by Visconti) that now rest on a green marble base. For the butch in you, set some time aside to visit the **Army Museum (Musée de l'Armée),** where suits of armor worn by the kings of France (including Louis XIV) are on display along with an amazing collection of swords and Napoleonic relics. In the **Museum of Scale Models (Musée des Plans-Reliefs),** you'll find a collection of French towns and monuments done in scale models.

Basilique du Sacré-Coeur. Place St-Pierre, 18e. ☎ **01-53-41-89-00.** Basilica, free; joint ticket to dome and crypt 30F ($6). Apr–Sept daily 9am–7pm; Oct–Mar daily to 6pm. Métro: Abbesses; then take the elevator to the surface and follow the signs to the funicular, which goes up to the church, for the price of one Métro ticket.

Montmartre, the hilly area surrounding this beautiful white marble Romanesque-Byzantine basilica (started in 1873 and consecrated in 1919), was known at the turn of the 20th century as the heart of Paris Bohemia (picture Mimi in *La Bohème* walking down these cobblestone streets). Many artists lived or worked in this neighborhood (Berlioz, Toulouse-Lautrec), and now the scene outside the basilica can be described as neo-Bohemia or turn-of-the-21st-century grunge (mostly teenage backpackers with beer cans and joints wearing unwashed jeans and fleece sweaters). Fight your way past the glazed-eyed crowd and peek at the elaborate mosaics and stained-glass windows decorating this house of worship. Take the steps up to the dome, where you get a wonderful view of the sacred heart's interior and a tremendous vista of the city's rooftops—on a clear day you can see all the way to the Eiffel Tower and beyond.

✪ **Musée Rodin.** 77 rue de Varenne, 7e. ☎ **01-44-18-61-10.** www.musee-rodin.fr. Admission 28F ($5). Apr–Sept Tues–Sun 9:30am–5:45pm; Oct–Mar Tues–Sun to 4:45pm. Métro: Varenne.

If you're in Paris for only 3 hours, spend at least one of them here. On a very Parisian street near the Hôtel des Invalides (above), this lovely museum occupies the Hôtel Biron, a grand 18th-century mansion that was Rodin's studio from 1910 until his death in 1917. (The house was built in 1728 for a wealthy Parisian wigmaker; it then became a dance hall and finally a residence for the ambassador of the tsar before being turned into studios; it opened as a museum in 1919.) Cocteau and Matisse worked here for a time too. You'll find Rodin's mainly bronze and white marble sculptures on display in the garden and inside the house, like *The Thinker* (in the courtyard, close to the main entrance), *The Kiss* (on the ground floor of the house), and his controversial nudes of Balzac (upstairs). There are several beautiful sculptures by his longtime

For Diana Fans

Place de l'Alma (Métro: Alma-Marceau) has been turned into a tribute to the late Diana, Princess of Wales, who was killed in an auto accident August 31, 1997, in the nearby underpass. The bronze flame in the center is a replication of the flame in the Statue of Liberty and was a 1989 gift by the *International Herald Tribune* to honor Franco-American friendship. Many bouquets, messages, and photographs are *still* placed around the flame, which seems to have come to represent the Princess.

Notre-Dame de Paris

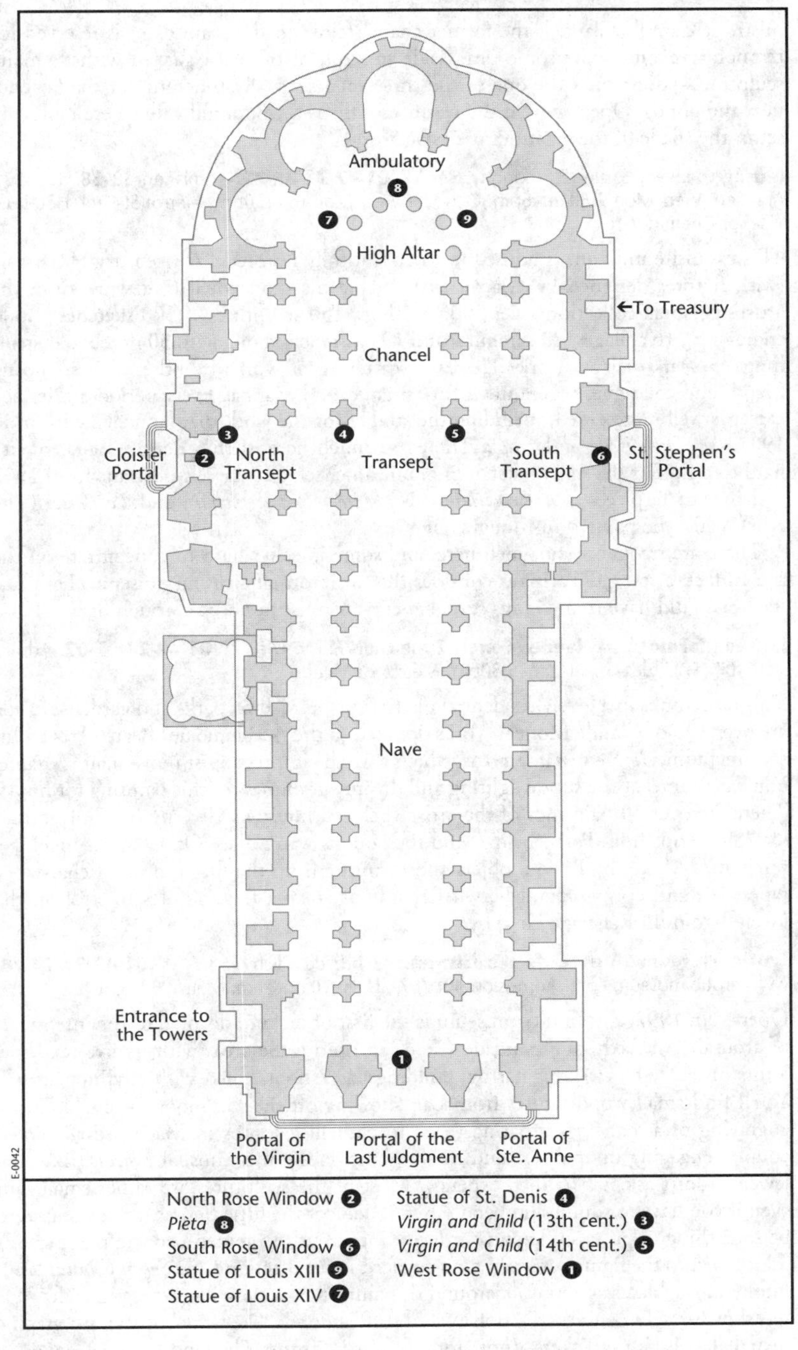
Ambulatory
High Altar
To Treasury
Chancel
Cloister Portal
North Transept
Transept
South Transept
St. Stephen's Portal
Nave
Entrance to the Towers
Portal of the Virgin
Portal of the Last Judgment
Portal of Ste. Anne
E-0042
North Rose Window 2
Pièta 8
South Rose Window 6
Statue of Louis XIII 9
Statue of Louis XIV 7
Statue of St. Denis 4
Virgin and Child (13th cent.) 3
Virgin and Child (14th cent.) 5
West Rose Window 1

mistress, Camille Claudel; the former chapel (close to the main gate) is reserved for temporary exhibits. Set some time aside to stroll in the back garden with its many sculptures—don't miss the one of the three men sensually touching (at the far end, near the pond). Open only in the warm months is a wonderful cafe where tables are set in the shade of the gigantic rose bushes.

Musée Picasso. 5 rue de Thorigny, 3e. ☎ **01-42-71-25-21.** Admission 30–38F ($6–$7). Apr–Sept Wed–Mon 9:30am–6pm; Oct–Mar Wed–Mon to 5:30pm. Métro: St-Paul, Hôtel-de-Ville, or Chemin-Vert.

This exquisite museum is housed in the beautifully restored 17th-century Hôtel Salé (with fixtures designed by Giacometti). In the mansion you'll find work from the artist's personal collection: over 200 paintings, 150 sculptures, 1,500 sketches, 1,600 engravings, 16 collages, 88 ceramics, and 19 bas-reliefs, along with 30 notebooks spanning 75 years of hard work. There's a scattering of works by other artists (mostly friends and colleagues): Cézanne, Miró, Braque, and Matisse. Every period of Picasso's career is well represented, including the studies for the work that launched cubism in 1907: *Les Demoiselles d'Avignon.* There's so much here, such a density of talent, it's hard to pinpoint the most outstanding, but do check out the self-portraits from 1901 and the masterpieces *The Crucifixion, Nude in a Red Armchair,* and *Le Baiser* (The Kiss), which he painted in Mougins in 1969.

There are frequently hot men here, and sometimes it's hard to concentrate on the art. In fact, a few gay Parisians consider this an informal cruising museum. Let's face it: Picasso did have tremendous sexual energy; it must just seep through his work.

Musée Marmottan–Claude Monet. 2 rue Louis-Boilly, 16e. ☎ **01-42-24-07-02.** Admission 40F ($7). Tues–Sun 10am–5:30pm. Métro: La Muette.

This museum is in a lovely residential district surrounded by parks and gardens. Inside are over 100 of Claude Monet's works donated to the Academie des Beaux-Arts by his son, including *Impression at Sunrise,* which gave the impressionist movement its name. You can marvel at the subtle lighting and dreamy graininess of this painting for hours. There are over 30 paintings of the artist's beloved house in Giverny (west of Paris—see "Side Trips from Paris" below) and the famous water lilies. Other works include a portrait of Monet by Renoir, objets and furniture from the first Empire, Renaissance tapestries, and crystal chandeliers. After leaving, take a few minutes to stroll in the lovely Jardin du Ranelagh close by.

Erotic Museum (Musée de l'Erotisme). 72 bd. de Clichy, 18e. ☎ **01-42-23-24-78.** www.erotic-museum.com. Admission 40F ($7). Daily 10am–2am. Métro: Blanche.

Opened in 1997, this quirky museum is the first of its kind devoted to the intense art of arousal. On seedy boulevard de Clichy in the Pigalle area (with its live sex-show joints on every block), this narrow building has 7 floors filled with anything sexual. You'll find small wood figures from Bali showing off their humongous erections, an engraving of a man masturbating (used to embellish tombs in Madagascar), carved couples engaging in anal sex, and many photographs and unusual objects, like anal jewelry (don't ask, it's hard to explain). Most of the sculptures are rather small, but even if you have to squint and bend down to look at the little figures, there's bound to be something to put a smile on your face. Check out the golden penis (a rich person's dildo) next to the figures of seven boys engaged in lurid action (*The Seven Capital Sins*). Funky music blares as you walk around this amusing sex shop cum museum; a few TV sets show straight couples in action. Weird stuff abounds, like wine bottles with graphic sexual labels, nutcrackers (not for walnuts!) from Thailand, and a wooden statue sporting yet another huge erection with a sign stating "a house without a lizard

Proust's Way: A Visit to Illiers-Combray

On the centennial of Marcel Proust's birth in 1971, the town of Illiers, 54 miles southwest of Paris and 15 miles southwest of Chartres, added a hyphen and "Combray" to its name to honor its most prized (gay) native. Proust called the town Combray in his masterpiece *A la recherche du temps perdu (Remembrance of Things Past),* and made it famous.

Proust mania is on the rise, and not exclusively with gay readers. Groupies come from all over the world to stroll around Illiers-Combray and of course to buy a madeleine or two and let these buttery little cupcakes melt in their mouths, eyes closed, hoping to remember something wonderful. Some critics claim it's because we're living in the age of the memoir that Proust's work has experienced such a fierce comeback. He invented involuntary memory, allowed us into his intimate world, and was always the perfect fairy—a typical mama's boy. In 1886, when Proust was 15, he paid his last visit to Illiers. His health deteriorated after that, and returning here was impossible. From then on it was memory that took over the images of this house and town he cherished. Proust thrived on memory for the rest of his life, not once returning to Illiers.

Renting a car would be the fastest way to get to Illiers-Combray, especially if you want to pass by Chartres to visit the cathedral (see "Side Trips from Paris" below). If you want to come by train, call the SNCF at ☎ **08-36-35-35-35** (daily 8am–7pm) for schedule information.

Once here, you may visit the **Musée du Marcel Proust,** 4 rue du Docteur-Proust (☎ **02-37-24-30-97;** open Jan 16–Dec 14 Tues–Sun for tours at 2:30 and 4pm; admission 30F [$6], which was Aunt Léonie's home in the novel. Upstairs is the bedroom where Marcel slept as a teenager, with its Empire-style bed and magic lantern next to it. You can also stroll around the garden. It's wise to call Anne Borrel, the museum manager, to confirm the hours before you make firm plans, since tours are sometimes suspended. After this, take your time to walk around the town and peek into the **Eglise St-Jacques,** where Proust as a boy played hawthorn on the altar. Signs will point out other Proustian sights and trivia.

is a house without happiness." Three of the floors are for temporary exhibits. At the gift shop, you can buy your very own wooden woody to take home.

✪ **Père-Lachaise Cemetery (Cimetière du Père-Lachaise).** 16 rue du Repos, 20e. ☎ **01-43-70-70-33.** Admission free. Mar 15–Nov 5 Mon–Fri 8am–6pm, Sat 8:30am–5:30pm, Sun 9am–5:30pm. Métro: Père-Lachaise.

Paris's largest cemetery is the eternal home for many famous artists, musicians, writers, and thinkers: Proust, Wilde, Stein and Toklas, Colette, Chopin, Rossini, Bizet, Ravel, Piaf, Montand and Signoret, Modigliani, Delacroix, Bernhardt, Balzac, Molière, Wright, and countless others. The most popular (and graffiti-covered) grave is Jim Morrison's—you'll always find a band of young hippies smoking joints and drinking whiskey in the vicinity (neither activity encouraged, but the security guards can do so much). Recent rumors that Morrison will be removed from Père-Lachaise haven't been confirmed.

Wilde's grave has a little sign stating it's "protected by law as an historic monument and was restored in 1992." Proust's is made of sleek black marble with only his name discreetly engraved (he wanted to be buried with his friend/lover, composer Maurice Ravel, but their families wouldn't allow it). Stein and Toklas are buried side by side (however, Toklas's grave has no stone—her name is engraved on the back of Stein's headstone). The crematorium (built in 1889) is an ominous section but worth a visit. About 2,800 cremations annually take place here. This is where Sylvia Beach was cremated in 1962. You'll need a few hours to stroll around this hilly and haunting place full of paths where the Jesuits loved to walk in the 15th century, when the cemetery was first founded. In the olden days, the top of the hill was nothing more than fields of wheat; grapes were grown on the southern slope. Buy a map from any of the cafes and newsstands on the streets leading to the cemetery to find the graves you're most interested in seeing. Bring violets for Marcel and green carnations for Oscar.

✪ **St-Eustache.** 2 rue du Jour, 1er. ☎ **01-42-36-31-05.** Admission free. Daily 9am–7:30pm, Sun mass at 11am; organ recitals 5:30pm. Métro: Les Halles or Rambuteau.

This mixed Gothic and Renaissance church from 1637 is one of the city's most beautiful. Early works by Berlioz and Liszt were performed here, and the church is known for its excellent choir and organ recitals, especially its moving Sunday mass, drawing the largest number of gay worshipers in Paris. The stone foundation for the church was set in 1532, but it took over 100 years for the work to be completed. The plans called for it to rival only Notre-Dame. Molière was baptized here in 1622, and in 1673, amid great controversy (the vicar didn't approve of an actor resting on holy ground), he was buried here; in the 18th century his remains were moved to Père-Lachaise (above).

Panthéon. Place du Panthéon, 5e. ☎ **01-44-32-18-00.** Admission 35F ($6). Apr–Sept daily 9:30am–6:30pm; Oct–Mar daily 10am–6:15pm. Métro: Cardinal-Lemoine or Maubert-Mutualité.

This neoclassical building with a huge dome was first the church of Ste-Geneviève (Paris's patron saint), commissioned by Louis XV in thanksgiving for his having recovered from a serious illness. Following the Revolution, it was renamed the Panthéon and rededicated as a necropolis for France's secular heroes. In the crypt beneath the dome are the tombs of Voltaire, Rousseau, Hugo, Braille (inventor of the reading system for the blind), Zola, and other outstanding figures. In the spring of 1995 the ashes of scientist Marie Curie were entombed here, "the first lady so honored in our history for her own merits," in the words of late president François Mitterrand. Most recently, French writer/politician/adventurer André Malraux was honored by a tomb here. A pendulum suspended from the central dome re-creates Foucault's 1851 demonstration proving the rotation of the earth.

Musée Jacquemart-André. 158 bd. Haussmann, 8e. ☎ **01-42-89-04-91.** Admission 47F ($8). Daily 10am–6pm. Métro: Miromesnil or St-Philippe-du-Roule.

Give Paris's best decorative-arts museum (calling all decorators!) at least 2½ hours. It derives from the André family, prominent Protestants in the 19th century. The family's last scion, Edouard André, spent most of his life as an officer in the French army

Adieu, Orangerie—For Now

Since 1984, the **Musée de l'Orangerie,** place de la Concorde (☎ **01-42-97-48-16;** Métro: Concorde), has housed the renowned Jean Walter and Paul Guillaume art collection. It comprises works by Cézanne, Renoir, Rousseau, Matisse, Derain, Picasso, and Soutine—but the highlight is undoubtedly the two oval rooms wrapped around with almost 360° of Monet's *Nymphéas,* the water lily series he painted especially for the Orangerie. It's partly in order to improve the presentation of the water lilies that the museum is undergoing a two-year overhaul. It'll be closed from August 1999 to August 2001.

stationed abroad, returning later to marry Nélie Jacquemart, a portraitist of government figures and aristocrats. They compiled a collection of rare French 18th-century decorative art and European paintings in an 1850s town house. In 1912, Mme André willed the house and its collections to the Institut de France. The collection's pride are works by Bellini, Carpaccio, and Uccello, complemented by Houdon busts, Gobelins tapestries, Savonnerie carpets, della Robbia terra-cottas, an awesome collection of antiques, and works by Rembrandt (*The Pilgrim of Emmaus*), van Dyck, Tiepolo, Rubens, Watteau, Fragonard, and Boucher. Take a break with a cup of tea, a salad, or a tart in Mme André's dining room, with 18th-century tapestries.

Musée de Cluny. 6 place Paul-Painlevé, 5e. ☎ **01-53-73-78-16.** Admission 30F ($5). Wed–Mon 9:15am–5:45pm. Métro: Cluny–La Sorbonne.

This is Paris's museum of medieval art. Wood and stone sculptures, brilliant stained glass and metalwork, and rich tapestries (including the famous 15th-century *Lady and the Unicorn,* with its representation of the five senses) are among the exhibits. The Hôtel de Cluny, in which the museum is housed, is one of the city's foremost examples of medieval architecture. Some parts date back to Roman times, and you can see the ruins of thermal baths.

Academie Française. 23 quai de Conti, 6e. Métro: Pont-Neuf. Not open for tours or visits.

The academy was founded by Cardinal Richelieu in 1635 to protect the French language and support the country's most influential writers. Weekly meetings are still held for the select group of members (usually numbering less than 50) at the Institut de France, with its domed hall overlooking the pont des Arts on the Left Bank. The building was designed by Le Veau (who worked on the Louvre), and membership is strictly by invitation only, restricted to the most accomplished writers, politicians, and doctors (usually at the end of their lives). Jean Cocteau and Julien Green were honorary members (Cocteau was the first openly gay member). Marguerite Yourcenar was the first woman (and the first lesbian) to be invited into this exclusive think tank of French literature and language. Though the building isn't open for visits, you can stroll around the courtyard Monday to Friday 9am to 5:30pm.

GAY PARIS

Le Marais lies at the heart of gay Paris. It developed as the gay area only in the mid-1980s, after the AIDS epidemic forced the involuntary dismantling of the older gay area, St-Anne. The Marais is a beautiful neighborhood known primarily as the old Jewish quarter, with magnificent 17th-century buildings, small streets, and cobblestone alleys. It extends from the Beaubourg (Centre Pompidou) to place des Vosges and from rue de Rivoli to rue de Turbigo. The gay area stretches farther to Les Halles, with its many cafes and gay bars, and to place de la Bastille, the youngest and most up-and-coming area.

The most convenient Métro stop is Hôtel-de-Ville. From rue de Rivoli, take rue des Archives north and as soon as you're 2 blocks in you'll begin seeing men (more than women)—walking hand-in-hand, shopping, dishing at cafes, you name it. The main queer streets are **rue St-Croix-de-la-Bretonnerie, rue des Archives,** and **rue Vieille-du-Temple,** plus the smaller alleys leading to them.

But the Marais is much more than just the gay area—in the 17th century it was the heart of aristocratic Paris, when its *hôtels particuliers* (mansions) were for the wealthy. As you stroll around, take a few minutes to walk into the courtyards of some of these amazing buildings. The most notable is the **Hôtel de Rohan,** 87 rue Vieille-du-Temple (☎ **01-40-27-60-96;** open Mon and Wed–Fri noon–5:45pm and Sat–Sun 2:45–9:45pm; admission 15F/$2.75), once occupied by the son of Louis XIV. Don't miss the stunning bas-relief of a nude Apollo and four horses.

The **Hôtel des Ambassadeurs de Hollande,** 47 rue Vieille-du-Temple (☎ **01-42-74-22-22**), where Beaumarchais wrote *The Marriage of Figaro*, isn't open to the public, but you can walk into the courtyard. Ironically, this was never the Dutch Embassy as the name suggests. Though the facade of the **Hôtel de Beauvais,** 68 rue François-Miron, was badly damaged during the Revolution, it's still charming; a plaque commemorates the fact that Mozart stayed here in 1763. And the **Hôtel de Bethune-Sully,** 62 rue St-Antoine (☎ **01-42-74-22-22**), with a relief-studded facade, was once home to the duc de Sully; it now contains the National Office of Historical Monuments and Sites (call for visiting days and hours).

Rue des Rosiers (Street of the Rose Bushes) is the oldest district in the Marais and what remains from the Jewish quarter. It's amazing what you'll see as you stroll here: orthodox rabbis with long beards walking alongside gay couples holding hands while straight teenagers make out in the doorways of hole-in-the-wall restaurants where North African immigrants serve plates of steaming couscous next to kosher shops selling sticky sweet almond cake. It makes you have faith that perhaps tolerance is still attainable . . . if only on one or two streets of a city.

You'll also find some interesting museums in the Marais. Next to the boy bars on rue des Archives is the **Hunting Museum (Musée de la Chasse),** 60 rue des Archives, 3e (☎ **01-42-72-86-43;** open Wed–Mon 10am–12:30pm and 1:30–5:30pm; admission 25F/$4.50), a specialized museum for those who like to hunt for sport. You don't find many gay boys here, though there's an excellent selection of hunting tapestries (of cannibalistic romps and such wild scenes to get your adrenaline pumping); there are rifles inlaid with pearls (some engraved with ivory) from the 17th century and other historical weapons. Paintings by Rubens, Oudry, and Corot, among others, are also on display.

In the same area is the **Museum of the History of France (Musée de l'Histoire de France),** 60 rue des Francs-Bourgeois, 3e (☎ **01-40-27-61-78;** open Wed–Fri noon–5:45pm, Sat–Sun 1:45–5:45pm; admission 15F/$2.75), devoted to the entire history of France, with exhibits showcasing major events like the occupation of Paris. Thousands of archives and important documents are housed here, dating as far back as the 7th century.

The most outstanding museum in the Marais is the ✪ **Musée Carnavalet,** 23 rue de Sévigné, 3e (☎ **01-42-72-21-13;** Métro: St-Paul or Chemin-Vert; open Tues–Sun 10am–5:40pm; admission 27F/$5), also known as the Musée de l'Histoire de Paris. It brings the history of Paris to life (from prehistoric times to the present), with interesting little details and reconstructions of the bedrooms and studios of some of the famous artists who lived in Paris, including a replica of Proust's cork-lined (thus soundproofed) bedroom, with his actual furniture and brass bed. The museum is housed in two splendid mansions: the Hôtel Le Peletier de St-Fargeau and the Hôtel Carnavalet, once the home of Mme de Sévigné, the 17th-century writer of masterful letters.

PARKS, GARDENS & SQUARES

The immense ✪ **Bois de Boulogne,** Porte Dauphine, 16e (☎ **01-40-67-90-82;** Métro: Porte Dauphine), is one of Europe's most beautiful parks. Just west of Paris, the park was once a forest kept for royal hunts, but now families come on weekends in the warmer months to picnic and joggers and bikers swarm the paths. It's so large it can never get really crowded: There are two lakes (boat rentals are available), a horseback-riding school, a zoological garden, and the Longchamp racetrack. The highly recommended (and utterly romantic) Le Pré Catelan (see "Romancing with a View" above) is also within the park's perimeter, as is the mansion once inhabited by the duke and duchess of Windsor and now owned by Mohammed al Fayed (Diana and Dodi visited briefly before heading to the Ritz on that fateful day).

The Marais

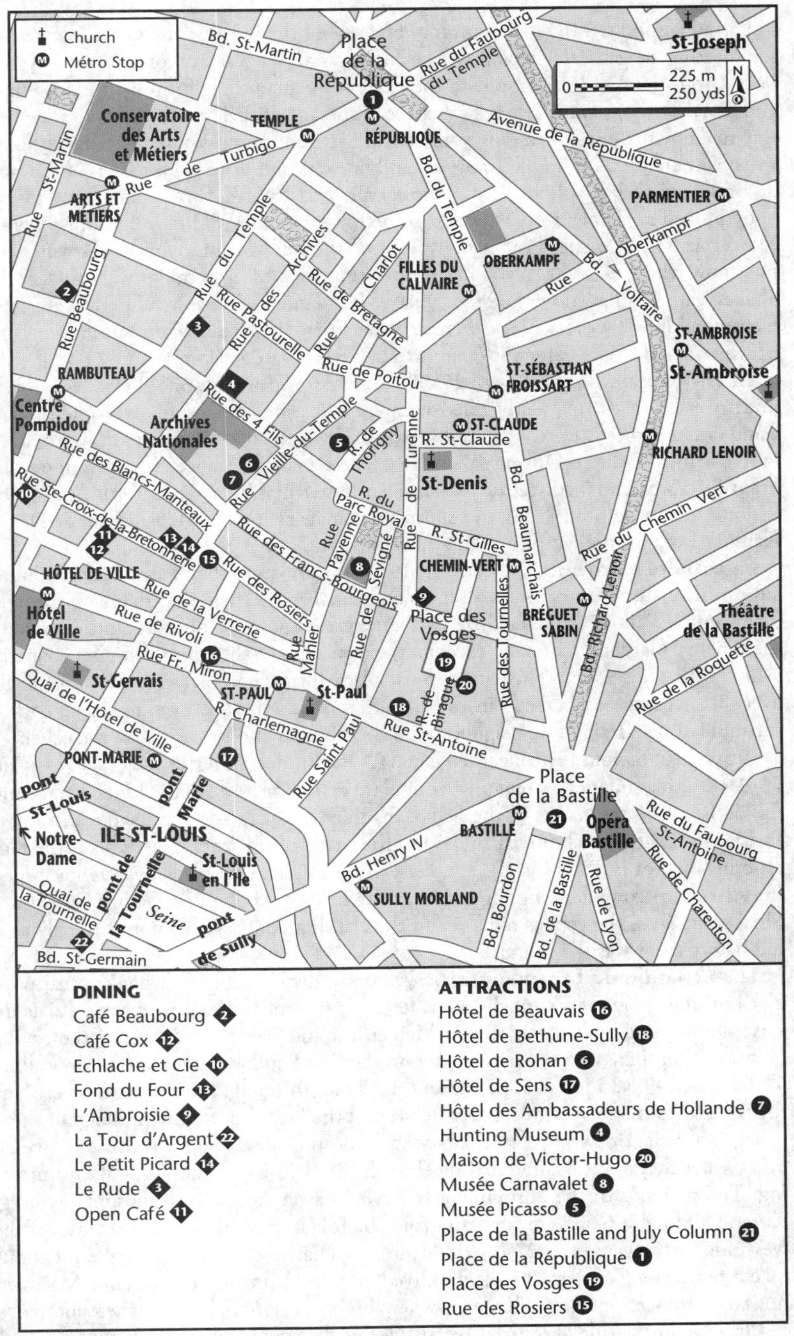

Church
Métro Stop
225 m
250 yds
0
N
Place de la République
Bd. St-Martin
Rue du Faubourg du Temple
St-Joseph
Conservatoire des Arts et Métiers
TEMPLE
RÉPUBLIQUE
Avenue de la République
Rue de Turbigo
ARTS ET MÉTIERS
Rue St-Martin
Bd. du Temple
PARMENTIER
Rue Oberkampf
OBERKAMPF
Bd. Voltaire
FILLES DU CALVAIRE
Rue Charlot
Rue des Archives
Rue de Bretagne
Rue du Temple
Rue Beaubourg
Rue Pastourelle
ST-AMBROISE
St-Ambroise
Rue de Poitou
ST-SÉBASTIAN FROISSART
RAMBUTEAU
Centre Pompidou
Archives Nationales
Rue des 4 Fils
ST-CLAUDE
R. St-Claude
RICHARD LENOIR
Rue Vieille-du-Temple
R. de Thorigny
Rue de Turenne
Rue des Blancs-Manteaux
St-Denis
Bd. Beaumarchais
Rue Ste-Croix-de-la-Bretonnerie
R. du Parc Royal
Rue du Chemin Vert
R. St-Gilles
Rue des Francs-Bourgeois
Rue Payenne
Rue de Sévigné
CHEMIN-VERT
HÔTEL DE VILLE
Rue des Rosiers
Hôtel de Ville
Rue de la Verrerie
Rue de Rivoli
Place des Vosges
BRÉGUET SABIN
Bd. Richard Lenoir
Rue des Tournelles
Théâtre de la Bastille
Rue de la Roquette
Rue Fr. Miron
Rue Mahler
St-Gervais
ST-PAUL
St-Paul
R. de Birague
Quai de l'Hôtel de Ville
R. Charlemagne
Rue Saint Paul
Rue St-Antoine
PONT-MARIE
Place de la Bastille
pont St-Louis
pont Marie
BASTILLE
Opéra Bastille
Rue du Faubourg St-Antoine
Notre-Dame
ILE ST-LOUIS
St-Louis en l'Ile
Bd. Henry IV
Rue de Charenton
Quai de la Tournelle
pont de la Tournelle
Seine
pont de Sully
SULLY MORLAND
Bd. Bourdon
Bd. de la Bastille
Rue de Lyon
Bd. St-Germain
DINING
Café Beaubourg 2
Café Cox 12
Echlache et Cie 10
Fond du Four 13
L'Ambroisie 9
La Tour d'Argent 22
Le Petit Picard 14
Le Rude 3
Open Café 11
ATTRACTIONS
Hôtel de Beauvais 16
Hôtel de Bethune-Sully 18
Hôtel de Rohan 6
Hôtel de Sens 17
Hôtel des Ambassadeurs de Hollande 7
Hunting Museum 4
Maison de Victor-Hugo 20
Musée Carnavalet 8
Musée Picasso 5
Place de la Bastille and July Column 21
Place de la République 1
Place des Vosges 19
Rue des Rosiers 15

Porte Dauphine is the main entrance and one of the most popular cruising areas—for meeting or gathering not hardcore fooling around. On the other hand, avenue Foch (from the Arc de Triomphe to the park) is the main drag for prostitution—male and female; on the south side is a transvestite cruising area. Though walking is the best way to enjoy the forest, bringing your car for a drive is permissible, especially at night, when certain areas are unsafe (muggers and hookers and drugs). Proust loved the Bois de Boulogne and in volume 1 of *Remembrance of Things Past* wrote about it: "Everybody looked as if they were there for something, but they didn't really know what." Marcel, if only you could see it now, with all the hunks running around—you can't not know what you want. If you have ample time to stroll, you might want to visit the Shakespeare Garden (near the Pré Catelan). It's planted with flowers, herbs, and trees mentioned in the writer's plays; there's a small open-air theater where summer performances are held. The garden is open for visits daily 3 to 5:30pm.

Parc Monceau, 8e (**☎ 01-42-27-39-56;** Métro: Monceau or Villiers), is a lovely midcity park that's frequently filled with mothers and their kids or businesspeople using it as a shortcut to rush from one side of town to another. The park was opened in 1778 by the duc d'Orléans, then the richest man in France. It's surrounded by beautiful 18th- and 19th-century mansions. Other highlights are a rotunda built by Ledoux and a column from the unfinished mausoleum of Henri II at St-Denis. Flaubert lived on rue Murillo overlooking the park.

Parc André-Citroën, 15e (Métro: Balard), is even larger than Parc Monceau but is almost futuristic, with ornamental lakes and canals, waterfalls, and thematic gardens. The Central Park is dominated by two large greenhouses (a mini-botanical garden), the Theme Gardens represent each of the five senses, and the Changing Gardens evolve with the seasons. This is a popular place for gays (mostly French and mostly over 30), who meet discreetly in the late afternoons and early evenings. The park is surrounded by a residential neighborhood on one side and the Seine on the other.

Paris's most famous formal garden is the ✪ **Jardin des Tuileries, 1e (☎ 01-44-50-75-01;** Métro: Tuileries), stretching from place de la Concorde to the Louvre and from rue de Rivoli to the banks of the Seine. It's filled with statues and chairs, and many Parisians eat their lunch on warm days in the shade of the leafy trees. This is the oldest cruising area in Paris (on the southern side, closest to the river), where local men (mostly older) come looking for action in the bushes. Though the action has diminished somewhat, the echoes remain and the cruising continues (if not as overtly as it did before there was the Marais).

The ✪ **Jardin du Luxembourg,** 6e (Métro: Odeon), is the Left Bank's most popular cruising spot, yet it's much more. It's a magnificent garden where the Palais du Luxembourg was built for Marie de Medici, the much-neglected wife of the roving Henri IV. You may visit the palace only on the first Sunday of each month by calling **☎ 01-44-33-99-83** for an appointment. Let's face it, though, the attraction here isn't the palace: it's the men who congregate around the beautiful fountain, many of them college students or tweedy professors who bring their books on a warm day (we all know what they're most interested in, though). It's laid-back and not at all intimidating. The presence of the Sorbonne a few blocks away keeps the atmosphere young, vibrant, and light. Gertrude Stein and Alice B. Toklas lived for many years just off the west side of the garden at 27 rue de Fleurus. Sylvia Beach (founder of the infamous Shakespeare and Company bookstore) lived with her companion, Adrienne Monnier, not far from here on rue de l'Odéon, where both of their bookstores where located.

Place de la Bastille, 12e (Métro: Bastille), is the square where on July 14, 1789 a mob of Parisians stormed the prison sparking the French Revolution (thus the name for Bastille or Independence Day). Nothing remains of the old structure and now the square is mostly known for its excellent Opéra de Bastille, opened in the last decade, which has breathed new life into this neighborhood. The young, trendy crowds flock here for the inexpensive cafes, restaurants and shops along rue de la Roquette. What St-Germain-des-Prés was for the 1960s and 1970s (the young and vibrant area) Bastille is now for the young happening scene. It's still not as clean or tidy as some other areas of Paris but that's exactly why it is up-and-coming. There are no set rules here and the young are creating their own. Many gays and lesbians come here, a spill-over effect from the nearby Marais, and almost anywhere you go here is gay-friendly.

✪ **Place de la Concorde,** 8e (Métro: Concorde) is the city's largest and most elegant square (constructed between 1755 and 1775), with an Egyptian obelisk dominating the center. The obelisk from Luxor is the oldest man-made object in Paris, carved in 1,200 B.C. and offered to Charles X by the viceroy of Egypt in 1829. The Hôtel de Crillon (formerly a palace) presides over this fancy square on one side (the U.S. Embassy is next to it), with the Tuileries gardens on the other; the Champs-Elysées and the Seine round up the surroundings. It was on this very square (then called place de la Révolution) that 1,300 heads were guillotined, most notably those of Louis XVI and Marie Antoinette, Danton, and Robespierre.

Paris's chicest square, ✪ **Place Vendôme,** 1e (Métro: Concorde or Opéra), dates back to the end of the reign of Louis XIV; Hardoin-Mansart designed the square facade in 1685. Now it's primarily known as home of the Hôtel Ritz and some of the fanciest shops in the world. The column in the center was commissioned by Napoléon to honor those who fought and won the Battle of Austerlitz, and 1,200 captured Austrian cannons were melted down and used in its construction. It was here at the Ritz that Diana and Dodi got in the backseat of their ill-fated Mercedes.

✪ **Place des Vosges,** 4e (Métro; Chemin-Vert or Bastille), is the heart of the Marais and the oldest square in Paris. Constructed under the reign of Henry IV, it was the first planned square on the continent, surrounded by shopping arcades and houses built with red brick and white stone. Henry II was killed in this square in 1559, and Victor Hugo lived here for many years. The lovely garden in the center is planted with chestnut and linden trees. You can visit the Maison de Victor-Hugo, 6 place des Vosges (☎ **01-42-72-10-16;** open Tues–Sun 10am–5:40pm; admission 17.50F/$3.20), which is now a museum and a literary shrine. Hugo lived here from 1832 to 1848. You'll find some of his furniture and some of his drawings (over 450 of them), illustrating scenes from his works.

WORKING UP A SWEAT

It's surprising there are no exclusively gay health clubs in Paris. There are gay gyms (meaning bathhouse), but no one hones anything more than their cruising techniques. A popular chain of well-equipped modern fitness centers is **Gymnase Club,** with over 15 locations in the city. Two draw a mainly gay crowd: The most popular (and the closest to the Marais) is at 147 bis rue St-Honoré, 1e (☎ **01-40-20-03-03;** Métro: Palais-Royal); the other is at 10 place de la République, 11e (☎ **01-47-00-69-98;** Métro: République), but the entrance is at 2 faubourg du Temple. Both branches charge a whopping 150F ($27) day fee. A booklet of 10 entries is 1,000F ($182). Hours for both gyms are Monday to Friday 7am to 10:30pm, Saturday 9am to 7pm, Sunday 9am to 5pm. It might be worth your while (and your wallet) to spend a little more for a hotel with a health club. But then again, you might miss the hot showers with the cuties.

The best pool (both for laps and hot bods) is the **Piscine des Halles,** 10 place de la Rotonde, 1e (☎ **01-42-36-98-44;** Métro: Châtelet–Les Halles). Pool hours are Monday 11:30am to 7:30pm; Tuesday, Thursday, and Friday 11:30am to 9:30pm; Wednesday 10am to 6:30pm; and Saturday and Sunday 9am to 4:30pm.

5 Hitting the Stores

Shopping in Paris is outstanding—from astronomical haute couture to cheap haute kitsch. Strolling down **avenue Montaigne** or **rue du Faubourg St-Honoré,** you can't help but think "this is where it all begins." On these streets and in these buildings, designers create, models strut, photographers make everything look beautiful for the mags, and salespeople try to convince you that you can't possibly live without a $1,000 tie or $5,000 sweater. This is one of the few cities where the fashion world congregates each season to give a thumbs up or thumbs down to the newest and most flamboyant haute couture and ready-to-wear. This is the city of Lagerfeld, Chanel, Dior, Gaultier, Lacroix, Saint Laurent, and hundreds of small independent designers trying to make a name for themselves.

The streets above are best for designer boutiques and high-fashion specialty shops. (At 29 rue du Faubourg St-Honoré, Cocteau visited Coco Chanel frequently while she designed costumes for many of his plays and films.) The **Champs-Elysées** and the streets around it also contain many upscale clothing stores. From **place Vendôme** to place de l'Opéra and on to place de la Madeleine is another dizzying concentration of shops. This is where the gourmet food shops are located, like Fauchon. Most younger Parisians shop in **St-Germain-des-Prés.** There the trendy shops aren't as expensive but are just as fashionable. The small streets all around the Hôtel Lutétia (between the Mabillon and Sèvres-Babylone Métro stops) carry great selections of shoes, designer jeans, suits, and so on. For inexpensive shops, head to **Les Halles,** where you can find imitation Nikes, imitation leather jackets, imitation anything—for cheap. In general, the large residential arrondissements (13e, 14e, and 18e) have huge boulevards lined with inexpensive shops. This is where middle-class Parisians shop.

Gay stores are concentrated in the **Marais** area (see "Gay Paris"), with a few in Les Halles and around place de la Bastille. They're mostly men's fashion, with the usual clubby black wear, sleek underwear, and skintight T-shirts so indispensable to a successful night of cruising (depending on whom you ask).

Shopping hours are generally Monday to Saturday 10am to 7pm. Smaller shops sometimes close for 2 hours at lunch; others don't open on Monday mornings, and still others don't open Monday at all. Always call ahead if you're making a special trek to a smaller store.

SHOPS A TO Z

ANTIQUES **Le Louvre des Antiquaires,** 2 place du Palais-Royal, 1e (☎ **01-42-97-27-00;** Métro: Palais-Royal), has the most fabulous collection of objets d'art (from crystal chandeliers to Limoges china), with over 250 dealers. Gay men abound (surprise, surprise), especially on Sunday. In the Marais, the **Village St-Paul,** 23–27 rue St-Paul, 4e (no phone; Métro: St-Paul; closed Tues–Wed), is a cluster of stands selling jewelry, crystal, and art deco objects. Sundays are hopping here too.

A good place for sterling silver and antique silver-plated tableware is **Argenterie des Francs-Bourgeois,** 17 rue des Francs-Bourgeois, 4e (☎ **01-42-72-04-00;** Métro: St-Paul), in the Marais. If you love antique clocks and watches, visit M. and Mme **Arvaud,** 23–25 rue du Cherche-Midi, 6e (☎ **01-45-48-25-88;** Métro: Sèvres-Babylone). M. Arvaud is the caretaker for all the clocks (and barometers and thermometers) at the presidential palaces—he personally adjusts President Chirac's clocks twice a year. There's a huge gay presence at the antique auction halls (Salle de Vente) at the **Drouot-Richelieu** location at 9 rue Drouot (☎ **01-48-00-20-20;** Métro: Richelieu-Drouot). Call for opening days and hours. Here's where you'll find outstanding bargains and mingle with older gay men who love antiques.

BOOKS The best gay and lesbian bookstore in France is **Les Mots à la Bouche,** 6 rue St-Croix-de-la-Bretonnerie, 4e (☎ **01-42-78-88-30;** Métro: Hôtel-de-Ville), with a small selection of English-language gay books and magazines. This is your best source for the free pamphlets advertising gay venues and events and for French magazines like *Têtu* that'll give you a peek into the everyday lives of French gays and lesbians.

One of the largest English-language bookstores is **W. H. Smith,** 248 rue de Rivoli, 1e (☎ **01-44-77-88-99;** Métro: Concorde), where you'll find the latest fiction and nonfiction mainstream books (most are British editions). Another large mainstream store is **Brentano's,** 37 rue de l'Opéra, 2e (☎ **01-42-61-52-50;** Métro: Opéra), where there's frequent readings by visiting poets and writers. The quaintest English-language store (Edmund White makes reference to it in several of his novels and frequently gives readings and book-signings here) is the **Village Voice,** 6 rue Princesse, 6e (☎ **01-46-33-36-47;** Métro: Mabillon); it sells an excellent selection of the latest hot novels (including some gay and lesbian titles).

CHOCOLATE One of the fanciest stores is **La Maison du Chocolat,** 225 rue du Fabourg St-Honoré, 8e (☎ **01-42-27-39-44,** Métro: Ternes), where you'll also find a delectable selection of chocolate pastries and a variety of chocolate-based products; there are five other locations in the city. For the best chocolate desserts, visit **Lenôtre,** 48 av. Victor-Hugo, 16e (☎ **01-45-02-21-21;** Métro: Victor-Hugo).

CLUBWEAR For the tightest T-shirts and the blackest pants (and underwear), drop by gay-owned **Factory's,** 3 rue St-Croix-de-la-Bretonnerie, 4e (☎ **01-48-87-29-10;** Métro: Hôtel-de-Ville). You'll find everything you need to paint the town red (or black), from Armani to Stephen Koskin.

The gay store in the Marais for a good selection of underwear is **Homme Sweet Homme,** 45 rue Vieille-du-Temple (☎ **01-48-04-94-99;** Métro: Hôtel-de-Ville). **Boy'z Bazaar,** 5 rue St-Croix-de-la-Bretonnerie (☎ **01-42-71-94-00;** Métro: Hôtel-de-Ville), also has good underwear and other tight gaywear.

DEPARTMENT STORES The most upcoming department store is **Le Bon Marché,** 38 rue de Sèvres, 7e (☎ **01-44-39-80-00;** Métro: Sèvres-Babylone). This was the first department store to open in Paris (the building was designed by Gustave Eiffel) and was neglected for a time. Now it has been renovated and boasts the fabulous Grande Epicerie, a gourmet grocery store/deli filled with goodies. This may well become the Fauchon of the Left Bank.

The two most famous department stores sit side by side in the 9e: **Galeries Lafayette,** 40 bd. Haussmann, 9e (☎ **01-42-82-34-56;** Métro: Chausée-d'Antin), is the largest and has a stupendous amount of products (over 75,000 brand names), from down comforters to women's hats to fondue pots. **Le Printemps,** 64 bd. Haussmann, 9e (☎ **01-42-82-50-00;** Métro: Havre-Caumartin), has an excellent new department for men and women's fashions, with many sales throughout the year offering great bargains. On Thursdays both stay open until 9pm.

FASHION In addition to the fancy boutiques lining **avenue Montaigne** (Calvin Klein, Valentino, Dolce & Gabbana) and the terribly upscale stores around **place Vendôme** and **Faubourg St-Honoré,** stroll around **rue du Cherche-Midi** in the 6e (Métro: Mabillon) to find some good bargains on designer wear.

If you want to dress like a preppie French boy, head to **Blanc Bleu,** 5 bd. Malesherbes, 8e (☎ **01-47-42-02-18;** Métro: Madeleine), where you'll find everything from navy-blue shirts and white pants to funky sneakers, all at reasonable prices. For a more chic look, drop by **The O Fil,** 238 rue de Rivoli, 1e (☎ **01-42-60-57-88;** Métro: Louvre), where an efficient staff will look after you with a smile (on a good day).

Though it's right on the Champs-Elysées, **Linea Nuovo,** 66 av. des Champs-Elysées, 8e (☎ **01-42-56-03-42;** Métro: Franklin-Roosevelt), has frequent sales—

Italian suits designed by the likes of Nino Denelli can go for as low as 3,500F ($636), a bargain in Paris. There are three floors of shoes, suits, and jackets, plus an all-male staff who need to learn to smile. For ultraexpensive/ultratrendy Italian-made suits, the hot spot is **Ermenegildo Zegna,** 368 rue St-Honoré, 1e (☎ **01-42-61-74-74;** Métro: Concorde), where you have to look really sharp or they won't even let you in.

Springfield, 12 bd. de la Madeleine, 8e (☎ **01-42-65-32-67;** Métro: Madeleine), sells Spanish-designed fashions (especially shirts and chenille sweaters) at reasonable prices. For the trendiest sports jackets at somewhat reasonable prices (pants, shirts, and shoes too), try **Hugo Boss,** 43 av. de l'Opéra, 2e (☎ **01-47-03-94-00;** Métro: Opéra). In the Marais, **Jean Chatel,** 29 rue des Francs-Bourgeois, 4e (☎ **01-44-78-80-71;** Métro: Hôtel-de-Ville), is a beautiful store where the original facade (of a pâtisserie) has been kept. Inside you'll find the trendiest sports jackets and sweaters and a few pairs of funky sneakers.

Rena Lange, 19 rue du faubourg St-Honoré, 8e (☎ **01-42-68-36-36;** Métro: Concorde), is one of the many top spots for women's ultrachic wear. And of course you remember *Ab Fab* Edwina and her Lacroix costumes. Sweetie darling, you can find similar outrageous designs at **Christian Lacroix,** 73 rue du faubourg St-Honoré, 8e (☎ **01-42-68-79-00;** Métro: Concorde). Lacroix!

In the Marais are several shops frequented by lesbians: **Une Affaire des Femmes,** 2 rue Parc-Royal, 4e (☎ **01-42-77-14-60;** Métro: Chemin-Vert), offers a good collection of ready-to-wear for both the butch and the femme. **Rev'elle et Vous,** 12 rue Ferdinand-Duval (☎ **01-44-59-39-00:** Métro: St-Paul), is filled with women's accessories, like handmade belts and scarves. And for slutty dancing skirts and red silk blouses, there's no better than **Nina Jacob,** 23 rue des Francs-Bourgeois, 3e (☎ **01-42-77-41-20;** Métro: St-Paul).

FOOD For anything related to gourmet food, you'll need only one address: **Fauchon,** place de la Madeleine, 8e (☎ **01-47-42-60-11;** Métro: Madeleine), a gourmand's dream. It has been open in some form since 1888 and now has over 300 employees and thousands of exotic offerings, from spices to canned foie gras. Don't expect to be helped, though. The number of visitors who flock here is staggering, and the staff can't keep up with their questions and requests. In the basement is a small cafe where you can taste some of their amazing pastries and other products. Avoid the needlessly overpriced restaurant Le 30.

The trendiest shop in Paris right now doesn't sell much, just bottled water in funky colored bottles and diet food that's all the rage with the toothpick model types who flock here. **Colette,** 213 rue St-Honoré, 1e (☎ **01-55-35-33-90;** Métro: Concorde), is worth a visit if only to ogle the good-looking men and women.

La Ferme St-Aubin, 76 rue St-Louis-en-l'Ile, 4e (☎ **01-43-54-74-54;** Métro: Pont-Marie), sells over 200 kinds of cheese from France and across Europe. The friendly staff will help you choose if they're not too busy. A less quaint place but more fabulous and expensive is **Androuët,** 83 rue St-Dominique, 7e (☎ **01-45-50-45-75;** Métro: Ecole Militaire or Invalides), which has been going strong since before World War I selling perfectly ripened sophisticated cheeses (a restaurant of the same name serves the shop's products). Take a few minutes to stroll around rue St-Dominique heading toward the Eiffel Tower—the street is lined with great bakeries, more cheese stores, and other gourmet shops.

JEWELRY You won't miss the fancy jewelry stores lining faubourg St-Honoré: Cartier, Piaget, Van Clef et Arpels, and so on. For something simpler and more original, head to the Marais to **Fugit Amor,** 11 rue des Francs-Bourgeois, 4e (☎ **01-42-74-52-37;** Métro: Hôtel-de-Ville), where 50 young jewelers (among them many gays and lesbians) display their creations. You'll find the funkiest rings, bracelets, earrings, and much more.

LEATHER The pedestrian-only streets at **Les Halles** are lined with shops selling fake and real leather jackets. A shop that has both is **Territoire Redskins,** 83 rue Rambuteau, 1e (☎ **01-40-26-21-64;** Métro: Rambuteau). For hard-core leather (human dog collars, chains), drop by the gay store **TTBM,** 16 rue St-Croix-de-la-Bretonnerie (☎ **01-48-04-80-88;** Métro: Hôtel-de-Ville), where you'll also find nipple pinchers and other tools and appliances for the butchest of the butch.

MARKETS The **Marché aux Puces de Clingancourt,** 17e (Métro: Porte-de-Clignancourt), is Paris's main seedy flea market, with several thousand stalls and vendors selling everything from antiques to used Barbie dolls. It's held Saturday, Sunday, and Monday 7:30am to 7pm. This isn't the safest area of Paris, so watch your pockets and purses and don't wear jewelry.

The **Marché aux Fleurs** (Métro: Cité) is a beautiful flower market on Ile de la Cité (place Louis-Lepine) held Monday to Saturday 8am to 1pm. On Sunday it sells birds and becomes the **Marché aux Oiseaux.**

Every arrondissement has its own **daily marché** for fresh produce, cheeses, meats, and baked goodies. Ask your concierge about the nearest one to your hotel or contact the **Cellules des Marchées** at ☎ **01-42-76-34-37** for a complete list.

SHOES For the latest in men's and women's footwear, drop by **J. Fenestrier,** 23 rue du Cherche-Midi, 6e (☎ **01-42-22-66-02;** Métro: Sèvres-Babylone). The trendiest store in the Marais for shoes and more is **Camper,** 9 rue des Francs-Bourgeois, 4e (☎ **01-48-87-09-09;** Métro: Hôtel-de-Ville); they carry both dressy and hiking boots.

WINE The main wine seller in Paris is **Nicolas,** 31 place de la Madeleine, 8e (☎ **01-42-68-00-16;** www.nicolas.tm.fr; Métro: Madeleine), with over 250 stores in the city. The staff is usually very knowledgeable, though not always available to answer questions. It's a busy shop, and locals and tourists fill this location next to Fauchon, making it one of the busiest. Their smaller neighborhood branches are more quaint and calm and all carry the same brands.

6 All the World's a Stage

The weekly French-language ***Pariscope*** and ***L'Officiel de Spectacle*** publish the most up-to-date listings for everything from movies to the opera to rock concerts. The ***International Herald Tribune*** also has a small section devoted to the cultural life in Paris (usually on Saturday).

For half-price theater tickets, go to the **Kiosque-Théâtre** at the northwest corner of the Madeleine church (Métro: Madeleine; open Tues–Sat 12:30–8pm and Sun to 4pm). You can buy tickets only for that same day's performance. There are also **ticket counters** in the Châtelet–Les Halles Métro Station and at Gare Montparnasse. For discounts of 20% to 40% on tickets for festivals, concerts, and the theater, try one of the two locations of the **FNAC department store** chain: 136 Rue de Rennes, 6e (☎ **01-49-54-30-00;** Métro: Montparnasse-Bienvenue), or in the Forum des Halles mall, 1–7 rue Pierre-Lescot, 1er (☎ **01-40-41-40-00;** Métro: Châtelet–Les Halles).

THE PERFORMING ARTS

OPERA, CLASSICAL MUSIC & BALLET The ✪ **Opéra Garnier,** place de l'Opéra, 9e (☎ **01-40-01-17-89;** Métro: Opéra; box office open daily 11am–6pm), is a rococo wonder designed by Charles Garnier in 1860, with a ceiling decorated by Chagall. This is still the sight of some of Paris's most exclusive performances, not only of opera but of ballet too. (This is where Nijinsky and Nureyev danced and dazzled the world.) Call way ahead of time for tickets, which range from 60 to 650F ($11 to $118); for credit card purchases, call ☎ **08-36-69-78-68.**

The magnificently modern **Opéra Bastille,** place de la Bastille, 12e (☎ **01-40-01-17-89;** Métro: Bastille; box office open daily 11am–6pm), was inaugurated in 1989 to commemorate the bicentennial of the Revolution and designed by the Uruguayan-Canadian architect Carlos Ott. It has fast become the premier spot for opera in Europe. Tickets run 60 to 650F ($11 to $118). Call ☎ **08-36-69-78-68** for opera and concert tickets, 01-43-43-96-96 for tape-recorded information, 01-47-42-53-71 for ballet tickets, and 01-44-73-13-99 for general information.

The **Cité de la Musique,** 221 av. Jean-Jaures, 19e (☎ **01-44-84-44-84;** www.cite-musique.fr; Métro: Porte-de-Pantin), boasts a fabulously modern concert hall, a music museum, and an amphitheater. The concert hall frequently pulls in some well-known names in the world of classic musical. Ticket ranges from 60 to 200F ($11 to $36). The cafe here is very popular with a gay and lesbian crowd, many of them musicians or researchers or just music lovers.

The Orchestre de Paris and world-famous philharmonics perform at the **Salle Pleyel,** 252 rue du faubourg St-Honoré, 8e (☎ **01-45-61-53-00;** Métro: Ternes; box office open Mon–Sat 10am–6pm). The busiest season is mid-September to early May; tickets range from 60 to 550F ($11 to $100).

Classical music concerts are given every summer in the Bois de Boulogne's lovely Parc de Bagatelle. There's usually a Chopin Festival for piano lovers. For details, contact the **Orangerie de Bagatelle,** Parc de Bagatelle, Bois de Boulogne, 16e (☎ **01-45-00-22-19**).

THEATER The beautifully renovated 300-year-old **Comédie-Française,** 2 rue de Richelieu, 1er (☎ **01-44-58-15-15;** Métro: Palais-Royal; box office open daily 11am–6pm, closed Aug–Sept 15), is where the grandest classics of Molière, Racine, and other French playwrights are staged—in French, *bien sur.* Prices average 100 to 250F ($18 to $45).

The **Théâtre des Champs-Elysées,** 15 av. Montaigne, 8e (☎ **01-49-52-50-50;** Métro: Alma-Marceau; box office open 11am–6pm), puts on more modern French plays, many by still-living playwrights. Tickets are 70 to 350F ($13 to $64). The most active season is October to May; in other months, there are limited venues and in August the theater is closed. The crowd tends to be young, trendy, and beautiful. The hip restaurant Maison Blanche (see "Romancing with a View" above) is on the top floor of the theater, affording panoramic views.

CABARETS & SUPPER CLUBS

The cabaret scene is alive and well in Paris, but it caters mostly to tourists who are disgorged by the busload every evening to attend these shows. If you've always dreamed of watching half-naked ladies (and bare-chested men) on a much more elegant scale than anything in Vegas, then skip the pricey and often bland food and just pay a cover to watch the show (the dancers are all professional models who come from around the world to be part of this lucrative business).

Henri de Toulouse-Lautrec immortalized the **Moulin Rouge,** place Blanche, 18e (☎ **01-53-09-82-82;** Métro: Blanche; cover 360F/$65, including two drinks), making it the subject of many of his colorful nocturnal paintings. The windmill and the cancan may still be here, but otherwise Henri would never recognize the place. In a slick revue, hot men and topless women shake their booties to choreographed moves. Shows begin nightly at 9 and 11pm.

The oldest such establishment in Paris opened in 1886, and visitors have flocked since to the **Folies-Bergère,** 32 rue Richer, 9e (☎ **01-44-79-98-98;** Métro: Cadet; cover 490–550F/$89–$100, including a glass of champagne), to watch the girls in action, though they're much less titillating here than at the Moulin Rouge. Josephine Baker sang here at the height of her career, shaking those bananas. Performances are Tuesday to Saturday at 9pm.

The ✪ **Lido de Paris,** 116 bis av. des Champs-Elysées, 8e (☎ **01-40-76-56-10;** Métro George V), is the most carefully choreographed and richly costumed cabaret show in Paris (it's also the most popular). To become a Lido dancer, girls must pass through a stringent training program (not unlike boot camp), and the result is a lot of sleek moves and a lot of beautiful faces and perfect bodies. You can watch from the bar by paying 375F ($68), which includes two drinks; or for a real seat, the show, and champagne you can pay 550F ($100). Shows are nightly at 10pm and midnight.

For a queeny, fun cabaret, head to the basement of **Banana Café,** 13 rue de la Ferronnerie, 1er (☎ **01-42-33-35-31;** Métro: Châtelet–Les-Halles; no cover), where several nights a week (call for exact schedule) at 11pm the boys present their *Priscilla, Queen of the Desert*–style act. Upstairs, a *très* gay crowd hangs out at the bar, munches on cheap food, and cruises.

LIVE-MUSIC CLUBS

Gay choirs come and go in Paris, so inquire at the **Centre Gai et Lesbien,** 3 rue Keller (☎ **01-43-57-21-47;** Métro: Bastille), as to the latest verdict on this men's choir.

You'll find the best jazz at **Jazz Club Le Villa,** in the Hôtel La Villa, 29 rue Jacob (☎ **01-43-26-60-00;** Métro: St-Germain-des-Prés; open Mon–Sat 9pm–2am; cover 150F/$27, including one drink), an upscale basement club with frequent big-name jazz artists from around the world. Concerts begin at 10:15pm; it's closed in August. For a more bohemian setting (with good blues), head to **Petit Journal St-Michel,** 71 bd. St-Michel, 5e (☎ **01-43-26-28-59;** Métro: Luxembourg; open Mon–Sat 9pm–2am; cover 20–50F/$3.65–$9), where a mainly student crowd comes to listen to jazz quintets and more; there's frequently a theme, such as an homage to Count Basie. It can get quite smoky here when it's crowded.

A jazzy place that attracts a solid gay and lesbian crowd is **Duc des Lombards,** 42 rue des Lombards, 1er (☎ **01-42-33-22-88;** Métro: Châtelet–Les-Halles; open Mon–Sat 9pm–2am; cover 20–25F/$3.65–$4.50), where an international collection of jazz artists performs several times a week. Concerts begin at 10pm.

7 In the Heat of the Night

Paris's bar scene is hopping, though bars here aren't as clearly defined as in other cities—they can be cafes and cafes can be bars, restaurants can be bars, and bars can also be clubs. It can get confusing. The best way to think about it would be not to let the name give you any preconceived notions of what the place might be like. (Café Marly, for example, is much more than just a cafe, and Buddha-bar is known more for its food than its cocktails.)

The trendy places are mostly located around the **Champs-Elysées, St-Germain-des-Prés,** and the **Marais.** Hard-core gay and lesbian bars still tend to be quite seedy, many times tucked away on small streets in iffy neighborhoods. The Marais, of course, has brought everything out of the closet, and the most popular bars are open, airy, friendly, and fun. Older gays and lesbians still frequent some of the faded bars that are fixtures in Paris, such as **Le Trap** (cruisy and older) and **Le Vagabond** (one of the city's oldest gay bars), but the new generation has made the Marais its main point of nocturnal interest.

Sex clubs are gaining popularity at an alarming rate—sometimes an entire bar is a "backroom," where unsafe sex frequently takes place on the darkened dance floor. (These clubs are scattered around the gay area, with none right in the Marais.) Dance clubs come and go with the seasons, and usually there are only two or three that are popular at any given time. Always ask around to get the latest scoop. Your best source of information on current events, hot spots, and weekly happenings (like the Bains

Mousse nights at Le Queen) is ***e.m@le Magazine,*** free at some gay bars or 8F ($1.50) at a newsstand or the gay bookstore, Les Mots à la Bouche (see "Hitting the Stores"). Other good sources are the ***Hyzberg Guide,*** also free; the ***Illico*** guides distributed at all the major bars and clubs; ***Gai Pied; Double Face; Lesbia;*** and ***Guide Lesbien Exes. Time Out Paris*** is a good weekly resource; ***WHERE Paris*** comes out monthly and is crammed with information.

Since the line between bar and cafe is so thin, **opening hours** aren't always very clear. Most of the bars below (except as noted) are open from early evening, usually around 7pm to at least 1 or 2am, though many open before noon and stay open until 2am. Harry's Bar stays open until 4am. Many places accept reservations even for a cocktail table if you don't want to just stand at the bar; call ahead (make sure you're not expected to order a full meal, though). And remember to dress well: Barfly is notorious for turning people away at whim; the more you look like a big spender, the less likely it is you'll be turned away. Some places specify "no blue jeans"; sneakers are also frowned on in many of the straight bars and clubs. Gay places are much more laid-back, and you can wear whatever to most of the bars and clubs.

MAINSTREAM BARS & PUBS

One of the trendiest places with a mixed crowd is ✪ **Barfly,** 49–51 av. George V, 8e (☎ **01-53-67-84-60;** Métro: George V). It boasts the longest bar in town and the most elegant crowd in Paris; fancy shirts and sports jackets are the norm, though on weekday evenings you'll see quite a few businessmen in suits. ✪ **Le Fumoir,** 6 rue de l'Amiral-Coligny, 1er (☎ **01-42-92-00-24;** Métro: Palais-Royal), is a breezy new place that's fast becoming tops with a straight cigar-smoking crowd; the small library lined with books is real cozy on a cold winter's night.

Near the Opéra Garnier, **Harry's New York Bar,** 5 rue Daunou, 2e (☎ **01-42-61-71-14;** Métro: Pyramides), is still going strong, serving the best Bloody Marys (they were created here) and martinis (with olives, thank you) since it opened in 1911, with Hemingway as one of its first customers. You'll find a mostly straight Anglo crowd. For a postperformance drink near the Opéra Bastille, there's no better choice than **The China Club,** 50 rue des Charenton, 12e (☎ **01-43-43-82-02;** Métro: Bastille), where French yuppies mingle on three levels amid a plush Indian and Far Eastern decor; there's a Chinese restaurant serving pricey dishes.

Wine is so abundant in France that wine bars haven't really been popular until now. **Willi's Wine Bar,** 13 rue des Petits-Champs, 1er (☎ **01-42-61-05-09;** Métro: Louvre), has become the hottest hangout for sophisticated Parisian 30- and 40-somethings. They congregate here for lunch or after work to sip on over 250 kinds of wine; the food isn't bad either, with daily specials and good deserts. If you're in the mood for a quiet romantic early-evening stroll, quench your thirst at **Le Bar du Caveau,** 17 place Dauphine, 1er (☎ **01-43-54-45-95;** Métro: Pont-Neuf; open daily noon-8pm), with a glass of wine and a snack.

Over in Montparnasse, **Le Select,** 99 bd. du Montparnasse, 6e (☎ **01-42-22-65-27;** Métro: Vavin), has been serving strong malt whiskies since the early 1920s. You won't find the trendy Parisians here (it's a mix of tourists and bohemians), but it's still a fun place to people-watch. This cafe/bar figured strongly in James Baldwin's *Giovanni's Room* and Baldwin himself came here often in the 1950s. Not far from the slightly cruisy park of André Citroën is a sleek modern bar popular with a mixed young crowd: **Zebra Square & Lounge Bar,** 3 square Clement-Ader, 16e (☎ **01-44-14-91-91;** Métro: Mirabeau). It boasts loud zebra-striped chairs and seems absurdly out of place in this quiet residential neighborhood with its 17th-century buildings.

Of all the hotel bars (many are excellent), the **Hemingway Bar** at the Ritz, 15 place Vendôme, 1er (☎ **01-43-16-30-30;** Métro: Louvre or Opéra; open

Dining in the Dark

Where to go at 3am for some decent food? The dancing boys coming out of Le Queen head to **La Maison d'Alsace,** 39 av. des Champs-Elysées, 8e (☎ **01-53-93-97-00;** Métro: George V; open 24 hours), for some sausage and *choucroute* (sauerkraut) and other hearty specials from the Alsace region. Main courses are 90 to 175F ($16 to $32), with a fixed-price menu at 123F ($22) after 10pm.

Boys and girls coming out of the bars and clubs in the Marais head to **Au Pied de Cochon,** 6 rue Coquillière, 1er (☎ **01-40-13-77-00;** Métro: Les Halles; open 24 hours), for some grilled pig's feet served with béarnaise sauce. If something lighter suits your fancy, there's seafood, chicken, and salads. Main courses run 78 to 150F ($14 to $27), with a fixed-price menu at 178F ($32).

Tues–Sat 6:30pm–1am), is the best, steeped in history. It's an intimate space with somber wood paneling where a somewhat older crowd lounges on leather chairs, puffs on cigars, and drinks whiskey or port. A bronze bust of Hemingway will greet you as you walk in.

GAY BARS

The three top gay bars are close to one another in the Marais (Métro: Hôtel-de-Ville) and are open daily 10am to 2am. Don't let their cafe names fool you—they're all bars, attracting men ages 20 to 40 from all over the world (usually more than half are Parisians).

✪ **Open Café,** 17 rue des Archives, 4e (☎ **01-42-72-26-18**), and ✪ **Café Cox,** 15 rue des Archives, 4e (☎ **01-42-72-08-00**), both get so busy in the early evening that the crowd stands out on the sidewalk. These places are where you'll find the most mixed gay crowd in Paris—from hunky American tourists to sexy Parisian men. Muscle dudes in white T-shirts and intellos (intellectuals) in tweed jackets all hang out here. The mood is especially flirtatious on Saturdays between 10pm and midnight, before the boys head to the dance clubs.

Amnesia Café, 42 rue du Vieille-du-Temple, 4e (☎ **01-42-72-16-94**), is laid-back, with more of a living-room feel and a slightly queenier crowd (less T-shirts and more scarves).

✪ **Le Quetzal,** 10 rue de la Verrerie, 4e (☎ **01-48-87-99-07**), attracts a lot of posers, cute boys with a constant bored look (pleading to be entertained), but that's only early in the evening. Later on, the place gets fun and slightly cruisy.

One of the oldest gay venues in the Marais, the **Bar Le Central,** 33 rue Vieille-du-Temple, 4e (☎ **01-48-87-56-08**), is tacky and a bit drab but still gets its share of hot tourists clutching guidebooks. Above the bar, Le Hôtel Central rents out seven simple rooms, most with shared baths; rates start at 495F ($90) double.

Paris's oldest gay bar is in the old gay district of St-Anne, **Le Vagabond,** 14 rue Thérèse, 1er (☎ **01-42-96-27-23;** Métro: Pyramides). It opened in the mid-1950s and for many years was the only venue in town. Now an older, tired group of men congregates in what's a landmark of French gay history.

Over in Les Halles, a new and successful place is **Le Tropic Café,** 66 rue des Lombards, 1er (☎ **01-40-13-92-62;** Métro: Châtelet–Les-Halles). The trendy good-looking crowd parties until dawn.

At **Banana Café,** 13 rue de la Ferronnerie, 1er (☎ **01-42-33-35-31;** Métro: Châtelet–Les-Halles), you'll find frequent cabaret shows in the basement as well as go-go boys; the action goes on until 6am.

For the most sedate and slightly intellectual gay bar in the city, head to **Le Duplex Bar,** 25 rue Michel-Le-Comte, 3e (☎ **01-42-72-80-86;** Métro: Rambuteau), where the men don't cruise but actually talk to one another (gasp!).

LESBIAN BARS

The largest lesbian bar in Paris is **La Champmeslé,** 4 rue Chabanais, 2e (☎ **01-42-96-85-20;** Métro: Pyramides; closed Sun). It has been popular for over 15 years with a mix of ages and styles.

A new restaurant with a bar fast becoming popular with women is **Okawa,** 40 rue Vieille-du-Temple, 4e (☎ **01-48-04-30-69;** Métro: Hôtel-de-Ville), where trendy lesbians (and some gay boys) sip drinks at Happy Hour.

The latest hot spot in the Marais for young women is **Les Scandaleuses,** 8 rue des Ecouffes, 4e (☎ **01-48-87-39-26;** Métro: St-Paul). It's sleek and contemporary and rocks with loud music.

✪ **Café Beaubourg,** 100 rue St-Martin, 4e (☎ **01-48-87-63-96;** Métro: Rambuteau), is one of the most popular bar/cafe/restaurants in Paris, attracting a steady stream of hip lesbians dressed in black.

LEATHER BARS

Le Transfert, 3 rue de la Sourdière, 1er (☎ **01-42-60-48-42;** Métro: Tuileries), doesn't even open until midnight, and the tough men don't arrive before 2am.

One Way Bar & Video, 28 rue Charlot, 3e (☎ **01-48-87-46-10;** Métro: République), draws big bearded (or goateed) bears in leather and offers a real friendly hairy staff. In the basement is a constant video show.

Le Trap, 10 rue Jacob, 6e (☎ **01-43-54-53-53;** Métro: St-Germain-des-Prés), attracts some men in leather at its very tame location on elegant rue Jacob. Come here very late; you'll have to ring to be let in. In the basement are several backrooms.

DANCE CLUBS

Expect to dish out a 50 to 100F ($9 to $18) cover, which more often than not also buys you a drink. Most clubs open at midnight and stay open until dawn. Weekly listings of theme nights and special events are published in ***e.m@le Magazine*** available free at gay bars and for sale at many gay shops in the Marais. For lesbians, the guide ***Exes Femmes*** publishes a free seasonal listing of lesbian bars and clubs.

GAY CLUBS The current hot spot for yuppie Parisian men is the ✪ **Gibus Club,** 18 rue faubourg-du-Temple, 11e (☎ 01-47-00-78-88; Métro: République), attracting a good-looking crowd of mostly 25- to 35-year-olds, with not as much attitude as you'll find elsewhere. Occasional morning parties start before midnight on Saturday and end at noon Sunday.

The oldest and most consistently popular gay dance club is ✪ **Le Queen,** 102 av. des Champs-Elysées, 8e (☎ **01-53-89-08-90;** Métro: George V). It employs a woman bouncer (along with two big guys) to explain to unsuspecting straight tourists that this is a gay club. The huge space fills with hot men from around the world (trendy Parisian gays dismiss it as passé, but everybody else seems to love it). Theme nights include Bain Mousse (bubble bath), when the dance floor fills with bubbles and the boys get wet and wild (bring extra clothes).

An interesting place that attracts a wide range of men (many over 40) is **Le London,** 33 bis rue des Lombards, 1er (☎ **01-42-33-41-45;** Métro: Châtelet–Les-Halles). This contemporary place is a restaurant until midnight, when it becomes a disco. Weekends can get real cruisy; it's a good place to find a daddy, young man.

LESBIAN CLUBS Recently acquired by a beautiful young woman, **Le Pulp,** 25 bd. Poissonnière, 2e (☎ **01-40-26-01-93;** Métro: Montmartre), attracts a crowd much like the owner.

More butch, **L'Enfer,** 34 rue du Départ, 14e (☎ **01-42-79-94-94;** Métro: Montparnasse), rocks with a huge crowd of trendy lesbians on Friday and Saturday; Thursdays are more mixed, with gay men welcome.

MIXED CLUBS ✪ **Les Bains, 7 rue du Bourg-l'Abbé,** 3e (☎ **01-48-87-01-80;** Métro: Reamur), draws a mixed trendy crowd that dresses up to dance at what used to be a bathhouse (thus the name). Monday nights are becoming increasingly gay.

Le Rex Club, 5 bd. Poissonnière, 2e (☎ **01-42-36-10-96;** Métro: Bonne-Nouvelle), offers a bit of everything, though theme nights can be exclusively gay; check the listings.

A mixed techno club welcoming both gays and lesbians is **Mixer,** 23 rue St-Croix-de-la-Bretonnerie, 4e (☎ **01-48-87-55-44;** Métro: Hôtel-de-Ville), but there's not much dancing here.

DOWN & DIRTY: CINEMAS, SAUNAS & MORE

The oldest cruising area is in the **Jardin des Tuileries** (on the southern end, closest to the river), where you'll find older men (some in raincoats, oh-so cliché), especially in the evenings. At the **Jardin du Luxembourg** (by the fountain) the men range from about 20 to 60. Late at night, around the **Eiffel Tower** are two cruising spots, both quite risky: On the Right Bank (on the sidewalk parallel to the small park) you'll see young hustlers waiting to be picked up; on the Left Bank, at the far end of Champ-de-Mars (facing the Ecole Militaire), men of all shapes and sizes prowl around looking for action.

SEX CLUBS An all-encompassing sex club (giant video screen, sauna, go-go boys, strippers, and more) is the huge **Univers Gym,** 20–22 rue des Bons-Enfants, 1er (☎ **01-42-61-24-83;** Métro: Palais-Royal; open Sun–Thurs noon–1am, Fri–Sat to 2am; admission 97F/$17), popular with a wide range of men. Live shows are on Saturday at 8pm; theme nights are held throughout the week.

Le Depot, 10 rue aux Ours, 3e (☎ **01-44-54-96-96;** Métro: Etienne-Marcel or Rambuteau; open daily noon–8am; admission 45F/$8, including one drink), is the newest and largest sex club. It claims to be all one backroom (several levels, that is) of hard-core cruising, with morning parties and theme nights weekly. **Les Docks,** 150 rue St-Maur, 11e (☎ **01-43-57-33-82;** Métro: Goncourt; open daily 4pm–2am), is real cruisy and hard-core, with video monitors, private cubicles, and slings. Theme parties include bizarre offerings like "tit work" nights—come shirtless with pierced nipples and they might waive the 45F ($8) admission. **L'Arène,** 80 quai de l'Hôtel-de-Ville, 4e (no phone; Métro: Hôtel-de-Ville; open daily 2pm–6am; admission 50F [$9]), was the most popular sex club until Le Depot opened; however, it still draws a steady stream of hungry men. There are live strip shows monthly.

IEM, 43 rue de l'Arbre-Sec, 1e (☎ **01-42-96-05-74;** Métro: Louvre; open Mon–Sat noon–10pm, Sun 2–10pm), is Paris's most respected sex shop for the best XXX videos (no viewing cabins), leather, latex, magazines, and sex toys. And at **Sex-Shop Video,** 21 rue des Lombards, 1er (☎ **01-40-27-98-09;** Métro: Châtelet–Les Halles), you'll find lots of young gays picking up supplies and viewing videos.

SAUNAS **Key West,** 141 rue de Lafayette, 10e (☎ **01-45-26-31-74;** Métro: Gare-du-Nord; open Sun–Thurs noon–1am, Fri–Sat to 2am; admission 95–135F/$17–$25), is one of the city's oldest gay saunas, pulling in a lot of out-of-towners of all ages.

IDM, 4 rue du Faubourg-Montmartre, 9e (☎ **01-45-23-10-03;** Métro: rue Montmartre; open Sun–Thurs noon–1am, Fri–Sat to 2am; admission 135F/$25), has a gym where actually a few people work out and offers free suntanning.

The smaller **Le Mandala,** 2 rue Drouot, 9e (☎ **01-42-46-60-14;** Métro: Richelieu-Drouot; open Sun–Wed noon–1am, Thurs–Sat to 6am; admission 135F/$25), offers a nonalcoholic bar and TV room in addition to the sauna, the steam room, the Jacuzzi, and relaxation rooms. A sauna popular with older gay businessmen is **Eden Form–Victor Hugo,** 109 av. Victor-Hugo, 16e (☎ **01-47-04-41-24;** Métro: Victor-Hugo; open Mon–Sat noon–9pm, Sun 1–8pm; admission 140F [$25]), with steam rooms, cubicles, and so on.

8 Side Trips from Paris: The Best of the Ile de France

After exploring Paris's wealth of treasures, you may be tempted to venture outside the city for a look at the attractions in the surrounding area, known as the Ile de France. All the following are easily reachable by car or public transport from Paris and make great day trips. Many of the tour companies (see "Exploring Paris" above) also offer day trips to the destinations below.

VERSAILLES

Louis XIV (reigned 1643 to 1715) commissioned the ✪ **Château de Versailles** (☎ **01-30-84-74-00;** www.chateauversailles.fr) and its vast grounds and gardens. Construction lasted for 50 years, transforming Louis XIII's simple hunting lodge into an extravagant palace. Fourteen miles southwest of Paris, Versailles is one of France's great attractions.

So he could keep an eye on the nobles of France (and with good reason), Louis summoned them to live at his court. Here he amused them with constant entertainment and lavish banquets. To some he awarded such tasks as holding the hem of his ermine-lined robe. While the aristocrats frivolously played away their lives, often in silly intrigues and games, the peasants on the estates sowed the seeds of the Revolution. Finally, on October 6, 1789, Louis XVI and Marie Antoinette were at Versailles when they were notified that mobs were marching on the palace.

The six magnificent **Grands Appartements** are in the Louis XIV style, each named after the allegorical painting on the room's ceiling. The largest is the **Hercules Salon,** with a ceiling depicting the Apotheosis of Hercules. In the **Mercury Salon,** the body of Louis XIV was put on display in 1715; his 72-year reign was one of the longest in history. The most famous room at Versailles is the 236-foot-long **Hall of Mirrors.** Begun by Mansart in 1678 in the Louis XIV style, it was decorated by Le Brun, with 17 large arched windows matched by corresponding beveled mirrors in simulated arcades. On June 28, 1919, the treaty ending World War I was signed here. Ironically, the German Empire was also proclaimed here in 1871.

The royal apartments were for show, but Louis XV and Louis XVI retired to the **Petits Appartements** to escape the demands of court etiquette. Louis XV died in his bedchamber in 1774, a victim of smallpox. In a second-floor apartment, which you can visit only with a guide, he stashed away first Mme de Pompadour and then Mme du Barry. Attempts have been made to return the Queen's Apartments to their appearance during the days of Marie Antoinette, when she played her harpsichord in front of specially invited guests. The **Clock Room** contains Passement's astronomical clock, encased in gilded bronze. Twenty years in the making, it was completed in 1753. The clock is supposed to keep time until the year 9999. At the age of 7, Mozart played in this room for the court.

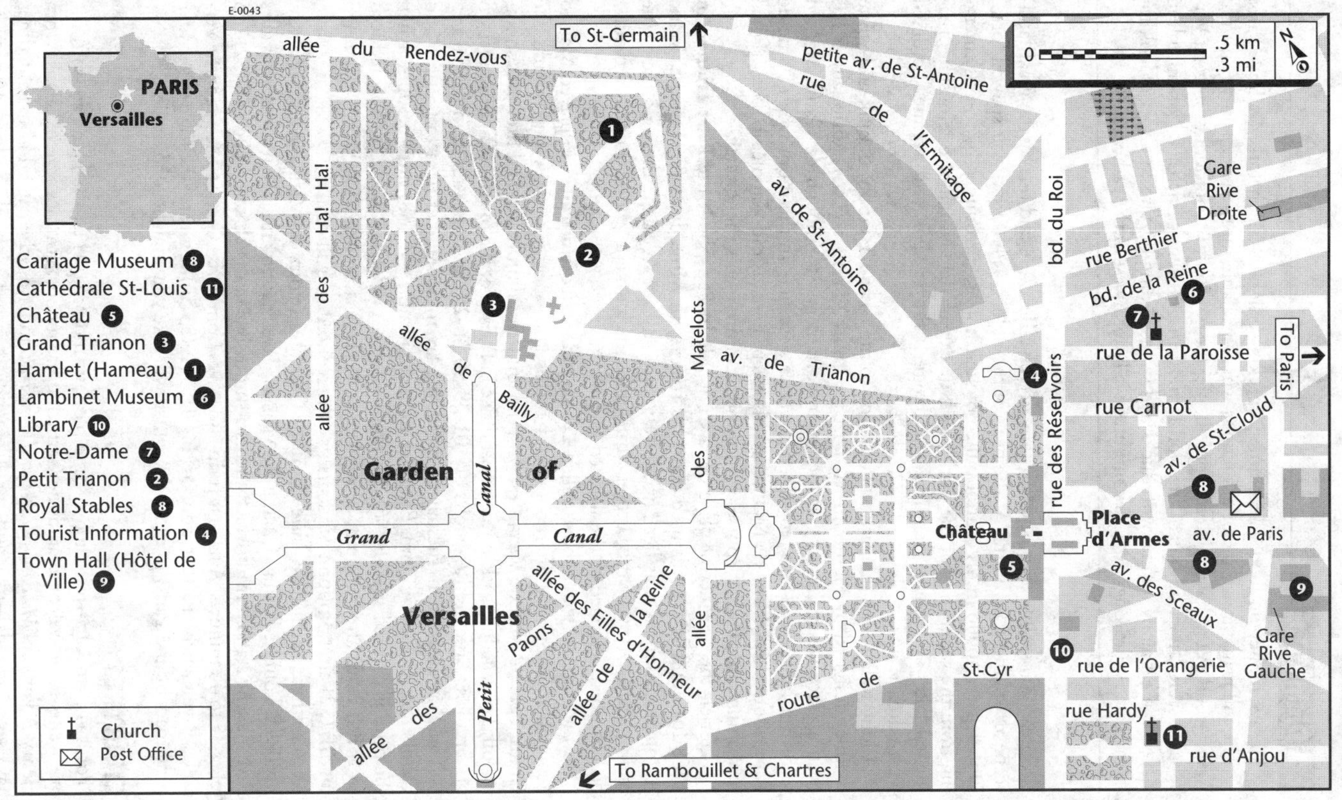
E-0043
To St-Germain
allée du Rendez-vous
petite av. de St-Antoine
rue de l'Ermitage
0
.5 km
.3 mi
PARIS
Versailles
Carriage Museum 8
Cathédrale St-Louis 11
Château 5
Grand Trianon 3
Hamlet (Hameau) 1
Lambinet Museum 6
Library 10
Notre-Dame 7
Petit Trianon 2
Royal Stables 8
Tourist Information 4
Town Hall (Hôtel de Ville) 9
Church
Post Office
allée des Ha! Ha!
av. de St-Antoine
bd. du Roi
Gare Rive Droite
rue Berthier
bd. de la Reine
rue de la Paroisse
To Paris
allée de Bailly
allée des Matelots
av. de Trianon
rue des Réservoirs
rue Carnot
av. de St-Cloud
Garden of Versailles
Grand Canal
Petit Canal
Château
Place d'Armes
av. de Paris
av. des Sceaux
Gare Rive Gauche
allée des Paons
allée des Filles d'Honneur
allée de la Reine
allée
route de St-Cyr
rue de l'Orangerie
rue Hardy
rue d'Anjou
allée des
To Rambouillet & Chartres

A Dining Tip

To save money on food, I recommend packing a light picnic before you leave Paris. The following are all major attractions where available meals are expensive and not very good. A few have cafeterias, but all offer the possibility of outdoor dining. At Versailles you can eat in one of the world's most magnificent gardens; at Fontainebleau you can eat along a canal with ducks and swans gliding by; and in Chartres look for the Parc André-Gagnon, a few minutes' walk norhtwest of the cathedral.

Spread across 250 acres, the **Gardens of Versailles** were laid out by the great landscape artist André Le Nôtre. At the peak of their glory, 1,400 fountains spewed forth. One depicts Apollo in his chariot pulled by four horses, surrounded by tritons emerging from the water to light the world. Le Nôtre created a Garden of Eden using ornamental lakes and canals, geometrically designed flower beds, and avenues bordered with statuary.

A long walk across the park will take you to the **Grand Trianon,** in pink-and-white marble, designed by Hardouin-Mansart for Louis XIV in 1687. Traditionally it has been a place where France has lodged important guests, though de Gaulle wanted to turn it into a weekend retreat. Nixon once slept here in the room where Mme de Pompadour died. Mme de Maintenon also slept here, as did Napoléon. The original furnishings are gone, of course, with mostly Empire pieces there today.

Gabriel, the designer of place de la Concorde in Paris, built the **Petit Trianon** in 1768 for Louis XV. Louis used it for his trysts with Mme du Barry. In time, Marie Antoinette adopted it as her favorite residence, a place to escape the rigid life at the main palace. Many of the current furnishings, including a few in her rather modest bedchamber, belonged to the ill-fated queen.

In the gardens, water shows called **Les Grands Eaux Musicales** are played May to September on Sunday afternoons, and there's also one night show per month, the **Grand Fête de Nuit de Versailles,** with the fountains illuminated and fireworks shooting off. For schedules, ask at the tourist office in Paris or at the **tourist office** in the town of Versailles, 7 rue des Réservoirs (☎ **01-39-50-36-22**), a short walk from the palace.

The château is open Tuesday to Sunday: May to September 9am to 6:30pm and October to April to 5:30pm. Entrance to the château is 45F ($8) until 3:30pm, when the price is reduced to 35F ($6). Entrance to the Grand Trianon is 25F ($4), reduced to 15F ($2.50) after 3:30pm; admission to the Petit Trianon is 15F ($2.50), lowered to 10F ($2) after 3:30pm. Students pay the reduced rate all day.

To get here, catch **RER Line C5** at the Gare d'Austerlitz, St-Michel, Musée-d'Orsay, Invalides, Pont de l'Alma, Champ-de-Mars, or Javel station and take it to the Versailles Rive Gauche station, from which there's a shuttle bus to the château. The 14F ($2) trip takes 35 to 40 minutes. A regular **train** also leaves from Paris's Gare St-Lazare for the Versailles Rive Gauche RER station, costing 19.50F ($3.50). By **car,** take the *périphérique* (ring road around Paris) to exit N10, which will take you straight to Versailles.

CHARTRES

"For a visit to Chartres, choose some pleasant morning when the lights are soft, for one wants to be welcome, and the Cathedral has moods, at times severe." Thus wrote Henry Adams in *Mont St-Michel and Chartres,* and, yes, the cathedral may at times have severe moods—gray and cold like winter weather in the Ile de France region—but it's always astoundingly beautiful, with its harmonious architecture and lofty stained-glass windows.

Notre-Dame de Chartres

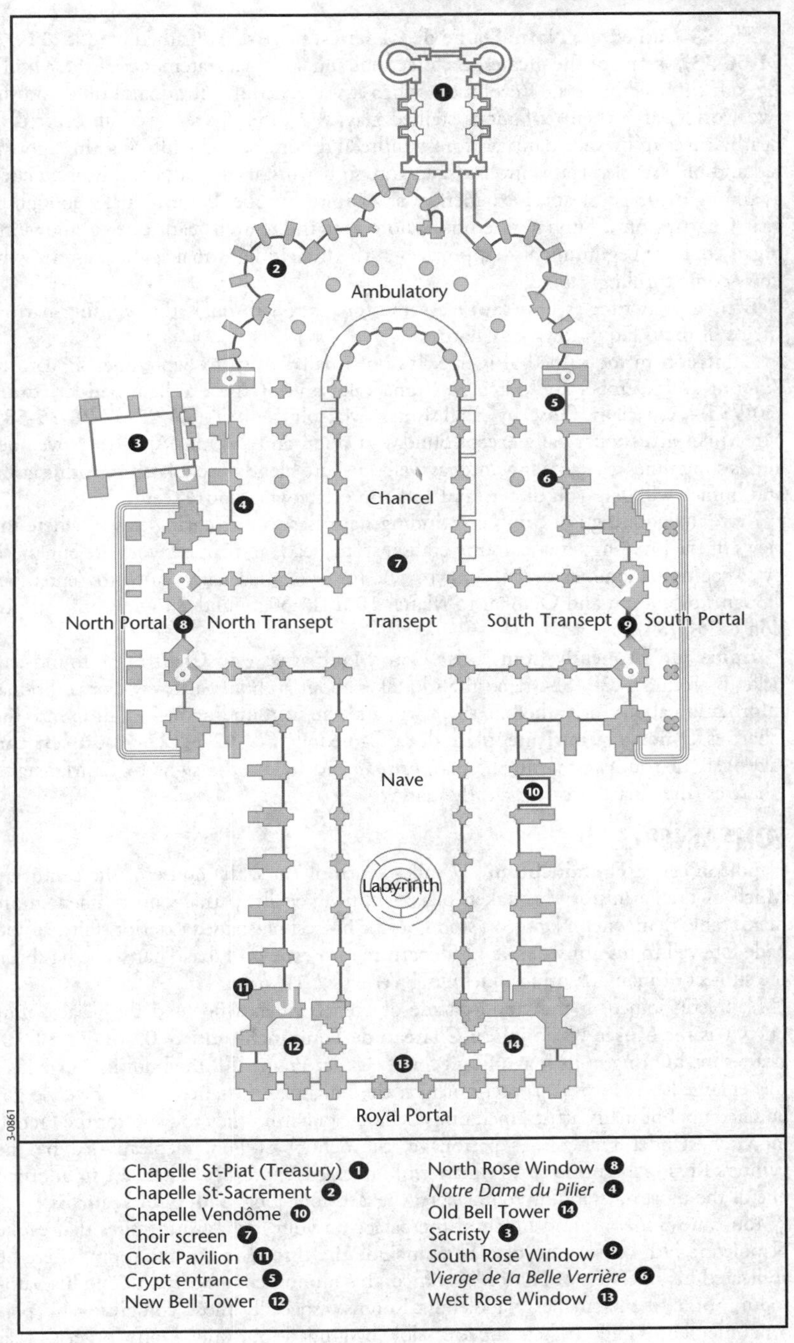
Ambulatory
Chancel
North Portal
North Transept
Transept
South Transept
South Portal
Nave
Labyrinth
Royal Portal
3-0861
Chapelle St-Piat (Treasury) 1
Chapelle St-Sacrement 2
Chapelle Vendôme 10
Choir screen 7
Clock Pavilion 11
Crypt entrance 5
New Bell Tower 12
North Rose Window 8
Notre Dame du Pilier 4
Old Bell Tower 14
Sacristy 3
South Rose Window 9
Vierge de la Belle Verrière 6
West Rose Window 13

The ✪ **Cathédrale Notre-Dame de Chartres,** place de la Cathédrale (☎ **02-37-21-56-33**), is one of the greatest architectural and spiritual statements of the Middle Ages. It survived both the Revolution, when it was scheduled for demolition, and the two world wars, when its famous stained glass was carefully removed and stored in nearby caves to prevent damage from gunfire and bombs. Light filtering through the red and blue stained glass onto the cold gray stonework of the cathedral is often cited as among the most mystical experiences of a trip to Europe. If you're lucky enough to visit Chartres on a Sunday afternoon, note that the church features free hour-long organ concerts beginning at 4:45pm, when the filtered light makes the western windows come thrillingly alive.

Even if your time is limited, save some for a stroll through the winding narrow streets of the tranquil town of Chartres.

Admission to the cathedral is free. It's open daily: April to September 7:30am to 7:30pm and October to March to 7pm. Take one of the excellent **guided tours** (30F/$5)—especially those by Englishman Malcolm Miller (☎ **02-37-28-15-58**). Mr. Miller gives tours daily except Sunday at noon and 2:45pm April to November and is sometimes available in winter as well. His rare blend of scholarship, enthusiasm, and humor will help you understand and appreciate what you're seeing.

More invigorating is a climb up winding staircases to the soaring **tower,** where the views of the building's meticulously crafted stone, lead, and copperwork are enhanced by sweeping panoramas over the town. The tower is open daily: April to September 9:30am to 5:30pm and October to March 10 to 11:30am and 2 to 4:30pm. Admission is 25F ($4).

Trains run frequently from Paris's Gare Montparnasse to Chartres. A round-trip ticket is around 142F ($24), and the trip takes about an hour each way. For additional information about the cathedral, the town, and the surrounding region, drop into the Chartres **Office de Tourisme,** place de la Cathédrale (☎ **02-37-21-50-00**). By **car,** take A10/11 southwest from the *périphérique* and follow the signs to Le Mans and Chartres (the Chartres exit is clearly marked).

FONTAINEBLEAU

Napoléon called **Fontainebleau,** 37 miles south of Paris, the house of the centuries. Much of French history has taken place within its walls, perhaps no moment more memorable than when Napoléon stood on the horseshoe-shaped exterior staircase and bade farewell to his army before his departure into exile on Elba. That scene has been the subject of many paintings, including Vernet's *Les Adieux.*

Napoléon joined in the grand parade of French rulers who used the palace, now known as the **Musée National du Château de Fontainebleau** (☎ **01-60-71-50-70**) as a resort, hunting in its magnificent forest. Under François I, the hunting lodge here was enlarged into a royal palace, much in the Italian Renaissance style. The style got botched up, but many artists, including Cellini, came from Italy to work for the French monarch. Under François I's patronage, the School of Fontainebleau (led by the painters Rosso Fiorentino and Primaticcio) increased in prestige. These artists adorned one of the most outstanding rooms here: the 210-foot-long **Gallery of François I.**

You can wander around much of the palace on your own, visiting sites that evoke Napoléon's 19th-century heyday. They include the throne room, the room where he abdicated his rulership of France, his offices, his monumental bedroom, and his bathroom. Some of the smaller Napoleonic Rooms, especially those containing his personal mementos and artifacts, are accessible by guided tour only. Don't forget to visit the gardens and, especially, the carp pond; however, they're not nearly as spectacular as those at Versailles.

Though Cocteau's main residence was an apartment close to the Palais Royal in Paris, he spent a considerable amount of time in the south of France (see "Cocteau on the Côte" in chapter 6) and kept a home outside Paris in Milly-la-Fôret, on the fringes of the Fontainebleau forest. He died there in 1963 and is buried at the town's cemetery.

The château's interior is open Wednesday to Monday: November to April 9:30am to 12:30pm and 2 to 5pm, May to October 9:30am to 5pm. Admission for the grands appartements is 35F ($6); admission for the Napoleonic Rooms is 16F ($3).

Trains to Fontainebleau depart from Paris's Gare de Lyon. The trip takes 35 to 60 minutes and costs 47F ($8). The Fontainebleau station is just outside the town in Avon, a suburb of Paris; a local **bus** makes the 2-mile trip to the château every 10 to 15 minutes Monday to Saturday (every 30 minutes Sunday). By **car,** from the *périphérique,* take A6 south from Paris, exit onto N191, and follow the signs.

GIVERNY

Even before you arrive at ✪ **Giverny,** 50 miles northwest of Paris, it's very likely you'll already have some idea of what you're going to see, since Claude Monet's paintings of his garden are known and loved throughout the world.

Monet moved to Giverny in 1883, and the water lilies beneath the Japanese bridge in the garden, as well as the flower garden, became his regular subjects until his death in 1926. In 1966, the Monet family donated Giverny to the Academie des Beaux-Arts in Paris, perhaps the most prestigious fine-arts school in France, and they subsequently decided to open the site to the public. It has since become one of the most popular attractions in France, but even the crowds can't completely overwhelm the magic of this place.

Though the gardens are lovely year-round, they're usually at their best in May and June and September and October. Should you yearn to have them almost to yourself, you should plan to be at the gates some morning when they first open. For more information, call ☎ **02-32-51-28-21.**

April to October, the gardens are open Tuesday to Sunday 10am to 6pm. Admission to the house and gardens is 35F ($6); admission to the gardens only is 25F ($4).

Trains leave Paris's Gare St-Lazare approximately every 45 minutes for Vernon, the town nearest the Monet gardens. The round-trip fare is roughly 134F ($22). From the station, buses make the 3-mile trip to the museum for 12F ($2) or you can go on foot—the route along the Seine makes for a nice walk. If you're coming by **car,** take A13 from Porte d'Auteuil to Bonnières and then D201 to Giverny.

6 Nice & the Côte d'Azur

The **Côte d'Azur** (Azure Coast) with its brilliant sunshine and deep-blue Mediterranean is fantastically romantic—from quaint hillside villages to palatial seaside resorts, from star-studded Cannes to glittering Monte Carlo to oh-so-gay St-Tropez, this land is everything you've heard about and more. It's the stuff wet dreams are made of (yes, those *hommes* and *femmes* in skimpy swimsuits or even less are real). Everyone from famous artists and writers to rock and movie stars (James Baldwin, Jean Cocteau, Joan Collins, Rupert Everett, F. Scott Fitzgerald, Elton John, Grace Kelly, Fernand Léger, Madonna, Henri Matisse, Pablo Picasso, Tina Turner, Marguerite Yourcenar, Frank Zappa) has come to partake of the beauty of this landscape. If there's anywhere in the world that reeks of glamour and romance, it's the French Riviera.

Though some people expect it to be a sleepy seaside town, **Nice** is France's fourth-largest city, a crowded, bustling place that's often used as a base for exploring the Riviera. It's framed to the south by the sparkling Bay of Angels (Baie des Anges), to the north by the Maritime Alps (Alpes Maritimes), to the west by the hills of the Massif de l'Estérel, and to the east by Italy, less than 40 miles away. It's a compact city, friendly and laid back. But expect what you would from any large urban area: traffic, noise, and hordes of tourists in July and August. If you're looking for a quiet beach vacation, this shouldn't be your first choice (St-Tropez or Cap d'Antibes might be more what you're after if you can afford them).

Nice's advantages are its central location along the coast, reasonably priced hotels and restaurants, and year-round nightlife, particularly gay. Though it boasts a solid gay and lesbian population, the city has no real community and no exclusively gay neighborhoods. Politically, it's conservative and has never been especially liberal, though the French attitude *il faut se montrer tolérant* (live and let live) translates into minimal discrimination. The current mayor leans to the far right and isn't very gay-friendly (the gay pride parade isn't held in Nice but in nearby Cannes, and he intends to keep it that way).

So perhaps it's not surprising that finding your way to Nice's gay restaurants, beaches, bars, and cruising areas isn't easy. Everything is a bit camouflaged. But I've done the work for you and discovered the places where you're most likely to enjoy the sun and the company of other gay men (lesbians are amazingly invisible all over the coast) . . . and where you'll definitely find some incredible art and architecture.

1 Nice Essentials

ARRIVING & DEPARTING

BY PLANE Nice's international airport, the **Aéroport Nice–Côte d'Azur,** is just 3 miles west of the city, its runways jutting out into the Mediterranean. This is France's second busiest airport (after Paris's Charles de Gaulle), and there are very competitive fares from around the world. The airport has two terminals: Terminal 1 is reserved for international arrivals, while Terminal 2 handles all the domestic traffic; for all airport information, call ☎ **04-93-21-30-30.** A free shuttle operates frequently between the two terminals, a mile apart.

From the United States, fares to Nice are only about $50 higher than they are to Paris, and in most cases you can fly into Nice and out of any other French or European city with just a minimal fare increase (ask for an open-jaw fare when planning your trip). Delta and Air France fly a combined daily nonstop from New York; British Airways and British Midland provide up to 12 daily arrivals from London. From Paris, there are flights every half an hour 6am to 10pm (AOM and Air Liberté have the lowest fares). There are six flights from Toulouse, plus daily nonstop flights from most European cities.

Many travelers rent a **car** at the airport, especially if they're not staying in Nice; there's a special exit directly to Autoroute A8, avoiding the city traffic altogether. (Note there's a 70–96F/$13–$17 airport surcharge for any car rented at the airport.) See below under "Getting Around" for more information.

Public bus no. 23 runs every half an hour (daily 6am–10:30pm) from Terminal 1 to the city center, terminating 25 minutes later at the downtown train station, the Gare SNCF. The fare is 8.50F ($1.50); you can buy a ticket on the bus. **Auto Nice Transport** at ☎ **04-92-29-88-88** operates air-conditioned buses from both terminals (daily 6am–11:40pm) to the Gare Routière, the coach station in the city center (where you can catch buses to most towns and villages in the South of France). On request, the bus will stop at predetermined points along the promenade des Anglais close to many major hotels. The one-way fare is 21F ($3.80); Monday to Saturday, the bus runs every 20 minutes, on Sunday and public holidays every 30 minutes. For the return trip, buses leave from platform 12 from the Gare Routière (☎ **04-93-80-08-70**) and at designated pick-up points at the major hotels along the promenade des Anglais; have your hotel call to request a pick-up. Hourly nonstop bus service is also available to Cannes and Monte Carlo operated by **Rapides Côte d'Azur,** 455 promenade des Anglais (☎ **04-93-39-11-39**). The one-way fare is 70F ($13) to Cannes and 80F ($15) to Monte Carlo. The trip to both destinations takes 40 minutes.

For ultra-speed and ultra-chic, there's **helicopter service** to Monte Carlo (and to St-Tropez and Cannes during high season). The one-way fare to Monte Carlo and Cannes is 370F ($67) for the 7-minute ride; St-Tropez is a 15-minute flight at 750F ($136). Frequency depends on the season (every 15 minutes July–Aug) and at least twice hourly during other months. Contact **Heli Inter Riviera,** Aéroport Nice–Côte d'Azur, 060056 Nice (☎ **04-93-21-46-46**).

Taxis are expensive. From the airport to Nice, plan on paying 160 to 200F ($29 to $36), depending on your destination. You'll pay around 450F ($81) to Monte Carlo and 370F ($67) to Cannes.

BY TRAIN Nice's main train station, the **Gare SNCF** (the Société National des Chemins de Fer is France's national rail company), is conveniently in the city center on avenue Thiers (☎ **04-93-87-50-50**). High-speed TGV (Trains de Grand Vitesse) trains arrive from Paris three times a day in high season and twice in winter for the 7-hour trip. Connections from London via the Chunnel are more convenient through

Lille, twice daily. Frequent service is also provided from many European cities; Milan is barely 4 hours away, Toulouse 7 hours. The train station is about 10 blocks from the sea, and though there are many hotels around the Gare, the area is known as the dumpiest neighborhood in the city. A **taxi** to major hotels will set you back anywhere from 80 to 150F ($15 to $27) depending on your destination. Buses to the seafront operate very frequently daily 6:30am to 9pm and cost 8.50F ($1.55); take bus no. 5, 12, or 17.

BY BUS Coaches from all over Europe, as well as domestic services from neighboring towns and cities, arrive at Nice's **Gare Routière,** 5 bd. Jean-Jaurés (☎ **04-93-80-08-70**), located off place Masséna, close to Vieux Nice.

BY CAR Autoroute A8 runs through the city's northern suburbs. Ignore the signs for Centre Ville (downtown) as it gets really confusing once you do get to the city center; follow the signs to the promenade des Anglais to get to the seafront, where you can get your bearings. Remember that in France you must always yield to cars approaching from the right.

BY BOAT The only scheduled service to the port of Nice is from Corsica; the **Société Nationale Maritime Corse Mediterranée,** Gare Maritime, Quai du Commerce, 06359 Nice (☎ **04-93-13-66-99**), has large high-speed ships (500 passengers and 150 cars) that make the 3-hour crossing daily to Ajaccio, Bastia, Calvi, and Ile Rousse from April to October. Cruise ships terminating or beginning Mediterranean cruises usually dock at the port of Villefranche, 3 miles east of Nice.

VISITOR INFORMATION

The **Office de Tourisme** is at 5 promenade des Anglais (☎ **04-92-14-48-00;** www.nice-coteazur.org; e-mail otc@nice-coteazur.org). There's also a branch at the airport's Terminal 1 (☎ **04-93-21-44-11**) and at the Gare SNCF (☎ **04-93-87-07-07**). Hours for these locations are daily: June to September 8am to 9pm (October to May to 7pm). The staff will help with hotel reservations if you arrive without one, the fee depending on the hotel booked.

GAY & LESBIAN EVENTS

JANUARY–FEBRUARY Nice's big event is **Carnavale,** beginning 2 or 3 weeks before Mardi Gras (Fat Tuesday), just before Ash Wednesday, the beginning of Lent. Depending on the religious calendar, Nice's Carnival season can begin in January or February; most of the action takes place on weekends. Festive decorations fill the city: by day, parades—the corsi and batailles de fleurs (flower battles)—with marchers and floats pass by reviewing stands in place Masséna; by night, parties and masked balls continue until all hours. On Mardi Gras, the last day of Carnavale, the city puts on a grand fireworks show over the Mediterranean. Many of the events surrounding Carnavale are free.

JUNE The local **Gay Pride Parade** is held not in Nice but in Cannes, usually on the third Sunday in June. Contact the Community Center Groupe Action Gay Côte

The Carte Musée Côte d'Azur

If you plan to visit several of the museums in Nice and along the Côte d'Azur, consider buying a **Carte Musée Côte d'Azur,** which gives you entry to over 60 museums and monuments from Cannes to Monte Carlo (including the exotic gardens in Eze). A 3-day pass is 70F ($13) and a 7-day pass 140F ($25); they're available from the Office de Tourisme branches and at larger museums. For details, call ☎ **04-93-13-17-51** or e-mail **cmca.niceAhol.fr.**

d'Azur (see "Fast Facts: Nice" below) for more details and to confirm the date, time, and location since it changes annually.

CITY LAYOUT

The easiest way to get oriented is by way of the **promenade des Anglais,** the seafront boulevard curving along the shore of the Baie des Anges. Heading west, the promenade leads to the airport, while to the east it changes names and becomes the **quai des Etats-Unis** before changing names once again to the **quai Rauba-Capeu** as it winds around the hill leading to the **port** of Nice. **Le Château,** with its panoramic views, is at the top of the steep hill; this is the spot where the ducs de Savoie built their castle, which was torn down in 1706.

One street inland from the quai des Etats-Unis is **Cours Saleya,** the main square of **Vieux Nice (Old Nice). Boulevard Jean-Jaurés** is at the northern fringes of the old city, where the **Gare Routière** is located. Walking south on Jean-Jaurés, back toward the waterfront, puts you on **place Masséna,** Nice's major square. Nearby is the pedestrian mall (***zone pietone***) area, with hundreds of shops and restaurants and sidewalk cafes; the *zone pietone* covers several blocks of rue de France, rue Halévy, rue Paradis, and rue Masséna, from which you can get to Nice's most commercial street, **avenue Jean-Médecin,** stretching all the way to the **Gare SNCF.**

Locals will tell you that the farther you go from the sea, the dumpier the area gets. That's true around the train station, but if you go farther north you'll reach the hilly suburb of **Cimiez** with its fancy homes and beautiful museums.

GETTING AROUND

BY BUS Nice's excellent bus system, **Sunbus,** operates all over the city, with most buses connecting at the **Station Centrale,** 10 av. Félix-Faure (☎ **04-93-16-52-10;** information office open Mon–Fri 7:15am–7pm, Sat to 6pm). Schedules and a route map are posted at all bus stops.

You can buy a **single ticket** on the bus for 8.50F ($1.50). The tourist office (see "Visitor Information" above) sells a **carnet of 10 tickets** for 72F ($13) and ***cartes touristique*** (tourist passes) good for 1, 5, or 7 days of unlimited travel; the 1-day pass is 22F ($4), the 5-day pass 85F ($15), and the 7-day pass 110F ($20). Remember to validate your ticket or pass in the machine as soon as you get on the bus.

Most buses stop running at 9pm, with only a handful of lines operating until 1am. There's no bus service at all on May 1 (Labor Day). On other holidays, the Sunday schedule is followed.

BY TAXI For some inexplicable reason, taxis are horrendously expensive in Nice. Within the city limits, the fare averages 80F ($15), with rates slightly higher 7pm to 7am. The good news is that they're available when you need them parked at taxi stands or by calling ☎ **04-93-13-78-78** (24 hours).

BY CAR Nice is full of cars and parking is difficult and very expensive. There are no meters, but you'll find ticket machines on each block: You insert 10F ($1.80) for 1 hour, push the button to get your ticket, and place the ticket on your dashboard. Parking structures provide covered spots but come at a hefty price—up to 160F ($29) per 24 hours in some downtown lots.

You don't need a car to see this compact city; rent one only to explore the surrounding areas. If you plan ahead you'll get the best rates and the option to pick up a car and drop it off in any city in France (and sometimes anywhere in western Europe) with no drop-off fees. To take advantage of this, you have to reserve, pay, and receive vouchers before leaving home. **Rail Europe** (☎ **800/4-EURAIL;** www.raileurope. com) has such a plan combined with a train pass allowing you to ride and drive all over the country, picking up and dropping off where and when you want.

In Nice, **Avis** has three locations: at the airport (☎ **04-93-21-36-33**), at the Gare SNCF (☎ **04-93-87-90-11**), and at 2 av. des Phocéens (☎ **04-93-80-63-52**). **Europcar** (National, Tilden) has a location at the airport (☎ **04-93-21-36-44**) and at 6 av. Suéde (☎ **04-93-88-64-04**). Ask for rates that include the exorbitant 20.6% value-added tax (called TVA in France) and full insurance. If you arrive without reservations, you can still bargain for a good all-inclusive rate if you're there in any month but July or August.

Go for a local company if you really want to save money. The cheapest is **Alloto Rent-A-Car,** 38 av. Aubert (☎ **04-93-86-69-69**; call 08-36-694-695 for reservations at its other locations). It offers all-inclusive rates as low as 199F ($36) per day for a tiny car like a Fiat Panda. The catch? The cheapest (very basic) cars come with advertising logos on the doors. In general, expect to dish out 300 to 400F ($55 to $73) per day for a compact or an intermediate car (no air-conditioning, of course). In France, car sizes are categorized by alphabet: A (subcompact), B (compact), C (compact 4-door), and so on. For ultimate luxury, most companies have Mercedes or BMWs (and more queeny sports cars like Z3 convertibles), fully automatic and air-conditioned. Rates begin at 1,600F ($290) per day.

For long-term rentals of at least 17 days, **Renault** has special tax-free rates only for tourists—as low as $500 for 17 days for a small Renault Twingo with insurance; a large air-conditioned Renault Laguna is $990. You have to book before leaving home by contacting Renault Eurodrive, 650 First Ave., New York, NY 10016 (☎ **800/221-1052;** www.eurodrive.net).

BY MOPED & BICYCLE Two-wheeling is a less expensive way to get around, but traffic is heavy and you have to be extra careful in the city. Helmets are required for any motorized bike. **Nicea Location Rent,** 9 av. Thiers (☎ **04-93-82-42-71**), rents both mopeds and bikes. **Arnaud,** 4 place Grimaldi (☎ **04-93-87-88-55**), has a large selection of mountain bikes too. For all rentals you'll need to cough up a 2,000F ($363) cash deposit (refunded when you return the bike in good shape) or a hold for the same amount on your credit card. Daily rates for a bike average 120F ($22), with mopeds starting at 175F ($32) per day. Thefts are rampant, so watch your bikes carefully and always lock up.

FAST FACTS: Nice

AIDS Organizations & Hot Lines The main 24-hour toll-free hot line is **SIDA Info Service** (AIDS in French is Sida) at ☎ **0-800-840-800.** Another service in English (located in Paris but serving the whole country) is **Anonymous AIDS/HIV Information and Support** at ☎ **01-44-93-16-69** (Mon–Wed and Fri 6–10pm). Also valuable is the **Association Médecins Gais** (Association of Gay Doctors); call ☎ **01-48-05-81-71** (Wed 6–8pm and Sat 2–4pm) for its referral service of gay doctors nationwide.

American Express The office is at 11 promenade des Anglais, at the corner of rue des Congrès (☎ **04-93-16-53-53;** open May–Sept Mon–Fri 9am–6pm, Sat to noon, and Oct–Apr Mon–Fri 9am–noon and 2–6pm, Sat to noon). The full-service travel agency can help you with any aspect of your travels, and the staff is young and fairly friendly.

Country & City Codes

The **country code** for France is **33.** The **city code** for Nice is **4;** use this code when you're calling from outside France. If you're calling Nice within Nice or from anywhere else in France, use **04,** which is now built into all phone numbers, making them 10 digits long.

Consulates All consulates and embassies are in Paris (see chapter 5). However, in Marseille you'll find a **U.S. consulate,** 12 bd. Paul-Peytral (☎ **04-91-54-92-00**), and a **U.K. consulate,** 24 av. Prado (☎ **04-91-15-72-10**).

Community Center Groupe Action Gay Côte d'Azur, 26 rue de la Cagne in Carron (☎ **04-93-29-06-73;** e-mail gagca@worldnet.net), organizes lectures and events, including gay pride in Cannes, usually the third Sunday in June. Call for events schedules and to confirm date of gay pride.

Currency Exchange Beware that many tourist exchange bureaus charge fees or a percentage to change money, so always ask before you hand your bills over. Banks (open Mon–Fri 8:30am–noon and 1:30pm–4:30pm) don't usually charge any fees and have the most competitive exchange rate. For after-hours exchange, try **Change Or,** 17 av. Thiers (☎ **04-93-88-56-80;** open daily 7am–midnight), or the **Money Shop,** 14 rue Centrale (☎ **04-93-80-38-02;** open daily 9am–midnight); be prepared for hefty fees of up to 25F ($4.50). The most convenient way to get French francs is by using your credit card; stop by any ATM scattered throughout the city (the exchange rate is always favorable and the fee, if any, if usually 10F/$1.80 or less). Be sure to get a PIN with the correct number of digits before leaving home.

Cybercafe The **Webstore** has an outlet at 12 rue de Russie (☎ 04-93-87-87-99; e-mail info@webstore.fr), where you can check your e-mail for 30F ($16) per hour.

Emergencies For police emergencies, dial ☎ **17;** for medical emergencies and to ask for an ambulance, dial ☎ **15;** to report a fire, dial ☎ **18.** The tourist department at the police station is ☎ **04-92-17-20-31** (lost passports must be reported in person at the main police station, 1 av. Maréchal-Foch).

Hospital The **Hôpital St-Roche** is at 5 rue Pierre-Devoluy (☎ **04-92-03-33-75**). For 24-hour doctor service, call **SOS Médecins** at ☎ **04-93-85-01-01** (they'll dispatch a doctor to come to wherever you are).

Magazines & Newspapers For the main publications, see "Fast Facts: Paris" in chapter 5. For Nice, pick up a free copy of ***Les Plans Exes,*** maps distributed at gay bars and clubs plotting the popular bars, restaurants, and beaches in Nice, Cannes, and St-Tropez. ***Le Zoom*** is a free little black book published monthly listing the gay venues along the entire coast.

Telephone All pay phones in France operate with phone cards (*télécartes*) that are available for purchase from all newspaper kiosks (*tabacs*) for 40F ($7) or 96F ($17), and many pay phones now accept credit cards; just swipe your card as directed and you can call anywhere domestically or internationally. From any phone you can dial the toll-free numbers of the various phone carriers to enable you to use your home phone card (such as AT&T and MCI). Hotels charge a fee on all calls made and exorbitant rates for long-distance calls. See "Fast Facts: Paris" in chapter 5 for more details.

2 Pillow Talk

It's basically like this: You'll be staying either on the promenade des Anglais facing the Mediterranean or a few streets inland on one of the side streets and around place Masséna. All the hotels below (with the exception of Palais Maeterlinck) are within walking distance of one another and most everything else. The hotels on the promenade, predictably, charge more for their sea-view rooms, which do have excellent views—but if you're picturing a quiet breakfast on a sun-splashed balcony, you'd better go elsewhere. The promenade comes complete with traffic jams, pollution, and noise. Traffic noise is a problem virtually anywhere in the city, but most hotels are soundproofed and have rooms facing a courtyard that are quieter than those overlooking the street. Visitors looking for peace and quiet should head to one of the hilly villages or seaside towns, such as St-Paul-de-Vence or Beaulieau (see "Side Trips from Nice" later in this chapter), and drive into Nice for nightlife and entertainment. However, remember that drinking and driving laws in France are strict.

November to March is when many hotels along the coast shut down, but hotels in Nice are open year-round. Christmas is a busy and festive time, and the Nice Carnavale held during the last 2 weeks of February attracts many out-of-towners. April is glorious, when the beaches are just beginning to prepare for summer and few tourists have arrived, but it's frequently not warm enough to swim. For a true beach vacation, pick May, June, or September. July and August are hot and crowded, but despite the crowds the beaches remain pleasant. I don't advise arriving without a reservation during those months; the French book their holidays a year in advance. If you do arrive without one, the Office du Tourisme can help you find a room (see "Visitor Information" above).

Nice's only gay-owned/gay-managed hotel is the very basic Meyerbeer, on a side street a block from the beach. Gays from around the world stay here, along with a growing number of lesbians. Around the train station are several hotels advertised in other guidebooks as gay, but I found them seedy and run down and haven't included them here. Though the Meyerbeer is a one-star hotel, it's well looked after and the care of the owners makes all the difference; it's also very well located. The Hôtel Windsor is Nice's most gay-friendly hotel (see below). However, rarely will gay couples raise eyebrows; the French attitude is whatever happens behind closed doors is nobody's business.

Breakfast is rarely included in the room rates in Nice, and hotels charge ridiculous prices for a simple continental breakfast: from a fair 28F ($5) to a whopping 130F ($24) for coffee, toast or croissant, and jam—and tax and service charge are added to those amounts. Chances are there's a cafe a block or two from your hotel where you can enjoy coffee and a croissant for 25 to 35F ($4.50 to $6).

ON THE PROMENADE

Flots d'Azur. 101 promenade des Anglais, 06000 Nice. ☎ **04-93-86-51-25.** Fax 04-93-97-22-07. 21 units. A/C TV TEL. 220–550F ($40–$100) double. MC, V. Bus: 9 or 10.

A Private Beach Tip

If you're staying at a hotel with a private beach, you're frequently not exempt from paying for mattress and umbrella rentals, from 50 to 100F ($9 to $18) per day. You can imagine the horror some guests find on their bill after a week on the beach. A lot of complaining goes on at check-out desks. Always ask at check-in what is extra and what is not; sometimes guests get a discounted rates at the hotel's private beach.

For clean accommodations on the promenade, this three-story villa is one of the least expensive choices. It's run by a friendly older couple who watch over everything to make sure their multinational guests of all ages are comfortable. The rooms are simple, varying in size and view; all windows are double-glazed to keep out noise, and the air-conditioning units are brand new. The basement rooms are larger and quieter but have no view. The most expensive rooms are the upper-level sea-view units, with large windows and clean baths; three have small balconies. Breakfast is served on the breezy terrace overlooking the sea, and the oleander bushes help block some of the traffic noise. Though parking is free on the hotel's narrow driveway, space isn't guaranteed; if all the spots are taken, you'll have to pay for parking on the street or in a nearby lot.

Hôtel Beau Rivage. 24 rue St-François-de-Paul, 06300 Nice. ☎ **04-93-80-80-70.** Fax 04-93-80-55-77. 118 units. 800–1150F ($145–$209) double; from 1,300F ($236) junior suite. AE, DC, MC, V. Bus: 6, 9, or 10.

Steps from Vieux Nice and across from the beach (the entrance is a block inland), this commanding white building dates from 1867 and was a coveted address in the early 1900s; both Matisse and Chagall stayed here. The interior (renovated in 1987) is rather bland, though, and service isn't a top priority. The rooms are soundproof, modern, and functional but rather small; even the Chambres de Prestige (the highest category of double) aren't spacious. Most rooms overlook the street (the seafront part of the building is private apartments) but are quiet and bright. All come with sparkling marble baths. This hotel advertises in some of the French gay press, so it gets a scattering of gay couples; the majority of guests are British and American tourists, middle-aged and straight. The hotel's private beach has a popular restaurant serving three meals; it moves indoors during winter.

Hôtel Méridien. 1 promenade des Anglais, 06000 Nice. ☎ **04-93-82-25-25.** Fax 04-93-16-08-90. 314 units. A/C MINIBAR TV TEL. 1,250–1,650F ($227–$300) double; from 2,850F ($518) suite. AE, DC, MC, V. Bus: 9, 10, or 12.

This 1960s hotel is one of Nice's largest, occupying the busiest block on the promenade next door to a large McDonald's and across from the Jardin Albert-1er. The Casino Ruhl is part of the building. The Méridien is one level up from the street; escalators carry you through the glass atrium to the reception. The staff is professional and helpful if a bit impersonal, and the rooms are modern and comfortable, with all the amenities you'd expect from a luxury chain; some have sea views. Promotional discounted rates are offered at various times, so be sure to ask. The hotel's best feature is the rooftop garden cafe (by the small pool) with its fabulous views and reasonably priced provençal dishes (open summer only). The more formal L'Habit Blanc serves excellent seafood year-round.

Hôtel Négresco. 37 promenade des Anglais, 06007 Nice. ☎ **04-93-16-64-00.** Fax 04-93-88-35-68. Email negresco@nicematin.fr. 141 units. A/C MINIBAR TV TEL. 1,300–2,150F ($237–$390) double; from 3,950F ($718) suite. AE, DC, MC, V. Parking 160F ($29) in garage. Bus: 6, 9, or 10.

This is the promenade's most eye-catching building, a belle-époque mansion designated a national monument (it was named for its founder, Henri Négresco, a Romanian who died francless in Paris in 1920). The first thing you'll note as you step inside the grand lobby are the bellboys sporting 18th-century costumes who'll escort you to your room (be good). No two rooms are alike, extraordinary for such a large hotel, and the owner, Mme Jeanne Augier (who was a friend of Matisse and Dalí), has personally selected the antique mirrors, sofas, chairs, and velvet and satin bedspreads adorning the rooms (she lives in the domed tower). Despite the opulence and meticulous upkeep, you'll likely feel the Négresco has passed its prime and needs a face-lift. The

Lifestyles of the Rich & the Fabulous

If you want the comfort and convenience of your own pad along the Côte d'Azur, consider renting a private home. **Occelli Top Vacances,** 20 rue Maréchal-Joffre, 06000 Nice (☎ **04-93-88-44-44;** fax 04-93-87-70-70; www.azur.fr/ocelli), offers a variety of rentals, from studios to luxury villas with pools. Price ranges from 3,000F ($545) for a simple studio for two to 50,000F ($9,090) per week for a luxury villa with a pool (you can request your own chef, gardener, and chauffeur too). They have rentals available in many areas from Menton to Cannes.

For simpler vacation homes, contact **Gìtes de France Alpes-Maritime,** 55 promenade des Anglais, 06011 Nice (☎ **04-92-15-21-30;** fax 04-93-86-01-06; www.crt.riviera.fr/gites06). The *gìtes* range from stone houses to large farmhouses but tend to be in rural areas (a few within an hour's drive of Nice) and get booked up to 1 year in advance. Rates begin at 2,900F ($527) per week.

painfully 1970s gaudy baths are all different; some have tubs speckled with gold, others green toilets seats. The public rooms are like a museum—in the Royal Salon is a 1-ton Baccarat chandelier that was delivered to the tzar of Russia. Le Chantecler restaurant with its two Michelin stars is the toast of the town (see "Whet Your Appetite" below); La Rotonde is more casual, with a large carousel in the center.

✪ **La Pérouse.** 11 quai Raubu-Capéu, 06300 Nice. ☎ **04-93-62-34-63.** Fax 04-93-62-59-41. E-mail lp@hroy.com. 64 units. A/C MINIBAR TV TEL. 745–1490F ($135–$271) double; from 1870F ($340) suite. AE, DC, MC, V. Parking 60F ($11). Bus: 6, 9, or 10.

This is the most charming and well-placed hotel on the seafront. On the hill at the foot of Le Château, facing the gay-friendly Castel Plage and steps from Cours Saleya, La Pérouse has been gaining popularity with gays and young French, Italian, and German straight couples for its elegant rooms and friendly laid-back atmosphere. All the rooms were renovated in 1996 and are bright and modern, with marble baths. The back wing offers no sea views but has spacious quiet rooms overlooking the rocky hill or the lovely pool in a garden. The restaurant (open May–Sept) serves provençal specialties in the garden or in the dining room with its colorful Matisse paintings and fireplace. If you're traveling alone, this should be your first choice—the hotel has single rooms with small baths at very attractive rates.

Primotel Suisse. 15 quai Rauba-Capéu, 06300 Nice. ☎ **04-92-17-39-00.** Fax 04-93-85-30-70. 42 units. A/C MINIBAR TV TEL. 400–590F ($73–$107) double; from 630F ($115) suite. AE, DC, MC, V. Bus: 6, 9, or 10.

Next door to the highly recommended La Pérouse (above), this is a less expensive choice. The Italian-style four-story Suisse was built in the early 1900s and faces west (it's where the road curves uphill), giving the sea-view rooms a breathtaking vista not only of the Mediterranean but also of all the promenade des Anglais lined with palm trees. Raoul Dufy stayed here, and the hotel management likes to think it was the view from the hotel that inspired him to paint and spend time in Nice. All the rooms are bland, however, and seem a bit dated, but they're clean and have been soundproofed (the front rooms are still a bit noisy). The inside rooms are quieter and smaller but an excellent bargain, especially if you're traveling alone. They get their share of older couples, mostly Swiss, German, and British. Don't expect too much service or elegance—but the location and low rates can make you overlook that.

Westminster Concorde. 27 promenade des Anglais, 06000 Nice. ☎ **04-93-88-29-44.** Fax 04-93-82-45-35. E-mail westminster@french-riviera.fr. 110 units. A/C MINIBAR TV TEL. 750–1,500F ($136–$272) double; from 1,500F ($272) junior suite. AE, DC, MC, V. Parking 100F ($18). Bus: 12 or 22.

When the British escaped the harsh northern winters at the turn of the century, they came to this elaborate seafront building with its marble terrace and lavish lobby and salons. The rooms have been renovated and modernized and are bright and pleasant. The standard rooms are the smallest, and they're a good bargain if you're looking for a first-class hotel on the promenade. The sea-view rooms are almost double the price and size, but only a handful have balconies. The guests tend to be older couples from northern Europe along with a growing number of Americans; due to the constant guest turnover, the staff doesn't give anyone much attention (good if you want to be anonymous). Le Farniente offers reasonably priced French cuisine, and you can have drinks and snacks on the fabulous terrace late into the night.

A FEW BLOCKS INLAND

✪ **Château des Ollières.** 39 av. des Baumettes, 06000 Nice. ☎ **04-92-15-77-99.** Fax 04-92-15-77-98. E-mail ollieres@riviera-isp.com. 8 units. A/C MINIBAR TV TEL. 950–1650F ($173–$300) double; from 1350F ($245) suite. AE, MC, V. Free parking. Bus: 38.

This sumptuous 1850s villa was the home of Russian Prince Lobanov-Rostowsky. It's close to the Musée des Beaux-Arts, the only other belle-époque palace in this hilly neighborhood, a 10-minute walk from the sea. Umbrella pines line the gravel drive leading to the castle, which sits on three parklike acres. Stepping into the reception salon, you'll feel you should be wearing a tux and top hat or a ball gown and tiara. The courteous staff speak in hushed whispers. The individualized guest rooms are so richly adorned it'll take you an hour just to marvel at the antiques and paintings. Of course, the smaller rooms have less space but are equally opulent. All contain marble baths. The most fabulous accommodation is the tower apartment with its private elevator opening directly into the living room, which in turns opens onto a private terrace; its marble bath is huge. About one wedding per week is held at the Ollières, so you can imagine most guests are straight, either honeymooners or wealthy retirees. The restaurant where breakfast and dinner are served boasts a veranda overlooking the park. Watch for the project slated to begin in 2000 that'll add a 34-room wing.

Grand Hôtel Aston. 12 av. Félix-Faure, 06002 Nice. ☎ **04-92-17-53-00.** Fax 04-93-80-40-02. 160 units. A/C MINIBAR TV TEL. 950–1300F ($173–$236) double. AE, DC, MC, V. Bus: 7, 9, or 10.

Facing place Masséna's beautiful fountains, this 19th-century hotel lives up to its name more in the facade than in the interior. The lobby is quite simple, and the slightly fading chairs in the public areas aren't too inviting. This is more a businessperson's hotel than a vacation destination, given its location across from the bus station and steps from Nice's major commercial street, avenue Jean-Médecin. The rooms are colorful and bright, with a hint of art deco, but not as luxurious or as carefully decorated as you'd expect from a grand hotel; the baths are functional and modern. Many rooms face the fountains, and all have balconies; despite the double-glazed windows, you can still hear the street noise, so light sleepers beware. The rooftop terrace offers good views of the Mediterranean, and Le Café de l'Horloge is a bustling brasserie-style place with prime people-watching tables on the sidewalk.

Hôtel de Flore. 2 rue Maccarani, 06000 Nice. ☎ **04-92-14-40-20.** Fax 04-92-14-40-21. E-mail flore@aacom.com. 63 units. A/C TV TEL. 450–650F ($82–$118) double; from 890F ($162) suite. AE, DC, MC, V. Bus: 3, 12, 14, or 22.

This fabulous hotel just off the *zone pieteone*, a 5-minute walk from the sea, was completely renovated in 1999 in a sophistocated Provençal style. The staff is noticeably younger than those at other hotels and refreshingly eager to make your stay as comfortable as possible. Though the rooms offer no view whatever, they have an elegant feel, with wrought-iron and wicker chairs, ceramic lamps, and Provençal pottery. The meticulous baths are small but sparkling clean. In good weather, breakfast is served on a terrace, or you can relax in a bright lounge. The guests are mostly French and tend to be young professionals, along with a few Americans and Brits in town for business.

Hôtel de la Fontaine. 49 rue de France, 06000 Nice. ☎ **04-93-88-30-38.** Fax 04-93-88-98-11. E-mail hotel-fontaine@webstore.fr. 29 units. A/C TV TEL. 530F ($96) double. AE, MC, V. Bus: 12 or 22.

This charming little hotel a block in from the sea has been welcoming guests since the 1940s and was completely renovated in the mid-1990s. It has a high number of repeat guests, American and European, and does get a small but growing number of gays. The owner has added a lot of little touches, from exotic plants to Provençal pottery to the delightful courtyard designed around the fountain that gives the hotel its name (breakfast is served here in summer). The English-speaking receptionists are young and trained to do what it takes to make you feel at home. The rooms are small but bright and colorful; the baths even have hair dryers. The rooms overlooking the courtyard are much quieter than those overlooking rue de France. A full buffet breakfast is served in the courtyard, and at night you can have a cocktail in the garden.

Hotel Meyerbeer. 15 rue Meyerbeer, 06000 Nice. ☎ **04-93-88-95-65.** Fax 04-93-82-09-25. E-mail hotel.meyerbeer.beach@wanadoo.fr. 20 units. TV TEL. 260F ($47) double. No credit cards. Bus: 12 or 22.

This simple gay hotel is a block from the promenade on a side street leading to the *zone pieteone*. The only one-star hotel I recommend in Nice and the only gay hotel, it occupies the first two floors of an older residential building; the lobby is on the second floor. Gays and lesbians from all over the world stay here, and Patrick and David look after everyone to ensure his or her comfort. The rooms have been recently renovated, and all come with small baths and kitchenettes. You're given your own key at check-in and then have the privacy of your own studio apartment, albeit a basic one—you can comfortably bring home a treat after the bars close down. A welcome basket is filled with info about local gay venues and events, and the gay staff is knowledgeable about area beaches and restaurants. This is a friendly, relaxed place if you like camaraderie. In the small dining area breakfast is served daily 8am to 8pm, so night owls can breakfast at dusk before heading out on the town.

✪ **Hôtel Windsor.** 11 rue Dalpozzo, 06000 Nice. ☎ **04-93-88-59-35.** Fax 04-93-88-94-57. E-mail windsor@webstore.fr. 57 units. A/C MINIBAR TV TEL. 400–680F ($73–$124) double. AE, MC, V. Bus: 12 or 22.

This is by far the best moderately priced hotel if you want to stay off the promenade a few streets inland. Built in 1880 as a private residence, it's now an oasis of calm in this bustling city. The exotic garden filled with palms and jasmine bushes (and two friendly parrots) is enough to make you never want to leave. The staff is multilingual and multinational, and Colvin, the gay son of the owner, can tell you anything you want to know about the scene (he and his dad live in the hotel). Predictably, they get their share of gays, but for the most part young American couples and British tourists are the crowd. Each of the artsy rooms is decorated differently; some have painted murals by well-known artists (Robert Indiana, Ben), others have zebra-striped walls

Nice Accommodations & Dining

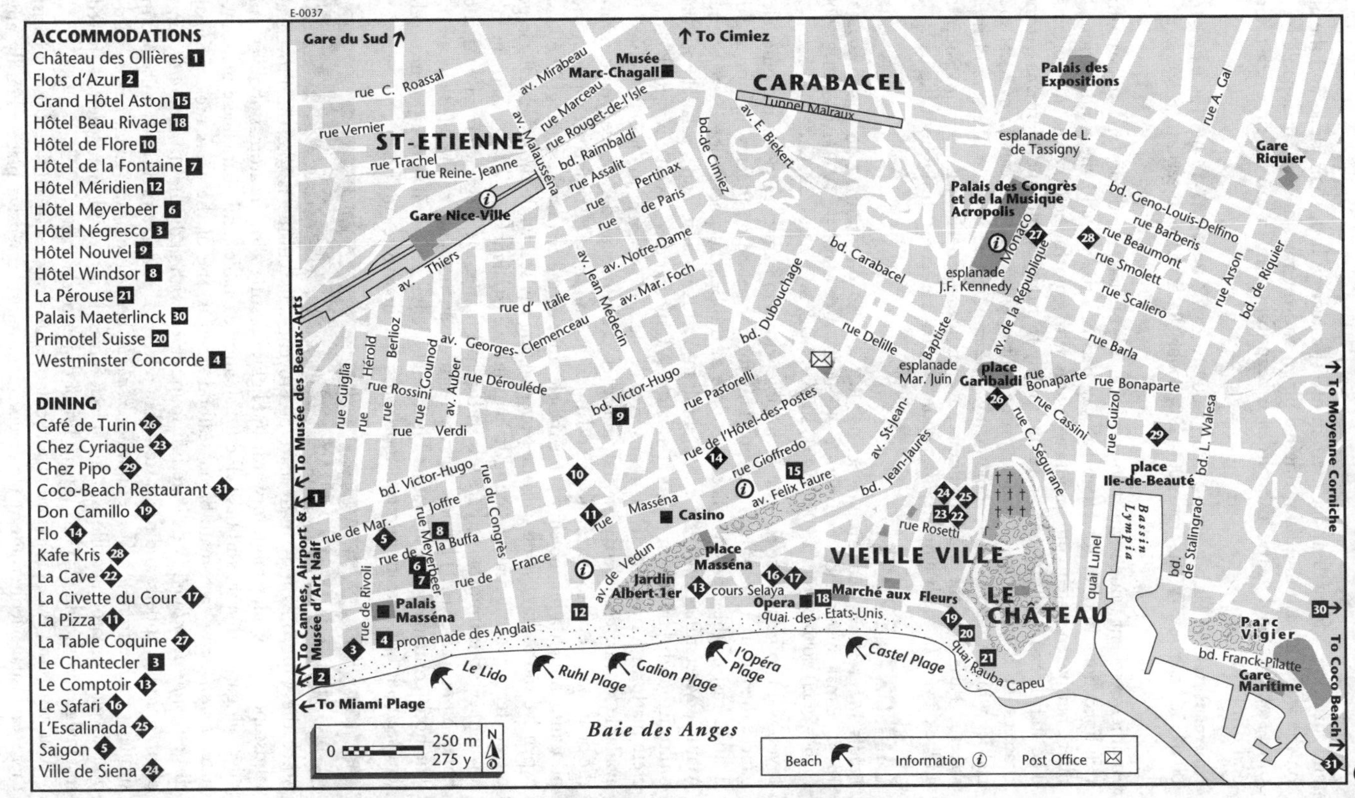

and furniture. Most fall under the minimalist category: bed, chair, desk, and the art on the walls. It's a fun, quirky, original place, and the rates are very reasonable for a three-star. The pool in the lush garden is beautiful, and you can have breakfast here and drinks at night.

Nouvel Hôtel. 19 bis bd. Victor-Hugo, 06000 Nice. ☎ **04-93-87-15-00.** Fax 04-93-16-00-67. 56 units. A/C TV TEL. From 500F ($90) double. Rates include breakfast. AE, MC, V. Bus: 12 or 15.

Another excellent value is this two-star hotel full of charm and comfort, on beautiful tree-lined boulevard Victor-Hugo halfway between the sea and the train station. It offers newly renovated contemporary rooms with colorful bedspreads and curtains. The staff is extremely friendly, catering mostly to straight Brits and Germans. At the Brasserie Le Boul Vic, occupying a prime spot of sidewalk, you can enjoy local specialties while watching the people go by. The atmosphere is more like a residential street in Paris than the south of France; avenue Jean-Médecin with its many shops is a block away. In the bright breakfast room, drinks are served throughout the day.

EAST OF THE PORT

Palais Maeterlinck. Basse Corniche, 06300 Nice. ☎ **04-92-00-72-00.** Fax 04-92-04-18-10. E-mail maeterlinck.@webstore.fr. 40 units. A/C MINIBAR TV TEL. 1,450–2,500F ($264–$455) double; from 2,700F ($491) suite. AE, DC, MC, V. Bus: 32. Closed Jan–Feb.

If you want to be as close to Nice as possible with panoramic sea views and quiet elegance, then you've found your haven. This former palace on 9 acres high on a cliff 2 miles east of the city was once the home of the Belgian poet/Nobel Prize winner Maurice Maeterlinck. In 1989 it was rebuilt into a luxury hotel and a palatial pool was built surrounded by Ionian pillars and palms. A funicular carries you down to the concrete platform jutting out to sea that serves as the hotel's beach; the hotel's sailboat is available for hire complete with crew and chef. (For ultimate decadence, you can hire the boat to nip over to Portofino or St-Tropez for a night.) The rooms are modern and pleasant, though a bit too simple for the elegance of the rest of the setting. The least expensive rooms have small balconies overlooking the sea, while the suites have large private terraces with chaises. Young Italians in love (straight) and a large German following keep the atmosphere here less stuffy than that at the Négresco or other grand hotels along the coast. The bar's terrace features terrific views of the Mediterranean. The hotel contains two restaurants: The casual Melisande is well known for its excellent seafood; Le Gastronomique is more posh, serving haute cuisine.

3 Whet Your Appetite

Since the Côte d'Azur is really part of Provence, its cuisine is like the Provençal landscape—colorful, straightforward, and light, bursting with the aromas of olives and olive oil, garlic, thyme, and basil. Fresh fish and vegetables and goat cheese predominate. *Bouillabaisse* (a tomato-based seafood stew) is one of the area's most popular dishes; *soupe de poissons* (a delicate fish soup served with garlic aïoli), *ratatouille* (eggplant, onions, peppers, and herbs stewed in olive oil), *pistou* (a rich basil-infused soup similar to minestrone), and the infamous *salade niçoise* (potatoes, green beans, hard-boiled eggs, tomatoes, scallions, tuna, black olives, lettuce, and mixed herbs, dressed in vinaigrette) should also be on your list of dishes to sample.

You won't find Nice's restaurants particularly stuffy or overpriced like those in Paris; there's a casual Mediterranean feel even to the most expensive places. Hardly any restaurants require jackets (a miracle in France), and dressing up for dinner here means

Dining with a View

Forget about dining on the promenade des Anglais with a to-die-for view: You'd think there'd be some good restaurants with a view here (Nice's best, Le Chantecler, lacks a terrace), but nothing is worth recommending—except for lunch in summer on the Hôtel Méridien's fabulous rooftop garden.

For restaurants with a view, you'll have to head to one of the surrounding towns, where there's no shortage of terribly romantic places with fabulous settings (and food and prices to write home about): Try Château Eza in Eze, La Bastide St-Antoine in Grasse, or La Réserve in Beaulieu (see "Side Trips from Nice" later in this chapter).

---

a shirt and trousers instead of shorts (for women, anything goes except jeans and tennis shoes).

Note: For the locations of the restaurants below, see the "Nice Accommodations & Dining" map on p. 229.

ON THE PROMENADE

✪ **Le Chantecler.** In the Hôtel Négresco, 37 promenade des Anglais. ☎ **04-93-16-64-00.** Reservations required at least a week in advance. Main courses 220F–340F ($40–$62); fixed-price menus 235F ($43) at lunch, 440F ($80) or 550F ($100) at dinner. AE, DC, MC, V. Daily 12:30–2:30pm and 7:30–10:30pm. Closed mid-Nov to mid-Dec. Bus: 9, 10, or 11. FRENCH.

Many food critics consider this opulent restaurant one of the top 10 in the world—and I agree. From the setting to the talented (and good-looking) chef, there are many reasons to splurge here. The dining room is fit for a Queen with its Louis XV decor, Aubusson carpet, and large portrait of the duchesse d'Orléans. The service is impeccable—the older maître d' will usher you in, and several handsome waiters will hover over you. Young chef Alan Llorca creates original dishes focusing on light natural flavors with a Mediterranean slant and uses a lot of seafood and locally grown vegetables and fruit. To begin, you might choose the exquisite artichoke salad with baby squid or the creamy risotto garnished with black truffles; the sea bass fried in aniseed and served with orange-flavored fish soup is to die for. For a main course, the Sisteron lamb with whole garlic cloves and delicate violet artichokes is out of this world, and for a more unique dish try the roast pigeon drizzled with honey and balsamic vinegar and served with candied onions. Dessert? You can't go wrong whatever you order, but the stewed apple and rhubarb in filo with wild strawberry sorbet is a perfect finish. The fixed-price lunch menu is a steal—you can bet the price will shoot up soon.

IN & AROUND VIEUX NICE

✪ **Café de Turin.** 5 place Garibaldi. ☎ **04-93-62-29-52.** Meals 100–200F ($18–$36). V. Daily 11:30am–11pm. Bus: 9 or 10. SEAFOOD.

Locals consider this sidewalk cafe, under the arcades on beautiful place Garibaldi, the only place in the south of France to enjoy *coquillage* (raw shellfish). Princess Caroline comes to eat here when she's in Monaco, and Italians trek all the way from Milan just for a meal. There's no English menu, so bring a dictionary to decipher all the choices. The way to eat is to order a sampling of the available shellfish (it changes daily according to what's fresh)—from sea snails and sea urchins to several kinds of oysters and clams. You could spend hours digging in shells with little forks. You've got to ask for bread and butter; order your white wine (the house is good and cheap) and wait for your shells to arrive with a slice of lemon. No salad, no appetizers. Apart from shellfish, they do serve a few cooked selections of shrimp and fish of the day and other *fruits de mer* (fruit of the sea). But everyone comes for the raw stuff, so you have to be real adventurous and patient; the service is slow, but the atmosphere can't be beat.

✪ **Don Camillo.** 5 rue des Ponchettes. ☎ **04-93-85-67-95.** Reservations required a week in advance in summer, a day in advance at other times. Main courses 138–160F ($25–$29); fixed-price menus 200–320F ($36–$58). AE, DC, MC, V. Mon 8–10pm, Tues–Sat noon–2pm and 8–10pm. Bus: 6 or 8. PROVENÇAL.

Franck and Veronique Cerutti run this sophisticated place just off Cours Saleya. When 30- and 40-something Niçois professionals want to treat their out-of-town visitors, they bring them here. The service is as refined and as crisp as the white tablecloths in this 10-table restaurant; don't come underdressed or you won't feel comfortable. The food is wonderful, meticulously prepared using the freshest local ingredients; fava beans, stockfish, cod, artichokes, and sheep's milk cheeses are used as staples. For an appetizer, try the *salade de chevre frais* (fresh goat cheese from a nearby farm served with tapenade on a bed of lettuce) or the amazing risotto with wild mushrooms (the best risotto in town). The main courses may include saddle of lamb (from a farm in Sisteron) with parmesan potatoes and vegetable sorbet and rabbit prepared differently every day. The wine list has a good selection of regional vintages; try the vin de Belet, made from grapes grown in the sunny hills northwest of Nice.

Kafe Kris. 3 rue Smolett (off bd. de la République). ☎ **04-93-26-75-85.** Meals 35–60F ($6–$11); daily special 60F ($11). No credit cards. Mon–Sat noon–3pm and 6–11pm. Bus: 3, 5, or 6. LIGHT MEALS/FRENCH.

This tiny cafe on a quiet side street north of Vieux Nice has just five tables inside and four on the sidewalk and keeps a loyal gay and lesbian crowd returning for its home-cooked food and incredibly low prices. Kris (a lesbian) hosts and waits tables, while the lone cook in the small kitchen whips up simple French specialties; the yummy *crêpe Popeye* (spinach and Swiss cheese) is guaranteed to make your biceps bulge; the *salade chevre chaud* (warm goat cheese on a bed of lettuce) is also good. The daily special is usually a traditional French dish like *coq au vin* or *boeuf bourguinon.* Dudes from the gym come here to load up on protein after their workouts, and many local gays

Three New Gay Spots

Gay restaurants are just beginning to pop up in Nice, but as in the rest of France they're not known for their food or service: Only **La Cave** (below) has been able to keep a loyal gay crowd coming back for excellent food and consistent service. A few restaurants around place Rossetti have opened recently, notably **Chez Cyriaque,** 1 rue Rossetti (☎ **04-93-92-68-47;** open daily noon–3pm and 7–11:30pm); it has a lively sidewalk setting and a cozy dining room, but the service is horrendous and you can wait hours for your food. I'm sure they'll get their act together; the food, once it arrives, is quite good.

La Table Coquine, 44 av. de la République (☎ **04-93-55-39-99;** open Tues–Sun noon–2:30pm and 7:30–10:30pm), is a new restaurant a few blocks north of Vieux Nice overlooking a parking lot; despite the bland setting, the owners are gay and friendly and use fresh local ingredients for their reasonably priced dishes.

At the tiny gay-owned/managed **CD Bar,** 22 rue Benoit Bunico, Vieux Nice (☎ **04-93-92-47-65;** open Tues–Sun noon–9pm), you can make your own salad at Nice's best salad bar. The very gay clientele is hip and oh-so buff.

drop in for a light meal. Fine dining this place is not, but you can get an inexpensive tasty meal and just might meet your very own French Popeye for dessert (well, blow me down!).

✪ **La Cave.** 6 rue François-Gallo (between Porte Fausse and place Rossetti), Vieux Nice. ☎ **04-93-62-48-46.** Reservations recommended. Main courses 85–120F ($15–$22); fixed-price menus 110–200F ($20–$36). MC, V. Daily 7–11:30pm. Bus: 1, 2, or 14. FRENCH.

This small gay restaurant is just off fashionable place Rosetti. Good food and good service keep a fun, trendy gay crowd coming back, both locals and visitors. The sidewalk tables fill up early (request one anyway when you reserve, though that doesn't guarantee anything, especially in high season, when the wait can get long even if you have a reservation). The cozy dining room is warmly decorated and does have a cavelike feel to it. Start with their special aperitif, *kir au mur* (kir with mulberry syrup instead of cassis); then sample the tangy *soupe de poissons* (fish soup) with aïoli and croutons. For a main course, the *magret de canard au miel et pêches* (duck glazed with honey and served with warm peaches) is their specialty; another winner is the *brochette mixte au thym et citron* (mixed grilled of chicken, beef, and lamb with thyme and lemon). The service sometimes is curt, especially when they're busy, but the camaraderie of the other diners will keep you occupied making new friends. For dessert, order the simple *fromage blanc au miel* (a creamy white cheese a lot like yogurt, served with honey) or the decadent *tarte au chocolat* with bananas.

Le Comptoir. 20 rue St-François-de-Paule (one street in from the promenade). ☎ **04-93-92-08-80.** Reservations recommended. Main courses 180–260F ($33–$47). AE, DC, MC, V. Mon–Sat noon–3pm and 7–11:30pm, Sun noon–3pm. Bus: 6 or 8. FRENCH.

The block this elegant restaurant occupies is one of the most beautiful in Nice, close to the Hôtel Beau Rivage and the Opéra. In summer, the sidewalk is filled with plants, flowers, and tables, and the dining room is very art deco with lovely mirrors and sleek black chairs. At lunch, you'll see quite a few businesspeople as well as straight Niçois yuppies. In the evenings, the place spills over with beautiful people (mostly over 30 and straight) who don't seem to mind the high prices because it's just so fabulous, dahling. You can expect to eat traditional French food. Start with the foie gras and a glass of sauterne or the smoked salmon that melts in your mouth. For the main course, go for one of the daily specials with salmon or duck breast, as it's guaranteed to be fresh and carefully prepared. Avoid the *soupe de poissons* (tasteless) and watch the wine list (unnecessarily pricey). Come with a sense of humor because despite their good looks, the waiters can be quite curt.

L'Escalinada. 22 rue Pairolière (from bd. Jean-Jaurés, take rue de la Tour toward Vieux Nice and turn left at rue Pairolière), Vieux Nice. ☎ **04-93-62-11-71.** Main courses 79–110F ($14–$20); fixed-price menus 110–125F ($20–$23). No credit cards. Daily noon–2:30pm and 6:45–11pm. Bus: 1, 2, or 14. NIÇOIS.

For true down-home Niçois cooking, this is your best bet. Tucked away on a charming corner of a cobblestone street are wooden picnic tables and colorful umbrellas and a mixed youngish crowd; the inside dining room is tiny, with tables so close together you can be assured of some kind of entertainment. If you're adventurous, you can go wild trying bizarre dishes like breaded mutton testicles (honest) and tripes (sheep intestines stuffed with rice and spices). Locals come in the spring to have the *omelette de poutine* (omelet made with bite-size baby fish eaten whole, head and all). Of course, you can have tame fare like handmade gnocchi with gorgonzola and ravioli with tomato or cream sauce and a variety of cod and lamb dishes. Ask for a local Côte de Provence, a nice chilled rosé that goes perfectly with anything you order on a warm summer day.

Street Eats

In Nice you'll find lots of "street food" (food you can have on the run or on the beach). Street-corner vendors bake trays of ***pissaladière***—thin-crust pizza with onions, herbs, anchovies, and black olives—and sell cut portions. Especially around Cours Saleya on market days, look for vendors offering ***socca,*** a savory sort of crêpe made with chickpea flour and baked on flat round pans; it's often eaten for breakfast. You might have to acquire a taste for *socca* and might need a beverage to go with it—but do try it.

You could live on healthy and delicious ***pan bagnat*** (a round bread loaf stuffed with salade niçoise–type goodies and moistened with olive oil) for the duration of your visit and barely put a dent in your wallet.

Le Safari. 1 Cours Saleya, Vieux Nice. ☎ **04-93-80-18-44.** Reservations recommended. Main courses 60–135F ($11–$25); fixed-price menu 150F ($27). AE, DC, MC, V. Daily noon–2:30pm and 7–11:30pm. Bus: 1, 2, or 14. PROVENÇAL/NIÇOIS.

Next to La Civette du Cours, the most popular cafe on Cours Saleya, is this extremely popular restaurant that has been serving Niçois specialties for many years and is the best restaurant out of the many on Cours Saleya. Still, more tourists than locals come here, and though the crowd is usually young and trendy, the place does get overrun (it's listed in so many guides). Sometimes, especially at lunch, it fills with tired travelers going down their list of must-eat-at restaurants. Come here in the evening, when the atmosphere is festive, whether you sit on the sidewalk or in the elegantly simple dining room with its black ceiling and terra-cotta floors. This is the place to have an authentic *salade niçoise* or the delicious conversation starter *merda de can* (dogshit), which is fresh spinach gnocchi with its unfortunate color. They usually offer several kinds of fish grilled to order, and, depending on the season, there might be local fresh sardines, grilled or fried and served with a slice of lemon.

Ville de Siena. 10 rue St-Vincent, Vieux Nice. ☎ **04-93-80-12-45.** Reservations recommended. Main courses 70–120F ($13–$22). MC, V. Mon–Sat noon–3pm and 6:30–11:30pm, Sun 6:30–11:30pm. Bus: 1, 2, or 14. ITALIAN.

This bustling Italian restaurant is on a tiny pedestrian-only street in the heart of Vieux Nice (here there's no shortage of Italian restaurants, but this is one of the more authentic). The owner is Italian and oversees everything with a smile; he might take your order in his sing-songy English. The pizza oven is on one side of the street and the main kitchen on the other, and you can spend the whole evening watching the waiters scurrying back and forth balancing trays over their heads. Tables are lined up against the old city walls in summer, and there's a cozy dining room filled with wine bottles when the weather turns cold. Start with one of the salads or fresh melon with *jambon de Parme* (thinly sliced Parma ham). Try the excellent yet simple Napolitaine pizza with olives and mozzarella or go for some ravioli or hearty lasagna; the gnocchi with gorgonzola is creamy and delicious. Equal numbers of locals and tourists come here, and the atmosphere is laid back and friendly. Avoid the house wine (it's nasty) and choose a bottle of Italian wine from the wide selection.

IN & AROUND THE *ZONE PIETONE*

Flo. 4 rue Sacha-Guitry (off place Masséna). ☎ **04-93-13-38-38.** Main courses 80–110F ($15–$20); fixed-price menus 106F ($19) at lunch and after 10pm, 153F ($28) at dinner. AE, DC, MC, V. Daily noon–3pm and 7pm–12:30am. Bus: 1, 2, or 5. FRENCH.

Though part of a chain, this is still a special place to dine if you're in the mood for a bustling Paris-style brasserie. It's located in what was a theater in the 1930s; now the curtain rises to reveal the kitchen on stage, and you can see the cooks at work. This place is popular with the local artists, and your gaydar will surely pick up on quite a few comrades, most of them young professionals. It's a lively place where the service is friendly—except during weekday lunch, when the waiters are often rushed. They serve hearty specialties like *choucroute* (sauerkraut from Alsace) and good steaks, but it's the fish that's the focus. The *carpaccio de thon rouge* (thin slices of raw tuna) is a delicate appetizer, as are the fresh oysters on their shell with lemon. The daily specials include several fish choices usually grilled and served with local vegetables. For dessert, the cinnamon ice cream is wonderful.

La Pizza. 34 rue Masséna (in the *zone pietone*). ☎ **04-93-87-70-29.** Meals 49–89F ($9–$16); pizza 45–59F ($9–$11). AE, MC, V. Daily 11:30am–2am. Bus: 3, 7, or 14. ITALIAN.

This is the most popular of the many sidewalk pizza restaurants in the pedestrian zone. The tables are squeezed in tight, providing for a loud communal atmosphere—when it's busy, boy it gets crazy with all kinds of people. This is definitely not a place for a quiet romantic dinner. The food is straightforward but good. The most popular item is the huge thin-crust pizza baked in the wood oven; there are no fancy toppings, just simple ingredients like olives, mushrooms, onions, and garlic. Try the pizza Marguerite with ham or the pizza à l'ognion if you like onions (and you're not planning to kiss anyone for a few hours). The salads and traditional pasta dishes (spaghetti Bolognese, ravioli, linguine al pesto) are good too. If you want heartier fare, the fettuccine Alfredo goes well with the house Chianti and the spaghetti Milanese comes with a thin veal fillet.

✪ **Saigon.** 26 rue de la Buffa. ☎ **04-93-87-56-93.** Main courses 70–90F ($13–$16); fixed-price menus 95–120F ($17–$22). MC, V. Wed–Mon noon–2:30pm and 7–11pm. Bus: 3, 12, 14, or 22. VIETNAMESE.

When the locals dine out, they tend to want something other than French and so head to this tiny family-run Vietnamese place. On a busy street a few blocks in from the promenade, this wonderful restaurant uses fresh local ingredients to create Indo-Chinese specialties. The Vietnamese-French family truly work together. Denise, the mother, cooks, while her daughter, Melanie, who speaks fluent English (she lived in the States for some years) hosts and takes orders; she'll explain everything to you. (Her handsome brother, Jean, does a little bit of everything, and some of the local boys come here and drool.) Start with the yummy *nems* (spring rolls stuffed with crab), which you wrap in lettuce and add fresh mint leaves before eating. Move on to the excellent chicken with Singapore curry (spicy but not too much—Melanie will ask how you like it). The almond chicken is good too, but before a night on the town, boys order the beef saté (thin slices of beef marinated in spices, then grilled), served sizzling on a griddle.

AROUND THE PORT

Chez Pipo. 13 rue Bavastro (at the port). ☎ **04-93-55-88-82.** 12F ($2.10) per portion. No credit cards. Daily 5:30–10pm. Closed Mar. Bus: 1, 2, 9, 10, or 32. NIÇOIS BAKERY.

For one of the least expensive and very authentic light meals, search out this gem on a side street behind the large church on the port. The focus of this simple place is the large wood oven where they bake Niçois specialties; there's no cooking and no kitchen, all they do is bake. Grab a table on the sidewalk and sip on a beer with the old ladies and young schoolchildren who come here for a quick snack. You can't have a hot meal, just drinks (inexpensive beers and wine) and slices of *pissaladière* and *socca* (see "Street

Eats" on page 234), but frankly you have to acquire a taste for *socca* (it's a bit dry, so you'll need a beverage). There's one choice for dessert: a tasty wheat tart with sugar and lemon. Bottles of wine go for 56F ($10). Two gay bars are very close by, and in the late evenings Pipo gets a few hungry men.

Coco-Beach Restaurant. 2 av. Jean-Lorrain (just past the port). ☎ **04-93-89-39-26.** Reservations recommended. Main courses 120–200F ($22–$36); fixed-price menu 220F ($40) at lunch. AE, MC, V. Tues–Sat noon–2:30pm and 7–10pm, Sun noon–3pm. Closed Dec. Bus: 32. PROVENÇAL/SEAFOOD.

This is one of the few places with a sea view, though be warned you're paying for the setting more than the food. A walkway gets you from the road to the dining room, which practically sits on the cliff with the crashing waves beneath. The waiters, like the clientele, are on the older and straight side. But a few gay men do find their way here (mostly couples) because one of the gay swimming areas (Coco Beach, what a surprise) is nearby. You can pick your live lobster from the water tank if you want to go all out or try the bouillabaisse (sometimes not available). A *salade verte* (green salad) and the grilled fish of the day is your best bet. Enjoy the view and don't forget to check the wine prices before you order—some of them are astronomical.

4 Exploring Nice

Nice boasts the largest concentration of museums after Paris, 16 in all, and most of them worth a visit. But let's face it: Most people come not for the museums but for the Mediterranean, the mild weather, and the fantastic landscape. On foot is the best way to explore Nice—from the **promenade des Anglais** to **Vieux Nice** (the old part of the city), to the ***zone pietone*** (pedestrian mall) near place Masséna, this city is made for strolling. (In-line skating along the promenade is also very popular.)

Many visitors coming from colder climates want to spend all their time outdoors, and there's no better place to do it than Nice. The pace is slower, the people smile, everyone is tanned (don't forget the sunscreen!), and boys in tank tops and shorts abound. This is the life. In cooler months, Nice moves indoors only at night. The days are sunny and pleasant even in midwinter, and having lunch outside or even stretching out (fully clothed alas) on the pebbly beach is still delightful. At this time of year, the French boys and girls put away their skimpy swimwear, don their tight ski pants, and head for the hills: There are several ski resorts within an hour and a half's drive from Nice (see "Boys & Their Poles" below).

A good way to get a quick feel for the city is to take a spin on the **Trains Touristique de Nice** (☎ **04-93-92-45-59**), vehicles resembling miniature trains that go around Vieux Nice, Cours Saleya, and the Château in a 40-minute ride. Trains leave every 30 minutes from the promenade des Anglais (opposite the Hôtel Méridien at

A Museum Tip

Most museums are closed on either Monday or Tuesday; some are closed Sunday mornings. All museums are closed on January 1, Easter Sunday, May 1, and December 25. Call the museum for its hours if you're visiting during one of France's many other public holidays. (In May, for example, there's one holiday per week.) For a complete list of museums and hours, get the free brochure *Les Musées de Nice* at the tourist office.

As a special treat, the city offers free admission to its museums on February 1 and 11, March 1, April 5 and 15, May 3, June 7 and 10, July 5, August 2, September 6, October 4, November 1, and December 6.

1 promenade des Anglais), and the fare is 30F ($5). There's no service on rainy days or in the slow winter months. For something totally different, there are four-wheel-drive excursions into the Alpes-Maritimes north of Nice. **Sunny Days,** 8 place des Amaryllis (☎ **04-93-71-10-75**), offers half- and full-day trips to the mountains starting at 550F ($100) per person.

THE HITS YOU SHOULDN'T MISS

IN CIMIEZ

Several of Nice's top museums, notably the Matisse and Chagall, are in the very posh hilly neighborhood of **Cimiez,** north of the train station, 2 miles from the promenade des Anglais. Cimiez, named Cemenelum by the Romans who founded it, was the main town of the province of the Maritime Alps from the 1st to the 4th century. All around the **Villa des Arènes** (which contains the Matisse Museum) are the ruins of the Roman city, including baths and a theater still used for performances. You can tour the **archaeological site** and its museum (see below). In the 19th century, Queen Victoria and her court made Cimiez their winter home.

Archaeological Site and Archaeological Museum (Musée d'Archéologie). 160 av. des Arènes de Cimiez. ☎ **04-93-81-59-57.** Admission 25F ($4.50). Apr–Oct Tues–Sun 10am–noon and 2–6pm; Nov–Mar to 5pm. Bus: 15 or 17 from place Masséna to Arènes.

Nice's archaeological museum was opened in 1989. Roman Cemenelum was the capital of the province of the Maritime Alps, an important passageway to Gallia and Hispania. Many artifacts found at local excavations are displayed here, including Bronze Age works, Greek and Etruscan pieces, and ceramics, coins, and jewelry from the Middle Ages. Enter the museum through the archaeological site on avenue Montecroce.

✪ **Matisse Museum (Musée Matisse).** 164 av. des Arènes de Cimiez. ☎ **04-93-53-40-53.** Admission 25F ($4.50). Apr–Sept Wed–Mon 10am–6pm; Oct–Mar to 5pm. Bus: 15 or 17 from place Masséna to Monastère.

Henri Matisse called Nice home from 1917 until his death in 1954, and this outstanding museum holds the best collection of his work from his early student sketches to the female nudes, Indian ink drawings, and silk screens of the last part of his life. The museum, surrounded by perfumed carob and umbrella pine trees, occupies a magnificent 17th-century Italian villa painted a deep red, as if in homage to Matisse's passion for color. A new wing was built in 1993, allowing for more work to be on permanent exhibit. In addition to pieces from every period of his life, there are photos of the artist at work, of his models, and of his bedroom in Nice. Many of his personal belongings, such as chairs and sofas, are scattered throughout. One of Matisse's final and largest works, *Fleurs et Fruits* (1953), painted for a California villa, now decorates the main reception hall. A large portion of his work centers around sketches of nude women (sorry, guys—not one naked man to be found), including *Nude in an Armchair with a Green Plant* (1937) and *Nymph in the Forest* (1935/1942). A restaurant is slated to open on the first floor.

Church and Monastery of Cimiez (Eglise et Monastère de Cimiez) / Franciscan Museum (Musée Franciscain). Place du Monastère. ☎ **04-93-81-00-04.** Admission free. Mon–Sat 10am–noon and 3–6pm. Bus: 15 or 17 from place Masséna to Monastère.

Most visitors stroll over here after they visit the Matisse Museum (above); the setting is beautiful, and in the olive groves surrounding the church is the cemetery where Matisse and Raoul Dufy are buried. The medieval monastery and museum provide an excellent glimpse into the Franciscan monks' lives between the 15th and the 18th century. You'll find paintings, sculptures, frescoes, prayer books, and a reconstructed chapel and monk's cell. Note that the giant marble cross in the church dates from 1477.

✪ National Biblical Message Marc Chagall Museum (Musée National Message Biblique Marc-Chagall). Av. du Docteur-Menard at bd. de Cimiez. ☎ **04-93-53-87-20.** Admission 38F ($7) Mon and Wed–Sat, 28F ($5) Sun. July–Sept Wed–Mon 10am–6pm; Oct–June Wed–Mon 10am–5pm. Bus: 15 from place Masséna.

This modern building, in its own small park, holds the largest permanent collection of Marc Chagall's work—over 400 drawings, engravings, lithographs, sculptures, pastels, and ceramics, plus a tapestry and three stained-glass windows. The focus of the museum, however, is the 17 paintings dealing with Chagall's vision of the Old Testament (thus the biblical name of the museum), inspired by his trip to the Holy Land in the early 1930s. The work can be viewed as somber or uplifting depending how you look at it; there are a lot of angels, fish, and birds. Most visitors love it or hate it. Don't miss the beautiful mosaic on a wall outside over the small pond. There are also various interesting photographs showing Chagall at work, one with his wife and daughter from 1924, and a few of him right before his death in Nice (Chagall was born in Russia but lived in Nice most of his adult life). This museum is popular in summer, with many tour buses unloading hordes; try to go early in the morning or late in the afternoon, when you can enjoy the lovely coffee shop overlooking the garden.

IN NICE

The wide **promenade des Anglais** fronts the bay. Split by "islands" of palms and flowers, it stretches for about 4 miles. Fronting the beach are rows of grand cafes, the Palais Masséna Museum, villas, hotels, and chic boutiques.

Museum of Fine Arts (Musée des Beaux-Arts). 33 av. des Baumettes, Baumettes. ☎ **04-92-15-28-28.** Admission 25F ($4.50). Tues–Sun 10am–noon and 2–6pm. Bus: 38 to Chéret (or 3, 7, 9, 10, 12, 14 or 22 and walk up short hill from rue de France).

On a hill in a quiet residential neighborhood is this wonderful museum housed in a sumptuous villa built for Ukrainian Princess Kotschoubey in 1876. You could come here for the grand marble staircase alone (just imagine what the princess wore as she descended to dinner), at the top of which you'll find the magnificently adorned "Piano of the Baroness Vitta" from the early 1900s. But start on the ground floor, where there's a good collection of 17th-century Italian art. Compare Francesco Pittoni's impressive *The Creation of Eve* (Adam is totally spent, God's hand is on Eve) and Ottavio Vanninni's version (Adam is virile and young, Eve seems old and haggard). What's up with that? The museum prides itself on Hendrick van Somer's *David Conquerer of Goliath,* also on the ground floor. On the upper level (past the piano), is a good collection of impressionists, mostly Degas, Sisley, and Manet; many of Jules Chéret's paintings, including *Le Déjeuner sur l'herbe* (the Manet version is at the Musée d'Orsay in Paris—see chapter 5); Rodin's *The Kiss;* and ceramics by Picasso. Raoul Dufy's work is well represented with 28 pieces.

Museum of Modern Art and Contemporary Art (Musée d'Art Moderne et d'Art Contemporain). Promenade des Arts. ☎ **04-93-62-61-62.** Admission 25F ($4.50). Wed–Thurs and Sat–Mon 11am–6pm, Fri to 10pm. Bus: 1, 2, 3, 5, 6, 16, or 25.

Frequently overlooked, this is a must stop for any lover of contemporary art, with a large selection covering the 1960s to the present. Opened in 1991 between place Masséna and Vieux Nice, this ultramodern glass-and-marble building is itself an homage to the avant-garde artists (there are also great views of Nice from the transparent walkways on the upper floors). You'll find mainly the work of European and American artists, but with particular attention to those who've lived or worked in Nice (Robert Indiana, Arman, Ben, Cesar). There's a room dedicated to Yves Klein and his magnificent blue version of the *Winged Victory* that's in the Louvre (see chapter 5). Andy Warhol's acrylic *Dollar Sign* from 1981 is also on display. Don't miss Claude

Nice Attractions

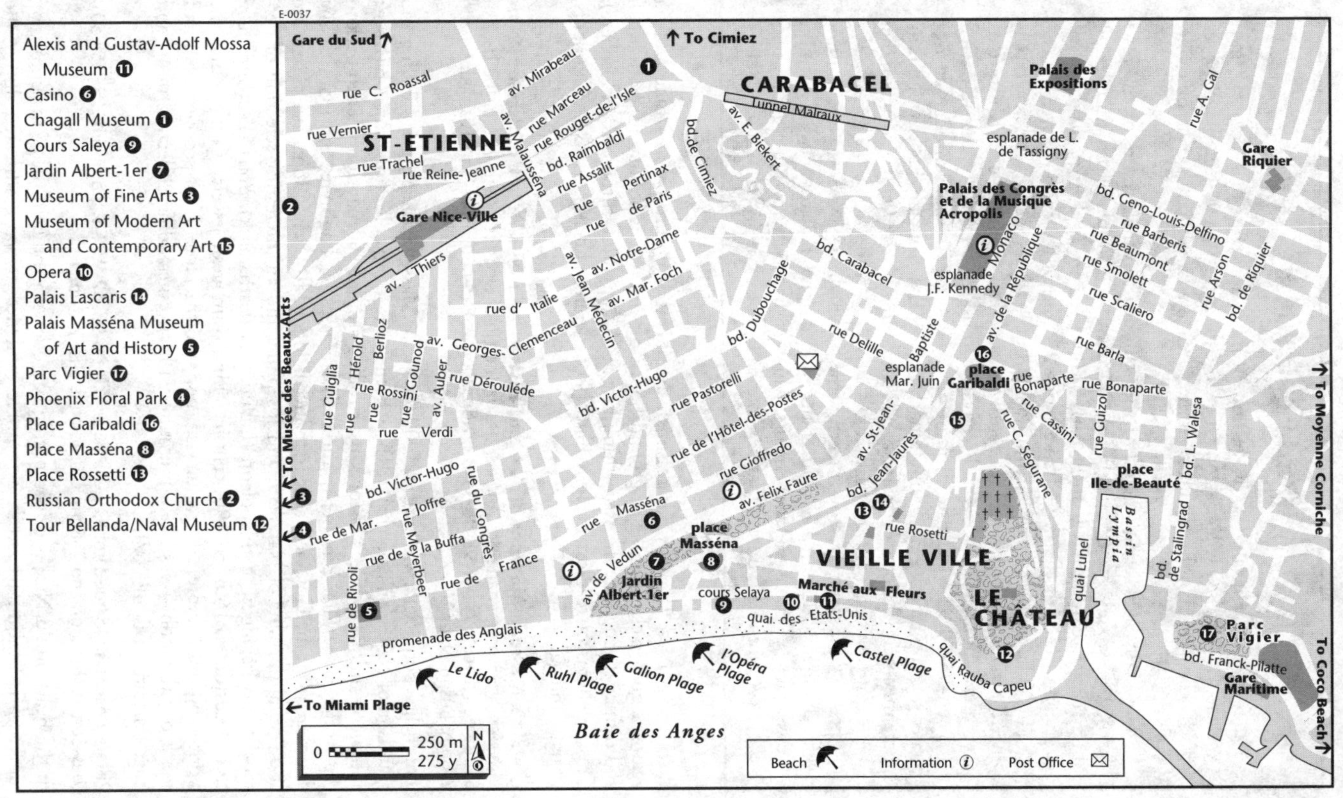

"Perching" in Peillon

The fortified medieval town of **Peillon,** 12 miles northwest of Nice, is the most spectacular "perched village" along the Côte d'Azur. At 1,000 feet above the sea, it's also unspoiled, unlike so many of the perched villages that have become filled with day-trippers and souvenir shops.

The main sightseeing interest is the semifortified architecture of the town itself. You can also visit the **Eglise du St-Sauveur,** a simple parish church built in a country-baroque style in the early 1700s, near the highest point of the village, and the 15th-century **Chapelle des Pénitents-Blancs,** on place Auguste-Arnuls. The parish church is always open, but local authorities don't encourage interior visits to the chapel, unless tours, usually for groups of art historians, are prearranged several weeks in advance through officials at the town hall (☎ **04-93-79-91-04**). Instead, most of the interior is visible through an iron gate. If you plunk 2F (35¢) into a machine near the iron gate, lights will illuminate the interior's noteworthy frescoes. Painted in 1491 by Jean Cannavesio, they represent eight stages of the passion of Christ.

Each of the town's narrow streets, some of which are enclosed with vaulting and accented with potted geraniums and strands of ivy, radiates outward from the town's "foyer," **place Auguste-Arnuls,** which is shaded by rows of plantain trees centered around a fountain that has splashed water from its basin since 1800.

Pascal's *Boy Nude* (for obvious reasons), a brilliant sculpture painted blue and set against a gold background. The ground-floor Café des Arts is popular for both lunch and dinner throughout the year (think art, think gay, think flirtatious atmosphere). This is where you're most likely to find Nice's young and hip artists and students, straight and gay.

✪ **Palais Masséna Museum of Art and History (Musée d'Art et d'Histoire Palais Masséna).** 35 promenade des Anglais, beside the Hôtel Négresco (entrance in the back at 65 rue de France). ☎ **04-93-88-11-34.** Admission 25F ($4.50). Tues–Sun 10am–noon and 2–6pm. Bus: 6, 9, or 10.

This belle-époque villa was built in 1900 for Victor Masséna, the prince of Essling and grandson of Napoléon's marshal. It's now home to a superb collection of decorative art and pieces unique to Nice's history. Just strolling around this mansion is a trip back to the world of the First Empire; in the halls are vases by Thomyre, and many of the doors are from the Govone Castle that once belonged to Lucien Bonaparte. There are also several portraits of Napoléon and Joséphine and an interesting selection of personal items belonging to Napoléon (including a death mask). You'll also find huge clocks, costumes, 16th- to 19th-century china (Limoges), jewelry from around the world, and much more. After your visit, pop into the Hotel Négresco next door and check out the lobby—it's like a museum, with an outstanding collection of art and huge portraits of Louis XVI.

Palais Lascaris. 15 rue Droite, Vieux Nice. ☎ **04-93-62-05-54.** Admission 25F ($4.50). Tues–Sun 10am–noon and 2–6pm. Closed Nov. Bus: 1, 2, or 14.

In the heart of old Nice is this imposing baroque villa. Built in the 17th century by the Lascaris-Ventimiglia family as a noble residence, it was confiscated during the French Revolution and almost destroyed. The city of Nice bought it in 1942, declared it a historic monument in 1946, and completely renovated it in the early 1960s. Inside this rather dark, somber villa you'll find a remarkable marble staircase adorned with

Once you've explored Peillon, consider a 2-hour, 7½-mile northward hike across the dry and rocky landscapes of eastern Provence to Peillon's remote twin, **Peille,** a smaller version of what you'll find in Peillon.

Few other towns in the area are as easy to reach by car and as inconvenient to reach by public transport. It's an easy **drive** northeast from Nice—take D2204 to D21 and you'll get there in about 20 minutes, depending on traffic. Only two **trains** a day stop near Peillon, at St-Techle. For rail information and schedules, call ☎ **08-36-35-35-39.** You'll find lots of dilapidated local color at St-Techle. Know in advance that no taxis will be waiting in line and there's no bus service; you'll have to walk the rest of the way.

The Santa Azur **bus** operates four buses that make the transit from Nice every day, with multiple stops en route and transit time of around 25 minutes each way. Don't expect it to be convenient, as you'll be dropped off about 2 miles from Peillon's center, at a tiny crossroads known as Le Moulin, and have to walk the rest of the way. For bus information, call Gare Routière in Nice ☎ **04-93-85-61-81.**

The **Syndicat d'Initiative** (tourist office) is in the village center (☎ **04-93-79-91-04**).

sculptures leading to rooms filled with 17th- and 18th-century furniture and art. Don't forget to look up at the painted ceilings (especially in the second-floor salon since—you guessed it—there are nude males) The top floor is the most interesting, loaded with miscellaneous items used in everyday life in the 17th century, like large clay jugs that held olive oil, early breadmakers, a lavender distiller, and traditional local costumes (check out the women's lingerie circa 1840).

Russian Orthodox Church (Eglise Orthodoxe Russe). Av. Nicholas II at bd. du Tzarevitch. ☎ **04-93-96-88-02.** Admission 12F ($2). Daily 9am–noon and 2:30–6pm. Bus: 17.

This is a magnificent church, richly ornamented and adorned with the onion-shaped domes you can see from afar. It was built during the belle époque, when droves of Russia's aristocracy, including the Romanovs, vacationed in Nice. It's said to be the most beautiful religious edifice of the Orthodoxy outside Russia, and there's still a large population of Russian immigrants living in Nice. Try to come on a Sunday morning when church services are held.

Alexis and Gustav-Adolf Mossa Museum (Musée Alexis et Gustav-Adolf Mossa). 59 quai des Etats-Unis. ☎ **04-93-62-37-11.** Admission 15F ($2.75), includes admission to Musée Raoul-Dufy. Tues–Sat 10am–noon and 2–6pm, Sun 2–6pm. Bus: 6.

This interesting museum used to be the Contemporary Art Gallery and was reopened in 1990 to honor one the city's most celebrated artists, Alexis Mossa, the creator of Nice's Carnavale parades. Models of floats from his early creations and many of his watercolors and painted scenes of the Carnavales are on display. His son, Gustav-Adolf, continued his father's work, though its definitely more surreal and there's much less symbolism. Lovers of parades and carnivals will have a ball. Admission to this museum also includes entry to the **Musée Raoul-Dufy** down the street at 77 quai des Etats-Unis (☎ **04-93-62-31-24;** same hours), where you'll find a good collection of Raoul Dufy's work, including paintings, drawings, watercolors, engravings, and ceramics.

GAY NICE

There's no specifically gay area in Nice, and that's not surprising given that the gay bars and clubs are scattered all over the city. The most gay-friendly area is **Vieux Nice,** a maze of streets and old squares, and the infamous **Cours Saleya,** where a century-old flower market is held every day but Monday. This long pedestrian-only street runs parallel to the sea, one block inland from the quai des Etats-Unis, and is lined with cafes, restaurants, and shops.

The gay, the straight, the young, and the hip head to Nice's most popular sidewalk cafe, ✪ **La Civette du Cours,** 1 Cours Saleya (☎ **04-93-80-80-59;** open daily 8am–2am); it shares the sidewalk and the address with Le Safari restaurant (see "Whet Your Appetite" above). This end of Cours Saleya is less touristy and ever so slightly cruisy, especially in the early evenings long before the boys even think of dressing for dinner. Some lesbians come here too, but like everywhere else in Nice, women couples aren't very visible. The tiny streets around Cours Saleya have their share of gay bars and gay-friendly restaurants, but rarely will you see two men holding hands or being intimate in public.

Early evenings on the **promenade des Anglais** is also a popular time for gay professionals who in-line skate, jog, or bike along the seafront (the stretch of sidewalk from the Hôtel Négresco westward is the popular area). When the locals want to get away, they go to St-Tropez, where anything goes and gay life is more visible. For gay pride, the Niçois boys and girls drive over to Cannes (during the last week of June) to participate in the parade.

BOYS & GIRLS ON THE BEACH

The gay beaches along the Côte d'Azur are either pebbly or rocky (with the exception of St-Tropez's beautiful sandy beaches), and most are quite a ways from the road. Bring good hiking shoes and supplies; most of these secluded beaches have no drinking water or food. Juan-les-Pins and Cannes both offer excellent sandy beaches, but none has a steady gay following.

✪ CASTEL PLAGE Though the promenade des Anglais is lined with miles of pebbly beaches, none of them is exclusively gay. **Castel Plage,** "the last beach in Nice" (past where the promenade changes names to quai des Etats-Unis just before winding uphill) is the most popular with gay men and the stray lesbian or two. On the easternmost side is the **private beach** where you can rent *matelas* (beach mattresses; 70F/$13 a day) and parasols (umbrellas; 15F/$2.75) and have the cute waiters wine and dine you right on your mattress (!); or you can walk the few steps to the shaded restaurant. Right next door is the **Plage Publique du Castel,** the most popular public beach with the local gay crowd. Friday afternoons and weekends is when both beaches are at their gayest, but they may seem quite straight a lot of the time. (Be patient, the boys do come.) The private beach is open mid-May to late September, and the restaurant is open daily noon to 4pm (a meal costs about 80F/$15); drinks are available until sunset in midsummer.

MIAMI PLAGE On the other side of town, toward the airport at 197 promenade des Anglais, you'll find **Miami Plage,** a family-run private beach that's pretty much straight, but everyone is very friendly and comfortable. Locals come for the reasonably priced (and very good) food served at the beach restaurant. At Sunday lunch, you'll usually find seniors with their poodles, young straight couples, and a few gay men (if you're lucky). The 85F ($15) prix-fixe menu is a steal; all is well prepared and fresh. Lunch is served daily noon to 3pm, sandwiches and drinks 10am to dusk. You can also spend the day right by the water, and the waiters will be happy to serve you anything from a sandwich to a three-course meal right on your beach mattress (and bring you buckets of ice to keep you cool). The beach is open late April to late September. Matelas rentals are 70F($13) per day, with umbrellas at 15F ($2.75).

COCO BEACH Sandless **Coco Beach** isn't really a beach but a jagged collection of big rocks and boulders where the boys scatter naked to catch the rays and then take a dip in the sea; it's the only gay nude spot in Nice. Coco is a pain to find, but once you're there you'll be surrounded by blue sea and sky and feel like you're a million miles away from the city. Follow the road that goes around the port past Parc Vigier (take bus no. 32 to Villa La Côte) to the **Coco-Beach Restaurant,** 2 av. Jean-Lorrain. Just past the restaurant, take the steps heading down to the water, go through the tunnel, and stay to your left, heading east. It's a good 10-minute walk along a jagged path hugging the coastline before you start seeing the boys on the rocks. Go as far as the path will take you and you'll see even more. On weekdays, it's pretty quiet, with a lot of men reading books or gazing out at the horizon; don't expect a great deal of entertainment. Weekends are busier, but it never gets as cruisy or hopping as Eze (see "Side Trips from Nice" later in this chapter), and the crowd is a tad older and less buff than elsewhere. It's a quiet, comfortable place to spend an afternoon. Bring water; there's nothing down here. (The Maeterlinck is the hotel closest to this area at the top of the cliff.)

OTHER AREA BEACHES Other gay and gay-friendly beaches are located at ✪ **Eze-sur-Mer** (the gayest on the coast), **St-Jean-Cap-Ferrat,** ✪ **St-Tropez,** and **Cannes.** See "Side Trips from Nice" later in this chapter for details.

PARKS, GARDENS & SQUARES

Le Château, the hill at the eastern end of the quai des Etats-Unis above Vieux Nice, is named after the castle built by the ducs de Savoie; it was torn down in 1706. Very little remains except for a beautiful park with panoramic views. An **elevator** from the eastern end of the quai des Etats-Unis carries you up the hill for 5F (90¢) round-trip (daily 10am–5:50pm); or you can climb the stairs. The **Tour Bellanda,** an old tower where Berlioz once lived, now houses a **Naval Museum** (☎ **04-93-80-47-61;** open Wed–Sun 10am–noon and 2–7pm, to 5pm Oct–May; admission 15F/$2.75). The eastern end of the park (where it overlooks the lighthouse) is semicruisy; the real action happens after dark when the park closes. The small paths leading down from the park eastward toward the cemeteries and the port get their share of anonymous goings-on. Note that it's a bit dangerous, not to mention illegal, to be in the park after closing.

One street in from the promenade des Anglais (at avenue de Verdun) is the **Jardin Albert-1er,** a small park full of exotic flowers, palm trees, and shade on a hot day. You'll find a lot of kids and seniors here. Open 24 hours.

For 17 acres of tropical plants, head to the **Phoenix Floral Park (Parc Floral Pheonix),** Nice's botanical gardens), 405 promenade des Anglais (☎ **04-93-18-03-33**). The park is home to one of Europe's biggest greenhouses, with over 2,000 kinds of tropical and subtropical plants. It's open daily: April to September 9am to 7pm (October to March to 5pm). Admission is 40F ($7).

On the other side of town at the port (Gare Maritime), is the small **Parc Vigier,** boulevard Franck-Pilatte. During the day it's full of screaming kids, but in the evenings it gets a bit cruisy since the road leads to Coco Beach (see above), and some of the boys returning home without a catch of the day will linger at the park after sunset. It's a nice place just to take in the view of the sea if nothing else.

Place Masséna is Nice's main square; it forms the heart of the city and is beautiful with its elegant Fontaine du Soleil (Fountain of the Sun) by Janoit surrounded by 17th-century buildings. There's a bit of everything (and everyone) here at all times of night and day. The most beautiful square is on the fringes of Vieux Nice, the baroque **place Garibaldi,** surrounded by Genoese-style arcaded houses from the 17th century.

There's not much going on here except for the popular Café de Turin (see "Whet Your Appetite" above).

Place Rossetti, though, is the hip and happening square in the heart of Vieux Nice (4 blocks north of Cours Saleya on rue St-Reparate). It's a beautiful old Italian square with cafes and ice-cream stands (Chez Fenocchio on the southwest corner has the best ice cream; open daily 11am–1am). This square is gaining popularity with local gays and visitors alike; several new gay-owned restaurants have opened recently within a block of here (see "Whet Your Appetite" above).

WORKING UP A SWEAT

It's surprising there aren't more gym bunnies or gyms in this city, but the boys tend to get their exercise outdoors on their bikes or in-line skates. Predictably, there are no gay gyms, but **Gold's Gym** (formerly The Universe), 6 rue de France (☎ **04-93-87-42-75**), is the most gay-friendly and is centrally located off the pedestrian mall (*zone pietone*); a day pass is 50F ($9).

5 Hitting the Stores

Shopping in Nice is unglamorous and refreshingly straightforward. (If you want designer wear and the convenience of shopping on one street while rubbing elbows with millionaires, go to Cannes and check out its rue d'Antibes). As with its hotels and restaurants, Nice is down to earth and reasonable when it comes to shopping. After all, most of the locals shop here too, so stores can't get away with "tourist" prices.

There are three areas for shopping in Nice: around the ***zone pietone*** off place Masséna, **Vieux Nice,** and **avenue Jean-Médecin.** The largest concentration of high-class boutiques and trendy clothing shops is in the *zone pietone,* in and around rue Masséna. Vieux Nice is the up-and-coming area for trendy (and gay) shops, and avenue Jean-Médecin is a run-of-the-mill commercial street lined with department stores, hardware stores, and reasonably priced (though not fashionable) clothes stores. There are only a few gay stores, all in Vieux Nice.

Shopping hours are generally Monday to Saturday 10am to noon and 3 to 7pm; some stores open Sunday mornings and close Mondays. Many bakeries, grocery stores, and produce stands are closed on Mondays too. During summer, many of the shops in Vieux Nice and in the *zone pietone* stay open to 9 or 10pm.

SHOPS A TO Z

ANTIQUES & ART The **Marché d'Art des Antiquaires** is the local antiques market held Tuesday to Saturday 9am to 5:30pm on several streets at the edge of Vieux Nice—rue Catherine-Segurane, rue Antoine-Gauthier, and rue Emmanuel-Philibert. Locals also consider gay-owned **Galerie Regards,** 20 rue Assalit (☎ **04-93-92-13-47**), as having the best collection of art deco antiques at reasonable prices.

If you're itching to spend your fortune on a Matisse or Chagall, you might want to call Jean Ferrero (he's a big art dealer in town) or one of his associates for an appointment at the **Galerie Ferrero,** 2 rue du Congrès (☎ **04-93-88-34-44**). If you just want to look around, try the **Boutique Ferrero,** 24 rue de France (☎ **04-93-82-56-79**), selling copies of lithographs and engravings from Picasso to Cesar that won't cost you your life savings.

BOOKS There are no gay bookstores in Nice, but **The Cat's Whiskers,** 26 rue Lamartine (☎ **04-93-80-02-66**), has a large selection of English-language books and is owned by an Englishwoman. **La Maison de la Presse,** 1 rue Massena (no phone), stocks a large selection of English-language magazines and newspapers.

CANDIED FRUIT & CHOCOLATE Candied fruit is a Nice specialty (how appropriate for a gay guide), and at the **Confiserie Florian du Vieux Nice,** 14 quai Papacino, near the port (☎ **04-93-55-43-50**), you can watch how the fruit is candied while you shop. At the **Confiserie Auer,** 7 rue St-François-de-Paule in Vieux Nice (☎ **04-93-85-77-98**), you can sample the candied fruit, pastries, and cakes at the *salon de thé* (tea salon) in the back. Both stores sell excellent chocolates too.

CERAMICS Almost every tiny souvenir shop sells some kind of ceramics, but for true Provençal work, head to **Terre à Provence,** 7 rue Massena (☎ **04-93-16-93-45**), where you'll find everything from simple pottery to hand-painted ceramic vases.

FASHION The very trendy ✪ **Zone Libre,** 2 rue St-Reparate (☎ **04-93-13-02-26**), is a large store with a wild selection of funky T-shirts, jeans, boots, shirts, and sweatshirts—it has a solid gay following. **Boys and Girls,** 2 rue Mascoinat (☎ **04-93-62-00-19**), is the local gay store, selling everything from tight T-shirts to funky platform shoes. **Un Monde à Part,** 12 rue Alexandre-Mari in Vieux Nice (☎ **04-93-13-94-53**), is gay-owned and has a cool selection of shirts, vests, and pants—anything and everything hip and tight, so be sure to starve yourself before shopping here.

Boy's Azur, 6 rue François-Gallo in Vieux Nice, off place Rossetti (☎ **04-93-92-20-97**), is the most popular gay-owned shop, with a good collection of undies, T-shirts, and shirts. **For Men,** 23 rue Masséna on the pedestrian mall (☎ **04-93-88-54-71**), is a tiny store selling elegant shirts and ties only; oh, yeah, the manager is cute.

JEWELRY **Barichella,** 14 av. de Verdun (☎ **04-93-16-29-16**), is one of the most elegant jewelry stores in Nice, with unique original designs from diamond rings to beautiful silver bracelets.

MARKETS The century-old **Flower Market (Marché aux Fleurs)** in Cours Saleya is one of France's best. It's held Tuesday to Sunday 6am to 5:30pm. On the same street and the same days but 7am to 1pm is the **marché** selling local products, from farm-fresh yogurt to honey and herbs. It's a good place to shop for a picnic lunch. The **flea market at Cours Saleya** is held every Monday (except on days before official holidays). Hours are 8am to 5pm. The **marche aux poissons** (fish market) is held every morning except Monday from 6am to 1pm on place Saint-Francois.

OLIVES & OLIVE OIL You can smell the wonderful aroma of crushed olives when you step into **Huilerie Alziari,** 14 rue St-François-de-Paule (☎ **04-93-85-76-92**), a tiny shop filled with anything you can eat or do with olive oil (well, almost) from soap to tapenade. They also have sacks of dried lavender and *herbes de provence* packed to go. They'll wrap anything for you to carry home.

PERFUME If you're looking for your perfect scent, head to **Aux Parfums de Grasse,** 10 rue St-Gaétan (☎ **04-93-85-60-77**), selling 80 scents in flasks and bottles costing 15F ($2.50) for a lipstick-sized container to 75F ($13) for 1 liter. The owner will help you combine various brands to create your personal fragrance.

PROVENÇAL SPECIALTIES If you fall in love with the magical colors of the Côte d'Azur, you can buy everything from napkins to wallpaper in the traditional Provençal style from **Les Olivades,** 7 rue de la Boucherie in Vieux Nice (☎ **04-93-85-85-19**). Provence is known for its *santons,* unique handmade decorations for Christmas trees and nativity scenes: **Au Coeur de Nice,** 11 rue Mascoinat (☎ **04-93-13-88-11**), sells the best collection.

SEX SHOP **Sexashop** in Vieux Nice at 8 Descente Crotti, off place Masséna (☎ **04-93-80-29-49**), is a large store with everything from dildos to videos (and private viewing cabins).

WINE The **Ducs de Gascogne,** 4 rue de France, at rue Halévy (☎ **04-93-87-48-20**), sells fine wines and champagnes as well as pâtés; they have attractive wicker baskets made especially for bottles—excellent gifts! **Canavin,** 4 bis rue Meyerbeer (☎ **04-93-82-05-20**), has a good collection of French wines, and the friendly English-speaking staff is quite knowledgeable.

6 All the World's a Stage

The **Jazz à Nice festival** brings world-renowned groups and vocalists every July to the Arène de Cimiez, and the **Carnavale de Nice** brings many eclectic shows and concerts. Nice's opera has an excellent fall and winter program.

To find out what's happening in the city when you arrive, pick up a copy of ***L'Officiel des Spectacles,*** which has weekly listings of concerts, theaters, and festivals. As might be expected from this conservative city, there are no gay theaters or musical groups at this time.

THE PERFORMING ARTS

The **Opéra de Nice,** 4 rue St-François-de-Paule (☎ **04-92-17-40-40;** box office open Tues–Sat 10am–6pm), offers an excellent program during its October-to-May season. The Nice Philharmonic also performs here regularly. Prices range from 40 to 380F ($7 to $69).

The **Théâtre de Nice/Centre Dramatique National Nice–Côte d'Azur,** promenade des Arts (☎ **04-93-80-52-60;** box office open Tues–Sat 1–7pm), hosts a busy October-to-April season with shows ranging from Lorca's *Blood Wedding* to a new version of *Pinocchio,* all in French, *bien sur.* Tickets range from 60 to 170F ($11 to $31).

The giant **Acropolis** convention center and concert hall, 1 Esplanade Kennedy (☎ **04-93-92-83-00;** box office open Mon–Sat 10am–5pm), hosts an eclectic selection of concerts and recitals, with tickets from 90 to 314F ($16 to $57). Late October to late April is when its calendar is fullest. On Sunday mornings, concerts are held at the hotel **Westminster Concorde,** 27 promenade des Anglais (☎ **04-93-88-29-44**); call for hours and program information.

At the **Fondation Kosma,** 24 bd. de Cimiez (☎ **04-92-26-72-20**), there's a free concert every Monday at 6pm October to April; admission is free. Throughout the year, jazz concerts are given at the **Cedac de Cimiez,** 49 av. de la Marne (☎ **04-93-53-85-95**); and at the **Forum Nice Nord,** 10 bd. Comte de Falicon (☎ **04-93-53-85-95**), there are frequent concerts by musicians from around the world. The **Théâtre de Nice,** Promenade des Arts (☎ **04-93-80-52-60**), is currently under the direction of Jacques Weber and hosts regular original national productions of French plays.

LIVE-MUSIC CLUBS

Chez Wayne, 15 rue de la Préfecture, off place Rossetti in Vieux Nice (☎ **04-93-13-46-99;** cover usually 20–50F/$3–$9, including a drink), is the current hot spot for live music (and a very straight bar scene); it's where the young and the beautiful go to listen to live rock, Beatles music, and the occasional jazz group. Live music begins nightly at 9pm (check for reduced winter program), and the bar/restaurant is open 3 to 11:15pm.

The **Jazz à Nice festival** runs for a week in mid-July at the Parc et Arènes de Cimiez (☎ **04-93-21-22-01**); three stages provide live music late into the night beginning at 6pm.

During the **Carnavale de Nice** in mid-February there are many concerts and shows all over town; programs are available from the Office du Tourisme.

A CABARET

Nice's humble attempt at competing with Monte Carlo's glitter is a small casino/cabaret, **Le Cabaret du Casino Roule,** at the Hôtel Méridien, 1 promenade des Anglais (☎ **04-93-87-95-87;** cover 90F ($16), including a drink). Las Vegas–style shows play nightly during the high season at 10pm. If you enjoy seeing feathery pseudo-drag wear, you might just have a laugh here.

7 In the Heat of the Night

Nice comes alive after dark, especially in summer, when people tend to stay at the beach until sunset; by the time they relax and shower, it's 9pm before anybody thinks of dinner. Vieux Nice is hopping with young people and tourists from early evening well into the night—it's the only area that stays somewhat lively after all the restaurants close at midnight. Many gay bars are located here, and they usually stay open until dawn in midsummer and at least 3am at other times. A moonlit stroll along the promenade is always a great end to a night of partying.

To find out about up-to-date happenings on the current gay scene, pick up a free copy of ***Exes,*** a small gay guide with a foldout map showing the bars and clubs. You can find it at any gay bar or store.

MAINSTREAM BARS

The bar at the **Hôtel Négresco,** 37 promenade des Anglais (☎ **04-93-16-64-00**), is a must if you feel like dressing up and watching wealthy Russians sip Kir Royals. If you're missing the guys back home (and their butts in tight jeans), go where the local straight boys drink beer, play pool, and watch soccer games: **L'Ideal's Bar,** 15 bd. Auguste-Raynaud (☎ **04-93-52-93-51**); it was recently bought by three young hets and renovated to resemble an American sports bar.

Chez Wayne, 15 rue de la Préfecture, off place Rossetti in Vieux Nice (☎ **04-93-13-46-99;** cover usually 20–50F/$3–$9, including a drink), is the hot spot for the young trendy crowd to drink, chow on Tex-Mex, and listen to live music. Also in Vieux Nice, **La Trappa,** 2 rue Jules-Gilly (☎ **04-93-80-33-69**), is another trendy bar whose artsy crowd sips wine and snacks on tapas.

Note that many bars double as cafes and serve light snacks and most cafes serve alcoholic drinks, so there's no fine line between the two.

GAY BARS

Nice's gay bar scene has two distinct faces. First, there are the smoky neighborhood bars, several of which are close to the port on dark side streets—they cater mostly to a hard-core bar crowd. Then you have the newer selections in Vieux Nice, where the crowd is hipper, younger, and more fit; these bars, Chez Edan and Le Boot's, are lively (as opposed to dark and somber) and full of a mixed gay crowd. And then there's Le Blue Boy, the oldest and only busy gay dance club in the city and absolutely *the* place where the boys end up at 1am. There usually is no cover at most bars; at dance clubs, 50F ($6) gets you in and gets you a drink.

There are two gay bars by the port of Nice on dark side streets where local barflies frequent. **Le Rusca,** 2 rue Rusca (☎ **04-93-89-46-25**), is owned by Jacques, who's 40-something and tends the smoky bar; it's cozy on a cold winter night, but in summer it's often empty. **L'Ascenceur,** 18 bis Emmanuel-Philibert (☎ **04-93-26-35-30**), is popular after midnight with men of different ages, mostly French. It's pretty dark and smoky, and there are a couple of backrooms. The level of cuteness isn't that high.

Tip Top, 30 quai Lunel (☎ **04-93-26-22-88**), advertises in the gay press and is trying to attract the boys. However, though it does boast a nice view of the port from the few tables outside, there's rarely anyone here but the older bartender. This is the bar closest to the two main cruising areas at the lighthouse (across the street) and the Château (just behind).

Close to the train station in the seedy Hôtel des Nations is the bar **Les Nations,** 25 av. Durante (☎ **04-93-88-30-58**). It attracts a gay grunge/Kate Moss crowd (black clothes, red lipstick, some nail polish); on Sunday evenings, though, the tea dance draws a more eclectic gay crowd.

In Vieux Nice, you'll find a trendier 20- and 30-something crowd. ✪ **Chez Edan** (☎ **04-93-62-82-85**), off Cours Saleya, is the happening place. You can have a light meal in the lush back garden before joining the boys in the front bar (the action starts around 10pm). Dan, the owner (Edan, get it?), will serve you shirtless but without a smile. (What's with the attitude, girl?) His clients are friendly, however, and this is a good place to practice your French (you know what I mean) with the local *garçons* and *hommes.*

A LESBIAN BAR

There used to be one lesbian bar in this city, but it closed down recently—it's astonishing that there's no place with a regular lesbian following, except on Sunday nights at **Oba Oba,** 73–75 quai des Etats-Unis (☎ **04-93-80-08-14**), when it's mixed gay/lesbian. On other nights, this place is very straight and there's samba dancing.

A LEATHER BAR

In Vieux Nice, you'll find Nice's only leather bar, **Le Boot's,** 5 place Vieille (☎ **04-93-62-89-82**); it's relatively new and attractive with hardwood floors and exposed stone walls. The top floor is quiet before 1am, but downstairs you'll find music blaring in the dungeonlike basement. (You have to ring the bell to be admitted; the men come late and stay until dawn.)

DANCE CLUBS

Wherever you are in Nice, it seems like all roads finally lead to ✪ **Le Blue Boy,** 9 rue Spinetta (☎ **04-93-44-68-24**), the city's oldest gay club (it's in a residential neighborhood between the promenade and the train station). It's a small club and frequently gets so crowded you'll have to rub elbows (and more) with more than one guy (thrilling to some, claustrophobic to others); try the less congested downstairs dance area if upstairs gets too much. You do get a large number of posers early on, but by 3am, the boys naturally work harder at making new friends. You'll find men of all ages and nationalities, but the majority are French and 25 to 45. The drag shows on weekends can be fun, but they're all in French. Le Blue Boy is the only happening gay dance club in town. Many new clubs try to compete but close down after a few months; the Boy reigns.

Not far from the *zone pietone,* **News Club,** 9 passage Emile-Negrin (☎ **04-93-87-76-30;** Wed–Sun only), was slated to open after this writing, so ask around when you arrive (it used to be known as Le Dauphin d'Argent).

The only other popular dance club this side of St-Tropez is Cannes's **Le Disco Sept,** 7 rue Rouguières (☎ **04-93-39-10-36**), where muscled young gays flex to techno until dawn.

L'Absolute, 6 rue Halévy (☎ **04-93-87-92-00;** open Wed–Sun 11pm–4am), opened in late 1998 and is gaining popularity with the local boys on Fridays. The question everybody is asking: Will it replace Blue Boy?

DOWN & DIRTY: CINEMAS, SAUNAS & MORE

The most popular cruising area is at the lighthouse, at the western end of the port; this is where it all happens between the huge rocks encircling the phallic bulge of the lighthouse. You'll also find some goings-on all along the pier leading to the lighthouse. From here, you have an excellent view of the fast boats to Corsica, among other things.

The pathway heading up to the Château across from the lighthouse pier is also cruisy in the evenings; cruising goes on along the promenade des Anglais just west of the Hôtel Négresco (the only stretch of promenade where cars are allowed to park), but there are always lots of tourists and seniors strolling along. Some of the men stay parked in their cars while the others come jogging by shirtless.

In Vieux Nice, **Sexashop** at 8 Descente Crotti (☎ **04-93-80-29-49;** open daily noon–10pm), has private video cabins for fun on the run. The cleanest and best-managed sauna is **Blue Gym's,** 7 av. Desambrois (☎ **04-93-80-71-11;** open daily 1pm–midnight), not far from the train station; it has a big Jacuzzi, video shows, and a snack bar. The largest sauna in Nice is **Bains Douches,** 7 rue Gubernatis (☎ **04-93-80-28-26;** open daily 1pm–10pm); it has four levels and close to avenue Jean-Médecin.

The cruisiest video club is **Traxx,** 11 av. du Maréchal-Foch (☎ **04-93-80-98-10;** open daily 2pm–2am).

8 Side Trips from Nice: The Côte d'Azur

The beauty along the **Côte d'Azur** is dazzling: azure skies and water, perched villages, Mediterranean views, orange groves, secluded coves and beaches, luxurious villas and resorts, lavender fields, yacht-filled harbors, and more—plus world-class art museums and romantic restaurants and hotels. Even the hideous overbuilding and mass tourism hasn't spoiled the area. Driving is the best way to get around, but if Nice is your base you could also use public transportation for day or overnight trips.

Trains and buses operate frequently to the coastal towns. If you're stopping off at one of the smaller seaside resorts (Beaulieu or Eze), make sure you don't board an express train or bus that runs from Nice to Monte Carlo (for eastbound travel) or Nice to St-Raphaël (calling at Antibes, Juan-les-Pins, and Cannes if you're going west). If you're heading to one of the mountain villages, the bus is your only choice. Both train and bus fares will run you 15 to 30F ($2.75 to $6) each way from Nice. Getting to St-Tropez is the trickiest. The closest train station is in St-Maxime or St-Raphaël, where you'll catch the bus to St-Tropez. Helicopter service is the quickest and chicest way to St-Tropez from Nice.

Nice—the fare is 950F ($173) one-way or 1,750F ($318) round-trip, with free shuttle service from the helipad to your hotel. Contact **Heli-Inter,** 11 Aéroport de Cannes Mandelieu (☎ **04-93-90-41-70;** fax 04-93-90-41-46).

If you base yourself in Nice, you'll have *so* many side-trip possibilities; I've mentioned the most beautiful and the most popular, including the best hotels and restaurants in each town. You'll note that some of the hotels and restaurants are exorbitantly expensive—but if there's anywhere in the world where you should obey the urge to splurge, it's here. Whenever possible I've included the good bargains as well, but this section is more about the best of the best and the few gay places along the coast.

Keep in mind that many of the hotels and restaurants in the smaller towns close for the winter season usually from late October to early April. Some, however, close only for a month or two; November and January are the slowest months. Hotels in Monaco, Cannes, and St-Tropez usually close only for short periods; most restaurants have annual closings of 1 to 2 months in midwinter, and December is generally busy, with many hotels reopening for 2 weeks during the holidays.

BEAULIEU-SUR-MER

The town of **Beaulieu-sur-Mer** is indeed a "beautiful place by the sea" and has been attracting vacationers since the belle époque. It's quiet and sleepy now, but with two of the Riviera's most sumptuous hotels located side by side and stately villas along the seafront promenade, this town packs a lot of sedate glamour (albeit behind closed doors).

The day-trippers who come here head to the amazing ✪ **Villa Kérylos,** rue Gustave-Eiffel (☎ **04-93-01-01-44**), designed by architect Emmanuel Pontremoli in the early 1900s. Its frescoes and mosaics are meant to replicate an ancient Greek palace much like what existed on the sacred island of Delos in the 2nd century B.C. (Archaeologist Theodore Reinach, an expert in ancient Greek history, was the force behind the building of the villa.) From the gardens on this rocky peninsula overlooking the Mediterranean to the elaborate designs on the water faucets in the baths, everything has been meticulously created. It's open Tuesday to Sunday: July and August 2 to 7pm (September and October and mid-December to 6pm). The 45F ($8) admission includes a guided tour and two films about the belle époque and the Roaring '20s on the coast.

For a memorable walk, stroll along **promenade Maurice-Rouvier.** The promenade runs parallel to the water, stretching from Beaulieu to St-Jean. On one side you'll see the most elegant of mansions set in well-landscaped gardens; on the other you'll get views of the distant Riviera landscape and the peninsular point of St-Hospice.

The **Office de Tourisme** is on place Georges-Clemenceau (☎ **04-93-01-02-21**).

PILLOW TALK **Le Métropole,** 15 bd. du Maréchal-Leclerc, 06310 Beaulieu-sur-Mer (☎ **04-93-01-00-08;** fax 04-93-01-18-51; e-mail metropole@relaischateaux.fr), was built at the end of the 19th century in the style of an Italian palace and occupies 2 prime acres on the sea, with a magnificent pool and terrace restaurant. Alas, the guests and the staff tend to be quite stiff (not in the good way). This is the kind of place where retired older couples dress staidly for dinner at 6pm and have cocktails while older waiters in crisp white jackets quietly putter about. The rates are 1,700 to 3,900F ($309 to $709) double and from 3,000F ($545) suite.

Next door, the pink Florentine-style 1880 villa ✪ **La Réserve de Beaulieu,** 5 bd. du Maréchal-Leclerc, 06310 Beaulieu-sur-Mer (☎ **04-93-01-00-01;** fax 04-93-01-28-99; e-mail reserve@webstore.fr), attracts a younger crowd that's more laid-back (50% of all guests are American). Here you'll see middle-aged professionals at 6pm taking a dip in the lovely pool while the energetic young staff readies the restaurant terrace for dinner. The grounds aren't as sumptuous as Le Métropole's, but you're more likely to run into Jack Nicholson; he's a regular. The rates are 1,500 to 3,200F ($273 to $581) double and from 3,800F ($691) suite.

WHET YOUR APPETITE The restaurant at ✪ **La Réserve de Beaulieu,** 5 bd. du Maréchal-Leclerc (☎ **04-93-01-00-01;** open daily noon–2:30 and 8–10:30pm), is one of the best along the Côte d'Azur, and whether you sit on the terrace overlooking the sea or in the Venetian dining room with its frescoed ceiling, you'll be very well looked after by the youngish and efficient waiters. Chef Christophe Cussac took over in 1997, and he's already acclaimed for his imaginative cuisine combining the best of traditional French recipes with a hint of Provence. His *pigéon a l'echalotes* (tender roasted pigeon with shallots) has won him many accolades, and he makes the best *soufflé au Grand Marnier* on the Riviera. (Hey, Jack, this is definitely as good as it gets.) The prix-fixe menu is 420F ($76); main courses are 220 to 340F ($40 to $62). Reserve at least a week in advance during summer or a day in advance at other times.

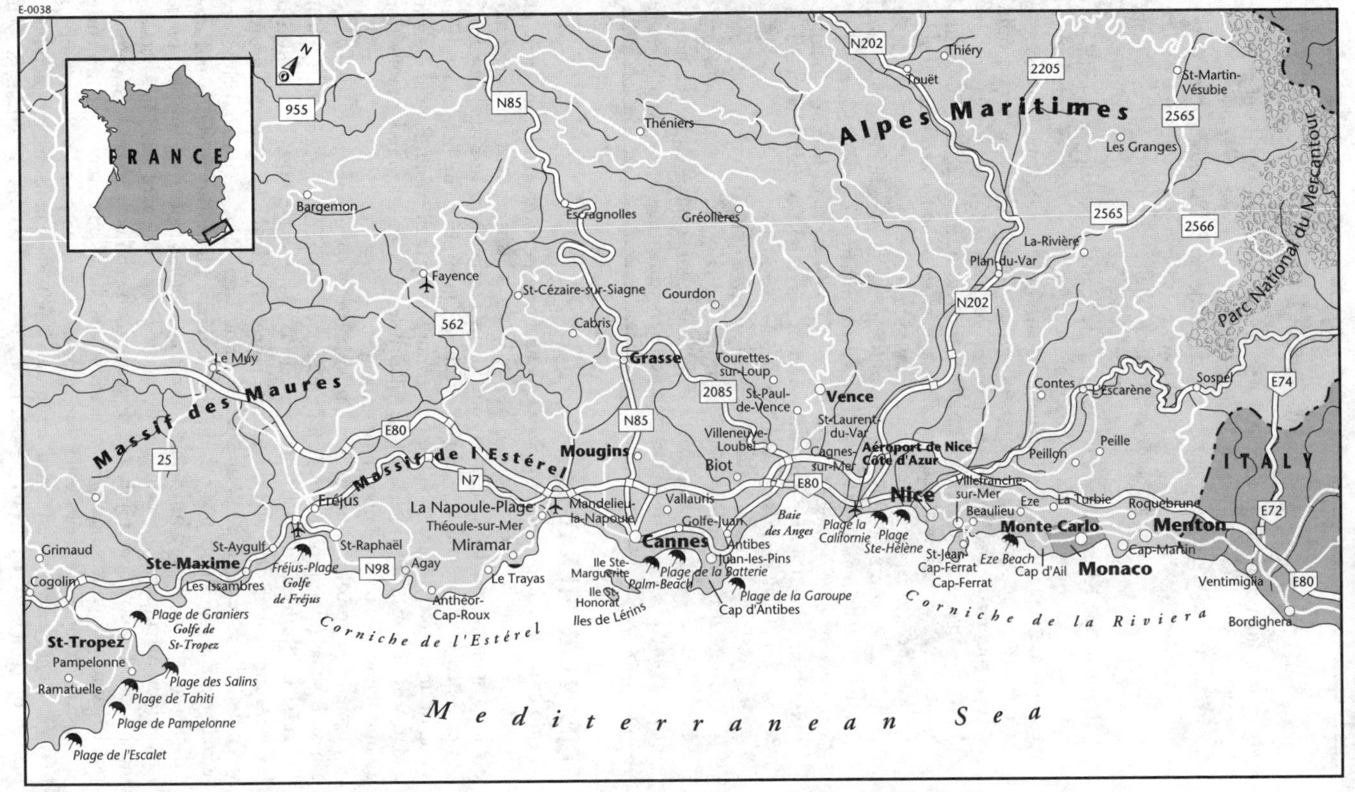

E-0038
FRANCE
Alpes Maritimes
Parc National du Mercantour
ITALY
Massif des Maures
Massif de l'Estérel
Mediterranean Sea
Corniche de l'Estérel
Corniche de la Riviera
N202
2205
2565
2566
N85
955
562
E80
25
N7
N98
2085
E74
E72
Thiéry
Touët
St-Martin-Vésubie
Les Granges
Théniers
Bargemon
Escragnolles
Gréolières
La-Rivière
Plan-du-Var
Fayence
St-Cézaire-sur-Siagne
Gourdon
Cabris
Grasse
Tourettes-sur-Loup
St-Paul-de-Vence
Vence
Le Muy
Contes
L'Escarène
Sospel
Peille
Peillon
St-Laurent-du-Var
Villeneuve-Loubet
Biot
Mougins
Aéroport de Nice-Côte d'Azur
Cagnes-sur-Mer
Nice
Villefranche-sur-Mer
Eze
La Turbie
Roquebrune
Menton
Beaulieu
Monte Carlo
Cap-Martin
Monaco
Cap d'Ail
Eze Beach
St-Jean-Cap-Ferrat
Cap-Ferrat
Ventimiglia
Bordighera
Plage la Californie
Plage Ste-Hélène
Baie des Anges
Vallauris
Golfe-Juan
Antibes
Juan-les-Pins
Cannes
Plage de la Batterie
Palm-Beach
Plage de la Garoupe
Cap d'Antibes
Ile Ste-Marguerite
Ile St-Honorat
Iles de Lérins
Mandelieu-la-Napoule
La Napoule-Plage
Théoule-sur-Mer
Miramar
Le Trayas
Anthéor-Cap-Roux
Agay
Fréjus
St-Raphaël
Fréjus-Plage
Golfe de Fréjus
St-Aygulf
Les Issambres
Ste-Maxime
Grimaud
Cogolin
Plage de Graniers
Golfe de St-Tropez
St-Tropez
Pampelonne
Ramatuelle
Plage des Salins
Plage de Tahiti
Plage de Pampelonne
Plage de l'Escalet

The Landscape of Desire

Nice and the surrounding area have long attracted an impressive list of artists—gay and straight, European and American. For the earliest travelers who came by coach the trip took 2 weeks from Paris and included a treacherous crossing of the Var River (the area separating the Savoie from the Alpes-Maritime); the women sometimes had to be carried across by the men. There were few hotels back then, and visitors who came stayed for the winter season.

The building boom came at the turn of the century and lasted until 1915—this is when all the grand luxury hotels began to appear. These years are known as the belle époque, when the British upper class, Russian aristocrats, and wealthy French and Germans came to escape the northern winters, looking for the mild weather that was believed to be good for lung disease.

But what kept this area so culturally fertile and nurtured it throughout the 20th century were the artists and thinkers and writers who flocked here, lured by the beauty of the landscape, the fragrant hillside villages, and the quaint seaside towns. **Berlioz** composed his overtures to King Lear in Nice (he lived at the top of Tour Bellanda by the Château); **Nietzsche** completed *The Will to Power* here (many historians now believe he was gay); **Picasso** came to live in Mougins; **Rodin** came to visit often; **Matisse** settled in Nice and **Chagall** in Vence; and **Renoir** spent the last years of his life in Cagnes-sur-Mer.

Nice lost its glory for a few years after World War I, but things picked up in the Roaring '20s, and by the early '30s the hotels finally realized they could market a whole new season in the south of France: summertime (until then hotels opened only in winter). It seemed absurd at the time that anyone would want

ST-JEAN-CAP-FERRAT

The tip of the 9-mile peninsula of **St-Jean-Cap-Ferrat,** crawling with pine trees, juts out to sea half-way between Nice and Monte Carlo. This is perhaps one of the most beautiful spots on the Côte d'Azur—not for its beach (there isn't one) but for its postcard-perfect views and excellent swimming. You could come here just to drive along the main road lined with villas and let your hair fly in the wind. Behind the walls and fences and security systems, these villas belong to the rich and famous from around the world and are empty most of the year.

Though you probably won't be going to visit somebody in one of those villas, you can still get a glimpse of a wonderfully preserved palace by the sea, the ✪ **Villa Ephrussi de Rothschild,** av. Denis-Séméria (☎ **04-93-01-33-09**), surrounded by seven magnificent gardens and the Mediterranean. Inside the belle-époque mansion you'll find all the baronne de Rothschild (sister of Baron Edouard de Rothschild) collected before her death in 1934. All the outstanding 18th-century furniture and art is still here in the salons and bedrooms and halls: Gobelins tapestries, rare Sexe porcelain, Clodion sculptures, drawings and paintings by Fragonard and Boucher, and much more. If you're here in July and August, inquire about the *Nuits d'Eté* (summer nights) events, when the villa is lit with a thousand lights and evening performances are hosted (about eight events each summer), ranging from piano recitals to operas (*The Barber of Seville* was performed in summer 1998). You can receive program information by calling ☎ **04-93-01-33-09,** faxing 04-93-01-31-10, or writing to Villa Ephrussi de Rothschild, 06230 St-Jean-Cap-Ferrat.

to come to Nice during its hot and humid season. But the idea caught on, and the seaside resorts thrived. This time the stars came by train on the luxurious Calais–Mediterranean Express (also known as the Train Bleu) with its 80 first-class compartments. From the **Fitzgeralds** (Zelda and Scott had many a drunken party at the Hôtel Belles-Rives in Juan-les-Pins and the Hôtel du Cap in Cap d'Antibes) to **Virginia Woolf** (who hated the casino in Monte Carlo, describing the players as a "sweaty, rather sordid crew"—sounds great to me). **Sylvia Plath** found the landscape "exquisite and fertile." **James Baldwin** settled in St-Paul-de-Vence, and **André Gide** spent time in Grasse toward the end of his life.

Nowadays it's the movie stars who come every year in early May to participate in the most covered media event in the world after the Olympics: the **Cannes Film Festival.** This is when Hollywood transplants itself to the Côte d'Azur for two glorious (or torturous) weeks. Many stars rent or own villas in Cannes, St-Tropez, and Cap d'Antibes. Among them are **Elton John** and his lover, **David Furnish,** who own a house in the hills overlooking the port of Nice; **Tina Turner,** who has a home in Villefranche; and **Joan Collins,** who has a home in Port Grimaud outside St-Tropez.

And perhaps not everybody remembers that **Dodi** and **Diana** fell in love in St-Tropez in July 1997. While vacationing on Dodi's private yacht, they descended on St-Tropez one evening for a good dinner. The photos of them in love on the yacht moored off the sparkling coast forever immortalizes the Côte d'Azur as one of the most romantic destinations in the world.

A light lunch and afternoon tea are served in the palatial *salon de thé* (tea salon) or on the spectacular terrace overlooking the bay of Villefranche (open June–Sept daily noon–5:30pm). The villa is open for visits daily 10am to 6pm (July and August to 7pm); admission is 45F ($8).

The **Office de Tourisme** is on avenue Denis-Séméria (☎ **04-93-01-02-21**).

BOYS ON THE BEACH Especially on weekends, guys (many of the local gay professionals with their dogs and friends) flock to the **"beach"** here—the rocks on the tip of the peninsula. The huge rocks are flat in spaces, and they spread their towels and skinny-dip in the Mediterranean. There's no cruising—it's much more sedate than the party scene at Eze. Mostly locals come here since it's so hard to find; parking is extremely difficult, and there's no public transportation. To find it? Get to the Cape of St-Jean by taking rue de la Phare (the road leading to the lighthouse), where you'll find a pathway running all around the peninsula. Walk southwest from the lighthouse until you're almost facing Villefranche (a 10-minute walk on the jagged path). That's the spot.

PILLOW TALK The **Grand Hôtel du Cap-Ferrat,** bd. du Général-de-Gaulle, 06230 St-Jean-Cap-Ferrat (☎ **04-93-76-50-50;** fax 04-93-76-04-52; e-mail: reserv@grand-hotel-cap-ferrat.com), is like a Rolls-Royce, terribly expensive and grand but not especially fashionable. At the tip of the cape on 14 glorious acres of pine trees and gardens, this white belle-époque palace boasts an Olympic-size pool, tennis courts, and two restaurants. An older, straight crowd and some honeymooners is mostly what you'll find, though in summer a few gay couples check in. Doubles begin at 3,100F ($564) and go up to 6,500F ($1,181), with suites beginning at 3,400F ($618).

In the village of St-Jean is the much more fashionable ✪ **La Voile d'Or,** 31 av. Jean-Mermoz, 06230 St-Jean-Cap-Ferrat (☎ **04-93-01-13-13;** fax 04-93-76-11-17; e-mail voiledor@calva.net), overlooking the marina and the fishing boats; it has two pools and an acclaimed restaurant. The views aren't the best on the Riviera, but the very professional and efficient staff carefully look after their privileged guests, who frequently come incognito with a pack of bodyguards (alas, those hunks don't hang out by the pool). Doubles are 1,050 to 1,850F ($190 to $336).

WHET YOUR APPETITE The restaurant at ✪ **La Voile d'Or,** 31 av. Jean-Mermoz (☎ **04-93-01-13-13;** open daily noon–2:30pm and 7:30–10:30pm), attracts some of the wealthiest diners on the coast, many of whom own villas on the cape (they come here to give their personal chef a night off). There's a quiet elegance on the terrace overlooking the sea and the passing boats; you'll want to take every one of the handsome waiters home (and after you pay the bill, you might feel entitled to). Expect to eat very well on a balanced cuisine of traditional French and Provençal dishes like succulent roasted saddle of lamb with pearl onions and string beans and delicate raviolis with foie gras. Main courses are 200 to 340F ($36 to $61); if you come at lunch, you can take advantage of the special fixed-price menu at 270F ($49). Reserve at least 2 weeks in advance during summer or a day in advance at other times.

If you want to dine well without depleting your wallet, head to **Le Sloop,** at the new port overlooking the yachts (☎ **04-93-01-48-63;** open summer Wed–Mon noon–2:30pm and 7–10pm). It's popular and lively and considered by locals to be the best bargain in the area for its fresh light cuisine. The chef knows how to make use of cool ingredients on a hot summer's day: delicious chilled lobster risotto, salmon tartare with baby onions, and an array of excellent salads using the freshest vegetables. The fixed-price menu at 155F ($28) is a steal; main courses run 130 to 240F ($24 to $44).

ANTIBES

Across the Baie des Anges from Nice, the port of **Antibes** was built on what used to be a Greek acropolis (the Greeks came in 400 B.C. and named it Antipolis; the Romans followed and changed the name to Antiboul, which then became Antibou and finally Antibes). This old Mediterranean town has a quiet charm unique on the coast. Its little harbor is filled with fishing boats and pleasure yachts, the marketplaces are full of flowers, mostly roses and carnations.

Presiding majestically over the town is the 12th-century **Château Grimaldi,** once home of the princes of Antibes of the Grimaldi family. You can see the fortlike granite structure from afar, and at night it's beautifully lit and the streets in this old part of town come alive (there are many shops, restaurants, and bars behind the fort).

Inside the château is the ✪ **Musée Picasso,** place Mariejol (☎ **04-92-90-54-20**). Picasso actually lived in the château for 6 months in 1946 and "worked like a madman"; when he left, he donated to the town of Antibes all the work he'd created during his stay. Later, the town added more of his work from different periods of his career as well as works of other artists, like Modigliani and Miró. The museum is open Wednesday to Sunday 10am to noon and 2 to 6pm. Admission is 30F ($5).

The **Antibes Jazz Festival** in July is held in Juan-les-Pins, officially part of Antibes (see below). Festival information is available from the **Office du Tourisme** at 11 place de Gaulle, 06600 Antibes (☎ **04-92-90-53-00;** fax 04-92-90-53-01).

PILLOW TALK In the newer part of town is the gay-owned/managed **Le Relais du Postillon,** 8 rue Championnet, 06600 Antibes (☎ **04-93-34-20-77;** fax 04-93-34-61-24), a 200-year-old coach house converted into a 15-room hotel; it's a short walk

Cocteau on the Côte

Jean Cocteau is one of the most famous gay artists who left his or her mark on this area. An acclaimed filmmaker, painter, and writer, he spent chunks of time on the Côte d'Azur, hanging out with the rich and famous from Picasso to Coco Chanel.

Cocteau was frequently a guest at Somerset Maugham's **Villa Mauresque,** on avenue Somerset-Maugham in St-Jean-Cap-Ferrat (the villa has long been sold and the new owners have done major renovations). At the **Grand Hôtel du Cap-Ferrat,** bd. Général-de-Gaulle (☎ **04-93-76-50-50**), you'll find the Somerset Maugham Piano Bar, where Cocteau sipped cocktails with the literati. It's a spectacular place, though the crowd now is more subdued and older. Cocteau and other artists also frequented the bar at Monte Carlo's **Hôtel de Paris,** place du Casino (☎ **377/92-16-30-00**); it's still there, though now is filled with a pretentious crowd dripping jewels. But Jean Cocteau left much more than gossip and stories (he was, after all, openly gay in mid-century and had a lover, actor Jean Marais); in addition to his films and books and paintings, he left some beautiful frescoes.

In Villefranche, he spent a year (1956–57) painting frescoes on the 14th-century walls of the Romanesque ✪ **Chapelle St-Pierre,** quai de la Douane/rue des Marinières (☎ **04-93-76-90-70**). He later presented it to the fishers of Villefranche. The chapel is open Tuesday to Sunday: July to September 10am to noon and 4 to 8:30pm, October to mid-November and mid-December to March 9:30am to noon and 2 to 5pm, and April to June 9:30am to noon and 3 to 7pm. Admission is 12F ($2).

In Menton (the last town before the Italian border), there's a small museum dedicated to Cocteau's work (he had a fondness for this little town). The **Musée Jean-Cocteau** is in a 17th-century fort at the Bastion du Port, quai Napoléon-III (☎ **04-93-57-72-30**). You'll find Cocteau's death portrait sketched by MacAvoy, plus several charcoals, watercolors, ceramics, pastels, and signed letters. The museum is open Wednesday to Monday 10am to noon and 2 to 6pm; admission is free.

Also in Menton, at the **Hôtel de Ville** (town hall), rue de la République (☎ **04-92-10-50-50**), Cocteau painted frescoes depicting the legend of Orpheus and Eurydice, among other things, in the Salle des Mariages. The room is used for civil marriage ceremonies and decorated with queeny red leather seats and even queenier leopard-skin rugs. It's open Monday to Friday 8:30am to 12:30pm and 1:30 to 5pm. Admission is 5F (90¢).

---

from old Antibes and the sea. All rooms are comfortable and clean, with phones and TVs. The gay French owner and his young attractive staff are friendly and will fill you in on the current hot spots. Doubles are 248 to 428F ($45 to $78).

WHET YOUR APPETITE ✪ **Le Relais du Postillon,** 8 rue Championnet (☎ **04-93-34-20-77;** open Tues–Sat noon–2:30pm and 7:30–10:30pm, Sun noon–2:30pm, Mon 7:30–10:30pm; closed Nov and Jan), is known more for its reasonably priced restaurant than for its hotel rooms. They don't promote it as a "gay restaurant" (most of their business is from straight tourists), but it does have a solid gay/lesbian following, mostly expat professionals. The cozy dining room with exposed brick and a fireplace seats only 25, so you're assured the attention of the hunky waitstaff (hand-picked by the gay owner; hands off). You're not likely to find such delicately made dishes at such low prices and know you're among family. The lobster ravioli with fresh basil or the baked oysters with truffle oil are excellent appetizers; the cod fillet with ratatouille and veal scallopini with tapenade (olive paste) are specialties of the young female chef; both cheese and dessert are included even in the least expensive fixed-price menu at 145F ($26). For a more elaborate meal, they offer fixed-price menus at 185 ($33) and 245F ($45).

HITTING THE STORES In the center of Antibes, not far from the above hotel, is a small sex shop (in case you're running low of essentials): **Eroshop,** 6 rue Vauban (☎ **04-93-34-09-04**).

JUAN-LES-PINS

More South Beach than south of France, **Juan-les-Pins** is the Riviera's party town (off-season, it's boarded up and resembles a ghost town). In summer, there's a carnival feel in the air at night as people dine on sidewalks and music blares from the mostly straight cafes, bars, and clubs. In August (the busiest month), the dancing spills out onto the streets as live bands perform at sidewalk cafes. This town rocks.

During the day the sandy beaches (yes, the beaches actually have sand!) teem with people of all shapes and sizes; boats pulling waterskiers, kids in paddleboats, and hunky windsurfers crowd the waters. There are no gay beaches, and nudity isn't permitted (toplessness is, though); you're as likely to be rubbing elbows with families on package tours as you are with sun-scorched college boys. There are both private (matelas rentals 70F/$13) and public beaches, with the most fun (and busy) beaches along boulevard Baudoin and boulevard Charles-Guillaumont.

The **Antibes Jazz Festival** in July (held in Juan-les-Pins, officially part of Antibes) attracts world-class artists and has been going strong since 1960 (the town is sometimes fondly referred to as New-Orleans-les-Pins); Ella Fitzgerald, Ray Charles, Dizzy Gillespie, and many others have performed here. Festival information is available from the **Office du Tourisme** at 11 place de Gaulle, 06600 Antibes (☎ **04-92-90-53-00;** fax 04-92-90-53-01).

The **Office de Tourisme** in Juan-les-Pins is at 51 bd. Charles-Guillaumont (☎ **04-92-90-53-05**).

PILLOW TALK The legendary **Hôtel Belles-Rives,** 33 bd. Baudoin, 06160 Juan-les-Pins (☎ **04-93-61-02-79**), is within a 5-minute walk from the town center. (When it was a holiday villa, Zelda and F. Scott Fitzgerald spent many summers and many drunken nights here; Josephine Baker and Edith Piaf stayed here too.) The 1930s villa has been recently renovated; some of the 41 art-deco rooms overlook the water. The popular (but overrated and overpriced) restaurant is on the breathtaking seaside terrace. Though it's on the sea, don't imagine a wide sandy beach (just a cement platform where you can jump into the water); a pretty pool and nice beaches are all less than a mile away. Doubles go for 1,100 to 2,450F ($200 to $445), with suites beginning at 3,240F ($589).

WHET YOUR APPETITE Every sidewalk in Juan-les-Pins is crammed with cafes and restaurants (the sidewalks seem to be made for tables rather than for pedestrians, who are frequently forced to walk on the street). There are plenty of pizza and pasta places and ice-cream shops, but the one place that keeps even locals coming back is a little crêpe stand serving the best dessert crêpes on the Riviera. At the ✪ **Crêperie Grand Marnier,** 14 bd. Baudoin (☎ **04-93-61-26-88;** open May–Oct daily 4pm–midnight), you can get a crêpe with as much liquor as you want doused on it for 22F ($4); the chocolate crêpe filled with creamy nutella is fantastic. The most popular spot in town in town for people-watching is ✪ **Pam Pam,** route Wilson

(☎ **04-93-61-11-05;** open daily 5pm–2am), serving humongous cocktails in coconut and pineapple shells; live Latin music lasts late into the night.

Depending on who you ask, the best bouillabaisse on the coast is dished up either at Restaurant de Bacon in Cap d'Antibes (below) or in Golfe-Juan (2 miles west of Juan-les-Pins) at **Chez Tétou,** av. des Frères-Roustand (☎ **04-93-63-71-16;** open daily noon–2:30pm and 8–10pm). In an unassuming cottage close to the main road and overlooking the marina, you'll feast on the best of what the sea has to offer, several kinds of fish and shellfish carefully prepared; the emphasis isn't on how the food looks but how it tastes—heavenly. Bouillabaisse runs 400 to 500F ($73 to $91), and fixed-price menus are 500–700F ($91–$127). You'll need at least 2 weeks advance reservations in summer.

CAP D'ANTIBES

Just east of Juan-les-Pins is **Cap d'Antibes,** a pine-covered hill that's home to some of the world's most expensive villas, all safely tucked away behind walls, palms, and security cameras. In *Tender Is the Night,* F. Scott Fitzgerald described it as a place where "old villas rotted like water lilies among the massed pines." There are a few coves for swimming along the curvy coast road, but the beaches aren't the attraction (besides, everybody has a pool). Take the road that winds around the cape to get a glimpse at a few of the fancy homes visible from the road.

PILLOW TALK The **Hôtel du Cap–Eden Roc,** bd. J.-F.-Kennedy, 06160 Cap d'Antibes (☎ **04-93-61-39-01;** fax 04-93-67-76-04; www.edenroc.hotel.fr), is where the stars stay when they come to the Cannes Film Festival. This is where Madonna had some wild parties in the 1980s and where you'd better look wealthy or beautiful (both is best) to get anybody's attention. Some claim that snobbery reigns on these 22 outstanding acres; what can you say about a hotel that changes your sheets twice a day whether or not you've slept on them? It's beautiful and opulent and sometimes feels like a Hollywood set, complete with producers with attitude. The amazing pool was blasted out of the cliffside at enormous expense, and the excellent Pavillon Eden Roc restaurant serves splendid views with its food. Doubles go for a mere 2,200 to 4600F ($400 to $836), with suites beginning at 4,800F ($873).

For less flash and pomp, the fabulous ✪ **Hôtel Imperial Garoupe,** 770 Chemin de la Garoupe, 06160 Cap d'Antibes (☎ **04-92-93-31-61;** fax 04-92-93-31-62), is a short walk from the popular Plage Garoupe. It's like staying at a super-rich relative's home. There are only 34 rooms in this Provençal villa furnished in the south's deep yellow and green, with lots of flowers and plants in handmade ceramic pots; the beautiful garden has a nice pool. The rooms are luxurious and spacious, and the crowd is mostly trendy straight French and Americans. Doubles are 1,200 to 2,000F ($218 to $364), with suites starting at 2,200F ($400).

Up the hill is the simpler and more affordable **Manoir Castel Garoupe Axa,** 959 bd. de la Garoupe, 06160 Cap d'Antibes (☎ **04-93-61-36-51**), a Mediterranean villa with a red-tiled roof and 27 spacious rooms, most with kitchenettes. This is the best value in this expensive area, with doubles at 700 to 1,050F ($127 to $190).

WHET YOUR APPETITE If you want to see how the other half lives, a meal at **Restaurant de Bacon,** bd. de Bacon (☎ **04-93-61-50-02;** open July–Aug daily 12:30–2:30pm and 8–10pm, Sept–June Tues–Sun only), is like being allowed into an exclusive club. If you don't pull up in a convertible Porsche, you might instantly feel out of place at this upper-crust seafood restaurant (you won't get a table in high season if you don't reserve at least a month in advance), but the beautiful people keep on coming back for the excellent bouillabaisse and the perfect *soupe de poissons*; if you order fresh fish they'll bring it to your table before grilling it. The portions are small, and if you don't have at least three courses you might leave hungry. Main courses run 250 to 400F ($45 to $73).

HAUT-DE-CAGNES & CAGNES-SUR-MER

Cagnes-sur-Mer is nothing special, but it leads to **Haut-de-Cagnes,** the old hilltop village crowned by the 14th-century fortress built by Rainier Grimaldi I, a lord of Monaco. If you're really interested in Prince Albert's roots (just why won't that boy get married?), visit the **Grimaldi Castle Museum,** place Grimaldi (☎ **04-93-20-87-29**), which in addition to the painted ceilings and elaborate marble arches has a gallery devoted to modern art and temporary exhibits. Check out the "boudoir," a collection of Suzy Solidor's portraits (she was a flamboyant cabaret singer who was painted by many artists, including Cocteau). The museum is open Wednesday to Monday: summer 10am to noon and 2 to 5pm and winter 10am to noon and 2:30 to 6:30pm. Admission is 20F ($3.60).

For many years, Renoir escaped the harsh Paris winters and lived in Cagnes-sur-Mer; in 1908, he bought a stone farmhouse on the hillside across the valley, **Les Collettes,** 19 chemin des Collettes (☎ **04-93-20-61-07**), where he lived until his death in 1919. There, surrounded by a garden that provided him and his family with food throughout the year, he spent the last and most cherished days of his life. He continued to sculpt, even though he was crippled by arthritis and had to be helped in and out of a wheelchair. He also continued to paint, with a brush tied to his hand and with the help of assistants. You can see one of his last paintings, *Rest After Bathing,* in the Louvre. The house has been lovingly preserved with his belongings (easel, wheelchair, brushes, and much more). From the terrace of Mme Renoir's bedroom is a stunning view of Cap d'Antibes and Haut-de-Cagnes. Call ahead for hours and directions.

The **Office de Tourisme** is located at 6 bd. Maréchal-Juin, Cagnes-Ville (☎ **04-93-20-61-64**).

WHET YOUR APPETITE The best gay-owned restaurant on the Côte d'Azur (but certainly not gay advertised or marketed) is the ✪ **Restaurant des Peintres,** 71 montée de la Bourgade (☎ **04-93-20-83-08;** open Mon 7:30-10:30pm, Tues and Thurs–Sun noon–2pm and 7:30–10:30pm), where Alan Llorca made his name before moving to the Négresco in Nice. Patrice Reignault (the young chef) and his partner, Jacques Madina (the gracious host/manager), took over this tiny restaurant that stays true to its name by constantly displaying the canvases of new young painters. The cuisine is steeped in Provence, and the menu changes with the seasons. In late summer, you might find delectable *foie gras aux deux figues* (one of the figs is served as is, plump and sweet; the other is mashed with walnuts, spices, and honey and returned to its shell) or chilled gazpacho with fresh mint; in winter, slightly heavier dishes prevail, like lamb with orange-butter sauce and the unique baked cod with chorizo served with puréed onions. The desserts are unorthodox: The *mousse au citron vert au basilic* (light white cheese with lemon and basil) has a wonderfully curious blend of salty and sweet—perfect for people who don't like too much sugar.

Perhaps the only drawback to this gem is the sometimes subdued atmosphere; they do need more gays in here to camp it up. The cute chef is shy and probably won't make an appearance unless you insist (be discreet, though, they're not entirely out). The 200F ($36) fixed-price menu is a great bargain. The 420F ($76) *ménu confiance* is a gourmand's dream and a good way to put your taste buds in the chef's hands (if only)—he chooses two appetizers, two entrees, and two desserts. Main courses are 140 to 200F($25 to $36); reservations are recommended a week in advance during summer but only a day or two in advance at other times. To get here, follow the signs to place St-Luce; where the restaurant's private van (call for reservations) will whisk you up the hill to the restaurant. (Parking is tough up there and the roads are very narrow and treacherous).

IN THE HEAT OF THE NIGHT An old bar that was popular with lesbians in the early 1990s, **Passeport,** av. de la Gare (☎ **04-93-22-66-66**), was slated at press time to reopen by the train station in the center of town. Cabaret shows are planned for the weekends, and it's being marketed as a gay and lesbian club.

GRASSE

Surrounded by jasmine, roses, and lavender, **Grasse** has been the perfume capital of the world since the 19th century. However, it's definitely not for anyone allergic to perfume or strong scents. You come to Grasse to use your nose. And also to dine at one of the best restaurants on the coast (see "Whet Your Appetite" below).

Today some three-quarters of the world's essences are produced here. Did you know that it takes 10,000 flowers to produce 2.2 pounds of jasmine petals? And that almost a ton of petals is needed to distill $1^1/_2$ quarts of essence?

Take a tour of the **Parfumerie Fragonard,** 20 bd. Fragonard (☎ **04-93-36-44-65**), and find out how the scent is extracted from flowers; visit the museum of the perfumery to see the history of scents dating back to ancient times, with a display of bottles and vases. Summer hours are daily 9am to 6:30pm; hours in the slower months are Monday to Saturday 9am to 12:30pm and 2 to 6pm.

You can create your very own scent at the ✪ **Parfumerie Galimard,** Rte. de Pegomas (☎ **04-93-09-20-00**), because the 200F ($36) 2-hour tour includes a 3-oz. bottle of the scent of your creation complete with a personalized label you create (a great gift for a heartthrob back home . . . or even your mother); call for tour hours and to ensure yourself a spot. (From Grasse, follow the signs to Pegomas and you'll see the signs for Galimard.)

André Gide, the outstanding French novelist who was one of the pioneers of gay literature, came to the south of France during the last part of his life to spend his holidays in Grasse. He loved the town of **Cabris,** the little perched village he could see from the window of his room at the Grand Hôtel. The hotel is no longer there, but Cabris is worth a stroll; to get there, take D4 southwest from Grasse for the 15-minute drive.

The **Office de Tourisme** is in the Palais des Congrès on place du Cours (☎ **04-93-36-66-66**).

PILLOW TALK ✪ **La Bastide St-Antoine,** 48 av. Henri-Durant (☎ **04-93-70-94-94;** fax 04-93-70-94-95; e-mail info@jacques-chibois.com), is a dreamy 17th-century *bastide* (three-story country house) that first became a celebrated restaurant and now offers 11 glorious rooms. Some have claw-footed tubs and original woodwork and some fireplaces and private balconies. All have terrific ceramic tile, CD players, antique pieces, and air-conditioning; every bed has an automatic mattress you adjust to suit your taste. The small touches make this place special, like the "Do Not Disturb" signs made out of sacks of dried lavender. At the pool, guests (mostly straight, youngish and wealthy) can take a dip before dinner. Doubles are a very reasonable 750 to 950F ($136 to $173). This would make an excellent base from which to discover the lovely hilltop villages surrounding Grasse, such as Gourdon and Cabris.

WHET YOUR APPETITE The restaurant at ✪ **La Bastide St-Antoine,** 48 av. Henri-Durant (☎ **04-93-70-94-94;** open daily noon–2:30pm and 8–11pm), has quickly become one of the most acclaimed in the area. Celebrated chef Jacques Chibois has chosen a romantic spot to continue his career after leaving the drab Gray d'Albion in Cannes. This is more like it—the hotel's lovely courtyard, surrounded by orchards, with the moon rising (if you're lucky) from between the olive trees to light up your evening. Be aware that men are given menus with prices, women menus without—how quaint. Two men together will both get menus with prices (they're not going to try to figure this one out) and two women together will create confusion. The tables facing the courtyard are the best, and you might be able to sneak in some hand-holding. The yummy waiters stay busy coming and going to refresh your water or wine and brush crumbs off your table. The girolles mushrooms with summer truffles layered with foie gras is a masterpiece; the lobster with aniseed tastes like angels dancing on your tongue. Many of the appetizers are more elaborate than the main courses—they both cost the same. The desserts are special too: The pistachio macaroons melt in your mouth, and the mango sorbet with fresh mint leaves is beyond wonderful. Call for reservations at least 2 weeks in advance. Main courses run 220 to 440F ($40 to $80), and the fixed-price menus are 280F ($51) at lunch and 480F ($87) and 660F ($120) at dinner.

MOUGINS

Among the hills a few miles outside Cannes, the pretty medieval village of **Mougins** is full of art galleries scattered deep within its cobblestoned alleys. Stop by the **Office du Tourisme** at the entrance of the village, 15 rue Jean-Charles Mallet (☎ **04-93-75-87-67**), and pick up a list of art galleries, museums, and churches to visit. Picasso spent the last 15 years of his life in Mougins; Jean Cocteau, Man Ray, and Yves Saint-Laurent also vacationed here.

Though Mougins looks serene and tranquil, it's actually part of the industrial park of Sophia Antipolis, a technological center where more than 1,000 national and international companies have offices.

If you happen to be into cars, check out the **Musée de l'Automobiliste,** Aire des Bréguières (☎ **04-93-69-27-80**). Founded in 1984 by Adrien Maeght, this ultramodern concrete-and-glass structure rises out of a green clearing. It houses temporary exhibits but also owns one of Europe's most magnificent collections of autos—more than 100 vehicles from 1894 until the present. It's open daily April–Sept 10am–7pm (Oct–March to 6pm); admission is 40F ($7).

PILLOW TALK One of the best values on the Côte d'Azur, ✪ **Le Manoir de l'Etang,** 66 Allée du Manoir-Bois de Font Merle (☎ **04-93-90-01-07;** fax 04-92-92-20-70), is a 19th-century Provençal house with 14 spacious rooms. The owner, Mme Gridaine, takes excellent care of her guests, who hail from around the world. Dinner is served around the pool in summer (the food is outstanding), and it's all perfectly romantic without costing a fortune. Doubles go for 600 to 1,000F ($109 to $182).

WHET YOUR APPETITE Right on the main square in the village, facing the fountain, **La Brasserie de la Mediterranée,** place de la Mairie (☎ **04-93-90-03-47;** open daily noon–2:30pm and 7–10:30pm), serves Provençal cuisine with a hint of North Africa; the *homard roti en tajine d'aubergine* (roast lobster with Tunisian eggplant stew) and the veal ravioli with coriander are simply delicious. Reasonable prices keep a loyal lively crowd coming back; main courses run 65 to 195F ($11 to $35), with fixed-price menus at 165 to 198F ($30 to $36).

Next door, **Le Relais à Mougins,** place de la Mairie (☎ **04-93-90-03-47;** open Tues–Sat noon–2:30pm and 7:30–10:30pm), is much pricier but has won accolades from many French and American critics. Chef André Surmain (who founded Lutèce in New York) creates light simple dishes like grilled monkfish with creamy risotto and duck breast with foie gras drizzled with balsamic vinegar. A mixed crowd of locals and returning visitors (mostly straight and middle-aged) keeps the place real busy in summer. Main courses are 150 to 350F ($27 to $40). Reserve at least a week in advance in summer.

It used to be that a table at the lovely olive-mill restaurant **Le Moulin de Mougins,** Notre-Dame de Vie (☎ **04-93-75-78-24;** open Tues–Sun noon–2:30pm and 8–10:30pm), was the most sought after on the coast. Then word got out that everything is in decline. Roger Vergé and his wife, Denise, seem to own Mougins with their food and wine shops, and perhaps that's why some critics have condemned him for commercializing food, packaging it for tourists to take home in jars (they certainly can't take home the perfect lemon soufflé). If you're a fan, you'll find that now it's a bit easier to get a table, but go for lunch to take advantage of the 250F ($45) fixed-price menu; dinner menus are 520 to 740F ($95 to $135). Reserve at least 2 weeks in advance during summer.

ST-PAUL-DE-VENCE & VENCE

The small hilltop town of **St-Paul-de-Vence,** probably the most famous of the "perched" villages, has become so popular with visitors in summer, you may get stuck in traffic jams just to get in and out of the parking lot. Its ramparts (allow about 30 minutes to circle them) overlook a peaceful setting of flowers and olive and orange trees. They remain somewhat as they were when they were built from 1537 to 1547 by François I. From the ramparts to the north you can look out on Baou de St-Jeannet, a sphinx-shaped rock that was painted into the landscape of Poussin's *Polyphème.*

The main attraction here is on a pine-covered hill just outside town: one of the best collections of contemporary art in Europe, the privately owned ✪ **Fondation Maeght,** founded by art dealer Aimé Maeght in 1964. Inside this avant-garde building (designed by José Luís Sert) you'll find sculptures by Giacometti and Miró, mural mosaics by Chagall, and stained-glass windows by Miró, Braque, and Ubac—plus much more. The foundation supports younger and still living artists with frequent temporary exhibits. The museum is open daily: July to September 10am to 7pm and October to June 10am to 12:30pm and 2:30 to 6pm. Admission is 40F ($7).

The town is also known for its olivewood work (salad bowls are the favorite item). You'll find the shops lining the narrow alleyways in the heart of the village. (To make sure what you're purchasing is pure olivewood, you should be able to smell olive oil when you put your nose to the wood.)

James Baldwin fell in love with St-Paul, bought a house, and spent the last part of his life there. The house is still owned by his brother and is right down the street from the Hôtel Le Hameau (see "Whet Your Appetite" below). It's a beautiful spot, surrounded by orchards, with a breathtaking view of the coastline. If you're really interested in Baldwin's life, book a room at the hotel and prod the owner for stories (he still knows Baldwin's brother). The author frequently dined at the fabulous La Colombe d'Or (see "Whet Your Appetite" below).

The **Office de Tourisme** in St-Paul is at the Maison Tour, rue Grande (☎ **04-93-32-60-27**).

A few miles north of St-Paul is **Vence,** a once-fortified walled town. Outside the town, along boulevard Paul-André, two olive presses carry on their age-old duties. But the charm here lies in the Vieille Ville (Old Town). Visitors invariably have themselves photographed on place du Peyra in front of the urn-shaped Vieille Fontaine (Old Fountain). However, the main attraction in Vence is the **Chapelle du Rosaire,** avenue Henri-Matisse (☎ **04-93-58-03-26**), which 77-year-old Matisse created and decorated for the Dominican nuns of Monteils (partly as a gesture of thanks to Sister Jacques-Marie, who nursed him back to health after a debilitating illness). He finished in 1951, 3 years before his death. From the front you might find it unremarkable and pass it by—until you spot a 40-foot crescent-adorned cross rising from a blue-tile roof.

The chapel is open only on Tuesday and Thursday 10am to 11:30am and 2:30 to 5:30pm. Admission is 10F ($1.80) and includes entrance to **L'Espace Matisse,** a gallery documenting the way Matisse handled the design and construction of the chapel. It also contains lithographs and religious artifacts that concerned Matisse in one way or another.

The **Office de Tourisme** in Vence is on place Grand-Jardin (☎ **04-93-58-06-38**).

PILLOW TALK A 200-year-old farmhouse in an orange grove, now the ✪ **Hôtel Le Hameau,** 528 rte. de la Colle (D107), 06570 St-Paul-de-Vence (☎ **04-93-32-80-24;** fax 04-93-32-55-75), is where James Baldwin first stayed when he came to St-Paul; room no. 6 was his. It's a wonderfully rustic 17-room auberge, very reasonable for this expensive area. Each room is unique, but all are comfortable, with phones and antiques; a few have terraces overlooking the olive trees and the sea. Several studios with kitchenettes face the pool. Doubles range from 430 to 660F ($78 to $120, with suites beginning at 750F ($136)).

If you want to stay in the heart of the medieval village, you're best choice is the excellent gay-friendly (several of the staff members are gay) ✪ **Hôtel Le St-Paul,** 86 rue Grande, 06570 St-Paul-de-Vence (☎ **04-93-32-65-25;** fax 04-93-32-52-94). This 16th-century village house has 15 Provençal-style rooms with all the amenities of a first-class hotel, plus lovely views of the valley and the Mediterranean. The restaurant is outstanding too. Doubles run 850 to 1,500F ($155 to $273), with suites starting at 1,750F ($318).

Most Americans choose the sprawling resort **Hôtel Mas d'Artigny,** Rte. de la Colle, 06570 St-Paul-de-Vence (☎ **04-93-32-84-54;** fax 04-93-32-95-36; e-mail mas.artigny@wanadoo.fr), just outside town. The most coveted accommodations are the 29 suites with their own private pools and panoramic sea vistas. (Hollywood stars frequently hide out here.) There's a wonderful restaurant too. Doubles are 640 to 1,200F ($116 to $218) and suites 1,760 to 2,700F ($320 to $491).

In Vence, Maurice Garnier and his wife, Josette, have restored a 100-year-old manor into the 14-room B&B-style ✪ **Hôtel La Roseraie,** 128 av. Henri-Giraud, 06140 Vence (☎ **04-93-58-02-20;** fax 04-93-58-99-31). Every item in the newly redone rooms (all with phones and minibars) has been handpicked by this hard-working couple, from the antique mirrors to the dried lavender potpourri; even the sheets on the four-poster beds are Provençal deep yellow dotted with green olives. The charming attic room is like an artist's studio with a skylight and window overlooking the old town. The owners support the arts by hosting sculpture exhibits in the courtyard shaded by a large magnolia (where breakfast is served until noon). The guests are mostly straight French and British couples (wait until one queen finds this place and spreads the word—will it be you?). Doubles are 480 to 730F ($87 to $133).

WHET YOUR APPETITE **La Colombe d'Or,** 1 place du Général-de-Gaulle (☎ **04-93-32-80-02;** open daily noon–2:30pm and 7:30–10:30pm), is the fabulously trendy restaurant James Baldwin frequented 30 years ago (they also have hotel rooms). It's as popular as ever, though now the clientele consists mostly of ladies over 65 and their ailing wealthy husbands in golf pants. Oh, you do get the incredibly good-looking Italian straight couples on their honeymoon and the occasional gay producers from Hollywood who are dairy intolerant and demand the impossible from the frazzled waitresses. The food is too simple for the exorbitant prices (Provençal specialties hastily prepared and hastily served). Main courses run 180 to 320F ($33 to $58). Reserve at least 2 weeks in advance during summer.

The connoisseurs who own homes in the area know to avoid La Colombe d'Or (especially in the high season) and head to ✪ **Le Diamant Rose,** Rte. de la Colle

(☎ **04-93-32-82-20;** open daily noon–2:30pm and 7–10pm, to 11pm July–Aug), where Nice's twinkling lights shine a thousand feet below. The views alone are worth the hefty prices, but the food is excellent if not as imaginative as you might expect from such a trendy place. Main courses are 220 to 360F ($40 to $65). Reserve at least 2 weeks in advance during summer.

EZE

The hamlet of **Eze** boasts a fortified feudal core high in the hills overlooking the Provençal coast. Clinging to the rocky hillsides around it are upscale villas, many of which were built since the 1950s by retirees from colder climes. Its medieval core contains art galleries, boutiques, and artisans' shops that have been restored.

Just off the Moyenne Corniche is the lovely perched village of **Eze.** You won't see much from the road; pull into the large parking lot at the village entrance and walk up to the village, where no cars are allowed. You're at 1,300 feet here, and the view from the cliff edge is awe-inspiring. Eze's leading attraction is the **Jardin Exotique,** boulevard du Jardin-Exotique (☎ **04-93-41-10-30**), a densely planted garden at the top of this medieval rock (check out the many kinds of cacti); the views are as beautiful as the flowers. Try to come as close to sunset as possible, when the colors are magnificent. It's open daily: July and August 8:30am to 8pm and September to June 9am to between 5 and 7:30pm (depending on the hour of sunset). Admission is 12F ($2.20).

The **Office de Tourisme** is on place du Général-de-Gaulle, Eze-Village (☎ **04-93-41-26-00**).

BOYS ON THE BEACH The gayest beach on the Côte d'Azur (with the exception of St-Tropez) is ✪ **Eze Plage** in Eze-sur-Mer (not to be confused with Eze village, a thousand feet up the cliff). This is where *everyone* goes, and it's such an ordeal to find the first time that you're really best off making a new friend so he can lead you here (I've provided detailed directions anyway).

This beautiful secluded cove is surrounded by rocks and bushes, and you'll find all sorts of goings-on; it's crowded and cruisy and full of men of all shapes and sizes and colors and ages, mostly nude. The men come for the sun, sea, and one another; they come to spread their towels on the pebbles, with hardly any room to stretch out, elbows touching; the tide slowly creeps higher, forcing everyone to bunch up in a ridiculously small space. There's a freshwater spring where the boys "shower" after a swim, giving everyone a thrill. Now you'd think there'd be a convivial atmosphere, but most of the time the mood is like a dance club's: Everyone is aloof until sunset, that magic hour when it's almost time to leave—then the guys start talking to one another. (The hard-core stuff goes on among the rocks just beyond the beach all day long, though.)

To get here, you can either drive or take the bus. If you're going by **car** from Nice, follow the signs from the port to the Basse Corniche heading to Monaco. You'll pass Eze-sur-Mer and go through a tunnel; slow down after the tunnel and make a left into the parking lot at St-Laurent d'Eze. There's a small shack, St-Laurent, in the middle of the lot. Park here and follow the path across the street down toward the coast. The beach is a good 15- to 20-minute walk (ask the dudes at the snack shack if you have doubts about the path or follow the boys). The narrow path winds down between fig and lemon trees and ends at the train tracks. Cross the tracks carefully and follow them to the right or take the next path down to the water and head south through the orchards and rocky terrain. You'll find two beaches: The first is straight, the second gay. If you're following the boys through the train tunnel, stay close to the wall (trains pass by at alarming speeds) and a few hundred feet after the tunnel turn left and down to the infamous Eze beach.

To reach St-Laurent d'Eze by **bus** from Nice, take the Monaco bus from Gare Routière and ask the driver to stop for you in St-Laurent; then follow the path down. The fare is 13.50F ($2.45) and includes a free return, so hold onto your stub. Buses run every half an hour 7am to 7pm.

CANNES

Blame it on Coco: When Coco Chanel went to **Cannes** and got a tan, returning to Paris bronzed, she startled the milk-white society ladies. However, they and their gentlemen quickly began copying her. And today you'll find bronzed bodies—male, female, whatever, in nearly nonexistent swimsuits—lining the sandy beaches of this resort. Especially at Film Festival time.

For most visitors, Cannes might as well consist of only one street, the **boulevard de la Croisette** (or just **La Croisette**), curving along the coast and split by islands of palms and flowers. On La Croisette is the **Palais des Festivals,** "the bunker," the epicenter of the Film Festival.

During the **Cannes Film Festival,** muscleheads in tank tops strut their stuff; Marilyn Monroe look-alikes (both men and women) cruise in convertibles up and down La Croisette hoping to become stars; and Big Names pose and pose and pose along the red carpet at the Palais des Festivals as the paparazzi swarm and snap shot after shot. For 2 weeks in May this town goes crazy with the glamour, decadence, and romance of the movies. At other times (except July and August, which are real busy), this palm-studded resort is a laid-backed albeit expensive town with a sizable gay community, good restaurants, shops, excellent beaches, and gay nightlife. In winter, Cannes becomes the convention center of the Côte d'Azur.

Come here in the warm months, when the beaches are hopping and the boys dine in the open air in the (somewhat) gay area (and most beautiful part of town) known as **Le Suquet.** To get there, cruise down La Croisette heading west, past the Palais des Festivals to the harbor; turn right and take rue de la République up the hill; it turns into rue du Suquet (you can't miss the area, there's a 14th-century tower at the top).

There aren't any fabulous museums in Cannes. The only one worth a visit is the **Musée de la Castre,** in the Château de la Castre, Le Suquet (☎ **04-93-38-55-26**), where you'll find 19th-century paintings and a good collection of relics from ancient Mediterranean civilizations from Crete to Corsica. The museum is open Wednesday to Monday; April to June 10am to noon and 2 to 6pm, July to September 10am to noon and 3 to 7pm, and October to March 10am to noon and 2 to 5pm. Admission is 10F ($1.80).

The **Office de Tourisme** is in the Palais des Festivals, boulevard de la Croisette (☎ **04-93-39-24-53**).

BOYS ON THE BEACH Try to spend at least half a day at one of the fancy resort's **private beaches** along La Croisette (pay the 100F/$18 mattress rental and you're in). It's a scream to guess which of the women (and men) hasn't had plastic surgery; the beach boys are cute (so are the sailors driving the speedboats that dock at the hotel piers). Cannes is very gay-friendly, and gays are much more visible here than in Nice. More than anywhere along the coast (except St-Tropez) anything goes here—no one bats an eyes.

In addition to the fine sandy beaches lining **La Croisette,** (several of them public and free, by the way), there's a nude gay beach off the N7 highway to Golfe-Juan. **Plage de la Batterie** is not really a beach but a jagged collection of rocks near the train tracks east of town. It's across from the Shell gas station (the only structure on that empty stretch of highway) about 2 miles out of town.

To get there, go under the train tracks and turn west, back toward Cannes. There's a parking lot if you're driving. If you're on foot, cross the parking lot and climb the rocks to get to the beach. All along the rocks on the jagged seashore you'll find nude men. The men vary from week to week, depending on the season; but there's a significant number of older men looking for action in the bushes. The local boys come on the weekends or late in the afternoons in summer.

PILLOW TALK During the Cannes Film Festival, the palatial **Hôtel Carlton Intercontinental,** 58 bd. de la Croisette, 06400 Cannes (☎ **04-93-06-40-06;** fax 04-93-06-40-25; www.interconti.com; e-mail cannes@interconti.com), is one of the hot spots for muscle dudes who hope to attract a producer (or a date); in midsummer it's shunned by "sophisticated travelers" and taken over by nouveaux-riche Russians and Saudis with servants and screaming kids. If you come in fall, it'll be perfectly calm. Big combo baths with hair dryers and luxurious appointments are standard. The most spacious rooms are in the west wing, and many of the upper-floor rooms have balconies fronting the Mediterranean. Doubles are 1,290 to 3,915F ($235 to $711), with suites beginning at 3,000F ($545).

Two blocks away is the newly renovated ✪ **Hôtel Martinez,** 73 bd. de la Croisette, 06406 Cannes (☎ **04-92-98-73-00;** fax 04-93-39-67-82; e-mail martinez@concorde-hotels.com), a grand art deco hotel that's much more elegant and gay. This is where the film critics and directors stay during the festival; the rest of the year, a sophisticated jet-set crowd checks in. The stretch of private beach across the street is the largest on La Croisette. The piano bar is fast becoming popular with local gay professionals (one of the pianists is gay). The most acclaimed restaurant in Cannes, La Palme d'Or (see "Whet Your Appetite" below) is in the hotel. All 430 units are luxuriously appointed in art deco style. Doubles range from 1,200 to 3800F ($218 to $691), and suites begin at 4,000F ($727).

On the other side of La Croisette, facing the Palais des Festivals, the ✪ **Hôtel Splendid,** 4 rue Félix-Faure, 06407 Cannes (☎ **04-93-99-53-11;** fax 04-93-99-55-02; e-mail hotel.splendid.cannes@wanadoo.fr), is the best bargain here. It's a grand white elephant of a building located in a young, trendy area of Cannes (it shares the block with Planet Hollywood). All the 62 spacious French-country rooms were renovated in 1997, with new baths installed in 1998; half the units have kitchenette, and all come with air-conditioning, TVs, and phones. You'll even find a welcome fruit basket (how appropriate) on your arrival. Doubles are 600 to 980F ($109 to $178).

One street in from the sea is the boutique-style ✪ **Hôtel America,** 13 rue St-Honore, 06400 Cannes (☎ **04-93-06-75-75;** fax 04-93-68-04-58; e-mail hotel.america@hol.fr), with excellent rates for its 28 air-conditioned and soundproofed rooms with marble baths. Doubles run 550 to 760F ($100 to $138). **Hôtel Touring,** 11 rue Hoche, 06400 Cannes (☎ **04-93-38-34-40;** fax 04-93-38-73-34), is a two-star gay hotel on a pleasant street close to the train station; the drab reception area is slated to be renovated soon but not the 27 rooms, where you'll find basic beds with thin mattresses, clean baths, TVs, and phones. Younger gay travelers and backpackers find their way to this friendly place. Doubles are 300 to 400F ($55 to $73).

WHET YOUR APPETITE Gays from all over the area come to Cannes to dine on **rue du Suquet,** the narrow cobblestone street (more like an alley) in Le Suquet area lined with restaurants that squeeze in as many tables as possible against the walls of the old town; it gets zooey, with tourists trying to get past the fuming waiters trying to deliver food to their waiting diners. What Cours Saleya is to Nice Le Suquet is to Cannes, but it's much more flamboyant here. It's the nature of the town—Cannes is glitzier than Nice, and so are the boys.

Though the street is packed with restaurants (most quite good), everyone still flocks to the most popular: ✪ **Le Marais,** 9 rue du Suquet (☎ **04-93-38-39-19;** in season open daily 7:30–11pm, call for off-season hours), named after Paris's gay neighborhood. The leopard-skin chairs do scream queer, and so do the flamboyant waiters and tables of tanned good-looking men of all ages. The food isn't the focus (everybody's so busy looking), but you can eat well enough on *fettuccine aux fruits de mer* (seafood fettuccine in light cream sauce) or *pavé de saumon* (pan-fried salmon fillet with baby parsley potatoes). Main courses are 90 to 160F ($16 to $29), with a fixed-price menu at 150F ($27).

The most acclaimed (and expensive) restaurant is **La Palme d'Or,** in the Hôtel Martinez, 73 bd. de la Croisette (☎ **04-92-98-74-14;** open June–Sept Tues–Sun 12:30–3pm and 7:30–10:30pm, closed Tues Oct–May), named after the film festival's highest award (what the Oscar is to Hollywood, the Palm d'Or is to Cannes). It's a fabulous art-deco dining room with photographs of stars on the walls and an equally fabulous crowd at the tables. The menu changes frequently but is focused on local themes, like tender red mullet fillets (small Mediterranean fish) with zucchini flowers in olive cream. The 295F ($54) fixed-price menu is served at lunch only; main courses are 220F to 480F ($40 to $87). Reserve at least 2 weeks in advance during summer or a day ahead at other times.

For the most delicious and reasonably priced meal in town, forego dining close to the water and head a few blocks inland (4 blocks north of the train station) to a small house overlooking a schoolyard. The ✪ **Côte Jardin,** 12 av. St-Louis (☎ **04-93-38-60-28;** open Tues–Sat noon–2:30pm and 7:30–10:30pm, Mon 7:30–10:30pm), charms with its flower-filled garden. Here's where you get five-star dishes at reasonable prices. Provençal specialties include delicate mushroom ravioli, lobster flan that's as light as a soufflé, and white-fish carpaccio marinated in olive oil. The bouillabaisse is great too. For dessert, the *gratinée des poires à la crème de pistache* (baked pear with pistachio cream) is super. Main courses run 80 to 180F ($15 to $33); fixed-price menus are 110F ($20) at lunch and 195F ($35) and 280F ($51) at dinner. Reserve at least a week in advance during summer or a day ahead at other times.

HITTING THE STORES All the trendy shops are on mile-long **rue d'Antibes,** which runs parallel to La Croisette, 2 blocks inland. Late afternoons is when the gay boys come to shop; you can't miss them—it's not a wide street and the narrow sidewalks are made for bumping. On **La Croisette** itself, you'll find the millionaire's jewelry stores and outrageously priced designer-wear shops. Shopping hours are 10am to 1pm and 3 to 7pm, with many shops staying open to 8pm in July and August.

Casual, dusty, and filled with the castaways from various estate sales, the **Marché Forville,** in the Marché Forville neighborhood near the Palais des Festivals, is a battered stucco structure with a roof and a few arches but no sides. It usually functions as the fruit-and-vegetable market, but Monday is *brocante* day, when the market fills with offhanded, sometimes strident antiques dealers selling everything from *grand-mère's* dishes to bone-handled carving knives.

IN THE HEAT OF THE NIGHT A lot goes on in Cannes at night in summer, with guys from all over converging on the several gay bars and clubs; in winter, the clubs come alive only on weekends with mostly local boys eager to meet a new face. Most bars open between 6 and 7pm and stay open to 2 or 3am; clubs open 10pm to 4am. There's only one happening dance club, Le Disco Sept. There are no lesbian bars.

Start your evening in Le Suquet, the quasi-gay neighborhood, at the sleek **Le Vogue,** 20 rue du Suquet (☎ **04-93-39-99-18**), and ask friendly owners Serge and Olivier anything you want to know about the gay scene (since it's in a touristy area, they get their share of unsuspecting straight couples, mostly young). It's small bar and a good place to meet a few trendy men. Up the street is the funky and very 1970s **Twiggy Records,** 3 rue des Suisses (☎ **04-93-99-13-32**), with its shiny green vinyl chairs; it's popular with young Cannois gays and lesbians, most with pierced noses, lips, or whatever.

At the top of the hill (by the parking lot) is the trendy **Barbarella,** 3 rue St-Dizier (☎ **04-92-99-17-33**), a bar/restaurant with Brazilian music and 20-something queens oozing attitude; it has been a gathering spot for local gays for several years. Down the hill closer to the port you'll find the down to earth **Le P'tit Zinc,** 85 rue Meynardier (☎ **04-93-39-38-32**), a good place to watch the people go by after dinner; the crowd is mixed, gays, some unsuspecting tourists, and the occasional lesbian.

A hip and happening bar, especially on Friday night with buff boys in white T-shirts, is **Le Scandale,** 7 rue Maréchal-Joffre (☎ **04-93-39-44-57**), one street in from La Croisette and close to the Palais des Festivals. In front of the Hôtel Splendid is the oldest gay bar, **Le Zanzibar,** 5 rue Félix-Faure (☎ **04-93-39-30-75**), attracting an older, smoky crowd; most gay visitors come here on their first night in town, if only for a quick drink (it's listed in all the gay guides) before going dancing.

If you want to dance, the hottest place in town is ✪ **Le Disco Sept,** 7 rue Rouguières (☎ **04-93-39-10-36;** cover 60–100F/$11–$18, includes one drink), where hot men from all over the Riviera come in skintight shirts to shake it and more. Don't bother coming before midnight; on summer Wednesdays to Saturdays they host "After Parties" 4:30 to 7am. A new gay and lesbian dance club was slated to open after this writing: **B.P.M.,** 8 rue des Frères-Pradignac (☎ **04-93-68-40-00**). When you arrive, ask around if it's worth a visit.

MONACO

Gays along the Côte d'Azur consider **Monaco,** the 370-acre principality ruled by Prince Rainier III, a place to avoid. There's not one gay bar or restaurant or anything openly gay in this sterile, glitzy, decadent principality (some attribute the lack of gay venues to the constant rumors about long-unmarried Prince Albert). However, Monaco is alluring for gay visitors, even if most come for short visits. The legend of Princess Grace (the former Grace Kelly, remember?) draws thousands to visit the palace and the gardens (and shops) she so loved. Now the most visible of her three children is Princess Stephanie, who stays involved in the commercial and cultural life of the principality.

If you're a first-timer, the first thing you'll notice is the amazingly tight security (there's a young policeman in white gloves at every major intersection). The government flaunts the fact that in Monaco "you can wear all your jewels in peace" (video cameras tape the action on all the major streets). And flaunt they do. The amount of custom-ordered Rolls-Royces, Lamborghinis, and Ferraris is mind-boggling. So much wealth in such a small area. (By the way, don't be fooled by the rainbow flags on the pedestrian mall in La Condamine port area; they're just colorful flags, not flags welcoming us.)

EXPLORING MONACO Monaco is 3 miles long, only half a mile wide, and less than 7 miles from the Italian border. It squeezes four neighborhoods into its territory: **The Rock,** also known as the **Vieille Ville** (old town), is part of **Monaco-Ville,** the oldest part of Monaco, on a rocky hillside graced by the Palais du Prince and the cathedral where Princess Grace is entombed under a marble slab reading gratia. **La Condamine** is the harbor district at the foot of the Rocher, surrounded by residential buildings, shops, and a pedestrian mall; this is where most of the Monégasques live. **Fontvieille,** by the helicopter pad, is the commercial area, with its convention center and large park. And just uphill from La Condamine is **Monte Carlo,** where the real glitz is; it stretches from the famous casino to the end of eastern border of the principality (most of the fancy hotels, clubs, and restaurants are here). The **Direction du Tourisme** is at 2A bd. des Moulins in Monte Carlo (☎ **92-16-61-16**).

At the top of the Rock, affording dramatic sea vistas, sits the ✪ **Palais du Prince,** where the Grimaldis still live when they're in town. You can visit the **Grand Apartments (Grands Appartements du Palais),** place du Palais (☎ **93-25-18-31**), in summer when part of the palace is open for visits. You'll be led on a guided tour of the Italianate salons decorated with elaborate frescoes, tapestries, and paintings; the Throne Room with its huge fireplace, where ceremonies have been held since the 14th century (notice the beautiful state portrait of Princess Grace); and the central courtyard of the fortress, dating back to the Renaissance, with its Carrara marble double staircase (performances are held here in summer).

The palace is open daily: June to September 9:30am to 6:30pm and October 10am to 5pm. Admission is 30F ($6). Be warned that at times visits are canceled due to security or special events. If you arrive just before noon, you'll witness the changing of the guard, a ceremony that has remained unchanged for over a century (some guards are older but some are terribly hunky in full uniform—white in summer, black in winter).

In the palace's south wing is the **Museum of Napoleonic Souvenirs and Collection of the Palace's Historic Archives (Musée des Souvenirs Napoléoniens et Collection des Archives Historique du Palais),** a collection of objects and documents linked to Napoléon and the history of the Grimaldis (they were relatives). June to September, the museum is open daily 9:30am to 6:30pm; October hours are daily 10am to 5pm; and December to May, it's open Tuesday to Sunday 10:30am to 12:30pm and 2 to 5pm. Admission, not included with that of the palace, is 20F ($3.65).

When you leave place du Palais, take the road on the right, Col. Bellando de Castro, which leads down to the **Cathédrale de Monaco** (☎ **93-30-87-70**), a marble beauty that holds the tomb of Princess Grace and other Grimaldis amidst 16th-century paintings and a gilded wooden altar from the Spanish Renaissance. If you're here September to June, come on Sunday at 10am to hear the choir boys light up the place with their gentle hymns. The cathedral is open daily 9am to 6pm; admission is free.

Across the street is an entrance to the **Jardins St-Martin,** a lush collection of exotic tropical plants with splendid views over the Mediterranean. The gardens were created by Prince Albert I, whose statue you can see here gazing at the sea, and are always open.

The gardens end at the ✪ **Oceanography Museum (Musée de l'Océanographie),** av. St-Martin (☎ **93-15-36-00**), which was built in 1910 and is home to 4,500 species of fish (you'll get dizzy looking at so many colors in so many aquariums). It's considered the best such museum in the world and was directed for some time by Jacques Cousteau. It's open daily: July and August 9am to 8pm, October and March 9:30am to 7pm, November to February 10am to 6pm, and April to June and September 9am to 7pm. The 60F ($11) admission includes screenings of films by Cousteau.

In Fontvielle you'll find the interesting **Prince's Collection of Antique Cars (Collection des Voitures Anciennes du Prince),** Les Terrasses de Fontvieille (☎ **92-05-28-56**), displaying 100 vintage vehicles belonging to Prince Rainier, including the 1952 Rolls-Royce Silver Cloud that carried him and the princess on their wedding day. It's open daily 10am to 6pm (closed November); admission is 30F ($6). South of the Auto Museum in the Fontvieille Park (opened in 1984), is the **Princess Grace Rose Garden (La Rosarie de Princesse Grace),** with 4,000 bushes and 150 varieties of roses. It's open sunrise to sunset, and admission is free.

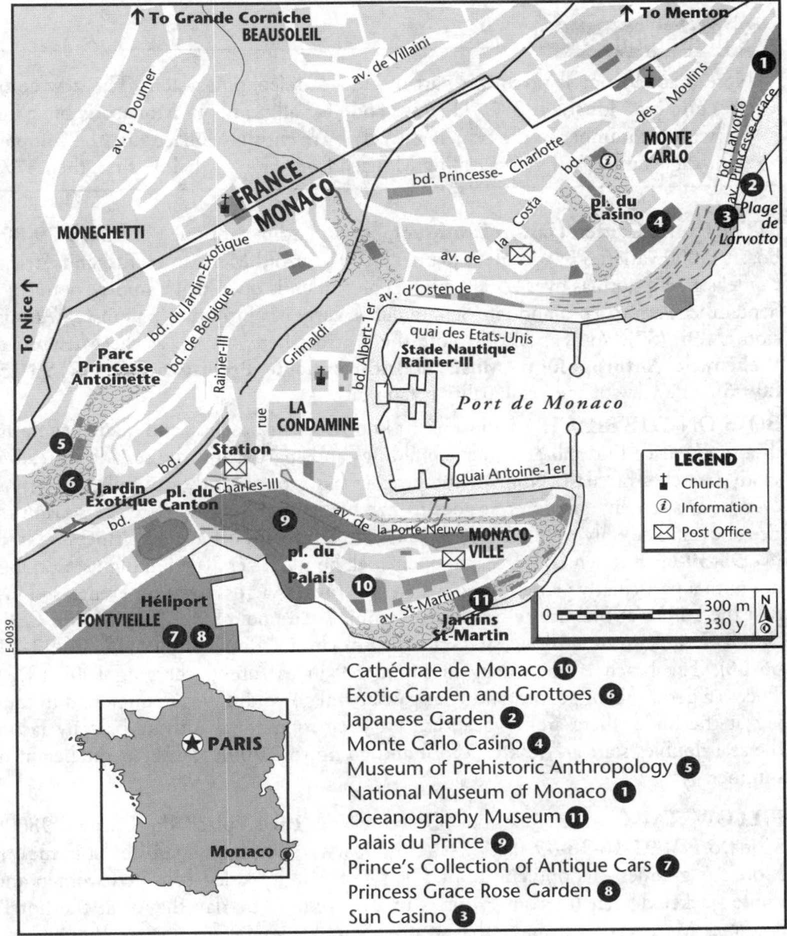

In Monte Carlo, the **National Museum of Monaco (Musée National de Monaco),** 17 av. Princesse-Grace (☎ **93-30-91-26**), has an amazing collection of mechanical toys and dolls in period costumes (no hunky Ken dolls here). The villa housing the museum was built by Charles Garnier (architect of Paris's Opéra Garnier), and to some the structure may be more interesting than the collection (including the lovely terraced rose garden strewn with sculptures). The museum is open daily: Easter to September 10am to 6:30pm and October to Easter 10am to 12:15pm and 2:30 to 6:30pm. Admission is 26F ($4.75).

South of the National Museum along avenue Princesse-Grace (just past boulevard Larvotto), is the **Japanese Garden (Jardin Japonaise),** a new addition to the gardens of Monaco, designed by Yasuo Beppu (an award-winning landscape artist), at the request of Prince Rainier. The concept of the garden comes from the "Zen thought which advocates meditation as a way of seeking beauty and serenity." Bamboo, parasol pine, cherry trees, fountains, ponds, and mini-waterfalls blend in beautifully with fences, gates, and lanterns all imported from Japan. There's a small area named the Garden of Grace to honor the late princess. The garden is open daily 9am to sunset.

Calling Monaco

Note that Monaco is no longer part of France's telephone system. The new **country code** for Monaco is **377.** The **city code** for all points in Monaco is built into every phone number in the principality. If you're within Monaco, use the complete eight-digit number. If you're calling Monaco from France, dial 00 first, then 377.

The **Exotic Garden (Jardin Exotique),** bd. du Jardin-Exotique (☎ **93-15-29-80**), boasts 7,000 varieties of succulent plants, a 100-year-old Mexican cactus, and African candelabra euphorbias over 25 feet high. The garden is open daily: mid-May to mid-September 9am to 7pm and late September to early May to 6pm (or sunset). Admission is 39F ($7). You can also explore the grottoes here, as well as the **Museum of Prehistoric Anthropology (Musée d'Anthropologie Préhistorique)** (☎ **93-15-80-06**). The view of the principality is fabulous.

BOYS ON THE BEACH Monaco isn't known for its beaches, and many people are disappointed to find tall apartment buildings and marinas on the seaside instead of sandy stretches of coast. None of the beaches has a particularly gay following (most everybody with any gay interest goes to Eze beach, 4 miles east—see the section on Eze above). The only public beach is **Plage de Larvotto,** off avenue Princesse-Grace (☎ **93-30-63-84**), which is free and open at all hours. It's crowded in high season, but not with a particularly glamorous crowd. That crowd is across town on French soil just past the border at the private beach or Olympic-sized pool of the glitzy **Monte Carlo Beach Hotel,** avenue Princesse-Grace–St-Roman in Roquebrune (☎ **04-93-28-66-66**). The beach is open daily in summer 9am to sunset, charging 100F ($18). There's a good mix of people, and your gaydar will go wild. If you're interested in staying at the hotel, there are 45 beautiful art deco rooms with private balcony facing the sea; doubles start at 1,850F ($336) and go up to 2,700F ($491) at the height of summer.

PILLOW TALK The infamous ✪ **Hôtel de Paris,** place du Casino, 98000 Monaco (☎ **92-16-38-49;** fax 92-16-38-50; www.sbm.mc; e-mail hp@sbm.mc), is Monaco's grandest, its opulent lobby filled with jewelry-laden coutured women and dinner-jacketed men (of course this is in the evening, by day they're at the hotel's Thermes Marins spa getting herbal wraps). Not everyone is glamorous, though, and the Paris does get its share of tourists who come to star-gaze and end up looking at one another. The hotel commands an excellent location facing the casino gardens; though its lobbies and restaurants are richly ornamented, the 198 rooms are modern and unpretentiously luxurious. Three of Monaco's top restaurants, Le Louis XV (see "Whet Your Appetite" below), Le Grill, and Restaurant Le Côte Jardin, are located here. Doubles go for 2,100 to 3,200F ($381 to $581), with suites beginning at 3,200F ($582).

For luxury by the sea at more affordable rates, try **Le Méridien Beach Plaza,** 22 av. Princesse-Grace, 98000 Monaco (☎ **93-30-98-80;** fax 93-50-23-14). It offers a minuscule private beach and is next to a fabulous sports center, the Sea Club, which gets its share of hot men. All 313 rooms have balconies (many with sea views) and are spacious and brightly furnished; there are three pools and two restaurants. Expect to see a lot of families during school holidays. Doubles are 890 to 2150F ($161 to $390), with suites starting at 2,950F ($536).

Close to the fancy hotels by the casino is the three-star **Hôtel Balmoral,** 12 av. de la Costa, 98006 Monaco (☎ **93-50-62-37;** fax 93-15-08-69), built at the end of the 19th century. It boasts antiques and good sea views but fading and dull rooms (50 of the 70 rooms have air-conditioning), all with TVs and phones. It's a friendly hotel with a mixed crowd, many Americans and most of them straight. Doubles are 550 to 1,000F ($100 to $182), with suites starting at 1,100F ($200).

If you're looking for a simple yet charming hotel close to the train station (and the palace), the **Hôtel Le Versailles,** 4 av. Prince-Pierre, MC 98000 (☎ **93-50-79-34;** fax 93-25-53-64), is your best bet. It looks slightly run down from outside, with faded blue shutters, but inside you'll find 15 clean, comfortable, but small rooms with phones and minibars. The staff is friendly and the clientele international and unpretentious. Doubles run 400 to 700F ($73 to $127).

The best bargain in Monaco (literally 3 feet from the invisible border—one side of the street is Monaco, the other France), is the **Hôtel Villa Boeri,** 29 bd. Général-Leclerc, 06240 Beausoleil (☎ **04-93-78-38-10;** fax 04-93-41-90-95), on a quiet street in a nice residential area only a 5-minute walk from the casino. Twenty-two of the 30 bright rooms have been renovated, and all come with air-conditioning, TVs, and phones; some are tiny but have good-sized windows, others are spacious with balconies. The guests are young, mostly northern Europeans, and seemingly straight. Doubles are 260 to 385F ($47 to $70).

WHET YOUR APPETITE ✪ **Le Louis XV,** in the Hôtel de Paris, place du Casino (☎ **92-16-30-01;** open July–Aug Tues–Wed 8–10pm, Thurs–Mon noon–2pm, and Sept–June Thurs–Mon noon–2pm and 8–10pm; closed Feb 17–Mar 4 and Dec 1–27), is one of the area's most celebrated restaurants. Master chef Alain Ducasse (the only Michelin six-star chef in France) continues to shuttle between here and his restaurant in Paris (see the introduction to "Whet Your Appetite" in chapter 5), winning even more raves for his light cuisine that promises no sauces, butter, or cream. He has revolutionized French food, infusing it with the scents and tastes of the south. Simplicity is what he's after—but why do we have to pay this much for simplicity? (And why should such simple dishes require such long names?) An example of two specialties: *légumes des jardins de Provence mijotes à la truffe noire écrasée* (Provençal garden vegetables simmered with crushed black truffles) or *poitrine de pigeonneau des Alpes de Haute-Provence et foie gras de canard sur la braise* (charcoal-grilled breast of baby pigeon from the high country served with duck liver)—he accentuates each ingredient by leaving out all the extras, and the results are a masterpiece. Is such a meal worth 1,000F ($182), though? Depends. It comes down to the setting, since you're paying as much for the surroundings and the service as you are for the food. If dining like a king or queen on Louis XV chairs in a palatial room (with waiters so professional they have no personality whatsoever) appeals to you, then there's no better place to blow your wad. The wine cellar holds thousands of bottles. Main courses are 400 to 600F ($73 to $109), with fixed-priced menus at 820F ($149) and 920F ($167). Reserve at least a month in advance during summer or 2 weeks in advance at other times.

L'Hirondelle, 2 av. de Monte-Carlo (☎ **92-16-49-47;** open Mon–Sat noon–2pm and 7–9:30pm, Sun noon–2pm), is a unique restaurant in the glass-and-pink marble complex of the Thermes Marins (seawater baths), where men and women from around the world check in for seaweed treatments, hydromassage, and a hundred other offerings; the complex is located between the Hôtel de Paris and the Hermitage. Chef Philippe Girard believes food is the ultimate pleasure, and though staying healthy (and losing weight) is the goal of many people who come here, "flavor must never be compromised and one must never leave the table hungry." And he fulfills his promise (at least the flavor part) as you dine on the spectacular terrace overlooking the port; for example, "feast" on trompe l'oeil prawn-and-artichoke salad (55 calories) or medallions of sole and scallops with vanilla-and-broccoli mousse (212 calories). There are also regular-calorie dishes that are richer but without added fat. Main courses run 160 to 280F ($29 to $51), with a fixed-price menu at 285F ($52). Reserve at least a week in advance during summer.

Perched 1,000 feet above the sea in the contemporary Hôtel Vista Palace, affording glorious views of Monaco, is the excellent **Le Vistaero,** just off the Grande Corniche in Roquebrune, France (☎ **04-92-10-40-00;** open daily 12:15–2:15pm and 8–10:15pm). This is yet another outlandishly expensive restaurant where you pay for the impeccable service and the unrivaled views (hang gliders float past during the day and get so close to the terrace you can almost reach out and touch). Chef Jean-Pierre Pestre combines French and Italian cuisine to create unique dishes; the prawns wrapped in pancetta and served with exotic fruit and sesame-crusted vegetables is fantastic, as is the exquisite grilled sea bass accompanied by wild mushrooms and olives with thyme and lemon. Main courses are 210 to 380F ($38 to $69), with fixed-price menus at 250 to 560F ($45 to $102). Reserve at least a week in advance during summer or a day ahead at other times.

For a good Italian meal, everybody heads over to the Rock, to the many restaurants between the Prince's Palace and the Monaco Cathedral. The most popular is **Le Pinocchio,** 30 rue Comte-Félix-Gastaldi (☎ **93-30-96-20;** open June–Sept daily 7:30pm–midnight and Oct–May Thurs–Tues 7:30–11pm). It's known for its delicious antipasti (like the carpaccio with parmesan); the ravioli with herbs in light cream sauce is delicious. Young Italians come here, and there's a small terrace good for people-watching. Main courses are 90 to 160F ($16 to $27).

Princess Stephanie has been busy with her new line of trendy shops selling men's and women's fashions. In Monaco, the shop is also a cafe where the young and hip (and wealthy) Monégasques grab a quick bite: **Replay Store and Café,** 47 rue Grimaldi (☎ **93-30-02-30;** open Mon–Sat 9am–midnight, but meals served only 11:30am–3pm and 7pm–midnight). Mixing French and Italian styles, the cafe offers an all-you-can-eat lunch buffet and an interesting vegetarian meal that includes a polenta pancake and vegetable cannelloni as a main course. Main courses are 45 to 75F ($8 to $13) and include an assortment of pastas and salads.

HITTING THE STORES If you're looking for fancy-schmancy stores, you'll find them around the Hôtel de Paris and lining the streets leading to the Hôtel Hermitage or across from the gardens at the minimal Park Palace. The **Allée Serge-Diaghilev** is just that, an alley, but a very tony one filled with designer shops. For less exalted shopping, stroll **rue Grimaldi,** the principality's main commercial street, and **boulevard des Moulins,** closer to the casino. There's also an all-pedestrian thoroughfare with shops less forbiddingly chic than those along boulevard des Moulins: **Rue Princesse-Caroline** is loaded with bakeries, flower shops, and the closest thing you'll find to funkiness in Monaco.

For the heart and soul of Monaco, get away from the glitz and head to place des Armes for the **fruit, flower, and food market** held daily 9am to noon; it has an indoor and an outdoor market with a fountain, cafes, and hand-painted vegetable tiles beneath your feet. While the outdoor market packs up promptly at noon, some dealers at the indoor market stay open to 2pm. If you prefer bric-a-brac, there's a small flea market, **Les Puces de Fontvieille,** held Saturday 9am to 6pm at the Espace Fontvieille, a panoramic open-air site near the heliport.

IN THE HEAT OF THE NIGHT Monaco is full of Italian tourists who cross the border for some gambling; the Italians like to have fun and live it up while on vacation, and they help keep Monte Carlo throbbing until the wee hours.

Of course, the center and core and heart of Monaco is the **Monte Carlo Casino,** place du Casino (☎ **92-16-21-21**), built at the end of the 19th century by Charles

Garnier (who built the Paris Opéra). Admission to the front part is free and doesn't require a jacket and tie; you can get as far as the slot machines before you're turned back if you're not dressed up. Beyond the slot machines, bring a lot of dough, your passport, and a tie and jacket (a tiara wouldn't hurt). The roulettes start at noon and the slot machines at 2pm; blackjack is offered from 9pm on weekdays and from 5pm on weekends. The action goes on until the early hours of the morning. Admission is 50F ($9) or 100F ($18), depending what rooms you're going to. The casino is also home to the **Opéra de Monte Carlo,** where many performances are held each year, and to a **Cabaret** where flashy shows are performed several times a week. Tickets are difficult to get for the opera; ask your concierge or inquire at the casino box office (☎ **92-16-22-99;** open Tues–Sun 10am–12:15pm and 2–5pm). For cabaret tickets, call ☎ **92-16-36-36.**

You can also gamble at the **Sun Casino,** in the sprawling Hôtel Loews Monte-Carlo, av. des Spélugues (☎ **92-16-20-82**); admission is free, and there's blackjack and slot machines.

You might want to start the evening at the **American Bar,** in the Hôtel de Paris, place du Casino (☎ **92-16-30-00**), where Cocteau and the gang sipped drinks and dished late into the night. Or you can people-watch at the **Café de Paris,** place du Casino (☎ **92-16-20-20**), occupying one of the many of the outdoor tables overlooking the action of the casino and the endless stream of fancy cars and fancy people.

Since there are no gay bars or clubs, you'll find a large number of gays, curious, lesbians, and bis at **Jimmy'z,** av. Princesse Grace, in the Sporting Club (☎ **92-16-22-66;** open daily 10:30–dawn but closed Mon–Tues Nov–Mar),one of the Côte d'Azur's largest and most popular clubs. After midnight on weekends is the busiest time, when all the boys and girls in Versace jeans seem like they just inherited an oil company or a bank (or both). If you want to see what the jet-set Gen-Xers look like, you'll find them at Jimmy'z and at **Paradyz's Disco,** av. Princesse Grace, in the Sporting Club (☎ **92-16-22-77;** open daily 11pm–dawn), where they're even younger and the place thumps with techno, rock, and 1970s disco, depending on the night. Bring cash (you might need to bribe the bouncers to let you in), a sports jacket (no blue jeans), and a convertible for the valet boys and you won't feel out of place. For both clubs, cover charges vary with the seasons and the days, but expect to cough up at least 100F ($18) and at least 45F ($8) per drink on top of that.

ST-TROPEZ

Fondly referred to as St-Trop (pronounced San Trop), **St-Tropez** is the ultimate playground not only of the rich and famous but also of the rich and not-so-famous gays. This is the ultimate beach destination on the coast, where even the city boys from Nice and Marseille come to escape for a weekend. It's not a gay destination like Ibiza, Sitges, or Mykonos, however, because the gays who come here don't necessarily come to be with other gays but with other over-the-top people. This is where you'll see a real ménage à trois in action or a swinging straight couple and their bisexual entourage. The prerequisite to be allowed into this seemingly exclusive vacation club is to be *un peu fou* and oh so fabulous (just like you).

Unlike Monaco or Cannes, St-Tropez feels like an island in the middle of the sea, belonging to no country or culture except the culture of decadence and frivolity. And just like an island, St-Tropez has retained its charm all these years because it's inaccessible. The nearest train station is an hour away in St-Raphaël and the nearest airport is in either Toulon or Nice, both almost a 2-hour drive. (No, the *stars* don't sit in a car for that long, they come by helicopter from Nice airport.) Despite the inaccessibility, 100,000 visitors per day find their way here during summer to stroll around the port, gawk at the fancy yachts, and watch the sunset turn the village a brilliant orange.

Though St-Tropez is cultured more in flesh than in art, there's one museum worth a visit, conveniently located facing the port in town (the second-floor balcony offers a postcard-perfect view). The 1568 Chapel of Notre-Dame was converted in 1955 into the ✪ **Musée l'Annonciade (Musée de St-Tropez),** at place Georges-Grammont (☎ **04-94-97-04-01**), and it's an homage to the many impressionist and avant-garde artists who flocked here in the first half of the 20th century. Painter Paul Signac (who said "a fateful wind blew me towards this eighth wonder of the world") was the first artist to live in St-Tropez (in 1892), and after him came a long troop of others attracted by the *laissez-faire* ambience. Pierre Bonnard, Edouard Vuillard, and Henri Matisse are all well represented in the small collection of paintings on the upper level; the lower level is reserved for temporary exhibits that change annually. The museum is open Wednesday to Monday: June to September 10am to noon and 3 to 7pm and October and December to May 10am to noon and 2 to 6pm. Admission is 30F ($5).

Colette lived in St-Tropez for many years, but it was Brigitte Bardot who put this fishing village on the map in the mid-1950s with images of her frolicking on local beaches in the movie *And God Created Woman.*

The **Office de Tourisme** is on quai Jean-Jaurès (☎ **04-94-97-45-21**).

Two miles from St-Tropez, **Port Grimaud** makes an interesting outing. If you approach the village at dusk, when it's softly bathed in Riviera pastels, it'll look like some old hamlet, perhaps from the 16th century. But this is a mirage. Port Grimaud is the dream fulfillment of its promoter, François Spoerry, who carved it out of marshland and dug canals. Flanking these canals, fingers of land extend from the main square to the sea. The homes are Provençal style, many with Italianate window arches. Boat owners can anchor right at their doorsteps. One newspaper called the port "the most magnificent fake since Disneyland."

BOYS ON THE BEACH The most beautiful beaches on the coast aren't exactly in St-Tropez—they're 2 miles south in **Ramatuelle,** along the bay of Pampelonne. This is where it all happens, over 3 miles of wide sandy beaches, restaurants, bars, shops, and hotels. (Two beaches are very gay, and nudity is not only tolerated but encouraged at most.) Expect to pay between 60F and 80F ($11 and $15) for a beach mattress (which in effect gives you access to these private beaches). If you're interested in hiking to the beaches, stop by the Office du Tourisme for a map and directions for the scenic 2- to 3-hour trek (you can take the bus back). Otherwise, you can go by car, bus, or bike.

✪ **Acqua Club,** part of the Plage de Pampelonne, Rte. de l'Epi (☎ **04-94-79-84-35**), is one of the two gay beaches. (Gay here means 50% to 75%, the rest straight and in-between.) It's a large beach with a separate restaurant/bar and a shop selling gay wear (Armani and Versace underwear and Dolce & Gabbana T-shirts). The men cover a wide age range, from early 20s to early 70s, and many come here for the whole summer every summer. It's not a very cruisy place, but it's friendly and eccentric. July and August, the restaurant is open daily 10am to 10:30pm; September, October, May, and June, it's hours are 10am to 8pm; and November to April, it's open Friday to Monday noon to 3pm. Main courses are 48 to 185F ($9 to $34). The shop is open in high season daily 10am to 7pm (☎ **04-94-79-88-81**).

A short walk down the beach is the cruisier and younger ✪ **Coco Beach,** Plage de Pampelonne, Rte. de l'Epi (☎ **04-94-79-83-25**), where a hunky crowd pumps up with a bench press and free weights at the "gym." Single men come here, and a testosterone cloud hangs over the boys (the ambience could very well be a dance club on Saturday night). In late afternoon, after a few beers, everyone loosens up and the mood gets jovial. The restaurant serves delicious salads for 55 to 68F ($10 to $12); April to October, it's open daily 10am to 8pm.

La Voile Rouge, part of the Plage de Tahiti, Rte. de Tahiti (☎ **04-94-97-18-02**), is the jet-set beach for the rich and famous. They come here from around the world, young couples from Rio and aging divorcées from Geneva, the male and the female, and everything in between (everything that can be surgically fixed is flaunted here). April to October, the beach, restaurant, and gigolo meeting point are open daily 10am to 8pm.

PILLOW TALK You can have two very different vacations here, so choosing where you stay is paramount to getting the most out of your vacation. Your choices: a hotel in the center of town or a hotel a mile or two away, closer to the beaches. In town, you're close to the nightlife, restaurants, and bars but are also close to the din, a problem if you're a light sleeper. You'll have to bike or drive to the beach from town. Or you can stay at one of the many hotels in Ramatuelle, a short walk to the beaches and drive into town for the nightlife. Many of the out-of-town hotels have gorgeous views of the olives groves and vineyards (few are right on the beach).

Only one hotel in St-Tropez has a private beach and is within walking distance of town, and that's the fabulous ✪ **Résidence de la Pinède,** Plage de la Bouillabaisse, 83990 St-Tropez (☎ **04-94-55-91-00;** fax 04-94-97-73-64; e-mail pinede@webstore.fr). It's a 36-room Relais & Châteaux hotel with personalized service and a loyal group of return visitors of all nationalities and persuasions, though the rates keep the age range closer to the senior levels. The restaurant has received one Michelin Star. Doubles range from 660 to 3795F ($120 to $690), with suites beginning at 1,760F ($320).

The only other over-the-top hotel is **Le Byblos,** avenue Paul-Signac, 83990 St-Tropez (☎ **04-94-56-68-00;** fax 04-94-56-68-01; e-mail saint-tropez@byblos.com), which every summer welcomes a very flamboyant and flaunty group of visitors who don't think twice about the exorbitant rates. Doubles go for 1,080 to 3,070F ($196 to $558), with suites starting at 2,800F ($509). The bar is a popular late-night stop for the jet-set crowd.

The most elegant place to stay if you want to be steps from all the restaurants (and the two gay bars) is the **Hôtel Le Yaca,** 1 bd. d'Aumale, 83992 St-Tropez (☎ **04-94-55-81-00;** fax 04-94-97-58-50), with its 26 luxurious rooms (some are really small, though) and professional staff. If you really want to splurge, go for the newly renovated house that has been turned into a huge suite. Doubles are 1,250 to 2,300F ($227 to $418) and suites 4,650 to 5,400F ($845 to $981).

If you like B&Bs, Blanche, you'll love **La Maison Blanche,** place des Lices, 93990 St-Tropez (☎ **04-94-97-52-66;** fax 04-94-97-89-23), offering 8 homey rooms with marble baths and lovely breakfast room overlooking bustling place des Lices. Doubles are 590 to 1,680F ($107 to $305).

The best bargain in town is a 5-minute walk up a tame hill: **Lou Troupelen,** Chemin des Vendanges, 93990 St-Tropez (☎ **04-94-97-44-88;** fax 04-94-97-41-76), is a charming country house that has been renovated into 44 comfortable rooms (all with TVs and phones). Many of the rooms have small balconies opening onto the quiet garden. Doubles are 390 to 499F ($71 to $91). Another great bargain is the 11-room **Hôtel Le Baron,** 23 rue de l'Aïoli, 83990 St-Tropez (☎ **04-94-97-06-57;** fax 04-94-97-58-72), close to all the action. The rooms are small but comfortable (all with TVs and phones). The owners, Pierre and Christine, are friendly and stay busy at all hours with the ground-floor pub, popular with the backpacking and transient college crowd. Doubles are 300 to 650F ($55 to $118).

The fanciest hotel a mile out of town is the **Château de la Messardière,** Rte. de Tahiti, 83990 St-Tropez (☎ **04-94-56-76-00;** fax 04-94-56-76-01; e-mail hotel@messardiere.com), a turn-of-the-century Italian Renaissance castle at the top of a hill about a 20-minute walk from all the beaches. The architecture of this special place blends many styles—from its Moorish columns and Spanish courtyard with a lovely pool to the terra-cotta tiles on the terraces overflowing with flowers. The 90 rooms and suites are luxurious without being overdone, decorated in greens, yellows, and oranges (the colors of a Mediterranean sunset); some have four-poster beds and most have plant-filled balconies overlooking the hillside. The guests hail from all over the world, with a large number of North Americans and a scattering of gays and lesbians (couples mostly). Le Restaurant du Château is getting rave reviews; meals are served around the pool in summer. Doubles are 1,100 to 3,200F ($200 to $582), with suites beginning at 2,700F ($491).

A 5-minute walk from the beach and overlooking a vineyard is the ✪ **Hôtel La Figuière,** Rte. de Tahiti, 83350 Ramatuelle (☎ **04-94-97-18-21;** fax 04-94-97-68-48), with spacious rooms, wondrous views, and a friendly staff. Room nos. 30 to 40 are the best (all with TVs, phones, and minibars), opening onto their own terraces overlooking the hillside (you can reach out and touch the grapes in late summer). The large baths have double sinks, and there's a gorgeous pool surrounded by olive trees. The guests are mostly French and Italian straight couples; many return year after year and ask for the same room. Doubles are 500 to 950F ($91 to $173).

WHET YOUR APPETITE The most popular gay-owned/managed restaurant on the Côte d'Azur is ✪ **Chez Maggy,** 7 rue Sybille (☎ **04-94-97-16-12;** open daily 7:30–11:30pm, bar to 1am), on a tiny pedestrian-only street in the town center. It's small, lively, and elegant, and about half the crowd is gay (the other half is a fun anything-goes mix). There's only one price for everyone and it's a bargain: 158F ($29) for three courses, including wine; the cuisine is a fusion of East and West, with specialties like chicken tandoori, couscous with fresh spicy tuna, salmon steak with sweet-and-sour berry sauce, and excellent lemon meringue pie. The bar is popular with gay singles.

The current hot spot is **Restaurant Joseph,** 1 place de l'Hôtel-de-Ville (☎ **04-94-97-01-66;** open daily noon–3pm and 7:30–11pm), right on one of the main squares. This is where Chez Nano (a gay restaurant) used to be (now it's a gay bar located elsewhere), and Joseph gets a fair amount of gays but also attracts older tourists. The terrace tables are the most sought after in town (so are the waiters). The food, however, is another story. The less expensive items seem to come from one kitchen and the "fancy" choices (like the wonderful lobster salad with warm green beans or aniseed-roasted scampi) from another. Main courses are 120 to 285F ($22 to $52); fixed-price menus are 99F ($18) at lunch and 160F ($29) at dinner.

The best seafood in St-Tropez is served close to the old fisherman's market at **La Ponche,** place du Revelin, port des Pêcheurs (☎ **04-94-97-02-53;** open daily noon–3pm and 7:30–11pm), which has been popular for over 50 years with a mainly French following. You'll find anything fresh that swims, prepared simply and excellently. Expect grilled fish with fresh vegetables and many kinds of salads. The friendly waiters are sometimes too harried to provide extra attention, so come late when the early dinner rush is over. Main courses are 110 to 230F ($20 to $42), with fixed-price menus at 130F ($24) at lunch and 180F ($33) at dinner.

At 9:15pm on July 20, 1997, Princess Diana ordered the Italian salad and the grilled fish of the day, princes William and Harry both ordered pizza, and Dodi asked for rosé wine. This all happened on the terrace of the low-key **La Renaissance,** place des Lices (☎ **04-94-97-02-00;** open daily noon–2:30pm and 7:30–10:30pm), when the four of them left Dodi's yacht to hit the town. Before this event, this restaurant wasn't on anybody's list and still isn't the best there is (pushy unfriendly waiters and mediocre food)—but what Diana fan can resist the connection? The pizza is good and inexpensive (57F/$10), and the banana split Diana is said to have had for dessert is better than the main courses. Dodi, in case you're interested, left a 300F ($55) tip.

The most enchanting restaurant is in Ramatuelle, 4 miles south of town, at ✪ **Ferme Ladouceur,** Quartier La Roullière (☎ **04-94-79-24-95;** open Wed–Mon 7:30–10:30pm). The "Farm of Tenderness" offers no-frills dining on a stone terrace overlooking a vineyard. You'll feel you've gone deep into the heart of Provence, and if you really like the place you can spend the night in one of the six basic rooms (doubles run 395F–525F/$72–$95). There's only one main course every night (not a good place for vegetarians or picky eaters), usually a traditional French specialty like boeuf bourguigon or coq au vin. The 170F ($31) fixed-price menu includes an excellent local wine.

IN THE HEAT OF THE NIGHT The most popular gay hot spot burned down in summer 1998 (some say it was hate motivated, others claim it was a personal tiff): **Le Bar à Vin,** 13 rue des Feniers (☎ **04-94-97-46-10**), is planning to rebuild and reopen, so ask around when you get to town.

For now, everybody starts the evening at **Chez Nano,** 2 rue Sybille (☎ **04-94-97-72-69;** open daily 7pm–3am), where a good mix of gays, bis, and straights live it up in this cozy bar with hunky bartenders. It feels more like a cocktail party with hors d'oeuvre trays being passed around and an air of friendliness and familiarity.

Chez Maggy (above) is another popular bar before midnight, that magic hour when the action shifts from these bars to **Le Pigeonnier,** 13 rue de la Ponche (☎ **04-94-97-36-85;** cover 50F/$9 Fri–Sat), a mixed bar with good music and a hip trendy crowd. The jetset gathers at **Les Caves du Roy** in the hotel Le Byblos, avenue Paul-Signac (☎ **04-94-56-68-00**), where bejeweled beauties lure the comte de this and marquis de that (the crowd is mixed but on the straight side). About 1am, the crowd divides into the straight/mixed clubs and the gay.

La Nacho Disco, 6 rue du Puits (☎ **04-94-59-88-81**), is popular with the young straight crowd, while the gays head to the infamous **L'Esquinade,** 2 rue du Four (☎ **04-94-97-87-45**), for some serious clubbing, dancing, cruising, and occasional drag shows (the Dolly Parties are popular in midsummer, when the boys dress up as blonde bimbos). The action goes on until the early hours.

4 Germany

Berlin Stories

by Donald Olson

Why call this part "Germany" when Berlin is the only city included? Well, what's the first place that comes to mind when you think of Germany? What German city has the most fascinating (and scariest) history? The widest cultural spectrum? The hottest gay nightlife? The most gays and lesbians? Berlin.

Hamburg, up in the cold Baltic north, is rich, rather haughty, and not particularly exciting (at least for those not into leather). Munich, to the southwest, is rich, beautiful, and irritatingly bourgeois. Frankfurt is a banking capital (so what?), and Düsseldorf can be exhausted in a day. Cologne has a great proactive gay scene and sits on the Rhine, but is it really where you want to spend your valuable vacation time? There are abundant reasons for visiting all these places, of course. But once you've been to Berlin, the rest of Germany seems pretty tame.

For international gay travelers, Berlin has long been a mecca, a hopping hot spot where it's impossible to be bored and potential adventures lie around every corner. In part, this is because Berlin welcomes the *Fremde, étranger,* stranger. You can dive into the city on all sorts of levels. It's as sophisticated or raunchy as you want it to be and accessible even if you don't speak German. There's an *immediacy* to Berlin because it's the one German city where everything is happening at once—past, present, and future meet and meld all over the place.

Now that the Wall has come down and Deutschland has been reunited, Berlin is once again the capital of the Federal Republic of Germany. The incredible cultural resources that were divvied up between the two sides of the city are now accessible to everyone. At Potsdamer Platz, the world's largest construction site, you can watch this city grow and reinvent itself. And if you tire of the urban scene, lakes and forests are minutes away by public transportation.

Berlin has a kind of inexhaustible energy, a fizz and a flair and a drive you'll find nowhere else. So go to those other cities in Germany—but only after you've experienced Berlin.

The German Mark

Money, as we all knew before seeing *Cabaret,* makes the world go round. Germany's currency is the **Deutsche Mark (DM).** One mark is made up of 100 **pfennigs.** Coins come in denominations of 5, 2, and 1 mark and in 50-, 10-, 5-, 2-, and 1-pfennig pieces. Bills come in denominations of 5, 10, 20, 50, 100, 200, 500, and 1,000 marks.

At this writing, 1.80DM was equivalent to $1 U.S., and that was the rate of exchange I used throughout. Prices over $5 U.S. have been rounded to the nearest dollar.

7

Berlin: Come to the Cabaret

Until 1989, every time I visited West Berlin I'd make a trip over to Communist East Berlin. It was fascinating but not exactly fun. First, you had to face hostile-looking guards with machine guns at Friedrichstrasse station. Then you had to get your passport stamped and obtain a day visa, which required you to exchange valuable West marks for worthless East marks. Going out into East Berlin was like entering a Third World country. It was filled with shoddy-looking Soviet-bloc buildings, lifeless memorials to Communist heroes, lousy food, and people who seemed grimly determined to make your stay as unpleasant as possible. You weren't supposed to talk to anyone, and taking photographs was *verboten.* All I can say in the East Berliners' favor is that they had a good recycling program for glass bottles.

The East Germans did have a social system that "protected" them from cradle to grave. And gay life did exist, even if it was discreet to the point of invisibility. Officially, homosexuality wasn't a crime. But in a system that rewarded conformity and gave its citizens extra money for every child they produced, there were few perks for the gay members of the proletariat. One of the worst aspects of life in the GDR was that it was riddled with spies and informers. You couldn't really trust anyone.

Now, 10 years later, all that's gone (at least physically), and reunited Berlin is once again Germany's political and cultural capital. There's no Wall and no border crossing, and all the decrepit and grimy buildings in the eastern part are being spic-and-spanned to perfection. But it'll take at least a generation for Berliners to deconstruct the Wall that still exists in their heads. Not everyone in the former East Berlin is overjoyed with a capitalist "market-driven" economy. It hasn't been easy for them to watch "their" city being rapidly taken over by slick politicians and businesspeople from the West. The division between "Westies" and "Osties" is real, if muted.

But when all is said and done, *"Berlin bleibt doch Berlin."* That's an old song lyric meaning "Berlin always remains Berlin." This is a city that has seen it all and survived to tell the tale. It's been the scene of Prussian power, artistic brilliance, endless political upheaval, and Nazi terror. By the end of World War II, much of it was reduced to smoldering rubble. For nearly 30 years it was divided by the Wall. Today? It's one of the most exciting cities in Europe. But, then, it always has been.

The Berliners, perhaps because they've seen so much, both triumph and horror, have always been a breed apart. Their cosmopolitan live-and-let-live attitude, laced with sharp-edged humor and sarcastic irreverence, gives the city an added bite. When you're in Berlin you'll see a city in transition—that's part of what makes it such an intriguing place to visit. But as it reinvents itself, yet again, *"Berlin bleibt doch Berlin."*

1 Berlin Essentials

ARRIVING & DEPARTING

BY PLANE Berlin is served by three airports, all with easy public transportation connections to the city at standard public fares.

Berlin-Tegel (☎ 030/410-11), the main airport, lies northwest of the city center. In the main hall is a tourist office where you can pick up general info on the city and buy tickets for the public transportation system (see below). Outside the terminal, **Express-Bus X9** (or **bus no. 109**) departs for central Berlin at frequent intervals, stopping along Kurfürstendamm and at Bahnhof Zoo; the trip takes less than half an hour. It's about a 20-minute ride into the city by taxi; expect to pay about 45DM ($25).

Berlin-Tempelhof (**☎ 030/695-111**), used for charters and inland flights, is in a residential area south of the city center. U-Bahn (subway) line **U6,** running north-south from Platz der Luftbrücke, connects with major subway-station interchanges at Mehringdamm, Hallesches Tor, and Friedrichstrsse. By taxi it's about half an hour to the city center; the ride costs around 55DM ($30).

Berlin-Schönefeld (**☎ 030/6091-5166**) lies in southeastern Berlin and handles flights from Eastern Europe and Asia. A shuttle-bus at the terminal will take you to S-Bahn (elevated train) line **S9,** which stops at Alexanderplatz, Friedrichstrasse, and Bahnhof Zoo (about 50 minutes). It's about 30 minutes into the city by taxi; the fare is about 55DM ($30).

BY TRAIN You can reach Berlin by train from everywhere in Europe. Most trains to destinations in Western Europe arrive at and depart from **Bahnhof Zoologischer Garten** (called **Bahnhof Zoo** or Zoo Station), centrally located close to Kurfürstendamm. Inside is the train travel office, **Fremdenverkehrsamt** (**☎ 030/313-9063;** open Mon–Sat 8am–11pm).

Trains to eastern European destinations use **Berlin Hauptbahnhof** (main train station), in the eastern part of the city. There's also a train travel office here (**☎ 030/279-5209;** open daily 8am–8pm).

Both stations are accessible by U-Bahn or S-Bahn.

Eventually, perhaps by 2000, all major trains will arrive at or depart from the Hauptbahnhof, which was Berlin's main station before the war. For 24-hour train information, call **Bundesbahn-Reiseauskunft** (German Train Information) at **☎ 030/194-19.**

BY BUS Berlin is served by over 25 bus lines with a number of destinations in Germany and throughout the rest of Europe. The main bus station for arrivals and departures is **Zentraler Omnibusbahnhof** (Central Bus Station), near the Funkturm (broadcasting tower) on the west side of the city (**☎ 030/301-8028**).

BY CAR Four **Autobahn** (freeway) routes enter Berlin from western Germany, three from the east. From Frankfurt or Munich it's about an 8-hour drive, depending on traffic. Once you're in the city, a car is something of a nuisance and you'd be better off keeping it parked at your hotel or in a garage. *Ja,* Berlin is a huge city, but unless you know it well, it's far easier to get around by public transportation than by car.

VISITOR INFORMATION

The main tourist information office is in the **Europa-Center,** Budapester Strasse 2 (☎ **030/626-031;** U-Bahn: Zoologischer Garten; open Mon–Sat 8am–10:30pm, Sun 9am–9pm). You can book a hotel room here for a fee of 5DM ($2.75). Other information offices are in the main hall of **Tegel Airport** (Bus: X-9 or 109; open daily 5:15am–10pm) and in the south wing of the **Brandenburg Gate,** Pariser Platz (U-Bahn: Unter den Linden; open daily 10:30am–7pm). You can also call the **Berlin-Hot Line** at ☎ **030/250-025** for information.

For current listings of everything that's going on, get a copy of ***Zitty,*** published every 2 weeks and available at all news agents for 4DM ($2.25), or ***Berlin Programm,*** costing 2.80DM ($1.50). Most gay bars, as well as Prince Eisenherz bookstore and Mann-o-Meter, the gay information center, have a large assortment of free gay magazines with gay listings (see later in this chapter for addresses).

BERLIN GAY & LESBIAN EVENTS

Like any major queer city, Berlin has its share of gay and lesbian events. The dates change, so it's best to call **Mann-o-Meter** at ☎ **030/216-808** or check the listings in the gay rags for exact dates and times.

JANUARY The city's big annual drag ball is the **Tuntenball.**

EASTER A **leather-scene event** is held on Easter weekend.

MAY The **Gay and Lesbian Run** draws queer guys 'n dolls who want to show off their legs and their stamina.

JUNE The annual **Leather Party Barbecue** in the Tiergarten brings together old friends and those new to the leather scene. **Motzstrassenfest** is a beerfest block party held on Motz Strasse in the gay village. And Berlin's **Gay Pride Day** takes place the last Sunday in June.

JULY The **Love Parade,** a big street party, features costumes and a queer carnival atmosphere.

OCTOBER Various arts and cultural events are held during **Berliner Lesbenwoche** (Lesbian week).

NOVEMBER The **Gay and Lesbian Film Fest** presents a program of new movies by gay and lesbian filmmakers.

CITY LAYOUT

Berlin is one of the world's largest cities—all of New York City's boroughs would fit into it with room to spare. For first-time visitors it can be difficult to get a handle on this sprawling metropolis, especially now that it's been reunified. Even though the Wall has come tumbling down, the first and simplest way to understand Berlin is to think in terms of the old political boundaries of "West" and "East."

From 1961 to 1989, West Berlin was basically an island of capitalism floating in the "red sea" of Communist East Germany. It was richer, showier, and wilder than its poor, repressed, unforgivably drab eastern counterpart. And it's where you'll probably want to find a hotel and spend most of your time.

West Berlin's glitziest artery was—and remains—the boulevard known as **Kurfürstendamm,** or **Ku-Damm** for short. The train station **Bahnhof Zoologischer Garten** (**Bahnhof Zoo** for short), near the Ku-Damm, is the major transportation hub on this side of the city and a good landmark for orienting yourself; it's just a few minutes from the station to the gay area around **Nollendorfplatz.** The zoo itself is part of the **Tiergarten,** a beautiful park (incidentally famous for its cruising grounds) stretching east and ending at the cultural center known as the **Kulturforum,** near Potsdamer Platz.

Charlottenburg, one of Berlin's most desirable neighborhoods, lies to the west of the Tiergarten. Here you'll find Charlottenburg Palace, several museums, and the Deutsche Oper (German Opera) house. The **Grunewald,** in the southwestern corner of the city, is a 15-square-mile forest bordered by the Havel River and a series of attractive lakes. **Kreuzberg,** a staunchly working-class neighborhood in south Berlin with a large population of Turks, was for years the "alternative" heart of the city. Some of its funkiness has disappeared now that gentrification has set in, but it remains a center of gay life.

Now let's talk "East Berlin," even though it doesn't really exist anymore. It's *physically* joined to the west but *psychologically* continues to be something of a separate entity. Eastern Berlin symbolically begins at **Potsdamer Platz** and the **Brandenburg Gate.** These areas, which stood behind the Berlin Wall, are now transitional zones lost in a bewildering maze of new construction. **Unter den Linden,** the grand boulevard that's the city's richest historical showcase, starts at the Brandenburg Gate (Pariser Platz) and extends east. It's lined with 18th- and 19th-century palaces (put to other uses) and monumental structures. The avenue and surrounding areas are the oldest sections of central Berlin and well worth exploring, particularly the beautiful neoclassical square called **Gendarmenmarkt.**

Friedrichstrasse, which intersects Unter den Linden, is in the process of restoring its prewar reputation as Berlin's preeminent shopping street. It's loaded with new luxury boutiques and department stores, but the commercial focus hasn't really shifted back here yet. **Friedrichstrasse train station,** where U-Bahn and S-Bahn lines converge, is the transportation hub of eastern Berlin. Before the war, this entire section of East Berlin was the traditional heart of the city, so it's referred to as **Mitte** (center) or **Stadtmitte** (city center) or **Berlin-Mitte.** Another part of East Berlin you may want to visit—mostly for its burgeoning gay scene—is the **Prenzlauer Berg** neighborhood, northeast of the Stadtmitte.

GETTING AROUND

Berlin's public transportation system—perhaps the best in the world—makes getting around fast, convenient, safe, and relatively inexpensive. It consists of subways (U-Bahn), elevated trains (S-Bahn), streetcars, buses, and even ferries. The fare is based on zones, and the same basic ticket price applies for all of them (except the ferries, which are run by a separate company). **Zone A** includes the central portion of the city (basically the area ringed by the S-Bahn lines), **Zone B** extends to the city borders, and **Zone C** is everything beyond.

There are several ticket options. A regular fare (**Einzelfahrscheine**) good for 2 hours in Zones A/B or B/C is 3.90DM ($2); for all three zones it's 4.20DM ($2.35). For short hops (three consecutive U- or S-Bahn stops or six stops on bus or streetcar) you can get a **Kurzstrecke** (short-stretch) ticket for 2.50DM ($1.40). A cheaper option is the 7.80DM ($4.50) **Tageskarte** (Day Ticket), good from validation until 3am the following day in all zones on all forms of transportation. An even better value is the ✪ **WelcomeCard,** which costs 29DM ($16) and is good for 72 hours. If you're going to be in Berlin for a few days, get a ✪ **7-Tage-Karte** (7-Day-Ticket) for 40DM ($22; Zones A/B), 42DM ($23; Zones B/C), or 48DM ($27; Zones A/B/C). Transfers between systems are free with these longer-term tickets.

The entire transportation system runs on an honor system. Buy your ticket at an U-Bahn station (windows or machines) or at the **BVG-Pavillion** (Hardenbergplatz, directly outside Zoo Station; open daily 8am–10pm). They'll also give you a free transportation map. Validate your ticket before boarding by sticking it into one of the red validation boxes on U-Bahn and S-Bahn platforms or inside busses and streetcars. (Long-term tickets are validated only once, before your first trip.) There are no turnstiles or collectors, but en route inspectors may appear to check everyone's ticket. If yours hasn't been validated, you're guilty of *schwarzfahren* (black travel) and fined 60DM ($33) on the spot.

BY SUBWAY The subway in Berlin is called the **U-Bahn** (think "underground"). There are 10 lines that criss-cross the city in all directions and extend out to the far reaches of Brandenburg. The stations are identified by a large U in a blue box, and the routes are clearly marked in all stations and in the trains. Service is fast and efficient, but after midnight only two lines, U9 and U2, run on a limited schedule; they intersect at Bahnhof Zoo. For general **U-Bahn information,** call ☎ **19449** (daily 6am–11pm).

BY ELEVATED TRAIN The venerable elevated train system in Berlin is called the **S-Bahn.** Thirteen lines cover most of central Berlin. The stations are identified by a large S in a green circle. S-Bahn and U-Bahn stations sometimes overlap, so you can change from one to the other. The S-Bahn is particularly handy if you're going from Bahnhof Zoo east to the Friedrichstrasse/Unter den Linden area or southwest to Grunewald and the lakes. Service is basically nonexistent after midnight. There's an S-Bahn **customer-service center** in Bahnhof Zoo (open Mon–Fri 6am–9pm, Sat–Sun 7am–9pm).

BY BUS Riding atop one of the double-decker buses (there are single-deckers too) is a fun way to see the city. One of the best and cheapest sightseeing routes is on **bus no. 100,** which leaves from Bahnhof Zoo and travels through the Tiergarten—passing Bellevue Palace (the Berlin residence of the German president), the Reichstag, and the Victory Column—to the Brandenburg Gate, Unter den Linden, Museum Island, and Alexanderplatz. **Night busses** leave every half an hour, going west and east, from **Bahnhof Zoo** and **Bahnhof Hackescher Markt** (near Alexanderplatz in the eastern section). Bus stops are identified by a green H (for *haltstelle,* or "stop") in a yellow circle; you can buy tickets from the driver and validate them on the bus. Buses are part of the transportation network and prices are the same as for the U-Bahn and S-Bahn.

BY TAXI Thousands of ivory-colored taxis cruise Berlin's main streets, and it's usually easy to hail one during the day (it takes longer at night). Cabs can be expensive, though, if you're going any distance. A new option that helps cut down on the cost is the **Kurzstrecke** (short-distance ride): For 5DM ($2.75), the driver will take you 2 kilometers (about 1.2 miles). You have to inform the driver you want a Kurzstrecke *before* the meter starts. To order a taxi, call ☎ **210-101.** Tip taxi drivers 1DM or 2DM.

BY STREETCAR Street cars, called **Strassenbahnen,** run in eastern Berlin only. Since you can get practically everywhere on the U-Bahn or S-Bahn, you probably won't be using the streetcar. Ticket prices are the same as for the U-Bahn, S-Bahn, and buses.

BY CAR Don't waste your time or your money renting *ein Auto* in Berlin. The public transport system will get you everywhere you want; if you're out very late, you can grab a cab to get back to your hotel. The only time a car may come in useful is if you want to explore the surrounding countryside. Both **Hertz** and **Avis** have offices at Budapester Strasse, close to Bahnhof Zoo. Avis is at Budapester Strasse 41 (☎ **030/230-9370**) and Hertz at Budapester Strasse 39 (☎ **030/262-1053**). The U-Bahn for both is Zoologischer Garten. Liability insurance is required to rent a car but is usually included in the rental charge (check to be sure). A national or international driver's license is required.

Berlin U-Bahn & S-Bahn

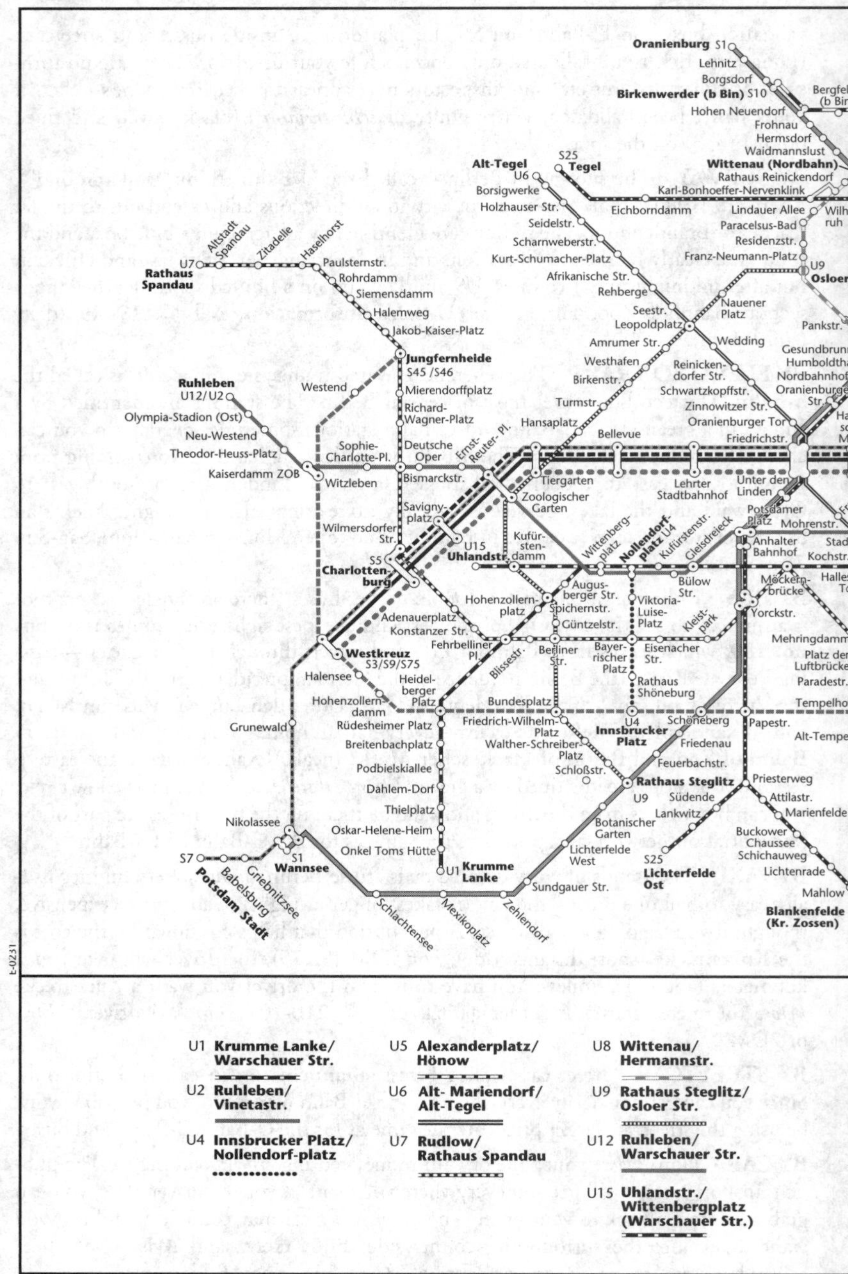

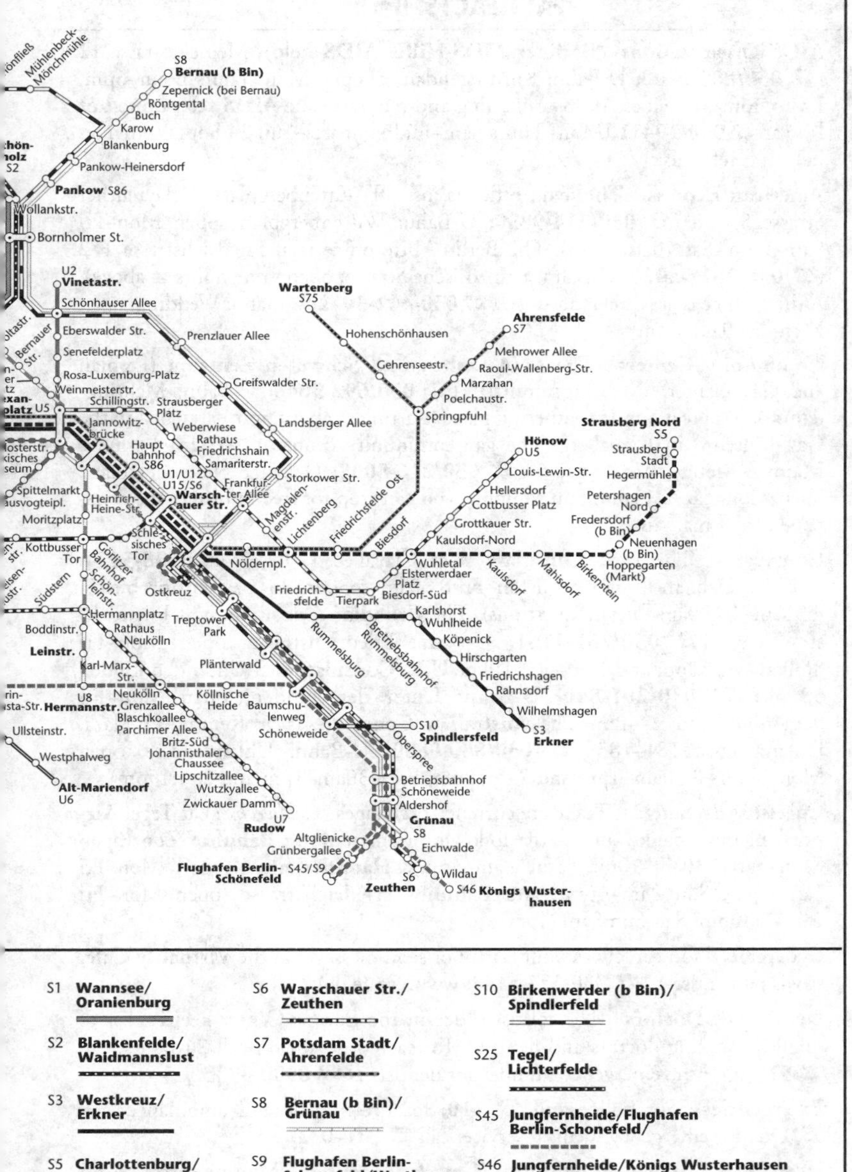

S1 **Wannsee/ Oranienburg**

S2 **Blankenfelde/ Waidmannslust**

S3 **Westkreuz/ Erkner**

S5 **Charlottenburg/ Strausberg Nord**

S6 **Warschauer Str./ Zeuthen**

S7 **Potsdam Stadt/ Ahrenfelde**

S8 **Bernau (b Bln)/ Grünau**

S9 **Flughafen Berlin-Schonefeld/Westkreuz**

S10 **Birkenwerder (b Bln)/ Spindlerfeld**

S25 **Tegel/ Lichterfelde**

S45 **Jungfernheide/Flughafen Berlin-Schonefeld/**

S46 **Jungfernheide/Königs Wusterhausen**

S75 **Westkreuz/ Wartenberg**

FAST FACTS: Berlin

AIDS Organizations **Berliner AIDS-Hilfe (AIDS help),** Meinekestrasse 12 (☎ **030/885-6400;** U-Bahn: Kurfürstendamm; open Mon–Thurs noon–6pm, Fri to 4pm), provides AIDS counseling and referrals. The **AIDS telephone hot line** at ☎ **030/19411** (Mon–Thurs 8am–midnight, Fri–Sun 24 hours) provides help and referrals.

American Express The main office is just off Wittenbergplatz at Bayreuther Strasse 37–38 (☎ **030/214-9830;** U-Bahn: Wittenbergplatz; open Mon–Fri 9am–6pm, Sat 10am–1pm). The Berlin-Mitte office is at Friedrichstrasse 172 (☎ **030/2017-4025;** U-Bahn: Französische Strasse; open same hours as above). A third office is at Müllerstrasse 16 (☎ **030/462-3072;** U-Bahn: Wedding; open Mon–Fri 9am–6pm).

Community Centers The **AHA-Lesben und Schwulen Zentrum** (Lesbian and Gay Center), Mehringdamm 61 (☎ **030/692-3648;** U-Bahn: Mehringdamm), is a great Sunday gathering place (starting at about 5pm) attached to the Gay Museum in Kreuzberg. The gay community center in western Berlin is **Mann-o-Meter,** Motzstrasse 5 (☎ **030/216-8008;** U-Bahn: Nollendorfplatz; open Mon–Sat 5–11pm, Sun to 9pm); you can stop for free information, newspapers, and magazines.

Consulates The **U.S. Consulate** is at Clayallee 170 (☎ **030/238-5174;** U-Bahn: Dahlem-Dorf; open Mon–Fri 8:30am–5:30pm for passport problems, 8:30am–10:30am for visa questions). The **Canadian Consulate** is at Friedrichstrasse 95 (☎ **030/261-1161;** U-Bahn: Friedrichstrasse; open Mon–Fri 8:30am–12:30pm and 1:30–5pm). The **U.K. Consulate** is at Unter den Linden 32–34 (☎ **030/201-840;** U-Bahn: Unter den Linden; open Mon–Fri 9am–noon and 2–4pm. The **Australian Consulate** is at Kempinski Plaza, Uhlandstrasse 181–183 (☎ **030/880-0880;** U-Bahn: Uhlandstrasse; open Mon–Thurs 8:30am–1pm and 2–5:30pm, Fri 8:30am–1pm and 2–4:15pm).

Currency Exchange There are currency exchanges (*Geldwechsel*) at **Tegel Airport,** in most banks, and at the following train stations: **Bahnhof Zoo** (open Mon–Sat 7:30am–10pm, Sun 8am–4pm), **Hauptbahnhof** (open Mon–Fri 7am–6pm, Sun 8am–4pm), and **Bahnhof Friedrichstrasse** (open Mon–Fri 7am–7:30pm, Sat–Sun 8am–4pm).

Cybercafe You can check your e-mail or send messages at the **Virtuality Café,** Lewishamstrasse 1 (☎ 030/327-5143; www.vrcafe.de).

Dentists & Doctors The tourist office in the Europa-Center keeps a list of English-speaking doctors and dentists. To reach a doctor on call 24 hours, call ☎ **310-031;** the emergency number for dentists is ☎ **8900-4333.**

Emergencies For police, call ☎ **110;** for fire brigade and ambulance, call ☎ **112;** for emergency medical service, call ☎ **310-031.**

Hot Lines **Schwulenberatung (Gay Counseling),** Mommsenstrasse 45 (☎ **030/3270-3040;** S-Bahn: Botanischer Garten; open Wed 3–5pm), offers free information, counseling, and therapy for every aspect of gay life; its phone helpline at ☎ **030/19446** is open Wednesday 5 to 8pm and Tuesday and Thursday 3 to 6pm. **Lesbian Advice and Counseling** at ☎ **030/615-7596** (Wed 7–9pm) or **030/215-2000** (Tues, Thurs 6–9pm, Fri 2–5pm) is a service organization dedicated to helping lesbians.

Country & City Codes

The **country code** for Germany is **49.** The **city code** for Berlin is **30;** use this code if you're calling from outside Germany. If you're within Germany but not in Berlin, use **030.** If you're calling within Berlin, simply leave off the code and dial only the regular phone number.

Magazines & Newspapers These magazines and periodicals are available at many gay bars. ***Siegesaüle* (Victory Column),** the largest gay city magazine in Europe, is published monthly for gays and lesbians. It has feature stories and is good for current gay Berlin gossip and listings, as is the bimonthly ***Die Andere Welt* (The Other World).** ***Sergej,*** another monthly, covers the gay male bar and club scene. News, facts, and calendar listings for Berlin, Hamburg, and Frankfurt can be found in the paper ***Gay Express.*** The magazine ***Hinnwerk*** covers the gay scene in all northern Germany. And ***First*** is a Germany-wide general-interest gay and lesbian newspaper.

Telephone Some telephones operate with coins—a local call costs 20 pfennig for the first 90 seconds; phones in restaurants and shops usually charge 50 pfennig. Other phones accept only **Telefonkarten** (telephone cards), which you can purchase in 12DM and 50DM denominations at any post office. You can also make long-distance calls from post offices. Berlin phone numbers may have from 5 to 8 digits.

2 Pillow Talk

You shouldn't have any trouble finding a hotel room in Berlin: There are currently 45,000 beds, with another 13,000 being added. In fact, there's a bit of a glut. Prices are generally less than in other major cities, but also check to see if the larger hotels offer special seasonal or weekend rates or a discount for longer stays. If you're traveling as a couple and want a double bed, ask for it. This is a liberal city and nobody will blink an eye. Breakfast (*Frühstuck*) is almost always included in the rates and typically consists of rolls (*Brötchen*), butter and jam, cheese, and cold cuts. Larger hotels often have buffets that include fresh fruit, yogurt, and cereal. English is spoken at all the hotels on this list.

My goal has been to give you the widest selection of choices in central areas. There are several top-notch gay or gay-friendly hotels and an excellent women-only hotel, plus luxury hotels, landmark hotels, small neighborhood hotels, and two modern hotels that show off the best in contemporary hotel design. Smaller bed-and-breakfast pensions are a time-honored tradition in Berlin; they're cheaper than hotels and have an intimacy no larger hotel can offer.

If you arrive in Berlin without a hotel room or the ones I've listed are full, the hotel service in **Mann-O-Meter,** Motzstrasse 5 (☎ **030/216-8008;** U-Bahn: Nollendorfplatz; open Mon–Sat 5–11pm, Sun to 9pm), can help you with gay choices. Ditto **Movin' Queer Berlin,** Liegnitzer Strasse 5 (☎ **030/618-6955;** U-Bahn: Görlitzer Bahnhof; open Mon–Fri 10am–4pm), another gay/lesbian travel service. Or you can go to the main **Tourist Information Office** in the Europa-Center, close to Bahnhof Zoo (entrance on Budapester Strasse); for 5DM ($2.75) they'll find you a room.

The prices quoted below include tax and service charge. They were correct as of press time but may go up a few marks during the lifetime of this edition.

WESTERN BERLIN

Alsterhof Ringhotel Berlin. Augsburger Strasse 5, D-10789 Berlin. ☎ **030/212-420.** Fax 030/218-3949. www.top-hotels.de/alsterhof. 195 units. MINIBAR TV TEL. 290–390DM ($161–$217) double. Rates include breakfast. AE, DC, MC, V. Garage parking 20DM ($11). U-Bahn: Bahnhof Zoo.

As it's just a few minutes walk from Bahnhof Zoo and the Ku-Damm, location is this hotel's greatest asset. But there's a kind of bland corporate feel to the place, perhaps because it's part of Germany's largest hotel chain and seeks to attract the widest possible clientele. If you're in Berlin on business, need a full-service hotel in a central location, and aren't looking for anything remotely gay or unique, this will do just fine. The rooms are comfortable and quiet and have lots of amenities though aren't particularly distinguished. All have trouser presses, safes, two phones (one in the bath), and hair dryers. On the sixth floor are a pool and sauna. There's a good breakfast buffet.

✪ **Arco Hotel.** Geisbergstrasse 30, 10777 Berlin. ☎ **030/235-1480.** Fax 030/211-3387. E-mail arco-hotel@t-online.de. 21 units. TV TEL. 120–170DM ($67–$94) double. Rates include breakfast. AE, DC, MC, V. U-Bahn: Wittenbergplatz.

The very gay-friendly Arco recently moved to this four-story turn-of-the-century building on a quiet street near the Ku-Damm. They renovated the entire structure and added a new wing, so it all has a fresh, clean look. The large doubles have high windows and are furnished with light-wood modern furniture; two street-facing rooms have balconies; and rooms on the ground floor look out into the garden. Some rooms on the top floors have a sitting area. There's no elevator, however. All the baths have showers; the 8 rooms in the new wing have hair dryers. One of the nicest features is the airy breakfast room, which looks out on a courtyard garden (you can eat outside in warm weather). The buffet breakfast includes bread, cereal, yogurt, cheese, cold cuts, juice, and excellent coffee. The English-speaking staff is friendly and helpful.

✪ **Artemisia.** Brandenburgischestrasse 18, 10707 Berlin. ☎ **030/873-8905** or 030/873-6373. Fax 030/861-8653. 9 units, 6 with bathroom. TV TEL. 170DM ($94) double without bathroom, 220DM ($122) double with bathroom. Breakfast buffet 10DM ($6). AE, DC, MC, V. U-Bahn: Konstanzerstrasse.

Located on the top floors of a large Berlin apartment block in Wilmersdorf, Artemisia is an excellent choice for lesbians (no men allowed). The rooms are large, light, and free of frou-frou but still have a warm feminine ambience heightened by splashes of color. Bold contemporary abstract paintings offset the pristine white walls in the public spaces. All rooms have showers; you can save money by renting one of the rooms sharing a toilet. The feeling throughout is one of restful repose. Best of all: There's a private roof terrace with wonderful views over Berlin; this becomes a gathering spot on warm afternoons and evenings.

✪ **Bleibtreu Hotel.** Bleibtreustrasse 31, 10707 Berlin. ☎ **030/3088-4740.** Fax 030/308-8474-444. www.savoy-hotel.com. E-mail info@bleibtreu.com. 60 units. MINIBAR TV TEL. 289–389DM ($161–$216) double; 499–699DM ($277–$388) suite. Rates include breakfast. AE, DC, MC, V. U-Bahn: Bahnhof Zoo. S-Bahn: Savignyplatz.

The ultra-cool Bleibtreu, on a sidestreet off the Ku-Damm, is one of Berlin's newest and most health-conscious hotels. If you're looking for chic, contemporary luxury combined with state-of-the-art technology, this is the best place in Berlin to find it. The rooms aren't particularly large but are beautifully designed and furnished. The furniture is hypoallergenic, and no chemicals of any kind are used for cleaning. The stylish bathrooms have tiled walls and tub and sinks of carved stone. The lights are operated by your room card or by remote control, the phones are wireless, there's a fax in every suite, and electric awnings are on the street-facing windows. You could spend hours just

Hey, Big Spender

If you've finally come into your trust fund and want to blow a wad on a Berlin hotel, there are many deluxe places that'll be more than glad to bend over backward for you. Be prepared to drop a minimum of $200 a night for a double at any of them.

The **Kempinski Hotel Bristol** and **Hotel Adlon,** two of the toniest, are listed in full below. Here are some others where you'll feel like a princess, no matter what sex you are:

Berlin Hilton, Mohrenstrasse 30, D-10117 Berlin (☎ **800/445-8667** in the U.S. and Canada, or 030/202-30; fax 030/2023-4269; www.hilton.com; U-Bahn Stadtmitte).

Four Seasons, Charlottenstrasse 49, D-10117 Berlin (☎ **800/332-3442** in the U.S., or 030/203-38; fax 030/2033-6166; www.fourseasons.com; e-mail kerstin.pundt@fourseasons.com; U-Bahn: Französische Strasse).

Grand Hotel Esplanade, Lützowufer 15, D-10785 Berlin (☎ **030/254-780;** fax 030/265-1171; www.esplanade.de; e-mail info@esplanade.de; U-Bahn: Kurfürstenstrasse, Nollendorfplatz, or Wittenbergplatz).

Schlosshotel Vier Jahreszeiten Berlin, Brahms-strasse 10, D-14193 Berlin-Grunewald (☎ **030/895-840;** fax 030/8958-4800; www.lhw.com/berlin/vierjahrenszeiten.html).

playing with the gizmos. Of course there's a "Wellness Center," where you can take a pore-cleansing sauna. Restaurant 31, to one side of the small lobby, lays out a healthy breakfast buffet. Its outdoor dining area sits on a bed of blue and white marbles.

Connection Cityhotel. Fuggerstrasse 33, 10777 Berlin. ☎ **030/217-7028.** Fax 030/217-7030. www.Connection-berlin.com. E-mail hotel@connection-berlin.com. 16 units, 3 with shower only. MINIBAR TV TEL. 140DM ($61) double without shower, 180DM (100) double with shower. Rates include breakfast. AE, MC, V. U-Bahn: Wittenbergplatz.

This gay-only hotel close to the gay center around Nollendorfplatz is used mostly by men, but women are welcome. The new owners took over what had been the Bols Hotel and began a complete refurbishment that'll be finished by the time this book hits the shelves. The large high-ceilinged rooms have been spiffed up with stylish contemporary furnishings. If you're into it, note that a regular leather contingent stays here. Downstairs, rented separately to groups for 800DM ($444) a night, is a new fetish room fitted out with so much paraphernalia it could be an S/M museum. It gave me the creeps, but if you want to check into a cage, here's your chance.

✪ **Hotel Brandenburger Hof.** Eislebener Strasse 14, 10789 Berlin. ☎ **030/214-050.** Fax 030/2140-5100. www.brandenburger-hof.com. E-mail info@brandenburger-hof.com. 86 units. AC MINIBAR TV TEL. 340–455DM ($189–$253) double. Rates include breakfast. AE, DC, MC, V. Garage 20DM ($11). U-Bahn: Kurfüstendamm or Augsburger Strasse. S-Bahn: Zoologischer Garten.

From the Le Corbusier chairs in the dazzling white-and-metal lobby to the Bauhaus fabrics and leather chairs in the rooms, this is a hotel where stylish luxury is a way of life. Occupying a turn-of-the-century mansion just a few steps from the Ku-Damm, the hotel opened in 1991. You don't have to love Bauhaus to appreciate the rooms, but that style, characterized by a sleek leather, wood, and chrome elegance, is used throughout. The sumptuous bathrooms are tiled in granite and have hair dryers.

Western Berlin Accommodations & Dining

Mierendorffplatz
Kaiserin-Augusta-Allee
Schlossgarten Charlottenburg
Mierendorffstrasse
Quedlinburgstrasse
Spree
Alt-Moabit
Schloss Bridge
Gotzkowsky Bridge
Levetzowstra.
Helmholtzstrasse
Charlottenburg Palace
Luisenplatz
Dovestrasse
Franklinstrasse
Spandauer-Damm
Otto-Suhr-Allee
Dove Bridge
Salzufer
Einsteinufer
Danckelmannstrasse
Christstrasse
Landwehrkanal
Schlossstrasse
Rich.-Wagner-Strasse
Magnus Hirschfeld Memorial
Cauerstrasse
Marchstrasse
Bachst
TIERGARTEN
Zillestrasse
Deutsche Oper Berlin
Ernst-Reuter-Platz
Strasse des 17. Juni
Kaiser-Friedrich-Strasse
Bismarckstrasse
Kaiserdamm
Krumme Strasse
Schillerstrasse
Wilmersdorfer
BAHNHOF ZOOLOGISCHER GARTEN
Knesebeckstr.
Hardenbergstrasse
Goethestrasse
Schlüterstr.
Pestalozzistrasse
Kantstrasse
Hardenbergpla
Savignyplatz
Kantst
CHARLOTTENBURG
Lewishamstr.
SAVIGNYPLATZ
Joachimstalerstrasse
Emperor William Memorial Church
Rönnestrasse
Sybelstrasse
Leibzitzstr.
Uhlandstr.
WESTKREUZ
Damaschkestrasse
Kurfürstendamm
Brandenburgische Str.
Lietzenburgerstr.
Ranke-platz
Kurfürstendamm
Konstanzerstr.
Pariser Strasse
Bundesallee
Seesener Strasse
bornerstrasse
Düsseldorfer Strasse
Hohenzollernplatz
Nachod strasse
Westfälische Strasse
Sächsische Strasse
Pauls-
Hohenzollernstrasse
To Dahlem
E-0232
BERLIN
Western Berlin
ACCOMMODATIONS
Alsterhof Ringhotel Berlin 18
Arco Hotel 25
Artemisia 13
Bleibtreu Hotel 14
Connection Cityhotel 27
Grand Hotel Esplanade 23
Hotel Brandenburger Hof 19
Hotel Charlottenburger Hof 2
Hotel Domus 15
Hotel Wilmersdorf 20
Kempinski Hotel Bristol 8
Pension Niebuhr 12
Pension Nürnberger Eck 24
Savoy Hotel 6
Schlosshotel Vier Jahreszeiten Berlin 3
Sorat Art'otel Berlin 17
Tom's House 33

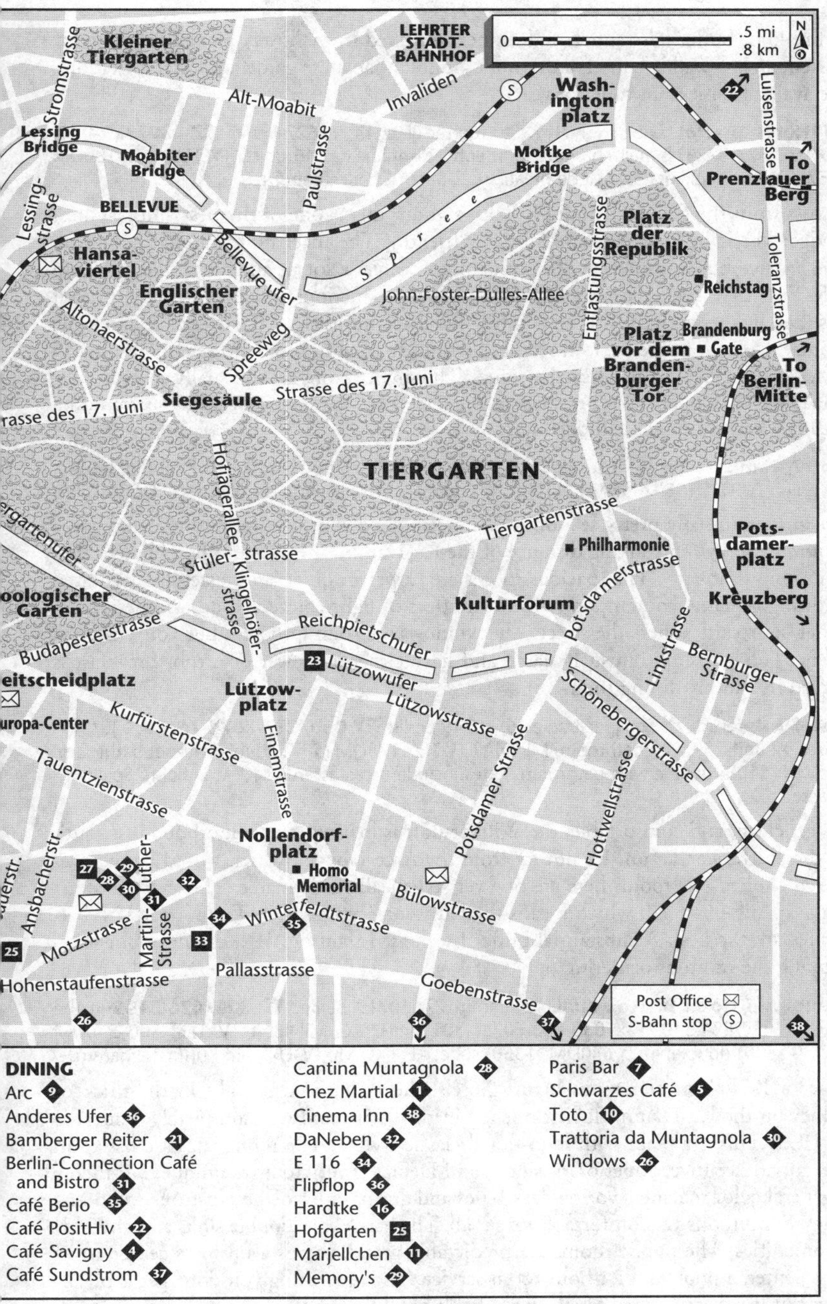

Kleiner Tiergarten
LEHRTER STADT-BAHNHOF
0
.5 mi
.8 km
N
Stromstrasse
Alt-Moabit
Invaliden
Wash-ington platz
Lessing Bridge
Moabiter Bridge
Paulstrasse
Moltke Bridge
Luisenstrasse
To Prenzlauer Berg
Lessing-strasse
BELLEVUE
Spree
Platz der Republik
Hansa-viertel
Bellevue ufer
Englischer Garten
John-Foster-Dulles-Allee
Entlastungsstrasse
Reichstag
Toleranzstrasse
Altonaerstrasse
Spreeweg
Platz vor dem Branden-burger Tor
Brandenburg Gate
To Berlin-Mitte
Siegesäule
Strasse des 17. Juni
rasse des 17. Juni
Hofjägerallee
TIERGARTEN
Tiergartenstrasse
Pots-damer-platz
Philharmonie
Stüler- strasse
Potsdamerstrasse
oologischer Garten
Klingelhöfer-strasse
Kulturforum
To Kreuzberg
Budapesterstrasse
Reichpietschufer
Linkstrasse
Bernburger Strasse
eitscheidplatz
Lützowufer
Lützow-platz
Lützowstrasse
Schönebergerstrasse
uropa-Center
Kurfürstenstrasse
Einemstrasse
Potsdamer Strasse
Flottwellstrasse
Tauentzienstrasse
Nollendorf-platz
Homo Memorial
Ansbacherstr.
Martin-Luther-Strasse
Bülowstrasse
Winterfeldtstrasse
Motzstrasse
Pallasstrasse
Hohenstaufenstrasse
Goebenstrasse
Post Office
S-Bahn stop
DINING
Arc 9
Anderes Ufer 36
Bamberger Reiter 21
Berlin-Connection Café and Bistro 31
Café Berio 35
Café PositHiv 22
Café Savigny 4
Café Sundstrom 37
Cantina Muntagnola 28
Chez Martial 1
Cinema Inn 38
DaNeben 32
E 116 34
Flipflop 36
Hardtke 16
Hofgarten 25
Marjellchen 11
Memory's 29
Paris Bar 7
Schwarzes Café 5
Toto 10
Trattoria da Muntagnola 30
Windows 26

A breakfast buffet (also lunch and dinner) is served in the lovely plant-filled Wintergarten, a glass-walled conservatory built around a Japanese garden. Special lower rates are available at certain times of year.

✪ **Hotel Charlottenburger Hof.** Stuttgarter Platz 14, 10627 Berlin. ☎ **030/329-070.** Fax 030/323-3723. E-mail charlottenburger.hof@t-online.de. 46 units. TV TEL. 120–180DM ($67–$100) double. Rates include breakfast. S-Bahn: Charlottenburg.

Across from the Charlottenburg S-Bahn station, this is one of the best and brightest budget hotels in town. It's also very gay-friendly. The nice thing about it is that it's inexpensive but unusually well decorated and offers a lot of amenities, like in-room safes, hair dryers, and laundry facilities. Miró reproductions and a constructivist motif inspired by the work of Russian painter Wassily Kandinsky set the overall design tone. Primary colors of blue, yellow, red, and white are used in some of the contemporary-styled rooms, six of which have balconies. The single rooms are unusually comfortable. You're given a voucher for breakfast at the Café Voltaire downstairs. The surrounding area is what you might call bustling.

Hotel Domus. Uhlandstrasse 49, 10719 Berlin. ☎ **030/880-3440.** Fax 030/8803-4444. 73 units. TV TEL. 198–265DM ($110–$147) double. Rates include breakfast. AE, DC, MC, V.

Set in an unusually pretty section of Wilmersdorf, down the street from St. Ludwig's Church and within walking distance of the Ku-Damm, this modern hotel has a calm, appealing simplicity. The spacious rooms are carpeted, quiet, and tastefully decorated with high-quality contemporary furniture (lots of light-colored wood). Some face an inner courtyard, others the street. The windows are soundproofed, but you can open them. The baths are unusually large and have either a shower or a tub. Breakfast is served in a lovely dining room.

Hotel Wilmersdorf. Schaperstrasse 36, 10719 Berlin. ☎ **030/217-7074-76.** Fax 030/217-7077. 42 units, 39 with bathroom. MINIBAR TV TEL. 175DM ($97) double without bathroom, 195DM ($108) double with bathroom. Rates include breakfast. AE, MC, V. U-Bahn: Spichernstrasse.

Large, clean, and comfortable, the Wilmersdorf is in a quiet neighborhood just south of the Kurfürstendamm. It's not far from the Arco (above), which would be my preferred choice. The rooms here are fine yet stylistically indefinable. The showers aren't glass- or tub-enclosed, which means the bathroom can get wet. The rooms with balconies are the best. A substantial buffet breakfast is laid out in a dining room overlooking the rooftops of Berlin.

Kempinski Hotel Bristol. Kurfürstendamm 27, 10719 Berlin. ☎ **800/426-3135** in the U.S. or 030/884-340. Fax 030/883-6075. 301 units. AC MINIBAR TV TEL. 390–540DM ($217–$300) double; from 630DM ($350) suite. AE, DC, MC, V. U-Bahn: Kurfürstendamm.

One of Berlin's most famous luxury hotels, the Kempinski is right in the thick of things on the Ku-Damm. It first opened in the 1950s and was completely renovated in 1991. This is a place with high-toned classic styling. The room rates are based on category: Executive, Superior, Business, and Deluxe. Every room is unique, but there's a general color scheme favoring dark blues and greens enlivened by lustrous wood finishes. Sumptuous yet comfortable says it all. The baths have double sinks and all kinds of amenities. The public rooms are predictably grand; there's a business center, a fitness center, a pool, and 24-hour room service. The only thing you don't get is breakfast, but if you can afford to stay here that'll hardly matter.

✪ **Pension Niebuhr.** Niebuhrstrasse 74, D-10629 Berlin. ☎ **030/324-9595.** Fax 030/324-8021. 12 units, 7 with bathroom. 120DM ($67) double without bathroom, 170DM ($94) double with bathroom. Rates include breakfast. AE, MC, V. S-Bahn: Savignyplatz.

This pleasant gay-friendly pension in Charlottenburg is one of the best deals in Berlin. It's 2 blocks from the S-Bahn and close to gay bars; the price is extremely reasonable; and the owner, Willi Heidasch, is very helpful. The rooms, all on the second floor of a turn-of-the-century apartment building, were renovated in 1994 and have a fresh, modest flair. The furnishings and color schemes are bright and cheerful. The rooms with baths come with TVs and phones; those without baths come with wash basins. Three street-facing rooms boast balconies, and the best single (no. 12) has a nifty loft bed. The rooms facing the courtyard (Hinterhof) can be a bit dark, but they're very quiet. One of the nicest features is that breakfast is brought up to your room.

Pension Nürnberger Eck. Nürnberger Strasse 24a, D-10789 Berlin. ☎ **030/235-1780.** Fax 030/2351-7899. 8 units, 5 with bathroom. TEL. 130DM ($72) double without bathroom, 150DM ($83) double with bathroom. Rates include breakfast. MC, V. U-Bahn: Wittenbergplatz or Augsburger Strasse.

This isn't a gay place, but if you're seeking an atmospheric old-fashioned pension—maybe the kind Christopher Isherwood or Sally Bowles would've stayed in—here it is. It's on the second floor of a building near the Europa-Center. Inside you'll get a glimpse of what old Berlin pensions often looked like: high-ceilinged rooms with heavy doors open off a long, dark hall. The rooms have patterned wallpaper, Oriental rugs, and big pieces of furniture, some reproduction Biedermeier. Though stylistically it's something of a mish-mash, it does convey a comfortable old-world charm. The baths are fine; there's a pleasant breakfast room.

Savoy Hotel. Fasanenstrasse 9–10, D-10623 Berlin. ☎ **800/223-5652** U.S. or 030/311-030. Fax 030/3110-3333. E-mail Info@Savoy-hotels.com. www.savoy-hotels.com. 145 units. MINIBAR TV TEL. 289–389DM ($161–$216) double; 520–900DM ($289–$500) suite. AE, DC, MC, V. U-Bahn: Kurfürstendamm.

The quietly elegant Savoy opened in 1930, about the time *The Blue Angel* first hit the screens. More than a few celebrities have stayed here over the years. It's just a skip from the Ku-Damm, so you can't beat it for location. The recently refurbished lobby is a luxe version of neoclassical styling. All the rooms are decorated uniquely and provide spacious and comfortable accommodation, with unusually large baths. Recently redecorated rooms on the air-conditioned sixth floor are the nicest. Fresh flowers, a sweet left on your pillow at turndown, and overnight shoe-shine service are a few of the special touches you can expect. A faxed edition of the latest *New York Times* will be waiting at your breakfast table if you want it. But speaking of breakfast, you won't get one unless you call and book directly from the hotel. A fitness room with a sauna and solarium completes the picture.

✪ **Sorat Art'otel Berlin.** Joachimstalerstrasse 29, D-10719 Berlin. ☎ **030/884-470.** Fax 030/8844-7700. 133 units. AC MINIBAR TV TEL. 275–395DM ($152–$219) double. Rates include breakfast. AE, DC, MC, V. U-Bahn: Kurfürstendamm.

If you love contemporary art and design or are looking for something really out of the ordinary, you'll appreciate this smart "art hotel" near the Ku-Damm. Designed by artist Wolf Vostell, it was Berlin's first "avant-garde" boutique hotel. The red-and-white 1990s lobby is graced by sleek Italian furniture. The halls are dark but dramatically lit: The room numbers are projected onto the floor in front of the doors, and art installations are set into the walls. The rooms aren't particularly large but are wonderfully modern, with patterned carpeting, red armoires, satin headboard insets, and groovy furniture. Uncompromisingly contemporary art hangs in every room. And the baths are equally fab, with suspended metal sinks, towels hidden behind the mirrors, and sleek hardware. The breakfast, on the other hand, is as filling and "old-fashioned" as you could wish. This isn't a place for every taste, but the unique decor and modern comforts will certainly appeal to design-conscious gays. Special weekend rates can cut the price dramatically.

Tom's House. Eisenacher Strasse 10, D-10777 Berlin. ☎ **030/218-5544.** Fax 030/213-4464. 8 units, sharing 3 toilets and showers. 140–170DM ($75–$94) double. Rates include breakfast. No credit cards. U-Bahn: Nollendorfplatz.

Boys will be boys at Tom's House—especially leather boys, who have been staying at this gay-only pension in the heart of gay Berlin for years. It's right above the famous (and a little worn) Tom's Bar, a landmark for Berlin's leather-and-denim crowd. The large high-ceilinged rooms are surprisingly well furnished, with contemporary leather (what else?) furniture and comfortable beds. Each has a wash basin, but otherwise you have to share toilets and showers. Breakfast is served in a darkish old-fashioned dining room. This is a place where you can do what you want to do—in fact, it's expected.

BERLIN-MITTE

For the locations of the hotels below, see the "Berlin-Mitte" map on p. 307.

Hotel Adlon. Unt er den Linden 77, D-10117 Berlin. ☎ **800/426-3135** U.S. or 030/2261-1111. Fax 030/2261-2222. www.hotel-adlon.de. E-mail adlon@kempenski.com. 337 units. AC MINIBAR TV TEL. 490–660DM ($272–$367) double; from 900DM ($500) suite. AE, DC, MC, V. U-Bahn: Potsdamer Platz or Friedrichstrasse; S-Bahn: Unter den Linden.

In prewar Berlin, the old Adlon, across from the Brandenburg Gate, was the most famous and glamorous hotel in the city. The new Adlon, built on part of the original site and completed in 1997, attempts to recapture the art deco glory of the former one. Everything about it is beautifully done and five-star deluxe; all it lacks is the soul of the original. Gold leaf gleams everywhere, there's an atrium with a stained-glass ceiling, a fountain splashes in the lobby, the woodwork and detailing are superbly crafted—yet it remains a version rather than the real thing. The rooms, however, are beautifully decorated and marvelously swish. I love the huge baths with double sinks. The service is everything you could wish for. The only other thing to wish for is that old Adlon was still around.

Westin Grand Hotel. Friedrichstrasse 158–164, D-10117 Berlin. ☎ **800/937-8461** U.S. or 030/20270. Fax 030/2027-3362. 358 units. AC MINIBAR TV TEL. 295–475DM ($164–$264) double. AE, DC, MC, V. U-Bahn: Franzosische Strasse. S-Bahn: Friedrichstrasse.

One of the last buildings erected in Communist East Berlin was, ironically enough, this five-star luxury hotel. It's a bit too much of everything for my tastes, but if you're interested in paying top dollar for the experience of staying in the newly chic Friedrichstrasse area, the Grand is—well, grand. The finishes throughout are beautiful, and the overall ambience tries to recapture the luxurious Grand Hotel era (dramatic staircases, chandeliers, glass-domed ceiling). There are restaurants, bars, and every amenity you can think of, including 24-hour room service, a fitness center, and a pool.

3 Whet Your Appetite

Berlin offers every kind of international cuisine. The local culinary tradition is fairly basic yet extraordinarily filling. Typical Berlin dishes are grilled or pickled herring with onions, fried potatoes, and bacon; pickled or roast pork (*Schweinefleisch*) or pork knuckles (*Eisbein*) with red cabbage and dumplings; meatballs (*Buletten*) with boiled potatoes; and pea soup (*Erbsensuppe*). A plate with various cold meats is a *Schlacteplatte.* Game like venison, duck, and wild boar appears seasonally; carp and trout are often available. Fancier restaurants often serve what's called *neue Deutsche Küche* (New

German cuisine), which uses the old standbys as a starting point but dolls them up with unusual ingredients and international touches.

Scattered all over town are vendors selling Berlin's classic fast-food snack: Currywurst (sausage with a glob of "curry" sauce) or fried Bratwurst. Grabbing a sausage (oh, you know what I mean) or eating at the stand-up counters of the fast-food snack shops (look for the signs that say IMBISS or SCHNELL-IMBISS) are a good way to save time and money.

You can always get soup, sandwiches, and lighter meals at one of the gay-friendly cafe/bars I've listed after the restaurants. And don't forget that in Germany, afternoon *Kaffee und Kuchen* (coffee and cake) is a time-honored tradition.

The service charge and value-added tax (VAT) are included in restaurant and cafe bills, but rounding out the total bill with an extra amount is expected. If the bill is 7.20DM, for example, round it up to 8DM. If the meal has cost more than 10DM, Berliners generally add a 15% tip.

WESTERN BERLIN

For the locations of the restaurants below, see the "Western Berlin Attractions & Dining" map on pp. 302–303.

✪ **Arc.** Fasanenstrasse 81A. ☎ **030/313-2625.** Reservations recommended for dinner. Main courses 19–33DM ($11–$18). AE, DC, MC, V. Mon–Thurs 10am–midnight, Fri–Sat to 1am (bar daily 10am–2am). U-Bahn: Zoologischer Garten. INTERNATIONAL/GERMAN/FRENCH.

Restaurant, bar, and cafe rolled into one, Arc is one of the nicest gay hangouts in the Ku-Damm area. It's tucked beneath the S-Bahn track at Fasanenstrasse, which adds to the "good vibrations." This is a great place to come for an English breakfast (bacon, eggs, and beans); it also offers a huge "Lovers" breakfast with champagne. For lunch, maybe you'll want just a bowl of potato soup with sausage or one of the many salads. Dinner? Homemade pasta (spätzle with cheese or rigatoni with pesto), roast beef, duck with cassis sauce, and tofu schnitzel are a few offerings. Everything is made with organically grown ingredients. There are daily specials, the staff is friendly, and there's outdoor seating in good weather. Club Banana, its cocktail bar, is next door (see "In the Heat of the Night" below).

✪ **Bamberger Reiter.** Regensburgerstrasse 7. ☎ **030/218-4282.** Main courses 52–60DM ($29–$33); fixed-price menu 145–185DM ($81–$103). AE, DC, MC, V. Tues– Sat 6pm–1am. Reservations required. U-Bahn: Spichernstrasse. CONTINENTAL.

One of the top choices for lovers of great food, Bamberger Reiter is small (maximum 35 diners) and rustic, with parquet floors, flowers, and lots of antiques. It opened in the early 1980s and is housed in a 100-year-old wine tavern two stops south of Bahnhof Zoo. Quality isn't an issue—everything is first-rate. The chef's *neue Deutsche Küche* approach extends to French, German, and Austrian dishes. The menu changes daily to take advantage of what's fresh and in season. That might mean cream of asparagus soup, roulade of quail, or bass with Riesling sauce. Vladimir Horowitz enjoyed the fresh Dover sole. If you want to splurge, you can safely do it here.

Cantina Muntagnola. Fuggerstrasse 33. ☎ **030/218-9179.** Main courses 21–37DM ($12–$21). AE, DC, MC, V. Daily 4pm–3am. U-Bahn: Wittenbergplatz. ITALIAN.

The same family that runs the Trattoria da Muntagnola a few doors down the street (see below) also runs this excellent cantina. The difference is that the trattoria serves traditional Italian fare, while the cantina cooks up creative versions of *nuova cucina italiana* (new Italian cooking). The menu changes daily. Pastas may include fusilli with lamb and pecorino cheese sauce or black tagliatelle in crayfish sauce. Stuffed smoked salmon fillet, lamb oven-baked in pastry crust, and beef with porcinis also make regular appearances. Fuggerstrasse is in the heart of the gay village.

✪ **Chez Martial.** Otto-Suhr-Allee 44. ☎ **030/341-1033.** Reservations essential. Main courses 28–31DM ($16–$17). No credit cards. Daily 6–11:30pm. U-Bahn: Richard-Wagner-Platz. FRENCH.

Top-quality products and superlative cooking have helped establish Chez Martial, in Charlottenberg, as one of Berlin's most popular French restaurants. Everyone is welcome in this intimate crowded bistro; it's not a jeans sort of place, but neither is it overly formal. Every dish is freshly prepared, so be ready to wait (while savoring a bottle of good French wine). If the weather is fine, try to get a table outside. The menu changes daily, but there are always about 15 main courses like fresh Atlantic fish, poultry, lamb, beef, and perhaps couscous. The fish soup, cooked in its own "foam," is exquisite. The lamb, served with polenta, is so tender it practically melts in your mouth. For dessert, try the chocolate or pumpernickel mousse.

Hardtke. Meinekestrasse 27A. ☎ **30/881-9827.** Reservations required. Main courses 15–30DM ($8–$17). No credit cards. Sun–Thurs 11am–midnight, Fri–Sat 11am–1am. U-Bahn: Kurfürstendamm. BERLINER.

Hardtke's, near the Ku-Damm, has been around for what seems like forever, and its continued success stems from the fact that it serves vast portions of good, traditional Berlin fare. The specialties include fresh black pudding and liverwurst on sauerkraut with potatoes, thick pea soup, and pig's knuckles. The wooden benches, chairs, and tables go well with this kind of macho food.

Hofgarten. Regensburger 5 (at the corner of Anspacher Strasse). ☎ **030/218-1883.** Main courses 17–32DM ($9–$18). AE, DC, MC, V. Daily 6pm–midnight. U-Bahn: Luise-Platz. FRENCH/GERMAN.

This recently opened corner restaurant is a 5-minute walk from the gay-friendly Arco Hotel. The decor is unobtrusively hip, with dark mahogany wainscoting, muted yellow walls, and interesting contemporary paintings. Actors and folks in the film business like it. The cooking is New German, the menu changes every 2 or 3 days, and only seasonally fresh local products are used. The soups are inventive and delicious: Recent offerings included squash with cream and kohlrabi with fresh tuna fish. Free-range chicken dishes are usually available, including one with port-wine sauce, and the lamb with rosemary, roast potatoes, and celery mousse is excellent. You can also get fresh fish and vegetarian dishes like asparagus with mushrooms and chicory in orange-gorgonzola sauce with noodles. The portions are large, but save room for the white chocolate mousse on blueberry coulis.

Marjellchen. Mommsenstrasse 9. ☎ **030/883-2676.** Reservations recommended. Main courses 20–40DM ($11–$22). AE, DC, MC, V. Mon–Sat 5pm–midnight. U-Bahn: Uhlandstrasse. EAST PRUSSIAN.

Ramona Azzaro, founder of this well-known restaurant, was born in Rome, but her grandmother came from East Prussia (where *marjellchen* means "young girl"). The dishes served are inspired by granny's old East Prussian recipes. For an appetizer you can try homemade aspic, smoked Pomeranian goose, or fried cockerel eggs. *Beetenbartsch* is a delicious red-beet soup with beef strips and sour cream, and there's also a scrumptious potato soup with shrimps and bacon. Main courses are something of an adventure: stewed pickled beef with green dumplings and stewed cabbage, smoked ham in cream sauce, pork kidneys in sweet-and-sour cream sauce, or roast of elk with chanterelles. There are also vegetarian dishes, like broccoli soufflé.

Paris Bar. Kantstrasse 152. ☎ **030/313-8052.** Main courses 29–45DM ($16–$25). AE. Daily noon–1am. U-Bahn: Uhlandstrasse. FRENCH.

The Paris Bar, between Savignyplatz and the Memorial Church, is a French restaurant that's a Berlin institution. A favorite hangout for artists and intellectuals, it has been around since the end of the last war and looks like the kind of unpretentious working-class bistro you used to see in Paris. If you're in the mood for onion soup, homemade pâté, escargots, or salade niçoise, go for it. They make a good omelet with fines herbes. Main courses are listed as *plats du jour* and change often. You might find asparagus with Hollandaise sauce, ham, and new potatoes; chicken breasts with mushrooms; braised veal; or grilled foie gras.

Toto. Bleibtreustrasse 55. ☎ **030/312-5449.** Main courses 14–38DM ($8–$21). EU. Daily noon–2am. S-Bahn: Savignyplatz. ITALIAN.

Toto (the trattoria, not Dorothy's dog) sits on the corner of Pestalozzistrasse, just down the street from Prinz Eisenherz, Berlin's premier gay bookstore. It's a good place to sit out on a warm afternoon and have lunch. (The interior, with wooden tables and benches, is nothing fancy.) The chef is Italian and knows his stuff. You can get a good plate of spaghetti with olive oil or spicy penne all'arrabiata. The bean soup is filling. Fresh fish, available every Tuesday and Friday (market days), includes grilled salmon with butter and lemon and grilled crayfish cooked in oil. There's a nice selection of Italian wines and aperitifs.

Trattoria da Muntagnola. Fuggerstrasse 27. ☎ **030/211-6642.** Main courses 15–36DM ($8–$20). AE, DC, MC, V. Reservations recommended. U-Bahn: Wittenbergplatz. ITALIAN.

Gays and lesbians are regulars at this popular Italian place. It's casually rustic, with braids of garlic hanging from the beamed ceiling, and can be a bit smoky. The menu is huge and the cooking generally reliable. Some of the pastas are made on the premises. The lasagna, if it's one of the daily specials, is worth trying. There are also all manner of meat dishes and some good seafood (calamari and scampi grilled or cooked with radicchio and rosemary in white-wine sauce). The pizzas are good too, particularly the Pizza della Mamma with bacon and Parma ham.

BERLIN-MITTE

For the locations of the restaurants below, see the "Berlin-Mitte" map on p. 307.

La Riva. Spreeufer 2. ☎ **030/242-5185.** Reservations recommended. Main courses 18–40DM ($10–$22). AE, MC, V. Mon–Fri 11am–11pm, Sat–Sun to midnight. U-Bahn: Klosterstrasse. ITALIAN/SEAFOOD.

One of the prettiest buildings in the restored Nikolaiviertel (St. Nicholas Quarter), just south of Alexanderplatz, is the Ephraim-Palais, a richly ornamented 1765 mansion. Part of it is a museum and part is occupied by this Italian-influenced restaurant, which sits right next to the Spree River. You'll want a table outside if the weather is fine. And you'll probably want to order fish, since that's what they do best. Choices include salmon with white-wine sauce; swordfish with fresh tomatoes, onions, and basil; and grilled or baked crayfish. If you simply must have pasta, that's available as well. They have a well-stocked wine cellar.

Restaurant Borchardt. Französische Strasse 47. ☎ **030/2038-7117.** Reservations recommended. Main courses 40–50DM ($22–$28); lunch specials 21DM ($12). AE, V. Daily noon–midnight. U-Bahn: Französische Strasse. FRENCH/INTERNATIONAL.

It's just amazing how unremittingly upscale dining has become in certain areas of formerly Communist East Berlin. You can recognize Borchardt, directly across from the Gendarmenmarkt, by its blood-colored awning and red sandstone facade. Inside it's huge, cool, spare, and elegant, with marble, gilding, and a bit of French moue attitude. The fashionable cell-phoners who eat here apparently like it that way. If you like it rich, go for the foie gras fillet with caramelized onions or the tender chicken breast stuffed with morels and sauced with cream and herbs. The humble carp is cooked in Riesling and finished with champagne. The best bet for lunch is one of the fixed-price specials.

Vau. Jägerstrasse 54–55. ☎ **030/202-9730.** Reservations essential. Main courses 28–38DM ($16–$21); set menus 119–179DM ($66–$99). AE, DC, MC, V. Mon–Sat noon–2:30pm and 7–10:30pm. INTERNATIONAL.

This sleek and unabashedly upscale gastronomic showcase opened near the Gendarmenmarkt in early 1997 and has already earned a Michelin star. The cooking has been accurately described as "upper-class free style." Vau is a very dress-up kind of place that's certainly not gay-oriented, but if you want a super-fancy lunch or dinner with impeccable service (including a sommelier), you'll find it here in spades. The menu choices are deftly prepared and can be surprisingly unfussy: classic Wiener schnitzel, loin of lamb with ratatouille, fennel-and-herb polenta (recommended), and salmon steak with lemon butter. You can sample it all with the three- to six-course set menus. All the power-eating and power-playing takes place in a long rather narrow room with an arched ceiling—everything is very precise, very modern, and very beautiful.

✪ **Zur Letzten Instanz.** Waisenstrasse 14–16. ☎ **030/242-5528.** Main courses 14–24DM ($8–$13). AE, DC, MC, V. Mon–Sat noon–1am, Sun noon–11pm. S-Bahn: Klosterstrasse. BERLINER.

There are now several trendy new restaurants in the former East Berlin, but over all the others I'd recommend this place, which happens to be Berlin's oldest restaurant, dating from 1525. It occupies two floors of a much-restored baroque building not far from Nikolaikirche, and the interior (and the menu) is as simple and atmospheric as you could wish. Main courses include old Berlin staples like grilled herring, meatballs, braised lamb knuckles with green beans and dumplings, pork-salmon escalope with carrots and boiled potatoes, and braised beef dumplings and red cabbage. For dessert, try the chocolate-covered pancakes filled with blueberries, vanilla ice cream, and whipped cream. They don't skimp on the portions. It's not nouvelle, but that's the point.

Zur Nolle. Beneath the arches of Friedrichstrasse S-Bahn station (S-Bahnbogen 30). ☎ **030/208-2655.** Main courses 13–20DM ($7–$11). AE, V. Mon–Thurs 11am–midnight, Fri–Sat to 1am. S-Bahn: Friedrichstrasse. GERMAN.

There's just something *so Berlin* about places built under S-Bahn tracks. A hundred years ago, Zur Nolle was a busy working-class beer hall. It closed in 1968 (GDR years) but reopened in capitalist-crazy 1993 as a bit of "Old Berlin" memorabilia with light brick walls and art deco accessories. The menu is unpretentious and the cooking reliable. Try the jacket potatoes with herb butter or herring/yogurt/apple/onion fillings. Vegetarian offerings include vegetable lasagna and roasted broccoli with a sharp cheese served on penne. For old-time's sake, I'd recommend the homemade meatballs, which come with a variety of sauces, spices, and additions (fried egg, bacon/onions/paprika, fresh mushrooms), or the roast bratwurst. Wash it (or them) down with a cold foamy beer.

GAY CAFE/BARS

Berlin is a city filled with cafes. These are places to go for breakfast (a fairly recent dining phenomenon in Berlin), a cup of coffee and a piece of *Kuchen*, or a light meal or snack. The cafes are also bars, so you can get a beer or a glass of wine as well.

The following is a list of gay or gay-friendly places in western Berlin and the Prenzlauer Berg neighborhood in eastern Berlin where gays and lesbians like to hang out, eat, read the paper, schmooze, write in their journals, and generally relax.

WESTERN BERLIN Frequented by gays and lesbians, ✪ **Anderes Ufer,** Hauptstrasse 157 (☎ **030/784-1578;** U-Bahn: Kleistpark; open daily 11am–2am), has been around since 1977 and is famous for its late-night breakfasts and afternoon cakes and coffee. The **Berlin-Connection Café and Bistro,** Martin-Luther-Strasse 19 (☎ **030/213-1116;** U-Bahn: Nollendorfplatz; open Mon–Sat 2pm–2am), is a gay/lesbo hangout both day and night.

Café Berio, Maassenstrasse 7 (☎ **030/216-1946;** U-Bahn: Nollendorfplatz; open daily 8am–1am), is a two-tiered cafe with a terrace much-favored by gays and lesbians; snacks, international breakfasts, and various sweeties are available. **Café PositHiv,** Alvenslebenstrasse 26 (☎ **030/216-8654;** U-Bahn: Bülowstrasse; open Tues–Sun 3–11pm), is a place for guys with and without HIV.

✪ **Café Savigny,** Grolmannstrasee 53–54 (☎ **030/312-8195;** S-Bahn: Savignyplatz; open daily 9am–1am), is a welcome hangout for gay artists, students, and intellectuals. **Café Sundstrom,** Mehringdamm 61 (☎ **030/692-4414;** U-Bahn: Mehringdamm; open Mon–Fri noon–midnight, Sat–Sun 24 hours), is a gay/lesbian cafe located in Kreuzberg, close to the Gay Museum. Also in Kreuzberg, **Cinema Inn,** Schlesische Strasse 29 (☎ **030/611-2670;** U-Bahn: Schlesisches Tor; open Mon–Fri 4pm–midnight, Sat–Sun 11am–midnight), has a mixed bar and movie-theme cafe.

✪ **DaNeben,** Motzstrasse 5 (☎ **030/217-0633;** U-Bahn: Nollendorfplatz; open Mon–Fri 10am–1am, Sat noon–1am, Sun 3pm–midnight), located next to Mann-o-Meter (the gay info center), and **E 116,** Eisenacher Strasse 116 (☎ **030/217-0518;** U-Bahn: Nollendorfplatz; open Mon–Thurs and Sun 8pm–1am, Fri–Sat 8pm–3am), are friendly gay cafe/bars in the gay village.

In Schöneberg, **Flipflop,** Kulmer Strasse 20a (☎ **030/216-2825;** U-Bahn: Kleistpark; open Mon–Sat 7pm–1am, Sun 11am–midnight), serves a popular Sunday brunch buffet. **Memorys,** Fuggerstrasse 37 (☎ **030/213-5271;** U-Bahn: Wittenbergplatz; open daily 4pm–1am), is a street cafe with a mixed male crowd. ✪ **Schwarzes Café,** Kantstrasse 148 (☎ **030/313-8038;** S-Bahn: Savignyplatz; open daily 24 hours), with its garden and round-the-clock breakfasts, is a long-time favorite with gays and lesbians.

And **Windows,** Martin-Luther-Strasse 22 (☎ **030/214-2394;** U-Bahn: Nollendorfplatz; open Mon–Sat 2pm–3am, Sun 11am–3am), a gay and lesbian cafe/bar/bistro, has a great terrace; a gay establishment of one sort or another has been in this location for decades.

PRENZLAUER BERG The **Altberliner Bierstuben,** Saarbrücker Strasse 17 (☎ **030/442-6130;** U-Bahn: Senefelder Platz; open daily noon–2am), is a bar/restaurant with a long history; it draws noncruisy gays (including leather types) and has a good à la carte menu. **Amsterdam,** Gleimstrasse 24 (☎ **030/448-0792;** U-/S-Bahn: Schönhauser Alle; open Mon–Sat 5pm–2am, Sun 3pm–1am), popular day and night, attracts a younger lesbigay crowd. **Café am Senefelder Platz,** Schönhauser Allee 173 (☎ **030/449-6605;** U-Bahn: Senefelder Platz; open Sun–Thurs 7pm–1am, Fri–Sat 8pm–2am), is a mixed local hangout with a gay contingent and good food.

✪ **Schall & Rauch,** Gleimstrasse 23 (☎ **030/448-0770;** U-Bahn: Schönhauser Allee; open daily 10am–3am), frequented by gays and lesbians, is a long narrow cafe with a hip, modern ambience and a good cafe menu. The **Biz-Café,** Rhinower Strasse 8 (☎ **030/ 449-7590;** U-Bahn: Schönhauser Allee; call for exact hours), is a multisexual sort of place that caters to everyone: Mondays are for youths, Tuesdays transsexuals, Wednesdays older gay men, and Fridays women only; the atmosphere is cozy and nonthreatening.

4 Exploring Berlin

Berlin offers so much to see and do you'd need a month to do it justice. It's particularly rich in museums (and cafes). Arm yourself with a good map—the Falk map is best. Choose a geographical area or cluster of sites you want to see, take the U-Bahn or S-Bahn there, and then spend some extra time exploring the neighborhood you're in. Allot at least a day to the former East Berlin, the oldest part of the city. Berlin is also blessed with lakes, rivers, and some remarkable green spaces. The parks mentioned toward the end of this section should also be considered an essential part of your tour. Wander through the Tiergarten or the Grunewald or spend an afternoon at the lakes.

You might want to orient yourself by taking one of the city sightseeing bus tours (*Stadtrundfahrten*) that leave from the Kurfürstendamm or close to it. Two principal tour operators are **Severin + Kuhn,** Kurfürstendamm 216 (☎ **030/883-1015**), and **Berolina Sightseeing,** Meinekestrasse 3 (☎ **030/882-2091**). Prices and times vary, but there are usually tours in English.

A good way to acquaint yourself with Berlin's history is by taking one of the English-language walking tours offered by **Berlin Walks** (☎ **030/301-9194**). "Discover Berlin" is a 3-hour introductory tour of the former East Berlin; "Infamous Third Reich Sites" (Sat–Sun) shows you sites associated with Nazi Berlin. Tours depart from the taxi stand outside the main entrance of Bahnhof Zoo daily at 10am, no reservations required. The price is 15DM ($9). For ✪ **gay sightseeing tours,** see "Gay Berlin," below.

From April to the end of October, **Stern und Kreis** (☎ **030/536-3600**) offers sightseeing boat trips on the Spree River and Havel and Wannsee lakes. Boats depart from Jannowitzbrücke in Berlin-Mitte and Schlossbrücke near Charlottenburg Palace. Call for details.

THE HITS YOU SHOULDN'T MISS

Brandenburg Gate (Brandenburger Tor). Pariser Platz. Admission free. U-Bahn: Potsdamer Platz or Friedrichstrasse; S-Bahn: Unter den Linden.

If you watched the televised fall of the GDR (German Democratic Republic) in 1989, you saw this historic monument, one of Berlin's most potent symbols, in every news clip. When the Wall came down, hundreds of thousands of East Germans walked freely through the Gate into West Berlin for the first time since 1961. The party is over now and some disgruntled Berliners wish the Wall would be raised again, but there, connecting the two formerly divided halves of the city, stands the freshly restored Brandenburg Gate. A neoclassical triumphal arch completed in 1791 as a terminating point for the grand boulevard Unter den Linden, the Gate is crowned by the famous ***Quadriga,*** a four-horse copper chariot drawn by the goddess Victor/Victoria. (That's a joke; did you know the Julie Andrews movie *Victor/Victoria* was based on an older German movie from the 1930s?) In the 19th and early 20th centuries, the Gate was the scene of Prussian military parades, triumphal marches, and glittering receptions. The revolutionary events of 1848 and 1918, like those in 1989, saw the Gate used as a symbolic gathering place. Too bad they've opened it to cars.

From the Gate, looking south, you can see the **Reichstag** (with a huge new dome being added to it), seat of the reunified German Parliament. Built in a pompous High Renaissance style between 1884 and 1894, it was partially destroyed by fire in 1933 and bombs in World War II—but it looked best when wrapped up like a bulky blue present by the artist Christo.

✪ **Charlottenburg Palace (Schloss Charlottenburg).** Luisenplatz. ☎ **030/320-911.** Palace tours Tues–Fri 9am–5pm, Sat–Sun 10am–5pm. Palace tour 8DM ($4.50); combined ticket (Tageskarte) for all buildings and historical rooms 15DM ($8). U-Bahn: Sophie-Charlotte-Platz or Richard-Wagner-Platz.

The oldest section of this lovely yellow palace was built in 1695 as a breezy summer abode for Sophie Charlotte, the hot and heavy wife of Friedrich I. Its present form, with additions by Eosander, Knobelsdorff, and Langhans, dates from 1790. You can see the palace only on a tour, and to take that tour you have to don huge felt slippers (so you're effectively polishing the wood floors as you slide around after the guide). The tour, incomprehensible unless you speak German or buy the English-language guide, includes the **Historical Rooms,** the living quarters of Friedrich I and Sophie Charlotte; the eye-catching **Porcelain Room;** and the **royal chapel.** With a combined ticket you can additionally visit, on your own, the **Galerie der Romantik,** with its fine collection of paintings from the neoclassical, Romantic, and Biedermeier periods, and the beautifully landscaped palace gardens, containing the charming **Schinkel Pavilion** and the **Belvedere** with its Rococo-to-Biedermeier porcelain collection. To see it all you need at least 3 or 4 hours.

Charlottenburg Museums. Schlossstrasse. U-Bahn: Sophie-Charlotte-Platz or Richard-Wagner-Platz.

Across from Charlottenburg Palace are three museums worth visiting. They're of manageable size, selective in what they show, and closed on Monday. An 8DM ($4.50) *Tageskarte* (day ticket) will get you into the first two and into all the city museums collectively called the Staatliche Museen zu Berlin, which include the Gemäldegalerie (Painting Gallery) in the Kulturforum and the museums on the Museumsinsel (see below).

The greatest treasure of the ✪ **Egyptian Museum (Ägyptisches Museum),** Schlossstrasse 70 (☎ **030/2090-5555;** open Tues–Fri 10am–6pm, Sat–Sun 11am–6pm), is the famous and fabulous bust of Queen Nefertiti, dating from around 1350 B.C.—it occupies a small room all its own. The riveting beauty of Nefertiti's painted limestone face (okay, so it's idealized and missing one eye) and profile are accentuated by dramatic glamour-portrait lighting. Note that some of the museum's collection will eventually be moved to the Bode Museum on Museum Island.

Across from the Egyptian Museum, the **Bergruen Sammlung Collection,** Schlossstrasse 1 (☎ **030/209-0555;** open same hours as Egyptian Museum), has a permanent collection called **Picasso und Seine Zeit (Picasso and His Era),** which showcases several important Picassos and some playful Klees.

You have to pay a separate admission of 8DM ($4.45) for the ✪ **Bröhan Museum,** Schlossstrasse 1A (☎ **030/321-4029;** open Tues–Sun 10am–6pm, Thurs to 8pm), which is privately operated and generally overlooked by visitors. However, inside you'll find one of the world's finest collections of Jugendstil (art nouveau) and art deco furniture, painting, sculpture, glass, silverware, and crafts, all from 1889 to 1939. Particularly to-die-for is the Suite Emile-Jacques Ruhlman, a completely decorated set of rooms from a luxurious private residence of the 1920s and 1930s.

Kulturforum, Painting Gallery (Gemäldegalerie), and New National Gallery (Neue Nationalgalerie). U-Bahn: Tiergarten or Potsdamer Platz; S-Bahn: Potsdamer Platz.

On the eastern edge of the Tiergarten, close to the chaotic construction site of Potsdamer Platz, is a group of buildings that collectively form a cultural center of international importance. The area is known as the **Kulturforum (Culture Forum).** Some of the buildings, like the **Philharmonie,** home of the Berlin Philharmonic, were completed over 30 years ago.

The newest addition is the **Gemäldegalerie,** Matthäikirchplatz 8 (☎ **030/2090-5555;** open Tues–Fri 10am–6pm, Sat–Sun 11am–6pm; admission 8DM/$4.50). The gallery, which moved to its new location here in 1998, houses Berlin's greatest collection of European painting, with an emphasis on medieval German and Dutch art

Western Berlin Attractions

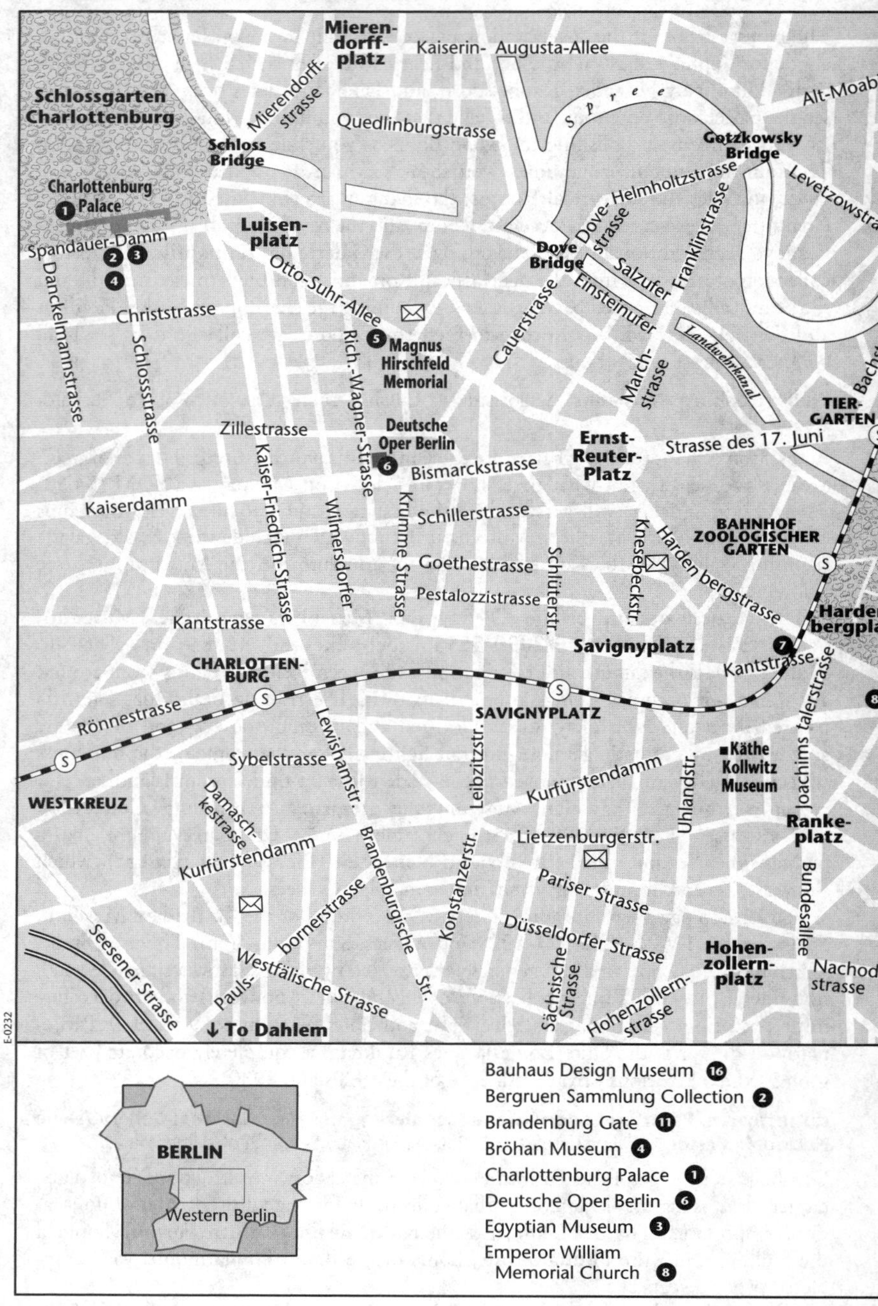

Mierendorffplatz
Kaiserin-Augusta-Allee
Schlossgarten Charlottenburg
Mierendorffstrasse
Quedlinburgstrasse
Spree
Alt-Moabit
Schloss Bridge
Gotzkowsky Bridge
Levetzowstrasse
Charlottenburg Palace
Helmholtzstrasse
Dove-strasse
Franklinstrasse
Luisenplatz
Spandauer-Damm
Dove Bridge
Salzufer
Einsteinufer
Otto-Suhr-Allee
Landwehrkanal
Danckelmannstrasse
Christstrasse
Cauerstrasse
Schlossstrasse
Rich.-Wagner-Strasse
Magnus Hirschfeld Memorial
Marchstrasse
TIERGARTEN
Zillestrasse
Deutsche Oper Berlin
Ernst-Reuter-Platz
Strasse des 17. Juni
Kaiser-Friedrich-Strasse
Bismarckstrasse
Kaiserdamm
Krumme Strasse
Schillerstrasse
Knesebeckstr.
Hardenbergstrasse
BAHNHOF ZOOLOGISCHER GARTEN
Wilmersdorfer
Goethestrasse
Schlüterstr.
Pestalozzistrasse
Hardenbergplatz
Kantstrasse
Savignyplatz
CHARLOTTENBURG
SAVIGNYPLATZ
Joachimstalerstrasse
Rönnestrasse
Lewishamstr.
Leibzitzstr.
Käthe Kollwitz Museum
Sybelstrasse
Uhlandstr.
WESTKREUZ
Damaschkestrasse
Kurfürstendamm
Rankeplatz
Brandenburgische Str.
Lietzenburgerstr.
Konstanzerstr.
Pariser Strasse
Bundesallee
Seesener Strasse
bornerstrasse
Düsseldorfer Strasse
Hohenzollernplatz
Nachodstrasse
Westfälische Strasse
Pauls-
Sächsische Strasse
Hohenzollernstrasse
↓ To Dahlem
E-0232
BERLIN
Western Berlin
Bauhaus Design Museum 16
Bergruen Sammlung Collection 2
Brandenburg Gate 11
Bröhan Museum 4
Charlottenburg Palace 1
Deutsche Oper Berlin 6
Egyptian Museum 3
Emperor William Memorial Church 8

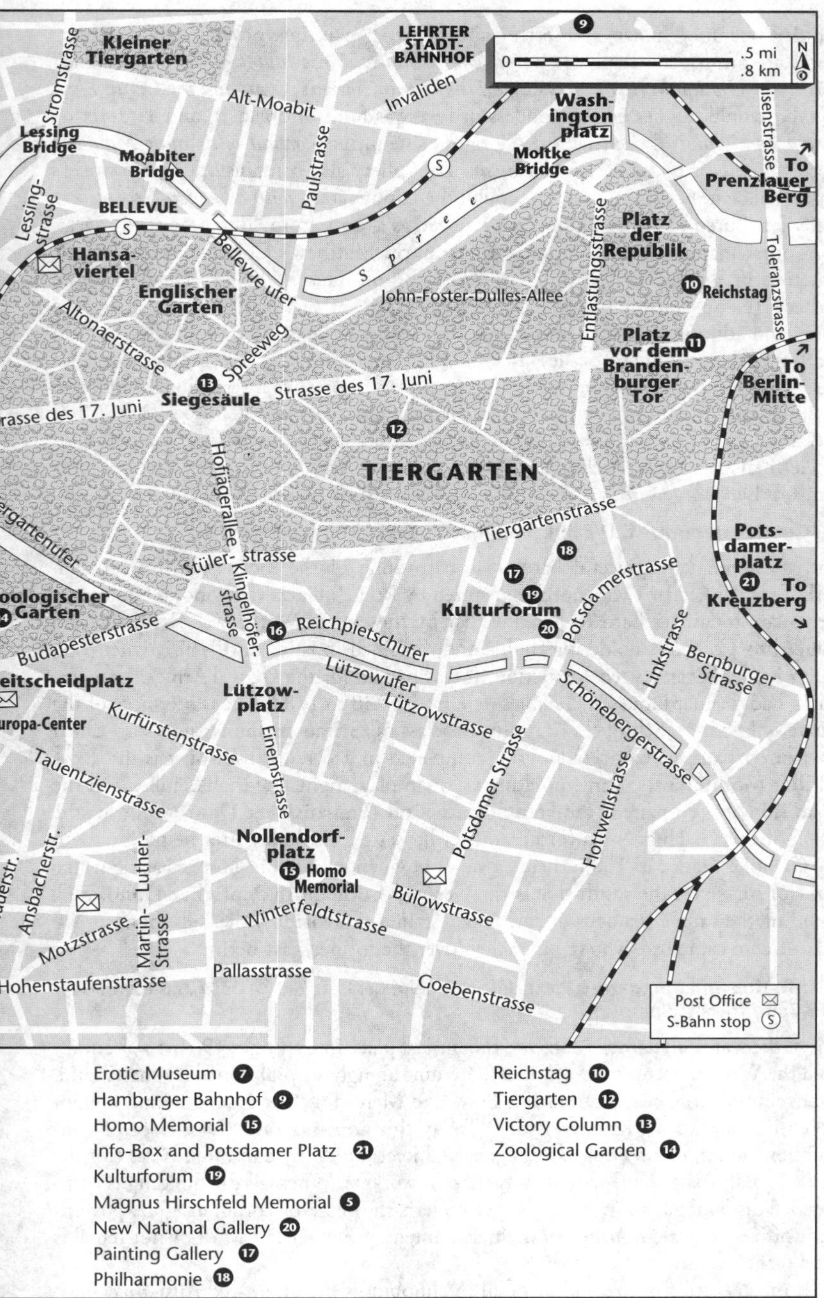
Kleiner Tiergarten
Stromstrasse
LEHRTER STADT-BAHNHOF
9
0
.5 mi
.8 km
N
Alt-Moabit
Invaliden
Lessing Bridge
Moabiter Bridge
Paulstrasse
Wash-ington platz
Moltke Bridge
To Prenzlauer Berg
Lessing-strasse
BELLEVUE
Spree
Hansa-viertel
Bellevue ufer
Entlastungsstrasse
Platz der Republik
Toleranzstrasse
Englischer Garten
John-Foster-Dulles-Allee
10 Reichstag
Altonaerstrasse
Spreeweg
Platz vor dem Branden-burger Tor
11
To Berlin-Mitte
13
Siegesäule
Strasse des 17. Juni
12
TIERGARTEN
Hofjägerallee
Tiergartenstrasse
Pots-damer-platz
21
To Kreuzberg
18
17
19
Kulturforum
20
Potsdamerstrasse
Stüler-strasse
Klingelhöfer-strasse
16
Reichpietschufer
Budapesterstrasse
Lützowufer
Linkstrasse
Bernburger Strasse
Lützow-platz
Lützowstrasse
Schönebergerstrasse
Kurfürstenstrasse
Einemstrasse
Tauentzienstrasse
Potsdamer Strasse
Flottwellstrasse
Nollendorf-platz
15 Homo Memorial
Ansbacherstr.
Martin-Luther-Strasse
Bülowstrasse
Winterfeldtstrasse
Motzstrasse
Pallasstrasse
Hohenstaufenstrasse
Goebenstrasse
Post Office
S-Bahn stop
Erotic Museum 7
Hamburger Bahnhof 9
Homo Memorial 15
Info-Box and Potsdamer Platz 21
Kulturforum 19
Magnus Hirschfeld Memorial 5
New National Gallery 20
Painting Gallery 17
Philharmonie 18
Reichstag 10
Tiergarten 12
Victory Column 13
Zoological Garden 14

and 16th-century Italian and 17th-century Dutch painting. Several Italian masterpieces are on display: Raphael's *Virgin and Child with the Infant St. John,* Bronzino's *Portrait of Ugolino Martelli,* Veronese's *Dead Christ,* Titian's *Venus and the Organ Player* (who would've guessed the goddess of love was fond of organs?), and Tintoretto's *Virgin and Child.* Also check out Giorgione's haunting *Portrait of a Young Man* and Correggio's seductive *Leda and the Swan.* The gallery also contains one of the world's largest collections of Rembrandts, though the famous *Man with a Golden Helmet,* formerly attributed to Rembrandt, is now tagged as a work from "Rembrandt's Circle."

Another major museum sits to one side of St. Matthew's Church, the only "old" structure in the aggressively modern Kulturforum. This is the ✪ **New National Gallery (Neue Nationalgalerie),** Potsdamerstrasse 50 (☎ **030/2090-5555;** same hours and admission as the Gemäldegalerie). Designed in 1968 by Ludwig Mies van der Rohe, the proponent of "less is more," the museum is an enormous expanse of glass windows and simple symmetry. It contains an impressive international collection of 20th-century painting and sculpture, including works by de Chirico, Dalí, Miró, and American abstractionists Rothko and Stella. Of special interest are the paintings by German artists Max Beckmann, Max Ernst, and Otto Dix and two bitter and brilliant oils by George Grosz that capture the decadent despair of the Weimar years.

✪ **Gendarmenmarkt.** U-Bahn: Stadtmitte; S-Bahn: Unter den Linden.

This monumentally graceful baroque square—one of the most beautiful spots in Berlin—is flanked by twin churches inspired by Rome's Piazza del Popolo. Looking at the square today, it's hard to imagine that by the end of World War II it had been reduced to a pile of smoldering rubble and remained in ruins until 1977, when East Berlin finally began its reconstruction. It was named for the Gens d'Armes regiment, which had its guardhouse and stables here from 1738 to 1782. The centerpiece of the square is Friedrich Schinkel's beautiful neoclassical **Schauspielhaus** (now also called the Konzerthaus, or Concert House), completed in 1821. In front of it is the 1871 **Schiller Monument,** commemorating German playwright Friedrich Schiller. On the north side of the square is the **French Cathedral (Französicher Dom),** built for the influx of French Huguenots (Protestants) who settled in Berlin after being forced to flee Catholic France in 1685; there's a small Huguenot Museum inside. Facing it like a mirror image on the south side is the **German Cathedral (Deutscher Dom).** Surrounding the square is a bevy of chic new restaurants favored by the cell-phone crowd of hard-core capitalists who've now taken over the former East Berlin.

✪ **Info-Box and Potsdamer Platz.** Info Box: Leipziger Platz 21. ☎ **030/226-6240.** Daily 9am–7pm, Thurs to 9pm.

Before the war, **Potsdamer Platz** was the busiest place in Berlin; in 1961 it was cut off from the Western sector by the Wall and became an ugly strip of mined no-man's-land. After reunification, corporations like Sony and Mercedes-Benz rushed in and bought the entire area for a (figurative) song. Today this area is a vast, chaotic sea of construction cranes, half-completed designer-architect buildings, enormous holes (for the future U-Bahn) and hard-hatted construction workers. When all the building is completed, Potsdamer Platz will be a supermodern showcase of corporate glitz, government offices, upscale housing, and entertainment. Whether it'll work or not remains to be seen.

Set on steel stilts in the middle of all the hubbub is the bright-red **Info-Box.** Basically a museum that explains what's going on, it contains scale models, drawings, interactive computers, and photographs of the way Potsdamer Platz used to look and the way it'll look at the dawn of the millennium. You can survey the surrounding construction areas from the windows or pay a small admission and go to the open viewing area at the top of the building. On the premises are an all-day cafe and a restaurant serving coffee, sandwiches, and sweets.

Kurfürstendamm. U-Bahn: Kurfürstendamm; S-Bahn: Zoologischer Garten.

The famous boulevard known as the "Ku-Damm" is Berlin's answer to Paris's Champs-Elysées. For years it hogged all the city's glamour because there was nothing in dreary East Berlin to rival it. Today, however, some of the glamour quotient is shifting back east to Friedrichstrasse. But the Ku-Damm will always remain one of Berlin's top shopping and entertainment streets; it's basically the heart of western Berlin. It began as nothing more than a humble log road, built in 1542 to make it easier for the Prince-Electors (Kurfürsten) to reach their hunting lodge in the Grunewald. From the turn of the century until World War II, it was the most brilliant, lively, and elegant street in this part of Berlin, filled with legendary cafes and renowned for its nightlife. It's still a good place to stroll, sit, and people-watch, and its central location close to the gay quarter around Nollendorfplatz makes it a street you'll want to know.

One of Berlin's most famous landmarks, the **Emperor William Memorial Church (Kaiser-Wilhelm-Gedächtniskirche)** sits on the Ku-Damm at Breitscheidplatz. A ponderous neo-Romanesque structure from the late 19th century, it was built to commemorate the 1871 establishment of the German Empire. At the end of World War II, only a ruined shell remained. This was preserved as a symbol of the ravages of war, and a new church complex was constructed around it between 1959 and 1961. A permanent, but rather boring, historical exhibition has been set up in the old church, which iconoclastic Berliners call *"der hohle Zahn"* (the hollow tooth).

Museum Island (Museumsinsel). Berlin-Mitte. U-/S-Bahn: Friedrichstrasse or Alexanderplatz.

Four museums on an island in the River Spree form the oldest museum complex in Berlin. The buildings, some dating back to the early and mid-19th century, were constructed after Frederick William III issued a decree stipulating that the privately owned artworks of the royal family should be made accessible to the public. The museums were the main attractions in old East Berlin, and boy were they ever grimy and decrepit. After reunification, a complicated process of restoring the buildings and reuniting various collections from the east and west began. What this means, alas, is that some of the museums, and portions of others, are currently closed. The hours are the same for all of them: Tuesday to Friday 10am to 6pm and Saturday and Sunday 11am to 6pm. And one 8DM ($4.50) admission will get you into the two that were open at press time.

As you approach along Unter den Linden, the first museum you reach is the **Altes Museum,** Bodestrasse 1–3 (☎ **030/203-550**). It resembles a Greek temple and was designed by Berlin's greatest architect, Karl Friedrich Schinkel. The museum's Antiquities Collection reopened in 1998 and mostly consists of Greek and Roman pottery, carved ivory, glassware, jewelry, and wood and stone sarcophagi. The 5th-century B.C. red-figure Attic vases are especially interesting—guess why. Next is the **Alte Nationalgalerie,** Bodestrasse, which looks like a Corinthian temple and is devoted to 19th-century painting and sculpture; it's closed until 2001.

Of all the museums on the island, the ✪ **Pergamon Museum,** Bodestrasse 1–3 (☎ **030/2090-5566**), is the one must-see, and what you must see is the Pergamon Altar, considered one of the Seven Wonders of the ancient world and still holding its own today. Part of the enormous Temple of Zeus and Athena, dating from 180–160 B.C., it was discovered in 1876 in Pergamon, a center of Late Hellenistic culture in western Turkey. Another showpiece is the ornate two-storied Market Gate of Miletus, a Roman building facade from the time of Emperor Marcus Aurelius (ca. A.D. 165).

Art, Design & Erotica: Three More Museums

Architects and design aficionados may want to spend an hour perusing the exhibits in the **Bauhaus Design Museum (Bauhaus Archiv–Museum für Gestaltung),** Klingelhoferstrasse 14 (☎ **030/254-0020;** U-Bahn: Nollendorfplatz; open Wed–Mon 10am–5pm; admission 5DM/$2.75), dedicated to the Bauhaus school, which sought to amalgamate art, design, and technology. The Bauhaus was founded in 1919 at Weimar, moved to Dessau, and finally settled in Berlin, before it disbanded in 1933. The museum, dating from 1979 and located in the Tiergarten, is one of the last works of great Berlin-born architect Walter Gropius. English-language texts describing the exhibits are available.

One of Berlin's newer museums, housed in a former train station, the **Hamburger Bahnhof,** Invalidenstrasse 50–51 (☎ **030/3978-3413;** S-Bahn: Lehrter Bahnhof; open Tues–Fri 10am–6pm, Sat–Sun 11am–6pm; admission 12DM/$7), is the place to go if you want to see contemporary art by artists living and working in Germany and around the world.

Berlin, the least stodgy of cities, has always been pretty upfront about sexual matters. Close to the hetero-porn arcades across from Zoo Station, the **Erotic Museum (Erotik-Museum),** at the corner of Kantstrasse and Joachimstaler Stasse (☎ **030/886-0666;** U-/S-Bahn: Zoologischer Garten; open daily 9am–midnight; admission 10DM/$6), looks a bit cheesy but has some fascinating exhibits. Of special interest to gays is the section devoted to the life and work of Magnus Hirschfeld, the pioneering granddaddy of homosexual rights in Germany. There are also Asian miniatures of coupling couples, titillating European paintings, humorous turn-of-the-century prints by Berlin's Heinrich Zille, and sections devoted to early erotic films, Rudolph Valentino, and Beate Uhse, who founded Germany's first sex shops back in the 1960s.

The domed neo-Baroque **Bode Museum,** at the far northern end of the island, will be closed from January 1999 until mid-2001. Since you can't get in, what can I say? It has a remarkably beautiful interior with marble walls and two curving staircases and houses a superlative Egyptian Museum, the Museum of Late Antiquity, and Byzantine sculpture.

✪ **Unter den Linden.** U-Bahn: Stadtmitte or Friedrichstrasse; S-Bahn: Unter den Linden.

Laid out in 1647 and extending about three-quarters of a mile east from the Brandenburg Gate, Unter den Linden is one of Berlin's most famous and historically significant streets. It got its name from the linden trees that were originally planted along it. This is the oldest and royalest boulevard in central Berlin, with several monumental buildings. Among them are the **Old Palace (Altes Palais),** completed in 1837 and used as a residence by Emperor Wilhelm I; the **Old Library (Alte Bibliothek),** dating from 1780 and called the Kommode, or "chest of drawers," by Berliners; the neoclassical **State Opera (Staatsoper),** the first opera house to occupy its own building, unattached to a palace or castle; the **Crown Prince's Palace (Kronprinzenpalais)** from 1733; Friedrich Schinkel's 1818 **Neue Wache,** which served as headquarters for the King's Guard and now contains the Tomb of the Unknown Soldier and the Tomb of the Unknown Resistance Fighter; and the **Armory (Zeughaus),** Berlin's largest baroque building and the first (1706) major building to be constructed on Unter den Linden (check out the 22 famous Masks of Dying Warriors in the interior courtyard).

Berlin-Mitte

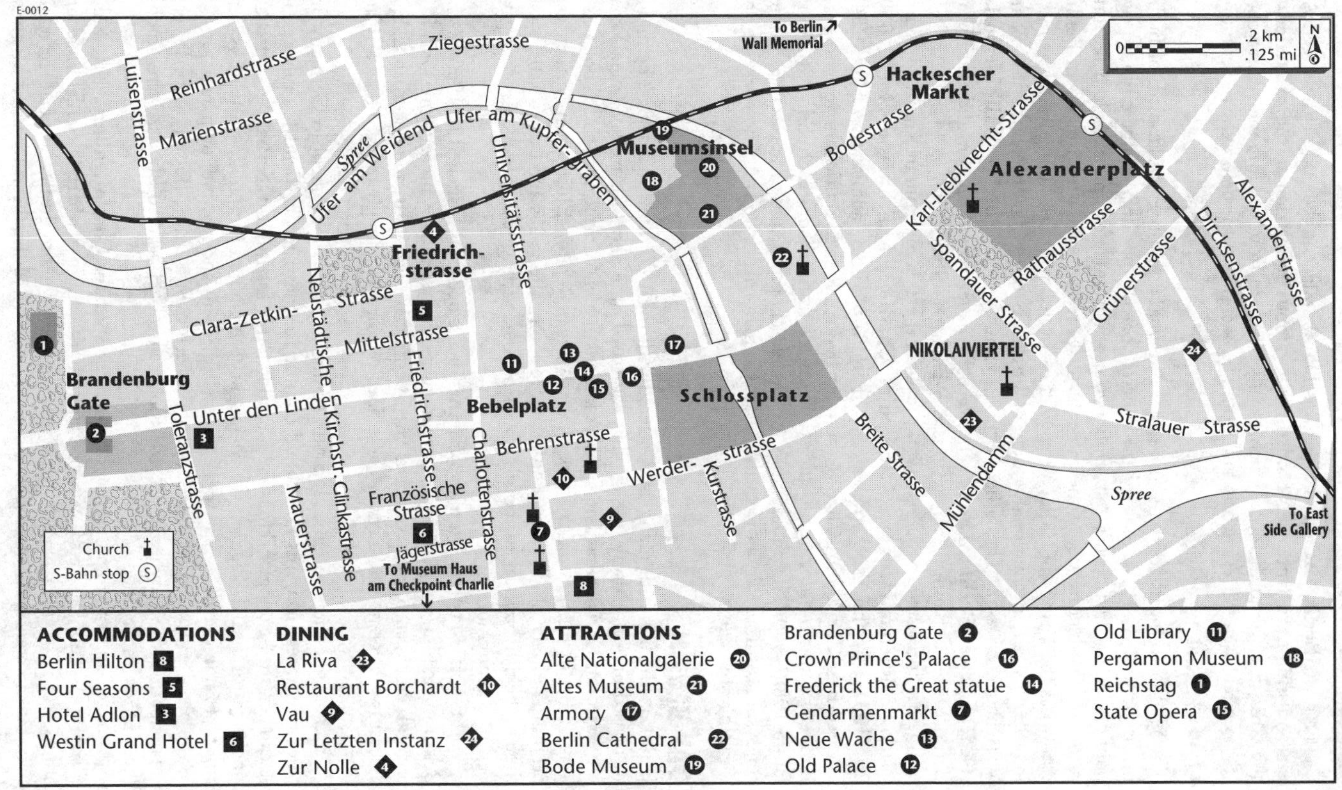

E-0012
0
.2 km
.125 mi
N
To Berlin Wall Memorial
To East Side Gallery
To Museum Haus am Checkpoint Charlie
Ziegestrasse
Reinhardstrasse
Luisenstrasse
Marienstrasse
Spree
Ufer am Weidend
Ufer am Kupfer-graben
Universitätsstrasse
Museumsinsel
Hackescher Markt
Bodestrasse
Karl-Liebknecht-Strasse
Alexanderplatz
Rathausstrasse
Spandauer Strasse
Grünerstrasse
Dircksenstrasse
Alexanderstrasse
Friedrich-strasse
Clara-Zetkin-Strasse
Neustädtische Kirchstr.
Mittelstrasse
Friedrichstrasse
Brandenburg Gate
Unter den Linden
Toleranzstrasse
Bebelplatz
Behrenstrasse
Charlottenstrasse
Schlossplatz
Werder-strasse
Kurstrasse
Breite Strasse
NIKOLAIVIERTEL
Stralauer Strasse
Mühlendamm
Französische Strasse
Jägerstrasse
Glinkastrasse
Mauerstrasse
Church
S-Bahn stop
ACCOMMODATIONS
Berlin Hilton 8
Four Seasons 5
Hotel Adlon 3
Westin Grand Hotel 6
DINING
La Riva 23
Restaurant Borchardt 10
Vau 9
Zur Letzten Instanz 24
Zur Nolle 4
ATTRACTIONS
Alte Nationalgalerie 20
Altes Museum 21
Armory 17
Berlin Cathedral 22
Bode Museum 19
Brandenburg Gate 2
Crown Prince's Palace 16
Frederick the Great statue 14
Gendarmenmarkt 7
Neue Wache 13
Old Palace 12
Old Library 11
Pergamon Museum 18
Reichstag 1
State Opera 15

The giant **Berlin Cathedral (Berliner Dom)** squats at the end of the street. All that's missing from Unter den Linden is the famous **equestrian statue of Frederick the Great** (one of our heroes), which usually stands in front of Humboldt University. It's been removed for restoration but should be back sometime before the millennium.

✪ **Berlin Wall.** Berlin-Mitte.

The Wall is no more. It's toast, zip, nada. But what a grimly essential piece of Berlin history it was! By 1990, most of the concrete barrier that divided one city into two political entities had been razed. Only two portions are left. One is a kilometer-long section on Mühlenstrasse on the banks of the Spree River in the former East Berlin. Known as the **East Side Gallery,** the Wall is covered with fast-fading murals painted in 1990 by an international group of artists (S-Bahn: Hauptbahnhof; U-Bahn: Warschauer Strasse). The other section, known as the **Berlin Wall Memorial (Gedenkstätte "Berlin Mauer)** is between Bernauer Strasse and Invalidenstrasse in Berlin-Mitte (U-Bahn: Bernauer Strasse; S-Bahn: Nordbahnhof).

If you're interested in the history of the Wall, there's a museum in Kreuzberg worth visiting: **Museum Haus am Checkpoint Charlie,** Friedrichstrasse 44 (☎ **030/251-1031;** U-Bahn: Kochstrasse; open daily 9am–10pm; admission 7.50DM/$4). Located near Checkpoint Charlie, the most frequently used traffic crossing into East Berlin, the museum documents the Wall's history from its construction in 1961 to its fall in 1989/1990. The photographs, newspaper clippings, and escape devices (sometimes successful, usually not) used by East Germans may give you a new take on the meaning of freedom.

GAY BERLIN

Berlin, in the minds of many, is associated with the 1972 movie *Cabaret.* The movie was based on a Broadway musical that was based on a play ("I Am A Camera") that was based on **Christopher Isherwood's** famous *Berlin Stories.* Isherwood's book was a look at Berlin in the waning years of the Weimar Republic, just when Nazism was beginning to take hold. The period he wrote about, the 1920s and early 1930s, was a time of hellish political turmoil but also of the startling sexual frankness that gave Berlin its reputation for "decadence."

Berlin-born **Marlene Dietrich's** international career was launched in 1930 by the Berlin-made film *The Blue Angel.* In many ways that legendary movie, along with Isherwood's book, encapsulates the era when Berlin was filled with raunchy cabarets, had at least two gay bars, and a cruisy eight-sided pissoir was jokingly referred to as a "Café Octogan."

At that time there was already a burgeoning gay-rights movement in Germany. Its chief activist was **Magnus Hirschfeld** (Auntie Magnesia to his friends), a pioneering researcher in "sexology." Hirschfeld founded the Institut für Sexual Wissenschaft (Institute for Sexual Science), which sought to enlighten the public on matters pertaining to homosexuality. He spoke out to Parliament about annulling paragraph 175 of the penal code, which made sodomy between men a crime. But any hope for gay emancipation ended when the Nazis took control. Hirschfeld's books were among those seized and burned in 1933.

A marker in front of a building opposite the **Rathaus Charlottenburg,** Otto-Suhr Allee 93 (U-Bahn: Richard-Wagner-Platz), marks the spot where Hirschfeld had his offices. For years, the gay community has tried to give him greater "official" recognition, but no statue has materialized and so far no street has been renamed Magnus-Hirschfeld-Strasse.

The Nazis, with their twisted obsession with "purity" and "normality," were determined to wipe out Jews, Gypsies, and homosexuals. In an infamous 1934 incident called the **Night of Long Knives,** they shot or imprisoned the head of the SA (storm troopers, or Brownshirts), his homosexual associates, and other political opponents. Hitler apparently made that decision because he was afraid he couldn't control the Brownshirts if they remained independent. But the public excuse for the murders was homosexuality: Hitler and Himmler talked openly about the need to purge "decadent elements" from the Nazi party. When they began arresting gays and shipping them to prison, the charge was violation of paragraph 175, which the Nazis had made more restrictive than ever. After release from prison, gays were put into SS workcamps where many of them died. Martin Sherman's play *Bent,* which starred Richard Gere on Broadway and was recently made into a movie, deals with this gruesome subject. In the end, we'll probably never know how many gays were killed by the Nazis between 1934 and 1945.

The irony of the postwar years was that homosexuality was officially not a crime in the Communist GDR, while paragraph 175 remained on the books in democratic West Germany until 1969. West German gay-rights groups organized and agitated for change. In 1973, the West German parliament made sex between men over the age of 18 legal. And in 1994 it completely abolished any reference to sex/gender whatsoever, so the age of consent (16) became the same for heteros and homos of either sex.

Gay life in Berlin today is so open and diverse it's easy to forget the contributions of early gay heroes like Hirschfeld and the horrors inflicted on gays during the Nazi past. But, in a way, it's a past every gay visitor to Berlin shares and would do well to remember.

Gay life goes on all over the city, but there are three main areas where gay bars and cafes are found in abundance. In western Berlin, the oldest gay neighborhood extends from **Nollendorfplatz** to **Wittenbergplatz. Kreuzberg,** long known for its healthy mix of "alternative lifestyles," is pretty homo-geneous as well. In eastern Berlin, the new gay beehive is **Prenzlauer Berg,** especially on and around Schönhauser Allee.

A great way to acquaint yourself with Berlin's incredible gay past is by taking the ✪ **gay sightseeing tour** (☎ **030/215-8008**) called "Von der Kaiserzeit zum Nationalsozialismus (From the Kaisers to the Nazis). It departs from Lutherkirche Dennewitzplatz (U-/S-Bahn: Yorkstrasse) at 3pm on Saturday and Sunday April to October and lasts about 90 minutes. Call for current price information and to verify times. **Frauen-Touren Unterwegs (Women's Tours)** (☎ **030/453-5304**), offers tours with gender-specific themes like "Women in the Middle Ages" and "Jewish Women"; you can request lesbian themes as well. Though these tours are given in German, the guides can clarify matters in English. Prices vary.

If there's another ✪ **Gay Museum (Schwules Museum),** Mehringdamm 61 (☎ **030/693-1172;** U-Bahn: Mehringdamm; open Wed–Sun 2–6pm; admission 12DM/$7), anywhere else in the world, I've never heard about it. This is the only one, and it's a must-see for all gays and lesbians (and anyone else) interested in gay history and the ongoing struggle for equality and freedom of expression. The museum is a gallery-like space with regular exhibits that deal—sometimes quite movingly—with different aspects of homosexual life and history. The primary emphasis is on gay life in Berlin and the rest of Germany, but the focus extends internationally. Exhibits are explained in German, so you need to ask for an English-language text at the front desk. The museum's impressive archive collection includes videos, recordings, and over 3,000 books.

If you didn't know what you were looking for, you might entirely miss the ✪ **Homo Memorial.** It's a plaque mounted on the outside southern wall of the Nollendorfplatz subway station, in the heart of what has been for decades the gay heart of Berlin. The simple inscription reads: *"Totgeschlagen-Totgeschiegen. Den Homosexuellen Opfern des National Socialismus"* ("Killed and Forgotten. The homosexual victims of National Socialism."). It's a poignant reminder—one of only two in the world (the

Falling in Love Again with Marlene

Every self-respecting queer knows who **Marlene Dietrich** is. The 1930 film *Die Blauen Engel (The Blue Angel)*, in which she played an amoral cabaret performer named Lola-Lola and sang the now-immortal "Falling in Love Again," catapulted the Berlin-born daughter of a Prussian military officer to international stardom. In Hollywood, she made several films (including *Morocco,* in which she wore a tuxedo and kissed a woman) and—according to her daughter's best-selling biography—had affairs with dozens of male and female celebs. Some Germans never forgave her for becoming an American citizen and entertaining American troops during World War II. Dietrich died in Paris at 91 and is buried in her hometown, in a cemetery on Fehlerstrasse in Friedenau (U-Bahn: Friedrich-Wilhelm Platz). Her simple headstone reads: MARLENE 1901–1992. HIER STEH ICH AN DEN MARKEN MEINER TAGE (Here I stand on the marker of my days).

UFA (later DEFA) Studios, founded in 1912, was the studio that produced *The Blue Angel.* It's now called **Babelsburg Studios,** August-Bebel-Strasse 26–53 (☎ **0331/721-2755;** tours Mar–Nov daily 10am–6pm; admission 28DM/$16). Marlene is long-gone, but you'll see movie sets, film props, and a special-effects display. It's not far from Potsdam, so you may want to combine the two for a day trip. Take the S-Bahn to Babelsberg station and then bus no. 690 to Grünstrasse. The studio entrance is on Grossbeerenstrasse.

Homomonument in Amsterdam is the other)—that the Nazis exterminated thousands of homosexuals in addition to their millions of Jewish, Gypsy, and other political victims. Stop for a moment, bow your head, and remember.

PARKS, GARDENS & SQUARES

Berlin's best-known and most popular inner-city park is the **Tiergarten.** Strasse des 17. Juni runs through it and around a phallic-looking column that has been a Berlin landmark since 1873 (it stood in front of the Reichstag until Hitler had it moved here in 1938). The **Victory Column (Siegesäule)** commemorates various Prussian military victories; coincidentally, Siegesäule is also the name of Berlin's oldest gay magazine. Maybe you remember the column from the beginning of the Wim Wenders's movie *Wings of Desire.* The angel was perched on top, beside the golden statue of Viktoria (or is it Viktor?).

Anyway, just past the cruisy rest room to the right of the column, down a footpath leading into the park, is one of Berlin's most popular gay sunbathing areas, called appropriately the **Queen's Meadow (Tuntenweise).** With the merest peep of sun, the local guys strip down to the teeniest of thongs. The busiest cruising area in the Tiergarten is around the **Löwenbrücke,** which spans the canal running through the park. The prettily landscaped **Zoological Garden,** in the park's southwestern corner, is home to one of the world's largest zoos. Those grunting sounds you hear behind the bushes are from four-legged beasts. The best way to get into the center of the park is by taking the S-Bahn to the Tiergarten stop.

How the nature-loving Germans love to walk—though when they go out for a brisk stroll in the **Grunewald** they often look like they're marching. Whole families take to the paths in this 15-square-mile forest that begins just beyond the western edge of the Kurfürstendamm. The Grunewald (green forest), Berlin's largest uninterrupted wooded area, is part of the Wilmersdorf and Zehlendorf districts. From Heerstrasse, it stretches some 6 miles south to the popular **Wannsee** lake. Havelchausee, the forest's western border, winds past several picturesque bays and beaches along the Havel River, while the eastern border is roughly marked off by four lakes: **Schlachtensee, Krumme Lanke, Grunewaldsee,** and **Schildhorn.** It's a good place to get away from the urban jungle, though on weekends you'll have plenty of company.

BOYS & GIRLS ON THE BEACH

When Berlin turns warm, the boys head for the hot nude beach on **Wannsee** in the Grunewald (see above). Here they exercise their skills in what the Germans somewhat hygienically call *Freie Körper Kultur* (free body culture, or FKK). No thongs here, baby; everything hangs out. To reach the beach, frequented mostly by gays but used by some women and heteros as well, take the S-Bahn to Nikolassee and then walk down Wannseebadweg to the lake. It's open May to September daily 8am to 8pm, and a small admission fee is charged. The FKK area is to the right, past all the shrieking children.

Another hot spot for beach life is the smaller **Grunewaldsee,** which doesn't have any opening or closing times. The FKK area called "Bullenwinkel" on the lake's western shore is where all the action is. To get there, take bus no. 119 or 186 to the Hagenplatz stop; from there's it's about half an hour's schlep via Königsallee and Forstamt Grunewald (the forest ranger's office) to the nudist area.

There's another FKK beach that attracts gay guys at **Müggelsee,** in the eastern borough of Köpenick. Take the S-Bahn east to Friedrichshagen station and change to the no. 60 streetcar. Get off at the Licht- und Luftbad Müggelsee station. You have to pay a small admission; the swimming area is open May to September daily 9am to 8pm.

WORKING UP A SWEAT

GYMS Used mostly by gay men, this full-service **Sport-Studio Apollo,** Hauptstrasse 150 (☎ **030/784-8203;** U-Bahn: Kleistpark; open Mon–Fri 10am–10pm, Sat–Sun 1–6pm; day use 20DM/$11), has machines, free weights, a cardiovascular section, and steam and sauna rooms. There's another branch offering the same services and hours: **Apollo Fitness World,** Borodinstrasse 16 (☎ **030/467-4231;** S-Bahn: Griefswalderstrasse).

SWIMMING Water sports (by which I mean swimming) are perhaps the most popular form of gay recreation in Berlin. As any gay Berliner will tell you, the city's public pools (and their shower and sauna areas) are cruisy to the max. So many gays frequent the ozone-disinfected **Strandbad Wilmersdorf,** Mecklenburgische Strasse 80 (☎ **030/821-0260;** U-Bahn to Heidelberg Platz, then follow signs for Stadtbad Wilmersdorf; open Mon–Fri 6am–11pm, Sat–Sun 8am–11pm), that it's unofficially called the "Tuntenaquarium" (Queen's Aquarium). The same hours apply at **Bad am Spreewaldplatz,** Spreewaldplatz (☎ **030/612-7057;** U-Bahn: Görlitzer Bahnhof), where lots of younger gays from Kreuzberg make a splash.

Meanwhile, the **Stadtbad Charlottenburg–Alte Halle,** Krumme Strasse 10 (☎ **030/3430-3214;** U-Bahn: Deutsche Oper), draws lots of gays on Tuesday and Friday 6 to 9pm; these are the hours reserved for nude swimming. This is Berlin's oldest pool, dating from 1898, and has a remarkable art nouveau interior.

There's a 5 or 6DM ($2.75 or $3.50) admission charge at all the pools.

5 Hitting the Stores

Most stores and shops open Monday to Saturday at 9 or 10am. Smaller stores and boutiques generally close at 6:30pm weekdays and 2pm Saturdays. Larger department stores may stay open some nights to 7 or 8:30pm, except Saturday, when there's an early closing. Nearly every store is closed on Sunday, so that's a good day to poke through the flea markets.

The main shopping area in the western part of the city is along the **Kurfürstendamm** and its side streets, which are loaded with boutiques, art galleries, designer clothing stores, jewelers, and antiques dealers. For the mall-minded, the **Europa-Center** on Breitscheidplatz (across from the Kaiser-Wilhelm Memorial Church on the Ku-Damm) has about 100 shops, boutiques, and restaurants. **Keithstrasse** in Schöneberg is known for its scores of *Trödelläden* (secondhand shops), crammed with gewgaws, doodads, knickknacks, and junk.

Don't forget that the east side of town (the old center, or Berlin-Mitte) has become a veritable retail wonderland of upscale chic now the socialists are gone. **Friedrichstrasse,** the main shopping drag, is lined with one luxury designer store after another.

SHOPS A TO Z

ART & ANTIQUES **Art Déco,** Belziger Strasse 36 (☎ **030/781-7384;** U-Bahn: Bayerischer Platz), sells designer furniture, lamps, and accessories from 1900 to 1980. **Galerie Janssen,** Pariser Strasse 45 (☎ **030/881-1590;** U-Bahn: Hohenzollernplatz), is a gay men's art and photo gallery with posters, postcards, videos, and assorted pop objects. **Pulz & Detering,** Wilhelmstrasse 140 in Willy-Brandt-Haus (☎ **030/2529-9871;** U-Bahn: Hallesches Tor), attached to an antiques store, specializes in rare books dealing with homosexuality.

BOOKSTORES One of the world's oldest gay and lesbian bookstores, ✪ **Prinz Eisenherz,** Bleibtreustrasse 52 (☎ **030/313-9936;** S-Bahn: Savignyplatz), stocks a vast array of new and rare fiction, nonfiction, art books, and magazines in German, English, and other languages. The staff is extremely knowledgeable and helpful. **Adam,** Gleimstrasse 23 (☎ **030/448-0767;** S-Bahn: Schonhauser Allee), carries gay and lesbian literature, newspapers, postcards, and videos. **Bruno's,** Nürnberger Strasse 53 (☎ **030/2147-3293;** U-Bahn: Zoologischer Garten), has books, videos, and CDs. **Lilith,** Knesebeckstrasse 86–87 (☎ **030/312-3102;** U-Bahn: Ernst-Reuter-Platz), is a women's bookstore. **Galerie Unter den Linden,** Unter den Linden 69d (☎ **030/2267-9203;** U-Bahn: Friedrichstrasse), isn't gay but has a good selection of art and architecture books, books on Berlin, and great postcards.

CONDOMS You can buy them at drugstores (*Apotheken*); for more variety, try **Condomi,** Kantstrasse 38 (☎ **030/313-5051;** U-Bahn: Zoologischer Garten).

DEPARTMENT STORES Western Berlin's biggest department store is **KaDeWe (Kaufhaus des Westens),** Tauentzienstrasse 21 (☎ **030/2120;** U-Bahn: Nollendorfplatz). If you're retailing in the Friedrichstrasse area, check out the new **Galeries Lafayette,** Französische Strasse 23 (☎ **030/209-480;** U-Bahn: Friedrichstrasse), with its four-story glass-cone centerpiece.

FLEA MARKETS Berlin's best-known and biggest flea market, the **Grosser/Berliner Trödelmarkt mit Kunstmarkt,** is just east of the Tiergrten S-bahn station on Strasse des 17. Juni; one side sells arts and crafts, the other antiques and junk. It's open Saturday and Sunday 8am to 4pm. The **Berliner Antik und Flohmarkt,** another good flea market, stretches out under the arches of the Friedrichstrasse S-Bahn station and is open Wednesday to Monday 11am to 6pm.

LEATHER & LATEX Fetishistical fashion-plates will find all kinds of "ouch-fits" at the following boutiques: **Fishbelly,** Grunewaldstrasse 71a (☎ **030/788-3015;** U-Bahn: Bayerischer Platz); **Hautnah,** Uhlandstrasse 170 (☎ **030/882-3434;** U-Bahn: Spichernstrasse); and **Schwarze Mode Berlin,** Grunewaldstrasse 91 (☎ **030/784-5922;** U-Bahn: Bayerischer Platz).

PIERCING & TATTOOING **Blut & Eisen (Blood and Iron),** Alte Schönhaser Strasse 6 (☎ **030/283-1982;** S-Bahn: Hackescher Markt), offers piercing, tattooing, and jewelry. **Crazy Ink,** Perleberger Strsse 5 (☎ **030/395-4786;** U-Bahn: Turmstrasse), does piercing and tattooing. **Piercing-Line Berlin,** Courbierestrasse 9 (☎ **030/218-2164;** U-Bahn: Nollendorfplatz), pierces in Playground, a gay sex shop. And **Tatau Obscur,** Solmsstrasse 35 (☎ **030/694-4288;** U-Bahn: Gneisen Strasse), tattoos, pierces, scarifies, and attaches rings and what-not.

6 All the World's a Stage

THE PERFORMING ARTS

Culture vultures take note: There's more going on in Berlin than in any other city in Germany. With three major symphony orchestras, three opera houses, ballet companies, and scads of theaters and cabarets, you won't be lacking for things to do. Check the listings in ***Zitty*** or ***Berlin Programm*** for schedules of what's going on where.

Unsold tickets for over 100 venues, including opera, classical concerts, and cabarets, are available for up to 50% off at **Hekticket,** with outlets at Kurfürstendamm 14 (☎ **030/883-6010;** U-Bahn: Kufürstendamm) and Alexanderplatz (☎ **030/242-6709;** U-Bahn: Alexanderplatz). You can also buy tickets at the box office or from ticket agencies, which charge a commission. **Theater Konzertkasse,** Kurfürstendamm 16 (☎ **030/852-4080;** U-Bahn: Kurfürstendamm), is one of the most centrally located agencies.

In Charlottenburg, the ✪ **Deutsche Oper Berlin,** Bismarckstrasse 35 (☎ **030/343-8401;** U-Bahn: Deutsche Oper; box office open Mon–Sat 11am to time of performance, Sun 10am–2pm), is the opera house that served the former West Berlin. Both opera and ballet are performed; tickets bought on the day of performance are half-price. The ✪ **Staatsoper Unter den Linden,** Unter den Linden 7 (☎ **030/2035-4555;** U-Bahn: Friedrichstrasse or Französichestrasse; S-Bahn: Unter den Linden; box office open Mon–Fri 10am–6pm, Sat–Sun 2–6pm and 1 hour before performances), is housed in a historic building in Berlin-Mitte. They also alternate opera and ballet performances. The **Komische Oper,** Behrenstrasse 55–57 (☎ **030/4702-1000;** S-Bahn: Unter den Linden; box office open Mon–Sat 11am–7pm, Sun 1pm to time of performance), is a famous and well-respected East Berlin house with a unique artistic identity, but it doesn't generally use internationally known stars; tickets bought on the day of performance are about 50% off.

In the Kulturforum complex, the renowned ✪ **Berlin Philharmonic Orchestra** plays in the acoustically outstanding **Philharmonie,** Matthäikirchstrasse 1 (☎ **030/2548-8132;** U-Bahn: Potsdamer Platz; box office Mon–Fri 3:30–6pm, Sat–Sun 11am–2pm). Chamber music concerts are given at the adjoining **Kammermusiksaal.** The historic Schauspielhaus in the former East Berlin has undergone a stunning transformation and is now the ✪ **Konzerthaus Berlin,** Gendarmenmarkt (☎ **030/203-09-2101;** S-Bahn: Unter den Linden; box office Mon–Sat noon–8pm, Sun to 4pm). The ✪ **Berlin Symphony Orchestra** and other classical music groups perform in this glittering pitch-perfect hall. The city's third major orchestra, the **Berlin Symphony,** performs at both the Philharmonie and the Konzerthaus.

Berlin's theater scene is outstanding—but guess what? The plays are performed in German. If you don't speak the language but still want to go to the theater, I suggest the famous **Berliner Ensemble,** Bertolt-Brecht-Platz 1 (☎ **030/282-3160;** U-Bahn: Friedrichstrasse; box office open Mon–Sat 11am–6pm, Sun 3–6pm and 1 hour before performance). This is the group formed by the great playwright Bertolt Brecht and his wife, Helene Weigel, and there's something to be said about seeing Brecht's plays performed in "his" theater.

GAY THEATER, CABARET & VARIETY SHOWS

Berlin has always been known for its cabaret and "variety" shows. The language barrier is less of an issue with these revues, which can be wickedly entertaining.

The cabaret ✪ **Bar jeder Vernunft** (roughly, "For No Reason"), with gay and lesbian artistes, performs in a mirrored turn-of-the-century circus tent called **Spiegelpalast,** Schaperstrasse 24 (☎ **030/883-1582;** U-Bahn: Spichernstrasse; admission about 30DM/$17). In Kreuzberg, cabaret shows (from drag to opera parodies) are performed on the small stage of **BKA (Berliner Kabarett Anstalt),** Mehringdamm 32–34 (☎ **030/251-0112;** U-Bahn: Mehringdamm; admission 35DM/$20 with a table, 29DM/$11 without). Shows usually begin at 8pm, and on weekends there's a disco starting at 10pm.

Another variety-cabaret show, this one with male strippers, acrobats, and drag numbers, is **Trottoir (Sidewalk),** Knesebeckstrasse 56–58 (☎ **030/883-9338;** U-Bahn: Uhlandstrasse; shows Wed–Sun 8pm). A famous and fairly fabulous drag revue, mostly attended now by visiting heteros but worth seeing if you're into cross-dressing at its most glamorous, is **Chez Nous Travestie-Theater,** Marburger Strasse 14 (☎ **030/213-1810;** U-Bahn: Wittenbergplatz; shows nightly 8:30 and 11pm; admission 15DM/$9). Note that there's a one-drink minimum of 35DM ($20) a gulp.

More down-to-earth, less expensive, and just as fun, is the drag show at **Lützower Lampe,** Witzlebenstrasse 38 (☎ **030/321-2097;** U-Bahn: Kaiserdamm; shows Fri–Sat 9 and 11pm; prices vary). Plays and theater pieces with gay themes are presented at the **Kleines Theater,** Sudwestkorso 64 (☎ **030/821-3030;** U-Bahn: Friedrich-Wilhelm-Platz).

7 In the Heat of the Night

There are so many gay bars in Berlin you're never going to make it to all of them. The following list is (of necessity) selective but gives a good choice of places west, east, and in-between. Some are favorite haunts that've been around for decades, some are new and trendy American-style bars, some have cruisy "darkrooms" (the new rage in Berlin), and others are quiet neighborhood "locals" (*Kneipen*). Bar-hopping is a late-night activity in Berlin (as in the rest of the world); things don't generally get going until midnight.

Although some of the bars in the former East Berlin (**Prenzlauer Berg** and **Berlin-Mitte**) are certainly worth visiting, it can be a hassle to get back to the western side of the city after midnight (when things are just revving up). The gay scene is more "international" in the area around **Nollendorfplatz,** which has had gay bars since the 1920s. **Kreuzberg,** becoming less countercultural and more capitalist by the day, is another hot gay borough with a fab-o selection of bars. I've organized this list by general area to make it easier for you.

GAY BARS

NEAR NOLLENDORFPLATZ U-BAHN ✪ **Andreas' Kneipe,** Ansbacher Strasse 29 (☎ **030/218-3257;** U-Bahn: Wittenbergplatz; open daily 11am–4am), is a long-standing and still popular favorite with an interesting mixed male crowd.

Blue Boy Bar, Eisenacher Strasse 3a (☎ **030/218-7498;** U-Bahn: Nollendorftplatz; open daily 24 hours), is used by hustling street boys.

Fugger Eck, Eisenacher Strasse 3a (☎ **030/218-3506;** U-Bahn: Nollendorfplatz; open Mon–Sat 1pm–3am), next to Blue Boy Bar, is a neighborhood local that's been around for ages.

Lenz, Eisenacher Strasse 3 (☎ **030/217-7820;** U-Bahn: Nollendorftplaz; open Mon–Fri 6pm–3am, Sat–Sun 8pm–3am), a few steps from Blue Boy Bar and Fugger Eck, is another popular meeting spot.

Eldorado, Motzstrsse 20 (☎ **030/2147-5550;** U-Bahn: Nollendorfplatz; open daily 24 hours), is a gay music bar. It's next to **Pinocchio,** Motzstrasse 20 (☎ **030/2137-5550;** U-Bahn: Nollendorftplaz; open daily 24 hours), used as an office for young hustlers. **Hafen,** Motzstrasse 19 (☎ **030/211-4118;** U-Bahn: Nollendorfplatz; open Mon–Sat 9pm–3am), is a favorite gay/lesbian guppy bar where you stand outside on warm evenings.

Another hustler joint is **Tabasco,** Fuggerstrasse 3 (☎ **030/214-2636;** U-Bahn: Nollendorfplatz; open Mon–Thurs noon–6am, Fri–Sun 24 hours), and I'd avoid it and Pinocchio unless you're into that scene.

Ma-Deuce, An der Urania 5 (☎ **030/214-1720;** U-Bahn: Nollendorftplatz; open daily 3pm–3am), is a small American-style men's bar with a cocktail menu.

On Courbierestrasse, one block east of An der Urania, is **Movie** (☎ **030/211-7702;** U-Bahn: Nollendorfplatz; open Tues–Fri 4pm–2am, Sat–Sun 2pm–2am), the newest gay bar in the gay village.

IN KREUZBERG ✪ **Roses,** Oranienstrasse 187 (☎ **030/615-6570;** U-Bahn: Kottbusser Tor; open daily 10:30pm–5am), has an overly plush ambience and is a favorite starting point for gays and lesbians partying in Kreuzberg.

Anal, Muskauer Strasse 15 (☎ **030/618-7064;** U-Bahn: Görlitzer Bahnhof; open daily 8pm–2am), is an alternative club for younger gays and lesbians; Monday nights are women only.

Dandy Club, Urbanstrasse 64 (☎ **030/691-9013;** U-Bahn: Hermannplatz; open Mon–Sat 4pm–3am), has a darkroom and a Friday-night safer-sex party.

Fogo, Arndtstrasse 29 (☎ **030/692-1465,** U-Bahn: Gneisenaustrasse; open daily 8pm–3am), is a mixed cocktail bar with loud decor and a louder international crowd.

Mondschein, Urbanstrasse 101 (☎ **030/932-355;** U-Bahn: Hermannplatz; open Mon–Thurs and Sun 8pm–3am, Sat 8pm–5am), is a gay pub with a darkroom.

O-Bar, Oranienstrasse 168 (☎ **030/614-2809;** U-Bahn: Kottbusser Tor; open daily 8pm–3am), is a hangout for gays and lesbians.

Bienenkönig, Luckauer Strasse 16 (☎ **030/614-1231;** U-Bahn: Kottbusser Tor; open daily 2pm–2am), is a small local that draws a more mature group.

Tunnel Bar, Schlesische Strasse 32 (☎ **030/6170-2003;** U-Bahn: Schlesisches Tor; open Mon–Sat 7pm–5am), is a gay/lesbian bar with a tunnel-like cellar that's dark and for men only.

ELSEWHERE IN WESTERN BERLIN **Action,** Lietzenburger Strasse 77 (☎ **030/882-5151;** U-Bahn: Kurfürstendamm; open daily 5pm–2am), is mostly for men, but lesbians are welcome.

✪ **Club Banana,** Fasanenstrasse 91a (☎ **030/313-3773;** S-Bahn: Savignyplatz; open daily 6pm–2am), a hip club for younger gays and lesbians, is located under the S-Bahn tracks next to the Arc restaurant.

Albrechtklause, Albrechtstrasse 125 (☎ **030/791-5621;** U-Bahn: Rathaus Steglitz; open Mon–Fri 2pm–2am, Sat–Sun 6pm–2am), is a quieter gay local.

CC 96, Lietzenburger Strasse 95 (☎ **030/883-2650;** U-Bahn: Uhlandstrasse; open Thurs–Tues 8pm–3am), is a gay bar in Charlottenburg with male strip shows.

Zufall, Pfalzburger Strasse 10 (☎ **030/83-2473;** U-Bahn: Uhlandstrasse; open Wed–Sun 10pm–3am), south of the Ku-damm, has served gays and lesbians for over 10 years.

Charly's BiBaBo, Pfalzburger Strasse 5 (☎ **030/883-2685;** U-Bahn: Hohenzollernplatz; open Mon–Sat 5pm–2am), is a small gay local in Wilmersdorf.

Die Espresso Bar, Joachimstaler Strasse 24 (☎ **030/881-9488;** U-Bahn: Kurfürstendamm; open daily 24 hours), is a favorite and centrally located gay hangout.

Quarx, Siegmunds Hof 21 (☎ **030/399-4763;** S-Bahn: Tiergarten; open Tues–Sun 7pm–2am), beams in gay and lesbian Trekkies—it's the city's first gay *Star Trek*–theme bar.

BERLIN-MITTE & PRENZLAUER BERG **Adonis,** Pappelallee 32a (☎ **030/447-9888;** U-Bahn: Eberswalder Strasse; open daily 8pm–8am), and **Dark Star,** Schönhauser Allee 39a (☎ **030/442-4213;** U-Bahn: Eberswalder Strasse; open daily 10pm–6am), are gay Prenzlauer Berg bars with darkrooms.

Besenkammer, Rathausstrasse 1 (☎ **030/242-4083;** U-/S-Bahn: Alexanderplatz; open daily 24 hours), tucked under the S-Bahn tracks, is a gay East Berlin historical landmark; the name means "broom closet" and that's about how big this place is.

Schoppenstube, Schönhauser Allee 44 (☎ **030/442-8204;** U-Bahn: Eberwalderstrasse; open daily 10pm–7am), East Berlin's oldest gay bar (it was here in GDR days), now has a darkroom and hosts different party nights.

Stiller Don, Erich-Weinert-Strasse 67 (☎ **030/445-5957;** S-Bahn: Prenzlauer Allee; open daily 6pm–2am), another East Berlin gay landmark, is a straight neighborhood pub (with food) during the early evenings; later on and during the weekends, it fills up with local gays and lesbians.

Oh-Ase, Rathausstrasse 5 (☎ **030/242-3030;** U-Bahn: Alexanderplatz; open Mon–Sat 10am–2am, Sun 2pm–2am), occupies the ground floor (Rathauspassage) of an office building and goes for a "tropical" theme.

Pick Ab!, Greifenhagener Strasse 16 (☎ **030/445-8523;** U-Bahn: Schönhauser Allee; open daily 24 hours), is a Prenzlauer Berg gay bar with a popular darkroom.

Romeo, Greifenhagener Strasse 16 (☎ **030/447-6789;** U-Bahn: Schönhauser Allee; open daily from 11pm–5am), is another gay bar not too far away.

Zum Burgfrieden, Wichertstrasse 69 (☎ **030/445-7279;** U-Bahn: Schönhauser Allee; open daily 7pm–6am), yet another hangover from commie days, has now gone capitalist and put in a darkroom; **Die Gruft,** next door (same phone as above; open daily 10pm–5am), is a jeans-and-leather bar.

LESBIAN CAFE/BARS

Begine, Potsdamer Strasse 139 (☎ **030/215-4325;** U-Bahn: Bülowstrasse or Kurfürstenstrasse; open daily 6pm–1am), is a women's cafe/disco.

Café Seidenfaden, Dircksenstrasse 47 (☎ **030/283-2783;** U-Bahn: Alexanderplatz; S-Bahn: Hackescher Markt; open Tues–Fri 11am–11pm, Sat noon–7pm, Sun 10am–9pm), a drug- and alcohol-free women's cafe, serves good breakfasts and snacks.

In Kreuzberg, **Futuro,** Adalbertstrasse 79 (☎ **030/615-2823;** U-Bahn: Kottbusser Tor; open daily 6pm–1am), is a women-owned cafe where men are welcome.

Pour Elle, Kalckreuthstrasse 10 (☎ **030/218-7533;** U-Bahn: Nollendorfplatz; open Sun–Mon and Wed–Thurs 7pm–2am, Fri–Sat 9pm–2am) is the city's oldest lesbian bar; it's plush and comfy and is frequented by dykes of every stripe; Monday and Wednesday men are welcome.

In Prenzlauer Berg, **Shambala,** Greifenhagener Strasse 12 (☎ **030/447-6226;** U-/S-Bahn: Schönhauser Allee; open daily 6pm–3am), is a lesbigay hangout with billiard tables and a jungle motif; it's women only on Monday.

Whistle Stop, Knackstrasse 94 (☎ **030/442-7847;** U-Bahn: Eberswalder Strasse; open Tues–Sat 6pm–midnight), is a comfortable bar/bistro/cafe popular with Prenzlauer Berg lesbians.

LEATHER BARS

Taking the U-Bahn or S-Bahn to the Schönhauser Allee stop will get you to the following three leather bars in Prenzlauer Berg:

Darkroom, Rodenbergstrasse 23 (☎ **030/444-9321;** open daily 10pm–5am), has a you-know-what for you-know-what. **Greifbar,** at the corner of Wichertstrasse and Greifenhagener Strasse (☎ **030/444-0828;** open daily 8pm–6am), is the neighborhood's newest leather cruise bar and has (appropriately) a construction theme. **Die Gruft,** Wichertstrasse 69 (☎ **030/445-7279;** open daily 10pm–5am), caters to leather, denim, and uniform queens and also has a darkroom.

Meanwhile, in the western part of the city, there are three leather bars near the Nollendorfplatz U-Bahn stop: **Knast,** Fuggerstrasse 34 (☎ **030/218-1026;** open daily 9pm–5am), is a famous "old" leather bar in the gay village. So is **Tom's Bar,** Motzstrasse 19 (☎ **030/213-4570;** open daily 10pm–5am), which has been around for ages and has a dark labyrinth down below. **New Action,** Kleiststrasse 35 (☎ **030/211-8256;** open Mon–Sat 8pm–5am, Sun 1pm–5am), is a newer leather-and-jeans bar with a darkroom. **Twilight Zone,** Welserstrasse 24 (☎ **030/218-1432;** open Fri–Sat midnight–6am), under Connection Disco, is a leather-and-jeans bar, also with a darkroom.

DANCE CLUBS

IN THE WEST Held in the huge Metropol hall now redecorated with an Egyptian theme, the ✪ **Angels Tea Dance,** Nollendorfplatz 5 (☎ **030/215-3569;** U-Bahn: Nollendorfplatz; admission 10–15DM/$6–$9), features top DJs, the Sisters of Perpetual Mercy granting indulgences, and several dance floors and bars—it's a real scene held twice monthly; call for info. **Connection,** Welserstrasse 24 (☎ **030/218-1432;** U-Bahn: Wittenbergplatz; open Fri–Sat 10pm; admission 10DM/$6), is big on techno and just plain big: It spreads out all over the place and has various "specialty areas" where you'll probably find whatever/whomever it is you're looking for.

SO 36, Oranienstrasse 190 (☎ **030/615-2601;** U-Bahn: Kottbusser Tor; never open before 10pm), is a trendy disco in Kreuzberg for a younger crowd; Monday is mixed, Wednesday is a lesbigay techno-fest, Sunday there's variety, and on the third Friday of every month there's a party for lesbians and drag queens. **SchwuZ,** Mehringdamm 61 (☎ **030/693-7025;** U-Bahn: Mehringdamm), located below the Gay Museum in Kreuzberg, has been the scene of lesbigay events for years; all sorts of things go on here—like special parties on Friday and disco on Saturday from 11pm.

Terminal Danceclub, at Tempelhof Airport, entrance at Columbiadamm 6 (☎ **030/6904-1367;** U-Bahn: Platz der Luftbrücke; opens Wed and Fri–Sun 10:30pm), is a bar/cafe/disco set up in the former officers' casino for the U.S. Air Force at the airport.

IN THE EAST **Die Busche,** Mühlenstrasse 11–12 (☎ **030/296-0800;** U-/S- Bahn: Warschauer Strasse; opens Wed and Fri–Sun 10:30pm), is a huge place (Berlin's largest gay disco) with big crowds and a somewhat provincial air.

DOWN & DIRTY: CINEMAS, SAUNAS & MORE

CINEMAS **Xenon,** Kolonnenstrasse 5–6 (☎ **030/782-8850;** U-Bahn: Kleistpark), is a real movie house that often shows real gay and lesbian films (plot, emotion, music, everything). In Prenzlauer Berg, gay movies show up on the programs at **Blow Up,** Immanuelkirchstrasse 14 (☎ **030/442-8662;** S-Bahn: Greifswalder Strasse).

FLICKS The following sex shops have porn with video cabins and cruising areas: **Bad Boy'z,** Schliemannstrasse 38 (☎ **030/440-8165;** U-Bahn: Eberswalder Strasse; open Mon–Sat 1pm–1am, Sun 3pm–1am); **Connection Garage,** Fuggerstrasse 33 (☎ **030/218-1432;** U-Bahn: Wittenbergplatz; open Mon–Sat 10am–1am, Sun

2pm–1am); **JAXX,** Motzstrasse 19 (☎ **030/213-8103;** U-Bahn: Nollendorfplatz; open Mon–Sat 11am–3am, Sun 2pm–3am); **Man's Pleasurechest,** Fuggerstrasse 5 (☎ **030/211-2015;** U-Bahn: Nollendorfplatz; open Mon–Sat 10am–1am, Sun 1pm–1am); **New Man,** Joachimsthaler Strasse 1–3 (no phone; U-Bahn: Zoologischer Garten; open Mon–Fri 10am–12:30am, Sat noon–12:30am); **Playground,** Courbierestrasse 9 (☎ **030/218-2164;** U-Bahn: Wittenbergplatz; open Mon–Sat noon–1am); **Pool Berlin,** Schaperstrasse 1 (☎ **030/214-1989;** U-Bahn: Kurfürstendamm; open Mon–Sat 10am–10pm).

SAUNAS **Apollo City Sauna,** Kurfürstenstrasse 10 (☎ **030/213-2424;** U-Bahn: Wittenbergplatz; open daily 1pm–7am; lockers 22DM/$12, cabins 34DM/$19), is one of the oldest and largest gay saunas in western Berlin and attracts a very mixed crowd. More mature machos climb the four flights of stairs to hang out at nearby **Steam,** Kufürstenstrasse 113 (☎ **030/218-4060;** open Mon–Thurs 11am–7am, weekends 24 hours; locker 23DM/$13, cabin 33DM/$18).

The two newest gay saunas, both very popular, are in former East Berlin. Close to the Brandenburg Gate is **Gate Sauna,** Wilhelmstrasse 80 (☎ **030/229-9430;** U-Bahn: Mohrenstrasse; open Mon–Thurs 11am–7am, weekends 24 hours; locker 21–27DM/$12–$15, cabin 29–37DM/$16–$21). Even more modern and luxurious is **Treibhaus,** Schönhauser Allee 132 (☎ **030/448-4503;** U-Bahn: Eberswalder Strasse; open Mon–Thurs 3pm–7am, weekends 24 hours; locker 21DM/$12, cabin 33DM/$18).

8 A Side Trip from Berlin: Potsdam & Sanssouci Palace

Did Frederick the Great, king of Prussia, dally with the boys? Well, he did play the flute awfully well (no slouch, he also united Germany for the first time). And is it true that the man Frederick's stern Prussian father (aka the "Soldier King") had put to death in 1730—an execution his son was forced to watch—was really Frederick's lover?

Straight historians will tell you one thing (or avoid the touchy subject entirely); gay historians will tell you another. Whatever the truth may be, Frederick the Great's **Sanssouci Palace** in Potsdam stands as a visual signature of a dominant personality in German history. Sanssouci is to Berlin what Louis XIV's Versailles is to Paris. Allow yourself a full day to visit this remarkable place, 15 miles southwest of Berlin, and maybe combine it with a tour of Babelsberg Studios (see above).

To get to Sanssouci, you must first get to **Potsdam,** a former garrison town on the Havel River that's now the capital of the state of Brandenburg. It couldn't be easier: **S-Bahn** lines S3 and S7 stop at the Potsdam Stadt station. From there it's half an hour's walk through the historic town center to the palace. Or you can hop on **bus no. 695** and go directly to the palace. Even better: From April to October, you can reach Potsdam by **boat** from Glienicker Brücke (bridge) in southwestern Berlin; for information contact **Weisse Flotte** at ☎ **030/280-4976.** And if you don't want to hassle with anything, you can take one of the **Potsdam–Sanssouci bus tours** offered by the sightseeing bus companies on Ku-Damm; the cost is generally 50 to 60DM ($28 to $33) for a half-day fast-track tour.

Potsdam celebrated its 1,000th anniversary in 1993, and there are several historic sites worth visiting in the city, including the old Dutch Quarter. Brochures and inexpensive guides are available at the **Potsdam Tourist Information office,** Friedrich-Ebert-Strasse 5 (☎ **0331/291-100**).

Potsdam didn't gain true importance until the "Great Elector" Friedrich Wilhelm (1620–1688) chose the lovely, leafy, lakey area to be his second seat of residence outside Berlin. From then on, Potsdam was a Hohenzollern hangout. To escape from the rigors of Berl318in court life, Frederick II (the Great; 1712–1786) built in Potsdam a "small" country palace where he could retire "sans souci" (without a care) and indulge his passions for music, poetry, and philosophy.

✪ **Schloss (Palace) Sanssouci** (☎ **0331/969-419**) is open Tuesday to Sunday 9am to 4pm (Nov–Mar) or to 5pm (Apr–Oct). You can see it only on a tour costing 10DM ($6) and requiring you to don huge felt slippers so you don't scuff those floors. The tour is given only in German, so you need an English-language guidebook. If you don't get there early, you may have to wait for a much-later tour. Use the time to wander through the magnificent landscaped gardens with their bevy of historic palaces and outbuildings, including the Orangerie and the adorably campy Chinese Teahouse. Freddy the Great created the original design for the grounds, and his planning is still evident in the restored vineyard terraces and the area immediately around the palace.

One of the greatest and most beautiful examples of European Rococo, Sanssouci was built between 1745 and 1747 as Fred's summerhouse. Here he could let his hair (or wig) down, talk turkey with French philosopher Voltaire and music with composer Johann Sebastian Bach. In short, this was a summer resort for an enlightened monarch. The palace is filled with all kinds of Rococo treasures. In 1991, Frederick the Great's remains were returned to be reburied on the grounds of Sanssouci, the palace he loved the most.

DINING **Aqua,** Zeppelinstrasse 136, in the Art'otel (☎ **0331/98150;** open daily 6:30–11pm), serves fish cakes and fondues, grilled meats, and fish in an upscale Havel-side dining room. **Arco,** Friedrich-Ebert-Strasse (☎ **0331/270-1690;** open daily 9am–midnight), is a small Italian restaurant in a historic 18th-century building. **Café Heider,** Friedrich-Ebert-Strasse (☎ **0331/270-5596;** open Mon–Fri from 8am, Sat from 9am, brunch Sun 10am–2:30pm), can be a bit of a scene, especially at the outside tables on a summer's night.

5 Greece

Where It All Began

by Haas Mroue

Greece is a land of contrasts—at once alluring and deceiving, welcoming and daunting. **Athens** is a big city of 6 million people and seems old, dusty, and impossibly crowded at first sight. But this ancient city is full of history, incredible archaeological sites, and excellent museums. It's also the only world capital where homosexuality was considered the norm thousands of years ago. But nowadays gay life isn't what Athens is known for, and many visitors are disappointed at the limited gay venues and the lack of community.

Mykonos, however, is a different story. It's a hedonist's paradise and the gayest beach destination in southern Europe. Nude beaches abound, and boy are there boys on this island that's fast becoming a gay Mecca as men from around the globe come and come.

Santorini is breathtakingly beautiful and attracts a sophisticated mixed crowd (as well as half the cruise ships in Europe). It's much more sedate and spectacular than any other Greek island with its villages hanging off cliffs and black pebbly beaches. **Folegandros** is unpretentious, incredibly simple, and uncluttered. There's only one taxi and one bus on the island, a few good tavernas and hotels, rugged hills for hiking, and secluded coves for swimming.

Some visitors find it convenient to fly into Athens, work their way south or east by boat, then fly out of Heraklion in Crete or even Istanbul. Athens is also a good place to begin a southern Mediterranean adventure to such places as Cyprus, the Holy Land, or even Egypt. Simple ferries and fancy cruise ships frequently plow the waters among these countries, docking at ports like Rhodes, Larnaca, Haifa, and Alexandria.

The Greek Drachma

The unit of currency is the **drachma** (*drachmi*, in Greek), abbreviated **Dr.** Coins come in denominations of 5Dr, 10Dr, 20Dr, 50Dr, and 100Dr (with old 1Dr and 2DR coins still occasionally surfacing). Bills come in denominations of 50Dr (blue), 100Dr (red) (both being taken out of circulation), 500DR (green), 1,000Dr (brown), 5,000Dr (mostly gray), and 10,000Dr (pinkish).

At this writing, the drachma was equivalent to 3¢ U.S. (or $1 = approximately 300Dr), and that was the rate of exchange I used throughout. Prices over $5 U.S. have been rounded to the nearest dollar.

8

Athens: Your First Taste of Greek

No one comes to Greece and stays only in **Athens (Athina).** For most visitors, it's a brief stop on the way to or from the islands. Be prepared for traffic and noise and smog. The summer heat is intense enough to drive many Athenians out of the city to the islands and mountains. And the winters are bone-chillingly cold; it snows in January and February.

Athenians (and the Greeks in general) aren't especially hospitable or warm. In fact, they come across as being quite unconcerned and indifferent. It takes them a while to warm up to visitors, especially since most foreigners come to Athens in a rush, with just enough time for a visit to the Acropolis. If you want to experience Athens, you have to take your time. Show some genuine interest, and the Greeks will warm up to you. Venture away from the commercial areas of Syntagma and Plaka to find quaint neighborhoods and many cafes crowded with people sitting on sidewalks. The Greeks prefer to sit outdoors as soon as the weather warms in April or May and as late as the first cold spell in November. That's the pleasure of Athens—so much happens on the streets. It's also very affordable, and you can dine well here for a fraction of what it would cost elsewhere in Europe.

However, if you're looking for hot gay nightlife, forget it—there are only a few bars and clubs. In ancient Greece, homosexuality was accepted as part of the culture. In fact, it was as normal for an older man to have a younger male lover as it was for him to be married to a woman. Now, though, things are much different. In Athens, discretion is the key word, and the gay clubs are somewhat dark places on dimly lit streets that aren't concentrated in one neighborhood. Since homosexuality isn't culturally accepted, gays tend to stay closeted. As in most cities, the more artsy places tend to have a heavy gay following. To save you time, I've sniffed out those places for you.

1 Athens Essentials

ARRIVING & DEPARTING

BY PLANE The layout of the Athens's **Ellinikon International Airport,** 7 miles south of Syntagma Square, is rather confusing. The three terminals are far apart, so it's important to know where you'll be landing or taking off from. The **West Terminal** is used solely by the national airline, Olympic. For flight information, call ☎ **01/936-3363.** The

Charter Terminal to the south is used by many unscheduled carriers flying mostly from Northern Europe.

Most visitors arrive at the **East Terminal,** used by all foreign scheduled airlines. For flight information, call ☎ **01/969-4466.** Early afternoon is the busiest time, with flights from every major European city arriving 2 to 4pm. Delta and TWA have nonstop flights from New York. Planes park away from the terminal and passengers descend using old-fashioned stairways. It's a grand way to start your vacation, adding a touch of old-world charm; you'll see the Mediterranean shimmering to the west before a bus whisks you to passport control. If you're connecting on to Mykonos or Santorini, you'll have to clear customs here (save time by changing money while waiting for your bags) and take the shuttle bus that runs to the West Terminal every half an hour 8:30am to 8:30pm. Be sure to allow plenty of time between your international arrival and domestic departure—at least 3 hours.

If you're heading into the city, a **taxi** is your best bet. It's quick (25 minutes if you don't hit traffic) and reasonable at 2,500Dr ($8) for the ride into downtown. The fare almost doubles 11pm to 5am. You can also take **bus** no. 091 to Syntagma Square in the center of the city. If you're going straight to the port of Piraeus to catch a ferry to the islands, a **taxi** costs about 3,000Dr ($10), but allow at least an hour during rush hour for the 7-mile journey. You can catch **bus** no. 019 to Piraeus from either the East or the West terminal. Buses run every half an hour 7am to 11pm, then every hour to 6am, with the trip lasting 30 minutes. The fare to both Syntagma Square and Piraeus is 200Dr (65¢) 6am to 11pm and 400Dr ($1.35) 11pm to 6am.

Don't expect to see any improvements at Ellinikon since a new airport, due to open in 2002, is being built at Spata, northeast of Athens.

BY TRAIN There are two rail stations in Athens. If you're coming from the west, crossing by ferry from Italy to Patras, you'll arrive at the **Peloponnese Station (Stathmos Peloponníssou)** about a mile northwest of Omonia Square. Trains from the north arrive nearby at the **Larissa Station (Stathmos Laríssis).** A taxi to Plaka, Kolonaki, or Syntagma from both stations shouldn't cost more than 750Dr ($2.50). For train schedules, dial ☎ **145** in Athens. The tourist offices also have detailed listings in English of current train schedules.

BY BOAT Arriving at the port of **Piraeus** is much more convenient than arriving at the port of Rafina, an hour east of Athens. Piraeus is a half-hour **taxi** ride or a 15-minute **metro** ride from the city center. If you don't have heavy bags, the subway is your best bet. It currently stops only at Thission, Monastiraki (a 10-minute walk from Plaka and Syntagma), and Omonia squares. The metro runs every 10 minutes 5am to midnight, costing 100Dr (35¢). You'll need to buy a ticket from the machine before entering the tracks. If you're taking a taxi, try walking past the waiting cabs when your ferry docks (they're a difficult bunch, charging tourists exorbitant amounts) and flag down a cab on one of the main streets. The metered rate into downtown Athens should be no more than 3,000Dr ($10). For ferry information, call the **Piraeus Port Authority** at ☎ **01/451-1311.**

BY CAR A car is a major headache in Athens, and it's dangerous if you're unfamiliar with the roads and the chaotic driving habits of the Greeks. On most summer days there's a partial curfew on cars in Athens. Cars with license plates ending with an even number are banned one day and cars with plates ending with an odd number are banned the next. This is to reduce traffic and pollution. The curfew lasts to 8pm, so many Athenians hit the roads after that and horrendous traffic jams at 10pm aren't uncommon.

An Orientation Tip

To get oriented while walking around the city, you can use two landmarks: the **Acropolis** and, to its northeast, **Lycabettus Hill,** with a small white church on top. Both are visible from practically anywhere in the city.

VISITOR INFORMATION

The **Greek National Tourist Organization** (known as EOT) has all the information you need on anything from bus schedules to up-to-the minute festival details, museum pamphlets, and city and island maps. Be sure to ask for a copy of ***Athens Today,*** a monthly listing of current events and lots of useful info that changes every season.

The main office is behind Syntagma Square at 2 Amerikis St. (☎ **01/322-3111;** open Mon–Fri 8:30am–1:30pm and 3–6:30pm, Sat 9am–2pm, Sun and holidays 10am–1pm). There's another branch at Syntagma Square right outside the National Bank of Greece (☎ **01/322-2545;** open Mon–Thurs 8am–2pm and 3:30–6:30pm, Sat 9am–2pm, Sun and holidays to 1pm).

If you need immediate assistance, contact the **tourist police** at ☎ **01/924-2700.**

CITY LAYOUT

The commercial center of Athens is the triangle formed by **Stadiou, Mitropoleos,** and **Athinas streets,** which link the main three squares, **Syntagma (Constitution), Omonia (Harmony),** and **Monastiraki (Little Monastery).** These three squares and the areas between them form the commercial center of the city. Syntagma and Omonia are the main hubs of life. Syntagma is close to Plaka, so most visitors use the banks, post office, and travel agencies here rather than at Omonia.

From Syntagma Square, **Plaka** is a 5-minute walk west on Ermou Street and then south on Voulis Street. Bordering the Acropolis, this is the oldest neighborhood in Athens, and it's a maze of many tiny streets—first-time visitors frequently get lost. Your best bet would be to buy a Plaka map available at any hotel or travel agency for 500Dr ($1.65). Otherwise, finding your way around Athens is pretty easy.

On the north side of Syntagma is Athens's trendiest neighborhood, **Kolonaki.** To get there from Syntagma, take Vasilissis Sophias Avenue east, going past the Parliament Building, then turn left toward Lycabettus Hill. Kolonaki is easy to find since it sits on the slope heading up to Lycabettus. If you head south from Syntagma on Amalias Avenue, you'll hit the National Gardens and Zappion Park and the area of **Makriyanni** (Amalias becomes Syngrou Avenue), where several gay bars and clubs are located. Continuing southeast will get you to the up-and-coming area of **Mets,** home to one of the city's best restaurants.

GETTING AROUND

BY METRO Athens has been one big construction sight in recent years as workers dig into the earth that'll eventually house a modern subway system. Construction is nearing completion, but for now only one line is open, running from Piraeus to Athens. The metro stops open in the city are Monastiraki, Omonia, and Thission. Trains run every 10 minutes 5am to midnight, and the trip to Pireaus from Athens is a quick 15 minutes. Tickets cost 100Dr (35¢). You'll need to validate your ticket in the machine as you enter the waiting platform. Metro and bus tickets aren't interchangeable.

BY BUS & TROLLEY BUS The **blue buses** run regular routes in Athens and its suburbs 5am to midnight. The **orange trolley buses,** powered by electric lines, run in the center of the city during the same hours. The fare for either bus service is 100Dr (35¢), and you must buy a ticket in advance from a news kiosk (there are plenty of those on every main street). When you board the bus, validate your ticket in the machine and hold on to it. Inspectors come on board regularly to check everyone's ticket, and you'll be fined if you don't have it or if you have it but it's not validated. For questions about **bus schedules,** call ☎ **185** (daily 7am–9pm).

BY TAXI Aside from walking, this is the most convenient and inexpensive way to get around. Taxis are plentiful, and most of the drivers are honest though not friendly. However, be sure the meter is on when you enter. At press time, the minimum fare was 200Dr (65¢).

Since Athens is so crowded, the taxi might already be carrying one or two passengers when the driver stops for you. If he's heading to your destination, then he can pick up as many passengers as his car can take. But remember to note what the meter says when you get in and adjust what you pay accordingly. Figuring out the total amount you owe can get pretty dicey, so be prepared to pay what's on the meter (within the city center it never amounts to more than 1,500Dr/$5). During rush hour, people stand on street corners calling out the names of their neighborhood to the drivers who slow down to listen, stop if they're so inclined, or continue on. In Athens, it's the taxi driver who decides where he's going—if you're going his way, he'll stop for you.

If you encounter any problems, call the **tourist police** at ☎ **171.** If you need to call for a taxi from your hotel, have the receptionist do it. Or you can try **Kosmos** at ☎ **01/809-9000, Express** at ☎ **01/993-4812,** or **Parthenon** at ☎ **01/581-4711.**

May to October, when the capital goes on its "summer hours," it's hardest to get a taxi between 2:30 and 4pm, when most Athenians are returning home after a day at work or school. Rush hours during winter are 5 to 7pm.

BY CAR If you want a permanent headache or are feeling suicidal, then by all means rent a car or a scooter in Athens. Traffic is crazy and parking close to impossible. But if you want to rent a car to explore the countryside, then you'll find many car-rental companies, most with offices around Syntagma Square. **Budget** is at 8 Syngrou Ave. (☎ **01/922-6666**) and **Hertz** at 12 Syngrou Ave. (☎ **01/922-0102**). For slightly cheaper rates, try the local companies, like **Just Rent-a-Car** at 43 Syngrou Ave. (☎ **01/923-9104**) or **Pappas Rent-a-Car** at 44 Amalias Ave. (☎ **01/322-0087**). Most companies charge about 14,000 to 16,000Dr ($46 to $53) per day. Make sure all taxes and a complete insurance package is included. It's helpful, though not required, to have an International Driver's License, which you can obtain before leaving home. Note that you'll save money by arranging for a car rental before leaving home.

FAST FACTS: Athens

AIDS Hot Line The AIDS helpline at ☎ **01/722-2222** is available daily 7am to 11pm. The operators don't always speak English, so if it's an emergency, call the U.S. Embassy (someone is available 24 hours a day) to get the name of a doctor or hospital they recommend.

American Express The office is at 2 Ermou St., on the southwest corner of Syntagma Square (☎ **01/324-4975;** open Mon–Fri 8:30am–4pm, Sat to 1pm).

Community Center The **Hellenic Homosexual Liberation Movement** is in the same building as the popular cafe Kirki, 31 Apostolou Pavlou St., in Thission (☎ **094/771-9291**). There are no regular activities, but call for more information.

Country & City Codes

The **country code** for Greece is **30.** The **city code** for Athens is **1;** use this code when you're calling from outside Greece. If you're within Greece but not in Athens, use **01.** If you're calling within Athens, simply leave off the code and dial only the regular phone number.

Currency Exchange In Greece, you can change money not only at banks but also at most travel agencies that offer currency exchange. Rates are pretty much the same everywhere, though some agencies will charge a fee of 500 to 2,000Dr ($1.65 to $7). If you use a credit card to get cash, most travel agencies charge a small fee, but on your card bill the advance will be listed as a purchase, which in most cases means a lower interest rate or a longer grace period for repayment. This is nice if you'll be away from home for a long period.

Cybercafe You can check your e-mail or send messages at the **Astor Internet Café,** 17 Patission St., a block of Omonia Square (☎ 01/523-8546; open Mon–Sat 10am–10pm, Sun to 4pm).

Embassies The **U.S. Embassy** is at 91 Vasilissis Sophia Ave. **☎ 01/721-2951;** after hours 01/729-4444). The **Canadian Embassy** is at 4 Ioannou Yenadiou St. (**☎ 01/725-4011**). The **U.K. Embassy** is at 1 Ploutarchou St. (**☎ 01/723-6211**). The **Irish Embassy** is at 7 Vasilissis Konstantinou Ave. (**☎ 01/723-2771**). The **Australian Embassy** is at 37 Dimitriou Soutsou St. (**☎ 01/644-7303**). The **New Zealand Consulate** is at 9 Semitelou St. (**☎ 01/771-0112**). The embassies and consulates are generally open Monday to Friday 9am to 1:30pm.

Emergencies Dial **☎ 100** for police assistance and **☎ 171** for the tourist police. Dial **☎ 166** for an ambulance, **☎ 150** for First Aid, or **☎ 199** for the fire department. **SOS Doctors** at **☎ 01/331-0310** will send out a doctor to wherever you are in the city within an hour. The charge is 20,000Dr ($66). Most of the doctors are young and speak decent English.

Hospitals Call your embassy for a list of hospitals they recommend. **Aretaeion,** 76 Vas. Sophias Ave. (**☎ 01/723-8511**), is one of the better state-owned hospitals that's close to most tourist areas. The **Greek Red Cross** is at 1 Erythrou Stavrou St. (**☎ 01/691-0512** or 01/693-1300).

Telephone The city's public phones mostly accept phone cards, which you can buy from newspaper stands and OTE offices. They cost 1,700Dr ($3.35) and are good for about a 10-minute call to the United States. Many hotel rooms now have dial-tone phones where you can use your calling card from home (AT&T, MCI, SPRINT). For hotels without dial tone, you can still use your phone cards, but you need to talk to your carrier's operator to connect you (AT&T 00-800-1311, MCI 00-800-1211, Sprint 00-800-1411). That's also the easiest way to call collect. For international calls, an English-speaking operator is available by dialing **☎ 161** or 169.

2 Pillow Talk

Think comfort and location and not service and luxury, and you won't be disappointed. In Athens, you have to choose your hotel carefully. If you're a light sleeper, be sure to get a room with air-conditioning to block out the street noise. If you like bathtubs, note that only the expensive hotels usually have them (baths most often come with small showers). Don't expect gushing hot water (it's more like a trickle in most places) and forget about smiling receptionists and a we'll-do-anything-to-please-you attitude, especially in the less expensive places. If you want a hotel with a pool, be sure to double-check when you book if the pool will be open during your stay. Some pools are open only June to September. Paying $350 for a room doesn't mean you'll have access to a health club (the Grande Bretagne has neither a pool nor a health club).

If you're traveling alone, you're in luck. Most hotels offer significantly lower rates for single rooms, so be sure to ask. If you're looking for rock-bottom prices, always ask for rates that don't include breakfast. And remember that most hotels require that you drop your key at the reception desk whenever you leave, so bringing back an unregistered guest after you've checked out the bars is pretty much out of the question, especially since if you're alone you're getting a single rate. (You'll have to revert to college-days dorm antics and be creative if you get lucky.)

There are no gay hotels in Athens. If you ask around, you might hear the Achilles Hotel close to Syntagma Square described as gay. It's not really. It's listed in other gay guides and thus gets its share of gay guests. But its location is drab, and the staff seem to be in a perpetual bad mood. I don't recommend it.

If you arrive without a reservation, check with the tourist office at the airport's East Terminal. Its staff can help you find a hotel, usually for a small fee. It's getting harder to find rooms here between May and September, so plan early. For help getting hotels at the best rate before you arrive, contact the **Greek Travel Supermarket,** 43 Voulis St., 105 57 Athens (☎ **01/323-1004;** fax 01/323-0881). Write or call with your request as early as possible. They get preferred rates and can also can arrange for transfers to/from the airport to your hotel.

SYNTAGMA & PLAKA

Acropolis House Hotel. 6–8 Kodrou St. (at the corner of Iperidou), Plaka, 105 58 Athens. ☎ **01/ 322-2344.** Fax 01/324-4143. 25 units, 15 with bathroom. TEL. 16,000Dr ($53) double without bathroom, 21,000Dr ($70) double with bathroom. Rates include continental breakfast. V.

For old-world charm and value, your best bet is this 150-year-old villa that's a family-run B&B-style hotel. The reception is tiny and dark, and as you go up to your room the stairs creak (there's an elevator in only the new wing). Charming for some, irritating for others. The newer wing (from the 1930s) has less character but more modern accommodations. All the rooms are furnished with the basics, and the baths are tiny but clean. Some rooms have air-conditioning, on request, for 4,000Dr ($13). Those without bath aren't an especially good value unless you really don't mind walking down the hall to do your business (the hall bath is tiled and clean). Don't expect to make loud nocturnal love noises, for the rooms are close together and the halls echo. But the Acropolis House is architecturally pleasing and the staff friendly enough.

Bedding Down

Note that double beds are hard to find anywhere in Greece. Most often you'll get two twin beds pushed together, leaving that awful gap between. Some hotels have true double beds, but few have queen- or king-size beds, so expect the worst and maybe you'll get lucky. Most hotels won't confirm bedding type, just room category.

✪ **Elektra Palace.** 18 Nikodimou St., Plaka, 105 57 Athens. ☎ **01/324-1401.** Fax 01/324-1875. 110 units. A/C MINIBAR TV TEL. 40,400Dr ($134) double. Rates include breakfast. AE, DC, MC, V.

This is where most savvy American travelers stay. At the edge of Plaka on a small busy street, the unassuming building at first might look a bit drab. But inside this excellent hotel the rooms are as luxurious as in five-star places, if a bit smaller, and they're soundproof (a blessing in this noisy neighborhood). The lower-floor rooms without balconies are more spacious, as are the rooms in back overlooking a schoolyard and rooftops. Advance planning is essential since the hotel is booked solid months ahead (everyone requests an Acropolis view). It doesn't confirm specific room types, so be prepared to take what you get. The breakfast buffet is hearty and served in the bright dining room, or you can have a continental breakfast delivered to your room for 350Dr ($1.15). The rooftop pool has an amazing view of the Acropolis (the best among all the hotels I recommend).

Hermes Hotel. 19 Apollonos St., Plaka, 105 57 Athens. ☎ **01/323-5514.** Fax 01/323-2073. 45 units. A/C TV TEL. 22,000Dr ($73) double. Rates include breakfast. AE, MC, V.

A 2-minute walk from the heart of Plaka on a small street, the new Hermes offers comfortable modern rooms. Most tourist-class hotels in this area are old and bleak, but this one is sparkling, with a bright facade and an amazingly cool (as in air-conditioned) reception. The guests tend to be young, with a high number of Northern Europeans and Americans. The rooms aren't too tiny and are clean and simply furnished (bed, chair, night table); those on the upper floors have good views of the rooftops. The staff is courteous, and there's a travel desk in the lobby to arrange for tours or transfers. The grocery store a block away stays open late.

Hotel Adonis. 3 Kodrou St. (at Voulis), Plaka, 105 58 Athens. ☎ **01/324-9737.** Fax 01/323-1602. 26 units. TEL. 14,500Dr ($48) double without A/C, 17,000Dr ($57) double with A/C. 1,000Dr ($3.35) per day discount for stays more than 2 nights. No credit cards.

This is an excellent value in the heart of Plaka, a few steps from the shops and restaurants. On a pedestrian-only street, the Adonis isn't beautiful as its name suggests but very functional. Many Americans stay here in summer, when you definitely need to splurge for air-conditioning. The rooms are comfortable if a bit aged, and the baths come with small showers. The rooms with balconies feel more spacious. Ask for a front room when making your reservation. The rooftop garden, where breakfast is served, has an excellent view of the Acropolis. If you're traveling alone, single rates here are exceptionally inexpensive. The staff isn't especially attentive.

Hotel Grande Bretagne. Syntagma Square, 105 63 Athens. ☎ **01/330-0000.** Fax 01/322-8034. 364 units. A/C MINIBAR TV TEL. 105,000–117,000DR ($350–$390) double; from 189,000Dr ($630) suite. AE, DC, MC, V.

For luxury and old-world elegance, you can't do better than the Grand Bretagne. Dating from 1842, this landmark hotel sits on Syntagma across from what will soon be one of the city's busiest subway stations. The service, like that everywhere in Athens, is quite haphazard. The staff gets overloaded when the place is full—which is often in the warmer months. They do try, but not quite as hard as you'd expect from one of the Leading Hotels of the World. The lack of same-sex couples is remarkable but hardly a reason not to stay here. Just don't expect camaraderie.

Given the steep rates, the crowd is older, with a lot of corporate jacket-and-tie action. The least expensive rooms are the smallest and have only inner courtyard views, but all have marble baths with tubs. The deluxe rooms are larger, and those on the upper floors have balconies with views. The slightly faded bedcovers and aging bath fixtures are tell-tale signs that a renovation is past due. The popular G.B. Corner Restaurant serves all meals in an English pub setting.

Hotel Nefeli. 16 Iperidou St. (at the corner of Hatzimihali), 105 58 Athens. ☎ **01/322-8044.** Fax 01/322-5800. 18 units. A/C TEL. 21,000Dr ($70) double. Rates include breakfast. AE, V.

This simple hotel in the heart of Plaka sits on a charming pedestrian-only street, across from the highly recommended De Profundis teahouse (see "Whet Your Appetite" below). Many excellent cafes and restaurant are within 2 blocks. Tasos, the manager, is always here to make your stay more enjoyable (and to keep a watchful eye on the front door). The rooms are functional and clean, and the recent addition of powerful air-conditioning in every room means you don't have to worry about sleeping with the window open (the streets echo at night). Five rooms have actual double beds, the rest have two twins pushed together. The baths are tiny but spotless. Many of the rooms overlook the street, where you can people-watch in the privacy of your room. This hotel is listed in many guides as an excellent value, so expect a lot of young Americans, some college age, some gay, plus a few lonely souls.

KOLONAKI

Andromeda Hotel. 23 Timoleontos Vassou St., Kolonaki, 115 21 Athens. ☎ **01/643-7302.** Fax 01/646-6361. 30 units. A/C MINIBAR TV TEL. 52,500–94,500Dr ($175–$315) double; from 61,500Dr ($205) suite. AE, DC, MC, V.

The Andromeda is Athens's only boutique hotel, on a hill on the fringes of Kolonaki, near the U.S. Embassy and overlooking the U.S. ambassador's residence. Elegance reigns, with authentic Persian rugs and an art deco reception. The individually decorated rooms are very spacious, with unusual colors like red velvet bedcovers and purple bedside lamps. Expect personalized service from a staff trained to provide whatever you need. The hotel has become so popular so quickly it gets booked up months in advance; only the most expensive suites at 132,000Dr ($440) sometimes remain available. Businesspeople on expense accounts stay here, and the majority of them are American. The White Elephant Bar is open all day and serves snacks, while the intimate restaurant specializes in Polynesian cuisine.

✪ **Athenian Inn.** 22 Haritos St., Kolonaki, 106 75 Athens. ☎ **01/723-8097.** Fax 01/724-2268. 28 units. A/C TEL. 28,200Dr ($94) double. Rates include breakfast. AE, V.

For value and a location that can't be beat, this should be your first choice. On a quiet residential street, this simple inn is just minutes from the elegant shops, restaurants, and cafes in this upscale neighborhood. The repeat clientele keep most of the rooms booked year-round, and the fact that the hotel is listed in many guides (gay and straight) keeps a mixed international crowd coming. The rates are an amazing value and can't stay this low for long; this hotel offers big savings for single travelers too, so be sure to request those rates. The rooms are simple but functional, with bright bedspreads and decent mattresses; a few rooms have old TVs. The baths are aging but very clean and come with tubs, which is unusual for a tourist-class hotel. Only one room has a balcony with a view of Lycabettus Hill (the manager insists he can't confirm requests for it, so don't ask).

✪ **Hilton Hotel.** 46 Vassilissis Sofias Ave., Kolonaki, 11 528 Athens. ☎ **01/725-0201.** Fax 01/725-3110. 453 units. A/C MINIBAR TV TEL. 90,000Dr ($300) double; from 135,000Dr ($450) suite. AE, DC, MC, V.

This is the best of the chains in Athens, if you want the familiarity of a Hilton (plus frequent-flyer miles) and the anonymity of a large hotel. Close to the U.S. Embassy on one of the city's busiest avenues, the hotel is known for its rooftop bar with loveseats from which to enjoy the spectacular views and boasts the largest outdoor pool in Athens. Kolonaki is a 10-minute walk away and Syntagma a half-hour walk along busy Vas. Sophias Avenue. Despite its size, the Hilton retains its elegance. All the rooms are modern and bright, with sliding French doors looking out over the city. The executive-floor rooms are more elegant and add nice touches like bathrobes and complimentary mineral water. The Byzantine restaurant serves an excellent buffet lunch of Greek and continental fare.

St. George Lycabettus Hotel. 2 Kleomenous St., Kolonaki, 106 75 Athens. ☎ **01/729-0711.** Fax 01/729-0439. E-mail stgeorge@mail.otenet.gr. 167 units. A/C MINIBAR TV TEL. 56,100Dr ($187) double without view, 77,000Dr ($256) double with Acropolis view. AE, DC, MC, V.

This is the only luxury hotel in the midst of upscale Kolonaki, on a hill overlooking the city, with shops and restaurants a 5-minute walk downhill. Stay here if you like peace and quiet and don't want to be where the crowds are. The standard rooms are rather small, but the balconies give them a more spacious feel. There are also less expensive inside rooms with no windows. All rooms are contemporary, containing the amenities you'd expect from a luxury hotel, including firm mattresses. The baths are small but well equipped. The clientele is made up mostly of American and Japanese tourists on package tours. The rooftop pool has great views, and the Mediterraneao Café is popular, especially in summer, when the garden terrace is open. The hotel prides itself for its fine dining Le Grand Balcon, but it's stuffy and overpriced.

MAKRIYANNI

Divani Palace Acropolis. 19–25 Parthenonos St., Makriyanni, 117 42 Athens. ☎ **01/922-2945.** Fax 01/921-4993. 267 units. A/C MINIBAR TV TEL. 52,000Dr ($173) double; from 78,300Dr ($261) suite. AE, DC, MC, V.

This is the luxury hotel closest to the Acropolis, a good choice if you're stopping just to visit the sacred rock. Many of the guests are older Americans on their way to/from cruise ships, so the staff has learned to be patient and friendly. The rooms are airy and sparkling. Instead of carpets, all have sleek marble floors and baths with the usual amenities, like hair dryers. Ask for a higher-floor room if it's available, as those have the best views and are brighter. The trademark here is the ruins that were found when the hotel was being built and are displayed below the lobby—they're sections of the actual walls built by Themistocles to protect Athens during the Persian Wars. The Socrates roof-garden restaurant is beautiful in summer, with a magnificent view of the Parthenon. But the pool is tiny and the basement Aspassia Restaurant nothing special.

Herodion Hotel. 4 Rovertou Galli St., Makriyanni, 117 42 Athens. ☎ **01/923-6832.** Fax 01/923-5851. E-mail vito1a@netor.gr. 90 units. A/C MINIBAR TV TEL. 37,700–40,500Dr ($109–$135) double. Rates include breakfast. AE, DC, MC, V.

If you want to stay at a small Greek hotel, away from the chains and large hotels, then you've found your home in this quiet residential area of Makriyanni, close to the Acropolis and to several gay bars and clubs I recommend. The rooms are small but extremely clean and very modern. Most have balconies offering limited views of the quiet street or a schoolyard. The baths were renovated in 1998 and come with hair dryers. The staff is friendly and tries harder than those at other hotels of the same class. There's a roof sundeck with the views you'd expect.

Philippos Hotel. 3 Mitseon St., Makriyanni, 117 42 Athens. ☎ **01/922-3611.** Fax 01/922-3615. 50 units. A/C TV TEL. 28,000Dr ($95) double. Rates include breakfast. AE, DC, MC, V.

Athens Accommodations & Dining

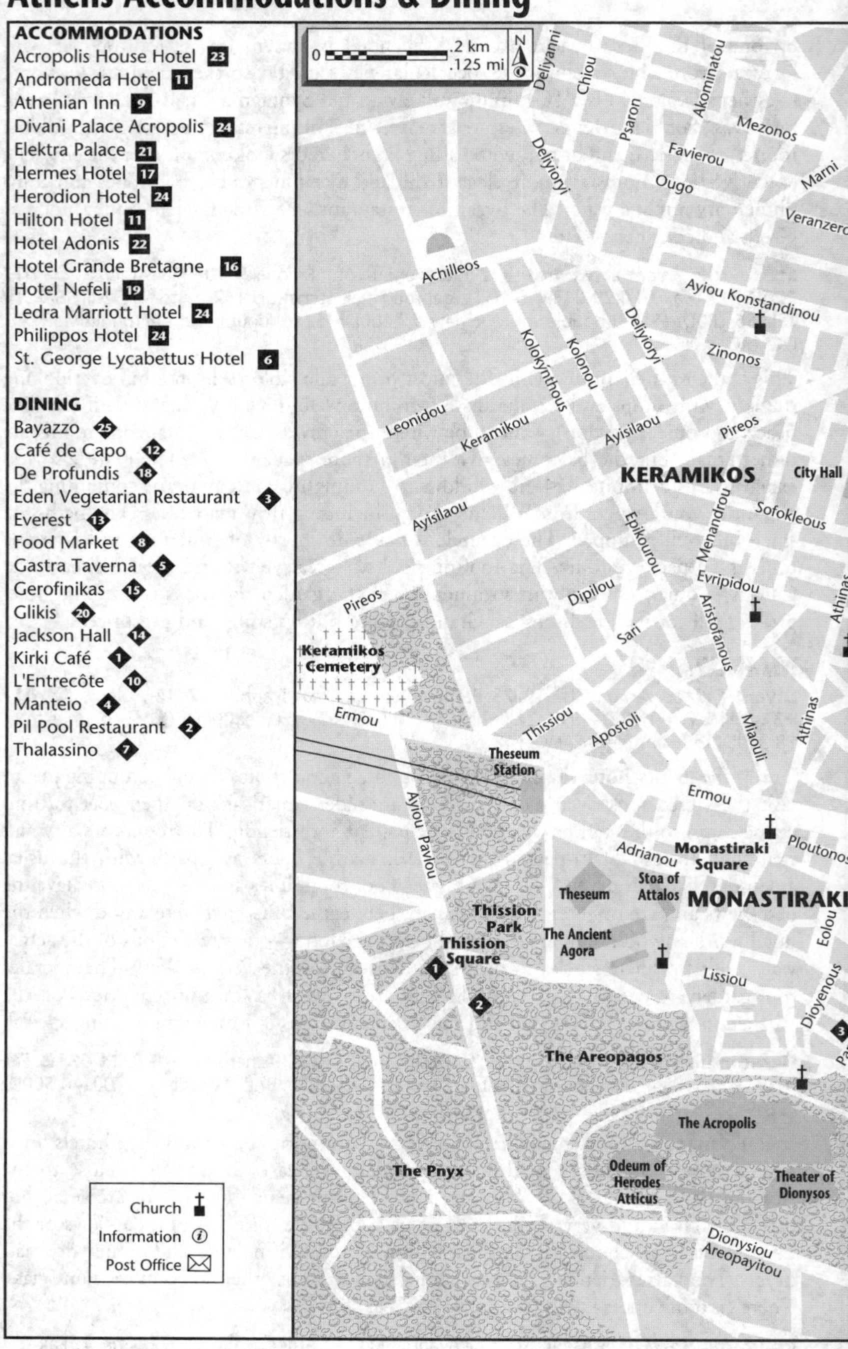

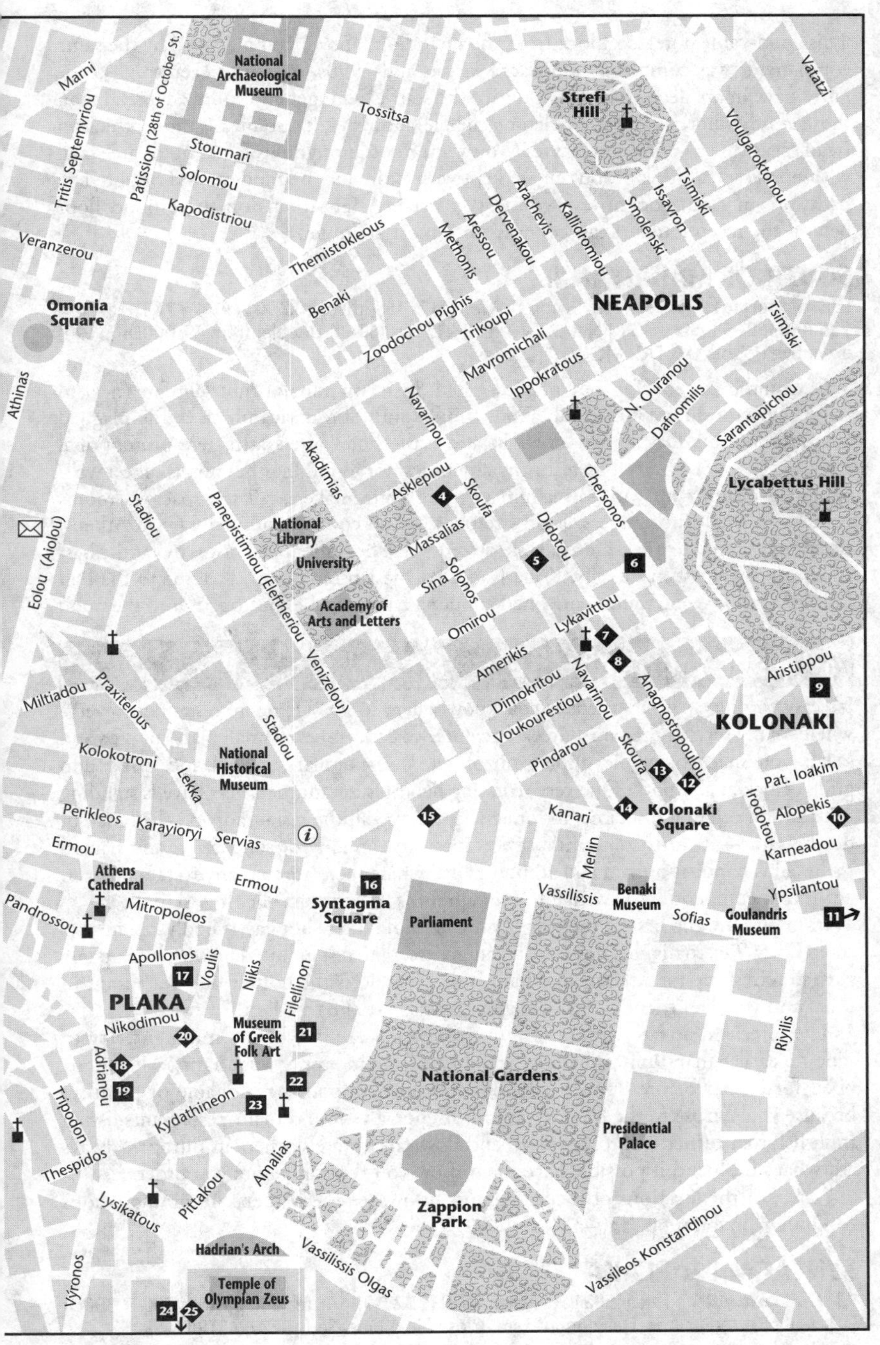
National Archaeological Museum
Marni
Patission (28th of October St.)
Tritis Septemvriou
Tossitsa
Stournari
Solomou
Kapodistriou
Veranzerou
Themistokleous
Strefi Hill
Vatatzi
Voulgaroktonou
Tsimiski
Issavron
Smolenski
Kallidromiou
Arachevis
Dervenakou
Aressou
Methonis
Benaki
Zoodochou Pighis
Trikoupi
Mavromichali
Ippokratous
NEAPOLIS
Omonia Square
Athinas
Navarinou
N. Ouranou
Dafnomilis
Sarantapichou
Akadimias
Asklepiou
Skoufa
Chersonos
Lycabettus Hill
Stadiou
Panepistimiou (Eleftheriou Venizelou)
National Library
University
Massalias
Didotou
Academy of Arts and Letters
Sina
Solonos
Eolou (Aiolou)
Omirou
Lykavittou
Amerikis
Dimokritou
Navarinou
Anagnostopoulou
Aristippou
Voukourestiou
Miltiadou
Praxitelous
KOLONAKI
Kolokotroni
Lekka
National Historical Museum
Pindarou
Skoufa
Pat. Ioakim
Irodotou
Alopekis
Perikleos
Karayioryi
Servias
Kanari
Kolonaki Square
Ermou
Karneadou
Athens Cathedral
Ermou
Merlin
Syntagma Square
Vassilissis
Benaki Museum
Ypsilantou
Pandrossou
Mitropoleos
Parliament
Sofias
Goulandris Museum
Apollonos
Voulis
Nikis
Filellinon
PLAKA
Nikodimou
Museum of Greek Folk Art
Adrianou
Riyilis
National Gardens
Tripodon
Kydathineon
Presidential Palace
Thespidos
Amalias
Lysikatous
Pittakou
Zappion Park
Hadrian's Arch
Vassilissis Olgas
Vassileos Konstandinou
Temple of Olympian Zeus
Výronos
4
5
6
7
8
9
10
11
12
13
14
15
16
17
18
19
20
21
22
23
24
25

This good-value hotel is a block from the Herodion (above) and managed by the same company. It was completely renovated in the mid-1990s, so expect everything to be fairly new, in art-deco style. You'll notice the staff is younger and more energetic than those at other hotels—what a welcome change. However, it also means more attention (read scrutiny), so don't come here if you want to be anonymous. The rooms are small with no views to speak of, but all are kept very clean and are modern and bright. The baths are tiny but contain everything you need. A few rooms on the ground floor behind the reception area can get noisy, but most are quiet.

SOUTH OF MAKRIYANNI

Ledra Marriott Hotel. 115 Syngrou Ave., 117 45 Athens. ☎ **01/934-7711.** Fax 01/935-8603. 266 units. A/C MINIBAR TV TEL. 48,150Dr ($160) double; from 57,000Dr ($190) executive double. AE, DC, MC, V.

This would be a gem if it were better located. It sits on a major thoroughfare (next to the Athenaeum Intercontinental) about a mile south of Makriyanni on traffic-plagued Syngrou Avenue. Despite the noisy location, the hotel offers attractive promotional rates and is very comfortable, featuring amenities not found in other hotels, like a well-equipped health club with sauna and in-room coffeemakers. All the spacious rooms come with small sitting areas. King-size beds (much coveted and very rare in Athens, except in expensive suites) are available on request. The buffet breakfast is by far the best American breakfast in the city. Kona Kai, a Polynesian restaurant, is home to the Bali Lounge with live entertainment. The Panorama bar is on the rooftop around the pool.

3 Whet Your Appetite

It's easy to dine well in Athens if you know where to go. There are restaurants everywhere, many serving the same Greek fare: Greek salad, *mezedes* (small plates of dips and salads you snack on while sipping ouzo), the ever-popular souvlaki and gyros, and grilled chicken and pork. One very irritating habit restaurant managers have is standing outside and offering discounts to foreigners, forcing all the restaurants on the block to do the same—it turns some little streets into a cacophony of solicitation and harassment. This happens only in and around Plaka, where there are so many restaurants and cut-throat competition. My rule: If a restaurant is so bent on soliciting, skip it.

In my list are the best of the best. And I've found a few hot gay-friendly restaurants too. Gastra Taverna is the closest you can get to a gay restaurant. The owner is openly gay (so refreshing for Athens) and flaunts it. Manteio is the hottest new restaurant in town and very gay-friendly. Pil Pool and Bayazzo are the trendiest.

The Greeks dine late, around 10pm, so few places close before midnight. Try to dine no earlier than 9pm, otherwise you'll be sitting in empty restaurants. Most don't open for dinner before 8pm. Lastly, don't assume seafood is reasonable or plentiful because you're close to the Mediterranean. It's not. I've found many restaurants listing fresh fish that turned out to be frozen and flown in from elsewhere in Europe. Always ask what's fresh and if possible have them show you the fish before you order.

Note: For the locations of the restaurants below, see the "Athens Accommodations & Dining" map on pp. 330–331.

SYNTAGMA & PLAKA

✪ **De Profundis.** 1 Hatzimihali St., Plaka. ☎ **01/323-1764.** Tea and pastries 700–1,300Dr ($2–$4). No credit cards. Daily noon–1am. Closed late June–Sept. TEA/PASTRIES.

Taking its name from Oscar Wilde's apology published by his literary executor, this interesting cafe on a charming Plaka street is a gay-owned teahouse. From old ladies to lonely tourists, this little place has the most cosmopolitan and mixed crowd in

Athens. Here's where two men can sit real close in broad daylight (!), perhaps even sneaking in a bit of hand-holding under the table. Dimitri, the soft-spoken owner, will make you instantly feel at home. Exotic teas from around the world (jasmine, ceylon, almond, apple) are served along with French and Greek pastries. Try the cookies with a swirl of apricot jam in the middle or the napoleons that melt in your mouth. There's also a limited amount of alcoholic drinks. This place is popular in the early evenings in the cooler months, when Dimitri plays his favorite operas and the atmosphere is cozy and warm. Since there's no terrace, it's closed in July and August.

Eden Vegetarian Restaurant. 12 Lissiou St. (at Mnissikleos St.), Plaka. ☎ **01/324-8858.** Main courses 1,500–2,800Dr ($5–$9). No credit cards. Daily noon–midnight. GREEK VEGETARIAN.

Tourists clutching guidebooks find their way here, many on their first night in Athens. This restaurant is listed in practically every travel guide to Greece not only because it's one of the city's only vegetarian restaurants but also because the food is consistently tasty and healthy. The energetic young staff speaks good English. The soy moussaka (layers of eggplant and cheese topped with béchamel sauce) is the most ordered dish. Meat eaters will hardly notice the difference between this and the real thing, and vegetarians can get a dose of this traditional Greek dish usually loaded with ground beef. The juices are made to order, and they have such unusual choices as fresh cucumber and watermelon. The Eden gets its share of gay diners and is always a good place to meet interesting people from around the world.

✪ **Gerofinikas.** 10 Pindarou St. (off Syntagma Sq.). ☎ **01/363-6710.** Reservations recommended. Main courses 4,000–7,000Dr ($13–$23). AE, DC, MC, V. Daily noon–1am. GREEK.

Since 1957, this traditional Greek restaurant has been serving excellent homemade dishes you won't find anywhere else. Ignore the plain exterior and walk through the long hall from the street to find yourself in a charming dining room with aging oak furniture and a captain ready to direct his staff to make you feel at home. You'll get service from waiters who've worked here for many years and food prepared with such care that many Greek families honor their out-of-town friends by bringing them for a festive lunch. Feast on cabbage stuffed with rice and herbs or lamb with artichoke hearts. Choose from a wide variety of fish (they'll tell you what's fresh) and meats grilled to order. This is the place to experiment. Try the pheasant cooked with onions or tender grilled quails. Sometimes even wild boar is available if you're feeling real adventurous. This is also the place to go all out and taste the local cheeses, but be sure to save room for dessert. The homemade ice cream is super.

Glikis. 2 Ag. Geronta St. (at the corner of Hatzimihali), Plaka. ☎ **01/322-3925.** Light meals 1,200–2,200Dr ($4–$7). No credit cards. Daily 10am–1am. GREEK MEZEDES/LIGHT MEALS.

Most Greek tavernas in Plaka cater to foreigners with food mass-produced and tasteless. This place, however, has a solid Greek following consisting mostly of young students. It's by far the best place in Plaka for *mezedes* and a glass of ouzo. Sit out under

A Taste of Ouzo

The most popular Greek hard drink is **ouzo,** an anise-flavored liqueur. Ouzo is taken either straight or with water, which turns it cloudy white. You may see Greek men drinking quarter- and even half-bottles of ouzo with their lunch; if you do the same, you'll find out why the after-lunch siesta is so popular.

A Toast for the Boys

Toast (pronounced *tost*) is the most popular meal for Athenian guys, usually eaten between 3 and 4am as they're on their way home after a night on the town. It's not just plain old toasted bread but what the Greeks call a toasted sandwich—a large roll stuffed with a variety of meats, cheeses, and vegetables and then, well, toasted.

The gathering spot is **Everest,** 14 Tsakalof St. in Kolonaki (☎ **01/361-3477;** open daily 11am–4am), the most popular location of this high-quality fast-food chain, popular with the young and the hip and the gay. Watch the macho types in tight jeans riding fancy Japanese bikes, engines revving, pull up noisily and fiddle with their helmets and keys as they stand in line to order.

The process might be confusing to a visitor, so here's what you do: Ask for tost from the guy standing behind the deli counter. Point to what you want to go inside your sandwich (you might want to stand around a bit to observe the process and get a feel for how it works). The most popular items to stuff your toast with are cheese, tomatoes, hard-boiled eggs, ham, crisp bacon, and French fries (yes, inside the sandwich). The roll, bulging with your ingredients, is then shoved in a toast-smasher, a contraption similar to a waffle iron. Meanwhile, pay the cashier, get your receipt, and wait. (You might take this opportunity to admire one of the boy's bikes and, if you're familiar with Suzuki or Kawasaki, perhaps even strike up a conversation.) When your sandwich finally emerges from the toaster miraculously flat, the deli boy will find a way to pry it open to douse it with the dressing of your choice and mustard, mayonnaise, or ketchup. Then grab a stool at one of the sidewalk high-top tables and watch the guys getting on and off their bikes.

the grapevine on traditional wood-and-wicker chairs and order the triple ouzo. For an amazing 1,700Dr ($6) you get ouzo, bread, and a plate loaded with appetizers—Greek sausage, salami, four kinds of dips, lima bean salad, and cheese. This is not fine dining by any means, and you can't have a hot meal. But you can be assured of freshness, as owner Michael Gianoussakis insists on quality. This is where Athenian college students hang out late into the night. *Glikis* means sweets, and they do have a good selection of Greek pastries dripping with honey. Many people, though, linger for hours over cups of coffee or glasses of freshly squeezed orange juice.

KOLONAKI

Food Market. 47 Agnastopolou St. ☎ **01/363-0373.** Light meals 1,200–3,000Dr ($4–$10). No credit cards. Mon–Sat 11am–1am. LIGHT MEALS.

This deli, the area's only gourmet takeout place, serves up excellent fresh salads, pastas, and sandwiches. On a quiet street across from Alexander's dance club, it's popular with gays and straights alike. The boys working behind the counter are cute and friendly and will take their time explaining what the daily specials are. The cold pastas are delicious—try the homemade cheese tortellini or the garlicky eggplant salad. Late in the evening you can spot guys loading up on carbos before heading over to Alexander's.

Gastra Taverna. 1 Dimaki St. (from Sina St., go north to the V in the road, take Itis St., then make the 2nd left; the taverna is at the corner of Itis and Dimaki). ☎ **01/360-2757.** Main courses 2,500–4,500Dr ($8–$15). Mon–Sat 8pm–1am. Closed June–Sept. No credit cards. GREEK/INTERNATIONAL.

Athens's best-known gay restaurant is hard to find. Owner Yannis Koulouris is gay and proud, very friendly, and knowledgeable about the city, so ask him anything you want to know. He always has stories. Yannis is here every night, as he's the sole waiter, along with two cooks. The food is straightforward and reasonably priced. Try the fried cheese pies or lamb stroganoff. The lamb with cardamom and chicken Kiev are the specialties, both quite good. This is an intimate place, with tables so close together you're almost forced to chat with your neighbors. The walls are lined with postcards from all over the world—an excellent conversation starter. Usually at least half the crowd is gay, but on some evenings the place can seem quite straight. Most patrons are young and intellectual, with a large number of writers and journalists.

Jackson Hall. 4 Millioni St. ☎ **01/364-0090.** Main courses 2,500–5,000Dr ($8–$16). AE, V, M. Daily noon–1am. AMERICAN.

If you're missing straight boys at a sports bar, a good cold beer, and a juicy burger with fries, this is the best in town. It's the most popular restaurant with the young trendy crowd. Upstairs are a bar and pool tables and several TVs. The dance floor gets busy only on weekend nights. Downstairs, the restaurant has a large menu serving all-American specialties, from cheeseburgers to chicken Caesar salad. At any given hour this place will probably be quite busy. The action moves outside in summer, when the pedestrian-only street is filled with tables and meals and drinks are served in the open air.

L'Entrecôte. 10 Ploutarchou St. ☎ **01/725-9091.** Reservations required. Fixed-price menu 8,900Dr ($30). MC, V. Tues–Sat 8pm–midnight. FRENCH.

This tiny restaurant follows the success of its Paris namesake, known for its juicy steaks and special secret sauce. A bright-orange facade is only an indicator of what you'll find as you descend the steps to this elegant dining room. There are only about 18 tables, most nights filled with who's who of Athenian society. Most come for the beef, entrecôte to be exact, a tender cut of sirloin with a special sauce resembling a béarnaise. The fixed-price menu includes a wonderful green salad with walnuts and a heavenly chocolate soufflé. Don't expect the aloof waiters to speak fluent English; pleasant service isn't their priority. This, after all, is one of the snobbiest places in town.

✪ **Manteio.** 4 Delfon St. (at Skoufa St.). ☎ **01/361-9682.** Reservations recommended on weekends. Main courses 6,000–9,000Dr ($20–$30). MC, V. Daily 8pm–1am. GREEK/INTERNATIONAL.

If you have only one night in Athens, you *must* dine at the trendiest and most gay-friendly restaurant in the city, on a tiny pedestrian-only street. You can opt to sit on the sidewalk, brushing up against the orange trees, or inside, where sleek art deco reigns. Since most of the crowd is Greek and young, no one dines before 11pm, even on weekdays. The menus are presented in huge plastic folders, but don't bother to look since as of this writing they're available only in Greek. The very friendly (and extremely cute) waiters will be more than happy to translate each item and explain it. The dishes are a mix of French and Italian and Greek. Anything Mediterranean, anything fresh. This is the place to have a Greek salad. The spaghetti al pesto, one of the simpler items, is immense and done correctly, with fresh basil and just the right amount of olive oil and Parmesan. The chicken with mustard sauce is yummy, as is the onion pie for an appetizer.

Thalassino. 36A Tsakalof St. ☎ **01/361-4695.** Reservations recommended. Main courses 4,000–9,000Dr ($13–$30). AE, MC, V. Mon–Sat 12:30–5pm and 8pm–1am. Closed early June–early Sept. SEAFOOD.

It's difficult to get fresh seafood in Athens, but once you've found this gem you'll have no reason to go anywhere else and pay exorbitant prices. On the second floor of a grand old building, this small restaurant is all about elegance. The parachute drapes covering the large wooden windows sway in the breeze, lending a romantic feel. The waiters are young and gay-friendly and speak good English. The menu, which varies daily, is simple in a sophisticated way, focusing on fish and vegetables. Start with the fresh squid and green salad or the tangy fish soup. For a main course, ask what the fresh fish is and it'll be grilled to order (the menu is translated so it reads "grilled fresh fishes"). The "figs dryly cooked in red sweet wine" (dry figs stewed in wine) is a delicious nonfat dessert. The house white wine served real chilled goes perfectly with your meal. Alas, this is one of the restaurants that closes all summer because there's no terrace.

THISSION

✪ **Pil Pool Restaurant.** 51 Apostolou Pavlou (at Thission Sq.). ☎ **01/342-3665.** Reservations required weekends. Main courses 6,000–11,000Dr ($20–37). AE, MC, V. Mon–Sat 8pm–1am. HAUTE CUISINE.

At the most glamorous restaurant in Athens, a small elevator whisks you up to the terrace of this meticulously renovated old house. The Acropolis view is breathtaking. But be prepared to pay steep prices for the infinite attention you'll receive. The service is stiff, but that's understandable given the older and rather traditional maître d'. The food, however, is exquisite. Start with the foie-gras terrine with passion-fruit sauce or the succulent grilled and sautéed mushrooms with grapes. Or go all out and order Sevruga caviar and icy vodka. You can dine well on traditional favorites like Caesar salad and Châteaubriand, but you can also be adventurous and try pheasant with raspberries. For a light, cool dessert the strawberry soup with lavender essence might make you squeal. Dine here late with the Greeks at 10pm to see the cream of Athenian society.

METS

✪ **Bayazzo.** 1 Tyrteou St. (at the corner of Anapafseos). ☎ **01/921-3013.** Reservations recommended. 20,000–25,000Dr ($67–$83) per person. AE, DC, MC, V. Mon–Sat 8pm–midnight. INTERNATIONAL/HAUTE CUISINE.

This intimate restaurant is one of Athens's most expensive, offering one of the best dining experiences. In a residential area southeast of the Olympic Stadium, it isn't easy to find, especially since there's no sign outside the renovated corner house (you'll want to take a taxi here). But open the front door (it's frequently closed) and get ready to be pampered, wined, and dined. In warmer months dinner is served in a small back garden, and in the front room antiques and hardwood floors give a cozy chalet-like atmosphere. The crowd can get stuffy, with many diplomats and executives on expense accounts. But here the emphasis is less on ambience and more on the art of fine dining. Chef Klaus Feuerbach creates new dishes every night, about 10 appetizers and 15 main courses. He mixes unique ingredients from several countries, mainly Germany and Greece, to create unique flavors. The lamb fillet and lobster on Greek coffee foam is a masterpiece. Try the olive-and-feta muffin or the roulade of fresh salmon in soy marinade for a starter. The young, gay-friendly staff will help you pick a perfect accompaniment to your meal from the excellent wine list.

4 Exploring Athens

The Acropolis, of course, is why most visitors come to this ancient city. Statistically, most people stay in Athens 2 days. That's probably just enough time to visit the Acropolis, stroll around Plaka, and maybe hit the National Archaeological Museum.

But Athens is more a place to experience than to visit. So try to put a bit of time aside to stroll around some residential neighborhoods, perhaps stopping at a cafe where the locals sip coffee or ouzo late into the night. Since this is one of the safest cities in Europe, you can venture almost anywhere at all hours and feel safe (except around Omonia Square, where it's dangerous after dark). Walking is the best way to feel the pulse of the city. If you have very little time, though, take taxis, which are cheap and plentiful.

A **Hop In Hop Out Sightseeing Bus** might be a good way to combine walking with visiting the sights. For 7,500Dr ($25), you get a 2-day pass on a comfortable air-conditioned bus that runs a specific route every 2 hours throughout Athens. Hop out at the designated stops (like Syntagma Square or the National Museum) and then hop on again 2 hours later. You can buy tickets from any travel agency or from **Hop In Sightseeing** at ☎ **01/428-5500.** You can contact them on the Internet at **www.travelling.gr/hopin.**

Key Tours, 4 Kalirois St. (☎ **01/923-3166**), offers half-day Athens sightseeing tours for 9,300Dr ($31), including a visit to the Acropolis and a drive-by tour of major sights. They also offer an Athens By Night Tour that includes the Sound-and-Light show at the Acropolis and Greek folk dancing. **G.O. (Greek Organized Tours),** 20 Athanassiou Diakou St. (☎ **01/921-9555**), also offers reliable half-day and full-day tours aboard air-conditioned buses.

Athens has many museums I don't list below, such as the Museum of the History of Greek Costume, the War Museum, and the Jewish Museum. More information is available from the Greek National Tourist Organization, which publishes a seasonal listing of museum and gallery hours, including admission prices and addresses. Many of the museums are free.

THE HITS YOU SHOULDN'T MISS

The Acropolis. South of Monastiraki Sq. ☎ **01/321-0219.** Admission (includes admission to Acropolis Museum) 2,000Dr ($7); free Sun and public holidays. Daily 8am–8pm (call for winter hours, usually to 5pm). The only entrance is on Dionysiou Areopayitou St., just west of the Odeum of Herodes Atticus (where the tour buses are parked).

The Athenians refer to it as their sacred rock, and visitors from all over the world come to climb up this hill. *Acropolis* in Greek means the highest point of a city, where the inhabitants watched for invasions. Now the only invasion anyone watches is that of the tour buses that charge in daily, disgorging thousands of visitors.

The first temple is believed to have been constructed here in the 8th century B.C., but no traces of that building remain. At the top of the hill still stand four monuments, the **Parthenon,** dedicated to Athena, patron goddess of Athens, the largest and most impressive. The Parthenon is visible from most areas of Athens, but up close it's breathtaking. Completed in 438 B.C., it was built using only marble excavated from Mount Penteli (northeast of Athens). In the early Christian era, it was turned into a church by Byzantine Emperor Theodosius II, and in the 15th century, the conquering Turks turned it into a mosque. It was damaged by Venetian canon fire in 1687, when the roof was torn off. It's currently undergoing renovations that'll help preserve it from the growing amount of pollution.

An Acropolis Tip

To avoid the worst of the crowds, come to the Acropolis either early in the morning, as soon as the site opens, or late in the afternoon, right before closing. Sunset is magical here, and on clear, crisp days you can see all the way to the Mediterranean.

A Warning

Strikes that close museums and archaeological sites can occur without warning. Decide what you most want to see and go there as soon as possible after your arrival. The fact that something is open today says nothing about tomorrow. If you're here in the off-season, check with the Greek National Tourist Organization for the abbreviated winter hours of sites and museums.

Three monuments surround the Parthenon: the **Propylaia,** which used to be the grand entryway worshipers used to gain access to the quiet sanctuary of the Acropolis; the **Erechtheum,** where Athena's burned olive tree was said to grow roots and come back to life; and the **Temple of Athena Nike,** which was completed in about 424 B.C. to commemorate the victory of the Greeks over the Persians and is positioned to overlook the right side of soldiers climbing the hill, carrying shields on their left arm. (Here's where you press play on your portable cassette/CD player and listen to Someone to Watch Over Me as you imagine the love the ancient Athenians had for their soldiers.)

Don't miss a quick visit to the **Acropolis Museum** (in a small building on the southeast corner; entrance included with that of the sight), where you can see some archaic remains and a few interesting statues, among them *The Calf Bearer,* a bearded 6th century B.C. youth carrying a calf on his shoulders.

April to October, catch the **Sound-and-Light spectacle,** when floodlights are aimed at the Parthenon and you can hear a commentary on the site and the city. For details, call ☎ **01/922-6210** or the **Athens Festival Box Office** at ☎ **01/322-1459.**

Ancient Agora & Museum. Just north of the Acropolis, at the edge of Monastiraki. ☎ **01/321-0185.** Admission 1,200Dr ($4) site and museum. Tues–Sun 8am–8pm. Enter from Monastiraki market and metro station.

Agora means market in Greek, but this huge area used to be more than just the central market. It was the gathering place in ancient times, the heart of the city, where all events from the religious to the athletic took place. The most impressive building is the best-preserved ancient temple in all Greece: the **Theseum** (or Thission as it's known in Athens), built between 449 and 449 B.C. and dedicated to the god of metallurgy, Hephaestus, since this area, the Western Agora, was known for blacksmiths and other metalworkers. To the east, the **Stoa of Attalos** was built in the 2nd century B.C. and reconstructed in the 1950s; it now contains the **Agora Museum,** one long room that was the sight of about 10 shops in ancient times. You can see bronze ballots and a marble allotment machine used in ancient courtrooms to decide the appointment of jurors. Many of the museum pieces are examples of items used in everyday ancient life.

Odeum of Herodes Atticus. Dionysiou Aeropayitou St. (next to the entrance to the Acropolis). Not open to the public, except evenings June-Oct for performances during the Athens Festival.

Called the Herodion in modern Greek, this theater was built from A.D. 161 to 171 by teacher/philosopher Tiberius Claudius Atticus Herodes. Herodes was a very competitive person and didn't want to be outdone by Emperor Hadrian, who built and renovated many buildings during his time. So Atticus built this theater on the slopes of the Acropolis after inheriting a great fortune from his father and dedicated it to the memory of his wife, Regilla. But Herodes had a young male lover (what Greek man didn't?) named Polydeukes who died prematurely, like Hadrian's Antinous (see the box "Hadrian & Antinous" below). Herodes was shattered after Polydeukes's death, and,

The Acropolis & Ancient Agora

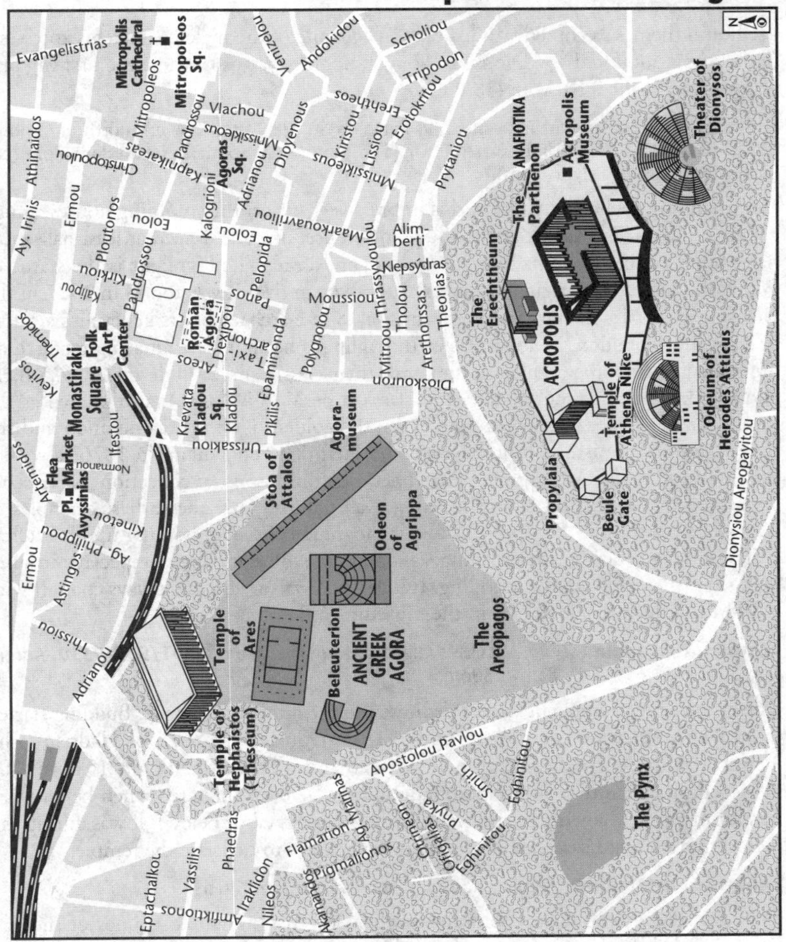

like Hadrian, wanted to leave something to his lover's memory. (Was this theater then built in memory of his wife or his lover? We'll never know for sure.) At that time, the theater seated 5,000 and boasted a cedar roof, white marble seats, and mosaic floors.

It's now home to the **Athens Festival,** where on most summer nights operas, ballets, concerts, or performances by Greek and international artists are held. For tickets (900–11,500Dr/$3–$38), call ☎ **01/322-2771** or 01/323-0049 or stop at the festival box office, 4 Odos Stadiou St., just off Syntagma Square (open daily 8:30am–2pm and 5–7pm). Tickets go on sale 2 weeks prior to each performance.

Theater of Dionysos. Dionysiou Areopayitou St. (on the southern slope of the Acropolis). ☎ **01/322-4625.** Admission 500Dr ($1.65). Daily 8am–2:30pm.

Built in 330 B.C., this is the world's oldest theater, where Sophocles, Euripides, Aeschylus, and Aristophanes first saw their tragedies and comedies staged. Back then the stage was made of wood, and it was reconstructed in the 4th century B.C. using the marble that's still visible. The theater seated 15,000, and on performance evenings practically the whole of Athens came. Aristophanes was the first-known playwright to use homo themes as comedy. In his play, *Wasps*, one of the male characters expresses a desire to be "mounted" by Dionysus. So, you might say, this is where the first gay play was ever performed, back in 438 B.C.

National Archaeological Museum. 44 Patission St. (28 October Ave.), north of Omonia Sq. ☎ **01/821-7717.** Admission 2,000Dr ($7). Mon noon–8pm, Tues–Sun 8am–8pm (call for winter hours, usually to 5pm).

Commanding a whole city block, this impressive 19th-century building houses a huge collection of ancient Greek art. If you're into museums, you'll need at least half a day here, but a couple of hours will give you a good taste. The highlight is the statue of Poseidon, one of few original bronze statues that survive. It was found in 1927 in the wreckage of a ship off the cape of Artemision. Some archaeologists believe it's a statue of Zeus, not Poseidon. Whoever he is, the tight abs he sports are amazing for such an old god. Look for the archaic statues with their classic smile (nude males, 625 B.C.) and the unsmiling statues of the early classical period (478 B.C.), also known as the severe period. Other noteworthy pieces are the golden mask of Agamemnon and the other treasures unearthed from Mycenae by Heinrich Schliemann in 1876 as well as the Jockey-Boy of Artemision. The Thera Exhibition is a collection of frescoes unearthed in Akrotiri on Santorini; these wall paintings are the earliest examples of large-scale painting in Europe. Check out the nude fisherman holding up his catch.

Try and come here in the morning, as soon as the museum opens, especially in summer, since there's no air-conditioning. If it gets too warm, you can always cool off with a cold drink in the shaded cafe in the museum garden.

Temple of Olympian Zeus. Vassilissis Olgas and Amalias aves. ☎ **01/922-6330.** Admission 500Dr ($1.65). Daily 8am–2:30pm.

This is the largest temple in Greece dedicated to the father of the gods. Building started in 515 B.C. but wasn't completed until A.D. 131 during the reign of Hadrian (who identified with Zeus, believing himself to be father of all emperors). Only 15 of the 104 tall Corinthian columns still stand. Hadrian must've been shattered when he returned here from Egypt following the death of Antinous (see the box below). It was during this period that Hadrian marched here with his entourage to dedicate the temple.

Panathenaic Stadium. Vassileos Konstandinou Ave. Daily 24 hours.

This impressive 60,000-seat stadium is where the first Olympic Games of modern times were held in 1896. It was built of white marble and is very similar to the original stadium at Olympia, where the ancient Olympic Games were held over 2,000 years ago (with most athletes competing in the nude remember). On summer evenings, Athenians stroll around the stadium. If you walk up a ways to the upper levels, you'll get a fabulous city view, especially at sunset. The National Gardens aren't far away, and you can glimpse the Temple of Olympian Zeus and, behind it, Hadrian's Arch.

Ilias Lalaounis Jewelry Museum. 4a Karyatidon St. (at Kalisperi). ☎ **01/922-1044.** Admission 800Dr ($3). Mon and Wed 9am–9pm, Thurs–Sat to 3pm, Sun 10am–3pm.

The 3,000 pieces on display are so spectacular that even nonjewelry lovers will enjoy this glitzy new museum, founded by one of Greece's most successful jewelry designers. The first floor has a boutique and small workshop. The second and third floors display pieces inspired by ancient, Byzantine, and Cycladic designs, as well as by plants and animals. The museum shop has copies of some of the displays, and jewelers in the workshop take orders, in case you want your own gold necklace inspired by insect vertebrae.

Goulandris Museum of Cycladic and Ancient Greek Art. 4 Neophytou Douka St. ☎ **01/722-8321.** Admission 800Dr ($3). Mon and Wed–Fri 10am–4pm, Sat to 3pm.

Hadrian & Antinous: Ancient Greek Love

Somewhere between A.D. 125 and 130, Emperor Hadrian of Rome fell head over heels for a 14- or 15-year-old Greek beauty named Antinous. Back then it was considered perfectly normal for an older man to take a younger man (even a teenager) as a lover. But Hadrian, who was then in his early 50s, became obsessed with the boy, showering him with gifts and insisting Antinous accompany him on all his travels. In A.D. 130, Antinous was barely 20 when he was found dead, drowned in the Nile in Egypt. To this day no one knows if his death was a suicide, a murder, or an accident.

Rumors abound. In one story, Hadrian is said to have ordered the castration of his lover to preserve his youthful beauty and Antinous died during the surgery. In another, Antinous's death is said to have been premeditated, a court conspiracy to get him out of the way because Hadrian's attraction to him had become an embarrassment. But the theory most historians believe is that Antinous died voluntarily, offering himself as a sacrifice meant to prolong the life of his ailing emperor: He died for love, for Hadrian. After Antinous's death, Hadrian was heartbroken. He surrounded himself with images of the young man preserved on coins and gems and as statues of the pretty boy with a buff chest and curly hair. Hadrian grieved for Antinous until his own death a few years later. Shortly after the boy's death, Hadrian's Arch was completed to honor the emperor and still stands on Amalias Avenue at the eastern edge of Plaka.

If you're interested in Hadrian's villa, see the end of the Rome chapter.

This handsome museum houses the astonishing collection of Nicolas and Aikaterini Goulandris, the largest collection of Cycladic art outside the National Archaeological Museum, with some 230 stone and pottery vessels and figurines from the 3rd millennium B.C. See if you agree with those who've compared the faces of the Cycladic figurines to the work of Modigliani. Be sure to go through the courtyard into the newest acquisition: the elegant 19th-century Stathatos Mansion, with some of its original furnishings.

GAY ATHENS

Let's face it, there isn't much in Athens that's openly gay. No rainbow flags or images of same-sex couples and only a few newsstands carrying gay magazines. Most of the gay clubs are tucked away on small side streets where the lights are dim and the boys safe behind closed doors. Masculinity and homosexuality don't seem to mix in this society except in secret dark areas.

Lesbians aren't visible either, even less so than gays, though the society better tolerates two women being intimate publicly.

Many of the trendy areas (like Kolonaki and Thission squares) are brimming with virile young men. There's definitely a flirtatious feel in the air in these neighborhoods, especially in the late afternoon and early evening in spring and fall. But don't be misled. Many of the men looking back at you are married. Maybe they're cruising, but they're not going to go any further (I'd be delighted if you proved me wrong). Be careful: The mating signs are different here. Some of these boys just *seem* gay, with their slicked black hair shining with gel and their tight jeans and the way they stand close to one another, touching. This is how it is here. It's Mediterranean. It's hot. Men are comfortable with one another, and it doesn't mean it gets sexual.

Athens Attractions

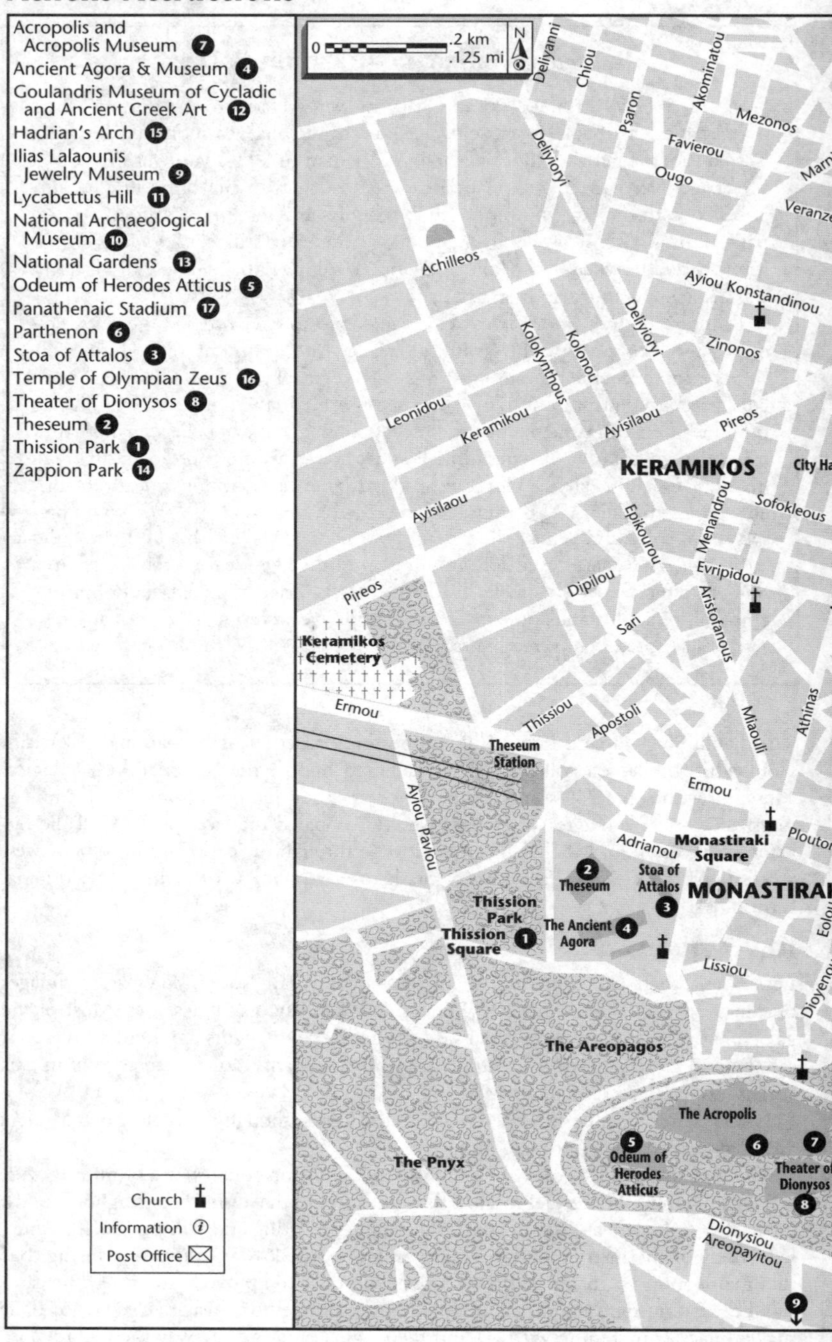

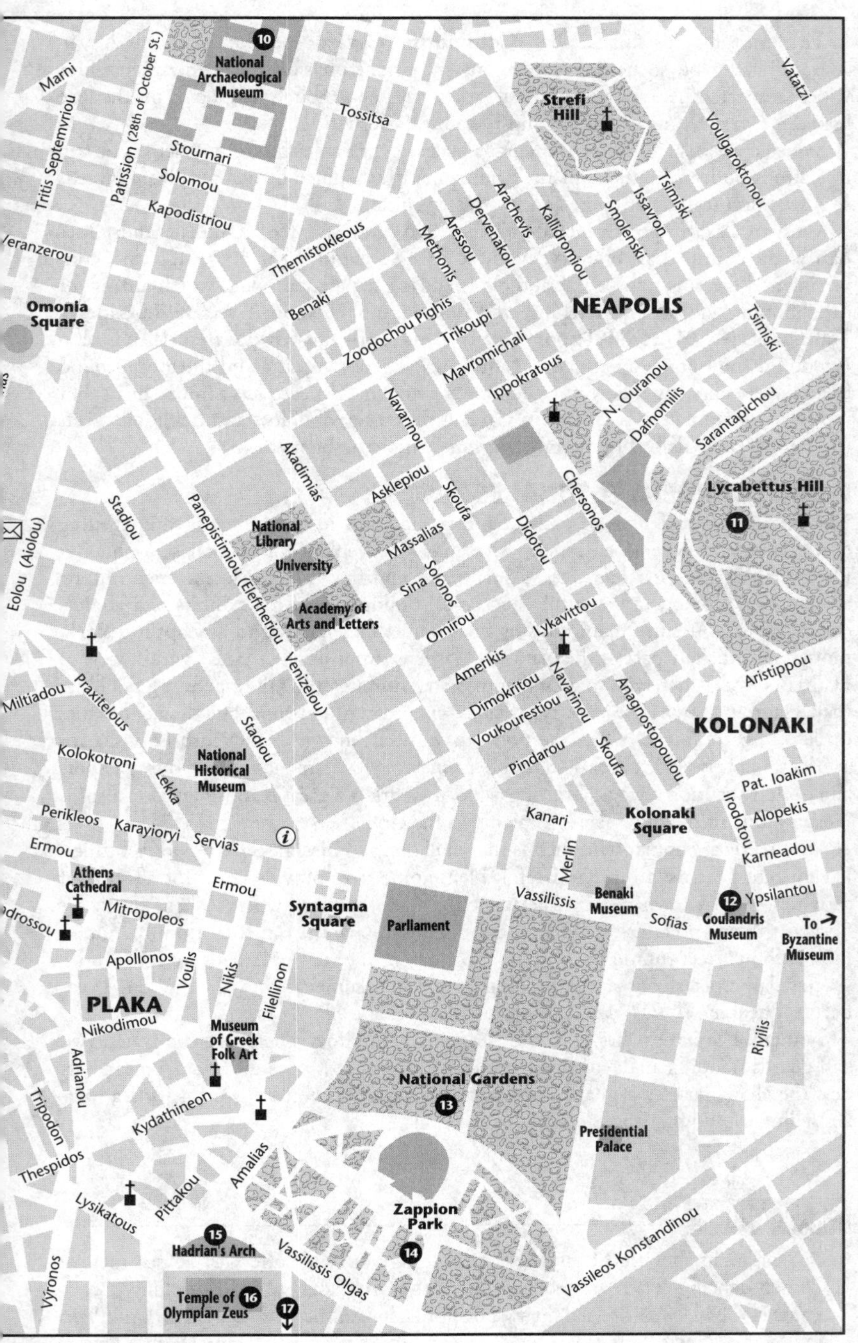
National Archaeological Museum
Strefi Hill
NEAPOLIS
Omonia Square
Lycabettus Hill
National Library
University
Academy of Arts and Letters
KOLONAKI
National Historical Museum
Kolonaki Square
Athens Cathedral
Syntagma Square
Parliament
Benaki Museum
Goulandris Museum
To Byzantine Museum
PLAKA
Museum of Greek Folk Art
National Gardens
Presidential Palace
Zappion Park
Hadrian's Arch
Temple of Olympian Zeus
Marni
Tritis Septemvriou
Patission (28th of October St.)
Tossitsa
Stournari
Solomou
Kapodistriou
Veranzerou
Themistokleous
Benaki
Zoodochou Pighis
Methonis
Aressou
Dervenakou
Arachevis
Kallidromiou
Smolenski
Issavron
Tsimiski
Voulgaroktonou
Vatatzi
Trikoupi
Mavromichali
Ippokratous
N. Ouranou
Dafnomilis
Sarantapichou
Navarinou
Akadimias
Asklepiou
Skoufa
Chersonos
Didotou
Massalias
Sina
Solonos
Omirou
Lykavittou
Amerikis
Dimokritou
Voukourestiou
Pindarou
Anagnostopoulou
Aristippou
Stadiou
Panepistimiou (Eleftheriou Venizelou)
Eolou (Aiolou)
Miltiadou
Praxitelous
Kolokotroni
Lekka
Perikleos
Karayioryi
Servias
Ermou
Kanari
Merlin
Irodotou
Pat. Ioakim
Alopekis
Karneadou
Ypsilantou
Vassilissis Sofias
Mitropoleos
Apollonos
Voulis
Nikis
Filellinon
Nikodimou
Adrianou
Tripodon
Kydathineon
Thespidos
Lysikatous
Pittakou
Amalias
Vassilissis Olgas
Vassileos Konstandinou
Riyilis
Výronos
10
11
12
13
14
15
16
17

The most famous Greek poet, **Constantine Cavafy,** spent most of his life in Alexandria, Egypt, so he didn't leave any important physical traces in Athens. He's widely respected here, but as a poet not as a *gay* poet, though his poems on the love between two men are among the most beautiful ever written.

Some gay visitors find it convenient to make Egypt a side trip from Athens. The trip to Cairo is under 2 hours by plane. And regularly scheduled boats travel from Piraeus to Alexandria (calling at Crete and Cyprus en route).

Many of Cavafy's poems include references to cafes. In Greece (and Alexandria) it's part of the culture, part of everyday life to spend a chunk of one's day at a cafe, conversing and meeting new people and old friends. The neighborhoods worth hitting for cafe-hopping and people-watching are Kolonaki and Thission. Try **Café de Capo,** 1 Tsakalof St. (☎ **01/243-3902;** open daily 9am–1am), and **Kirki Café,** 31 Apostolou Pavlou St. (no phone; open daily 11am–2am). These two cafes and the areas around them have a solid gay following, albeit not very open. Kirki attracts some lesbians, but the place for women to try is **Berlin Café,** at the corner of Nileos and Iraklidon streets (no phone; open daily 11am-2am), with its feminist/lesbian crowd.

PARKS, GARDENS & SQUARES

The **National Garden** is an oasis of green and calm in the center of this bustling city. There are several entrances, the most convenient on Amalias Avenue at Hadrian's Arch. Other than trees, a small lake, and fresh air, you'll find men milling around the Zappion (a beautiful neoclassical building used for exhibits and conferences). This is Athens's main cruising area, sometimes referred to as **Zappion Park,** though it's officially part of the National Gardens. Appropriate that it's within view of Hadrian's Arch—here you may find your own Antinous (though hopefully a tad older than Hadrian's boy). The park is officially open dawn to 10pm, but the action goes on late into the night, when the police have been known to pay surprise visits for a "document or ID check"—a euphemism for harassment. Take your passport and exercise caution always. Cruising aside, the park is a great place to relax on a summer day, one of the only places to picnic in the city.

Another park popular with men is the small one at **Thission Square,** off Apostolou Pavlou Street (across from Kirki cafe). Dense pine trees provide cover for all sorts of activities. Across town, up **Lycabettus Hill** is another spot where Athenians go for fresh air (there's no cruising here, though). You can take the funicular from the top of Ploutarchou Street (uphill from Kolonaki Square). The view of Athens from the top is spectacular, especially at sunset on clear days. On summer nights, the outdoor **Lycabettus Theater** (☎ **01/722-7209**) hosts concerts and plays.

Syntagma Square is home to the Parliament Building, where you can watch two stiff guards standing all day wearing traditional Greek costumes. At 6pm, you can witness the changing of the guards. **Monastiraki Square** is best known for its flea market selling everything from antiques to olive oil.

A Warning

Day or night, beware of anyone approaching you with offers to go see men or women dancing. There have been numerous stories lately of visitors falling prey to scams involving well-dressed men who approach unsuspecting tourists around Plaka and Syntagma with offers of a good time and free entrance to a great "club." They're insistent but not dangerous—just ignore them or say you'll call the police if they don't stop harassing you. They usually give up quickly if you show no interest.

Omonia Square is the seediest part of town, with hundreds of small thrift shops, newsstands, and cheap cafes. Young Albanian immigrants have been known to hustle here at night, when this area becomes dangerous for most Athenians. It's the only place locals avoid after sunset. **Kolonaki Square** is the exact opposite. This small square with its cafes and high-priced shops hops well into the night with a mix of people of all ages. It's the most expensive area of Athens.

WORKING UP A SWEAT

Work-out mania is just hitting Athens, and small neighborhood gyms are opening (and closing) with the seasons. The largest and best equipped health club is **Universal Studios,** 126 Twenty-fifth of March St., Peristeri (☎ **01/577-2490**). You'll find everything from free weights to a large pool, squash courts, tennis courts, and 185 aerobic and universal machines. This is the only club in Athens open 24 hours. There's also massage, a sauna, and a steam room.

Since there's no gay area, there are no gay gyms. But ask the bouncers at the dance clubs Alexander's and Lambda where the current pumping hot spot is. Gay boys go where it's trendy, and it changes often.

5 Hitting the Stores

Shopping isn't why most people come to Athens. Designer labels tend to be overpriced. The flea market at Monastiraki Square and the hundreds of tiny stores in Plaka have an interesting collection of trinkets, replicas of Greek statues, sandals, rugs, and many touristy souvenirs. But Plaka is where everybody goes.

To get a taste of shopping like an Athenian, head to the pedestrian-only **Ermou Street** off Syntagma Square. Walk south on it and you'll come to where most middle-class Athenians shop. Many department stores, like Marks & Spencer, are on Ermou. The streets around **Omonia Square** house hundreds of cheap clothing stores, and that's where the rock-bottom prices are.

For a taste of how the upper-crust shop, head to **Kolonaki Square.** That's where you're most likely to run into gay shoppers and quite a few gay-owned stores, though they don't advertise as such and in this closeted society don't want to be known as gay. Like everything else here, the trendy shops in the trendy areas tend to be more mixed and gay-friendly. The stores here usually have younger sales help who will struggle in their broken English to help you find what you need. But don't expect especially friendly service. This is a snobby area, and the shop owners can act very unconcerned toward all shoppers. A take-it-or-leave-it attitude prevails.

Generally, **store hours** are Monday, Wednesday, and Saturday 9am to 3pm and Tuesday, Thursday, and Friday 9am to 2pm and 5 to 8pm. Department stores are open longer hours; check with the individual stores. All stores are closed on Sunday, except in the tourist areas in and around Plaka.

SHOPS A TO Z

ANTIQUES Your best bet is the **Monastiraki open-air flea market** (from Syntagma Square, take Ermou Street south until you hit Monastiraki Square). You'll find everything from tiny antique mirrors to handmade bedside tables. Closed Monday.

BOOKS There are no gay bookstores in Athens yet. But at Athens's largest bookstore, **Eleftheroudakis,** 17 Panepistimiou Ave., near Syntagma Square (☎ **01/331-4180**), you'll find a large selection of books in English and occasionally an Edmund White paperback. At **Compendium,** 28 Nikis St., near Plaka (☎ **01/322-1248**), there's a small collection of English titles.

CERAMICS ✪ **Ergastiri,** 23 Iperidou St., across from the Hotel Nefeli (☎ **01/324-4360**), displays hand-painted ceramics by Greek artists. The owner of this tiny store, Christine Drakou, works closely with all the artists she represents to ensure the highest quality. Many of the bowls and plates are very reasonably priced, and you won't find anything like them anywhere else. Closed Monday and Wednesday and January 15 to March 1.

CHOCOLATE, SWEETS & WINE **Aristokratikon,** 9 Karagiorgi Servias St., near Syntagma Square (☎ **01/322-0546**), has an excellent selection of handmade chocolates. The facade of this elegant store looks like it belongs on a street in Paris. Your mouth will water at the delicately displayed chocolates in the window. **Matsouka,** 6 Apollon St., behind Syntagma Square (☎ **01/323-3604**), sells Greek sweets and desserts packaged for the traveler, plus a good selection of local wines and ouzos.

FASHION The hippest, trendiest, and most expensive stores are in Kolonaki on the small streets heading up the hill, north from the square. Here you'll find **DKNY, Bally, Charles Jourdan,** and **Armani.** This is the Rodeo Drive of Athens.

My favorite store is ✪ **Mohnblumchen,** 7 Dexaminis St., at the corner of Spefsippol Street (☎ **01/723-6960**). If you've ever wanted to be a supermodel, you'll love this: There's a large runway where you can model your potential purchases to loud disco music. Work it, girl. This place feel more like a nightclub than a unisex clothing store. For a great selection of shirts and summer T-shirts as well as underwear for men, stop at **Sarafees,** 5 Patriarchi Ioakim St. (☎ **01/722-5319**). The young energetic staff is refreshingly helpful.

If you're looking for men's designer wear, drop by **Boutique Gianfranco Ferré,** 4 Anagnostopoulou St. (☎ **01/723-1654**). The sleek salesmen can't manage a smile but can easily sell you a couple of Versace shirts that'll cost more than your flight.

JEWELRY If you're heading to Mykonos after Athens and want some jewelry, you'd be better off waiting until you get there. But your best bet in Athens is to visit **Anna Mari,** 4 Hatzimihali St., next door to the Hotel Nefeli (☎ **01/331-2237**). She designs most of the jewelry she sells, and it's all reasonably priced. For the ultimate queenness, check out her special tiaras that turn into necklaces (don't ask, it's hard to explain).

MUSEUM REPLICAS At **The Centaur,** 4 Vas. Irakliou St., across from the National Archaeological Museum (☎ **01/432-3200**), you'll find everything from frescoes to vases of Corinth to beautiful marble chessboards, all at reasonable prices and all exact museum replicas.

RUGS **Karamichos Mazarakis,** 31–33 Voulis St., between Syntagma Square and Plaka (☎ **01/322-4932**), has the best selection of traditional hand-woven Greek flokati rugs as well as silk carpets and funky Berbers. Check out the collection of rugs with designs by Andy Warhol.

6 All the World's a Stage

Summertime is when Athens comes alive, with outdoor music and dance festivals and the unique open-air movie theaters. October to May is opera, jazz, and concert season. There's always a lot going on in the music scene. Your best source of performance listings is the bimonthly ***Now In Athens,*** distributed free at the major hotels and at the tourist offices. For a more detailed listing, pick up a copy of ***Athenscope.*** It's no longer available in English, but you can ask the receptionist or concierge at your hotel to translate the listings you're interested in. As of this writing, there are no gay-specific companies or theaters.

In summer, most performances move outdoors to the many festivals in and around Athens. The most popular is the **Athens Festival** held at the foot of the Acropolis at the Odeon of Herodes Atticus (☎ **01/322-1459**). The festival, running June to October, has been staging Greek plays, concerts, ballets, and modern dance performances since 1955. Maria Callas and Luciano Pavarotti have sung here. A program is available at the theater box office and at the ticket outlet on Syntagma Square, 4 Stadiou St.

The June-to-October **Lycabettus Festival** is host to many cultural events, including plays, musicals, and dance performances. Inquire at the Athens Festival box office or by calling ☎ **01/722-7209.**

THE PERFORMING ARTS

The **Greek National Opera House,** 59–61 Academias St. (☎ **01/361-2461;** box office open Mon–Fri 9am–1pm and 5–8pm and Sat–Sun 10am–1pm and 5–7pm), is where Maria Callas first sang and is now also home to the National Ballet Company. The season runs October to May. If you're interested in Greek folk dancing, the **Dora Stratou Dance Theater,** on Philopappou Hill (☎ **01/324-4395** or ☎ 01/921-4650 daily 5:30–10pm; box office open daily 8am–2pm), hosts performances May to September.

The **Megaron Mousikis (Athens Concert Hall),** 89 Vassilissis Sofias Ave. (☎ **01/728-2333;** box office open Mon–Fri 10am–6pm, Sat to 2pm and Sun 6–8:30pm), is the sight of most of the city's classical concerts, symphonies, and recitals. There are daily programs, sometimes two different performances per day September to June. The concert hall, opened in 1991, is acclaimed for its outstanding acoustics. Tickets are available from the Megaron box office, but it might be easier to get them from **The Arcade,** 4 Stadiou St., at Syntagma Square (☎ **01/322-1459;** open Mon–Sat 8:30am–2pm and 5–7pm, Sun 10am–1pm).

LIVE-MUSIC CLUBS

The jazz scene is flourishing in Athens. But note that many of the live-music clubs close in summer.

In the residential area of Mets, the **Half Note Jazz Club,** 17 Trivonianou St. (☎ **01/921-3310**), changes its program weekly. If you're in the mood for blues, call the **Blues Hall,** 44 Arditou St., also in Mets (☎ **01/924-7448**), where there are frequent appearances by Greece's leading blues/rock band, Socrates.

For a louder, livelier crowd, consider spending an evening at the **An Club,** 13–15 Solomou St., in Exarchia (☎ **01/330-5056**), where you'll find everything from rock to disco bands nightly during the season. If you're into mixing folk and rock and everything in between, **Rodon Live,** 24 Marnis St. (☎ **01/524-7427**), has an unusual lineup, from the latest big names on the Greek music scene to a string quartet from Finland. And at **Café Asante,** 78 Damereos St. (☎ **01/726-0102**), the choices might be traditional Armenian songs one night, Argentine tangos the next, and a singer from Peru to wrap up the week.

OPEN-AIR MOVIE THEATERS

This is a Greek tradition. As soon as the weather is warm enough (usually by late May or early June), rooftops and gardens are turned into outdoor movie theaters. It's a romantic way (but don't get *too* romantic) to spend an evening with the locals under the stars. The foldout chairs can get uncomfortable, but the setting will make up for it. Most movies come from Hollywood and are in English with Greek subtitles.

In the heart of Plaka is **Cine Paris,** at the corner of Thespidos and Adrianou streets (☎ **01/322-2071**). In Kolonaki, there's the **Athinai,** 50 Haritos St. (☎ **01/721-5717**). At Thission Square is the **Thission,** 7 Apostolou Pavlou St. (☎ **01/347-0980**). Most shows start at 9pm, with an additional show at 11pm on Friday and Saturday.

7 In the Heat of the Night

The Greeks are nocturnal people. The streets come alive after dark, and traffic jams at midnight in Athens aren't uncommon. Since the Greeks dine late (no earlier than 10pm), the clubs don't get going before midnight. In fact, most dance clubs don't bother opening until midnight, and usually it's about 2am before it gets crowded.

To get the scoop on what's happening, your best bet is to ask at the gay bars I mention below. There are no publications in English listing gay venues, so it's hard to find up-to-date info. But the bartenders and bar owners at a few places, notably The Guys and Aleko at Aleko's Island will be more than happy to fill you in on the hot scene.

MAINSTREAM BARS & PUBS

Since all cafes serve alcohol in Greece, often there's no fine line between a cafe and a bar. At Kolonaki and Thission squares, as well as in Plaka, this holds true in the popular bar/cafes serving both coffee and cocktails.

Most hotels have good bars, many located on the roof garden with views of the Acropolis. The Hilton's **Galaxy Bar,** 46 Vassilissis Sofias Ave., Kolonaki (☎ **01/725-0201**), is lined with loveseats so you can truly lounge. And the popular **GB Corner Bar** at the Grande Bretagne Hotel, Syntagma Square (☎ **01/330-0000**), is reminiscent of an English pub.

GAY BARS

For such a large city, Athens has few gay bars. They're concentrated in three areas: Kolonaki, Thission, and Makriyanni.

The friendliest bar in town is ✪ **Aleko's Island,** 42 Tsakalof St. (no phone). This is a fun place where you can actually have a conversation with the local and foreign men who come here. Aleko knows his city well, so ask him what's new and hot.

A 10-minute walk from Kolonaki, heading downhill on Skoufa Street (turn right at Delfon), you'll find the very hip **Delfis Bar,** 5 Delfon St. (no phone). Although it's not advertised as a gay bar, the crowd is heavily gay and gets densest after 1am.

Across town in Makriyanni is a small dark street that's home to two gay bars. **The Guys,** 8 Lembessi St. (☎ **01/921-4244**), is run by the owner, Theodore. This is a neighborhood bar where many local gay men of varying ages go. Ask Theodore for the latest dirt on the bar upstairs from him. It changes names every few months and has been known as Aquarius and Endohomeno. It's pretty seedy now, so do ask before venturing up there.

Down the street is **Granazi,** 20 Lembessi St. (☎ **01/324-4585**). It attracts a louder, livelier, and younger crowd than the other bars and half the clientele is Greek, so this is the place to go if you want to meet local guys.

On the other side of the Acropolis, at Thission Square, you'll find **Kirki,** 31 Apostolou Pavlou St. (no phone). It's a lively bar/cafe with a mainly gay crowd, especially early on Sunday evenings. Light snacks are served, and the crowd sips ouzo and is more intellectual and less cruisy than that on Lembessi Street.

LESBIAN BARS

Porta, 10 Phalirou St., in Makriyanni (☎ **01/924-3858**), is the only true lesbian bar in town. Whereas the boy bars play mostly techno music, Porta is strictly rock, and the female staff is very friendly to the gay men who venture in.

On the southeast corner of Thission Square, **Café Berlin** (no phone) is very lesbian-friendly and has a mainly female crowd. You won't miss it: It's the one with the bright red chairs outside and is as sleek as a SoHo cafe.

DANCE CLUBS

Dance clubs usually charge about 2,500Dr ($8) admission, which includes one drink.

Drag Clubs Koukles, at the corner of Zan Moreas Street and Syngrou Avenue in Makriyanni, behind the Olympic Airways building (☎ **01/921-3054**), has occasional drag shows after midnight and is known for its fun-loving transgender crowd. While you're here, ask for directions to the transvestite cruising area nearby.

GAY CLUBS There are two gay dance clubs that are popular and have been around for a while. **Lambda,** 15 Lembessi St., in Makriyanni (☎ **01/922-4202**), is hip and trendy now with the young locals who come around 2am. There's a backroom too.

In Kolonaki, the well-established **Alexander's,** 4 Anagnostopoulou St. (☎ **01/364-6660**), has two bars. Upstairs they play Greek music occasionally and downstairs it's rock. Don't expect to see anyone but the bartenders before 1am.

Zone DK, 8 Keleshrou St., at Syngrou Avenue (☎ **01/922-0245**), was slated to open after this writing. Ask around if it has taken off.

MIXED CLUBS Dance clubs (both gay and straight) come and go in Athens like the seasons. Word of mouth is your best bet to get the scoop on up-to-date information.

Booze, close to Plaka at 57 Kolokotrani St. (☎ **01/324-0944**), has a young crowd of locals and foreigners, but it's more straight than mixed.

Mercedes Rex, 48 Panepistimiou St., behind Syntagma Square (☎ **01/361-4591**), has a slightly more diverse crowd, but you still can't really call it mixed.

DOWN & DIRTY: CINEMAS & MORE

There are no gay movie houses in Athens, but the very seedy **Athenaikon** on Athena Street (by the old town Hall at Omonia Square) is largely gay and very cruisy. This is a questionable area, though, and frequent muggings have been reported after dark. Be careful.

A brand-new video and sex shop, **Videoland,** is now open on the second floor at 65 Panepistimiou St., between Syntagma and Omonia squares (no phone). It has individual cabins showing gay videos.

Most of the **saunas** and **bathhouses** are around Omonia Square, an area I don't recommend. **Athens Relax,** 8 Xouthou St. close to Omonio Square (☎ **01/528-8800**), is said to have mainly a gay clientele and some hustlers.

8 Side Trips from Athens: Delphi & the Peloponnese

DELPHI

The most popular day trip from Athens is **Delphi,** known in ancient Greece as the "center of the earth." If you're traveling by **car,** Delphi is a 3-hour drive northwest of Athens. **Buses** leave from Bus Terminal B at 260 Liossion St. (☎ **01/831-7096**). There are seven buses daily, the first leaving at 7:30am. The round-trip fare is 5,700Dr ($19).

Consider taking a tour bus: You'll save a lot of time and ride in air-conditioned comfort with a guide who speaks English. Both **G.O. Tours** (☎ **01/921-9555**) and **Key Tours** (☎ **01/923-3166**) have convenient day trips to Delphi, departing Athens at 8:30am and returning at 6:30pm. The current rate is 17,000Dr ($56), which includes a stop in the scenic town of Arachova on the slopes of Mount Parnassus.

Once in Delphi, you'll feel the magic of this beautiful sight. This is the city of the oracle: Know Thyself and Nothing In Excess were the two precepts inscribed on the Delphic oracle. The admission is 1,500Dr ($5), and the site is open Monday to Friday 7:30am to 6:30pm and Saturday, Sunday, and holidays 8:30am to 3pm.

Head first to the **Sanctuary of Apollo,** beginning a few hundred feet after you enter the archaeological site. You'll first be walking down the **Sacred Way,** which used to be lined with bronze statues, before arriving at the **Temple of Apollo.** The ancient Greeks believed that here they stood in the presence of the gods, and the words of Apollo were believed to have been heard here. The **theater** above the Temple of Apollo was completed in the 2nd century B.C. and seated 5,000 spectators. Climb up through the pine trees to the **stadium.** The best-preserved stadium in Greece, it's known for its chariot races during the quadrennial Pythian Games, begun in 582 B.C.

Between the Temple of Apollo and the Temple of Athena Pronaea is the **Castalia Fountain,** where pilgrims to Delphi purified themselves by washing their hair with water from Mt. Parnassus. The water is still potable and icy cold, fresh from the nearby mountain. Walk a few minutes farther down, past the tourist cafe, and you'll reach the **Temple of Athena Pronaea,** built in the 4th century B.C. and visited by pilgrims before entering the Sacred Precinct. Beyond it is the circular monument known as **Tholos,** built in 380 B.C. From here you have a wondrous view of the ruins and what's left from the ancient Greek world.

End your day at the **Delphi Museum,** west of the Temple of Apollo (☎ **0265/82-1313**), where you'll find one of the best-preserved sculptures of Hadrian's lover, Antinous, along with the famous bronze charioteer and a valuable collection of friezes and sculptures. The museum is open Monday 11am to 6:30pm; Tuesday to Friday 7:30am to 6:30pm; and Saturday, Sunday, and holidays 8:30am to 3pm. Admission is 1,500Dr ($5).

THE PELOPONNESE

Many tour companies offer day trips into the Peloponnese—to **Corinth,** with its famous Doric temple and Greek and Roman ruins; **Mycenae,** the city of Agamemnon, with the ruins of the royal citadel and the eerie "beehive" tombs where Mycenaean royalty were buried; and **Epidauros,** where you can visit the sanctuary of the healing god Asclepios and the best-preserved ancient theater in Greece, which seats 14,000 and is still used each summer for performances in the Festival of Epidauros. If you want to see a show, try to find a tour company that gets you there early, so you can visit the site before the performance begins.

Buses for these and other destinations on the Peloponnese Peninsula leave from Bus Terminal A, 100 Kifissiou St. (☎ **01/512-9233**). To reach it, take local bus no. 051 at Zinonos and Menandrou streets, 3 blocks southwest of Omonia Square

Delphi Site Plan

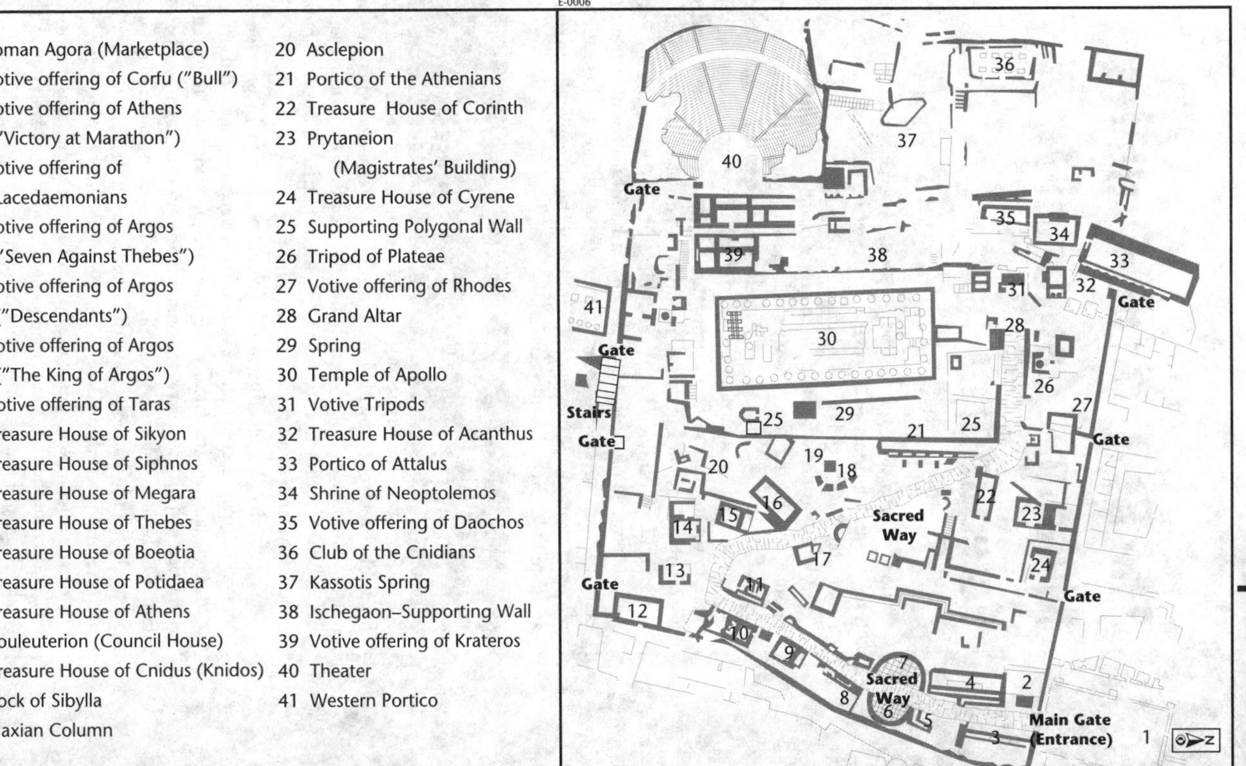

E-0006
1 Roman Agora (Marketplace)
2 Votive offering of Corfu ("Bull")
3 Votive offering of Athens ("Victory at Marathon")
4 Votive offering of Lacedaemonians
5 Votive offering of Argos ("Seven Against Thebes")
6 Votive offering of Argos ("Descendants")
7 Votive offering of Argos ("The King of Argos")
8 Votive offering of Taras
9 Treasure House of Sikyon
10 Treasure House of Siphnos
11 Treasure House of Megara
12 Treasure House of Thebes
13 Treasure House of Boeotia
14 Treasure House of Potidaea
15 Treasure House of Athens
16 Bouleuterion (Council House)
17 Treasure House of Cnidus (Knidos)
18 Rock of Sibylla
19 Naxian Column
20 Asclepion
21 Portico of the Athenians
22 Treasure House of Corinth
23 Prytaneion (Magistrates' Building)
24 Treasure House of Cyrene
25 Supporting Polygonal Wall
26 Tripod of Plateae
27 Votive offering of Rhodes
28 Grand Altar
29 Spring
30 Temple of Apollo
31 Votive Tripods
32 Treasure House of Acanthus
33 Portico of Attalus
34 Shrine of Neoptolemos
35 Votive offering of Daochos
36 Club of the Cnidians
37 Kassotis Spring
38 Ischegaon–Supporting Wall
39 Votive offering of Krateros
40 Theater
41 Western Portico
Gate
Stairs
Sacred Way
Main Gate (Entrance)
N

9

The Best of the Cyclades: Mykonos, Santorini & Folegandros

The **Cyclades**, after the Acropolis, is what Greece is famous for. Picturesque and unique, each of these islands in the Aegean south of Athens has a different flavor and landscape.

Mykonos is known for its wide sandy beaches, its large cruisy gay population, and the quaint town of Hora, with windmills and designer shops. **Santorini** is spectacular, with its volcanic terrain, whitewashed villages stacked on a mountainside, and infamous mules lugging supplies up the hundreds of stairs from the old port to town. **Folegandros** is one of the last sleepy and nontouristy islands left in the Cyclades. You can hike for miles on its rugged hills and not see another soul, and you can lounge on beaches where only a handful of visitors venture each summer. So close to one another yet so different, these islands offer a very unique experience. Combining the three would give you an incredible Greek island vacation.

1 Mykonos: Decadence & Debauchery Unlimited

So you've heard of **Mykonos,** the quintessential Greek island, the jewel of the Cyclades with its windmills, whitewashed villages, and outstanding beaches. You've probably also heard of the nude beaches, the dancing in the streets, and the all-night parties at Super Paradise Beach. Mykonos is all that and much more.

Gays from all over the world (very few lesbians) converge on Mykonos, men of every shape and size, of every age, race, and profession. Germans are statistically the most frequent visitors, followed by the British. This is a very seasonal island—nothing is open before Easter or beyond the end of October. The best months are May, June, September, and October, when the island is at its gayest, the weather perfect, and everything less expensive. July and August are very crowded with a mixed tourist crowd. Hip young Athenians escape the city and come here too, and it gets so crowded that walking in the small village of Hora is immensely frustrating.

Some travelers complain of the noise and traffic, others say the gay scene is too much like an endless circuit party. But the great thing about Mykonos is that with so many beaches, all large and sandy, with sparkling blue water, you can still find some peace and quiet if you want. But in the end, Mykonos isn't about reading a book under a beach umbrella—it's about decadence and debauchery (you'd be better off reading somewhere cheaper anyway). The rhythm is party until dawn, sleep until noon, then hit the beach, dine at 10pm, and repeat.

MYKONOS ESSENTIALS

ARRIVING & DEPARTING

BY PLANE This is the easiest way to reach Mykonos, especially if you're not planning to visit Athens. During the high season, up to 14 flights arrive at **Mykonos International Airport** from Athens (a 20-minute hop aboard large propeller planes) and one from Santorini, Rhodes, and Heraklion. You can reach **Olympic Airways** in Athens at ☎ **01/966-6666** and in Mykonos at ☎ **0289/22-490.**

The runway has recently been lengthened to accommodate large jets, and now several charter flights a day arrive from Amsterdam, Frankfurt, and Vienna, among other European cities. To make a reservation on a charter flight, contact **Windmills Travel** in Mykonos at ☎ **0289/23-877** or e-mail windmills@travelling.gr. Taxis meet all incoming flights. If you have a reservation at any hotel, advise them of your arrival flight and they'll send a free shuttle van to pick you up. This is a nice touch, and most hotels offer this perk with the room price.

BY BOAT This is the most popular way of getting to Mykonos. From Piraus, there are several **ferries** a day. The fast ferry, simply called High Speed, usually leaves in mid-afternoon and takes 3 hours. This service is operated by **Minoan Lines** (☎ **01/751-2356**). The slow ferries take about 6 hours, making several stops along the way (usually in Syros and Tinos). **Ventouris Ferries** (☎ **01/482-5815**) has a morning departure and adds an evening departure during summer.

Ferries from Santorini run at least once a day, with hydrofoil service added during the peak months, including four weekly trips from Folegandros. Call the **Mykonos Port Authority** for schedules at ☎ **0289/22-218.** You can also check schedules online at **www.gtpnet.com.**

BY PRIVATE YACHT The only other way to arrive on Mykonos (apart from private jet) is on a private yacht. Yeah, it sounds extravagant and glamorous, but it's also surprisingly affordable if you have a group of six or more. Sleep on-board the yacht, save hotel bills, and sail to a different beach or island every day. Design your own itinerary (most start and end in Athens). **Valef Yachts** at ☎ **01/428-1920** in Piraeus has offices worldwide and a variety of yachts available for hire. Or contact the **Greek Yacht Brokers & Consultants Association** at ☎ **01/985-0122** for a complete list of companies.

VISITOR INFORMATION

The **Mykonos Tourist Office** is at the port, near the excursion boats to Delos (☎ **0289/23-990;** open daily 9am-2pm and 5-9pm). They also have a counter at the airport that'll help with hotel reservations. Purchase a Skymap of Hora (Mykonos Town) at any travel agency or hotel for 500Dr ($1.65).

ISLAND LAYOUT

The heart of the island is **Mykonos Town,** known as **Hora.** Ferries arrive at the port at the edge of town, with cafes and shops lining the waterfront. The center of Hora is a maze of small streets. Originally built to confuse pirates, it still manages to frustrate visitors, who frequently find themselves going round in circles. It's a beautiful town to get lost in, though, with hundreds of small shops, whitewashed buildings, and laundry hanging from balconies. People do live here, though at first sight it might seem overrun with tourists.

Matoyanni is the main street, running south from Taxi Square (officially Mando Mavroyenous Square), and is lined with shops and bars. The "square" where most of the gay nightlife happens is just off Matoyanni, one street in from the port. Kalogera intersects Matoyanni, and if you head east here you'll reach a neighborhood known as **Tria Pigadia (Three Wells).** These wells used to be the town's only fresh water source. This is where you'll find the **Nautical Museum** and **Lena's House.** South on Mitropoleos from here takes you to the area known as **Laka,** followed by **Fabrica,** which is where the south bus station is located. If you go north on Mitropoleos, you'll get to the **Greek Orthodox cathedral (Mitropolis)** and, on its right, the **Roman Catholic cathedral.**

Continuing north from the cathedral, you'll reach **Little Venice,** known as the perfect place to view the sunset. Little Venice and the area around it has many bars and restaurants I recommend. The **windmills,** circular structures painted in white with a wooden roof and Mykonos's most unique landmarks, are on the waterfront just south of Little Venice. These mills used to grind all the wheat used on Mykonos. Four out of 15 still stand, facing the sea and the wind that blows about 300 days of the year. From Little Venice, head north on Ayion Anaryiron and you'll get to the old **Venetian Kastro** and the **Folk Art Museum.** Behind them is the **Panayia Paraportiani church,** famous not only for its four chapels but also as the premier gay cruising spot in town.

GETTING AROUND

The only way to get around Hora is on foot. Most of the town is a national landmark, and cars are banned. There are many hotels of all categories within a 20-minute walk from town, so you don't need any other form of transport except to get to the beaches. The most irritating part of walking on the main roads is that there are so many cars and scooters you feel you're going to get run over every time you hit the road. That's not a way to live on vacation. So walking to the beaches, though some are only a half-hour walk from town, isn't pleasant.

BY BUS The bus system on Mykonos is excellent, and this is your best means of transportation for longer distances. Some bus service is available late at night on the most heavily traveled routes (to Ornos Beach and Platis Yialos). Buses to the south beaches (Ornos, Platis Yialos, Paradise) leave from the south bus station at the edge of town, just off the main road. Buses heading north to Ayios Stephanos depart from the bus stop just north of the port, close to the Leto Hotel. For **schedule information,** call ☎ **0289/23360.** You buy tickets on the bus once it's moving. The drivers are impatient and will just wave you aboard but an attendant will come around to collect the fare, which ranges from 250 to 360Dr (85¢ to $1.20), depending on the destination.

BY TAXI Taxis fares are all predetermined and posted each season by the taxi stand on taxi square. It's not cheap, with the average fare around 2,500Dr ($8). It's easier to find taxis at night at the south bus stop than at the main taxi square where the rest of the island is waiting for a ride. Or you can call for a cab at ☎ **0289/23-700** or 0289/22-400.

BY SCOOTER This is a very dangerous albeit convenient way to get around. Though many people opt to rent one for their entire stay, note that there's currently no insurance coverage with a scooter rental, so you're liable for whatever happens to it. The roads on the island are treacherous, with many blind curves and buses and cars going at incredible speeds. If you still want to rent a scooter, your best bet would be to shop for a good price from the rental shops lining the road to Ornos by the south bus stop. Rates range from 3,000 to 6,000Dr ($10 to $20) a day depending on the type. **Moto Speed** at ☎ **0289/25-990** has several rental locations.

A Note on Streets

Many streets on Mykonos don't have numbers, and some don't even have names. They go by name of the area.

BY CAR You're safer in a car than you are on a scooter, but in many ways a car is a nuisance since parking in Hora is practically impossible. Expect to pay anywhere from 10,000 to 17,000Dr ($33 to $57) per day, including insurance, for a small manual car like a Fiat Cinquecento or a Nissan Micra. A good plan would be to rent a car in the morning and return it in the late evening (most agencies are open pretty late). In town, try **Autorent** at ☎ **0289/25990** or **Avis** at ☎ **0289/22960,** which also has an office at the airport (☎ **0289/27-580**). If you're staying in one of the beach towns, consider renting your car from there. **Moto Speed** in Platis Yialos (☎ **0289/25-990**) has rates slightly lower than those at the bigger agencies in town. Like hotels, car rentals are much more expensive in July and August than other months.

BY CAIQUE Caiques are small wooden boats that make regular runs to several beaches, especially the more secluded ones, like Super Paradise and Elia. Caiques leave from Platis Yialos (take the bus there) about every 20 minutes daily 9am to 6pm. Buy a ticket from the attendant at the small port. Price varies according to your destination: 700Dr ($2.35) to Paranga, 800Dr ($2.65) to Paradise or Super Paradise, and 1,000Dr ($3.35) to Agrari or Elia. Hold on to your ticket for the return trip, and note that the return boat leaves at 6pm or you'll be stranded on the beach.

PILLOW TALK

Expensive and not particularly luxurious is how I characterize most hotels on Mykonos. The high season from late June to late August is when the island is busiest and hotels charge exorbitant rates. Planning a trip in early June or mid-September would be best. The island is busy without being overrun, and you'll benefit from fantastic weather. Some hotels are limiting their off-season rates, though, since bookings have been so strong the past few summers.

To preplan your accommodations, contact Pam at **Windmills Travel** (☎ **0289/23-877;** fax 0289/22-066; e-mail windmills@travelling.gr). Pam and her girlfriend are constantly visiting various properties and can give you firsthand info about hotels. They'll let you know which have the best deals at any given time. All hotels offer free transportation from the airport or harbor, so be sure to let them know of your arrival time and call again the day before, if possible, to confirm your ride.

If you're traveling on a tight budget, there are hundreds of rooms to let all over the island and especially in town, but you can't reserve ahead for the best deals. If you're not traveling in July and August and really want a bargain, I suggest reserving a hotel for your first night and then spending a few hours bargaining for a cheap room. You'll see signs everywhere for rooms, so simply ring the doorbell to talk to the owners. Most rooms are in private homes, but many come with their own entrance and shower. Ask to see the room and then offer what you can afford. They'll take it or leave it. These rooms are simple but clean and come with fresh linen. You can find small rooms in and around town for as little as 5,000Dr ($17) a day. If you're staying longer than a week, the price might be even lower.

In & Around Town

The Elysium. School of Fine Art area, 846 00 Mykonos. ☎ **0289/239-52.** Fax 0289/23-747. www.elysium@otenet.gr. 45 units. A/C MINIBAR TV TEL. Summer 39,000Dr ($130) double; 55,000Dr ($183) suite; off-season 31,000Dr ($103) double; 46,000Dr ($153) suite. Rates include full breakfast. AE, DC, M, V.

Country & City Codes

The **country code** for Greece is **30.** The **city code** for Hora and all of Mykonos is **289;** use this code when you're calling from outside Greece. If you're within Greece but not on Mykonos, use **0289.** If you're calling within Mykonos, simply leave off the code and dial only the regular phone number.

The effervescent Vassili, owner/manager of this gay hotel, jokes that the Elysium is straight-friendly, though the crowd is 90☎ gay. Located up a steep hill, a few minutes' walk from town, the Elysium offers sweeping vistas from its spectacular pool and bar. Many of the rooms have excellent sea views, but most are rather small. The suites are spacious and have king-size beds (hard to find on this island). The staff is very friendly and helpful, arranging sunset happy hours, helping you plan your day and find your way around, and directing you to the hottest beaches and hippest bars of the season. The fully equipped gym means you won't have to venture far to work out. Singles get a discounted rate, so be sure to ask when you make a reservation.

Hotel Alex. Tourlos, 846 00 Mykonos. ☎ **0289/230-30.** Fax 0289/231-93. 44 units. A/C TV TEL. Summer 26,000Dr ($86) double; off-season from 13,000Dr ($43) double. MC, V.

This family-run hotel has been around for some 20 years, and the owner builds a new annex every few years. Since the Alex now has 44 rooms and is a 30-minute walk outside town (halfway to Aghios Stephanos), it tends not to be full except in July and August. It offers bargain rates when the hotel isn't overrun with tourists on package tours. Unofficially, a double, when available, goes for as little as 10,000Dr ($33). But don't expect to call or fax ahead and get this rate. It's worth a shot once you arrive if you have trouble finding anything else cheaper. The rooms are clean and modern, and the pool, at the top of the hillside, is a great place to relax before a night on the town. They've seen it all here, so everyone is comfortable.

Hotel Matina. Fournakia, 846 00 Mykonos. ☎ **0289/223-87.** Fax 0289/245-01. 14 units. Summer 28,000Dr ($93) double; off-season 19,600Dr ($65) double. Rates include continental breakfast. No credit cards.

This is the best hotel in the center of town. But remember that you'll have to lug your luggage a ways, since cars are banned from the heart of town. The simple Matina has a beautiful garden that insulates the rooms and makes them quieter than at others in town. The manager is very friendly, and Frommer's has recommended the Matina for many years. Most guests are American, and many are young straight couples. You'll get a small simple room and bath; don't look for any amenities. You're paying for the location.

Hotel Rochari. Near the south bus station, 846 00 Mykonos. ☎ **0289/231-07.** Fax 0289/243-07. 60 units. A/C TV TEL. Summer 26,000Dr ($86) double; off-season 13,000–22,000Dr ($43–$73) double. Rates include full breakfast. AE, MC, V.

This is your best bet for a reasonably priced hotel with a pool that's right in town. You can get to all the restaurants and bars using pedestrian-only streets, making this a nice stop if you're planning to enjoy the nightlife (and not have windy roads to negotiate and major hills to climb as you stumble back at dawn). On the edge of town, close to the south bus stop, the family-run Rochari is a favorite hangout for the local gay community, who come for lunch and a swim. There are many repeat visitors, and the staff is well trained to keep everybody happy. The rooms are simply furnished, most with two twin beds pushed together, and all come with small baths. Many of the rooms have sea views.

Mykonos Town

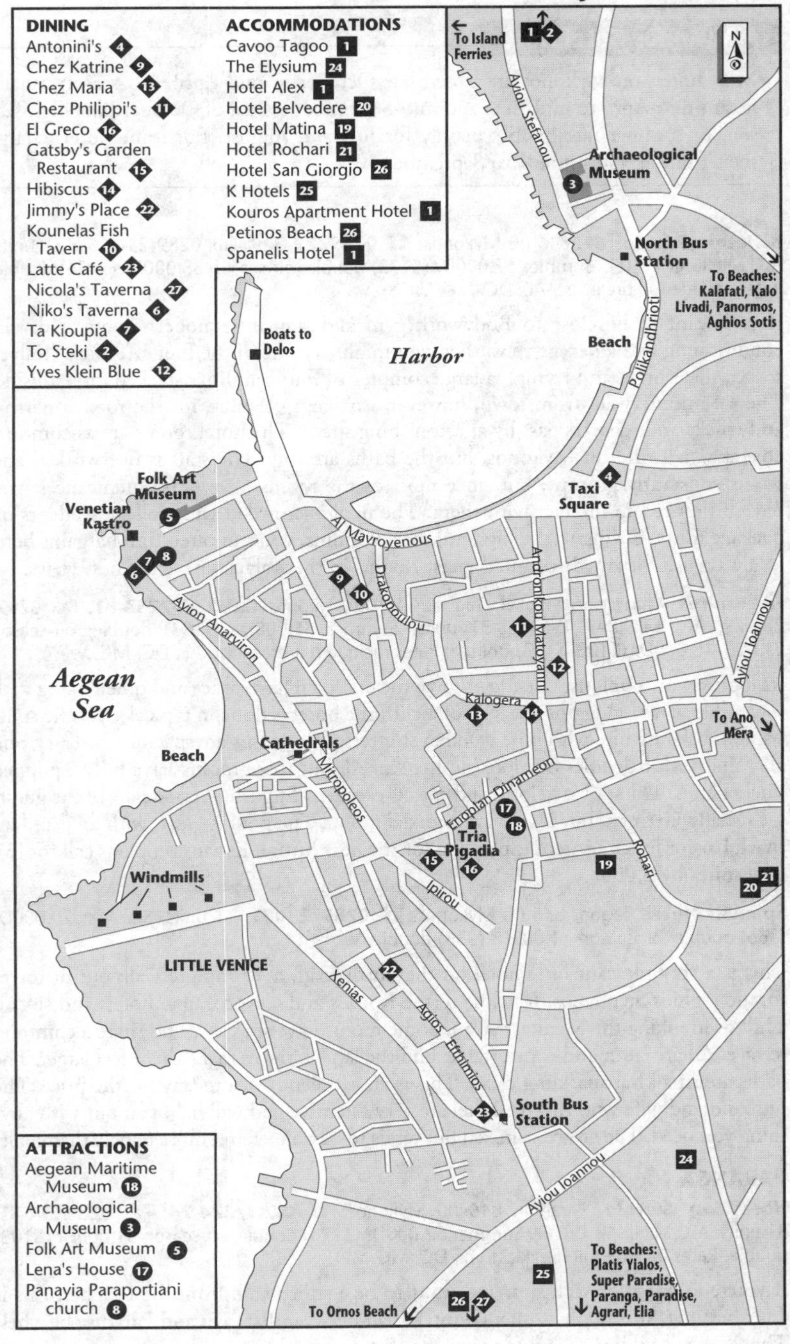

DINING
Antonini's 4
Chez Katrine 9
Chez Maria 13
Chez Philippi's 11
El Greco 16
Gatsby's Garden Restaurant 15
Hibiscus 14
Jimmy's Place 22
Kounelas Fish Tavern 10
Latte Café 23
Nicola's Taverna 27
Niko's Taverna 6
Ta Kioupia 7
To Steki 2
Yves Klein Blue 12
ACCOMMODATIONS
Cavoo Tagoo 1
The Elysium 24
Hotel Alex 1
Hotel Belvedere 20
Hotel Matina 19
Hotel Rochari 21
Hotel San Giorgio 26
K Hotels 25
Kouros Apartment Hotel 1
Petinos Beach 26
Spanelis Hotel 1
ATTRACTIONS
Aegean Maritime Museum 18
Archaeological Museum 3
Folk Art Museum 5
Lena's House 17
Panayia Paraportiani church 8
To Island Ferries
Ayiou Stefanou
Archaeological Museum
North Bus Station
To Beaches: Kalafati, Kalo Livadi, Panormos, Aghios Sotis
Beach
Polikandhrioti
Boats to Delos
Harbor
Folk Art Museum
Venetian Kastro
Taxi Square
Al Mavroyenous
Drakopoulou
Andronikou Matoyanni
Ayion Anaryiron
Ayiou Ioannou
Aegean Sea
Kalogera
To Ano Mera
Beach
Cathedrals
Mitropoleos
Enoplan Dinameon
Tria Pigadia
Rohari
Ipirou
Windmills
LITTLE VENICE
Xenias
Agios Efthimios
South Bus Station
Ayiou Ioannou
To Beaches: Platis Yialos, Super Paradise, Paranga, Paradise, Agrari, Elia
To Ornos Beach

A Mykonos Hotel Note

Most hotels on Mykonos are closed late October to mid-April. Off-season usually means mid-April to mid-June and mid-September to end of October. The high season, or summer rates, apply mainly for July and August. But some hotels charge their summer rates June 1 to September 30.

K Hotels. P.O. Box 64, 846 00 Mykonos. ☎ **0289/22-929.** Fax 0289/23-455. 135 units. A/C MINIBAR TV TEL. Summer 52,000Dr ($173) double; off-season 38,000Dr ($126) double. Rates include full breakfast. AE, DC, MC, V.

If you want to be close to Bodywork gym and stay in a modern room with air-conditioning and a decent view, then you might try one of the four K Hotels (Kalypso, Kohili, Korali, and Kyma), a large complex of four buildings stacked on a hillside. The 10-minute walk from town, however, isn't very pleasant, for the road is narrow and trucks and scooters pass by at astonishing speed. The hotel rooms are as comfortable as you'll find on Mykonos, but the baths are tiny. The staff is overworked and seems constantly grumpy, but since most of the rooms have outside entrances, you have little need to interact with them. The pool is crowded with college students on package tours. Owing to the high number of rooms, you can often find bargains here, so always ask for any discounted rates. Rooms in the Kalypso have the best views.

✪ **Kouros Apartment Hotel.** Tagoo, 846 00 Mykonos. ☎ **0289/253-81.** Fax 0289/253-79. A/C MINIBAR TV TEL. 31 units. Summer 55,000Dr ($183) double; off-season 31,000–46,000Dr ($103–$153) double. Rates include full breakfast. AE, DC, MC, V.

Its location on a hill just outside of town means you'll have peace and quiet, along with incredible views. Hugging the side of a cliff, the hotel is done in typical Cycladic style, painted bright white with blue wooden shutters. The rooms are spacious and airy, and all come with balconies overlooking the sea. All but three rooms have fully equipped kitchenettes. The staff is helpful and speaks excellent English. A good part of the guests are usually German, but it's always a mixed group. The pool is great, with an excellent snack bar for lunch. A gym is planned for the near future. Expansion plans call for five new suites by 2,000.

Spanelis Hotel. Tagoo, 846 00 Mykonos. ☎ **0289/23081.** 11 units. Summer 20,000Dr ($66) double; off-season 11,000Dr ($36) double. V.

This is a very pleasant little hotel on the north road, a 15-minute walk out of town, toward Aghios Stephanos. It's close to the Kouros and Cavoo Tagoo hotels and sits on a hill overlooking the Mediterranean. Some rooms have sea views and share a common terrace. All are clean and comfortable, and the large terraces make them feel larger. The baths are small but sparkling clean. This is an excellent place to stay for the price. The husband and wife who run the hotel are very attentive and will help you out with anything you need. The crowd is mixed but tends to be quieter and more female than male.

PARANGA

Hotel San Giorgio. Paranga, 846 00 Mykonos. ☎ **0289/274-74.** Fax 0289/274-81. 31 units. A/C MINIBAR TV TEL. Summer 52,000Dr ($173) double; off-season 31,000Dr ($103) double. Rates include full breakfast. AE, DC, MC, V.

If you're looking for seclusion and want to be a short walk from the beaches, this is your best bet, sitting on a quiet country road between Paranga and Paradise beaches. The 2-story buildings are done in stone and painted blue and white, conforming to true Cycladic architecture. The mosaic tile in the spacious rooms and well-equipped

Hey, Big Spender: Over the Top on Mykonos

For true luxury, you have to splurge for the highest category of rooms and suites. Every hotel seems to have good deals on its smallest rooms, which have no views and/or baths so tiny your elbows are bruised by the time you finish showering.

If you want space and privacy, there's nothing more luxurious than your own private villa at the **Santa Marina Hotel,** on a hill near Ornos Beach, Ornos Bay, 846 00 Mykonos (☎ **0289/232-20;** fax 0289/234-12). It offers 30 villas, some with private pools and sweeping sea views. Or for something really different, ask for the Cycladic windmill that has been turned into a 3-story suite. There's also a private beach, a health club, and a good restaurant. Rates for villas start at 82,500Dr ($275).

Nearby, the exclusive 30-unit **Kivotos Club Hotel,** Ornos Bay, 846 00 Mykonos (☎ **0289/24-094;** fax 0289/22-844), is considered by locals to be the most luxurious. Its set on a bluff overlooking the sea and has a private beach, fitness center, sauna, Jacuzzi, and squash court. Expect to pay no less than 118,000Dr ($393) for the top rooms, which are beautifully furnished with antique wrought-iron beds and mirrors.

Closer to town, a suite at **Cavoo Tagoo,** built on the side of a hill, Tagoo, 846 00 Mykonos (☎ **0289/23-692;** fax 0289/24-923), comes with a four-poster bed and fantastic views. It's popular with American couples both straight and gay and has won awards for its unique architecture. Sea-view suites start at 78,000Dr ($260).

Hotel Belvedere, on the edge of town (☎ **0289/25-122;** fax 0289/25-126), is a good bet if you come in the cooler months. The large suites with fireplaces go for 81,000Dr ($270).

baths is elegant without being overdone. In high season, you can catch the bus to town in front of the hotel; a 20-minute walk away is Platis Yialos beach, where there's more frequent bus service and caiques to other beaches. The clientele is made up mainly of middle-aged straight couples and singles who enjoy the calm of this place. Very few gays stay here because of its secluded location, though if you're looking for privacy there can't be a more special place. An excellent buffet breakfast is served on the flagstone terrace, and the magnificent pool and bar is a great place to spend the day.

ORNOS

Ornos Beach Hotel. Ornos Beach, 846 00 Mykonos. ☎ **0289/232-16.** Fax 0289/222-43. 25 units. A/C MINIBAR TV TEL. Summer 36,000Dr ($120) double; off-season 19,000–24,500Dr ($63–$81) double. Rates include full breakfast. AE, MC, V.

If you want to be as close to Mykonos Town as possible yet be steps from a sandy beach, then recently renovated blue-and-white Ornos is for you. The rooms are simply furnished with dark wood and wicker, and each has its own balcony with blue shutters to keep the heat out. The baths are small but functional. If you get a room overlooking the sea, you can hear the gentle Mediterranean waves at night. The staff is young, energetic, and gay-friendly, but the crowd is predominantly straight and there's no nudity on the beach. D'a Massimo, the hotel's beachfront Italian restaurant, is a romantic spot for dinner. There's a new circular pool surrounded by palm trees just steps from the beach.

Platis Yialos

Petinos Beach. Platis Yialos, 846 00 Mykonos. ☎ **0289/22-913.** Fax 0289/23-680. E-mail petinos@vacation.forthnet.gr. 19 units. A/C MINIBAR TV TEL. Summer 47,000Dr ($156) double; off-season 29,000Dr ($96) double. AE, MC, V.

This elegant hotel is just a few steps away from the little port where the caiques depart for the beaches. Most rooms are spacious and come with sea views and baths with showers. The hotel tends to attract a very eclectic mix of people and has a solid gay following. The bus to town leaves frequently from right in front. There are several tavernas and restaurants on the beach nearby, so you don't have to go into town every night for dinner. The hotel restaurant is pleasant, with wonderful sea views.

WHET YOUR APPETITE

There's no shortage of restaurants on Mykonos. It's finding the outstanding that's difficult. The restaurants in general are more expensive than those elsewhere in Greece, and the food at best is mediocre. Forget the cafes and restaurants lining the waterfront at the harbor, where the food is generally low quality and the prices are ridiculous.

The only taverna considered good by locals near the port on taxi square is **Antonini's** (no phone; open daily noon–1am), where the inexpensive Greek food is well prepared and the prices are very reasonable. **Niko's Taverna,** near Paraportiani church (no phone; open daily noon–1am), has become very popular in recent summers with the gay crowd; the food is good and inexpensive but the service hurried and unfriendly. Across from Niko's, **Ta Kioupia** (☎ **0289/22-866;** open daily noon–1am) serves the same food for the same prices, with friendlier service.

After a night on the town, head to **Jimmy's Place,** Aghios Efthimios Street (☎ **0289/22-630;** open daily noon–4am), for a gyros sandwich. The best chicken salad sandwiches are found at **Latte Café,** at the south bus stop (☎ **0289/23-574;** open daily 9am–9pm); it also serves the best omelet's for breakfast and is gay-managed. If you're craving croissants or want to try a slice of Mykonian walnut cake, try **Hibiscus,** 19 Kalogera St. (☎ **0289/24-889;** open daily 8am–10pm).

The top two places for an elegant night out have remained the same for several years: **Chez Katrine,** at Odos Ayios Yerasimos Street (☎ **0289/22-169**), for French cuisine, and **Chez Philippi's,** off Matoyanni Street (☎ **0289/22-294**), for refined Greek food. Chez Katrine is the most expensive restaurant on the island, and the atmosphere can be quite stuffy, with many older couples, men in suits, and ladies with big hair. Expect to pay no less than 20,000Dr ($66) per person. Chez Philippi's garden is beautiful and the crowd a bit younger and gayer. Prices are more reasonable, with main courses at 6,000 to 12,000Dr ($20 to $40).

Note: For the locations of the restaurants below, see the "Mykonos Town" map on p. 357.

In Town

Chez Maria. 30 Kalogera St. ☎ **0289/27-565.** Main courses 3,700–7,500Dr ($12–$25). AE, MC, V. Daily 8pm–1am. GREEK.

A Fish Warning

Fish is expensive on Mykonos and not always fresh. Almost all good restaurants will have at least one type of local fish, but ask to see it before they cook it to make sure it's fresh. Price is normally by the kilo.

Maria greets and hovers over you, making sure all is as well as can be in this romantic setting, its garden filled with flowers, plants, and candles. A lot of gay couples come here before hitting the "square." You'll find Frenchmen dressed in Armani sports jackets, Germans in tight black T-shirts, and Americans in sweatshirts. Chez Maria's special stuffed souvlaki is to die for: Served on a large wooden carving board, the pork, beef, and chicken fillets are marinated, stuffed with feta cheese, and then charcoal-grilled. Don't miss Maria's delicious salad dressing with the salad named after her, and for dessert try the fabulous chocolate mousse.

El Greco. Tria Pigadia. ☎ **0289/22-074.** Main courses 1,700–5,900Dr ($6–$20). AE, DC, MC, V. Daily 8pm–1am. GREEK.

Grab a sidewalk table and people-watch while you dine on quality Greek food at this popular restaurant in the middle of bustling Three Wells square. Start with the home-style Greek lemon soup or the excellent Khoriatiki salad (cucumbers and tomatoes with feta). Then try the delicious veal cutlets with eggplant or the grilled fish of the day with a steaming side of sautéed potatoes and vegetables. The mezedes are excellent. Dip your bread in the tangy *tsatsiki* (yogurt-and-garlic dip) or *taramosalata* (fish roe, garlic, and spices). It gets very busy during high season, so be prepared to wait a while before you're seated. For dessert, the yogurt with fresh fruit is light and yummy.

Gatsby's Garden Restaurant. Odos Fournakion St. ☎ **0289/26-217.** Reservations only for parties of 6 or more. Main courses 1,900–4,900Dr ($6–$16). MC, V. Daily 8pm–1am. INTERNATIONAL.

The garden here is nice for a casual dinner. The crowd is young and mixed and the staff (mostly German and British) hip and friendly. If you want a break from Greek food, you'll find a reasonable selection of Italian and continental dishes. The pasta with sun-dried tomato pesto is good fuel for a night of dancing, and the penne arabiata isn't too spicy. For dessert, the tiramisu is excellent. Most evenings, a performer sings Barbra Streisand hits and queeny classics like "Don't Cry for Me, Argentina." Their wines by the glass are better than most. Gatsby's is good value for your money and popular with the local expat gay and lesbian community.

Kounelas Fish Tavern. Off Drakopoulou St. ☎ **0289/28-220.** Fish portion 3,000–4,900Dr ($10–$16). No credit cards. Daily 7pm–midnight.

Ask until you find this gem of a place in a tiny alley two streets in from the port. With reasonably priced fresh fish so hard to find on Mykonos, it's surprising that this simple taverna exists at all. Before you get a table, the manager will show you a bucket with the fish of the day and quote you the price per kilo. Tell him how you want it cooked and it'll be brought to your table with a salad and a few plates of mezedes. Red snapper is usually the catch of the day, and sometimes that's all they have. You'll dine among locals and old fishermen tired from their day at sea.

✪ **Yves Klein Blue.** Aghios Saranta St. ☎ **0289/27-391.** Reservations recommended at least a week in advance. Main courses 4,000–5,900Dr ($13–$20). Daily 8pm–1am. MC, V. ITALIAN.

This tiny restaurant with walls painted the same deep blue Yves Klein is famous for has become all the rage. Candles melt on the bar and opera blares from the speakers. There are just a few tables on the terrace and a few on the cobblestone street, so getting a reservation requires at least a week's notice. The crowd is mostly gay and everyone oh-so-trendy trying desperately not to dunk hunks of bread into the giant bowls of mussels in white wine and parsley sauce. You can't help but dunk. The gnocchi with gorgonzola melts in your mouth, and the veal scallopini with artichoke hearts will make you want to sing along with the tenors. The wine list has only Italian wines, with a few selections under 6,000Dr ($20). It's rare for a place that looks so good to have such excellent food. You can only hope it'll stay consistent in coming seasons. If you can't get a reservation, try coming at 8pm or midnight and you might score a table.

Outside Town

✪ **Nicola's Taverna.** Agia Anna Paranga (a 5-minute walk from Platis Yialos and Paranga). ☎ **0289/23-566.** Main courses 900–2,900Dr ($3–$10). No credit cards. Daily noon–10pm. GREEK.

In a small cove halfway between Platis Yialos and Paranga is this charming beach taverna. Nicola's is more like a shack with a few tables under a makeshift bamboo roof, but it's one of the most genuine places on the island. Grab a table on the sand and spend the afternoon drinking ouzo and eating mezedes. The husband and wife who run this place don't speak very good English but try hard to make everyone feel at home. Go into the kitchen and point at what looks good from the selection of salads. The black-eye pea salad is excellent, as are the dolmades (grape leaves stuffed with rice). If you're feeling adventurous, try the octopus salad—it's delicious, marinated in lemon and olive oil. Then choose a meat or fresh fish and they'll grill it for you.

To Steki. Tourlos. ☎ **0289/25-458.** Main courses 2,900–6,000Dr ($10–$20). Daily noon–1am. MC, V. GREEK.

This excellent traditional restaurant could well serve the best Greek food on the island, but it has an inconvenient location, right on the road to Ayios Stephanos, about a 25-minute walk from town. But it's worth every effort it takes to get here. The emphasis is on freshness and quality, and the owners handpick the vegetables and meat at the market every morning. The moussaka is served in ceramic pots, and they have such hard-to-find Greek specials as lettuce leaves stuffed with rice and lamb and breaded tomato slices with saganaki cheese. The selection of wines is excellent, including the local rose and white Paraportiano, named after the cruisy church area in town.

EXPLORING MYKONOS

You don't come to Mykonos to soak up Greek culture. There really isn't much here in terms of archaeological sites except the sacred island of Delos nearby (see below). Mykonos is for the hedonist looking for sun, sea, and nightlife. The main attraction is the men. Men from all over the world—old and young, blond and dark, single and married, and certainly the curious. Men hold hands and even kiss in the tiny streets while old Greek women out shopping for vegetables pretend they don't notice. Or if they do, they roll their eyes ever so slightly, knowing there's not much they can do.

On several occasions throughout the year, the U.S. navy brings its ships, and its randy seamen, for a weekend getaway on Mykonos. (Don't ask and I won't tell why they picked Mykonos.) But you can imagine the mayhem of locked-up straight boys and the confusion they and their hosts endure. Yes, Mykonos does get zooey. And everything seems to be about sex, gay and straight and whatever. There's a feeling, especially on weekends in midsummer, that the town is overrun and everything is out of control. You wait for a table at restaurants, you wait for a drink at the bar, you wait to take a few steps trying to walk in the streets and then wait for a taxi.

However, barely a few miles away are empty stretches of beach waiting to be discovered. You can have the best of both worlds on Mykonos: You can enjoy the cruising and the dancing. You can watch the queens posing in the square and the navy boys chasing local girls (not many of those). But right outside of town you can spend an evening on a quiet beach just listening to the waves and counting the stars with the man of your dreams.

Boys on the Beach

SUPER PARADISE You'll probably hear of **Super Paradise Beach,** the gayest on Mykonos, long before you arrive. The second stop on the caique from Platis Yialos, it's a secluded stretch reachable only by boat or four-wheel-drive vehicle (and scooter if you're into potential suicide and permanent back damage). If you arrive on the small boat, you'll notice that on the right side of the beach the scene is meat-market hetero and partly nude and the left side almost exclusively gay and mostly nude. You can just imagine what goes on at all hours among the rocks and cliffs and trails behind the beach (of course, you're not interested in that, are you?). The music blares, it gets real crowded by early afternoon, and the boys like to stare. Don't expect any seclusion, just lots of cruising action. The **Super Paradise Restaurant and Bar** (no phone; open daily 11am–9pm) is right above the beach on the rocky cliff and has a small freshwater pool. In addition to all kinds of cocktails, the bar serves fresh fruit juices. The restaurant is a bit overpriced for its mediocre food; expect to pay 2,500Dr ($8) for drinks and 6,000Dr ($20) for a meal.

PARANGA A 10-minute hike from Platis Yialos or the first stop on the caique if you request it when you buy your ticket, ✪ **Paranga Beach** is a beautiful stretch of sand big enough for you to choose the spot you want according to your mood. The south side is calm and sedate, with many people reading and lounging in the nude. Here you'll find many returning visitors and local gays who don't want to deal with the crowds at Super Paradise. You can rent chaise lounges for 500Dr ($1.65) and an umbrella for the same price. It's a very mixed beach, with equal numbers of gays and straights. On the north side, the tavernas play music and serve drinks. **Barbra & Yannis Restaurant and Bar** (☎ **0289/23-552;** open daily 11am–9pm) serves excellent homemade Greek food at amazingly reasonable prices. Have lunch at one of their tables in the shade of the grapevine before venturing back out to your chaise for an afternoon of swimming and sunbathing.

PARADISE Between Paranga and Super Paradise, **Paradise Beach** is the second stop (sometimes the first) on the caique (or buses run several times a day from the south bus stop). This is the hetero version of Super Paradise. Here music blares and the young and the seemingly straight party day and night. You'll find mostly northern European tourists and American college students, beer in hand. It's a fun, boisterous crowd if you're into the Mazatlan-meets-Mykonos spring-break scene. A large complex with a beach bar, pool, and restaurant, **Cavo Paradiso** (☎ **0289/26-124;** open daily 10am–2am) is on the hill above the beach. There's also a gym where you can pump it up with the college boys. On midsummer nights, parties are held here, and the whole beach resembles one huge disco, with people dancing on the rocks, on the sand, around the pool, and on the cliffs around the beach. The dancing and drinking continues until way past sunrise.

AGARARI & ELIA Side-by-side ✪ **Agrari and Elia beaches,** the third and fourth stops on the caique (or take the bus to Elia during high season from the north bus station), are large and sandy and perfect for a quiet afternoon of swimming. Agrari is mellow, and Elia has a variety of tavernas and bars and water sports. Here you can windsurf, water-ski, or parasail. For lunch or drinks, **Desire Restaurant & Bar,** at the northern end (☎ **0289/71-207**), has fresh salads and cute waiters. Expect to pay 1600Dr ($5) for drinks and 2,600Dr ($9) for a light meal (the octopus salad is delicious). **Watermania,** on a hillside behind Elia (☎ **0289/71-685**), is a huge aqua park where a party atmosphere reigns daily 10am to 9pm. There are two huge pools, a variety of slides, and boat rides. Admission is 3,500Dr ($12) for the day.

KALAFATI & KALO LIVADI You'll need a scooter or a car to get to the less-crowded **Kalafati and Kalo Livadi beaches,** but there is limited bus service from the north bus stop. On days when the meltemi winds blow hard, Kalo Livadi is your best bet, since it's one of the few pebbly beaches on Mykonos. In Kalafati you'll find the new **Paradise Aphrodite Beach Hotel** (☎ **0289/71-367**), with 148 rooms and a large pool; doubles begin at 38,000Dr ($127). Despite its hugeness, it's a good place to have lunch and a swim. The beach is sandy and over a mile long and has the cleanest water in Mykonos.

ORNOS The closest good beach to Mykonos Town is **Ornos Beach,** where buses from the south bus stop run every half an hour. Lined with tavernas, restaurants, bars, and hotels, it can get packed in high season. This beach is usually overrun with families and tourists on package vacations, and there's absolutely no nudity. But it's still possible to have a nice swim and people-watch while you relax on your chaise, which you pay 500Dr ($1.65) to rent for the day.

PLATIS YIALOS **Platis Yialos,** to which buses run every 20 minutes from the south bus station, is the hub of beach life in Mykonos. This is where the buses bring hordes of people every half an hour to catch the caiques to the outlying beaches. The sandy beach is jammed with taverna after taverna and hotel after hotel. Only visitors staying in hotels seem to swim at this beach, for it's just too busy most of the time. If you're staying here and have asked for a seafront or sea-view room from any of the hotels, be prepared for noise. Many visitors hoping to hear the waves from their beach hotels end up with screeching scooter noise and clanging dishes instead.

OTHER BEACHES The beach closest to Mykonos Town on the north side is **Aghios Stephanos,** with many hotels and tavernas. It's too crowded to be enjoyable. Farther north, accessible only by car or scooter, are several pretty beaches. Take the road north heading to the town of Ano Mera (the only other town on Mykonos apart from Hora) to get to **Panormos,** the largest and most popular of the northern beaches. **Panormos Restaurant,** on the hillside (☎ **0289/25-182**), serves fresh fish. Close to Panormos are many small coves and secluded beaches. **Aghios Sotis** is the farthest beach north reachable by car and is gaining popularity with the local gay population; nudity is permitted.

A Few Sights to See

Note: For the locations of the sights below, see the "Mykonos Town" map on p. 357.

The **Archeological Museum** is located to the west of the port, by the OTE office and the north bus stop (☎ **0289/22-325;** open Wed–Sat 9am–3:30pm and Sun and holidays 10am–3pm; admission 500Dr/$1.65). Founded at the turn of the century, this five-room museum features a limited collection of vases and funerary jewelry and grave ornaments found mostly on the small neighboring island of Rhenia. A statue of Hercules sculpted from marble from the nearby island of Paros is on display.

The **Folk Art Museum,** in the Kastro area, by the excursion boats to Delos (no phone; open Mon–Sat 4–8pm, Sun 5–8pm; admission free), is full of interesting objects depicting life on ancient Mykonos. There's everything from musical instruments to lace-making devices to antique four-poster beds to old farmhouse utensils and traditional costumes.

For another look at past life in Mykonos, check out **Lena's House,** in the Tria Pigadia area (☎ **0289/225-91;** open daily only 7–9pm; admission free). It's an authentic middle-class Mykonian residence of the 19th century, complete with a drawing room, furnished bedrooms, and two courtyards. If you're into antiques, tapestries, old mirrors, and painted plates, you'll love it.

If you're into the history of the high seas, check out the **Aegean Maritime Museum,** in the Tria Pigadia area (☎ **0289/22-700;** open daily 10:30am–1pm and 6:30–9pm; admission 500Dr/$1.65). Founded by ship owner George N. Drakopoulos, it houses model ships from the pre-Minoan period to the 19th century, as well as maps and navigational instruments and tools and a rare ancient coin collection.

The **Panayia Paraportiani church** commands a prime location at the edge of the Kastro district, by the water close to the departing boats to Delos. It's really four separate chapels erected over a period of time, but it appears from the outside as one church. It's also the main cruising area. All around it, especially in the late evenings, men cruise. The stray tourists pass innocently by at all hours gawking at the church, shielding themselves from the breeze on windy days and oblivious of the action going on behind the white-washed walls and in the tiny alleys nearby.

Working Up a Sweat

Dive Adventures, on Paradise Beach (☎ **0289/265-39**) offers a full range of diving equipment and certification programs. Windsurfing is very popular on Myknonos because of the constant strong winds. Elia and Paradise beaches both have windsurf rentals by the hour or the day.

If a romantic horseback ride is your idea of working up a sweat with your man, then contact Pam at **Windmills Travel** (☎ **0289/23-877**) to arrange your sunset ride.

There's only one good gym, **Bodywork Gym** (☎ **0289/22-225;** open Mon–Sat 8:30am–9:30pm), and it recently moved to its new location a few minutes from town on the road to Platis Yialos. There are free weights and several cardio machines. If you want to work out with the straight boys, come early in the day, otherwise it gets hopping with a predominantly gay crowd in the late afternoon. A day pass is 2,500Dr ($8), including a towel. There's a small changing room and a tiny shower.

HITTING THE STORES

Shopping on Mykonos is fun because all the stores are concentrated on the narrow streets of Hora and there's a carnival atmosphere, especially in the evenings. But don't expect any bargains. Everything is expensive. You'll find popular shops like **DKNY, Benetton,** and **The Body Shop** next to quaint little stores selling local handicrafts and handmade jewelry. And there are several gay-owned stores, from art galleries to funky clothing stores.

Generally, **stores hours** are daily 10am to 2pm and 5:30 to 11pm. During the high season, some stores stay open to midnight or 1am.

Shopping A to Z

ANTIQUES & ART **Rarity Art & Decor,** 22 Kalogera St. (☎ **0289/25-761**), offers a great selection of rare religious icons, clocks, and a unique collection sculptures of male faces by Greek artists. **Domingo Art & Design Gallery,** 4 Kalogera St. (☎ **0289/26-614**), has the largest selection of Cycladic art and hand-painted porcelain. Ask for Domingo and he'll show you around.

The newest and most glamorous art gallery in town is **Minima,** in the Tria Pigadia area (☎ **0289/23-236**); it specializes in modern Greek Art. **Orama Art Gallery,** Fournakia (☎ **0289/26-339**), displays beautiful paintings of the Cyclades by local artists.

BEACHWEAR Yos and Soto own the very popular **Phenomenon Boutique,** 8 Zouganeli St., behind Pierro's (☎ **0289/24-105**). If you're looking for sexy swim shorts, you'll find them here.

BOOKS **International Press** on Kambani Street (☎ **0289/23-316**) is the only store in town that has some English books and magazines.

CERAMICS Hand-painted ceramics from the only such workshop on Mykonos are on sale at **Selini,** Aghios Saranta Street (☎ **0289/24-038**).

FASHION For the latest Versace or Moschino designs, head to **Boutique Armonia** in Lakka (☎ **0289/27-022**). **Booze,** also in Lakka (☎ **0289/25-350**), is owned by a gay couple and they have everything from Guess and Valentino jeans to Replay underwear.

The funkiest store on the island is **Zapp** on Drakopoulou Street (☎ **0289/25-208**), with everything from orange platform shoes to bright red plastic undies. **Diesel,** 44 Matoyanni St. (☎ **0289/24-495**), and **Post,** 2 Mitropoleos St. (☎ **0289/28-007**), have a great selection of jeans and denim shirts.

At **Remember Fashions** in Lakka (☎ **0289/23-907**), you'll find colorful Greek-made shirts and sweatshirts. **Thio Peppe,** 17 Matoyanni St. (☎ **0289/24-022**), also has fun shirts and sweatshirts. You'll find the funkiest T-shirts in town at **Zoe** in Lakka (☎ **0289/28-378**). And **Hi-Tek Designs** in Little Venice (☎ **0289/24-584**) offers a good selection of shoes and boots.

JEWELRY **Aries,** 26 Dynameon St. (☎ **0289/23-573**), is a gay-owned jewelry shop with a wide selection of silver, gold, and watches. **Templo,** in Kastro (☎ **0289/26-823**), sells many original designs made at its local workshop. **La Magia,** in Little Venice (☎ **0289/24-698**), is known for its unique and expensive creations.

A SEX SHOP It's simply called **Sexy Shop** and is close to the port at 18 Fioroy Zouganeli St. (no phone). You'll find all the necessary accessories, from dildos to lubricants.

IN THE HEAT OF THE NIGHT

On Mykonos, there's a thin line between straight and gay. You'll always find gays at the straight bars and vice versa. Even the patrons at the gay bars are usually about 70☎ gay. As Jody, co-owner of the Montparnasse Piano Bar, put it, "There's always enough variety that my mother feels comfortable here."

Until midnight, that is. Midnight is the magic hour, when anyone with any gay interest heads to the "square," in front of an old church, one street in from taxi square on Matoyanni street. There are three bars: Pierrot's, Manto's, and Ikarus, the three most famous gay bars in all Greece. Most of the posing, cruising, and drinking actually happens right outside the bars, on the square. By 1am, the crowd is so thick it takes quite a bit of shoving and pushing to squeeze through the lycra T-shirted boys to get inside to the bar for a drink (talk about a contact sport).

Where are the gay men before midnight? There's only one happening place and that's the Montparnasse Piano Bar in Little Venice. It's most fun between 10pm and midnight, before the boys start thinking of going dancing and looking for other pursuits.

Mainstream Bars

The action starts at sunset in Little Venice, where all the bars lining the waterfront are hopping. **Galleraki** (☎ **0289/27-188**) gets the young college students on vacation, as does **The Verandah** (☎ **0289/23-290**), on the first floor of an old building nearby.

If it's a windy day, head to **Katerina's** (☎ **0289/23-084**), where you can watch the sunset from the large picture windows inside this elegant bar. On Matoyanni Street, **Bar Uno** (☎ **0289/26-144**) gets busy after the sun goes down with straight middle-aged couples sipping sugary cocktails, but the crowd grows younger and louder as the evening progresses.

Anchor Bar (☎ **0289/24-273**) has been around for a long time and is popular for its almost topless waitresses. **Apaggio** (☎ **0289/27-462**) down the street plays Greek music until the early hours. Near the Paraportiani church, the **Scandinavian Bar** (no phone) overflows with an international beer-drinking hetero crowd.

Outside of town, the **Hard Rock Cafe** (☎ **0289/72-162**), with a free shuttle service from the port, hops with college students on vacation. And at **Tropicana,** on Paradise Beach (☎ **0289/23-582**), the young and the straight and the sexy sip daiquiris and dance on the bar.

Gay Bars

The friendliest bar on Mykonos is the ✪ **Montparnasse Piano Bar** (☎ **0289/23-719**) in Little Venice. It's mellow at sunset but picks up after 9pm, when the singing starts. By midnight, Phyllis Pastore is bringing the house down with her rendition of "There's Not a Straight Man in the House." The owners, Jody and Nikos (both male, an American-Greek couple), will make you feel instantly at home, introduce you around, and mix you a cocktail. This is usually any gay man's first stop on Mykonos.

Nearby at **Kastro Bar** (☎ **0289/23-072**), you can watch the sunset while listening to classical music. The men here are older and mellower.

Near Paraportiani church, **Porta** (☎ **0289/27-087**) is a new bar that's fast becoming a popular gay hangout. It's small and intimate and an easy place to make new friends as you elbow your way to the bar. Like Montparnasse, boys and men of all ages come here.

After midnight, most of the action shifts to the "square," where **Manto Bar** (☎ **0289/22-177**) becomes the hottest spot in town.

Lesbian Bars

There are no strictly lesbian bars on Mykonos yet. But both **Montparnasse Piano Bar** and **Porta** get their share of lesbian clientele, as does **Manto.**

Dance Clubs

Admission to the dance clubs is usually 2,500Dr ($8), including one drink.

GAY CLUBS Next door to Manto (same management) on the "square," **Pierrot's** (☎ **0289/22-177**) is where most gays and some lesbians and heteros go to dance after midnight. The dance floor is chock-full of beautiful men dressed in the latest fashions. The dancing spills out onto the square, and the partying goes on until the early hours. Other dance clubs come and go, but they never make it longer than a season. Pierrot's remains the queen of dance.

Upstairs from Pierrot's at **Ikarus** (no phone), also on the "square," the boys hang off the balcony, and the stairs are the most coveted people-watching spot on the island. There are occasional drag shows here.

The only other gay dancing occurs at special parties during summer on **Super Paradise Beach,** especially during the last week of August and first week of September. Look for flyers at the above bars and clubs.

MIXED CLUBS More straight than mixed, **La Mer** (☎ **0289/24-192**) in Little Venice rocks all night with a young beautiful crowd. **Four Roses** on Ag. Monis Square (☎ **0289/23-350**) plays only Greek dance music after midnight, and on a busy night locals of all ages dance on the bar until dawn. At **Cavo Paradiso** (☎ **0289/26-124**) on Paradise Beach, the dancing spills out onto the sand and half the crowd is under 21.

A Side Trip to Delos

Delos is one of the richest archaeological sites in Greece. This tiny island, a 40-minute boat ride from Mykonos, was the most sacred spot in ancient Greece and the birthplace of Apollo. It forms the absolute center of the Cyclades, the other islands wrapping around it as if to protect it from harm. Now Delos is uninhabited and open only to day-trippers.

Several boats every morning depart from Mykonos, by the Paraportiani church, beginning at 8am and continuing to 11am. **Sea & Sky Travel (☎ 0289/22-853)** is one of the many agencies offering a 3-hour tour (shades of *Gilligan's Island*). You can choose to pay the 1,700Dr ($6) for the round-trip boat ride right before departure at the dock or prepay 8,500Dr ($28) at any travel agency the day before for a tour that includes the boat ride, the entrance fee, and a guide. The entrance fee to the site is 1,200Dr ($4), and it's open Tuesday to Sunday 8:30am to 3pm. Return boats depart from Delos beginning at 11am, with the last boat leaving at 3pm. Go early to avoid the midday heat and the crowds.

If you arrive early in the morning, hit the **Archaelogical Museum** (at the eastern end of the island; admission included with that of the site) before the crowds. Here you'll find a good collection of Cylcadic art, sculptures, and jewelry. Next door, in the **Tourist Pavilion,** is a cafe serving snacks (you can buy bottled water) as well as the only toilets on the island.

Heading north from here, you'll find the filled-in **Sacred Lake** where Leto is said to have given birth to Apollo. On the **Terrace of the Lions,** beautiful guardian lions sit imposingly facing the lake. Head south toward **Mt. Kynthos** and you'll find the **Sanctuary of the Syrian Gods,** the **Terrace of the Foreign Gods,** the **Temple of Serapis,** the **Shrine of the Great Gods,** and other temples. Heading up the hill you'll find the **Sacred Cave,** once an oracle of Apollo. Take a few minutes to go up beyond the cave to the top of the mountain. From here, the view of the sea dotted with islands is fabulous. The sun is strong at midday; bring a hat. Don't miss the **House of Masks** with its famous treasure, a superb colored mosaic of Dionysus on a panther.

2 Santorini: Spectacular & Mellow

Santorini is one of the world's most spectacular islands, achingly beautiful, with whitewashed villages hanging at the top of cliffs and a magnificent bay that's the largest caldera (volcanic crater) on earth. The island was shaped over 3,000 years ago by a volcanic eruption that sank parts of it into the Mediterranean. The first settlers around 2,000 B.C. named it Kallisti (beautiful). The Dorians in the 10th century B.C. called it Thira, and the Venetian crusaders who occupied the island from the 13th to the 16th century called it Santorini. Many Greeks still call it Thira or Thera (not to be confused with Fira, the main village).

If you arrive by sea, you'll be stunned by the view of the villages of Ia and Fira, 900 feet above sea level, clinging to the side of the reddish cliffs. The eastern side of Santorini is remarkably flat, with long stretch of black-sand beaches. Two of the most beautiful beaches have a heavy gay following and one is nude. Apart from them, there's no visible gay life outside Fira. Even in Fira, there's no exclusively gay hotel or restaurant, but several gay-friendly places attract a mixed crowd.

Santorini attracts the slightly older and more mellow gay visitor. Many gay singles and couples who claim to be "over" the Mykonos scene come to Santorini, perhaps hydrofoiling to Mykonos for a couple of days of round-the-clock partying but spending the bulk of their vacation here.

SANTORINI ESSENTIALS

ARRIVING & DEPARTING

BY PLANE **Santorini International Airport,** on the eastern side of the island near the beach of Monolithos (**☎ 0286/31-525**), has recently been enlarged to handle jets from various European cities, and now charters arrive frequently from Paris, Amsterdam, and Frankfurt. **Olympic Airways** (☎ **0286/22-493** on Santorini) continues to be the sole operator of domestic flights, with four to six flights daily from Athens, one flight daily from Mykonos, and two flights weekly from Heraklion. These are booked months in advance for the high season, so it's essential to plan ahead.

From the airport, the most convenient way to get to Fira or any other town is by **taxi** (usually shared), costing about 3,000Dr ($10) for the 15-minute ride to Fira. Some **hotel vans** are usually on hand to greet most arriving flights. **Bus** service from the airport isn't reliable and fairly sporadic.

BY FERRY There are several ferries a day from Piraeus, the trip taking 9 to 10 hours. Usually there's one ferry departing Athens in the morning, one ferry in the late afternoon, and an overnight service. **Agapitos Lines** in Piraeus (☎ **01/429-5020**) and **Agapitos Express Ferries** (☎ **01/412-5249**) are the main operators.

From Mykonos, there's at least one ferry per day in the high season; contact **Amorgos Lines** in Pireaus (☎ **01/429-4852**). The **Santorini port authority** can be reached at ☎ **0286/22-239.** Updated ferry schedules are available on the Internet at **www.gtpnet.com.**

Alas, the new port isn't as spectacular as the old port at Skala, where mules carried baggage up the hundreds of steps to Fira. The new port, **Athinios,** is a 20-minute drive from Fira. Buses wait for every arrival and charge 350Dr ($1.15) for the ride into town, where you can change buses to practically anywhere else on the island. **Taxis** are hard to find around the port; they charge 3,500Dr ($12) into Fira. **Buses** depart Fira 1 hour prior to every ferry or hydrofoil departure throughout the day (check night schedules at the bus station), making the return to the port very convenient. Those buses have ample room for baggage storage in their hold.

BY HYDROFOIL Hydrofoil service is available daily in summer to and from Mykonos, reducing travel time from 6 hours to 4. This service includes a stop on Folegandros twice a week. High winds frequently delay these services though, and if you're on a tight schedule you're better off going by slow ferry. For schedule information, call the **Santorini port authority** at ☎ **0286/22-239** or stop by one of the travel agencies in town.

Visitor Information

At the port is a **hotel reservation kiosk** that'll help you find a room if you arrive without reservations. The fee depends on the price of the room. There's no official government tourist office on Santorini, but every travel agency in town has maps and travel info. Buy a copy of the **Santorini Sky-map** for 500Dr ($1.65) and pick up a copy of ***Santorini Today*** from one of the travel agencies on the main square in Fira.

The most helpful agency with an English-speaking staff is **Santorama Travel,** 3 blocks west of the main square in Fira, by the Olympic Airways Office (☎ **0286/23-177**). **Pelican Travel,** on the main square (☎ **0286/22-220**), also has a friendly staff who'll answer any questions. If you're visiting in July and August, you definitely need to make plans ahead of time; don't arrive without hotel reservations and expect to find a room.

Island Layout

Fira is Santorini's main village, hanging to the edge of the cliff with spectacular views of the caldera. Most hotels are on the caldera side, and the streets in the heart of town are narrow and cars are banned. The central square, a few blocks to the east of the caldera, is the hub of the commercial action, with banks, travel agencies, and taxi and bus stations. Fira is where most visitors stay. It's the most diverse village on the island and the only place with a semblance of gay nightlife.

Country & City Codes

The **country code** for Greece is **30.** The **city code** for Fira and all of Santorini is **286;** use this code when you're calling from outside Greece. If you're within Greece but not on Santorini, use **0286.** If you're calling within Santorini or from Folegandros, simply leave off the code and dial only the regular phone number.

From Fira, follow Odos M. Nomikou (Nomikos Street) north on the edge of the caldera to **Firostephani,** home to many attractive hotels and my favorite restaurant. Another 10 minutes on the same path gets you to **Imerovigli,** with more excellent hotels. **Ia** is the northernmost village, reachable by a winding mountain road.

The eastern side of the island is where the best beaches are. The village of **Kamari** is the largest of the beach villages but is overrun with straight tourists on package tours. **Perissa,** just to the south, is popular with the backpacking crowd and is rather ugly and run down. South of Perissa are the two main gay beaches, at **Cape Exomitis** and at **Vlihada Bay.** The archaeological site of **Akrotiri** and **Red Beach** are to the southwest. The main villages in the heart of the island are **Megalohori, Emborio,** and **Pyrgos,** which is the highest village on the island.

Getting Around

BY BUS Santorini has an excellent bus system, with frequent departures to most areas of the island. The main bus station is by the central square in Fira. From here, buses depart every 20 to 30 minutes 7am to 11:30pm to the main towns. Schedules are posted. There's limited service to the out-of-the-way beaches, like Vlihada and Exomitis. Fares are 300 to 900Dr ($1 to $3), depending on your destination. Conductors collect the fare after the bus has departed.

BY TAXI Next to the central square in Fira is the main taxi stand. Rates are fixed but rarely posted. From Fira to one of the gay beaches at Exomitis or Vlihada, the rate ranges from 3,000 to 3,500Dr ($10 to $12). Negotiate it with the driver or dispatcher before you get in. To call a taxi, dial ☎ **0286/22-555.**

BY CAR Rental cars are plentiful in Santorini and bargains are easy to come by except in July and August. For really good deals try the smaller companies. **Halaris Rent A Car** in Firostephani (☎ **0286/25-209**) has small cars for as little as 9,000Dr ($30) per day including insurance. The roads here are easier to maneuver than those on Mykonos. The two gay beaches aren't easily accessible by public transport and a car would make your beach excursions easier. **REA Rent A Car** in Fira (☎ **0286/22-616**) rents four-seater convertible beach jeeps starting at 18,000Dr ($60) per day. **Budget** (☎ **0286/33-290**) rents Suzuki jeeps and has an office at the airport. Remember to get an International's Driver's License before leaving home; though it's not required, having one speeds up the rental process.

BY MOPED It's a dangerous way to get around but cheap and practical. Expect to pay 3,500 to 6,000Dr ($12 to $20) per day. **Tony's** in Firostephani (☎ **0286/22-863**) has the largest selection. Officially you must have a motorcycle license to rent mopeds, but this rule is rarely enforced; your regular driver's license will suffice most of the time.

PILLOW TALK

Staying in **Fira** or at least within walking distance of town is your best bet for a relaxing vacation. Most good restaurants and all gay-friendly bars, clubs, and restaurants are in Fira. It offers breathtaking views, and the rooms overlooking the caldera are

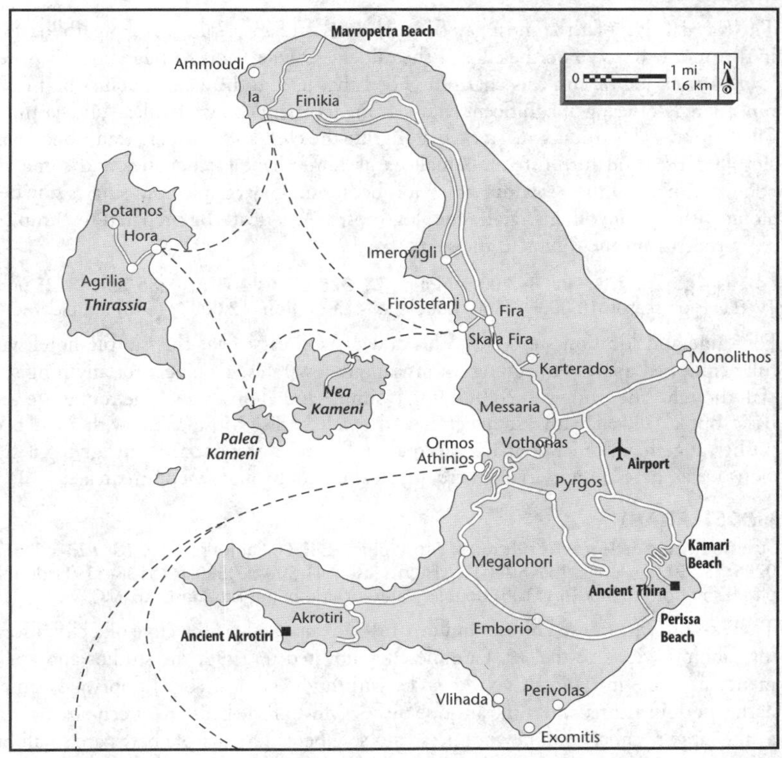

always more expensive. **Hotel Kavalari** right in town should be your first choice. The gay couple who runs it are friendly and helpful, and the guests are an interesting mix of nationalities and persuasions.

Consider staying in **Firostephani** or **Imerovigli,** within walking distance, for quieter rooms and fabulous views. **Ia** mostly has overpriced hotels, except the excellent **Flower Pension.** If you want to be within walking distance of the gay beaches, the luxurious **Veggara** in **Perissa** should be your choice.

FIRA

Hotel Atlantis. Fira, 847 00 Santorini. ☎ **0286/22-232.** Fax 0286/22-821. E-mail atlantishotel@santonet.gr. 25 units. A/C MINIBAR TV TEL. High season 46,000Dr ($153) double; off-season 40,000Dr ($133) double. AE, MC, V.

Brilliantly white and commanding an excellent location on the caldera, the Atlantis offers sparkling clean rooms with marble baths. But there's not much charm, and you're paying a lot for the location and the views (which are truly magnificent). Stay here if the Kavalari (below) is full or if you're just passing through for a night. A lot of couples just off cruise ships overnight here. There's a small pool and a bar open all day.

✪ **Hotel Kavalari.** P.O. Box 17, Fira, 84 700 Santorini. ☎ **0286/22-347.** Fax 0286/22-603. E-mail kavalari@santonet.gr. 20 units. MINIBAR TEL. High season 29,000–45,000Dr ($96–$150) double; off-season from 25,000Dr ($83) double. Rates include continental breakfast. AE, MC, V.

The Kavalari is by far the most gay-friendly hotel on Santorini, with a superb location in the middle of town on the edge of the caldera. Owner Fanis Kavalari and his American partner, James, run this charming hotel that used to be a sea captain's house. It's multitiered, offering magnificent views from its many bougainvillea- and jasmine-filled terraces. The rooms are stacked alongside the cliff, and most are traditional, with simple dark wood furniture and small baths; some have kitchenettes and some air-conditioning, and there's a unit with a loft bedroom. Gay couples and singles stay here along with lots of young straight couples, mostly American. Be prepared to climb the steep stairs from the rooms to the street.

Loizos Apartments. Fira, 847 00 Santorini. ☎ **0286/24-046.** Fax 0286/25-188. 23 units. TV TEL. High season 18,000Dr ($60) double; off-season from 12,000Dr ($40) double. MC, V.

For value and location steps from the caldera, you can't beat this simple hotel with fully equipped apartments going for amazingly low rates. Don't expect anything special, though. The whitewashed building is simple and almost ugly. The rooms are very basic but clean, all with kitchenettes and small baths. Most come with twin beds pushed together. A nice touch is the marble floors in every apartment, giving a spacious feel. There are no services here, just a small lobby and reception area.

FIROSTEPHANI

Sun Rocks Traditional Residences. Firostephani, 847 00 Santorini. ☎ **0286/23-241.** Fax 0286/23-991. 26 units. MINIBAR TEL. High season 41,500–57,500Dr ($138–$191) double; off-season from 32,000Dr ($106) double. Rates include buffet breakfast. AE, MC, V.

These traditional domed houses built in 1993 are stacked on the edge of a cliff affording fabulous views of the sea. Completely renovated in 1998, the studios and apartments are done in typical Cycladic style, with high ceilings, coved doorways, simple dark wood furniture, and some antique pieces. Most of the beds are queen-sized owing to the large number of honeymooners who stay here. The marble baths are small but functional. Every unit has a fully equipped kitchenette, and a few larger units come with loft bedrooms and two baths. A large number of guests are British and German and mostly straight. There's a great pool.

✪ **The Tsitouras Collection Hotel.** Firostephani, 847 00 Santorini. Reservations ☎ **01/362-2326.** Fax 01/363-6738. Other inquiries ☎ 0286/23-747. Fax 0286/23-918. 5 units. TEL. 120,000–140,000Dr ($400–$466) villa for 2. Rates include breakfast. AE, DC, MC, V.

This 1870s house that was converted in 1985 into five separate one-bedroom houses is by far the most opulent and unique hotel you'll find in all the Cyclades. Each house has a separate living room and bedroom, all meticulously furnished with antiques and period pieces. The House of Portraits, filled with portraits of Lord Byron, is very much 19th century; it boasts decorative objects like Russian icons, ancient oil lamps, and a bust of Sappho. The House of Porcelain is filled with 19th-century porcelain plates displayed in an authentic china cabinet from the same era. The House of the Winds has high vaulted ceilings and is furnished with Santorinian period furniture and decorated with Venetian oil and wooden lamps. The House of the Sea has an authentic ceramic piece by Picasso. The most modern and airy house is the House of Nureyev, perched above the other houses and filled with sketches of the famous dancer. This is the only house with a private veranda; the others have shared terraces.

IMEROVIGLI

Chromata. Imerovigli, 847 00 Santorini. ☎ **0286/24-850.** Fax 0286/23-672. 18 units. A/C MINIBAR TEL. High season 48,000–60,000Dr ($133–$200) double; off-season from 39,000Dr ($130) double; from 64,000Dr ($213) suite. Rates include buffet breakfast. AE, DC, MC, V.

The Chromata is carved out of the cliffs just below the main square of Imerovigli. No two units are alike but all have domed cavelike walls and terraces with spectacular sea views. The smallest are studios, some with loft bedrooms. The apartments have separate sitting areas and the suites four-poster beds and stone baths with Jacuzzi tubs. All have fully equipped kitchenettes and air-conditioning, which is rarely found in these traditional hotels. The guests are mostly northern Europeans; Americans haven't yet discovered this beautiful place. The small pool hangs off the side of the cliff. The friendly staff can arrange for rental cars.

IA

✪ **Flower Pension.** Finikia, Ia, 847 00 Santorini. ☎ and fax **0286/71-130.** 12 units. High season 11,500Dr ($38) double; off-season from 7,500Dr ($25) double. No credit cards.

A 10-minute walk outside Ia, on the main road to Fira, sits this absolute gem run by Flora Halari, her sister, and her parents. The brand-new two-story structure housing the rooms is next door to the Halaris' own house. You'll feel this is more like a B&B than a hotel. The rooms are simple but sparkling clean, and all come with small refrigerators and baths with shower; most have balconies, some with a view of the vineyards and the sea. The garden, encircling the handsome pool, is full of geraniums and flowers. (It's not named Flower Pension for nothing.) You can have breakfast in the family dining room for 1,000Dr ($3.35). The bus to Fira stops right in front of the pension, and Flora will give you detailed directions to wherever you want to go.

PERISSA

Veggara Hotel. Perissa, 847 00 Santorini. ☎ **0286/82-060.** Fax 0286/82-608. 41 units. A/C MINIBAR TV TEL. High season from 48,000Dr ($160) double; off-season from 39,000Dr ($130) double. MC, V.

The Veggara is your best choice if you want a beach vacation. Located on the black-sand beach at Perissa, the neoclassical building houses the most luxurious hotel on this side of the island. The happening beach of Perivolas is a 15-minute stroll away, and the gay beach at Exomitis is another 15 minutes farther south. There are varying categories of rooms, suites, and apartments with wildly fluctuating rates, so be sure to get your category confirmed in writing when making a reservation. Most of the rooms are spacious and feature marble baths and balconies overlooking the sea. The apartments have fully equipped kitchenettes. There are two beautiful pools, one with a bar.

MEGALOHORI

Vedema Hotel. Megalohori, 847 00 Santorini. ☎ **0286/81-796.** Fax 0286/81-798. E-mail vedema@oneworld.net. 42 units. High season 75,000Dr ($250) 1-bedroom apt, 106,000Dr ($353) 2-bedroom villa, 170,000Dr ($566) 3-bedroom villa; off-season 55,000Dr ($183) 1-bedroom apt, 70,000Dr ($233) 2-bedroom villa, 125,000Dr ($416) 3-bedroom villa. Rates include breakfast. AE, DC, MC, V.

The luxury Vedema offers Cycladic-style villas and exceptionally attentive service, but its location isn't convenient for a beach vacation or nightlife and the atmosphere is stuffy. Privacy is the key word, and they get their share of Hollywood stars and other celebs. The hotel was built to resemble a small traditional Greek village, with white-washed buildings surrounded by olive and pistachio trees. The villas have high ceilings and are furnished in a minimalist elegant style, and most have kitchens for guests who desire their own personal chef. Most baths have no tubs, only large showers. There's a shuttle to the hotel's private beach, a 15-minute drive downhill. But most of the young, straight wealthy guests stay around the pool, where the Pergola restaurant serves three meals a day in a casual setting. The Vedema Restaurant, however, is so exclusive it serves only about 15 people a night (jackets required). There's a wine tasting every evening in the hotel's 300-year-old winery, the Canava Wine Bar.

WHET YOUR APPETITE

Santorini is known for its giant capers, succulent tomatoes, delicious chora cheese, and excellent wines. **Fira** offers the most diverse selection of restaurants, a few of which specialize in traditional Greek and Santorinian specialties. Fira is also home to the oldest restaurant on the island, **Nicholas Taverna,** still serving the best inexpensive Greek food.

Ia offers few choices but below the town, in **Ammoudi,** is where you'll find a beautiful cove lined with tavernas just a few feet from the water. Ammoudi is the place to have fresh fish (it's guaranteed to have been swimming a few hours before they cook it). **Firostephani** is home to my favorite restaurant, **Vanillia,** which offers the best culinary experience on the island: Excellent food, breathtaking views, a casual yet elegant setting, and an extremely gay-friendly staff. I could easily dine there every night.

FIRA & ENVIRONS

Archipelagos. Fira. ☎ **0286/23-673.** Main courses 2,300–5,900Dr ($8–$20). MC, V. Daily noon–1am. GREEK.

This attractive restaurant has one of the best locations in Fira, right in town, next to the better known but inconsistent Sphinx restaurant. Archipelagos attracts a young, casual crowd who linger for hours, relaxing on the terrace and enjoying the terrific view with an ouzo and mezedes. The food is old Greek, mixing traditional recipes with modern ingredients. Try the lettuce leaves stuffed with rice and spices and baked or the special Santorinian tomato soup. Even the simple Greek salad is excellent and the *shrimp saganaki* (shrimp with warm sharp cheese) delicious. The prices are reasonable considering the prime location, and the staff is energetic and friendly.

Koukoumavlos Restaurant. At the end of Fira, just past the Hotel Atlantis. ☎ **0286/23-807.** Main courses 3,500–7,000Dr ($11–$23). MC, V. Daily noon–1am. GREEK.

Opened in summer 1998, Koukoumavlos is at the end of town, below the Hotel Atlantis and tucked away in a plant-filled courtyard. You'll feel as if you've stepped into the garden of a wealthy relative where you can have a leisurely meal of Santorianian specialties. Try the crushed fava beans with almonds, tomatoes, and onions for a truly local appetizer. The keftedes in *kopanisti* sauce (minced lamb and veal made into patties and served with spicy kopanisti cheese from Santorini) are heavenly. Considered by locals a bit on the expensive side, this restaurant is frequently filled with out-of-towners.

Mama's Restaurant. Just outside Fira on the road to Ia. ☎ **0286/23-032.** Main courses 1,300–2,100Dr ($4.35–$7); breakfast 800–1,200Dr ($2.65–$4). No credit cards. Daily 8am–midnight. INTERNATIONAL.

If you have a craving for a strong cup of American coffee and pancakes with syrup, come here between 8am and 1pm, when a real American breakfast is served. For lunch and dinner, there's large portions and very reasonable prices. This the only place in town serving barbecued ribs. There's also excellent roasted chicken and homemade lasagna. Many of the diners are college students staying at the youth hostel down the street, but locals come here too. The staff is extremely friendly, and if Mama (a boisterous woman) is there she'll come around to chat with you.

✪ **Nicholas Taverna.** Erythrou Stavrou St., Fira. ☎ **0286/24-550.** Main courses 900–3,000Dr ($3–$10). No credit cards. Mon–Sat noon–4pm and 6–10pm, Sun 6–11pm. GREEK.

This tiny hole in the wall on "nightclub row" is the oldest taverna on the island and the most authentic. Basic service and down-to-earth Greek food with a lot of flavor is what you can expect. There's a vegetarian main course daily, special dishes the Greeks make during lent, like stuffed tomatoes and peppers cooked with onions and olive oil. There's no menu, but the old waiter will tell you what the few dishes are since they change daily. There's always an excellent Greek salad, several grilled meat and chicken dishes, and a traditional Greek dish like moussaka or veal with eggplant stewed in tomatoes and onions.

Selene Restaurant. Below the Hotel Atlantis, Fira. ☎ **0286/22-249.** Main courses 4,200–6,500Dr ($14–$22). M, V. Daily noon–11:30pm. GREEK.

The setting is superb, right on the cliff with unobstructed caldera views. The black-clothed tables are scattered on two fabulous whitewashed terraces. Selene is known for its Santorinian specialties using vegetables grown on the island, such as capers and tomatoes and local cheeses. Service is quietly subdued, as if in respect to the heavenly views. You might begin with an octopus-and-eggplant salad or olive bread with a puree of tomatoes and green peppers. For a main course, the monkfish on caper leaves and rabbit in lemon sauce are specialties. Or try the Bordado, a fisherman's stew with squid and calamari. End with a selection of cheeses from Ios, Crete, and Santorini served with a local dessert wine. With three courses and wine, the bill does add up, but it's worth it even for the view alone.

✪ **Vanilia.** On the path heading from Fira to Firostephani. ☎ **0286/22-706.** Main courses 2,400–3,900Dr ($8–$13). No credit cards. Daily noon–1am. GREEK.

This is the island's most magical restaurant. Recently opened by a cook, a host, and a bartender, this old stone house on the cliff offers amazing caldera views. Charming and handsome Dimitri will greet you warmly (Manos tends bar and Vassillis cooks in the back). You can sit on one of the two whitewashed terraces or inside the cozy rooms with thick stone walls, which are adorned with rugs and antiques from the owners' villages in northwest Greece. The food is truly authentic, an interesting mix of dishes you might not find elsewhere, like Al Basan Taba, a Greek-Turkish dish of tender lamb baked in yogurt. Many of the local gay boys come here, and the atmosphere is very relaxed and laid back. This is a place to linger over ouzo at sunset and stay for dinner when the terraces are lit with candles. The owners truly care about making everyone's meal special.

IA

Ammoudi Tavern. Ammoudi, below Ia (last tavern on the right). ☎ **0286/71-606.** Main courses 1900–5,000Dr ($6–$17). MC, V. Daily noon–midnight. SEAFOOD.

Just below Ia, the charming tiny cove of Ammoudi is lined with tavernas that all look alike. The one at the end, away from the road, is the best. For 10 years, a Greek man and his American wife have owned and managed this fantastic taverna. Here you're eye level with the small fishing boats bobbing up and down in the water just a few feet away. You can feel, smell, and hear the sea while eating what the fishers caught earlier. If you come during the day, you can watch them unloading their catch. If you're lucky, there'll be grouper for your main course, grilled to order and served simply with lemon. Sip an ouzo and order a few mezedes before you plunge into your meal. The grilled calamari are to die for, and the wild greens with lemon is a truly local specialty.

Minim's Patisserie. Just south of the church square, Ia. ☎ **0289/71-149.** Breakfast and light meals 700–1900Dr ($2.35–$6). No credit cards. Daily 9am–11pm. LIGHT MEALS.

Ia has several high-priced and touristy restaurants perched on top of the village affording great views. But Minim's is your best bet for a light lunch or an afternoon tea with delicious pastries as you linger on the terrace. The bakery is just below the cafe, and you can venture down there and see what's coming out of the oven (usually pizza, pie, and cakes). For a light lunch, try the spankopita (filo pastry filled with feta cheese and spinach). The walnut cake is delicious, and they have the best gourmet coffee and largest selection of exotic teas on the island.

EXPLORING SANTORINI

Akrotiri is the one site any traveler to Santorini must visit. One of the most important archaeological finds of the 20th century, Akrotiri is being excavated to this day. The Dorian remains of **Ancient Thira** on the slopes of the hillside of Mesa Vouna, is probably the second most frequently visited site.

The volcanic island of **Nea Kameni** and its hot springs is the most advertised excursion, followed by the sunset at **Ia.** Unless you enjoy swimming in the sulfur-green water of a hot spring, you won't see much on this excursion, and it's known by locals as the tourist trap tour (you hike up a dirt path, see some black dirt, and swim in smelly water). The sunset at Ia is as special as the sunset from Fira, and you don't need a tour to get there.

Unless you're extremely pressed for time, you can get to all the worthwhile sights on Santorini by bus. However, several tour companies offer half-day and full-day tours of the island. Most of them include a guided visit of Akrotiri and a wine-tasting stop at a local vineyard. **Kamari Tours** at ☎ **0286/32-751** offers excursions at 4,000 to 7,000Dr ($13 to $23), and **Ifestos Travel** at ☎ **0286/31-871** has several itineraries.

For sheer romance, consider a sunset cruise on the sailboat ✪ ***Bella Aurora.*** This replica of a 19th-century schooner sails around Santorini and the volcanic islands surrounding it. You'll witness a spectacular sunset while sipping ouzo and will find countless photo ops for capturing magnificent angles of the islands. (Yes, the crowd consists mostly of straight couples, but, hey, if two men decide to hold hands and somebody doesn't like it, they're free to jump overboard). The Belle Aurora leaves from Athinios Port daily at 4:30pm and returns at 9:30pm. The price is 7,500Dr ($25) per person (includes ouzo and appetizers). Reserve through your hotel's reception or any travel agency in town.

BOYS ON THE BEACH

VLIHADA BAY Off the road to Perissa, beautiful and secluded ✪ **Vlihada Bay** is the most popular gay beach. In July and August, buses run several times a day from Fira to Vlihada. In other months, take the Perissa bus (operates every half an hour) and get off at the Vlihada turnoff. It's a half-hour walk to the beach.

Vlihada is a long beach, and nudity is tolerated by the few straights who venture far enough south. At the first stretch of sand, where the paved road ends, you'll frequently find families with children. Walk south, toward the more cliffy part. There's only a bumpy dirt road leading to this area, and curious Greek boys ride their bikes and check out the action. (You might see a few of them later in town at a dance club passing as straight.) This beach is great in the afternoon, when the sun is at a perfect angle.

Late in the afternoon, climb back up to the paved road for a glass of ouzo and mezedes at the **Vlihada Tavern** (☎ **0286/82-531**); it has a nice terrace with a stone barbecue, and the food is cheap. Owner Dimitris rents rooms in a building behind the tavern for 10,000Dr ($33) for two with bath. Or he can call a taxi for your ride back to town.

CAPE EXOMITIS Halfway between Vlihada (above) and Perivolas (below) is ✪ **Cape Exomitis,** the second most popular gay beach. Take the bus to Perivolas and walk south on the beach from there. From Perissa it's a 30-minute walk south on the beach.

This beach is slightly cruisier than Vlihada since the shrubs and bushes separating the dirt road from the beach provide cover for all sorts of activities, but Exomitis is narrower and not as beautiful. Here you're at the island's southernmost tip, and the water is a bit rougher. A Byzantine fortress (the best preserved such building in the Cyclades) looms behind the beach.

South of Exomitis, close to the ugly new port that's being built, is one of the most charming tavernas on the island. Two elderly sisters (who speak just a few words of English) run the simple **Paradiso Tavern** (no phone). They grow their own greens, tomatoes, and capers in the back garden. It's one of the most authentic spots on Santorini, and cheap too. You might have to use sign language to communicate, but it's worth the effort.

PERISSA & PERIVOLAS Buses run hourly to these beaches from Fira, or you can follow the sign for Perivolas from the road to Perissa.

Perissa is a rundown village filled with backpackers, cheap rooms, and tavernas. The beach is okay, with many hotels and bars jammed next to one another. It's kind of pointless to come here when a short walk south along the beach gets you to **Perivolas,** which is trendier and prettier. Perivolas is popular with a young straight crowd, and it's where the local boys get their tans.

You'll find them playing volleyball on the sand in front of the **Wet Stories Bar-Restaurant** (☎ **0286/82-990**). Wet indeed! If you want to stay close to Perivolas, the **Santorini Nine Muses Hotel** (☎ **0286/81-781**) has doubles from 40,000Dr ($133). Set slightly back from the beach, it boasts a magnificent pool on a huge flagstone terrace and bungalow-style units with lofts.

KAMARI The huge cliffs at Cape Mesa Vouno separate Perrisa Beach from **Kamari Beach.** Buses run every 30 minutes from Fira for the 20-minute ride. Kamari is the island's largest beach town. Its beach is a 4-mile stretch, wide and pebbly, and tavernas and hotels are lined across the street from the beach. Many tourists on package tours from northern Europe come here, and the whole town is very touristy and straight and filled with families and kids.

However, you can get very good deals on hotels and rooms, and if you're looking for a beach-town atmosphere, you might be happy making Kamari your base. The **Roussos Beach Hotel** (☎ **0286/31-590**) is a good choice, with doubles from 25,000Dr ($83) and a friendly staff. For very basic accommodations, your best bet is **Esperides Rooms** (☎ **0286/31-670**), a few blocks from the beach, with doubles starting at 15,000Dr ($50).

Hook Bar (☎ **0286/33-441**) on the beach is listed in some guides as a gay bar. It's not but is frequented by a young mixed crowd. For authentic Greek cuisine, forget the beachfront tavernas and head to **Amalthia** (☎ **0286/32-780**) near the bus stop to Fira. You'll dine in an orchard of pistachio trees, and they always have excellent fresh fish.

RED BEACH Popular with young college students on vacation (mostly straight), **Red Beach** gets its name from the reddish volcanic sand. Take the bus to Akrotiri; from the bus stop walk on the lower road for 15 minutes. Many visitors combine a visit to Akrotiri with a refreshing swim here afterward.

Nearby, the **Dolphins Taverna** (☎ **0286/81-151**) has tables right on the water (from Akroriti, take the upper road a quarter of a mile, you'll see a sign for Dolphins on your left). This family-run restaurant guarantees the fish is fresh, brought in by its own fishermen every morning. Try the tender red mullet at about 9,000Dr ($30) a kilo.

OTHER BEACHES **Monolithos,** north of Kamari and close to the airport, is nothing special, and neither are the rest of the east coast beaches. Down the steep cliff from Ia is the small cove of **Ammoudi,** lined with tavernas serving fresh fish. Follow the path south around the corner and you'll find rocky platforms from which you can dive into the shimmering blue water. There are several tiny pebbly coves where nudity is the norm.

Some Sights to See

ARCHAEOLOGICAL SITES & A MUSEUM The remains of the amazing Minoan city of ✪ **Akrotiri** is a covered excavation site, on a hill in the southeast corner of the island. It's a half-hour bus ride from Fira, with buses running regularly throughout the day. The site is open daily 8:30am to 3pm, and admission is 1,250Dr ($4.15).

You'll need less than an hour to visit the small site, but what you'll see is astonishing: a city dating back as far as 3,000 B.C. that was seemingly so advanced the houses had toilets and drainage systems. You can see the remains of the two-story houses where the ground floors were used for storage and the upper floors as apartments. Large clay jars were found with remains of barley seed and olive oil, giving a glimpse of how truly advanced the Minoans were. Beautiful frescoes decorated every house (they're now in Athens's National Archaeological Museum). But no human remains were found, only part of a pig skeleton. Where the inhabitants escaped to remains a mystery, but it seems they had ample warning of the volcanic eruption that buried the city in ash in 1,520 B.C. There has been a lot of debate among archaeologists and historians as to whether Santorini is actually the legendary lost city of Atlantis.

The other major archaeological site on the island, albeit much less frequently visited, is **Ancient Thira.** (Consider hiking up the 1,200 feet from Kamari Beach; it's a beautiful 1-hour hike.) The site is open Tuesday to Sunday 9am to 2:30pm, with an admission of 1,250Dr ($4.15). You'll see a few Byzantine remains and Doric columns, but most of what's visible dates back to the Hellenistic era. Find the southern end of the site, a terrace that was used for religious practices. Stone tablets were found here dating back to 800 B.C., listing the names of the boys who danced naked (!) in homage to Dionysus. The view from here toward Kamari and Perissa is spectacular. (If you want to pay your own tame homage to the god of wine on your way back, stop by the **Santos** or **Canava Roussos** winery for a tasting of Santorini wines.)

At the northern edge of Fira, at the beginning of Ypapantis Street (known as Gold Street), is the **Archaeology Museum** (☎ **0286/22-217;** open Tues–Sun 8:30am–3pm; admission 800Dr/$2.65), home to some interesting vases from Ancient Thira and some finds from Akrotiri. Nearby is the cable car that goes down to the old port of Skala every 15 minutes.

INLAND VILLAGES To get a feel for a traditional Greek village, stroll around **Emborio,** at the turnoff to Perissa—its houses are built inside the ruins of a Venetian fortress. **Pyrgos,** the oldest and highest village on the island, is also worth a quick visit. The **Pyrgos Taverna** (☎ **0286/31-346**) is a good choice for lunch.

Though the ultrachic **Hotel Vedema** has put the village of **Megalohori** on the map, it still retains much of its old charm. Take a few minutes to stroll around this medieval village if you have some time. The **Boutari winery,** south of Megalohori, offers wine tastings. **Messaria** and **Karterados** are other inland villages south of Fira popular for their pottery workshops and traditional tavernas.

Working Up a Sweat

There's one gym in Fira where everybody goes (including all the boys with any gay interest), and that's **Santorini Gym,** by the Olympic Airways office (☎ **0286/251-96**). It's well equipped and the only decent place in town to lift weights. Call for hours since they change with the seasons.

For scuba diving and other watersports, the most fun and well-equipped location is Perivolas's **Yaya Beach Club** (☎ **0286/82-946**).

HITTING THE STORES

The tiny streets of **Fira** are lined with jewelry, ceramic, and Greek decorative art shops. There are also many clothes shops, some carrying Greek-made cotton shirts and sweatshirts at reasonable prices. The **main shopping area** is the streets all around the main square and the narrow alleys close to the steps leading down to the old port.

Ia has one "main" street with many unique and interesting shops. Some visitors claim Ia is much more elegant (and expensive) than Fira. It is. And it caters mostly to foreign visitors, while Fira has a more eclectic mix of people and shops.

Shopping hours are generally daily 9am to 2pm and 5 to 10pm. Some stores stay open to midnight during July and August. Many streets don't have names or numbers, so ask or call if you have trouble finding a shop.

SHOPPING A TO Z

ART & ANTIQUES **Roloi** in Ia (☎ **0286/71-303**) stocks an excellent collection of unique bronze vases and old kilims in perfect condition.

✪ **Armonia,** on the steps to the old port in Fira (☎ **0286/24-040**), carries an unusual selection of hand-blown glass, limited handmade bronze work, and unique old window frames from Santorini; Jackie Ranger, the English owner, will be glad to ship any of your purchases back home. **Kisiris,** just off the main square in Fira (☎ **0286/23-929**), has the most beautiful collection of wind chimes and hand-painted mugs. In Ia, **Replica** (☎ **0286/71-916**) sells the best collection of museum-endorsed replicas of Hellenic art.

CERAMICS Santorini boasts several excellent ceramic workshops and galleries. **Work Shop Ceramics** in Karterados, just south of Fira (☎ **0286/25-220**), is the largest workshop, with hundreds of vases and jugs. For a more refined collection, stop by the new **GEA Workshop & Gallery** in Kamari, one street in from the beach on the road to Fira (☎ **0286/32-421**); it carries the work of seven local Greek artists.

FASHION There isn't much when it comes to expensive name-brands like Armani or Versace. Try **Betini,** behind the main square in Fira (☎ **0286/24-032**), if you're looking for Tommy Hilfiger shirts or Diesel jeans. The **American Store** in Fira (☎ **0286/22-227**) has the largest selection of jeans and sweatshirts. The newest and hippest clothes store on the island is **Cliff** in Ia (☎ **0286/71-910**), with everything from boots to T-shirts.

JEWELRY One out of three stores in both Fira and Ia is a jewelry shop. Locals consider **Greco Gold,** by Café Classico in Fira (☎ **0286/22-460**), the best. Owner Stefanos Keramidas is known for his expert knowledge and honest prices.

IN THE HEAT OF THE NIGHT

Santorini's nightlife is limited to Fira and in midsummer to some of the beach bars in Perivolas, Perissa, and Kamari. Ia is quiet at night and, beyond a few cafes, offers no nightlife. Fira is where you want to be. Nothing in Fira is exclusively gay, but most everywhere is gay-friendly.

Franco's (☎ **0286/22-881**) is Santorini's most famous bar, with magnificent sunset views and extra-comfortable lounge chairs. The prices are steep and the crowd tends to be straighter and older than at ✪ **Tropical,** just above Franco's (☎ **0286/23-089**), the gay-friendliest bar in town; its small terrace offers an equally stunning view. Most of the action happens inside this cozy bar where Genie makes her special coffees all afternoon until Michael takes over in the evening and the crowd switches from caffeine to alcohol. If you're going to meet any interesting people (especially the young and the gay), you'll do it at Tropical. It's also popular with the local restaurant owners and hotel managers (several of them gay). Ask Michael for pointers; he's the most knowledgeable person on the island about the gay scene. Tell him I sent you.

Around 1am is when the dancing starts at the several clubs on Erythrou Stavrou Street (two streets up from Tropical heading toward the main square). **Trip** (no phone) is the most popular disco, with a mixed crowd dancing to rock and British Top 20 hits. At the **Casablanca Club,** above Trip (☎ **0286/24-008**), the music is just a tad mellower and the guests a tad older, and there's a small terrace where you can chat up your nightly catch.

Next door, the **Koo Club** (☎ **0286/22-025**) is huge, with two indoor bars and three outdoor bars and people dancing in the gardens and on the terrace. The crowd is definitely younger, many college students on vacation and some too young to be out this late. Another happening place on the same street is ✪ **Town Club** (☎ **0286/22-820**), popular with young Greek guys with slicked black hair and tight butts. They play Greek music here, and when everyone's sufficiently loaded with alcohol there's wild dancing on the bars. Even the bartenders join in the fun. Two men can dance with complete freedom. A gay club? Not quite, but the boys are definitely curious. **Engima Club,** farther up the street (☎ **0286/22-466**), is also popular with a young crowd.

3 Folegandros: Sun & Seclusion

Folegandros is a true Greek island, as yet unspoiled with resorts and huge hotels and souvenir shops and formula tavernas. The beaches are outstanding if you enjoy seclusion, the hiking is superb, and the prices are very reasonable. It gets crowded from mid-July to late August, but otherwise the island is quiet, the pace is slow, and you can truly unwind.

There's nothing openly gay on Folegandros, but the space and freedom it provides ensure privacy. The locals are friendly to all visitors. Quite a few Greek and foreign gay couples who want to get away from Mykonos or Santorini come here for a few days of sun and silence. Once you've been to Folegandros, the phrase "getting away from it all" will take on a whole new meaning.

FOLEGANDROS ESSENTIALS

ARRIVING & DEPARTING

The only way to arrive on Folegandros is by sea. **Ferries** from Athens run four to six times a week April to October, with service dropping to two to three times a week in winter. Ferries usually depart Piraeus in the morning for the 8- to 9-hour trip. From Folegandros, ferries depart three to four times weekly to Santorini and Mykonos.

During summer, **Ilio Lines** operate the *Flying Dolphins* hydrofoils two to three times a week to Mykonos and Santorini. For more information, contact the **Sottovento Tourism Office** on Folegandros (☎ **0286/41-444**). Schedules are also available on the Internet at **www.gtpnet.com.** A bus meets all scheduled arrivals and chugs up the hill to the main village of Hora.

There had been no **taxi** service on Folegandros, but as of 1998 there's one cabbie, George, who'll be at the port to greet all incoming ferries.

VISITOR INFORMATION

There's no official tourist office, but Flavio Facciolo (an Italian from Torino), his beautiful wife, and his sister operate the main travel agency on the island, the **Sottovento Tourism Office** (☎ **0286/41-444;** fax 0286/41-430). Call or fax before your arrival and they'll arrange for a hotel and greet you at the harbor. Or drop by once you've arrived and they'll give you a map and answer questions. Flavio knows just about everyone in town and everything remotely connected to tourism on the island.

Country & City Codes

The **country code** for Greece is **30.** The **city code** for Hora and all of Folegandros is **286;** use this code when you're calling from outside Greece. If you're within Greece but not on Folegandros, use **0286.** If you're calling within Folegandros or from Santorini, simply leave off the code and dial only the regular phone number.

Island Layout

The port town of **Karavostassi** is nothing more than a harbor with a couple of tavernas, three small grocery stores, and a bar. The main town, **Hora,** is about 2 miles up the hill, and all the hotels are in or around the town. The other small village is **Ano Meria,** and you can take the bus there and then hike to many of the best beaches. **Angali Beach** is the largest and easiest to reach.

Getting Around

The **bus** makes regular runs from the port to Hora and from Hora to Ano Meria, where there's a path to Angali Beach. The frequency depends on the seasons, but there's always several buses in the morning and several in the afternoon. Schedules are posted at the main bus stop in the square.

Just a year ago there weren't any **scooters** for rent. Now you have a choice of two rental locations, **Jimmy** at the port (☎ **0286/41-448**) or **Venetia** in Hora (☎ **0286/41-316**). Expect to pay from 2,500 to 5,000Dr ($8 to $16) per day depending on the season.

There was no **taxi** on the island until summer 1998. Now there's one. You'll find George with his brand-new car greeting every arriving ferry and hydrofoil.

To get to the more secluded beaches, small **boats** depart from the port in summer. Ask at the port for the daily schedule.

PILLOW TALK

There's not much to talk about. Basically, there are three hotels and then a selection of cheap rooms. If you like space and views, you have only one choice: the fantastic **Anemomilos Apartments.** For a cozy B&B-style hotel in the heart of town, there's the **Castro,** and the **Polikandia** is the largest tourist-class hotel.

Call Flavio at **Sottovento Tourism Office** (☎ **0286/41-444**) and he'll reserve a hotel and greet you at the port—see "Visitor Information" above.

✪ **Anemomilos Apartments.** Hora, 840 11 Folegandros. ☎ **0286/41-309.** Fax 0286/41-407. 17 units. MINIBAR TEL. High season 28,000Dr ($93) double, off-season from 16,000Dr ($53) double. MC, V.

This could well be one of the most beautiful and peaceful hotels in the Cyclades. The two-story structures built in 1993 conform to traditional Cycladic style, perched at the top of the cliff overlooking the sea, steps from Hora's main square. The studio apartments are sparkling and spacious; all have fully equipped kitchenettes, orthopedic mattresses, antique mirrors, and radios from the 1930s. The baths are modern and even have hair dryers. Dimitri Patelis and his friendly wife live next door in the small house where breakfast is served all day and where there's a small bar for guests to enjoy a cocktail at sunset. They'll try hard to make you feel at home. There's one wheelchair-accessible unit.

Athineos Pension. Outside Hora, set slightly back on the road to the port, 840 11 Folegandros. ☎ and fax **0286/41-232.** 7 units. High season 12,000Dr ($40) double; off-season from 6,000Dr ($20) double. No credit cards.

This large recently built stone villa is a good choice if you can't find a room in town. The rooms and baths are large and most have shared patios; those in back overlook the hills and fields of Folegandros. Strattos, the friendly manager, will meet you at the port if you call ahead, and he serves breakfast. Across the street next to the old stables, Strattos also has 14 very basic rooms he rents (mostly to backpacking college students), with rates start at 5,000Dr ($17) double. You won't find anything cheaper.

Hotel Castro. Hora, 840 11 Folegandros. ☎ **0286/41-414.** Fax 0286/41-230. 12 units. TEL. High season from 16,000Dr ($53) double; off-season from 10,000Dr ($33) double. No credit cards.

This charming hotel in the town center has been owned and managed for generations by the hospitable Danassi family. No two rooms are alike. The front rooms overlook the small narrow street for a truly authentic village view; some have small patios. The back rooms (more expensive) have great views of the sea, hundreds of feet below. There's a magnificent rooftop terrace for sunbathing and relaxing.

Polikandia Hotel. Hora, 840 11 Folegandros. ☎ **0286/41-322.** Fax 0286/41-323. 31 units. MINIBAR TEL. High season 17,000Dr ($56) double; off-season from 9,000Dr ($30) double. Rates include breakfast. No credit cards.

Surrounding a beautiful courtyard of plants and palms, the Polikandia is the island's largest hotel. The two-story structure is just steps from the third square in Hora. All the simple rooms have either a village or a mountain view and baths with showers. A full buffet breakfast is served. Dimitri, the doting manager, will be more than happy to mix you a cocktail in the evening at the bar.

WHET YOUR APPETITE

Expect to eat Greek, to eat simply, to eat fresh, to eat cheap, and to eat well. Most of the restaurants are on one of Hora's five squares and on the few streets leading to them. Some of the beaches also have tavernas serving decent food.

Remember that it's busy on this island only in July and August and that many of the restaurants can be rather empty (and close shortly after dark) in the slower months.

Apanemo. Next to Sottovento Trave, near the bus stop to Ano Meria. ☎ **0286/41-443.** Main courses 700–1,800Dr ($2.35–$6). No credit cards. Daily 9am–11pm. GREEK.

This family taverna is run by George Spinggos, while his wife cooks and George Jr. bakes the pizza. The pizzas are excellent; try the shrimp and feta. There's a large variety of homemade Greek dishes, from moussaka to *pastisio* (pasta baked with béchamel sauce and ground beef). For something really different, try *gardouba,* the Greek version of liver and onions. Mrs. Spinggos always has some homemade dessert, so be sure to leave room for baklava along with a strong cup of Greek coffee.

Greco Cafe. Next to the bus stop to Ano Meria. ☎ **0286/41-456.** Light meals 1,500–1,900Dr ($5–$6). No credit cards. Daily 8am–3am. GREEK/BAR/CAFE.

This popular spot is the only happening place late in the evening and has the youngest crowd in town. Harris, a young Greek guy and his English girlfriend, Sarah, run this hip joint. Enjoy the best coffees on the island (if you're craving a real Italian espresso, go here) and the best omelets and sandwiches all day and night. Harris plays classical music in the morning, switches to international in the afternoon (Greek, British, and the like), and then ends with strictly rock music in the evening, when the dancing begins.

Melissa. On Hora's third square. ☎ **0286/41-067.** Main courses 900–1,700Dr ($3–$6). No credit cards. Daily 8am–1am. GREEK.

This old taverna has been serving excellent food for years and considers its cuisine to be "old Greek." Breakfast, lunch, and dinner are served inside the cozy taverna with its wooden tables and chairs or on the square filled with jasmine bushes. Try the *rabbit stifado* (rabbit stewed with onions and spices) or giant baked beans. The *piperofai* (eggplant and peppers with feta) is usually hard to find in restaurants and is excellent here.

Piatsa. On Hora's third square. ☎ **0286/41-274.** Main courses 900–2,300Dr ($3–$8). No credit cards. Daily 8am–1am. GREEK.

Because of its excellent location (under the almond tree in the center of the square), this is one of the busiest tavernas in summer, but the owners work hard to keep the quality high. Try the grilled swordfish kebabs, Greek meatballs, or traditional moussaka. This is the place to enjoy a sweet Greek coffee in the late afternoon while watching the people walk by.

Pounta. On bus stop square. ☎ **0286/41-063.** Main courses 950–1,600Dr ($3–$5). No credit cards. Daily 8am–1am. GREEK.

This wonderful little restaurant run by the friendly Takis has a delightful garden in back. This place is known for its excellent zucchini pie (thick pie crust filled with zucchini, onions, and tomatoes). The stuffed tomatoes are delicious, as are the *marides* (small fried fish) when in season. The freshly baked walnut and apple cakes are heavenly.

EXPLORING FOLEGANDROS

SOME SIGHTS TO SEE

The village of **Hora** is beautiful; it feels like a mountain town, yet on one side the cliffs descend straight into the sea. The brilliantly white **Panayia Church** sits at the top of the hill above town, where there are incredible views of the Mediterranean. The **Kastro** in town was built in the 13th century and has been inhabited ever since. The village is centered around five squares with a few shops and tavernas and rooms for rent along its narrow streets.

The only other town on the island (apart from the tiny port of Karavostassi, where the ferries dock) is the hilltop village of **Ano Meria.** It's hardly a town, with a few stone houses, farms, and fields, but this is the last stop on the bus route. From here, you can hike to many of the island's secluded coves and beaches.

BOYS ON THE BEACH

It's more like no boys on the beach, since you come here for the seclusion, isolation, and quiet . . . and the very stray and very rare gay boy. Most of the beaches are pebbly, and large rocks jut out of the water, making diving dangerous. However, the snorkeling is great. The water sparkles at all the beaches and is incredibly clean.

Angali, heading west from Ano Meria, is the largest beach, with a few tavernas and rooms for rent. ✪ **Ayios Nikolaos,** farther west, is home to one of the most charming tavernas on the island: The Mezzalira family runs the ✪ **Pappalaki Tavern** on the small hill above the beach (☎ **0286/41-413**); you'll eat octopus and whatever fish the fishermen caught in the morning. If you're backpacking, there's free camping close to the beach at Ayios Nikolaos. Even farther west, **Livadaki** is another good beach.

On the southern end of the island is the beautiful beach of **Katergo,** with large boulders jutting out of the sea. Katergo is best reached by boat or it's an hour hike from the port town of Karavostassi.

If you don't want to take the bus and hike to the beaches, (or ride your scooter and hike), the only other way to get to the good beaches is by boat. From the harbor, **taxi boats** leave sporadically to some of the secluded coves, including the picturesque beach of **Katergo.** Inquire at the harbor.

Flavio, owner of the **Sottovento Tourism Office** (☎ **0286/41-444**), organizes special excursions on a large private boat. He can put together a great itinerary, so call ahead if beach-hopping (minus the hiking) is what you're after. In high season, a 7-hour excursion leaves the harbor at 10am, goes around the famous caves, and then stops at four or five beaches for a delicious swim (and lunch). The beaches include Livadaki, Ayios Nikolaus, and Katergo. On windy days (and those winds blow often in summer), the boat heads south to the protected beaches around Ampeli. The price for the whole day, including lunch, is 6,500Dr ($21) per person; it most often includes transportation from Hora down to the harbor.

HITTING THE STORES

There aren't many shops on the island—all are in Hora and most sell jewelry and souvenirs. Drop by and visit **Diamantina Gorgona,** on Hora's third square (☎ **0286/41-082**); she has some interesting originally designed jewelry and unique handmade puppets. **Gold Creations** nearby (☎ **0286/41-319**) is the main shop selling beautiful silver and gold bracelets and earrings. Shopping till you drop on Folegandros takes about 20 minutes.

IN THE HEAT OF THE NIGHT

There's not much nightlife on Folegandros. In July and August, you can find the northern European and Greek tourists partying at the **Greco Cafe** (☎ **0286/41-456**) with Harris and Sarah (see "Whet Your Appetite" above). At **Rakendia** (☎ **0286/41-431**) there's a terrace bar with beautiful sea views, and a mellow group gathers in the early evening for drinks.

Astarti, close to the bus stop square (no phone), is the best place to enjoy Greek music. And nearby **To Kellari** (no phone) is a little wine bar with an excellent wine list.

6 Italy

In the Gay Footsteps of Michelangelo & Leonardo

by Donald Olson

Raise your hand if you've never dreamed of going to Italy. Just as I thought: I don't see a single hand.

Your first introduction to "Italy" may have been through movies by Italian directors like Rossellini, Fellini, Visconti, Zefferelli, and Pasolini, who've shaped our cinematic perceptions of the country. So have gladiator flicks and Roman epics like *Spartacus* and *Ben-Hur* and that TV favorite *I, Claudius.* More recently, you may have drooled over the scenery (and other things) in the adaptations of E. M. Forster's *A Room with a View* and Henry James's *The Wings of the Dove* and laughed and cried with Roberto Benini's *Life Is Beautiful.*

For gay travelers, Italy's artistic heritage can have a very special meaning. After all, some of the country's greatest and most universally venerated artists—Michelangelo, Leonardo da Vinci, Sandro Botticelli, Benvenuto Cellini, and Caravaggio among them—were homosexual.

If you're an opera lover, you may yearn to hear an opera by Verdi or Puccini in one of Italy's many opera houses (though, sadly, La Scala will be closing sometime soon for renovations). Or maybe you just love to *mangia*, in which case you can look forward to delicious food and wine. And you can't overlook the beauty of the Italians themselves. Whether sauntering haughtily down the street in a tailored Armani suit and talking on a cell phone, or squeezed into tight jeans and a T-shirt and racing through the ancient streets on a Vespa, Italian men know how to cut *una bella figura.* The women? Equally gorgeous but more mysterious, with penetrating eyes, husky voices, and an elegant flair and secret power of their own.

You can appreciate Italy on so many levels it's pointless to enumerate them all. And though just about every town and region has something to recommend it, in this guide I've limited myself to the four great cities: **Rome, Florence, Venice,** and **Milan.** Each represents a very different aspect of Italy. Each is singular in terms of its art, architecture, history, cuisine, and overall atmosphere. And, more important, three of the cities—Venice being the exception—have developed a gay social network of political organizations, bookstores, social groups, bars, and clubs.

Gay life in Italy is a complex subject that often confuses gay visitors from more

The Italian Lire

Italian currency is the **lira,** plural **lire (L).** Notes come in denominations of 1,000, 2,000, 5,000, 50,000 and 100,000 lire. (Caravaggio is on the 100,000L note.) There are 50-, 100-, 200-, and 500-lire coins.

At this writing, 1,800L was equivalent to $1 U.S., and that was the rate of exchange I used throughout. Prices over $5 U.S. have been rounded to the nearest dollar.

Queer Tips for Italian Hotels

There are very few specifically "gay hotels" in Italy, and those that advertise in the various gay magazines aren't always the best places to stay. "Gay-friendly" is another matter. In Milan, Florence, Venice, and Rome you probably won't encounter any problems. But if you're traveling as a couple and book a double room (*doppio*), you're inevitably going to get twin beds. If you want a double bed, you must ask for a *matrimoniale* (the Italian word for double bed presupposes that only married couples sleep in them).

For single gay travelers, potential problems can arise if you book a room, meet someone, and want to take him or her back to your hotel. In classier places, non-paying guests must register on entering. If you're in a pensione, you may have your own key, but in most Italian hotels you must leave your room key at the front desk and pick it up again when you return. If you come back late at night with a "nonpaying guest," the hotelkeeper may not take kindly to it.

"open" countries. The Italians, in the most general sense, don't "proclaim" their sexuality. Only in recent years has the subject been openly talked about. The Catholic church, with its emphasis on procreation and long-standing condemnation of gays and lesbians, continues to exert a tremendous influence on everyday attitudes. Its official stance now is that it's okay to be queer so long as you never "act" on it (the "suffering is good for you" syndrome). Italian AIDS activists consider the church (with its inflexible attitudes regarding the use of condoms to prevent HIV) to be a real foe in the arena of public health policy. Another factor to consider is that Italy—and Mediterranean cultures in general—are family-oriented societies where the male-macho ethic runs strong. Under these conditions it's more difficult for gays to come out; many opt instead to lead a double life.

But homosexuality isn't illegal in Italy. The legal age of consent for everyone is 16. Just remember this: Sex, whether homo or hetero, must be kept private. Any sexual act performed in "public" is potential grounds for a 3-year prison term. "Public" means any place you can be seen, including—if one stretches the point—a private room others can see into. (Maybe that's why the Italians so often keep their shutters closed.) Though rarely enforced, this law is on the books. Nowadays an offender of public morality is more likely to be fined instead of thrown into the slammer.

Still another thing to keep in mind is that many Italian gays and lesbians don't have their own apartments. High rents and high unemployment tend to keep the unmarried members of society at home with their parents. This economic tourniquet can add a level of frustration (or adventure) to the logistics of gay desire. It may also help to explain why so many Italian men seem to favor the secretive quickie. They either don't have a room of their own or they do—and maybe share it with a wife and bambini. It's equally difficult for Italian lesbians to establish personal and financial autonomy outside the home. Although strong lesbian social networks do exist and the society as a whole is slowly loosening up, there's still a stigma attached to unmarried childless women.

But this isn't a country lacking in gay pride or gay history. Homosexuality in ancient Rome—and even earlier, among the Etruscans—was an accepted fact of life. It did, however, adhere to the classical Greek model of dominant older lover with submissive younger beloved. Hadrian, one of the greatest Roman emperors, not only loved pretty buff Antinous but also elevated his male lover to the status of a god.

All this changed once the Empire fell apart and Christianity emerged triumphant. Sex of any kind was almost psychotically vilified by the early church fathers. But none of this long deterred the boys from being boys. Renaissance Florence was as queer as New York's Chelsea or San Francisco's Castro. It was *so* queer, in fact, that the German verb for sodomy at the time was *florenzen.*

In 1870, after centuries of gay persecution (castration, hanging, fines), the newly unified republic of Italy adopted the Napoleonic Code. Church and state were separated. Homosexuality, though still excoriated, was "legal." (Grand Duke Ferdinand III, a Medici, decriminalized homosexuality in Tuscany in the late 18th century.)

However, it took another century before the first steps were taken toward gay liberation. Gay political agitation began in the turbulent early 1970s with a revolutionary gay group called F.U.O.R.I ("Out"), spearheaded by Mario Mieli and Corrado Levi. A brutal rash of homophobic violence forced more of the Italian gay community out of the closet and led, in the early 1980s, to the formation of a national gay organization known as **Arci-Gay Arci-Lesbica.** There are now 40 Arci centers throughout Italy, selling yearly membership cards, called the **Arci Gay Uno,** for 20,000L ($11). These cards are required for admittance to many gay bars, discos, and saunas. As a foreigner you may be exempted, but having an Arci membership is a good way to show your support. Often you can buy the Arci Uno card at the bar or disco itself.

Gays and lesbians in Italy today have basic constitutional protections against discrimination in the home and in the workplace. (Wish I could say the same for the U.S.A.) In some cities, same-sex couples can register as domestic partners. These aren't national laws, so same-sex couples cannot adopt children—but, in time, anything is possible.

Note: In summer 1998, as part of an experimental program, many Italian museums lengthened their opening hours to 11:30pm. As of press time there was no official announcement that the program would be repeated in summer 1999 and other summers thereafter, but it seems likely, especially considering the hordes expected in 2000. The later opening hours are in effect only during summer. Check with the local tourist office when you arrive for more details.

10 Rome: Where *La Dolce Vita* Began

Of all the great cities in Italy, **Rome (Roma),** at least for me, is the most intoxicating. For one thing, it hasn't turned into a theme park, which is the impression you sometimes get in Florence and Venice. Roma remains a real city, inhabited by a large and lively resident population. Many northern Italians consider the Romans coarse and vulgar, yet I find them earthy and theatrical. Watch their dazzling repertoire of conversational hand gestures and facial expressions and you'll know what I mean.

Tradition has it that Rome was founded on the Palatine Hill by Romulus, the first of seven kings, in 753 B.C. Its very antiquity makes it unique and mysteriously compelling. Woven into the urban fabric of everyday Rome are fragments from its ancient Imperial and Republican past and churches from the earliest years of Christianity. Standing cheek-by-jowl on the streets are medieval, Renaissance, Baroque, Neoclassical, and art nouveau buildings. Century is spread on century, style on style, in a dazzling historical palimpsest. In that sense, Rome is a city of endless discovery. Self-discovery too, for it challenges you to think about time and the changing fortunes of civilizations.

The capital of Italy has never looked better or been more accessible to visitors as it prepares for the **Papal Jubilee 2000.** The city government has been working hard to clean up and revitalize areas like Piazza dei Cinquecento in front of the train station. Monuments and fountains have been restored, new museums have appeared, opening hours have been extended, a new tramline is operating, and you can now walk into the Roman Forum without paying an admission. (Be prepared, though—some major sights may be obscured behind scaffolding when you arrive.) In preparation for the year 2000, which the Catholic church has declared a Holy Year (it's also the year when gay Rome will host the first-ever **World Pride**), the church has pumped millions into cleaning and restoring its major churches. Facades formerly encrusted with centuries of grime are now gleaming white. The only thing that hasn't changed for the better is the traffic. Since many Romans drive home for lunch and an afternoon siesta before heading back to work, the city has four rush hours instead of two.

In ancient times, it was said that "Africa begins at Rome." That's another part of its appeal. In Rome you're aware of being in *southern* Italy, in a different climate, closer to the heart of the great civilizations of Greece and Egypt, both of which influenced the development of Rome. Naples, to the south, is only a couple of hours away by high-speed train. From there you can visit Pompeii and Herculaneum, cities buried by the eruption of Mount Vesuvius in A.D. 79, or take a boat to the fabled isle of Capri, where emperors Tiberius and Caligula led their debauched lives and which has been a haunt of gays and lesbians for well over a century (and is, I suppose, where Capri pants came from). Southern Italy is visibly poorer and less industrialized than the north, but its landscape, cities, islands, and ancient sites have a remarkably evocative power of their own.

When I first visited Rome, I was amazed at how small the old city actually is. This, after all, was the capital of the vast Roman Empire, which once stretched from England to Africa and east into Asia Minor. It was the most powerful city in the Western world. But, unlike cities today, it was built on a walkable human scale, and that scale has remained intact. Instead of skyscrapers you see domes and spires. Or maybe the silhouette of a palm tree, standing above the ruins of the Forum against an orange-and-magenta twilight sky. Time goes ricocheting backward at such moments, but Rome, for all its ancient majesty, isn't a city locked in the past. It's very much a city of today. For over 2 millennia it has drawn people from all over the civilized (and uncivilized) world. You, the lucky traveler, are part of a long, long tradition.

One thing to remember when you're planning your trip to Rome (or anywhere in Italy): August isn't a good month. Not just because it can get infernally hot, but because many Romans close up their shops and restaurants and head for cooler climes.

1 Rome Essentials

ARRIVING & DEPARTING

BY PLANE Rome's **Aeroporto Leonardo da Vinci** (☎ **06-65-951** or 06-6595-3640 for information), also called **Fiumicino,** handles international and domestic flights. It's about 18 miles from the city center. There's a nonstop train service between the airport and Stazione Termini, Rome's main train station. From Termini, service begins at 6:54am and runs every hour 7:22am to 9:22pm; from the airport, service begins at 7:38am and runs every hour 8:08am to 10:08pm. Tickets are 15,000L ($8), and the trip takes about 30 minutes. A taxi to central Rome from the airport costs 90,000 to 108,000L ($50 to $60) and also takes about 30 minutes, though heavy traffic can make it much longer.

Charter flights land at **Ciampino** airport (☎ **06-794-941**). To get into the city, take a COTRAL bus (departing every half an hour) to the Anagnina stop of the Metropolitana Line A, which will take you to Stazione Termini. The cost is 2,000L ($1). The entire trip should take about 45 minutes.

BY TRAIN & BUS Trains and buses arrive at **Stazione Termini,** Piazza dei Cinquecento (☎ **1478-880-881**). This is the city's major transportation hub (there's a subway stop here as well). The building has been cleaned up in recent years and offers many services, including a *cambio* (currency exchange), train information, and a tourist office. Most city buses begin their journeys at Piazza dei Cinquecento, in front of the station; you'll also find a taxi line here.

BY CAR Autostrada del Sole (A1) enters Rome from the north via Milan and Florence. A2 heads south from Rome to Naples. Both feed into the Grande Raccordo Anulare, a ring road encircling the city. Rome isn't an easy city to drive in, and a car is generally far more hassle than help.

VISITOR INFORMATION

The **Ente Provinciale per il Turismo,** the tourist office at the main train station, Stazione Termini (☎ **06-487-1270;** open daily 8:15am–7:15pm), is your best bet for maps, brochures, calendar listings, and so on. There's another tourist office at Via Parigi 5 (☎ **06-4889-9253;** Metro: Repubblica; open Mon–Fri 8:15am–7:15pm, Sat 8:15am–2:15pm).

More helful, and stocking maps and brochures, are the offices maintained by the **Commune di Roma** at 13 sights around the city. You can identify them because they have red-and-orange or yellow-and-black signs saying COMMUNE DI ROMA—PUNTI DI INFORMAZIONE TURISTICA. They're staffed daily 9am to 6pm, except the one at Termini, which is open daily 8am to 9pm. Here are the addresses and phone numbers of the best six locations: in Stazione Termini (☎ **06-4890-6300**); in Piazza Pia, near Castelo Sant'Angelo (☎ **06-6880-9707**); in Piazza San Giovanni in Laterano (☎ **06-7720-3598**); along Largo Carlo Goldoni (☎ **06-6813-6061**), near the intersection of Via del Corso and Via Condotti; on Via Nazionale, near the Palazzo delle Esposizioni (☎ **06-4782-4525**); on Largo Corrado Ricci, near the Colosseum (☎ **06-6992-4307**); and in Trastevere, on Piazza Sonnino (☎ **06-5833-3457**).

Enjoy Rome, Via Varese 39 (☎ **06-445-1843;** fax 06-445-0734; e-mail info@enjoyrom.com; www.enjoyrome.com), was begun by a young couple, Fulvia and Pierluigi, with a simple but bright idea, and it's the answer to many travelers' dreams. In their English-speaking, visitor-friendly office near the station, they dispense information on just about everything in Rome and are far more pleasant and organized than the government-run Board of Tourism. They also find hotel rooms at rock-bottom to moderate prices (hostels to three-star hotels) free of charge. Summer hours are Monday to Friday 8:30am to 7pm and Saturday 8:30am to 1:30pm; winter hours are Monday to Friday 8:30am to 1:30pm and 3:30 to 6pm.

For information on the Web, try **www.informaroma.it.**

A MAJOR GAY & LESBIAN EVENT: THE FIRST WORLD PRIDE

The first-ever ✪ **World Pride** will take place in Rome in the year 2000. This historic event, to be held from June 28 to July 9, will honor gays, lesbians, bisexuals, and transgender peoples from throughout the world and focus on international homo civil rights. A host of art exhibits, gay and lesbian performances, and cultural and political events will take place throughout the 12-day period, culminating in a mass demonstration in downtown Rome on Saturday, July 8, 2000.

Rome was selected as the site for World Pride by the International Association of Lesbian & Gay Pride Coordinators from 20 countries. If you've been thinking about a trip to Rome, this might be the most exciting incentive you'll ever have.

There's no specific phone number or Web site as yet, but **www.europride.se** is a good site for general Pride information.

CITY LAYOUT

Rome was built on seven hills on the east and west sides of the **Tiber River (Fiume Tevere).** In A.D. 271, the **Great Aurelian Wall** was constructed to protect the city (unsuccessfully, as it later turned out) from barbarian invasions. Much of this wall, with its monumental gates, remains intact, and most of what you'll want to see is contained within its perimeters.

The **Forum,** the **Colosseum,** and other principal archaeological sites from ancient Rome lie on the east side of the Tiber, most of them on or near **Via dei Fori Imperiali.** On the east side of the river you'll also find the palaces and churches of Renaissance and Baroque Rome and the city's most famous and beautiful piazzas. The entire area composes the ***centro storico*** (historic center) of Rome.

From **Piazza Venezia,** dominated by the Palazzo Venezia and the late-19th-century Vittorio Emanuele monument (known as the "wedding cake" because of its ornate tiers of glaring white Brescian marble), **Via del Corso** runs north to **Piazza del Popolo.** West of Via del Corso (called "Il Corso") lie the Pantheon, Piazza Navona, Campo dei Fiori, and the Tiber. East of it are the Spanish Steps, the Trevi Fountain, and the Borghese Gardens. **Via Nazionale,** another main artery, runs east from Piazza Venezia to **Piazza dei Cinquecento** in front of Stazione Termini.

St. Peter's Basilica, Vatican City (which includes the Vatican Museums and is a separate entity, not part of Rome), and **Castel Sant'Angelo** lie on the west side of the Tiber. So does the old Roman neighborhood of **Trastevere** (the name means "across the Tiber"), and the **Janiculum (Giancolo),** one of Rome's seven hills and a wonderful place to get a panoramic view of the city.

GETTING AROUND

Rome's public transportation system consists of buses, subways, and trams, all run by **ATAC** (Azienda Tramvie e Autobus del Commune di Roma*)*. A **one-way ticket** for any of them, good for 75 minutes and one transfer (including between systems), costs 1,500L (80¢). A booklet of **11 bus/Metro tickets** is 15,000L ($8). A **24-hour daily bus/Metro ticket** is 6,000L ($3). A **weekly bus/Metro pass** is 24,000L ($13); a **monthly pass** is 50,000L ($28). You can buy tickets at any *tabacchi* (tobacconist) or newsstand. Validate your ticket at the entry turnstiles in the Metro stations or in the validation boxes on buses. For information, contact **ATAC** at ☎ **06-4695-4444** (Mon–Sat 8am–8pm).

Walking remains the best way to see Rome, but do get a good map to help you navigate (as usual, the Falk map is best). And remember to watch out for all that traffic!

BY BUS Rome's public bus service is comprehensive, reliable, fairly easy to use, and often slow because of traffic. At peak hours, the buses can be extremely crowded—but that's part of the fun (if you don't mind personal contact). In general, buses remain the preferred mode of transportation in the center of Rome.

The major bus hub is **Piazza dei Cinquecento** in front of Stazione Termini. Rome buses are orange and have three doors; you can enter the front and rear doors but not the one in the center. Buy your ticket before you enter and validate it once on board. One important bus to know about is the **no. 64,** which leaves from Termini and goes all the way to St. Peter's; if you take it to Piazza Venezia you're within easy walking distance to the Forum and the Colosseum; from the Largo Argentina stop you can walk to Piazza Navona, the Pantheon, and Campo dei Fiori. The no. 64 is known as the "Pickpocket Express," so watch for nimble hands trying to take liberties.

BY SUBWAY The Roman subway system is called the **Metropolitana,** and its stations are marked with a red M. The stations are functional and fairly unattractive, and directions to the trains aren't always easy to decipher. There are two lines, A and B, running in roughly an X shape (the only place they intersect is Stazione Termini). Service begins at 5:30am and continues to 11:30pm. You may think the Metro is more

A Bus Warning

Any map of the Roman bus system will likely be outdated before it's printed. Many buses listed on the latest map no longer exist; others are enjoying a much-needed rest, and new buses suddenly appear without warning. There's also talk of completely renumbering the whole system soon, so be aware that the route numbers listed in this chapter may have changed by the time you travel.

convenient than the buses, but this isn't really the case, especially in the city center. The Metro has a stop at the Colosseum (Colosseo) and near the Spanish Steps (Spagna), but it doesn't otherwise penetrate the *centro storico* where many top sites are located.

BY TRAM There's a useful new tramline (no. 8) that runs from Largo Argentina to Trastevere. Service begins about 6am and continues until midnight. The older lines cover routes you'll probably not be using.

BY TAXI Licensed Roman taxis are white or yellow, have a name and an ID number, and are equipped with a taxi meter. The meter must be turned on upon departure and starts at 4,500L ($2.50, though this may be higher in 1999), and the first display lasts 9 minutes or 3 kilometers. After that it goes up 200L (11¢) every 150 meters. There's an additional charge of 5,000L ($3) for night service (10pm–7am); each piece of luggage costs 2,000L ($1).

In the city center there are taxi stands in Piazza dei Cinquecento, Piazza della Repubblica, Piazza Venezia, and Largo Argentina. To call a taxi, dial ☎ **3570,** 4994, or 88177; if you do this, the meter is turned on when the taxi picks up the call.

BY BICYCLE OR SCOOTER Rome's traffic can be ferocious and its streets difficult to maneuver, so think twice before renting bikes or scooters. You can get both at **Bici e Baci,** Via del Viminale 5 (☎ **06-482-8443;** open daily 8am–7pm), near Stazione Termini (the nearest Metro stop). You can rent scooters by the day for about 80,000L ($44) from **Scooter Center,** Via in Lucina (☎ **06-687-6455;** open daily 9am–7:30pm), near the Parliament building (Metro: Barberini). You'll need to have a valid driver's license for scooter rentals and will pay a hefty but refundable deposit.

BY CAR Save yourself a nightmare and don't drive in Rome. If you want to rent a car for excursions outside the city, **Avis** has an office in Stazione Termini (☎ **06-481-4373;** Metro: Termini); **Hertz** is near the Villa Borghese at Via Vittoria Veneto 156 (☎ **06-321-6831;** Metro: Spagna); and **Budget** is at Via Ludovisi 60 (☎ **06-482-0966;** Metro: Spagna). Of course, it's best to arrange for the rental before leaving home.

FACT FACTS: Rome

Note: The gay and lesbian organizations below are primarily set up for residents of Rome and its environs. If you call, don't automatically expect to find English speakers. The one exception is the Arci-Gay Pegaso information hot line.

AIDS Organizations **Positifs,** Viale di Valle Aurelia 111 (☎ **06-638-0365**), a group for those with HIV, has an AIDS phone line (hours vary).

American Express The Rome branch is at Piazza di Spagna 38 (☎ **06-6764-2413;** open Mon–Fri 9am–5:30pm, Sat 9am–3pm).

Community Centers The **Centro Sociale Garage,** Via Gustavo Modena 92, near Piazza Sonnino in Trastevere (no phone), holds gay meetings on Sunday and provides counseling services on Thursday 6 to 9pm. The **Coordimento Lesbiche Italiano (Cli),** Via San Francesco di Sales (☎ **06-686-4201;** Bus: 23, 30, 280; hours vary), is a separatist lesbian group with one of the largest lesbian archives in Italy; it sponsors cultural activities and publishes *La Bolletina del "Cli,"* a lesbian newsletter.

Currency Exchange There are currency exchange services in the main train station, in most banks, and at American Express.

Cybercafe You can check your e-mail or send messages at **Thenetgate,** Piazza Firenze 25 (☎ **06-689-3445;** open Mon–Sat 10:30am–12:30pm and 3:30–10:30pm in summer, daily 10:40am–8:30pm in winter).

Rome Metropolitana

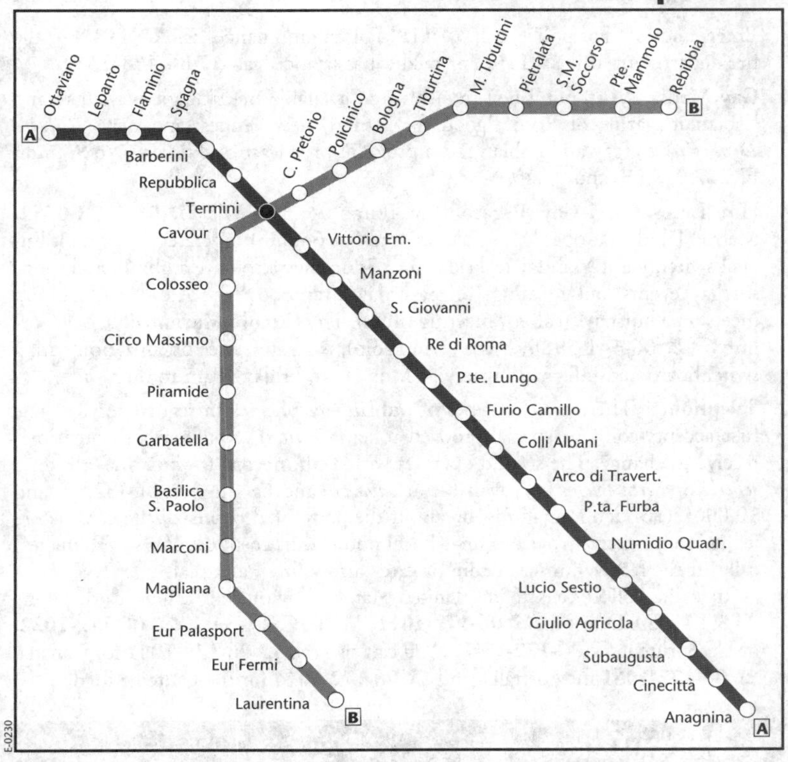

Doctors & Dentists The U.S. Embassy (below) will provide a list of English-speaking doctors and dentists. There are English-speaking doctors on duty 24 hours at the **Rome American Hospital,** Via Emilio Longoni 69 (☎ **06-22-551**). **MEDI-CALL Sr 1,** Studio Medico, Via Salaria, 300 Palazzina C interno 5 (☎ **06-844-0113;** Bus: 38, 319), is a Medical Society providing private assistance to foreigners in Rome. For 24-hour English-speaking home medical services, try **Med-Line** at ☎ **06-808-0995.**

Embassies & Consulates The **U.S. Embassy** is at Via Veneto 119A (☎ **06-46741;** Metro: Barberini; open Mon–Fri 8:30am–5:30pm). The following are open Monday to Friday about 9:30am to 12:30pm and 2 to 4pm: The **Canadian Embassy,** Via G.B. DeRossi 27 (☎ **06-445-981;** Metro: Bologna); the **U.K. Embassy,** XX Settembre 80A (☎ **06-482-5441;** Metro: Repubblica); the **Australian Embassy,** Via Alessandria 215 (☎ **06-852-721;** Bus: 36, 37); the **Irish Embassy,** Piazza Campitelli 3 (☎ **06-697-9121;** Bus: 81, 95); the **New Zealand Embassy,** Via Zara 28 (☎ **06-440-2928;** Bus 36, 37).

Country & City Codes

The **country code** for Italy is **39.** The **city code** for Rome is **06.** You must now use both digits whenever you call Rome—whether you're outside Italy, inside Italy but not within Rome, or even within Rome.

Emergencies For police, call ☎ **112.** For an ambulance, call ☎ **118.** For the fire department, call ☎ **115.** For medical assistance, call ☎ **06-488-2371.**

Gay Media ***Aut,*** published monthly and available free at bars, is the gay and lesbian magazine of Rome, good for listings, new venues, and news. ***Effetto Diversità*** is a gay and lesbian radio program broadcast on Fridays 7 to 8pm on FM 87.9, 93.3, and 93.45.

Hot Lines **Arci-Gay Pegaso,** Via Primo Acciaresi 7 (☎ **06-4173-0752;** Metro: Tiburtina; open Mon, Thurs, and Sat 6–8pm), operates a gay multilingual switchboard Monday to Friday 3 to 7pm; they also have a library and sponsor gay events and meetings on Saturday afternoons; the Arci-Lesbica group meets on Thursdays (call for meeting times). The **Circolo Mario Mieli,** Via Corinto 5 (☎ **06-541-3985;** Metro: San Paolo), is a gay service organization with a switchboard and information service Monday to Friday 10am to 6pm.

Telephone There are two types of **public pay phones** in regular service. The first accepts coins or special grooved tokens *(gettoni),* which you'll sometimes receive in change. The second operates with a **phonecard** (to buy one, ask for a *scheda* or *carta telefonica*), available at *tabacchi* and bars in 5,000L ($2.80) and 10,000L ($6) denominations; break off the perforated corner of the card before using it and insert arrow end first. Local phone calls cost 200L (11¢). To make a call, lift the receiver, insert a coin or card (arrow first), and dial.

To make collect calls to the United States, or with your calling card, phone AT&T's USA Direct at ☎ **06-172-1011,** MCI's Call USA at ☎ **06-172-1022,** or US Sprint at ☎ **06-172-18-77.** You can also call ☎ **06-172-1001** for Canada, ☎ **06-172-1061** for Australia, and ☎ **06-172-0044** for the United Kingdom.

2 Pillow Talk

Rome is a year-round destination (except maybe August), so it's important to book a hotel early. There are only a couple of hotels that could be classified as openly "gay-friendly," but it's unlikely you'll encounter any difficulties on this front unless you bring someone home at night (see the box "Queer Tips for Italian Hotels" on p.386). In some hotels, visitors must register at the front desk, which ensures they won't be spending the night for free. The city has hundreds of hotels in all categories and in every neighborhood. There are hotel-booking services in the main train station and at Enjoy Rome (see above).

NEAR STAZIONE TERMINI

The area around the train station isn't the most atmospheric part of Rome, but it's central and convenient. The following five hotels, all operated by the Bettoja family, are no more than a couple of blocks from the station, and you can expect high standards of professional service. All but one of them (the Nord) are classified as four stars, and all have purposefully retained as much as possible of their original period furnishings. I find this comforting and rather unique, but some may find the furniture and color schemes a bit glum. Each hotel offers a fairly lavish breakfast buffet.

Hotel Atlantico. Via Cavour 23, 00184 Roma. ☎ **800/223-9832** in U.S. or 06-610-556. Fax 06-610-556. 80 units. AC MINIBAR TV TEL. 370,000L ($205) double. Rates include breakfast. AE, DC, MC, V. Metro: Termini.

This 19th-century hotel was rebuilt in 1935 and renovated in the 1960s, when its lobby lost some of its art deco fixtures. It has the largest rooms of all the Bettoja hotels,

Hey, Big Spender

If you've finally come into your trust fund and want to blow a wad on a Rome hotel, there are many deluxe places that'll be more than glad to bend over backward for you. Be prepared to drop a minimum of $200 a night for a double at any of them.

The **Hotel Mediterraneo** and **Hotel d'Inghilterra,** two of the toniest, are listed in full below. Here are some o`thers where you'll feel like a princess, no matter what sex you are:

Excelsior, Via Vittorio Veneto 125, 00187 Roma (☎ **800/325-3589** in the U.S. and Canada, or 06-47-081; fax 06-482-6205; Metro: Piazza Barberini).

The Hassler, Piazza Trinità dei Monti 6, 00187 Roma (☎ **800/223-6800** in the U.S., or 06-699-340; fax 06-678-9991; e-mail hasselroma@maclink.it; Metro: Piazza di Spagna).

Hotel de la Ville Inter-Continental Roma; Via Sistina 67–69, 00187 Roma (☎ **800/327-0200** in the U.S. and Canada, or 06-67-331; fax 06-678-4213; www.interconti.com; e-mail rome@interconti.com; Metro: Piazza di Spagna or Barberini).

Hotel Eden, Via Ludovisi 49, 00187 Roma (☎ **800/225-5843** in the U.S., or 06-478-121; fax 06-482-1584; www.forte-hotels.com).

Hotel Lord Byron, Via G. de Notaris 5, 00197 Roma (☎ **06-322-0404;** fax 06-322-0405; www.italyhotel.com/roma/lord-byron; e-mail lord.byron@italyhotel.com; Metro: Flaminio).

Le Grand Hotel, Via Vittorio Emanuele Orlando 3, 00185 Roma (☎ **800/325-3589** in the U.S. and Canada, or 06-47-091; fax 06-474-7307; Metro: Piazza della Repubblica).

Mecenate Palace Hotel, Via Carlo Alberto 3, 00185 Roma (☎ **06-4470-2024;** fax 06-446-1354; www.venere.it/home/roma/mecenate/mecenate.html; e-mail mecenate@venere.it; Metro: Termini).

and they're furnished with original pieces from the 1930s and 1940s (with modern conveniences) and have marble baths. Four rooms have terraces. The Atlantico is connected to the bar/restaurant of the Hotel Mediterraneo next door (below).

Hotel Massimo d'Azeglio. Via Cavour 18, 00184 Roma. ☎ **800/223-9832** in U.S. or 06-487-0270. Fax 06-482-7386. 210 units. AC MINIBAR TV TEL. 430,000L ($239) double. Rates include breakfast. AE, DC, MC, V. Metro: Termini.

The flagship of the Bettoja chain, the Massimo d'Azeglio was built in 1878 and occupies a rather grand neoclassical building across from the Mediterraneo (below). It has been refurbished many times but in the elegant public areas retains some of its late-19th-century character. The gleaming wood-paneled lobby, halls, bar, and restaurant house a collection of Risorgimento-era paintings and prints. The guest rooms are very large and have a 1950s-ish look, with wooden desks and built-in armoires. The marble baths are particularly nice. The hotel's restaurant serves excellent Roman cuisine.

Hotel Mediterraneo. Via Cavour 15, 00184 Roma. ☎ **800/223-9832** in U.S. or 06-488-4051. Fax 06-474-4105. 270 units. AC MINIBAR TV TEL. 480,000L ($267) double; from 575,000L ($319) suite. Rates include breakfast. AE, DC, MC, V. Metro: Termini.

The 10-story Mediterraneo was built on the Esquilino, the highest of the seven hills of Rome, in 1939. It's the area's tallest building and a landmark of the period. The exterior looks a bit grim (stripped-down classicism) and functional, but the giant marble-clad lobby with its arched ceiling is a showpiece of original art deco style. All the fixtures and furnishings are original. The marble busts are from the collection of the Bettoja family, and the rooms are likewise furnished in their original 1930s and 1940s style. Some have intriguing "built-ins" like wood-frame beds with drawers and shelves for slippers. Bedside rugs were rewoven to the original patterns. On the 10th floor is a wonderful roof garden with panoramic views of Rome. The suites, with large terraces, have fabulous views as well.

Hotel Nord. Via G. Amendola 3, 00185 Roma. ☎ **800/223-9832** in U.S. or 06-488-5441. Fax 06-481-1763. 159 units. AC MINIBAR TV TEL. 300,000L ($167) double. Rates include breakfast. AE, DC, MC, V. Metro: Termini.

The Nord is the only three-star Bettoja hotel, but it's a cut above most hotels in this category and a good place to know about. It serves many government employees who aren't allowed to stay in four-star hotels but want to. The room rates are cheaper because it's less grandiose, but it still has all the amenities. The six-story hotel was renovated in 1992 and has parquet and terrazzo floors. Each room is unique; some baths are marble, others are tiled, but all have hair dryers. The windows are soundproofed, and some rooms are no-smoking. The Nord faces the new Roman Archaeological Museum and is across from the Museum of the Baths of Diocletian and the Rome Opera.

Hotel San Giorgio. Via Giovanni G. Amendola 61, 00185 Roma. ☎ **800/223-9832** in U.S. or 06-482-7341. Fax 06-488-3191. 186 units. AC MINIBAR TV TEL. 370,000L ($205) double. Rates include breakfast. AE, DC, MC, V. Metro: Termini.

The San Giorgio is next to the Massimo d'Azeglio (above) and connected to that hotel's restaurant. It opened in 1940 and still has much of its original furniture. The public rooms are light, spacious, and attractive. The guest rooms are very comfortable, old-fashioned, and quiet; you won't feel cramped in one of the singles. The doubles on the sixth floor have terraces (no additional charge).

NEAR PIAZZA DELLA REPUBBLICA

✪ **Hotel Ranieri.** Via Venti Settembre 43, 00187 Roma. ☎ **06-481-4467.** Fax 06-481-8834. 40 units. AC MINIBAR TV TEL. 200,000–260,000L ($111–$144) double. Rates include breakfast. AE, MC, V. Metro: Piazza della Repubblica.

This three-star hotel near Piazza della Repubblica, the train station, and the Rome Opera was completely renovated in 1998. It's gay-friendly without advertising the fact—maybe just plain friendly would be a better way to describe it. When it comes to fresh interiors and loads of amenities, the Ranieri wins hands down. I don't know of any other hotel in this price range that offers so much. The rooms, all with new natural wood furniture, have trouser presses, hair dryers, safes, and double-glazed windows. The singles aren't the dark dinky closets you get at some places. You might find the new ceilings and light fixtures a bit strange looking—but chalk it up to contemporary Italian design. The hotel, occupying the upper floors of a 19th-century building, is impeccably maintained and has a multilingual staff.

NEAR THE SPANISH STEPS

Hotel Alexandra. Via Vittorio Veneto 18, 00187 Roma. ☎ **06-488-1943.** Fax 06-487-1804. www.venere.it/roma/alexandra. E-mail alexandra@venere.it. 45 units. A/C MINIBAR TV TEL. 350,000L ($195) double; 430,000L ($239) triple; 470,000L ($261) suite. Rates include buffet breakfast. AE, DC, MC, V. Parking 35,000L ($19). Metro: Piazza Barberini.

This is one of your few chances to stay on Via Veneto without going broke (though it's not exactly cheap). Behind the dignified stone facade of a 19th-century mansion, the Alexandra offers immaculate rooms filled with antique furniture and modern conveniences. Rooms facing the front are exposed to the traffic of Via Veneto; those in back are quieter but with less of a view. The breakfast room is especially appealing: Inspired by an Italian garden, it was designed by noted architect Paolo Portoghesi.

Hotel Cecil. Via Francesco Crispi 55A, 00187 Roma. ☎ **06-679-7998.** Fax 06-679-7996. 41 units. AC TV TEL. 380,000L ($211) double. Rates include breakfast. AE, MC, V. Parking 25,000–30,000L ($17). Metro: Piazza Barberini.

The Cecil is close to everything, including the Trevi Fountain, Piazza di Spagna, and the train station. The 17th-century building has been a hotel for about 300 years and has played host to the likes of Casanova and Ibsen, but you won't find or feel much historic resonance today because it has been completely renovated. The well-kept rooms are large, with high ceilings and hardwood floors. They're comfortable and not unattractive, but some rooms feel a bit sparse (or streamlined, depending on your point of view) and others are on the darkish side. The baths are tile and marble. Double windows keep the sound down. The rooftop terrace boasts a panoramic view.

Hotel d'Inghilterra. Via Bocca di Leone 14, 00187 Roma. ☎ **06-69981.** Fax 06-6992-2243. 100 units. AC MINIBAR TV TEL. 506,000–594,000L ($281–$330) double; from 759,000L ($422) suite. AE, DC, MC, V. Metro: Piazza di Spagna.

The d'Inghilterra (Italian for "England") is between the fashionable shopping streets of Via Condotti and Via Borgognona, just a few minutes' walk from the Spanish Steps. A former princely guest house (it's part of the Palazzo Torlonia), it was transformed into an exclusive hotel in 1850. European nobility and artists like Liszt, Mendelssohn, and Hemingway have all stayed here. The period decor is outstanding: Every room has antique furniture, sumptuous fabrics, and rich colors. Minute care has been applied to every detail. The baths, with beautiful inlaid marble tubs, are to die for. If you want Old Roman elegance, look no further. On top of the steep room rates, you have to pay a 33,000L ($18) if you want a buffet breakfast.

Hotel Gregoriana. Via Gregoriana 18, 00187 Roma. ☎ **06-679-4269.** Fax 06-678-4258. 19 units. A/C TV TEL. 340,000L ($189) double. Rates include breakfast. No credit cards. Parking 35,000L ($19). Metro: Piazza di Spagna.

The small Gregoriana has some loyal fans, including guests from the Italian fashion industry. The matriarch of an aristocratic family left the building to an order of nuns in the 19th century, but they moved to other quarters—you might find an elevated spirituality in Room C, as it used to be a chapel. The smallish rooms provide comfort and fine Italian design. The elevator cage is a black-and-gold art deco fantasy, and the door to each room bears a reproduction of an Erté print whose fanciful characters indicate the letter designating that room.

✪ **Hotel Scalinata di Spagna.** Piazza Trinità dei Monti 17, 00187 Roma. ☎ **06-679-3006** or 06-6994-0896. Fax 06-6994-0598. 16 units. AC MINIBAR TV TEL. 200,000–450,000L ($111–$250) double. Rates include breakfast. AE, MC, V. Metro: Piazza di Spagna.

At the top of the famous Spanish Steps, close to where Mrs. Stone had her Roman spring (watch the movie *The Roman Spring of Mrs. Stone*, based on a story by Tennessee Williams, if you don't know what I'm talking about), this charming small hotel has a loyal gay following. It's certainly the best gay-friendly hotel in Rome, maybe in all Italy. It underwent a complete renovation in 1998, and the results are quite elegant. Blue and gold are the overall color scheme, with chandeliers and coffered ceilings. The

Rome Accommodations & Dining

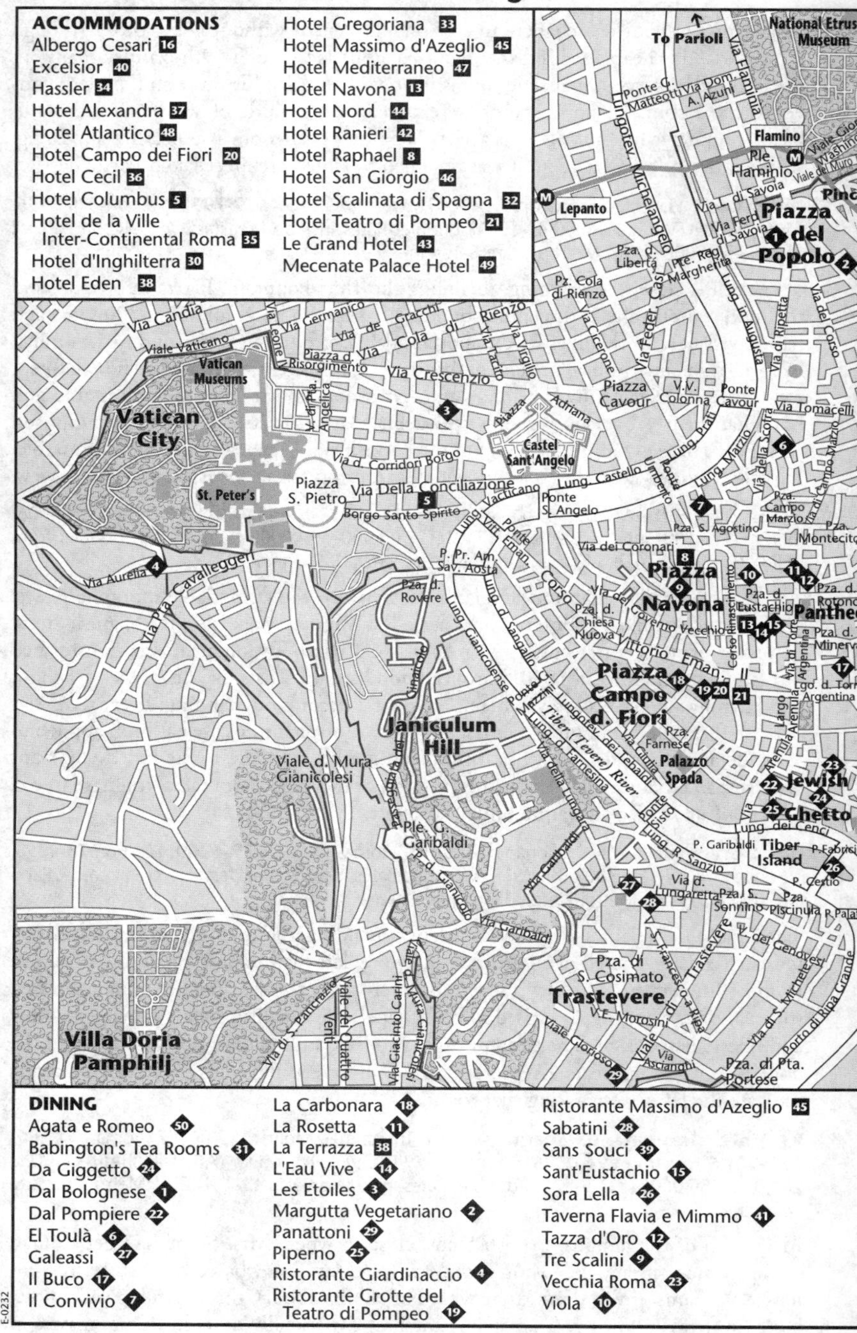
ACCOMMODATIONS
Albergo Cesari 16
Excelsior 40
Hassler 34
Hotel Alexandra 37
Hotel Atlantico 48
Hotel Campo dei Fiori 20
Hotel Cecil 36
Hotel Columbus 5
Hotel de la Ville Inter-Continental Roma 35
Hotel d'Inghilterra 30
Hotel Eden 38
Hotel Gregoriana 33
Hotel Massimo d'Azeglio 45
Hotel Mediterraneo 47
Hotel Navona 13
Hotel Nord 44
Hotel Ranieri 42
Hotel Raphael 8
Hotel San Giorgio 46
Hotel Scalinata di Spagna 32
Hotel Teatro di Pompeo 21
Le Grand Hotel 43
Mecenate Palace Hotel 49
To Parioli
National Etruscan Museum
Flamino
Lepanto
Piazza del Popolo
Vatican Museums
Vatican City
St. Peter's
Piazza S. Pietro
Via Della Conciliazione
Castel Sant'Angelo
Piazza Cavour
Piazza Navona
Pantheon
Piazza Campo d. Fiori
Palazzo Spada
Jewish Ghetto
Tiber Island
Tiber (Tevere) River
Janiculum Hill
Ple. G. Garibaldi
Trastevere
Villa Doria Pamphilj
Via Aurelia
Via Crescenzio
Via Cola di Rienzo
Via del Corso
Corso Vittorio Emanuele II
Viale Trastevere
Via Garibaldi
DINING
Agata e Romeo 50
Babington's Tea Rooms 31
Da Giggetto 24
Dal Bolognese 1
Dal Pompiere 22
El Toulà 6
Galeassi 27
Il Buco 17
Il Convivio 7
La Carbonara 18
La Rosetta 11
La Terrazza 38
L'Eau Vive 14
Les Etoiles 3
Margutta Vegetariano 2
Panattoni 29
Piperno 25
Ristorante Giardinaccio 4
Ristorante Grotte del Teatro di Pompeo 19
Ristorante Massimo d'Azeglio 45
Sabatini 28
Sans Souci 39
Sant'Eustachio 15
Sora Lella 26
Taverna Flavia e Mimmo 41
Tazza d'Oro 12
Tre Scalini 9
Vecchia Roma 23
Viola 10
E-0232

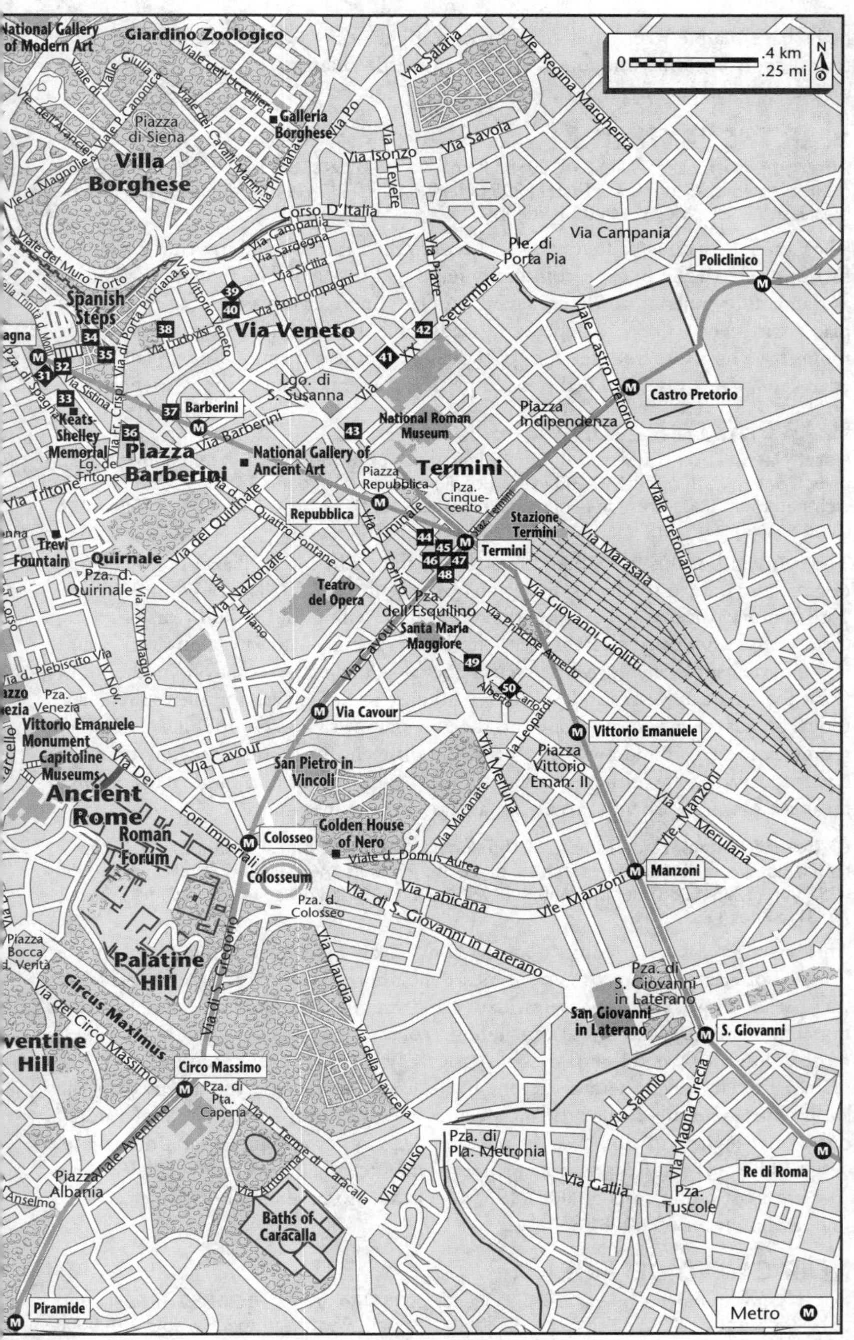
National Gallery of Modern Art
Giardino Zoologico
Galleria Borghese
Villa Borghese
Piazza di Siena
Spanish Steps
Via Veneto
Barberini
Keats-Shelley Memorial
Piazza Barberini
National Gallery of Ancient Art
National Roman Museum
Termini
Piazza Repubblica
Repubblica
Stazione Termini
Trevi Fountain
Quirinale
Pza. d. Quirinale
Teatro del Opera
Santa Maria Maggiore
Via Cavour
Vittorio Emanuele
Castro Pretorio
Policlinico
Piazza Indipendenza
Vittorio Emanuele Monument
Capitoline Museums
Ancient Rome
Roman Forum
San Pietro in Vincoli
Golden House of Nero
Colosseo
Colosseum
Palatine Hill
Circus Maximus
Aventine Hill
Circo Massimo
Baths of Caracalla
San Giovanni in Laterano
S. Giovanni
Manzoni
Re di Roma
Piramide
Piazza Vittorio Eman. II
Pza. di Pla. Metronia
Pza. Tuscole
Piazza Albania
Ple. di Porta Pia
Metro
.4 km
.25 mi
Via Salaria
Viale Regina Margherita
Via Po
Via Savoia
Via Isonzo
Corso D'Italia
Via Campania
Via Piave
Via XX Settembre
Via Boncompagni
Via Sicilia
Via Ludovisi
Via Sistina
Via Barberini
Via Tritone
Via del Quirinale
Via Nazionale
Via Milano
Via Quattro Fontane
Via Viminale
Via Torino
Via Principe Amedeo
Via Giovanni Giolitti
Via Marsala
Viale Castro Pretorio
Viale Pretoriano
Via Merulana
Via Labicana
Via di S. Giovanni in Laterano
Via Claudia
Via della Navicella
Via di S. Gregorio
Via del Circo Massimo
Viale Aventino
Via Druso
Via Gallia
Via Sannio
Via Magna Grecia
Via Manzoni
Vle. Manzoni
Via Dei Fori Imperiali
Viale d. Domus Aurea
Via Antonina
Via D. Terme di Caracalla

baths have marble walls. And though you're right next to one of the most popular tourist spots in Rome, the rooms are very quiet. Breakfast is served in your room or on the wonderful roof garden.

NEAR THE PANTHEON

Albergo Cesari. Via di Pietra 89A, 00186 Roma. ☎ **06-679-2386.** Fax 06-679-0882. E-mail cesari@venere.it. 47 units. AC TV TEL. 205,000–300,000L ($114–$167) double. Rates include breakfast. AE, DC, MC, V. Metro: Barberini.

The Cesari, on a quiet pedestrian street between the Pantheon and the Trevi Fountain, first opened in 1787 but was completely renovated in 1996. The rooms are classified as standard or superior, the latter having minibars and hair dryers. It's a pleasant little place, with wood floors, wooden bedsteads, and dramatic draperies. Some of the rooms have furniture from the turn of the century, others are more functionally modern. A roof garden is scheduled to open in 1999. Several antiques shops are nearby.

NEAR PIAZZA NAVONA

Hotel Navona. Via dei Sediari 8, 00186 Roma. ☎ **06-686-4203.** Fax 06-6880-3802. 30 units, 25 with bathroom. 150,000 ($83) double without bathroom, 160,000L ($89) double with bathroom. Rates include continental breakfast. AE, DC, MC, V. Bus: 64 from Termini to Largo Argentina.

The courtyard of this lively budget hotel near the south end of Piazza Navona is the original entrance to the Baths of Agrippa (first century B.C.). The building itself is a 15th-century palazzo, and some of the rooms have ceilings nearly 700 years old. It's a clean, simple, and very pleasant place run by an Australian-Italian family with seemingly inexhaustible energy. Most recently they've added eight rooms on another floor (which was part of Keats's and Shelley's first house in Rome); ask for one of these new rooms because they're nicely done and the only ones with air-conditioning. The other rooms (scattered around a warren of halls on different floors, some looking onto the quiet courtyard) are pleasant, high-ceilinged nooks. There's a large refectory-like breakfast room. It's essential you book at least 90 days in advance.

✪ **Hotel Raphael.** Largo Febo 2, 00186 Roma. ☎ **06-682-831.** Fax 06-687-8993. www.raphaelhotel.com. E-mail info@raphaelhotel.com. 73 units. AC MINIBAR TV TEL. 495,000–695,000L ($275–$386) double; 660,000–760,000L ($367–$422) suite. AE, DC, MC, V. Bus 70, 81, 87, or 115.

This ivy-covered hotel occupies a former convent on a secluded cobblestoned square just west of Piazza Navona. It's one of the loveliest hotels in Rome and caters to a select well-heeled crowd that appreciates luxury and fine details. The lobby is a veritable museum of antiques and fine art, including a collection of Picasso ceramics. The guest rooms, with their wood floors, are not particularly large, but they're sumptuously decorated. Roman travertine and elegant hand-decorated ceramic tile are used in the baths. There's a state-of-the-art fitness center and a Finnish sauna. The roof garden, one of the highest in Rome, looks out over the cloister of Santa Maria della Pace, designed by the great Renaissance architect Bramante, and offers an unparalleled view. The breakfast buffet costs 31,000L ($17); you can also have lunch or dinner at their fine restaurant for 60,000L ($33).

NEAR CAMPO DEI FIORI

Hotel Campo dei Fiori. Via del Biscione 6, 00186 Roma. ☎ **06-6880-6865** or 06-687-4886. Fax 06-687-6003. 27 units, 4 with shower only, 9 with bathroom; 8 apts. 140,000L ($78) double without bathroom, 160,000L ($89) double with shower only, 200,000L ($111) double with bathroom; 200,000–280,000L ($111–$156) apartment. Rates include breakfast. MC, V. Bus: 46, 62, or 64 from Termini to Museo di Roma.

The rooms at this popular budget hotel are small and rather cramped, but they're a good value for the area. Don't expect any amenities or much in the way of excess furniture. That's not to say this narrow six-story elevatorless hotel is lacking in charm. It has a frescoed front hall, some of the rooms have brick walls, and there's a very pleasant roof garden overlooking the busy outdoor market in Campo dei Fiori. If you want more space and privacy, book one of the eight apartments near the hotel. The smallest sleeps two and has a bed, kitchen, and bath; the largest has a living room as well.

✪ **Hotel Teatro di Pompeo.** Largo del Pallaro 8, 00186 Roma. ☎ **06-6872-2812** or 06-6830-0170. Fax 06-6880-5531. 12 units. AC TV TEL. 290,000L ($161) double. Rates include breakfast. AE, DC, MC, V. Metro: Termini. Bus: 46, 62, or 64.

This elegant small hotel, on a quiet little piazza close to Campo dei Fiori, resonates with history. It's built on top of the ruins of the Theater of Pompey, dating from 55 B.C. The breakfast room is actually tucked into a subterranean portion of the ancient ruins. The building itself is more than 500 years old. Third-floor rooms with sloping wooden roofs are the coziest and most atmospheric, but all the rooms are fine. They have tiled floors, a safe, and good-sized tiled baths with hair dryers. The decor throughout is contemporary. You need to book early for this little gem.

NEAR ST. PETER'S

Hotel Columbus. Via della Conciliazione 33, 00193 Roma. ☎ **06-686-5435.** Fax 06-686-4874. 92 units. MINIBAR TV TEL. 370,000L ($206) double. Rates include buffet breakfast. AE, DC, MC, V. Free parking. Bus: 62.

The Columbus was once the palatial home of the cardinal who became Pope Julius II and tormented Michelangelo into painting the Sistine Chapel. The cobbled entrance leads to a reception hall with massive furniture, then on to a series of baronial public rooms. The guest rooms are considerably simpler than the tiled and tapestried salons, done in soft beiges and furnished with comfortable modern pieces. All are spacious, but a few are enormous and still have such original details as decorated wood ceilings and frescoed walls. Only some rooms are air-conditioned, though.

3 Whet Your Appetite

Roman cuisine is simple and hearty, and—*mamma mia!*—is it ever good! I've never been the same since I first tasted *spaghetti alla carbonara.* Invented in Rome, it's pasta with a creamy egg-yolk sauce enlivened with pepper and bits of pancetta (bacon). Other specialties are *saltimbocca alla romana* (escalope of veal topped with sage leaves and prosciutto), *trippa alla romana* (tripe in a tomato sauce, sometimes with a bit of mint), *abbacchio* (baby lamb seasoned with rosemary and garlic), and *osso buco* (the Roman version has a creamy tomato-and-onion sauce).

For some really good classic Roman food, I suggest you visit one of the restaurants in the Jewish Ghetto. Here you'll find a unique appetizer called *carciofi alla guidia.* These are small artichokes boiled in olive oil and then carefully opened or smashed between hot bricks; you eat the whole things (no spines). And if you're in Rome between February and early April, be sure to try a crisp seasonal salad called *puntarelle.* It's shaved from a thick vegetable stalk, soaked in water, and served with an anchovy sauce. Regional wines worth trying include Colli Albani, Castelli Romani, Velletri, and the sweeter Frascati.

Dining out in Rome, I'm happy to report, isn't as expensive as it is in other world capitals. On the other hand, there are no specifically gay or gay-friendly restaurants where you and your inamorato/inamorata will feel comfortable holding hands. The macho-male ethic being what it is, Roman waiters might turn surly if you have a nelly attack or show overt signs of your same-sex preferences.

A Dining Note

In some restaurants you may be charged a *pane e coperto* (bread and cover charge), from 1,000 to 3,000L (60¢ to $1.75) per person. It's a charge you'll have to pay simply for the privilege of eating there. Also note that a *servizio* (tip) of 10% to 15% will often be added to your bill or included in the price, though patrons often leave an extra 1,000 to 3,000L (60¢ to $1.75) as a token.

Romans tend to eat late, especially in summer, when dinner might start at 10pm and go on well past midnight. As with all the restaurant listings in this chapter, the quoted price range starts with the least expensive *primo* (first course) and ends with the most expensive *secondo* (second or main course). This isn't representative of the cost for a full meal, which may be four or five courses. It's best to reserve at all the restaurants listed below.

Note: For the locations of the restaurants below, see the "Rome Accommodations & Dining" map on pp. 398–399.

IN THE JEWISH GHETTO

The ancient Jewish Ghetto is roughly demarcated by Via Arenula on the west, the Capitoline Hill on the east, Via della Botteghe Oscure on the north, and the Tiber on the south. Pope Paul IV ordered Rome's Jewish population to move into this area in 1556; its walls weren't torn down until 1849. It boasts dozens of restaurants, many serving traditional Roman cuisine. These are my faves.

Note: There are no Metro stops in this area. To reach the heart of the Jewish ghetto from Termini, take bus no. 64 to Largo Argentina and then walk southwest on Via Arenula and east on Via di Pianto. Make sure you have a detailed street map with you.

Da Giggetto. Via del Portico d'Ottavia 21A–22. ☎ **06-686-1105.** Reservations recommended. Main courses 12,000–26,000L ($7–$14). AE, DC. MC, V. Tues–Sun 12:30–3pm and 7:30–11pm. Closed Aug 1–15. ROMAN.

Beside the ancient Portico d'Ottavia, Giggetto is a third-generation trattoria specializing in traditional Roman cuisine. It's nonswank but well known. The lofty ceiling is hung with dried herbs, and wine bottles line the walls. As an antipasto, try the *carciofi all giudia* (whole edible artichokes boiled in olive oil) or the equally delicious *fiori di zucchini ripieni* (zucchini flowers stuffed with mozzarella and anchovies). They serve a wonderful cannelloni and fettuccine with porcinis and artichokes. For your secondo, I'd recommend the *vitello* (veal), *bauletti* (veal rolls stuffed with mushrooms, ham, and mozzarella), or *zuppa di pesce* (fish soup). Braver hearts than mine might want the various offal dishes that are an essential part of old Roman cuisine: *trippa alla romana, coratella con carciofi* (mixed offal of lamb with artichokes), and *fritto di cervello* (fried brains with mushrooms, zucchini, and artichokes).

✪ **Dal Pompiere.** Via S. Maria dei Calderari 38, 2nd floor. ☎ **06-686-8377.** Reservations essential. Main courses 16,000–20,000L ($9–$11). AE, MC, V. Mon–Sat 12:30–2:30pm and 7–11pm. ROMAN.

In an ancient building east of Via Arenula, near Piazza dei Scoie, Pompiere ("fireman") is one of my favorite restaurants in Rome. The high-ceilinged white dining rooms are decorated with Piranesi prints, old Roman street lanterns, and two stuffed stags' heads. Everything is wonderful. Pasta lovers might try the excellent *tonnarelli con carciofi* (with a creamy artichoke sauce). If you like seafood, there's fresh fish, *seppioline alla griglia* (grilled cuttlefish), and octopus in tomato sauce. Other typical Roman dishes are *polpetti in umido* (steamed meatballs) and rice balls with peas and mushrooms.

The Best Cappuccino in Rome

In my never-ending quest to find a *buonissimo* cappuccino, I've tracked down two outstanding Rome coffee bars that deserve your fully caffeinated attention.

Tazza D'Oro, Via degli Orfani (☎ **06-678-9792;** Bus: 64), is just around the corner from the Pantheon (Piazza della Rotonda). **Sant'Eustachio,** Piazza San Eustachio (☎ **06-686-1309;** Bus: 64), is a short walk south of Tazza D'Oro, between the Pantheon and Piazza Navona. As in all Italian coffee bars, you pay for your drink at the cashier first, then present the receipt to the *barrista.* If he says "Zuccherato?" that means "Do you want sugar?" (Shake your head yes or no.) Both places sell their coffee, but it would be hard to duplicate back home.

Scallopine alle Pompiere is slices of veal cooked in whisky and cream. The *saltimbocca* (ham on top of veal in a light sauce of sage and onion) and *osso buco* (beef shank with tomato-and-onion sauce) are marvelous.

Piperno. Monte de' Cenci 9. ☎ **06-6880-6629.** Reservations essential. Main courses 20,000–32,000L ($14–$18). V. Tues–Sat 12:30–2:30pm and 7–11pm, Sun 12:30–2:30pm. Closed Aug. ROMAN.

Piperno, closer to the Tiber, is a much fancier version of Da Giggetto (above). Its walls are green and frescoed, and a table loaded with luscious antipasti sits beside the front door. It too specializes in old Roman cuisine, but there's a bit more flair to the cooking, and the overall ambience is slightly overstuffed. Many of the dishes are the same as at Da Giggetto (artichokes, zucchini flowers, offal); the prices are about 25% higher. Two dishes worth trying are *farfalle in salsa di spigola* (pasta in sea-bass sauce) and *gnocchi al ragù* (in ragu sauce).

✪ **Vecchia Roma.** Piazza Campitelli. ☎ **06-686-4604.** Reservations essential. Main courses 17,000–28,000L ($9–$16). AE, DC. Thurs–Tues 1–4pm and 8pm–1am. Closed 3 weeks in Aug. ROMAN/ITALIAN.

Vecchia Roma ("Old Rome"), one of the city's best restaurants, sits on a lovely narrow Baroque square. It's swank in a nicely old-fashioned way. The four dining rooms have vaulted ceilings, stone arches, and pale walls hung with paintings. One of its most delicious specialties is *strozzapreti,* a handmade pasta with pancetta bacon, *taleggio* (a special gorgonzola), and arugula. Another handmade pasta, *stringhelli,* is served with a sauce of fresh tomatoes, basil, and pecorino cheese. There's a marvelous celery, potato, and shrimp soup and one made with beans and calamari. Any fish dish on the menu is worth trying: It may be *baccala* (dried salt cod), a fillet of scorpionfish, grilled baby calamari, or sole cooked in an earthen pot with oregano, olives, and butter. The meat specialties include veal kidneys in a sweet sauce and liver cooked in a bittersweet sauce with onions, carrots, and asparagus.

ON OR NEAR CAMPO DEI FIORI

✪ **La Carbonara.** Campo dei Fiori 23. ☎ **06-686-4783.** Reservations essential. Main courses 10,000–24,000L ($6–$13). AE, MC, V. Wed–Mon noon–2:30pm and 6:30–10:30pm. Closed 3 weeks in Aug. Bus: 64. ROMAN.

Occupying a prominent spot on the north side of Campo dei Fiori, La Carbonara is named for the famous pasta dish it claims was invented here. Even if it wasn't, I'd urge you to try it—this version is made with penne rather than spaghetti. If the weather is decent, eat out on the piazza so you can people-watch. Inside is a warren of dining rooms on two floors. Other recommended pasta dishes are tagliatinni with porcinis and ravioli with ricotta. *Abbacchio arrosto* (roast baby lamb), *cinghiale* (wild boar) in a sweet-and-sour sauce, *fegatini di pollo alla salvia* (chicken livers with sage), and *vitello alla tonne* (cold veal in a tuna-fish sauce) are all worth trying. If you're in the mood for seafood, there's usually *scampi al grati* (with cheese) and sometimes salmon and pickled mussels.

Ristorante Grotte del Teatro di Pompeo. Via del Biscione 73–74. ☎ **06-6880-3686.** Main courses 10,000–18,000L ($6–$10). AE, DC, MC. V. Tues–Sun 12:30–3pm and 7:15–11:15pm. Bus: 64. ITALIAN.

A few steps north of Campo dei Fiori, this trattoria does a thriving tourist trade in large part because of its very reasonable prices. The owner claims that Julius Caesar was assassinated on this spot (before it became a restaurant). The food is good and the menu has something that'll appeal to everyone. Pasta dishes include *fettuccine Mari e Monti* (with a sauce of seafood and mushrooms), tortellini in cream sauce, and green fettuccine with gorgonzola. The *risotto* (rice) dishes are more tempting: there's one with seafood, one with cuttlefish in their own ink, one with wild mushrooms, and one with zucchini flowers. Roast veal, lamb, and chicken come with roasted potatoes. Vegetarians can try the *melanzane alla parmigiana* (baked eggplant with mozzarella, parmesan, and tomatoes) or roasted wild mushrooms. The restaurant is attractive, with beamed ceilings, brick arches and wainscoting, and burgundy damask tablecloths.

ON OR NEAR PIAZZA NAVONA

L'Eau Vive. Via Monterone 85. ☎ **06-6880-1095.** Fixed-price menus 15,000L, 22,000L, 30,000L, and 50,000L ($8, $12, $16, and $28). AE, MC, V. Mon–Sat 12:30–2:30pm and 7:30–10:30pm. Closed Aug 1–20. Bus: 64. FRENCH/INTERNATIONAL.

Here's an unusual place that could exist only in Rome. However, remember that you're supporting the Catholic church's missionary efforts by dining here. The restaurant, run by sweet, smiling lay missionaries who wear native frocks and break into heavenly song at 10pm, is southeast of Piazza Navona (just south of Piazza Sant'Eustachio). If you can bear the treacly organ music, reminiscent of a funeral parlor, you're in for some good food. Fixed-price menus are all that's offered; they change weekly and are a good bargain. For your *primo* (depending on price) you might get carrot salad, vegetable soup, crêpes with mushrooms, or onion soup. That could be followed by hacksteak (steak that's been pounded to tender it), veal Cordon Bleu, grilled entrecôte, or fillet of duck with mushrooms and cognac. Dessert, fruit or ice cream, follows. It's camp, but the girls don't know it—and if you tell them you're gay they might start praying for your soul.

Tre Scalini. Piazza Navona 30. ☎ **06-687-9148.** Reservations essential. Main courses 18,000–32,000L ($10–$18). AE, DC, MC, V. Daily 12:15–3pm and 7–11pm. Closed Dec–Feb. Bus: 64. ROMAN.

I'm recommending Tre Scalini only if you can get a table out on Piazza Navona, on a languid evening in late spring or summer. The food is nothing to sneeze at, but it's the view of the piazza with its Baroque church, Bernini's illuminated fountain, and hundreds of milling visitors that'll linger in your memory. Also, Tre Scalini isn't quite as bitchy as the other Navona restaurants, though it serves just as many tourists. House specialties are risotto (rice) with porcinis, *spaghetti con vongole* (with clams), roast duck with prosciutto, saltimbocca, and roast lamb. If you decide to skip dinner here, at least stop in the bar for a *tartufo*—a chocolate-covered ice-cream confection so famous it's doled out like something at a Dairy Queen. Get one to go for 5,000L ($3) and take it out into the piazza; if you sit down, it costs 17,000L ($9).

Take a Gelato Break

If you're hankering for a good gelato (ice cream), head for ✪ **Giolitti,** Via Uffici del Vicario 40 (☎ **06-699-1243;** open daily 7am–2am), the city's oldest ice-cream shop. The choices include *gianduia* (chocolate hazelnut), strawberry, chocolate, coffee, and vanilla, as well as *cassata Siciliana* and *zabaglione,* a rich custard-based concoction.

Close behind is **Tre Scalini** (see full entry above), celebrated for its rich chocolate tartufo. The century-old **Palazzo del Freddo Giovanni Fassi,** Via Principe Eugenio 65–67 (☎ **06-446-4740;** open Tues–Sun noon–12:30am) whips up delectable specializes made from rice ice cream.

If you're fond of fruity, frothy frulatti (Italian frappes), head to **Pascucci,** Via Torre Argentina 20 (☎ **06-686-4816;** open Mon–Sat noon–1am), where blenders churn fresh fruit into smooth, refreshing drinks. For frozen yogurt, try **Yogofruit,** P. G. Tavani Arquati 118 (☎ **06-587-972;** open daily noon–1:30pm), just off Piazza Sonnino in Trastevere; they blend their tart frozen yogurts with fruit from the countryside.

ON OR NEAR PIAZZA DI SPAGNA & PIAZZA DEL POPOLO

Babington's Tea Rooms. Piazza di Spagna 23. ☎ **06-678-6027.** Main courses 18,000–38,000L ($10–$21); daily brunch 48,000L ($27). AE, DC, MC, V. Daily 9am–8:30pm. Metro: Spagna. ENGLISH/INTERNATIONAL.

Babington's first served the needs of all the Brits who swarmed to the Piazza di Spagna area in the 19th century; it has been in its present location, to one side of the Spanish Steps, since 1896. Quaint and overpriced, it's one of the few places open "nonstop" (as the Italians say) daily. Maybe you just want a pot of English tea and a hot buttered muffin ($12). Brunch, served at all hours, includes fresh juice, eggs Benedict, pancakes, and tea or coffee. You can also order various kinds of hamburgers, salads, egg dishes, and even Welsh rarebit or shepherd's pie.

Dal Bolognese. Piazza del Popolo 1–2. ☎ **06-361-1426.** Reservations required. Main courses 18,0000–28,000L ($10–$16); fixed-price menu 60,000L ($33). AE, V. Tues–Sun 12:30–3pm and 8:15pm–1am. Closed 20 days in Aug. Metro: Flaminio. BOLOGNESE.

Chic and often a bit haughty, Dal Bolognese is *the* restaurant on Piazza del Popolo. Sitting outside at one of the coveted see-and-be-seen sidewalk tables is the way to do it (the interior is a bit too pink and gilded for my tastes). The best dishes are derived from the Bolognese style of cooking, which favors tomato sauces. Begin with *misto de paste* (a sampling of various handmade pastas, each with a different sauce), *tortellini al ragù,* or lasagna. Veal (*vitello*) makes a good secondo, either the *cotolette alla bolognese* (topped with cheese) or the *lombatina ai ferri* (roasted). You can also get roast beef or fresh fish. Other noteworthy dishes are *polpettini* (meatballs) and *seppie con piselli* (cuttlefish with peas). Note that at press time Piazza del Popolo was under restoration and filled with scaffolding; hopefully, the job will be completed by the time you arrive.

✪ **La Terrazza.** In the Hotel Eden, Via Ludovisi 49. ☎ **06-478-121.** Reservations recommended. Main courses 42,000–72,000L ($23–$40); fixed-price menu 120,000L ($67). AE, DC, MC, V. Daily 12:30–2:30pm and 7:30–10:30pm. Metro: Barberini. Metro: Spagna. ITALIAN/INTERNATIONAL.

This restaurant serves distinctive international (as opposed to Roman) cuisine and provides a sweeping view over St. Peter's from the fifth floor of the Eden. The service manages to be formal and flawless yet not intimidating. The seasonally changing menu might include a warm salad of grilled vegetables lightly toasted with greens in balsamic vinegar, red tortelli (whose pink coloring comes from tomato mousse) stuffed with mascarpone and drizzled with lemon, or grilled tagliata of beef with eggplant and tomatoes.

✪ **Margutta Vegetariano.** Via Margutta 118. ☎ **06-3265-0577.** Reservations recommended. Main courses 10,000–16,000L ($6–$9); tasting menu 40,000L ($22); tourist menu 20,000L ($11). AE, DC, MC, V. Daily noon–midnight. Closed 2 weeks in Aug. Metro: Flaminio. VEGETARIAN.

When it first opened in 1980, Margutta was the only vegetarian restaurant in Rome. It's grown steadily and has been in its new expanded location for 2 years. The interior is lovely: light and airy, with big windows and constantly changing artwork on the walls. The menu uses Italian pastas and produce in delicious new ways. Recommended first courses are the *acquacotta alla Toscana* (Tuscan-style soup), risotto with pumpkin and almonds, and tagliatelline with mushrooms. A characteristic Roman dish is potato gnocchi, here served with a vegetable ragù. For your meatless second, try the stuffed artichokes or the vegetable torte with broccoli and smoked provola cheese. There's a wonderful selection of fresh salads. Desserts include crème brûlée, chocolate hazelnut mousse, lemon cream cup with fruit, and ice cream. This is a very pleasant spot with excellent food and reasonable prices.

NEAR STAZIONE TERMINI

Ristorante Massimo d'Azeglio. In the Hotel Massimo d'Azeglio, Via Cavour 14. ☎ **06-481-4101.** Main courses 14,000–40,000L ($8–$22); fixed-price menu 45,000L ($25). AE, DC, MC, V. Mon–Sat 12:30–3pm and 7–11:30pm. Metro: Termini. ROMAN/ITALIAN.

Just a block from the train station, the Massimo d'Azeglio hotel and its restaurant were founded in 1875. Both have very high standards of service. The cooking is a bit too upscale to be called rustic, but there are many old Roman and Italian standards on the menu. The fixed-price daily menu (*menu del giorno*) is a tasty bargain. It might start with *spaghetti alla tarantina* (with seafood), *sedanini* pasta with prosciutto and peas, or Milanese-style minestrone soup. After that may come loin medallions flavored with juniper and wine or beef carpaccio with celery and Parmesan, both served with seasonal vegetables. The restaurant serves very good fish dishes (skewered prawns, sole, swordfish steak), and the daily specials are always worth trying. Fresh fruit or cheese and coffee round out the meal.

Taverna Flavia e Mimmo. Via Flavia 9. ☎ **06-474-5214.** Reservations recommended. Main courses 16,000–45,000L ($9–$25). AE, DC, MC, V. Mon–Fri 12:30–3pm and 7:30–11pm, Sat 7–11pm. Metro: Barberini. ROMAN/ITALIAN.

It's a bit out of the main tourist circuit and not as chic as it was once was, but the Taverna Flavia e Mimmo is still a good place to eat. North of Piazza della Repubblica and a block west of Via XX Settembre, it's a fancyish pink-tablecloth place known for its special porcini and truffle dishes. Anything with precious truffles is going to be expensive. The "Verushka" (remember her?) salad, for instance, consists of lettuce, cheese, and truffles. There's also a fettuccine with truffles (or with porcinis). Risotto with crayfish or four cheeses is worth trying. Regional dishes include a recommendable *abbacchio* (lamb) with potatoes, *saltimbocca alla romana, osso buco* with peas, and a good fillet with porcinis. You can get grilled meat dishes as well as fresh fish.

NEAR THE PANTHEON

Il Buco. Via San Ignazio 8. ☎ **06-679-3298.** Reservations recommended. Main courses 11,000–25,000L ($6–$14); tourist menu 35,000L ($19). AE, DC, MC, V. Tues–Sun 12:30–3:30pm and 7–11pm. Bus: 64. TUSCAN.

Il Buco, east of the Pantheon and just off Piazza del Collegio Romano, is a fairly upscale restaurant with a red-and-white tile floor, ivory walls, and a barrel-vaulted ceiling. It's been around for a long time and remains a highly reliable place for a good meal. It specializes in Tuscan cuisine and, like the Taverna Flavia e Mimmo (above), dishes using truffles and porcinis. If you didn't get a chance to sample *bistecca alla fiorentina* or *ribollita*, the Tuscan bread soup, you can try them here. The ravioli with nut sauce and pappardelle with rabbit sauce are both worthy of your attention. Il Buco also serves seasonal game dishes like wild boar with chocolate, partridge, guinea fowl with artichokes, and rabbit with truffles.

Viola. Via della Maddalena 16–18. ☎ **06-6880-2067.** Main courses 7,000–12,000L ($4–$7). AE, MC, V. Wed–Mon 6:30pm–1am. Bus: 64. BAR/PIZZERIA/ITALIAN.

Viola is one tourist trap you can really enjoy. Just north of the Pantheon, it has lots of tables set out alongside a narrow pedestrian street that's wonderful for people-watching (Romans as well as tourists). Since it's also a bar, it's open early for coffee and pastries. I'd recommend it for a late lunch after you've exhausted yourself looking at the sights. The prices are extremely reasonable and the food is good. I like the crackly-crust pizzas, especially the capricciosa with tomatoes, mozzarella, mushrooms, artichokes, and ham. Others are topped with beans, sausage, tomatoes, and mozzarella cheese, calamari, tuna fish, corn, and salmon. You can also get a respectable plate of spaghetti—carbonara, one topped with cheese and peppers, or one with clams, tomatoes, and basil.

ON THE ISOLA TIBERINA

✪ **Sora Lella.** Via Ponte Quattro Capi 16. ☎ **06-686-1601.** Reservations recommended. Main courses 15,000–26,000L ($8–$14). AE, MC, V. Tues–Sat noon–2:30pm and 7:30–11pm, Sun noon–2:30pm. Closed Aug. Tram: 8 from Largo Argentina to Piazza Belli. ROMAN.

The Isola Tiberina is a tiny island in the Tiber between Trastevere and the Jewish Ghetto. In ancient times, it was the site of a healing temple dedicated to Aesclepius. This old-fashioned small trattoria, the only restaurant on the island, has been around since 1943 and serves wonderful Roman cuisine. Start with *tonnarelli,* a pasta with a sauce of sausage, walnuts, egg, and cream, or *gnocchi all'Amatriciana* (with a tomato, bacon, and Roman cheese sauce). Recommended meat dishes are beef fillet in a green pepper, cream, and brandy sauce; and lamb in a creamy lemon, egg, parmesan, and parsley sauce. A typical Roman dish is tripe with tomato and cheese. They make a wonderful fish stew with mussels and clams and have an unusual squid casserole with artichoke sauce. If *puntarelle* is available, do try it as your salad course (after the main course).

IN TRASTEVERE

Trastevere is the old Roman working-class quarter across the Tiber. It has been "discovered" and gentrified in recent years, but it's still a great place to go for dinner, especially on a warm summer evening when young Romans play soccer in front of the church of Santa Maria and tables are set out on the streets and piazzas.

The new no. 8 tramline at Largo Argentina will take you across the Garibaldi Bridge to Piazza Belli (the first stop across the Tiber); from there, walk west on narrow Via della Lungaretta to Piazza Santa Maria in Trastevere, where all these restaurants are found.

Gay-Friendly in Trastevere

Panattoni, Viale Trastevere 53 (☎ **06-580-0919;** open Thurs–Tues 6pm–midnight), is a no-frills pizzeria frequented by gays and lesbians.

Galeassi. Piazza Santa Maria in Trastevere 3. ☎ **06-580-9898.** Reservations recommended. Main courses 14,000–30,000L ($8–$17). AE, MC, V. Tues–Sun 12:30–2:30pm and 7:30–11pm. ROMAN.

I once watched Gore Vidal picking his teeth (maybe they were dentures) after a plateful of Galeassi's *spaghetti alla carbonara,* and that image always comes back to me when I dine here. This is one of two famous restaurants on Piazza Santa Maria in Trastevere, and if you eat outdoors at either one of them you can look up at the floodlit church with its ancient golden mosaics. The menu at Galeassi is geared to all the popular Roman dishes. If you don't want carbonara, try spaghetti with clams or with tomatoes, mussels, and tuna. They also serve penne with salmon, rigatoni with tomato-and-bacon sauce, and risotto with creamy shrimp sauce. Classic specialties are *saltimbocca* (escalopes with ham, mushrooms, and sage), *scaloppine al marsala,* chicken with tomato sauce and peppers, *osso buco,* turkey fillet, and eggplant parmigiana. Roast chicken and lamb, grilled steak, and veal with tuna-fish sauce are also available. A strolling guitar player sometimes serenades diners—but if you're part of a same-sex couple he may avoid you.

Sabatini. Piazza Santa Maria in Trastevere 13. ☎ **06-581-2026.** Reservations recommended. Main courses 20,000–42,000L ($11–$23). AE, DC, MC, V. Daily noon–3pm and 8pm–midnight. Closed 2 weeks in Aug. ROMAN/SEAFOOD.

Sabatini is the other famous restaurant on Piazza Santa Maria in Trastevere; it's more prominent than Galeassi (above) and generally so crowded you have to wait for a table even if you've called ahead to reserve. The menu features some of the same dishes found at Galeassi but with more emphasis on seafood. I can recommend any of the fresh fish dishes, but they're the most expensive items on the menu.

NEAR ST. PETER'S

Ristorante Giardinaccio. Via Aurelia 53. ☎ **06-631-367.** Main courses 12,000–20,000L ($7–$11). AE, DC, MC, V. Wed–Mon 12:15–3:30pm and 7:15–11pm. Bus: 60. ITALIAN/MOLISIAN/PIZZERIA.

If you're in the vicinity of St. Peter's, this is a good spot for lunch, attracting a lot of families and tourist groups. This rustic-looking place has low ceilings, wood walls, and dining rooms on two levels and is unusual because it specializes in dishes from Molisia, a region in southeastern Italy. This isn't a stylish cuisine but more like peasant food, but when done right it's awfully tasty. So if grilled goat, quail, or mutton goulash sounds appealing, try it. The pastas are great too, particularly the taglialini with asparagus, ravioli with ricotta and spinach, and tacconelle with lamb sauce. Plus, they serve over a dozen kinds of pizza.

4 Exploring Rome

There's so much to see it can be a bit overwhelming, especially if you're in Rome for only a couple of days. Allow a full day to visit St. Peter's, the Vatican Museums, and Castel Sant'Angelo, all on the west side of the Tiber. It's a good idea to go to the Vatican Museums first and get there early. On my last visit, it took an hour to get to the door and another hour to reach the restored Sistine Chapel. You can easily spend another day exploring ancient Rome—the Forum, the Palatine Hill, and the Colosseum—and the adjacent Capitoline Museums.

I'd highly recommend taking a morning or an afternoon to visit the newly reopened and overwhelmingly beautiful Galleria Borghese in the Villa Borghese park, but you must make a reservation to get in. Piazza Navona, the Pantheon, the Spanish Steps, and Piazza del Popolo could all be part of another partial-day itinerary. The one place you *don't* have to visit is Via Veneto. Many visitors think this boulevard, made famous by Fellini's film *La Dolce Vita,* still retains its cafe-life glamour. It doesn't.

If you're really pushed for time, you can hit the highlights with a guided bus tour—but doing so you won't get a feel for Rome, only for other tourists. **American Express** (**☎ 06-6764-2413**) offers English-language bus tours (see "Fast Facts: Rome" above), as does **Green Line Tours,** Via Farini 5A (**☎ 06-482-7480**). The public bus company offers a 2-hour **City Bus Tour** on bus no. 110 Monday to Saturday at 3:30pm (autumn/winter at 2:30pm), with departures from the ATAC information office at Piazza dei Cinquecento (in front of Stazione Termini); there's no guide, and the cost is 15,000L ($8).

If you want an official tourist guide to show you around, contact the **Sindacato Nazionale delle Guide Turistiche,** Via Santa Maria alle Fornaci 80 (**☎ 06-639-0409;** open Mon–Fri 9am–2pm, Sat 9am–noon).

THE HITS YOU SHOULDN'T MISS

The Frommer's star system for highlighting truly must-see sights just doesn't work in Rome. All the sights I've listed can be considered starred attractions.

St. Peter's Basilica (Basilica di San Pietro). Piazza San Pietro. Basilica free; treasury 5,000L ($3); dome 6,000L ($3). Daily 7am–7pm. Metro: Ottaviano–S. Pietro.

We all know what the Catholic church thinks of gays and lesbians, but don't let that deter you from visiting St. Peter's (or any other Roman church). After all, one of the greatest gay artists of all time—Michelangelo, of course—designed the majestic dome rising 375 feet above the headquarters of the Roman Catholic Church. St. Peter's Basilica is a gargantuan structure that stands in St. Peter's Square at the end of an elliptical colonnade designed by Bernini. An ancient Egyptian obelisk rises from the center of the square, where crowds of up to 300,000 sometimes gather to receive the blessing of the Pope (called "Papa" in Italy). The present basilica, a remarkably dignified High Renaissance structure with Baroque flourishes, was constructed over a much earlier basilica that was purportedly built over the tomb of the crucified St. Peter. The cavernous interior, as big as two football fields, is a marvel of marble, gilt, and mosaic work. In the first chapel to your right, Michelangelo's *Pietà,* created when he was still in his 20s, stands behind a wall of reinforced glass—a sad reminder of the lunatic who attacked the sculpture in the 1970s. If you're devout and aren't worried about germs, you may kiss the toe of the 13th-century bronze statue of St. Peter at the far end of the nave. Directly beneath Michelangelo's dome, resting on the papal altar,

The Socius Urbus Card

At press time I'd just gotten word that a new Rome museum pass, the **Socius Urbus Card,** was about to be instituted. It costs 25,000L ($14) and is good for the Capitoline Museums and several of the less-visited museums and archaeological sites in Rome. Alas, there was no specific information on where to obtain the pass, so check with the tourist office when you arrive.

A St. Peter's Fashion Alert

A dress code for men and women prohibiting shorts, bare arms and shoulders, and skirts above the knee is strictly enforced at all times in the basilica. You *will* be turned away. You also must remain silent and cannot take photographs.

is a curious Baroque structure called the *baldaicchino,* designed by Bernini. Unless you're terrifically interested in reliquaries, chalices, and papal vestments, skip the treasury and instead take the elevator up to the dome. Here you can look down into the basilica and walk outside for a superlative view of the Eternal City.

Vatican Museums and Sistine Chapel (Musei Vaticani and Cappella Sistina). Viale del Vaticano. ☎ **06-6988-3333.** Admission 15,000L ($8). Free the last Sun of every month (8:45am–1:45pm). Nov–Mar 14 Mon–Fri 8:45am–1:45pm; Mar 16–Oct 8:45am–4:45pm, Sat 8:45am–1:45pm. Closed Jan 1–6, Feb 11, Mar 19, Apr 13, May 1 and 29, June 29, Aug 15, Dec 25–26. Metro: Ottaviano. Bus: 64.

It's impossible to give you an adequate rundown of the countless treasures amassed by the Vatican and displayed in its vast museums (there are 4½ miles of corridors). The magnificent collections span the centuries and include masterpieces of Egyptian, Etruscan, Roman, Renaissance, and Baroque art, as well as later works by Canova, Dalí, and Chagall. Keep in mind that the earlier you arrive, the faster you'll get in, that there are an enormous number of galleries, and that the crowds can be suffocatingly dense. Four **color-coded itineraries** (A, B, C, D) allow you to choose what you'll see based on your interests and the amount of time you have (from 1½ to 5 hours). Some of the lavishly decorated rooms you pass through from one gallery to the next were actually once papal apartments.

There are some fascinating pieces in the **Etruscan-Gregorian Museum,** including the Regolini-Galassi tomb from Cerveteri and the *Mars of Todi*, a 5th-century-B.C. bronze. You'll probably want to linger longer in the **Pio Clementino Museum,** for it contains masterpieces of Greek and Roman sculpture. The abs and pecs on the 1st-century-B.C. Greek *Belvedere Torso* are admirable, and the famous *Apollo of Belvedere* is a classic figure of male beauty. The giant statue of Antinous, the emperor Hadrian's deified lover, is a marvel. Eventually, on your crowded, complicated way to the Sistine Chapel, you come to the **Raphael Rooms,** the rooms of Julius II decorated by the great painter Raphael between 1508 and 1524. Raphael's glorious painting of *The School of Athens* is in the next room.

Finally, after many turnings and twistings, you come to the magnificent **Sistine Chapel.** No paltry words of mine can describe the overwhelming genius apparent in

A Vatican Tip

On the left side of the piazza is the **Vatican Tourist Office** (☎ **06-6988-4466;** open Mon–Sat 8:30am–7pm). It sells maps and guides that'll help you make more sense of the incredible riches you'll be seeing in the museums, accepts reservations for tours of the Vatican Gardens, and tries to answer any questions you might have.

A **shuttle bus** leaves from in front of this office for the entrance to the Vatican Museums daily every 30 minutes 8:45am to 1:45pm in summer and 8:45am to 12:45pm in winter; the fare is 2,000L ($1.20). (Take it: It's a long and generally uninteresting walk to the museum entrance; from the bus's route you'll pass through some of the Vatican's' lovely gardens.)

Vatican City

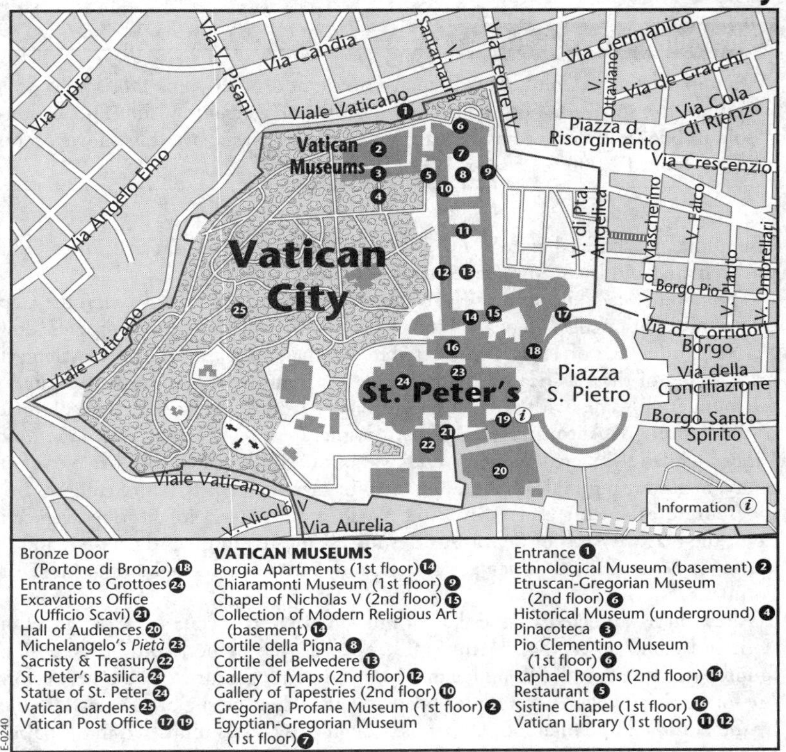

Michelangelo's ceiling frescoes depicting the stories of Genesis and the Expulsion from the Garden of Eden, which he labored over for 4 years, ruining his eyesight in the process. Or his enormous wall painting of the *Last Judgment*, painted when he was in his 60s. Recently cleaned, the paintings glow with intense life and color. To best appreciate these masterpieces, be sure to bring along binoculars.

The secluded **Vatican Gardens** are 58 acres of beauty, but you can visit them only on a guided tour arranged by the Vatican Tourist Office (see above). You have to reserve far in advance (no phone reservations accepted). Tours are limited to 33 people at a time, cost 18,000L ($10), and take place Monday to Tuesday and Thursday to Saturday at 10am.

Roman Forum (Foro Romano) and Palatine Hill (Palatino). Largo Romolo e Remo, entrance from Piazza del Colosseo. ☎ **06-699-0110.** Forum free; Palatine Hill 12,000L ($7). Daily 9am–an hour before sunset. Metro: Colosseo.

As you walk along the paving stones of the **Via Sacra (Sacred Road)** into the Roman Forum, you're entering the very heart of ancient Rome. It may be difficult to reconstruct in your mind's eye all the dazzling temples and civic structures that once stood in this nucleus of Roman power. Only fragments remain to give you an idea of what it looked like, so you have to use your imagination. Think of it as incredibly busy. Religious and civic functions (one and the same) took place here, business was transacted, emperors and senators orated to the crowds, vendors sold their wares, whores plied their trade, and centurions patrolled. Roman triumphs—with chained captives and plundered loot—made their way past pagan temples served by priests and priestesses.

The Ruins Before & After

To appreciate the Colosseum, Roman Forum, and other ruins more fully, buy a copy of the small red book called ***Rome Past and Present*** (Vision Publications), sold in bookstores or on stands near the Forum. Its plastic overleafs show you how things looked 2,000 years ago.

The smoke of sacrificed animals filled the air. It was in the Forum that Julius Caesar was cremated and Marc Antony delivered his funeral speech.

The Forum was built up over the centuries in the marshy land between the Capitoline and Palatine hills. Here are some of the highlights you'll see you progress down Via Sacra: the **Arch of Titus,** constructed to commemorate the sack of Jerusalem; the brick arches of the **Basilica of Constantine;** the **Temple of Romulus,** dedicated to the founder of Rome (with original doors from A.D. 306); the freestanding colonnade of the **Temple of Antoninus and Faustina;** the **Temple of Vesta,** where the Vestal Virgins tended the sacred flame (a Vestal was put to death if she broke her vow of virginity; men were put to death if they entered the sacred precincts); three columns from the **Temple of Castor and Pollux;** the **Basilica Julia,** used for hearing civil court cases; the massive **Arch of Septimius Severus,** dedicated in the 3rd century; and the **Curia,** or Senate House, which is really the only intact ancient building in the entire Forum.

After you've wandered around the Forum, you can retrace your steps, pay an admission, and climb up to the **Palatine Hill.** The Palatino is the traditional site of the founding of Rome under Romulus in 753 B.C. In later centuries it became a favored site for patrician villas (Cicero lived here) and after that the site of royal palaces built by some of the more infamous emperors: Caligula (who was murdered in his palace), Nero, Tiberius, and Domitian. The most interesting sights to visit are the **Hippodrome,** where private games were held for the imperial family; the **House of Livia** (scheming grandmother of Claudius), with its beautiful blue frescoes; and the **Farnese Gardens,** which look out over the Forum below.

Colosseum (Colosseo) and Imperial Forums (Fori Imperiale). Piazza del Colosseo, Via dei Fori Imperiale. ☎ **06-700-4261.** Admission to Colosseum 10,000L ($6). Summer daily 9am–7:30pm (winter to 5pm). Metro: Colosseo.

The ancient Romans loved their circuses, but the emperors were hardly Shriners when it came to devising public entertainments. In the Colosseum, built in A.D. 72, 50,000 spectators could watch horse races, mock sea battles, wild animal fights, and gladiators hacking one another to death. Of course, we all know from the movies (*Quo Vadis?* and the like) how the early Christian martyrs were fed to the lions. Some historians now dispute this, but given the blood-thirst of the crowds and the emperors it doesn't seem unlikely. So, although the Colosseum is the symbol of Rome and one of the greatest architectural monuments from ancient times, it's not exactly a place brimming over with good karma. Originally the four-tiered elliptical-shaped amphitheater had a retractable saillike roof so the Romans could watch their gory spectacles without the sun glaring in their eyes. The Colosseum is now a shell, the marble adorning its facade stripped away long ago and put to other uses. It's always a thrill to see it (especially when it's lit up at night), and lately two hunks dressed as ancient Roman centurions (helmets, skirts, and sandals) have been posted on photo-op duty near the entrance.

Next to the Colosseum is another famous Roman monument, the **Arch of Constantine,** erected in A.D. 315 to honor the defeat of the pagan Maxentius by Constantine (the first Christian emperor). For years it was hidden by scaffolding, but you

Jumpin' for the Jubilee

The year 2000 will not be just another year in Rome or merely the start of a new millennium. It'll be a **Papal Jubilee Year,** and that means all heaven's gonna break loose across the city. In A.D. 1300, Pope Boniface VIII first adapted the Holy Year from a Judaic tradition, declaring a Papal Jubilee, a year during which pilgrims could come to Rome and make the rounds of all four great basilicas—San Giovanni in Laterano, Santa Maria Maggiore, San Paolo Fuori le Mura, and St. Peter's—*and* receive a plenary indulgence (the Superbowl of going to confession).

Estimates are that over 29 million visitors will clog Rome in 2000, entailing an additional 2,000 tour buses and 400,000 cars daily. And I'm sure that doesn't include the thousands of queers coming over for the first **World Pride** in summer! (I hear the pope is so thrilled with the World Pride event he's opening at the Vatican a cafe called the Sissy Chapel.) Expect monuments and museums to stay open longer, lines to take forever, crowds to be thicker than you'd ever imagined, prices to soar, tempers to be short, and spirits to be high.

For details, you can check the Web at **www.romagiubileo.it,** visit the information stand planned to go up on Via San Pietro in Carcere (off Via dei Fori Imperiali), or contact the **Comitato Centrale del Grande Giubileo del 2000** at Borgo Sant'Angelo 23, 00193 Roma (☎ **06-6988-1561;** fax 06-6988-2181), for a list of events in English.

can now see the intricate well-preserved carvings and bas-reliefs. The entrance to the Roman Forum is in Piazza del Colosseo, to one side of Constantine's Arch.

If you cross Via dei Fori Imperiali and walk northwest along it, then cut off onto Via Alessandrina, you'll past some massive brick ruins. These are the **Imperial Forums.** The first one you pass is the **Forum of Augustus,** with the remains of a monumental wall and temple. Continue on and you'll come to the more-interesting **Forum of Trajan.** When it was built at the beginning of the 2nd century, Trajan's Forum was considered one of the wonders of the classical world. It had a temple and libraries and was a commercial marketplace. The only part of it that gives some idea of its former grandeur is **Trajana's Column (Colonno Traiano),** carved from bottom to top with an intricate series of bas-reliefs showing highlights of the emperor's military career.

Capitoline Museums (Musei Capitolini). Piazza del Campidoglio. ☎ **06-6710-2071.** Tues–Sat 9am–7pm (Sun to 1:30pm). Admission 10,000L ($6). Bus: 64 to Piazza Venezia.

On the Capitoline hill, adjacent to the Forum and Palatine Hill, is the beautiful **Campidoglio,** an elliptical piazza designed by Michelangelo in 1536 for the reception of the Holy Roman Emperor Charles V. In the piazza's center is the most famous equestrian bronze of the ancient world, the **statue of Marcus Aurelius.**

Flanking the statue are the Caitoline Museums: the **Museo Capitolino** and the **Palazzo dei Conservatori,** two 17th-century structures constructed according to plans by Michelangelo and housing the greatest collections of classical sculpture in the world. To the rear of the piazza is the **Palazzo del Senatore.** Michelangelo designed the piazza and the golden-hued palaces as a theatrical setting for Renaissance pomp and ceremony, and after several years of restoration the Campidoglio is once again one of the most breathtaking sites. It's wonderful to see it for the first time at night, when the whole is brilliantly illuminated.

Rome Attractions

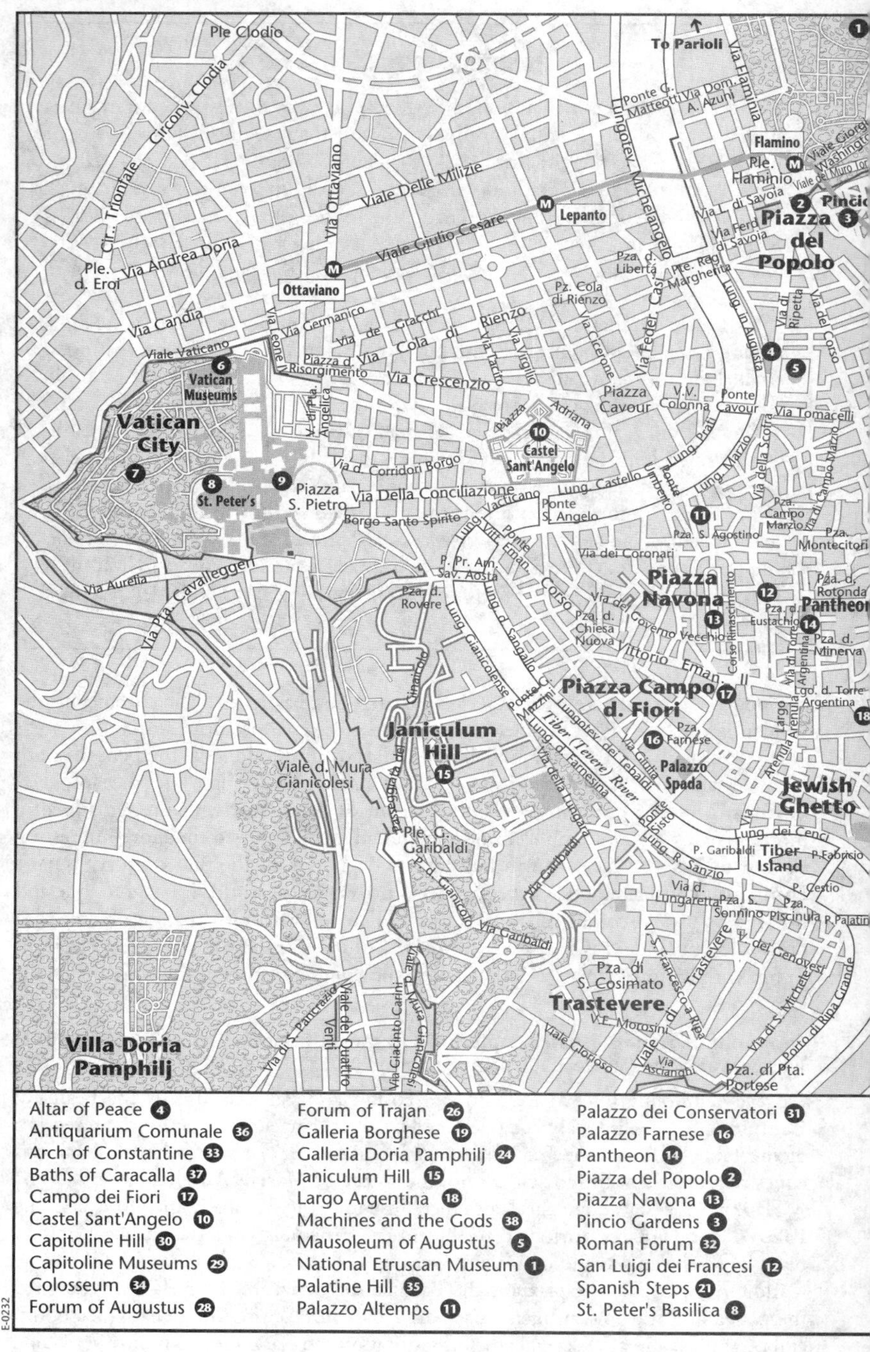

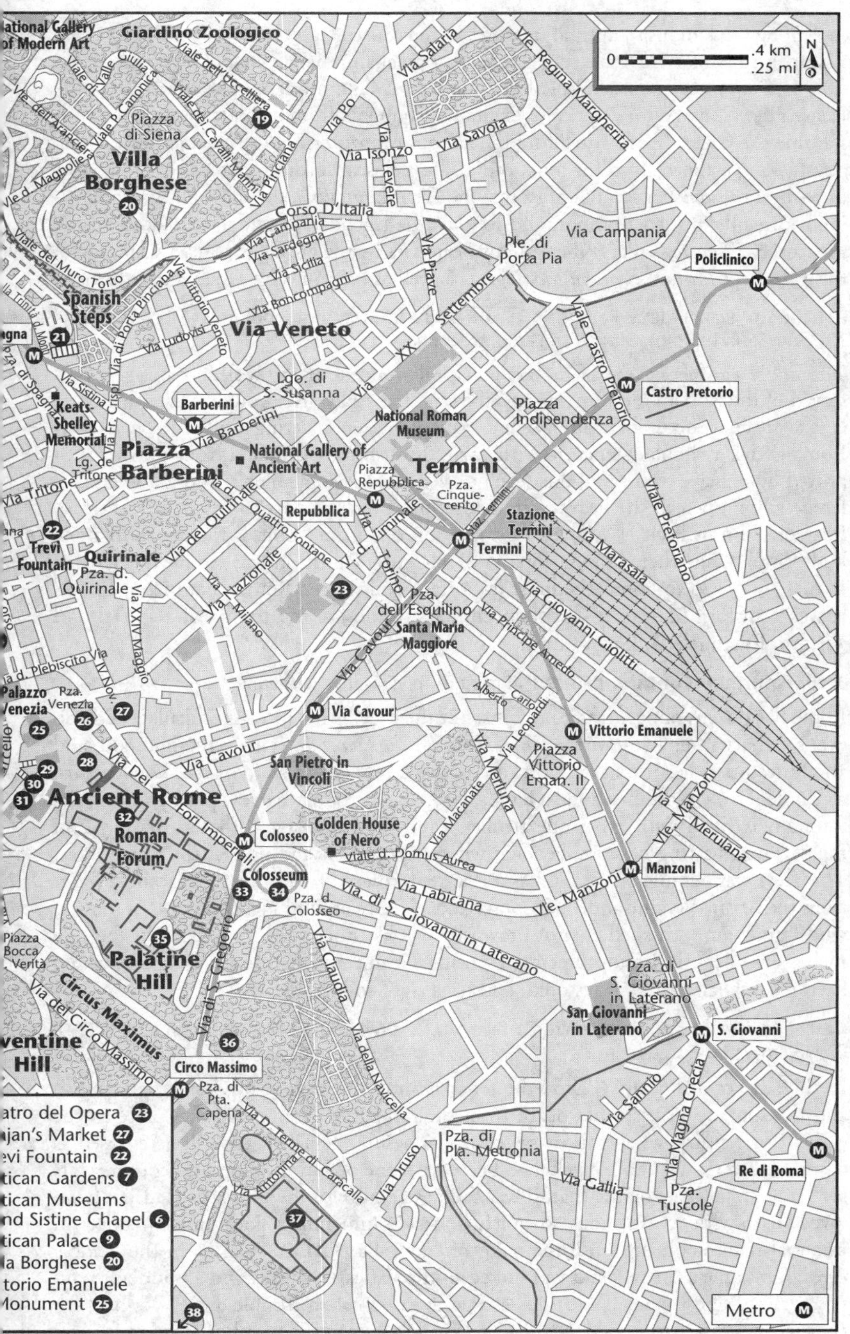
Giardino Zoologico
Villa Borghese
Spanish Steps
Via Veneto
Keats-Shelley Memorial
Piazza Barberini
National Gallery of Ancient Art
National Roman Museum
Termini
Stazione Termini
Trevi Fountain
Quirinale
Santa Maria Maggiore
Via Cavour
Vittorio Emanuele
San Pietro in Vincoli
Ancient Rome
Roman Forum
Golden House of Nero
Colosseo
Colosseum
Palatine Hill
Circus Maximus
Circo Massimo
San Giovanni in Laterano
Manzoni
S. Giovanni
Re di Roma
Policlinico
Castro Pretorio
Barberini
Repubblica
Metro

Among the famous sculptural treasures in the Museo Capitolino are the *Dying Gaul*, a Roman copy of a 3rd-century-B.C. Greek original and the *Capitoline Venus*, the classical world's quintessential symbol of feminine beauty and modesty. The courtyard of the Palazzo dei Conservatori, opposite, contains fragments from a colossal statue of Constantine the Great. Inside you'll find the famous bronze *Lo Spinario*, depicting a young boy picking a thorn from his foot, and a rare Etruscan bronze that has over the centuries become another symbol of Rome, the *Lupa Capitolina*, the she-wolf that, according to legend, suckled Romulus and Remus, the legendary founders of Rome. In the Pinacoteca (Picture Gallery) there are two canvases by the great gay painter Caravaggio, the *Fortune-Teller* and *St. John the Baptist*, as well as paintings by Titian and Rubens.

Pantheon. Piazza della Rotonda. ☎ **06-6830-0230.** Admission free. Mon–Sat 9am–12:30pm (Sun to 1pm). Bus: 64 to Largo Argentina.

The noble Pantheon, one of the architectural wonders of the world, is the best preserved of the Roman monuments and the one that really gives you an accurate picture of the scale, structural ingenuity, and remarkable engineering skills of the ancient Romans. It's a circular structure with two 20-ton bronze doors, a front portico supported by massive stone columns (each carved from a single block) and a domed coffered ceiling open to the heavens. The inscription on the portico reads "M. Agrippa. L.F.Cos. Terium Fecit" ("Marcus Agrippa, son of Lucius, Consul for the third time, built this"). Constructed by Agrippa in 27 B.C., the Pantheon was rebuilt by Hadrian in A.D. 117–125 to honor the most important gods in the Roman pantheon. In 608 it was transformed into a Christian church. Inside are the tombs of Raphael and Vittorio Emanuele II, king of Italy.

Trevi Fountain (Fontana di Trevi). Piazza di Trevi. Metro: Barberini.

Rome has dozens of beautiful fountains, but the Trevi is the most spectacular. Did you ever see that rather awful movie *Three Coins in the Fountain?* This is the fountain, and an old tradition has it that if you turn your back on it and toss in a coin, you'll return to Rome. I *always* do this, and so far it's worked. The rather narrow piazza around the fountain is filled with grotesque trinket stands and buzzing with tourists day and night. There's a ring of stone benches where you can sit and gaze at the water show. The Trevi was completed in 1762 and is a masterpiece of Baroque theatricality. Water from the Acqua Vergine aqueduct sprays and splashes around Neptune, god of the sea, who stands on a sea-shell chariot drawn by winged horses led by tritons. In the side niches are allegorical sculptures representing Health and Fertility. The fountain has been recently cleaned and restored, and it's a sight to behold.

Castel Sant'Angelo. Lungotevere Castello 50. ☎ **06-6880-5148.** Admission 8,000L ($4). Daily 9am–7pm. Bus: 64.

In the last act of Puccini's *Tosca*, the tenor is shot on the roof of Castel Sant'Angelo and the soprano leaps to her death from the ramparts. The opera takes place in the early 19th century, when this massive fortress beside the Tiber was still being used as a prison. But Castel Sant'Angelo had been the scene of various plots and counterplots for some 1,700 years before that. It was built as a tomb for the Emperor Hadrian (who loved his boyfriend Antinous so much he made him into a god) and remained an imperial mausoleum up until the reign of Caracalla (A.D. 211–217). In the Middle Ages, it became a fortress and was linked to the Vatican by walls and an underground passageway. The Papacy could thus escape to safety when trouble arose. By the 14th century, it was a papal residence. Michelangelo's patron, Pope Julius II, used it. And so did Pope Alexander VI, who didn't take his vows of celibacy too seriously: He was the father of those legendary monsters Cesare and Lucrezia Borgia. Today you can visit

Tosca in Rome

Puccini's opera *Tosca*, a masterpiece of musical melodrama, takes place entirely in Rome. The first act is set in the splendid Baroque church of **Sant'Andrea delle Valle,** just west of Largo Argentina on Corso Vittore Emanuele. The church, completed in the late 17th century, has the second-highest dome in Rome after St. Peter's. *Tosca*'s second act takes place in Baron Scarpia's apartments in the **Palazzo Farnese** on the piazza of the same name. Completed in 1589, the palazzo is the greatest Renaissance palace in Rome; it has been the French Embassy since 1871. The opera's tragic denouement takes place in **Castel Sant'Angelo** (see listing). Maria Callas's recording of *Tosca* is probably the best known. Recently the entire opera was filmed on location, starring Catherine Malfitano and Plàcido Domingo.

the castle's Renaissance apartments, view its collection of arms and armor, and descend to the cells that once echoed with the screams of tortured prisoners. Benvenuto Cellini, the famous sculptor and goldsmith, was once locked up here. He's the troublemaker who was also fined in Florence for homosexual activities. The rooftop terrace, from which Floria Tosca leapt to her death, provides a spectacular panorama of Rome.

Galleria Borghese. In the Villa Borghese, Piazza Scipione Borghese. ☎ **06-328-101.** Admission by reservation only, 12,000L ($7). Tues–Sat 9am–5pm (Sat to 1pm). Metro: Barberini, then bus no. 56.

After 13 years of painstaking restoration, the Galleria Borghese reopened in 1997, and the results are truly breathtaking. The number of visitors allowed in at any one time is limited, so it's essential you call and reserve a space. If you're staying at a hotel, ask the concierge to call for you; you can also go directly to the ticket office on the lower level and find out when you can get in. I assure you, it's worth the effort. When the Galleria was built in 1613 to hold Cardinal Scipione Borghese's fabulous collection of art, the concept of an art gallery was very different from today's. Every inch of wall and ceiling space is richly decorated, so the rooms themselves can almost overwhelm the artworks. You may experience sensory overload.

Giovanni Bernini (1598–1680) was one of the most important artists to work in 17th-century Rome. His most famous sculptural creations in the Galleria Borghese are *Apollo and Daphne, David*, and *The Rape of Persephone.* They're all vigorous, physically intense, larger-than-life works. The well-known sculpture of Pauline Borghese by Antonio Canova (1757–1822) is a very different kettle of fish. Called *Venus Victorious,* it shows Napoléon's scandalous sister (she was married to Prince Cesare Borghese) reclining nude on a chaise longue; here the physical contortions of the Baroque (epitomized by Bernini) have given way to a somewhat remote neoclassicism. Two ancient works may tickle your fancy: the *Sileno danzante* (Dancing Silenus), clapping his cymbals as he dances naked, and the *Satiro delfino* (Satyr on a Dolphin), a nude youth poking his hand into a dolphin's mouth. Both look like they're having a good time, even though their marble members were removed by censorious Church Fathers. On the upper floor, which is the picture gallery, you might want to track down the three paintings by the gay artist Caravaggio. His *Davide con la testa di Golia* shows a handsome boy David holding the severed head of Goliath—which happens to be a self-portrait of Caravaggio. *Giovane con canestro di frutta* (Boy with a Basket of Fruit) is a languorously sensual homo work. Weirder, but just as powerful, is the *Bacchino malato* (Sick Bacchus), in which a yellow-skinned god of wine looks as though he's suffering from hepatitis.

Other Museums & Monuments of Note

Both a museum and an archaeological storehouse, the **Antiquarium Comunale,** Via del Parco del Celio 22 (☎ **06-700-1569;** Metro: Circo Massimo; open summer Tues–Sat 9am–7pm, Sun to 1:30pm and winter Tues–Sat 9am–5pm, Sun 9am–1:30pm; admission 3,750L/$2), has a fascinating permanent exhibit on "Daily Life in Imperial Rome."

The **Altar of Peace (Ara Pacis),** Lungotevere in Augusta (☎ **06-6880-6848;** Metro: Spagna; open Tues–Sun 9am–5pm; admission 3,750L/$2), housed in a glass enclosure beside the Tiber, was consecrated in A.D. 9 by Caesar Octavian to celebrate the conquest of peace in the Empire. A complex figurative frieze showing mythological and allegorical figures decorates the altar.

The ✪ **Machines and the Gods (Macchine e gli Dei),** Art Center Acea in the Montemartini power plant, Viale Ostiense 106 (☎ **06-575-4207;** Metro: Piramide; open Tues–Fri 10am–6pm, Sat–Sun to 7pm; admission 12,000L/$7), is Rome's most exciting new museum, set up inside a former power plant (the city's first); it houses over 400 pieces of sculpture from the Capitoline Museum. The splendidly eclectic setting combines classical art with industrial archaeology.

For a look at what it was like to live in an 18th-century palace, head to the **Galleria Doria Pamphilj,** Piazza del Collegio Romano 2, off Via del Corso (☎ **06-679-7323;** Bus: 64; open Fri–Wed 10am–5pm; admission gallery 13,000L/$7, apartments 5,000L/$2.80). The upper floors are leased to tenants and there are shops on the street level—but you'll overlook this after entering the grand apartments of the Doria Pamphilj family, which traces its lines to before the great 15th-century Genoese admiral Andrea Doria.

And you thought you knew what a bathhouse looked like: The monumental **Baths of Caracalla (Terme di Caracalla),** Via delle Terme di Caracalla (☎ **06-575-8626;** open Sun–Mon 9am–2pm, Tues–Sat to an hour before sunset), dating from Rome's imperial era, were where men of leisure gathered to steam, do business, and monkey around. The baths used to be the site of a fabled summer grand-opera season, but damage to the ruins caused the cancellation of major staples like *Aïda.* Some opera and ballet performances still occasionally take place here (check with the tourist office).

✪ **National Etruscan Museum (Museo Nazionale Etrusco).** In the Villa Giulia, Piazzale di Villa Giulia 9, in the Villa Borghese. ☎ **06-322-6571.** Admission 8,000L ($4.50). Tues–Sat 9am–7pm, Sun to 2pm. Metro: Flaminio, then bus no. 48.

The superlative Etruscan Museum is housed in a 16th-century palazzo and contains artifacts from the Etruscan settlement at Cerveteri, north of Rome. The mysterious Etruscans (nobody seems to know exactly where they came from) predated the Romans and were known for their sophisticated art and design. In room 7 is a remarkable 6th-century-B.C. *Apollo* (clothed, for a change), a *Dea con Bambino* (Goddess with a Baby) and a mutilated but still powerful *Hercules with a Stag.* One of the world's most important Etruscan art treasures is the 6th-century-B.C bride and bridegroom sarcophagus in room 9. Another masterpiece, the 4th-century-B.C. Cista Ficoroni, a bronze urn with paw feet and three figures, is in room 33. There's also Etruscan jewelry and a reconstructed temple.

Ancient Rome & Environs

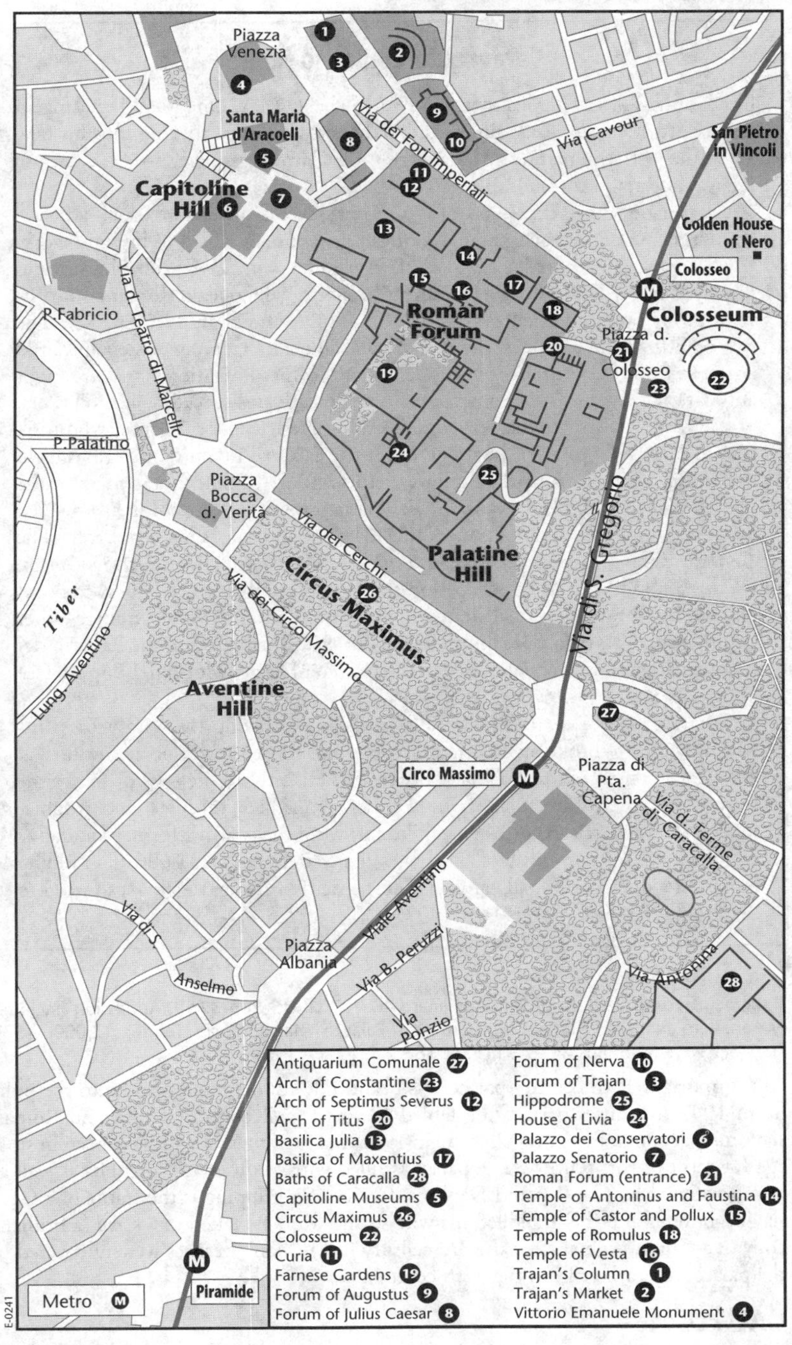

Caravaggio Comes to Rome

In the annals of gay genius there are two Michelangelos. One was Michelangelo Buonarotti, the sculptor, painter, and architect who kept working into his 80s. The other was the painter **Michelangelo da Caravaggio** (1573–1610), whose life was short and tumultuous.

Caravaggio came to Rome at 16. After several poverty-stricken years, a churchman gave the young man a room in his house in which to live and work. Here Caravaggio painted a *Flight into Egypt* and a *Magdalen*, probably the ones displayed in the **Galleria Doria Pamphilj,** Piazza del Collegio Romano (☎ **06-679-4365;** Bus: 64; open Fri–Wed 10am–5pm; admission 12,000L/$7). The two paintings and a third of *John the Baptist* illustrate Caravaggio's evolution as an artist from the simplicity of his early days to the dramatic *chiaroscuro* (light and dark) effects that were to become his trademark and copied by his followers.

Later, the artist met the powerful Cardinal Francesco del Monte, who took him to live in his palazzo. In about 1597, the cardinal procured for Caravaggio the commission to paint the famous pictures of St. Matthew that hang in the church of **San Luigi dei Francesi,** Via Santa Giovanna d'Arco (open Fri–Wed 8am–12:30pm and 3:30–7pm, Thurs 8am–12:30pm; admission free). The *Calling of St. Matthew, St. Matthew and the Angel,* and the *Martydom of St. Matthew,* found in the last chapel on the left, are probably the largest canvases painted by Caravaggio; their dramatic intensity is almost overwhelming. Other paintings by Caravaggio are found in the **Galleria Borghese** and the **Palazzo dei Conservatori** (both above) as well as the church of **Santa Maria del Popolo** (see Piazza del Popolo, below).

Caravaggio's use of realistic detail—such as portraying the Virgin or saints with dirty feet—broke all artistic precedent and roused many people to fury at what they considered to be a lack of respect. His private life—wild, to say the least—didn't help him make friends either. A drinker, carouser, and trouble-maker, he was arrested for offenses like throwing rocks at his former landlady's windows and hurling a dish of artichokes at a waiter's head. In 1606, after killing a man in a duel after a ball game in Campo dei Fiori, Caravaggio was forced to flee Rome. He died 4 years later at 37.

Palazzo Altemps. Piazza di Sant'Apollinare 46–48. ☎ **06-683-3759.** Admission (includes entrance to National Roman Museum and Palazzo Massimo alle Terme) 12,000L ($7). Tues–Sat 9am–5pm. Bus 70, 87, 119, or 186.

This important 15th-century palace was beautifully restored and opened to the public in 1997. It houses part of the fabled Ludovisi Collection of Greek and Roman sculpture, acquired by the Italian state in 1901; many of these works have been in storage for most of this century. The palace is filled with Venuses and nymphs as well as homoerotic works like Pan and Daphnis. Particularly gripping is the statue of a Gaul slaying himself after he has killed his wife so she won't be taken as a slave (a brilliant copy of a Greek original from the 3rd century B.C.). Many frescoes were uncovered in the palace, the earliest from the 12th century.

GAY ROME

Rome isn't as gay as you might think. At least not openly. There are an active gay political scene and a gay social network, but when it comes to cruising this is a city of frequently mixed signals. When a Roman flashes his dark eyes in your direction and gives you the once-over, it doesn't necessarily mean he's sexually interested. More likely, he's simply curious (and checking out your clothes). You may see men strolling down a street with their arms around each other. It doesn't mean they're lovers, but simply affectionate friends. The signals may be clearer in gay bars and discos . . . and clearest of all in the men's rest room at the train station.

Caution: I want to warn you about outdoor cruising and especially about picking up hustlers. Over the years there have been several gay-related homicides in Rome. The standard (but as yet unproven) theory is that they were committed by hustlers. So please be alert and use common sense.

PARKS, GARDENS, SQUARES & ROMAN MONUMENTS

Rome boasts some of the most beautiful parks and piazzas in the world. Splashing fountains and acanthus-filled gardens shaded by palm trees and umbrella pines form an essential part of the city's urban fabric. They also help cool it down when the scorching scirocco winds from Africa start to blow. And they're definitely people places.

✪ **Piazza Navona,** a short walk north from Campo dei Fiori across Corso Vittorio Emanuele, is one of Rome's greatest piazzas. A long rectangle with semicircular ends, its shape was determined by its former use as the Circus of Domitian (ca. A.D. 90). In the center is Bernini's fabulous Fountain of the Four Rivers, which allegorically depicts the Nile, Danube, Ganges, and Rio de Plata (note that the face of the Nile figure is covered because its source was unknown at the time). The Baroque church of Santa Agnese in Agone, built by G. Rinaldi and Borromini, occupies part of the west side of the piazza. People gather here day and night, sitting at outdoor restaurants along the fringe and strolling past the artists who set up their easels near the fountain.

✪ **Piazza del Popolo,** at the northern end of Via del Corso, is a remarkable architectural composition of monumental proportions. Carlo Rinaldi designed the twin churches of Santa Maria di Monte Santo and Santa Maria de' Miracoli that stand between Via Ripetta, the Corso, and Via del Babuino on the south end. In the center is the second-oldest obelisk in Rome, dating from the 13th century B.C. and brought to Rome by Augustus. An arch in the Aurelian Wall at the northern end of the piazza marks the beginning of Via Flaminia, which in Roman times led to all points north. In her famous 1655 entry into Rome, Queen Christina of Sweden—who was a king because the Swedish sovereign was always a king, regardless of sex—passed through the gate after renouncing the Swedish throne and converting to Roman Catholicism. Beside the gate is the 11th-century church of Santa Maria del Popolo. It was built over the Domitian family tomb which, according to legend, was haunted by Emperor Nero and has two paintings by Caravaggio: *Saul on the Road to Damascus* and *The Crucifixion of St. Peter.* The piazza has a couple of famous restaurants and is a popular meeting place.

Overlooking Piazza del Popolo are the **Pincio Gardens,** laid out in 1810. A path beside Santa Maria del Popolo leads up to a high terrace with a superb view of Rome with St. Peter's in the distance.

The **Spanish Steps (Scalinata di Spagna)** rise in graceful curves from Piazza di Spagna at the end of Via Condotti, one of Rome's most fashionable shopping streets. Throngs of tourists gather on the steps, which begin at the Barcaccia, a small barge-shaped fountain designed by Bernini, and culminate at the church of Trinità dei Monti, built by the kings of France on the hill above. The piazza and its environs were a thriving tourist and artists' center by the 17th century; so many Brits came to the area that in the 19th century it was known as "the English ghetto." Keats died in a house beside the steps (today the Keats-Shelly Memorial). Every time I visit the Spanish Steps I'm reminded of the movie version of Tennessee Williams's *The Roman Spring of Mrs. Stone:* Across from the Keats-Shelly Memorial is the house where Mrs. Stone (played by Vivien Leigh) had her Roman spring (with the gigolo played by a young beauty Warren Beatty).

The grounds of the **Villa Borghese** (which houses the Galleria Borghese and the Etrusan Museum) form a giant park that's a perennially popular outdoor oasis. Pathways and broad avenues wend their way past statuary, fountains, and landscaped garden areas.

Campo dei Fiori, off Corso Vittorio Emanuele and just behind the church of Sant'Andrea delle Valle, is lined with shops, restaurants, and Renaissance buildings. And on Monday to Saturday it's the sight of a lively outdoor food market. Come before noon to have a look at the produce, cheeses, flowers, and other foodstuffs. At night it's a wonderful place to sit and have an aperitif or dinner at La Carbonara. A historic footnote: Julius Caesar was assassinated in this vicinity in 44 B.C.

Largo Argentina, west of Piazza Venezia at the beginning of Corso Vittorio Emanuele, sits below street level in the center of a busy traffic area. There's more life around it than in it. In 2nd-century-B.C. Republican Rome, this was an important sacred area. Set among a paved square are the restored fragments from four temples.

The **Mausoleum of Augustus (Mausoleo di Augusto),** on Piazza Augusto Imperatore on the east bank of the Tiber, is the dynastic tomb of the emperor Augustus and his family. Augustus had the circular tomb built in A.D. 29 on what was a grass-covered tumulus. You can't enter the mausoleum, but it's surrounded by a small park.

Two splendid parks are found on the west side of the Tiber. The **Janiculum (Gianicolo),** one of Rome's seven hills, covers the high ground behind Trastevere to the Vatican. Starting at the beautiful Fontana del Paola, walk north on Passegiata del Gianicolo past the Giuseppe Garibaldi monument to an area of panoramic overlooks and leafy garden paths. If you head west from the Fontana Paola along Via di San Pancrazio, you'll eventually enter the landscaped grounds of the **Villa Doria Pamphilj.** Paths meander past the Baroque villa, with its formal garden area, to a grove of umbrella pines carefully planted in rows on the sloping hillside.

5 Hitting the Stores

Romans know how to cut *una bella figura* (literally, a beautiful figure), and there are plenty of high-fashion shops and designer boutiques to supply them with all the requisite goods. The most fashionable streets for shopping are **Via Condotti, Via Borgognona,** and **Via Babuino** in the vicinity of Piazza di Spagna and the Spanish Steps. The shops along **Via del Corso** are less chic and therefore more affordable. For antiques browsing, **Via dei Coronari** is the place to go.

June to September, general **store hours** are Monday to Friday 9am to 1pm and 4 to 8pm and Saturday 9am to 1pm. The rest of the year, shops are usually closed Monday mornings. There's no Sunday shopping in Rome at any time of year.

SHOPS A TO Z

ANTIQUES & OBJETS D'ART The **Galleria Marmi Line,** Via dei Coronari 113 (☎ **06-689-3795;** Metro: Cavour), sells antique busts, columns, and tables and reproductions in marble and onyx. **Polyedra,** Via della Scrofa 46 (☎ **06-687-3259;** Metro: Cavour), stocks collectors' items from every era in every style.

BOOKS **La Bancarella di Andy Capp,** Piazza Alessandria 2 (☎ **06-8530-3071;** Metro: Repubblica), near Porta Pia, has a large assortment of erotic comics and magazines and gay and lesbian publications. The **Libreria Babele,** Via dei Banchi Vecchi 116 (☎ **06-687-6628;** Bus: 46 or 62), is Rome's only all-gay/lesbian bookstore. **Rinascita,** Via delle Botteghe Oscure 1 (☎ **06-679-7136;** Bus: 26 or 44), has a gay and lesbian section for fiction, poetry, and essays.

The **Anglo-American Bookshop,** Via della Vite 102 (☎ **06-679-5222;** Metro: Spagna), stocks books in English. And the **Economy Book and Video Center,** Via Torino 136 (☎ **06-474-6877;** Metro: Termini), also caters to English readers and sells new and used hardcovers and paperbacks.

CLOTHING The following are gay-friendly and popular. **Antinoo,** Via Genova 12, at the corner of Via Nazionale (☎ **06-474-3323;** Metro: Termini), stocks current fashion trends for men. **Eventi,** Via dei Serpenti 134 (☎ **06-484-960;** Metro: Cavour), is a place to go if you're looking for that perfect retro disco suit. **Marco Polo,** Via Nazioale 205 (☎ **06-488-2705;** Metro: Repubblica), is another store that carries trendy men's fashions.

Storm, Via Nazionale 182 (☎ **06-4890-3657;** Metro: Repubblica), is a clothing store for both men and women. **Symbol,** Via Salaria 21 (☎ **06-8542-2534;** Metro: Barberini), is a fashion clothing store mostly for women. And **Vintage,** Via dei Pastini 117 (☎ **06-6994-2135;** Bus: 64), sells fashionable cast-offs.

For higher-end designer fashion options try the following: **Fiorucci,** Via Mario de Fiori 41 (☎ **06-678-7877;** Metro: Barberini), carries mostly women's clothes and accessories. **Gianfranco Ferré Jeans,** Piazza di Spagna 70 (☎ **06-678-6797;** Metro: Spagna), offers luxurious casual clothes and accessories for both sexes. **Giorgio Armani,** Via dei Condotti 77 (☎ **06-699-1460;** Metro: Spagna), has a women's store selling understated, elegant daywear and evening clothes. And **Gianni Versace,** Via Bocca de Leone 26–27 (☎ **06-678-0521;** Metro: Spagna), carries the signature Versace line of clothes, household items, and jewelry; you'll find his sportier, younger line at **Versace Jeans Couture,** Via Frattina 116 (☎ **06-678-7680;** Metro: Spagna).

GAY SHOPS **Cobra** sells gay and lesbian what-nots and erotica, videos, and magazines at three locations: Via Barletta 23 (☎ **06-3751-7350;** Metro: Ottaviano), Via Aureliocotta 22–24 (☎ **06-764-357;** Metro: Numidio Quadrato), and Via G. Giolitti 307–313 (☎ **06-4470-0636;** Metro: Vittorio). **Europa 92,** Via Boezio 96 (☎ **06-687-1210;** Metro: Vittorio), offers sexy underwear, perfumes, gay gifts, and videos.

Eurosex Italia, Via G. Bagnera 49 (☎ **06-559-4376;** Metro: Marconi), has gay videos and toys for boyz. And **Ville Rouge,** Via Pigafetta 48 (☎ **06-575-6495;** Metro: Garbatella), stocks erotic gadgets, gay videos, and gifts.

JEWELRY **Alternatives,** Via d'Ascanio 19 (☎ **06-6830-8233;** Bus: 64), is the only store in Rome to specialize in contemporary jewelry created by international designers. **Epifanio,** Via del Pie di Marmo 35 (☎ **06-699-0007;** Bus: 64) carries gold jewelry set with ancient bronze and silver coins, precious stones, and antique glass.

SHOES **Re Mishelle,** Via del Corso 526 (☎ **06-361-0194;** Metro: Barberini), stocks luxury shoes from top Italian designers for both men and women. **Sergio Rossi,** Piazza di Spagna 97–100 (☎ **06-678-3245;** Metro: Spagna), sells his hot styles of men's and women's footwear and accessories in a shop near the Spanish Steps.

TOILETRIES In Rome you'll find a branch of the **Officinia Profuma-Farmaceutica di Santa Maria Novella,** the most fabulous soap and scent shop in Florence; it's at Corso Rinascimento 47 (☎ **06-687-9608;** Bus: 64), between Piazza Navona and the Pantheon.

6 All the World's a Stage

The **Teatro dell'Opera,** Piazza Beniamino Gigli (☎ **06-481-601;** Metro: Termini or Repubblica), is the home of the Rome Opera and also presents ballet performances. The **Accademia Filarmonica Romana (Roman Philharmonic Academy)** gives concerts at the **Teatro Olimpico,** Piazza Gentile da Fabriano 17 (☎ **06-323-4890;** Bus: 48, 910, or 911), and the **Sala Casella,** Via Flaminia 18 (☎ **06-323-4890;** Bus: 48, 910, or 911). The orchestra of the **Accademia Nazionale di Santa Cecilia** gives concerts at the **Auditorium of Via della Conciliazione** near St. Peter's (☎ **06-6880-1044;** Metro: San Pietro; Bus: 64).

For a rundown of performing arts groups and venues, check the listings in the monthly magazine ***Un Ospite a Roma (A Guest in Rome),*** available free at the tourist office and in many hotels.

7 In the Heat of the Night

Ever heard of a "drink card"? That's what you'll get in many Roman bars. It's presented to you at the door, and your drinks are duly noted by the bartender. You turn in the card and pay when you leave. There may be a one-drink minimum. The cost of a drink generally starts at 5,000 to 10,000L ($3 to $6); hard drinks and fancy cocktails will cost considerably more.

GAY BARS

You need to buy a 5,000L ($3) membership to enter the **Apeiron Club,** Via dei Quattro Cantoni 5 (☎ **06-482-8820;** Metro: Cavour; open Mon–Thurs and Sun 10:30pm–2am, Fri to 3am, Sat to 3:30am), which features an all-the-rage maze, darkroom, and giant video screens; women are welcome, but the crowd is mostly male.

Hangar, Via in Selci 69 (☎ **06-488-1397;** Metro: Cavour; Wed–Mon 10:30pm–2am), is a cruisy jeans-and-leather cruise bar around the corner from the Apeiron; there's free admission to everyone but transvestites, who aren't allowed (go figure). It contains two rooms, one with New York–style disco DJs; the crowd is generally young and trendy and in a party mood.

There's no admission to get into the lesbigay **Frutta e Verdura (Fruit and Vegetables),** Via Principe Umberto 36 (☎ **06-446-4862;** Metro: Vittorio; open Wed–Mon 10pm–3am), but they make it obvious you're supposed to drink; there are nightly shows in this bilevel bar, a gropey underground tunnel, a video room, and a tearoom (the kind that serves tea).

An Arci membership card is required for entrance to **Incognito 2000,** Via Casilina Vecchia 146 (☎ **06-784-3567;** open daily 7pm–3am; Metro: Ponte Lungo), but they may let you in anyway; inside is a darkroom (hence the "incognito"?) and a hustler service; it's in an outlying area where you'll also find the Oxy Theatre and K-Man's Club.

The **Oxy Theatre,** Via Dulceri 30 (☎ **0338-348-7819;** open Tues–Sun 11pm–4am), is a go-go bar and male-strip joint way out in the 'burbs; there's no Metro nearby so you'll have to cab it.

A disco/backroom bar, the **Officina Fans Club,** Via Ignazio Danti 20 at Via Casilina (☎ **06-275-3508;** Metro: Largo Ale; Bus: 105 or 50N; open daily 10pm–late), has maxi-screen videos, karaoke, and various theme nights.

Skyline, Via degli Aurunci 26–28 (☎ **06-444-0817;** Metro: Policlinico; open Wed–Mon 10pm–2am and Sun 5–8:30pm in winter), an American-style gay and lesbian bar close to Stazione Termini and the San Lorenzo church, is more popular on weekends than weekdays; it has the obligatory backroom on an upper floor, a hardcore video room, snacks, and shows.

Located in Trastevere, **Shelter Club,** Via dei Vascellari 35 (☎ **06-588-0862;** Tram: 8; open daily 8pm–4am), is a lesbigay hangout that's a great little spot for an American-style cocktail and a bite to eat. Also in Trastevere, **Garbo,** Vicolo di Santa Margherita 1A (☎ **06-581-6700;** Tram: 8; open daily 10pm–3am), is a cocktail bar with free membership.

LESBIAN BAR

Le Sorellastre, Via San Francesco di Sales 1 (☎ **06-686-4201;** Metro: Piramide; then bus no. 23 in the direction of Piazzale Clodio), is a women's bar.

LEATHER BAR

In Casalina, **K-Men's Club,** Via Amato Amati 6–8 (☎ **0347-622-0462;** Bus: 105 or 50N from Stazione Termini; open daily 10pm–2am), is a men-only leather sex club.

DANCE CLUBS

L'Alibi, Via di Monte Testaccio 39–44 (☎ **06-574-3448;** Metro: Piramide; open Wed–Sun 11pm–4am; admission generally free Thurs and Sun, about 15,000L/$8 Fri–Sat), is a popular two-story disco, about a 10-minute walk from the pyramid, and was throbbing long before the Testaccio area became trendy; it features a great summer terrace and attracts a younger mixed gay/lesbian crowd.

The popular all-ages gay **Max's Bar,** Via Achille Grandi 7A (☎ **06-7030-1599;** Metro: Vittorio Emanuele; open Tues–Sun 10:30pm–late; admission 15,000L/$8 Fri–Sat, mandatory drink card weekdays), near the Porta Maggiore, was recently renovated and expanded; on some nights there are performances. You can also get something to eat and watch videos.

L'Angelo Azzuro, Via Cardinal Merry del Val 13 (☎ **06-5800-4782;** Tram: 8; open Fri–Sun 11pm–5am; admission 20,000L/$11 Sat, 10,000L/$6 Fri and Sun), was recently reopened after a fire. The venerable and upscale Blue Angel in Trastevere holds a women-only disco on Friday and is a mixed gay/lesbian disco on Saturday and Sunday.

Muccassassina, Via del Commercio 36 (☎ **06-541-3985;** Metro: Piramide; open Fri 10:30pm–4am; admission 20,000L/$11). This Friday-night event, held in the Alpheus club, is sponsored by the Mario Mieli Group to raise funds for gay social services.

New Superstars, Vicolo de Modelli 51 (☎ **06-679-1909;** Metro: Barberini; open Wed 10:30pm–4am, Thurs–Sun to 7am), is a late-hours gay/lesbian disco near the Trevi Fountain; it's men only on Wednesday, and free membership is issued at the door.

In Rome's African quarter, **Jolie Coeur,** Via Sirte 5 (☎ **06-8621-5827;** Bus: 38, 58; open Wed and Sat from 11pm; admission 15,000L/$8 Wed, 10,000L/$6 Sat), is open to a mixed crowd, including gay men, on Wednesday but on Saturday, it's lesbians only. It has pool tables, video screens, karaoke nights, and a snack bar; if you're in a dance-cruise mood, I recommend the other discos over this one.

DOWN & DIRTY: CINEMAS, SAUNAS & MORE

Keep in mind the potential dangers of outdoor cruising and picking up hustlers. All of these places are AYOR: Behind the Colosseum on **Via del Colle Oppio** cruising is done in cars. Cruising on foot is done at the **Colosseo Quadrato,** in the gardens near Palazzo Civiltà dei Lavoro; on **Monte Caprino,** in the Villa Caffarelli park on the Campidoglio (the city council has been trying to restrict access so it may be closed); and near the **Piramide di Gaio Cestio,** beside the walls of the Protestant Cemetery (in the vicinity of the gay disco L'Alibi).

CINEMAS If you go to a first-run movie in Italy, it'll be dubbed in Italian. Movies in their original languages are shown on Monday at **Alcazar,** in Trastevere on Via Mery del Val 14 (☎ **06-588-0099;** Tram: 8), and every day at the **Pasquino,** Vicolo de Piede 19 (☎ **06-580-3622;** Tram: 8), also in Trastevere.

For X-rated movies (not always gay, but usually with gays in the audience), try the **Ambasciatori Sexy Movie,** Via Montebello 101 (☎ **06-494-1290;** Bus: 60, 81, 61); **Blue Moon,** Via dei Quattro Cantoni 53 (☎ **06-474-3936;** Metro: Cavour); and **Pussycat,** Via Cairoli 98 (☎ **06-446-4961;** Metro: Vittorio). The busiest is **Tiffany,** Via A. de Pretis 11 (☎ **06-488-2390;** Metro: Termini).

SAUNAS The big new **Europa Multiclub,** Via Aureliana 40 (☎ **06-482-3650;** Metro: Repubblica; open Sun–Thurs 3pm–midnight, Fri–Sun 1pm–2am), is popular with a mostly younger crowd; on three floors you'll find dry and wet sweat facilities, a whirlpool tub, a little pool, a barber, and a solarium and garden bar. **Mediterraneo,** Via Pasquale Villari 3 (☎ **06-7720-5934;** Metro: Manzoni; open daily 2–11pm), is a full-service facility on three floors with dry and wet saunas, tanning beds, a whirlpool tub, a masseur, a video room, a full bar with food, and free condoms.

The **Terme di Roma Internazionale,** Via Persio 4 (☎ **06-718-4378;** Metro: Arco di Travertino; open Sun–Thurs 3pm–midnight, Fri–Sat to 2am), is in the outer burbs, making it something of a hassle to reach, but this is one of the largest and certainly the best-equipped saunas in Rome. It features a "mega-Jacuzzi," Turkish and Finnish sauna areas, a dark room and labyrinth, a masseur, a gym, a barber, and video and chill-out rooms—and it takes credit cards.

8 Side Trips from Rome: Tivoli, Ostia Antica & Pompeii

TIVOLI: HADRIAN'S VILLA & THE VILLA D'ESTE

Tivoli, called Tibur by the ancient Romans, is the site of two famed attractions: the Villa d'Este and Hadrian's Villa. The town is 20 miles southeast of Rome on Via Tiburtina. To get there, take Metro Line B to Rebibbia, the last station, and from the station take an Acotral bus (departing about every 20 minutes) to the town. American Express and other bus-sightseeing companies offer day trips to Tivoli as well.

The bus from Rebibbia in Rome stops right at the entrance to the 16th-century **Villa d'Este,** Piazza Trento, Viale delle Centro Fontane (☎ **0774-312-070**), built by Cardinal Ippolito d'Este. It's not the villa itself you want to visit but the superb gardens, designed by Pirro Ligorio, with their world-famous fountains. This splashy hillside paradise has artificial cataracts, waterfalls, and spouting gargoyles and lilies. On the grounds and along the promenade are some 100 spraying fountains, the most spectacular of them designed by Ligorio, Claude Veanard, and Bernini. The villa and grounds are open daily: November to February 9am to 4pm, March to mid-April to 5:30pm, and mid-April to October to 6:30pm. Admission is 8,000L ($4).

The no. 2 or 4 bus from Tivoli will take you about 3 miles southwest of town to what's a must-see attraction for gay travelers: the ✪ **Villa Adriano (Hadrian's Villa),** Via di Villa Adriana (☎ **0774-530-203**). Historians and guidebook writers always conveniently "overlook" the fact that Emperor Hadrian (A.D. 76–138) was as queer as they come. The fact is, after the mysterious death by drowning of his lover Antinous, Hadrian elevated the young man to the status of a god and had statues of him erected throughout the Roman Empire (there's one in the Vatican Museums). (For more on Hadrian and Antinous, see the box in chapter 8.) The highly cultured Hadrian, an incessant world traveler, spent the last 3 years of his life in this villa, which was a spectacular world unto itself, with theaters, temples, baths, fountains, and gardens. There were statues of Antinous as the Egyptian god Osiris and the mythological Greek Ganymede, so beautiful that he was abducted by Zeus. At the villa's entrance is a model of what the place once looked like, and scattered around the grounds are fragments of some of the buildings and statuary, including the Marine Theater, the Canopus, and the Great Baths. Hadrian's villa has been called the "queen of the villas of the ancient world"—with no pun intended. If you want to bone up before visiting, read Marguerite Yourcenar's brilliant novel *The Memoirs of Hadrian.* The villa is open daily 9am to sunset, and admission is 8,000L ($4).

OSTIA ANTICA

A well-preserved ancient Roman city, **Ostia Antica** was once the busy commercial port of Rome and its major sea-faring military base. In their pastoral setting, the ruins of Ostia help capture the essence of Imperial Rome in its heyday. Founded in the 4th century B.C., it was gradually abandoned in the 4th and 5th centuries A.D. when the harbor silted up. The city of 100,000 eventually followed Rome into decline. Ostia is now inland (a full 1.9 miles from the sea), and wasn't excavated until before World War II on orders of Mussolini.

Ostia is worth visiting if you won't have a chance to visit Pompeii, for here you'll get a good idea of how an ancient city was laid out and how it looked. Preserved details of Roman building styles include mosaic floors, marble walls, and a few wall paintings. Just south of the excavations is the **Lido di Ostia,** a beach resort on the Tyrrhenian Sea (though I wouldn't recommend swimming in those polluted waters).

Ostia Antica is open daily: March to September 9am to 7pm (the rest of the year to 5pm). Last entrance is 1 hour before closing, and admission is 12,000L ($7).

Just 16 miles southwest of Rome, Ostia is Rome's most convenient day trip. To get there, take the Metro Line B to the Magliana station and transfer to a suburban Lido train connecting with Ostia Antica (STAZIONE DI OSTIA ANTICA) in half an hour. To reach the excavations *(scavi),* walk across a bridge over a highway and continue straight in that direction for 5 to 10 minutes. The same train goes all the way to Stazione Lido di Roma (the beaches). There *is* a nude gay beach (*Spiaggia libera*), called **Il Buco,** but it's a bit difficult to reach from Lido di Ostia; it's on Via Aurelia on the Anzio highway (look for the km. 46 marker).

FARTHER AFIELD TO POMPEII

Once a thriving city of 30,000, the Roman colony of **Pompeii** was virtually buried alive in A.D. 79 when nearby Mount Vesuvius erupted, burying it beneath 20 feet of scalding cinder and volcanic ash (not lava as is commonly thought). It was "rediscovered" in the 16th century, but systematic digs didn't begin until 1860. Today, some two-thirds of the 160-acre site have been excavated, and work still goes on. Much of the remarkable frescoes, mosaics, and statuary you've seen photographed has wound up in Naples's Museo Archeologico Nazionale, but enough has been left to make these Europe's most fascinating and best-preserved 2,000-year-old ruins.

Day-long trips from Rome to Pompeii (150 miles southeast) have always been doable, but you've got to catch the 2-hour express train to Naples and connect with the local Circumvesuviana train to Pompeii—a 4-hour adventure if all runs smoothly (it rarely does). **Enjoy Rome** (see "Visitor Information" above) has now launched a daily air-conditioned minivan that whisks eight passengers from Rome to the gates of Pompeii in 3 hours, leaving several days a week (usually weekends) at 8:30am and returning at 6:30pm. The round-trip costs 70,000L ($42) and includes maps and a guidebook but not tour or site admission.

11

Florence: Renaissance Homo Hangout

Florence (Firenze), the City of the Lily, was the birthplace of the Renaissance. That 15th-century flowering (or explosion) of the arts and humanities drew the greatest artists in Italy to this city on the Arno. Today it draws tourists—hundreds of thousands of them, all eager to see for themselves the works of Michelangelo, Leonardo da Vinci, Sandro Botticelli, Benvenuto Cellini, and others. Though the summer crowds can at times be a little overwhelming, it's difficult not to appreciate and enjoy the beauties of Florence, which is first and foremost a city of art and culture.

Tuscany, the province of which Florence is the capital, lies almost in the center of Italy. Its landscape of sun-drenched hills brushstroked with vineyards, olive groves, tall cypress trees, and villas half hidden in verdant green groves glows with an imperturbable elegance.

1 Florence Essentials

ARRIVING & DEPARTING

BY PLANE Florence's **Aeroporto Amerigo Vespucci (☎ 055-30-615)**, lies about 3½ miles northwest of the city; it's also called **Peretola.** There are daily flights to and from Milan, Rome, London, Amsterdam, Paris, Vienna, and other domestic and international cities. A local A.T.A.F bus (no. 62) connects the airport and the city's Stazione Santa Maria Novella train station and takes about 30 minutes. By taxi it's about 15 minutes, costing approximately 36,000L ($20).

Some U.S. flights with connections in Rome fly into Pisa's **Galileo Galilei Airport** (**☎ 050-500-707**), 58 miles west of Florence. Between 6 or 7am and 7 or 8pm, there's shuttle train service every hour or two between the airport and Florence's Stazione Santa Maria Novella; the trip takes about an hour and costs 9,200L ($5).

BY TRAIN Florence's train station, **Stazione Santa Maria Novella** (**S.M.N.** to natives), on Piazza della Stazione, adjoins Piazza Santa Maria Novella and isn't far from the historic town center. Florence is a major train junction with frequent (often hourly) service to Rome, Milan, Venice, and other Italian cities. For train information, call **☎ 166-105-050.** There are buses and a taxi rank directly outside the station and a currency exchange and tourist office within.

BY BUS Two long-distance bus companies offer coach service to Florence from other cities in Italy: **SITA,** Viale Cadorna 103–105

(☎ **055-483-651**), and **Lazzi Eurolines,** Piazza della Stazione 4–6 (☎ **055-215-154**). Many long-distance buses arrive at Piazze delle Stazione, in front of the train station.

BY CAR There are good autostrada connections between Florence and the rest of Italy. Autostrada A1 runs north-south. A11 heads west to the Tyrrhenian coast (an hour away). I don't recommend driving to Florence since much of the inner city is closed to cars.

VISITOR INFORMATION

The tourist office, **Azienda di Promozione Turistica Firenze,** has a small office in Stazione Santa Maria Novella (☎ **055-212-245;** open daily 8:15am–7:30pm in summer and Mon–Sat 8:15am–1:45pm the rest of the year); at Vespucci Airport (☎ **055-315-874**); and at Borgo Santa Croce 29R (☎ **055-234-0444**). The largest and most helpful branch is on Via Cavour 1R (☎ **055-290-832;** open Mon–Sat 8:15am–7:15pm, Sun to 1:45pm).

CITY LAYOUT

Piazza della Signoria, the sculpture-laden heart of Renaissance (and contemporary) Florence, sits just north of the Arno River in the historic inner city (*centro storico*) and is adjoined by the Uffizi Gallery. **Piazza del Duomo,** the other main gathering point, is about a 10-minute walk north. Neighborhoods are roughly demarcated by major churches: **Santa Croce** to the east of Piazza della Signoria; **Santa Maria Novella,** to the west (near the train station); and **Santo Spirito** (Oltrarno), on the south side of the Arno, are three of the most important.

The **Arno River** splits the city into north and south. It's spanned by eight bridges, the most famous being the **Ponte Vecchio (Old Bridge).** Most of the monuments and sights you'll want to see are on the north ("right") side of the river. The major attractions on the south ("left") bank are the Pitti Palace, the Boboli Gardens, and the Belvedere fort with its panoramic overlook.

GETTING AROUND

Florence is a walking city, and though some treks may seem rather long (especially on hot summer days), the city is fairly compact and walking remains the best way to see the sights.

BY BUS I find Florence's buses more confusing than useful. If you want to ride the bus, buy your tickets at a *tabacchi* (tobacconist) before boarding. A **single fare** is 2,000L ($1) and is good for 70 minutes on any city bus. The local bus company is **A.T.A.F.** (☎ **055-565-0222**); the main bus station is at Piazza del Duomo, and the train station is another major bus hub. Bus routes are marked at each stop.

BY TAXI You'll find taxis at all the major piazzas and outside the train station. The fare starts at 6,500L ($3.60), with extra supplements for baggage and at night, and

The Red & the Black

Finding an address in Florence can be frustrating. There are two systems of street numbering: red and black (sometimes blue). Red numbers, signified by an *R* after the street number, are used for commercial businesses like restaurants and shops. Black (blue) numbers are used for private homes, apartment buildings, offices, and hotels. To confuse matters further, numbers don't always run consecutively along one side of the street. Your best defense is a Falk map and a good pair of shoes.

Country & City Codes

The **country code** for Italy is **39.** The **city code** for Florence is **055.** You must now use all three digits whenever you call Florence—whether you're outside Italy, inside Italy but not within Florence, or even within Florence.

---

goes up 1,350L (75¢) per kilometer. To call a radio taxi, dial ☎ **4390-4499** or **4798-4242.** From the train station to the Ponte Vecchio, the fare is about $15. New price increases for taxis will probably be in effect by the time you arrive.

BY CAR Don't rent a car for driving in Florence: It's a pain in the butt since most of the city is closed to traffic and completely unnecessary since the city is entirely walkable. If you want to rent a car for excursions into Tuscany, you can find one at **Avis,** Borgo Ognissanti 128R (☎ **055-213-629**) or **Hertz,** Via del Termine 1 (☎ **055-307-370**). Of course, it's best to arrange for the rental before leaving home.

FACT FACTS: Florence

AIDS Organizations See "Community Centers" below.

American Express The offices are at Via Dante Alighieri 20–22R (☎ **055-50-981**) and Via Guicciardini 49R (☎ **055-288-751**). Both are open Monday to Friday 9am to 5:30pm and Saturday 9am to 12:30pm.

Community Centers & Gay Organizations **Arci-Gay/Arci-Lesbica Firenze,** Via San Zanobi 54R (☎ **055-476-557;** open Mon–Sat 4–8pm), offers a new community center that's a good place for all sorts of information. It holds meetings on Mondays at 9:30pm, has free HIV testing on Wednesday 4 to 6pm, and a group for young gays on Saturday 4 to 7pm. Women meet Thursday at 9pm. Gay counseling is available Monday to Friday at ☎ **055-288-126.** This group also sponsors a gay/lesbian youth group, a Catholic gay group, and lesbigay hiking.

Ireos, Via del Ponte all'Asse 7 (☎ **055-353-462;** open Mon–Sat 4–7pm), is a queer community-service center with a help line and free psychological and medical counseling Monday 4 to 7pm. It sponsors Coordinamento Queer, a consortium of various gay/lesbian groups. And **L'Amandorla** at ☎ **0360-311-058** (after 8pm), a women's separatist group, holds meetings on Wednesdays at 9:30pm; call for times and details.

Consulates The **U.S. Consulate** is at Lungarno Amerigo Vespucci 46 (☎ **055-239-8276;** open Mon–Fri 9am–2pm). The **U.K. Consulate** is at Lungarno Corsini 2 (☎ **055-284-133;** open Mon–Fri 9:30am–12:30pm and 2:30–4:30pm).

Currency Exchange There are currency-exchange services in most banks and at American Express. The **Ufficio Informazione** booth at the train station is another currency exchange (open daily 7:30am–7:40pm). Money can also be exchanged at the post office.

Cybercafe You can check your e-mail or send messages at **Internet Train,** Via dell'Oriuolo 25$, a block east of the Duomo (☎ **055-263-8963;** e-mail info@fionline.it; www.fionline.it; open daily "till late at night").

Doctors & Dentists Contact your consulate for a list of English-speaking doctors and dentists. Or call **Tourist Medical Service,** Via Lorenzo il Magnifico 59 (☎ **055-475-411**).

Emergencies For police, call ☎ **113.** For an ambulance, call ☎ **118.** For the fire department, call ☎ **115.**

Gay Media ***Quir,*** the Florentine gay and lesbian magazine, is available free in bars and at Arci-Gay; it's in English as well as Italian. They also publish ***The Pink Lily Gay & Lesbian Guide to Florence & Tuscany.*** A Florentine monthly with a gay section, ***Viva Piazza,*** is available at newsstands, as is ***Babilonia,*** the national gay magazine.

Telephone Public **pay phones** accept either coins (100L, 200L, or 500L coins) or a phonecard (sometimes only one or the other). The latter, a *carta telefonica* (or *scheda telefonica*), is available at post offices and *tabacchi* (tobacconists) in 5,000L ($2.80), 10,000L ($6), and 15,000L ($9) denominations and can be used for local or international calls. Break off the perforated corner of the card before using it. **Local phone calls** cost 200L (11¢), enough to put you in contact with AT&T, MCI, or Sprint's direct-dialing international operators—see "Fast Facts: Rome" in chapter 10. To make a call, lift the receiver, insert a coin or card, and dial. You may find old pay phones that still accept special tokens, *gettoni,* which you'll sometimes receive in bars in exchange for change, though this is now rare.

You can place **long-distance and international phone calls** at the Telecom office north of the Duomo at Via Cavour 21R (open daily 8am–9:45pm). Several countries also have direct-operator service, allowing callers to use AT&T or MCI calling cards or call collect (reverse charges) from almost any phone, including pay phones.

2 Pillow Talk

Guess what? There are more authentically gay-friendly hotels in Florence than anywhere else in Italy. Keep this in mind if you want to keep your lire exclusively pink. The city has lots of good "straight" hotels too, and with the number of queers blowing through town you'll be welcomed at all of them.

However, the old caveat applies: Book early if you're traveling from June to September or during Easter week. If you arrive roomless, you can go to the **Consorizio ITA office** in Stazione Santa Maria Novella (open daily 9am–9pm) for help finding a place. Low rates usually indicate off-season accommodation (Nov–Mar).

BETWEEN THE DUOMO & PIAZZA DELLA SIGNORIA

All the places below are gay or particularly gay-friendly.

✪ **Dei Mori.** Via Dante Alighieri 12, 50122 Firenze. ☎ and fax **055-211-438.** E-mail deimori@bnb.it. 6 units, 3 with bathroom. TEL. 120,00L ($67) double without bathroom, 140,000L ($78) double with bathroom. Rates include breakfast. AE, MC, V.

This small gay-run B&B, centrally located between Piazza del Duomo and Piazza della Signoria, opened in 1996 and is a good place if you want a friendly, comfortable accommodation in a homolike setting. The B&B occupies the second floor of an 1820 building. Daniele Dei, the owner, prefers to call his B&B "people-friendly"—meaning straights are as welcome as gays. The rooms are on the small side but nicely furnished, with standard double beds. The three rooms without bath have a sink and share two large bathrooms; the other rooms have showers. Daniele is a very attentive host and goes out his way to make his guests feel welcome. The parlor is filled with books and art, and guests have the use of the kitchen, which doubles as a breakfast room.

Hey, Big Spender

If you want to blow a wad on a Florence hotel, there are many deluxe places that'll be more than glad to bend over backward for you. Be prepared to drop a minimum of $200 a night for a double at any of them.

The **Hotel Bristol & Helvetia** and **Torre di Bellosguardo,** two of the toniest, are listed in full below. Here are some others where you'll feel like a princess, no matter what sex you are:

Grand Hotel, Piazza Ognissanti 1, 50123 Firenze (☎ **800/325-3589** in the U.S. and Canada, or 055-288-781; fax 055-217-400; Bus: B, C, or 9).

Grand Hotel Villa Medici, Via il Prato 42, 50123 Firenze (☎ **055-238-1331;** fax 055-238-1336; www.venere.it/firenze/villa_medici.html; e-mail sina@italyhotel.com; Bus: 9, 13, 16, 17, or 26).

Hotel Excelsior, Piazza Ognissanti 3, 50123 Firenze (☎ **800/325-3535** in the U.S. and Canada, or 055-264-201; fax 055-210-278; Bus: B, C, or 9).

Savoy Hotel, Piazza della Repubblica 7, 50123 Firenze (☎ **055-283-313;** fax 055-284-840; www.italyhotel.com/hotelm/3839.html; e-mail savoy@florenceallegro. it; Bus: 22, 36, 37).

✪ **Hotel Morandi alla Crocetta.** Via Laura 50, 50121 Firenze. ☎ **055-234-4747.** Fax 055-248-0954. www.dada.it/Hotel.Morandi. E-mail Hotel.Morandi@dada.it. 10 units. AC MINIBAR TV TEL. 220,000L ($122) double. AE, MC, DC, V.

This charming gay-friendly hotel, behind the Archaeological Museum and 2 blocks from the Accademia, has been a favorite of gays and lesbians for some time. It's considerably more distinguished than the smaller Dei Mori (above) but has less of a "gay-family" atmosphere. An unprepossessing entrance conceals a stylishly comfortable hotel on the second floor of the former convent of the Crocetto. You enter a large, lovely entrance hall with white walls and a heavy beamed ceiling. Original architectural elements have been retained whenever possible. Every room is differently laid out; all are beautifully furnished with original antiques and have safes. One room has a small balcony, another fragment of fresco from the convent. A great deal of atmosphere for an extremely reasonable price.

Hotel-Pensione Medici. Via dei Medici 6, 50122 Firenze. ☎ **055-291-098.** Fax 055-216-202. 40 units, 32 with bathroom. TEL. 100,000–250,000L ($54–$139) double with bathroom. Rates include breakfast. AE, MC, V.

This gay-friendly hotel is centrally located and offers a lot of nice things for a very low price. It's an economy hotel, so don't expect super-luxe accommodations. You'll be very comfortable, though, and the management is pro-gay all the way. First, see if you can get one of the four rooms with a balcony—they and some of the other rooms open out to fabulous views of the Duomo. So does the breakfast room and the narrow, somewhat vertigo-producing terrace (you're up several floors). The rooms vary in size

Beware the Zanzare

One- and two-star hotels rarely offer air-conditioning, and open windows mean Florentine mosquitoes (*zanzare*), a local problem that can prove most annoying. Most hotels carry mosquito-repellent coils you burn to keep the buzzers at bay.

and decor, and those on two of the floors have TVs. Some have a sink and shower but no toilet, others have just a sink, but most have baths with toilet and shower. If you're traveling alone you might try for the tower room, a single with a sloping roof; it's the only room with air-conditioning.

Hotel Porta Rossa. Via Porta Rossa 19, 50123 Firenze. ☎ **055-287-551.** Fax 055-282-179. 81 units. MINIBAR TV TEL. 240,000–270,000L ($133–$150) double. Higher rates include breakfast. AE, DC, MC, V.

This gay-friendly hotel, about halfway between Piazza della Repubblica and the Arno, was an inn in the 14th century, rebuilt in the 15th century, and passed to the Torrigiani family in the 16th century. You won't see evidence of its ancient history today. It is, however, a great old building, with a look that hasn't changed much since around the turn of the century. It's the kind of hotel that used to cater to business travelers looking for a simple room at a low price. You may find it moderately charming or merely faded and tatty, but it's close to everything, including gay bars. The rooms are hardly glamorous but are serviceable. (The single light bulbs hanging from a cord have got to go, though.) The baths are tiled and have a shower. It's fine for a day or two, but I doubt you'd want to stay much longer.

NEAR SANTA CROCE

✪ **Romantik Hotel J and J.** Via di Mezzo 20, 50121 Firenze. ☎ **055-234-5005.** Fax 055-240-282. E-mail jandj@dada.it. 24 units. AC MINIBAR TV TEL. 350,000–600,000L ($194–$333) double or suite. Rates include breakfast. AE, DC, MC, V.

Romantik is the name of the hotel chain, and *romantic* certainly fits the hotel itself. This is one of Italy's most beautifully designed small hotels. It opened in 1990; 400 years earlier it was a monastery. Its tranquillity envelops you the minute you walk in. Original features—frescoes, plasterwork, vaulted and beamed ceilings, and a cloister with a well and stone columns—have been skillfully incorporated into the modern hotel. Every room is unique and unusually spacious, furnished with antiques and carefully chosen contemporary furniture. The bathrooms are wonderful. You look out onto old roofs or the cloister. What more do you want?

NEAR THE PONTE VECCHIO

✪ **Hermitage Hotel.** Vicolo Marzio 1, Piazza del Pesce, 50122 Firenze. ☎ **055-287-216.** Fax 055-212-208. www.italyhotel.com/firenze/hermitage. E-mail hermitage@italyhotel.com. 29 units. AC TV TEL. 280,000–330,000L ($156–$183) double. Rates include breakfast. MC, V.

This charming and immaculately kept three-star hotel is around the corner from the north end of the Ponte Vecchio. Its rooms are scattered over six floors (the reception desk is on the fifth floor). Ten rooms have a view of the Arno, but if yours doesn't all you need do is go up to the wonderful rooftop sun terrace. Though not large, the rooms boast high ceilings and are well furnished with Tuscan antiques and reproductions. The beds are comfortable, and the tiled baths have semicircular shower stalls and hair dryers. Second-floor rooms come with whirlpool baths. Some of the courtyard-facing rooms can be noisy in the early morning, when the garbage trucks appear, so request one with a river view. In summer, breakfast is served in the lovely rooftop garden, and you can also sit outside with a drink. The staff all speak English and are unusually helpful.

Hotel della Signoria. Via delle Terme 1, 50123 Firenze. ☎ **055-214-530.** Fax 055-216-101. E-mail Dellasignoria@italyhotel.com. 27 units. AC TV TEL. 230,000–285,000L ($128–$158) double. Rates include breakfast. AE, DC, MC, V.

Like the Hermitage (above), which is in the same vicinity, this is a three-star hotel. It's a nice place and very well situated, but it lacks the Hermitage's charm and overall style.

Florence Accommodations & Dining

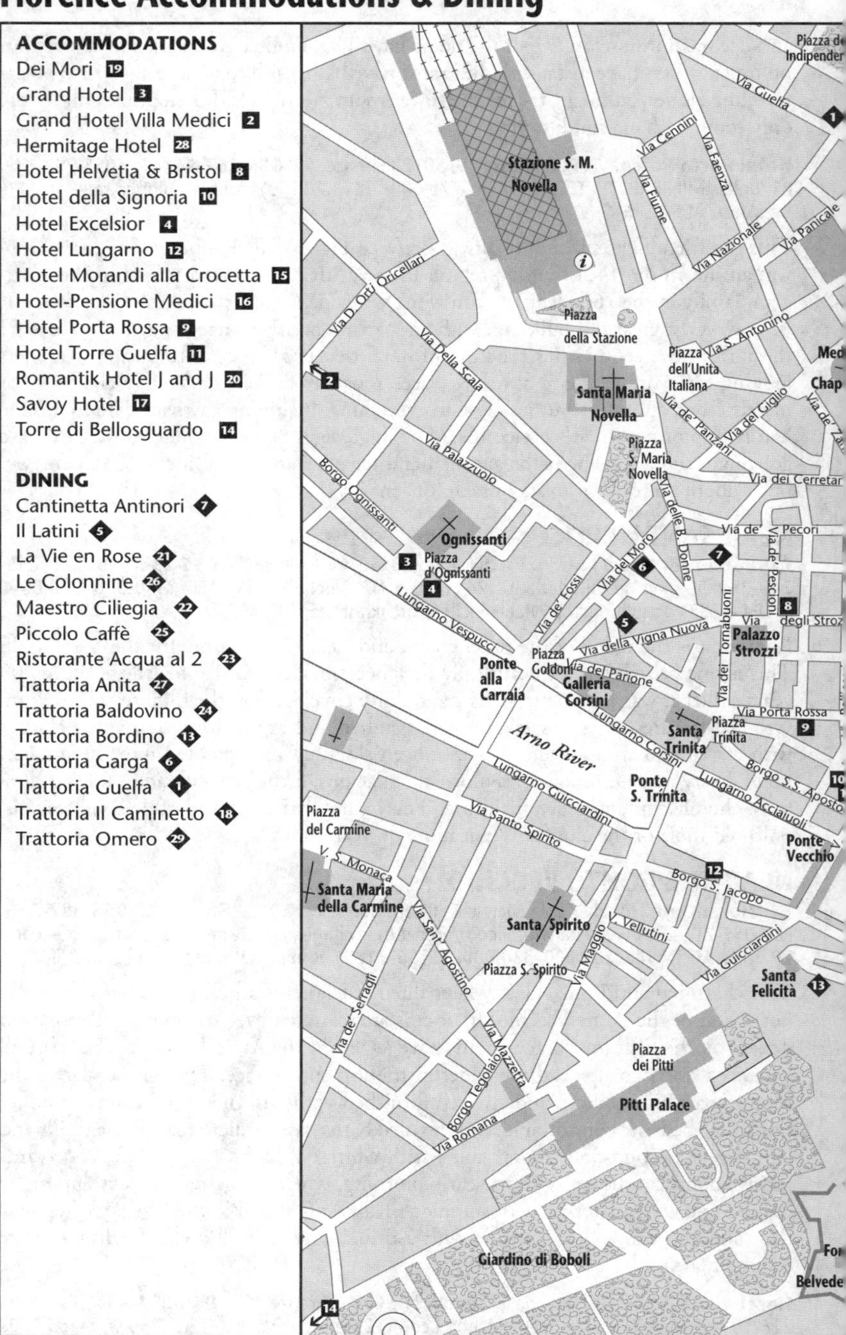

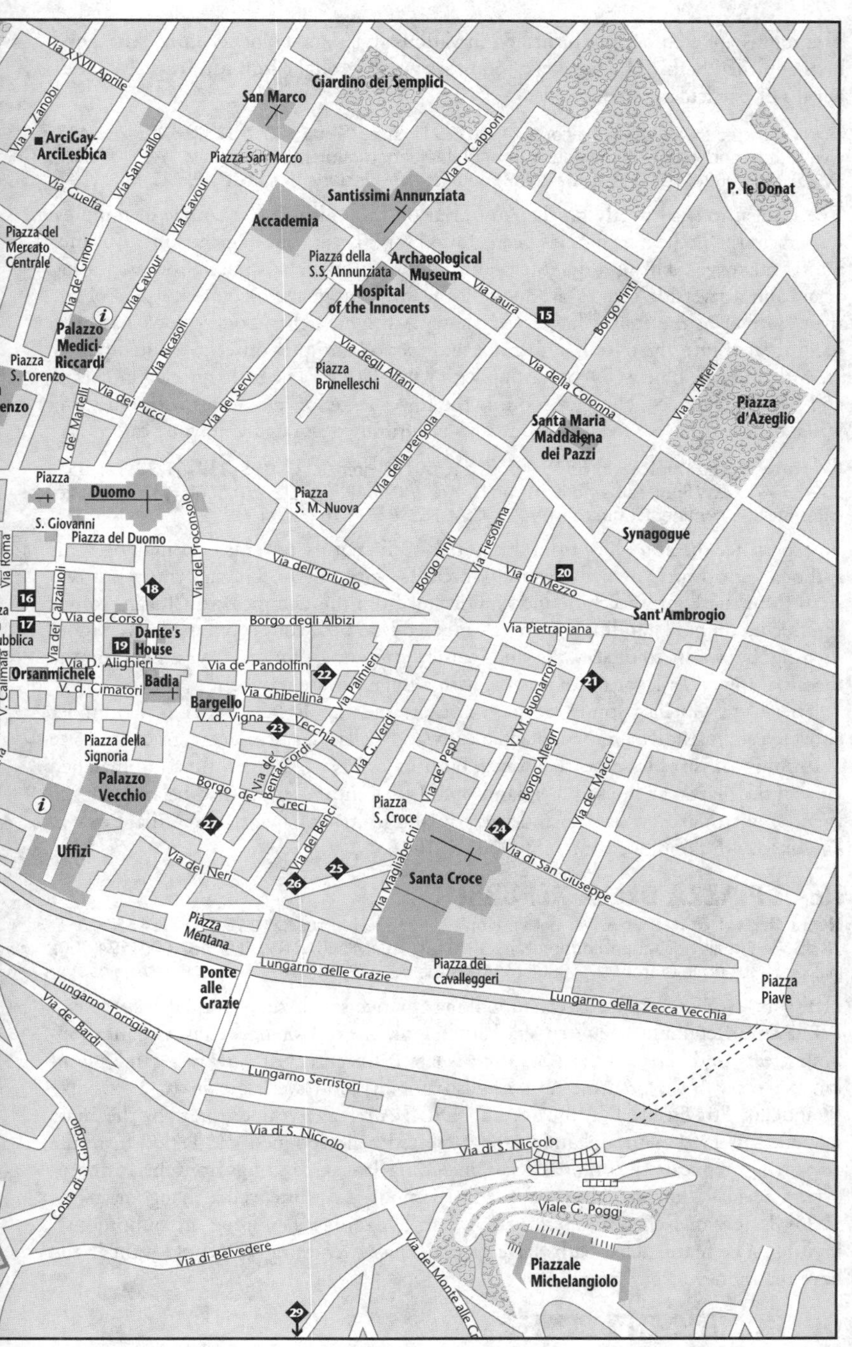

Via XXVII Aprile
Giardino dei Semplici
San Marco
Via S. Zanobi
ArciGay-
ArciLesbica
Via San Gallo
Piazza San Marco
Via G. Capponi
Via Guelfa
Via Cavour
Santissimi Annunziata
P. le Donat
Piazza del
Mercato
Centrale
Accademia
Via de' Ginori
Via Cavour
Piazza della
S.S. Annunziata
Archaeological
Museum
Hospital
of the Innocents
Via Laura
15
Borgo Pinti
Palazzo
Medici-
Riccardi
Via Ricasoli
Via degli Alfani
Piazza
S. Lorenzo
Piazza
Brunelleschi
Via della Colonna
Via V. Alfieri
Piazza
d'Azeglio
Via de' Pucci
Via dei Servi
V. de' Martelli
Via della Pergola
Santa Maria
Maddalena
dei Pazzi
Piazza
Duomo
Piazza
S. M. Nuova
S. Giovanni
Piazza del Duomo
Via del Proconsolo
Borgo Pinti
Via Fiesolana
Synagogue
Via dell'Oriuolo
20
Via di Mezzo
Via Roma
Via dei Calzaiuoli
18
16
17
Via del Corso
Borgo degli Albizi
Sant'Ambrogio
Via Pietrapiana
Dante's
House
19
Via D. Alighieri
Orsanmichele
Via de' Pandolfini
22
Via Palmieri
V. d. Cimatori
Badia
Via Ghibellina
21
Bargello
V. M. Buonarroti
V. d. Vigna
23
Vecchia
Via G. Verdi
Via de' Pepi
Borgo Allegri
Piazza della
Signoria
Via de' Bentaccordi
Palazzo
Vecchio
Borgo de' Greci
Via de' Macci
Piazza
S. Croce
27
Via dei Benci
24
Uffizi
Via di San Giuseppe
Via de' Neri
25
26
Santa Croce
Via Magliabechi
Piazza
Mentana
Ponte
alle
Grazie
Lungarno delle Grazie
Piazza dei
Cavalleggeri
Piazza
Piave
Lungarno della Zecca Vecchia
Lungarno Torrigiani
Via de' Bardi
Lungarno Serristori
Via di S. Niccolo
Via di S. Niccolo
Costa di S. Giorgio
Viale G. Poggi
Via di Belvedere
Piazzale
Michelangiolo
Via del Monte alle Cr
29

The rooms are comfortably furnished in various styles and color schemes, with good beds and tiled baths. The breakfast room has white wrought-iron furniture. It's pleasant if not particularly memorable.

Hotel Lungarno. Borgo San Jacopo 14, 50125 Firenze. ☎ **055-272-61.** Fax 055-268-437. www.lungarnohotels.it. E-mail lungarnohotels@lungarnohotels.it. 66 units. AC MINIBAR TV TEL. 400,000–510,000L ($222–$283) double. Rates include breakfast. AE, DC, MC, V.

The Lungarno sits directly on the Arno, but on the south side, a couple of minutes' walk from the Ponte Vecchio. It's been around for 30 years but reopened in 1997 after a total makeover. This is a quiet, elegant hotel with marvelous public rooms, seating areas, and a riverside terrace overlooking the swift cappuccino-colored waters of the river. Several of the rooms have river views. A bright, light, modern look has been incorporated into the overall ambience, with period antiques offset by contemporary artwork and pale-blue walls contrasting with white fabrics. The baths are clad in marble and have hair dryers. The best room is the tower suite, on two levels with old stone walls; it doesn't have a river view but is so beautifully decorated you won't care.

✪ **Hotel Torre Guelfa.** Borgo SS. Apostoli 8, 50123 Firenze. ☎ **055-239-63-38.** Fax 055-239-85-77. www.firenzealbergo.it. 12 units. A/C MINIBAR TV TEL. 290,000L ($161) double. Rates include continental breakfast. AE, MC, V. Bus: 6, 11, 36, 37, or 68.

To experience the 360° view from this hotel's 13th-century tower is breathtaking. This is the tallest privately owned tower in Florence's *centro storico.* Though you're just two steps from the Ponte Vecchio (and equidistant from the Duomo), you'll want to put sightseeing on hold and linger in your canopied iron bed, your room made even more inviting by warm-colored walls and paisley carpeting (for a view similar to the medieval tower's, ask for room no. 15, with a huge private terrace).

The Torre Guelfa's young owners have created the **Relais Uffizi** (call number above), a sibling hotel a few cobbled lanes away. Similar in spirit, decor, price, and size (11 rooms), it isn't blessed with a tower, but it does have a lounge with an unmatched view of the piazza, all housed in a handsome 14th-century refurbished palazzo. Or ask them about their new Tuscan hideaway in the heart of Chianti, the **Villa Rosa** in Pansano, with doubles costing 180,000L ($100).

NEAR PIAZZA DELLA REPUBBLICA

Hotel Bristol & Helvetia. Via dei Pescioni 2, 50123 Firenze. ☎ **055-287-814.** Fax 055-288-353. E-mail hbf@charminghotels.it. 52 units. AC MINIBAR TV TEL. 462,000–594,000L ($257–$330) double; from 979,000L ($544) suite. AE, DC, MC, V.

Here's an excellent choice if you're looking for five-star luxury, located just west of Piazza della Repubblica between Via Tornabuoni, one of Florence's most elegant shopping streets, and Piazza Strozzi. Built in the late 19th century, it quickly became a fashionable place for Florentine and English nobility and well known to artists like Pirandello, Stravinsky, D'Annuzio, and Duse. After a 3-year restoration, the hotel reopened in 1991 with a glamorously re-created belle-époque look. Period furniture and fittings replicate the original decor, including Tuscan paintings from the 15th century. The glass-domed Winter Garden, a famous artist/intellectual hangout in the 1920s, is now an exclusive American-style bar. The rooms, all unique, are sumptuously inviting. The marble-clad baths have Jacuzzi tubs. Everything you could want if you have the money to pay for it.

OUTSIDE THE CITY CENTER

✪ **Torre di Bellosguardo.** Via Roti Michelozzi 2, 50124 Firenze. ☎ **055-229-8145.** Fax 055-229-008. 16 units. TEL. 390,000–450,000L ($217–$250) double; 490,000–650,000L ($272–$361) suite. AE, V.

A stay at the Bellosguardo may prove to be one of your most memorable experiences in Italy. It's about 2 miles southwest of the city center, in the hills west of the Porta Romana. You'll have to take a taxi or drive to get there, but the walk back to Florence is beautiful, taking you past vineyards, olive groves, and panoramic views. The hotel, which opened in 1988, occupies a 13th-century Tuscan tower and a 15th-century palazzo surrounded by hilltop gardens with a pool. The setting is grand and the hotel a gem of tranquillity, with no TVs or modern gadgets to intrude on its historic personality. The enormous rooms are furnished with a few choice period antiques but retain a look of medieval simplicity. Breakfast is an extra 30,000L ($17). It's hard not to fall in love with this place.

3 Whet Your Appetite

Love that Tuscan food! It may be hearty *ribollita* (thick soup made with vegetables and bread) or *bistecca alla fiorentina* (pan-fried beefsteak sliced thin and sprinkled with arugula). It may be *pappardelle al coniglio* (pasta with rabbit sauce), *arista* (roast pork with garlic and rosemary), or veal with lemon sauce. The Florentines are blessed with the riches of the land, especially superb olive oil and wonderful produce. The wines, from nearby Chianti, Orvieto, and San Gimignano, are superb. Dessert specialties include *biscotti di Prato* (almond biscuits dipped in sweet *vin santo*) and *zuccotto* (sponge cake and chocolate pudding soaked in liqueur).

As for all the restaurant listings in Italy, the price range starts with the least expensive *primo* (first course) and ends with the most expensive *secondo* (second or main course). This isn't representative of the cost for a full meal, which may be four or five courses.

One other nice thing about Florence: There are more gay-friendly restaurants here than in any other Italian city. This doesn't mean gays are the primary clientele but that same-sex couples won't feel uncomfortable. That is true for most restaurants in this tolerant city, but I'm giving primary coverage to "ours."

Note: For the locations of the restaurants below, see the ""Florence Accommodations & Dining"" map on pp. 434–435.

NEAR SANTA CROCE

✪ **La Vie en Rose.** Borgo Allegri 68R. ☎ **055-245-860.** Reservations recommended for dinner. Main courses 10,000–18,000L ($6–$10). AE, MC, V. Mon–Fri noon–2pm; Wed–Mon 7:30pm–12:30am. CREATIVE TUSCAN.

La Vie en Rose, a few minutes' walk north of the church of Santa Croce, may be the only restaurant in Italy where you and your sweetie can have a truly romantic meal, holding hands between courses if you feel like it. The chef is an exponent of "nuova cucina Toscana" (new Tuscan cuisine), which means less butter, less oil, and less pepper. The restaurant is a small narrow room lined with tables on two sides and pale pistachio-colored walls dominated by large contemporary paintings. Antipasti offerings include homemade pâté with orange jelly, salmon pâté, and endive-and-shrimp salad with cognac. There are some adventurous pastas: tortelli stuffed with leeks and cottage cheese, ravioli stuffed with pears and pecorino cheese, and tagliatelle with arugula and clams. Main courses (served with fresh vegetables) include curried turkey stew, rabbit with herbs, salmon fillet with yogurt, stuffed chicken, and steamed vegetables with balsamic vinegar.

Le Colonnine. Via dei Benci 6R. ☎ **055-234-6417.** Main courses 8,000–22,000L ($4–$12). AE, MC, V. Bar Tues–Sun 7am–2am; restaurant Tues–Sun noon–3:30pm and 7:30pm–2am. ITALIAN/PIZZA.

Other Gay-Friendly Spots to Graze

The following restaurants advertise in the local gay papers, or I've picked up their names from other gay sources. I haven't eaten at them, so I can't give you a personal recommendation; chances are they're all good.

Gaugain, Via degli Alfani 24R (☎ **055-234-0616;** open Mon–Sat 8–11pm), is a gay-owned vegetarian restaurant near the university; main courses run about 8,000L ($4). **Maestro Ciliegia,** Via Matteo Palmieri 34R (☎ **055-293-372;** open Tues–Sun noon–3pm and 7pm–midnight), is a Tuscan trattoria and pizzeria in the *centro storico;* it's in the 15,000L-to-30,000L ($8-to-$17) price range. And **Trattoria Guelfa,** Via Guelfa 103R (☎ **055-213-306;** open Thurs–Tues noon–2:30pm and 7–10:30pm), east of the train station near the Fortezza da Basso, serves Tuscan cuisine.

This lively and unpretentious bar/restaurant sits on a corner just west of the church of Santa Croce. It's not really gay but draws a lot of students, younger visitors who don't frequent Florence's fancier restaurants, and locals. The front area is a bar where you can get a good sandwich or have a stand-up breakfast of pastry and coffee. Behind this is a large restaurant. For lunch it serves only pizza, or you can help yourself to the buffet spread. The pizzas run the gamut from a simple *margherita* with tomato, mozzarella, and basil to *frutti di mare* (seafood). You can also get focaccia and calzones. At night you'll find a full menu of pastas, salads, and meat dishes. This isn't gourmet cooking, but it's filling and easy on the pocketbook. Also, the place is open late—not often the case with Florence restaurants.

Piccolo Caffè. Via Borgo Santa Croce 27. ☎ **055-241-704.** Main courses 5,000–8,000L ($3–$4). No credit cards. Sun–Thurs 9:30am–1am, Fri–Sat to 2:30am. ITALIAN/TUSCAN.

This cafe/bar where pop music is always playing, around the corner from the church of Santa Croce, has been a longtime favorite of gays and lesbians. The overall atmosphere is, shall we say, colorful: black floor, chrome stools, and yellow, green, and magenta walls. You can get a good simple meal (or a cappuccino or glass of wine) for not much money. Dishes include lasagna, a good tortelloni with cream and bacon, ravioli with red-radish-and-cream sauce, and an unpretentious spaghetti with basil. There's also a special pasta with soft cheese and spinach, mixed salads, cheese plates, and a yummy sausage-and-fennel plate. The pizzas include a *margherita* (with ham) and *caprese* (carpaccio with Parmesan, salt, pepper, and lemon).

Trattoria Baldovino. Via San Giuseppe 22R ☎ **055-241-773.** Main courses 10,000–30,000L ($6–$17). AE, DC. Wed–Mon 12:30–3pm and 7:30–11pm. NEW ITALIAN.

Creative homestyle cooking is the order of the day (and night) at Baldovino, on the north side of the church of Santa Croce. A first course might be linguine with scampi and zucchini; spaghetti with oil, eggplant, and pecorino cheese; fettuccine with arugula and brie; or hearty meat soup (*zuppa di polpo*). From there you can go on to lamb with yogurt, chicken breasts with kiwi, or veal scallopini cooked in sweet *vin santo.* All this takes place in a pretty L-shaped room with marble-topped tables, ivory-colored walls, and low lighting.

NEAR PIAZZA DELLA SIGNORIA

Ristorante Acqua al 2. Via della Vigna Vecchia 40R. ☎ **055-284-170.** Reservations recommended. Main courses 10,000–25,000L ($6–$14). AE, MC, V. Daily 7:30pm–1am. CREATIVE ITALIAN.

Take a Gelato Break

Opened in the 1930s and today run by the third generation of the Vivoli family, the ✪ **Gelateria Vivoli,** Via Isola delle Stinche 7R (☎ **055-292-334;** open Tues–Sun 8am–1am; closed 3 weeks in Aug), produces some of Italy's finest ice cream and provides the gelati for many of Florence's restaurants. Buy a ticket first and then select your flavor—blueberry, fig, melon, and other fruits in season, as well as chocolate mousse or coffee ice cream flavored with espresso. You can also choose from a number of *semifreddi*—an Italian ice cream using cream as a base instead of milk. The most popular flavors are almond, *marengo* (a type of meringue), and *zabaglione* (eggnog). Others are *limoncini alla crema* (candied lemon peels with vanilla ice cream) and *aranciotti al cioccolate* (candied orange peels with chocolate ice cream). Prices range from 3,000 to 16,000L ($1.75 to $9).

Of all the centrally located gelaterie, **Festival del Gelato,** Via del Corso 75R, just off Via dei Calzaiuoli (☎ **055-239-4386;** open Tues–Sun, 8am to 1am in summer and 11am to 1am in winter), has been the only serious contender to Vivoli, offering about 50 flavors along with pounding pop music and bright neon.

This popular "nuova cucina Italiana" (new Italian cooking) restaurant is just east of the Bargello museum. There are tables with benches in front and another dining room in back. Just about everything on the menu is worth trying. If you like risotto, there's a dish with gorgonzola, a second with savory green sauce (*sugo verde*), and a third with mushrooms. If you're looking for *carne* (meat), try the wonderful beef fillet cooked with balsamic vinegar or the one made with bilberrys. You can also have grilled veal or chicken breasts with curry, artichoke, or mushroom sauce.

Trattoria Anita. Via del Parlascio 2R (at the corner of Via Vinegia). ☎ **055-218-698.** Main courses 7,000–18,000L ($4–$10). AE, MC, V. Mon–Sat noon–2:30pm and 7–10:15pm. TUSCAN.

A lot of locals frequent this old trattoria serving solid Tuscan food. It has a nice, simple ambience with brown-wood wainscoting and a row of wine bottles on a shelf above. You might want to start with the *antipasto Anita* (bread, salami, and black olives). For a *primo,* try the *talgierini all'Anita,* a pasta dish of thin noodles with ham, mushrooms, Parmesan, and cream. They serve one Florentine dish many Americans eschew rather than chew: *trippa* (tripe). You might be more comfortable with *osso buco* (veal shank). My personal favorite is *lombatina al limone* (thin slices of veal with lemon sauce).

NEAR THE DUOMO

Trattoria Il Caminetto. Via dello Studio 34R. ☎ **055-239-6274.** Main courses 10,000–25,000L ($6–$14). No credit cards. Thurs–Tues 12:30–3pm and 7pm–midnight. TUSCAN.

Heavenly smells emanate from this charming old-fashioned trattoria just south of the Duomo. It's a cozy spot, with arched brick passageways, coffered ceilings, blue tablecloths, and paintings covering every inch of wall space. There are different specials every day (like artichoke salad) as well as delicious Tuscan standards like *ribollita* and *osso buco.* One pasta worth trying is the tagliatelle with fresh peas. If *spada* (swordfish) is on the menu, go for it. Or try the herbed roast pork. The place isn't openly gay, but if you behave yourself you'll be fine.

NEAR SANTA MARIA NOVELLA

Cantinetta Antinori. Piazza Antinori 3. ☎ **055-292-234.** Reservations recommended. Main courses 25,000–32,000L ($14–$18). AE, DC, MC, V. Mon–Fri 12:30–2:30pm and 7–10:30pm. Closed Aug and Dec 24–Jan 6. Bus: 6, 11, 36, 37, or 68. FLORENTINE/TUSCAN.

In the 15th-century Palazzo Antinori is this popular restaurant and one of the city's few top-notch wine bars. It's a showplace for the vintages of the most distinguished wine company in Tuscany, Umbria, and Piedmont, and you can sample these by the glass at the bar or by the bottle with the meals served at wooden tables. The cookery is standard but satisfying, especially the sausages with white haricot beans, fresh Tuscan ewe's cheese, and thick oven-roasted Chiana beef (even if it is a bit pricey).

✪ **Trattoria Garga.** Via del Moro 48R. ☎ **055-239-8898.** Reservations required. Main courses 20,000–45,000L ($11–$25). AE, DC, MC, V. Tues–Sat 12:30–3pm and 7:30pm–midnight. CREATIVE TUSCAN.

One of Florence's top restaurants, known for its adventuresome cooking, Trattoria Garga is a few minutes' walk east of Santa Maria Novella. It's a fashionable hangout, featuring several small rooms decorated with murals painted in Tuscan reds and blues. One first course definitely worth trying is the *taglialini magnifico* made with pasta, orange and lemon rind, cognac-flavored cream, and Parmesan. Simpler, but just as good, is the taglialini with porcinis and olive oil. Escalopes of veal with lemon are tart and sweet, or there's a heartier version with artichokes. The menu also has some unusual seasonal game dishes, like wild boar with juniper berries and grilled marinated quail. Finish your meal with biscotti dipped in *vin santo.* A meal here is pricey but worth it.

ACROSS THE ARNO

Trattoria Bordino. Via Stracciatella 9R. ☎ **055-213-048.** Reservations recommended. Main courses 6,000–20,000L ($3–$11). AE, MC, V. Mon–Sat noon–2:30pm and 7:30–10:30pm. TUSCAN.

To find this friendly trattoria, cross to the south side of the Ponte Vecchio, then turn left up Via dei Bardi and right on Via Stracciatella. The dining room, with old brick walls and wrought-iron lighting fixtures, is often jammed with Italian families doing the "mangia, mangia, mangia" thing, so enter into the spirit of the place. They have a *forno* (oven) for grills. But first, how about a plate of penne with smoked salmon or spaghetti with lobster and tomato sauce? The chicken breast with cream and capers and the carpaccio (thinly sliced raw beef) with artichokes and Parmesan are great. You can also get rib of veal with mushrooms, olives, and cream. If you want a grilled main course, try the *lombatina di vitello* (veal loin) or *bistecca alla fiorentina.* This is a good place for grilled trout—but they also do a sole with champagne and cream.

✪ **Trattoria Omero.** Via Pian del Giulari 11R, Arcetri. ☎ **055-220-053.** Reservations essential. Main courses 10,000–45,000L ($6–$25). AE, DC, MC, V. Wed–Mon noon–2:30pm and 7:30–10:30pm. TUSCAN.

Communal Eating

There are some good inexpensive restaurants where you can't reserve and are seated at communal tables. This can be fun if you've had a glass of wine and like meeting new people but a nightmare if you're misanthropic or on a tight schedule. One of the most popular, and most boisterous, is **Il Latini,** Via Palchetti 4, west of Piazza della Repubblica. It's open for dinner only, and the crowd starts congregating outside at about 5 or 6pm; it opens around 7pm. Tuscan food is served from a limited menu.

If you want to have a truly outstanding Tuscan meal, this is the spot. Omero is secreted away in the hills about 15 minutes south of the *centro storico* and you need a taxi to get there (about $15). You'd never guess that hiding behind the inconspicuous exterior—marked by a tiny sign—is one of the finest restaurants in the region. The front area is a delicatessen that sells Tuscan delicacies. Behind, on two levels and spilling out to a grape-arbored terrace, are lovely dining rooms with sublimely beautiful views of hills dotted with villas, olive groves, and cypress trees. The restaurant is frequented by well-heeled Italians who know of it by reputation; its elegance is understated. Start with a selection of *crostini* covered with liver and artichoke pâtés and served with Tuscan sausages. Then go on to the *ribollita,* a thick, traditional Tuscan bread soup, the ravioli, or the penne with meat sauce. (They can give you a sampling of each.) Other Tuscan specialties include fried chicken, fried rabbit, and a superb *tagliata con rucola* (thin slices of grilled beef steak topped with arugula). For dessert there is a refreshing fruit salad, chocolate torte, and cream pie with raspberry sauce. The restaurant has a huge wine cellar with 250 types of Tuscan wines; choose a Chianti to go with your meal and you'll be in heaven.

4 Exploring Florence

If you're an itinerary nut, with dozens of places you have to visit every day, keep in mind that many churches and museums close in the early part of the afternoon and reopen later. The Uffizi Gallery will no doubt be high on your list of must-sees, but even with the new reservation system you could spend more than an hour waiting in line to get in. However, if you show up later in the day—after 5pm, say—you can often get in immediately.

One general rule for sightseeing in Florence: The earlier the better. Lines for major attractions such as the Duomo can be endless; get there early or part of your day will be wasted.

You can arrange for special guided tours through the **Ufficio Guide Turistiche,** Viale Gramsci 9a (☎ **055-247-8188**). **American Express** (☎ **055-50-981**) and **SitaSightseeing** (☎ **055-214-721**) offer half-day guided bus tours of the major sights, but unless you're disabled this isn't a good way to see Florence.

THE HITS YOU SHOULDN'T MISS

✪ **Uffizi Gallery (Galleria degli Uffizi).** Piazzale degli Uffizi 6. ☎ **055-238-85;** reservations ☎ 055-294-882. Admission 12,000L ($7). Tues–Sat 8:30am–10pm, Sun to 8pm.

Because of the long, long lines at the Uffizi (only a certain number of people are allowed inside at any one time), it's a good idea to reserve your tickets as far in advance as possible with a credit card (MasterCard and Visa only); you must pay for them at least 5 days before entrance and can pick them up at the tourist information office on Via Chiasso Baroncelli on the morning of the reserved date. The other alternative is to arrive about 2 hours before closing, when you can often get in immediately. The gallery suffered major damage in a 1993 terrorist bomb attack: Some 200 paintings were damaged, 3 were destroyed. As a result, some of the rooms may still be closed.

Now to the good stuff. This is one of the greatest art galleries in the world. The collection, assembled over 3 centuries by the Medici family for their private delectation, contains many world-famous Italian and European masterpieces. Gay pride of place goes to the Renaissance paintings and sculpture. Though no mention is made of any of the artists' sexuality, at least four of them—Botticelli, Leonardo, Michelangelo, and Caravaggio—were full- or part-time same-sexers.

A Tip on Seeing *David*

The wait to get in to see Michelangelo's *David* can be an hour or even more. Try getting there before the museum opens in the morning or an hour or two before closing.

There's far too much here to enumerate. The first room is classical sculpture. Next come works by Cimabue and Giotto, who rebelled against the constraints of the iconic Byzantine style. The Botticelli rooms showcase several of his most important paintings, including *Birth of Venus* (often called "Venus on the Half Shell"), *Minerva Subduing the Centaur*, and *Primavera* (Spring). Leonardo's *Annunciation* and his unfinished *Adoration of the Magi* are farther on. After passing works by Giorgione, Bellini, Mantegna, Perugino, and Dürer, you come to Michelangelo's *Holy Family* and eventually Caravaggio's *Bacchus*. Women take note: There's a painting of *Judith* by Artemisia Gentileschi, the great female artist whose life was the subject of the recent film *Artemisia*. This is but the sparsest inventory of the treasures you'll find in the Uffizi; give yourself as much time as possible.

✪ **Academy Gallery (Galleria dell'Accademia).** Via Ricasoli 60. ☎ **055-238-8609;** reservations ☎ 055-294-882. Admission 12,000L ($7). Tues–Sat 8:30am–10pm, Sun to 8pm.

Though there are other paintings and sculptures on display here, there's one work that literally towers above all the others: Michelangelo's ***David.*** I once overheard a hideous teenaged girl say of this piece: "Nice body, but tiny wiener." I could've beaned that stupid little size queen. The length of David's organ isn't the issue here or even relevant. The 17-foot figure, carved from a block of Duccio marble, possesses an Apollonian perfection that's breathtaking. This sculpture (nicknamed Il Gigante) originally stood in Piazza della Signoria but was moved here in 1873 (a life-size copy stands in its place on the piazza and another stands in Piazzale Michelangiolo), but now it has star status beneath the rotunda of the main room built specifically for its display. A Plexiglas screen surrounds the base so you can't get close enough to suck *David*'s toe (or hack it off as someone once tried to do), but the screen in no way obstructs the total view. The adjacent picture gallery contains works by various Tuscan masters, including our gay brother Sandro Botticelli.

✪ **Duomo, Campanile, and Duomo Museum (Museo dell'Opera del Duomo).** Piazza del Duomo. ☎ **055-230-2885.** Cathedral free; cupola 10,000L ($6); campanile 10,000L ($6); Duomo Museum 4,000L ($2). Cathedral Mon–Sat 10am–5pm, Sun 1–5pm. Cupola Mon–Fri 8:30am–6:20pm, Sat 8:30am–5pm. Campanile summer daily 9am–6:50pm; winter daily to 4:20pm. Duomo Museum summer Mon–Sat 9am–6:50pm; winter Mon–Sat to 6:20pm.

Santa Maria del Fiore (St. Mary of the Flowers), Florence's cathedral, is graced by one of the most magnificent domes in the world. Like the adjacent Baptistery, the cathedral was built with geometric bands of pink, white, and green marble in Florentine Gothic style. The enormous edifice was started in the late 13th century and consecrated in 1436—but work continued into the 19th century. Renaissance architect Filippo Brunelleschi labored long and hard to get the commission for the dome. It's a work of structural genius, ribbed but constructed without supports. You can climb up into this cupola for a fabulous view. The interior of the cathedral is rather spartan and disappoints many visitors, but the quiet serenity of the space is moving in its own way.

The peerless beauty of Brunelleschi's dome is matched by the cathedral's adjacent 274-foot-high **campanile (bell tower).** This masterpiece of Tuscan Gothic, banded with colored marble, was designed by the great Florentine artist Giotto, the first artist to free painting from the stiff formality of Byzantium. He was working on it at the time of his death in 1337. Andrea Pisano (who designed the famous Baptistery doors) saw the work to its completion. It's a hefty climb to the top, but once there you'll have an incomparable view of Florence and the surrounding villa-dotted hills.

The **Duomo Museum (Museo dell'Opera del Duomo),** across the street from the cathedral, contains the originals of Pisano's bronze Baptistery doors and other pieces of sculpture removed from the cathedral and campanile to protect them from air pollution.

Baptistery (Battistero San Giovanni). Piazza San Giovanni. ☎ **055-230-2885.** Admission 5,000L ($3). Mon–Sat 1:30–6:30pm, Sun 8:30am–1:30pm.

The octagonal baptistery, built in the 11th and 12th centuries, was named for St. John the Baptist, patron saint of Florence. This Romanesque structure, with its alternating bands of pink, white, and green marble, is the oldest building in Florence. Its most famous features are two sets of gilt-covered bronze doors representing scenes from the Bible, a nearly life-long project by Lorenzo Ghiberti. He began work on the east doors (scenes from the New Testament) in 1501, when he was 23, and completed them nearly 20 years later. He then labored over the west doors (scenes from the Old Testament) for another 27 years, completing them in 1452, just 3 years before his death. (The doors you see are actually copies; the originals are in the Duomo Museum.) Even older are the south doors, created by Andrea Pisano and completed in 1336. These show the "Virtues" and scenes from the life of St. John the Baptist. The interior dome of the Baptistery is decorated with 13th-century mosaics.

Medici Chapels (Cappelle Medicee). Piazza Madonna degli Aldobrandini. ☎ **055-238-8602;** reservations ☎ 055-294-882. Admission 10,000L ($6). Tues–Sat 8:30am–5pm, Sun to 1:50pm.

Michelangelo was chosen by the ruling Medicis to create their family mausoleum adjacent to the Basilica of San Lorenzo. The great gay Renaissance artist worked for 13 years (1521–34) to create the various sculptural groups found in the dark and gloomy **New Sacristry.** In the process, he paved (or chiseled) his way to a style that prefigured the Baroque. Was Michelangelo being ironic when he sculpted Lorenzo II, the deranged duke of Urbino, as a "thinker"? Or just thinking about his commission? Allegorical figures called *Dawn* (a woman) and *Dusk* (a man) are also found on Lorenzo's tomb. More famous are the powerful figures called *Night* (a woman in need of Excedrin P.M.) and *Day* (a hunk facing the rigors of the day). Michelangelo's female figures always look like men with breasts to me; what do you think? A trap door and winding staircase lead to a deeper chamber where Michelangelo used the walls as a kind of sketchpad.

✪ **Bargello Museum (Museo del Bargello).** Via del Proconsolo 4. ☎ **055-238-8605;** reservations ☎ 055-294-882. Admission 8,000L ($4). Tues–Sun 8:30am–1:50pm.

Yet another treasure house of Renaissance sculpture, the Bargello is near Piazza della Signoria. Michelangelo sculpted not one *David,* but two: The *David* on display here was done about a quarter-century after the *David* in the Accademia. This one is less virile—an indication of Michelangelo's changing style if not his mastery with a chisel. An earlier work, *Bacchus,* is also on display. Another artist to pay attention to here is Donatello, one of the greatest talents of the early Renaissance. His bronze *David* was the first freestanding nude sculpture to be created since classical antiquity and thus deserves a special place in art history. This is no macho giant slayer, however. Donatello's *David* is a somewhat coy and very stylish little gent, posing so prettily (naked except for a hat and boots) he almost looks like a wet dream of Aubrey Beardsley.

Florence Attractions

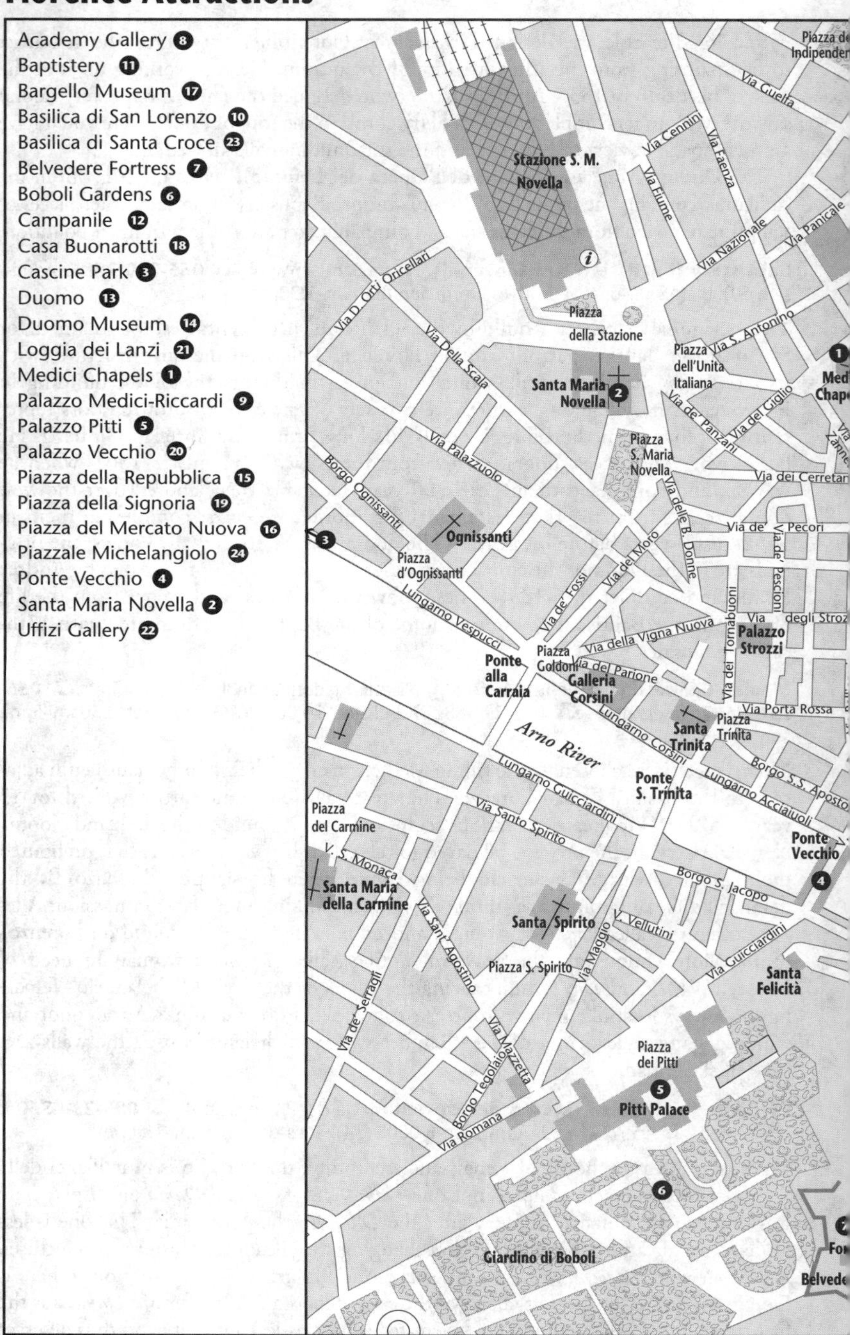

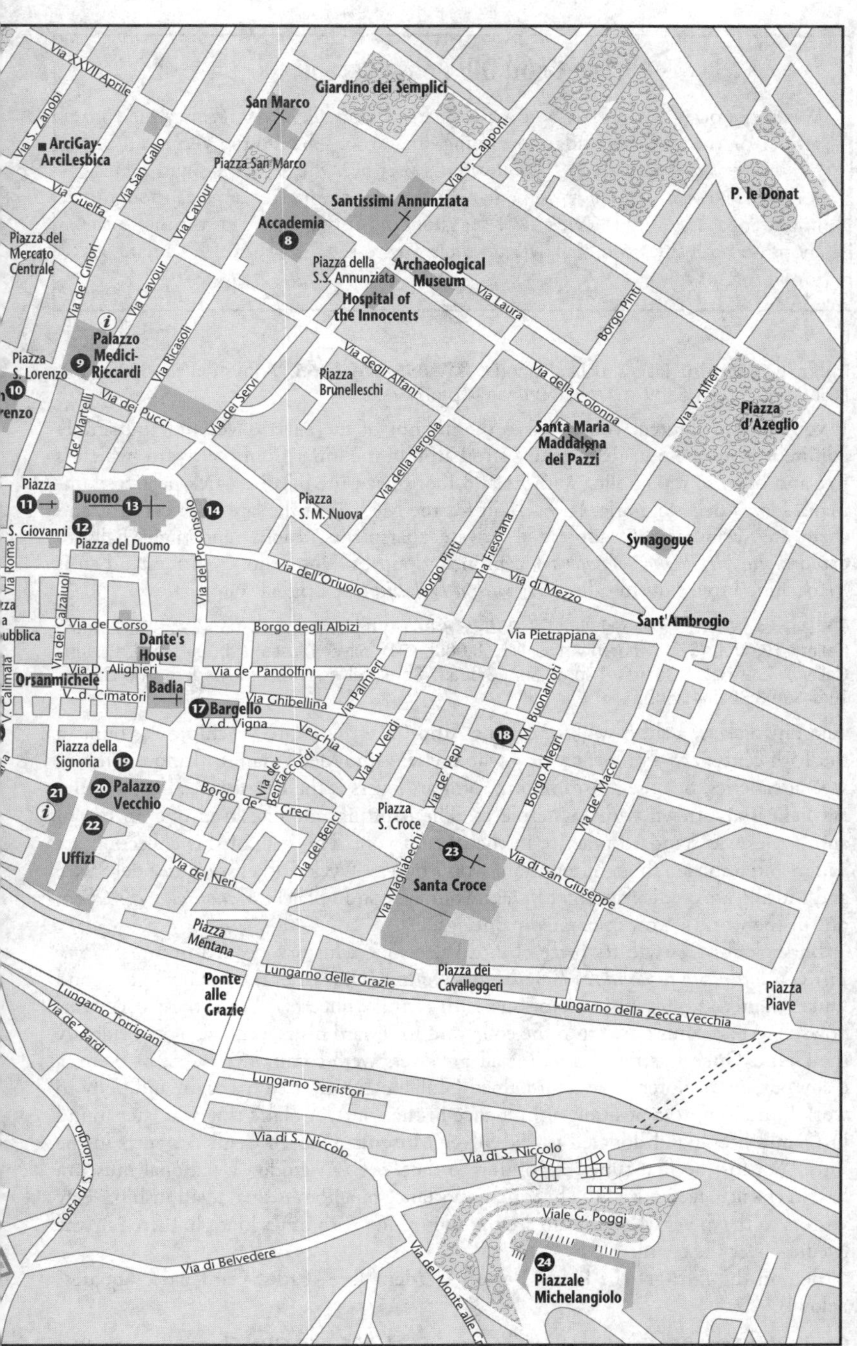

Via XXVII Aprile
Via S. Zanobi
ArciGay-ArciLesbica
Via San Gallo
San Marco
Giardino dei Semplici
Piazza San Marco
Via G. Capponi
P. le Donat
Via Guelfa
Via Cavour
Santissimi Annunziata
Accademia
8
Piazza del Mercato Centrale
Via de' Ginori
Piazza della S.S. Annunziata
Archaeological Museum
Hospital of the Innocents
Via Laura
Borgo Pinti
Palazzo Medici-Riccardi
9
Via Ricasoli
Piazza S. Lorenzo
10
Via degli Alfani
Piazza Brunelleschi
Via della Colonna
Via V. Alfieri
Piazza d'Azeglio
Via dei Pucci
Via dei Servi
Via de' Martelli
Santa Maria Maddalena dei Pazzi
Via della Pergola
Piazza
11
Duomo
13
14
Piazza S. M. Nuova
S. Giovanni
12
Piazza del Duomo
Via del Proconsolo
Synagogue
Via dell'Oriuolo
Borgo Pinti
Via Fiesolana
Via di Mezzo
Via Roma
Via dei Calzaiuoli
Via del Corso
Borgo degli Albizi
Sant'Ambrogio
Via Pietrapiana
Dante's House
Via D. Alighieri
Via de' Pandolfini
Orsanmichele
V. d. Cimatori
Badia
Via Ghibellina
Via Palmieri
17 Bargello
V. d. Vigna
Vecchia
V. M. Buonarroti
18
Via G. Verdi
Via de' Pepi
V. Calimala
Piazza della Signoria
19
Via de' Bentaccordi
Borgo Allegri
Via de' Macci
20 Palazzo Vecchio
21
Borgo de' Greci
Piazza S. Croce
22
Via dei Benci
Uffizi
23
Via di San Giuseppe
Via del Neri
Via Magliabechi
Santa Croce
Piazza Mentana
Ponte alle Grazie
Lungarno delle Grazie
Piazza dei Cavalleggeri
Piazza Piave
Lungarno della Zecca Vecchia
Lungarno Torrigiani
Via de' Bardi
Lungarno Serristori
Via di S. Niccolo
Via di S. Niccolo
Costa di S. Giorgio
Viale G. Poggi
Via di Belvedere
Via del Monte alle Croci
24
Piazzale Michelangiolo

The Good Old Ponte Vecchio

When the occupying Nazis beat a retreat from Florence in 1944, they blew up several of the historic bridges spanning the Arno. The **Ponte Vecchio (Old Bridge)** was spared. In 1966, floodwaters swept over the top of it—and again it survived. Now it's closed to vehicular traffic but at times it seems as though it might collapse under the weight of the thousands of tourists who throng to the shops on both sides and pass over on their way to the Pitti Palace. It's a hangout for all sorts.

Palazzo Vecchio. Piazza della Signoria. ☎ **055-276-8465.** Admission 10,000L ($6). Mon–Wed and Fri–Sat 9am–7pm, Sun 8am–1pm.

If your time is limited, you can skip the interior of the Palazzo Vecchio and simply admire it from the outside or take a stroll around the inner front courtyard, which is free and open to the public. With its 308-foot tower, the massive brick palazzo dominates Piazza della Signoria. It was built for the Medicis in the late 13th century, and there are various richly appointed private apartments, salons, and giant halls to explore. *Judith Slaying Holofernes*, a bronze group by Donatello, is inside, and so is Verocchio's bronze putto called *Boy with a Dolphin* (the original Flipper).

✪ **Palazzo Pitti.** Piazza dei Pitti. ☎ **055-238-8614;** reservations ☎ 055-294-882. Palatina Gallery 12,000L ($7); Modern Art Gallery 8,000L ($4); Silver Museum 4,000L ($2). Palatina Gallery, Tues–Sat 8:30am– 10pm, Sun 8:30am–8pm. Silver Museum/Modern Art Gallery, Tues–Sun 8:30am–1:50pm.

The Pitti Palace, a short walk across the Arno (take the Ponte Vecchio), was built in the 15th century as a residence for—whom else?—the Medici family. It now contains several galleries, but the most important for art lovers is the **Palatina Gallery (Galleria Palatina),** strewn with masterpieces. The paintings are displayed one on top of another, as was standard practice in the days of yore. The stars of this collection are Titian and Raphael, though important works by Van Dyck, Rubens, Andrea del Sarto, and Murillo are on display. You can feast your eyes on Raphael's *Madonna of the Chair*, one of the world's most celebrated paintings.

But now for an itty-bitty piece of Pitti Palace queer history gleaned from *The Pink Lily Gay and Lesbian Guide to Florence and Tuscany.* The last of the Medici line, Grand Duke Gian Gastone, was a notorious 18th-century queerola. From the palace windows, he'd toss coins down into the courtyard to reward his favorite gigolos. Evidently the Grand Duke was into trade, for all his lovers were commoners. One of them, a dishy but smart Florentine youth named Giuliano Dami, used his brain and body to work himself up to a position of influence in the court. A man's ring was later found in Dami's house and donated to the **Silver Museum (Museo degli Argenti)** in the Pitti. "So, for the first time," according to the *Pink Lily* guide, "a national museum has, in essence, recognized the historic importance of a homosexual relationship." Gay visitors to the Silver Museum can see the ring, along with other loot plundered by the Medicis over the centuries.

Behind the Pitti are the lovely **Boboli Gardens** (see "Parks, Gardens & Squares" below).

Basilica di Santa Croce. Piazza Santa Croce 16. ☎ **055-244-619.** Church, free; cloisters and church museum, 4,000L ($2.40). Church, daily 8am–12:30pm and 3–6:30pm. Museum and cloisters, Mar–Sept Thurs–Tues 10am–12:30pm and 2:30–6:30pm; Oct–Feb daily 10am–12:30pm and 3–5pm. Bus: B, 13, 23, or 71.

This Franciscan church, a kind of Tuscan Westminster Abbey, contains the tombs of Michelangelo, Machiavelli, Dante, and Galileo, who at the hands of the Inquisition "recanted" his concept that the earth revolves around the sun. In the right nave (first tomb) is the Vasari-executed monument to Michelangelo, whose 89-year-old body was smuggled back to his native Florence from Rome, where the pope wanted the revered "Mike" to remain. A prune-faced Dante, a poet belatedly honored in the city that exiled him, looks down rather forbiddingly in the next memorial. Farther on, still on the right, is the tomb of Niccolò Machiavelli, whose *The Prince* (about Cesare Borgia) became a virtual textbook on power politics. Nearby is Donatello's lyrical bas-relief *The Annunciation.*

The 13th-century frescoes are reason enough for visiting Santa Croce—especially those by Giotto to the right of the main chapel. In the left transept is Donatello's once-controversial wooden Crucifix—too gruesome for some Renaissance tastes.

Inside the monastery the Franciscan fathers established a **Leather School** (no, not *that* kind of leather) at the end of World War II. The purpose of the school was to teach young boys the art of Florentine leather work. The school has flourished and produced many fine artisans who continue their careers here. Stop in and see the work when you visit the church.

Santa Maria Novella. Piazza Santa Maria Novella. ☎ **055-210-113.** Admission free. Mon–Fri 7am–noon and 3–6pm, Sat 7am–noon and 3–5pm, Sun 7am–12:15pm and 3–6pm.

Space limitations have kept me from mentioning any of Florence's superb churches, except for the Duomo, Santa Croce, and this one, which might be the first sight you see on leaving the train station. It was begun in 1278 for the Dominicans, but its striking geometric facade of green and white marble was designed by Leon Battista Alberti in the late 15th century. The interior is vast and rather awesome. One of its treasures is a large fresco by Masaccio, the *Trinity.* Another is the wooden *Christ on the Cross* by Brunelleschi (who designed the Duomo's dome). There's also a 15th-century fresco cycle by Ghirlandaio, one of Michelangelo's teachers. The cloisters are also worth visiting.

✪ **Casa Buonarotti.** Via Ghibellina 70. ☎ **055-241-752.** Admission 10,000L ($6). Wed–Mon 9:30am–1:30pm.

Why is it so many heterosexuals can't bear the thought that a great genius, such as Michelangelo Buonarotti, was homosexual? Charlton Heston (new president of the National Rifle Association) played the artist in the movie version of Irving Stone's *The Agony and the Ecstasy*—and you can't get much straighter than that. Sorry, straight folks—Mike was a hardworking homo, a genius who happened to be queer. He bought this house, not far from Santa Croce, for his nephew, which shows he was generous and not adverse to family values. The Buonarotti descendants later turned the casa into a museum dedicated to the Great One. There are some very early works, like the *Madonna of the Stairs,* which he sculpted when he was 16, and a lively bas-relief of the *Battle of the Centaurs.* The museum displays many Michelangelo drawings, including a portrait of his lover, Tommaso Cavalieri, as *Cleopatra.* Alas, that's not on display, but you can get a postcard reproduction.

Palazzo Medici-Riccardi. Via Camillo Cavour 1. ☎ **055-276-0340.** Admission 6,000L ($3.40). Mon–Tues and Thurs–Sat 9am–12:30pm and 3–6pm, Sun 9am–noon. Bus: 1, 6, 7, 11, 17, 33, 67, or 68.

This palace, a short walk from the Duomo, was the home of Cosimo de' Medici before he took his household to the Palazzo Vecchio. Art lovers visit chiefly to see the mid-15th-century frescoes by Benozzo Gozzoli in the **Medici Chapel** (not to be confused with the Medici Chapels above). Gozzoli's frescoes, depicting the journey of the Magi, form his masterpiece—they're a hallmark in Renaissance painting. Though taking a

Catching the View from Piazzale Michelangiolo

For a view of the wonders of Florence below and Fiesole above, climb aboard bus no. 12 or 13 at the Ponte alla Grazie (the first bridge east of the Ponte Vecchio) for a 15-minute ride to ✪ **Piazzale Michelangiolo,** an 1865 belvedere overlooking a view seen in many a Renaissance painting and on many a modern-day postcard. It's best at dusk, when the purple-fringed Tuscan hills form a frame for Giotto's bell tower, Brunelleschi's dome, and the tower of Palazzo Vecchio. A copy of Michelangelo's *David* dominates the square and gives the *piazzale* (wide piazza) its name. Round out your trip with a gelato at the **Gelateria Michelangiolo** (☎ **055-234-2705;** open daily 10am–1am).

Warning: At certain times, the square is overrun with tour buses and peddlers selling trinkets. If you go at these times, often midday in summer, you'll find the view of Florence is still beautiful—but you may be struck down by a Vespa or crushed in a crowd if you try to enjoy it.

religious theme as his subject, the artist turned it into a gay (you know what I mean) romp, a pageant of royals, knights, and pages, with fun mascots like greyhounds and even a giraffe. It's a fairy-tale world come alive, with faces of the Medicis along with local celebrities who were as famous as Madonna in their day but are known only to scholars today.

GAY FLORENCE

The beautiful Renaissance capital of Tuscany has attracted gays for centuries. In terms of gay culture, openness, and political activism, Florence is right up there with Milan.

The city has long enjoyed a reputation for gay tolerance. There once was evidently so much action that the medieval Florentine state formed an official militia—the Uffiziali Notte (Night Officials)—whose duty it was to repress queer sex. (I wonder how bribes worked back then.) In Germany, Florence's reputation as "Sodom City" was so great that the term for sodomy was *florenzen.* Then came the Renaissance, and we all know that queers were at least partially responsible for that. These Renaissance men did everything: sculpted, painted, wrote poetry, designed buildings, and had gay sex. Some of the world's greatest gay artists—Leonardo da Vinci, Sandro Botticelli, and Benvenuto Cellini—were nabbed by the Night Officials and fined. Michelangelo and Donatello were evidently more discreet. But as you explore Florence, admiring the masterpieces produced by these Renaissance artists, remember how much of the gay spirit is behind the city.

Tuscany, ruled by the Medicis, was ahead of the rest of Italy in decriminalizing homosexuality. Grand Duke Ferdinand III repealed the antihomosexual laws in 1795. News like this spreads, of course.

In the 18th and 19th centuries, Florence was an essential part of every gay gentleman's "Grand Tour" (that era's party circuit). Drawn by the spirit of the Renaissance—and because they could be imprisoned in their own countries—many gays and lesbians came to Florence and never left. Gay Brits were particularly fond of Florence and established a regular enclave. E. M. Forster's *A Room with a View* is perhaps the most famous work inspired by Florence—the novel isn't gay, but Forster sure was.

So gays and lesbians have been around Florence for a long, long time. In the Etruscan Tomb of the Bulls at Tarquinia is a fresco of penetrating power. This would seem to indicate that homosexuality has been known in Tuscany since perhaps 500 B.C. That's 2,500 years, kids. The lily symbolizing Florence may be white, but it's also very pink.

PARKS, GARDENS & SQUARES

✪ **Piazza della Signoria,** dominated by the enormous Palazzo Vecchio, is the center of Renaissance Florence. There are magnificent nudes, in every conceivable position, everywhere you look. Sculptures, I mean. You don't have to be homo to find them erotic, but it does help.

After Masaccio liberated the human body in art by painting a nude Adam and Eve (in the Brancacci Chapel), Renaissance sculptors followed (birthday) suit. They obviously gloried in the newfound freedom to portray the human body. First to catch your eye will likely be the copy of Michelangelo's *David* (the real young stud is in the Accademia). The **Fountain of Neptune (Fontana di Nettuno)**—the sea god, surrounded by satyrs and nymphs indulging in water sports—is a work by Ammannati, who later said he was sorry to have sculpted Neptune unclothed (since when do sea gods wear bathing suits?). The **Loggia dei Lanzi,** to one side of the square, is an outdoor sculpture gallery (because of excavations you can admire the statues only at a distance). Benvenuto Cellini (1500–1571), a gay goldsmith/sculptor, created the loggia's famous *Perseus,* holding aloft the head of Medusa (this *Perseus* is a replica—the original has been removed for restoration). The piazza is usually packed tight with gawking tourists staring up at various parts of the human anatomy; it's quite a show.

Piazza della Repubblica, about midway between Piazza della Signoria and the Duomo, doesn't have much aesthetic élan but does boast a couple of famous old cafes: the Giubbe Rosse, dating from 1888, and Caffè Gilli, from 1733.

The ✪ **Boboli Gardens (Giardini Boboli),** behind the Pitti Palace on the south bank of the Arno, were laid out for the Medicis in the 16th century. They're classically landscaped and a must for any garden lover. Wander the gravel paths, past statuary and fountains, and maybe have a picnic lunch, then climb higher to the Belvedere (below). Admission to the gardens is 5,000L ($3). They're open daily: April, May, and October 8:30am to 6:30pm; June to September to 7:30pm; and November to March 9am to 5:30pm.

The ✪ **Belvedere Fortress (Fortezza di Belvedere),** on the south ("left") bank of the Arno, is a bit of a hike but worth every gasp. From the grounds you have an unparalleled view of Florence, the Duomo, and the surrounding hills. The three-story fort was built in the 16th century and is surrounded by star-shaped bastions. Today the building and grounds are used for major art exhibits, some of which include grandiose pieces of outdoor sculpture. A road from the Boboli Gardens winds up to the Belvedere (which means "beautiful view").

5 Hitting the Stores

Florence is a famous shopping city, known for all kinds of luxurious goodies: leather, marble, ceramics, jewelry, handmade papers (not the rolling kind), and fashion in general. Though it's often unbearably crowded, stroll along the **Ponte Vecchio** for a look at some of the shops. You'll find enticing shops along **Via dei Tornabuoni, Via Vigna Nuova, Via Porta Rossa,** and **Via degli Strozi.** Don't expect to find bargains in Florence, though.

Shopping hours are generally Monday 4 to 7:30pm and Tuesday to Saturday 9 or 10am to 1pm and 4 to 7:30pm. In summer, stores are usually open Monday mornings as well. In August, many shopkeepers leave town.

SHOPS A TO Z

ANTIQUES None of the historical goodies at the following stores on Via Maggio will be cheap, but you might want to have a look anyway. **Adriana Chellini,** Via Maggio (☎ **055-213-479**), specializes in 16th- and 17th-century furniture (small and large pieces) and glass and porcelain. Art deco and 19th-century pieces are sold at **Bottega San Felice,** Via Maggio 39R (☎ **055-215-479**). **Guido Bartolozzi,** Via Maggio 18R (☎ **055-215-294**), carries furniture, tapestries, china, and glassware from the 16th to the 19th centuries.

BOOKS The **Libreria delle Donne,** Via Fiesolana 2B (☎ **055-240-384**), is a women's bookstore with a lesbian section. The **Libreria Marzocco,** Via de' Martelli 22R (☎ **055-282-873**), has a gay section; the bookstore is near the train station. **Paperback Exchange,** Via Fiesolana 31R (☎ **055-247-8154**), stocks English and American books, including some gay titles. The oldest English bookstore in Florence, with a great selection in all genres, is **Bm Bookshop,** Borgo Ognissanti 4R (☎ **055-294-575**).

CLOTHING **Gerard,** Via Vacchereccia 18–20R (☎ **055-215-942**), stocks clothes for both genders. **Il Giardino d'Inverno (Summer Garden),** Via del Melancio 8 (☎ **055-211-391**), specializes in sexy men's and women's undies. And **Sandro P.2,** Via de' Tosinghi 7R (☎ **055-215-063**), carries new and retro-fit men's and women's clothing.

FABRIC Fabric connoisseurs—I mean all you girls with sewing machines at home—will find a huge selection of high-quality linen, silk, wool, and cotton at **Casa di Tessuti,** Via de' Pecori 20R (☎ **055-215-961**). For fine Florentine embroidery, check out **Cirri,** Via por Santa Maria (☎ **055-215-961**).

GAY SHOPS **Frisco,** Via F. Veracini 15 (☎ **055-357-351**), sells leather and S/M apparel, gay videos, and toys for boys. **Magic America,** Via Guelfa 89–91R (☎ **055-212-840**), has a large selection of gay goods, including magazines and videos. **Studio Blu,** Via delle Panche 8R (☎ **055-422-3767**), features leather togs for flogs, undies, toys, and magazines.

JEWELRY You'll find enameled antique silver boxes, cameos, and modern 18-carat gold jewelry at **Rudolfo Fallaci,** Ponte Vecchio 10 and 22 (☎ **055-294-981**). High-priced handcrafted pieces are sold at **Mario Buccellati,** Via dei Tornabuoni 69-71R (☎ **055-239-6579**).

LEATHER The **Ponte Vecchio Leather Factory,** Borgo San Jacopo 38R (☎ **055-215-654**), sells leather fashions and accessories (not S/M).

MARKETS Monday to Saturday 9am to 7pm, **Piazza del Mercato Nuovo,** close to Piazza della Signoria, offers market stands with all manner of goods: straw and leather items, frames, embroidery, and so on. The **Mercato Centrale,** on Borgo San Lorenzo near the train station, is another well-known market; there's a bit of everything: leather goods, clothing, souvenirs, T-shirts, and so on. Mid-March to October, the market is open daily 9am to 7pm (closed Sunday and Monday the rest of the year). Take my word for it: A lot of the stuff at both markets is nothing more than tourist-oriented junk.

PAPER & STATIONERY ✪ **Giulio Giannini & Figlio,** Piazza Pitti 37R (☎ **055-212-621**), sells beautiful handmade papers and stationery items. **Pineider,** Piazza della Signoria 13R (☎ **055-284-4655**), is the oldest stationery store in Florence; there's another branch at Via dei Tornabuoni 76 (☎ **055-211-605**).

SHOES **Ferragamo,** Via dei Tornabuoni 16R (☎ **055-292-123**), sells high-end ultrafashionable shoes for men and women at his Florence headquarters. Guys 'n gals will find high-quality leather shoes from many designers (and in American sizes) at **Lily of Florence,** Via Guicciardini 2R (☎ **055-294-748**).

TOILETRIES A friend turned me onto the ✪ **Officina Profumo-Farmaceutica di Santa Maria Novella,** Via della Scala 16 (☎ **055-216-276**), a truly must-visit shop, and I've never smelled the same since. Founded in 1542 by the Dominican friars, it's one of the oldest pharmacies in the world. They still make pure flower- and herb-based products from original recipes, including colognes, soaps, face creams, body milks, tonics, and shampoos. One of their specialties is pomegranate soap and talc. I also love the toothpaste made from iris root. This place is perfect for finding unusual gifts. It's very close to the train station and not well marked from the street; let your nose guide you.

6 All the World's a Stage

The tourist office publishes a free cultural calendar called ***Avvenimenti/Events,*** listing musical events, theater programs, and art exhibits. Concerts are given around the city, often in churches and historic buildings. The city's yearly cultural bash is the **Maggio Musicale Fiorentina** (for tickets and information, Via Solferino 16, 50123 Firenze; ☎ **055-27-791**), which presents a wide range of opera, ballet, concerts, and recitals from May to July.

The **Teatro Comunale di Firenze,** Corso Italia 16 (☎ **055-211-158**), Florence's main theater, has an opera and ballet season from September to December and a concert season from January to April. From May to July it's a venue for the prestigious music and arts festival, Maggio Musicale Fiorentina. The **Teatro Verdi,** Via Ghibellina 99 (☎ **055-212-320**), has all kinds of events going on: opera, ballet, musicals, films, and symphony and pop music concerts.

The **Teatro di Rifredi,** Via Vittorio Emanuele 303 (☎ **055-422-0361**), often presents plays and performances with gay themes.

7 In the Heat of the Night

Many of the gay watering holes require an **Arci Gay Uno** card for admittance, but foreigners can sometimes get around this or buy a card at the door. The cards, available at the Arci-Gay Arci-Lesbica Center, cost 20,000L ($12) and are required for admittance to many gay bars, discos, and saunas throughout the country. You may have to buy an obligatory drink in the bars and discos.

GAY BARS

Crisco Club, Via San Egidio 43R (☎ **055-248-0580;** open Wed–Mon 10:30pm–3:30am, Fri–Sat to 6am), is a no-holds-barred bar with darkroom, videos, drag shows, and male strippers. Men only on weekends.

The cafe/bar **Finisterrae,** Via San Zanobi (☎ **055-476-557;** open Wed–Mon 9pm–1am), in the new gay and lesbian community center, is a good informal gathering spot that sponsors various events. Thursday is women only.

In the Santa Croce neighborhood, near the Verdi Theater, is **Satanassa,** Via Pandolfini 26R, second floor (☎ **055-243-356;** open Tues–Sun 10pm–5am, Fri–Sat to 6am); this trendy bar has a darkroom, videos, and live shows on Saturday. Women only on Friday.

MIXED CAFE/BARS

Bar Stop, Via Ghibellina 145R (☎ **055-238-2648;** open Mon–Sat 8am–1am, Sun 5–11pm), offers pasta, salads, and board games.

The **Cabiria Café,** Piazza Santo Spirito 4R (☎ **055-215-732;** open daily 7am–1am), is a mixed gay/straight hangout. At the ✪ **Piccolo Café,** Borgo Santa Croce 23R (☎ **055-241-704;** open Tues–Sun 4pm–1am), you'll find a mixed crowd but lots of lesbigays; there's a coffee and snack bar and sometimes cabaret shows and art exhibits.

Polly Magù, Via Panicale 27R (☎ **055-230-2259;** open Tues–Sat 10am–1am), is a popular cafe/bar near Piazza del Mercato Centrale; Thursday is gay/lesbian night, but we're there the rest of the week as well. **Rose's,** Via del Parioe 26R (☎ **055-287-090;** open Mon–Sat 1pm–1am), is a good place for a light gay lunch.

And **Zut Rockcaffé,** Via Il Prato 58R (☎ **055-283-749;** open Tues–Sun 10am–1am), is a relatively new Internet cafe with a bit of food and a lot of beers; the crowd is trendy and mixed, with cyber-gays among them.

A DANCE CLUB

I don't like to promote "selection clubs" (if you're wearing a dress or aren't adequately dishy they don't want you), but if you're sufficiently hot (and your night vision is good) you'll no doubt enjoy the other hot numbers cruising around the maze and darkroom at **Tabasco,** Piazza Santa Cecilia 3R (☎ **055-213-000;** open Sun–Fri 10pm–4am, Sat to 6am). Tabasco was the first gay-only club in Italy. Disco is featured on Friday and Saturday nights; otherwise it's a bar.

DOWN & DIRTY: CINEMAS, SAUNAS & MORE

If you're out cruising, stay alert, steer way clear of junkies and any skinhead types, and don't carry cash and credit cards. An evening *passaggiata* (walk) from Piazza della Repubblica to Piazza Santa Croce, through Calimala, Via Porta Santa Maria, Via Vacchereccia, Piazza della Signoria, and Via de'Neri, may yield interesting results.

From the late afternoon into the evening, large **Cascine Park (Parco delle Cascine),** west of the city center on the north bank of the Arno, can be pretty busy, especially in the parking lot, along Viale delle Cascine near the Agriculture School, and around Viale Lincoln-Washington on the bike path between the Ponte della Vittoria and the Ponte all'Indiano (the two bridges); be very careful here because it's a druggie hangout. The **Stadio Campo di Marte,** a park northeast of the city center, has a night-cruising area in front of the Palasport building that houses the pool; during the day, gay guys hang out in the pool area (surprised?).

CINEMAS **Cinema Astro,** Piazza San Simone (near Santa Croce), shows current films in English every night except Monday. **Cinema Goldoni,** Via dei Serraghli (☎ **055-222-437**), screens English-language films on Wednesday. And **Italia,** Piazza Alinari (☎ **055-211-069**), shows fag flicks on Wednesday.

SAUNAS The **Florence Baths,** Via Guelfa 93R (☎ **055-216-050;** open daily 2pm–1am, Sat to 2am), is a 5-minute walk from the rail station. This private sauna/gym club has an American bar with a Turkish bath, a Finnish sauna, a whirlpool, a video room, and a chill-out area.

8 Side Trips from Florence: Fiesole & the Tuscan Countryside

FIESOLE

The countryside around Florence is a remarkably beautiful landscape of green wooded hills, villas, tall cypress trees, silvery olive groves, and terraced vineyards. If it looks somehow familiar, it's probably because you've been looking at it in the works of various Tuscan masters in the art galleries.

Fiesole, one of the prettiest of the hill towns, is an easy side trip from Florence—only 25 minutes by bus no. 7 from Piazza San Marco. The bus ride is wonderful in and of itself: Winding up into the hills, it passes fountains and gardens and provides memorable views. The town, dating back to the Etruscan era (6th century B.C.), boasts some worthwhile sights, all within walking distance of the main square.

Fronting the main square is the **Cathedral of San Romolo (Cattedrale di San Romolo),** Piazza Mino da Fiesole (open daily 7:30am–noon and 4–7pm; admission free), built a thousand years ago and altered during the Renaissance. Just west of here, atop the steep hill, the **Museum of the Convent of San Francesco (Museo Missionario Francescano Fiesole),** Via San Francesco 13 (open Mon–Fri 9am–noon and 3–6pm, Sat 3–6pm; admission by donation), is housed in the 15th-century convent church; it contains a good collection of Florentine paintings and an ethnological museum with an Etruscan-Roman section. The **Roman Theater (Teatro Romano),** Via Portigiani 1 (open daily 9:30am–6:30pm; admission 6,000L/$3), is the ruins of a 1st-century-B.C. theater and contains an interesting Etruscan-Roman museum. It's just northeast of the cathedral.

TOURS IN THE TUSCAN COUNTRYSIDE

Florence-based ✪ **I Bike Italy** (☎ **055-234-2371** or 0347-419-8288; e-mail i_bike_italy@compuserve.com; www.ibikeitaly.com), staffed with Americans, Brits, Danes, New Zealanders, and Australians, offers professionally guided single-day rides in the countryside. The rides are deliberately designed to meander past olive groves, vineyards, crumbling castles, and vine-covered estates from the Renaissance.

The company provides a shuttle service to carry you in and out of the city, use of a 21-speed bike, helmets, water bottles, and a bilingual bike guide to show you the way, fix any flats, and deal with any problems. All tours cover from 15 to 20 scenic miles (the average speed is a leisurely 3.2 mph) and return the same day to Florence between 4:30 and 5pm. The cost is 95,000L ($55) per person, lunch and equipment included. The same company leads less-extensive walking tours in Tuscany. Priced at 75,000L ($44) for a 3-hour walk, they end in Fiesole and include 4 to 5 miles of trekking with supervision by a British, American, Italian, or Danish guide.

If biking doesn't appeal but you want a focused guided tour, consider the offerings of **Custom Tours in Tuscany,** 206 Ivy Lane, Highland Park, IL 60035 (☎ **847-432-1814;** fax 847-432-1889), with up to 10 well-trained bilingual staff members, each intimately familiar with Tuscany's art and culture. The company listens carefully to what you want to see and do, then tailors a day-long guided tour for you. Its staff can help you visit Florence's important monuments, guide you through labyrinths of less-often-visited alleyways, and show you where to buy antiques, gold jewelry, leather, extra-virgin olive oil, or bed and table linens at a fraction of the regular prices.

The company's day tours in Tuscany include visits to Lucca, Siena, San Gimignano, and Pietrasanta. They begin and end in Florence but may be expanded into longer countryside trips. In Florence, plan to do a lot of walking; outside Florence, the guides will accompany you in your own rented car or arrange for a car and driver. Fees are $325 per day for Florence tours or $425 for tours in the Tuscan countryside (6–7 hours) for up to two people. Extra persons are $25 each. Transportation, meals, highway tolls, museum admissions, and gratuities aren't included.

12 Venice: La Serenissima

There's no other place on earth like **Venice (Venezia),** a city of shimmering, seductive beauty where the interplay of light and water on old stone buildings never ceases to entrance the eye. Somewhere in the background is always the sound of lapping waves. This is an intimate and sensual city with a touch of slightly melancholic decay that adds to its mysterious flavor. It's true that Venice is sinking—by an estimated 2½ inches a year. That's actually part of its emotional allure. It's a place you always feel you're saying good-bye to. (And then, on the next trip, it's there, as wonderful as ever.)

Few cities can so instantly capture the imagination. Your first glimpse of Venice will probably be on a *vaporetto* ride from the train station to your hotel. The panorama that unfolds as the boat makes its way down the Grand Canal can be literally breathtaking. Some visitors never leave; most of us want to stay longer but can't. It's one of those cities where you can't imagine anyone ever taking it for granted.

In its seafaring heyday, Venice was one of the richest cities in the world. It was *La Serenissima*, a serene republic unto itself—proud, self-assured, and extremely powerful. The legacy of those treasure-laden years is everywhere around you in Venice. The city was built on commerce and conquest, but that it was built at all—and that it's still standing—is the real miracle.

But I do have to warn you: Venice is one of the most crowded cities in Europe. Creeping through its labyrinth of narrow streets, among thousands of other tourists, you might feel like you're in an ant farm. Once you actually see Venice, you'll understand the reasons for its popularity. What's never talked about is the inevitable loss of "soul" that goes along with an almost exclusively tourist-driven economy. The ticket booths now set up in many of the churches are just one example. Yes, the money helps to defray the cost of maintenance, but gone is the sense of spiritual peace and quiet discovery.

In Venice, there's nothing that hasn't been discovered, nor do you particularly get the sense the city has much of a "real" life beyond the commercial one set up for tourists. It does, of course, but you won't find it on any of the main streets. The real life of Venice is hidden away, kept to itself, a mystery few visitors can ever penetrate.

1 Venice Essentials

ARRIVING & DEPARTING

BY PLANE Flights arrive at **Marco Polo Aeroporto** (☎ **041-260-9260**) at Mestre, the hideous industrial area connected to Venice by a causeway. From the airport, *moto-scafi* (shuttle boats) operated by the **Cooperative San Marco** (☎ **041-522-2303**) depart for their terminal near Piazza San Marco; the fare is 15,000L ($8) and takes about an hour. The *motoscafo* stops at Murano and the Lido before reaching San Marco.

Another option for getting into the city is to take a ***taxi acquei*** (water taxi); they're useful if you have a ton of luggage and a ton of money. The fare from the airport to Piazza San Marco is 107,000L ($59); from Piazzale Roma to Piazza San Marco it's 80,000L ($44). There are additional surcharges at night and for baggage. A porter will take you to the water-taxi stand, or you can phone **Radio Taxi** at ☎ **041-522-2303.**

A 5,000L ($3) shuttle-bus link between the airport and Piazzale Roma, across the Grand Canal from Venice's main train station, is operated by **Azienda Trasporti Veneto Orientale** (☎ **041-520-5530**). Local **ACTV** (☎ **041-780-111**) buses depart hourly for Piazzale Roma as well; the trip costs 1,500L (80¢) and takes about an hour. Piazzale Roma is a vaporetto stop, so once there you can board one of the city boats to your hotel.

BY TRAIN The **Stazione di Santa Lucia** (☎ **1478-880-88**), across from Piazzale Roma, is Venice's train station. Inside is a tourist office, a hotel-booking service, and a currency exchange. Step outside and you're on the Grand Canal. A vaporetto is the cheapest way to get from the station to or near your hotel; there's a vaporetto stop directly in front of the station.

BY CAR Venice is directly linked by autostrada to the rest of Italy. Obviously you can't drive in the city. There are several large parking garages at Mestre, Tronchetto, and near Piazzale Roma in case you arrive by car.

VISITOR INFORMATION

The tourist office, **Azienda di Promozione Turistica di Venezia,** is in the Palazzina del Santi in the San Marco quarter (☎ **041-522-6356;** open daily 9:30am–6:30pm in summer, to 3:30pm off-season). There are branches in the train station and at the airport.

CITY LAYOUT

Venice is an archipelago of islands—some 117 of them to be exact—linked by 400 bridges, set in the middle of the Adriatic lagoon. It's connected to **Mestre,** on the mainland, by a 2½-mile-long causeway. The Adriatic Sea begins at the south shore of the **Lido,** an island 1½ miles south. The city "streets" in Venice, as I'm sure you know, are mostly canals. The most famous is the **Grand Canal (Canal Grande),** winding through Venice like a watery intestine and dividing the city in two. Three bridges span the Grand Canal: the **Ponte Rialto,** the **Ponte Accademia,** and the **Ponte degli Scalzi.**

The city is divided into six quarters, or *sestieri.* To the east of the Grand Canal, from north to south, they're **Cannaregio, San Marco,** and **Castello;** to the west, **Santa Croce, San Polo,** and **Dorsoduro.** You'll find that each address in this chapter is followed by the quarter name. The tourist epicenter of Venice is **Piazza San Marco.**

A Note on Addresses

Within each sestiere is a most original system of numbering the palazzi, using one continuous string of 6,000 or so numbers. The format for addresses I've used in this chapter is the name of the street or campo, followed by the sestieri name and then the building number—for example, Salizzada San Moisé, San Marco 1471. Be aware that San Marco 1471 may not be found close to San Marco 1475 and that many buildings aren't numbered at all.

It lies at the mouth of the Grand Canal and it's the only piazza in the entire city; all the other open spaces in Venice are called *campos.* Many visitors never leave the Piazza San Marco area, but you'll never get to know the city unless you do.

The long, mostly residential island of **Giudecca** lies across the Canale delle Giudecca. To the east, forming a barrier against the open sea, is the beach-resort island called the **Lido.** There are four small islands in the Venetian lagoon north of Venice: these are **Murano, Burano, Torcello** (the three visited by tourists) and **Sant'Erasmo.**

GETTING AROUND

Go by foot whenever possible and be sure to have a highly detailed map. The Falk map is best. Otherwise, do as the Venetians do and take a vaporetto.

BY VAPORETTO The city's main form of public transport is the ***vaporetto*** (plural, *vaporetti*). Operated by **ACTV (Azienda del Consorzio Trasporti Veneziano; ☎ 041-528-7886**), these water buses ply the Grand Canal, circle the city, and cross over to the island of Giudecca and to the Lido. Though not always fast, they are cheap and fun and provide unbelievably scenic sightseeing opportunities. An ***accelerato*** is the equivalent of a "local" and makes every stop. A ***diretto*** makes only express stops. Note that in early 1999 the **vaporetto** lines were renumbered, so if you have an old map showing the lines, disregard it. The stops, however, have stayed the same.

Vaporetti provide daily service 7am to midnight, then run hourly. You can pick up a map of the entire system at the tourist office. A single **one-way fare** is 1,400L (80¢) and a **return fare** 2,500L ($1.50). There are special discount tickets you can buy at the vaporetto stations: The **Biglietto 24 Ore,** good for 24 hours of unlimited travel on any vaporetto, is 15,000L ($8); the **Biglietto 3 Giorni,** good for 3 days, is 30,000L ($17); and the **Biglietto 7 Giorni,** good for 7 days, is 55,000L ($30).

If you're on foot and need to cross the Grand Canal but aren't close to one of its three bridges, look for a ***traghetto.*** Moored at the end of passageways called Calle del Traghetto, these boats make direct trips from one side of the Grand Canal to the other for 1,000L (60¢).

BY WATER TAXI Venice has many private motor launches, called ***taxi acquei,*** and they're good if you don't want to use the often-crowded vaporetti. Water taxis are expensive, however, and you may share the boat with other passengers. In the *centro storico* (historic center of town), water taxis operate at a fixed rate of 27,000L ($15) for

Country & City Codes

The **country code** for Italy is **39.** The **city code** for Venice is **041.** You must now use all three digits whenever you call Venice—whether you're outside Italy, inside Italy but not within Venice, or even within Venice.

7 minutes and 500L (27¢) for every 15 seconds thereafter. You can phone **Radio Taxi** at ☎ **041-522-2303;** but be aware that this will add at least another 8,000L ($4.50) to the rates above.

BY CAR You can't drive in Venice, but you may want to rent a car for excursions into the Veneto and beyond. You can do so at **Europcar,** Piazzale Roma 496H (☎ **041-523-8616**), or **Avis,** Piazzle Rma 496G (☎ **041-522-5825**). Both offices are open Monday to Friday 8:30am to 12:30pm and 2:30 to 6pm and Saturday 8:30am to noon. Of course, it's best to arrange for the rental before leaving home.

FAST FACTS: Venice

American Express The office is on Salizzada San Moisé, San Marco 1471 (☎ **041-520-0844;** Vaporetto: San Marco; open May–Oct Mon–Sat 8am–8pm for currency exchange, 9am–5:30pm for all other transactions and Nov–Apr Mon–Fri 9am–5:30pm, Sat 9am–12:30pm).

Community Centers **Arci-Gay/Arci-Lesbica Nove,** Campo San Giacomo dell'Orio, Santa Croce 1507 (☎ **041-721-197;** Vaporetto: Riva di Biasio; open Tues–Sun 6pm–midnight), is the city's one and only gay-and-lesbian center. It provides information and assistance.

Consulates There's no **U.S. Consulate** in Venice; the closest is in Milan (see below). The **British Consulate** is at Dorsoduro 1051 (☎ **041-522-7207;** open Mon–Fri 10am–noon and 2–3pm).

Currency Exchange American Express and many banks have currency exchanges.

Dentists & Doctors American Express and the U.K. Consulate have lists of English-speaking doctors and dentists. Or have the concierge at your hotel call to set up an appointment.

Emergencies For police, call ☎ **113.** For an ambulance, call ☎ **523-0000.** For the fire Station, call ☎ **520-0222.** For first-aid emergencies, call ☎ **118.**

Hospitals The **Civili Riuniti di Venezia,** Campo Santi Giovanni e Paolo, Castello (☎ **041-529-4111;** Vaporetto: Fondamenta Nuove), is staffed with English-speaking doctors 24 hours a day.

2 Pillow Talk

A word of warning: If you're traveling to Venice for Carnevale, during Easter Week, or between June and September, reserve your hotel as far in advance as possible. You may otherwise arrive and find that virtually every hotel, *pensioni*, and *locanda* (small inn) is already booked solid. If that happens you'll be forced to stay in Mestre, the gruesomely ugly industrial area on the mainland. However, many new hotels have been opening of late (like the Locanda Vivaldi), so you may have a better chance of getting a room.

Keep in mind that a luxury hotel in Venice is going to be extremely expensive and in smaller hotels any room with a view is going to be more expensive. Many of the low rates quoted below are for off-season.

There are no identified gay or gay-friendly hotels in Venice, but you shouldn't have a problem. Hoteliers here, as in the rest of Italy, cannot discriminate against guests.

If you do arrive without a room, check with one of the **AVA (Hotel Association) reservations booths.** Their main office is at Piazzale Roma, near the train station (☎ **041-921-638;** Vaporetto: Piazzale Roma), but there are locations at the airport

Hey, Big Spender

If you've finally come into your trust fund and want to blow a wad on a Venice hotel, there are many deluxe places that'll be more than glad to bend over backward for you. Be prepared to drop a minimum of $200 a night for a double at any of them.

The **Hotel Gritti Palace, Hotel Londra Palace,** and **Hotel des Bains,** three of the toniest, are listed in full below. Here are some others:

Danieli Royal Excelsior, Riva degli Schiavoni, Castello 4196, 30122 Venezia (☎ **800/325-3535** in the U.S. and Canada, or 041-522-6480; fax 041-520-0208; www.ittsheraton.com; Vaporetto: San Zaccaria).

Excelsior Palace, Lungomare Marconi 41, 30126 Lido di Venezia (☎ **800/325-3535** in the U.S. and Canada, or 041-526-0201; fax 041-526-7276; www.ittsheraton.com; Vaporetto: Lido, then bus A, B, or C).

Hotel Cipriani, Isola della Giudecca 10, 30133 Venezia (☎ **800/992-5055** in the U.S., or 041-520-7744; fax 041-520-7745; Vaporetto: Zitelle).

and in the train station. You'll be required to put down a deposit for a room, but this is rebated on your final hotel bill. All hotel booths are open daily 9am to 9pm.

NEAR PIAZZA SAN MARCO & LA FENICE

Hotel Ala. Campo Santa Maria del Giglio, San Marco 2494, 30124 Venezia. ☎ **041-520-8333.** Fax 041-520-6390. E-mail alahtve@gpnet.it. 86 units. AC MINIBAR TV TEL. 200,000–290,000L ($111–$161) double. Rates include breakfast. AE, DC, MC, V. Vaporetto: Santa Maria del Giglio or San Marco.

The luxurious Gritti Palace is the star hotel of the Campo Santa Maria del Giglio area, but there are two charming (and considerably less expensive) smaller hotels in the same vicinity, the Ala and the Bel Sito (below). The back rooms at the Ala overlook a canal (Rio delle Ostreghe), and the front rooms at the Bel Sito open onto the brilliant white facade of the Santa Maria del Giglio church. Though I prefer the dramatic church views and overall ambience of the Bel Sito, a canalside room at the Ala will provide plenty of romantic atmosphere. You do have to get past a suit of armor in the lobby, however. Some of the rooms are a bit dark; some are carpeted, others have lovely inlaid floors and beamed ceilings. All have safes and good tiled baths. There's a wonderful rooftop terrace as well.

✪ **Hotel Bel Sito.** Campo Santa Maria del Giglio, San Marco 2517, 30124 Venezia. ☎ **041-522-3365.** Fax 041-520-4083. 38 units. AC MINIBAR TV TEL. 190,000–295,000L ($106–$164) double. Rates include breakfast. AE, DC, MC, V. Vaporetto: Santa Maria del Giglio or San Marco.

This small three-star hotel lies between Piazza San Marco and La Fenice opera house on a typical Venetian *campo* (open square). It's extremely well kept and a good value for its location and charm. The lobby, with patterned gold wallpaper and dark wood antiques, is more florid than the rooms. Those are done in light colors and scattered with reproductions of 18th- and 19th-century pieces. For a truly memorable view, request a room looking out on the Santa Maria del Giglio church. All the rooms are air-conditioned, but you have to pay a 13,000L ($7) supplement to stay cool in the hot summer.

Hotel Do Pozzi. Via XXII Marzo, San Marco 2373, 30124 Venezia. ☎ **041-520-7855.** Fax 041-522-9413. 35 units. AC MINIBAR TV TEL. 190,000–260,000L ($106–$144) double. Rates include breakfast. AE, DC, MC, V. Vaporetto: Santa Maria del Giglio.

The location, in a *campiello* (small, quiet square) just minutes from Piazza San Marco and the Grand Canal, is unbeatable and the price excellent. This is a small three-star hotel with a pleasant garden courtyard for breakfast and other meals (lunch or dinner is offered for 40,000L/$22). Rooms facing the street are subject to the passing parade below; the ones looking onto the courtyard are quieter. There's a nice mix of antiques and reproductions. The tiled baths are fairly small.

Hotel Gritti Palace. Campo Santa Maria del Giglio, San Marco 2467, 30124 Venezia. ☎ **800/325-3589** in U.S. or 041-794-611. Fax 041-520-0942. 93 units. AC MINIBAR TV TEL. 850,000–1,000,000L ($472–$556) double; from 1,900,000L ($1,056) suite. AE, DC, MC, V. Vaporetto: Santa Maria del Giglio.

If you can grit your teeth and bear the price, this ultrafamous hotel/palazzo on the Grand Canal will accommodate you in very high style indeed. Kings, queens (of every sort), prime ministers, presidents, and just about every famous person who has come to Venice has stayed at the Gritti. (It was Ernest Hemingway's home away from home.) The rooms are all decorated in the same sumptuous style but with different furnishings, and the baths are marble and have two sinks. You'll find lots of Venetian terrazzo, luxurious fabrics, splendid antiques, and artwork. The rooms overlooking the Grand Canal are the most expensive; a few of these have balconies. The public rooms possess a grandeur unequaled by any other grand hotel in Venice. Service is discreet and efficient.

Hotel Kette. San Marco 2053, 30124 Venezia. ☎ **041-520-7766.** Fax 041-522-8964. 56 units. AC TV TEL. 200,000–340,000L ($111–$189) double. Rates include breakfast. AE, MC, V. Vaporetto: San Marco.

Another good choice in the San Marco/La Fenice area is this quiet canalside charmer, one street north of Via XX Marzo, a couple of minutes west of San Marco. Of course you want a room overlooking Rio delle Veste, the small canal. There's nothing to dislike about this hotel, which has been recently renovated and offers comfortable accommodations. The rooms boast parquet floors with Oriental area rugs and fine decor, plus safes. The baths come with hair dryers. A nice find.

Hotel La Fenice et des Artistes. Campiello de la Fenice, San Marco 1936, 30124 Venezia. ☎ **041-523-2333.** Fax 041-520-3721. 69 units. TV TEL. 220,000–340,000L ($122–$189) double. Rates include breakfast. AE, DC, MC, V. Vaporetto: San Marco.

One of the best things about this hotel is its location just yards from La Fenice opera house. Unfortunately, the opera house was destroyed by fire and won't reopen until at least 2000. But the hotel is still a good choice. It occupies two adjacent buildings in a small quiet square (*campiello*) about 10 minutes from San Marco. Stylistically it's hard to get a grip on the place. The rooms in the newer building have a gold, pink, and green color scheme with modern furniture (plus 1960s-era posters and "artwork"); three have private terraces. The furnishings in the older building are more ornate. The baths throughout are decent sized and have showers; all will be renovated during the next 2 years. A generous buffet breakfast buffet is served. The staff is friendly and very helpful.

✪ **Hotel Londra Palace.** Riva degli Schiavoni, Castello 4171, 30122 Venezia. ☎ **041-520-0533.** Fax 041-522-5032. E-mail: info@hotelondra.it. www.hotelondra.it. 70 units. AC MINIBAR TV TEL. 375,000–810,000L ($208–$450) double; 520,000–1,000,000L ($289–$556) suite. Rates include breakfast. AE, DC, MC, V. Vaporetto: San Zaccaria.

Facing directly onto the Venetian lagoon, a 5-minute walk east from the piazzetta, this six-story gabled manor is one of the loveliest hotels in Venice. Tchaikovsky, the great Russian composer (who happened to be gay but was tortured about it), stayed here in 1877 when he was working on his Fourth Symphony. The entire hotel was recently

Venice Accommodations & Dining

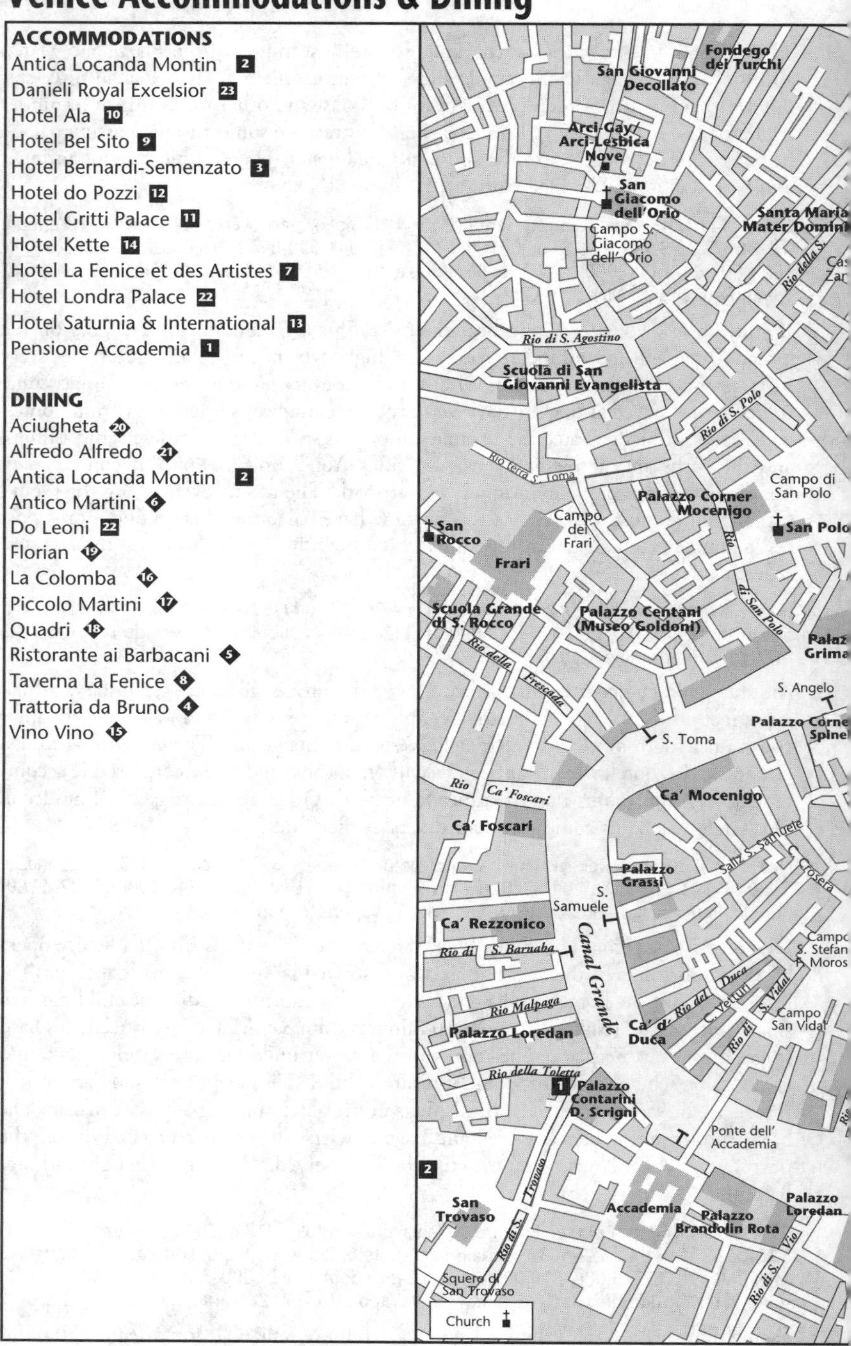

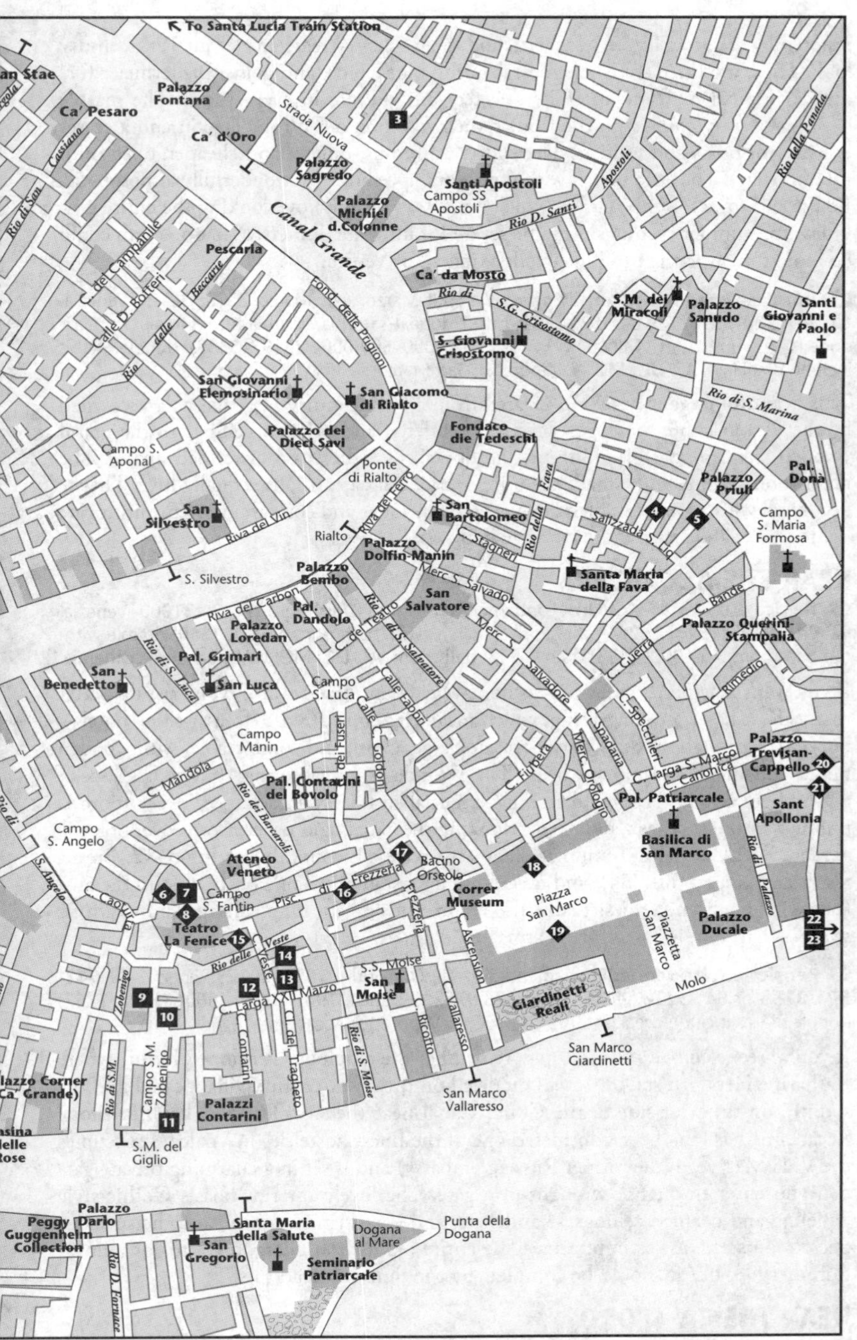

To Santa Lucia Train Station
Palazzo Fontana
Ca' Pesaro
Ca' d'Oro
Strada Nuova
Palazzo Sagredo
Santi Apostoli
Campo SS Apostoli
Palazzo Michiel d.Colonne
Canal Grande
Pescaria
Ca' da Mosto
S.M. dei Miracoli
Palazzo Sanudo
Santi Giovanni e Paolo
S. Giovanni Crisostomo
San Giovanni Elemosinario
San Giacomo di Rialto
Palazzo dei Dieci Savi
Fondaco die Tedeschi
Campo S. Aponal
Ponte di Rialto
Palazzo Priuli
Pal. Donà
Campo S. Maria Formosa
San Silvestro
San Bartolomeo
Rialto
Palazzo Dolfin-Manin
S. Silvestro
Palazzo Bembo
Santa Maria della Fava
San Salvatore
Pal. Dandolo
Palazzo Loredan
Palazzo Querini-Stampalia
Pal. Grimari
San Benedetto
San Luca
Campo S. Luca
Campo Manin
Palazzo Trevisan-Cappello
Pal. Contarini del Bovolo
Pal. Patriarcale
Sant Apollonia
Campo S. Angelo
Basilica di San Marco
Ateneo Veneto
Bacino Orseolo
Campo S. Fantin
Correr Museum
Piazza San Marco
Teatro La Fenice
Palazzo Ducale
Piazzetta San Marco
S.S. Moise
San Moisè
Giardinetti Reali
Molo
San Marco Giardinetti
San Marco Vallaresso
Palazzi Contarini
Campo S.M. Zobenigo
S.M. del Giglio
Palazzo Dario
Peggy Guggenheim Collection
San Gregorio
Santa Maria della Salute
Dogana al Mare
Punta della Dogana
Seminario Patriarcale
Rio della Panada
Rio D. Santi
Rio di S. Marina
Salizzada S. Lio
C. Larga S. Marco
C. Canonica
Merc. Orologio
Frezzeria
Larga XXII Marzo
Riva del Vin
Riva del Carbon
Riva del Ferro
Rio di S. Luca
Rio dei Barcaroli
Rio delle Veste
C. Mandola
Rio di Palazzo
Rio D. Fornace
1 2 3 4 5 6 7 8 9 10 11 12 13 14 15 16 17 18 19 20 21 22 23

restored by architect Ettore Mochetti, and the results re-create an elegant 19th-century look. There are three color schemes, favoring blues, reds, and golds. Biedermeier furniture, original oils, and carefully selected antiques are in every room. The marble baths are *benissimmi.* From the front rooms you look out on the lagoon and a ceaseless flow of boats and tourists. The courtyard rooms, quieter and cheaper, open onto rooftop views. The attic rooms with their sloping ceilings are wonderfully atmospheric. Best of all is the rooftop terrace (called an *al tana* in Italy) overlooking the entire city. On warm summer evenings it can be set up for intimate dinners. What on earth could be more romantic than to dine overlooking all of Venice?

✪ **Hotel Saturnia & International.** Via XXII Marzo, San Marco 2398, 30124 Venezia. ☎ **041-520-8377.** Fax 041-520-7131. http://doge.it/saturnia/saturnia.htm. E-mail saturnia@doge.it. 95 units. A/C MINIBAR TV TEL. 345,000–690,000L ($192–$383) double. Rates include breakfast. AE, DC, MC, V. Vaporetto: San Marco.

This beautiful elegant hotel was created from a 14th-century Venetian palazzo owned by the Pisano family of doges. From the coffered and beamed ceilings to the grand wooden staircase and gleaming marble floors, it's a showcase of refined luxury. The guest rooms, some with small balconies overlooking a canal, are equally luxe. They're decorated with a gorgeous blend of Venetian antiques and contemporary furniture, are lighted by chandeliers, and have large baths.

NEAR THE ACCADEMIA

✪ **Antica Locanda Montin.** Fondamenta Eremite, Dorsoduro 1147, 31000 Venezia. ☎ **041-522-7151.** Fax 041-520-0255. 9 units, 5 with bathroom. 90,000 ($50) double without bathroom, 150,000L ($83) double with bathroom. AE, DC, MC, V. Vaporetto: Accademia.

If you want to experience an old-fashioned Venetian *locanda* (inn), you can't do better than this. It has a one-star rating, which means it's considered a "fourth-class" hotel—but don't worry about that. The rooms are large, clean, and comfortable, with wooden floors and big old-fashioned beds. The locanda isn't glamorous, but it has lots of atmosphere and is very popular so it's essential to reserve in advance. Every room is unique. Number 5 has a terrace overlooking the canal, and other rooms overlook the garden. Poet Gabriel D'Annunzio slept with actress Eleonora Duse in no. 12. Breakfast is an extra 8,000L ($4), and the adjoining restaurant is one of the best in the area (below). The locanda doesn't advertise its presence except for a carriage lamp with its name—that, too, is part of its charm.

✪ **Pensione Accademia.** Fondamenta Bollani, Dorsoduro 1058, 30123 Venezia. ☎ **041-521-0188** or 041-523-7846. Fax 041-523-9152. 29 units. 190,000–300,000L ($106–$167) double. Rates include breakfast. AE, DC, MC, V. Vaporetto: Accademia.

If you've seen *Summertime* you may remember the fabulous "Pensione Fiorini" where Katharine Hepburn stayed. It was modeled on this 17th-century villa located in Dorsoduro, on the west side of the Grand Canal near the Accademia Gallery. Pensione Accademia has long been considered one of the finest hostelries in Venice. It occupies the Villa Maravege (the former Russian embassy) and is set in a charming private garden you enter through a wrought-iron gate. The lovely interior boasts Gothic-style paneling and beamed ceilings, chandeliers, and Victorian furniture, and the spacious guest rooms are just as impressive. The entire place was undergoing a major renovation in 1998, but it should be complete by the time you read this.

NEAR THE CA' D'ORO

Hotel Bernardi-Semenzato. Calle de l'Oca, Cannaregio 4366, 30121 Venezia. ☎ **041-522-7257.** Fax 041-522-2424. Hotel, 18 units, 10 with bathroom; annex, 8 units, 1 with bathroom. A/C TV TEL. 85,000L ($47) double without bathroom, 130,000L ($72) double with bathroom. MC, V. Closed Nov 20–Dec 10. Vaporetto: Ca' d'Oro.

From the outside, this weather-worn palazzo doesn't hint of its full 1995 renovation, which left hand-hewn ceiling beams exposed, air-conditioned rooms with coordinated headboard/spread sets, and baths modernized and retiled. The English-speaking owners, Maria Teresa and Leonardo Pepoli, aspire to three-star style and have just received a two-star rating, but they offer one-star rates (which are even less off-season). The addition of an annex 3 blocks away offers the chance to feel as if you've rented an aristocratic apartment. (To get the rates above, be sure to mention you're a Frommer's reader when you're booking.)

ON THE LIDO

Hotel des Bains. Lungomare Marconi 17, 30126 Lido di Venezia. ☎ **800/325-3535** in U.S. or 041-526-5921. Fax 041-526-0113. 210 units. A/C MINIBAR TV TEL. 429,000–660,000L ($238–$367) double; from 660,000L ($367) suite. AE, DC, MC, V. Closed Dec–Feb. Vaporetto: Lido, then bus A, B, or C.

Thomas Mann stayed in this grand old resort hotel and used it as the setting for his famous novella *Death in Venice*, in which an aging writer, Gustav Aschenbach, falls hopelessly in love with a beautiful young boy named Tadzio. Visconti shot part of the film version here. With its spacious, airy, old-fashioned public rooms and creaking wooden floors, the place quickly transports you back to another era. The question is: Do you want to be transported? The pastel-hued guest rooms face the sea (most expensive) or the garden. They're large, filled with light, and have marble-clad baths and small dressing rooms. Details are understated rather than overblown. A private beach with cabanas lies across the road and is accessible by an underground tunnel, but you'll probably want to do your swimming in the beautiful pool beside the hotel. Special rates in March/April and October/November bring the price down dramatically.

3 Whet Your Appetite

As you might expect, fish (*pesce*) is the trademark food of Venice. It's usually pretty expensive, though. Venetian kitchens also receive plenty of fresh produce from the mainland, and there are some excellent regional wines to sample. In high season it's absolutely essential to book.

The price range for main courses starts with what's usually considered a *primo*, or first course (usually pasta), and goes up to the most expensive *secondo* (second or main course). In nearly all these places you'll be charged a *coperto* (cover) as well.

Note: For the locations of the restaurants below, see the "Venice Accommodations & Dining" map on pp. 460–461.

NEAR SAN MARCO & LA FENICE

Aciugheta. Campo SS Filippo e Giacomo, San Marco. ☎ **041-522-4292.** Reservations recommended. Main courses 10,000–30,000L ($6–$17); tourist menu 22,000–39,000L ($12–$22). AE, MC, V. Daily noon–2pm and 6–10:30pm. Vaporetto: San Marco.

The little Campo SS Filippo and Giacomo, a few minutes' walk east of Piazza San Marco, is a busy place. This and a few other restaurants in the vicinity are often jammed with tourists, and it isn't a place where you'll want to linger: I'm talking high-volume turnover. With its brick walls and beamed ceiling, Aciugheta is a pleasant enough spot, but if you dine outside you'll have more air. The selection of Veneto and Italian wines by the glass is amazing and cheap. The food? It's decent but not great. My one recommendation is not to order any of the frozen fish dishes; the fresh ones are far better. And they serve a couple of fresh fish dishes many tourist restaurants don't: sea-wolf and stewed cuttlefish. You can also get a good pizza, and there's a tourist menu whereby you get soup

A Note on Fresh Fish

The fish merchants at the Mercato Rialto (Venice's main open-air market) take Monday off, which explains why many restaurants are closed on Monday. Those that are open on Monday are sometimes selling Saturday's goods—beware!

or pasta, followed by chicken, fish, roast veal, or grilled sole and a mixed salad or fresh seasonal vegetables.

Alfredo Alfredo. Campo San Filippo e Giacomo, Castello 4294. ☎ **041-522-5331.** Main courses 12,000–26,000L ($7–$15); fixed-price menu 22,000L ($12). AE, DC, MC, V. Thurs–Tues 11am–2am. Vaporetto: San Zaccaria. VENETIAN/INTERNATIONAL.

This place is nothing fancy and better for a quick inexpensive lunch than dinner. The setting is Italian coffee shop and the food is on the same level. At these prices you get fast and simple, not gourmet. You can carb up on your daily dose of pasta (mostly simple spaghetti dishes with various sauces); the *lasagna alla bolognese* is great. Also available are freshly made salads, omelets, and grilled meats (including veal scallopini). For the fixed-price menu you get spaghetti or lasagna and a scallopina, a cotoletta, or maybe scampi with fried zucchinis. A *piatto unico* (one-plate meal) of spaghetti with tomato sauce and a mixed salad comes in at 17,000L ($9).

Antico Martini. Campo San Fantin, San Marco 1983. ☎ **041-522-4121.** Reservations required. Main courses 26,000–68,000L ($14–$38); fixed-price menus 70,000–126,000L ($39–$70). AE, DC, MC, V. Thurs–Mon noon–2:30pm and 7–11pm, Wed 7–11:30pm. Vaporetto: San Marco or Santa Maria del Giglio. VENETIAN/INTERNATIONAL.

This restaurant, housed in a palazzo, opened in 1720 as a cafe. Since 1921 it has belonged to the Baldi family, and they've made it into one the city's top restaurants, where dedicated gourmands will find Venetian cooking elevated to its highest level. The "international" fare is less successful. *Pappardelle dello Chef,* one of the least expensive dishes, is also one of the best: large pasta noodles with scampi and sweet peppers. There's a superb *risotto di frutti di mare* (seafood risotto). One of the specialties is *chicche del nonno* (tiny dumplings filled with spinach). The tasty *fegato alla veneziano* is liver fried with onions. Whatever's fresh and in season will show up as a chef's suggestion.

✪ **Do Leoni.** In the Hotel Londra Palace, Riva degli Schiavoni, Castello 4171. ☎ **041-520-0533.** Reservations required. Main courses 30,000–48,000L ($17–$27). AE, DC, MC, V. Daily noon–2:30pm and 7–11pm. Vaporetto: San Marco. VENETIAN/INTERNATIONAL.

Do Leoni ("Two Lions") has been in existence since the Londra Palace opened in 1860. It's a very elegant place with wonderful food, top-quality service, and high prices, and it's a good place to know about if you want a special "dress-up" lunch or dinner. The dining room juts out along the Riva degli Schiavoni, so you're assured of a passing parade of people to watch. At night, a piano player softly tickles the ivories. You won't feel rushed. The menu is very selective and features some wonderful Venetian-style dishes. For antipasti, try the fresh smoked salmon, boneless marinated sardines, or fresh tuna carpaccio. For a first course there are different kinds of risotto, tagliatelle with fresh scampi and asparagus, gnocchi with lobster sauce, and a rice-and-bean soup from an ancient recipe. There's always a fresh grilled fish of the day. Meat courses include calves' liver, veal scallops, and duck fillet. One particularly divine dessert is the marscapone with fruit.

La Colomba. Piscinia Frezzeria, San Marco 1665. ☎ **041-522-1175.** Reservations recommended. Main courses 16,000–45,000L ($9–$25). AE, DC, MC, V. Apr–June and Sept–Oct

Take a Gelato or Pastry Break

If you're in the mood for some tasty gelato (ice cream), head to the **Gelateria Paolin,** Campo San Stefano, Dorsoduro 2962A (☎ **041-522-5576;** open June–Sept daily 7:30am–midnight and Oct–May Tues–Sun 7:30am–8:30pm), offering 18 flavors. It has stood on the corner of this busy square since the 1930s, making it Venice's oldest ice-cream parlor. You can order your ice cream to go or pay more and eat it at one of the sidewalk tables.

One of the city's best-respected pastry shops is the **Pasticceria Marchini,** Ponte San Maurizio, San Marco 2769 (☎ **041-522-9109;** open daily 8:30am–8:30pm), whose cakes, muffins, and pastries are sold by the piece for on-the-spot eating at the bar (there are few tables) or by the kilogram for eating elsewhere. The pastries include traditional versions of *torte del Doge,* made from almonds and pine nuts; *zalleto,* made from a mix of cornmeal and eggs; and *bigna,* akin to zabaglione, concocted from chocolate and cream.

daily noon–3pm and 7–11pm; closed Wed other months. Vaporetto: San Marco. VENETIAN/INTERNATIONAL.

On a quiet, narrow street between San Marco and La Fenice, La Colomba ("The Dove") is a decidedly upscale restaurant with a kitchen oriented toward Venetian specialties. The chic interior, with light-colored walls, linen and crystal table settings, and contemporary artwork, is lovely (there's also seating outside). Generally you'll find five daily specials based on what's fresh and in season. There's a good selection of pastas, including cannelloni, tagliatelle, ravioli, and risotto with mushrooms. The restaurant is known for its fried, grilled, and boiled fish dishes. Try the carpaccio of salmon if it's available or the exotic *baccala alla vicentina* (dry cod simmered in milk and seasoned with onions, anchovies, and cinnamon).

Piccolo Martini. Frezzaria, San Marco 30124. ☎ **041-528-5136.** Reservations recommended. Main courses 19,000–42,000L ($11–$23). AE, DC, MC, V. Daily noon–2:30pm and 7–11pm. Vaporetto: San Marco. VENETIAN.

Small *(piccolo)* and smart, this place is less than 5 minutes west of Piazza San Marco. It's on a well-traveled tourist beat, but once inside you'll feel extremely cozy. In summer, you'll be grateful for the air-conditioning. Some specialties are spaghetti with crayfish, tagliolini with shrimps and arugula, and pasta-and-bean soup. There are also a wonderful fish soup and French oysters (for the libido). The grilled mixed-fish plate comes with sea bass, lobster, and salmon. I'd recommend, if it's on the menu, *orata con punte di asparagi* (sea bass with asparagus tips). There's also a nice and spicy veal dish called *churrasco Porteno.*

✪ **Ristorante ai Barbacani.** Calle del Paradiso, San Marco 5748. ☎ **041-520-4691.** Reservations recommended. Main courses 10,000–33,000L ($6–$18); special menu 35,000L ($19). AE, DC, MC, V. Tues–Sun noon–2:30pm and 7–10pm. Vaporetto: Rialto or San Marco. VENETIAN.

Occupying a building from around 1400 and darkly gleaming with lots of old wood, this restaurant is a lovely place to linger over a fine Venetian meal. It specializes in fish. Start with Venetian-style spaghetti with squid or spider crab or a risotto cooked with seafood, squid, or lemon (which is more Florentine than Venetian). Order more fish for your main course, perhaps oven-baked turbot with olives and capers (for two), Venetian-style squid with polenta or salt cod, or a special fresh fish baked in foil. You'll do very well with the tourist menu, which may include fish soup, grilled salmon, fresh vegetables, and tiramisu. Order a light white wine to go with your fish feast and you should come away contented. The atmosphere is a little fancy, so it's a good idea to wear something other than shorts or jeans. The restaurant is about midway between the Rialto and the Grand Canal.

✪ **Taverna La Fenice.** Campiello de la Fenice, San Marco 1939. ☎ **041-522-3856.** Reservations required. Main courses 20,000–45,000L ($11–$25). AE, DC, MC, V. Aug–Apr Mon 7–10:30pm, Tues–Sat noon–2:30pm and 7–11pm; May–July daily noon–3pm and 7–10:30pm. Vaporetto: San Marco. ITALIAN/VENETIAN.

On the same quiet square as the Hotel La Fenice et des Artistes (and accessible from the hotel), this is a romantic spot with extremely good food. It's been serving artists, travelers, lovers, and patrons of La Fenice since 1907. The interior has a coffered wood ceiling, damask walls, terrazzo floors, and pink tablecloths, but eat outside on the terrace if the weather is fine. One good seasonal dish is gray shrimps with polenta. The fish risotto and the risotto with black cuttlefish are delicious. Handmade pastas include gnocchi (with prawn sauce), tagliolini (with crab sauce), pappardelle (with porcinis and truffles), and tagliatelle (with fish eggs). There are many seasonal fish dishes on the menu.

Trattoria Da Bruno. Salizzada San Lio, Calle del Paradiso, San Marco 5731. ☎ **041-522-1480.** Main courses 14,000–25,000L ($8–$14); fixed-price menu 25,000L ($14). AE, DC, MC, V. Wed–Mon noon–3pm and 6:30–11pm. Closed 1 week in Jan. Vaporetto: San Marco or Rialto. VENETIAN.

This is a place where Italians go to eat, though you'll inevitably encounter other tourists as well. The trattoria is on a narrow street about midway between Piazza San Marco and the Rialto Bridge. Hopefully you'll be wearing something that goes with the pink walls and tablecloths. The ceiling is beamed and the floors are terrazzo. For the price it's an excellent choice; the fixed-price menu (soup or pasta; veal, chicken, or fish; french-fried potatoes or salad; and dessert) counts as a true bargain in a generally bargainless city. For starters, there's a good antipasti table and wonderful prosciutto. Some of the meat dishes are grilled on an open-hearth fire. They also do very good seasonal game dishes, like *capriolo* (roebuck) and *fagiano* (pheasant). Of course you can always fall back on Venetian fish soup.

Vino Vino. Ponte delle Veste, San Marco 2007A. ☎ **041-523-7027.** Main courses 7,000–15,000L ($4–$8). AE, MC, V. Wed–Mon 10am–midnight, Sat to 1am. Vaporetto: San Marco. VENETIAN/ITALIAN.

This little hole-in-the-wall wine bar is just north of Via XXII Marzo, close to La Fenice. It's absolutely no frills and a bit dark, but that's why I like it. And it's open "nonstop" (as the Italians say), so you can get something to eat (or a glass of wine) when everything else is closed. There's a small selection of daily pasta and vegetable dishes, plus salads, and that's it. You choose what you want from the counter. A very large selection of fine Italian and imported wines is available by the glass or the bottle.

NEAR THE ACCADEMIA

✪ **Antica Locanda Montin.** Fondamenta Eremite, Dorsoduro 1147. ☎ **041-522-7151.** Reservations required. Main courses 10,000–30,000L ($6–$17). AE, MC, V. Thurs–Mon 12:30–2:30pm and 7:30–10:30pm, Tues 12:30–2:30pm. Vaporetto: Accademia. VENETIAN/ITALIAN.

I described the *locanda* (inn) above, and this is the inn's restaurant. It's one of the best-loved dining spots in Dorsoduro and with good reason. Try as a first course the handmade tortelloni stuffed with radicchio or artichokes and you'll know what I mean. Several meat dishes are available, including *fegato* (veal liver) *alla veneziana* (with onions) or with butter and sage. Most people come for the fish: Sea bass with artichokes, grilled giant scampi or sole, and fried sardines are some of the possibilities. For a fishy bit of everything, order the *grigliata mista Montin.* The place is always pretty crowded, and you may end up being seated almost, but not quite, at the same table with other members of your party. It's casual, but you won't feel out of place if you're dressed up.

ON THE LIDO

Al Fortunale. Gran Viale 49. ☎ **041-526-1612.** Main courses 8,000–13,000L ($5–$8); fixed-price menu 12,000L ($7) at lunch, 22,000L ($12) at dinner. AE, DC, MC, V. Tues–Sun 11am–10:30pm. Closed Dec. Vaporetto: Lido. PIZZA/ITALIAN.

This is a very casual, very pleasant pizzeria with outside seating under a bright yellow-and-white-striped canopy. It's on the main street running from the vaporetto stop to the Lido beach. Antipasti include a good Caprese (mozzarella with oil and fresh tomatoes) and *gamberetti salsa rosa* (shrimp cocktail). Pizza is the specialty and what I recommend. The pies are cooked individually and so may arrive at different times, and they have wonderful thin, flaky crusts. There's also a daily selection of *primis* (first courses) for 10,000L ($6). You might find spicy *penne all'arrabbiata,* tortelli with radicchio, or tortellini with prosciutto.

4 Exploring Venice

Venice is a complicated city to find your way around in, but with a detailed map you'll be able to do it. Yes, you'll become lost—but what better place to get lost in? Street numbers exist, but they make little if any sense to non-natives, so it's best to get detailed instructions and have your destination marked on a map. Use the Grand Canal and Piazza San Marco as your main landmarks or watermarks and orient yourself at the vaporetto stops.

If you want an authorized guide to show you around, have your concierge call for one at ☎ **041-523-9902** or **041-520-9038.**

THE HITS YOU SHOULDN'T MISS

✪ **St. Mark's Basilica (Basilica di San Marco).** Piazza San Marco, San Marco. ☎ **041-522-5205.** Basilica free; treasury 4,000L ($2); presbytery 3,000L ($2); galleria 3,000L ($2); Marciano Museum 3,000L ($2); campanile 8,000L ($4). Basilica and most interior attractions Apr–Sept Mon–Sat 9:45am–4:30pm, Sun 2–5pm; Oct–Mar Mon–Sat 9:30am–5pm, Sun 1:30–4:30pm. Campanile daily May–Oct 9am–8pm; Nov–Apr 9:30am–3:45pm. Vaporetto: San Marco.

St. Mark's Basilica is one of the most famous churches in the world, and it gives its name to one of the most famous piazzas in the world. The cathedral's style is primarily Byzantine, characterized by a huge center dome and smaller side domes, but the whole is overlaid with Gothic fretwork and Romanesque elements. The cathedral was built to contain the body of St. Mark the Evangelist, which was smuggled out of

A Note on Street Designations

As you wander, be prepared for a lot of unfamiliar street designations. A broad street running along a canal is a *fondamenta,* a narrower street running along a canal is a *calle,* and a paved road is a *salizzada, ruga,* or *calle larga.* A *rio terra* is a filled canal channel now used as a walkway, and a *sottoportego* is a passage beneath buildings. And you'll often encounter the word *campo* when you come to an open-air area—that's a reference to the fact that such a place was once grassy, and—in days of yore—cattle grazed there.

A St. Mark's Fashion Alert

A dress code for men and women prohibiting shorts, bare arms and shoulders, and skirts above the knee is strictly enforced at all times in the basilica. You *will* be turned away. You also must remain silent and cannot take photographs.

Alexandria and brought to Venice in 832. Work continued up until the 18th century. On the balcony *(loggia)*, directly over the center door, are copies of the four famous bronze horses (the originals are in the Marciano Museum) carted back as booty from the sack of Constantinople in 1204. The cathedral's **campanile (bell tower)** is a slender brick skyscraper rebuilt (with an elevator) after the original collapsed in 1902. There's a viewing platform on the top.

At peak hours you'll need to line up to get inside the cathedral, and once there you have to follow a set path unless you're paying for the "extras." Dark and richly adorned, glittering with gold mosaics and rare marbles, the basilica was once the private chapel of the doges, the rulers of Venice. It's chief treasure is the **Pala d'Oro,** a 10th-century gold altar screen inset with enamel and jewels. I recommend you skip the **treasury (tesoro)** and other sidelights (unless you're an art historian) and go up to the **Marciano Museum (Museo Marciano)** to view the originals of the four bronze horses, dating from the 4th century. From there you can step out to the **Loggia dei Cavalli** for a panoramic view of St. Mark's Square.

✪ **Ducal Palace (Palazzo Ducale) and Bridge of Sighs (Ponte dei Sospiri).** Piazzetta San Marco, San Marco. ☎ **041-522-4951.** Admission 17,000L ($10), includes admission to Museo Civico Correr below. Daily 9am–7pm (ticket office closes 5:30pm). Vaporetto: San Marco.

The powerful rulers of Venice were not dukes, they were doges. The Palace of the Doges, where they lived and worked, is the most popular attraction in Venice after St. Mark's. As you're facing the cathedral, the entrance to the palace (the 15th-century Porta della Carta) is to your right, just off the piazzetta. Built of pinky-red marble and white Istrian stone and covered with a lacy fretwork of Gothic intricacy, the palace is one of Italy's great civic monuments. Much of the first palace, erected in 1309, was destroyed by a fire in the 16th century. During its restoration, several great Venetian artists contributed to the grandeur you see today. From the Renaissance courtyard, the **Giant's Stairway (Scala dei Giganti)** leads up to the loggia (it was called this because of its two giant mythological figures carved by Sansovino).

Inside, you pass through several public rooms before reaching the **Anti-Collegio Salon (Sala di Anti-Collegio),** dominated by Veronese's *Rape of Europa* and Tintoretto's paintings of the *Three Graces* and *Bacchus and Ariadne.* There are more works by these two artists in the adjacent rooms. The **Salon of the Council of Ten (Sala del Consiglio dei Dieci)** is appropriately creepy; it was here that the Council of Ten picked up and read their "mail"—bills of accusation placed in the mouth of a stone lion—and decided who was in need of what particularly hideous punishment.

Downstairs are more rooms to explore, including the **private apartments** of the doges. Tintoretto's *Paradise,* in the enormous **Grand Council Chamber (Sala del Maggior Consiglio),** is reputedly the largest oil painting in the world. From the Council Chamber, with Veronese's allegorical-propagandical ceiling fresco *The Triumph of Venice,* you can cross the famous **Bridge of Sighs (Ponte dei Sospiri).** It connects the palace to an adjacent prison, where all that Venetian triumph turned into unmitigated terror.

✪ **Peggy Guggenheim Collection (Collezione Peggy Guggenheim).** Palazzo Venier dei Leoni, San Gregorio, Dorsoduro 701. ☎ **041-520-6288.** Admission 12,000L ($7). Wed–Mon 11am–6pm. Vaporetto: Salute.

Basilica di San Marco

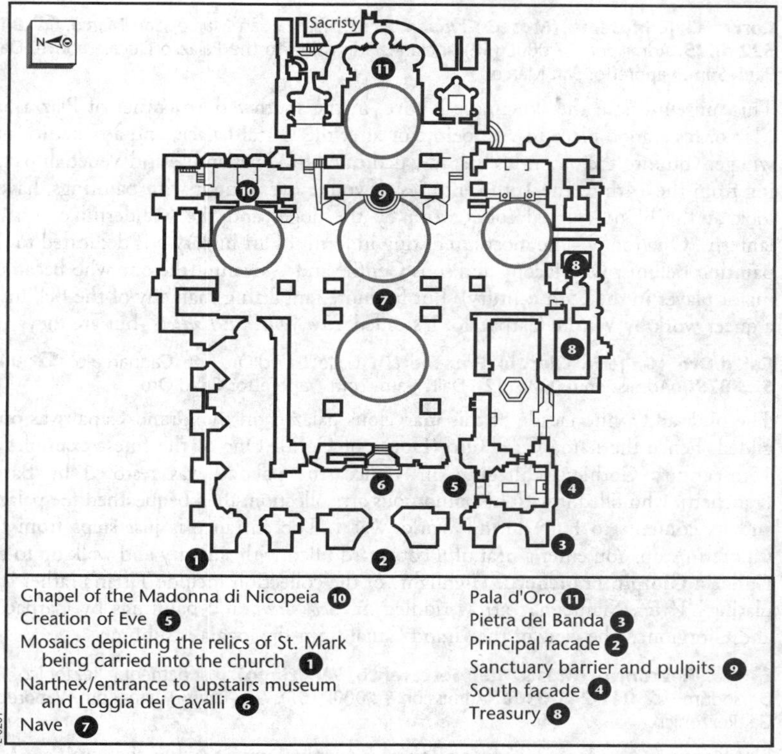

If you're a fan of modern art or even if you're not, this is one collection you must see. The bulk of it was assembled between 1938 and 1947 by Peggy Guggenheim, an American heiress who was a great patron of contemporary artists (Max Ernst was her second husband). Since 1976, the museum has been administered by the Guggenheim Foundation, New York. It is, quite simply, the best museum of modern art in all Italy, housed in Peggy Guggenheim's stunningly beautiful palazzo on the Grand Canal. (She died in 1979 and is buried in the sculpture garden.) Premiere examples of cubist, abstract, surrealist, and abstract expressionist art are on display. Major European and American artists from Picasso to Pollock are represented. And if you're interested, copies of Peggy's trademark sandals and carnival sunglasses are for sale in the gift shop.

Academy Gallery (Galleria dell'Accademia). Accademia, Dorsoduro, at the foot of the Accademia Bridge. ☎ **041-522-2247.** Admission 12,000L ($7). Tues–Sat 9am–10pm, Sun 9am–2pm. Vaporetto: Accademia.

Some of the world's best-known artists lived and worked in Venice. The Accademia is dedicated to their paintings, which compose the "Venetian School." The collection covers a 400-year period, from the 14th to the 18th centuries, and includes masterpieces too numerous to enumerate. Highlights are Bellini's *Madonna and Saint Sebastian,* Giorgione's *La Tempesta* (the most famous painting here), *Banquet in the House of Levi* (not the jeans manufacturer) by Veronese, Mantegna's *St. George,* and four enormous canvases by Tintoretto based on the life of St. Mark. Also search out the Venetian scenes by Canaletto, Bellini, and Carpaccio.

Correr Civic Museum (Museo Civico Correr). Piazza San Marco, San Marco. ☎ **041-522-5625.** Admission 17,000L ($9), includes admission to the Palazzo Ducale above. Daily 9am–5pm. Vaporetto: San Marco.

This museum is in the Procuratie Nuove, in the southwestern corner of Piazza San Marco. It's a good place to visit before or after the Ducal Palace, and a ticket for one will get you into the other. It's basically dedicated to Venetian life and Venetian painting from the 14th to the 16th centuries. If you've overdone it with paintings, have a look at the blood-colored robes worn by the doges and the wonderful old street lanterns. One room—the most interesting in terms of art history—is dedicated to the painting Bellinis: Dad Jacopo and sons Gentile and Giovanni (the one who became a major player in the 15th-century). But far more tantalizing than any of the Bellinis is a queer work by Vittore Carpaccio: It's called *Two Venetian Ladies*—but are they?

Ca' d'Oro (Galleria Giorgio Franchetti). Calle Ca' d'Oro, 4L Cannaregio. ☎ **041-523-8790.** Admission 4,000L ($2). Daily 9am–2pm. Vaporetto: Ca' d'Oro.

The pink-and-white facade of this marvelous palazzo on the Grand Canal was once gilded, hence the name Ca' d'Oro (House of Gold). One of the finest examples of 15th-century Gothic architecture in Venice, the palazzo was restored by Baron Franchetti, who filled it with his sumptuous art collection, then bequeathed the palazzo and its contents to Italy during World War I. The entrance is just steps from the vaporetto stop. You enter a beautiful courtyard filled with statuary and walk up to the **Galleria Giorgio Franchetti.** Highlights of the collection include Titian's rather "titillating" *Venus*, Mantegna's arrow-riddled *St. Sebastian*, and paintings by Carpaccio and Giorgione. The view of the Grand Canal from the loggia is sublime.

✪ **Ca' Rezzonico (Museo del Settecento Veneziano).** Fondamenta Rezzonico, 7H Dorsoduro. ☎ **041-241-0100.** Admission 12,000L ($7). Sat–Thurs 10am–4pm. Vaporetto: Ca' Rezzonico.

Hardly anyone reads the poetry of Robert Browning anymore, but that eminent Victorian lived and died in this palazzo on the Grand Canal. (Browning's the one who was married to poet Elizabeth Barrett, remember?) Now dedicated to the Venetian Settecento (1700s), the 17th- and 18th-century palazzo is a treasure trove of baroque paintings and furniture. It gives you a good idea of the kind of heavy Venetian style that has never quite gone out of fashion: brocaded walls, glass chandeliers, dark portraits, and gilded furnishings. Tiepolo painted the ceiling allegories in the Throne Room (no, I don't mean the water closet). In the first-floor salons are some paintings unmatched for their *bizarrerie*. In one, which seems to be a Baroque version of a hetero S/M fantasy, a tribe of half-naked Amazons is pummeling a naked man with pitchforks and even a violin. In another, a woman is pounding a spike through a man's skull. I'm afraid these weird paintings are more memorable than the masterpieces by Guardi and Canaletto. Only Pietro Longhi's *The Lady and the Hairdresser* can compete.

Note: In 1998 only the first floor of the palazzo was open; the rest may be open by the time you arrive.

Basilica di Santa Maria Gloriosa dei Frari. Campo dei Frari, San Polo. Tel. **041-522-2637.** Admission 3,000L ($1.75); free Sun. Mon–Sat 9am–6pm, Sun 3–6pm. Vaporetto: San Tomà.

Known simply as the Frari, this Venetian Gothic church is only a short walk from the Scuola di San Rocco (below) and filled with some great art. The most dazzlingly dramatic work is Titian's *Assumption* over the main altar—a masterpiece depicting Mary being sucked up to heaven on a cloud. On the first altar to the right as you enter is Titian's second major work here—a *Madonna Enthroned*, painted in 1526. Raphael's tomb is a large, latter-day neoclassical model on the opposite wall. Facing it is a memorial to Canova, the Italian sculptor who led the neoclassical revival. In the sacristy is a

The Venice International Film Festival

The Venice International Film Festival, held on the Lido during the first 2 weeks of September, isn't as famous as the Cannes festival but is just as starry. Events center around the Casino on the Lido, but films are also screened in squares around Venice and on the Grand Canal itself (talk about a *son-et-lumière* show!).

If you're in town when Hollywood comes to Venice (and West Hollywood is strongly represented), get into your coolest drop-dead clothes and crash all the showbiz parties. This isn't so difficult to do in Italy: Just look important, bored, and say you're with Disney. It's your chance to rub up against the stars.

1488 Giovanni Bellini triptych on wood; the Madonna is cool and serene, one of Bellini's finest portraits of the Virgin. Also see the almost primitive-looking wood carving by Donatello of St. John the Baptist.

Scuole Grande di San Rocco. 6G Campo San Rocco, San Polo 3058. ☎ **041-523-4864.** Admission 8,000L ($4). Daily 9am–5:30pm. Vaporetto: San Tomà.

I'm putting this place in just in case you've fallen in love with the works of Tintoretto. You'll find prime examples of allegorical cycles, the *Life and Passion of Christ,* and scenes from the Old and New Testament.

GAY VENICE

Don't be shocked, but there *is* no gay Venice. At least not in the sense that there's a gay Milan, a gay Florence, and a gay Rome. Gays live and work in Venice, of course, and there's an Arci-Gay center, but otherwise, there's no specifically gay social network of bars, clubs, cafes, and shops.

This might seem odd, given the numbers of gay and lesbian travelers who descend on Venice every year. But if you walk around the city at night you won't come across many straight bars or discos either. The city is actually fairly quiet, not what you'd call a party town. Touristic nightlife generally consists of dining at a restaurant and sitting down for a coffee or a drink at one of the large outdoor cafes around Piazza San Marco. There's nothing gay or straight about it—until someone sitting a few tables away catches your eye.

The nearest gay bars are in Padua (see the end of this chapter). What gay life there is in Venice (at least for the tourist) revolves mostly around outdoor cruising. One time-honored late-night cruising ground, used mostly by a younger crowd, is **Muro del Pianto,** the lagoonside promenade off Piazza San Marco. The area is just behind the Marciana Library and around the Reali Gardens (Giardini Reali). The **Rialto Bridge** is another cruising area. **Riva dei Martiri** and **Viale Trieste,** waterside promenades near the Public Gardens (Giardini Pubblici) and the Biennale exhibit hall on the eastern end of the island, are active in the early evening; the area extends down the naval barracks (of course) on Viale Piave. **Zattere,** the area along the island of Giudecca's canalfront (Fondamenta Zattere up to the promontory, Punto della Dogana) is cruisy in the late afternoon and after 9pm; hustlers show up after 11pm. Petty crime isn't uncommon, so be careful.

Campo Santa Barnaba and **Campo Santa Margherita,** both in the university district, are busy from 10:30pm on. And **Campo San Giacomo dell'Orio** and **Calle Stroppe,** around Arci-Gay headquarters, are active 6pm to midnight. On the **Isola di San Giorgio Maggiore,** walk along the waterfront next to the moored yachts on the left side of the cathedral; take the path from the Biblioteca Marciana annex (behind

Venice Attractions

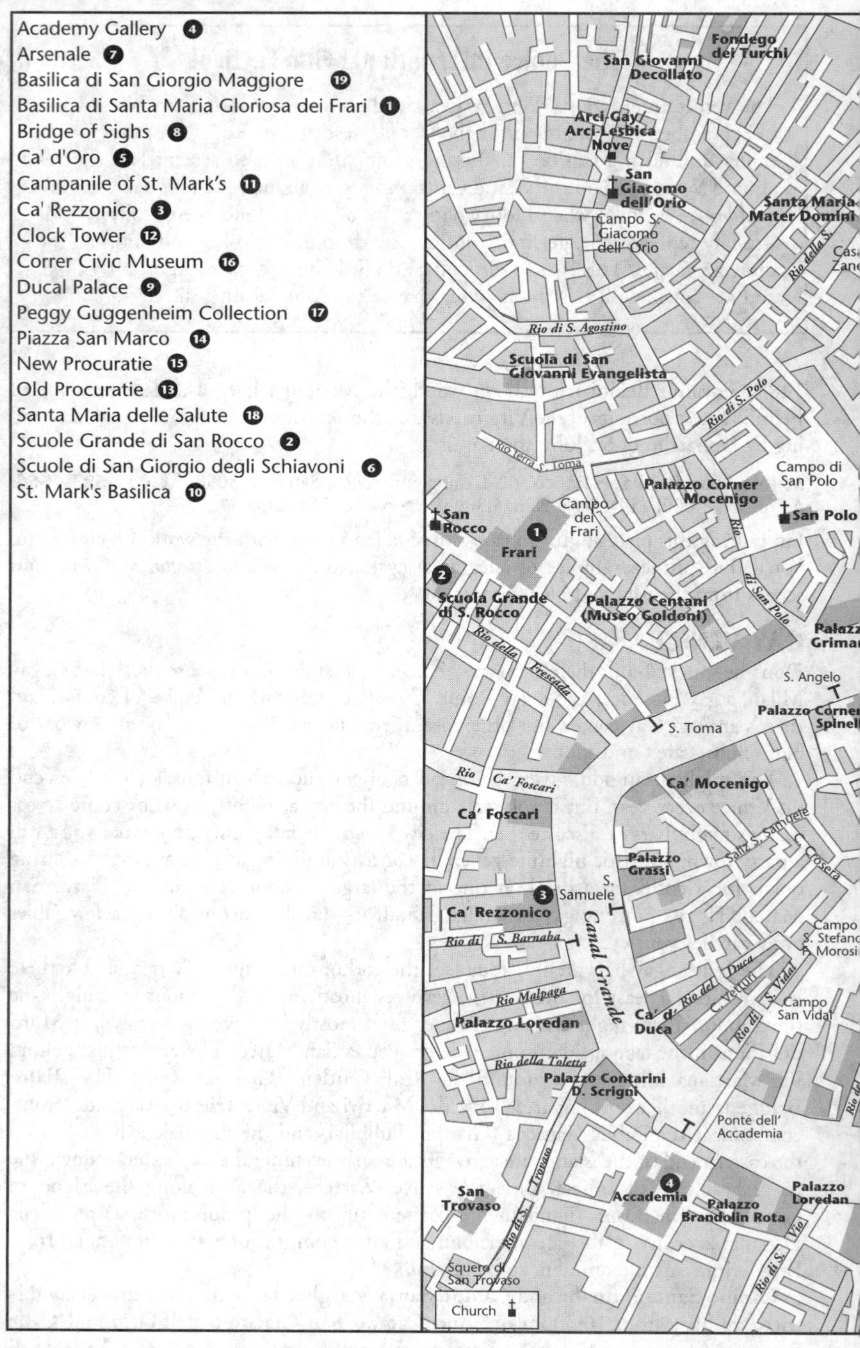

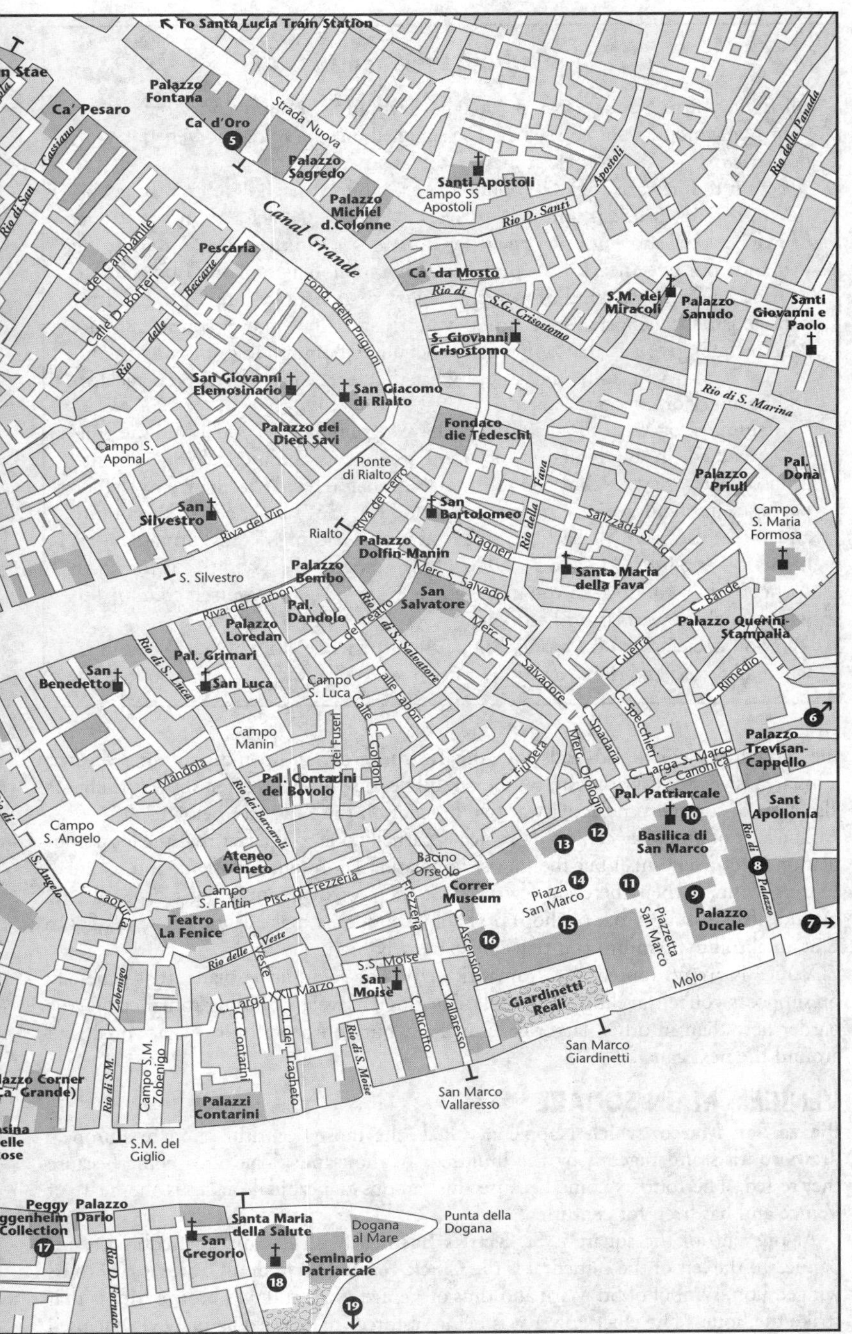

To Santa Lucia Train Station
Palazzo Fontana
Ca' Pesaro
Ca' d'Oro
Strada Nuova
Palazzo Sagredo
Santi Apostoli
Campo SS Apostoli
Palazzo Michiel d.Colonne
Canal Grande
Rio D. Santi
Apostoli
Rio della Panada
Pescaria
C. del Campanile
Calle D. Botteri
Beccarie
Fond. delle Prigioni
Ca' da Mosto
Rio di
S.G. Crisostomo
S.M. dei Miracoli
Palazzo Sanudo
Santi Giovanni e Paolo
S. Giovanni Crisostomo
Rio delle
San Giovanni Elemosinario
San Giacomo di Rialto
Rio di S. Marina
Palazzo dei Dieci Savi
Fondaco die Tedeschi
Campo S. Aponal
Ponte di Rialto
Riva del Ferro
Fava
Palazzo Priuli
Pal. Donà
San Silvestro
Riva del Vin
San Bartolomeo
Rio della
Salizzada S. Lio
Campo S. Maria Formosa
Rialto
Palazzo Dolfin-Manin
C. Stagneri
S. Silvestro
Palazzo Bembo
Merc S. Salvador
Santa Maria della Fava
Riva del Carbon
San Salvatore
C. Bande
Pal. Dandolo
Palazzo Loredan
Rio del Teatro
Merc. S.
Palazzo Querini-Stampalia
Pal. Grimari
di S. Salvatore
C. del Teatro
Salvadore
C. Guerra
Rio di S. Luca
San Benedetto
San Luca
Campo S. Luca
Calle Fabbri
C. Rimedio
Calle
dei Fuseri
C. Goldoni
C. Specchieri
Campo Manin
Spadaria
Palazzo Trevisan-Cappello
C. Mandola
C. Fiubera
C. Larga S. Marco
C. Canonica
Pal. Contarini del Bovolo
Merc. Orologio
Pal. Patriarcale
Sant Apollonia
Rio dei Barcaroli
Basilica di San Marco
Campo S. Angelo
Rio di Palazzo
S. Angelo
Ateneo Veneto
Bacino Orseolo
C. Caotorta
Campo S. Fantin
Pisc. di Frezzeria
Frezzeria
Correr Museum
Piazza San Marco
Piazzetta San Marco
Palazzo Ducale
Teatro La Fenice
Rio delle
Veste
C. Ascensione
S.S. Moise
Zobenigo
San Moisè
Molo
C. Larga XXII Marzo
Giardinetti Reali
Rio di S. Moisè
C. Contarini
Cl. del Traghetto
C. Ricotto
C. Vallaresso
San Marco Giardinetti
Campo S.M. Zobenigo
Rio di S.M.
San Marco Vallaresso
lazzo Corner Ca' Grande)
Palazzi Contarini
asina elle ose
S.M. del Giglio
Peggy ggenheim Collection
Palazzo Dario
Santa Maria della Salute
Dogana al Mare
Punta della Dogana
San Gregorio
Seminario Patriarcale
Rio D. Fornace
5
6
7
8
9
10
11
12
13
14
15
16
17
18
19

Cruising the Canals

All right, you're here as a couple, maybe celebrating an anniversary or even on your honeymoon. And you've heard so much about the romantic Venetian gondolas that you're determined to have a ride in one.

I want to forewarn you: The gondoliers are a pretty macho group, comparable to construction workers and truck drivers. Maybe you'll get a really sweet one, or maybe you'll suss out a gay one (they must exist). On the other hand, putting you and your sweetheart in the hands of a homophobic gondolier isn't going to provide you with the kind of romantic memories you're looking for. I'm all for consciousness-raising and for claiming your right to do whatever you want to do. All I'm telling you is that you might encounter homophobic jokes and comments. Even if you don't understand what they are, you'll get the general drift and be angry or uncomfortable.

Assuming you want to go ahead and have a gondola ride, you'll find the gondolas "parked" in stands all over the city. This is a very commercialized "romance industry," with set fees, but you must establish beforehand exactly what you'll be paying. The standard price is currently 120,000L ($67) for the first 50 minutes and 60,000L ($33) for each extra 25 minutes. The night rate (8pm–8am) is higher by 30,000L ($17) and 15,000L ($8), respectively. The price is for up to six people in a gondola, so you may—to your horror—find yourself crammed in with straight tourists from Dubuque.

If you decide to go for a ride, I hope the experience is a wonderful one. It is, when all is said and done, a unique way to see Venice with the one you love.

the cathedral), which also leads into the Teatro Verde, an open-air summer theater. This area is very cruisy at night, but be careful because druggies often show up. There's also a lot of summertime activity at two beaches on the **Lido** (see below).

The lack of other gay centers in Venice is partially due to the fact that the local population is relatively small but the tourist population enormous, transient, and seasonal. During winter, when there are few visitors, the cost of maintaining a "specialized" business (such as a gay bar or shop) probably just doesn't make economic sense. Space is at an absolute premium and rents are extremely high.

Venice is always touted as a "romantic" city. For gays and lesbians, that generally presupposes you're traveling as a couple. For single travelers, finding romance may be harder here than in other, larger cities in Italy, but you never know what you'll find around the next canal.

VENICE'S MAIN SQUARE

Piazza San Marco, which Napoléon called "the most beautiful salon in Europe," draws tourists and pigeons by the hundreds of thousands. The birds come because they're fed. The tourists come because this famous trapezoidal piazza is the heart of Venice and has been for centuries.

At one end of the square is **St. Mark's Basilica,** with its adjacent redbrick campanile. To the left of the cathedral is the **Clock Tower (Torre dell'Orologio),** with its winged lion, symbol of St. Mark and thus of Venice itself, and two bronze Moors that strike the hour. (The clock tower was being restored in 1998.) The piazza is enclosed on the north by the **Old Procuratie (Procuratie Vecchie).** Dating from 1514, this was the building where the procurators who looked after the basilica and its properties lived. Opposite it stands the **New Procuratie (Procuratie Nuove),** built in 1640.

Piazza San Marco

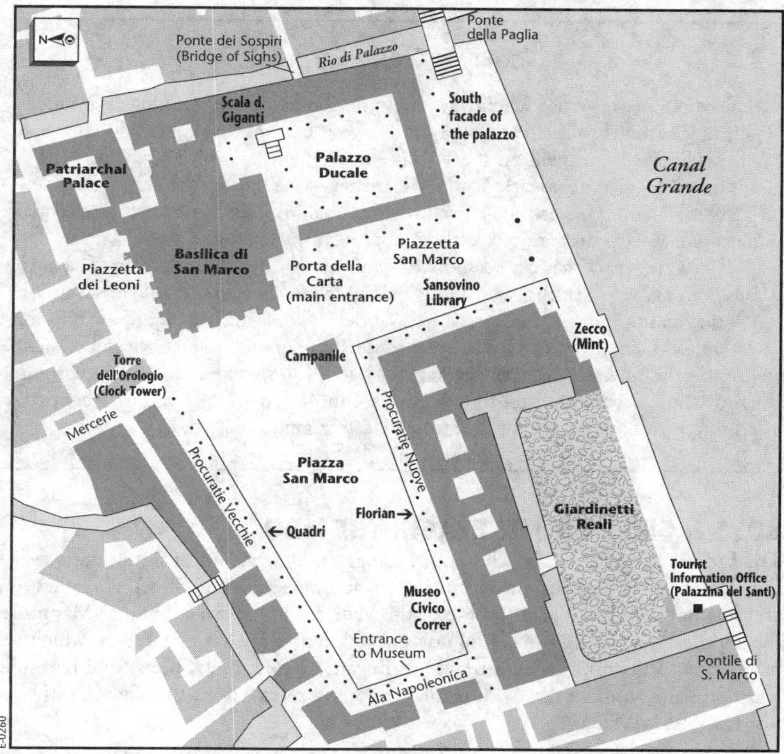

Napoléon connected the old and new buildings and enclosed the square with the neoclassical **Ala Napoleonica,** where a staircase leads up to the Museo Civico Correr. Arcades run along the sides of all these buildings; in and alongside one of them is **Caffè Florian,** one of Venice's most famous gathering spots. The piazza is the site of evening concerts in summer, and in winter it's frequently flooded by the rising tides and raised walkways are put out.

Piazzetta San Marco is the adjacent open-ended square running from St. Mark's to the Grand Canal. On the left is the **Ducal Palace,** on the right is the **Sansovino Library.** Directly across the Grand Canal, framed by twin columns topped by the lions of St. Mark and St. Teodoro, is the gleaming white church of **San Giorgio Maggiore,** occupying its own little island at the eastern tip of the island of Giudecca. It was designed by the great 16th-century architect Andrea Palladio, and its interior is massive but bare, since Palladio wasn't big on ornamentation. The broad lagoonside walkway along the Grand Canal is called the **Molo.** You can follow it (it changes names) all the way to the eastern tip of the city.

Many movies have been shot here. If you want a highly romantic look at St. Mark's Square and the Piazzetta, rent the movie *Summertime.* Filmed on location in the 1950s, directed by David Lean, and starring Katharine Hepburn and Rossano Brazzi, it's a glorious Technicolor tribute to Venice (just don't fall into a canal like Kate did). Also evocative is the recent film adaptation of Henry James's *The Wings of the Dove,* starring Helena Bonham Carter and Linus Roache. Nicholas Roeg's film version of Daphne du Maurier's *Don't Look Now,* with Julie Christie and Donald Sutherland, casts the city in a scary, haunted light.

Campy & Cruisy Carnevale

The one time in Venice when it's okay to display same-sex affection in public is during **Carnevale (Carnival).** You can bet your booties that gays make the most of this yearly event, held on the 10 days before Lent (at which time everyone is supposed to give up meat). Venice's Carnevale isn't gay in the sense that New Orleans's Mardi Gras is, but it's so cruisy and camp it's a must for international party-seekers (finding a hotel is the one problem).

Everyone wears masks and most dress up in costume (for the best places to buy a mask, see "Hitting the Stores" below). Street bars and cafes are set up on all the main squares, and everyone wanders about the city stopping off for *un'ombra* (local wine) or *un vin brulé* (mulled wine) and a *porchetta* (roast suckling pig) sandwich. All ages participate, but it's mostly the chic 30-something crowd and resident college-student population. If you're lucky you may be invited to a private party, maybe even one held in a grand old palazzo.

BOYS & GIRLS ON THE BEACH: THE LIDO

The **Lido** is famed for its beaches, but I'd suggest you stay out of the Adriatic even if they haven't posted pollution warnings. This fashionable island resort, 7½ miles long and just half a mile wide, is the site of the Venice Film Festival. Thomas Mann used the Lido as the setting for his homoerotic masterpiece *Death in Venice*, which was made into a Visconti movie starring Dirk Bogarde. The Lido is an easy and refreshing jaunt on a hot summer day, with regular vaporetto service from the San Zaccaria stop just east of San Marco.

Some of the beaches along the Lido are private enclaves set up with cabanas. The **Lido degli Alberoni** is a well-known gay nude beach (mostly men) and it's free. To get there, take bus B for Alberoni from the Lido bus station next to the vaporetto stop. This is a public beach with rolling dunes, bushes, and pine woods, very popular with Italian and foreign gays. Obviously the action takes place only in summer, and it's on the right side of the beach going toward the lighthouse. There's another gay beach, also free, on the western end of the Lido, close to the airport and on the opposite side of the Lido degli Alberoni. This is the **Lido San Nicolò,** and bus B (for San Nicolò) will take you there.

For an accommodations and a dining choice on the Lido, see earlier in this chapter.

5 Hitting the Stores

Venice is known for its lace, glass (manufactured on the island of Murano), and endless and often rather tacky Carnevale masks. You'll find these items, in varying degrees of price and authenticity, everywhere you look. You really do need to be discerning or you'll end up with a shoddy product that was manufactured in Eastern Europe. The places listed below are all reliable dealers. Be aware that there are absolutely no gay shops in Venice.

Shopping hours are generally Monday to Saturday 9am to 12:30pm and 3 to 7:30pm. In winter, shops are closed on Monday mornings; in summer, they sometimes close on Saturday afternoon.

SHOPPING A TO Z

ART OBJECTS At **Osvaldo Bohm,** Campo San Moisé, san Marco 1349–1350 (☎ **041-522-2255;** Vaporetto: Vallaresso), look especially for his little bronze masks, the nicest I've found in Venice.

CARNEVALE MASKS Venetian masks, considered collectors' items, originated during Carnevale. In the old days there was a good reason to wear masks during the riotous Carnival: They helped heterosexual wives and husbands cheat on one another, lecherous priests break their vows of chastity, and the rest of us (I hope) to get in some fun without being recognized. Things got so orgiastic that Carnevale was banned in the late 18th century. When it came back, the masks went on again.

You can find shops selling masks practically on every corner. As with glass and lace, however, quality varies. For every mask that's beautifully realized there are hundreds that are no more than shoddy, tacky tourist souvenirs. The most sought-after mask is the *Portafortuna* (luck bringer), with its long nose and birdlike visage. *Orientale* masks evoke the heyday of the Serene Republic and its trade with the Far East. The *Bauta* was worn by men to assert their machismo, and the *Neutra* is androgynous, blending the facial characteristics of both sexes.

The best place to buy Carnevale masks is the **Laboratorio Artigiano Maschere,** Barbaria delle Tole, Castello 6657 (☎ **041-522-3110**), which sells handcrafted masks in papier-mâché or leather. It has a particularly good selection, including masks depicting characters of the Commedia dell'Arte.

Also good is **Mondonovo,** Rio Terrà Canal, Dorsoduro 3063 (tel. **041-528-7344**), where talented artisans labor to produce copies of both traditional and more-modern masks, each of which is one-of-a-kind. Prices range from 30,000L ($17) for a fairly basic model to 3,000,000L ($1,740) for something you might display on a wall as a piece of sculpture.

GLASS **Anticlea,** Campo San Provolo, Castello 4719 (☎ **041-528-6949;** Vaporetto: San Zaccaria), sells antique and reproduction glass beads, strung or unstrung. **The Domus,** Fondamenta dei Vetrai 82, Murano (☎ **041-739-215;** Vaporetto: 12 or 13 to Murano), stocks a good selection of handblown drinking glasses, bowls, vases, and jewelry produced by top artisans. **L'Isola,** Campo San Moisé, San Marco 1468 (☎ **041-523-1973;** Vaporetto: Vallaresso), specializes in glass works by Carlo Moretti, one of the world's best-known glass artisans.

Pauly & Co., Ponte Consorzi, San Marco (☎ **041-520-9899;** Vaporetto: San Zaccaria), features 21 salons devoted to artistic glassware; most of their work is made-to-order. **Venini,** Piazzetta Leoncini, San Marco 314 (☎ **041-522-4045;** Vaporetto: San Zaccaria), another top name in art glass, features lamps, bottles, and vases with a distinctive swirl pattern.

LACE **Jesurum,** Mercerie del Capitello, San Marco 4857 (☎ **041-520-6177;** Vaporetto: San Zaccaria), is an elegant shop that's been in business for over 120 years; both handmade and machine-made lace and embroidery are available.

6 All the World's a Stage

A great cultural tragedy struck Venice in January 1996 when a fire broke out in the city's celebrated—and extremely beautiful—opera house, **La Fenice,** Campo San Fantin, San Marco 1965. The interior was entirely destroyed. Scaffolding now surrounds the exterior, and though a reopening was scheduled for 1999 it now looks like sometime in 2000 is more likely. There's still a full opera, ballet, and concert season, but performances are now held in the **Palafenice** theater on the Isola Nuova Tronchetto, to the west of the train station. Information is available by calling ☎ **06-3265-8010.** Or check out Teatro La Fenice on the Internet at **www.tin/fenice.** The box office, at Campo Santa Luca, is open Monday to Friday 8:30am to 1:30pm. Check with the tourist office for a list of other concerts and performances in the city.

I've told you about Carnevale and the Venice Film Festival. The third big event in Venice is the **Biennale Arts Festival.** It's held every other year on odd-numbered years, but a special biggie is planned for 2000, after which it'll switch over to even-number years. Events center around the Esposizione Nazionale d'Arte, where there's an exhibit of international paintings and sculpture.

7 In the Heat of the Night

With an absence of gay bars, clubs and discos, what's a queer in Venice to do after dark? Well, you can always wander around those cruising areas I discuss under "Exploring Venice." Or you can go to Padua (see below), which has a bit of a gay scene. Or you can relax and take a seat at a cafe in Piazza San Marco, like Kate Hepburn does in *Summertime,* and watch the passing parade (you never know who'll pass by). The vaporetto stop for the three cafes below is San Marco.

THE TOP CAFES

The most famous cafe in Venice is **Florian,** Piazza San Marco 56–59 (☎ **041-528-5338;** open Thurs–Tues 9am–midnight), on the south side of St. Mark's Square. It dates from 1720 and is a series of salons with red plush banquettes and outdoor tables (Apr–Oct). An espresso costs about $4 and an alcoholic drink about $12, and there's a music surcharge of 5,000L ($2.75) if you sit outside when music is playing.

Opposite Florian, on the north side of the square, is **Quadri,** Piazza San Marco 120–124 (☎ **041-522-2105;** open Wed–Sun noon–2:30pm and 7–10:30pm), founded in 1638. Opera nuts take note: Wagner stopped in here when he was working on *Tristan und Isolde.* The prices are about the same as at Florian, but the music charge is 4,000L ($2.25).

The more intimate **Gran Caffè Lavena,** Piazza San Marco 133–134 (☎ **041-522-4070;** open daily 9:30am–7:30pm; closed Thurs in winter), is also popular but doesn't have the late(r)-night scene of the other two. If you sit at a table, a coffee will cost about $3.50, plus the 5,000L ($2.75) music surcharge; if you stand at the bar it's about $1.

GAY LIFE IN PADUA

There are no gay bars or saunas in Venice, but you'll find both in nearby **Padua (Padova).** This lovely old city is about 35 minutes from Venice by train. Trains leave from Venice about every half hour or so; the round-trip fare is 6,800L ($3.75).

Padua is famous for its university, as old and prestigious as Oxford. The gay crowd is mostly college students. From the front of Padua's train station, take the no. 18 bus to reach **Fiera,** the gay area. To get into the clubs and saunas you'll need an Arci-Gay membership card (20,000L/$11), obtainable at the door. The card is valid in nearly all gay venues throughout the country.

The **Flexo Videobar,** Via N. Tommaseo 96B (☎ **049-807-4707;** opens Tues–Sun 9:30pm), is a sex club for gays spread out over four floors. You get to choose from bars, videos, playrooms, darkrooms, a meeting zone, and private cabins. It's *the* place for gays in Padua and the Veneto and is always busy. The second Saturday of each month is Leather Night; other theme parties are announced from time to time. **Tiratardi,** Via Palermo 20 (☎ **049-661-052**), is a bar/cafe popular with lesbians.

Next door to the Flexo, the **Olympus Club Sauna,** Via N. Tommaseo 96A (☎ **049-807-5834;** open Mon–Tues 1pm–2am, Wed and Sat–Sun 2–11pm), is very active, with Turkish baths, a whirlpool, massage, relaxation rooms, and a labyrinth (for that Minotaur you're hoping to meet). The **Metro Sauna Club,** Via Turazza 19

(☎ **49-807-5828;** open Wed and Sat 8pm–2am, Thurs–Fri 2pm–2am, Sun 4:30pm–2am), is another popular sauna, this one with a darkroom.

8 Boat Trips to the Lagoon Islands

Besides the Lido (above), there are three islands in the Venetian lagoon you can easily visit. There's daily ferry service to all three on line no. 12, which leaves from Fondamenta Nuova, or on line no. 14, which leaves from Santa Zaccaria.

Murano, less than a mile northeast of Venice, has been a famous glassmaking center since the 13th century. There's a glass museum, the **Museo Vetrario di Murano,** Fondamenta Giustinian (☎ **041-739-586;** open Apr–Oct Mon–Tues and Thurs–Sat 10am–5pm, closes 1 hour earlier the rest of the year; admission 8,000L/$4.50), with a stunning collection of Venetian glass, both antique and contemporary. On the island are shops where you can observe the glassmaking process (and buy the products). You can have lunch at one of the island's restaurants.

Torcello, about 5½ nautical miles northeast, was settled in the 9th century and was at one time the most populous island in the Venetian lagoon. It's now pretty much deserted. The **Cattedrale di Torcello** (☎ **041-730-084;** open Apr–Oct daily 10am–12:30pm and 2:30–6:30pm, closes 1 hour earlier the rest of the year; admission 1,500L/$1), with its Byzantine mosaics, is well worth visiting. It sits in a meadow beside an 11th-century campanile and has, like the rest of the island, a rather lonely, melancholic appeal.

Burano, close to Torcello, was a major European lace-making center in the 16th century, and lace is still made there today. It's sometimes referred to as the "Rainbow Island"—but this has nothing to do with the gay rainbow. Rather, it refers to houses, painted in vivid pinks, blues, yellows, and reds. The island is still inhabited by fishing families, and the trattorie are famous for their seafood.

13

Milan: For the Fashion & Opera Queen

The truth is, **Milan (Milano)** is the least "romantic" of Italian cities. The most "modern" of Italian cities, it's big, busy, and dedicated to hard work and commerce. Attitudinally, there's a world of difference between nose-to-the-grindstone Milan and the more languorous *dolce vita* of Rome and southern Italy. And Milan isn't as completely tourist-dominated as Venice and Florence. It's a fashion-and-design center of international importance and culturally one Italy's most vital cities. Historically too, it's an interesting place. But the remnants of old Milan—basilicas, city gates, palazzi, even a ducal palace—are often wedged in among newer buildings that tend to obscure them. You have to look a little harder and use some extra imagination in order to appreciate what Milan has to offer.

Located in the fertile Po Valley between the Adda and Ticino rivers, Milan is the capital of Lombardy, a northern Italian region dominated by the Italian Alps. It was originally Gallic but was captured by the Romans in 222 B.C. and by the 4th century had become a principle archbishopric of the Western Roman Empire. In the 14th and 15th centuries, under the rule of the Viscontis, it emerged as a powerful duchy and shared control of northern Italy with Venice. Under the patronage of Ludovico Il Moro (1452–1508), great artists like Leonardo da Vinci and Donato Bramante came to work in Milan. Under the Sforzas, Milan became a pawn in French-Hapsburg rivalries, was taken over by the Spanish, and then was ceded to Austria. Still later it became the capital of Napoléon's Cisalpine Republic and the Kingdom of Italy. After Napoléon's defeat, the city reverted back to the Austrians.

It wasn't until 1860 that Lombardy—and Milan, its most important city—became part of a new Italian Republic. The city was heavily damaged by Allied bombs during World War II, and at war's end the Milanese strung up Mussolini and his mistress by their heels and vented their fury on their corpses. About 50 years later, Alessandra Mussolini, Il Duce's niece and a leader of the Italy's "new" Fascist party (Alleanza Nazionale), went on the record as a supporter of equal rights for same-sex couples. *Brava!*

Milan isn't necessarily a city where you'll want to spend a great deal of time. Some people "do" it in a day. If you give yourself a little longer, you may begin to discover aspects of this sophisticated metropolis that you can't discern with a cursory glance.

1 Milan Essentials

ARRIVING & DEPARTING

BY PLANE Milan is Italy's primary airport hub. Most international flights arrive at **Aeroporto della Malpensa,** 31 miles northwest of the city. The **Malpensa Shuttle Bus** (☎ **02-6698-4509**) connects the airport to Stazione Centrale, Milan's main train station; it departs every half an hour 7am to 4pm, hourly 4 to 9pm, and hourly 10:15pm to 7am. The fare for the 50-minute trip is 13,000L ($7). A new rail service, the **Malpensa Express,** is scheduled to open in summer 1999; the trip will take about 35 minutes. Metered **taxis** outside the arrivals hall can also get you into the city; the 45- to 50-minute trip generally costs about 130,000L ($72).

Aeroporto di Linate, about 4½ miles east of the city center, is used for flights within Italy and Europe. **City (ATM) bus** no. 75 runs from the airport to Piazza San Babila at 6, 7, and 7:30am, then every 20 minutes to 7pm and every 30 minutes 7 to 11:30pm; the cost is 1500L (80¢) and the trip time about 30 minutes. There's also a **STAM bus** (☎ **02-6698-4509**) from Stazione Centrale to Linate that runs every 20 to 30 minutes 5:30am to 9pm; the cost is 4,500L ($2.50).

For information about both airports, call ☎ **02-7485-2200** (7am–11pm).

BY TRAIN Milan has the best rail connections in Italy. Trains arrive at **Stazione Centrale,** Piazza Duca d'Aosta (☎ **02-1478-88088**), just northeast of the city center. Inside the station is a National Railways information office (☎ **02-63711;** open daily 7am–11pm). There's almost hourly fast-train service to Florence (trip time: about 2 hours), Venice (2½–3 hours), and Rome (about 4 hours). Trams, buses, and the Metro (subway) link the station to Piazza del Duomo, the heart of the city; the Metro stop is Stazione Centrale (Centrale F.S. on some subway maps).

BY CAR The main east-west autostrada route for Milan is A4. A8 comes in from the northwest, A1 from the southeast, and A7 from the southwest. Note that in the city center there are waiting and parking restrictions that could result in fines and wheelclamps. For street parking, you'll need to buy and display a **Sostomilano** parking permit, available from tobacconists, newsstands, and bars; call ☎ **02-1670-16857** for more information.

VISITOR INFORMATION

The tourist office, **Azienda di Promozione Turistica del Milanese,** Piazza del Duomo at Via Marconi 1 (☎ **02-7252-4300;** Metro: Duomo), is a good source for maps and advice. The office in Stazione Centrale (☎ **02-7252-4360;** Metro: Stazione Centrale), is a bit difficult to locate (it's in the front of the station, to your left as you're leaving the train tracks), but the staff there can give you lots of printed brochures and find you a hotel room. Both offices are open Monday to Friday 8:30am to 7pm and Saturday and Sunday 9am to 1pm and 2 to 5pm.

CITY LAYOUT

Piazza del Duomo, the heart of Milan, sits in the historic inner city (*centro storico*). This roughly circular area is demarcated by the **Cerchia dei Navigli,** a ring road following the outline of the city's medieval walls, which had canals (*navigli*) running alongside them. Beyond that is a second ring road, the **Bastioni** or **Viali,** following the outline of the 16th-century Spanish walls (it's now a tram route). The **Circonvallazione,** the third and outermost ring road, connects to the main arteries coming into the city.

You'll probably spend most or all of your time in the *centro storico.* From Piazza del Duomo it's a 5-minute walk north to La Scala, the city's world-famous opera house, and the beginning of **Via Manzoni,** one of the city's most important streets. It runs northeast to the busy traffic hub of **Piazza Cavour.** From the piazza, **Via Fatebenefratelli** heads west into the lively **Brera** district, a student quarter with lots of bars, clubs, and restaurants. The **Public Gardens (Giardini Pubblici)** lie just beyond Piazza Cavour; at their north end lies **Piazza della Repubblica** and **Via Vittorio Pisani,** which leads north to Stazione Centrale. The historic **Sforza Castle (Castello Sforza)** and its surrounding park are northwest of Piazza del Duomo. **Corso Vittorio Emanuele,** another main street, runs east from Piazza del Duomo to **Piazza San Babila,** the high-fashion district.

GETTING AROUND

BY PUBLIC TRANSPORTATION Milan's network of subways (Metropolitana), buses, trams, and streetcars is run by Azienda Trasporti Municipali (ATM). The cost of above- and underground transportation is the same, with a **single ticket** costing 1,500L (80c); it's valid for 75 minutes on all forms of transport (but can't be used twice in the subway). You can buy tickets at newsstands, bars, tobacconists, and automatic vending machines, but not in buses. Public transportation runs about 6am to midnight.

At newsstands in the subway stations you can buy a **24-hour ticket** for 6,000L ($3) or a **48-hour ticket** for 9,000L ($5). For information on urban transport, call ☎ **02-1670-16857** or the **ATM office** in the Duomo subway station at ☎ **02-4803-2403** (open Mon–Sat 8am–8pm).

If your time in Milan is limited and you're hitting only the main sights, walk it.

BY TAXI Milanese taxis are white and park in ranks throughout the city. There's a 6,000L ($3) charge on entering and additional surcharges at night, on holidays, and for luggage. The actual meter charge changes fairly frequently; rates are posted inside the cab. To call a cab, dial ☎ **6767** or 8585.

BY CAR Driving in Milan isn't fun, and I wouldn't recommend doing so. If you want to rent a car for excursions to outlying areas in Lombardy, **Avis** has an office in Stazione Centrale (☎ **02-669-0280;** open Mon–Fri 7:45am–9pm, Sat 7:45am–1pm), and so does **Hertz** (☎ **02-2669-0061;** open Mon–Fri 8am–1pm and 2–6pm, Sat 8am–2pm). Of course, it's best to arrange for the rental before leaving home.

FACT FACTS: Milan

AIDS Organizations The **Servizio AIDS del Comune di Milane,** Via Fiamma 6 (☎ **02-716-845** or 02-738-2765; Bus: 60, 73), is the AIDS service organization for Milan. The **AIDS counseling switchboard** is open Monday to Friday 11:30am to 1:30pm. HIV tests are available during the same hours. Don't expect English speakers.

American Express The office is at Via Brera 3 (☎ **02-876-674;** Metro: Monte Napoleone; open Mon–Fri 9am–5pm).

Community Centers **Arci-Gay/Centro d'Iniziativa Gay,** Via Torricelli 19 (☎ **02-8940-1749;** Metro: Romolo; open Mon–Fri 8:30–11pm, Sun 3–11pm), provides general info; has gay magazines, a library, and archives; and arranges various gay events. If you're going to be in Italy for some time, you might want to buy an Arci-Gay membership card, available here. It's called **Arci Gay Uno,** it costs 20,000L ($11), is good for a year, and provides admittance to many bars, clubs, and discos throughout Italy.

Country & City Codes

The **country code** for Italy is **39.** The **city code** for Milan is **02.** You must now use both digits whenever you call Milan—whether you're outside Italy, inside Italy but not within Milan, or even within Milan.

Consulates The **U.S. Consulate** is at Via Principe Amedeo 2–10 (☎ **02-290-351;** Metro: Turati; open Mon–Fri 9am–noon and 2–4pm). The **Canadian Consulate** is at Via Vitto Pisani 19 (☎ **02-67581;** Metro: Repubblica; open Mon–Fri 9am–5pm). The **U.K. Consulate** is at Via San Paolo 7 (☎ **02-723-001;** Metro: Duomo; open Mon–Fri 9:15am–12:15pm and 2:30–4:30pm). The **Australian Consulate** is at Via Borgogna 2 (☎ **02-777-041;** Metro: San Babila; open Mon–Thurs 9am–noon and 2–4pm). Citizens of New Zealand and Ireland should contact their consulates in Rome.

Currency Exchange There are two currency exchange services in the Departure Hall of Stazione Centrale: **Exact** (open daily 7am–8pm) and **Centro Servizi Pantheon** (open daily 7am–11pm). American Express and many banks also have currency exchanges.

Cybercafe You can check your e-mail or send messages at **Hard Disk Cafe,** Corso Sempione 44 (☎ **02-3310-3666;** e-mail info@hdc.it; www.hdc.it/foto. htm; open Mon–Sat 8pm–2am, Sun 5pm–midnight).

Doctors & Hospitals For the city emergency doctor service, call ☎ **34567.** **Ospedale (Hospital) Maggiore Policlinico,** Via Francesco Sforza 35 (☎ **02-55-031;** Metro: Missori or Crocetta), has English-speaking doctors.

Emergencies For **police,** call ☎ **113.** For an **ambulance,** call ☎ **118.** For the **fire brigade,** call ☎ **115.** For the **city emergency doctor service,** call ☎ **34567.** For **police headquarters,** foreigners department, call ☎ **02-6226-3400.**

Gay & Lesbian Organizations The lesbian separatist group **CDM** meets Sundays 3 to 8pm at Via Cicco Simonette 15 (☎ **02-805-1808;** Metro: S. Agostino). A gay Christian group, **Gruppo del Guado** (☎ **02-284-0369**) meets Wednesdays 9 to 11pm; call for information. The **Leather Club Milano** (☎ **02-837-5427**) publishes information on the leather scene and meets on the first Saturday of the month; call for information. Big bears and their fans can call **Magnum Club** (☎ **0360-536-273**), for information on activities in Milan. Don't assume there'll be English speakers at any of these organizations.

Gay Media ***Orabuca*** is a free Milan monthly with lots of gay listings. ***Guide*** is a gay-and-lesbian monthly that has listings for all of Italy. And ***Babilonia,*** the national gay magazine, is available at many newsstands.

Hot Lines The **Linea Lesbica Amica** at ☎ **02-2952-1109** (open Thurs 7–9pm), is a lesbian switchboard with information on women's events in Milan. The **Linea Amica Trans** at ☎ **02-8940-1749** (Wed 8–10pm) is a volunteer counseling line for transsexuals and transvestites. And **Telefono Amico Gay** at ☎ **02-8940-1749** (Mon–Tues and Thurs–Fri 8pm–midnight) is a volunteer-staffed phone line offering advice and counseling for gay men. Again, don't assume you'll hook up with an English-speaking staff person.

Telephone See "Fast Facts: Rome" in chapter 10.

2 Pillow Talk

Oddly enough, the hotels in this design-conscious, business-oriented city are often decor-challenged. Don't expect much in the way of glamour unless you're booking into a five-star luxury place. When breakfast (*colazione*) is included, it's usually continental: coffee, a *cornetto* (croissant), rolls, butter, and jam. The luxury hotels generally don't include breakfast in their room rates.

The only gay-friendly hotel worth considering is the Durante (see below). You may find ads for others in the gay magazines and other gay guides, but the two I checked out turned out to be used as whorehouses (no, I didn't stay). You shouldn't encounter any difficulties at any "straight" hotel.

The **Information and Accommodation (I.A.T.) offices** in Piazza del Duomo and Stazione Centrale can help you find a hotel room. Both offices are open Monday to Friday 8:30am to 7pm and Saturday and Sunday 9am to 1pm and 2 to 5pm; this is a walk-in service only. You can also contact **Milano Hotels Central Booking** at ☎ **02-805-4242** (daily 9am 6pm).

✪ **Antica Locanda Solferino.** Via Castelfidardo 2, 20121 Milano. ☎ **02-657-0129.** Fax 02-657-1361. 11 units. TV TEL. 200,000L ($111) double. Rates include breakfast. AE, DC, MC, V. Parking 25,000–30,000L ($14–$17) nearby. Metro: Moscova or Repubblica.

In the arty Brera district north of the Duomo, this small *locanda* (inn) opened in 1976. It's charming without being cute, centrally located, and inexpensive: Ergo, it's very popular and you need to book in advance. The smallish guest rooms, simply decorated with printed fabrics and turn-of-the-century furnishings, are graced with original Daumier engravings. The baths are modern. It's gay-friendly without advertising the fact.

Excelsior Hotel Gallia. Piazza Duca d'Aosta 9, 20124 Milano. ☎ **800/225-5843** in the U.S. or 02-6785. Fax 02-6671-3239. 250 units. AC MINIBAR TV TEL. 460,000–510,000L ($256–$283) double; from 700,000L ($389) suite. AE, DC, MC, V. Parking 30,000–50,000L ($17–$28). Metro: Stazione Centrale.

Built in 1932 across from the train station, this monumental Liberty-style (art nouveau) building was extensively renovated in 1994. It's tasteful and comfortable but not overly luxurious, boasting grand-sized public rooms, stained-glass windows, marble floors, and a smartly decorated bar. Some guest rooms have modern furnishings while others have kept their old-fashioned ambience. The big baths come with marble tubs and surrounds. There's a sauna and fitness room on the premises, and the rates are cheaper on weekends when the businessfolk are home with the family.

✪ **Four Seasons Hotel Milano.** Via Gesù 8, 20121 Milano. ☎ **800/332-3442** in the U.S. or 02-77088. Fax 02-7708-5000. 98 units. A/C MINIBAR TV TEL. 660,000–905,000L ($367–$503) double; from 995,000L ($553) suite. AE, DC, MC, V. Metro: San Babila or Montenapoleone.

For its fabulous but understated luxury and truly snap-to-it staff, the Four Seasons rates more than just a star—how about a tiara? If you want a five-star deluxe hotel in the heart of the fashion district, close to where Donatella Versace and all the big-name designers live, this is the one I'd recommend above all others—because there are no others. A hotel since 1993, the Four Seasons occupies a cloistered convent from the early 15th century. All that's left from that period is a fragment of fresco and the enormous columns in the lobby. The former sacristy is now the hotel bar. The guest rooms? Let's just say *bellissimi.* Most of them face the tranquil inner *cortile* (courtyard), and each has a to-die-for marble bath with separate bath and glass shower and a toilet in its own marble sanctuary. No detail has been overlooked. Il Teatro, their restaurant, rates equally high (see "Whet Your Appetite" below).

Milan Accommodations & Dining

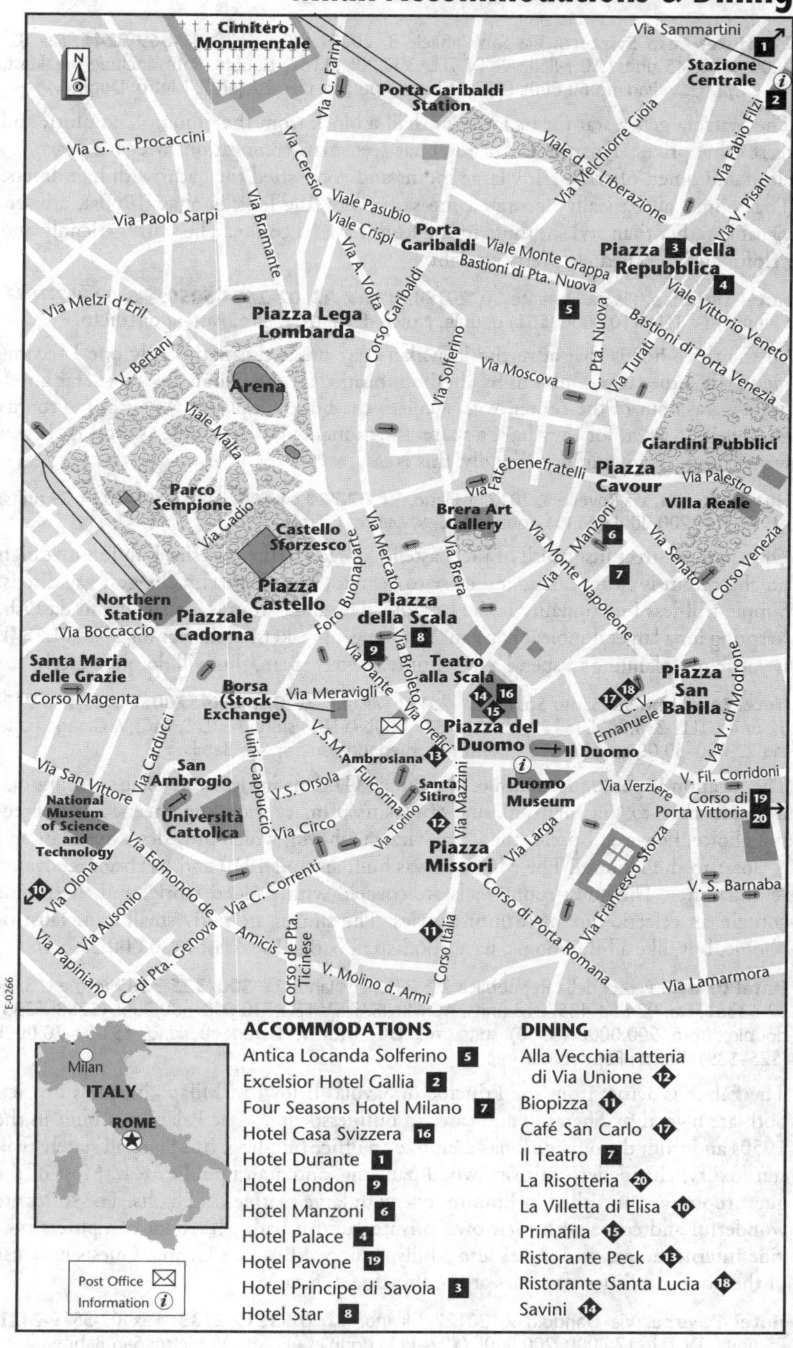

Cimitero Monumentale
Via Sammartini
Stazione Centrale
Porta Garibaldi Station
Via C. Farini
Via G. C. Procaccini
Via Ceresio
Viale d. Liberazione
Via Melchiorre Gioia
Via Fabio Filzi
Via V. Pisani
Via Paolo Sarpi
Via Bramante
Viale Pasubio
Viale Crispi
Porta Garibaldi
Viale Monte Grappa
Bastioni di Pta. Nuova
Piazza della Repubblica
Via A. Volta
Viale Vittorio Veneto
Via Melzi d'Eril
Piazza Lega Lombarda
Corso Garibaldi
Bastioni di Porta Venezia
C. Pta. Nuova
Via Turati
Via Solferino
V. Bertani
Arena
Via Moscova
Viale Malta
Giardini Pubblici
Via Fatebenefratelli
Piazza Cavour
Via Palestro
Villa Reale
Parco Sempione
Via Cadio
Brera Art Gallery
Via Manzoni
Castello Sforzesco
Via Mercato
Via Brera
Via Monte Napoleone
Via Senato
Corso Venezia
Foro Buonaparte
Northern Station
Piazza Castello
Piazza della Scala
Via Boccaccio
Piazzale Cadorna
Via Dante
Via Broletto
Santa Maria delle Grazie
Teatro alla Scala
Piazza San Babila
Corso Magenta
Borsa (Stock Exchange)
Via Meravigli
Via Orefici
C. V. Emanuele
Via V. di Modrone
Piazza del Duomo
Il Duomo
Via Carducci
V.S.M. Fulcorina
Ambrosiana
Via San Vittore
San Ambrogio
luini Cappuccio
V.S. Orsola
Santa Sitiro
Duomo Museum
Via Verziere
V. Fil. Corridoni
Corso di Porta Vittoria
National Museum of Science and Technology
Università Cattolica
Via Circo
Via Torino
Via Mazzini
Via Larga
Via Edmondo de Amicis
Piazza Missori
Via Francesco Sforza
Via Olona
Via C. Correnti
Corso di Porta Romana
V. S. Barnaba
Via Ausonio
Via Papiniano
C. di Pta. Genova
Corso de Pta. Ticinese
V. Molino d. Armi
Corso Italia
Via Lamarmora
E-0266
Milan
ITALY
ROME
Post Office
Information
ACCOMMODATIONS
Antica Locanda Solferino 5
Excelsior Hotel Gallia 2
Four Seasons Hotel Milano 7
Hotel Casa Svizzera 16
Hotel Durante 1
Hotel London 9
Hotel Manzoni 6
Hotel Palace 4
Hotel Pavone 19
Hotel Principe di Savoia 3
Hotel Star 8
DINING
Alla Vecchia Latteria di Via Unione 12
Biopizza 11
Café San Carlo 17
Il Teatro 7
La Risotteria 20
La Villetta di Elisa 10
Primafila 15
Ristorante Peck 13
Ristorante Santa Lucia 18
Savini 14

✪ **Hotel Casa Svizzera.** Via San Raffaele 3, 20121 Milano. ☎ **02-869-2246.** Fax 02-7200-4690. 45 units. AC MINIBAR TV TEL. 300,00L ($167) double. Rates include breakfast. AE, DC, MC, V. Parking 60,000L ($33). Closed Aug and Dec 20–Jan 7. Metro: Duomo.

The Svizzera gets a star for its location (half a block from the Duomo), comfort, and reasonable prices. This three-star hotel has seen many renovations over the years. It's clean and quiet, offering fairly large rooms and good-sized tile baths with hair dryers. The rooms, all basically decorated the same way (the look is quasi-1960s), are serviceable rather than stylish; those in the front have balconies. The staff is friendly and helpful and the clientele pretty straight.

Hotel Durante. Piazza Durante 30, 20130 Milano. ☎ **02-2614-5050.** Fax 02-282-7673. 12 units. TV TEL. 110,000L ($61) double. No credit cards. Metro: Pasteur or Loreto.

Of the three hotels that advertise in Milan's gay press, this is the only one I recommend (the other two double as by-the-hour brothels). The Durante is a one-star hotel, quite a ways out of the center, with a cut-to-the-bone simplicity. As far as the rooms go, this is an asset, for they have a spare, functional look that's rather soothing. If you want cheap, clean, and gay-friendly, this is it.

Hotel London. Via Rovello 3, 20121 Milano. ☎ **02-7202-0166.** Fax 02-805-7037. 29 units. AC TV TEL. 200,000L ($111) double. MC, V. Metro: Cairoli.

On a narrow street just south of the Castello Sforzesco, the two-star London isn't high on charm but is clean, quiet, and close to Segreto, one of the city's biggest gay discos. Simple frill-less functionality is the keynote. The single rooms are small and darkish, so spring for a larger double if you can. You can get breakfast at the bar for 12,000L ($7). If you're not planning to spend a lot of time in your room, this will do quite nicely.

Hotel Manzoni. Via Santo Spirito 20, 20121 Milano. ☎ **02-7600-5700.** Fax 02-748-212. 52 units. TEL. 235,000L ($131) double; 325,000L ($181) suite. AE, DC, MC, V. Garage parking 22,000–50,000L ($12–$28). Metro: Montenapoleone or San Babila.

The location is good: just south of the Public Gardens in the heart of the fashion district and close to Via Manzoni, one of Milan's primary shopping streets. For a three-star choice, however, I prefer the Casa Svizzera (above), which provides a breakfast and is closer to the Duomo. The Manzoni was built around 1910 and has been renovated several times. The guest-room walls are covered with padded fabric, and the rooms contain an eclectic mix of furniture styles. The singles are fairly small and claustrophobic, but, like all the rooms, have good-sized baths. Breakfast is 20,000L ($12).

Hotel Palace. Piazza della Repubblica 20, 20124 Milano. ☎ **800/325-3589** in the U.S. or 02-63361. Fax 02-654-485. 216 units. AC MINIBAR TV TEL. 510,000–600,000L ($283–$333) double; from 900,000L ($500) suite. AE, DC, MC, V. Garage parking 45,000–70,000L ($25–$39). Metro: Repubblica.

The Palace is across from the Principe di Savoia (below) in Milan's business district; both are owned by Sheraton and cater to businesspeople. The Palace was built in the 1950s and from the outside looks a bit like an office building. Inside it's all stately five-star luxury: chandeliers, mirrors, wood paneling, and grand public areas. Most of the guest rooms are furnished in Empire style with large marble-clad baths. The suites are wonderful and come with their own private Turkish baths. In-room computers provide Internet access, and there's also a fully equipped Business Center. Guests have use of the pool and fitness facilities at the Principe di Savoia.

Hotel Pavone. Via Dandolo 2, 20122 Milano. ☎ **02-5519-2133.** Fax 02-5519-2421. 25 units. TV TEL. 175,000–200,000L ($97–111) double. AE, MC, V. Metro: San Babila.

This two-star hotel (without elevator) is on a peaceful street a few minutes' walk southeast of San Babila, the fashion district, and just west of the Porta Vittoria.

Everything in the *centro storico* is within walking distance. It's a good, clean, functional hotel, nothing fancy or glamorous, but a cut above many hotels in the same category. The rooms are relatively large and airy, with tile floors, colorful bedspreads, and modern furniture (the overhead lights have to go, however). The baths are small.

Hotel Principe di Savoia. Piazza della Repubblica 17, 20124 Milano. ☎ **800/325-3589** in the U.S. or 02-62301. Fax 02-659-5838. 299 units. AC MINIBAR TV TEL. 590,000–760,000L (328–$422) double; from 1,100,000L ($611) suite. AE, DC, MC, V. Parking from 60,000L ($33). Metro: Repubblica.

Until the Four Seasons opened (above), this was considered by many to be Milan's premiere luxury hotel. It remains right up at the top of the five-star firmament, but at these prices you'd think they'd at least throw in free breakfast. Dominating Piazza della Repubblica, it was built in 1927 and completely restored in 1991. A massive stained-glass ceiling dominates the grandiose public rooms with their inlaid multicolored marble floors and wood paneling. You'll have no complaints about the spacious guest rooms, decorated in a 19th-century Lombard style with marble-clad baths and double sinks; some look out on the Alps. On the new 10th floor are a pool, a state-of-the-art health club, and a mind-boggling Presidential Suite, where Michael Jackson stayed but was afraid to leave, lest his fans tear him to bits.

✪ **Hotel Star.** Via dei Bossi 5, 20121 Milano. ☎ **02-801-501.** Fax 02-861-787. 30 units. AC MINIBAR TV TEL. 260,000L ($144) double. Rates include breakfast. AE, MC, V. Closed Aug and Christmas. Metro: Cordusio.

This friendly, comfortable, well-run hotel is 2 blocks from La Scala. The lobby, with its wood and marble-clad walls and Oriental rugs, has a pleasant seating area with tufted leather chairs and sofa. The singles here are larger than in most hotels. All rooms have light-colored walls, parquet floors with bedside rugs, and in-room safes. The good-sized baths (some tiled, others marble) are equipped with hair dryers. There's a fresh, clean feeling throughout.

3 Whet Your Appetite

Milanese *cucina* (cooking) has been influenced by the French and Austrians and the butter-based (rather than olive oil–based) cooking of northern Italy. Lombardy is Italy's richest agricultural region, famed for its wheat, rice, and meat and dairy products. *Spaghetti milanese,* one local dish, has a thick tomato-and-meat sauce. *Osso buco milanese,* another favorite, is braised veal shanks in tomato sauce. *Risotto milanese* is a creamy rice dish flavored with saffron.

At most Italian restaurants you'll be charged a *coperto* (cover) for bread. Service is generally included in the bill. Prices given throughout this chapter for "main courses" means either pizza, pasta (usually considered a *primo,* or first course), or a *secondo* (second) course, typically meat or fish. The highest prices will nearly always be for fish. Please bear in mind that the quoted prices will not get you an entire meal, only one course. Italian meals are typically three or four courses—*antipasto, primo, secondo,* followed by *dolce* (sweet) or *frutta* (fruit). House or table wines are generally available.

As with hotels, there are no exclusively gay restaurants in Milan, but La Risotteria and La Villetta di Elisa (both below) are very gay-friendly.

Note: For the locations of the restaurants below, see the "Milan Accommodations & Dining" map on p. 485.

Alla Vecchia Latteria di Via Unione. Via dell'Unione 6. ☎ **02-874-401.** Main courses 10,000–18,000L ($6–$10). No credit cards. Mon–Sat 11:30am–3:30pm. Metro: Missori. VEGETARIAN.

Here's your chance to experience some authentic, nontouristy atmosphere at lunch. This friendly family-run restaurant is a six-table hole-in-the-wall just off busy Via Torino, south of Piazza del Duomo. The vegetarian menu is simple but imaginative. In addition to fresh soups and salads, you'll find a yummy cannelloni made with zucchini, cheese, and pine nuts; rice with radicchio; tofu scallopini; and pasta with beans. On my last visit mamma was doing the cooking and papa was the waiter.

Biopizza. Corso Italia 16. ☎ **02-805-3819.** Pizzas 8,000–15,000L ($4–$8). Mon–Sat 11am–3:30pm and 6:30pm–12:30am. AE, MC, V. Metro: Missori. PIZZA.

You may not think of pizzas as "health food," and certainly the gooey versions served in America aren't. At Biopizza, however, it's a different story. The ingredients are organic, the pastas are made with filtered water, the yeast is natural, even the olive oil is extra virgin (just like me). The restaurant itself is cool, hip, and modern, with copper columns, stone walls, and low lighting. No wonder gays like it, particularly at lunchtime, when healthy business "suits" drop in for a pie. I won't give you a laundry list of the pizza possibilities—suffice it to say that all the bases are covered.

Café San Carlo. Vorso Vittorio Emanuele II. ☎ **02-7602-3116.** Main courses 15,000–20,000L ($8–$11). MC, V. Mon–Sat 7am–8pm. Metro: San Babila. MILANESE.

This is a good place for breakfast, a simple lunch, or an afternoon coffee break. There are two floors for indoor seating, but in warm weather it's more fun to sit outside and people-watch. Many of the office workers in the surrounding area come here, so at peak lunchtime hours service can be hard and fast. The menu is fairly minimal: a pasta dish, a meat dish, salads, and sandwiches. It's tasty, no-nonsense food.

✪ **Il Teatro.** In the Four Seasons Hotel Milano, Via Gesù 8. ☎ **02-77088.** Reservations essential. Main courses 26,000–42,000L ($14–23); gourmet menu 85,000L ($47). AE, DC, MC, V. Mon–Sat 7:30pm–midnight. Metro: San Babila or Montenapoleone. MEDITERRANEAN.

A dinner at Il Teatro is a true culinary event, something you'll tell all your friends about. To begin with, the restaurant itself, beneath the ancient convent courtyard of the Four Seasons Hotel, is a spacious example of contemporary Italian design, with beautiful woods, leather walls, and glass lighting fixtures from Murano. You'll feel out of place if you're not reasonably well dressed. But the staff, though extraordinary attentive, isn't at all haughty. Sergio Mei, the chef, takes old regional dishes and lightens them, cooking just enough to bring out the flavors. The results are superb, so superb that I recommend eating your way through the six-course gourmet menu. It might go something like this: ricotta cheese with black truffles, fresh bean salad with crayfish, asparagus soup with bruschetta, sea-bass scallops, fillet of beef with peppers, and caramel custard with strawberries and vanilla.

✪ **La Risotteria.** Via Dandolo 2. ☎ **02-5518-1694.** Main courses 10,000–23,000L ($6–$13). AE, DC, MC, V. Mon–Fri noon–11pm, Sat 8–11pm. Tram: 12 or 23. Bus: 37 or 43. MILANESE/RICE.

This place gets a star for wonderful food, stylish atmosphere, and being gay-friendly to boot. As you might've guessed from its name, La Risotteria specializes in rice dishes. Rice is a major crop in Lombardy, and here it's cooked in every variation you can imagine—including traditional *risotto alla milanese* with saffron. You can also have it with lemon, pepper, asparagus, scampi, or even strawberries. You won't find glorified rice but will find rice glorified in the large paintings on the walls. The interior is green with pink tablecloths and a terrazzo floor. The diners constitute a very mixed crowd, but if you want to keep your lire pink, you can do it here and be assured of a good meal.

La Villetta di Elisa. Viale E. Bezzi 86, on the corner with Piazza Tripoli. ☎ **02-435-293.** Main courses 9,000–30,000L ($5–$17). AE, MC, V. Wed–Sun 7pm–3am. Metro: De Angeli. Bus: 1, 58, 67, or 90. ITALIAN.

This restaurant is a bit out of the way but definitely is gay/lesbian friendly, and the cooking is dependable. The well-rounded Italian menu lists a bit of everything: pizzas, spaghetti with clams, tagliolini with salmon, rice with seafood or strawberries, beef, chicken, and fish. One unusual dish (for Milan) is Hungarian goulash with polenta. You can also order vegetarian—perhaps the grilled vegetable plate or the omelet with cheese or spinach. The decor is informally rustic, and there's a patio for summer dining.

Primafila. Via Ugo Foscolo 1. ☎ **02-862-020.** Reservations recommended. Main courses 16,000–35,000L ($9–$19). AE, DC, MC, V. Thurs–Tues noon–3pm and 5pm–1am. Metro: Duomo. ITALIAN.

Milan may be sophisticated, but it's still difficult to find a good meal after 11pm. So here's a place you might want to consider after an evening at La Scala (when it reopens) or a concert; it's about midway between the opera house and the Duomo. Large and somewhat commercialized, Primafila feels more impersonal than many restaurants. But the sea of pink tablecloths, the wall covered with autographed photos of visiting opera stars and celebs, and the late-night crowds make for a lively night-on-the-town ambience. The cooking is good if not inspired. Pastas include a hot and simple spaghetti rosa with olive oil, garlic, and spicy peppers and a Milanese version of carbonara made with pancetta, onions, and saffron. You can get *scaloppa* (veal) *alla milanese* as well as various beef and fish dishes and grilled mozzarella.

✪ **Ristorante Peck.** Victor Hugo 4. ☎ **02-876-774.** Reservations essential for restaurant. Main courses 20,000–42,000L ($11–$23); fixed-price menu 70,000–90,0000L ($39–$50). AE, DC, MC, V. Bar and cafeteria Mon–Sat 7:30am–9pm; restaurant 12:15–2:30pm and 7:15–10:30pm. Closed part of Jan and July 1–21. Metro: Duomo. MILANESE/ITALIAN.

You want to know about Peck because, first of all, you can get the best cappuccino in Milan at the stand-up bar. The self-service (but decidedly upscale) cafeteria off to one side is an excellent place for lunch, and downstairs is one of the best restaurants in Milan. All these places, along with a fabuloso gourmet food store across the street, are under the aegis of Peck, Milan's most famous purveyor of gourmet delicatessen foods. The restaurant is light, spare, and elegant, the food impeccable in both preparation and presentation. Specialties are classic Milanese versions of risotto, minestrone, and osso buco, as well as wonderful pasta and fish dishes from other areas in Lombardy and throughout Italy. There are two tasting menus—one offering more traditional fare, the other a more adventurous assortment of delights. French and Italian vintages make up the bulk of the impressive wine list.

Ristorante Santa Lucia. Via San Pietro all'Orto 3. ☎ **02-7602-3155.** Reservations recommended. Main courses 13,000–40,000L ($7–$22). DC, MC, V. Tues–Sun noon–2:30pm and 7:30pm–2:30am. Closed Aug. Metro: San Babila. MEDITERRANEAN/SEAFOOD.

Milan's Best Cappuccino

At Ristorante Peck, you'll find the best cappuccino in the city. Not only is it delicious, it's sometimes artistic. When I was last there, the barrista somehow managed to create a beautiful leaf pattern in the foam on top. For a quick cup you can head to the stand-up bar in front, but you can get the same coffee in the restaurant. At the bar (good for breakfast or a snack) they also sell *cornetti* (croissants) and pastries.

Santa Lucia is known for its fish and seafood. It boasts wooden wainscoting, cream-colored walls, Tuscan red ceilings, and celebrity photos plastered all over. What do all those celebs eat? Savory fish soup, fried baby squid, sole, grilled scampi, and fried calamari. But you can also get good calzones and pizzas here.

Savini. In the Galleria Vittorio Emanuele, Piazza del Duomo. ☎ **02-7200-3433.** Reservations required. Main courses 18,000–40,000L ($10–$22); fixed-price menu 70,000L ($39) at lunch, 80,000L ($44) at dinner. AE, DC, MC, V. Mon–Fri noon–2:30pm and 7:30–10:30pm, Sat 7:30–10:30pm. Closed Dec 24–Jan 2 and Aug 10–25. Metro: Duomo. LOMBARD/INTERNATIONAL.

Savini's has been around since 1867. It has a reputation to uphold, and it upholds it very well indeed. This is where you go if you want to dress up and eat well in lovely old-fashioned surroundings or out on the terrace. Everyone from Puccini to Pavarotti has dined here. Two Lombardy specialties are worth considering: *costoletta alla milanese* (veal coated with egg batter and bread crumbs and fried) and *risotto alla milanese* (rice cooked in broth and flavored with saffron). Or, if it's on the menu, try the ravioli stuffed with sea bass. Another delectable dish is pan-fried veal kidneys with sweet garlic. Several fishes are available every day. Sometimes even baked pigeon shows up.

4 Exploring Milan

You can reach most if not all of Milan's main sights on foot, especially if you're staying around the Duomo area. The city **tourist office,** Via Marconi 1, at the corner of Piazza del Duomo (☎ **02-7252-4300;** Metro: Duomo), offers a 3-hour English-language bus tour leaving Tuesday to Sunday at 9:30am from their office; the cost is 50,000L ($28), and you can buy tickets at the office. Contract them for information on walking tours as well.

Ambrosiana (☎ **02-475-883**) offers a 4-hour English-language bus tour costing 60,000L ($33) and leaving from Piazza della Repubblica (at the corner of Via Turato) Friday to Sunday at 8:30am; you can buy tickets on the bus. The **Ciao Milano Tourist Tram** (☎ **02-805-5323**) departs from Piazza Castello and makes a 1¾-hour circuit; tickets are on sale in the tram, and headphones provide English commentary.

THE HITS YOU SHOULDN'T MISS

✪ **Duomo and Duomo Museum (Museo del Duomo).** Piazza del Duomo. Duomo, admission free; admission to roof 6,000L ($3) by stairs, 8,000L ($4) by elevator; global ticket for roof and Duomo Museum 12,000L ($7). Duomo Museum alone 10,000L ($6). Duomo daily 9am–5:30pm. Duomo Museum Tues–Sun 9:30am–12:30pm and 3–6pm. Metro: Duomo.

One thing is certain: You can't miss the Duomo. The sheer size of Milan's great cathedral, one of the largest in Europe, is mind-boggling. The facade is busy, busy, busy: Built of Candoglia marble, it's the apotheosis of the International Gothic style. Every inch is decorated with sculpted ornamentation, including 3,400 statues. Recently cleaned, it now gleams like an ornate wedding cake covered with sugary white frosting. Work on this delicate behemoth began in 1386 and wasn't truly completed until nearly 600 years later. In 1966, the last bronze portal on the main facade was installed. The cathedral is unique in that it combines Lombard and northern European characteristics, for in the early stages of construction, architects from France and Germany worked alongside their Lombardian counterparts.

It's an experience just walking through the vast five-naved interior, but there's not much art to linger over. Hidden at the top of the apse's vaulted roof is a relic known as the Sacred Nail of the Cross. On the second Sunday in September, the archbishop is wafted aloft in a strange cloud-shaped lift and takes it out for 2 days of public display.

Pay the extra dollar and take the elevator up to the roof for great views of the city and the Alps. Then, if you want to learn more about the cathedral, visit the **Duomo Museum (Museo del Duomo),** in the Palazzo Reale at Piazza del Duomo 14 (☎ **02-860-358**). Here you'll also find the **Civic Museum of Contemporary Art (Museo Civico d'Arte Contemporaneo).**

✪ **Chiesa di Santa Maria delle Grazie (*The Last Supper*).** In the Chiesa di Santa Maria delle Grazie, Piazza Santa Maria della Grazie 2. ☎ **02-498-7588.** Admission 12,000L ($7). Tues–Sun 8am–1:45pm. Metro: Cadorna or Conciliazione.

You'd never forgive yourself if you came to Milan and didn't see its most famous attraction, would you? But just how much of it you can actually see is another matter. As everyone knows, Leonardo da Vinci (1452–1519) was one of the world's greatest artists. And he was gay, despite what legions of straight art historians will tell you. Commissioned by Ludovico the Moor, he painted ***The Last Supper (Cenacolo Vinziano)*** on a wall of the refectory next door to the 15th-century Gothic church of Santa Maria della Grazie, completing the 28- by 15-foot fresco in 1497. Almost immediately it began to disintegrate. It has been completely repainted twice, in the 1700s and the 1800s, and it was—can you believe it?—exposed to the elements for 3 years during World War II when a bomb demolished the roof (a new roof was finally built at the end of the war). And in a controversial effort, the fresco was recently "restored" yet again. What you see today is basically Leonardo's faint "outline" of the painting. That it has (or had) a powerful grandeur is indisputable; so is the fact that it's vanishing. Only 25 people are allowed in at one time, and you must first pass through *Star Trek*–like filtration chambers supposedly to remove dust and pollutants that could further damage the work. Ten minutes is what you're given, so make the most of it.

✪ **Ambrosiana Art Gallery and Library (Biblioteca-Pinacoteca Ambrosiana).** Piazza Pio XI 2. ☎ **02-806-921.** Admission 12,000L ($7). Tues–Sun 10am–5:30pm. Metro: Duomo or Cordusio.

Near the Duomo, the palazzo housing the Ambrosiana Art Gallery and Library reopened in 1997 after years of restoration. The library (*biblioteca*), commissioned by Cardinal Federico Borromeo in 1607, was Europe's first "public library." Bibliophiles will cream over its treasures: the Virgil manuscript with miniatures by Simone Martini that once belonged to Petrarch, a 1353 copy of Dante's *Divine Comedy*, and the *Atlantic Codex*, a collection of notebooks, sketches, and drawings by Leonardo da Vinci. Works exhibited in the art gallery (*pinacoteca*) include the *Portrait of a Musician* attributed to Leonardo, Raphael's cartoon for the *School of Athens* in the Vatican, and Caravaggio's famous *Basket of Fruit.*

Museo Poldi-Pezzoli. Via Manzoni 12. ☎ **02-794-889.** Admission 10,000L ($6). Tues–Fri 9:30am–12:30pm and 2:30–6pm, Sat 9:30am–12:30pm and 2:30–7:30pm, Sun 9:30am–12:30pm and 2:30–6pm (closed Sun afternoon Apr–Sept). Metro: Duomo or Montenapoleone.

This fabulous museum is done in great taste and is rich with antique furnishings, tapestries, frescoes, and Lombard wood carvings. It also displays a remarkable collection of paintings by many of the old masters of northern and central Italy, like Andrea Mantegna's *Madonna and Child,* Giovanni Bellini's *Cristo Morto,* and Filippo Lippi's *Madonna, Angels, and Saints.* One portrait that enjoys the same fame in Milan that the *Mona Lisa* does worldwide is Antonio Pollaiolo's *Portrait of a Lady,* a work of haunting beauty. One room is devoted to Flemish artists, and there's a collection of ceramics and also one of clocks and watches. The museum grew out of a private collection donated to the city in 1881.

Sforza Castle (Castello Sforzesco). Piazza Castello. ☎ **02-6208-3940.** Admission free. Tues–Sun 9:30am–5:30pm. Metro: Cairoli.

For centuries, until the French kicked them out, the Sforza family was the most powerful dynasty in Milan. They were, in fact, the dukes of Milan, and this was their imposing palace. Construction of the castle—initially a military fortress—began in 1450. It has a square plan with massive corner towers and three internal courtyards: The first was used as a parade grounds, the second is in Renaissance style, and the third, the ducal court, was the official residence of the dukes. After the family demise, the castle was turned into a barracks. Restored early in the 20th century, it now houses the eminently browsable **City Art Museum (Civici Musei d'Arte),** with several good collections: Lombard painting, sculpture from the Middle Ages to the 1700s (including Michelangelo's *Pietà Rondanini*), decorative arts, furniture, tapestries, and an important Egyptian art section. The Sala delle Asse (not what you think—it means the Room of the Boards), with its ceiling frescoes of intertwined oak leaves, was decorated by none other than Leonardo (an interior decorator as well as an artist and a scientist).

Brera Art Gallery (Pinacoteca di Brera). Via Brera 28. ☎ **02-722-631.** Admission 8,000L ($4). Tues–Sat 9am–5pm, Sun 9am–12:30pm. Metro: Cairoli, Lanza, or Montenapoleone.

Every guidebook will tell you that the Brera is one of Italy's greatest art galleries, but I've always found it a bit of a bore. In the courtyard, as you enter, you'll see Canova's nude statue of Napoléon posing like a pompous Roman emperor: Its colossal proportions (in all respects) would indicate that the runty Napoléon (or Canova) was a real size queen. Of course, there are some truly great Italian paintings on display: Bellini's *Madonna and Child,* Mantegna's *Dead Christ,* and Bronzino's *Andrea Doria.* The *Saint Sebastian,* painted by someone in the "school of Carvaggio," is a gay pinup with arrows. There are endless numbers of gloomy religious paintings. More interesting (at least to me) are the Modigliani portraits, the Braque still life, and the works of the Italian Modernists.

Galleria Vittorio Emmanuele II. Piazza del Duomo. Metro: Duomo.

I'm putting this in just in case you don't have much time and want to stay right in the center of town. The Galleria is across from the Duomo. Completed in 1877, it's perhaps the largest and most impressive shopping arcade in Italy, with high vaulted glass ceilings. Some of its old glamour has gone now that a McDonald's has moved in (across from a new Prada—only in Italy), and scads of desperate-looking people from Southeast Asia and Africa hawk designer rip-offs (scarves and purses) and cheap toys. But the Galleria is still filled with cafes, restaurants, boutiques, and bookstores, and it pulses with life.

National Museum of Science and Technology (Museo Nazionale della Scienza e Tecnica). Via San Vittore 21. ☎ **02-4801-0040.** 10,000L ($6). Tues–Fri 9:30am–4:50pm, Sat–Sun 9:30am–6:20pm. Metro: San Ambrogio.

Why, you might ask, would I list the Museum of Science and Technology as a top sight in a gay guidebook? It's quite simple: The museum has a Leonardo Gallery. Leonardo was gay. And it's about time we all claimed this universal genius as one of ours. You've may have seen his notebooks in the Ambrosiana Library and may have seen his *Last Supper.* Here, in the Leonardo Gallery, you can see models of the various machines designed by this great artist/scientist, as well as the original drawings.

La Scala Opera House Museum (Museo Teatrale alla Scala). In the Teatro alla Scala, Piazza della Scala. ☎ **02-805-3418.** Admission 6,000L ($3). Nov–Apr Mon–Sat 9am–12:30pm and 2–5:30pm (also Sun May–Oct). Metro: Duomo.

This isn't for everyone—but it's a must for opera queens and music lovers. The museum covers the history of Italy's most important opera house, with costume and set displays, two rooms devoted to Verdi, and all sorts of miscellaneous memorabilia (Rossini's

Milan Attractions

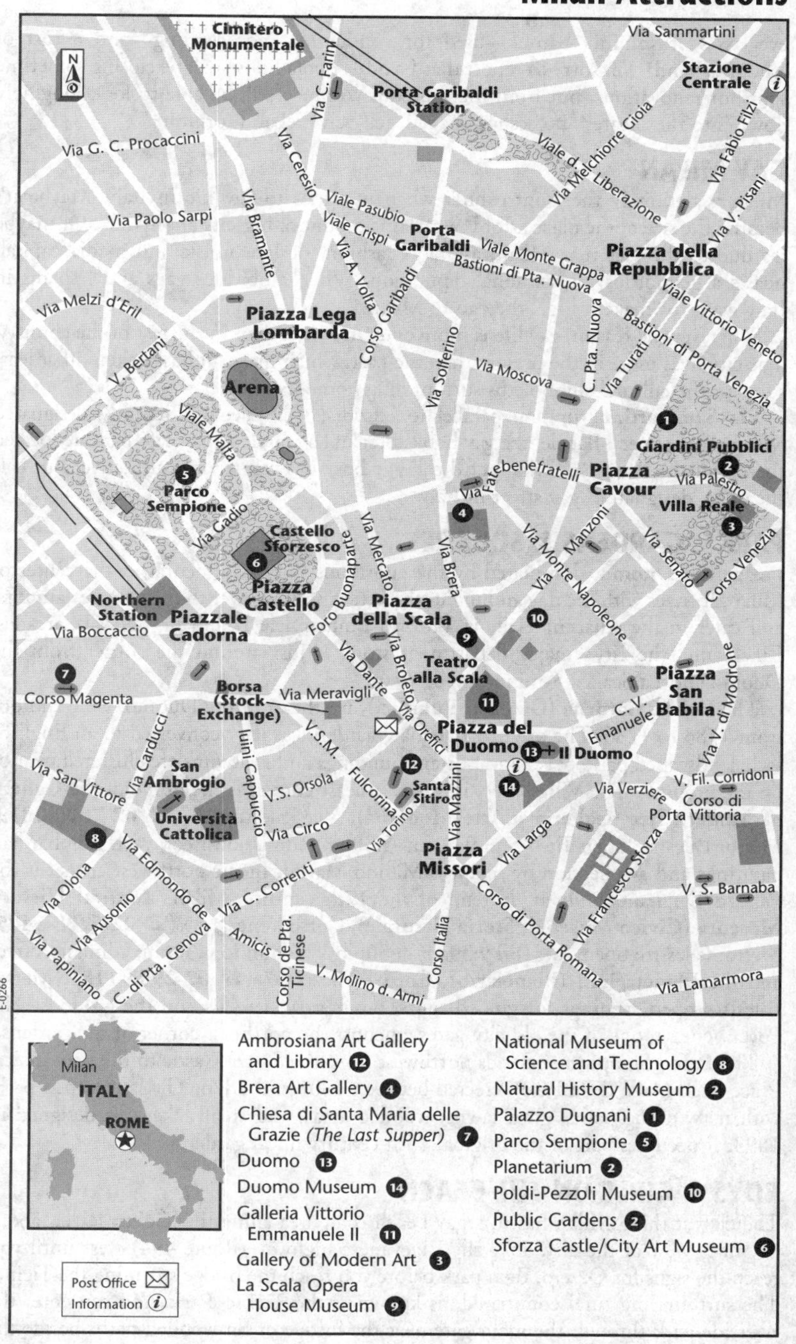

Cimitero Monumentale
Via Sammartini
Stazione Centrale
Porta Garibaldi Station
Via C. Farini
Via G. C. Procaccini
Via Ceresio
Viale d. Liberazione
Via Melchiorre Gioia
Via Fabio Filzi
Via V. Pisani
Via Bramante
Viale Pasubio
Viale Crispi
Via Paolo Sarpi
Porta Garibaldi
Viale Monte Grappa
Bastioni di Pta. Nuova
Piazza della Repubblica
Via A. Volta
Corso Garibaldi
Viale Vittorio Veneto
Bastioni di Porta Venezia
Via Melzi d'Eril
Piazza Lega Lombarda
Via Solferino
C. Pta. Nuova
Via Turati
V. Bertani
Arena
Via Moscova
Viale Malta
Giardini Pubblici
Via Fatebenefratelli
Piazza Cavour
Via Palestro
Villa Reale
Parco Sempione
Via Cadio
Castello Sforzesco
Via Mercato
Via Brera
Via Manzoni
Via Monte Napoleone
Via Senato
Corso Venezia
Northern Station
Piazza Castello
Foro Buonaparte
Piazza della Scala
Piazzale Cadorna
Via Boccaccio
Teatro alla Scala
Via Dante
Via Broletto
Piazza San Babila
Corso Magenta
Borsa (Stock Exchange)
Via Meravigli
Via Orefici
C. V. Emanuele
Via V. di Modrone
Piazza del Duomo
Il Duomo
Via Carducci
Iuini Cappuccio
V.S.M. Fulcorina
San Ambrogio
Via San Vittore
V.S. Orsola
Santa Sitiro
Via Mazzini
V. Fil. Corridoni
Via Verziere
Corso di Porta Vittoria
Università Cattolica
Via Circo
Via Torino
Via Larga
Piazza Missori
Via Olona
Via Edmondo de Amicis
Via C. Correnti
Via Francesco Sforza
V. S. Barnaba
Via Ausonio
Corso di Porta Romana
Via Papiniano
C. di Pta. Genova
Corso de Pta. Ticinese
V. Molino d. Armi
Corso Italia
Via Lamarmora
E-0266
Milan
ITALY
ROME
Post Office
Information
Ambrosiana Art Gallery and Library 12
Brera Art Gallery 4
Chiesa di Santa Maria delle Grazie (The Last Supper) 7
Duomo 13
Duomo Museum 14
Galleria Vittorio Emmanuele II 11
Gallery of Modern Art 3
La Scala Opera House Museum 9
National Museum of Science and Technology 8
Natural History Museum 2
Palazzo Dugnani 1
Parco Sempione 5
Planetarium 2
Poldi-Pezzoli Museum 10
Public Gardens 2
Sforza Castle/City Art Museum 6

eyeglasses, Toscanini's batons—used for conducting, not twirling—and a cast of Chopin's hand). I'm sorry to report that La Scala opera house will be closing sometime soon for renovations, but from the museum you may still be able to look longingly down into the theater's horseshoe-shaped, red-velveted auditorium.

GAY MILAN

Milan is definitely the front-runner when it comes to gay life in Italy. Maybe it's because the size of the place affords a certain amount of big-city anonymity. Or maybe it's due to the fact that Milan, as Italy's fashion, design, music and media capital, boasts a glamorous international reputation. When ambitious gays and lesbians in Italy want to "make it big," they go to Milan.

Whatever the reason, gay life is more open in Milan than in the rest of the country. The city lives more in the present than the past, which means it has shaken off at least some of the cultural shibboleths surrounding homosexuality.

Via Sammartini, running parallel to Stazione Centrale, was recently designated Milan's "gay street." Babele, the gay bookstore, and a couple of gay cafe/bars are located there, but the street isn't what you'd call gay busy or even terribly attractive. But it is the only "designated" gay street in Italy.

PARKS, GARDENS & SQUARES

Piazza del Duomo, dominated by the enormous Gothic cathedral, is the center of Milan. It fizzes with life day and night, the action spilling over to the bars, restaurants, and cafes in the adjacent Galleria Vittorio Emmanuele II and its sidewalk arcades. Rinascente, the city's major department store, is just around the corner from the Duomo and La Scala a 5-minute walk away.

The **Public Gardens (Giardini Pubblici),** northeast of the Duomo, were laid out from 1783 to 1786. The original Italianate garden was later converted to an English-style landscaped park. Several important buildings and museums are clustered near or on the grounds. The Villa Reale, in the southeast corner, is the home of the **Gallery of Modern Art (Galleria d'Arte Moderna),** Via Palestro 16 (☎ **02-7600-2819;** Metro: Palestro; open Tues–Sun 9:30am–5:30pm; admission free), with Lombardian paintings and a collection by sculptor Marino Marini. In the northwest corner is the Palazzo Dugnani, built at the end of the 17th century. Milan's **Natural History Museum (Civico Museo di Storia Naturale),** Corso Venezia 55 (☎ **02-6208-5405;** Metro: Palestro; open Tues–Fri 9:30am–5:30pm, Sat–Sun to 6:30pm; admission free) and the **Planetarium (Planetario),** Corso Venezia 57 (☎ **02-2953-1181;** Metro: Palestro; open evenings for guided tours, hours vary), are also on the grounds. The Porta Venezia, one of the old city gates, anchors the northeast corner of the gardens.

The **Parco Sempione** extends northwest from the Sforza Castle to the neoclassical Peace Arch (Arco della Pace), erected between 1807 and 1826. The landscaped park, with its winding paths, great lawns, wooded areas, and small lake, was designed in 1893. It occupies part of the original 15th-century ducal gardens.

BOYS & GIRLS ON THE BEACH

The closest thing Milan has to a gay beach is an area along the **Ticino River,** about 16 miles west of the city. Take the Vigevanese highway (Route 494) west until you reach the signs for Ozzero, then park before you reach the bridge spanning the Ticino. The surrounding rural countryside is known as the **Ticino Park.** You can enter the riverside park through the main gate near the bridge or on wooded paths beside the highway. Walk along the river until you come to the sandbars that form an alfresco tanning salon. Note that the beach isn't exclusively homo.

WORKING UP A SWEAT

If you're a swimmer, you may want to contact Milan's gay swimming and diving club, **Gruppo Pesce,** at ☎ **02-4895-3254;** they meet Tuesdays at 8pm and Sundays at 4pm at the pool at Linate Airport. Soccer buffs can contact the **Kaos Soccer Team** at ☎ **02-7012-3607** for information on gay soccer events. If you want to hit the slopes with other gay skiiers, call **Ski Group Milano** at ☎ **02-5810-0871** (7–11pm). Don't expect English speakers at any of them.

5 Hitting the Stores

Milan is the fashion capital of Italy and the headquarters for many of the country's most famous designers. In the exclusive designer boutiques you'll pay top prices (but still less than in New York) and be treated to a lot of retail attitude, but these places are still fun to visit.

Corso Vittorio Emanuele, now a pedestrian zone, is Milan's "high street," with cinemas, bookshops, and fashion shops in abundance. The Corso runs from Piazza del Duomo, with the Galleria Vittorio Emanele II (see "Exploring Milan" above) fronting the piazza, to Piazza San Babila. Elegant designer showrooms line the streets around **Piazza San Babila** and along **Via Montenapoleone,** which runs northwest from Piazza San Babila to **Via Manzoni,** another major shopping street.

Store hours are generally Tuesday to Saturday 9:30am to 1pm and 3:30 to 7:30pm. On Monday morning, many shops are closed (except during the Christmas season); they open between 3:30 and 7:30pm. Department stores and some of the shops in the center stay open all day, without the afternoon break.

SHOPS A TO Z

BOOKS The **Libreria Babele,** Via Sammartini 23 (☎ **02-669-2376;** Metro: Stazione Centrale), is a gay bookshop with Italian and imported books (fiction, nonfiction, poetry), calendars, postcards, and magazines. The **Libreria della Donne,** Via Dogana 2 (☎ **02-874-213;** Metro: Duomo), is a women's bookstore. The **American Bookstore,** Via Camperio 16 (☎ **02-878-920;** Metro: Cairoli), sells American and English books.

CLOTHING **Buba International Designer,** Via Spallanzani 6 (☎ **02-2940-9634;** Metro: Porta Venezia) is a gay-friendly store that sells designer garb and accessories. Ditto **Se Ti Va è Cosi,** Via Porpora 5 (☎ **02-2682-7743;** Metro: Loreto). You can find all sorts of secondhand clothing (and since this is Milan, fashion capital of Italy, you might luck out) at **Ware House,** Via G. Giardino, near the Duomo (☎ **02-878-832;** Metro: Duomo).

Milan is a center of international fashion, and many top designers have their headquarters and showrooms in the San Babila district. These showrooms, often dazzlingly chic, are fun to visit, but the clerks can show attitude (especially if it's obvious you're not buying anything).

Here's a roster of exclusive designer shops: **Armani,** Via Durini 24 (☎ **02-7600-3030;** Metro: Montenapoleone); **Cacharel,** Via Verziere 11 (☎ **02-7600-6411;** Metro: Duomo); **Dolce e Gabbana,** Via della Spiga 2 (☎ **02-7600-1155;** Metro: Montenapoleone); **Ermenegildo Zegna,** Via P. Verri 3 (☎ **02-795-521;** Metro: Montenapoleone); **Fendi,** Via Sant'Andrea 16 (☎ **02-7602-1617;** Metro: San Babila); **Fiorucci Store,** Galleria Passarella 1 (☎ **02-7600-3276;** Metro: Montenapoleone); **Gianfranco Ferré,** Via della Spiga 11 (☎ **02-794-864;** Metro: Montenapoleone); **Kenzo,** Via Sant'Andrea 11 (☎ **02-7602-0929;** Metro: San Babila); **Laura Biagiotti,** Via Borgospesso 19 (☎ **02-799-659;** Metro: Montenapoleone); **Missoni,** Via

Sant'Andrea 9 (☎ **02-7600-3555;** Metro: San Babila); **Moschino,** Via Sant'Andrea 12 (☎ **02-7600-0832;** Metro: San Babila); **Prada,** Galleria Vittorio Emanuele 63 (☎ **02-876-979;** Metro: Duomo); **Salvatore Ferragamo,** Via Montenapoleone, at the corner of Via Borgospesso (☎ **02-7600-6660;** Metro: Montenapoleone); **Ungaro,** Via Montenapoleone 27 (☎ **02-784-256;** Montenapoleone); **Valentino,** Via Montenapoleone 10 (☎ **02-7602-0285;** Metro: Montenapoleone); **Versace,** Via Montenapoleone 11 (☎ **02-7600-8528;** Metro: Montenapoleone).

DRAG Try **Europa OKI,** Via Vitruvio 22 (☎ **02-2940-6693;** Metro: Stazione Centrale), for those extra-long and extra-wide women's shoes.

GAY SHOPS **Bushido,** Via Andrea Doria 48A (☎ **02-670-6420;** Metro: Caiazzo), carries magazines, videos, latex and leather clothes, underwear, and gadgets. The **Erotika Shop,** Via Melzo 19 (☎ **02-2952-1849;** Metro: Porta Venezia), stocks imported magazines, leather and fetish gear, underwear, and various erotic condiments. **Europa 92,** Via G.B. Sammartini 21 (☎ **02-6698-2448;** Metro: Stazione Centrale), sells condoms, videos, leather items, and toys.

Lovecity, Corso di Porta Ticinese 105 (☎ **02-5810-5472;** Metro: S. Ambrogio), has books, condoms, clothing, and toys. **Magic America,** Via Legnone 19 (☎ **02-608-1109;** Bus: 90, 91), carries gay videos, magazines, and clothing. The **Men Store,** Via C. Imbonati 5 (☎ **02-668-4600;** Metro: Zara), is a new all-purpose gay emporium with books, videos, and all sorts of sexy accessories. **Sex Sade,** Via Santa Maria Valle 1, at the corner of Via Torino (☎ **02-804-880;** Metro: Missori), sells leather and rubber fetish clothing and accessories. **Studio Know-How,** Piazza Duca d'Aosta 12 (☎ **02-669-870;** Metro: Stazione Centrale), is the only exclusively gay sex shop in Italy.

PIERCING **Body & Soul,** Via Vigevano 11 (☎ **02-837-3051;** Metro: Porta Genova), is Milan's oldest and most experienced piercing studio.

TOILETRIES **Aqua di Parma,** Via Gesù 3 (☎ **02-7602-3307;** Metro: Montenapoleone), sells its delicious line of soaps and cologne across from the Four Seasons Hotel.

6 All the World's a Stage

If you're a fan of opera, I don't need to tell you the ✪ **Teatro alla Scala (La Scala)** Piazza della Scala (☎ **02-7200-3744** for information; www.lascala.milano.it), is Italy's preeminent opera house and has been for over 200 years. No one seems to know exactly when La Scala will close for refurbishment; it seems at press time that this will happen sometime in 2000. The season (Dec–July) will continue, but at different venues. The ticket office is in the arcade in Via Filodrammatici, on the left side of the opera house; hours are generally 10am to 6pm. They've recently instituted a new telephone-booking service that's so complicated I'm only going to give you the number and wish you good luck if you use it: For nonresidents of Milan, it's ☎ **02-860-787.**

Besides opera, this is where the Filarmonia della Scala presents concerts; there are also vocal and chamber music recitals. Check with the tourist office to find out what musical and performing events are happening and where.

7 In the Heat of the Night

A "bar" in Italy can be a bar-bar where alcohol is served or a coffee-bar where you go for a stand-up cappuccino (and also order an *aperitivo* or *digestivo*). In the gay bars and discos, the scene begins late. Some require an **Arci Card Uno** for admittance, but foreigners can generally get around this. You can obtain an "Uno" card at Libreria Babele or at the Arci-Gay Center (see above for both) or at the bars themselves. It costs 20,000L ($11) and is good for 1 year.

GAY BARS

Across from Stazione Centrale, **After Line,** Via G.B. Sammartini 25 (☎ **02-669-2130;** Metro: Stazione Centrale; open Wed–Mon 9pm–2am, Sun from 3pm), is a good-sized bar with a disco, a women's area, and video games.

Alexander's Bar, Via Pindaro 23 (☎ **02-255-0220;** Metro: Villa San Giovanni; open Fri–Sat 2–5am), is a sauna by day; it turns into a late-late-night bar with darkroom and maze on Friday and Saturday; it's located on the outskirts of town, but the Metro doesn't run at these hours.

The **Argos Club,** Via Resegone 1 (☎ **02-607-2249;** Tram: 3 or 8; open Sun–Thurs 10pm–3am, Fri–Sat to 6am), is raucho-sleaze, with glory holes, cubicles, a darkroom, strippers on Thursdays, and occasional theme parties; it's a "private club," which means you should have an Arci membership card or be prepared to plead your case.

At the **Company Club,** Via Benadir 14 (☎ **02-282-9481;** Metro: Cimiano; open Tues–Sun 10pm–2:30am, Fri–Sat to 6am), visitors are welcome, but you might lose all sense of nationality in the three darkrooms; the place is popular with leathermen, bears, and other nocturnal heat-seeking mammals.

L'Elephante, Via Melzo 22 (☎ **02-2951-8768;** Metro: Porta Venezia; open Tues–Sat 9pm–late, Sun brunch noon–4pm), is a trendy bar/restaurant with a popular Sunday brunch, loud music, and a mixed uncruisy crowd.

Sponsored by Arci-Gay, ✪ **Querelle,** Via de Castillia 20 (☎ **02-683-90;** Metro: Gioia; open Thurs–Sun 9pm–2am, Sat to sunrise), is one of Milan's oldest gay meeting spots, featuring theme parties, video shows, and lectures; early Saturday morning they serve breakfast.

Mister Sister, Via Calabria 5 (☎ **02-376-1531;** Tram: 3; Mon–Sat 9pm–2am, Sun from 6pm), attracts a mixed gay/lesbian crowd, with women sometimes outnumbering men.

Next Groove, Via Sammartini 23 (☎ **02-6698-0450;** Metro: Stazione Centrale; open Wed–Mon 5pm–3am), is a friendly cafe/bar on Milan's "gay street" beside Stazione Centrale.

LESBIAN BARS

Cicip e Ciciap, Via Gorani 9 (☎ **02-867-202;** Metro: Cordusio; open Wed–Sun 10:30pm–late), is a late-night women-only bar-cafe with pool tables.

No Ties, Via G. Giacoa 58 (☎ **02-261-9089;** Metro: Pasteur; open Thurs–Sun 9:30pm–2am), is a large bar/cafe with an outdoor summer patio; it's open only to women and transvestites.

Up two flights of stairs, **Sottomarino Giallo,** Via Donatello 2 (☎ **02-2940-1047;** Metro: Loreto; open Wed–Fri 10pm–2:30am), is a women-only disco.

MIXED CAFE/BARS

The following are trendy and sometimes theme-oriented gay-friendly cafe/bars with a mixed homo/hetero crowd.

Aquarius is a cocktail/snack bar with two smoky locations: Corso Sempione 49 (☎ **02-331-5093;** Metro: Moscova) and Via Foppa 21 (☎ **02-4800-5147;** Metro: Agostino); both are open Monday to Saturday to 1am.

A small romantic cocktail bar, **Atmosfera,** Via Teodosio 44 (no phone; Metro: Lambrate; open Sun–Fri 8am–midnight), features candlelight, good coffee, and a summer garden.

Birreria Uno, Viale Pasubio 14 (☎ **02-659-2164;** Metro: Garibaldi; open Wed–Mon 7:30pm–3am), is a multimedia bar with telephones and computers on every table.

Eclisse Café, Via Teodosio 92 (☎ **02-2614-3110;** Metro: Lambrate; open Mon–Sat 7am–2am), is a nice place to get wired on an espresso.

Film Cafe, Viale Zara 63 (☎ **02-608-1134;** Metro: Zara; Mon–Sat 6pm 1am, happy hour 6–10:30pm), has a black-and-white decor inspired by noir movies.

Frescobar, Via Bramante 9 (☎ **02-349-4576;** Metro: Moscova; open Tues–Sun 7:30am–2am), offers breakfast, lunch, a 6:30-to-9pm happy hour, and Sunday brunch.

Molto, Via Borgogna 7 (☎ **02-7602-4512;** Metro: San Babila; open Tues–Sun 7pm 2am), is a huge fave with a 7-to-10pm happy hour.

DANCE CLUBS

✪ **After Line Disco Bar, Via G.B. Sammartini 25 (☎ 02-669-2130;** Metro: Stazione Centrale; open Thurs–Sat 7pm–3am, Sun 3pm–3am; admission free), is a popular all-purpose bar/disco across from the train station; it serves alcoholic and nonalcoholic drinks and snacks, sponsors a "Lesbo Party" every Wednesday, and has go-go boys on Sunday.

HD, Via Tajani 11 (☎ **020-718-990;** Metro: Piola; open Fri–Tues 9pm–3am), is a small dance club with American music and male strippers on Mondays.

✪ **Killer Plastic, Viale Umbria 120 (☎ 02-733-996;** Metro: Romana), offers a hot men-only gay night on Thursday (11pm–6am) called **Man 2 Man.** It's mixed on Friday and Saturday.

On Sunday nights (11pm–4am) only men are allowed into **Papè Satan,** a popular one-night-disco on Via Baracchini 1 (no phone; Metro: Duomo); the crowd tends to be 20- to 30-somethings with retro-fashion fetishes. Admission is free, but you have to order at least one drink.

The largest gay disco in Italy is **Nuova Idea International,** Via de Castillia 30 (☎ **02-6900-7859;** Metro: Garibaldi; open Thurs–Sun 9:30pm–2am, Sat to 3am); there are two dance floors (one for disco, one for everything from waltzes to polkas), live bands on weekends, and cabaret shows on Thursday. Everyone from young gay singles to older gay couples and dragsters enjoy this place; Saturday night is the best time to go.

A cavernous underground space with a medieval dungeon "theme," **Segreta,** Piazza Castello 1 (☎ **02-860-307;** Metro: Cairoli; Wed and Fri–Sat from 10:30pm), is across from the Sforza Castle and attracts a younger fashionable crowd; there are video shows and dancing boys. **Zip Club,** Corso Sempione 76 (☎ **020-331-4904;** Metro: Moscova; open Tues–Sun midnight–6am), is a disco with a darkroom and male strippers on Thursdays, Saturdays, and Sundays.

DOWN & DIRTY: CINEMAS, SAUNAS & MORE

If you're looking to cruise, you might want to try the **Porta Venezia,** on the northeast corner of the public gardens, and within the gardens, especially in summer. For the macabre, try the **Cimitero Maggiore (Musocco Cemetery),** near the front (why anyone would want to cruise around a graveyard, I have no idea). Two more choices are **La Fossa (the Trench)** on Via Zola, in the park behind Stazione Ferroviana Nord near Castello Sforza (don't fall in the trench), and **Piazza Leonardo da Vinci** (appropriate, huh?), near the gas pumps on Viale Romagna.

As I've said in all the Italy chapters, *please be careful if you go cruising in Milan or anywhere in Italy.* Cruising spots are frequented by the hot and horny, but they are also hangouts for drug addicts and maladjusted psychos. In recent years there has been a flood of immigrants from Arab and Eastern European countries, particularly Romania, and some of these guys work as hustlers. They want money and can be murderously homophobic, especially if you in any way "challenge" their "masculinity." Is it worth it?

CINEMAS For first-run films in their original language, check out the offerings at **Mexico,** Via Via Savona 57 (☎ **02-4895-1802;** Metro: Porta Genova). **Roxy,** Galleria di Corso Lodi 130 (☎ **02-569-2304;** Metro: Corvetto; open daily 2:30–11:30pm), is a porn movie theater that sometimes shows hard-core gay films. If it's a gay video arcade you're looking for, try **Ambra,** at the corner of Via Clitumno and Via Padova (☎ **02-2682-2610;** Metro: Loreto; open daily 2:30pm–midnight), or **Zodiaco,** Via Padova 179 (☎ **02-256-7602;** Metro: Loreto; open daily 2–11:30pm).

SAUNAS At **Alexander's Club & Bar,** Via Pindaro 23 (☎ **02-255-0220;** Metro: Loreto; open Sun–Thurs 2pm–1am, Fri–Sat to 2am), you'll find steam and dry saunas, video and TV rooms, a solarium, a darkroom, and a full bar. **Body Gym,** Via Lesmi 9 (☎ **02-8940-2049;** Metro: S. Ambrogio; open daily noon–midnight), is a large, clean gym/sauna with steam and dry heat, a whirlpool, a darkroom, a bar (non-alcoholic drinks only), and free condoms.

Magic Sauna, Via Maiocchi 8 (☎ **02-2940-6182;** Metro: Porta Venezia; open Wed–Mon noon–midnight), offers dry and wet saunas, tanning booths, videos, and a large solarium; English is spoken. And at **Thermas,** Via Bezzecca 9 (☎ **02-545-0355;** Metro: San Babila; open Fri–Wed noon–midnight), you'll find steam and dry saunas, a gym, tanning booths, a darkroom, and a video room.

The Netherlands

Tulips & Tolerance

by Todd Savage

Think of visiting the **Netherlands** (aka **Holland**) as a way to time-travel to a kinder, gentler future. When it comes to social issues, this tiny country is a few steps more highly evolved than much of the world. Holland is a place where poverty has been largely eliminated, flower arranging is a national pastime, women can safely walk alone at night, and gays and lesbians are so accepted they're no longer trendy. (Okay, so maybe we're not ready to jump *that* far into the future.) It's amazing how such a small country has done so much with so little.

The country is burdened with all sorts of cultural clichés (warning: obligatory joke ahead), from tulips to wooden shoes to Hans Brinker, and you may wonder how the Dutch keep their cool after the umpteenth joke about whose finger was stuck in what *dyke*, I mean, *dike*. But when you travel outside Amsterdam, it's surprising how much the country—an utterly flat landscape dotted by windmills, medieval churches, and fields of grazing sheep—still resembles all those Dutch landscapes stored away in our mental databanks. While this country of 15 million people, who occupy a landmass half the size the state of Maine, is a global business center with the world's busiest port, much of the physical landscape still reflects the prosperity of the 17th-century Golden Age glory.

Who knows why such a tiny country ended up populated by the world's seemingly tallest people? Perhaps, like one of their beloved flowers, they're trying to rise above the clouds for a glimpse of sun on all those rainy days (weather is definitely not one of the country's selling points). Not only are they statuesque, but also the Dutch have got to be some of the world's most coordinated people: just watch them ride their bicycles. Here's a country where dykes on bikes is an everyday sight. There's a kind of grace about people who handle their bikes with one hand, or no hands, while doing any number of other things (keep your minds out of the gutter)—including shielding themselves from the driving rain with a tattered umbrella, talking on a mobile phone, and balancing all kinds of impossible things on their handlebars or rear rack. And could there be anything more romantic than being carried on the back of a bike by a Dutchman or -woman? (Anyone who asks if you want a ride home one evening may want to give you more than a lift.)

Tolerance has been a national source of pride ever since the country became a safe haven for refugees in the 17th and 18th centuries. There are some spotty patches on its record, but Holland and the political and cultural capital of Amsterdam have shown a willingness to live and let live. In these modern times, that philosophy extends to the lives of gays and lesbians. While queer Dutch still must come out like the rest of us, gays and lesbians in the Netherlands don't face many of the same cultural taboos. They surely have a sophisticated gay social life, but because they don't encounter much political or religious opposition to their existence, they don't have the same idea

The Netherlands on the Net

Look for the latest on Amsterdam by perusing a few helpful gay-themed Web sites, such as the comprehensive listing geared to tourists at **www.gayamsterdam.com,** with an updated calendar of events, and the site of *Gay News* at **www.gaynews.nl.** And there's **www.dds.nl/plein/homo,** an excellent source of information with links to the city's gay and lesbian switchboard.

For general information on Amsterdam and the Netherlands; check out the Netherlands Board of Tourism's site at **www.visitholland.com** and the city's official site at **www.amsterdam.nl.** Architecture fans can get a sneak preview of the city's streetscape at **www.amsterdam.nl/bm2/adam/adam_e.html.**

of a gay identity that homos in other parts of the West, particularly the United States, have developed. Surely one of the thrills of spending time in the Netherlands is viewing the world from thousands of miles and an ocean away from Jerry Falwell, Pat Robertson, and friends.

Whatever the private attitudes of the Dutch, the law of the land puts gays on par in nearly every way with straights. That's not to say there haven't been some rough spots over the centuries. Gay men have been convenient scapegoats, and during the "worm scare" of the 1700s in Amsterdam—when worms began eating away at the wooden foundations that supported the dikes, causing flooding—gays took the blame. Intermittent raids on homosexual social circles were carried out, and records show that dozens of men were executed throughout the century. Laws prohibiting homosexuality were lifted in 1811. The country's gay-rights organization, **COC (Cultur en Ontspannings Centrum),** traces its roots to efforts that were under way before World War I, but it wasn't until 1971 that gays and lesbians achieved equal legal rights in employment, housing, and taxation. Holland has continued to show the world that gays and lesbians aren't the hobgoblins they're often portrayed as. Dutch queers serve openly in the military, and while gays and lesbians have the right to the same kind of quasi-marriage domestic partnership that's legal in many Scandinavian countries, the government is moving toward a new world first: the right to a full Dutch civil marriage and the right to adopt native-born children. Gays are so much a well-accepted part of life they're on their way to becoming downright boring.

(The queen herself may want to check out a PFLAG meeting sometime. Deprived of a royal family of their own, the Germans obsess about the Dutch monarchy, and while it's not reported in the local Dutch press, the German gay rags have kept alive the rumor that Queen Beatrix's second-oldest son, who lives in London, is cohabitating with another man. Shhhh.)

In some countries, it would be impolite to rush into a conversation in English with a stranger without at least extending the courtesy of asking whether they speak it. In Holland, especially Amsterdam, there's hardly a need. In fact, the Dutch are so fluent with English they might even take mild offense to such a query. They learn it from an early age (and many are also versed in French and German) and probably speak it better than some of your friends. Not only that, but their English is so darn cute! Expect to overhear English (Engels in Dutch) everywhere, from besotted people belting out drinking songs on the tram to the slightly depressing sight (if you're a hopeless monolinguist) of Dutch people speaking it to each other.

The Dutch Guilder

The Dutch currency is the **guilder** (or **gulden**), abbreviated **NLG** or **fl** or **DFL** (a holdover from the days when the Dutch currency was known as the florin). Each guilder is divided into 100 cents. The colorful guilder banknotes come in denominations of 10DFL (blue), 25DFL (red), 50DFL (yellow), 100DFL (brown), 250DFL (purple), and 1,000DFL (green). There are also 5¢, 10¢, 25¢, and 1DFL, 2½DFL, and 5DFL coins.

At this writing, the U.S. dollar was equivalent to 1.9DFL, and this was the exchange rate I used throughout. Prices over U.S.$5 have been rounded to the nearest dollar.

Amsterdam, long known as the Gay Capital of Europe, so dominates the country that it's a veritable city-state, and while you can be forgiven for letting inertia get the best of you once you master the city, you'll never know why they call it the Netherlands (Low Country) until you get out of town and see just how unceasingly flat it is. The country is small enough and transportation so convenient you can reach the far corners of the Netherlands in 1 or 2 hours. Consider an excursion to such postcard-perfect Dutch towns as **Delft** and **Haarlem** and to the flower auction at **Aalsmeer** and the cheese market at **Alkmaar.**

14

Amsterdam: Letting It All Hang Out

The Dutch capital of **Amsterdam** is a city that experiences marvelous mood swings. Sometimes it's thrillingly crazy and exotic and about to come undone, and then you turn around and find it's a transcendent picture of harmony and grace. By day, you may witness a convoy of techno-blasting flatbed trucks brimming with dancing prodrug activists, and by night you may be charmed by the chime of church bells and the gentle rattle of bicycles on cobblestone. The city is *all that.*

No matter how depraved or deliciously sinful you find it, Amsterdam offers you a rare chance to see life in an honest light. In fact, of its many charms, the city's greatest appeal may be its disarming, refreshing humanity. People and life are complicated and messy, and the city doesn't try to hide this or clean it up (of course, some mandatory pooper-scoopering might be nice). Urges and aspirations are acted out in public. The city's closet door is always swung wide open.

Amsterdam's rep as a kind of 20th-century Sodom and Gomorrah is legendary: People—or rather, some horny guys—want to get their rocks off and some enterprising women are willing to make a trade, so get the red neon flowing! Human beings have a natural curiosity to alter their consciousness drinking, smoking funny cigarettes, and spinning in circles, so turn the taps and let the people puff away. Some women fancy women, some men take a liking to other guys—no big deal! Mind you, it's not always a pretty picture, from the tackiness of the Red Light District to some pretty skanky darkrooms to the suburban big hairs in Rembrandtplein. But then Amsterdam also offers you a view of the refined, uplifting side of humankind, from the masterful works of Dutch painters in the Rijksmuseum to the engineering marvels of the waterways to the wonderfully multilingual residents.

Pretenders like London, Paris, and Berlin may make claims to the mantle of Gay Capital of Europe, yet Amsterdam has a long track record as a city that tolerates and even celebrates gays and lesbians. When organizers of the Gay Games chose a site for their first competition outside the States, it was only natural to give the nod to Amsterdam. Talk about bringing out the Welcome Wagon: Months before the games began in August 1998, straight businesses flew the rainbow colors (confusing queens all over town about where to drink and shop), and the Dutch government not only endorsed the Games but also kicked in millions of guilders to support them. The gay Amsterdam business community was even inspired to begin an annual pride celebration with what's now a legend-in-the-making Canal Parade. Amsterdammers were enthusiastic about the attention brought by the games, but they didn't always understand the need for a queer-only competition. Many straights and even some gays in Amsterdam, who live such integrated lives, viewed the event's self-imposed segregation as a step back for the gay movement. As a result, gay organizers found it easier selling the event to the larger community as a big party (the Dutch love parties) rather than as a quasi-cultural-political event. In the end, the games only enhanced and expanded the city's reputation as a home away from home for homos the world over.

Amsterdam has endured decades of heavy tourism, so it's well organized for visitors; the local population—English-speaking, congenial and good-humored—have long ago extended their well-honed tolerance to tourists. (They can have a lot of fun with it too: eavesdropping in English and then talking openly about you in Dutch.) Of course, the city is ready for us crazy gay people too. Gay travelers can and do go there as everything from serious cultural mavens to Bangkok-style sex tourists. There are dozens of gay bars, clubs, and special parties; more than two dozen gay hotels; and an array of gay cafes and restaurants. But even with such a sophisticated scene, this is one city where you need not keep to the gay ghettos. In fact, if you do you'll miss out on what makes Amsterdam such an idyllic destination for gay travelers. This is a place where you can go where you want to go and do what (and whom) you want to do.

1 Amsterdam Essentials

ARRIVING & DEPARTING

BY PLANE You get your first taste of Dutch efficiency at the up-to-date **Schiphol International Airport** (☎ **06/350 340 50;** www.schiphol.nl), about 11 miles from the center of Amsterdam.

You have a variety of options for getting to the city. The one-way **taxi** fare will run you around 60DFL ($32), and the trip will take about 25 minutes. KLM offers a **shuttle bus** from the airport to many of the major hotels in the city center. Buses leave every 20 minutes during the day and less frequently in the evening until 10pm, taking about half an hour to reach most hotels. The cost is 17.50DFL ($9) each way or 30DFL ($16) round-trip. A third option is taking the Amsterdam CS **train,** costing 6.25DFL ($3.30) and departing every 15 minutes 6am to midnight and on the hour after midnight; the trip to Centraal Station takes about 15 minutes. The airport also has the full range of **car-rental agencies** (see below).

The airport planners installed a bunch of **duty-free shops** so you can spend your first few guilders as soon as you hit the ground or your last few before you take off.

BY TRAIN Travelers arriving in Amsterdam over land pull into **Centraal Station** (☎ **020/624 8391**), a grand old station recently restored with its back to the river IJ and imperiously looking down toward the city center. In summer, the station is filled with young 'uns burdened with scruffy overstuffed backpacks, so expect big lines everywhere from the Amsterdam Tourist Office to the frozen yogurt counter. There are places to eat, get money, and stow luggage. Outside in the front of the station (slightly to your left) is a GVB public transit office, where you can buy tram tickets (see below). There are VVV tourist offices both inside and outside the station as well. You'll immediately realize Centraal Station's importance as a transportation hub: about a zillion bicycles are locked up here, and many of the yellow trams originate their routes in front of the station.

BY CAR Cars are pretty much the low man on the traffic totem pole in Amsterdam. Pedestrians and bicyclists rule the road. Parking is scarce and roads are narrow, so a car won't be much of a friend when you're traveling within the city.

VISITOR INFORMATION

The official source for info on all things Amsterdam is one of several **Amsterdam Tourist Offices** (☎ **900/400 40 40;** 1DFL/53¢ per minute; fax 020/625 2869; e-mail vvvadam@pi.net; www.visitholland.com; hours vary, but most are open at least daily 9am to 5pm), known as VVV (Vereniging voor Vreemdelingen-Verkeer, or Association for Foreigners' Travel). There are offices both outside and inside Centraal Station (at platform 2), at Schiphol Airport, and at the corner of Leidsestraat and Leidseplein. Here you can gather brochures and maps, make hotel reservations, book canal cruises, exchange money, plan excursions, and buy tram passes, theater and concert tickets, and telephone cards.

AMSTERDAM GAY & LESBIAN EVENTS

APRIL Queens sure know how to throw a party. **Queen's Day** (April 30), the day-long celebration of Queen Beatrix's birthday (Koninginnedag), is one of the best times of year to experience Amsterdam. (She was actually born in January, when it's far too cold to party, but she continues to keep the holiday fixed to her mother's birthday.) It's an epic street extravaganza that's Mardi Gras, Gay Pride, and a giant yard sale all rolled into one. Go to the usual queer entertainment zones, as well as the Homomonument, to revel with your gay and lesbian comrades.

MAY On **Memorial Day** (May 4), the victims of World War II and the end of that war are commemorated. While Queen Beatrix lays a wreath at the National Monument in Dam Square on Memorial Day, the gay community leaves flowers at the Homomonument to remember the gay victims of the war. On the next day, **Liberation Day,** parties are held around the Monument.

AUGUST The first weekend in August brings **Amsterdam Pride:** The city's gay-pride fest began only 4 years ago, inspired by the then-upcoming Gay Games and organized by Gay Business Amsterdam. Parade floats here actually float. The highlight of the day-long festival is the Canal Parade along Prinsengracht, with dozens of festive barges and boats and plenty of hard-body go-go boys. Of course, this is one of the most entertaining events of the year (they've toned it down a bit; the first year there were naked go-go boys). For more details, contact the Gay and Lesbian Switchboard at ☎ **020/623 6565.**

The Culture & Leisure Pass & the Museumkaart

Serious culture mavens may find it cost-effective to buy an **Amsterdam Culture & Leisure Pass,** containing more than 30 coupons good for free entry or discounts to many of the city's museums and other attractions, including the Rijksmuseum, the Vincent van Gogh Museum, and several tours and restaurants. The pass is 36.75DFL ($19) and sold through the VVV Amsterdam Ticket Office and many hotels.

One of the best all-around discounts is the **Museumkaart (National Museum Card),** giving free admission to more than 400 museums all over the Netherlands for 1 year for 55DFL ($29). If you plan to visit more than five or six museums in Amsterdam, you'll save money with this card, available from museum ticket windows and at the tourist office in front of Centraal Station. You'll need a passport-size photo to attach to it, which you can get in photo booths at Centraal Station. Note that the Anne Frankhuis, one of Amsterdam's most popular museums, doesn't honor this card.

The third Monday in August is **Heart's Day,** a festival held since the Middle Ages on the Zeedijk in the Red Light District. On this day, which was banned during World War II by the Germans and only recently revived, men and women do drag, and each year the most beautiful man or woman in drag is crowned.

OCTOBER In late October, the leather community celebrates **Amsterdam Leather Pride.** This 10-day event, sponsored by several leather/rubber fetish shops, is one of the world's largest leather festivals, with more than 5,000 participants from all over. Dozens of hotels, bars, fetish and sex clubs, and restaurants get involved, and there are lots of special events, a leather expo, and parties, including women's events and the European Mr. Drummer finals. For more details, contact **Amsterdam Leather Pride,** P.O. Box 2782, 1000 CT Amsterdam (☎ **020/422-3737**) or check out **www.freeyellow.com/members/alp** or **www.gayplanet.nl/lpn** on the Internet.

CITY LAYOUT

Amsterdam has a reassuring human scale that often makes it feel more like an overgrown village than a major cosmopolitan capital. This city of three-quarters of a million people is one of the most densely populated in the world, and the vast majority of them walk, bike, or take the tram to wherever they need to go. While finding your way among the canals requires some study, once you grasp how a few squares and major streets connect, you'll find getting around Amsterdam is fairly simple.

The city is laid out like a series of ever-expanding horseshoes, and everything seems to build out from **Centraal Station.** Many visitors arrive here at the magnificent old train station, so it serves as a helpful landmark when you're developing a sense of direction. From the station, the city spills down along the **Damrak,** a flashy commercial thoroughfare lined with touristy shops and fast-food joints, and deposits you into **Dam Square,** the main square. From here roads lead in several directions: east into the notorious **Red Light District** and the equally notorious **gay leather strip;** south toward the **Kalverstraat** pedestrian shopping street or continuing on the Damrak and then the Rokin along the Amstel River toward **Muntplein;** or west behind the Royal Palace toward the **Anne Frankhuis** and the **Homomonument.** The city center also embraces attractions like the Amsterdam Historical Museum as well as high-profile hotels and restaurants.

Much of the city's historic heart is cradled in a series of four major canals: **Singel, Herengracht, Keizersgracht,** and **Prinsengracht** (*gracht* is the Dutch word for canal and requires you to utter one of the language's least lovely sounds). Here you'll find Amsterdam's collection of handsome 17th-century **canal houses,** put up by the wealthy classes during Holland's Golden Age. The canal ring also contains the **flower market;** shopping on **Leidsestraat;** the antiques district of **Nieuwe Spiegelstraat;** the busy social hub of **Rembrandtplein** and **Leidseplein** with their cafes, theaters, bars, and restaurants; and the gay nightlife ghettos along **Reguliersdwaarsstraat, Kerkstraat,** and the **Amstel River.** On the southern side of the city is a fashionable residential area blessed with the verdant **Vondelpark; Museumplein,** a freshly renovated square that bridges the trio of the Rijksmuseum, the Vincent van Gogh Museum, and the Stedelijk; and the shopping enclave along **P. C. Hooftstraat** and **Van Baerlsestraat.**

Things are less uptight in a couple of neighborhoods celebrated for their eclectic flair and diversity. The gentrified old working-class area known as the **Jordaan** (your-*dawn*), west of Dam Square and north of the Westerkerk, is a wonderful place for strolling among the curious shops and *gezellig* corner cafes and is especially popular with gays and lesbians. Somewhat grungier is **de Pijp** (deh **pipe**), a funky neighborhood south of Vondelpark that's home to the city's largest general market, the Albert Cuyp, and a growing number of interesting restaurants and bars.

GETTING AROUND

Central Amsterdam is pleasantly compact, so you can easily reach most of your destinations on foot. Since the trams stop running at midnight, sometimes you'll have little choice but to hit the pavement. Even when walking, you've got to keep your eyes on the road to avoid getting run down by trams, buses, cars, or bicyclists (who'll gently alert you with a chime of their bells).

BY TRAM, SUBWAY & BUS Amsterdam's extensive public transport system (☎ **0900/9292**) is served by 17 **tram** lines, 3 underground **subways,** and numerous **buses.** You'll spend most of your time on the trams, which crisscross the city and make frequent stops. The subway and bus systems are good for getting to the outer reaches of the city not served by tram lines.

Though you can buy tickets on board from a tram or bus driver, it's less expensive to buy them in advance at a VVV office or the GVB metro office outside Centraal Station. You can buy passes, **dagkaarts,** good for unlimited travel in all zones for up to 9 days. A 1-day card is 12DFL ($6) and available on buses and trams as well as at tobacco shops, newsstands, and post offices. At the ticket office at Centraal Station it's only 10DFL ($5). You can also buy 2- to 9-day dagkaarts for 15 to 43DFL ($8 to $22), but these aren't available on buses or trams. You need to take a lot of trams for a dagkaart to be worthwhile, but if you're staying outside the town center, a day or multiday pass may be your best bet.

You can also buy a **strippenkaart,** which you have stamped according to the number or zones you're traveling through. (Most attractions are in the central zone.) Strippenkaarts come in denominations of 2, 3, 8, 15, and 45 boxes. Before boarding a bus or tram, consult the map posted at every stop to determine how many zones you'll be traversing. Fold your strippenkaart so that one more box than the number of zones you're traveling through is facing up and stick this end into the yellow box near the door as you enter. The machine will stamp your card. On buses, have the driver stamp your card. The ticket includes transfers to other tram, bus, and Metro lines within 1 hour. If you don't have a strippenkaart, you can buy 2-, 3-, and 8-strip cards from the driver, but this is a more expensive option.

When taking a tram, board at the rear of the car, where you need to get your ticket validated by the attendant or the yellow stamping machine. (It's not a good idea to try to freeload: You risk a fine of 60DFL ($32) from a ticket inspector who may ask to see your validated ticket.) Tickets are stamped according to the number of zones (there are 11 in the city) you'll pass through on your ride. You'll need to stamp one additional ticket for each zone, but most of the major attractions in Amsterdam fall within the Centrum zone. If you're confused, tell the conductor or driver where you're going and he or she will tell you the number of zones you should calculate.

The city has tried to simplify things by establishing **Circle Tram 20.** The tram originates at Centraal Station and makes a wide loop in both directions through the city and over the major canals, stopping by Museumplein, the Anne Frankhuis, and many of the other major attractions and hotels. It departs every 10 to 12 minutes and runs daily 9am to 6pm. A Circle Tram pass is also valid on other public transport lines. Tickets for 1 to 9 days are available; prices run from 10 to 43DFL ($5 to $23).

The subways and trams run until midnight, and a number of night buses run about every 30 minutes.

BY BICYCLE When in Amsterdam, do as the Dutch do: Two-wheeling is the way to go native. Numerous rental shops will lend you a sturdy one-speed (though many bear dorky signs letting everyone know you're an out-of-towner). Rentals usually run about 12.50DFL ($7) per day, with discounts for multiple-day rentals; be aware that most bikes have pedal brakes. A deposit of a passport and cash or credit-card imprint is usually required. Two convenient companies are **MacBike,** Mr. Visserplein 2, near Waterlooplein (☎ **020/620-0985;** Tram: 4, 9, 14, or 20; open daily 9am–6pm), and **Damstraat Rent-A-Bike,** Damstraat 22–24 (☎ **020/625-5029;** Tram: 4, 9, 16, 20, 24, or 25; open daily 9am–6pm).

A few pointers: Be sure to keep your bike locked, ring your bell early and often to give pedestrians a heads-up, and watch out for the ferocious tire-eating tram tracks.

BY CANAL BIKE Amsterdam offers another pedal-powered means of transport—**canal bikes.** These are small pedal boats for two to four that are available on Leidseplein, near the Rijksmuseum, on Westerkerk and the Anne Frankhuis, and on Keizersgracht near Leidsestraat. Canal bikes are available daily 10am to 4pm in spring and autumn (to 10pm in summer). Rates are 19.50DFL ($10) per hour for a two-person boat and 29.50DFL ($16) per hour for a four-person boat. There's also a 50DFL ($26) refundable deposit.

BY TAXI It can be tricky finding taxis in Amsterdam. By law, they're required to queue up at cabstands, but if you see one with its cab light illuminated by all means try to flag it. Better yet, call ahead if you know you're going to need a lift. There's a central dispatch at ☎ **020/677-7777.** Rates start at 5.80DFL ($2.95) and increase by 2.80DFL ($1.40) per kilometer.

BY BOAT With miles of waterways winding through the city, an obvious way to navigate Amsterdam is by boat. The best option is the **Museum Boat** (☎ **020/622-2181**), which stops near virtually all Amsterdam's museums and attractions. The boats leave from behind the tourist office in front of Centraal Station every 30 minutes daily 10am to 5pm. Tickets are available at the Lovers Canal Cruises counter near the dock. A day ticket is 25DFL ($13). The ticket also allows reduced admission at most museums. There are English-speaking guides on the boats.

BY CAR Drivers approach from Belgium and Germany on major European expressways like E19, E35, E231, and E22, then reach Amsterdam exits on A4, the major expressway connecting the city to The Hague and Rotterdam. Believe me, you *don't* want to drive in Amsterdam. If you happen to arrive by car, you'll find several large garages in the center of town, including ones at Centraal Station, at de Bijenkorf department store, and at the Muziektheater under Waterlooplein. There's free parking in park-and-ride lots outside the center, or better yet, put your car in the secure underground lot outside the city at the ArenA soccer stadium. A one-day ticket is 12.50DFL ($7) and includes two round-trip public transit tickets to the center. When traveling on the A1, A2, and A9 toward Amsterdam, follow the signs to "Transferium ArenA."

If you want to explore the areas around Amsterdam, you'll find the major car-rental companies here, including **Avis,** 380 Nassaukade, near Leidseplein (☎ **020/430-9611;** Tram: 1, 2, 5, 6, 7, or 10); **Budget,** Schiphol Airport and Overtoom 21 (☎ **0800/023-8238;** Tram: 1 or 6); **Hertz,** Engelse Steeg 4, near Centraal Station (☎ **020/623-6123;** Tram: any tram); and **Europcar Interrent,** Schiphol Airport and Overtoom 51–53 (☎ **070/381-1891;** 1 or 6). Please be sure to stow any valuables in the trunk of your car to avoid tempting any would-be thief.

Country & City Codes

The **country code** for the Netherlands is **31.** The **city code** for Amsterdam is **20;** use this code when you're calling from outside the Netherlands. If you're within the Netherlands but not in Amsterdam, use **020.** If you're calling within Amsterdam, simply leave off the code and dial only the regular phone number.

Fast Facts: Amsterdam

AIDS Organizations & Hot Lines Amsterdam's toll-free AIDS line at ☎ **0800/022-2220** (open Mon–Fri 2–10pm) provides information about HIV/AIDS and safe sex, referrals, and support. The organization **SAD-Schorerstichting,** P.C. Hooftstraat 5 (☎ **020/662-4206;** Tram: 2, 5, or 20), offers gay-specific resources and HIV prevention advice and provides a range of health services.

American Express The main travel center is at Damrak 66 (☎ **020/520-7777;** Tram: 4, 9, 16, 20, 24, 25; travel office open Mon–Fri 9am–5pm, Sat–Sun to noon), a short walk from Centraal Station. For a lost or stolen card or traveler's checks, call the 24-hour hot line at ☎ **0800/022-0100** or 020/504-8666.

Community Centers Amsterdam has an active gay community center, **COC-Amsterdam,** which is one of the 30 local branches of the national gay organization COC (Organization for the Integration of Homosexuality). Operating out of a turn-of-the-century building in the Jordaan at Rozenstraat 14 (☎ **020/626 30 87;** www.xs4all.nl/~nvicoc; Tram: 13 or 17), the group provides a range of services, from legal aid to a comfortable meeting place for a variety of gay/lesbian groups. There's a first-floor cafe (open Wed–Sat 1–5pm) where you can stop by to find out the latest on gay happenings, a theater, and a disco (see "In the Heat of the Night"). The city also has a gay and lesbian switchboard (☎ **020/623 65 65;** open daily 10am–10pm) that offers information, support, and referrals. If you want to see the way things used to be over the centuries, the COC has an extensive gay historical **library and archives** known as **Homodok,** Oudezijds Achterburgwal 185 (☎ **020/525 2601;** www.homodok.nl; open Wed–Fri 10:30am–4:30pm). There's also a center specifically documenting the lesbian herstory called **Lesbian Archives Amsterdam,** near Leidseplein at Eerste Helmersstraat 17 (☎ **020/618 5879;** www.dds.nl~laa; open daily 1–4:30pm; Tram: 1, 2, 3, 5, 6, 10, 11, or 12). The archives also has a guidebook (published only in Dutch) of self-guided walking, biking, and boat tours that reveal some of the culture and history of lesbians in Amsterdam.

Consulates & Embassies The **U.S. Consulate** in Amsterdam is at Museumplein 19 (☎ **020/575-5309;** Tram: 2, 5, or 16; open Mon–Fri 8:30am–noon); the **U.S. Embassy** is in The Hague at Lange Voorhout 102 (☎ **070/310-9209;** www.usemb.nl). The **U.K. Consulate General** in Amsterdam is at Koningslaan 44 (☎ **020/676-4343;** Tram: 2; open Mon–Fri 9am–noon and 2–3:15pm; the **U.K. Embassy** is in The Hague at Lange Voorhout 10 (☎ **070/364-5800**). In The Hague, the **Canadian Embassy** is at Sophialaan 7 (☎ **070/311-1600;** open Mon–Tues and Thurs–Fri 10am–noon and 2:30–4pm), the **Australian Embassy** at Carnegielaan 4 (☎ **070/310-8200;** open Mon–Fri 8:30am–4:50pm); and the **New Zealand Embassy** at Carnegielaan 10 (☎ **070/346-9324;** open Mon–Fri 9am–12:15pm and 1:30–5:30pm).

Currency Exchange You can get competitive rates with amazingly no commission at Amsterdam Tourist Offices (VVV), as well as at the small exchange booth on the northwest corner of Rembrandtplein. Other places with good rates are the 24-hour GWK bank in Centraal Station and Schiphol Airport and the post offices at Singel 250 and Oosterdokskade 3 and the 24-hour GWK bank in Centraal Station.

Cybercafe There are free public Internet terminals in the cafe at **In De Waag,** Nieuwmarkt 4 (☎ **020/422-7772;** e-mail indexwaag@xs4all.nl; Metro: Nieuwmarkt; Tram: 4, 9, 14, 16, 20, 24, or 25; open daily 10am–1am).

Emergencies For any kind of emergency, dial ☎ **112** to make a request for police, fire, or ambulance attention. For a police nonemergency, call ☎ **020/559-9111.**

Gay Media On your radio dial, **MVS** (106.8 FM and 103.8 on cable) broadcasts 3 hours of gay and lesbian programming daily in Amsterdam. Programs air 6 to 9pm, with a variety of English and Dutch music and talk. Programs are all English on Sundays, with a 2-hour live program called "Alien," hosted by two ex-pats chatting up gay issues, local news, books, movies, and whatever they feel like gossiping about (sex is often heavy on their minds). It's followed by another program called "Radio 2 Puff," hosted by "Black American MoFo's," with more news and gossip of special interest to the black community. For more information, call ☎ **020/620 0247,** or check the station's Web site at **www.mvs.nl.**

Hospitals Foreign visitors can seek 24-hour emergency medical and dental services by calling ☎ **020/612-3766.**

Hot Line The city's gay and lesbian switchboard at ☎ **020/623-6565** (open daily 10am–10pm) offers info, support, and referrals.

Newspaper & Magazines Several gay papers in Amsterdam have articles in Dutch and English, including the monthly newspapers ***Gay News*** and ***Gay & Night,*** which carry handy maps of all the gay bars, clubs, restaurants, and hotels. You can find most of these gay periodicals free in bars and gay bookstores (occasionally they're for sale). Also keep your eyes opened for the free newsletters **"Queer Fish"** and **"Shark,"** self-published by a British expat lesbian. Each week she gives an insider's scoop on the bar scene, as well as film and restaurant picks, with emphasis on the alternative, squat, and queer world.

The Amsterdam Tourist Office produces a sharp monthly guide called ***What's On in Amsterdam*** (4DFL/$2.10) that includes a calendar of cultural happenings. The American improv group **Boom Chicago** publishes its own quarterly newsletter offering tips on what's new; pick it up at the group's theater (see "All the World's a Stage" below) or the VVV.

There's no English-language newspaper geared to expats or visitors, but you can find all kinds of English-language periodicals at the **American Book Center,** Kalverstraat 185 (☎ **020/625-5537;** www.abc.nl; Tram: 1, 2, 5, 9, 14, 16, 20, 24, or 25).

Telephone Public telephones are plentiful. A **local phone call** costs .50DFL (25¢) for 3 minutes, but watch out for numbers that begin with 06 or 0900, as they can be more expensive. Telephone instructions are in English, and though some machines accept coins, most will accept only phonecards. You can buy stored-value phonecards at VVV offices, the post office, and many newsstands. For **international phone calls,** you can use any of the phone booths spread all over town by using plastic phonecards selling for 5DFL ($2.50), 10DFL ($5), or 25DFL ($13). You can also reach an AT&T operator by dialing **06** (wait for the tone), then **022-9111.** For local directory assistance, dial ☎ **0900/0808.**

2 Pillow Talk

With Amsterdam's summer sun shrinking the hours of darkness, its happening bar scene, and its "very friendly" guys and gals, the adventurous visitor could probably get away without even bothering to bed down in a hotel ("Your place or mine?" . . . "Yours."). How's that for a budget travel tip? However, for the rest of us who aren't likely to get so lucky or act so trashy, it's a smart idea to consider paying for a place to stay.

As a sophisticated capital containing more than 300 hotels, Amsterdam presents you with some choices. Will it be luxury or budget? On the canals or not? Gay or non-gay? Budget leather or luxury leather? (Told you you had choices.) Amsterdam offers a great diversity in the types of housing options, and many of the city's hotels and guesthouses deliver tons of atmosphere. Amsterdam is compact enough that most anywhere you stay you'll be able to get from there to wherever you want to go in a leisurely walk or on one of the many tram lines. Staying at one of the large hotels in the heart of the city, near Centraal Station and Dam Square, will position you well for your explorations. But you also should consider staying in an old canal house where you'll have a better feel for the city—not to mention your calves, since you should expect to be climbing up steep, skinny stairways, a signature of the centuries-old buildings.

The summer tourist season is heavy, so unless you want to end up camping out in Dam Square (as has happened in years past when all the hotels were filled), it's crucial that you make reservations a couple of months in advance, especially if you hope to book a special place. Some hotels, especially popular gay spots, fill up half a year in advance for events like the Queen's Day celebration in April.

Don't expect anyone at a mainstream hotel to blink an eye at same-sex guests checking in. They're quite accustomed to gay travelers—after all, Amsterdam is known as the gay capital of Europe. After 1998's Gay Games, there isn't a hotel here that hasn't been inundated with queers. About two dozen hotels advertise in the gay papers and guides that they're "gay" or "gay-friendly." They may or may not be gay-owned, may book varying mixes of guests, and may just want to get friendly with your wallet, so it's worth asking some questions if you have a preference. It's also a good idea to abandon some old stereotypes: Never assume because it's gay it's automatically tasteful. Some homos just don't have the touch. At the end of this section I've grouped many of the smaller gay hotels and guesthouses.

A couple of centralized services can assist with booking rooms if you arrive without a reservation. Try **the Netherlands Reservations Center,** Postbus 404, 2260 AK Leidschendam (☎ **070/317 5454;** fax 070/320 -2611; www.hotelres.nl), and the **Amsterdam Tourist Office** (known as the VVV), which has up-to-date listings of room availability and can book a hotel for a small fee the day of your arrival. VVV offices are found inside and outside Centraal Station, at Leidseplein/Leidsestraat, and at the Holland Tourist Information counter at Schiphol Airport. For more information, call ☎ **900/400-4040** (1DFL/53¢ per minute).

OVERLOOKING THE AMSTEL RIVER

Amsterdam House. Office at Amstel 176, 1017 AE Amsterdam. ☎ **800/618-1008** in the U.S. or 020/626-2577. Fax 020/626-2987. www.amsterdamhouse.com. 30 units. MINIBAR TV TEL. From 295DFL ($155) houseboat. AE, DC, EU, MC, V. Tram: 4, 9, 14, or 20.

Follow the lead of thousands of eccentric Amsterdammers and you won't be able to get much closer to the canals than on a furnished houseboat. This company has a fleet of

Hey, Big Spender

If you've finally come into your trust fund and want to blow a wad on an Amsterdam hotel, there are many deluxe places that'll be more than glad to bend over backward for you. Be prepared to drop a minimum of $200 a night for a double at any of them.

The **American, Pulitzer, Hotel de l'Europe, Schiller,** and **Doelen,** some of the toniest, are listed in full below. Here are some others where you'll feel like a princess, no matter what sex you are:

Amstel Inter-Continental Amsterdam, Prof. Tulpplein 1, 1018 GX Amsterdam (☎ **800/327-1177** in the U.S. and Canada, or 020/622-6060; fax 020/622-5808; e-mail amstel@interconti.com; Tram: 6, 7, 10, or 20).

Golden Tulip Barbizon Palace, Prins Hendrikkade 59–72, 1012 AD Amsterdam (☎ **800/327-1177** in the U.S. and Canada, or 020/556-4564; fax 020/624-3353; www.goldentulip.com; e-mail sales@gtbpalace.goldentulip.nl; Tram: Any tram to Centraal Station).

Grand Hotel Krasnapolsky, Dam 9, 1012 JS Amsterdam (☎ **020/554-9111;** fax 020/622-8607; www.krasnapolsky.nl; e-mail book@krasnapolsky.nl; Tram: 4, 9, 16, 20, 24, or 25).

Radisson SAS, Rusland 17, 1012 CK Amsterdam (☎ **800/333-3333** in the U.S. and Canada, or 020/520-8300; fax 020/623-1231; e-mail info@amszh.rdsas.com; Tram: 4, 9, 16, 24, and 25).

Renaissance Amsterdam, Kattengat 1, 1012 SZ Amsterdam (☎ **800/HOTELS1** in the U.S. and Canada, or 020/621-2223; fax 020/627-5245; www.renaissancehotels.com; Tram: 1, 2, 5, 13, 17, or 20).

Sofitel Amsterdam, Nieuwezijds Voorburgwal 67, 1012 RE Amsterdam (☎ **800/221-4542** in the U.S. and Canada, or 020/627-5900; fax 020/623-8932; e-mail faw@euronet.nl; Tram: 1, 2, 5, 13, 17, or 20).

10 one-, two-, and three-bedroom houseboats that put you at water level along the Amstel near Rembrandtplein and along Prinsengracht. They're available for short- or long-term visits (a minimum stay may be required depending on availability and season). The company owners are straight, but they have gay staff and are definitely savvy to gay travelers—if the dozen gay guides behind the reception desk are any indication. All boats have fully equipped kitchens and are heated for use in winter. Though the level of accommodations varies, one of the luxury houseboats boasts parquet floors, living and dining rooms with leather sofas, a complete entertainment center including a VCR, an antique table, live houseplants, a small bedroom, and a bath with tub and shower, plus a small outdoor deck. The company provides a 24-hour emergency number in case you drop your keys in the canal or have any problems when the reservation office is closed. Amsterdam House also offers 20 private furnished apartments for rent (175DFL/$97) and runs a small hotel on the north bank of the Amstel (115DFL/$64 double).

Doelen Hotel. Nieuwe Doelenstraat 24. ☎ **020/554-0777** or 020/554-0600. Fax 020/622-1084. 85 units. A/C MINIBAR TV TEL. 420–530DFL ($221–$279) double; from 530DFL ($279) suite. AE, DC, MC, V. Tram: 4, 9, 14, or 20.

The Krasnapolsky hotel chain recently unveiled a renovation of the historic Doelen. You can't get much more central, right on the Amstel near Waterlooplein and

Rembrandtplein—and you definitely pay for it. The standard rooms are cozy (a kind way of saying there's barely enough room to walk around the beds), but many have high ceilings and are nicely furnished with pediment-shaped headboards, a couple of chairs and a small writing desk, gilt-framed mirrors, and large draped windows; they also come with hair dryers, coffeemakers, and safes. The white-tile baths have both tubs and showers but aren't large or luxurious. One of the hotel's selling points is the handful of deluxe suites (or salons, named for notable guests like Sarah Bernhardt) that are spacious, with king-size beds, antique furnishings, marble-top nightstands, mirrored dressing tables, and large armoires. Art-history buffs should take note that the Doelen was the home for Rembrandt's masterpiece *The Night Watch* (now in the Rijksmuseum) for a while, and its former location is noted on the ground floor.

Hotel de l'Europe. Nieuwe Doelenstraat 2–8. ☎ **020/531-1777.** Fax 020/531-1778. www.leurope.nl. 100 units. A/C MINIBAR TV TEL. 580–680DFL ($305–$358) double; from 820DFL ($431) suite. AE, DC, MC, V. Valet parking 50DFL ($26). Tram: 4, 9, 14, or 20.

This is the kind of grand hotel every major world city seemed to build back in the heyday of rail travel. Today you pay for the fabulous in-the-heart-of-it-all location and the ooh-ahh factor of the hotel name—but, you know, these dowagers are always on the frumpy side. The lobby impresses, the Amstel laps at the hotel's front door, and the rooms are spacious and well furnished, with extras like gift baskets of fruit and Dutch candies. But for the big bucks you're shelling out, the rooms—even with their half-canopied beds, gilt-trimmed chairs, and yards of window drapery—still look like some houses do when their owners gave up on redecorating, say in the 1970s. Each room has two phones, and the marble-clad baths are roomy, often with two sinks, and come with terry robes. The Excelsior is the hotel's elegant restaurant, which requires men to don dinner jackets.

Liliane's Home. Sarphatistraat 119, 1018 GB Amsterdam. ☎ **020/627-4006.** 7 units, 2 with bathroom. TV TEL. 130DFL ($68) double without bathroom; 185–260DFL ($97–$137) private apt. Rates include breakfast. No credit cards. Limited parking 35DFL ($18). Tram: 6, 7, or 10.

Liliane Maesen's home is Amsterdam's only guesthouse exclusively for women. Liliane opened up rooms in her place, an early 1900s house not far from the Amstel and a 10-minute walk from Rembrandtplein, a few years ago to give women a place where they could let it all hang out. Lesbian travelers constitute the majority of her guests, but the place is open to all women (children and pets, however, aren't welcome). You have your own key and separate entrance from Liliane's residence. Five rooms accommodate up to three guests, and two apartments sleep four, including an especially spacious one with a kitchen and balcony. Room guests share a bath on the hall; apartment renters have private baths. The rooms vary in size and come with old-fashioned homey furnishings (there's carpeting in some). A Dutch breakfast is offered each morning (8:30–9:30am), and Liliane (who trained for her first marathon during 1998's Gay Games—you go, girl!), will help you navigate maps and clue you into the women's scene.

NEAR THE CENTER

✪ **Black Tulip.** Geldersekade 16, 1012 BH Amsterdam. ☎ **020/427-0933.** Fax 020/624-4281. www.blacktulip.nl. 9 units. MINIBAR TV TEL. 325DFL ($171) double; from 425DFL ($224) deluxe fantasy suite. Rates include breakfast. AE, DC, EU, MC, V. Tram: 4, 9, 16, 20, 24, or 25.

It's late morning at the Black Tulip, the world's only luxury leather hotel. Guests arrive in the breakfast room with its stainless-steel appliances and wood-beam ceiling and are greeted by Tchaikovsky playing and fresh flowers lending their perfume. The meal of fresh-squeezed orange juice, coffee, and a spread of meats and cheeses is served by one of the proprietors, smartly attired in a leather apron. This unusual boutique hotel is for the guy who'd stay at the Ritz but doesn't want to parade in and out in full leather. Home to prominent Dutch writers in the 17th century, this elegant canal house near Centraal Station and the leather district was renovated in 1998 by owners Frank and Eelco and named after a novel by French writer Alexandre Dumas *père*. They've left the name off the house, adorned with gay pride and leather flags and a gilt leaf over the door, to avoid any awkward moments in case Harvey and Gladys from Iowa ring the bell. They'd sure get an eye-opener: Though the rooms offer "normal" amenities like baths, safes, and coffeemakers, other standard features are bondage hooks, slings over the beds, and adult cable channels. The rooms, in grays, blacks, and reds, have been creatively furnished with military-style lockers, custom-made chairs, and camouflage-print curtains (with black-out blinds). The deluxe suite—the Black Body fantasy room–is furnished with . . . , well, I'll leave that to your fantasies. Many rooms come with galvanized steel cages (padlocks are available), and there's a boot rental "for the light traveler." The owners, a couple whose families were the first guests to stay in the hotel when it opened, have thought of everything. Well, apparently not: Alas, they weren't able to please the guy who complained he couldn't see the TV from his cage. The building was extensively remodeled to ensure soundproofing, and the owners have pledged to maintain a high level of cleanliness.

Rainbow Palace Hotel. Raadhuisstraat 33, 1016 DC Amsterdam. ☎ **020/625-4317.** Fax 020/420-5428. 9 units, 2 with shower only. MINIBAR TV TEL. 100DFL ($53) double without shower; 150DFL ($79) triple with shower. Rates include breakfast. AE, DC, JCB, MC, V. Tram: 13, 14, or 17.

A simple gay-owned hotel that welcomes gays with pride flags out front but takes in everybody, the Rainbow is in a landmark building on a busy street between the Royal Palace in Dam Square and the Westerkerk, my favorite church in Amsterdam (the site of Rembrandt's unmarked grave), the Homomonument, and the Anne Frankhuis. You can definitely skip your Stairmaster routine if you stay here and are forced to work the steep stairway. The rooms are pretty small and simple, all with radios, sinks, and safes. The cozy little breakfast room is the kind your grandmother had, with lace on the table, an old chandelier, and artwork of Dutch life. The owner lives on site.

Schiller Hotel. Rembrandtplein 26–36, 1017 CV Amsterdam. ☎ **020/554-0777** or 020/554-0700. Fax 020/624-0098. 92 units. A/C TV TEL. 420DFL ($221) double; from 750DFL ($395) suite. AE, DC, JCB, MC, V. Tram: 4, 9, 14, or 20.

Another grand old dame, the Schiller has overlooked Rembrandtplein since 1912. After a major renovation in 1997, it's looking better than ever, with stained-glass windows and hundreds of paintings throughout created by the hotel's namesake. The rooms boast rich colors and contemporary furnishings, including a couple of sitting chairs and a desk. Some of those facing the square have French balconies; less appealing are the top-floor rooms, with sloped ceilings and small windows. The baths are clean and up-to-date, with slate floors and wood detailing on the tub and toilets; all come with hair dryers. The Schiller is a place to stay if you want to be part of the action; Rembrandtplein is lively until the wee hours in summer. You're also steps from the only lesbian bar and blocks from the gay ghettos along the Amstel and Reguliersdwarsstraat. The morning after, you have a range of choices for your coffee at the cafes lining the square. Even if you have no plans to stay here, try the hotel's stylish brasserie, evoking the early 1900s with handsome paneling, art deco fixtures, and a terrace.

Tulip Inn. Spuistraat 288–292, 1012 VX Amsterdam. ☎ **800/344-1212** in the U.S. and Canada or 020/420-4545. Fax 020/420-4300. www.goldentulip.com. 209 units. TV TEL. 290DFL ($153) double. AE, DC, MC, V. Parking 50DFL ($26). Tram: 1, 2, or 5.

Opened in 1994, the Tulip Inn is part of an international Dutch hotel chain, Golden Tulip. It occupies five adjoining 1920s buildings in the Amsterdam School style, with entrances on both Singel and Spuistraat. That explains the unusual flow of the interior spaces, which have extra-wide corridors and irregularly (you could even say queerly) shaped rooms that are quite spacious and have two walls of windows. (Ask for a view on the Spui side so you're not stuck with a back-of-the-building view.) The rooms are contemporary and fresh, decorated with light-blond furniture, including a nice-size desk and a pair of chairs and a table. The clean white-and-black tile baths have either a tub or a shower. You can start your day perked and pumped since all rooms come with hair dryers and coffeemakers. In the lobby are a breakfast room, a skylit lounge with bar service and some stylish club chairs, and a full-service Italian restaurant. The hotel is perfectly situated, around the corner from Dam Square, near shopping and nightlife, and with a variety of top-notch restaurants and bars right out the door on Spuistraat. The KLM airport shuttle makes a stop outside the hotel.

AT LEIDSEPLEIN & MUSEUMPLEIN

✪ **American Hotel.** Leidsekade 97, 1017 PN Amsterdam. ☎ **800/327-0200** in the U.S. and Canada, or 020/624 53 22. Fax 020/625 32 36. E-mail: american@interconti.com. 188 units. A/C MINIBAR TV TEL. 325DFL ($171) double; 675DFL ($355) junior suite with canal view. Rates include breakfast buffet. AE, DC, EU, JCB, MC, V. Tram: 1, 2, 5, 7, or 10.

The castlelike American has been a landmark for its clock tower and Dutch art nouveau theatrics since it was built in the early 1900s. The hotel's Café Americain (see "Cafe Culture" below) has been a gathering place for artists, intellectuals, and homos for decades and still is popular for high tea and Sunday jazz brunch. This isn't a cookie-cutter hotel: The rooms are of different sizes and have some mild art deco styling; some have stained-glass windows, balconies with flower boxes, and views overlooking the canal and Leidseplein. The baths have granite counters, cosmetic mirrors, and hair dryers. The Nightwatch Bar has an old Wurlitzer jukebox, and the summer terrace gives you an entertaining view of the action on Leidseplein.

Amsterdam Marriott Hotel. Stadhouderskade 12, 1054 ES Amsterdam. ☎ **800/228-9290** in the U.S. and Canada, or 020/607-5555. Fax 020/607-5511. 392 units. A/C MINIBAR TV TEL. 325–445DFL ($171–$234) double. Rates include breakfast buffet. AE, DC, JCB, MC, V. Underground parking 50DFL ($26). Tram: 1, 2, 5, 7, or 10.

Given all the charming housing options in Amsterdam, nothing sounds more boring than a Marriott. But if you aren't looking for any surprises or can't take steep, twisting stairs in canal houses, then this expense-account hotel may be for you, especially since it has an excellent location near Leidseplein and the Rijksmuseum. At the reception desk, you'll be greeted by a smiling queen (a portrait of Queen Beatrix) and a friendly staff (well, maybe some queens too—not sure). The generously proportioned rooms got a freshening up in 1998, so they look pretty good. The standard doubles are furnished with two double beds or a king-size, a chair with an ottoman, and a desk with all the latest phone gadgetry. As in all good American-style hotels, the rooms also have irons, safes, and hair dryers. If you choose one of the executive-level rooms, you'll get floor-to-ceiling windows, more-deluxe furnishings, and a fluffy robe. The hotel has a bar and two restaurants, including an all-you-can-eat American Sunday brunch. The Marriott gets big points for creativity: Steps from Vondelpark, it provides early-morning joggers a table stocked with towels, ice water, and a route map and offers a special biking package that includes use of a bike and a prepared box lunch.

Hotel Orfeo. Leidsekruisstraat 14 (at Prinsengracht), 1017 RH Amsterdam. ☎ **020/623-1347.** Fax 020/620-2348. 23 units, 7 with bathroom. MINIBAR TV TEL. 115DFL ($61) double without bathroom, 185DFL ($97) double with bathroom. Rates include breakfast. AE, MC, V. Tram: 1, 2, or 5.

Central Amsterdam Accommodations & Dining

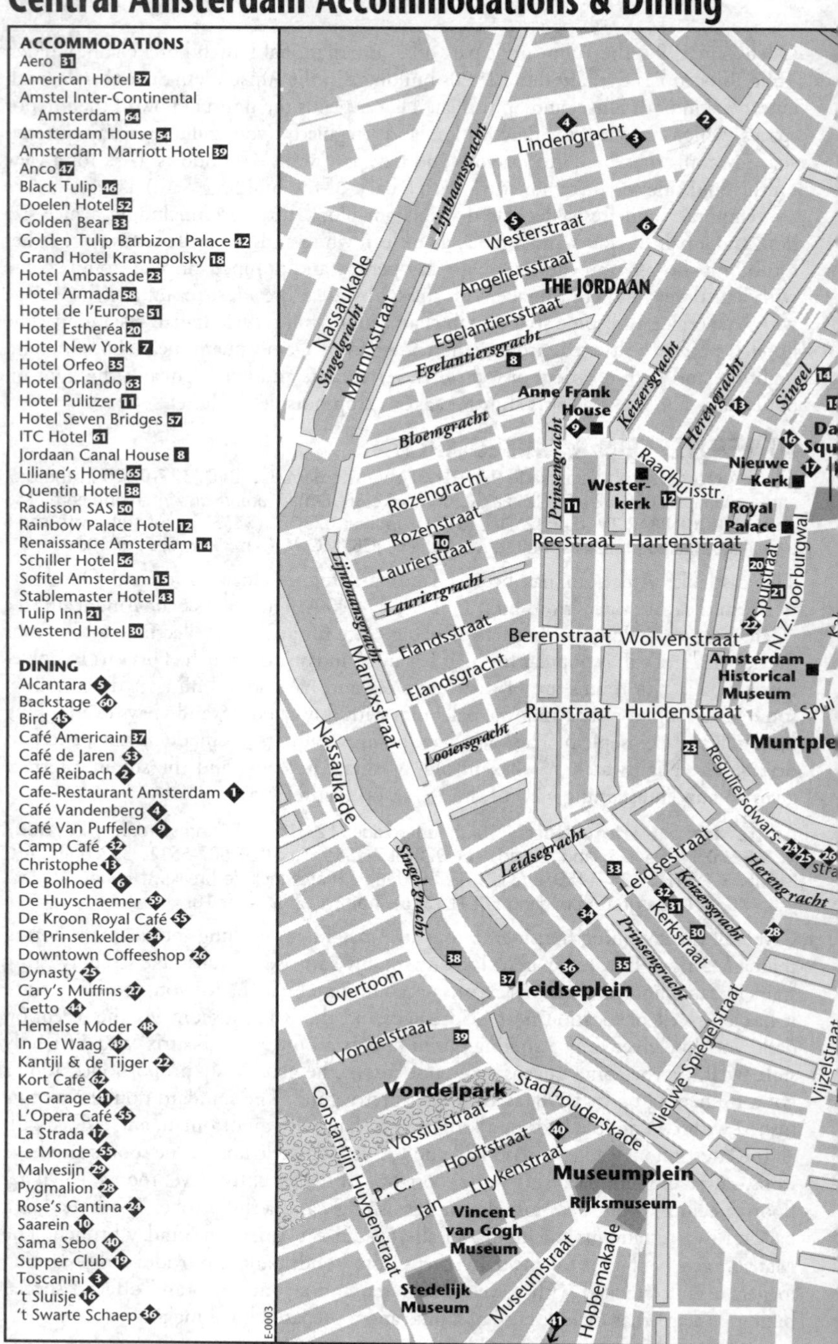

ACCOMMODATIONS
Aero 31
American Hotel 37
Amstel Inter-Continental Amsterdam 64
Amsterdam House 54
Amsterdam Marriott Hotel 39
Anco 47
Black Tulip 46
Doelen Hotel 52
Golden Bear 33
Golden Tulip Barbizon Palace 42
Grand Hotel Krasnapolsky 18
Hotel Ambassade 23
Hotel Armada 58
Hotel de l'Europe 51
Hotel Estheréa 20
Hotel New York 7
Hotel Orfeo 35
Hotel Orlando 63
Hotel Pulitzer 11
Hotel Seven Bridges 57
ITC Hotel 61
Jordaan Canal House 8
Liliane's Home 65
Quentin Hotel 38
Radisson SAS 50
Rainbow Palace Hotel 12
Renaissance Amsterdam 14
Schiller Hotel 56
Sofitel Amsterdam 15
Stablemaster Hotel 43
Tulip Inn 21
Westend Hotel 30
DINING
Alcantara 5
Backstage 60
Bird 45
Café Americain 37
Café de Jaren 53
Café Reibach 2
Cafe-Restaurant Amsterdam 1
Café Vandenberg 4
Café Van Puffelen 9
Camp Café 32
Christophe 13
De Bolhoed 6
De Huyschaemer 59
De Kroon Royal Café 55
De Prinsenkelder 34
Downtown Coffeeshop 26
Dynasty 25
Gary's Muffins 27
Getto 44
Hemelse Moder 48
In De Waag 49
Kantjil & de Tijger 22
Kort Café 62
Le Garage 41
L'Opera Café 55
La Strada 17
Le Monde 55
Malvesijn 29
Pygmalion 28
Rose's Cantina 24
Saarein 10
Sama Sebo 40
Supper Club 19
Toscanini 3
't Sluisje 16
't Swarte Schaep 36
E-0003
Lindengracht
Lijnbaansgracht
Westerstraat
Angeliersstraat
THE JORDAAN
Egelantiersstraat
Egelantiersgracht
Nassaukade
Singelgracht
Marnixstraat
Anne Frank House
Keizersgracht
Herengracht
Singel
Bloemgracht
Prinsengracht
Raadhuisstr.
Nieuwe Kerk
Wester-kerk
Rozengracht
Royal Palace
Rozenstraat
Reestraat
Hartenstraat
Lauriersstraat
Lauriergracht
Spuistraat
N.Z. Voorburgwal
Elandsstraat
Berenstraat
Wolvenstraat
Amsterdam Historical Museum
Elandsgracht
Runstraat
Huidenstraat
Spui
Looiersgracht
Muntple
Reguliersdwars-
Leidsegracht
Leidsestraat
Kerkstraat
Overtoom
Leidseplein
Nieuwe Spiegelstraat
Vondelstraat
Vondelpark
Stadhouderskade
Vijzelstraat
Constantijn Huygenstraat
Vossiusstraat
P. C. Hooftstraat
Jan Luykenstraat
Museumplein
Rijksmuseum
Vincent van Gogh Museum
Hobbemakade
Museumstraat
Stedelijk Museum

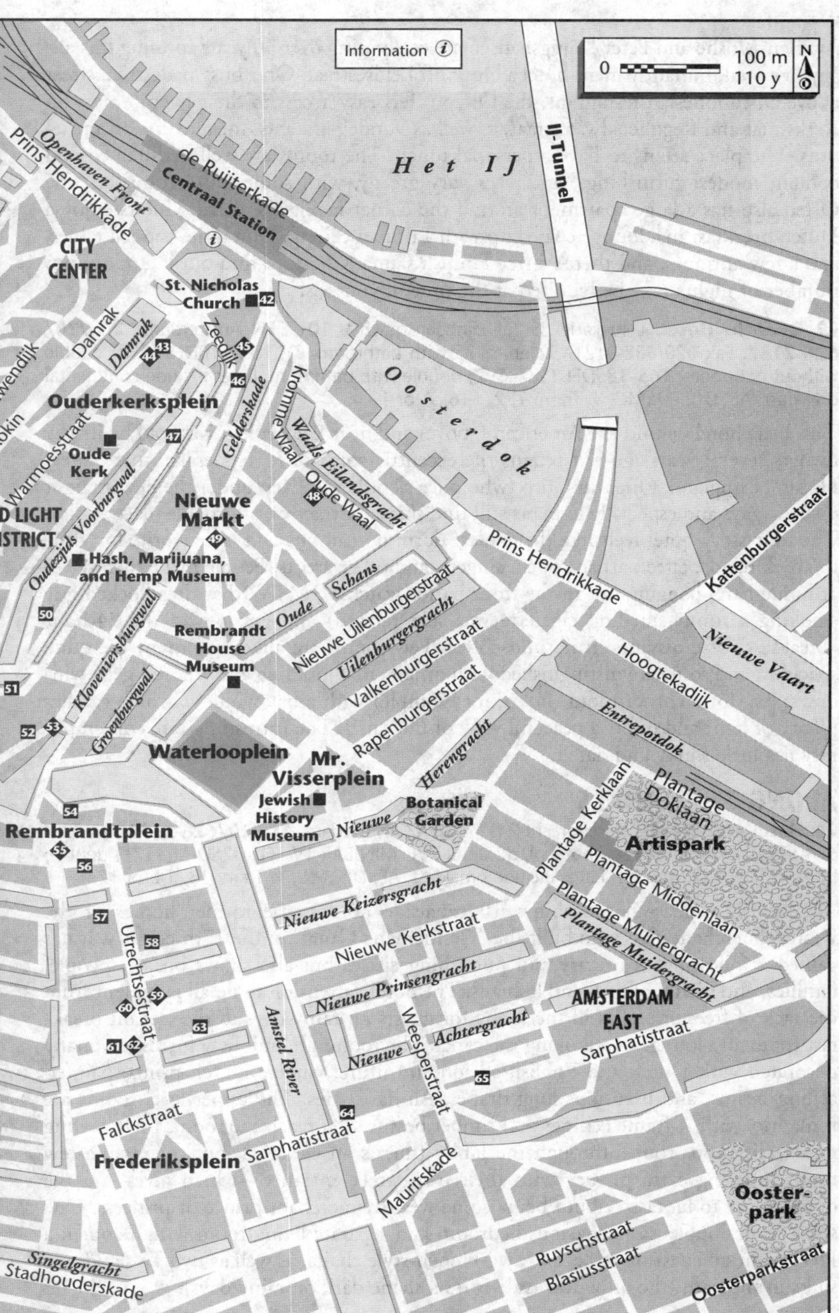
Information
0
100 m
110 y
N
Het IJ
IJ-Tunnel
de Ruijterkade
Centraal Station
Openhaven Front
Prins Hendrikkade
CITY CENTER
St. Nicholas Church
Damrak
Zeedijk
Oosterdok
Kromme Waal
Waals Eilandsgracht
Oude Waal
Gelderskade
Ouderkerksplein
Warmoesstraat
Oude Kerk
Oudezijds Voorburgwal
RED LIGHT DISTRICT
Nieuwe Markt
Hash, Marijuana, and Hemp Museum
Prins Hendrikkade
Kattenburgerstraat
Schans
Oude
Nieuwe Uilenburgerstraat
Uilenburgergracht
Rembrandt House Museum
Kloveniersburgwal
Groenburgwal
Valkenburgerstraat
Rapenburgerstraat
Hoogtekadijk
Nieuwe Vaart
Entrepotdok
Herengracht
Waterlooplein
Mr. Visserplein
Jewish History Museum
Nieuwe
Botanical Garden
Plantage Kerklaan
Plantage Doklaan
Artispark
Rembrandtplein
Plantage Middenlaan
Plantage Muidergracht
Nieuwe Keizersgracht
Nieuwe Kerkstraat
Utrechtsestraat
Nieuwe Prinsengracht
AMSTERDAM EAST
Amstel River
Weesperstraat
Nieuwe Achtergracht
Sarphatistraat
Falckstraat
Sarphatistraat
Frederiksplein
Mauritskade
Ooster-park
Ruyschstraat
Blasiusstraat
Oosterparkstraat
Singelgracht
Stadhouderskade
42 43 44 45 46 47 48 49 50 51 52 53 54 55 56 57 58 59 60 61 62 63 64 65

Avi Ben-Moshe and Peter Königshausen are celebrating over 30 years running this all-gay (it's predominantly men) hotel a block off Leidsestraat. On a busy pedestrian street above an Indonesian restaurant, the Orfeo offers easy access to the gay epicenters on Kerkstraat and Reguliersdwarsstraat, as well as Vondelpark and Amsterdam's art museums. The place seems to have a personal touch. The rooms are well maintained and contain modest furnishings, and sizes vary greatly, with some quite compact. The Orfeo also has a large apartment around the corner facing the canal. Guests enjoy a Dutch breakfast in a lounge cozied up with a timber ceiling, Dutch tile-topped tables, and a few antiques, and there's a free Finnish sauna. Check to find out if a minimum number of nights may be required at the time of your visit.

✪ **Quentin Hotel.** Leidekade 89 (at Lijnbaansgracht), 1017 PN Amsterdam. ☎ **020/626-2187.** Fax 020/622-0121. 32 units, 25 with bathroom. TV TEL. 110DFL ($58) double without bathroom, 165–185DFL ($87–$97) double with bathroom. Rates include continental breakfast. AE, DC, EU, MC, V. Tram: 1, 2, 5, 6, 7, or 10.

This little hotel behind the American (above) and near Leidseplein was sold by its gay owners several years ago but retains the eccentric spirit of its namesake, that Stately Homo of England, Quentin Crisp (who once slept here). Even under the new straight owners, gays and especially lesbians still find this an attractive, affordable place to stay. The four-story hotel feels like the coolest dorm on campus and is a favorite for visiting rock bands, tattoo artists, opera singers, and other artists. People make themselves at home here, hanging out in the front parlor watching MTV (that dreadlocked guy smoking a funny-smelling cigarette was sure relaxed) and grazing on the 24-hour "breakfast" of croissants, fruit, and coffee. Few rooms are alike, but many are quite spacious, and some are distinguished with ornamental molding and colored-glass windows. Ask for a corner room (no. 5, for example) with a bay window, which catches plenty of light and offers a peaceful view of the canal. The furnishings are contemporary if a little funky and dated.

ALONG THE CANALS

✪ **Hotel Ambassade.** Herengracht 241, 1016 AZ Amsterdam. ☎ **020/626-2333.** Fax 020/624-5321. www.ambassade-hotel.nl. 52 units. A/C MINIBAR TV TEL. 325DFL ($171) double; from 425DFL ($224) suite. Rates include breakfast. AE, DC, MC, V. Tram: 13, 14, or 17.

The stylish Ambassade combines 10 canalside houses, the former homes of the wealthy merchant class who built the "Gentleman's Canal" in the 17th century. It has gained a following in literary and publishing circles but also draws businesspeople, families, and plenty of gays and lesbians. The hotel's attention to detail is evident from the rack of free umbrellas in the lobby for guests on rainy days to the elegant breakfast room and lounge overlooking the canal. The rooms are uniquely furnished, many decorated with Dutch and English antique furniture, vintage Dutch prints, painted ceiling beams, and luxurious long drapes. All have safes. The upper-level rooms are romantic, with A-frame ceilings and timber beams. You reach the rooms by following rather circuitous routes through the lobby (there's an elevator), but there are a few rooms offering extra privacy with their own street entrance—which gives you the opportunity to fantasize about being some wealthy merchant prince or princess. One street-level double has a spacious bedroom and separate living room with a couch, a French antique writing table, and two French-style chairs, as well as two TVs and two sinks in the bath (the only downside is it's a shade dark on rainy days).

Hotel Armada. Keizersgracht 713–715 (at Utrechtsestraat), 1017 DX Amsterdam. ☎ **020/623-2980.** Fax 020/623-5829. 27 units, 4 with bathrooms. TV TEL. 125–155DFL ($66–$82) double without bathroom, 135–165DFL ($71–$88) double with bathroom. Rates include breakfast. AE, MC, V. Tram: 4.

The Armada has got to have some good queer karma. After all, in a former life in the last century it was a house for wealthy unmarried women, and you can imagine what kind of mischief went on there. The mostly gay-run hotel now attracts lots of young travelers, including a fair amount of gays. With 25-plus years in business, the hotel is traditional and perhaps showing its age, but the staff is friendly and accommodating, and the location is in the heart of the canal rings, around the corner from some restaurant hot spots, and within blocks of Rembrandtplein and the flower market. Many rooms overlook the canal, and the ground-floor rooms have exceptionally high ceilings. The breakfast room is decorated in Dutch fashion with Oriental rugs on the tables, fringe lamps, and nautical-themed artwork playing out the hotel's name.

Hotel Estheréa. Singel 303–309, 1012 WJ Amsterdam. ☎ **800/223-9868** in the U.S., or 020/624-5146. Fax 020/623-9001. E-mail: estherea@xs4all.nl. 70 units. MINIBAR TV TEL. 230–385DFL ($121–$203) double. Rates include breakfast. AE, DC, EU, JCB, MC, V. Valet parking 60DFL ($32). Tram: 1, 2, or 5.

It's a family affair at the Estheréa, a hotel near Dam Square that was started by a war widow, run by her children, and recently passed down to her grandchildren. Over the last half century, the hotel has spread to six neighboring 17th-century canal houses. It has the personal feel of a family-run operation but is big enough so you have a little breathing room. The two sisters and brother running the show have a slightly hip sensibility and have begun slowly renovating the rooms to add a dash of panache. One of the new designs in the deluxe rooms is romantic, with wrought-iron canopy beds, an antiquish fold-down desk, and fleur de lis–patterned drapes; another design is more contemporary and subdued, and yet another is enlivened with van Gogh prints and bright Dutch-colored walls. The room sizes do vary, and you should avoid the smallish center rooms; the 25 rooms with canal views are obviously the most popular and costly. Breakfast is served in a charming paneled lounge.

Hotel New York. Herengracht 13 (at Brouwersgracht), 1015 BA Amsterdam. ☎ **020/624-3066.** Fax 020/620-3230. 20 units. TV TEL. 200–250DFL ($105–$132). Rates include breakfast. AE, DC, EU, MC, V. Limited indoor parking 35DFL ($18). Tram: 1, 2, 5, 13, or 17.

This well-known gay hotel in the Jordaan occupies three connected 17th-century houses, but you really wouldn't know it from the inside because everything has been thoroughly modernized. The New York's setting on a quiet street overlooking the Milk Maid's Bridge will definitely give you a feeling for Amsterdam. The rooms, all with hair dryers and safes, are clean and efficient and decorated with art prints and furniture that does the job but not much more. The sizes and layouts vary and include some with a second-floor sleeping loft. Four rooms face the canal side of the building, and the others look onto other buildings in back. While the clientele is predominantly gay men, some women do stay there.

✪ **Hotel Orlando.** Prinsengracht 1099 (at Amstel River), 1017 JH Amsterdam. ☎ **020/638-6915.** Fax 020/625-2123. 5 units. MINIBAR TV TEL. 145–225DFL ($76–$118) double. Rates include breakfast. AE, DC, MC, V. Tram: 4, 6, 7, or 10.

Wouldn't you love to have a couple of tasteful friends living in Amsterdam in an impeccably restored 17th-century canal house? Well, if you did, you'd be staying with them and wouldn't be reading this section. But since you do need a place to stay, consider the Orlando, a quiet spot popular with visiting opera singers and classical musicians and a mix of gay and straight tourists. This centrally located old family home is a spectacular value. The house was restored in 1994 by Paul Westerman and Paul Lodder, who live on the upper floors and are gracious hosts: They offer pointers on attractions (if you're nice, Westerman, an architect, may even give an ad-hoc architectural tour of the neighborhood), help make dinner reservations, and serve a full breakfast in a basement lounge (you can also opt to take the meal in your room). While you're down there, note the poster for the film *Orlando:* It's interesting that this hotel was named for the novel by Virginia Woolf and that the Quentin Hotel (above) was named for Quentin Crisp, who played Queen Elizabeth in the film of Woolf's book. Each room has its own character, but they're all furnished with elegant touches (however, take a pass on the basement room). The owners are enthusiastic furniture collectors and have installed antique Dutch and Belgian armoires, pieces by Philippe Starck, designer Italian lights, and even cabinets Westerman designed himself, as well as original contemporary artwork. The most spacious apartment (room no. 17), decorated with art deco pieces, has got to be one of the nicest places in Amsterdam, especially for the money: three sunny rooms with oak floors and a wonderful tree-framed view of the canal. Since the hotel is so small and popular, I advise you to book at least 2 months in advance, especially if you want a canalside room.

✪ **Hotel Pulitzer.** Prinsengracht 315–331, 1016 GZ Amsterdam. ☎ **800/325-3535** in the U.S. and Canada or 020/523-5235. Fax 020/627-6753. 224 units. AC MINIBAR TV TEL. 455–540DFL ($239–$284) double; 1,075DFL ($566) suite. AE, DC, JCB, MC, V. Valet parking 42.50DFL ($22). Tram: 13, 14, or 17.

The Pulitzer gives you the illusion of staying in one of Amsterdam's gabled canal houses while still enjoying the comforts of a traditional luxury hotel. One of Amsterdam's more unusual hotels, it's a collection of 24 17th-century houses along Prinsengracht and Keizersgracht that have been creatively combined to form a hotel around a pretty brick courtyard. The unusual configuration means few rooms are alike; some have lofted ceilings, others have views onto a garden. In 1998 the Pulitzer completed a major renovation that brightened up the lobby and upgraded about a third of the units into what are known as deluxe rooms, with dark woods, warm masculine colors, two-poster beds, and decorative Dutch tile in the baths. Other rooms are decorated with rustic woods and wicker. All have hair dryers, safes, and dataport connections. There's an intimate restaurant and cafe for dining. The Pulitzer also operates a vintage saloon boat known as *The Tourist* that takes guests on daily city tours (for an extra charge).

✪ **Hotel Seven Bridges.** Reguliersgracht 31, 1017 LK Amsterdam. ☎ **020/623-1329.** 11 units, 6 with bathroom. 140–160DFL ($74–$84) double without bathroom, 200–300DFL ($105–$158) double with bathroom. Rates include breakfast. AE, EU, MC, V. Tram: 16, 24, or 25.

The secret is out about the Seven Bridges, a luxurious inn nestled on a quiet stretch of canal where there are indeed seven identical bridges. This family home about 2 centuries old has been cared for by Pierre Keulers and Gunter Glaner, who offer wonderful touches like enormous vases of flowers (you've never seen such decadent displays of lilies) and a full breakfast in bed served every day on a different set of bone china. This couple of real antiques queens are charming and happy to tell you how they've spared no expense filling the house with beautiful objets, from imported Italian drapes to vintage furniture drawn from sales at French châteaux and Sotheby's auctions. The rooms are all unique—from a large high-ceilinged first-floor room to the sloped-roof attic rooms with shared baths, and many have handsome hardwood floors covered with Oriental rugs and timber-beam ceilings. Most rooms have TVs, and while you don't have your own phone, you're free to use the phone at the reception desk or borrow a mobile. From the hotel, it's easy to hit the art museums at Museumplein by day and hit the bars near Rembrandtplein at night.

ITC Hotel. Prinsengracht 1051 (at Utretchtsestraat), 1017 JE Amsterdam. ☎ **020/623-0230.** Fax 020/624-5846. www.itc-hotel.com. 15 units. TV TEL. 140–170DFL ($74–$89) double. Rates include breakfast. AE, DC, EU, JCB, MC, V. Tram: 4.

One of Amsterdam's oldest gay hotels, the ITC was known by the discreet name of the International Travel Club when it opened in 1971 (the owners claim the old hotel bar was the first in the city to show porn videos). In an 18th-century canal house, the simple ITC has a wonderful location on Prinsengracht and is around the corner from some of the city's best restaurants on Utrechtsestraat. The rooms are no great shakes (you may want to skip the basement rooms), but they're clean and have all the basics, including twinned double beds, dressers, sinks, and wall-mounted TVs. The staff is easygoing, and breakfast is served (daily 9am–noon) in the pleasant sitting room, with its little library of magazines and books.

✪ **Jordaan Canal House.** Egelantiersgracht 23, 1015 RC Amsterdam. ☎ **020/620-1545.** Fax 020/638-5056. http://ourworld.compuserve.com/homepages/hanspluygers. 5 units. TV TEL. 195–295DFL ($103–$155) double. Rates include breakfast. AE, MC, V. Tram: 10, 13, 14, 17, or 20.

You may have to walk past this B&B on a picturesque canal in the Jordaan a couple of times before you know you're in the right place. It looks deceptively like any of the other charming housefronts, which in typical Dutch fashion offer the world an open view into the homes. So look for a bunch of guys sitting around a breakfast table and you're there. In 1997, Hans Pluygers, a good-humored Brit of Dutch parentage (who updates his chatty Web site), and his Dutch husband opened this exclusively male gay guesthouse not far from the Anne Frankhuis and Homomonument. Carved out of a gabled three-story wool warehouse from 1629, it's an intimate dollhouse of a place, so be prepared to get to know the other guests, and tall guys will need to remember to duck when they're taking the stairs. All the rooms are completely idiosyncratic, but each is homey in its own way. Particularly wonderful is the roomy first-floor suite, the Garden Room, decorated with warm touches like an Oriental rug, a comfy sofa, an upright piano, and even a private garden. One of the upstairs rooms is pretty romantic, with a four-poster bed, a glass-block shower, and a sofa. Details give the place its charm—snapshots stuck to the kitchen fridge (always stocked with free munchies, beer, and other beverages), piles of magazines, well-stocked bookshelves (Flaubert, Jane Austen), fresh flowers, and rustic wooden furniture. Each morning you're treated to an ever-changing breakfast of hot and cold dishes round the kitchen table.

OTHER PLACES TO STAY GAY

The following hotels are small and the rooms basic, with minimal furnishings. They're the kind of places you use to store your stuff and sleep and not much else. Room rates generally run 100 to 195DFL ($53 to $103).

Dating from 1948, the city's oldest gay hotel, formerly the Unique, recently got friendly new owners, Theo and Jörg, and a new name, the **Golden Bear,** Kerkstraat 37, at Leidsestraat, 1017 GB Amsterdam (☎ **020/624-4785;** fax 020/627-0164; www.goldenbear.nl; Tram: 1, 2, or 5). Theo and Jörg are indeed bears (and members of a local social club, the Netherbears), but they're welcoming to all kinds of gays, big and small, men and women, furry and smooth. After buying the business in 1997, they began making improvements, brightening up the small lobby, where a complimentary breakfast is served, with sunny gold walls and fresh lilies. The 17 singles and doubles are simple, clean, and decent sized (if still a bit bland), but only a few have baths and TVs. They're all furnished with sinks, side tables, and a couple of chairs. The stairs are steep, Amsterdam style, but the desk staff is on its toes to assist you. The location near Leidseplein puts you close to the museums and the Reguliersdwarsstraat bars and the flower market. (Watch the address closely lest you em-bear-ass yourself mistaking the neighboring day-care center, which displays a teddy-bear flag, with the hotel.)

Another longtime gay hotel is the **Aero,** Kerkstraat 49, 1017 GB Amsterdam (☎ **020/622-7728;** Tram: 1, 2, or 5), which seems positively entombed in the early 1970s—from the groovy furniture to the feather-haired boys in the soft porn artwork in some of the 19 doubles (about half with baths). It's the kind of place you could imagine Jon Voight checking into if *Midnight Cowboy* had been set in Amsterdam. Even though the staff can be a bit curt, the place is smack in the middle of one of the city's gay areas, right off Leidsestraat.

Another option on the street is the **Westend Hotel,** Kerkstraat 42, 1017 GM Amsterdam (☎ **020/624-8074;** fax 020/622-9997; e-mail: westendhotel@wxs.nl; Tram: 1, 2, or 5). Things don't get much more basic than this five-room setup. You get four bare white walls, a ceiling, a bed, a TV, and a safe, and there's a shared bath down the hall. The kindly owner, Herman Sjouwerman, has run the place for 20 years and also owns the downstairs late-night bar, Cosmo.

With a history stretching back to the 1960s, the oldest hotel in Amsterdam catering to leathermen and a fairly international crowd is the **Anco,** Oudezijds Voorburgwal 55, 1012 EJ Amsterdam (☎ **020/624-1126;** fax 020/620-5275; Tram: 4, 9, 16, 20, 24, or 25). In a black-painted 17th-century canal house in the Red Light District, the hotel has 14 rooms (plus some dorm-style beds) that are simple, small, and clean (a few were a bit musty-smelling); some have canal views, beam ceilings, and blond-wood paneling and furnishings. All have TVs with 24-hour gay video and sinks (showers and phones are on the hall). Forget what you may have heard about the hotel bar, where a free continental breakfast is served—it's still rebounding from a reputation years ago when the hotel was known as "the sleaze pit" and few guests ever slept. However, Kees Duis, who took over in 1996 and lives next door, has eliminated the darkroom and is steadily upgrading the guest rooms.

Another place popular with the leather community is the **Stablemaster Hotel,** Warmoesstraat 23, 1012 JE Amsterdam (☎ **020/625-0148;** Tram: 4, 9, 16, 20, 24, or 25), a no-frills affair in a 17th-century house with eight rooms (shared baths) and two apartments (with baths) right on the busy leather street. The rooms have TVs, minibars, and coffeemakers. The place is best known for its bar, where there are nightly jack-off parties (hotel guests do have a separate entrance, up a perilously steep stairway). The owner, Bryan Derbyshire, who used to own a London bar called The Block, runs a leather shop across the street and was happy to host the American wrestling team during the Gay Games. Wouldn't you have?

3 Whet Your Appetite

Say what you will about Holland's colonial past, but without those global explorations Amsterdam's culinary offerings would be rather dull. The city's options mirror its diverse worldly population, and you'll find everything from ultrafine dining to a rainbow of ethnic storefront restaurants. The Dutch kitchen has long labored under the shadow of its French neighbors, but it boasts a few staples that are unique to the country. The Dutch score points for combining things that wouldn't occur to most cultures. After all, these are the people who insist on drizzling mayonnaise on their french fries.

The Dutch have a long fishing tradition, so you'll encounter a host of seafood, including the local delicacy of raw or pickled herring, eel, and mussels. They also have a notoriously sweet tooth, so be prepared to fatten up. Bread is a breakfast staple, often coated with butter that's then topped with chocolate sprinkles to make ***hagelslag.*** For lunch or snacking, the local equivalent of croissants is ***broodjes,*** butter rolls filled with your choice of deli meats and cheese. Another popular snack is ***kroketten*** (croquettes), fried meat- or cheese-filled balls garnished with a spicy mustard. Alongside their homegrown dishes, the Dutch proudly embrace Indonesian food, and the two cultures and cuisines have mingled for several hundred years. The signature dish is a ***rijsttafel*** (see "A True Amsterdam Dining Experience" below). Another common dish is ***saté*** (satay), grilled kebabs of varying types of meats accompanied by a delicious peanut sauce.

Of course, you want to drink like a Dutchman or Dutchwoman too, and there's nothing more traditional than a shot of **jenever,** a Dutch gin made from juniper berries that's served cold as an aperitif or as a chaser with beer.

When you want to hold hands across the table, you'll find a variety of restaurants with a heavy gay and lesbian following. Since they're neighbors with some of Amsterdam's trendiest gay bars, just about any of the restaurants on Reguliersdwarsstraat (including a few I haven't covered, like Santorino and the cleverly named Garlic Queen) draw gay diners galore. Sometimes it's hard to find a hetero in these places, but again, gays and lesbians are everywhere in Amsterdam, so there are few places where you won't feel at ease.

The Dutch don't eat out as much as Americans, but when they do they make plans. It's often difficult to get seated without reservations, especially on weekends, when some popular restaurants are booked weeks in advance. Dutch service is pleasant but often aloof. Of course, how you view it makes all the difference: You can get annoyed that your waitperson has seemingly abandoned you, or you can slow down and enjoy the meal knowing no one is going to rush you out.

Note: For the locations of the restaurants below, see the "Central Amsterdam Accommodations & Dining" map on pp. 516–517.

NEAR THE CENTER

Bird. Zeedijk 77. ☎ **020/420 62 89.** Main courses 12.50–22.50DFL ($7–$12). No credit cards. Daily 3–10pm. Tram: 4, 9, 16, 20, 24, or 25. THAI.

A tiny inauspicious storefront with half-a-dozen tables, a row of windowside stools, and a few decorative Thai tapestries, this spot in the Red Light District is named for its gay owner, who cooks up delicious Thai dishes on a small open grill. Select from a voluminous menu offering starters like spring rolls and coconut chicken soup to entrees like zesty curry dishes and Thai squid with basil. The place is always packed with hungry folks who know a good thing when they find it. To accommodate the crowds, they've opened across the street a new full-service restaurant of the same name (☎ **020/620-1442;** open daily 4–10:30pm) that accepts credit cards and serves liquor.

✪ **Getto.** Warmoesstraat 51. ☎ **020/421-5151.** Reservations recommended. Main courses 18.50–27.50DFL ($10–$14). AE, DC, MC, V. Wed–Sat 4pm–1am, Sun 1pm–midnight (kitchen open to 11pm). Tram: 4, 9, 14, 16, or 20. ECLECTIC.

This hip Red Light District cafe/bar, with a decor of kitchsy art and lamps and table toys, could be dropped into any American gay ghetto and easily fit in. One of the gayest restaurants in town, it's savvy to the leather district's tourist traffic, offering a menu written in English (no Dutch!) on a large chalkboard in the dining room and an up-front bar where American cocktail culture reigns with Cosmopolitans, Manhattans, and Margaritas. Expect to hear fun up-tempo music and a lot of English from the clubby crowd displaying plenty of piercings and chaps. The menu, which changes regularly, features house standards like the Getto BBQ Burger with homefries and salad, the Argos rib eye with roast garlic sauce, and a warm salad of thyme potatoes, smoky bacon, spring onions, and gorgonzola sauce. Other entrees may be items as varied as kangaroo fillet, Thai red curry, and sautéed red sea bass. Look for desserts like Cuban bread pudding and homemade apple strudel. A kind of community center, Getto presents several special events each week, including a women-only night (Tues 7pm–closing), drag-queen bingo (Thurs), and a popular Sunday brunch.

✪ **Hemelse Moder.** Oude Waal 9. ☎ **020/624-3203.** Reservations recommended. Main courses 45–57.50DFL ($24–$30). AE, DC, EC, MC, V. Tues–Sun 6–10pm. Tram: 4, 9, 16, or 20. ECLECTIC/DUTCH.

What began as a squat place more than a decade ago has grown into a fairly sophisticated restaurant popular with gays and straights alike. The group of owners (many gay) recently expanded again in this storefront space not far from Centraal Station. Named for a Dutch chocolate mousse dessert (it's on the menu), Hemelse Moder has a pleasant minimalist decor of weathered hardwood floors and blond-wood furnishings. Though it's a casual restaurant, you'll find a few special touches—from the meal starter of a bowl of Spanish olives and piping hot bread to the congenial servers who keep your wine chilled tableside. Choose from a handwritten menu of creative dishes like goat-cheese-filled tomato surrounded by grilled eggplant and oregano dressing; carpaccio of roast beef with a marinade of sesame oil, soy sauce, and ginger; grilled swordfish; and escalope of veal wrapped in Italian ham and sage. Go for the namesake dessert, a sorbet, or a summer pudding.

✪ **In De Waag.** Nieuwmarkt 4. ☎ **020/422-7772.** E-mail indewaag@xs4all.nl. Reservations recommended. Main courses 28–37DFL ($15–$19); fixed-price meals 47.50DFL ($25) for two courses, 55DFL ($29) for three courses. AE, DC, EU, MC, V. Daily 10am–1am. Metro: Nieuwmarkt. Tram: 4, 9, 14, 16, 20, 24, or 25. ECLECTIC.

A historic tower built in 1488 as a public weighing house serves as the unusual setting for this hip restaurant/cafe. The romantic dining room with high ceilings, long wooden tables, and brick floors is lit by more than 300 candles, giving it the feel of a minimalist medieval banquet hall. But the restaurant is very much ahead of the times with Internet-equipped computers available free in the cafe (with the purchase of a drink). The creative menu contains many appealing choices, from appetizers like timbale of sweet potatoes and spinach and potato truffle salad and hickory smoked ham to entrees like lamb with asparagus, monkfish with sorel/watercress sauce, and sausage with sage and watercress.

Kantjil & de Tijger. Spuistraat 291–293. ☎ **020/620-0994.** Main courses 25–50DFL ($13–$26). AE, DC, EU, MC, V. Daily 4:30–11pm. Tram: 1, 2, or 5. INDONESIAN.

"The Antelope and the Tiger" is a softly lit casual-chic restaurant with a stylized art deco decor and simple flavorful food. While hungry folk can go for the full-blown *rijsttafel,* the menu offers a mini-*rijsttafel* (25DFL/$13) with about 10 items and rice on one plate. It's a satisfying meal and a good introduction to the celebrated dish. Some of the other popular choices are any of the satés, especially the lamb; *gago gado,* a mix of steamed vegetables with peanut dressing; and ultra-spicy *pepesan oedang,* steamed prawns wrapped in banana leaves.

La Strada. Nieuwezijds Voorburgwal 93. ☎ **020/625-0276.** Reservations recommended weekends. Main courses 27.50–31.50DFL ($14–$17). AE, DC, MC, V. Sun, Tues–Thurs 4pm–midnight, Fri–Sat noon–1am. Tram: 1, 2, 5, or 20. CONTINENTAL/ASIAN.

A True Amsterdam Dining Experience

While you're here, you simply *must* have at least one Indonesian ***rijsttafel*** dinner, a traditional "rice table" banquet of as many as 20 succulent and spicy foods served in tiny bowls. Pick and choose from among the bowls and add your choice to the pile of rice on your plate. It's almost impossible to eat all the food set on your table, but give it a shot—it's delicious. For an abbreviated version served on one plate, try *nasi rames.* At lunch, the standard Indonesian fare is *nasi goreng* (fried rice with meat and vegetables) or *bami goreng* (fried noodles prepared in the same way).

In a 17th-century building that leans precipitously in classic Amsterdam fashion, La Strada has long been popular among gays and lesbians. The restaurant opens to the street, and the yellow-and-red interior boasts stained-glass tulip-shaped lights. The seasonal menu, reflecting touches of Asian, French, and Italian, features grilled entrecôte with basil-garlic sauce, pike perch in a spicy sauce, and guinea fowl stuffed with smoked salmon and seawood. For appetizers there might be spicy Thai chicken soup, snail-stuffed mushrooms, and traditional-style carpaccio. The desserts include apple pie, crêpes, and white chocolate mousse. There's occasional live entertainment, from a pianist to a DJ to some campy show.

Supper Club. Jonge Roelensteeg 21 (just off the Rokin near Dam Square). ☎ **020/638-0513.** Reservations recommended. Fixed-price menus 65–95DFL ($34–$50). AE, DC, MC, V. Sun–Thurs 8pm–1am, Fri–Sat to 3am. Tram: 4, 9, 14, 16, 20, 24, or 25. ECLECTIC.

Here's a restaurant where you can go to bed on the first date and not feel too cheap. In fact, you can have a three-way or even a group scene at the Supper Club. That's because at this offbeat restaurant you're invited to take off your shoes and dine sprawling on beds like guests at a Roman bacchanal. Plan on making an entire night of a dining experience at this arty restaurant, where the chef working in an open kitchen at the head of the room prepares a four- to six-course meal that's often full of surprises; there may even be some sort of poerformance, like live music or even a painter at a canvas. The menu, which is handwritten in a large book you pass around, spans the globe, with special attention to Asian influences. You might begin with a trio of oysters on seaweed and a mixed-herb salad with smoked eel, then follow with tuna with carmelized spinach and duck liver capped with elderflower sorbet and vanilla sauce. Part of the fun here is the sense of discovery.

't Sluisje. Torensteeg 1. ☎ **020/624-0813.** Reservations recommended. Main courses 24.50–37.50DFL ($13–$20). AE, DC, EU, JCB, MC, V. Sun and Wed–Thurs 6pm–1am, Fri–Sat to 3am. Tram: 1, 2, 5, 7, 13, or 20. CONTINENTAL.

This restaurant serves up steaks as the main course and drag queens as a side dish. Apparently hungry for drag, gay, and straight diners sit elbow to elbow at wooden tables in the cramped space, with an open kitchen on one side and a tiny stage with a mirrored disco ball in back where performers work their magic nightly from 8pm. The appetizers embrace everything from onion soup to egg rolls, the house specialty is sliced steak with onions and mushrooms, and main attractions are spareribs, tenderloin, fish and chips, and a variety of satays. For dessert, there are several decadent-sounding delights, like *la travestiata* (basically a banana sundae), naughtily advertised as the choice "for those with a big mouth." Two seatings are scheduled on Friday and Saturday, at 6 and 9pm.

NEAR LEIDSEPLEIN

Camp Cafe. Kerkstraat 45 (at Leidsestraat). ☎ **020/622-1506.** Main courses 19.50–26.50DFL ($10–$14). AE, EU, MC, V. Daily 11am–1am. Tram: 1, 2, or 5. CONTINENTAL.

Camp Cafe is a casual gay-owned/hetero-friendly place with Parisian cafe chairs and a ceiling of backlit Dutch Master reproductions from the Rijksmuseum. The changing menu is listed daily on a chalkboard but usually features a fish entree (perhaps grilled swordfish), chicken satay in curry sauce, lamb, and turkey breast with lobster sauce. The chef, who'll happily prepare a tasty vegetarian dish on request, is aiming to present quality food without outrageous prices. The lunch menu features flat-bread Italian sandwiches and salads.

Sama Sebo. P.C. Hoofstraat 27. ☎ **020/662-8146.** Reservations recommended. Main courses 30–60DFL ($16–$32). AE, DC, EU, MC, V. Mon–Sat noon–3pm and 6–10pm. Tram: 2, 5, or 20. INDONESIAN.

Cafe Culture

In the 1950s, the terrace at the American Hotel was a popular Sunday afternoon meeting place for gay Amsterdammers. But the most poopular gay hangout these days is the hotel's **Café Americain,** Leidsekade 97 (☎ **020/624-5322;** Tram: 1, 2, 5, 6, 7, 10, or 20; open daily 8:30am–1am), a lovely art deco space with gorgeous stained-glass windows, is still a fashionable spot. The Sunday jazz brunch (noon–3pm) is a big draw, with a full buffet, champagne, and coffee for 59.50DFL ($31).

But the most popular gay hangout now is the **Downtown Coffeeshop,** Reguliersdwarsstraat 31 (☎ **020/622-9958;** Tram: 1, 2, or 5; open daily 10am–7pm), which despite its name isn't a smoking coffee shop (the kind where grass and hash are the specials of the day). Supercruisy and supercozy, the tiny storefront makes it easy to get talking to others because you're practically sitting in your neighbor's lap, whether you're seated in the window or on the stepped-up gallery. The place buzzes all day with pumped-up tunes, a bouncy staff, and a menu of American and English breakfasts, sandwiches, quiches, salads, and soups, as well as shakes and excellent apple pie. On nice days, the scene spills onto the sidewalk for more ogling, no doubt inspired by the sculpture of a reclining nude hunk next to the cafe's wall.

Big and theatrical, the **Café de Jaren,** Nieuwe Doelenstraat 20 (☎ **020/625-5771;** Tram: 4, 9, 14, or 20; open daily 10am–1am), translates as "Years Cafe," and you could spend a lot of them here. The light-filled bilevel place with a sunny dockside terrace on the Amstel is a prime place to observe all manner of cafelike behavior: people skimming magazines from the well-stocked reading table, engaging in study-group political discussions, waiting for late companions, or perfecting their smoke rings. The menu includes couscous with lamb, veggie lasagna, quiche, soups, broodjes, pies, and coffees (the upstairs restaurant has an expanded menu).

Le Monde, Rembrandtplein 6 (☎ **020/626-9922;** Tram: 4, 9, 14, or 20; open daily 8am–11pm), is a gay-owned cafe, but its location in straightsville Rembrandtplein makes the crowd definitely mixed. Three meals daily are served, with a menu of burgers, broodjes, and salads (breakfast is served to 4pm).

For a seat above all the square's commotion, try **De Kroon Royal Café,** Rembrandtplein 17 (☎ **020/625-2011;** www.dekroon.nl; Tram: 4, 9, 14, or 20; open Sun–Thurs 10am–1am, Fri–Sat to 2am). This grand space offers prime balcony seats that attract everyone from punks in steel-toed boots to moms with babies for a spot of afternoon tea. By day, De Kroon is rather studiously sedate, but by night music livens it up like a nightclub. The airy room is fun and funky, with big chandeliers, colorful velvety Empire chairs, and sponge-painted walls. Most curious of all is the gorgeous old horseshoe-shaped bar backed with curio cases displaying

After a day exploring the Rijksmuseum or an afternoon shopping chi-chi P. C. Hoofstraat, a gut-filling *rijsttafel* is a well-earned treat. Celebrating over 30 years in Amsterdam, Sama Sebo is a popular choice, giving you the options of eating in the casual bar/lounge or the small dining room where the ceiling is decorated with brass pots and pans and where you'll be waited on by older Indonesian men in native jackets and ties. The restaurant's proximity to the ritzy shopping street does mean you may have to contend with a bit of a 'tudy tone from the waiters, but the food is some of the best Indonesian fare in town.

what appears to be leftovers from a defunct natural science museum: a collection of butterflies, beetles, grasshoppers, snakes, lizards, and a giant ram's head. The cafe serves all the usual coffee drinks, big cups of hot chocolate, and a full bar with a dozen-and-a-half beer selections, plus edibles like salads, broodjes, and cakes.

A third option on the square is **L'Opera Café,** Rembrandtplein 27–29 (☎ **020/620-4754;** Tram: 4, 9, 14, or 20; open Mon–Fri 10am–1am, Sat–Sun to 2am), a cafe at ground level, both literally and figuratively. The crowd in this beautiful art deco space, carved out of what was once an opera house (be sure to check out the second floor), is more sophisticated and staid, with a grand piano and Toulouse-Lautrec imagery. Besides coffee, cocktails, and desserts, the menu offers everything from morning croissants to crêpes, broodjes, soups, and salads for lunch and more substantial dinner dishes like lamb chops, cannelloni, and a fish special. There's also a rack of magazines for solo travelers or pairs just fed up with each other.

A welcome alternative to all the usual greasy late-night horrors is **Gary's Muffins,** Reguliersdwarsstraat 53 (☎ **020/420-2406;** Tram: 1, 2, or 5; open Sun–Thurs noon–3am, Fri–Sat to 4am), a nice way to lick the late-night munchies since this branch of the local gay-owned bread shop is open so insanely and wonderfully late. Choose from a wide assortment of muffins, bagels, cookies, cakes, and other baked goods. Take two: one to devour on the stumble home and another for whenever you wake up. There are three other locations, including one at Prinsengracht 454, just off Leidsestraat.

You may feel as if you've landed on a set of *Pee-Wee's Playhouse* when you step into the Technicolor **Backstage,** Utrechtsedwarsstraat 67 (☎ **020/622-3638;** Tram: 4, 6, 10, or 20; Mon–Sat 10am–5:30pm). Backstage draws a quirky crowd who comes for the food and drink but mostly for the eccentric 60-something owner, Gary Christmas, who easily fills up the space with his outgoing personality (he asks new customers, "What do you want? Besides my body!"). Originally from Boston, he and his brother (who sadly died 2 years ago) were a showbiz team who moved to Amsterdam 25 years ago and eventually set up this cafe, where they also sold their original knitwear designs. The small space is decorated with kitschy memorabilia (look in the unisex bathroom for nudie magazine pics and a giant penis blowup), and the menu lists items like "Hot and Heavy" espresso and the "Smile, Say Cheese" sandwich.

In one of the prettiest corners of the hip Jordaan, the **Café Reibach,** Brouwersgracht 139 (☎ **020/626-7708;** Tram: 3; Mon–Sat 10am–6pm, Sun 11am–6pm), is a quintessential neighborhood spot that draws an interesting arty mix. The cozy gay-owned cafe offers broodjes, cheeses and meats, salads, desserts, and a variety of yummy milkshakes.

't Swarte Schaep. Korte Leidesdwarstraat 24. ☎ **020/622-3021.** Reservations recommended. Main courses 40–55DFL ($22–$31). AE, DC, JCB, MC, V. Daily noon–11pm. Tram: 1, 2, 5, 6, 7, or 10. FRENCH.

On the second floor of a 17th-century taxhouse, the old-fashioned Black Sheep has the feel of a French country inn. Its romantic room contains 10 tables, a rustic beamed ceiling, and gold-plated chandeliers, and soft classical music plays. The menu is traditional French cuisine with equal parts fish and meat courses, including a combination dish of lobster and asparagus with chives, poached turbot with truffle butter sauce, veal sirloin with goose liver sauce, and stuffed quail prepared in a light nutmeg sauce. For dessert, there are decisions to make: a pear tarte with caramel ice cream, crème brûlée with orange liqueur, and exotic nougat ice cream with fruit sauce.

ALONG THE CANALS

Café Van Puffelen. Prinsengracht 375–377. ☎ **020/624-6270.** Reservations recommended. Main courses 26.50–34.50DFL ($14–$18); three-course fixed-price menu 49.50DFL ($26). AE, DC, EU, V (for credit card, tab must exceed 50DFL). Daily 6–11pm. Tram: 13, 14, 17, or 20. DUTCH/CONTINENTAL.

Big and bustling, the Van Puffelen is a casual restaurant that began as a brown pub, one of the traditional Dutch taverns. Its series of cozy unfolding rooms boasts high ceilings, large copper light fixtures, and dark-paneled walls adorned with original paintings and posters of local art shows and concerts. Diners, who are mostly locals attired from dressy to casual (some even arrive by boat), sit at old weathered tables. There's always one meat and one fish special, plus a fixed-price menu. For starters, there are selections like gazpacho, warm goat cheese with honey-lemon dressing, and terrine of smoked salmon with dill-pesto sauce. Main courses include salmon fillet with stroganoff sauce, vegetarian stir-fry, beef fillet with duck mousse and cherry sauce, and salad van Puffelen (tandoori chicken, seafood, terrine of smoked ostrich, and marinated mushrooms). The tempting desserts, like chocolate brownie with fudge sauce and lemon bavarois with strawberry mint sauce, are nicely presented. Often a live jazz combo performs. The bar area offers a menu of Spanish tapas. The owners run a second, smaller restaurant, **Proeverij** (☎ **020/421 1848**), a rather intimate alternative and slightly more upscale restaurant down the canal at Prinsengracht 274.

✪ **Christophe.** Leliegracht 46. ☎ **020/625-0807.** Reservations recommended. Main courses 55–70DFL ($29–$37); four-course prix-fixe menus 85–110DFL ($45–$58). AE, DC, EU, MC, V. Tues–Sat 6:30–10:30pm. Tram: 3. FRENCH/INTERNATIONAL.

One of the city's finest restaurants, Christophe is a sophisticated spot in the Jordaan. The handsome split-level room is done in muted earthy tones with a prominent painting of roses by a contemporary Dutch artist; banquette seating is in back, with tables up front. Chef/owner Jean Christophe is gay, but that's beside the point since his food is so outstanding; he offers a modern take on classic French cuisine with a nod to his Algerian upbringing. Specialties include starters like warm oysters with saffron and caviar, quail risotto with truffle oil, and white and green asparagus soup and main courses like beef sirloin and roasted duckling with olives and turnips. For dessert, you might be so lucky to try crème brûlée with honey and saffron, roasted fresh figs with thyme ice cream, or black chocolate fritters with a sauce of tea and mint. There's also an extensive wine list.

De Bolhoed. Prinsengracht 60–62 (at Tuinstraat). ☎ **020/626-1803.** Main courses 14.50–25.50DFL ($8–$13). No credit cards. Sun–Fri noon–10pm, Sat 11am–10pm. Tram: 13, 14, or 17. VEGETARIAN.

You can get your daily allowance of twigs and weeds at this canalside veggie cafe. Look for a basic menu of small dishes like Greek salad, quiche with mixed salad, and hummus with pita bread and main dishes like corn enchiladas with beans and feta cheese and veggie casserole. At lunch, there's a special pasta of the day and a featured soup. About 95% of this sunny two-room restaurant's produce is organic, and there's always a daily vegan special. The desserts include a variety of seasonal fruit pies and a delicious chocolate brownie with honey. De Bolhoed also serves fresh juices.

✪ **De Huyschaemer.** Utretchsestraat 137. ☎ **020/627-0575.** Main courses 20.50–25.50DFL ($11–$13). AE, DC, JCB, MC, V. Mon–Thurs 11am–1am, Fri to 3am, Sun 1pm–1am; kitchen to 11pm daily. Tram: 4, 6, 7, 10, or 20. ECLECTIC.

Gay and straight commingle at this funky neighborhood corner storefront. The straight owner has fashioned an arty industrial-chic backdrop in the high-ceilinged space, and the congenial gay/lesbian staff keeps things lively for the diners, who include lots of cute same-sex couples on dates. It's a homey place, true to its name ("The Living Room"), with hip tunes from a pile of CDs stacked behind the counter playing on the stereo (Abba to acid jazz). The menu is as global as the decor: Look for burritos, broodjes, and salads on the lunch menu, and dinners with appetizers like tasty soups and ceviche and main dishes like fettuccine with tuna and artichokes; salad with smoked turkey, goat cheese, and honey; and Mexican pancake stuffed with potatoes, beans, and cheese. There's the usual complement of coffees, wine, and beer, plus a full bar.

✪ **De Prinsenkelder.** Prinsengracht 438 (at Leidsestraat). ☎ **020/422-2777.** Reservations recommended. Main courses 17.50–36.50DFL ($9–$19). AE, DC, EU, JCB, MC, V. Daily 5:30–10:30pm. Tram: 1, 2, or 5. FRENCH/ITALIAN.

True to its billing, "The Prince's Cellar" occupies a garden-level dining room with a low-timbered ceiling in a 17th-century building—it's one of the best-known restaurants in Amsterdam, open over 30 years. A gay Irishman took over 2 years ago and has revamped the menu and the decor; the room feels more relaxed, yet some fresh energy is stirred up by the new chef in the kitchen and the eclectic mixed crowd at the tables. The engaging servers will help you sort through the menu. To start, you may consider the wild mushroom risotto with green asparagus and Parmesan, the tartlet of crispy fried prosciutto with smoked guinea fowl and avocado, or one of the soups. Then you can get serious with wing of ray with herb provençale, basil, and Parmesan; rack of Dutch lamb coated with herb and mustard crust; and vegetarian ravioli filled with wild spinach, goat cheese, and sweet bell pepper confit.

✪ **Dynasty.** Reguliersdwarsstraat 30 (at Leidsestraat). ☎ **020/626-8400.** Reservations recommended. Main courses 69.75–98DFL ($37–$52). AE, DC, MC, V. Wed–Mon 5:30–11pm. Closed Jan. Tram: 1, 2, or 5. ASIAN.

No, you won't find Alexis or Krystle or Blake here (not even gay Stephen). The name of this elegant Pan-Asian restaurant in the heart of the trendy gay street has a nice double meaning that's purely accidental but irresistible nonetheless. A place to celebrate a special occasion, Dynasty is one of the prettiest rooms in the city, with bamboo chairs, colorful geisha murals by Chinese artist Walasse Ting, and inverted Oriental parasols covering the ceiling. The menu is roughly half-Chinese and half-Thai but sprinkled with a few other Asian specialties, like Indian pappadams and Vietnamese spring rolls. There are several two-person specialty dinners with several courses: The Royal Table (98DFL/$54) includes fried goose liver and shark fin soup, lobster, salmon, spicy ox, and a dessert of tropical fruit sorbet; the Taste of Siam (69.75DFL/$39) includes tom yum soup, lemon chicken, shrimp curry, fish, Thai hot beef, crispy Thai noodles, and tropical fruit sorbet.

✪ **Kort Café.** Amstelveld 12. ☎ **020/626-1199.** Reservations recommended. Main courses 17.50–36.50DFL ($9–$19); 3-course daily menu 49.50DFL ($26). AE, DC, EU, MC, V. Sun–Thurs 11:30am–10pm, Fri–Sat to 11pm. Tram: 4, 6, 7, 10, or 20. FRENCH/ITALIAN.

Part of the oldest wooden church in Amsterdam has been converted into the Kort Café, a cozy restaurant along the Prinsengracht and a lovely brick terrace in the shadows of a small grove of linden trees—it's one of Amsterdam's best locations for brunch. Inside, the restaurant gathers its warmth from the tabletop candelight and funky original artwork on the walls. The Kort, managed by the president of Gay Business Amsterdam, has drawn an increasingly gay following but is popular with a diverse set of diners. The menu offers appealing dishes like fried pheasant fillet and strudel of salmon, tuna fillet, and ricotta with olives.

Malvesijn. Prinsengracht 598. ☎ **020/638-0899.** Main courses 19.50–31.50DFL ($10–$17). AE, DC, EU, JCB, MC, V. Daily 10am–midnight; kitchen to 10pm. Tram: 1, 2, 5, 16, 24, or 25. DUTCH.

At this good-humored restaurant you may find a Tammy Wynette soundtrack, an autographed *Ab Fab* T-shirt on the wall, and friendly owners Paul and Willy, partners of 2 decades. In a homey corner spot on the canal, Malvesijn has the feel of a small-town lunch counter and serves pretty traditional fare with the love and care of a home-cooked meal. The bilingual menu, decorated with images of Hollywood legends, features lots of meat, including half a dozen steaks, lamb, calf's liver, and duck breast. There are always soup and salads and two special entrees each night. Lunch is a variety of breads, quiches, and salads.

Pygmalion. Nieuwe Spiegelstraat 5. ☎ **020/420-7022.** Reservations recommended. Main courses 25.50–36.50DFL ($13–$19). AE, DC, MC, V. Mon 11am–3pm, Tues–Sat to 10pm. Tram: 1, 2, 5, 6, 7, or 10. SOUTH AFRICAN.

In the Spiegelhof Arcade, this cute storefront restaurant flying a gay pride flag is perfect for a lunch break on the city's antiques row. The gay owners (a Brit and a South African) have put together a menu with South African, French, and Malay influences. Look for exotic dishes like crocodile tail in pineapple barbecue sauce, *springbok* (a gazelle found in southern Africa) casserole, and ostrich fillet marinated in ginger and mint. For lunch, choose from half a dozen salads, some delicious soups (among them sweet pumpkin and tomato curry), quiches, and Dutch broodjes. There's also a variety of fresh juices. Desserts include a warm rhubarb pie and pancakes with warm caramel mango sauce. The service is friendly and warm.

Rose's Cantina. Reguliersdwarsstraat 38–40. ☎ **020/625-9797.** Main courses 24.50–42.50DFL ($13–$22). AE, DC, JCB, MC, V. Mon–Thurs 5pm–10:30pm, Fri–Sat to 11:30pm. Tram: 1, 2, 4, 5, 9, or 14. MEXICAN.

You know it's going to be a late night when you start out at this noisy Mexican restaurant, oh-so-conveniently located on one of Amsterdam's gay party streets. They start pouring the Margaritas the minute you walk in the door of this sprawling bilevel place, and that's a smart strategy when there's a long wait in the bar. The food is pretty good, with all the typical Mexican offerings (burritos, fajitas, quesadillas, tacos), with seafood making a strong showing, as in the flautas with catfish, crab, and shrimp and the prawn fajitas. The bar stocks Mexican beers and prepares a bunch of classic cocktails.

IN THE JORDAAN

Alcantara. Westerstraat 186. ☎ **020/420-3959.** Reservations recommended. Main courses 24.50–37.50DFL ($13–$20). No credit cards. Wed–Sun 6–11pm. Tram: 3. PORTUGUESE.

One of those places you wish were in your own neighborhood, this popular Portuguese restaurant/tapas bar operates out of a large skylit room that apparently was originally a small cinema house (though it's hard to see how). Save for candles along one wall, the decorations are few in a room of weathered wooden floors and a large open kitchen. Big groups of people gather for the wonderful food, which is lots of grilled fish and steak.

Café Vandenberg. Lindengracht 95. ☎ **020/622-2716.** Reservations recommended. Main courses 18.50–27DFL ($10–$14). No credit cards. Sun–Thurs 5–10pm, Fri–Sat 10am–10pm. Tram: 3. DUTCH.

This lesbian-owned bar/restaurant is an easygoing spot where you can linger all night (it's open until well past midnight after the kitchen closes). Steaks are the house specialty, but wanna-be vegetarians can feel a bit easier knowing all the meat is free range and vegetarian selections (like oven-baked lentils with fresh spinach) are offered. Other entrees are beefsteak with mushrooms, grilled leg of lamb, and pork satay with peanut sauce. There are always several fish items and soups and salads.

✪ **Toscanini.** Lindegracht 75. ☎ **020/623-2813.** Reservations recommended. Main courses 13.50–30DFL ($7–$16). AE, DC, MC, V. Daily 6–10:30pm. Tram: 3. ITALIAN.

Simple and chic, Toscanini has white tablecloths and hardwood floors and reverberates with the clattering from the open kitchen at the back. The menu changes every few months, but there are always two daily specials, plus a soup and a risotta of the day. Start with one of the fresh salads or an appetizer like asparagus with prosciutto and Parmesan; then choose from half a dozen homemade pastas (small or large portion) and consider entrees like stewed rabbit with baby artichokes, oven-roasted lamb chops, and grilled calf's T-bone steak with pepper-and-tomato sauce. The chef can also prepare a three- or four-course "surprise" menu (ask your waitperson). It's a very popular spot and often requires a week's notice to get a table on the weekend.

ELSEWHERE

Cafe-Restaurant Amsterdam. Watertorenplein 6. ☎ **020/682-2666.** Reservations recommended. Main courses 17.50–36.50DFL ($9–$19). AE, DC, EU, MC, V. Sun–Thurs 11am–1am, Fri–Sat 11:30am–2am; kitchen to 11:30pm nightly. Tram: 10. Bus: 18. FRENCH/DUTCH.

What's said to be the largest restaurant in the Netherlands, Cafe-Restaurant Amsterdam, west of Centraal Station, contrasts sharply with the typical tiny Dutch restaurants. The setting is dramatic: The brasserie-style place is housed in the converted engine room of a turn-of-the-century brick pumping station, with one of the giant diesel engines intact, and lighting is provided by floodlights taken from two soccer stadiums. It's definitely a good place for making an entrance, as the hostess leads you on a long walk to your table. The huge open space means plenty of good sightlines and a casually cool crowd seated on long tables where you'll no doubt notice a few eyes looking your way. The trio of women owners is forward-looking, and the staff are equipped with palm pilots to record orders; the menu already provides euro conversion rates. There's no music but the rumble of conversation. Though the place is trendy (I spied Dutch actor/director Jeroen Krabbé and his family), the food is as simple old-fashioned Dutch as you can get. It features everything from steaks and lamb chops to a selection of fish and seafood to a few pastas, plus salads and soups (like mussel), cheese croquettes with spicy mustard, and cold and hot broodjes with everything from tuna to smoked halibut to *haselslag* (chocolate sprinkles, a Dutch childhood treat). Also offered are a pool table, a reading table, and an outdoor terrace. And there's free parking after 7pm.

Le Garage. Ruysdaelstraat 54–56. ☎ **020/679 71 76.** Reservations recommended. Main courses 18.50–97.50DFL ($10–$54); fixed-price meals 59.50 ($33) for 2 courses, 75DFL ($39) for 3 courses. AE, DC, JCB, MC, V. Mon–Fri noon–2pm and 6pm–1am, Sat–Sun 6pm–1pm. Tram: 3, 5, or 12. FRENCH/INTERNATIONAL.

When he's not camping it up on his weekly TV cooking program, Holland's flamboyant celebrity chef Joop Braakhekke is overseeing his kitchen at Le Garage in south Amsterdam. The cosmopolitan restaurant's namesake has been thoroughly gutted to create this showy room ringed with bright-red banquettes and mirrors so the fashionable crowd can see who's here or admire themselves. You can select a two- or a three-course meal from the menu, which is peppered with dishy comments that hype the offerings, or order à la carte. Start with fish soup, one of the house specialties, or asparagus with vinaigrette and foie gras; then move on to a fish course of tuna with peppers from Madagascar or Dutch cod with jenever-based butter sauce or a meat course of wood-fired rib eye, Indian lamb curry stew, or French rotisserie chicken.

Meals end with a selection of cheeses and crème brûlée or banana in caramel with Szechuan pepper and coconut ice cream. The à la carte side dishes include Iranian caviar, smoked salmon, and terrine de foie gras. As a souvenir, you can pick up one of the chef's cookbooks on sale. Reservations can be a bit of a challenge on short notice.

4 Exploring Amsterdam

It's only natural to find yourself a bit disoriented by Amsterdam, and that's even without indulging in any of the funny-smelling stuff. First, the street names are impossibly long strings of vowels and consonants (try wrapping your mouth around Reguliersdwarsstraat, one of the gay streets), and you can be forgiven if you can only grasp about the first five or six letters before they all blur. Then there's the inner ring of gracefully curving canals lined with brown-brick canal houses that all start to look familiar, especially when you think you're walking one way on the canal and it turns out you're walking another. Call it getting lost or call it going with the flow, but there's so much to discover as the city unfolds along the way. It won't take long in Amsterdam before you find your favorite bend in the canal, gabled roof, or church tower.

Make the canals your friend: One of the best ways to find your orientation (you've already handled the one orientation that matters, so this should be cake) to this city, which has been shaped geographically and historically by its sophisticated network of man-made waterways, is to take a ✪ **canal tour.** The prerecorded commentary may not be the most scintillating, but you'll spend so much time walking over and along the canals that it only makes sense to reverse your perspective and see things from the water. You have the opportunity to study the canal houses, bridges, and streets with greater care and detail. Tours are typically about an hour and include the port, the inner ring of canals, and the Amstel River. Many of the operators dock their glass-topped boats (*rondvaart*) near Centraal Station. Tours are given during the day, and there are after-dark dinner cruises as well.

Canal Bus, Weteringschans 24 (☎ **020/623-9886**), runs a tour allowing you to get on and off all day at any of six stops. Day passes, sold on the boat, are 22DFL ($12). The same company also rents four-seat pedal boats for 10 to 12DFL ($5 to $6) per person and even offers discounts on museum admissions. One operator runs a **Museum Boat** (☎ **020/622-2181;** running daily 10am–5pm), which departs from Centraal Station and makes seven stops that put you at the doorsteps of most of the city's museums and cultural attractions. The ride includes substantial discounts on museum admission. A day ticket costs 25DFL ($13).

After you've worn out some shoe leather on the brick streets, you may want to try two-wheeling it like the natives, on either a guided or a self-tour. There are several agencies where you can rent a bike for a day or a week, and **MacBike,** Mr. Visserplein 2, near Waterlooplein (☎ **020/620-0985;** Tram: 4, 9, 14, or 20; open daily 9am–6pm), has developed a series of maps for day trips in Amsterdam, including a gay tour. The 2-hour gay trip, detailed in the map (1.50DFL/79¢), takes you on a self-guided tour that includes gay/lesbian historical sites, gay bars and clubs, and other background. Bikes are 12.50DFL ($7) per day, with discounts for multiple-day rentals.

You'll no doubt see groups of cyclists in yellow rainsmocks and yellow bikes tooling about town, and if you don't think you'd feel too ridiculous traveling in a similar manner, consider contacting **Yellow Bike Guided Tours,** Nieuwezyds Kolk (☎ **020/620-6940;** Tram: 1, 2, 5, 13, 17, or 20). The company offers both 3-hour city tours (29DFL/$15) that hit all the major sites and 6-hour excursions into the countryside north of Amsterdam (42.50DFL/$22), with stops at a windmill and wooden-shoe factory. Considerably less conspicuous are the day trips organized by **Mike's Bike Tours**

(☎ **020/622-7970**), which meet every day during summer at 11:30am and 4pm at the west entrance to the Rijksmuseum (in early spring and fall at 12:30pm only). The company offers tours of both the city (37DFL/$19) and the countryside (59DFL/$31).

THE HITS YOU SHOULDN'T MISS

There's a new Web site for Dutch museums: **www.hollandmuseums.nl.**

✪ **Rijksmuseum.** Stadhouderskade 42, halfway between Leidseplein and Weteringplantsoen. ☎ **020/673-2121.** E-mail info@rijksmuseum.nl. Admission 15DFL ($8). Daily 10am–5pm. Tram: 2, 5, 6, 7, 10, or 20.

The Rijksmuseum (State Museum), a stately 1885 neo-Gothic building by P. J. H. Cuypers, is the country's treasure trove of painting, sculpture, and decorative arts from the Middle Ages to the 19th century. If you want to learn anything about Dutch history and culture, there's no better way than spending a few hours strolling among the Rembrandts, Vermeers, Hals, Steens, and van Eycks of this internationally renowned collection. Talk about masters.

Rembrandt's *The Night Watch,* a soaring and dramatic canvas set at the end of the large Gallery of Honour, is the museum's star attraction. Painted in 1642 and correctly titled *The Shooting Company of Captain Frans Banning Cocq* and *Lieutenant Willem van Ruytenbuch,* this canvas was commissioned as a group portrait to hang in a guildhall. In the small galleries leading up to it are the work of Holland's great 17th-century painters, plus several of Rembrandt's most beautiful works, like *The Jewish Bride and Self-portrait as the Apostle Paul.* A few of these Golden Age paintings lend themselves to revisionist history and a little fun-making for the gay museumgoer, with plenty of divinely dressed militiamen in pantaloons, ribbons, bows, and lace collars; assorted strapping nude studs; and various cavorting half-clothed or naked nymphs in drag or engaged in other provocations. If you can manage to get to the museum early, head straight to gallery 221a, off to the left of *The Night Watch,* so you can have a few minutes of unobstructed time with four paintings by Jan Vermeer: *View of Houses in Delft, The Kitchen Maid, Woman Reading a Letter,* and *Love Letter.* The museum also has collections of Delft porcelain (look for a wonderful tile collection in the stairway off gallery 260), 17th-century dollhouses, and Asian art, plus a wing devoted to a survey of Dutch history. Theere are also handsome gardens, fountains, sculptures, and interesting architectural ruins.

In 1998, the Rijksmuseum introduced ARIA, an interactive multimedia system, so you can learn more about the collections. By touching a screen, you can access information about more than 1,200 artworks, including text, illustrations, video, and animation.

✪ **Anne Frank House (Anne Frankhuis).** Prinsengracht 263. ☎ **020/556-7100.** www.annefrank.nl. Admission 10DFL ($5). Daily Apr–Aug 9am–9pm, Sept–Mar to 7pm. Tram: 13, 14, or 17.

You know her story and have probably seen the Patty Duke–Anne Bancroft movie. But nothing brings *The Diary of Anne Frank* alive quite like walking through the cramped

Size Doesn't Matter: The World's Smallest Art Museum

The world's smallest art museum is now in Amsterdam, **Reflex,** Weteringschans 79A, opposite the Rijksmuseum (☎ **020/627-2832**). It's only 13.2 square meters large and displays 1,500 miniature paintings, graphics, sculptures, and pictures, including works by Picasso, Lichtenstein, Oldenburg, and Christo. Admission is free, and it's open Tuesday to Saturday 11am to 6pm.

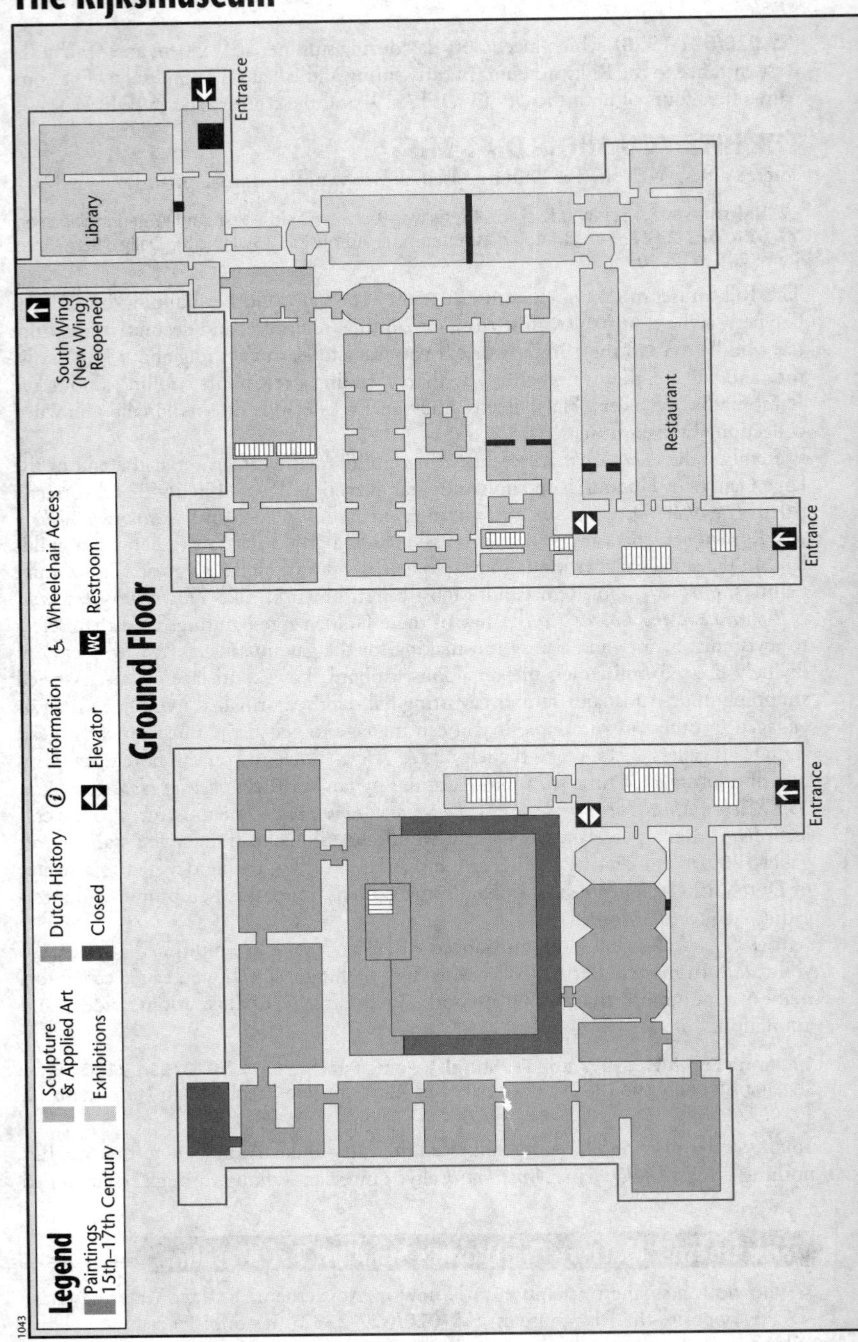
Ground Floor
Legend
Paintings 15th–17th Century
Sculpture & Applied Art
Exhibitions
Dutch History
Closed
Information
Elevator
Wheelchair Access
WC Restroom
Entrance
Library
South Wing (New Wing) Reopened
Restaurant
Entrance
Entrance
1043

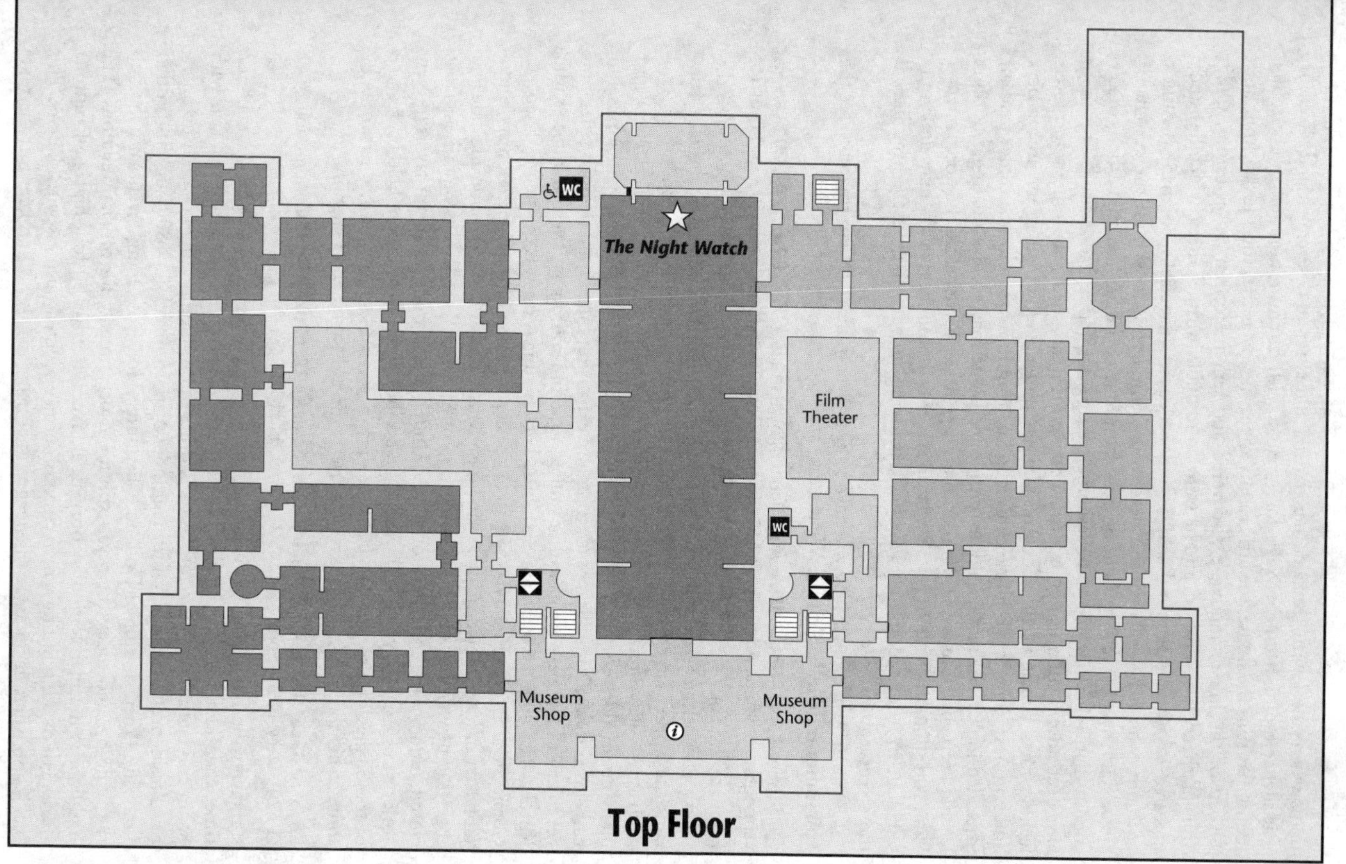

WC
The Night Watch
Film
Theater
WC
Museum
Shop
Museum
Shop
Top Floor

rooms where the Jewish teenager, her parents and sister, and several friends lived in near-silence hiding from the Nazis for 2 years. With careful restoration by the foundation that runs the house, the attic rooms appear nearly as they did the day Anne and the rest of the inhabitants were discovered and sent to concentration camps. Only Anne's father, Otto, survived, and he went on to publish Anne's diary, which has since appeared in 51 languages and sold 13 million copies. Especially poignant is Anne's bedroom, where the walls are still decorated (behind glass now) with the cutouts of movie stars she adored. Was Anne on our team? One of the most recent editions of her famous diaries has restored some lesbonic passages her father had excised. They may have been adolescent musings, but Anne does write unabashedly about her unexplored feelings for a female friend. The museum has undertaken an expansion into a new building next door that'll house exhibit space, a multimedia resource center, and an expanded lobby. The perpetual line outside the house may be intimidating, but don't let that keep you from a visit. If you can manage to get there before the doors open at 9am, you should be able to get a jump on the crowds and, best of all, may find yourself alone in Anne's room long enough to contemplate what life must've been like all those years in this hideaway.

Of course, while you're here you have to head over to nearby Westermarkt to see the **Homomonument,** behind the Westerkerk (see "Gay Amsterdam" below).

✪ **Vincent van Gogh Museum.** Paulus Potterstraat 7. ☎ **020/570-5200.** www.vangoghmuseum.nl. Admission 12.50DFL ($7). Daily 10am–5pm. Tram: 2, 3, 5, 12, or 16.

Here are the potato eaters, the golden sunflowers and wheatfields, the bedroom, the earless self-portraits—from the darkest to the most vivid, this impressive museum contains the world's largest collection of works by Vincent van Gogh (pronounce it correctly now—it's *van Khokh*). Included are more than 200 paintings, 500 drawings, and many personal letters, all of which were inherited by van Gogh's family. The museum had closed for a $20-million renovation and expansion but should be open when you get to town. The new wing, with a vaulted titanium roof by Japanese architect Kisho Kurokawa, will house temporary exhibits. The opening show was devoted to Theo van Gogh, the artist's brother, who was an art dealer, a patron of the impressionists, and a supporter of his troubled sib. The van Gogh Museum also has a gift shop and cafe and is getting new grounds with the renovation of Museumplein. While the museum was closed, much of the collection toured the United States, but even if you saw it in New York or Los Angeles, you'll still want to take a look since the museum held back some of the biggies. It also has 400 Japanese drawings van Gogh so loved, plus works by some of his contemporaries, like Toulouse-Lautrec, Monet, and Gauguin.

Royal Palace (Koninklijk Paleis). Dam Square. ☎ **020/620-4060.** Admission 7DFL ($3.70). Daily 12:30–5pm. Tram: 1, 2, 4, 5, 9, 11, 13, 17, or 20.

Originally the Town Hall, this imposing building was begun in 1648 during a euphoric time when Holland was enjoying a well-deserved breather from its 80-year war with Spain and had reached its zenith as the world's undisputed trading power. It became a royal residence when the country fell under Napoléon's rule in 1808, and his brother Louis lived there as king of Holland. The Dutch House of Orange eventually took up the building, and today the royals still use it occasionally for official functions. The highlight is the marble-floored Burgerzaal, a vast nearly 100-foot-high hall running the length of the building where citizens once conducted business with the city. This hall is also where gay men often engaged in cruising rituals . . . and later met their fate in court for sodomy.

Stock Exchange (Beurs van Berlage). Damrak 243. ☎ **020/530-4113.** E-mail info@bvb.nl. Admission 6DFL ($3.20). Tues–Sun 10am–4pm. Tram: 4, 9, 14, 16, 20, 24, or 25.

A New Museumplein

The Rijksmuseum, Vincent van Gogh Museum, and Stedelijk Museum of Modern Art are conveniently clustered around **Museumplein,** the big open square just south of the old city. Museumplein has just undergone a total transformation, and now motorized traffic through the square is abolished.

Most of the rebuilt square consists of open green areas bordered by avenues of linden trees and gardens that can be used for major outdoor events. Walkways and bicycle paths pass through. At the north end are sports and play areas and a long pond that serves as an ice-skating rink in winter.

You don't have to get stuck in the 17th century in Amsterdam. One of the most important Dutch buildings of the 20th century is this graceful clean-lined brick one built as the city's stock exchange (*beurs*) in 1903 by influential Dutch architect Hendrik Petrus Berlage. While Frank Lloyd Wright was doing his thing in the United States, Berlage, considered the father of modern Dutch architecture, was making his name as one of the precursors of the Amsterdam School. This splendid building, containing some wonderful murals, is now a venue for concerts and special exhibits. A permanent exhibit chronicles the building's history, and you'll find a panoramic city view from the tower.

Rembrandt House Museum (Museum het Rembrandthuis). Jodenbreestraat 4–6. ☎ **020/624-9486.** www.rembrandthuis.nl. Admission $7.50DFL ($3.95). Mon–Sat 10am–5pm, Sun 1–5pm. Tram: 9, 14, or 20.

The house where Holland's Golden Age golden boy lived and worked is now a museum to his life and work. Taking up residence here in 1639 at the height of his fame, Rembrandt called it home for the next 20 years. During that time, he created most of his most famous masterpieces, including *The Night Watch,* in the first-floor studio. The museum contains 250 Rembrandt etchings and drawings, including many self-portraits, as well as paintings by many of his predecessors and pupils.

Stedelijk Museum of Modern Art. Paulus Potterstraat 13. ☎ **020/573-2911.** www.stedelijk.nl. Admission 9DFL ($4.75). Apr–Sept daily 11am–6pm (Oct–March to 5pm). Tram: 2, 3, 5, 12, 16, or 20.

After hours spent gazing on still lifes of flowers, naval armadas, and crows over wheatfields, you should find the Museum of Modern Art a refreshing change. In this neo-Renaissance building from the late 19th century, down the street from the van Gogh Museum, are cavernous skylit galleries suited to the large contemporary works displayed. Curators explore the 20th century through paintings and drawings, graphic art, photography, video, and industrial design, and the museum's permanent collections includes works by early moderns like Mondrian, Malevich, and Chagall, as well as the developments of postwar artists like Karel Appel and Willem de Kooning. There's also a restaurant and gift shop. Sundays seem to attract an especially queer crowd.

✪ **Amsterdam Historical Museum (Amsterdam Historisch Museum).** Kalverstraat 92/ Nieuwezijds Voorburgwal 359. ☎ **020/523 18 22.** Admission 9DFL ($4.75). Mon–Fri 10am–5pm, Sat–Sun 11am–5pm. Tram: 1, 2, 4, 5, 9, 14, 16, 20, 24, or 25.

Amsterdam itself is a kind of open-air museum spanning the centuries, and there's plenty to absorb about its past with careful attention as you wander among the canals and narrow medieval lanes. But when your curiosity is nagging at you, an afternoon at the Historical Museum will greatly broaden your understanding of what you see around town. The museum, housed in a 17th-century orphanage, traces the city's history from its beginnings as a fishing village to the wacky, weird place it is today.

Central Amsterdam Attractions

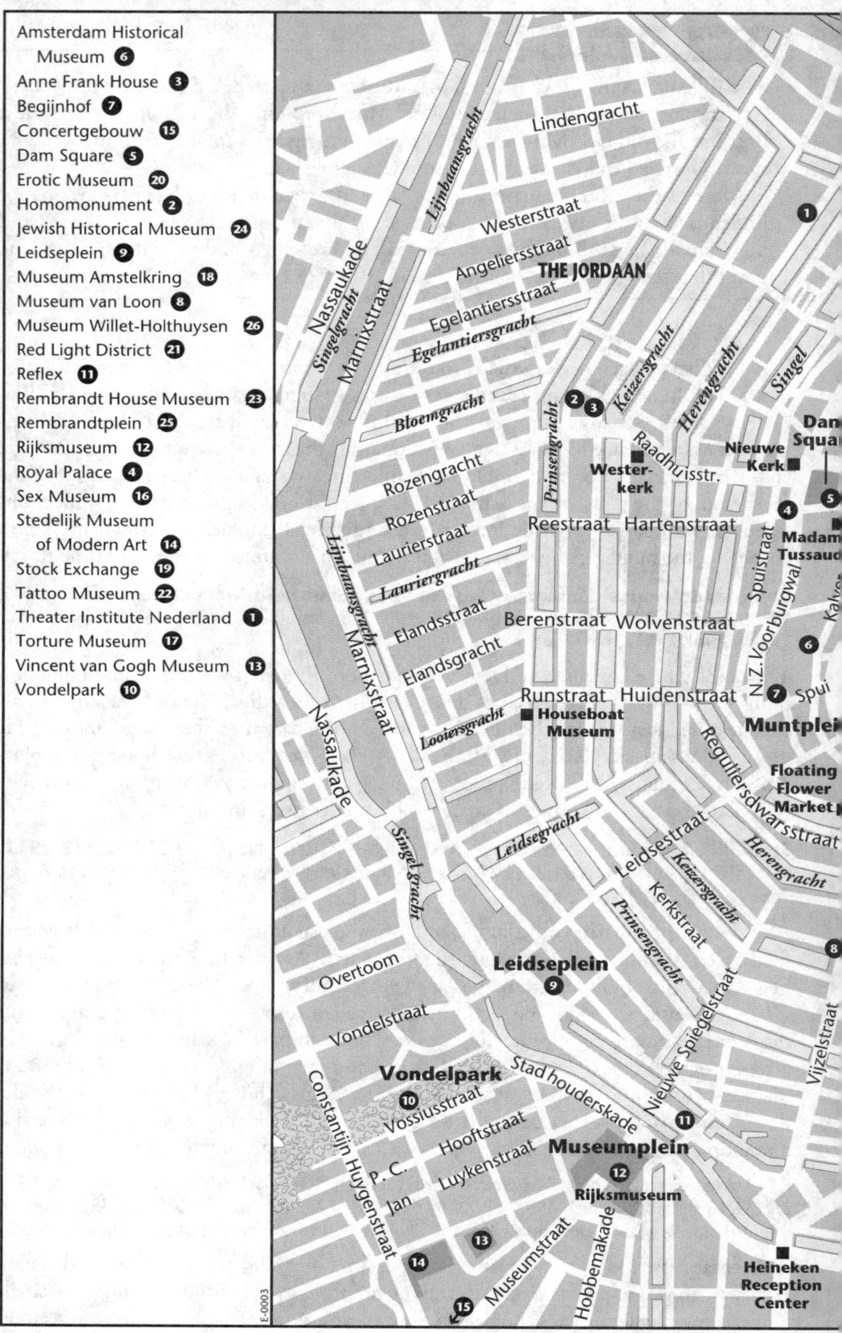

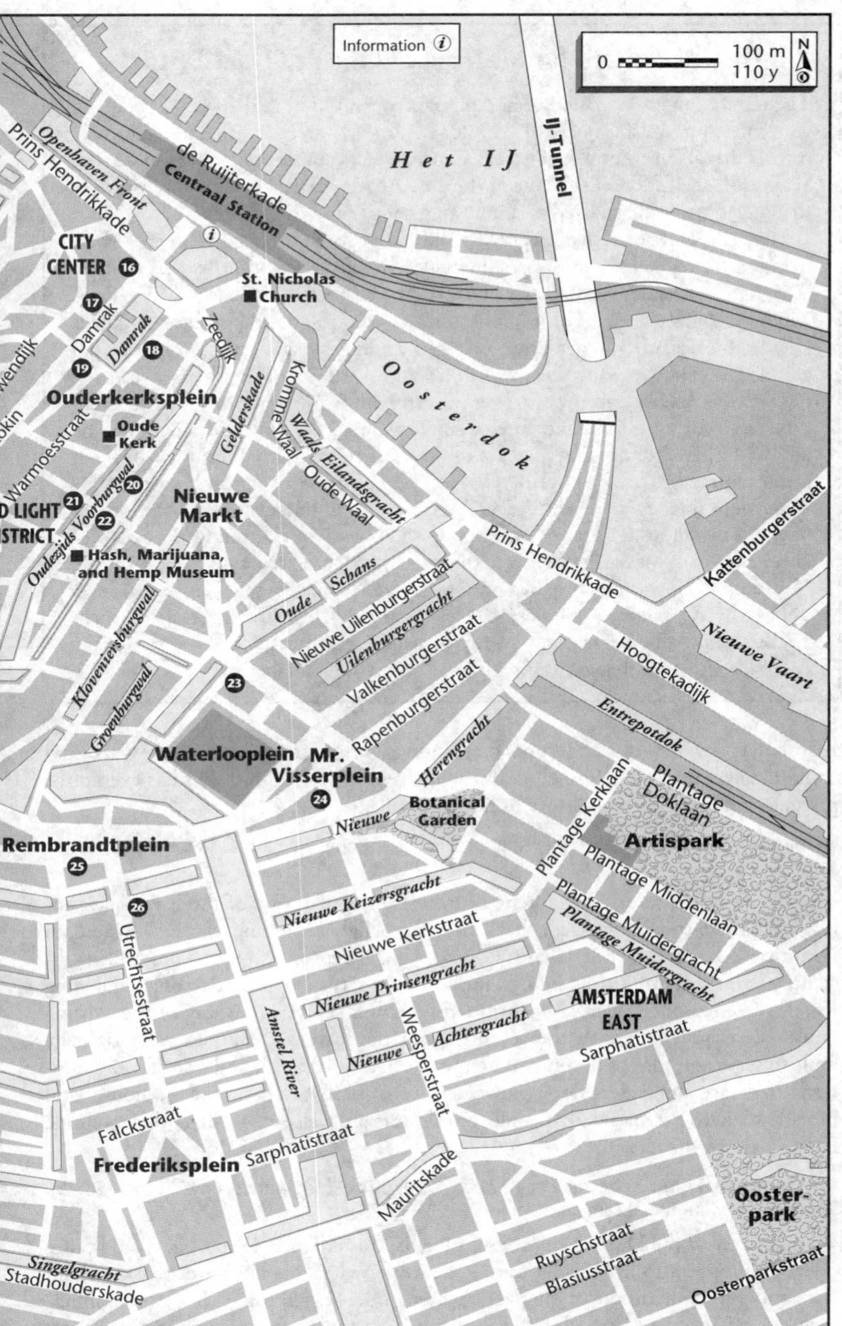

Information
100 m
110 y
N
Het IJ
IJ-Tunnel
de Ruijterkade
Centraal Station
Openhaven Front
Prins Hendrikkade
CITY CENTER
16
17
18
19
St. Nicholas Church
Damrak
Zeedijk
Ouderkerksplein
Oude Kerk
Warmoesstraat
Gelderskade
Kromme Waal
Waals Eilandsgracht
Oude Waal
Oosterdok
Nieuwe Markt
20
21
22
Oudezijds Voorburgwal
Hash, Marijuana, and Hemp Museum
Oude Schans
Nieuwe Uilenburgerstraat
Uilenburgergracht
Valkenburgerstraat
Rapenburgerstraat
Prins Hendrikkade
Kattenburgerstraat
Nieuwe Vaart
Hoogtekadijk
Entrepotdok
Kloveniersburgwal
Groenburgwal
23
Waterlooplein
Mr. Visserplein
24
Herengracht
Botanical Garden
Nieuwe
Plantage Kerklaan
Plantage Doklaan
Artispark
Plantage Middenlaan
Plantage Muidergracht
Rembrandtplein
25
26
Nieuwe Keizersgracht
Nieuwe Kerkstraat
Nieuwe Prinsengracht
Utrechtsestraat
Amstel River
Weesperstraat
Nieuwe Achtergracht
AMSTERDAM EAST
Sarphatistraat
Falckstraat
Frederiksplein
Sarphatistraat
Mauritskade
Ooster-park
Ruyschstraat
Blasiusstraat
Oosterparkstraat
Singelgracht
Stadhouderskade

They Work Hard for the Money in the Red Light District

The reputation of this 'hood of ill repute, between Oude Zijds Voorburgwal and Kloveniersburgwal (Tram: 4, 9, 16, 20, 24, or 25), precedes it. An area of narrow medieval streets and canals near Centraal Station and east of the Rokin, the **Walletjes** (the little walls) is one of the oldest parts of Amsterdam, and for more than a century it has hosted an interesting social experiment.

Here the glow of red neon serves notice that some of Amsterdam's hardest-working entrepreneurs are open (literally) for business. Scantily clad women advertise their wares on the street in little rented rooms behind glass windows, while their horn-dog customers look for one who catches their fancy. Lesbians may find it titillating to get a free look at these lingerie-clad gals, some of whom are absolutely gorgeous, if they don't mind rubbing shoulders with the testosterone-fueled frat guys trolling the streets. (Two or more women together probably won't be bothered, but a single woman walking around might be harassed.) Note that taking pictures of the women is strictly forbidden—one of the strapping "guards" will gladly dispose of your camera for you if you try.

Beyond the sex for sale, the area is highly commercial (with sex shows, naughty toy shops, and greasy fast food) and boasts an all-around sleazy ambience. Gay bars have always been tolerated here; two remained open during World War II because the area was off-limits to occupying German troops. Today the city's leather bars are clustered on the fringes of the district. Pickpockets know the area attracts plenty of wide-eyed tourists, so be wary on the dark side streets and always keep close tabs on your valuables.

Featured is a wonderful collection of paintings, prints, maps, porcelain, glass, and archaeological finds. The museum also stages temporary exhibits and has even done presentations on the city's history of homosexuality.

✪ **Begijnhof.** Gedempte Begijnensloot at Spui. No phone. Free admission. Daily to sunset. Tram: 1, 2, or 5.

There's not much to do or see here, but the Begijnhof is one of those you-have-to-know-it's-there-to-find-it places that's always a delight. Entering via the Amsterdam Historical Museum's Civic Guard Gallery, you're deposited into a peaceful 14th-century courtyard of little old houses, including the city's oldest (one of only remaining wooden-fronted ones) at no. 34, surrounding a well-kept lawn. Many of the existing houses were built later over the centuries, but the medieval complex was originally built to serve an order of devout women who cared for the sick and poor for the nunnery that once stood next door (now the museum). Today many of the houses still provide shelter to poor elderly people, but visitors are welcome to share their solitude in this oasis in the city.

Museum van Loon. Keizersgracht 672. ☎ **020/624-5255.** Admission 7.50DFL ($3.95). Sun 1–5pm, Mon–Tues 11am–5pm. Tram: 16, 24, or 25.

Wondering how the Dutch kept house? One of Amsterdam's elegant old canal houses offers a glimpse into life during the Golden Age, when the city's wealthy merchant class put up their mansions along the Grachtengordel (Canal Ring). The van Loon residence is one of two identical houses built in 1672 that today contains period rooms with furnishings, sculpture, and art, as well as more than 50 portraits of the colorful families who resided there over the centuries. There's also a formal rose garden looking onto a classical 18th-century coach house.

What Matters Isn't the Length but the Width

You can see the **narrowest house** in Amsterdam (and maybe even the world) at **Singel 7.** It's just 1 meter wide—barely wider than the front door. However, it's a cheat: Only the front facade is really so narrow; behind that the house broadens out to more normal proportions.

The genuine narrowest house is at **Oude Hoogstraat 22,** between Dam Square and Nieuwmarkt. With a typical Amsterdam bell gable, it's 2.02 meters wide and 6 meters deep. A close rival, 2.44 meters wide, is nearby at **Kloveniersburgwal 26;** this is the cornice-gabled **Kleine Trippenhuis,** also known as Mr. Trip's Coachman's House. It faces the elegant Trippenhuis at no. 29, which at 22 meters is the widest old Amsterdam house and was built in 1660 for the wealthy merchant Trip brothers. The story goes that the coachman exclaimed one day, "Oh, if only I could be so lucky as to have a house as wide as my master's door." His master overheard this, and the coachman's wish was granted.

Museum Willet-Holthuysen. Herengracht 605. ☎ **020/523-1822.** Admission 5DFL ($2.65). Mon–Fri 10am–5pm, Sat–Sun 11am–5pm. Tram: 4, 9, 14, or 20.

Dating to 1687 and undergoing several renovations until the family gave the museum to the city in the late 19th century, the Willet-Holthuysen house has rooms representing several time periods, from 18th-century French to Victorian. There are also displays of French earthenware, Chinese vases, a to-die-for silver collection, and a 275-piece porcelain dinner service. An interesting historical film on the ground floor offers some context.

✪ **Jewish Historical Museum (Joods Historisch Museum).** Jonas Daniël Meijerplein 2–4. ☎ **020/626-9945.** www.jhm.nl. Admission 8DFL ($4.20). Daily 11am–5pm. Tram: 9, 14, or 20.

Amsterdam has been a center of Jewish life for 4 centuries, but sadly much of the community was devastated by the Holocaust. Today the city's former Jewish quarter is home to a museum preserving and protecting the legacy of a community that long played an active role in the country's livelihood. The museum complex, which opened in 1987, has been uniquely formed by joining with steel and glass four former synagogues from the 17th and 18th centuries. The extensive collection contains antique objects, paintings, photographs, and other artwork, including articles used in Jewish ceremonies in home and synagogues. The museum also hosts temporary exhibits that explore themes related to the Jewish experience in the Netherlands and worldwide. The only synagogue that remains active in the neighborhood is the nearby **Portuguese Synagogue,** which is worth a visit after spending time here.

Museum Amstelkring ("Our Lord in the Attic"). Oudezijds Voorburgwal 40. ☎ **020/624-6604.** Admission 7.50DFL ($3.25). Mon–Sat 10am–5pm, Sun 1–5pm. Closed Jan 1.

Though Amsterdam has been known as a tolerant city for centuries, just after the Protestant Reformation Roman Catholics fell into disfavor. Forced to worship in secret, they devised ingenious ways of gathering for services. In an ordinary-looking 17th-century canal house in the middle of the Red Light District is the most amazing of these clandestine churches, known as "Our Lord in the Attic." The three houses composing this museum were built in the 1660s by a wealthy Catholic merchant specifically to house a church. Today they're furnished much as they would've been in the mid–18th century. Nothing prepares you for the minicathedral you come on when you climb the last flight of stairs into the attic. A large baroque altar, religious statuary, pews to seat 150, an 18th-century organ, and an upper gallery complete this miniature church.

Theater Institute Nederland. Herengracht 168. ☎ **020/551-3300.** Admission 7.50DFL ($3.25). Tues–Fri 11am–5pm, Sat–Sun 1–5pm. Tram: 13, 14, or 17.

Splendid marble corridors, wall and ceiling frescoes, and ornate plasterwork make this patrician canal house one of the city's most beautiful. Richly ornamented roof gables of different styles were a sign of wealth during Amsterdam's Golden Age, and crowning this building is the oldest extant example of an ornate neck gable. Though it's worth visiting this museum simply to see how the wealthy once lived, there are also many interesting exhibits pertaining to theater in the Netherlands over the centuries. Be sure to press the buttons of the miniature stage sets: You'll see how waves once rolled across the stage and other effects. Perfect for drama queens!

Sex Museum. Damrak 18. ☎ **020/622-8376.** Admission 4.50DFL ($2.40). Mon–Sun 10am–11:30pm. Tram: 4, 9, 16, 20, 24, or 25.

Sex is so out in the open here, you won't be surprised to find not one but two museums dedicated to carnal urges and desires: the Sex Museum and the Erotic Museum (below). These aren't serious research institutions by any stretch of the imagination—they're much closer to carnival sideshows than anything. But since sex may be so much on your mind in Amsterdam (and everywhere else), you may find them an amusing diversion. The Sex Museum, centrally located on a strip of tourist-oriented shops and restaurants on the Damrak, explores erotic art from the Greek and Roman times to the present through paintings, sculpture, photography, and film. Some of the more interesting items are carved wooden phalluses and other fertility symbols from South America, India, and Indonesia as well as early nude and porn photography, including images of 1920s bondage, women in compromising positions, and a bunch of fun-loving guys on a camping trip. The museum also has campy dioramas, including Marilyn Monroe on the subway grate, a trench-coated flasher, and a sailor in the Red Light District doing something . . . interesting. There's some mention of homosexuality, including an 18th-century Dutch book containing a list of men accused of sodomy and sentenced to death, plus the various execution methods.

Erotic Museum. Oudezijds Achterburgwal 54. ☎ **020/624-7303.** Admission 5DFL ($2.65). Sun–Thurs 11am–1am, Fri–Sat 11am–2am. Tram: 1, 2, 4, 5, 9, 16, 20, 24, or 25.

The Erotic Museum covers much of the same territory as the Sex Museum (above) and is worth wandering into only if you happen to be checking out the Red Light District and feel the need to look at some knee-high carved phalluses. The five-floor "museum" is nothing more than a tourist distraction, with no attempts to offer any explanations. The collection is largely hetero (the only nod to homos are some woman/woman scenes) and contains erotic prints, drawings (some by John Lennon), and photos (check out the bondage shots of Betty Page), as well as some cheesy lifesize scenes of a Red Light District alley and a bondage room.

GAY AMSTERDAM

Nothing epitomizes the openness of Amsterdam than the ✪ **Homomonument,** the world's first memorial to gays and lesbians. It occupies a highly visible site behind the Westerkerk, on the banks of Keizersgracht. Designed by Karin Daan, the monument is made of three triangles of pink granite spread over different levels that together form one larger triangle, a reference to the symbol homos were forced to wear by the Nazis. Each of the sides represents the past, present, and future of the international gay movement. One triangle, pointing toward the Anne Frankhuis as a reminder of gay persecution, is engraved with the words of gay poet Jacob Israel de Haan: "Such an immense longing for friendship." A second triangle, pointing toward the Amsterdam office of COC, the country's pioneering gay-rights organization, calls attention to the future. The triangle's third corner juts out over the water and embodies the present.

A Little T 'n' T: For Those into Tattoos or Torture

The president and curator of the **Tattoo Museum,** Oudezijds Achterburgwal 130, in the Red Light District (☎ **020/625-1565;** Tram: 4, 9, 16, 20, 24, 25; open summer daily noon–6pm, other periods closed Mon; admission 5DFL/$2,65), is Henk Schiffmacher (aka Henky Penky), a tattoo enthusiast of long standing; he has his own suite of personal decorations peeking out of bare arms to prove it. His museum chronicles the history and practice of tattooing internationally and in its modern Western variations, with exhibits from all over the world he has gathered himself. It includes a library and an archive for researchers and features regular demonstrations of the art.

You enter the **Torture Museum,** Damrak 20–22 (☎ **020/639-2027;** Tram: 4, 9, 16, 20, 24, or 25; open daily 10am–11pm; admission 7.50DFL/$3.95), through an appropriately long and gloomy tunnel and emerge with a new appreciation of why the framers of the U.S. Constitution outlawed cruel and unusual punishment. Yet one suspects the motives of the Torture Museum—and its visitors?—aren't purely educational. There's a horrible fascination about devices like the Inquisition chair, the guillotine, and assorted grotesque implements of torture, punishment, and "redemption" favored by the civil and ecclesiastic authorities in times not so far past.

Since it was dedicated in 1987, the monument has become a rallying point for gays and lesbians on many holidays and special occasions, such as Memorial Day and Liberation Day (May 4 and 5), Queen's Day, and the annual gay Canal Parade, which originates here. You'll often find flowers piled at the water's edge: In past years, these were usually brought to remember friends and family who had died of AIDS, but now they're often left by gay wedding celebrants floating down the canal. The bridge over the canal was recently renamed in honor of Nico Engelschman, one of the founders of COC. The Homomonument is a short walk from Dam Square and also reached by tram lines 13, 14, and 17.

The monument is not the only site of gay significance in Amsterdam. An active way to learn more about the city's gay history is to get a firsthand look on a bicycling tour. The bike-rental agency **MacBike** (see above) provides a map detailing a self-guided tour of gay and lesbian sites of yesterday and today, including the city. The route takes about 2 hours.

The bike tour will introduce you to Amsterdam's four gay ghettos. Gay and lesbian Amsterdammers inhabit all corners of the city, and that means the nightlife strips tend to be places gay people go but don't necessarily live near. The gay zones are conveniently themed according to homo-stereotype (see "In the Heat of the Night"), so leather studs (**Warmoesstraat**), show-tune queens (**Amstel**), beauty boys (**Reguliersdwarsstraat**), and regular guys (**Kerkstraat**) can proceed directly to their preferred environs without much worry about where to go. When it comes to home, fancy fags and dykes take their place along with the rest of Amsterdam's fashionable set living along the city's main canals, but more-bohemian queers have made a few neighborhoods like the Jordaan and de Pijp into enclaves of gay living.

PARKS, GARDENS & SQUARES

Greenery is scarce in Amsterdam, so locals have great affection for **Vondelpark** (Tram: 2, 5, 7, or 10), a 19th-century English-style park named for classical Dutch dramatist Joost van den Vondel. This long, narrow haven of ponds, gardens, broad lawns, and

Tiptoe Through the Tulips

Many of the city's loveliest gardens are hidden from view in the well-tended plots behind the facades of the handsome canal houses. You get your chance to do some snooping around in June during an annual **canal garden walk.** Contact the Amsterdam Tourist Office (see "Visitor Information" above) for details.

patches of both sun and shade is where locals go to commune with nature and kick off their wooden shoes for a day of picnicking, Frisbee-tossing, and lolling in the sun. In summer, it's an especially lively scene as joggers, in-line skaters, and dog walkers populate its winding paths and frequent concerts are given at the park's open-air bandshell. The park, slightly southwest of Leidseplein and near the Rijksmuseum, also has several cafes and restaurants. The rose garden is a popular gay sunbathing spot, as well as a cruising destination.

Amsterdam contains several large public squares (*plein* in Dutch) that serve as exuberant gathering places. The largest and most significant is **Dam Square** (or the **Dam**), a broad treeless plaza directly south from Centraal Station—this is the site of the original dam across the Amstel River that gave the city its name. In summer the Dam overflows with visitors and pigeons (take your pick of which to avoid); its "walls" are formed by several important institutions representing the trinity of state, church, and shopping. Taking up one flank is the classically inspired **Royal Palace (Koninklijk Paleis),** built in 1648 as Amsterdam's town hall; under Napoléon's rule it became a royal residence. Next door is the **Nieuwe Kerk,** a venerable church that's the site of royal coronations. And on the north side is the grand **De Bijenkorf department store,** where you'll find same-sex couples dutifully paying their respects on Saturday afternoons. The site of the country's World War II monument (predictably phallic), the Dam has significance in the pages of Amsterdam's gay history. In the 18th century, gay men used the central gallery of the palace as a rendezvous point, taking it as a friendly invitation if another man brushed their elbow. The palace also has been the site of frequent public hangings, including a number of "sodomites" who were executed in the 18th century.

Though the Dam performs many of city's official obligations, Amsterdam has two squares that are charged with more frivolous duties. They're both mini–Times Squares if you will: **Rembrandtplein** (where the poor statue of the great Master looks a little lost amid the flashing neon) and **Leidseplein** (farther south near Vondelpark and the museum quarter) are both playgrounds crowded with restaurants and cafes, bars, coffee shops, and movie theaters.

BOYS ON THE BEACH

When summer finally decides to appear in the Netherlands (June if you're lucky), the beaches at the North Sea resort of **Zandvoort** are where gays play. Trains leave from Amsterdam's Centraal Station every half an hour for the 40-minute trip that in summer is a direct route to the beach (it requires a change in Haarlem the rest of the year). From the station, walk toward the left to the southern end of the beach promenade. The walk takes about half an hour (or you can try to grab a cab). The beach near the Havana beach pavilion is gayish, but most sun bunnies prefer the more private **gay nude beach** a little farther south (shy types need not fret; not everyone goes au naturel). Keep walking for another 15 minutes or so along the beach or follow the path heading inland through the dunes. You'll eventually arrive at a pair of beach pavilions with terraces equipped with cafes, lounging chairs, bathrooms, and showers.

The folks who run the gay saunas in Amsterdam have a beachside operation here called **Thermos aan Zee (☎ 023/573-0141;** www.thermos.nl), and next to it is a popular pavilion called **El Dorado** (☎ **023/571-8229**). Both are open daily 8am to midnight in summer. Ambitious types can easily bike to the beach from Amsterdam. The ride takes about an hour and a half, but it's a fairly scenic route, with its own dedicated bike path taking you past windmills, woodsy glens, and the historic city of Haarlem. At the beach, there's an attended bike lot across the dunes from Thermos and El Dorado.

WORKING UP A SWEAT

One of the larger parks in Amsterdam, **Vondelpark** gets a lot of use from Amsterdammers on foot, bike, and blade. The meandering paths are a good place for all manner of exercise, and in summer the park is packed with Amsterdammers desperate for a little open green space. The asphalt paths are a fine surface for in-line skating, and you can **rent skates** near the Pannekoekenhuis (Pancake House). Rates are 7.50DFL ($3.95) for 1 hour and 17.50DFL ($9) per day, including pads. A deposit of a passport, credit card, or driver's license plus 50DFL ($26) is required. For more information, call ☎ **020/693-9574.**

If you have access to a car or bike, you can disappear into the **Amsterdam Forest (Amsterdamse Bos),** a more sylvan setting in the southern region of the city that's popular with joggers and anybody who wants to get away from the madding crowds (take the Amstelveensweg exit on A4 and A10 freeways).

When Amsterdam is its usual brooding, rainy self, you can seek shelter at a couple of indoor pools. **Marnixbad,** Marnixplein 9 (☎ **020/625-4843;** Tram: 10; call for hours; admission 4.50/$2.40), has special times set aside for lap swimmers, men, women, seniors, and nudists (the Monday-night swim is especially popular with gay men). Naturally, the night swims have the cruisiest vibe. Near Museumplein, the **Zuiderbad,** Hobbemastraat 26 (☎ **020/671-0287;** Tram: 2, 5, or 20; call for hours; admission 5DFL/$2.65), is a grand old pool with mosaics, relief sculptures, and other architecturally rich details. If you want to work your body while you're away, **A Bigger Splash,** Looiersgracht 26–30 (☎ **020/624-8404;** Tram: 1, 2, 5, 7, 10, or 20; open daily 7am–midnight; day card 35DFL/$18, weekly pass 67DFL/$35), is well equipped with weight-lifting hardware and a social scene that includes a dollop of gay members. The club also has cardio equipment, a sauna and Turkish bath, aerobics, a juice bar, and doors that open onto the canal.

For a gay environment, there's the small all-male gym **Mandate,** Prinsengracht 715, at Leidsestraat (☎ **020/625-4100;** Tram: 1, 2, or 5; open Mon–Fri 11am–10pm, Sat noon–6pm, Sun 2–6pm; day rates 18–63DFL/$9–$33 for 1–6 days). It has Nautilus-style and free weights, a sauna, and a coffee bar. (The gym was changing hands in 1998, so change may be afoot.) Another big health club is **Sporting Club Leidseplein,** Korte Leidsedwarsstraat 18 (☎ **020/620-6631;** Tram: 1, 2, 5, 6, 7, 10, or 20; open Mon–Fri 9am–midnight, Sat–Sun 10am–6pm; day pass, Mon–Fri only, 25DFL/$13), a full-service gym with weights, aerobics, squash courts, a sauna, and a bar.

5 Hitting the Stores

Thanks to the Dutch's history as enthusiastic and savvy traders, you'll find plenty of things to buy here. Some of life's simple pleasures are so plentiful and so inexpensive you might be tempted to stuff your suitcase full of tulips and candles. The city's small scale makes it ideal for aimless wandering among the picturesque canals and side streets where you'll find a curious mix of merchants and markets.

Amsterdam has two **main walking streets,** basically suburban mall–type stores laid out end to end; all that's missing is a roof. A few interesting upscale shops are mixed in, but most are geared to suburban kids shopping for the latest fashion statement.

Kalverstraat kicks off at the southern end of Dam Square and arcs slowly east until it hits **Leidsestraat,** which then marches on across the city's ring of canals until it ends at Leidseplein. Both of these streets are packed on Saturdays as Amsterdammers race out to do a week's shopping in a day. A number of galleries, antiques shops, and high-fashion retailers, including agnès b. and the upscale department store Maison de Bonneterie, are sprinkled along the western side of the **Rokin,** the wide road running from the Dam to the Amstel. The chi-chi, poo-poo enclave is **P.C. Hooftstraat,** a few blocks in the Museumplein area and adjacent to Vondelpark. This upscale street boasts all the big names—Hugo Boss, Gianni Versace, Emporio Armani, DKNY, Cartier—and several homegrown boutiques carrying a range of designers from Comme des Garçons to John Galliano.

The toniest antiques row in Amsterdam, and some would say in Europe, is ✪ **Nieuwe Spiegelstraat,** a few short blocks leading up to the Rijksmuseum between Prinsengracht and Herengracht. On this street and some of the surrounding side streets are nearly 70 antiques and art dealers carrying hand-painted clocks, old Delft fireplace tiles, Russian icons, old Masters prints, Oriental art, and heirloom jewelry.

There's been a big push to promote what is known as the ✪ **"9 little streets,"** a succession of intimate lanes between the canals on the western side of the city ring, below Raadhuisstraat. You can wander here for hours browsing in a variety of small independent shops and designer boutiques selling everything from picture frames and pottery to imported teak tables and made-to-order dresses. You'll also find several gay and lesbian bookshops and a variety of fetish shops specializing in quality leather and rubber wear, whether for day or for night. Of course, straight guys who say they hate shopping don't seem to mind "window-shopping" for hours in the Red Light District, where the blushingly bold window displays of the "toy shops" are always within your field of vision.

Shopping hours are generally Monday to Friday 9am to 6pm and Saturday 9am to 5pm (some closing earlier). Most everything, except for tourist-trade shops and downtown department stores, is closed on Sunday.

SHOPS A TO Z

ART & ANTIQUES Other than the shops on Nieuwe Spiegelstraat, a must-browse is the ✪ **De Looier Antique Market,** Lijnbaansgracht 193, at Elandsgracht (☎ **020/624-9038;** www.looier.nl; Tram: 10, 17, or 20; open Sun–Thurs 11am–5pm), one of those labyrinthine malls where it's easy to become disoriented after about 5 minutes of wandering among the diverging rows of booths and cases of antiques, art, and assorted curiosities. Some of the 150 stalls are staffed by their dealers, who are often willing to deal. On Wednesday, Saturday, and Sunday, more dealers set up tables with jewelry and other small items. **Silver Plate,** Nes 89, at Grimburgwal (☎ **020/624-8339;** Tram: 4, 9, 16, 20, 24, or 25), is on a medieval lane below Dam Square; it specializes in turn-of-the-century silver-plated (duh!) items from old Dutch, and some English, hotels. Look for cutlery, tea services, bowls, trays, candelabras, and other necessities of fine living.

BOOKS The city's gay and lesbian bookstore is **Boekhandel Vrolijk,** Paleisstraat 135 (☎ **020/623-5142;** www.xs4all.nl/~vrolijk; Tram: 1, 2, or 5). The shop, near Dam Square, carries novels, biographies, erotica, humor, and poetry, as well as cards, magazines, and even Billy dolls. Nearby is **Intermale,** Spuistraat 251 (☎ **020/625-0009;** Tram: 1, 2, or 5), limited to books, magazines, and videos for the boys. The girls will find books of their own at **Xantippe Unlimited,** Prinsengracht 290 (☎ **020/623-5854;** www.dds.nl/xantippe; Tram: 13, 14, or 17), a general-interest shop with strong sections of lesbian fiction and nonfiction and women's studies (the shop was started by a feminist collective and is now lesbian-owned).

The largest English-language used bookstore in Amsterdam is the **Book Exchange,** Kloveniersburgwal 58 (☎ **020/626-6266;** Tram: 4, 9, 14, or 20), on the fringes of the Red Light District. For new stuff, the **American Book Center,** Kalverstraat 185 (☎ **020/625-5537;** www.abc.nl; Tram: 1, 2, 5, 9, 14, 16, 20, 24, or 25), is a four-level store with books and magazines from the United States and the United Kingdom. There's also a large and well-chosen gay and lesbian section in the basement, plus gay mags and greeting cards.

CHOCOLATE Serious chocoholics will want to know all about what Ans van Soelen does with chocolate in her bonbon boutique ✪ **Puccini Bonbons,** Staalstraat 17 (☎ **020/626-5474;** Tram: 4, 9, 14, or 20), near the Hotel de l'Europe. After all, as she says, who wants to sit on the couch on a rainy day eating same-tasting bonbon after bonbon? In the main shop, where you can watch bonbon elves at work in the kitchen through a window, a bountiful table displays the chocolates in every permutation, from amaretto to thyme to mint to nutmeg. There's a second shop behind the Royal Palace at Singel 184 (☎ **020/427-8341;** Tram: 1, 2, 5, 13, 17, or 20).

CONDOMS **Het Gulden Vlies,** Warmoesstraat 141 (☎ **020/627-4174;** www.condomerie.com; Tram: 4, 9, 16, 20, 24, or 25), is smart to be located in the Red Light District, with sex on sale or given away all around in the walk-up windows, dildo shops, and backrooms. The cute, inviting "Golden Fleece" offers hundreds of varieties of condoms from all over the world, special carrying cases, and gift-wrapping services, and it even has a museum case of condoms through the years (remember the quaint old days when they were rubbers?). Look for inspired window displays: During the 1998 World Cup, the shop offered gift sets of condoms in the team's orange colors.

DEPARTMENT STORES Every big city has a big department store with everything under one architecturally magnificent roof, and in Amsterdam it's **De Bijenkorf (The Beehive),** Dam 1 (☎ **020/621-8080;** Tram: 1, 2, 5, 13, 17, or 20). Other major department stores are upscale **Maison de Bonneterie** on the Rokin and **Metz & Co.** on Leidsestraat.

FASHION The Dutch have a modest style all their own, but Amsterdam is not the place to do heavy-duty shopping for high fashion. You're better off finding stuff that looks good on the street, atop a bicycle, or at a nightclub. If you forgot to pack your clingy T-shirt to show off your perfect pecs, make an emergency run to **De Nieuwe Kleren van de Keizer** (The Emperor's New Clothes, Runstraat 29 (☎ **020/422-6895;** Tram: 1, 2, 5, 7, 10, or 20), a bright little shop that carries T-shirts and tank tops from American circuit-boy seamstresses like Body Body, as well as some German and French designers. It's owned by a couple of boyfriends who know the bar scene well. Worth including if only for the name is **Sissy Boy,** a Gap-like chain with an outlet on the Kalverstraat (☎ **020/638-9305;** Tram: 4, 9, 14, 16, 20, 24, or 25).

Men who take their underwear seriously shop at **Mantalk,** Reguliersdwarsstraat 39 (☎ **020/627-2525;** Tram: 1, 2, or 5), a trendy boutique located among a group of gay bars that sells fashionable labels of undies and swimwear. Down the street is another shop where strippers and exhibitionists can add to their minimalist wardrobes: **Stringslip** ("The String Brief"), Reguliersdwarsstraat 59 (☎ **020/638-1143;** Tram: 1, 2, or 5). Women can find all kinds of exciting erotic lingerie, clothing, and "accessories" at **Female and Partners,** Spuistraat 100 (☎ **020/620-9152;** Tram: 1, 2, or 5).

FURNITURE & DESIGN The spacious bilevel showroom of **Frozen Fountain,** Prinsengracht 629 (☎ **020/622-9375;** Tram: 1, 2, 5, 13, 14, or 17), presents a wide range of contemporary furniture and home accessories, from the work of young Dutch designers to the latest lines from Italian designers and even 19th-century Shaker reproductions. Typical of the funky cultural crossroads Amsterdam has always been is

Fanous Ramadan, Runstraat 33, between Prinsengracht and Keizersgracht (☎ **020/423-2350;** Tram: 1, 2, 5, 7, 10, or 20), where the Egyptian-born owner has packed his tiny storefront with imported lanterns and lamps inspired by the ones used by children during the Muslim holy month and made to his design by artisans in his native country. The shop shimmers with light from the hanging lamps, frames, jewelry, perfume bottles, vases, glassware, and other hand-crafted shiny objects.

GIFTS & TOYS Looking for postcards depicting something besides tulips and windmills? Prepare to be overwhelmed by selection at ✪ **Art Unlimited,** Max Euweplein 58 (☎ **020/627-6606;** Tram: 1, 2, 5, 7, 10, or 20), the shop in Leidseplein that's the retail arm of a postcard publishing house. They carry 50,000 postcards, greeting cards, and posters with art from the Rijksmuseum and the van Gogh Museum, and thousands of other images from the silly to the sublime. You'll find cute handmade wooden toys, mobiles, and other decorative pieces, all very reasonably priced, at **'t Winkeltje,** Spuistraat 257 (☎ **020/624-9391;** Tram: 1, 2, or 5), a tiny shop (thus its name, The Little Shop) near Dam Square that carries the work of several artists.

A quintessentially European toy shop is ✪ **Mechanisch Speelgoed,** Westerstraat 67 (☎ **020/638-1680;** Tram: 3), in the Jordaan. It brims with an eye-boggling number of interactive old-fashioned playthings, ranging from tin windup figures to paper masks to dollhouse accessories. It may seem silly to buy things from Mexico while in Holland (many of those tacky souvenirs are made in China anyway), but one of the most offbeat shops around is **Kitsch Kitchen,** Bloemdwarsstraat 21–23 (☎ **020/428-4969;** Tram: 13, 14, 17, or 20), near the Westerkerk. The owners, who began their trade in one of the city markets, have cornered the market on Day-Glo plastic items from Mexico. One never knows when one is going to need colorful brushes and brooms, flowery laminated aprons and tablecloths, aluminum cups, beaded curtains, Virgin Mary shrines, Mexican tiles, and other fun trinkets. They recently opened an adjunct, **Kids Kitsch Kitchen,** nearby at Rozengracht 183 (☎ **020/622-8261;** Tram: 13, 14, 17, or 20).

LEATHER, RUBBER & FETISHWEAR When it comes to leather and rubber gear, Amsterdam is the capital of kink. You can buy off the rack or get measured for a made-to-order piece. Serious leather daddies (and perhaps a few mommies) know the name ✪ **RoB,** Weteringschans 253, at Reguliersgracht (☎ **020/625-4686;** www.rob.nl; Tram: 4, 6, 7, 10, 16, 24, or 25), a standard-bearer that has been dressing Toms of Finland (and Germany, England, the United States, and everywhere else) since the late owner, Rob Meier, a big proponent of leather liberation, opened a small leather tailor business 25 years ago. The well-regarded manufacturer has retail outlets in London and New York City, publishes *Drummer* magazine, and cosponsors Amsterdam's annual Leather Pride. The shop's slightly out-of-the way location—a 5-minute walk from the Rijksmuseum—guarantees a more serious crowd of shoppers than some of the leather shops in touristy areas. Look for everything from leather pants and chaps, jackets, vests, and boots to all kinds of rubber, latex, and other "twisted gear" (with helpful labels illuminating where all these things go) in the slightly spooky basement, including a hall of harnesses. The shop's big-ticket item is a steel cage that collapses to fit under your bed (all tools included for assembly!).

✪ **Mr. B,** Warmoesstraat 89 (☎ **020/422-0003;** www.mrb.nl; Tram: 4, 9, 16, 20, 24, or 25), is a stylish trilevel shop with a prominent Red Light District location right on the street with all the leather bars. Mr. B, opened by an ex-RoB employee, has a less intimidating atmosphere and attracts plenty of curiosity seekers. The sales counter often functions as an unofficial gay tourist center since the staff answers questions and makes recommendations. The shop also has tattoo artists and piercers available for consultation. Rubber enthusiasts should bounce over to **Black Body,** Lijnbaansgracht 292, off Spiegelgracht (☎ **020/626-2553;** e-mail welcome@blackbody.nl; Tram: 6, 7, 10, 16, 24, or 25), a well-stocked store near the Rijksmuseum. From jocks to jeans, tanks tops to trench coats, every possible garment is rendered in rubber and leather, and there are even hard-to-find "total enclosure" apparel and equipment. The shop's catalog makes for a fun souvenir (be sure to ask for the 50-color hanky chart).

A couple of merchants specialize in custom-made designer leather. The tailoring team of **Robin & Rik,** Runstraat 30 (☎ **020/627-8924;** Tram: 1, 2, 5, 7, 10, or 20), has been designing leatherwear for 25 years and carries a full line of leather and suede garments and accessories, including jackets, pants and chaps, caps, waistcoats, shirts, belts, caps, wristbands, and backpacks. Whether for day or night, leather is serious fashion at designer Joyce van Heek's boutique ✪ **Lust for Leather,** Brouwersgracht 226b, at Prinsengracht (☎ **020/627-0778;** e-mail info@lustforleather.nl; Tram: 3). This hip showroom in the Jordaan draws both gay and straight, amateur fetishist and professional. Van Heek will definitely help you sex up your wardrobe. She has one of the widest selections of provocative garments for women, including halter tops and bras, skirts that lace up the backside, and chaps with side lacing; men can shop for pants, jackets, G-strings, wallets (some especially made for darkroom excursions), caps, and harnesses.

MARKETS Shopping any of the city's two dozen markets beats browsing the usual retail scene for surprise and local color. The most celebrated of the open-air markets is the ✪ **Singel Flower Market,** between Leidsestraat and the Munt Tower (Tram: 1, 2, or 5; open Mon–Sat 9:30am–5pm), a floating bazaar along the canal that derives from the days when flowers were delivered by boat (nowadays flowers are brought by truck and the stalls are all permanently docked barges). About a dozen sweet-smelling stalls sell bouquets of fresh flowers, packets of tulip bulbs in all their myriad permutations, and other colorful flora. The flowers are so inexpensive you really can't resist buying: Brighten up that hotel room with a bunch of sunflowers or tulips or impress that tall stranger you've been eyeing on Regulierdwarstraat.

A couple of other busy markets are the eclectic **Waterlooplein flea market,** behind the City Hall and City Opera (Tram: 9, 14, or 20; open Mon–Sat 9am–5pm), a longstanding tradition that attracts dozens of dealers hawking racks of recycled and new clothing, including suede and leather jackets and tie-dyed T-shirts, record albums, Dutch prints, hardware and kitchen implements, and assorted junk. One of the largest and best general markets is the ✪ **Albert Cuyp Market,** in the de Pijp neighborhood on Albert Cuypstraat, between Ferdinand Bolstraat and Van Woustraat (Tram: 4, 16, 20, 24, or 25; open Mon–Sat 9:30am–5pm), an ethnic parade of blocks and blocks of merchants dispensing with everything to keep Amsterdammers fed and clothed, including cheese, meats, fish, produce, nuts, flowers, and clothing . . . even feather boas. There are several specialty markets, including the **secondhand/antiquarian book market** on the Spui Fridays 10am to 6pm (Tram: 1, 2, or 5), and the **antiques market** Mondays 9am to 1pm outside the Noorderkerk in the Jordaan (Tram: 13, 14, 17, or 20).

6 All the World's a Stage

Amsterdam has rich and funky cultural offerings worthy of its diverse population—from opera and classical music to avant-garde performance art and engaging street performers. No matter when you're planning a visit, there's bound to be something interesting playing on stage, and in summer, the pace of cultural life picks up with a variety of festivals and other special events.

For the latest of what's on stage in Amsterdam, scan the listings in ***What's On in Amsterdam,*** a biweekly entertainment guide sold at the VVV Amsterdam Tourist Office for 4DFL ($2.10). Concert and theatrical tickets are sold by the **Amsterdam Uit Buro (AUB),** which has an office at Leidseplein 26, at Marnixstraat (☎ **020/621-1211** for phone orders Mon–Sun 9am–9pm; www.aub.nl; Tram: 1, 2, 5, 6, 7, 10, or 11; open Mon–Sun 10am–5pm); or at any of the VVV Amsterdam Tourist Offices (see "Visitor Information" above).

THE PERFORMING ARTS

Cultural opportunities abound in June, when the international **Holland Festival** (☎ **020/530-7110**) busies the stages of more than a dozen venues with an enormous variety of music, theater, dance, opera, and film over a 3-week stretch. For a complete rundown of events, visit the festival headquarters at the **Stadsschouwburg (Municipal Theater),** Leidseplein 26 (☎ **020/624-2311;** Tram: 1, 2, 5, 6, 7, 10, or 11).

THEATER The large resident population of English speakers means that Amsterdam, more than most European cities, offers theatrical offerings staged in English on a regular basis, including a lot of musicals and plays spun off from London and New York. Many of these big shows are held at the **Stadsscchouwburg** (see below) and the **Royal Carré Theatre,** Amstel 115 (☎ **020/622-5225;** Tram: 4, 9, or 14; box office open Mon–Sat 10am–7pm, Sun 1–7pm).

For theater with a queer bent, check with the gay community center **COC-Amsterdam,** Rozenstraat 14 in the Jordaan (☎ **020/623-4079;** Tram: 13, 14, or 17), which has an upstairs theater space where English-language plays are often performed. One of Amsterdam's most successful theatrical exports is the progressive performance art troupe known as **Dogtroep,** blending music, dance, and performance to create something visually striking and wholly original. Check with the VVV to find out when and where the widely touring group is scheduled to perform.

Amsterdam has always been welcoming to outsiders, and perhaps that explains the success of **Boom Chicago,** Leidseplein 12 (☎ **020/423-0101;** www.boomchicago.nl; Tram: 1, 2, 5, 6, 7, 10, or 20), a group of young actors that has exported the Windy City's famed Second City style of comedy improv. You can come for a 6:30pm dinner or show up later for shows that usually begin at 8:15pm (nights vary by season). The show is 27.50 to 29.50DFL ($14 to $16), excluding dinners and drinks. The theater also has special "best of Boom" and late-night shows. During the Gay Games, it hosted a Second City touring group's special gay-themed program. (Not that it matters, but since this is a gay guide . . . one of the founders of Boom Chicago is the son of Charles Moskos, the Northwestern University sociologist who's the architect of the U.S. military's "Don't Ask, Don't Tell" policy. But his good-humored son is working on dad.)

The last thing you may want to do on vacation is watch a movie, but seeing a film in Amsterdam's most famous cinema, **Tuschinski,** Reguliersbreestraat 26 (☎ **020/626-2633** or 020/626-2637; Tram: 4, 9, 14, 16, 20, 24, or 25), is a thrill. Right off Rembrandtplein and not far from the bars on Reguliersdwarsstraat, the 1921 theater is dripping in art nouveau excess. It's always interesting to see how people in other countries go to the movies. Here the concession stand serves coffee or any hot drink in cups and saucers, and there's usually an intermission (or *pauze*), an appropriate time for scoping the crowd. All films in Holland are screened in their native language, with Dutch subtitles. Gay and lesbian films from around the world are often screened at the art house **Desmet,** Plantage Middenlaan 4A (☎ **020/627-3434;** Tram: 7, 9, or 14).

OPERA & CLASSICAL MUSIC The city's big-league opera company, the **Netherlands Opera Society (De Nederlandse Opera),** works through a repertoire of classics and a few adventurous works during its September-to-March season at the modern marble-and-glass **Muziektheater,** Waterlooplein 22 (☎ **020/625-5455;** Tram: 4, 9, 14, 16, 24, or 25; box office open Mon–Sat 10am–6pm, Sun 11:30am–6pm), part of the sleek city hall complex along the Amstel River and Waterlooplein. The country's leading orchestra, the **Royal Concertgebouw (Koninklijk Concertgebouworkest),** is known for performances of Wagner, Bruckner, Mahler, and Strauss, as well as a repertoire of 20th-century and contemporary masterpieces. It performs in the acoustically divine **Concertgebouw,** Concertgebouwplein 2–6 (☎ **020/671-8345;** www.concertgebouw.nl; Tram: 2, 3, 5, 12, or 16; box office open daily 10am–7pm), an elegant neo-Renaissance edifice that has been home to classical concerts since it opened in 1888. Another major group, the **Netherlands Philharmonic Orchestra (Nederlands Philharmonisch Orkest),** shares the hall.

Music and dance recitals, as well as touring theatrical shows, are often held in the intimate **Stadsscchouwburg (Municipal Theater),** Leidseplein 26 (☎ **020/624 23 11;** Tram: 1, 2, 5, 6, 7, 10, or 11; box office open daily 10am–6pm), an ornate old theater that's the former home of the national opera and dance companies. Several classical music groups perform in a concert hall at the **Beurs van Berlage,** the city's old stock exchange, Damrak 243 (☎ **020/627-0466;** Tram: 4, 9, 16, 20, 24, or 25; box office open Tues–Fri 12:30–6pm, Sat to 5pm).

In late August, the city's canal houses and waterways provide a romantic backdrop for a series of outdoor concerts during the annual **Canal Festival** (☎ **020/523-5235**). What began years ago with a piano performance on a canal barge has evolved into an elaborate weekend of classical music concerts and recitals in gardens, on rooftop terraces, and atop boats along both Prinsengracht and Keizersgracht. The festival traditionally begins on Thursday night with a concert performed from boats on the canal opposite the Pulitzer Hotel on Prinsengracht. Another place to go looking for musical interludes is one of the city's many beautiful **churches,** which provide the right atmosphere for baroque chamber music and organ concerts.

DANCE The dance scene has grown ever more vibrant in Amsterdam, and the major company is the **Dutch National Ballet (Het Nationale Ballet)** (☎ **020/625-5455**), a troupe whose repertoire embraces both classical and modern works, including those by George Balanchine. The company makes its home at the **Muziektheater** (see above) for eight productions each season, accompanied by a live orchestra. There's also another world-class company, the **Netherlands Dance Theatre (Nederlands Dans Theater),** as well as a variety of modern-dance companies in Amsterdam.

LIVE-MUSIC CLUBS

The place for jazz and experimental music is **Bimhuis,** Oude Schans 73–77 (☎ **020/623-1361;** www.bimhuis.nl; Tram: 9 or 14; open Thurs–Sun from 9pm; cover 15–25DFL/$8–$13), a venerable club that has witnessed all the big names, from Charlie Mingus to Max Roach. For blues, jazz, and rock, stop at **Bourbon Street,** Leidsekruisstraat 6–8, off Leidsestraat (☎ **020/623-3440;** Tram: 1, 2, or 5; open Sun–Thurs 10pm–4am, Fri–Sat to 5am; cover 2.50–5DFL/$1.30–$2.65), an intimate earthy room decorated in New Orleans style with musical instruments as wall art and an eclectic standing-room-only crowd that's equal parts visitors and locals.

The multicultural, multimedia, multiroom **De Melkweg,** Lijnbaansgracht 234a, near Leidseplein (☎ **020/624-1777;** www.melkweg.nl; Tram: 1, 2, 5, 6, 7, 10, or 11; shows begin at 9pm; cover 15–30DFL/$8–$16), is a former dairy that has occupied a place on Amsterdam's musical and theatrical edge for 2 decades. "The Milky Way" is a labyrinthine trilevel space reached via a little bridge over the canal—it contains two concert halls, a cinema and video room, a small concert studio, a tearoom, and a gallery cafe. On its big stages, Melkweg showcases everything from DJ extravaganzas to hard-core music fests to the latest alt-rock bands; concerts begin at 9pm. It's the site of an array of music festivals and special events throughout the year, including the Amsterdam Roots Festival, an annual 2-week celebration of world music held in June.

Another place for big shows is **Paradiso,** Weteringschans 6–8 (☎ **020/626-4521;** www.paradiso.nl; Tram: 1, 2, 5, 6, 7, 10, or 11; open 8pm for concerts, midnight for dance nights; cover 10–30DFL/$5–$16), a former church retrofitted for kids who come here to worship their fave bands or a hot DJ. Come summer, the **open-air theater in Vondelpark** (Tram: 2, 5, 7, 10, 20) is a popular place to enjoy free concerts, which span the musical spectrum, rock and jazz jam sessions to Brazilian bossa nova. On weekends from late May to late August, performances are scheduled both afternoon and evening. The Royal Concertgebouw presents an annual outdoor concert on a lawn in the center of the park. For more information, call ☎ **020/673-1499.**

7 In the Heat of the Night

Great beer, long summer light, and rooms full of beautiful Dutch men and women—who in their right mind would stay home at night in Amsterdam? Perhaps this explains the city's lively and rich nocturnal world, featuring everything from decadent of-the-moment nightclubs to supercozy neighborhood pubs to sweet-smelling coffee shops (where coffee isn't to be found—wink, wink) to wacky Dutch sing-along bars. Of course, the city's gay nightlife is well known. Though there are nearly 50 gay and lesbian bars, taverns, pubs, and clubs covering every possible predilection, everybody tends to find a handful of favorites and stick with them.

Turn to ***Gay News*** and ***Gay & Night*** for up-to-date listings, including maps that are helpful navigation tools. Two alternative freebies, **"Queer Fish"** and **"Shark,"** are also insightful guides in plotting your course in Amsterdam.

MAINSTREAM BROWN CAFES

Think of how much your clothes smell after a night in a smoky bar (not to mention a European bar). Ever wonder about the bar walls? Consider the ***bruine kroeg*** (brown cafe): This venerable Dutch institution is so called because its walls are coated with layers of tobacco residue from smokers over the centuries. Today these neighborhood watering holes point with pride to their dark walls. They're what adds to their sense of charm and tradition.

Dating to 1670, **Café Hoppe,** Spui 18–20 (☎ **020/420-4420;** Tram: 1, 2, or 5; open Sun–Thurs 8am–1am, Fri–Sat 8am–2am), manages to honor its history with sand on the floor (another sure sign of a brown cafe), leaded-glass windows, and older gentleman barkeeps in crisp white shirts and ties while at the same time attracting a fashionable set to its high-ceilinged airy room decorated with a big funky painting. They've kept it dark and dusty at **Café de Dokter,** Rozenboomsteeg 4 (☎ **020/626-4427;** Tram: 1, 2, or 5; open Tues–Sat 4pm–1am), a tiny candlelit bar near the Spui where the chandeliers are covered with cobwebs that've most likely been here since the place was opened by a pharmacist in 1798. It's crammed with all sorts of curious bric-a-brac, from a stuffed bird in a cage to vintage musical instruments. The current owners keep jazz playing and maintain one of Amsterdam's largest selections of whiskey.

Cafe 't Smalle, Egelantiersgracht 12 (☎ **020/623-9617;** Tram: 13, 14, 17, or 20; open daily 10am–1pm), dates back 2 centuries yet is still very much a vital part of the community in the Jordaan. Inside the corner cafe, it's warm and cozy, with pretty leaded-glass windows, high ceilings, and dark-paneled walls, and outside there's seating on a canal dock. Beside a well-stocked bar, the cafe offers a menu of broodjes, salads, and a soup of the day. One of the city's very oldest brown cafes is **Pieper,**

Prinsengracht 424 (☎ **020/626-4775;** Tram: 1, 2, 5, or 20; open Sun–Thurs 4pm–1am, Fri–Sat to 2am), dating from the 1660s. You definitely feel the history of this neighborhood place: It's like a dollhouse with a low-slung ceiling, colored-glass windows, and sand scattered over the creaky wooden floors.

GAY BARS

Consider your mood and your taste when planning a night on the town. Gay bars are clustered in four areas of the city, and each area bubbles (or sometimes staggers) with its own distinct personality. Think of these areas as the four legs of a fabulous Biedermeier table.

REGULIERSDWARSSTRAAT: ALL ABOUT HAIRCUTS The trendy pretty-boy bars are on **Reguliersdwarsstraat** (immediately off Leidsestraat and a block south of Singel; Tram: 1, 2, or 5), the mouthful-of-a-street that's busy with hip bars and restaurants. The crowd circulating through the gay bars here—a night on the Reguliersdwarsstraat usually involves hopping between April and Havana and ending up at the disco Exit—is young, social, fun, and *very tall.* (The owners don't care where you spend your money; they own all three places.) Wherever you're chatting up new friends or acquaintances, you can't help but wonder if there's more excitement, more energy, and cuter guys (it's mostly men) a few doors down. So go find out. The scene spills out onto the street during happy hour on late Sunday afternoons.

Start your tour at ✪ **April,** Reguliersdwarsstraat 37 (☎ **020/625-9572;** open Sun–Thurs 2pm–1am, Fri–Sat to 3am), a sleek modern bar that'll feel familiar to any American barfly. There's always a large international contingent in the good-looking crowd, which includes everyone from club kids to muscle boys, all jostling for personal space on weekends. April has a central bar up front, where you'll get looked over by the assembled masses, and in back is a DJ and a revolving bar—while you're trying your luck waving down one of the busy bartenders, you may actually end up on the other side of the room as the bar makes its slow circuit.

Down the block at **Havana,** Reguliersdwarsstraat 17 (☎ **020/620-6788;** open Sun 2pm–1am, Mon–Thurs 4pm–1am, Fri to 3am, Sat 2pm–3am), the tunes are a little more high energy and the crowd is younger and more self-possessed (though you'll see many of the faces you saw moments ago at April). The layout of the colorful split-level room, with booths lining one side, seems to encourage less mingling; a small third-floor dance floor is open on weekends.

Farther down the street, heading toward Rembrandtplein, is a whole different scene at **Reality,** Reguliersdwarsstraat 129 (☎ **020/639-3012;** open daily 8pm–3am), a neighborhood bar whose crowd is largely black (including a fair number of residents from former Dutch colonies); there's always a lively sing-along with bartenders and customers alike.

While you're bar-hopping on Reguliersdwarsstraat, look for other gay attractions: the disco **Exit,** the cruisy cafe **Downtown,** the gay hash bar **The Other Side,** and several **clothing shops.**

KERKSTRAAT: THE OLD STANDBYS If you want to duck the straight partying at Leidseplein, choose among the group of bars clumped together on **Kerkstraat** (between Keizersgracht and Prinsengracht; Tram: 1, 2, or 5), an area that has been home to gay life since the 1960s. The bars are laid back and untrendy, tend to draw a somewhat older crowd of locals, and offer something for everyone.

For a little bit of leather and jeans, there's **de Spijker,** Kerkstraat 4 (☎ **020/620-5919;** open Mon–Thurs 1pm–1am, Fri–Sat to 3am), a slightly sinister-seeming bar with a giant nail penetrating the building's facade (hence the name, the Spike) and an interior that's dim and getting dimmer. A good choice for an early-evening drink,

Beware the Bathroom Lady

Many Dutch bars and nightclubs (even some restaurants) staff their johns with door minders who supposedly watch out that things stay clean and orderly (keep your eyes and hands to yourself, young man). It's customary to leave a tip of 50 Dutch cents ($.25) when you use one of these bathrooms. (Interestingly, 18th-century Amsterdam authorities paid poor widows and children to spy on men who met in the pissoirs that were once located under bridges in the city.)

---

it's best known for its creative pairing of TV fare over the bar: hard-core porn on one, cartoons on the other. A lot of regulars, a range of looks and ages, gather here to play pool and check out the second-floor darkroom.

On the same block but closer to Leidsestraat is the **Cosmo Bar,** Kerkstraat 42 (☎ **020/624-8074;** open Sun–Thurs midnight–3am, Fri–Sat to 4am), an eclectic spot that's conveniently located near the night sauna (see "Down & Dirty" below). It's a mellow place with an interior of red velvety walls, mirrors, and old-fashioned street lights that appears carefully preserved for decades.

Other bars in the area are **Meia Meia,** Kerkstraat 63 (☎ **020/623-4129;** open daily noon–1am), a simple cocktail bar that seems trapped in the 1970s, and **Mankind,** Weteringsstraat 60 (☎ **020/638-4755;** open Sun–Thurs 11am–1am, Fri–Sat to 2am), a cafe with seating along Lijnbaansgracht.

REMBRANDTPLEIN: STRIKE UP A TUNE Show-tune and sing-along enthusiasts should start warming up on their way to the shiny, happy pubs radiating out from **Rembrandtplein** (Tram: 4, 9, 14, or 20). Here along the Amstel River and on a couple of side streets are half a dozen bars that encourage everyone to participate in true Dutch style.

One of the city's oldest bars (gay or otherwise) is ✪ **Amstel Taveerne,** Amstel 54 (☎ **020/623-4254;** open Sun–Thurs 4pm–1am, Fri–Sat to 3am), an old-fashioned corner bar that provides an authentic Dutch experience. The rathskeller, with a century-old beer tap, dates back to the 1700s but went gay only sometime in recent decades. It's a friendly, enthusiastic pub where the patrons, who are a range of ages but not especially fashionable, gather around the U-shaped bar and sing out their lungs to all their favorite Dutch songs. It's especially popular on Sunday afternoons, when the crowd overflows into the street along the river.

Around the corner at ✪ **Montmartre,** Halvemaansteeg 17 (☎ **020/624-9216;** open Sun–Thurs 4pm–1am, Fri–Sat to 3am), a spirit of fun pervades, with blasting music, a twirling disco ball, and a preening younger crowd. The bar is *so* gay (in the junior-high sense of the word). The decor with its mural singing the praises of the Parisian jazz age may be an ode to gay Paree, but the bartenders are typically Dutch: They're often much more concerned with cueing up the next cheeseball tune on the stereo than keeping up with your drink order.

Across the street are a couple of alternatives if Montmartre is too crowded or not crowded enough: **Café de Steeg,** Halvemaansteeg 10 (☎ **020/626-4510;** open Sun 4pm–1am, Mon–Thurs 5pm–1am, Fri to 3am, Sat 4pm–3am), a sleek successor to the well-known Chez Manfred; and **Entre Nous,** Halvemansteeg 14 (☎ **020/623-1700;** open Sun–Thurs 8pm–3am, Fri–Sat to 4am), a small dim tavern filled up with a row of Naugahyde stools along the bar and decorated with *Hello, Dolly!* and *Kiss of the Spider Woman* posters and various bric-a-brac. Feel free to barhop among the bars along the Amstel too: They're mostly small places with loyal followings but rather indistinguishable.

One of the silliest bars in Amsterdam has got to be **Mix Café,** Amstel 50 (☎ **020/ 420-3388;** open Sun–Thurs 8pm–3am, Fri–Sat to 4am), where a cute boy-and-girl staff (the boys seem to be gay, the girls straight) will never let a disparaging word be said about the Spice Girls. As the name says, the crowd is mixed and loves to sing.

Other canalside bars are **Gaiety,** Amstel 14 (☎ **020/624-4271;** open Sun and Tues–Thurs 3pm–1am, Fri–Sat to 2am), an intimate black-box space that draws a mix of ages and a lot of older/younger pairings; **Milord,** Amstel 102 (☎ **020/622-8335;** open Sun–Thurs 6pm–1am, Fri–Sat to 3am), with British pub stylings; **Monopole Taveerne,** Amstel 60 (☎ **020/624-6451;** open Sun–Thurs 4pm–1am, Fri–Sat to 3am), another very traditional Dutch pub; and **de Krokodil,** Amstelstraat 34 (☎ **020/626-2243;** open Sun–Thurs 4pm–1am, Fri–Sat to 2am), with nearly half a century in business and the kibitzing regulars who've been there since the start, plus occasional travesty (drag) shows.

One block parallel to the sing-along bars is a smallish alleylike street, **Paardenstraat,** home to several bars that are hangouts for hustlers. They're known to be good places to make a paid acquaintance, but often the boys are kicking back "after work." The bars are **Cupido,** Paardenstraat 7 (☎ **020/622-1789;** open Sun–Thurs 8pm–2am, Fri–Sat to 3am); **Music Box,** Paardenstraat 19 (☎ **020/620-4110;** open Sun–Thurs 8pm–2am, Fri–Sat to 3am); and **Festival,** Paardenstraat 15 (☎ **020/ 623-1217;** open daily 1pm–2am), noteworthy for its interior designed by the architect of Amsterdam's landmark art nouveau movie theater Tuchinksi.

THE WARMOESSTRAAT: LOVE YOU IN LEATHER Moving from happiness and light to darkness and sleaze, the city's fourth gay zone is the **Warmoesstraat,** a narrow street near Centraal Station in the Red Light District (Tram: 4, 9, 16, 20, 24, or 25)—this is Amsterdam's celebrated leather alley. For a raw update on the leather and rubber scene, including special events, call **Leather Pride Nederland** at ☎ **020/ 422-3737** or visit its Web site at **www.gayplanet.nl/lpn.**

Because most of the leather bars open late, the place to start a night out on Warmoesstraat is ✪ **Casa Maria,** Warmoesstraat 60 (☎ **020/627-6848;** open Sun–Thurs noon–1am, Fri–Sat to 2am), with an unbeatable location. Sit in the large picture window and look down Lange Niezel for an entertaining view at the leather boys, college-kid stoners, junkies, and sweatsuited tourists all merrily strolling about the Red Light District. Since it's down the street, you may want to take a look into **Monico Bar,** Lange Niezel 15 (no phone; hours vary), what's considered the oldest operating gay bar in Amsterdam. Dating to 1935, it doesn't seem to have retained any trace of its history and is now a pretty decrepit place that may appeal to people who have a fondness for eccentrics.

The oldest leather bar in Europe and the most heavy-duty leather bar in Amsterdam is ✪ **Argos,** Warmoesstraat 95 (☎ **020/622-6595;** open Sun–Thurs 10pm–3am, Fri–Sat to 4am). The bar started in 1958, has moved several times, and is now owned by a Brazilian named Eduardo (don't go looking for him; if you're lucky he'll find you). The bar is decorated with a head of its namesake, various hooks and chains dangling from the ceiling, and just the right lighting; though there's no dress code, this is the place to pull out all your leathers if you packed them (it's not unusual to see men, mask to boots in leather, bellying up to the bar for a beer). Downstairs is a fully equipped darkroom.

If you want to wait for things to warm up at Argos, make your first stop of the night **Amsterdam's Eagle,** Warmoesstraat 90 (☎ **020/627-8634;** open Sun–Thurs 10pm–4am, Fri–Sat to 5am), with the same kind of reddish glow as at Argos and standard leather-bar decor, a pool table, and a darkroom.

Filling out the roster on the block are **Club Jaecques,** Warmoesstraat 93 (☎ **020/622-0323;** open Sun–Thurs 8:30pm–3am, Fri–Sat to 4am), which is always pretty slow but picks up for its safe-sex parties the first weekend of the month; and the charmingly named **Dirty Dick's,** Warmoesstraat 86 (☎ **020/627-8634;** open Fri–Sat 10pm–4am), owned by the same folks as the Eagle, with a buzzer outside for admittance (the bar looks so rundown from the street you might not even think it's open).

Are they bars with darkrooms or darkrooms with bars? That's a good question for several other spots nearby.

The British owner of the **Stablemaster,** Warmoesstraat 23 (☎ **020/624-5573;** open Sun–Mon and Thurs 8pm–1am, Fri–Sat 2pm–2am), a bar annex to the hotel of the same name (see "Pillow Talk" above), is no dummy: He knows you gotta have a theme. Jack-off parties, which begin at 8pm, are the Stablemaster's claim to fame. "An orgy with a cocktail bar," he brags. (Hotel guests have a separate entrance.) A couple of popular after-work destinations are the **Cuckoo's Nest,** Nieuwezijds Kolk 6 (☎ **020/627-1752;** open Sun–Thurs 1pm–1am, Fri–Sat to 2am), a bar with expansive underground darkroom; and **The Web,** St. Jacobsstraat 6, between Nieuwendijk and N.Z. Voorburgwal (☎ **020/623-6758;** open Sun–Thurs 1pm–1am, Fri–Sat to 2am), a super-seedy trilevel bar with hard-core porn on the TV, a frisky Levi's-and-leather crowd, and a very dark darkroom.

A new bar in the neighborhood that's quickly gained a following is the ✪ **Queen's Head,** Zeedijk 20 (no phone; open Sun–Thurs 5pm–1am, Fri–Sat to 3am). Look for the chorus line of Ken dolls in the window (and one Barbie) and an orgy of Billy dolls behind the bar. Dusty and Johan, a couple of bald-headed guys who are veterans of de Trut (below), opened the bar in 1998 and modeled it after an old pub with red velvety walls and Oriental runners on the tables. They gave it the name of an extinct Dutch gay bar, hoping to draw older customers who so often are banished from most youth-worshipping places. The owners have set a homey mood, from the friendly drag-queen bingo night (hosted by none other than Dusty and her big wig) to the resident dog, a Jack Russell terrier named Bingo; they've attracted a diverse but slightly left-of-center, unpretentious crowd. There's an open-mike night and a Club Positive night for people with HIV and their friends.

DRAG VENUES

The drag (or "travesty") industry has diversified itself in Amsterdam. Home to some certifiable stars on the scene over the years (American Nicki Nicole made a big splash here), the city boasts a drag restaurant, **'t Sluisje** (see "Whet Your Appetite" above), occasional performances at several bars and nightclubs (like **the iT** and **Exit**), and popular drag-queen bingo nights at the **Queen's Head** with Dusty on Tuesdays and at **Getto** (see "Whet Your Appetite" above) with hostess Jeanne P'Arc on Thursdays.

New to the scene is a full-time drag bar, **Lellebel,** Utrechtsestraat 4 (☎ **020/427-5139;** Tram: 4, 9, 14, or 20; open Mon–Thurs 9pm–3am, Fri–Sat to 4am, Sun to 3am). Unabashedly located in the straight mix on Rembrandtplein, the small narrow room festooned with lacy women's undergarments is a pretty modest corner bar—definitely no La Cage aux Folles. Shows are held mostly on weekends, special guests are occasionally booked, and the girls work the bar on other nights.

A MIXED BAR

A feminist institution in Amsterdam, **Saarein,** Elandstraat 119 (☎ **020/623-4901;** Tram: 7 or 10; open Tues–Thurs and Sun 3pm–1am, Fri–Sat to 2am), has opened the doors to men after more than two decades as a women-only cafe. Now this bilevel corner spot in the Jordaan will be run as a gay and lesbian bar. The new crowd is exptected to be younger and trendier.

Feeling Your Way in the Dark

Miss Manners doesn't seem to have ruled on the etiquette for conducting yourself in one of Amsterdam's ubiquitous darkrooms (I'm not talking places where photos are developed), so I'll offer a few tips gleaned from experienced locals.

First and foremost: Play safely.

Darkrooms are varied and cater to every demand: dark, darker, and darker still; small and large; tame and rough and some seriously creepy. For example, the exceedingly popular room at the disco **Cockring** (up a short flight of stairs near the bathrooms, by the way) is nearly pitch black, stifling steamy, and overflowing with guys, while the darkroom at **Cuckoo's Nest** is a little too bright for comfort (the idea, after all, is not to have to consider what some of these guys really look like). Occasionally there are condom dispensers near the entrance to darkrooms, but you usually need to bring with you whatever you think you'll need.

A few rules of common sense apply: Darkrooms are always gratis, but bars have got to pay the bills. It's rude and rather ungrateful to freeload, so buy a drink before you make a beeline for the backroom. This also gives you time to see who's who, make some meaningful eye contact, and follow (or lead) the one of your choice into the darkroom. Pickpockets are a hazard: These spaces are dark, after all, and while you may want to invite some roaming hands, you don't want them taking more than you're willing to give. It's a good idea to leave your wallet behind. (Several leather shops sell "darkroom wallets" specially designed to keep your stuff secure.) Give your eyes a moment to adjust and watch your head. Some rooms are so dark that a friend (not me) actually ran into a door that I—I mean, he—thought was a hallway. Remember to stay calm: If some unwelcome hand comes your way, it's best to gently push it away.

LESBIAN BARS & CLUBS

Even in the homo heaven of Amsterdam, you'll hear the familiar lesbian lament about the dearth of nightlife for women. The sole lesbian bar in the city is **Vivelavie,** Amstelstraat 7 (☎ **020/624-0114;** Tram: 4, 9, or 14; open Sun–Thurs 3pm–1am, Fri–Sat to 2am), a convivial little corner spot on Rembrandtplein. As at many of its gay neighbors, the women (and a few men) here raise their voices and occasionally dance to the Europop tunes and old Dutch classics. This is a good place to check in to find out what special parties or events are scheduled around town when you're visiting.

A lifeline to the women's scene are parties held at **COC-Amsterdam,** Rozenstraat 14 (☎ **020/623-4079;** Tram: 13, 14, or 17), the gay/lesbian community center in the Jordaan. The organization hosts a big women's party on Saturday (10pm–4am) and other monthly special nights for women of different ages. The cooler-than-thou nightclub **RoXY** (see below), Singel 465 (☎ **020/620-0354;** www.roxy.nl; Tram: 4, 9, 14, 16, 24, or 25), hosts a lesbian party called the Pussy Lounge the third Sunday of the month (8pm–midnight).

Girls into leather will want to find out about S&M parties organized by **Wild Side** (☎ **071/512-8632;** e-mail: wildside@dds.nl).

Some of the "men's bars" where women show up are **April, Havana,** and **Exit,** but then you have to try to sort out the real girls from the fag hags. About a third of the hip alternative crowd at the weekly party at **de Trut** (see "Special Party Nights" below) are lesbians, and cute ones at that (as a homo accused of being a lesbian at heart, you'll have to take my word for it); the door staff eliminates any potential confusion by screening out nongays.

DANCE CLUBS

Amsterdammers like the nightlife, they like to boogie, and they like to disco down, so they're willing to submit themselves to the sunglassed eyes of the snooty fashion police guarding the door. Many of them fail to measure up, so come prepared packing feather boa and eyeliner or be ready to calm yourself with a little Stewart Smally pep talk when you're cast out as hopelessly square and American (basically the same thing, after all).

GAY CLUBS For a full-time gay disco, you've got a couple of choices. ✪ **Exit,** Reguliersdwarsstraat 42 (☎ **020/625-8788;** Tram: 1, 2, or 5; open daily 11pm–5am), is the next logical stop after bouncing between the stand-and-pose bars April and Havana on Reguliersdwarsstraat (see above). You can continue standing in Exit's ground-floor sing-along bar or get your body moving with reckless abandon upstairs on the sweat-inducing dance floor (or in the darkroom). The crowd is diverse and on the young side but united in their hopes of a wild night out.

The Dutch are a direct-talking people, so I guess it's no surprise they'd name a disco ✪ **Cockring,** Warmoesstraat 96 (☎ **020/623-9604;** www.clubcockring.com; Tram: 4, 9, 16, 20, or 24; open Sun–Thurs 11pm–4am, Fri–Sat to 5am). This supercruisy dance club in the city's leather row casts a soft dim light so everyone starts looking like a porn star. The dance bar is busy every night (there's never a cover) with everything from a DJ soundtrack ranging from trance to techno to Sunday-night strip shows. There are several levels—a bar and small but well-used dance floor up front, a too-popular darkroom, and back bar with porn videos up one flight.

MIXED CLUBS The most fun and fabulous of Amsterdam's dance palaces is ✪ **the iT,** Amstelstraat 24 (☎ **020/625-0111;** Tram: 4, 9, 14, or 20; open daily 11pm–5am; admission 12.50DFL/$7), a longtime legend with big lights, bigger sounds, and often even bigger costumes. Created by the late flamboyant nightlife mogul Manfred Langer, the extravagant multilevel, multiroom dance arena near Rembrandtplein has long attracted the outrageous, and if you need tips on what to wear check the photos in the display windows outside the club. The most energetic night is the all-gay party on Saturday, when the tight T-shirts don't stay on for long and the dancing to the frenzied house beat doesn't slow until the early morning. These guys never seem to tire. How do they do it? If you don't have some wild or revealing ensemble to get you in the door, grab hold of someone with one of the club's membership cards.

Another important name on the club circuit is the **RoXY,** Singel 465 (☎ **020/620-0354;** www.roxy.nl; Tram: 4, 9, 14, 16, 24, 25; open Sun, Wed–Thurs 11pm–4am, Fri–Sat to 4am; admission 12.50–20DFL/$7–$11), a barrel-vaulted old theater that hasn't shown signs of tiring after a decade in business. The club has a big dance floor dominated by a cluster of disco balls and a chill-out area in the balcony where there are a few tire swings for propping up your feet. Wednesdays are gay nights and your knock on the club's heavy door will likely have more success in gaining admittance on that night than on others, when the club has a very strict door policy. The crowd is a middle-of-the-week mix with everyone from rough-looking leather types to cutie college boys.

The young raver sets fill up **Mazzo,** Rozengracht 114 (☎ **020/626-7500;** www.xs4all.nl/~mazzo; Tram: 7, 10, 13, 14, or 17; open Wed–Sun midnight–4am; admission 10–20DFL/$5–$11), a club with an underground feel near Westermarkt. The crowd seems mostly straight, but you never know who you'll find. The club is a long narrow room with a DJ overseeing all the action on the dance floor and a variety of lounge spaces for mingling and mixing it up to the fast-beat tunes. The club does have a membership, so sometimes you might have to sweet-talk the doorman to get inside.

Amsterdam's Famous Dyke on a Bike

One of Amsterdam's most fascinating bars hasn't been open for decades, but it's a monument—one of the first gay bars in the city—worth paying your respects to. You'll find the facade of **'t Mandje,** Zeedijk 63 in the Red Light District, preserved as a kind of museum to the bar's legendary butch dyke owner, **Bet van Beeren.** She was the flamboyant motorbike-riding woman who took over the bar from her family in the 1920s and made it a safe haven for gays and lesbians, prostitutes, and other misfits. The bar remained open throughout the Nazi occupation, and van Beeren employed a few tricks to keep it that way. Since prostitutes were forbidden to wait for customers, van Beeren often kept bags of groceries behind the bar so if police dropped by, the women could take the bags and look busy by sorting through them. She also had in the bar an owl-shaped light that served as a warning when straights were coming. Even today, "owl" is still a slang term for straights among old-time gays in Amsterdam.

Each year on Queen's Day, van Beeren allowed women to dance with women and men to dance with men. She was famous for riding her motorbike around town, and when she was feeling ornery was said to have a driver take her to Centraal Station to watch steamer ships arrive and pick out a pretty girl from the arriving passengers; her straight male driver might end up with the woman if van Beeren struck out, but she usually got her way. She died in 1967, but her sister continued to run the place for many years. Before a recent clean-up effort helped turn around an area overrun with drug trafficking, the bar finally closed in 1981. The sister lives upstairs, continues to keep the place intact, and briefly reopened the bar for a week during the Gay Games in 1998. Look for photos of the "Queen of the Zeedijk" in the window.

SPECIAL PARTY NIGHTS

COC-Amsterdam, the city's gay/lesbian community center, holds several parties and special events that are an integral part of Amsterdam nightlife. All the parties are run by volunteers, charge a modest fee to nonmembers (but free before 10pm), and are held in COC's building at Rozenstraat 14 (☎ **020/626-3087;** www.xs4all.nl/~cocasd; Tram: 13, 14, or 17) in the Jordaan.

Fridays (10pm–4am) are billed as "mixed" parties but attract mostly men under 40 and their girlfriends for a lively dance party that feels like a wholesome high school dance. The guys are good-looking and social, but it's not especially cruisy, since most of the crowd is here to party with their pals. On **Saturdays,** the women take over with a cafe and dance party (10pm–4am), and there are special women's events (for over-45s, for example) at other times during the month. There also are parties for a variety of specific groups, including the **Sunday Arabian disco** (8pm–12:30am), which draws a lot of young North Africans for a night of intoxicating *rai* music and seductive dancing with handkerchiefs. **Thursdays** are HIV nights (8pm–12:30am) for people with HIV and AIDS. The COC also regularly hosts some lively leather parties; call to find out what's scheduled. You're welcome to stop by COC's ground-floor cafe (open Wed–Sat 1–5pm).

One of the hippest nights is the Sunday party at ✪ **de Trut** (11pm–4am; Tram: 3 or 12; admission 2.50DFL/$1.30). A collective of volunteers has run this event, which is as much a cause as a club, for a dozen years from its early days as a squat. They've since gone legit, but the club has retained an underground feel, both literally and figuratively, and the decor is funky amateurish. A sign above the bar says "Heteros Go Homo." The organizers are leery of overexposure, so to find it you'll have to do a little research when you get to town (I'll say it's somewhere on Bilderdijkstraat and leave it at that). The door minders screen out straights to keep the club a safe friendly queer space. Get there on the early side; the doors open at 11pm and often close by midnight, when the occupancy of the space maxes out.

If you're heading to Amsterdam for unadulterated sleaze, plan a trip so you hit town on the third Saturday of the month. That's the monthly bacchanal known as **Club Trash** (☎ **020/639-2335;** www.xs4all.nl/~trash; open 10pm–4am), a wild party that gives the people what they want—everything from private cabins to a sling room, from a bondage room to a dance floor, from a chill-out area to darkrooms. The dress code is leather, rubber, uniform, and just plain kinky (no jeans, please). The venue is just east of the city center along the harbor, and bus service is provided from the Barbizon Palace Hotel near Centraal Station. Advance tickets are sold at Mr. B and RoB (see "Hitting the Stores" above) for 25DFL ($13); tickets at the door are 30DFL ($16).

Your boots and jeans will be welcomed at the **Gay Western Saloon** (☎ **020/683-7333;** Tram: 4, 9, 14, 16, 24, or 25; admission usually 7.50DFL/$3.95); a country-western night is often held the last Sunday of the month at the Crea Café at the University of Amsterdam (☎ **020/626-2412**), on Grimburgwal, at the edge of the Red Light District.

A GAY COFFEE SHOP

In a city known for its gay life and permissive drug policy, it's no surprise there's even a gay "coffee shop" (the local tag for places with hash and grass and rarely any coffee on the menu). **The Other Side,** Reguliersdwarsstraat 6 (no phone; Tram: 1, 2, or 5; open daily 11am–1am), is a compact storefront on Amsterdam's trendy gay strip. A high-intensity gay beat pulses through the shop, where there are a few tables, a friendly crowd, and a staff who'll help you make your selection from the menu of grass and hash (you can also borrow a pipe if you forgot to pack yours).

DOWN & DIRTY: CINEMAS, SAUNAS & MORE

Amsterdam has a variety of cruising spots. There are few hang-ups about public sex here, and the biggest cruising area in the Netherlands is **De Nieuwe Meer,** a rather desolate area south of the center city off the Amsterdam–The Hague (A4) freeway (take the Sloten exit) and behind the Mercure Hotel. Look for other cars near the water and you're there. You really need a car to get here, and it's active both day and night. Closer to the city are several parks, including **Vondelpark** (Tram: 2, 5, or 20), where, far better than stinky bathrooms, is the rose garden, which is busy at night and sometimes even during the day (when it's a popular gay sunbathing area). Other spots are **Sarphatipark** (Tram: 3 or 20), near the baseball field in de Pijp neighborhood, and **Oosterpark** (Tram: 3, 7, or 10), in the middle of the park. The dunes near the gay nude beach at **Zandvoort** are also a sure thing for cruising under the sun. As always, be especially cautious in parks to avoid getting hassled by junkies or even mugged.

SAUNAS Amsterdam has definitely taken the sauna to new heights of sophistication. Local laws prohibit businesses from being open 24 hours, so a clever business operator has opened night and day saunas known as Thermos.

✪ **Thermos Day,** Raamstraat 33 (☎ **020/623-9158;** Tram: 1, 2, 5, 7, or 10; Mon–Thurs noon–11pm, Fri–Sat to 10pm; admission 30DFL/$16), is a veritable megaplex that's clean and well appointed and hugely popular on Sunday afternoons. The sauna is spread over three floors, boasting a pool and a whirlpool with a large-screen TV, a bar and cafe, plenty of cushioned semiprivate cabins, a steamroom, a very dark dry sauna, and even a beauty salon and massage services. Condoms are available at the front desk.

Looking a little more dated but still very popular is **Thermos Night,** Kerkstraat 58 (☎ **020/623-4936;** www.thermos.nl; Tram: 1, 2, or 5; open daily 11pm–8am; admission 30DFL/$16, but 22.50DFL/$12 for those under 24), near Leidseplein and a 5-minute walk from the day sauna. The trilevel complex is equipped with a sauna and steamroom, a bar, and numerous cabins. Condoms are available here too.

CINEMAS There are several sex shops with cinemas and general merchandise. In the leather district is **Adonis,** Warmoesstraat 92 (☎ **020/627-2959;** Tram: 4, 9, 16, 20, 24, or 25; open Sun–Thurs noon–midnight, Fri–Sat midnight–3am), which has private cabins, a 40-seat theater with a darkroom and even soft-drink concession, and a small video and porn shop. Look out front for a list of the day's films; entry is 12.50DFL ($7) all day. Near Rembrandtplein, **B1 Cinema,** Reguliersbreestraat 4 (☎ **020/623-9546;** Tram: 4, 9, 14, or 20; open daily 10am–1am), is an equal-opportunity movie house. There are straight flicks on the first floor, gay films on the second, and sex toys for everybody on the ground floor. There's an all-day rate of 12.50DFL ($7).

Near Leidseplein is the **Bronx,** Kerkstraat 53–55 (☎ **020/623-1548;** Tram: 1, 2, or 5; open daily noon–midnight; all-day admission 11DFL/$6), selling mags, videos, and toys. The cinema costs 11DFL ($6), and the private screening rooms cost 11.50DFL ($6.40) per half an hour and 22.50DFL ($12.50) per hour. Straight tourists are in for a surprise when they walk inside to pay for the postcards they innocently chose in the kiosks outside **Drake's,** Damrak 61 (☎ **020/627-9544;** Tram: 4, 9, 16, 24, or 25; open daily 9am–12:30am): They find the shop's main business is gay skin mags and movies. There are private cabins upstairs, and with a location in the center of town, the cinema is especially busy during the lunch and rush hours. Prices are 15 to 30DFL ($8 to $16) from 15 minutes to more than an hour.

In an area near the Spui (Tram: 1, 2, 5, 13, or 17), historically the setting for Amsterdam's gay brothels, there are the cinemas **Man to Man,** Spuistraat 21 (☎ **020/625-8797;** open daily 11am–1am), and **Le Salon,** Nieuwendijk 20–22 (☎ **020/622-6565;** open daily 10am–midnight). All-day admission is 15DFL ($8).

While women are front and center behind glass in the Red Light District (and nary a man), the guys all work behind closed doors in one of the few all-male brothels. The oldest and best known is the **Blue Boy Club & Why Not Bar,** Nieuwezijds Voorburgwal 28 (☎ **020/627-4374;** www.whynot.nl; Tram: 1, 2, 5, 13, or 17; open daily noon–2am), which brings in the crowds with free strip shows and nude dancing and a not-free live-sex show (40DFL/$22) that gives you a chance to look over the staff studs (mostly non-Dutch and supposedly over 18, costing 22DFL/$125 per hour). You're also invited to browse through a scrapbook at the upstairs bar to better familiarize yourself with all your options. Besides the two bars, there are "luxury relax rooms," an S&M room, and a cinema. Credit cards are cheerfully accepted.

Possession Is Nine-Tenths . . .

While you're free to light up in one of the city's ubiquitous smoking coffee shops, you may be surprised to learn it's technically illegal to possess such funny stuff.

8 Side Trips from Amsterdam: Delft, Haarlem & More

If Amsterdam is your only stop in the Netherlands, try to make at least one excursion into the countryside. Dikes, windmills, and some of Holland's quaintest villages await you just beyond the city limits.

DELFT

Yes, **Delft,** 38 miles south of Amsterdam, is the city of the famous blue-and-white earthenware. And, yes, you can visit the factory of De Porceleyne Fles, as long as you realize it's only a visit to a showroom and not the painting studios and other workrooms. But don't let Delftware be your only reason to visit. Not only is this one of the prettiest small cities in Holland, Delft is also important as a cradle of the Dutch Republic and the traditional burial place of the royal family. Plus, it was the birthplace (and inspiration) of the 17th-century master of light and subtle emotion, painter Jan Vermeer. Delft remains a quiet little town, with flowers in its flower boxes and linden trees bending over its gracious canals.

There are **several** trains per hour from Amsterdam's Centraal Station. The trip takes about 1 hour and 10 minutes and costs 32DFL ($16) round-trip. For **bus** information, call ☎ **020/651-2793.** If you're **driving,** take A13 in the direction of The Hague and watch for the Delft exit.

The house where Vermeer was born, lived, and painted is long gone from Delft, as are his paintings. Instead, you can visit the **Oude Kerk,** at Roland Holstlaan 753, where he's buried (open Apr–Oct Mon–Sat 10am–5pm). You might want to visit the **Nieuwe Kerk,** on Markt near the VVV office, where Prince William of Orange and all other members of the House of Orange–Nassau are buried (open Mon–Sat 11am–5pm; tower open May–Sept Tues–Sat 10am–4:30pm).

The **Prinsenhof Museum,** Sint-Agathaplein 1 (☎ **015/260-2358;** open Tues–Sat 10am–5pm, Sun 1–5pm; admission 5DFL/$2.50), on the nearby Oude Delft canal, is where William I of Orange (William the Silent) lived and had his headquarters in the years during which he helped found the Dutch Republic. It's also where he was assassinated in 1584 (you can still see the musket-ball holes in the stairwell). Today, however, the Prinsenhof is a museum of paintings, tapestries, silverware, and pottery.

In the same neighborhood you can see a fine collection of old Delft tiles displayed in the wood-paneled setting of a 19th-century mansion museum called **Lambert van Meerten,** at Oude Delft 199 (☎ **015/260-2358;** open Tues–Sat 10am–5pm, Sun 1–5pm; admission 3.50DFL/$1.75). Or to see brand-new Delftware and a demonstration of the art of hand-painting it, visit the showroom of **De Porceleyne Fles,** Rotterdamseweg 196 (☎ **015/256-9214;** open Mon–Sat 9am–5pm, Apr–Oct also Sun 9:30am–5pm; admission 5DFL/$2.65).

WHET YOUR APPETITE Delft has a full panoply of Dutch and international restaurants. The best is **Spijshuis de Dis,** Beestenmarkt 36 (☎ **015/213-1782;** open Thurs–Tues 5–9:30pm), where a meal is about 35DFL ($18). Though the specialty is steak, the pork fillet with vegetables and the lamb fillet are delicious. And try the homemade mushroom soup. **Stadsherberg de Mol,** Molslaan 104 (☎ **015/212-1343;** open Tues–Sun 6pm–midnight), is a large fun place with live music and dancing that offers a 39DFL ($20) fixed-price menu. The food is served medieval style in wooden bowls, and you eat with your hands.

HAARLEM

Haarlem, 13 miles west of Amsterdam, is a graceful town of winding canals and medieval neighborhoods that also boasts several fine museums. The best time to visit is Saturday, for the market in Grote Markt, or in tulip season (March to mid-May), when the city explodes with flowers.

Haarlem is only an hour from Amsterdam by **train,** and one leaves every hour from Centraal Station. A round-trip ticket is 10.50DFL ($5). There are also frequent **buses;** call ☎ **0900/9292** for information. If you go by **car,** take A16.

Haarlem is where Frans Hals, Jacob van Ruysdael, and Pieter Saenredam were living and painting their famous portraits, landscapes, and church interiors while Rembrandt was living and working in Amsterdam. It's also a city to which both Handel and Mozart made special visits just to play the magnificent organ of the **Church of St. Bavo,** also known as Grote Kerk, Oude Groenmarkt 23 (open Mon–Sat 10am–4pm). Look for the tombstone of painter Frans Hals and for a cannonball that has been imbedded in the wall ever since it came flying through a window during the 1572–73 siege of Haarlem. And, of course, don't miss seeing the famous **Christian Müller Organ,** built in 1738. You can hear it at one of the free concerts given on Tuesday and Thursday April to October. It has 5,068 pipes and is nearly 98 feet tall. The woodwork was done by Jan van Logteren. Mozart played the organ in 1766, when he was just 10.

From St. Bavo's, it's an easy walk to Holland's oldest and perhaps most unusual museum, the **Teylers Museum,** Spaarne 16 (☎ **023/531-9010;** open Tues–Sat 10am–5pm, Sun noon–5pm; admission 10DFL/$5). It contains a curious collection: drawings by Michelangelo, Raphael, and Rembrandt; fossils, minerals, and skeletons; instruments of physics and an odd assortment of inventions, including the largest electrostatic generator in the world (1784) and a 19th-century radarscope.

Saving the best for last, visit the **Frans Halsmuseum,** Groot Heiligeland 62 (☎ **023/511-5775;** open Mon–Sat 11am–5pm, Sun noon–5pm; admission 10DFL/$5), where the galleries are the halls and furnished chambers of a former pensioners' home and the famous paintings by the masters of the Haarlem School hang in settings that look like the 17th-century homes they were intended to adorn.

WHET YOUR APPETITE You'll find reasonably priced meals at **Café Mephisto,** Grote Markt 29 (☎ **023/532-9742;** open daily at 9:30am, meals begin at noon; closes 2am). At this comfortable brown cafe, the decor is art nouveau and the music leans toward classic jazz. The kitchen turns out very good broodjes and a respectable chicken saté.

AALSMEER FLOWER AUCTION

The Netherlands is the world's largest exporter of cut flowers, and nearly 50 percent of the flowers that leave the country are sold at the massive **Aalsmeer Flower Auction** (☎ **0297/393939**), held in the lakeside community of Aalsmeer, near Schiphol Airport. Nothing could adequately prepare you for the sight of these acres of cut flowers stacked three tiers high on moving carts. In two auction halls, hundreds of buyers compete for the best flowers at the lowest prices. The auction is open Monday to Friday 7:30 to 11am. Admission is 7.50DFL ($3.25).

To reach the auction in Aalsmeer, take **bus** no. 172 from in front of the Victoria Hotel across the square from Centraal Station. The trip will take five strips on your *strippenkart.* If you're **driving,** take A4 and follow the signs to Aaalsmeer.

8 Portugal

Breaking Down the Closet Door

by David Andrusia

Portugal is at war—with itself. On one hand, it's a country still trying to revel in its golden age of navigation and imperialism; on the other, Portugal understands its status as the poor stepchild of Western Europe, trying desperately to play catch-up before the Euro is introduced. When a nation suffers at once from hubris and an inferiority complex, a very odd national character results.

How to describe the Portuguese? Fans of Brazilian music will undoubtedly be familiar with the concept of *saudade*, which translates literally as "sadness" yet means ever so much more. (The German word *Weltschmerz* comes closer to the mark.) It's a kind of nagging nostalgia, mixed with a healthy dose of fatalism, that imbues virtually every nook and cranny of the Portuguese spirit. And it's this ubiquitous national psyche, much more than mere monuments, that'll color your trip to this historic and fast-changing land.

Indeed, there's much to fall in love with in Portugal; just don't expect the natives to lead you there. From five-star hotels to the tourist board itself, I was never less than amazed by the lack of ardor the Portuguese hold for their native land. Ask a Frenchman for a restaurant recommendation and you'll come away with 10; inquire directions of a Dane and he'll walk you to your destination, sharing the entire history of Denmark along the way. Yet the Portuguese are oddly reserved, offering no more information than you've specifically requested—and even then, often only under duress.

No matter: You'll find your own way just fine. (Of course, I'll see to that!) And, if you're lucky, you'll find more than your way. The Portuguese can be comely and kind; if outwardly undemonstrative, they're romantics to the core. Partly because of this and partly because the opportunities for chance encounters here are more limited than in other parts of Europe, the gay people seem more

The Portuguese Escudo

The Portuguese currency unit is the **escudo,** written **1$00**. Hundredths of an escudo (**centavos**) follow the $; for example, 100 escudos is written 100$00. (However, in this chapter I've omitted the final 00.) Coins are minted in 50 centavos, and 1, 5, 10, 20, 50, 100, and 200 escudos. Notes are printed in 500, 1,000, 2,000, 5,000, and 10,000 escudos.

At this writing, the dollar compared extremely favorably to the escudo: 182$ is equivalent to $1 U.S., and that was the rate of exchange I used throughout. Prices over $5 U.S. have been rounded to the nearest dollar.

interested in forming attachments than in promiscuous partnering—and I say hooray for that. The Portuguese may be a bit hard to get to know at first, but once you do, you'll be a friend for life.

The following chapter focuses on **Lisbon,** which as the capital and largest city is at the heart of Portugal's gay life. I also fill you in on **Cascais** and **Estoril,** the pretty seaside resorts that are a quick (and cheap!) train ride from the heart of Lisbon. Not only does visiting these towns make for a fun day's excursion, but Estoril also boasts a cruisy beach area.

Lisbon, of course, is where you'll spend the lion's share of your time in this historic country, which, while struggling to find its place in modern Europe, continues to offers visitors of all persuasions a glimpse of its treasures, old and new.

15 Lisbon: The Heart of Portugal's Gay Life

Of all Western European cities, **Lisbon (Lisboa)** has a closet door that's still most pronouncedly closed. Forget the hysteria that's London, the in-your-face attitude of Paris's Marais district, or even the relative tolerance of the Scandinavian lands. While gays in Lisbon are no longer the personae non gratae they were even 10 years ago, they still know not to make waves in this traditional ultra-Catholic country.

However, that isn't to say Lisbon is without a gay presence or there aren't ample meeting grounds. You just won't find a gay ghetto or parades featuring half-naked revelers all fired up on X. And if falling into a K hole is your idea of fun, you'd better leave your heart in San Francisco, sweetie.

Of course, all that may soon change as Portugal places kinship with the European Union above its traditional mores. For now, two gay groups—Associacão Abraco and ILGA Portugal—have made inroads, at least in Lisbon; these are the pioneers on whose shoulders the future of gay life in Portugal partly rests. You go, guys!

So that's the obligatory preamble to the gay scene. But there's far more to do in Lisbon (or anywhere, for that matter) than bars and baths. This is the birthplace of modern Romance languages and the city from which explorers literally found the New World. (Don't even mention Columbus here. Vasco da Gama is the name to know.) So it only stands to reason that Lisbon's sense of history is wide and deep.

The city, in fact, is arguably the oldest in all Europe; it certainly contains a greater concentration of 17th-century buildings than any other capital, and this contributes in large part to Lisbon's unique feel—for better and for worse. The central square, Praça Dom Pedro IV (known as the Rossio), looks distinctly Third World and might make you want to run screaming to Madrid and points west. But stick around to experience the up side of antiquity, which manifests itself in the centuries-old Bairro Alto, perched high above Lisbon, or in the steep cobbled streets of the upmarket Lapa district.

And that's just the start: Lisbon's museums, restaurants, and breathtaking natural setting provide more than enough treasures for a visit of several days. It's this city's special combination of history and promise that makes Lisbon a travel destination you really shouldn't miss.

1 Lisbon Essentials

ARRIVING & DEPARTING

BY PLANE All flights land at **Portela Airport** (☎ **01/840-20-60**), 4 miles from central Lisbon. The **airport bus** costs 420$ ($2.30) and runs to the Cais do Sodré train station daily 7am to 9pm, leaving in either direction every 20 minutes. Along the way, it stops at 10 major points in Lisbon, including Praça dos Restauradores and Praça do Comércio.

You can also take a **taxi,** which is far cheaper than in any other Western European capital—typically, about 2,000$ ($11) to the center of town. A surcharge of 300$ ($1.70) is added for each piece of luggage. But beware: Lisbon taxi drivers are arguably the most unscrupulous in Europe, per my experience and that of my friends. One of my gal pals was driven to an outlying area and almost raped, escaping by the grace of God and college-track-runner legs. I myself, driven to one of the nicest hotels in town, was asked to pay 5,000$ ($27), which I steadfastly refused. The doorman whittled the price down to 4,000$ ($22), which I also refused, thanks to having read *Frommer's Portugal.* I gave him 2,000$ ($11) and asked to see the director of the hotel, which set things straight.

Note: Even if you're driven slightly out of the way by a taxi driver when in Lisbon, it's no big deal, as no fare will cost you more than $5.

BY TRAIN International trains (typically, from Paris or Madrid), arrive at the **Estação de Sana Apolónia,** Avenida Infante Dom Henrique in the Alfama. Two trains run daily from Madrid to Lisbon (a 10-hour trek only the most intrepid are advised to make); trains from northern and eastern Portugal also stop here. The other principal rail stations are the **Estação do Rossio,** right downtown off Praça dos Restaudores, where you get trains to Sintra, and the **Estação do Cais do Sodré,** near Praça do Comércio, which is the place for trains to Cascais and Estoril (see the end of this chapter).

BY BUS The **Rodoviaria da Estremadura,** Av. Casal Ribeiro 18B (☎ **01/54-54-35**), is about 30 minutes by foot from Praça dos Restauradores; or you can take bus no. 1, 21, or 32 to Rossio. A minimum of 5 buses per day go from Lisbon to Faro and Porto, more in heavy tourist season. Don't, however, expect the kind of shiny, spotless autobuses you see in Germany and France; you may luck into a gorgeous new coach, but chances are you won't—and smoking en route is the rule, not the exception.

BY CAR Look at a map and it'll be clear there's only one way to arrive—through Spain. Passing at the border is painless, given Portugal's place in the European Union, though you'll have to show your passport and papers for your rented car. Happily, Portuguese roadways are exponentially better than they were even 10 years ago, and the highways in and around Lisbon are flawless and less congested than in other Continental capitals. However, do not, I repeat, not, try to drive in Lisbon. If you arrive by car, either return it to the rental agency on your arrival or find a garage and leave it there until you're ready to leave.

VISITOR INFORMATION

The principal **tourist office** is at the Palácio da Foz, on Avenida da Liberdade at Praça dos Restauradores (☎ **01/346-33-14;** Metro: Restauradores; open Mon–Sat 9am–8pm, Sun 10am–6pm). Not far away is **Lisboa Turismo,** Rua do Jardin do Reqedor 50 (☎ **01/343-36-72;** open Mon–Fri 9am–6pm, Sat–Sun 9am–1pm and 2–6pm), a municipal tourist office selling the Lisboa Card.

The Lisboa Card

The **Lisboa Card** provides free admission to 25 museums and free, unrestricted access to all forms of public transport. Discounts of 10% to 50% are also given by a variety of other places and services, like sightseeing companies, the Port Wine Institute, and the National Ballet. The cards are valid for periods of 24, 48, and 72 hours and cost 1,700$ ($9), 2,800$ ($15), and 3,600$ ($20), respectively. You can buy the card at Lisboa Turismo (see "Visitor Information" above).

CITY LAYOUT

On your first glance at a Lisbon map, you're likely to go running for the nearest glass of port wine. (I did, but then I'm not a well woman anyway.) Calm down! Three-quarters of the neighborhoods shown are residential or outlying districts you won't be visiting; and while it's true that the major tourist areas' streets are twisty and turny, there are only a couple of neighborhoods you really need to worry about. At any rate, cabs are so cheap that if you throw your hands up in despair (as I did more than once), you can just spend a few bucks to get back to your hotel and be done with it.

So here's what you need to know. Think of **Praça do Comércio,** best known for its monumental arch, as ground zero. This square, just north of the Tagus River (Rio Tejo in Portuguese), is also a major transportation hub, the heart of many bus and tram lines. At the other end of this square is **Praça Dom Pedro IV,** commonly known (though nobody could explain why) as the **Rossio,** the central core of downtown. The Rossio, in turn, abuts two other squares, the larger of which, **Praça dos Restauradores,** is dotted with cafes, tourist shops, and the throb of daily Lisbon life.

Between the Rossio and Praça do Comércio lies an area known as the **Baixa** (Lower Town, pronounced "*bye*-shah"), a shopping district that's the busiest part of the city, home equally to marauding tourists and local business folk. Directly west of the Rossio is **Chiado** ("*shya*-doh"). Though much of this was destroyed in a horrible 1988 fire, the restored Chiado remains Lisbon's classiest shopping district; this area is also a link between the low-lying Baixa and the heights of the **Bairro Alto** (Upper Town) above. By the way, walking from Chiado to the Bairro Alto is the best butt-tightener I know; heavy smokers may wish to take the funicular tram or the Elevador Santa Justa.

Just east of the Baixa is where the historic **Alfama** district begins. Block by block, building by building, this is the oldest part of Lisbon, having escaped damage in the 1755 earthquake that leveled much of the city; you'll practically see the ghosts of Moors hiding in the back alleyways and windings lanes.

To the north of downtown (generally recognized as the Baixa and Chiado), via **Avenida da Liberdade** (which tries, but fails, to be a kind of Portuguese Champs-Elysées), is the modern city. The central artery here is **Avendida da Roma,** boasting an upmarket scene of shops, businesses, and cafes.

To the west of the Rossio is the historic town of **Belém (Bethlehem),** a must-do day trip via a fun-if-slow tram line. Just northwest (reachable by tram lines 25 and 28) is the embassy-laden nabe of **Lapa,** where you'll rub shoulders with local and international gentry. And that, in a nutshell, is Lisbon, friends.

GETTING AROUND

Like most European cities, Lisbon offers cut-rate repeat-use passes for its municipal transportation system. These represent a great bargain and are valid on all city buses, trams, subways, the Santa Justa Elevator, and the funicular. At press time, a **daily pass** costs 430$ ($2.40), a **2-day pass** 1,000$ ($6), a **4-day pass** 1,640$ ($9), and a **7-day pass** 2,320$ ($13).

BY METRO Yes, Lisbon has a metro system. But unlike that in Paris or Madrid, which represents the major (and easiest) way to get around, Lisbon`s is a mere accessory compared with its far more colorful trams. The Lisbon subway system comprises two main north-south routes, which are far more important in the inbound-outbound shuttling of commuters than for getting around town. In fact, the only time you'll probably have to use the Lisbon subway is to get from downtown to the Avenida da Roma shopping district uptown—in itself an optional, not obligatory, trip. The system runs daily 6:30am to 1am.

BY BUS In all my visits to Lisbon (four, at last count), I've never once set foot in a bus. First, they're always packed to the gills and look superuncomfortable. Second, and more germanely, as a tourist you probably won't need to use them. The buses, like the subway, are geared more toward taking residents to outlying districts than for getting visitors around town. As you'll see, I offer both bus and tram routes for most listings; take the bus if you must, but the trams are almost always a much better choice. The buses run daily 6am to 1am.

BY TRAM Every city should have public transportation as cute, fun, and—at times—death-defying as Lisbon's trams. They're the perfect way to get around this old town's serpentlike hilly cobblestone lanes. The tram drivers are abject daredevils, screaming obscenities and very nearly running into all manner of cars, buses, and pedestrians. If San Francisco's cable cars are Geo Metros, these monsters are Ferraris! The trams run daily 6am to 1am.

BY TAXI Jackpot! Any city where even a freelance writer can afford to dart around town in cabs is okay by me. A cab from the airport will set you back only about 2,000$ ($11), a bit more for excess luggage, and you can hardly pay more than 5 bucks for a ride anywhere within the tourist area—usually even less. (There's a 20% sur-charge 10pm to 6am.) Plus, most of the cabs are brand-new Mercedes; don't we love that?

What you won't love is that many of the taxi drivers are major rip-off artists. Always negotiate your price to/from the airport, as cited above, before getting in the cab. You should do the same when traveling in town, though here it's hard to do major damage. Your best defense is to get a good lay of the land, though admittedly that's difficult; even if you're ripped off a little, however, it'll only be by a buck. In that case, forget about a tip; if your driver is nice, tip well—15% or 20% extra means little to even modest American budgets but will mean a lot to him.

BY CAR As I said above, don't think of driving in Lisbon. But if you want to rent a car to explore the countryside, you'll find all the major multinationals are represented: **Avis,** Av. Praia da Vitoria 12C (☎ **01/346-26-76;** open daily 8am–7pm); **Hertz,** Qto. Frangelha Baixio (☎ **01/346-26-76;** open Mon–Fri 8am–7pm, Sat–Sun 9am–1pm and 2–7pm); and **Budget,** Av. Visconte Valmar 36 (☎ **01-796-10-28;** open Mon–Sat 8am–8pm, Sun 8am–6:30pm). Of course, it'll be less expensive if you arrange for the car rental before leaving home.

Rentor emptor, however—and then some! My friend and I rented a car from one of the above for a 1-day fee of $29, per the toll-free number we called before leaving home. The local office, however, tried to tack on hidden charges, bringing the fee up to over $100. We refused to sign and had an attorney call their headquarters, to positive effect, but do you really want to go through this? Spanish and Portuguese car-rental companies are the major offenders, according to all the major travel magazines, so think twice before renting a car. My advice is to take public transportation in these countries and spare yourself the headache and letter-writing campaigns.

FAST FACTS: Lisbon

AIDS Organizations Portugal, the least developed of Western European countries, isn't known for its medical treatments of any kind. Thus, if you have AIDS or any other serious disease, I very strongly suggest checking with your doctor before visiting. If you absolutely need urgent treatment, your best bet is to contact the gay organization **Associacão Abraco,** Travessa do Noronha 5, 4th floor (☎ **01/603-835** or 01/395-79-21; Metro: Cais do Sodré; hours variable).

American Express The Am Ex office, Av. Duque de Loulé 108 (☎ **01/315-58-77;** Metro: Rotunda; open Mon–Fri 9:30am–1pm and 2:30–-6:30pm), is managed by a company called Top Tours.

Currency Exchange American Express traveler's checks always have the best rate of exchange if you cash them at a bank or bureau of exchange. I always prefer to change money at my hotel, since it's done there without the commission rate both banks and commercial agencies charge. But if you're a big spender and the exchange rate is important, do the math and then decide what's best for you.

Cybercafe You can check your e-mail or send messages at **Cyberbica,** Duques de Bragança 7, in Chiado (☎ 01/342-17-07; e-mail cyberbica@telepac.pt).

Embassies Lisbon is home to the embassies of many countries, including the **United States,** Avenida das Forças Armadas (☎ **01/726-66-00**); the **United Kingdom,** Rua São Domingos à Lapa 37 (☎ **01/396-11-91**); **Canada,** Av. da Liberdade 144–56 (☎ **01/347-48-92**); and **Australia,** Av. da Liberdade 244 (☎ **01/353-25-55**). They're all open Monday to Friday, usually 9 or 9:30am to 12:30 or 1pm and 2 or 2:30 to 5 or 5:30pm, but call ahead before making the trip.

Emergencies To call the police or to arrange emergency medical help, dial ☎ **115.**

Hospitals The **British Hospital,** Rua Saraiva da Carvalho 49 (☎ **01/395-50-67;** Tram: G), is the best bet, for all the obvious reasons. Most good hotels also keep the names of English-speaking doctors on file, should you so require.

Telephone My traveling companion and I are both graduates of Ivy League colleges and speak decent Portuguese. Neither of us, however, could figure out how to use a pay phone in Lisbon. We tried, over the course of half an hour, to make the damn thing work, utilizing an unending permutation of coin-drop techniques, to no avail. Some phones in tourist-infested neighborhoods even have English-language instruction, to no avail. We did hear a fascinating symphony of noises and dial tones, none of which exists in the United States or Canada, and one phone even had a flashing light to tell us we were screwed.

At one point, we thought we'd actually completed a call, only to be told by an electronic message display that we hadn't deposited enough coins. Our connection was then terminated at once—probably by some Ernestine-like sadista. What can I tell you? Make the calls from your hotel. You'll live longer, surcharges be damned.

Country & City Codes

The **country code** for Portugal is **351.** The **city code** for Lisbon is **1;** use this code when you're calling from outside Portugal. If you're within Portugal but not in Lisbon, use **01.** If you're calling within Lisbon, simply leave off the code and dial only the regular phone number.

2 Pillow Talk

The number of hotels in Lisbon seems to have doubled during the past 10 years. This is partly due to Expo '98, the world's fair that'll already have taken place by the time you read this, and partly due to the city's expansion and EU membership.

Travel writers everywhere rue the passing of supercheap hotel rooms in Lisbon—after Spain went as a bargain destination, Portugal was the last stop for budgeteers. That said, there are still cheap *pensãoes* to be had if price is your object.

Note that in this conservative city, there are no gay hotels per se. And don't assume that overnight guests are as easily accepted as they are in the States. In the larger hotels you should have no problem; in the smaller ultra-Catholic inns, a prayer before smuggling in your friend might work wonders.

✪ **As Janelas Verdes.** Rua das Janelas Verdes 47, 1200 Lisboa. ☎ **01/396-81-43.** Fax 01/396-81-44. 17 units. A/C TV TEL. 27,300$–40,000$ ($150–$219) double. AE, DC, MC, V. Bus: 27, 40, 54, or 60.

This may well be my favorite hotel in Lisbon, so replete is it with charm. The Janelas Verdes is located in a 19th-century mansion, and today it hardly feels less luxe than it did back then. You'll love the marble baths, period furniture, and (on the top floors) gorgeous river views. Though it isn't the most central hotel in town, its evocative atmosphere and very nice staff more than make this an excellent choice.

✪ **Casa de São Mamede.** Rua da Escola Politecnica 159, 1250 Lisboa. ☎ **01/396-31-66.** 28 units. 13,125$–15,750$ ($72–$87) double. No credit cards. Bus: 9 or 22. Tram: 24.

Originally a private town house from the 18th century, this is a charming pensão with a true Portuguese feel and shabby-genteel allure. The people who work here were most kind, and the São Mameda is a doable walk from all the bar action in the Bairro Alto. For those reasons, a highly recommended spot.

Hotel Borges. Rua Garrett 108, 1200 Lisboa. ☎ **01/346-19-51.** Fax 01/342-66-17. 30 units. 17,500$–20,000$ ($96–$110) double. AE, DC, MC, V. Metro: Chiado.

I love that this little French-style hotel is practically right next to the fabulous A Brasileira cafe—so convenient for a tryst should you meet the man of your screams over coffee. The old bat at the front desk wouldn't let me look at the rooms, but assume they're fine if not exactly luxurious. Plus, the Bairro Alto is just a short (if totally uphill) walk away.

Hotel Britania. Rua Rodrigues Sampaio 17, 1250 Lisboa. ☎ **01/315-50-16.** 30 units. A/C MINIBAR TV TEL. Fax 01/315-50-21. 18,000$–37,000$ ($99–$203) double. Rates include breakfast. AE, DC, MC, V. Metro: Avenida.

There's definite old-world charm at the Britania, a hotel that's expensive but not exorbitant. The rooms were recently redone in a kind of nondescript international middle-class style; I'm guessing the previous shabby chic was preferable. I like the Britania anyway, not least of all because the manager had actually heard of Frommer's and didn't look at me as if I were a convicted child molester.

✪ **Hotel da Lapa.** Rua do Pau de Bandeira 4, 1200 Lisboa. ☎ **01/395-00-05.** Fax 01/347-16-30. 102 units. A/C MINIBAR TV TEL. 32,500$–87,500$ ($179–$481) double; 94,500$ ($519) suite. Weekend specials about 15% less. AE, DC, MC, V. Bus: 13 or 27.

Put simply, this is *the* place to stay for business travelers or trust funders. A former palace, the Lapa (as it's commonly known) is luxe and then some. The rooms are huge, the baths larger than my apartment at home, and the free toiletries fabu. But it's the gardens that truly set the Lapa apart—walking down by the outdoor pool, I felt like a Finzi-Contini gone bad. A tad pissy, but then what five-star hotel isn't?

Hey, Big Spender

If you've finally come into your trust fund and want to blow a wad on a Lisbon hotel, there are several deluxe places that'll be more than glad to bend over backward for you. Be prepared to drop a minimum of $200 a night for a double at any of them.

The **Hotel da Lapa** and **Ritz Inter-Continental,** two of the toniest, are listed in full below. Here are some others where you'll feel like a princess, no matter what sex you are:

Hotel Tivoli, Av. da Liberdade 185, 1298 Lisbon (☎ **01/314-11-01;** fax 01/352-42-04; Metro: Avenida; Bus: 1, 2, 9, or 32).

Le Méridien, Rua Castilho 149, 1070 Lisbon (☎ **01/383-04-00;** fax 01/387-04-72; Metro: Rotunda; Bus: 1, 2, 9, or 32).

Sofitel Lisboa, Av. da Liberdade 123, 1250 Lisbon (☎ **01/342-92-02;** fax 01/342-92-22; Metro: Avenida).

✪ **Hotel Lisboa Plaza.** Travessa do Salitre 7, 1200 Lisboa. ☎ **800/528-1234** in the U.S. or 01/346-39-11. Fax 01/347-16-30. 118 units. A/C MINIBAR TV TEL. 25,000$–$31,000$ ($137–$170) double; 37,800$–48,300$ ($208–$265) suite. AE, DC, MC, V. Metro: Avenida. Bus: 1, 2, or 44.

I can't say enough good things about the Lisboa Plaza, owned by the same people who own As Janelas Verdes (above). It's an art nouveau wonder—classy without being stuffy at all, decorated without being overdone. It's central yet a nice bit removed from the hysteria of downtown; indeed, a gorgeous garden is across the way. There's even a good Portuguese restaurant on the premises.

Hotel Metropol. Praça Dom Pedro IV 30, 1100 Lisboa. ☎ **01/346-91-64.** Fax 01/346-91-66. 36 units. A/C TV TEL. 18,800$–20,800$ (103$–$114) double. AE, MC, V. Metro: Rossio.

Charming the Metropol ain't; central it is. The rooms are spare, modern, and serviceable, if without personality of any kind. The same can easily be said of the desk staff, who were among the least hospitable folks I met. If it weren't so well situated, I'd never give the Metropol the time of day; but it is, Blanche, it is!

Mundial Hotel. Rua Dom Duarte 4, 1100 Lisboa. ☎ **01/866-31-01.** Fax 01/887-57-77. 152 units. A/C TV TEL. 19,000$ ($104) double; 29,000$ ($159) suite. AE, DC, MC, V. Tram: 28.

This is a nondescript modern hotel that's nonetheless recommendable for its central location and great views from its upper floors (and yes, I admit it, the way-cute front-desk clerk I couldn't help but ogle). If you like the French Novotel chain, you'll like this place. Nothing fancy or special . . . except for sexy João.

Pensão Galicia. Rua do Crucifixo 50–54, 1100 Lisboa. ☎ **01/342-84-30.** 10 units. 4,000$–$8,000 ($22–$44) double. No credit cards. Metro: Baixa-Chiado.

Since the entrance to this pension is through a shoe-repair kiosk, you may think about checking out before you check in. Don't. The rooms themselves are quite cozy, and some even have balconies—a steal at the price. And the woman at the desk was awfully nice.

✪ **Pensão Globo.** Rua do Teixeira 37, 1200 Lisboa. ☎ **01/346-22-79.** 14 units. 4,000$ ($22) double. No credit cards. Bus: 100. Tram: 28.

This pleasant pension occupies a private house in a central location just west of the Bairro Alto. The Globo is fairly bare bones—slightly shabby, even—but a good bargain at the price, and the front-desk staff was surprisingly nice. I was assured all rooms have baths, but the fact that I saw someone coming out of her room to use the shower belies this. Though at this price, beggars can't be choosers.

✪ **Pensão Londres.** Rua Dom Pedro V 53, 1200 Lisboa. ☎ **01/346-22-03.** 39 units, 8 with sink/shower only, 15 with bathroom. 3,675$–11,000$ ($20–$60) double. DC, MC, V. Tram: 20, 24, or 28. Bus: 15.

Ask gay travelers where to stay in Lisbon, and the Londres is always among the first places mentioned. There's nothing fancy here and the baths are the size of a Chihuahua, but the Londres's location—a hop, skip, and a jump from the Bairro Alto—makes this a winner if you're looking for some action. (Both the bars and the infamous Parque Principe Real are a stone's throw away.)

Ritz Inter-Continental. Rua Rodrigo de Fonseca 88, 1200 Lisboa. ☎ **800/327-0200** in the U.S. or 01/383-20-20. Fax 01/383-17-83. 284 units. 23,000$–43,000$ ($126–$236) double; 34,000$–46,000$ ($189–253) suite. AE, DC, MC, V. Metro: Rotunda. Bus: 1, 2, 9, or 32.

From far away, this posh hotel looks rather like a Communist-era high-rise in Moscow, and up close it doesn't look much better. But when you go inside, you find antiques, fancy rugs, marble, and all manner of ritzy furnishings. The Ritz is a little off the beaten path, but that's of no concern to the monied travelers who stay here. One special note: While taking people to your room can be a tricky proposition in Lisbon, it's no problem here—or so said a randy MBA I met in a bar.

3 Whet Your Appetite

At first blush, Lisbon may not seem to offer the myriad dining choices of Paris or Milan. And certainly it's true that, while the gastronomic situation has improved vastly over the past 10 years, Lisbon isn't yet a world-class town for restaurant snobs. However, there's a happy flip side: The prices for dining here are more reasonable than those in any other Western European capital. Whether it's at an informal haunt or an old elegant classic like Gambrinus, you'll be paying less dish for dish . . . and, as Martha Stewart reminds us, that's a good thing. The other good news is that Lisbon finally has some places for the trendy crowd, and I duly note them below.

Truth be told, Portuguese cuisine has long been given short shrift, and I think that's grossly unfair. To be sure, it doesn't have the finesse of French or the culinary elan of Chinese—and Lord knows, the fat grams practically dance off your plate—but it's tasty fare indeed.

Fish is what the Portuguese do best. **Sardines** are probably the fish most commonly associated with Portugal, served fried or in oil, usually as appetizers. Equally commonplace is ***bacalhau*** (cod), typically salted and cooked with greater variety than any other type of fish. It can be fried (perhaps the most typical preparation), stewed with olives and potatoes, or barbecued churrasco style. The national dish is garlicky and delicious ***caldeirada,*** a Portuguese bouillabaisse. Its exact contents change from restaurant to restaurant, depending on what's freshly caught that day. Shellfish is wonderful but increasingly expensive and thus usually served in only the priciest restaurants. In fact, the prices are usually left off the menu, as they can change from day to day. But if you're rich or on an expense account, go ahead and enjoy a super seafood meal.

Portuguese wines are typically less expensive than their French and Italian counterparts and can be quite good indeed. ***Vinhos verdes*** (green wines) are among the most

Dining Notes

The practice of charging a *couvert* (cover) is common. It's a charge for bread, butter, and the little tins of pâté typically set on each table, and most places add it to the bill whether or not you consume those items. Some restaurants, however, will skip the charge if the extras remain untouched. In many *cafetarias,* customers are expected to prepay for snacks or beverages to be taken at the bar. Look for the sign PRÉ-PAGAMENTO near the cashier. Tell her what you want, pay, and take the receipt to the bar.

---

popular and certainly the most unique. But, naturally, **port** is what's most commonly associated with this country, and its manufacture is the main industry of Porto, the second-largest city. By the way, many people think port is always sweet, but that's not so—some of this wine is rather dry and can be drunk with a meal, though it's more commonly drunk as an aperitif or liqueur. Finally, there's **madeira,** wine fortified with brandy that makes a perfect late-afternoon libation.

Note: For the locations of the restaurants below, see the "Lisbon Accommodations & Dining" map on p. 575.

✪ **A Tasquinha.** Largo do Contador. No phone. Main courses 1,600$–3,000$ ($9–$14). MC, V. Mon–Sat 12:30–2:30pm and 7–10:30pm. Tram: 28. PORTUGUESE.

My Lisbon contact called this a hidden secret, and she was right: Nestled on a street at the foothills of the São Jorge Castle, A Tasquinha is far from the madding crowd of tourists. The Portuguese food is traditionally prepared and very reasonably priced, and a table on the outdoor terrace makes this a combination of note.

Bizarro. Rua da Atalaia 133. ☎ No phone Reservations recommended. Main courses 2,400$–4,000$ ($13–$22). AE, DC, MC, V. Mon–Fri 12:30–3pm and 7–11pm. Tram: 28. PORTUGUESE/CONTINENTAL.

It doesn't quite live up to its name, but Bizarro is a fashionable meeting spot for Lisbon's TV, magazine, and advertising folks. The food is Portuguese with a continental/fusion slant, and the results are mixed. (The owner has obviously spent some time in California; the color of the sauces is the only odd thing here.) Still and all, Bizarro is smack in the middle of the Bairro Alto.

Bonjardim. Travessa de Santo Antão 10. ☎ **01/342-74-24.** Main courses 1,100$–2,700$ ($6–$15). AE, DC, MC, V. Daily noon–11pm. Metro: Restauradores. Tram: 28. PORTUGUESE.

This cheapie has been around about a year less than Vasco da Gama, and tourists have been happy about that for decades on end. *Frango,* the delicious roasted chicken that's well-nigh the Portuguese national dish, is the star; it'll set you back a grand total of $4 (of course, the fabu greasy fries are $1.50 extra). We could do without the black pit that's the toilet, but for a great cheap meal, Bonjardim can't be beat.

Bota Alta. Travessa da Queimada 35. ☎ **01/342-79-59.** Main courses 1,400$–2,400$ ($8–$13). AE, DC, MC, V. Mon–Fri noon–2:30pm and 7–10:30pm, Sat 7–10:30pm. Tram: 28. Bus: 58. PORTUGUESE.

Always packed (with tourists and locals alike), Bota Alta is a great place to get to know Portuguese bonne femme cuisine. The preparations are honest, and though the place isn't superfancy, it's got a nice rustic Iberian touch. I love the *bife Bota Alta,* a tough piece of meat with mushrooms and gravy galore, plus the requisite greasy fries; you'll find the ubiquitous Portuguese fried codfish too. (Much ado about nothing, methinks.) Anyway, you'll leave with enough money to traipse through the nearby bars after dinner.

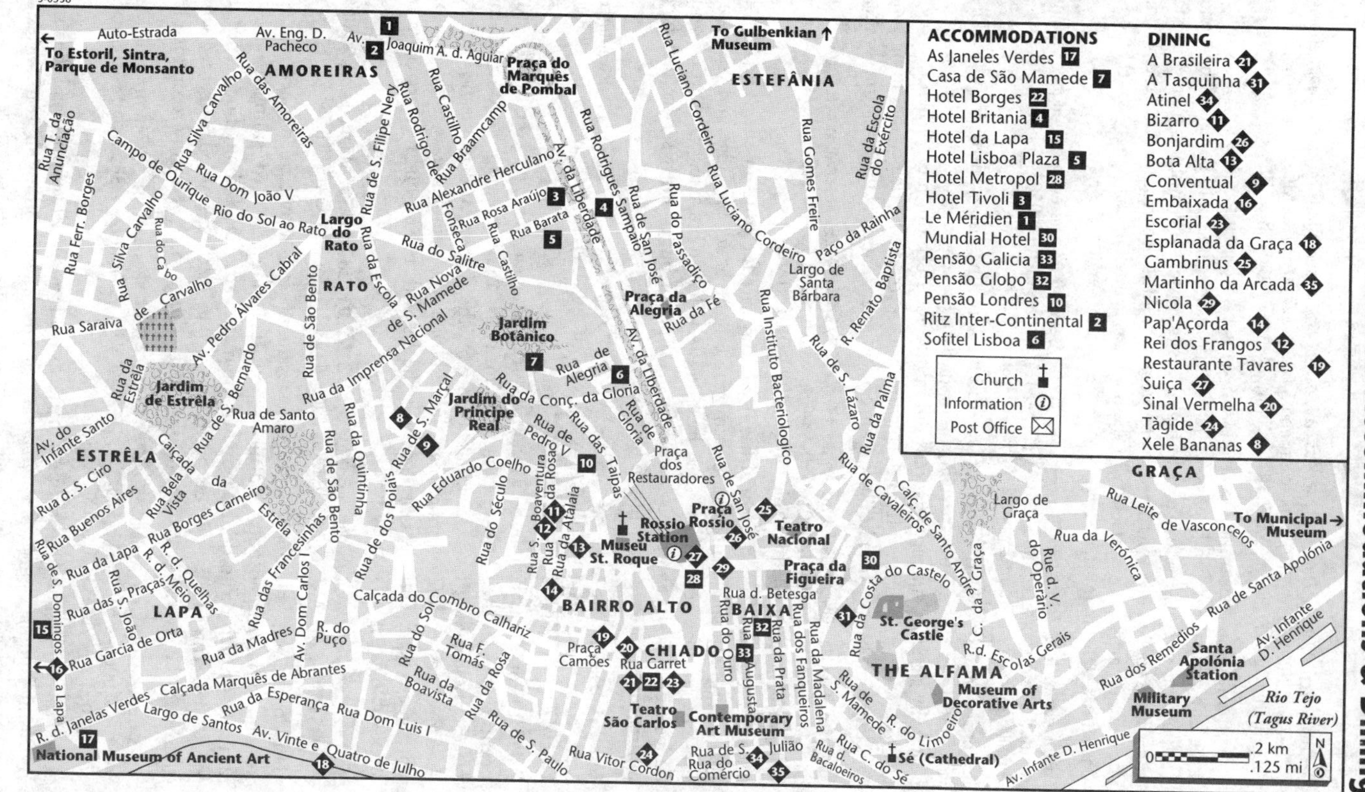
ACCOMMODATIONS
As Janeles Verdes 17
Casa de São Mamede 7
Hotel Borges 22
Hotel Britania 4
Hotel da Lapa 15
Hotel Lisboa Plaza 5
Hotel Metropol 28
Hotel Tivoli 3
Le Méridien 1
Mundial Hotel 30
Pensão Galicia 33
Pensão Globo 32
Pensão Londres 10
Ritz Inter-Continental 2
Sofitel Lisboa 6
Church
Information
Post Office
DINING
A Brasileira 21
A Tasquinha 31
Atinel 34
Bizarro 11
Bonjardim 26
Bota Alta 13
Conventual 9
Embaixada 16
Escorial 23
Esplanada da Graça 18
Gambrinus 25
Martinho da Arcada 35
Nicola 29
Pap'Açorda 14
Rei dos Frangos 12
Restaurante Tavares 19
Suiça 27
Sinal Vermelha 20
Tàgide 24
Xele Bananas 8
To Estoril, Sintra, Parque de Monsanto
Auto-Estrada
To Gulbenkian Museum
To Municipal Museum
AMOREIRAS
ESTEFÂNIA
RATO
ESTRÊLA
LAPA
BAIRRO ALTO
CHIADO
BAIXA
GRAÇA
THE ALFAMA
Praça do Marquês de Pombal
Praça da Alegria
Jardim Botânico
Jardim do Principe Real
Jardim de Estrêla
Largo do Rato
Rossio Station
Praça Rossio
Teatro Nacional
Praça da Figueira
Museu St. Roque
Teatro São Carlos
Contemporary Art Museum
St. George's Castle
Sé (Cathedral)
Museum of Decorative Arts
Military Museum
Santa Apolónia Station
National Museum of Ancient Art
Largo de Santa Bárbara
Largo de Graça
Praça Camões
Praça dos Restauradores
Av. Eng. D. Pacheco
Av. Joaquim A. d. Aguiar
Av. da Liberdade
Rua Rodrigues Sampaio
Rua de San José
Rua do Passadiço
Rua Luciano Cordeiro
Rua Gomes Freire
Rua Instituto Bacteriologico
Rua de S. Lázaro
Rua da Palma
Rua da Escola do Exército
Rua Castilho
Rua Braamcamp
Rua Alexandre Herculano
Rua Rodrigo de Fonseca
Rua do Salitre
Rua da Escola Politécnica
Rua de São Bento
Rua da Quintinha
Rua de dos Poiais
Rua do Século
Rua da Rosa
Rua de S. Paulo
Rua das Amoreiras
Rua Silva Carvalho
Rua Saraiva de Carvalho
Rua Dom João V
Rua Buenos Aires
Rua da Lapa
Av. do Infante Santo
Calçada da Estrêla
Av. Dom Carlos I
Av. Vinte e Quatro de Julho
Rua Dom Luis I
Calçada Marquês de Abrantes
Rua da Madalena
Rua dos Fanqueiros
Rua da Prata
Rua Augusta
Rua do Ouro
Rua Garret
Rua Vitor Cordon
Rua da Costa do Castelo
Rua dos Remedios
Rua de Santa Apolónia
Rua Leite de Vasconcelos
Rua da Verónica
Av. Infante D. Henrique
Rio Tejo (Tagus River)
0 .2 km
.125 mi
N
3-0538

✪ **Conventual.** Praça das Flores 45. ☎ **01/60-91-96.** Reservations required. Main courses 2,300$–3,500$ ($13–$19); prix-fixe menu 5,000$ ($27). AE, DC, MC, V. Mon–Fri 12:30–3:30pm and 7:30–11:30pm, Sat 7:30–11:30pm. Metro: Avenida. Bus: 100. PORTUGUESE.

For fashionistas and gastronomes alike, Conventual is where it's at. In fact, many folks in the know say if you can have just one meal in Lisbon, it should be here. The scene is important, of course (a mélange of high-class trendsters and business folk), but the food glitters too: a kind of updated Portuguese with influences from around the world. The stewed partridge is a specialty of the house, as is duck in champagne sauce. Conventual is a definite must.

Embaixada. Rua do Pau de Bandeira 4. ☎ **01/395-00-05.** Reservations highly recommended. Main courses 2,700$–7,900$ ($15–$43); tasting menu 8,050$ ($44). AE, DC, MC, V. Daily noon–3pm. Tram: 25 or 28. PORTUGUESE/FRENCH.

Pretentious and posh, this is the place to take someone you want to impress. The very nature of the menu—part Portuguese, part French, part God knows what—practically signals a culinary faux pas. Indeed, the food is hit or miss: When it's good, it's great; when it's bad . . . you get the picture. Still, if you meet a rich count during your trip, this is probably where he'll take you. Super desserts, notably the black forest cake.

Escorial. Rua das Portas de Santo Antão 47. ☎ **01/346-44-29.** Reservations recommended. Main courses 3,700$–8,000$ ($20–$44); prix-fixe menu $5,700 ($31). AE, DC, MC, V. Daily noon-midnight. Metro: Rossio. SPANISH/CONTINENTAL.

Like Gambrinus (below), Escorial has been a favorite for years on end. The food is Spanish rather than Portuguese and invariably quite good; partridge and paella are constant cravings here. There's also fresh lobster—lovely but likely far beyond your budget. Best of all, Escorial is known for its superior but unstuffy service. For food purists, an experience that's not to be missed.

Gambrinus. Rua das Portas de Sato Antão 25. ☎ **01/342-14-66.** Reservations required. Main courses 4,500$–10,000$ ($25–$55). AE, MC, V. Daily noon–2am. Metro: Rossio. SEAFOOD/PORTUGUESE.

Ask 10 people for their Lisbon restaurant recommendations, and you'll find Gambrinus always on their list—as it has been for years. You'd be hard pressed to call this place trendy; rather, it's a perennial favorite for the richie rich/haut business crowd. The food, respected even more than the clubby, woodsy ambience, is seafood with a Portuguese bent. Perhaps best known is the eel with bacon, but regulars claim it's impossible to get a bad meal here.

✪ **Martinho da Arcada.** Praça do Comércio 3. ☎ **01/887-92-59.** Main courses 2,200$–4,800$ ($12–$26). AE, DC, MC, V. Mon–Sat 7–11pm. Tram: 25. PORTUGUESE.

This lovely, very traditional Portuguese restaurant is a wonderful respite from the trying-too-hard trendspots and noisy tourist haunts. Refined simplicity is the attitude—which is, no doubt, why Martinho's has attracted Lisbon's finest since the days when writer Fernando Pessoa dined here. The fish and seafood, presented without fuss (I luvved the grilled swordfish) are the things to get. Heartily recommended.

Pap'Açorda. Rua da Atalaia 57. ☎ **01/346-48-11.** Reservations recommended. Main courses 2,000$–4,600$ ($11–$25). AE, DC, MC, V. Mon–Fri noon–2:30pm and 7–10pm, Sat 7–10pm. Tram: 28. PORTUGUESE.

I first saw this restaurant listed in a Spartacus guide about 10 years ago and then stole it for my landmark guide *Gay Europe*; at that time, it was nothing short of *the* restaurant for Lisbon`s ultracloseted gays. Today, it still attracts a gay crowd, as well as a nice mix of fashion types, locals out on the town, and German tourists crowing about how

Cafe Culture

As in all Mediterranean cities, Lisbon boasts a thriving cafe culture. I wish I could report that these cafes are as full of life as those in Spain and France, but they aren't. (That dour Portuguese character again.) But even though the locals don't look too thrilled to be there, you should be, especially on a sunny day—and at the right cafes. These are the ones you shouldn't miss:

The most famous coffeehouse in Lisbon is **A Brasileira,** Rua Garret 120 (☎ **01/46-95-41;** Metro: Chiado; open daily 8am–2am). Its position on one of Chiado's busiest seats truly lets you watch the city go by. The pastries and sandwiches look abysmal and the inside is truly depressing, but the outside tables are populated by local trendies, tourists, and (especially during early evening) some supercute gay guys. If you visit only one cafe, A Brasileira should be the one.

After A Brasileira, **Suiça,** Praça Dom Pedro IV 105 (☎ **01/342-80-92;** Metro: Rossio; open daily 8am–9pm), is probably the best known of Lisbon's cafes, and it's packed from dusk till dawn. Happily, there are tons of outdoor tables; and if the panorama isn't as scenic as at Atinel (below), Suiça is still a great place to watch Lisbon go by.

Always busy, **Atinel,** Praça do Comércio (no phone; Tram: 25; open Mon–Fri 6am–9:30pm, Sat to 8:30pm), is a bar/cafe alongside the ferry terminal. It affords an unbeatable view of the Tagus River to set your reveries in motion—a dream world even the too-loud German tourists can't destroy. **Nicola,** Praça Dom Pedro IV 24 (☎ **01/346-05-79;** Metro: Rossio; Tram: 25; open daily 8am–11pm), is a fine place to take a load off during the day. The drill is simple: Tourists grab the tables outside, locals (mainly lunching businessmen) the tables inside. Very cute waiters here, usually. Nicola is a daytime haunt; don't even bother at night.

The **Esplanada da Graça,** on the Esplanada de Graça (no phone; Tram: 25; open daily 10am–2am), is currently a big in-spot for local youth patronizing the clubs by the dock; given this fact, it's best to avoid this place on weekends. At night, they play music (at press time, techno) really loud—something of a drawback, but the river view is too good to pass by.

cheap everything is. Though it's rather more expensive than it once was, Pap'Acorda is still a Bairro Alto treat. I do, however, caution against ordering the eponymous dish, a not entirely pleasant compote of bread, garlic, olive oil, and God knows what kind of fish entrails.

Rei dos Frangos. Travessa de Bon Jardim. No phone. Main courses 1,000$–2,600$ ($5–$14). No credit cards. Mon–Sat 12:30–3:00pm and 7–11pm. Metro: Restauradores. PORTUGUESE.

Purists argue whether this place or Bonjardim (above) serves the best roast chicken. I say it's six of one, half a dozen of the other. Though this place has even less ambience than its competitor, I think the chicken and fries are both better here—or maybe it was the tableful of cute French guys that caught my eye. Lunch (or dinner) don't come much cheaper than this.

Restaurante Tavares. Rua da Misericorida 37. ☎ **01/342-11-12.** Reservations required. Main courses 6,200$–8,200$ ($34–$45); prix-fixe meal 10,000$ ($55). AE, DC, MC, V. Mon–Fri 12:30–3pm and 8–10:30pm. Bus: 15. Tram: 28. PORTUGUESE/CONTINENTAL.

This restaurant has been around for centuries, having originally been a cafe in (gasp!) 1784. It was for many years Lisbon's keynote restaurant and still stands at the top of many people's must-do list. The decor is trés Versailles, with faux gold leaf and chandeliers galore. (If Liberace were still alive, this is where he'd dine.) The menu highlights seafood—really, the thing to have—as well as the kind of Portuguese specialties you can get cheaper elsewhere. While this is a magnet more for businesspeople than for hipsters, Tavares is enough of a tradition to merit a visit.

✪ **Sinal Vermelha.** Rua das Gaveas 89. ☎ **01/36-12-52.** Reservations recommended. Main courses 2,000$–3,500$ ($11–$20). AE, DC, MC, V. Mon–Fri 12:15–3pm and 7:15–11:30pm. Metro: Chiado. PORTUGUESE.

As of this writing, this is a hands-down trendspot for fashion and communications types from Lisbon and beyond. The biggest surprise, though, is the food, which is surprisingly classic Portuguese fare, lovingly prepared. Among the best dishes are the liver and (most especially) the rabbit in wine sauce. Recommended strongly, whether food or fashion is your thing.

Tàgide. Largo da Academic Nacional de Belas Artes 18. ☎ **01/342-0702.** Reservations required. Main courses 3,000$–$3,900$ ($1.60–$2); prix-fixe menu 7,000$ ($38). AE, DC, MC, V. Mon–Fri 12:30–3:00pm and 7:30–10:30pm. Metro: Rossio. Bus: 15. PORTUGUESE.

The splendid view of the docks is reason enough to eat here (book well in advance for a window seat!); the ambience, a kind of upscale traditional Portuguese decor, is another. But the real star is the food, as it has been for years. (The fish is superb.) All Lisbon's movers and shakers come to roost here—and you will too, if you've got the bucks.

✪ **Xele Bananas.** Praça das Flores 29. ☎ **01/395-25-15.** Reservations recommended. Main courses 1,800$–3,800$ ($10–$21). AE, DC, MC, V. Mon–Fri 12:30–3pm and 8–1pm, Sat 8–11pm. Metro: Restauradores. Tram: 28. INTERNATIONAL.

Bananas, as it's lovingly called, would be on anyone's Top 10 list of chic Lisbon eateries, and there's always an upmarket gay presence of fashion victims and their ilk. The Brazilian/tropical decor is a bit tired (think any Holiday Inn in the Midwest), but the food, a kind of world fusion theme, is very good, if not classically Portuguese.

4 Exploring Lisbon

Lisbon offers an ample, if not overpowering, array of sightseeing attractions—enough, surely, to keep you engaged for several days. (More than three would be pushing it.) If you've got a fourth day to roam about, head for Estoril and Cascais.

I'm the last person in the world to pooh-pooh city tour buses; I think they're a great way to explore a new town your first day. Thus, I strongly recommend doing the **Circuito Tejo (Tagus tour),** operating May to September daily 11am to 4pm and costing 2,000$ ($11) for an all-day pass. The bus departs several times an hour, and you can get on and off at your heart's content.

There's also a narrated tram tour called the **Circuito Colinas (hills tour),** operating March to October and costing 2,800$ ($15). It's an interesting 90-minute ride from Praça do Comércio through the Alfama, Chiado, and environs.

Call ☎ **01/363-93-43** for more information on both of the above tours.

THE HITS YOU SHOULDN'T MISS

St. George's Castle (Castelo São Jorge). Rua da Costa da Castelo, the Alfama. Free admission. Apr–Sept daily 9am–9pm (Oct–Mar to 7pm). Tram: 28. Bus: 37.

Although this former residence of kings has been reduced to a mere shadow of its former self—no more than a shell, really—it's nonetheless worth seeing. To some extent,

A Sightseeing Tip

It's always a good idea to call ahead about opening hours, since the Portuguese notion of holidays is elastic, even taking in such occasions as Halloween and Fat Tuesday, the last day before Lent.

---

in fact, this is Lisbon's most obvious architectural symbol. At the main entrance is a statue of Afonso Henriques, who tried unsuccessfully to defend Lisbon and its inhabitants from the Crusaders and Moors. The view of the city from the towers is still spectacular, and the cafe in front of the entrance is a fine place to while away an hour writing postcards and such. It's a steep uphill walk from the nearest bus and tram stops, so you might want to take a taxi to the castle entrance and then walk back down, especially if you're sporting fancy footwear.

✪ **Sé (Cathedral).** Largo da Sé, the Alfama. Free admission. Mon–Sat 10am–5pm, Sun 10am–noon. Cloisters closed Sun. Tram: 28. Bus: 37.

Equal parts cathedral and fortress, the Sé was completed in the 12th century to commemorate Lisbon's reconquest from the Moors. The Romanesque architecture is at once elegant and reticent, unlike the ornate baroque influence that infects more recent cathedrals. The cloister, replete with tombs and other treasures, is semi-interesting; either pay the 120$ (70¢) to get in or just walk on in (no one really much cares). Just opposite the Sé is the church of Santo Antonio, which, according to legend, was built on the very spot on which the city's patron saint was born.

Belém Tower (Torre de Belém). Off Avenida Brasília, Belém. Admission 400$ ($2.20). Tues–Sun 10am–1pm and 2–5:30pm. Tram: 15 or 17. Bus: 43 or 49.

Constructed from 1515 to 1520, this almost-fantastical turreted tower looks rather like something you'd find Rapunzel hanging out of and makes a marked impression on the Portuguese coast. The Moorish influence is undeniable; in fact, the tower's architect, Francisco de Arruda, also designed Portuguese forts in Morocco. B&D enthusiasts will want to go inside the tower to get a gander at the prison used by Dom Miguel in the early 19th century; it's said to have been among the ghastliest dungeons in the world (after my apartment on New York's Lower East Side, of course).

You might also want to amble several hundred yards along Avenida Brasília to the **Monument of the Discoveries (Monumento dos Descobrimentos),** built in 1060 to commemorate the 500th anniversary of the death of Prince Henry the Navigator. In the pavement is a map chronicling Portuguese discoveries from 1427 to 1541. An elevator can take you to the top of the monument for 275$ ($1.50) on Tuesday to Sunday 9:30am to 7pm.

✪ **Naval Museum (Museu da Marinha).** In the west wing of the Jerónimos Monastery (Mosteiro dos Jerónimos), Praça do Império, Belém. ☎ **01/362-00-19.** Admission 300$ ($1.65); free Sun mornings. June–Sept Tues–Sun 10am–5pm (Oct–May to 4pm). Tram: 15. Bus: 27, 28, 43, 49, or 51.

In the huge foreboding **Jerónimos Monastery,** this museum is for anyone who loves the Smithsonian's Transportation wing. It's a tribute to Portugal's seafaring tradition and even features real vessels (as well as reconstructions thereof) used by the country's navigators in centuries past. There are excellent explanatory notes throughout, plus a couple of curiosities: a pageant of maritime uniforms and a replica of the queen's stateroom on the royal yacht *Carlos I.* Even if you think this isn't your thing, I urge you to visit this fascinating museum.

The Ups & Downs of Tram No. 28

Can a tram ride be a tourist attraction? In the case of the famous no. 28 line, I vote a resounding yes. This is the best 160$ (90¢) you'll ever spend—and maybe the scariest. Coney Island's Cyclone roller coaster has nothing on this little doozy that starts in the Lapa district (don't miss the nifty little public garden before hopping aboard) and ends up rumbling up and down hills that make San Fran look as flat as Kansas. Along the way you'll pass the Baixa District, the Bairro Alto, and the Sé. So nice you'll want to do it twice!

While you're at the monastery, built to express gratitude for the discoveries of Vasco da Gama (who's buried here) and other Portuguese navigators, you may want to explore the Gothic-Renaissance **Santa Maria,** famed for its deeply carved stonework. Entrance to the church is free, but you'll pay 400$ ($2.20) to see the cloisters.

National Museum of Ancient Art (Museum Nacional de Arte Antiga). Rua das Janelas Verdas 9, Lapa. ☎ **01/396-41-51.** Admission 500$ ($2.75); free Sun mornings. Tues 2–6pm, Wed–Sun 10am–6pm. Bus: 27, 40, 49, or 60.

Though not as large as the Gulbenkian (below), this museum in the fashionable Lapa district is very much Portugal's national gallery. It contains the largest collection of 15th- and 16th-century Portuguese artists in the world but also boasts a grand collection of European painting from the 1400s to today. (Bosch, Velazquez, and Corbet are all represented.) The museum is gorgeously set in a 17th-century palace and features meticulous gardens and a marvelous Tagus River view. There's also some auxiliary stuff like silver- and goldware and that famous filler of the art world, Flemish tapestries (yawn).

✪ **Gulbenkian Foundation Museum (Museu da Fundação Calouste Gulbenkian).** Av. de Berna 45. ☎ **01/396-41-51.** Admission 500$ ($2.75). Tues 2–6pm, Wed–Sun 10am–6pm. Metro: Palhavà. Tram: 24. Bus: 16, 26, 31, 46, 51, or 56.

The Portuguese analog to the Getty Museum, this is said to be the largest private collection of art anywhere. Indeed, the Gulbenkian is immense, so it's best to know exactly what you're after before taking this behemoth on. In general, there are two important halves: the antiquities area (really, Egyptian, Greek, Roman, Islamic, and Oriental art) and the European area. Knowing this—and utilizing the helpful directory—will allow you to tackle the Gulbenkian head-on. Those of you into Egyptology and Asiana will know what to do. If you're a cretinous Eurocentric slob like me, look for exceptional collections of Flemish art, canvases by Rembrandt and Gainsborough, and—best of all—an amazing selection of 19th- and 20th-century Frenchies, notably Manet, Monet, Degas, and Renoir. Finally, there's a wide selection of furniture, jewelry, and textiles in this mind-bending tribute to the creative spirit.

Botanical Garden (Jardim Botânico). Largo de Julio Castilho. Admission 250$ ($1.40). Tues–Sun 10am–6pm. Bus: 1 or 36.

Large but not forebodingly huge, these gorgeous gardens are among Europe's finest, ostensibly boasting over 20,000 plants. The flora are identified for botany buffs; the rest of us will be content to saunter through the greenery, escaping the constant construction and noise that's modern Lisbon. Lovely!

Santa Justa Elevator (Elevador Santa Justa). Linking Rua do Ouro in Baixa with Praça do Carmo I in the Bairro Alto. Admission 150$ (82¢). Daily 7am–11pm. Metro: Rossio.

This art-nouveau beauty is a throwback to years gone by; today it's still the best way to go from the flats of Baixa to the Bairro Alto in one swift swoop. Built in 1902 and

Lisbon Attractions

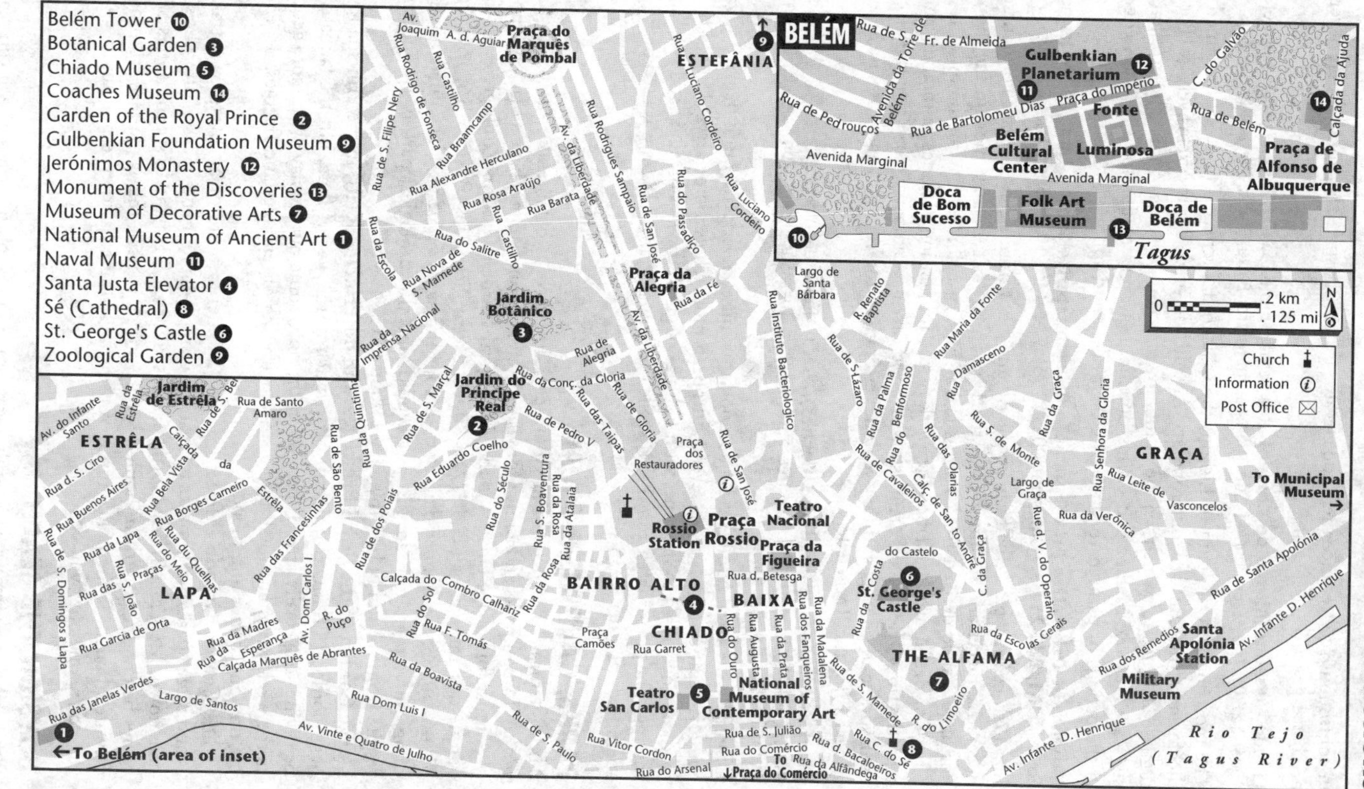

in continuous service since then, the elevator is proof positive that some things never need change.

Chiado Museum (Museo do Chiado). Rua Serpa Pinto 6. ☎ **01/343-21-48.** Admission 400$ ($2.20). Tues 2–6pm, Wed–Sun 10am–6pm. Metro: Baixa. Tram: 28. Bus: 58 or 100.

The most modern museum in Lisbon, the Chiado has replaced (indeed, subsumed) the former Museum of Contemporary Art. It's devoted almost exclusively to Portuguese art, most of which will be as unknown to you as it was to me. The excellent cityscapes by Jose Malhoa and Carlos Botelho, however, require no prior knowledge of the periods or painters to appreciate their talent and appeal.

Museum of Decorative Arts (Fundação Ricardo Espírito Santo). Largo das Portas do Sol 2. ☎ **01/886-21-83.** Admission 500$ ($2.75). Wed–Mon 10am–5pm. Tram: 28. Bus: 37.

In a 17th-century palace halfway up the Alfama hill, this museum displays Portuguese decorative pieces and furniture from the 17th and 18th centuries, most in the Indo-Portuguese style derived from Portugal's Far Eastern colonies. On the premises is a school of decorative arts, since the work of the foundation includes restoration and reproduction. The artisans are masters of wood carving, cabinetry, inlay, painting, lacquerwork, and gilding, and they've done restorations for Versailles and Fontainebleau as well as for the Rockefellers.

Coaches Museum (Museu dos Coches). Praça Afonso de Albuquerque. ☎ **01/363-80-22.** Admission 450$ ($2.50); free Sun morning. Tues–Sun 10am–1pm and 2:30–5pm. Tram: 15. Bus: 14, 27, 43, or 49.

Originally the royal family's riding school, this museum displays more than 70 royal and aristocratic coaches from several European monarchies. Some are as long as railroad cars, decorated to the nines with lashings of gilt and swags of velvet and swirls of carving. The oldest dates from 1581, while the youngest, from 1824, was used by Elizabeth II during her 1958 state visit.

PARKS, GARDENS & SQUARES

The Botanical Garden **(Jardim Botanico),** described in detail above, is the *ne plus ultra* of Lisbon parks and a must for visitors (even if you, like me, have a black thumb).

A must for foliage fanatics is the **Zoological Garden (Jardim Zoologico),** in the Parque dos Laranjeiros (☎ **01/726-80-41;** Metro: Sete Rios; Bus: 15, 16, 16C, 26, 31, 46, 58, 63, or 68; open daily 9am–8pm; admission 550$/$3). The animals are the thing, but the grounds are just as splendid, and this zoological park is a wonderful respite from the hubbub of the daily Lisbon din.

The **Garden of the Royal Prince (Jardim do Principe Real),** in the Principe Real neighborhood (Tram: 28), doesn't offer much in the way of flora, but the fauna can be divine—especially after 10pm, when the boyz come out to play, with more action as the week wears on. You'll find a sexy smattering of rentables and freebies, depending on your money and mood.

The **Campo Grande** (Metro: Campo Grande) is more of an overgrown traffic island than a park, but it makes for heavy cruising—on foot and in cars—after the sun goes down. Me, I'm a 'fraidy cat (my friends joke that I demand to see someone's SAT scores before dragging them home), but if you're a tomcat, this is the place to prowl. Beware, though: If the police throw you in the slammer, as they're not unknown to do, you're on your own.

BOYS ON THE BEACH

Praia 19 is the premier—nay, only—gay beach in Lisbon proper, and you can reach it easily in 15 minutes via tram no. 17, 18, or 19. It's quite the hot spot from late spring to early fall; though the water is often too polluted to swim in, the cruising never ends. While I can't testify under oath, my sources tell me there's an amazing amount of action under piers and behind bushes after the sun goes down.

Praia do Tamariz in Estoril is also supercruisy during summer. See the end of this chapter for information on the beach resorts of **Cascais** and **Estoril.**

WORKING UP A SWEAT

If you think you're going to find a Portuguese version of a big-city gay gym, forget it; there's no such animal here. For the few days you're in town, you should use your **hotel gym** (if it has one and it's a good one) or see about a guest pass at the **Hotel Lapa,** which has a nice (if not huge) pool and passable workout area. The people I asked about this were a bit shocked: Do Americans have to work out every day—even on vacation? My sentiments precisely; pass the pastry, please.

Horseback riding appeals to this Maryland boy. If it does to you too, try the **Penha Longa Country Club** outside the city (☎ **01/24-90-33**). Horses are rented for about 3,500$ ($19) per hour.

Golf is a big deal here, and the courses (especially those near Estoril) are quite something. The best and classiest are in Linhó, near Sintra: **Caesar Park,** Estate da Logoa Azul (☎ **01/924-90-11**), and the **Penha Longa Golf Club,** Quinta da Penha Longa, on the site of a former monastery (☎ **01/924-90-22**). If they're booked, contact the **Estoril Golf Club** at ☎ **01/468-01-76.**

BULLFIGHTING

See the bulls at the **Praça de Touros,** Campo Pequeno (☎ **01/793-20-93;** Metro: Campo Pequeno). In Spain, the bulls ultimately die, but that's not the object here; instead of one matador, Portuguese bullfights feature a man on a horse and an on-foot cavalry of 8 macho men who try to wrestle the bull to the ground. (Me, I'd like to wrestle the guys to the ground.)

5 Hitting the Stores

While Lisbon's shopping scene is vastly better than it was during my first visit 10 years ago, it still leaves a lot to be desired. The best stores for clothing (with a few exceptions, noted below) are still local branches of trans-European chains, but even then you won't find a lot to write home about. I'm not a shopaholic, but if you are, I suggest you supplant your desire with other activities while in town; either that or go through withdrawal as best you see fit.

If that sounds like too great a cross to bear, take a cab to the **Amoreiras** shopping center (yes, malls have invaded Europe in force). There's nothing extrafabulous here, but you'll find the usual suspects like Benetton and Body Shop.

If you really must buy something, antiquities, tiles, and booze are the things to go for. Maybe it's because I live in a New York City tenement, but I still have no clue as to why people feel compelled to lug Portuguese tiles back home. Even my friend Robin, who bought some for her mother, had no idea what she wanted them for. Trivets? Coasters? Oversized medallions? Write and let me know.

Most shops are said to open daily 10am to 10pm, but each really sets its own hours. Call first if you want to be sure.

SHOPS A TO Z

ANTIQUES **Rua Dom Pedro V** in the Bairro Alto is the place to go for authentic antiques. My favorite shop is ✪ **Carvalho & Gil,** Rua da Escola Politécnica 31–33 (☎ **01/346-94-17;** Tram 15 or 28). *Diversos objectos de arte,* their business card proclaims, and that's just about right. This old-world shop has all kinds of fancy stuff and comes replete with a crusty dowager/proprietress. Since my entire life's possessions include a laptop and five old Psychedelic Furs tapes, I'm no expert, but the antiques look pretty good to me. Or maybe I just liked the ancient broad's moxie—you will too.

ARTS & CRAFTS The Baixa and Bairro Alto are awash in tacky crafts shops; buy AYOR. If you're willing to spend a bit more for real Portuguese artifacts, head to ✪ **Fabrica Sant'ana,** Rua do Alecrim 95 (☎ **01/342-25-37;** Metro: Chiado). This is kind of a factory outlet for the aforementioned tiles (no further comment), as well as ceramics and other doodads. Though not as highly regarded as Sant'Ana, the tile shop **Fabrica Viuva Lamego,** Largo do Intendente 25 (☎ **01/885-24-08;** Metro: Intendente; Tram: 17, 19, or 28), is a lot closer to the center of town. You be the judge.

✪ **Olaria do Desterro,** Rua Nova do Desterro 14 (☎ **01/885-03-29;** Metro: Jardim Botanico), is a family-owned shop and company that has been producing high-quality Portuguese ceramics and pottery for a century and a half. Lovely stuff, perfect for gifts.

BOOKS The **Livraria Bertrand,** Rua Garrett 73 (☎ **01/346-86-46;** Metro: Chiado), is a wonderful large bookstore with titles in English and other foreign languages, plus a large supply of gifty books and a knowledgeable staff. The **Livraria Portugal,** Rua do Carmo 70 (☎ **01/347-49-82;** Metro: Chiado), is another bookstore with titles in English as well as Portuguese. Kinda cruisy too.

FADO & OTHER MUSIC A little fado goes a long way. But if you're hell-bent on taking home a CD or cassette, **Valentim de Carvalho,** Praça Dom Pedro IV 57 (☎ **01/342-02-05;** Metro: Rossio). The staff, like most Portuguese sales help, is vastly unhelpful, though, so it's good to know what you want before you stop in. Not that it matters: It all sounds the same.

FASHION **Atalaia 31,** Rua da Atalaia 31 (☎ **01/346-20-93;** Tram: 28), sells high-fashion men's clothing, including some by local designers, plus the usual retinue of accessories and colognes. I didn't buy anything, though I certainly would've liked to have taken the shop clerk home.

✪ **Jose Antonio Tenente,** A. do Ultra Mar 13C (☎ **01/482-0451;** Tram: 28), is the most interesting of the new breed of homegrown designer shops that've been popping up around the Bairro Alto. Both men's and women's clothes are on display, as are some funky accessories and assorted doodads. The duds are made with what my designer friend Jerry calls loving fingers. This shop is definitely worth a look. **Massimo Dutti,** Av. Guerra Junqueiro 13D (☎ **01/846-56-68;** Metro: Roma Portugal), is awash with branches of this Italian men's clothing chain. This is hardly alternawear (think upper-middle-class Eurotrash), but the clothes are well made and the price points excellent. Plus, there's always at least one way-cute guy on the sales staff you can invite into the try-on room for personal advice.

Often called the new Benetton, **Zara,** Rua Garret 9 (☎ **01/47-18-23;** Metro: Chiado) and Av. Junquerio 16A (☎ **01/847-07-11;** Metro: Roma), is a now-international chain of Spanish stores with branches galore in Portugal. The clothes range from very stylish to preppie chic; they're well made, well merchandised, and very well priced. Several suits, priced at $250, would make a perfect addition to anyone's wardrobe.

FLEA MARKET On Tuesday and Saturday the ✪ **Fiera da Ladra** ("Thieves" or Flea Market) goes on from 9am to 6pm in Campo de Santa Clara behind the Igreja São Vicente. Take bus no. 12 from the Santa Apolónia Station.

SHOES **Annabella C,** Rua do Carmo 67C (☎ **01/346-3875;** Metro: Rossio), is a nicely merchandised shoe emporium. It isn't avant-garde, but you'll find good-quality contemporary shoes at super prices; the staff is knowledgeable and nice. Remember, Clarisse: A good bag and cheap shoes will never do.

SPIRITS & FOODSTUFFS You can hardly travel to Portugal without bringing back good local wines, and the porto varieties should be at the top of your list. **Mercearia Liberdade,** Av. da Liberdade 207 (☎ **01/354-70-46;** Metro: Avenida; Bus: 41, 44, or 45), is the shop everyone recommends, despite its alternately bored and surly staff. While the wines tend to be upmarket (you can buy supercheapos anywhere), they're expertly picked and sensibly displayed.

I love the small, ancient **Manuel Tavares,** Rua da Betesga (☎ **01/342-11-12;** Metro: Rossio), a kind of one-stop shop for foodstuff gifts. The wines are popularly priced to expensive, and there's a wide range of chocolates, cheeses, coffees, and more.

6 All the World's a Stage

The best newspaper to consult for listings is ***Capital.*** Also good is ***What's On in Lisbon.*** Both are available at most newsstands.

THE PERFORMING ARTS

The gorgeously ornate ✪ **Teatro Nacional de São Carlos,** Rua Serpa Pinto 9 (☎ **01/346-59-14;** Tram: 24 or 28; Bus: 15 or 100), is worth a look even if you're a cultural philistine. Of course, if you're not, you'll want to check the local listings to see who's performing—both Portuguese national companies and traveling troupes from around the world have wowed audiences here. Tickets run 2,500$ to 9,600$ ($14 to $53).

At the **Teatro Municipal de São Luis,** Rua Antonio Maria Cardoso 40 (☎ **01/342-12-79;** Metro: Cais do Sodré; Tram: 10 or 28), you'll find orchestral music of all kinds and occasional dance performances. The Lisbon papers tell who's on and when. Tickets run 1,000$ to 2,500$ ($5 to $14).

Additionally, you should know that there are **free recitals** at the Carmo and São Roque churches in the Bairro Alto most Saturday nights; listings are posted, but there's no phone number to call. Periodically, the Sé also hosts chamber music; again, if this interests you, check during your visit there.

If you speak Portuguese, you may want to visit Lisbon`s version of the Comédie-Française, the **Teatro Nacional de Dona Maria II,** Praça de Dom Pedro IV (☎ **01/342-84-49;** Metro: Rossio; Bus: 21, 31, 36, or 41). If you don't, you won't.

FADO & OTHER MUSIC CLUBS

This is the place where every guidebook waxes poetic about **fado,** the ages-old Portuguese song tradition. I'm supposed to say that this is every bit as important as American blues, how it reflects the national character, how it influenced contemporary Brazilian music, blah, blah, blah.

Well, fasten your seat belts, because I'm going to go against the grain—far against it. First, a little bit of fado goes a long way. A good point of reference: How many mariachi songs can you stand in a row? Three? Four? (One, if it's Linda Ronstadt singing.) That's about how many fados you'll be able to listen to before you start wondering whether Céline Dion really isn't that bad. Second, fado just isn't something that interests young 'uns anymore; go and you'll be surrounded by a lot of tourists and maybe a few depressed oldsters out for a night on the town. I asked loads of Portuguese under 40 if they ever went to fado clubs and didn't get a single positive response. Last, and perhaps most important, fado clubs are huge rip-offs—the price you pay is indirectly related to the amount of fun you'll have. As Nancy Reagan once said, "Just say no."

If you feel you absolutely *must* go to a fado club, I recommend ✪ **Timpanas,** Rua Gilberto Rola 24 (☎ **01/397-24-31**), which is a bit off the beaten path and most favored by residents. It's not cheap but not a tourist trap either, and aficionadi claim the songs and stylists are quite good.

I say you forget fado and visit one of Lisbon's African or Brazilian music clubs instead. Either choice is less touristy, less expensive, and much more likely to be populated by some cute guy out for a night with friends. The best choices for African sounds are **B.leza,** Largo Cone-Barão 50 (no phone; Metro: Cais do Sodré); **Kussunguila,** Rua dos Luisadas 5 (☎ **01/363-35-90;** Bus: 22, 27, 40, 42, or 56); and **Lontra,** Rua de São Bento 157 (☎ **01/369-10-83;** Metro: Rato). Brazilian music hot spots include **Bipi-Bip,** Rua Oliveira Martins 6 (☎ **01/797-89-24;** Metro: Martim Moniz), and **Pe Sujo,** Largo de São Martinho 6 (☎ **01/886-56-29;** Bus: 37).

Rocksters will want to hit the mosh pit (just kidding) at **Cinearte,** Largo de Santos 2 (☎ **01/396-53-60;** Metro: Cais do Sodré; Bus: 44, 45, or 82), which hosts bands, mostly Portuguese, every night except Sunday and Monday, and **Gartejo,** Av. da Ceuta 38–48 (☎ **01/395-59-77;** Bus: 14, 22, 27, 32, 38, 40, or 43), a performing place for bands from Europe and (sometimes) the States. If you're a jazz baby, check out **Hot Clube de Portugal,** Praça de Alegria (☎ **01/346-73-69;** Metro: Avenida; Bus: 40 or 43), unanimously regarded as the city's best jazz club.

7 In the Heat of the Night

Anyone who's stared a list of gay nightlife in London, Paris, or New York in the face knows—and I believe Ringo Starr said this first—it don't come easy. The choices are endless, a situation that could throw someone as anal as me into a real tizzy. You'll thus be cheered to know that finding your fave spot in Lisbon is mere child's play: In a couple of nights you can hit virtually all the city's clubs and watering holes. (Of course, that's less welcome news if you actually have to live there.)

Virtually all Lisbon's gay sites are entered by pressing a buzzer outside and waiting for someone to let you in. It's a deliciously louche touch that makes you think you're entering a forbidden den of iniquity. But such is not the case. Lisbon's bars are tame affairs by international standards: No drug deals, gyrating go-go boys, or dark-corner activity. No matter—you'll find plenty else to occupy your time, especially on weekends, when gazing at the local gentry is good eye candy indeed.

Note that the bars' happy hours begin at 11pm; most have two-for-one drink specials until midnight. And don't even think about popping into a disco 'til the clock strikes 12 (1am is better still if you don't want to be the only one in the place). Here's where to hang.

GAY & LESBIAN BARS

✪ **Agua-no-Bico,** Rua do São Marçal 170 (☎ **01/347-72-80;** Tram: 24; Bus: 15, 58, or 100), is a sexy little grotto with Day-Glo orange walls and work by local artists (given the size of this place, that usually means about two large canvases). As in most Lisbon bars, you can order coffee as well as booze. The bartenders, who refused to relinquish their names, are the sexiest in town, and the crowd tends toward the boho side (if only slightly perceptibly).

Another tiny Eurobar, ✪ **106,** Rua do São Marçal 106 (☎ **01/342-73-73;** Tram: 24; Bus: 15, 58, or 100), has a modern decor and less pretty, bitchier staff. The crowd is the most yuppified of all the Bairro Alto bars, though since everybody barhops anyway—and you'll undoubtedly do the same—the distinction may ultimately be moot.

Tattoo, Rua de São Marçal 15 (no phone; Tram: 24; Bus: 15, 58, or 100), is billed as a leather bar, and from the name, I was willing to believe it was true. Alas, I didn't see any evidence of that. What I did see was a semisleazy crowd and hustlers plying their trade.

Reputed to be the oldest ongoing gay bar in Lisbon, **Harry's Bar,** Rua São Pedro de Alcântara 57–61 (☎ **01/346-07-60;** Tram: 24; Bus: 15 or 100), has the luck of the Irish: Every time I've visited Lisbon, there's a rumor the place is soon going to close, yet it refuses to die. The crowd is a little bit of everything (gays, slumming straights, whatever), with a downward slant on the socioeconomic meter. Whether the patrons were druggies, hustlers, or what passes for counterculturists in a city like Lisbon was beyond me; I didn't stick around long enough to find out. Not recommended, except perhaps for gay historians.

The minuscule **Finalmente,** Rua da Palmeira 38 (☎ **01/347-26-52;** Bus: 15, 58, or 100; Tram: 24), calls itself a disco, but there's just a bit of hubris in that; in fact, Finalmente is so crowded on weekends there's barely room to breathe. On a tiny stage (I'm talking about 2 feet square), a drag show begins at about 12:30am. While said performers sometimes ape Liza or Madonna, they more frequently mimic a European diva I didn't know—or maybe no one specific at all. The place is nothing special and is just too cramped on weekends, but perhaps it's worth a quick look during the week.

DANCE CLUBS

✪ **Kings & Queens,** Rua de Cintura do Porto de Lisboa, at the Alcantara Docks (no phone; Tram: 15; admission 1,000$/$5), is arguably the hottest gay dance club in town. In fact, though it opened as a gay place, the breeders have moved in, and the mix is now about 70%/30% (still in our favor). Kings & Queens is the latest brainstorm from nightlife impresario Pedro Luz, and it's a winner—a huge glittering disco with an industrial decor and the latest international dance sounds. The crowd is young, pretty, and hip; if you're a dance freak or trendster, this is the place.

Until the opening of Kings & Queens, **Frágil,** Rua da Atalaia 128 (☎ **01/346-95-78;** Bus: 15 or 100; Tram: 28; admission 1,000$/$5), was Lisbon's top mixed fashion crowd haunt; its allure may have been distilled somewhat, yet it's still a very hip place to go, especially during the week, when only the hard-core clubbers venture out. The quality of the patrons tends to be high, as the drinks are pricey and a tacit door policy is in effect, keeping dealers, hustlers, and other trashoids at bay.

In the narrow streets of the Bairro Alto, the **Memorial Bar,** Rua Gustavo de Matos Sequeira 42A (☎ **01/396-88-91;** Bus: 58 or 100; admission 1,000$/$5), is tops in the lesbian community. Around 60% of the crowd is usually lesbians, the rest gay men (but gays seem to be moving on elsewhere, so the number of women keeps growing). Newcomers will feel especially welcome. Twice a week there's usually live entertainment—comedy, cross-dressing, and the like.

Kremlin, Escadinhas da Praia 5 (☎ **01/60-87-68;** Bus: 32 or 37; admission 1,000$/$5), is a kind of latter-day Area (the defunct New York club famous for new installations as the owner's whims arose), with a trendy fashionable young crowd of all persuasions. It's more het than homo, but the gay scenesters (from Lisbon and beyond) certainly make their presence known. If you're the type to high-hat gay bars in favor of mixed dance palazzi, Kremlin is for you. Caveat emptor: There`s a door policy to keep out the old, ugly, and suburban, but it's more dutifully enforced on weekends than during the week.

A Lisbon tradition, **Trumps,** Rua da Imprensa Nacional 104B (☎ **01/397-10-59;** Bus: 58; admission 1,000$/$5, including one drink), is the longest-running gay dance club, and it's still fun (even if the crowd is no longer exclusively gay/lesbian). Recently remodeled, this is a large but not daunting two-tiered affair, with raging music and a (generally) good-looking crowd. Plus, since Trumps is less pretentious than Kremlin, it's easier to hook up—especially during the week, when the crew definitely looks to be on the prowl.

Rather nondescript, **Bric-a-Bar,** Rua Cecilio de Sousa 84 (☎ **01/342-89-71;** Bus: 15, 58, or 100), is a small dance bar that has fallen on hard times since the opening of other joints. The staff is cute, the patrons far less so and definitely on the unfashionable side. Still, if you're in the Bairro Alto on a horny lone night, it's worth popping in. Ya never know.

A SAUNA

From late afternoon to all hours of the early morning (especially on weekends), **Spartacus,** Praça da Misericordia 1 (no phone; Bus: 15 or 100; Tram: 24), is the sauna of record in Lisbon. My friend Adolph reports that many of the patrons are married, since this is still the preferred state of affairs in Portugal. Anyway, this sauna is fairly modest—it's smaller and less elaborate than it is overdone, almost elegant analogs in Paris or Madrid. Still, Spartacus is clean, cruisy, and centrally located to the Bairro Alto clubs and certainly worth a visit if the baths are your thang.

8 A Side Trip to Estoril & Cascais

Alone among European capitals, Lisbon boasts a bustling beach scene wonderfully close at hand. What's more, the twin towns of **Estoril** and **Cascais** are superaccessible: From Lisbon's Cais do Sodre station, trains leave every 20 minutes daily 5:30am to 2:30am and cost the princely sum of 185$ ($1).

ESTORIL

Of the two, **Estoril** is Portugal's answer to Palm Beach and maintains its position as the home of choice of dispossessed royalty from around the world. While I saw neither king nor queen, I did see a lot of fancy houses, ranging from the truly magnificent to the kind of god-awful monstrosity favored by Persian internists in Beverly Hills. Part of the Costa do Sol or Portuguese Riviera (at least by the tourism commission), Estoril features a casino (calling Suzanne Somers!), good golf courses, and luxury hotels.

Estoril is also the home to a major gay beach, the ✪ **Praia do Tamariz.** While the entire beachfront is obviously not exclusively gay (this isn't Fire Island), the homo presence is easy to discern—just look for the tiniest trunks and biggest baskets. (The occasional beacon of badly blonded hair will offer another important clue.)

Since much of Estoril's entertaining takes place in private homes/mansions, its street life is rather less interesting than that in Cascais; apart from the beach and casino, there aren't scads to do. With one exception: the **Parque Estoril,** a beautiful public garden that recalls similar spaces in the south of France.

If you're planning to spend the night in Estoril, beg, steal, or borrow to stay at the ✪ **Palacio,** Rua do Parque, 2765 Estoril (☎ **01/468-04-00**). It beckons from on high as soon as you come anywhere near Estoril, and it's indeed the coastal spot for celebs, politicians, and rich folks. A recent remodeling has left this five-star beauty in most excellent shape, and the bar would seem to be a prime place to find a trust-funded hubby or date. Rates are 42,000$ ($231) double or 48,000$ ($264) suite.

Estoril's restaurants tend to be expensive and snotty; if you end up here rather than Cascais for lunch or dinner, **A Mare** (☎ **01/468-55-70;** open daily noon–3pm and

7–11pm), with excellent just-off-the-boat fish, is definitely the best choice. And if you're planning to shake your groove thang, get on over to **Absurdo,** Praia do Tamaris, open every night except Monday; this small club attracts a glittery Eurotrash crowd after midnight.

CASCAIS

Much more fun than Estoril is **Cascais,** the neighboring town (4 miles west), which you can reach by cab or, better still, a leisurely walk along the beachfront promenade. Not quite the small fishing village it once was, the town still boasts daily auctions of the catches of the day; and behind the glossy veneers of the boutiques, in smaller travessas near the docks, you can still find the kind of trashy street types you'd expect to hang around this kind of place.

Cascais also offers more shopping opportunities, cheaper restaurants, and a younger nightlife scene than Estoril. The main artery is **Rua Fredeco Arouca,** the street around which shops, eateries, and other commerce are based. For shopping enthusiasts, there's enough to do here to while away a couple of hours.

But there are also sights to be seen. Chief among these is the **Igrega da Assunção,** Largo do Assunção (no phone; open daily 9am–1pm and 5–8pm), whose tile work has remained intact (a major earthquake notwithstanding) since the mid-1700s. Just beyond the church is the charming **Parque Municipal da Gandarinha** (open daily 10am–5pm), a lovely place for a stroll or a troll. At one end of the park is the **Conde Castro Gimaraes Library Museum (Museu Biblioteca Conde Castro Gimaraes),** on the grounds of an old mansion (no phone; open Tues–Sun 10am–5pm; admission 250$/$1.40). Decorator queens will love the furniture, art, and other curios that pepper the house. At the opposite end of the park is the **Maritime Museum (Museu do Mar)** (no phone; open Tues–Sun 10am–5pm; admission 200$/$1.10), a small but worthwhile look at Portugal's maritime glory.

If you decide to stay in Cascais, do whatever necessary to make the ritzy-but-unstuffy **Hotel Albatroz,** Rua Frederica Arouca 100, 2750 Cascais (☎ **01/483-28-21**), your temporary home. This swank beach hotel is rather like something an Anita Brookner character would end up in. Naturally, you'll want to request a room with a view. A modern behemoth teeming with French (and other) tour groups is the **Estoril Sol,** Parque Pamela, 2750 Cascais (☎ **01/483-28-31**), whose balconied rooms afford great ocean views. A double goes for 33,000$ ($181). If you're on a budget, the **Pensão Palma,** Av. Valbom 15, 2750 Cascais (☎ **01/438-77-97**), is ace—a charming little place with a private garden and supernice staff.

Where to eat? For the expense-accounted, the **Restaurant Albatroz** in the eponymous hotel, Rua Frederica Arouca 100 (☎ **01/483-28-21;** open daily noon–3pm and 7–11pm), is a must. The food is continental/updated, with nods to Portuguese fish and game. The **Adega do Goncalves,** Rua Afonso Sanches 54 (no phone; open daily 7–11:30pm), is unpretentious and cheap and serves big portions of traditional Portuguese food with minimal interference from German tourists. And priced somewhere between the previous two, **O Muchaxo,** Praia da Guincho (☎ **01/487-01-21;** open daily noon–3pm and 7–11pm), boasts fresh fish and seaside vistas that combine to produce the best choice of all.

What to eat? Try the strippers at **Coconuts,** Estrada Do Guincho 126, (☎ **01/483-01-73;** on Wednesday nights. (As Joan Rivers would say, "Oh, grow up!") This place isn't gay, but it's where queers in Cascais go out to join the other trendies who call Coconuts home. **News,** Estrada da Malveira (no phone), is a dance hot spot from which the more intrepid among you can certainly drag home a confused local or two.

9 Spain

Olé España!

by David Andrusia

As a travel writer, I'm constantly asked one general question by friends and acquaintances alike: What's the hot place to go in Europe this year? For the past decade, my answer has been the same: Spain.

Why am I so bullish on what I consider to be the most fabulous country on earth? Some would say I've watched Madonna's "Take a Bow" and "You'll See" videos one too many times (you know, the ones with that totally cute matador in those totally tight pants). But my love affair with Spain has blossomed not out of unrequited love but out of firsthand experience: I've never gone anywhere in the country and had less than a glorious time. Which is why I feel so confident in recommending this hot, happening, and hip land to one and all.

Quite simply, Spain has it all: culture, great cities, nightlife, beaches, and a joie de vivre that's more infectious than what you'll find anywhere else I've ever been. Couple this with an economy that in the past 20 years has grown by leaps and bounds—Spain now has one of the 10 largest GNPs in the world—and the result is a progressive country whose newfound affluence provides a counterpoint to the tradition and character of its glorious past.

Indeed, contemporary Spain is among the most progressive societies on the planet, and nowhere is this more apparent than in the flowering of gay life. Even small cities have gay bars and saunas, and when it comes to the big guns, Madrid and Barcelona, the scene is as wild and frenzied as any elsewhere. In Spain today, anything goes—and does!

Of course, this wasn't always the case. When I first visited as a student nearly 20 years ago, I thought Spain a dusty, dreary place. And having just shorn the shackles of Franco's repressive regime, it was dusty and dreary, especially when compared to the rest of Western Europe. But everything's different now.

Where to go in Spain? It depends, of course, on the amount of time you have and where your interests lie. A friend of mine, a beautiful circuit boy, recently spent a week on Ibiza without ever visiting Barcelona or Madrid; but then he thinks the Prado is an Italian designer.

The Spanish Peseta

The unit of currency is the Spanish **peseta (P),** with coins of 1, 5, 10, 25, 50, 100, 200, and 500 pesetas. Be aware that the 500P coin is easily confused with the 100P coin, and that the old 25P coin has been replaced with a smaller brass coin with a hole in the center. Notes are issued in 1,000P, 2,000P, 5,000P, and 10,000P denominations.

At this writing, 150P is equivalent to $1 U.S., and that was the rate of exchange I used throughout. Prices over $5 U.S. have been rounded to the nearest dollar.

Reserving Your Hotel on the Web

Jordí De Vernet, whom I met at the ultracheap, totally delicious restaurant Egipte in Barcelona, has his own company, **Vernet & Partners,** which arranges hotel reservations in Spain via the Web. (Jordí specializes in his hometown of Barcelona.) The Web address is **http://members.tripod.com/~devernet,** or send an e-mail to **devernet@maptel.es.** This sounds like a wonderful and cost-effective alternative to phoning across the Atlantic; plus, you can get scads of good information on individual hotels and rates.

Unless you're a total vulgarian or hate the sun (hello, Morrissey), I recommend a combo of city and shore. This is a combination most easily achieved by hitting beautiful **Barcelona** and swingin' **Sitges,** which, most conveniently, are only 40 minutes apart from each other by train.

Naturally, a grander tour of Spain would be even more fun, in which case you should visit the capital, **Madrid** (which, with the 1993 opening of the Thyssen-Bornemisza Museum, has become one of the world's great art centers), and **Ibiza,** an island so enchanting that even hordes of tourists can't make it less so.

Enchanting, by the way, is a word that could easily describe the men of Spain, quite possibly the best looking anywhere and as hip, sexy, and sweet as they come. They're just part of the reason that, if you're anything like me, your first visit to this festive country most certainly won't be your last. And sisters of Sappho will go ga-ga over *las chicas,* among the most desirable women in the world.

16

Madrid: Let's Party Muchacho!

As my cab pulled into **Madrid** in the wee hours of a Sunday morn, I was struck by all the sexy young guys waiting for buses and taxis in the dawn light. How sweet, I thought, they're going to mass. I smiled as wide as some beatific Church Lady, thinking I had my opening sentence nailed down: "Despite all the advances in Spain's economy and society, the institutions of family and church are what remain at the heart of life in this charming land."

Then I realized the truth: These cute (if slightly shopworn) guys aren't going to *church*. They're going *home*—after a night of depravity and drugs in the clubs.

So let me rethink that lead sentence. How about: "The only shrine most young Madrileños worship at these days is that of the holy trinity of clothes, clubs, and cash. Heady, hedonistic, and very hot, modern Madrid is every bit as dizzy and daring as an Almodóvar film."

Oh, well—a bit heavy on the alliteration (not to mention hyperbole) but you get the point. What was once a dusty old-world capital has become a major international city of note, on a par with Paris, London, and New York. But you can't really get a good feel for Madrid unless you throw the Castillian character into the mix. These are people not on the verge of a nervous breakdown but folks constantly diving head first into a love affair with life. And so it has been since Franco left power, an event that produced the spunky, punky socioartistic free-for-all known as La Movida.

Unlike Barcelona, which assiduously asserts its connections with hard-working Europe, Madrid is happy to let you know you're still in Spain. Early to bed? Hardly—the clubs and restaurants are packed every night with social critters of all ages. Early to rise? This is Madrid—probably not.

And that attitude has both its assets and its liabilities. On the negative side, you'll find that, despite its grandeur, large parts of Madrid appear a bit down at their heels (once you visit ultraprosperous Barcelona, you'll feel the difference at once), somewhat mired in centuries past. On the positive side, the city's pleasure principle means you'll find lots of places to play and have a great time doing it. And when all is said and done, isn't that what great cities are really all about?

1 Madrid Essentials

ARRIVING & DEPARTING

BY PLANE **Barajas Airport (☎ 91-305-8343)** is Madrid's main air terminal, serving as the major air connection from the capital to the rest of the world. A wonderful little **bus** speeds you to the city for just 350P ($2.35); daily 4:45am to 1:30am, it leaves every 15 minutes and lets you off at Plaza de Colón, a convenient subway stop.

Here's the rub: Madrid **taxis** can charge you for luggage by the piece, so unless you can walk to your hotel from Colón or know the subway system well, I advise you to take a cab from the airport to your hotel. It should cost no more than 2,100P ($14) and take about 30 minutes—unless you're traveling during peak traffic times—just a little bit more expensive than the bus/cab combo in town.

BY TRAIN There are three main train stations. **Atocha** is the place to go for trains leaving for Lisbon and points in-between; **Chamartín** has trains going to Barcelona and Bilbao; and **Principe Pio** goes to Galicia and other points in northwest Spain. If you need information, call RENFE (the Spanish rail system) at **☎ 91-328-90-20** and they'll tell you not only the schedules but also where to catch the train. On the Internet, you can book your train at **www.renfe.com.**

BY BUS The largest bus station is the **Estación Saur de Autobuses,** Canarias 17 (**☎ 91-468-45-11**). But with the now-excellent Spanish national train system, I can't imagine why you'd want to travel by bus. (In fact, I recommend you don't, especially since most of these buses still allow smoking and you could die of emphysema before you got to your destination.)

BY CAR Spain's superhighways rival the best and most modern roads in the world. But even if you've rented a car to tour other parts of the country, I must advise you to perish the thought of tooling around Madrid in a car. Traffic and parking are horrendous, the Metro system is fine, and cabs are cheap. End of story.

VISITOR INFORMATION

There's an excellent travel office at **Barajas Airport** (**☎ 91-305-83-44;** open Mon–Fri 8am–8pm, Sat 8am–1pm). In the city, the largest and most helpful tourist office is in the **Torre de Madrid,** Plaza de España (**☎ 91-541-23-25;** Metro: España; open Mon–Fri 9am–7pm, Sat 9am–1pm).

A GAY PRIDE EVENT

Madrid's **Gay Pride Parade** is usually coordinated with the rest of the civilized world's Pride events, on the last weekend in June. Each year the march is committed to a cause—for example, 1998's was centered around the fight for same-sex domestic partnership benefits. The Pride March, on Saturday, starts at the Puerta de Alcalá with the usual floats full of drag queens alternating with floats of muscle boys getting the crowd worked up with lots of loud disco music. The procession heads across La Castellana and to the Puerta del Sol. In a society like Spain's, where a great many gays and lesbians still live a very closeted life at the same time the community is more visible every day, the Pride Parade fulfills an important purpose. It's worthwhile noting that the parade has grown enormously every year since it began. But maybe that could be because of the muscle boys flashing their flawless assets from atop the floats.

CITY LAYOUT

A map of Madrid looks rather daunting; this isn't a small city by any means. And Madrid provides a fine example of poor urban planning, the city having long since seeped past its original border into one hideous suburban sprawl. Happily, however, the portions of the city that are of interest to visitors remain in a very doable area, so take a deep breath and don't think you have to know every locus on that huge map from the tourist office.

Start with the **Puerta del Sol,** the heart and soul of Spain. (All road distances in Spain are still measured from this central square.) More than any other plaza, this one matches the mental image you probably have of Spain if your high school Spanish-language textbook was printed any time before 1985. Frankly, the Puerta del Sol is just kind of Third World–like and creepy, more important as a bus depot (and a center of sleazy male prostitution if street trash is your thang) than anything else. Locals claim that Sol has been cleaned up as of late, but I haven't seen the difference.

South of Sol is **Plaza Mayor,** the best remaining symbol of old-time Madrid. It's a huge powerful square that really lets you know you're in Spain, even if the immediate neighborhood is peppered more with McDonald's and tourist traps than real Madrileño haunts.

To the south of Mayor, however, are the so-called ***barrios bajos,*** which are much more representative of life in Madrid. Here you'll find working-class life, to be sure, especially as you enter the Arco de Cuchilleros and the huge weekend flea market that seemingly extends from Madrid to Moscow and back.

If you take Calle Alcalá from Sol due west, you'll run into Madrid's grandest boulevard, the **Paseo del Prado,** which turns into the **Paseo Recoletos** at Plaza la Cibeles. Not only will you find Spain's greatest museum, the Prado, on this strip, but also, between Cibeles and **Plaza de Colón,** you'll see Madrid at its social best: From spring to fall, the outdoor terraces on this strip go on virtually nonstop, and it's something of a gay cruising ground as well.

From Alcalá to the north and east is the **Gran Vía,** and it once was precisely that. While it's still a major thoroughfare, today the Gran Vía has lost much of its luster; it's more or less a down-market entertainment center, with cinemas, undistinguished restaurants, and largely uninteresting shops its current calling cards.

Finally, to the northwest of the Gran Vía is **Chueca,** or gay central. If Spain has anything close to a gay ghetto, this working-class neighborhood is it: The lion's share of bars, clubs, and gay cafes are here. Much has been made of how unsafe the area is, but the situation is actually much better than it was even 5 years ago. Yes, there's still a lot of drug trade (especially on the downtrodden Plaza de Chueca itself), yet the crowds are so throbbing at night that, above and beyond any normal city precaution, you don't have much to worry about.

GETTING AROUND

Because most of Madrid isn't laid out in any kind of recognizable grid, finding your way around can be difficult at times; a good sense of direction really helps. If you don't mind walking, you can get around a lot on foot, though the public transport system is excellent (if not the easiest in the world to figure out).

For general information on public transport, call the **Consorcio de Transportes** at **☎ 91-580-19-80.**

BY SUBWAY At first glance, Madrid's Metro system looks quite scary, but the fact is that many of the lines are suburban ones you won't need to know. Basically, a map (available at your hotel or tourist office) notates the lines by color, so getting from one place to another is very easy indeed.

Madrid Metro

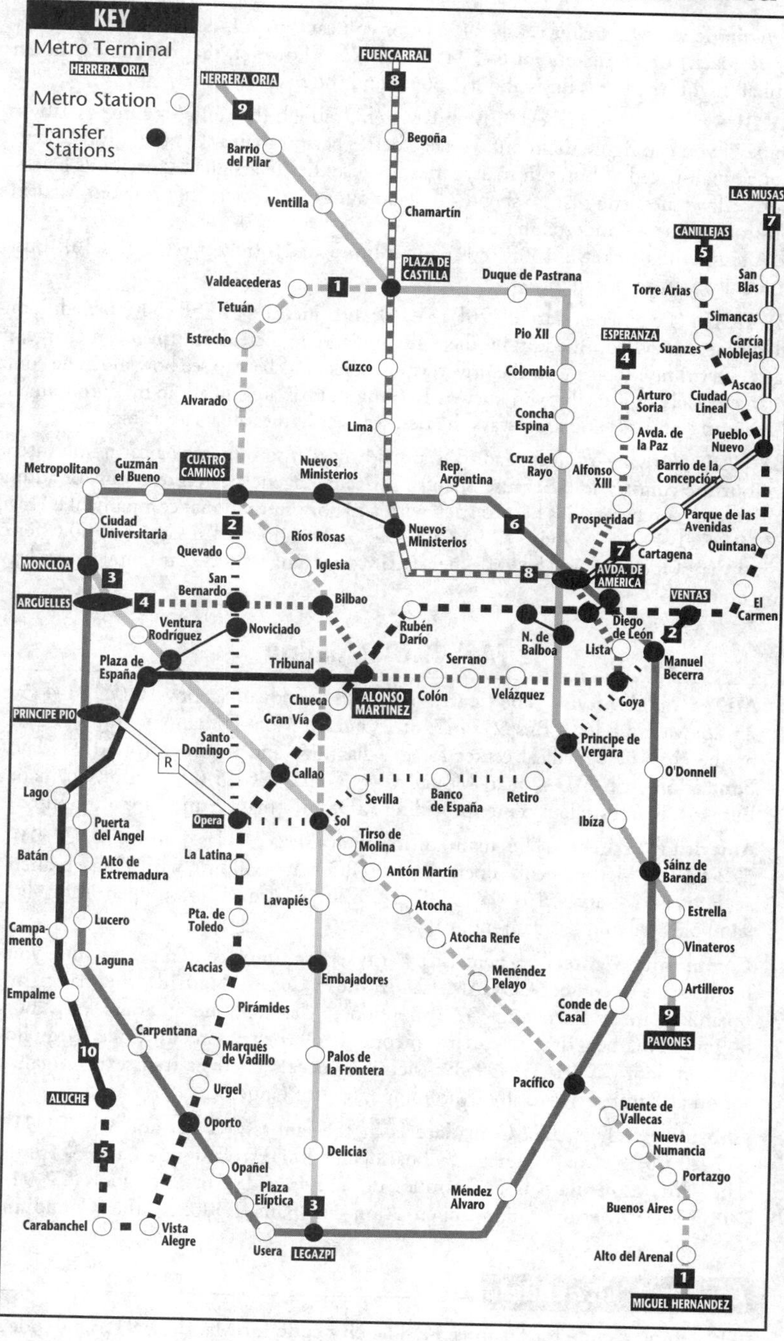

A **single subway ticket** is 140P (95¢), or you can buy a much more cost-effective ***bono* (pack) of 10 tickets** for 645P ($4.30). Note, however, that the subway doesn't run all night; the last train is about 1:30am and the first at 6am.

BY BUS Madrid has an extensive bus system, though the routes are utterly labyrnthine; if you can figure them out, you're a better person than I. On the upside, they're not as snail-paced as buses in many cities because they're assigned special bus lanes—but, really, unless you plan to spend a long amount of time here, figuring out Madrid's bus routes isn't an undertaking I advise.

A **single bus ticket** is 130P (80¢) and a **bono of 10 tickets** 645P ($4.30). Buses run daily 6am to midnight.

BY TAXI Taxi meters start at 170P ($1.15), then increase by 75P (50¢) per additional kilometer traveled. In addition, there are myriad fare increases a driver can charge; in fact, every time I took a taxi, the driver would consult a chart to see how much he could charge (legally or illegally, who knew?). Regardless, taxis are still cheap by European and American standards and are always the best way get home safely late at night.

BY CAR Driving around Madrid is a major hassle, so only rent a car if you intend to tour the countryside. Because Spanish car-rental agencies are notorious for adding mysterious surcharges, it's best to stick with a major international company like **Hertz** (☎ **91-541-99-24**) or **Avis** (☎ **91-205-42-73**), both located at Gran Vía 60 (Metro: Gran Vía). Of course, it'll be less expensive if you arrange for the car rental before leaving home.

FAST FACTS: Madrid

AIDS Organizations The **Centro Sanitario Sandoval,** Sandoval 7 (☎ **91-445-23-28;** Metro: Bilbao; Bus: 21, 147, or 149; open Mon–Fri 9am–noon), is said to be the city's best medical center for the diagnosis and treatment of AIDS. The **Fundación Anti-SIDA,** Juan Montalvo 6 (☎ **91-536-15-00;** Metro: Guzman; Bus: 44), is an excellent center providing AIDS information and support groups.

American Express The main office is at Plaza de las Cortes 2 (☎ **91-572-03-03;** Metro: Sevilla; open Mon–Fri 8:30am–4:30pm), with a busy branch at Francisco Gervás 10 (☎ **91-572-03-20;** Metro: Cuzco; open Mon–Fri 9am–5:30pm and Sat 9am–noon).

Community Centers There isn't a gay community center per se, but you might want to contact **COGAM (Coordinora Gay de Madrid),** the major gay organization, at Fuencarral 37 (no phone; Metro: Chueca; hours vary, but 5–9pm is the best time to catch someone there); or try **Crecul,** Calle Barquillo 44, 2nd floor (☎ **91-319-39-89;** Metro: Chueca). There's a transsexual organization at Barbieri 3, 3rd floor (no phone; Metro: Chueca).

Consulates The **U.S. Consulate** is in the embassy at Serrano 75 (☎ **91-577-40-00;** Metro: Núñez de Balboa; open Mon–Fri 9am–noon and 3–5pm). The **U.K. Consulate** is at Marqués de la Ensenada 16, 2nd floor (☎ **91-308-52-01;** Metro: Colón; open Mon–Fri 8am–2:30pm). the **Canadian**

Country & City Codes

The **country code** for Spain is **34.** The **city code** for Madrid is **91.** This code has now been incorporated into all phone numbers, so you must always dial it, whether you're outside Spain, within Spain but not in Madrid, or even within Madrid.

Consulate is in the embassy at Núñez de Balboa 35 (☎ **91-431-43-00;** Metro: Velázquez; open Mon–Fri 9am–12:30pm). The **Australian Consulate** is at Castellana 143 (☎ **91-579-04-28;** Metro: Cuzco; open Mon–Thurs 8:30am–1:30pm and 2:30–4:45pm and Fri 8:30am–2:15pm). The **New Zealand Embassy** is at Plaza de la Lealtad 2 (☎ **91-523-02-26;** Metro: Banco de España; open Mon–Fri 9am–1:30pm and 2:30–5:30pm).

Currency Exchange Madrid offers both commercial money exchanges and bank change centers, both charging commission (thus, it's always better to change money in fairly substantial amounts, lest the favorable exchange be eaten up by fees). The airport and train stations all have currency-exchange offices too.

Cybercafe You can check your e-mail or send messages at **La Ciberteca,** Perón 32 (☎ **91-556-67-73;** e-mail info@ciberteca.cs; Metro: Lima or Neuvos Ministerios).

Emergencies For the police, call ☎ **091;** for the fire department, call ☎ **080;** for an ambulance, call ☎ **91-522-22-22.**

Hospitals If you need a doctor, the best thing to do is inform the powers-that-be at your hotel; they always have a number of someone to call. Otherwise, two main hospitals in Madrid **Hospital La Paz,** Castellana 261 (☎ **91-73-26-00;** Metro: Begoña), and **Hospital 12 de Octubre,** Carretera de Andalucía, km 5.4 (☎ **91-390-80-00**).

Telephone If you need to call abroad, you'll be pleasantly surprised to find public phones that provide instruction in several languages—including, of course, ours. These accept a *tarjeta telefonica,* which you can buy at post offices, the central phone office (Plaza de Colón), or tobacco shops. Some even let you use your credit card, though you may want to tear your hair out before you can actually complete a call. (See my section on using the public phone in Lisbon if you don't believe me.) Local calls cost 15P (10¢).

To **make collect or calling-card calls,** dial ☎ **900/99-00-11** to access **AT&T's USA Direct** (to do so from a public phone might require coins or a phone card) or ☎ **900/99-00-14** to access **MCI's Call USA.** When calling from a hotel, check first to make sure there's no service charge or surcharge or at least how much it is.

To make **international calls** to the United States and Canada, dial 07, wait for another tone, then dial 1, followed by the area code and number. The average cost of a 3-minute call to the United States is 1,800P ($12).

2 Pillow Talk

Not too long ago, Madrid didn't have the range of deluxe hotels you'll find in Paris, London, or Rome. Well, that's very different now, and the old guard (the Ritz and the Palace) are just the leaders of an impressive pack. At the bottom end you'll find innumerable *hostals* (the Spanish equivalent of a French pension or an Italian pensione—a small guest lodging typically located on one or two floors of a residential or sometimes commercial building).

In just 2 decades' time, Spain has gone from the repressive Franco regime to a swinging country where practically anything goes—Mr. Almodóvar and his Movida friends saw to that. So you can drag the object of your desires back to your room, *sin embargo.* Who cares if the person at the front desk looks at you askance? (At pricier hotels, nobody will say anything.)

Hey, Big Spender

If you've finally come into your trust fund and want to blow a wad on a Madrid hotel, there are many deluxe places that'll be more than glad to bend over backward for you. Be prepared to drop a minimum of $200 a night for a double at any of them.

The **Ritz,** one of the toniest, is listed in full below. Here are some others where you'll feel like a princess, no matter what sex you are:

Castellana Inter-Continental Hotel, Castellana 49, 28046 Madrid (☎ **800/327-0200** in the U.S., or 91-310-02-00; fax 91-319-58-53; Metro: Rubén Darío).

Hotel Palacio Santo Mauro, Zurbano 36, 28010 Madrid (☎ **91-319-6900;** fax 91-308-5477; Metro: Rubén Darío or Alonso Martínez).

Hotel Villa Real, Plaza de las Cortés 10, 28014 Madrid (☎ **91-420-37-67;** fax 91-420-25-47; www.derbyhotels.es; e-mail ifo@derbyhotels.es; Metro: Plaza de la Cibeles).

Palace, Plaza de las Cortés 7, 28014 Madrid (☎ **800/325-3535** in the U.S., 800/325-3589 in Canada, or 91-360-80-00; fax 91-360-81-00; www.ittsheraton.com; Metro: Banco de España).

Park Hyatt Villa Magna, Castellana 22, 28046 Madrid (☎ **800/223-1234** in North America, or 91-587-12-34; fax 91-431-22-86; www.travelweb.com/hyatt.html; Metro: Rubén Darío).

Eurobuilding. Padre Damián 23, 28036 Madrid. ☎ **91-345-45-00.** Fax 91-345-45-76. 520 units. A/C MINIBAR TV TEL. 29,500P ($197) double; from 34,000P ($231) suite. AE, DC, MC, V. Parking 2,500P ($17). Metro: Cuzco.

It's hard to know what to make of the Eurobuilding, so I'll just present the facts. What it is: supermodern, somewhat impersonal, and architecturally stunning. What it isn't: old world, supercentral, or full of charm. Continentals seem to like swank new places like this white marble palace of two buildings linked by a courtyard, and it certainly has everything a business traveler would need. If you're looking for a dose of Old Spain, stay elsewhere; but if you're on the lookout for a Euroyuppie with a cell phone, this is the place.

✪ **Gran Hotel Reina Victoria.** Plaza Santa Ana 14, 28012 Madrid. ☎ **91-531-45-00.** Fax 91-522-03-7. 201 units. A/C MINIBAR TV TEL. 25,000P ($167) double; from 60,000P ($400) suite. AE, DC, MC, V. Parking 1,750P ($12). Metro: Tirso de Molina or Puerta del Sol.

The namesake of Juan Carlos II's grandmother, this was for many years Spain's most famous hotel. Thanks to a recent renovation by the Tryp Hotel consortium, it's as fabulous as ever and a nice alternative to the pushier Ritz and Palace. Behind a historic stone facade, the Reina Victoria is a world unto itself, even though it's a stone's throw from busy Puerta del Sol. The rooms are spacious and elegantly decorated, and the lobby is full of bullfighting memorabilia.

Hostal Avenida. Gran Vía 15, 4th floor, 28013 Madrid. ☎ **91-522-63-60,** Madrid. 12 units. TEL. 5,300P ($35) double. MC, V. Metro: Gran Vía.

There's nothing spectacular about this hostal, except that it's very cheap and clean and the owners are extremely nice—all of which sound to me like good reasons to stay here. Some of the rooms are postage stamp–sized, but hey, you get what you pay for.

Two Hostal Tips

If you arrive in Madrid and haven't had the foresight to get a room beforehand, I'd advise heading to the building that contains the **Hotel Avenida:** Gran Vía 15, otherwise known as hostal central. There are no less than six fairly identical cheap hostals contained within, and unless there's a convention in town, you're pretty likely to find a room for at least one night.

Many of Madrid's hostals occupy one or two floors of mixed-use buildings, and they're rarely on the ground floor. To gain entrance, it's often necessary to press a button and then respond to a shouted "¿Sí?" or "¡Digame!" on the intercom. Keep your answer simple—your last name or "Frommer's!" will nearly always get you buzzed in.

Hotel Alcalá. Alcalá 66, 28009 Madrid. ☎ **91-435-10-60.** Fax 91-435-11-05. 153 units. TV TEL. 16,700P ($111) double. AE, DC, MC, V. Metro: Banco.

This charming old hotel is a nice midway point between standard-issue hostals and expensive hotels. The rooms, recently refurbished, are a very nice size, and there's a lovely garden that the inside rooms overlook. The location is close to the museums and cafes of Recoletos/Paseo del Prado, and the exclusive shops of Salamanca are just a short walk away.

Hotel Emperador. Gran Vía 53, 28013 Madrid. ☎ **91-341-28-00.** Fax 91-547-28-17. E-mail hemperador@sei.es. 232 units. A/C MINIBAR TV TEL. 26,500P ($177) double. AE, DC, MC, V. Metro: Gran Vía.

The Gran Vía's most elegant hotel, the Emperador is indeed fit for an emperor. In fact, the decor of the large rooms is French Empire—classy but not pushy. There's also a great work-out room and wonderful rooftop pool. You can have it all: the lap of luxury and Chueca proximity too!

✪ **Hotel Gaudí.** Gran Vía 9, 28013 Madrid. ☎ **91-531-22-22.** Fax 91-531-54-69. E-mail cataloni@hoteles-catalonia.es. 88 units. A/C MINIBAR TV TEL. 21,900P ($146) double. AE, DC, MC, V. Metro: Gran Vía.

A majestic turn-of-the-century building at the more elegant end of the Gran Vía was transformed into this near-luxury hotel. Plaza Mayor and the Prado and Thyssen museums are within walking distance, as are Chueca's bars. A very good restaurant and stylish bar are pluses. Don't get this place confused with the Hotel Residencia Gaudí, below.

✪ **Hotel Paris.** Alcalá 2, 28009 Madrid. ☎ **91-521-64-91** or 91-521-64-96. Fax 91-531-01-88. 121 units. TV TEL. 11,900P ($79) double. AE, DC, MC, V. Metro: Sol.

I've recommended this hotel forever, and no one's been less than charmed. Right off the Puerta del Sol, the Paris has a wonderful Old Spanish feel that really lets you know you're in Madrid. The rooms are fairly Spartan and the decor hasn't been changed for years, but you'll forgive that as soon as you open your balcony and see all of Spain whizzing by. You may even break into a few strains of "Don't Cry for Me, Argentina."

Hotel Residencia Gaudí. Hortaleza 17, 1st floor, 28013 Madrid. ☎ **91-521-99-56.** 16 units. 5,000P ($33) double; 6,500P ($43) triple. No credit cards. Metro: Gran Vía or Chueca.

For those on a very tight budget, the Residencia Gaudí is a good choice. At these prices, there's nothing at all fancy here—austere is more like it—but you can practically fall out of bed and skip into Chueca's bars and cafes. Don't look too closely at the bed linens, though.

Hotel Residencia Santander. Echegaray 1, 28014 Madrid. ☎ **91-429-95-51.** Fax 91-369-1078. 36 units. TEL. 7,000P ($47) double. MC, V. Metro: Sol.

Madrid Accommodations & Dining

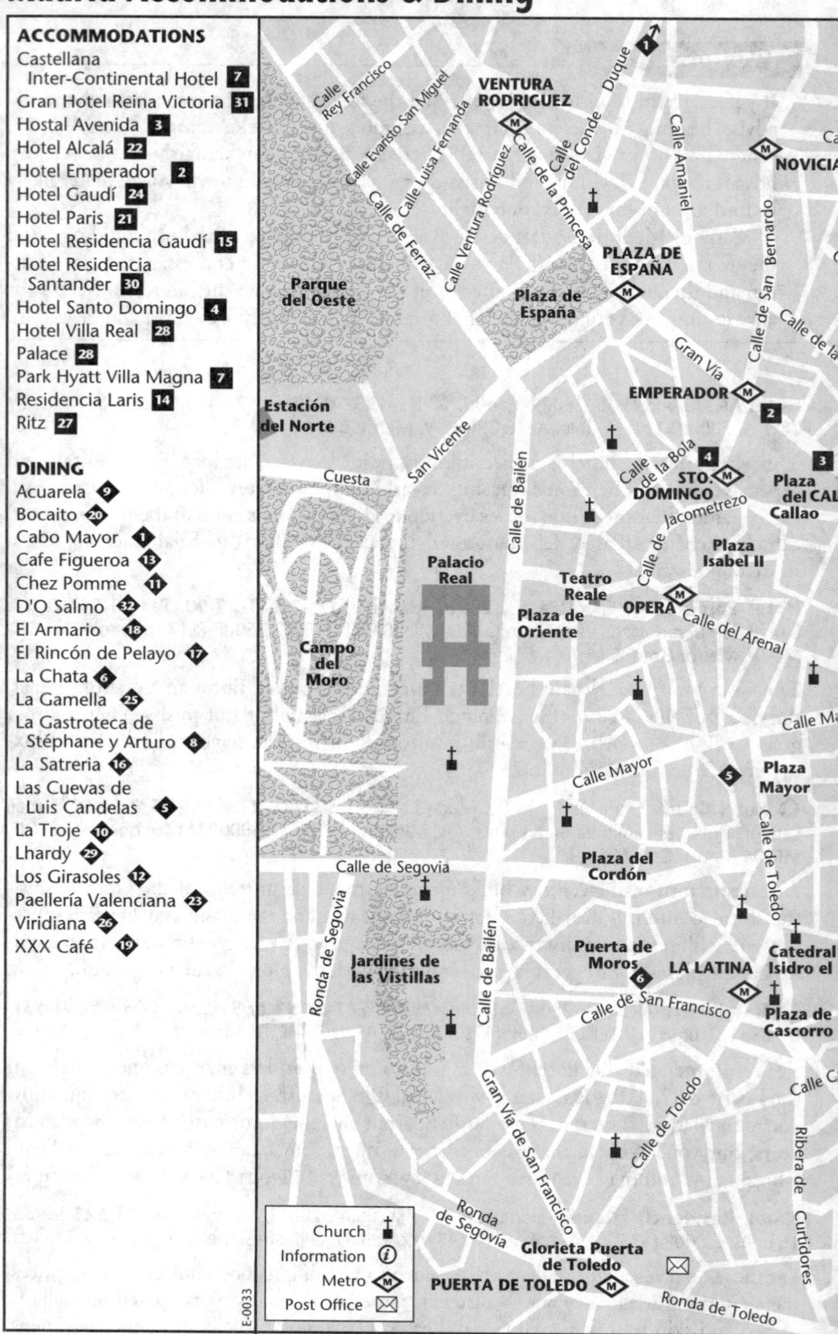

ACCOMMODATIONS
Castellana Inter-Continental Hotel 7
Gran Hotel Reina Victoria 31
Hostal Avenida 3
Hotel Alcalá 22
Hotel Emperador 2
Hotel Gaudí 24
Hotel Paris 21
Hotel Residencia Gaudí 15
Hotel Residencia Santander 30
Hotel Santo Domingo 4
Hotel Villa Real 28
Palace 28
Park Hyatt Villa Magna 7
Residencia Laris 14
Ritz 27
DINING
Acuarela 9
Bocaito 20
Cabo Mayor 1
Cafe Figueroa 13
Chez Pomme 11
D'O Salmo 32
El Armario 18
El Rincón de Pelayo 17
La Chata 6
La Gamella 25
La Gastroteca de Stéphane y Arturo 8
La Satreria 16
Las Cuevas de Luis Candelas 5
La Troje 10
Lhardy 29
Los Girasoles 12
Paellería Valenciana 23
Viridiana 26
XXX Café 19
Calle Rey Francisco
Calle Evaristo San Miguel
Calle Luisa Fernanda
Calle de Ferraz
Calle Ventura Rodríguez
VENTURA RODRIGUEZ
Calle de la Princesa
Calle del Conde
Duque
Calle Amaniel
NOVICIA
Calle de San Bernardo
PLAZA DE ESPAÑA
Plaza de España
Parque del Oeste
Gran Vía
EMPERADOR
Estación del Norte
San Vicente
Cuesta
Calle de la Bola
STO. DOMINGO
Plaza del Callao
Calle de Jacometrezo
Plaza Isabel II
Calle de Bailén
Palacio Real
Teatro Reale
OPERA
Plaza de Oriente
Calle del Arenal
Campo del Moro
Calle Mayor
Plaza Mayor
Calle de Toledo
Plaza del Cordón
Calle de Segovia
Ronda de Segovia
Jardines de las Vistillas
Puerta de Moros
LA LATINA
Calle de San Francisco
Plaza de Cascorro
Gran Vía de San Francisco
Calle de Toledo
Ribera de Curtidores
Ronda de Segovia
Glorieta Puerta de Toledo
PUERTA DE TOLEDO
Ronda de Toledo
Church
Information
Metro
Post Office
E-0033

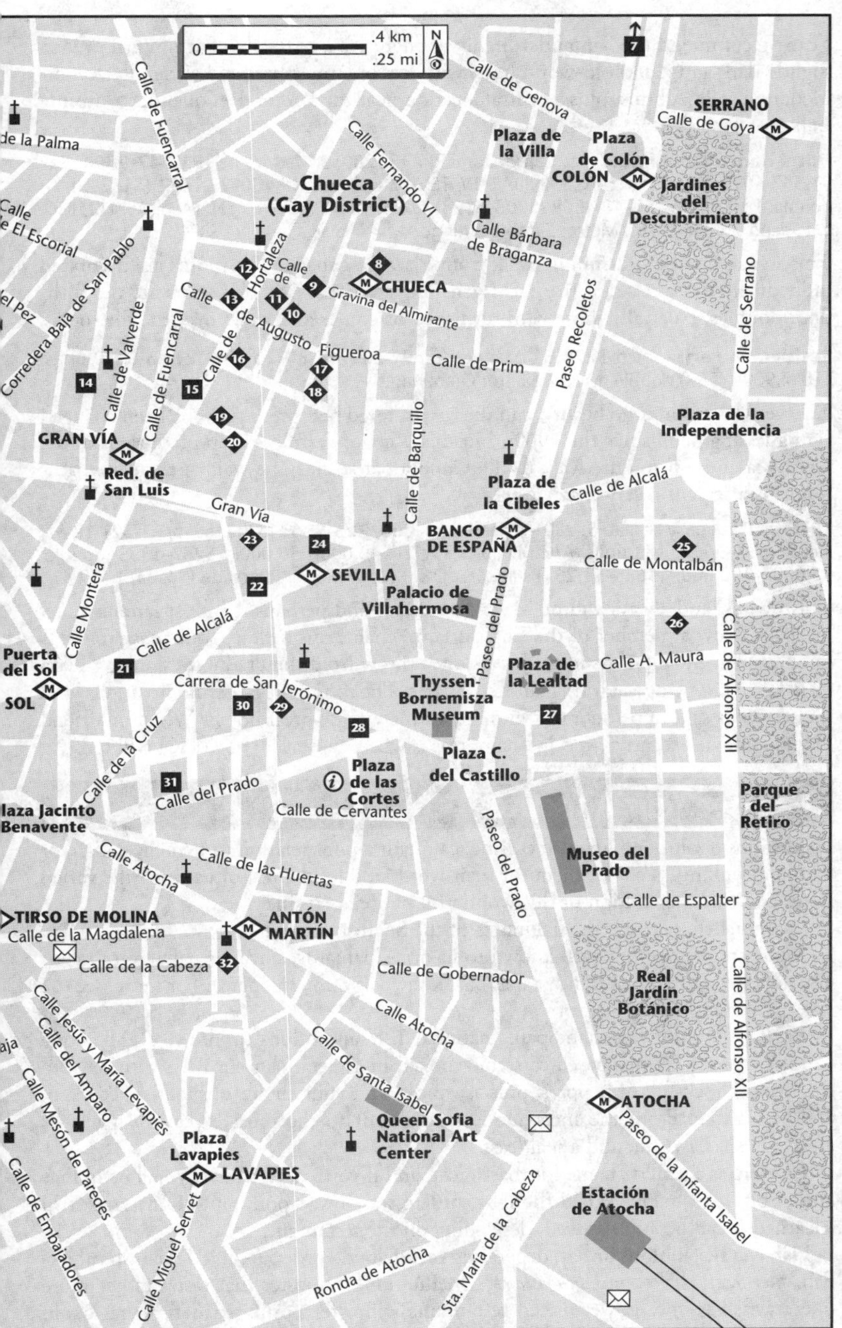

0
.4 km
.25 mi
N
Calle de Fuencarral
Calle de Genova
SERRANO
Calle de Goya
de la Palma
Calle Fernando VI
Plaza de la Villa
Plaza de Colón
COLÓN
Jardines del Descubrimiento
Chueca (Gay District)
Calle de El Escorial
Calle Bárbara de Braganza
Corredera Baja de San Pablo
Calle de Hortaleza
Calle de Gravina del Almirante
CHUECA
Calle de Augusto Figueroa
Calle de Serrano
Paseo Recoletos
Calle de Prim
Calle de Valverde
Calle de Fuencarral
Calle de Barquillo
Plaza de la Independencia
GRAN VÍA
Red. de San Luis
Plaza de la Cibeles
Calle de Alcalá
Gran Vía
BANCO DE ESPAÑA
Calle de Montalbán
Calle Montera
SEVILLA
Palacio de Villahermosa
Paseo del Prado
Calle de Alcalá
Puerta del Sol
SOL
Plaza de la Lealtad
Calle A. Maura
Carrera de San Jerónimo
Thyssen-Bornemisza Museum
Calle de Alfonso XII
Calle de la Cruz
Plaza C. del Castillo
Plaza de las Cortes
Calle del Prado
Calle de Cervantes
Plaza Jacinto Benavente
Parque del Retiro
Calle Atocha
Calle de las Huertas
Paseo del Prado
Museo del Prado
Calle de Espalter
TIRSO DE MOLINA
ANTÓN MARTÍN
Calle de la Magdalena
Calle de la Cabeza
Calle de Gobernador
Real Jardín Botánico
Calle Jesús y María Levapiés
Calle del Amparo
Calle Atocha
Calle de Santa Isabel
Calle de Alfonso XII
Calle Mesón de Paredes
ATOCHA
Queen Sofia National Art Center
Plaza Lavapies
LAVAPIES
Paseo de la Infanta Isabel
Estación de Atocha
Calle de Embajadores
Calle Miguel Servet
Ronda de Atocha
Sta. María de la Cabeza

I can't recommend the Santander highly enough: It's a cozy and charming (if ever so slightly dark and dank) old-world hotel with lots of atmosphere and a friendly accommodating staff. All this, plus a central location near the Puerta del Sol and a 5-minute walk from the Prado.

Hotel Santo Domingo. Plaza Santo Domingo 13, 28013 Madrid. ☎ **91-547-9800.** Fax 91-547-5995. 120 units. A/C MINIBAR TV TEL. Mon–Thurs 19,750–22,175P ($132–$148) double; Fri–Sun 16,250–18,450P ($108–$123) double. Breakfast free Sat–Mon. AE, DC, MC, V. Parking 2,400P ($16). Metro: Santo Domingo.

This stylish hotel is a 2-minute walk from Plaza de España. The rooms are decorated individually in pastels and the baths generally spacious. The best units are the fifth-floor doubles, especially those with furnished balconies and views over the tile roofs.

Residencia Laris. Barco 3, 28013 Madrid. ☎ **91-521-46-80.** Fax 91-521-46-8. 20 units. TEL. 7,900P ($53) double. MC, V. Metro: Gran Vía.

This very basic inn is no beauty, and the rust-colored bedspreads haven't been changed (I'm guessing here) since the 1960s, but this is a wonderfully cheap place right of the Gran Vía and a 5-minute walk to the Chueca bar scene. The wallpaper in the bathrooms is a scream—very *Brady Bunch.*

✪ **Ritz.** Plaza de la Lealtad 5, 28014 Madrid. ☎ **800/225-5843** in the U.S. or 91-521-18-57. Fax 91-532-87-76. 183 units. A/C MINIBAR TV TEL. 40,000P–50,000P ($267–$333) double; 95,000P–190,000P ($633–$1,267) suite. AE, DC, MC, V. Metro: Banco de España.

This is, was, and always will be Madrid's big gun and perhaps the most famous hotel in Spain. Now a member of the English Forte chain, this belle-époque masterpiece is once again at the top if its form. It's a stone's throw from the Prado, overlooking Plaza de la Lealtad, one of Madrid's grandest squares. The rooms are large and luxurious, and the service is said to be on a par with any of the world's great hotels. When my friend Doug, a movie executive, was in Spain, this is where he stayed; one day, I will too.

3 Whet Your Appetite

Food snobs pooh-pooh Spanish cuisine, calling it a poor relation to French, Italian, or Chinese cooking. Well, let them eat their words and let the rest of us enjoy the varied tastes and fine preparation of this wonderful national cuisine.

In a nutshell, here are the hallmarks of the Spanish kitchen:

Tapas are increasingly well known to us non-Spaniards, since virtually every major city now has at least one trendy tapas bar (known as *tascas* in Spain). For more, see the box, "Taste My Tapas" below.

Paella is nothing less than Spain's national dish, and I don't think I've ever had one I didn't enjoy. It's a rice-based casserole cooked in a metal pan; flavored with saffron, the rice is chock-full of peppers, onions, spices, and your choice of shellfish, chicken, and/or sausage. From the most modest restaurant to the most expensive, paella is always fresh, flavorful, and a real feast.

Cordero is a generic name for roast meat, and if you're a carnivore, you'll be in love at first bite. For many years, I thought cordero was always pork, but on my latest trip I learned it can be lamb as well, depending on the restaurant.

Fish can be fabulous or flat, depending on what you order. *Rape* is a Spanish monkfish, *merluza* is hake, and *langosta* is a Mediterranean lobster that tastes rather more like crayfish to me. Lower-priced restaurants will offer boring fried fish that could emanate from any junior-high cafeteria, so buyer beware. Instead, git yerselves to the restaurants I note specifically as fish-famous.

Note: For the locations of the restaurants below, see the "Madrid Accommodations & Dining" map on pp. 600–601.

Taste My Tapas

The traditional time to eat tapas is after work with friends or coworkers—especially since dinner is eaten late, usually at 10pm. Standard tapas are *bacalao* (balls of codfish) fried in garlic and oil, *empanadillas* (tuna- or chicken-filled pastries), eggs in mayonnaise or in fritterlike concoctions called *tortillas*, fried *chorizo* or *salchichón* (sausages), or just plain olives. Sardines—sometimes lightly battered and fried, sometimes served simply in olive oil—are almost always the best you'll ever have.

Areas to begin exploration of this delectable Spanish invention are the streets on and around Plaza Santa and Calle Victoria, which leads to it, and down Calle San Miguel, which borders Plaza Mayor on the west.

Perhaps the best place to start is **Bocaito** (see below). Other good tascas are **Antonio Sánchez,** Mesón de Paredes 13 (☎ **91-539-78-26;** Metro: Tirso de Molina); Hemingway's haunt, **Cervecería Alemania,** Plaza de Santa Ana 6 (☎ **91-429-70-33;** Metro: Alonso Martín or Sevilla); and **Taberna Toscana,** Ventura de la Vega 22 (☎ **91-429-60-31;** Metro: Puerta del Sol or Sevilla).

✪ **Bocaito.** Libertad 4–6. ☎ **91-532-12-19.** Main courses 750–1,500P ($5–$10). AE, MC, V. Mon–Sat 1–4pm and 8:30pm–midnight. Metro: Gran Vía or Chueca. TAPAS.

Here's a great place to get initiated into the cult of tapas—and so close to the Chueca bars! There are many more locals than tourists here, and they tend to congregate at the large bar where you can order tapas (including a great fried *bacalao*) one by one. Most likely, you'll have so much fun eating them you won't get anywhere near the dining room—I didn't.

Cabo Mayor. Juan Ramon Jiminez 37. ☎ **91-350-87-76.** Reservations required. Main courses 1,400–2,300P ($9–$15). AE, DC, MC, V. Mon–Sat 1:30–4pm and 9pm–midnight. Metro: Cuzco. BASQUE/SEAFOOD.

Once a favorite of the higher-echelon participants in La Movida, today Cabo Mayor is still going strong. The decor has a marine theme, and while this restaurant is chic, it still manages not to be snotty. The emphasis is on nouvelle preparations of seafood and Basque dishes, a combination that continues to win accolades from even the most discriminating diners from Madrid and beyond.

Chez Pomme. Pelayo 4. ☎ **91-532-1646.** Main courses 700–350P ($5–$9). AE, MC, V. Daily 1–4pm and 9–11:30pm. Metro: Chueca. SPANISH/VEGETARIAN.

In the heart of Chueca, this stylish little eatery is a vegetarian's paradise, featuring recipes from Spain and beyond. Me, I could eat a whole suckling pig in one sitting; but if the veggie scene's your thing, Chez Pomme does the trick nicely, thank you.

D'O Salmo. Leon 4. ☎ **91-429-39-52.** Main courses 800–1,850P ($5–$12). AE, MC, V. Tues–Sun 1–4pm and 9pm–midnight. Metro: Anton Martin. Bus: 6, 32, or 57. SPANISH/GALICIAN.

If you've ever wanted to sample traditional Galician fare but were afraid to ask, D'O Salmo is a great place to start. There's nothing fancy about this restaurant—nor is there anything remotely touristy about it—but that's a recommendation in my book. So are the seafood cocktails and Galician wines.

El Armario. San Bartolome 7. ☎ **91-532-83-77.** Main courses 900–1,900P ($6–$13); lunch buffet 1,200P ($8). AE, DC, MC, V. Tues–Sun 1:30–4pm and 9pm–midnight. Metro: Chueca. SPANISH.

Cafe Culture

Acuarela, Gravina 10 (Metro: Chueca), is a cozy, eclectically decorated dark cafe that's a true afternoon delight, a fabu pit stop after your shopping expeditions on nearly Almirante. You can also find all the gay rags and other papers on display for your reading pleasure. Coffee, tea, and wine, but (oddly) not a thing to eat. How very gay.

The oldest of Madrid's cafes, the bilevel **Cafe Figueroa,** Augusto Figueroa 17 (Metro: Chueca), is a welcoming place to while away an hour in late afternoon or early evening. The young, hip crowds have moved on (see below), but the Figueroa legend lives on.

Mixed, young, and uberhip, **La Satreria,** Hortaleza 74 (Metro: Chueca), is one of Madrid's trendiest cafes for the fashionista crowd. It's the perfect place to meet friends before dinner in early evening or to meet up with that cute guy you met last night—at least if he's a hipster.

La Troje, Pelayo 26 (Metro: Chueca), is a bar/cafe popular from early evening on; it makes a great first stop for the evening, whether you're flying solo or with friends. Cute young crowd, strong coffee, and (usually) errant fashion mags to peruse.

The **XXX Café,** Clavel 2 (Metro: Gran Vía), is a new bar aimed at trendy young 'uns. Though it's still finding its crowd, early signs are that this will be a real winner; the Friday-night drag shows are already popular.

This is a traditional Spanish restaurant that attracts a very large gay clientele. It boasts a welcoming updated decor and very nice staff—led by a drag queen named Mimi—who wants business from the boys. The Spanish food is far better than it needs to be, given that the scene is really the thing.

El Puchero. Larra 13. ☎ **91-445-05-77.** Main courses 900P–2,000P ($6–$13). AE, MC, V. Mon–Sat 1:30–4pm and 9–11:30pm. Metro: Tribunal or Bilbao. Bus: 3. SPANISH.

This basement eatery is off the beaten path for most visitors but absolutely worth a special trip. Both the decor and the menu are utterly traditional. There's wonderful *cordero,* though the daily specials (usually game and fish) are the things to get at this modestly priced, terrifically tasty gem I can't recommend highly enough. Not a scene, just fabulous food.

El Rincón de Pelayo. Pelayo 19. ☎ **91-521-84-07.** Prix-fixe menu 1,100P ($7) at lunch, 1,600P ($11) at dinner. AE, MC, V. Daily 1:30–4pm and 9pm–midnight. Metro: Chueca. SPANISH/ECLECTIC.

This cute Chueca restaurant is a perennial favorite among the boys, as much for its excellent prices as for its charming decor and attentive staff. The food tends to be more vegetable-oriented than much traditional Spanish cuisine, and the fish (generally grilled) is quite good.

La Chata. Cava Baja 24. ☎ **91-366-14-58.** Reservations recommended. Main courses 1,600–2,400P ($11–$16). AE, MC, V. Daily 12:30–5pm; Sun–Mon 7pm–midnight. Metro: La Latina. SPANISH.

Working-class Madrileños come here for tapas, which are good and hearty enough for a main meal, but I suggest you save room for the main courses offered in the dining room. All the Spanish classics are here, like *cordero* and *bacalao,* and the suckling pig is said to be among the very best in Madrid.

La Gamella. Alfonso XII 4. ☎ **91-532-45-09.** Reservations required. Main courses 2,400–4,300P ($16–$29). AE, DC, MC, V. Mon–Fri 1:30–4pm; Mon–Sat 9pm–midnight. Metro: Retiro. Bus: 19. SPANISH/NOUVELLE.

It had to happen: California cuisine has come to Spain. Dick Stephens, an American, opened this way-posh restaurant 10 years ago, and the chic crowds haven't stopped coming. Housed in a historic building, La Gamella serves nouvelle/Californian renditions of Spanish dishes, with duck the culinary star. If you want to dine with the crème de la crème of Madrid and beyond, this fancy outpost is where to go.

✪ **La Gastroteca de Stéphane y Arturo.** Plaza de Chueca 8. ☎ **91-532-25-64.** Reservations recommended. Main courses 1,100–2,300P ($7–$15). Mon–Sat 2–3:30pm and 9:30–10:30pm. Metro: Chueca. Bus: 3, 40, or 149. FRENCH.

The Spanish/French couple of Stephane and Arturo has created a wonderfully chic little outpost in Chueca, one of the nicest eateries in this part of town. The menu is updated French, with a few Spanish touches thrown in. A great place for an upscale date.

La Playa. Magallanes 24. ☎ **91-446-84-76.** Main courses 950–1,900P ($6–$13). No credit cards. Daily 11am–4:30pm and 8:30pm–midnight. Metro: Quevedo. SPANISH.

Totally unpretentious, this family-run eatery is all about classic, hearty Spanish fare, with nothing new or superficial added. The *albondigas* (meatballs) are bathed in a tangy tomato-and-pepper sauce, and the daily fish specials reflect the catch of the day—usually served swimming in a gorgeous sea of olive oil and garlic. Yummy!

Las Cuevas de Luis Candelas. Cuchilleros 1. ☎ **91-366-54-28.** Reservations recommended. Main courses 1,500–3,500P ($10–$23). DC, MC, V. Daily 1–4pm and 8pm–midnight. Metro: Puerta del Sol. SPANISH/CONTINENTAL.

In this traditional neighborhood near Plaza Mayor lies one of Madrid's longest-running restaurants. The house provides a medieval feel, and the dishes (no nouvelle here) probably haven't changed much since then: roast lamb (*cordero*), suckling pig, and daily fish specials are the things to have. Slightly touristy but worth a trip nonetheless.

✪ **Lhardy.** San Jeronomo 8. ☎ **91-521-33-85.** Reservations required. Main courses 1,900–5,000P ($13–$33). AE, DC, MC, V. Daily 1–3:30pm and 9–11:30pm. Metro: Sevilla or Sol. FRENCH.

In continuous operation for well over 100 years, this is one of the most expensive restaurants in town, a place designed to impress—and it does. If you're on an expense account (or have an independent income), you'd be wise to take a meal at Madrid's fanciest French restaurant, where nouvelle preparations have failed to infest the classic haute cuisine.

Los Girasoles. Hortaleza 106. ☎ **92/308-44-94.** Main courses 850–1,990P ($6–$13). AE, DC, MC, V. Daily 1–4pm and 8pm–midnight. Metro: Chueca. SPANISH.

This is a semitrendy little restaurant in the heart of the gay district that's quite nice indeed. Los Girasoles serves up classic Spanish fare like *bacalao* and *entrecôte* with pimentos at moderate prices and with a definite gay atmosphere. A great date place.

Paellería Valenciana. Caballero de Gracia 12. ☎ **91-531-17-85.** Reservations recommended. Main courses 1,250–2,500P ($8–$17); fixed-price menus 1,250–1,600P ($8–$11). AE, MC, V. Mon–Sat 1:30–4:30pm. Metro: Gran Vía. SPANISH.

This lunch-only restaurant is a super value. The specialty is paella, which you must order by phone in advance. Once you arrive, you might begin with homemade soup or the house salad, then follow with the paella, served for two or more. The chef's special dessert is razor-thin orange slices flavored with rum, coconut, sugar, honey, and raspberry sauce—scrumptious but best avoided before a night of dancing or sauna fun.

✪ **Restaurante Belagua.** In the Hotel Palacio Santo Mauro, Zurbano 36. ☎ **91-319-69-00.** Reservations recommended. Main courses 2,400–4,000P ($16–$27). AE, DC, MC, V. Mon–Sat 1–4pm and 8:30–11:30pm. Metro: Ruben Dario or Alonso Martinez. BASQUE.

For well-paid trendies, the Belagua is a key place to meet and greet—a hip modern restaurant in a tony part of town. Though the menu claims to be Basque, it looks rather more nouvelle inspired than what I imagine peasants in northeastern Spain to be eating around a wooden table. But that doesn't mean you shouldn't.

Viridiana. Juan de Mena 14. ☎ **91-523-44-78.** Reservations recommended. Main courses 4,000–9,000P ($27–$60). AE, MC, V. Mon–Sat 1:30pm–4pm and 9pm–midnight. Metro: Banco. INTERNATIONAL.

Viridiana—named after the 1961 Luis Buñuel classic and decorated with stills from Buñuel films—is one of Madrid's up-and-comers, known for the creativity of chef/part-owner Abraham García. Examples of the stylish cooking are chicken pastilla with cinnamon, baby squid with curry on a bed of lentils, and roasted lamb in puff pastry with fresh basil. For foodies, an absolute must.

4 Exploring Madrid

The very heart and soul of Spain, Madrid has emerged from its sleepy days under Franco to become a European capital of note. Indeed, Madrid beckons with every hallmark of a world-class city: grand boulevards, great restaurants, stellar museums, and a dizzying nightlife.

What's more, despite rampant modernization, Madrid, much more than Barcelona, retains a definite old-world feel. This is Spain as you might know it from Carlos Saura movies—a city whose frenzy is assuaged only by its traditional roots. It's a somewhat schizophrenic juxtaposition to be sure, but it's the one that makes Madrid one of the world's most charismatic cities.

The **Madrid Vision Bus** makes 14 stops at major museums, plazas, and avenues all year. For the full 1,800P ($12) ticket you can get off and reboard as many times in 1 day as you wish; the cost is 2,200P ($15) for 2 days. Or take the 1½-hour tour, boarding at any point but without the on/off option, for 1,500P ($10). The air-conditioned buses carry multilingual guides who provide info over earphones. Departures are Tuesday to Sunday 10am to 6:15pm. Convenient places to pick up the bus are at the Prado, the Puerta del Sol, or El Corte Inglés department store. For details, contact **Trapsatur,** San Bernardo 23 (☎ **91-541-63-20**).

THE HITS YOU SHOULDN'T MISS

✪ **Prado Museum (Museo del Prado).** Paseo del Prado. ☎ **91-420-28-36.** Admission 450P ($3). Admission includes entrance to Casón del Buen Retiro, an annex 3 blocks east up Calle de Felípe IV. Tues–Sat 9am–7pm, Sun and holidays to 2pm. Metro: Banco de España. Bus: 10, 14, 17, 34, 37, or 45.

One of the great museums of the world, the Prado is reason enough to visit Madrid for art historians and avocational aficionados alike. Happily, after major reorganization during the past few years, the museum is once again entirely open, with all its prime properties on view.

Tackling the Prado in all its enormity could be baffling if the museum weren't as well organized as it is. (Get a floor plan when you enter the main hall.) Virtually every period of art is represented, though the 20th century is given much more space at the Thyssen and the Reina Sofía (below). Certainly, the work of the Spanish masters—Velázquez (his classic *Las Meninas*), El Greco, Goya, and Murillo—is seen in greater depth and breadth here than anywhere else in the world. There are also numerous

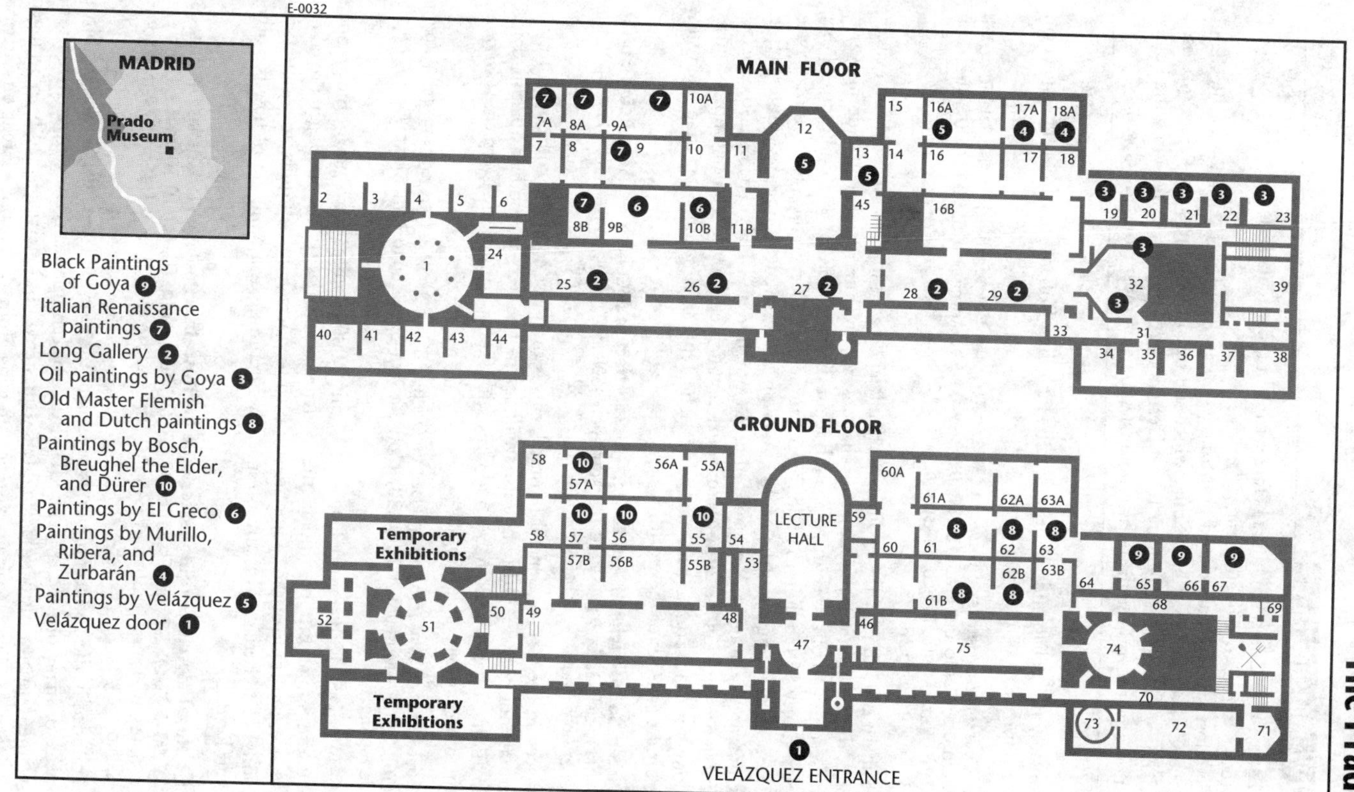
E-0032
MADRID
Prado Museum
Black Paintings of Goya 9
Italian Renaissance paintings 7
Long Gallery 2
Oil paintings by Goya 3
Old Master Flemish and Dutch paintings 8
Paintings by Bosch, Breughel the Elder, and Dürer 10
Paintings by El Greco 6
Paintings by Murillo, Ribera, and Zurbarán 4
Paintings by Velázquez 5
Velázquez door 1
MAIN FLOOR
GROUND FLOOR
LECTURE HALL
Temporary Exhibitions
Temporary Exhibitions
VELÁZQUEZ ENTRANCE

Two Museum Tips

Always check museum hours before setting out, particularly at the smaller ones, for they're prone to sudden changes.

Most museums are closed on Monday, so save for that day the Palacio Real and the Centro de Arte Reine Sofía, which are open. Most museums are also closed January 1, Good Friday, May 1, and December 26, but many, including the Prado, now stay open through the afternoon siesta, when most stores are closed.

---

works by the Italian and Flemish masters, including Rubens, Botticelli, Fra Angelico, and Raphael.

✪ **Thyssen-Bornemisza Museum (Museo Thyssen-Bornemisza).** In the Palacio de Villahermosa, Paseo del Prado 8. ☎ **91-369-01-51.** Admission 650P ($4.30). Tues–Sun 10am–7pm. Metro: Banco de España. Bus: 1, 2, 5, 9, 10, 14, 15, 20, 27, 34, 45, 51, 52, 53, 74, 146, or 150.

Formerly a holding of the eponymous family and based in a villa in Lugano, Switzerland, the Thyssen was the subject of the most violent international art bidding war in the second half of this century. Spain bought the collection for $350 million and then spent nearly $50 million to build this monumental gallery in the Villahermosa Palace. European painting from the Middle Ages on is displayed; among the painters represented are Caravaggio, Watteau, Dürer, Rembrandt, and Hals. There's also an excellent representation of 20th-century art, highlighted by the French impressionists, along with Picasso, Sargent, and others. The Thyssen is nothing less than one of the great art galleries of the world.

Queen Sofía National Art Center (Museo Nacional Centro de Arte Reine Sofía). Santa Isabel 52. ☎ **91-467-50-62.** Admission 450P ($3). Mon and Wed–Sat 10am–9pm, Sun to 2:30pm. Metro: Atocha. Bus 6, 14, 26, 27, 32, 45, 57, or C.

Placed in the former General Hospital, this is the most complete collection of modern art not only in Madrid but also in all Spain. The stars are modern Spanish artists, including Picasso, Dalí, Miró, and Gris, with Picasso's antiwar masterpiece, *Guernica,* the most famous tableau of all.

Royal Palace (Palacio Real). Plaza de Oriente, Bailen 2. ☎ **91-542-00-59.** Palace 900P ($6); Carriage Museum 200P ($1.30). Mon–Sat 9am–6pm, Sun to 3pm. Metro: Opera or Plaza de España.

Begun in the 18th century for Felípe V, this 2,000-room palace is one of the grandest buildings in all Europe. Initially the residence of Charles III, it's no longer a royal residence, but some of the rooms are still used for formal and administrative state functions. The Carriage Museum is especially interesting as a reminder of how the other half lived.

✪ **Royal Monastery (Monasterio de las Descalzas Reales).** Plaza de las Descalzas 3. ☎ **91-542-00-59.** Admission 650P ($4.50) Tues, Wed, Fri, Sat 10:30am–12:45pm and 4–5:45pm, Thurs 10:30am–12:45pm, Sun and holidays 11am–1:45pm. Metro: Sol or Callao.

Founded in the 16th century, this royal convent near the Puerta del Sol was the birthplace of Juana of Austria, Felipe II's sister. For centuries, this convent sheltered royal women, usually aristocratic daughters sequestered until marriages had been arranged. They didn't live a spartan existence, judging from the wealth of religious artwork around, including tapestries, sculptures, and paintings by Rubens, Brueghel the Elder, and Titian. You can visit 16 of the 32 chapels (count 'em!).

National Archaeological Museum (Museo Arqueológico Nacional). Serrano 13. ☎ **91-577-79-12.** Admission 400P ($2.70); free on Sat 2:30–8:30pm and Sun. Tues–Sat 9:30am–8:30pm, Sun to 2:30pm. Metro: Serrano or Retiro. Bus 1, 9, 19, 51, 74, or M2.

You don't have to be an archaeologist to dig the relics presented here. Many of them, like the Iberian statue the *Lady of Elche,* dating from the 4th century B.C., are Spanish in origin; others have been culled from points as far away as ancient Rome. The cave paintings from northern Spain are of great interest too.

Museum of America (Museo de América). Avenida de los Reyes Catolicos 6. ☎ **91-549-2641.** Admission 400P ($2.70). Tues–Sat 10am–3pm, Sun to 2:30pm. Metro: Moncloa.

An unorthodox choice, perhaps, but a fascinating one, this museum is devoted to relics and artifacts of ancient North and South American civilizations. But it also has excellent textual references explaining the cultures and their societies/religious beliefs that put this beyond the pale of most archaeology exhibits.

Municipal Museum (Museo Municipal). Fuencarral 78. ☎ **91-588-86-72.** Admission 300P ($2). Tues–Fri 9:30am–8pm, Sat–Sun 10am–2pm. Metro: Bilbao or Tribunal. Bus 3, 7, 40, 147, or 149.

This is a fascinating look at the history and development of Madrid as a municipality, city state, and seat of Spanish culture. Period re-creations of city scenes via models and actual tapestries are the calling cards here.

Goya Tomb (Panteón de Goya). San António de la Florida 5. ☎ **91-547-79-21.** Admission 200P ($1.35). Tues–Fri 10am–2pm and 4–7pm, Sat–Sun 10am–2pm. Metro: Norte. Bus: 41, 46, 75, or C.

Carlos IV commissioned Goya to decorate the domed ceiling of the chapel in this 1797 hermitage. His frescoes tell the story of St. Anthony of Padua and are populated with plump cherubs and voluptuous angels modeled after members of the Spanish court and Madrid society. Some of the women were rumored to have rented themselves by the hour. Goya is buried here, but somehow his head got lost in transit from Bordeaux, where he was first interred.

Royal Academy of Fine Arts of San Fernando (Real Academia de Bellas Artes de San Fernando). Alcalá 13. ☎ **91-522-14-91.** Admission 300P ($2.05); free Sat–Sun. Tues–Fri 9am–7pm, Sat–Mon 9am–2pm. Metro: Sol or Sevilla. Bus: 3, 5, 15, 20, 51, or 52.

This center, in a recently restored building east of the Puerta del Sol, offers a wide variety of works by artists like El Greco, Zurbarán, Sorolla, Ribera, Murillo, Rubens, and Fragonard, plus one room filled with Goyas, produced in his mature years. After a showy display of these heavyweights, the rooms in back contain a diversity of Chinese terra-cottas, Egyptian bronzes, and small sculptures.

Museum of Decorative Arts (Museo de Artes Decorativas). Montalban 12 (off Plaza de las Cibeles). ☎ **91-522-17-40.** Admission 400P ($2.70). Tues–Fri 9am–3pm, Sat–Sun 10am–2pm. Metro: Banco de España. Bus: 14, 27, 34, 37, or 45.

This museum is crammed with furniture, leatherwork, wall hangings, ceramics, rugs, porcelain, glass, jewelry, toys, clothes, and lace. After the first floor, it progresses in chronological order, tracing the development of Spanish interior decoration from the 15th to the 19th century. Calling all interior decorators . . .

Funicular (Teleferico). In the Parque de Atracciones, Paseo del Pinto Rosales. ☎ **91-541-74-40.** Fare 350P ($2.30) one way, 500P ($3.30) round-trip. Mar–Oct daily noon–9pm; Nov–Feb Sat–Sun noon–9pm. Metro: Plaza de España or Arguelles. Bus: 74.

Unless you're a kid, the Parque de Atracciones probably won't hold much interest for you, but this funicular will; it affords a great view of the city and is thrilling besides. There are placards designating what's where in the park, or (easier still) just ask for

Madrid Attractions

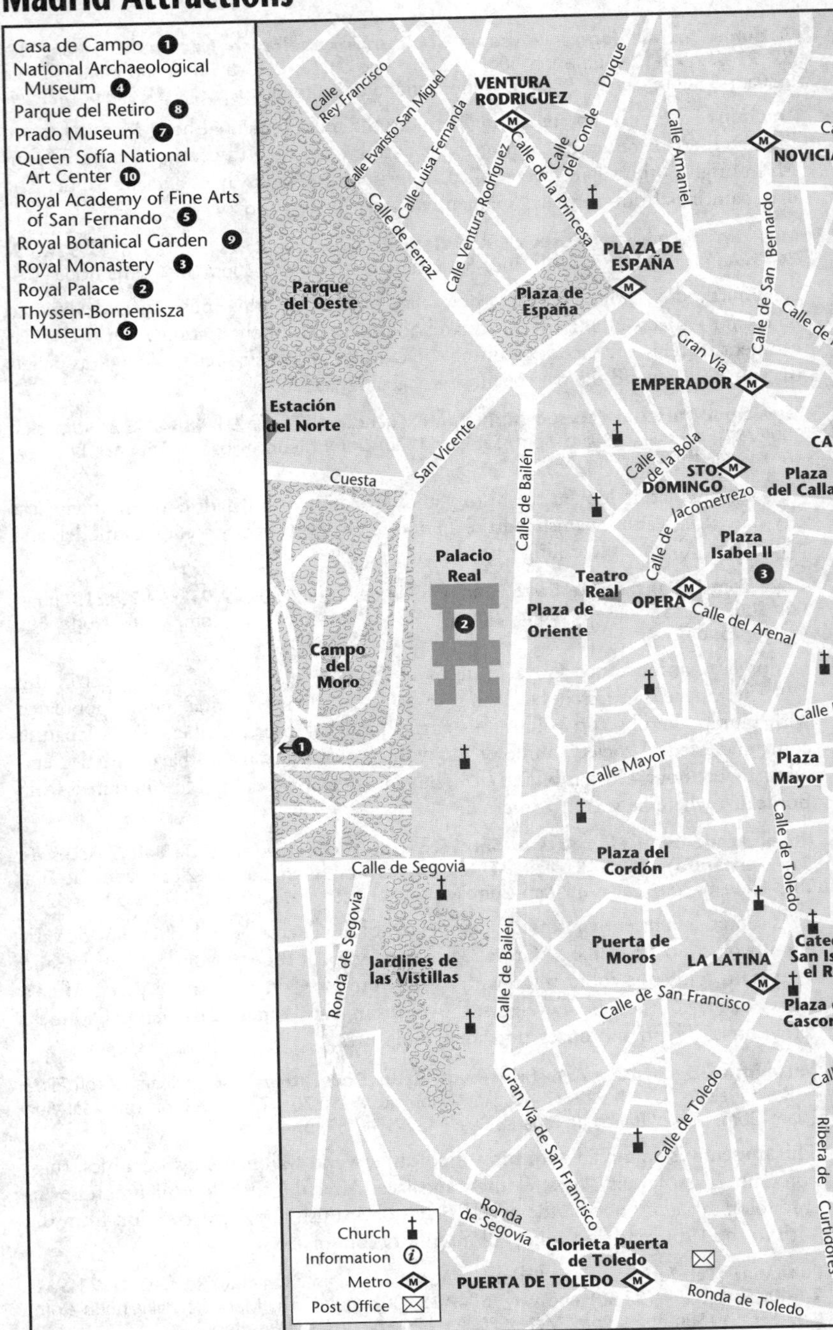

Casa de Campo 1
National Archaeological Museum 4
Parque del Retiro 8
Prado Museum 7
Queen Sofía National Art Center 10
Royal Academy of Fine Arts of San Fernando 5
Royal Botanical Garden 9
Royal Monastery 3
Royal Palace 2
Thyssen-Bornemisza Museum 6
Calle Rey Francisco
Calle Evaristo San Miguel
Calle Luisa Fernanda
VENTURA RODRIGUEZ
Duque
Calle del Conde
Calle de la Princesa
Calle Ventura Rodríguez
Calle de Ferraz
Calle Amaniel
Calle de San Bernardo
PLAZA DE ESPAÑA
Plaza de España
Parque del Oeste
Gran Vía
EMPERADOR
Estación del Norte
San Vicente
Cuesta
Calle de Bailén
Calle de la Bola
STO. DOMINGO
Plaza del Callao
Calle de Jacometrezo
Plaza Isabel II
Palacio Real
Teatro Real
OPERA
Plaza de Oriente
Calle del Arenal
Campo del Moro
Calle Mayor
Plaza Mayor
Calle de Toledo
Plaza del Cordón
Calle de Segovia
Ronda de Segovia
Jardines de las Vistillas
Puerta de Moros
LA LATINA
Calle de San Francisco
Gran Vía de San Francisco
Ribera de Curtidores
Ronda de Segovia
Glorieta Puerta de Toledo
PUERTA DE TOLEDO
Ronda de Toledo
Church
Information
Metro
Post Office

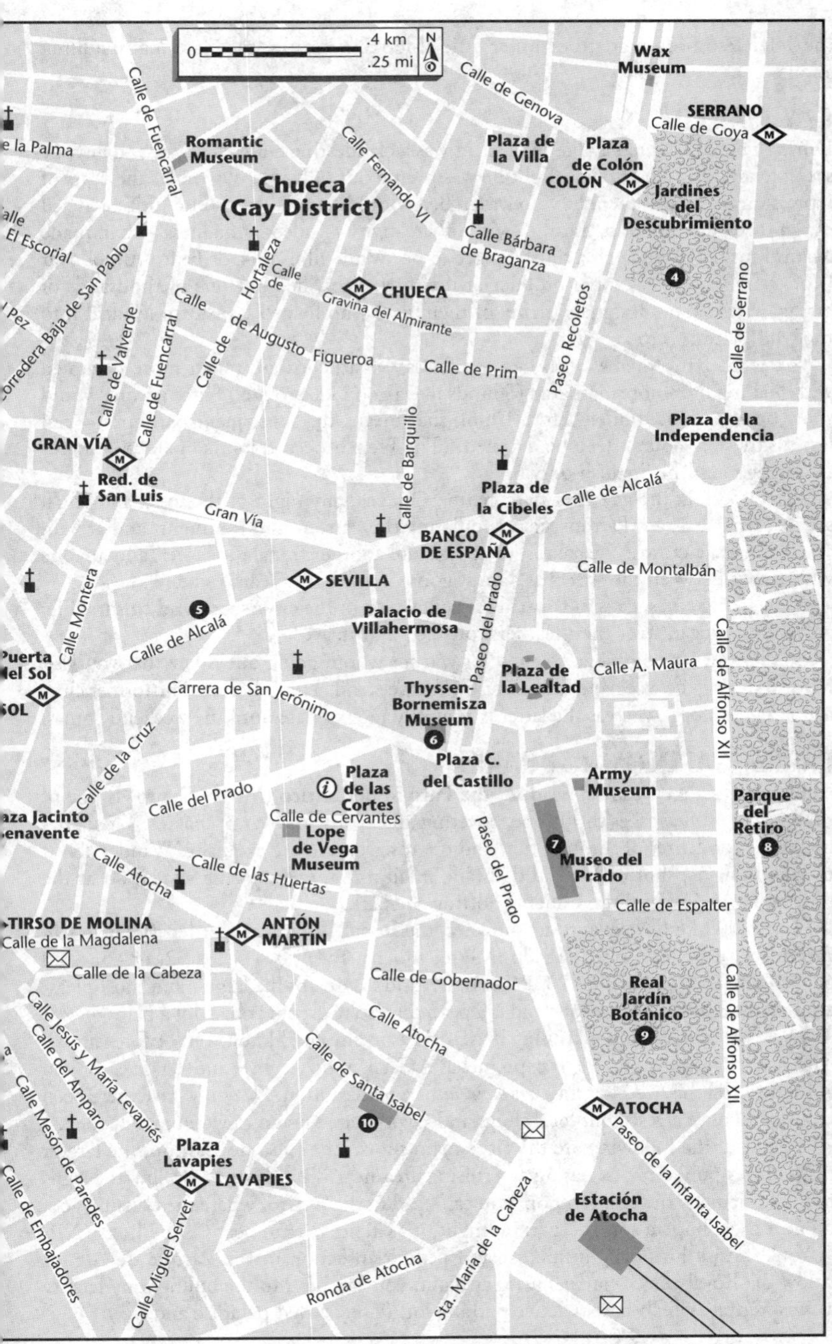

0
.4 km
.25 mi
N
Wax
Museum
SERRANO
Calle de Goya
Calle de Genova
Plaza de
la Villa
Plaza
de Colón
COLÓN
Jardines
del
Descubrimiento
Romantic
Museum
Chueca
(Gay District)
Calle Fernando VI
Calle de Fuencarral
e la Palma
alle
El Escorial
Corredera Baja de San Pablo
Pez
Calle Bárbara
de Braganza
Calle
de
Hortaleza
CHUECA
Gravina del Almirante
Calle
de Augusto
Figueroa
Calle de Prim
Paseo Recoletos
Calle de Serrano
Calle de Valverde
Calle de Fuencarral
Calle de
Calle de Barquillo
Plaza de la
Independencia
GRAN VÍA
Red. de
San Luis
Gran Vía
Plaza de
la Cibeles
Calle de Alcalá
BANCO
DE ESPAÑA
Calle de Montalbán
SEVILLA
Calle Montera
Calle de Alcalá
Palacio de
Villahermosa
Paseo del Prado
Plaza de
la Lealtad
Calle A. Maura
Puerta
del Sol
SOL
Carrera de San Jerónimo
Thyssen-
Bornemisza
Museum
Calle de Alfonso XII
Calle de la Cruz
Plaza C.
del Castillo
Calle del Prado
Plaza
de las
Cortes
Calle de Cervantes
Army
Museum
Parque
del
Retiro
aza Jacinto
enavente
Lope
de Vega
Museum
Paseo del Prado
Museo del
Prado
Calle Atocha
Calle de las Huertas
Calle de Espalter
TIRSO DE MOLINA
Calle de la Magdalena
ANTÓN
MARTÍN
Calle de la Cabeza
Calle de Gobernador
Real
Jardín
Botánico
Calle Atocha
Calle Jesús y María Levapiés
Calle del Amparo
Calle de Santa Isabel
Calle de Alfonso XII
Calle Mesón de Paredes
ATOCHA
Paseo de la Infanta Isabel
Plaza
Lavapies
LAVAPIES
Calle de Embajadores
Calle Miguel Servet
Ronda de Atocha
Sta. María de la Cabeza
Estación
de Atocha

the Teleferico from a guard or other official-looking person; there are many milling about.

GAY MADRID

During Franco's reign, gay life in Madrid was a clandestine closeted affair, and anyone seeking anything close to gay nightlife was plumb out of luck. No wonder the years of repression under this dictator who was in bed with Hitler and Mussolini ultimately led to La Movida, the hip, heady swirl of creativity—indeed, madness—that made Madrid in the 1980s such a terrific place to be. While film director Pedro Almodóvar is of course the best-known product of the movement, he's but one of thousands of artists, writers, and designers (many of them gay) who helped transform Madrid into the wild place it is today.

Yes, wild. Barcelonans work like the Swiss; Madrileños are much more occupied with making life a nonstop party. (Sounds like a good idea to me.) Since no one would show up for a chic dinner before 10pm, that means the subsequent barhopping can last till the wee hours, sleep be damned. (The French need 8 hours of sleep, a popular saying goes; the Spanish only 6.)

Take a peek at the gay after-dark center, **Chueca,** any night of the week and you'll see just what I mean. Patrons start populating the bars around midnight, and at 3am you'll still see a crowd. Weekends, of course, are another thing altogether, and anyone who crawls between the sheets at 4am is going home early. Yeah, right.

As in all big cities, gays in Madrid are a vital part of the city's social and cultural life, and they now can strut their feathers, prosper, and thrive.

By the way, I recommend to those of you for whom going out is key that you visit Madrid during the week and Barcelona on the weekend. This is because the former city's action never stops, whereas the latter is relatively more sedate until the weekend comes.

PARKS, GARDENS & SQUARES

Though set right in central Madrid, the **Parque del Retiro** (Metro: Retiro) is one of the largest public spaces in Europe, covering an expanse of over 350 acres. The park's huge lake is a center of summer fun, and the rose gardens are exquisite. Wander about to take in a snapshot of Madrid daily life in all its varieties, gazing as you do at the statues, fountains, and monuments dotting the park.

Over 3,000 kinds of plants are grown at the **Royal Botanical Garden (Real Jardín Botánico),** just south of the Prado (Metro: Atocha; Bus: 10, 14, 19, 32, or 45; open daily 10am–8pm; admission 200P/1.33). Madrid's is one of the largest and most pleasant botanical gardens in Europe and is a peaceful respite even if you're not a plant queen.

There's as much outdoor cruising in Madrid as in any city I know. But be forewarned: This isn't Barcelona, where the progressive Catalan police live and let live. If you absolutely feel the need to cruise *en plein air*, exercise caution. Not only have there been reports of police arrests, but local thugs and Gypsies are known to victimize gay men.

That said, the following are the city's main spots: The **Casa de Campo,** the largest of Madrid's public parks, has a gay cruising area near the Teleferico (follow the signs to the funicular). In the afternoon, you can head to the **Retiro,** where the cruising goes on near the Chopera sports center; at night, it switches over to near Calle Alfonso XII.

You'll find a lot of nighttime car and pedestrian action in the **Parque de Atenas** below the Royal Palace gardens. Also at night, you can head to the bullfighting facility at **Las Ventas,** which has an active parking lot. (They paved paradise and . . .)

WORKING UP A SWEAT

In the gay district of Chueca, **City Sport,** Hortaleza 41 (no phone; Metro: Gran Vía or Chueca), is a small but very central gym for those who can't do without their daily workouts. The crowd tends to be gayer at City Sport than at **Bodhiharma,** Moratines 18 (☎ **91-517-28-16;** Metro: Embajadores), a popular large gym for men and women offering a weekly guest membership for 2,300P ($15).

Madrid offers a plethora of well-run public pools, and the ones in the **Casa de Campo** (☎ **91-463-00-50;** Metro: Lago; Bus: 33), are rather cruisy (for all the obvious reasons). They're closest to Avenida del Angel. There's a nude sun-worshipper's area at the pool in the outlying district of **Barrio del Pilar,** Calle Montforte de Lemos (☎ **91-314-79-43;** Metro: Barrio del Pilar; Bus: 83 or 128).

5 Hitting the Stores

It wasn't too long ago that shopping in Madrid was light-years behind that in other major European capitals. Everything's different now: Madrid presents a dizzying gamut of possibilities for the committed shopper—everything from the poshest international boutiques to groovy local designers to funky vintage shops.

Salamanca is hands-down the sexiest shopping area, the place where monied Madrid goes to buy (especially clothes). **Calles Serrano, Goy,** and **Velázquez** are the key streets. On the other side of Recoletos, abutting the Chueca district, is **Almirante,** where local talent shows their wares in funky SoHo-style shops. **Chueca** itself, once virtually unknown as a shopping district, has begun to host (in addition to the obvious gay-oriented stores) vintage clothing stores and other fun shops.

Spain is the country where the term siesta was born, and shopping hours generally reflect this tradition. Throughout the country, shops close from about 2 to 4pm, though the exact hours are at the discretion of the owner. However, some stores do stay open continuously. In fact, this is a growing trend, especially among upscale stores.

ANTIQUES The **Galerias Riquer,** Ribera de Curtidores 29 (no phone; Metro: La Latina), contains more than 20 individual stores and thus represents a kind of one-stop shop for antiques hounds. The **Nuevas Galerias,** Ribera de Curtidores 12 (no phone; Metro: La Latina; Bus: 17, 18, or 23), is another upmarket antiques arcade, this one with 10 stores; it's a quick walk from the Riquer.

ART GALLERIES One of the city's most respected galleries, ✪ **Antonio Machon,** Conde de Xiquena 8 (☎ **91-532-40-93;** Metro: Chueca), deals in established artists like Tapíes and Bonifacio, with exhibits of emerging painters as well.

A darling of the fashion and art worlds, ✪ **Elba Benitez, San Lorenzo 11** (☎ **91-308-04-68;** Metro: Tribunal; Bus: 3, 37, or 149), owns this gallery housed in an old mansion; it's equally devoted to foreign artists and young Spanish talent, many from Catalonia. La Movida practically got started at **Moriarty,** Almirante 5, first floor (☎ **91-531-43-65;** Metro: Chueca), and many of its founding members (the ones who are still alive) exhibit here, including Ouka Lele (!), Mireia Sents, and Mariscal. A must for lovers of the wild, weird, and wonderful.

BOOKS Madrid's gay bookstore, ✪ **Berkana,** Gravina 11 (☎ **91-32-13-93;** Metro: Chueca), is a bit small but is well stocked with Spanish editions of gay books, as well as international magazines and a few gifties. The guys who work here are excellent sources of info on what's happening in the gay community. **Turner,** Principe de Vergara 206 (☎ **91-563-69-430;** Metro: Concha Espina; Bus: 16, 19, 52, or 122), is Madrid's largest English-language bookstore and is also a great way to keep up with the English-language community (crappy jobs, apartment shares, and such dot the bulletin board) if you're in Madrid for a while.

CLUBWEAR At **Condoms,** Colón 3 (no phone; Metro: Tribunal; Bus: 3, 40, or 149), guess what you can buy? Why have I put this under Clubwear? Because Madrid's clubs are so top heavy (ha, ha) with backrooms that you really should bring some along to slip into casually when the time is right. And nowhere has as broad a collection as this store, though the li'l rubber things are far cheaper back home. Everything a club kid's heart could desire is on sale at **Glam,** Fuencaral 35 (☎ **91-522-80-54;** Metro: Gran Vía or Chueca; Bus: 3 or 40), from platform shoes to mod belts and more. Sadly, however, no Hello Kitty was on display.

The family-run ✪ **Odd!,** Leon 35 (☎ **91-429-05-70;** Metro: Anton Martín; Bus: 6, 26, 57), is upbeat and friendly, with a range of clothes (many of them English) to wear if you want to look like Baby Spice. Some of this transcends clubwear, and you could actually wear it in on the street (unless you're a stockbroker). At gay-run **Top,** Hortaleza 27 (☎ **91-23-57-10;** Metro: Chueca), sexy see-through underwear, skintight shorts, and other unmentionables are the key items. All this, plus the usual assortment of gay gift items and toys.

FASHION ✪ **Asuntos Infernos,** Fuencarral 2 (☎ **91-32-32-99;** Metro: Gran Vía), is Madrid's biggest men's emporium, featuring Diesel, Dominguez, and Basi, plus more mainstream mid-to upper-range international names. The lower floor is a great place to buy sexy European underwear, swimwear, and men's accessories. (The name means Internal Affairs—duh.)

Massimo Dutti, Princesa 79 (☎ **91-543-74-22;** Metro: Moncloa; Bus: 1 or 44), is the flagship branch of this now-international Spanish designer. The clothes aren't supertrendy, but they're kind of an updated Spanish Brooks brothers style—handsome, well-made, and well-priced, with a modern if not avant-garde feel.

Zara, Princesa 45 (☎ **91-541-09-02;** Metro: Areguelles or Moncloa; Bus: 1 or 44), a Spanish chain of clothes for men, women, and children, stands poised to become the world's next Benetton—which is fine, 'cuz I like 'em better. These are mid-priced, well-made fashions ranging from fairly mainstream stuff to knockoffs of designer trends; highbrows trash Zara, but their price-quality ratios is generally very high.

FOOD ✪ **Casa Mira,** San Jeronimo 30 (☎ **91-429-67-96;** Metro: Sevilla), is probably the most famous sweets store in town; the specialty is *turron,* a Spanish nougat I don't much care for (though it makes an easily transportable, almost indestructible gift). There are lots of other kinds of sweets and cakes, many packaged for trans-Atlantic travel. If you're a cheese queen like me, you'll agree that cheese has every right to have its own palace. The wonderful old-world **El Palacio de los Quesos,** Mayor 53 (☎ **91-548-16-23;** Metro: Sol), has just about every Spanish (and foreign) cheese made, plus loads of wines and other gourmet foods to take home.

At ✪ **Mendez, Ayala 65 (☎ 91-402-43-78;** Metro: Lista; Bus: 32, 26, 29, 53, or 61), products from Galicia are the stock-in-trade, with many kinds of cheeses, olives, meats, and canned fish. Spanish wines too. The **Museo del Jamon,** San Jeronimo 6 (☎ **91-521-03-46;** Metro: Sol), is the original and largest of the several museums dedicated to ham, a staple of tapas of various kinds. While ham (packaged to take across the pond, if you wish) is the star, there are other delicacies for your—or your friends'—munching pleasure.

GIFTS If you're in the market for Iberian ceramics and pottery, **Ceramica El Alfar,** Claudio Coello 112 (☎ **91-411-35-87;** Metro: Nuñez de Balboa; Bus: 9, 51, or 6l), is the place to go. Though the emphasis is on traditional designs, some more modern pieces are available too.

Potters from the north of Spain are the calling card at the charming **Sargadelos,** Zarbano 4 (☎ **91-310-48-30;** Metro: Ruben Dario; Bus: 5, 7, 16, 61, or 147). Unlike at most stores of this type, the focus is on unique modern work rather than on the far more typical reproductions of classic Spanish designs and motifs. Straight out of an Almodóvar film, ✪ **Almirante 23,** Almirante 23 (☎ **91-308-12-02;** Metro: Chueca; Bus 5, 14, 27, 37, or 53), is a little shoebox of a store selling all manner of campy stuff, both Spanish and otherwise. Perfect for kitschy things to put in your kitchen, bathroom, or office or to give as gifts.

LEATHER The Gucci of Spain (if lacking a Tom Ford), **Loewe,** Gran Vía 8 (☎ **91-522-68-15;** Metro: Banco de España), is the only place Madrid's elite shops for handbags, luggage, and shoes. Not ultrafashionable, but the kind of conservative chic rich folks love.

A MARKET The expansive outdoor ✪ **El Rastro,** Ribera de Curtidores (Metro: Latina; Bus: 17, 18, 23, 35, or 148), is much more interesting as a slice of Madrid life than as a serious place to buy; in fact, many of the dealers have the same kind of things (odd 1960s holdouts like macramé and incense, bad clothes) as icky street fairs in New York (and, I assume, any American or Canadian city). In fact, some of the stalls on the market's fringe are little more than makeshift booths (milk cartons and the like) with whatever crap the vendor could find in the garbage heap that day. Still, it's a fun thing to do on a Sunday morning or afternoon. Note: Watch your wallets, as pickpockets abound.

TATTOOS If you attempt to check out the **Biotek Body Experience Shop,** Santa Lucia 2 (☎ **91-521-30-93;** Metro: Noviciado or Tribnal; Bus: 3, 40, or 147), be scared . . . be very scared. This isn't a shop for the faint of heart or those of you who needed four Darvons to get your ears pierced at the mall. Instead, the folks at Biotek (note odd pseudolaboratorical name) specialize in tattoos in places where the sun don't shine. Don't ask—I didn't.

6 All the World's a Stage

THE PERFORMING ARTS

As befits any major capital, Madrid is fairly awash in both the popular and the high performing arts. Of course, unless your Spanish is up to snuff, you'll be fairly limited in your choices of any involving the spoken word, but there are plenty of music and dance options from which to choose.

To find out what's happening during your stay, look at the newspaper ***El País.*** Your other option is to pick up the ***Guia del Ocio,*** sold at news kiosks throughout the city, for the events of the week. And ***Shangay,*** Madrid's gay newspaper (found free at most of the gay places in this chapter, especially the cafes), lists events and performances of gay interest.

In 1997, the big cultural news was the reopening of the 1,750-seat ✪ **Teatro Real (Royal Opera House), Plaza de Oriente** (☎ **91-558-87-87;** Metro: Opera), after almost a decade of false starts and slow construction costing $157 million. It hadn't experienced an operatic performance for over 70 years, opening and closing irregularly over that time to serve as a orchestral concert hall. Guided tours of the grand renovation are available Saturday, Sunday, and holidays, every 30 minutes 10:30am to 1:30pm.

The modern **Auditorio Nacional de Musica,** Principe de Vergara 146 (☎ **91-337-01-00;** Metro: Cruz de Rayo), is home base for Spain's National Orchestra and National Chorus. There are three rooms for performances ranging from small recitals to full symphony events.

The **Auditoria del Parque de Atracciones,** Casa de Campo (No phone ; Metro: Lago or Batan), is located in a large amusement park. It hosts performers ranging from Pavarotti to Patti Smith. Check the local listings to find out who's playing and when.

Work That Skirt: Flamenco!

People either love or hate **flamenco.** Dance purists find this typically Spanish form flashy and even vulgar, but the rest of us can enjoy this soulful art.

Flamenco's origins are unknown, though Andalusia (southern Spain) is most generally cited as its source. Jewish, Moorish, and Gypsy origins are also claimed. What doesn't change is the basic premise: A company of guitarist(s), castanet players, and clappers form the melody and (mostly) rhythm to which one or more performers dance. By nature, it's a sensual, ritualistic dance, performed mainly by prostitutes in its early days; flamenco is considered to have low-brow roots and thus still scorned by the Spanish upper crust.

While it's understandable to want to see flamenco here, don't expect to be surrounded by hot, hip youth. Young people in Spain are supercool and would rather hear pop music or go to a disco than hit the dwindling flamenco scene. Some would argue that hot-bodied Joaquin Cortes (Naomi Campbell's ex) is fronting a flamenco renaissance, but his special version is so married to classical and modern dance it's more a one-man hybrid than anything else.

All that having been said, there are far worse ways to spend an evening than watching a bunch of women working their ruffled skirts and guys traipsing around in crotch-splitting pants, *verdad*?

Casa Patas, Canizares 10 (☎ **91-369-04-96;** Metro: Tirso de Molina), is a fine place to see flamenco performed by artists from all over Spain. Dinner is available too, but it's overpriced and of more interest to packaged tours than anyone else. A dinner theater cum performance space, the **Cafe de Chinitas,** Torija 7 (☎ **91-559-51-35;** Metro: Santo Domingo; Bus 1 or 2), is a well-known place to see flamenco acts of high repute. It's somewhat touristy, though local aficionados are here as well.

The unique **Circulo de Bellas Artes,** Marqes de Casa Rivera 2 (☎ **91-531-77-00;** Metro: Banco de España or Sevilla), is a testament to Madrid's forward thinking, a performance place dedicated to new music of all kinds. It also hosts a couple of musical festivals, which the local newspapers will fill you in on. Really worth a trip if experimental and modern music are your passions.

Spain's national theater company (the direct analog of the Comédie-Française) is based at the **Teatro de la Comedia,** Principe 14 (☎ **91-521-49-31;** Metro: Sevilla; Bus: 15, 20, or 150). Classic Spanish drama is the ticket, but only if your Spanish is *bueno.* The **Teatro Español,** Principe 25 (☎ **91-429-62-97;** Metro: Sevilla), is another highly respected troupe offering Castillian-language drama.

The ✪ **Compañia Nacional de Danza,** with artistic director Nacho Duato, is one of Spain's premier arts organizations, with a very high profile on the international dance scene. Sensuous and lyrical, as well as stunningly musical, Duato's works demand dancers of the highest caliber and that's exactly what he has. The company has strong roots in the classical tradition, but the repertory reads like a who's who of today's foremost contemporary dance. In fall, look for the company to perform at either the **Teatro Real** (see above) or the **Teatro La Zarzuela,** Jovellanos 4 (☎ **91-524-54-00;** Metro: Banco de España or Sevilla). In spring it heads out to the **Teatro de Madrid** in La Vaguada (Metro: Barrio de Pillar). Be on the lookout for the company's annual workshop benefit performance for Apoyo Positivo, a local AIDS support network, held at the Teatro de Madrid.

LIVE-MUSIC CLUBS

The music at **Cafe Populart,** Huertas 22 (☎ **91-429-84-07;** Metro: Anton Martin or Sevilla; Bus: 6 or 60; admission 600P/$4), begins with jazz, then branches out to Brazilian, African, and other world sounds depending on the performer and night. It doesn't have a gay clientele per se but may be attractive to those of you seeking to scope out sounds you can't hear at home.

Clamores, Albuqerque 4 (☎ **91-445-79-38;** Metro: Bilbao; Bus: 6, 26, 32; admission 600P/$4), claims to be the largest of Madrid's jazz clubs, and it certainly attracts key names from around the world. But you'll also find musical acts from other genres performing here.

Malasana was the neighborhood at the heart of La Movida, and **Maravillas,** San Vicente Ferrer 33 (☎ **91-523-30-71;** Metro: Tribunal; Bus: 3, 40, or 149; admission varies), is a holdover from those days that's still going strong (albeit with a totally different, younger crowd). Alternative rock is the thing here, and there are bands on most (but not all) nights.

Oba Oba, Jacometrezo 4 (no phone; Metro: Callao; admission varies), is a small, usually packed, very hip Brazilian music bar where you can drink *cachaça* (a superpotent rum, the Brazilian national alcoholic beverage, aka *pinga*—and we all know what that means) to your heart's content. Typically, the evening starts off with softer sounds (Veloso, Nascimento) and deteriorates into a mad frenzy of Afro-Caribbean and samba beats.

7 In the Heat of the Night

"In the Heat of the Night" is an appropriate heading for the dizzy, dazzling scene that's gay nightlife in Madrid. *Restraint? Sleep?* Neither word is in the vocabulary of young Madrileños, who can be seen dancing, drinking, and doin' the wild thang in the capital's clubs night after night. Rest when you get home; get set for nonstop action here!

GAY & LESBIAN BARS

Black & White, Libertad 34 (no phone; Metro: Chueca), may well be Madrid's longest-running gay bar. As of late, though, it has fallen on hard times and tends to be a place older men pick up rent boys. There are extratrashy strip shows from Thursday to Sunday night.

Another old standby, ✪ **Cruising,** Perez Galdos 5 (no phone; Metro: Chueca), continues to pack 'em in. The upper floor features an underutilized bar and a small movie theater with dirty goings-on; but the real action takes place downstairs, where a small dance floor is the cover for major backroom action. One could hardly accuse Cruising of being trendy, but when the mood strikes . . .

Open from 9pm, ✪ **La Lupe,** Torrecilla del Leal 12 (☎ **91-527-50-19;** Metro: Anton Martin; Bus: 6, 26, 32, or 57), is an alternative spot run by the group Radical Gai and attracts a boho crowd of lesbians and gays. Convivial and friendly, this may well be a prime meeting spot for those turned off by conventional gay bars.

Isis, Plaza de Chueca (no phone; Metro: Chueca), is one of the few exclusively women's bars in Madrid. Men, often of the flamboyant variety, occasionally show up, but it's mainly a place where ladies meet. The decor is a bit campy, with flaming torches. Patrons range from young lipstick beauties to older women who'd like to break in the new arrivals.

Hot, Infantas 9 (no phone; Metro: Chueca), is a spot that can't quite decide what it wants to be—a leather bar, an after-work meeting spot, or a strip-show palace. It's in the middle of everything, thus worth a look, though Lord knows how hot this will be by the time you read this.

Another chameleon, **LL Bar,** Pelayo 11 (☎ **91-523-31-21;** Metro: Chueca), takes on different guises at different times of the week. On weekdays, it's full of rent boys and older gents, some of whom conduct their business in the darkroom downstairs. On weekend nights, a more diverse gay crowd congregates for the trashy strip shows that take place around 1am.

✪ **Rick's,** Clavel 8 (no phone; Metro: Chueca), is a small American-style drinking bar (read: no disco and no backroom), and at 'round midnight it starts reeling in a supercute young crowd who (maybe thankfully) are turned off by the shadier goings-on at many of Madrid's bars. Rick's is perhaps a nice harbinger of the younger generation's growing preference for socializing before indiscriminate playtime.

Video Show Bar, Barco 32 (no phone; Metro: Gran Vía or Chueca), is a weird hybrid joint that starts out with a small bar in front, then devolves into a video arcade where lots of naughtiness goes on. It's busiest, the owner tells me, after work, 7 to 9pm. On Sundays at 9pm, there are striptease shows, the quality of which I can't attest to (sorry).

MIXED BARS

The alternative set hangs at the trendy mixed **El Mojito,** Olmo 6 (no phone; Metro: Tirso de Molina), and it's loads of fun. There are often photographic exhibits that further support this bar's arty air. A breath of fresh air far in attitude and location from the standard Chueca-based gay scene.

On those nights when you're in mixed company, trendy **Priscila,** San Bartlome 12 (no phone; Metro: Chueca), is a nice place to hang, especially during the week (on weekends, the crowd's just too-too thick). Why? This small downstairs haunt plays fabu music, from 1960s Motown to 1970s glam, and the hip young crowd (practically no one over 25) can't get enough.

LEATHER BARS

Madrid's premier leather bar, the **Sling,** Valverde 6 (no phone; Metro; Gran Vía), attracts a crowd of leather devotees from early evening on. If you're a queer into *cuiro*, the Sling's your thing. The **Eagle,** Pelayo 30 (no phone; Metro: Chueca), is Madrid's most serious leather bar. Gawkers aren't appreciated, but you'll be if you show up at this dark, dank spot in full regalia. (But leather in Madrid's blazing midsummer heat? Puh-leeez!)

A misnomer, the **New Leather Bar,** Pelayo 42 (☎ **91-308-14-62;** Metro: Chueca), has been around for more than a few years, but it continues to attract a leather crowd; the backroom is said to be a mondo bizarro unto itself. (Vanilla, I didn't partake.)

DANCE CLUBS

Madrid's cutest young guys can't get enough of ✪ **Refugio,** Doctor Cortezo 1 (☎ **91-369-40-38;** Metro: Tirso de Molina; admission 1,500P/$10), where the music has its finger on the pulse of whatever's hottest on the international dance circuit. I'm sorry to report that some of the States' most vapid trends (underwear and foam parties) have made their way here, but this is one of Spain's best gay club spots anyway.

Sponsored by the eponymous gay magazine, the way-cool ✪ **Shangay Tea Dance,** Mesonero Romanos 13 (☎ **91-531-48-27;** Metro: Callao or Gran Vía; admission free), takes place Sundays 9pm to 2am and features some of the best music and hottest bods in town. For circuit queens, a must.

Talk about late: **Goa After Hours,** Mesnero Romanos 13 (☎ **91-531-48-27;** Metro: Callao or Gran Vía; admission 1,000P/$7, including one drink), doesn't even happen till 6am Saturday and Sunday mornings! Everyone here gets a little help from their (powdered) friends, natch. The dance music rages, but only hard-core partyers need apply.

Heaven, Veneras 2 (no phone; Metro: Sol; admission 1,000P/$7), is a crapshoot during the week (though it, like practically every club in Madrid, is trying to spice things up with strip shows) but a very popular weekend after-hours spot. (I'm talking 5am minimum.) The music is house and the boys are hot and hedonistic.

Why Not?, San Bartolomé 6 (☎ **91-523-05-81;** Metro: Gran Vía; admission 1,000P/$7, including one drink), is one of Madrid's trendiest night scenes. This mixed club roars, with dancing, drinking, and general partying with much less posing than you'd see in Stateside clubs. After all, girls just want to have fun—but not till at least 1am, and the club is open till 8am.

Calling the **Strong Center,** Trujillos 7 (☎ **91-41-54-14;** Metro: Opera; admission 1,000P/$7), a disco is a bit much, since the tiny dance floor—rarely used—is just a cover for the huge backroom that's the real draw. The admission treats you to two free drinks Monday to Wednesday. Trashy as they come, and about as much fun.

SAUNAS

Comendadores, Plaza Comendadores 9 (☎ **91-532-88-92;** Metro: Noviciado; Bus: 21), is one of Madrid's perennially popular bathhouses, one of the largest and busiest. It's a bit off the beaten path but worth the visit—especially in the late afternoon or after work, if married men are your thing. **Men,** Pelayo 25 (☎ **91-531-25-83;** Metro: Gran Vía or Chueca), is among the smallest of Madrid's saunas. It's very basic and not the cleanest and seems to stay in business mainly on the strength of unsuspecting tourists who wander in because it's in the heart of Chueca. Try it only if you're too tired to go anywhere else.

Another popular spot, **Paraiso,** North 15 (☎ **91-522-43-32;** Metro: Noviciado), is a medium-sized clean and well-staffed sauna with a massage therapist on duty most of time. You can also pay extra to sit in the sun beds, if you're a tanaholic type. Recently renovated, the **Principe,** Principe 15 (☎ **91-429-3949;** Metro: Sol or Tirso de Molina), attracts a hot crowd, especially in the late afternoon and early evening.

8 Side Trips from Madrid: El Escorial & Segovia

EL ESCORIAL

Felípe II commissioned Juan Bautista de Toledo and his assistant, Juan de Herrera, to build **El Escorial** on this hillside in the Sierra de Guadarrama 34 miles northwest of Madrid. Its purported intent was to commemorate an important victory over the French in Flanders, but the likely real reason was that the ascetic Felípe was increasingly unnerved by the stress of overseeing an empire that bridged four continents. (And I can't even balance my checkbook!) This retreat insulated him from the pressures and intrigues of the Madrid Court. He ruled the troubled empire from his largely unadorned cells here for the last 14 years of his life.

Trains for El Escorial leave frequently from Madrid's Atocha, Chamartín, Recoletos, and Nuevos Ministerios stations. They take under 1 hour and cost 775P ($5) round-trip. **Buses** leave from Empresa Herranz, Isaac Peral 10, Moncloa (☎ **91-543-36-45**), and cost 750P ($5) round-trip; buses drop off closer to Felípe's royal monastery.

SEEING THE PALACE The squared-off monastery/palace is known for its brooding simplicity. That impression will be altered when you step inside, where you can appreciate its considerable size and wealth of accoutrements. The extraordinary library reflects the scholarly king's intellectual interests, with thousands of volumes and rare manuscripts in many languages and representative of the three primary religions that had existed in Spain. Also in the building is a sizable church with a large frescoed dome, beneath which is a royal pantheon whose sarcophagi contain the remains of most of Spain's monarchs since Carlos V. Museums and royal apartments contain canvases by El Greco, Titian, Tintoretto, Rubens, and Velázquez.

An all-inclusive ticket is 850P ($6). The monastery is open Tuesday to Sunday and holidays 10am to 6pm (to 5pm in winter). The **tourist office** at El Escorial can be reached at ☎ **91-890-59-05.**

A pleasant town has grown up around the monastery/palace. Its full name is San Lorenzo de El Escorial and it's not nearly as touristy as you might expect, given its proximity to Madrid. Avoiding weekends is a good idea, however.

WHET YOUR APPETITE There are a number of appealing bars and cafes, some with outside tables, at which to have a snack or sandwich. For a complete meal, a popular inn is the 18th-century **La Cueva,** San Antón 4 (☎ **91-890-15-16;** open Tues–Sun 1–4:30pm and 8:30–11pm).

SEGOVIA

If you have time for a 2-day, 1-night adventure out of Madrid, spend the first day exploring **El Escorial,** then continue on to **Segovia** for the night**.**

As is true throughout Spain, **buses** are preferable to **trains** for almost all trips under 100 miles. Between Segovia and Madrid, the bus takes 90 minutes but the train 2 hours, and the bus leaves you at the terminal at Paseo de Ezequile González 10, much closer than the rail station on Paseo Obispo Quesada. There are up to 15 buses daily from Madrid; a one-way fare is 810P ($5).

SEEING THE SIGHTS In Segovia you'll find what may be Spain's most recognizable structure: the ✪ **Acueducto Romano.** A spectacular engineering feat even if it were contemplated today, the double-tiered aqueduct cuts across the city to the snow-fed waters of the nearby mountains. Almost 2,400 feet long and nearly 95 feet at its highest point at the east end of town, it boasts over 160 arches fashioned of stone so precisely cut that no mortar was used. Probably completed in the 2nd century A.D. (though some sources date it as many as 3 centuries earlier), it has survived war and partial dismantling by the Moors. Amazingly, it carried water until only a few years ago.

The layout of Segovia routinely evokes comparison with a ship. Using that image, the aqueduct marks the stern. The land rises from there, accommodating several Romanesque churches and a Flamboyant Gothic **cathedral** begun and completed in the 16th century. Its spires are the ship's "riggings." Constructed at the command of Carlos V to replace one destroyed during the Communero Revolt against his policies, it deserves at least a brief tour. More interesting, if only for historic reasons, is the attached 15th-century **cloister.** After the earlier cathedral was razed by rebels, its cloister was moved stone by stone and reassembled here. It contains a small museum. Admission to the cathedral is free, but the cloister and museum cost 250P ($1.60). They're open daily: June to September 10am to 6pm and October to May 10am to 1pm and 3:30 to 6pm.

The cathedral abuts Plaza Mayor; at no. 10, opposite, is the **tourist information office** (☎ **921/46-03-34**). It hands out good maps and can help with lodging and bus and train schedules. Continuing west, the "prow" of the raised old town rears above the confluence of the rivers Clamores and Eresma and that dramatic position is held by the **Alcázar,** almost as familiar a symbol of Castilla (Castile) as the aqueduct. Satisfying though it is as fulfillment of "castles in Spain" fantasies (at least from the outside), the Alcázar is really a late-19th-century replica of the medieval fortress that stood here before a devastating 1868 fire. Admission is 375P ($2.50), and it's open April to September daily 10am to 7pm (to 6pm the rest of the year). But since the interior is of only modest interest, my suggestion is to take your photos of the exterior and save the admission fee for dinner.

The town is truly walkable, so take your time on the way back to Plaza de Azoguejo and the aqueduct. These narrow medieval streets suffer less from the ravages of mass tourism (except on weekends and holidays) than other destinations in Madrid's orbit and reveal much about what life must've been here 500 years ago. To many eyes, the several Romanesque churches of the 12th and 13th centuries are more visually appealing than the later Gothic temples. Seek out **San Esteban** (on the plaza of that name), **La Trinidad** (on the street of that name), and **San Juan de los Caballeros** (on nearby San Agustin).

PILLOW TALK If you want to stay the night, one of the best hotels in town, regardless of price, is **Los Linajes,** Dr. Velasco 9, 40003 Segovia (☎ **921/46-04-75**). Behind its 11th-century facade lies a thoroughly modern facility, with a bar and lounge and terraces bestowing fine views. Its 55 units have TVs and bathrooms. Doubles are 10,500P ($72), perhaps a little lower off-season with negotiation.

WHET YOUR APPETITE Segovia is celebrated as the locus of the "zone of roasts," meaning incredibly tender suckling pig (*cochinillo asado*) and young lamb (*cordero*). The traditional place to sample these is the **Mesón de Candido,** Plaza del Azoguejo 5 (☎ **921/42-59-11;** open daily 12:30–4:30pm and 8–11:30pm). Layers of authentic atmosphere and views of the aqueduct add to the experience, and the *menú del día* is a not-bad 2,700P ($18). Less expensive, with similar food but at no great markdown in quality, is **Casa Duque,** Cervantes 12 (☎ **921/43-05-37;** open daily 12:30–5pm and 8–11:30pm). The *menú del día* is 1,900P ($13).

17

Barcelona: Gaudí Reigns, but the Boys Rule

There are a million good reasons to visit **Barcelona** . . . and just one reason why you shouldn't—because, quite simply, you may never want to come back.

This inevitably is what happens. You plan on spending a week in Spain, devoting 2 days each to Barcelona and Madrid and the rest of the time at one of the majorly fun gay beach resorts. Understood. But then there's that hitch, one I've seen happen time and time again: You fall in love. With a guy or gal, maybe (and Lord knows, with all the beauties here, that's easy enough to do); but with Barcelona, beyond a shadow of a doubt.

Think I'm going overboard, a bit on the starstruck side? Then consider my friend Jack. He took 2 weeks off from his job as administrator of an arts center to bum around Spain in 1987 and still hasn't come back. (Jack even gave up his $600-a-month New York apartment—now, that's commitment to living forever in the big B!) And his can't be considered an isolated act. During my frequent trips to Barcelona, I've met more than a few Americans who took one look at this glorious city, its even more glorious men and women, and its heady social and cultural mix, and then shoved their passports deep into a drawer.

You may be tempted to do the same. Because, friends, there are very few cities blessed with Barcelona's immediate and powerful draw. Some need to grow on you, carefully asserting their special appeal; a few rare others grab you from behind and never let go. Paris is one and San Francisco another—and beauteous Barcelona is very much in their league.

Why does the city possess this undeniable force? First and foremost is its spellbinding natural setting, nestling as it does the country's busiest port. (Barcelona's oceanfront prominence also explains its—and Catalonia's—centuries-old position as the richest trading center in Spain.) It's a cardinal rule: Any visually thrilling city needs to have water somewhere in the picture. It also needs to have a historic district, and that's where the Barri Xinés (Chinese Quarter) and Barri Gòtic (Gothic Quarter) come in. Original structures from as far back as the late 1600s still stand, imparting the spirit of glory past.

And there must be a grand boulevard—while Barcelona has several, none comes close to the pomp and circumstance of Les Rambles (in Catalan; La Rambla in Castillian Spanish), made up of five individually named sections. The city's main stroll, it begins at the harbor and

The Barcelona Card

You can buy the **Barcelona Card** at the subterranean **Centre d'Informació,** under the southeast corner of Plaça de Catalunya (☎ **93-423-18-00;** Metro: Catalunya; open daily 9am–9pm). The card gives discounts of 30% to 50% off admission to over museums and other attractions and smaller discounts at a selection of shops and restaurants. Cards are good for periods of 24, 48, or 72 hours and cost 2,500P ($17), 3,000P ($20), and 3,500P ($23), respectively.

continues a couple of miles northward through posher districts uptown. All along the way, Les Rambles boasts shady trees, shops, and a plethora of cafes from which to watch the city amble by. A world-class city must also show financial strength, and Barcelona feels so damned affluent it hurts. The Catalans have always been the economic miracle workers of Spain, and today the city feels progressive and rich enough to make Gotham feel downright Third World!

Finally, a city of the world needs a solid social scene, and Barcelona's is dizzying. Not in Madrid's slightly madcap, ragtag fashion, but in an elegant European way. "We don't go out every night," my new friend Jordí sniffed. "Unlike the rest of Spain, we work." Catalan superiority complexes aside, there's truth to this; and indeed, the clubs are much more packed on weekends than during the week. (Since Madrid's are always busy, if you're a denizen of the night, you might wish to travel to that city in the earlier part of the week, then hit Barcelona for the *fin de semana* to make the most of its after-dark scene.)

But in the end, the bounties of Barcelona taken together are much more than the sum of their parts. This is a gorgeous, thriving, culturally brilliant city that works, breathing life into everything it does. It's the kind of place we all wish we lived in; and maybe, just maybe, you'll pull a Jack and never come back. (Just call me about that Manhattan apartment first.)

1 Barcelona Essentials

ARRIVING & DEPARTING

BY PLANE Only one American carrier, TWA, flies directly to Barcelona from the States, leaving from JFK in New York. Iberia, the excellent national carrier, offers daily flights to Madrid from several American cities, with ongoing service to Barcelona.

Barcelona's international airport, **El Prat de Llobregat** (dig that Catalan name!), is less than 8 miles from town, and getting to/from the city is a breeze. There are two options. The first is a **train** operated by the excellent regional RENFE system, which costs an average of 300P ($2) depending on the day of travel; the train runs daily 6:14am to 10:44pm, and the trip takes 20 minutes. The second is a **bus** that leaves the airport every 15 minutes daily 5:30am to 10pm and costs only 375P ($2.50). The latter leaves you off at several key points of the city; for most travelers, Plaça de Catalunya is the most reasonable place to disembark (after about 30 minutes), and from there you can walk or take a short cab ride to your hotel. Since you probably don't want to arrive in a new city and start figuring out the underground train system (I know I don't), the clean, fast bus is typically the better choice.

If you elect to take a **cab** from the airport to your hotel, know that it won't break the bank: It'll cost 2,100P ($14) when there's no traffic and no more than 3,000P ($20) during rush hour.

BY TRAIN This all depends where you're coming from and going. Most cross-country treks require a train change at the Spanish–French border, though this isn't necessary for the Barcelona–TALGO, a service running from Barcelona to Paris in less than 12 hours. (Do yourself a favor: take the overnight train and rent a couchette.)

Most of the long-distance trains (both within Spain and to other countries) leave from Barcelona's main terminal, **Estació de França,** in the quaint Barceloneta district. Unlike many skeevy American train stations, this one is nearly an entertainment center in and of itself, with cute shops, good places to eat, and—yes!—even a busy men's room. (Calling George Michael . . .) Places like Union Station in my hometown of D.C. try to mimic the vitality of European train stations but don't even come close.

For shorter jaunts, such as the RENFE trains along the coast to the beach resort of Sitges, you can go directly to the **Estació Central de Barcelona-Sants,** commonly known as Sants, in the western part of the city.

BY BUS The mere thought of long-distance bus travel—the fumes, the noise, and the smoke—makes me want to puke. (Remember that ghastly scene in *Midnight Cowboy*?) While in college, I took a bus from Paris to Amsterdam and wished I were dead.

Though there are long-distance buses, European trains (yes, now even Spanish ones!) are so wonderful and comparatively inexpensive that there's no sane reason to take a bus on a cross-country trip—unless, of course, you're an abject masochist. In a word: Don't.

BY CAR If you arrive in Barcelona by car, I suggest you immediately return it to the rental company or garage it until you leave. If your hotel has no garage, there are usually nearby lots or facilities; one of the easiest to find is the garage beneath the plaza in front of the cathedral.

VISITOR INFORMATION

Both rail stations and the airport contain excellent English-speaking **visitors' offices** that are strong sources of info for the new and seasoned guest both. In fact, if you arrive in town without a firm reservation—never a good idea, but potentially treacherous in summer—they can help you get one at everything from the cheapest to the costliest hotels.

After you've arrived in town, you might want to head over to the **Oficina de Informació Turistica,** Gran Vía des Corts Catalants 658 (☎ **93-301-74-43;** Metro: Catalunya; open Mon–Fri 9am–7pm, Sat to 2pm). The multilingual staff is unfailingly courteous, and you'll find a plethora of information on every aspect of the tourism scene.

CITY LAYOUT

On top of all its other pleasures, Barcelona's layout is really easy to figure out. I tend to get lost and flustered easily in new cities (not a good trait for a travel writer!), but I took to Barcelona like a duck to water, and you will too.

Start with the port, where a monument to Columbus is erected. Proceeding directly northward is **Les Rambles (La Rambla),** the tree-lined superbusy main drag I described in the intro to this chapter. This forms the heart of the **Ciutat Vella (Old Town).**

Due east of La Rambla—the Spanish is much easier to pronounce!—is the **Barri Xinés (Chinese Quarter),** though nobody quite knows why it's called this. Much has been made of how dangerous this neighborhood is, especially at night, but I think the stories are overblown. (Try tripping down New York's Avenue C at 4am and you'll know what feeling scared is all about.) And during the day, it's positively humming, with funky shops, cool and traditional restaurants, and all manner of street life. The **Plaça Reial,** a large medieval-style square, is the heart and soul of this district.

Barcelona Metro

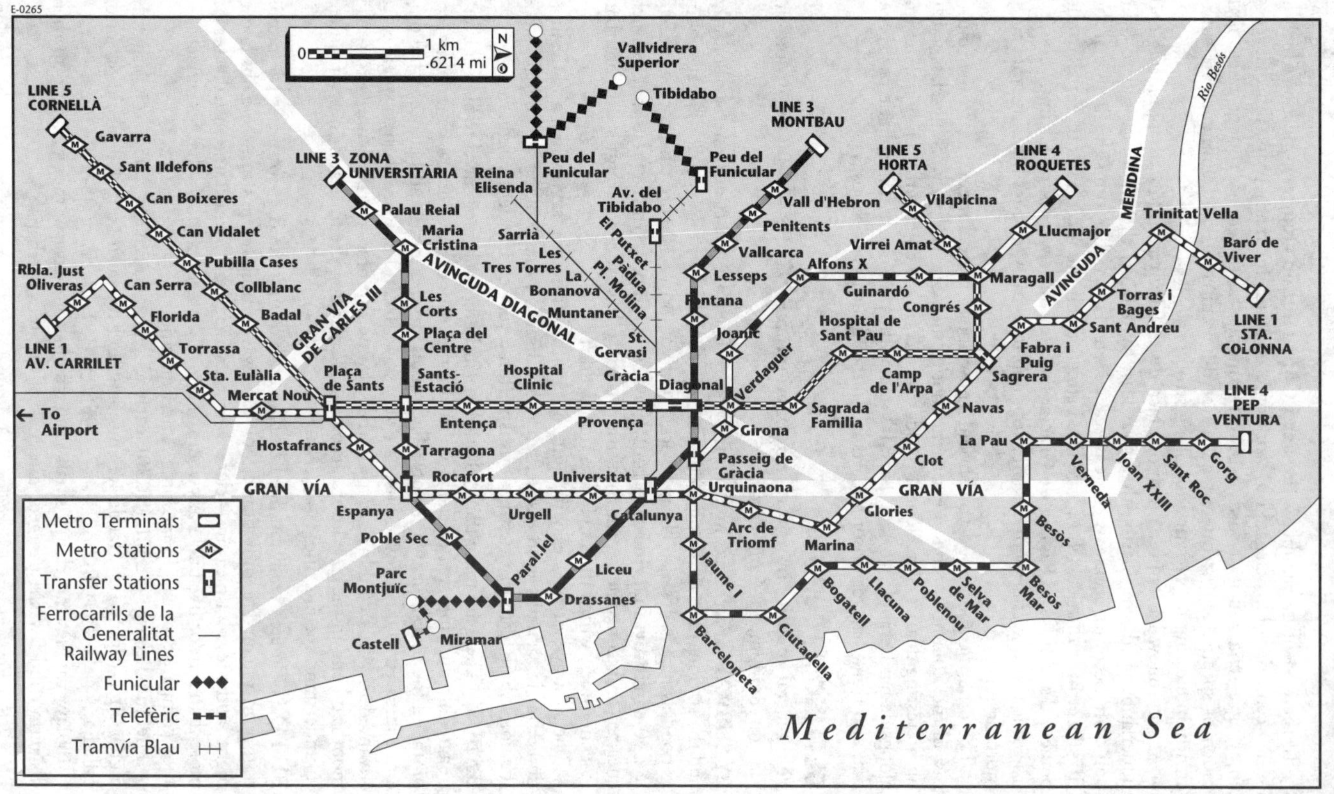

To the west of La Rambla is the **Barri Gòtic (Gothic Quarter),** most of which is over 3 centuries old. Relegated to working-class status for many years, this district is enjoying a renaissance of sorts, especially among the bohemian young. There isn't much of specific tourist interest here, but the architecture and ambience are sufficiently interesting to warrant a nice long stroll.

As you follow La Rambla north of **Plaça de Catalunya**—oddly disappointing and underlandscaped, considering this is (at least by default) the main city square—the boulevard becomes decidedly more upscale. Here, La Rambla forms the lifeline of the ritzy **Eixample** district, whose tree-lined streets recall the nicer parts of Paris. To the boulevard's west is the **Passeig de Gràcia,** Barcelona's answer to the Champs-Elysées; it's a fine broad avenue with elegant shops and tony cafes, and it's bustling from early morning on.

The other neighborhood you should know about, **Barceloneta,** lies to the southeast of the Columbus monument at the foot of the port. Long a working-class, fairly uninteresting district, Barceloneta is today reemerging as chic, with trendy restaurants alongside hardscrabble workers' bars. It's one of the city's most atmospheric parts, one that also (for whatever reason) boasts lots of fabulous pastry shops.

GETTING AROUND

For general **public transport information,** call ☎ **93-412-00-00** (Mon–Fri 7:30am–8:30pm, Sat 8am–2pm).

BY SUBWAY Barcelona's Metro is truly a joy. The trains are clean, quiet, and orderly, and the stations have music piped in. For anyone who's lived in New York, that's about as good as it gets. It's also cheap, especially if you buy a **10-ride card** for only 650P ($4.30); an **individual ride** costs 140P (95¢). In addition to the fact that they're much cheaper and convenient, the multiride cards allow you to transfer to suburban (S-code) lines, which the single-fare tickets don't.

The subway system is easy to figure out, with distinctly marked lines and destinations. But it's actually even easier than you'd think on first looking at the map, since the lion's share of tourist destinations is within a very clearly delineated area.

BY BUS There are more than 50 bus lines in Barcelona; they travel to almost every imaginable outlying area of the city. But to get around Barcelona, I can't really recommend the buses, for two reasons: The routes are circuitous and hard to figure out, and compared to the subway, buses are very slow. In candor, there wasn't a single place I wanted to visit I couldn't get to on the subway; so unless you're planning to spend months on end in the city, I don't recommend spending the time and energy required to understand the bus lines.

BY TAXI There's really no need to take taxis during the day, so fine is the public transport system. The only time I took cabs was coming home from the clubs late at night, and they're a pleasure—clean Mercedes that whisk you home, usually for no more than four or five bucks anywhere in central Barcelona (how's that for service?)—a joy compared to taxis in most big American cities.

The initial charge is 250P ($1.70); each additional kilometer is 95P (65¢), slightly higher after 10pm. Taxi stands are abundant and cabs can be hailed on the street or called at ☎ **93-433-10-20,** 93-357-77-55, 93-391-22-22, or 93-490-22-22.

By law, cabbies can charge small supplements for baggage, though it's up to their discretion and I wasn't charged. The luck of the draw, perhaps.

BY CAR Drive around Barcelona? Are you mad? Don't even consider this option. (Besides, even if you could, wouldn't you really rather see this gorgeous city—and every one of its nooks and crannies—by foot?)

If you're planning to rent a car to tool around Spain, you can contact **Budget,** Travessa de Grácia 71 (☎ **93-201-29-99;** Metro: Gràcia), or **Avis,** Casanova 209 (☎ **93-209-95-33;** Metro: Urgüell). Renting cars in Europe is, however, not cheap, and tales of hidden extras being tagged on to the final bill are legendary—even in a country as nice and generous as Spain. Of course, you'll get a better deal if you reserve the car before leaving home.

FAST FACTS: Barcelona

American Express Barcelona's main office is at Passeig de Gràcia 101 (☎ **93-217-00-70;** Metro: Diagonal; open Mon–Fri 9:30am–6pm, Sat 10am–noon).

Community Centers The following gay associations exist should you require specific legal or health needs: **Casal Lambda,** Ample (☎ **93-412-72-72**); **Col-lectiu Gai de Barcelona,** Paloma 12 (☎ **93-318-16-66**); and **FAGC,** Villaroel 62, third floor (☎ **93-454-63-98**).

Consulates The **U.S. Consulate** is at Reina Elisenda 23 (☎ **93-280-22-27;** Metro: Reina Elisenda; open Mon–Fri 9am–12:30pm and 3–5pm). The **Canadian Consulate** is at Traveserra de les Corts 265 (☎ **93-410-66-99;** Metro: Plaça Molina; open Mon–Fri 10am–noon). The **U.K. Consulate** is at Diagonal 477 (☎ **93-419-90-44;** Metro: Hospital Clinic; open Mon–Fri 9:30am–1:30pm and 4–5pm). The **Irish Consulate** is at Gran Via Carles III 94 (☎ **93-491-50-21;** Metro: María Cristina; open Mon–Fri 10am–1pm). The **Australian Consulate** is at Gran Via Carles III 98 (☎ **93-330-94-96;** Metro: María Cristina; open Mon–Fri 10am–noon). The **New Zealand Consulate** is at Travessera de Gràcia 64 (☎ **93-209-03-99;** Metro: none nearby; open Mon–Fri 9am–2pm and 4:30–7pm).

Currency Exchange All banks (generally open Mon–Fri 8:30am–2pm, Sat 8:30am–1pm), have an exchange section. In addition, commercial *cambio* offices (exchange bureaus) pepper the streets of Barcelona, especially around La Rambla, and their commission may actually be lower than banks'. (I was able to find no rhyme or reason to fees and commissions in Barcelona; oddly, they tend to be higher than at the beach resorts.) If you're planning on exchanging a large amount of money, do some comparison shopping first.

The airport and two main train stations also have currency exchange offices, and the former keeps longer hours than anywhere else—usually 7am to 11pm.

Cybercafe You can check your e-mail or send messages at **El Café de Internet** (see "Whet Your Appetite" below).

Emergencies For fire, call ☎ **080;** for police, call ☎ **092;** for ambulances, call ☎ **061.**

Hospitals The largest emergency rooms are at **Hospital Clinic i Provincial,** Casanova 143 (☎ **93-454-60-00;** Metro: Urgüell), and **Hospital Sant,** Sant Antoni Maria Clarer 167 (☎ **93-347-31-33;** Metro: Sants). Of course, the best

Country & City Codes

The **country code** for Spain is **34.** The **city code** for Barcelona is **93.** This code has now been incorporated into all phone numbers, so you must always dial it, whether you're outside Spain, within Spain but not in Barcelona, or even within Barcelona.

thing to do is jump in a cab and ask for the nearest hospital, which the driver will surely know.

Telephone Local calls are 15P (10¢). If you need to call long-distance and aren't on an expense account, you may want to go to the **main phone office** at Fontanella 4 (Metro: Catalunya; open Mon–Sat 8:30am–9pm). For more details, see "Fast Facts: Madrid" in chapter 16).

2 Pillow Talk

Barcelona boasts scores of hotels to fit every budget and taste; as a frequent visitor to this wonderful city, I think these are the best in each range. Happily, because Barcelona is such a sophisticated city, you should have no trouble bringing your new love (or whatever) back to your hotel.

BARRI GÒTIC & BARCELONETA

Hotel California. Raurich 14, 08002 Barcelona. ☎ **93-317-77-76.** Fax 93-317-54-74. www.seker.es/hotel_california. E-mail hotel_california@seker.es. 31 units. TV TEL. 8,500P ($57) double. AE, DC, MC, V. Metro: Liceu.

My, my, how times have changed. When I first stayed here 10 years ago, the California was the fleabag of all time; today it has its own Web site. It has also added a (huh?) Corinthian feel to the lobby, replete with marble and (crappy) leather chairs. The rooms now actually contain clean linens, though the beds are as low-rent as always. The breakfast room still looks like a penitentiary in Georgia—the country, not the state. That aside, I still vote yes for this classic Old Town choice; and if you're a budgeteer, so will you.

Hotel Oasis. Plaça Palacia 17, Barcelona. ☎ **93-319-43-96.** Fax 93-310-48-74. 49 units. TV. 7,000P ($47) double; 10,000P ($67) triple. MC, V. Metro: Barceloneta.

This supercheapy is at the mouth of the Barceloneta neighborhood, a quick walk to the França train station, the Picasso Museum, the Gothic Quarter, and the zoo. The rooms are clean yet depressing enough to make you want to kill yourself—but wait, the goon at the front desk will probably do that for you. Listen, you get what you pay for.

Hotel Rialto. Fernando 42, Barcelona. ☎ **93-318-52-12.** Fax 93-318-52-74. 137 units. TV TEL. 14,000P ($93) double. AE, MC, DC, V. Metro: Liceu.

The Rialto is definitely the nicest of the downtown hotels—not luxe, but a step up from the California and the like. The lobby is modern nondescript, but the rooms, though not especially large, are much more tasteful—an inoffensive mix of gold-toned Old Spain bedspreads and Miró prints on the wall. And you're just a stone's throw from the wonderful Schilling Cafe (see "Hitting the Stores" below), downtown shopping, and the all-important Liceu subway stop.

A Pension Warning

I want to let you know there's a pension called **La Nau** that advertises in the gay papers. However, the staff was indescribably rude to me when I showed up (they refused to believe I wasn't trying to sell them advertising space), and thus I can report only that the place exists. If you insist on calling, you can do so at ☎ **93-245-10-13.** *Suerte!*

Hey, Big Spender

If you've finally come into your trust fund and want to blow a wad on a Barcelona hotel, there are many deluxe places that'll be more than glad to bend over backward for you. Be prepared to drop a minimum of $200 a night for a double at any of them.

The **Ritz,** one of the toniest, is listed in full below. Here are some others where you'll feel like a princess, no matter what sex you are:

Barcelona Hilton, Diagonal 589, 08014 Barcelona (☎ **800/445-8667** in the U.S. and Canada, or 93-495-77-77; fax 93-495-77-00; www.hilton.com; Metro: María Cristina).

Claris, Pau Claris 150, 08009 Barcelona (☎ **800/888-4747** in the U.S., or 93-487-62-62; fax 93-487-87-36; www.derbyhotels.es; e-mail info@derbyhotels.es; Metro: Passeig de Gràcia).

Hotel Arts, Marina 19–21, 08005 Barcelona (☎ **800/241-3333** in the U.S., or 93-221-10-00; fax 93-221-10-70; www.ritzcarlton.com; Metro: Ciutadella–Vila Olímpica).

Le Meridien Barcelona, La Rambla 111, 08002 Barcelona (☎ **800/543-4300** in the U.S., or 93-318-62-00; fax 93-301-77-76; Metro: Liceu or Plaça de Catalunya).

Hotel Roma Reial. Plaça Reial 11, Barcelona. ☎ **93-302-03-66.** Fax 93-301-18-39. 102 units. TEL. 4,500P–7,800P ($30–$52) double. AE, DC, MC, V. Metro: Liceu.

This user-friendly hotel offers clean if uninspired rooms. (And what, pray tell, is the rationale behind the Navajo bedspreads?) Still, there's something undeniably romantic about staying right on Plaça Reial, especially if you plan to hit the boho bars on Caller Raurich at night.

✪ **Marina Folch.** Mar 16, Barcelona. ☎ **93-310-37-09.** Fax 93-310-53-27. 11 units. TV. 6,000P ($40) double. AE, MC, V. Metro: Barceloneta.

Totally unique, this is a fun and charming little hostal run by a family with a restaurant down the block. The rooms are small but modern and supercute, all decorated in nautical blues; six have harbor views (really, the reason to stay here). Not all rooms have TV and none have phones; the Marina Folch isn't a business hotel. But as it's a local charmer with an upbeat character all its own, you'll love the Folch.

PASSEIG DE GRACIA & CATALUNYA

✪ **Condes de Barcelona.** Passeig de Gràcia 73–75, 08008 Barcelona. ☎ **93-488-2200.** Fax 93-487-14-42. www.gulliver.es/publicit/condesbcn. 183 units. A/C MINIBAR TV TEL. 20,000P ($133) double. AE, DC, MC, V. Metro: Passeig de Gràcia.

If you've got the bucks, the Condes is an awfully good place to stay: an old art nouveau edifice in which modern style meets classic architecture and succeeds with élan. The lobby has an almost Oriental reticence; then you turn around and see a curved staircase of superb art-nouveau style. The rooms preserve the original architectural integrity but are updated with sophisticated tones of yellow wood and beige. The entire effect is one of rich asceticism, a hat-trick design queens will love.

Duques de Bergara. Bergara 11, 08002 Barcelona. ☎ **93-301-51-51.** Fax 93-317-34-42. E-mail cataloni@hoteles-catalonia.es. 150 units. A/C MINIBAR TV TEL. 20,900P ($140) double. AE, DC, MC, V. Metro: Universitat.

Barcelona Accommodations & Dining

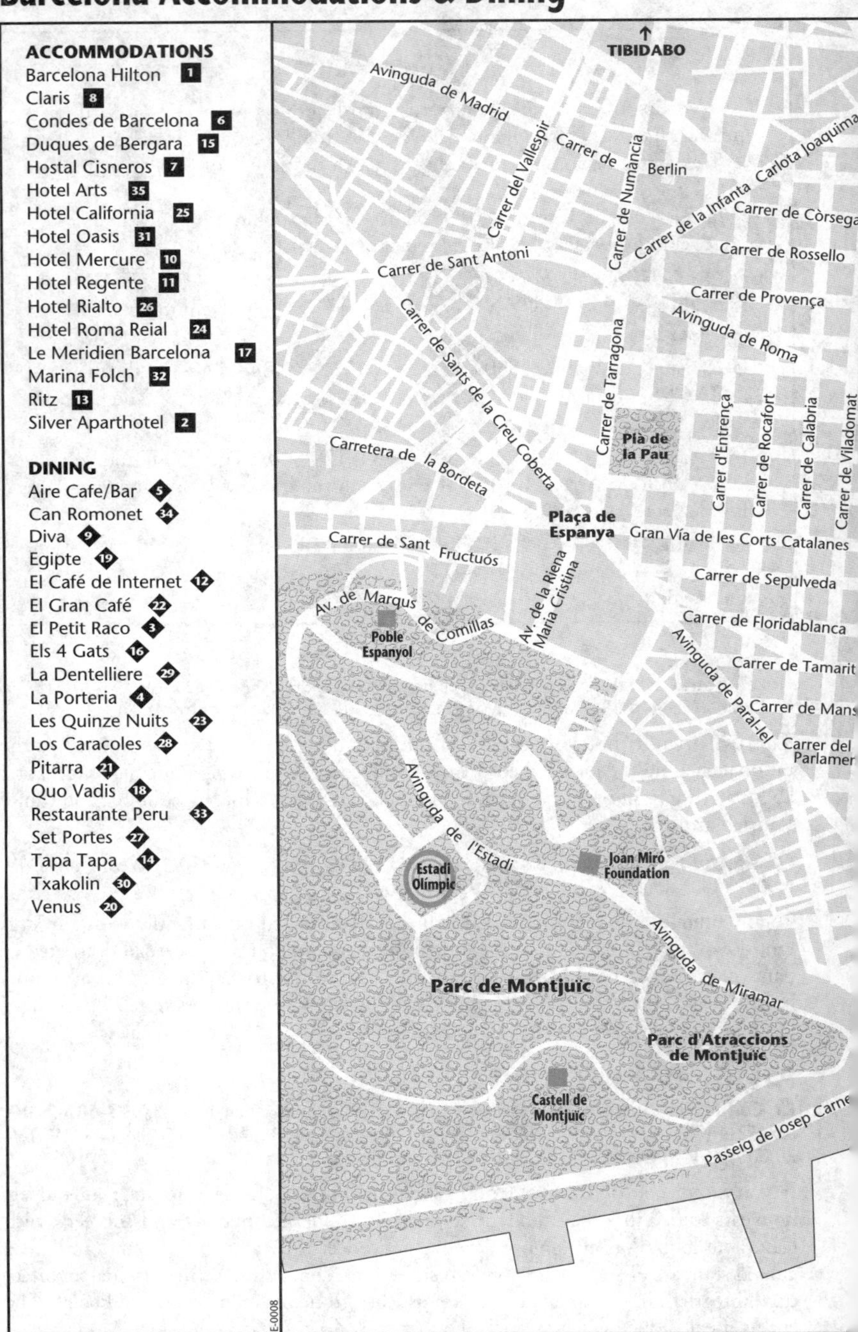

ACCOMMODATIONS
Barcelona Hilton 1
Claris 8
Condes de Barcelona 6
Duques de Bergara 15
Hostal Cisneros 7
Hotel Arts 35
Hotel California 25
Hotel Oasis 31
Hotel Mercure 10
Hotel Regente 11
Hotel Rialto 26
Hotel Roma Reial 24
Le Meridien Barcelona 17
Marina Folch 32
Ritz 13
Silver Aparthotel 2
DINING
Aire Cafe/Bar 5
Can Romonet 34
Diva 9
Egipte 19
El Café de Internet 12
El Gran Café 22
El Petit Raco 3
Els 4 Gats 16
La Dentelliere 29
La Porteria 4
Les Quinze Nuits 23
Los Caracoles 28
Pitarra 21
Quo Vadis 18
Restaurante Peru 33
Set Portes 27
Tapa Tapa 14
Txakolin 30
Venus 20
TIBIDABO
Avinguda de Madrid
Carrer del Vallespir
Carrer de Berlin
Carrer de Numància
Carrer de la Infanta Carlota Joaquima
Carrer de Còrsega
Carrer de Rossello
Carrer de Sant Antoni
Carrer de Provença
Avinguda de Roma
Carrer de Sants de la Creu Coberta
Carrer de Tarragona
Pla de la Pau
Carrer d'Entrença
Carrer de Rocafort
Carrer de Calabria
Carrer de Viladomat
Carretera de la Bordeta
Plaça de Espanya
Gran Via de les Corts Catalanes
Carrer de Sant Fructuós
Carrer de Sepulveda
Av. de Marqus de Comillas
Av. de la Riena Maria Cristina
Carrer de Floridablanca
Poble Espanyol
Avinguda de Paral-lel
Carrer de Tamarit
Carrer de Mans
Carrer del Parlamer
Avinguda de l'Estadi
Joan Miró Foundation
Estadi Olimpic
Avinguda de Miramar
Parc de Montjuïc
Parc d'Atraccions de Montjuïc
Castell de Montjuïc
Passeig de Josep Carne
E-0008

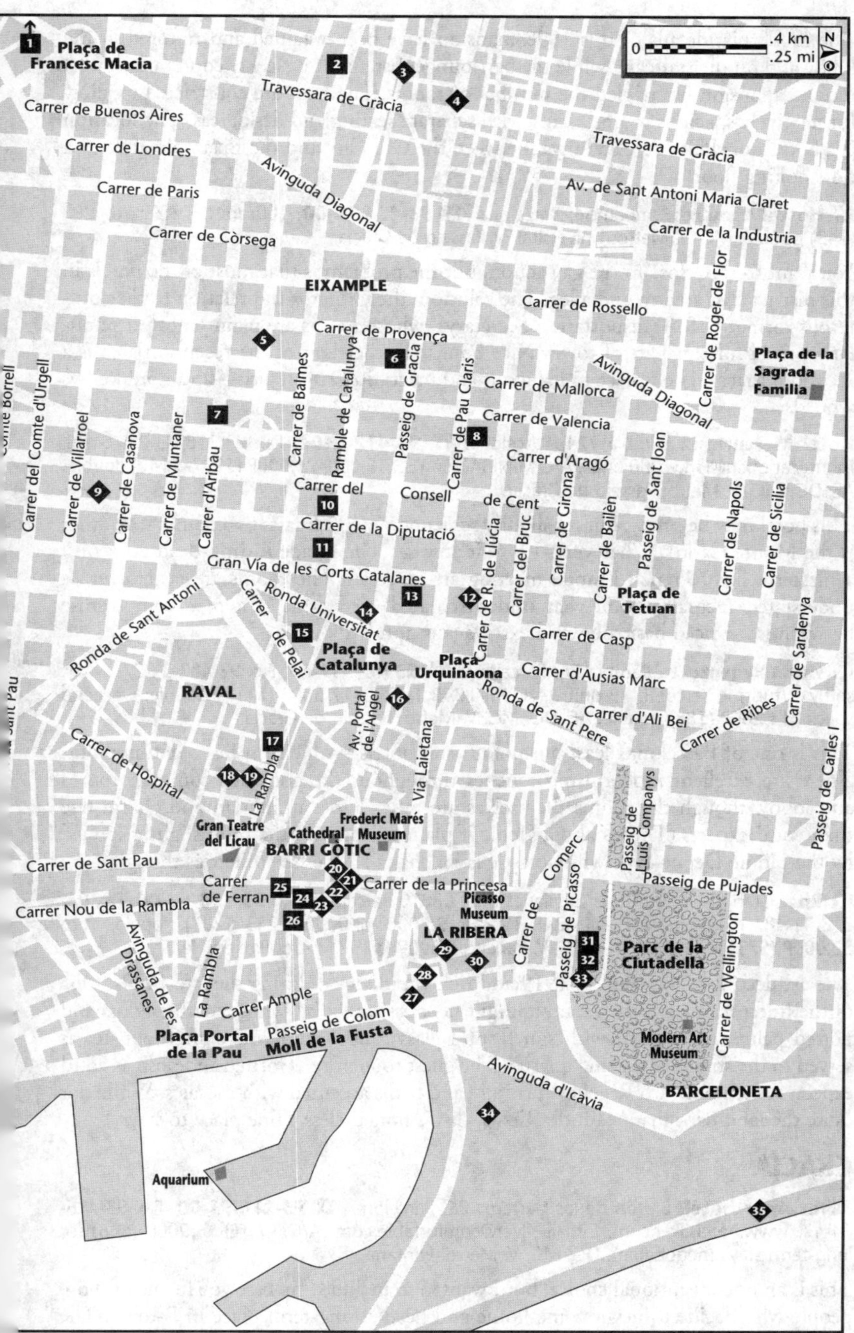

Plaça de Francesc Macia
Travessara de Gràcia
Carrer de Buenos Aires
Carrer de Londres
Carrer de Paris
Avinguda Diagonal
Carrer de Còrsega
Av. de Sant Antoni Maria Claret
Carrer de la Industria
EIXAMPLE
Carrer de Rossello
Carrer de Provença
Carrer de Roger de Flor
Plaça de la Sagrada Familia
Carrer de Mallorca
Carrer de Valencia
Carrer d'Aragó
Carrer del Consell de Cent
Carrer de la Diputació
Gran Vía de les Corts Catalanes
Ronda Universitat
Ronda de Sant Antoni
Carrer de Pelai
Plaça de Catalunya
Plaça Urquinaona
Plaça de Tetuan
Carrer de Casp
Carrer d'Ausias Marc
Carrer d'Ali Bei
Ronda de Sant Pere
Carrer de Ribes
Carrer de Sardenya
Passeig de Carles I
RAVAL
Carrer de Hospital
La Rambla
Av. Portal de l'Angel
Via Laietana
Gran Teatre del Licau
Cathedral
Frederic Marés Museum
BARRI GÒTIC
Carrer de Sant Pau
Carrer de Ferran
Carrer Nou de la Rambla
Carrer de la Princesa
Picasso Museum
LA RIBERA
Carrer de Comerc
Passeig de Picasso
Passeig de Lluís Companys
Passeig de Pujades
Parc de la Ciutadella
Carrer de Wellington
Modern Art Museum
Avinguda de les Drassanes
Carrer Ample
Passeig de Colom
Plaça Portal de la Pau
Moll de la Fusta
Avinguda d'Icàvia
BARCELONETA
Aquarium
Carrer del Comte d'Urgell
Carrer de Villarroel
Carrer de Casanova
Carrer de Muntaner
Carrer d'Aribau
Carrer de Balmes
Ramble de Catalunya
Passeig de Gràcia
Carrer de Pau Claris
Carrer de R. de Llúcia
Carrer del Bruc
Carrer de Girona
Carrer de Bailèn
Passeig de Sant Joan
Carrer de Napols
Carrer de Sicilia
0 .4 km .25 mi
N
1 2 3 4 5 6 7 8 9 10 11 12 13 14 15 16 17 18 19 20 21 22 23 24 25 26 27 28 29 30 31 32 33 34 35

The modernist details of this 1898 mansion have been retained and restored in the lobby and on the staircase, while the bar/lounge/restaurant is sleekly contemporary. A recent expansion has tripled the number of rooms. The halls are constricted to allow for relatively spacious rooms, many with separate seating and desk areas. The location is a bonus, off Plaça de Catalunya, between the Old City and the Eixample. There's a no-smoking floor.

✪ **Hostal Cisneros.** Aribau 54, Barcelona. ☎ **93-454-18-00.** 100 units. TV TEL. 6,420P ($43) double. MC, V. Metro: Universitat or Passeig de Gràcia.

You want to stay close to the gay action, but the problem is that most of the hotels in this district cost an arm and a leg. The solution: the Cisneros (no relation to the adulterous former U.S. Transportation Secretary), whose rooms are plain Janes yet popularly priced for this part of town. Nice bonus: To the right of the reception area is a rec room that's a good place to hang out and meet hip Danish girls—and Lord knows who else.

Hotel Mercure. La Rambla 124, Barcelona. ☎ **93-412-0404.** Fax 93-318/73-23. E-mail montecarlobcn@i3d.es. 80 units. A/C MINIBAR TV TEL. 16,000–21,000P ($107–$140) double. AE, DC, MC, V. Metro: Passeig de Gràcia.

This hotel may be pretty, but it's slightly schizophrenic: It boasts two names (the other is the Monte Carlo). Whatever—I love it anyway. The facade is drop-dead gorgeous, a masterpiece of French Empire meeting art nouveau. The rooms are tasteful in an understated (actually, somewhat underdecorated) way; this is a nice compromise between low-priced basic digs and extravagant uptown joints.

✪ **Hotel Regente.** La Rambla 76, Barcelona. ☎ **93-487-59-89.** Fax 93-487-32-27. www.softly.es/turismo/sercotel. 79 units. A/C MINIBAR TV TEL. 17,500P ($117) double; weekend special 13,200P ($88) double. AE, DC, MC, V. Metro: Passeig de Gràcia.

This is one of Barcelona's least pushy four-star hotels—which I see as a definite plus. There are excellent modernismo touches throughout the gorgeous common rooms and lobby, though the rooms themselves are much more utilitarian and charm-free than you'd expect. (There's also a scenic if plain balcony on the roof, slightly spoiled by the Home Depot–type white plastic lawn chairs.) Nice free toiletries though.

✪ **Ritz.** Gran Vía de les Corts Catalanes 668, 08010 Barcelona. ☎ **93-318-52-00.** Fax 93-318-01-48. 161 units. A/C MINIBAR TV TEL. 35,000–43,000P ($233–$287) double; from 80,000P ($533) suite. AE, DC, MC, V. Parking 3,500P ($23). Metro: Passeig de Gràcia.

The art-deco Ritz was built in 1919 and richly remodeled during the late 1980s. One of the finest features is the cream-and-gilt neoclassical lobby, whose marble floors and potted palms are flooded with sun from a glass canopy and where afternoon tea is served to the strains of a string quartet. The guest rooms are as formal and posh as you'd expect, sometimes with Regency furniture and baths accented with mosaics. While not quite the landmark that Madrid's Ritz is, this is nonetheless a fine place to stay.

GRACIA

Silver Aparthotel. Breton de los Herreros 26, Barcelona. ☎ **93-218-91-00.** Fax 93-416-14-47. www.hotelsilver.com. E-mail silver@comfortable.com. A/C TV TEL. 6,900P ($46) for long-term stays (negotiable). DC, MC, V. Metro: Fontana.

This is an unconventional choice, but I wanted to include it in case you're one of those people who decide to never come home and need a long-term place in B-town. The studios are surpassingly large and actually kinda homey in a conventual kind of way. Best yet, you can walk to two gay bars, the Roma and the Cafe de la Calle, both located in this upscale uptown nabe.

3 Whet Your Appetite

Barcelona's restaurants have long enjoyed an infusion of continental (mainly French) influences, and Catalan nationalists would argue that this represents an entirely separate culinary style. That's a stretch, but it's true that restaurants here often have a decidedly "fusion" bent.

Barcelona offers anything you could hope for, from superexpensive businesspeople's places to modest holes in the wall with wonderfully prepared food. There's even a gay restaurant, with cuisine that's much better than it should be. The following are my personal favorites based on many visits to this wonderful city; but by all means, have fun finding places to call your very own.

Note: For the locations of the restaurants below, see the "Barcelona Accommodations & Dining" map on pp. 630–631.

✪ **Aire Cafe/Bar.** Enrique Granados 48. ☎ **93-451-84-62.** www.alaval.com. Main courses 500–800P ($3–$5). MC, V. Daily 1–4pm and 9pm–midnight. Metro: Passeig de Gràcia. SPANISH.

This gay-operated bar/cafe is a new addition to the Barcelona scene, and a most welcome one. It's a bright, cheery place to hang out, especially at lunch or before the bars open. You'll find a nice selection of light fare—from traditional tapas to American-style sandwiches and yummy desserts. At press time, this new place promised daily Spanish specials for those interested in more hearty fare.

Can Romonet. Maquinista 17. ☎ **93-319-30-64.** Fax 93-319-70-14. Main courses 750–2,800P ($5–$19). AE, DC, MC, V. Daily 1–4pm and 8–11:30pm. Metro: Barceloneta. CATALAN.

This unprepossessing tavern bills itself as the oldest in the port area—and who am I to disagree? Neither trendy nor excessively touristy, this is a marvelous place to sit down to a whole meal or—better still—pig out on tapas to your heart's delight. Best of all are the sardines with pimento in olive oil and the daily croquette specials. Scene queens will probably want to stay away, but those in search of the truly Spanish will want to stop by, at least for a tapa or two.

✪ **Diva.** Diputac3io 172. ☎ **93-454-63-98.** Main courses 1,225–2,095P ($8–$14). AE, DC, MC, V. Daily noon–4pm and 9–12:30am. Metro: Universitat. MEDITERRANEAN.

An utterly charming somewhat kitschy decor and a way-cute waitstaff join with a strong menu to make this Barcelona's best gay restaurant (with a name like Diva, you had any doubts?). The cuisine is Mediterranean, which means the start-off point is Catalan fare, with French and Italian specialties on a daily basis. Open late and located around the corner from the clubs, Diva is the perfect solution to that age-old question, What do I do till the bars start hopping at 1am?

✪ **Egipte.** La Rambla 79. ☎ **93-317-95-45.** Fax 93-318-15-44. Main courses 900–2,325P ($6–$16); lunch menu 985P ($7). AE, DC, MC, V. Daily 1–4pm and 8pm–midnight. Metro: Liceu. SPANISH.

Some Barcelonans may hold the old Egipte around the corner (now called El Convent, on Jerusalem 3) dearer to their hearts, but this huge extension of the original continues the traditonal in force. Hear ye, hear ye: Egipte's 985P menu is nothing short of the best $7 lunch in the Western world. It includes both a first course (the *fabes à la Catalana,* fava beans with sausage Catalan style, is a must—especially with a good Chianti) and an entree (*carn al estil Egipte,* beef with pimento sauce, is fine), plus bread, a carafe of wine, and dessert. (If you're traveling solo, you can eat at the counter.) There are many people who can't tear themselves away and eat lunch here every day of their stay in Barcelona; I'd be lying if I said I could blame them. A terrific tradition and an absolute must.

El Café de Internet. Gran Vía de les Corts Catalanes 656. ☎ **93-412-19-14.** Main courses 440P–1,800P ($2.90–$12); *menú del día* 900P or 1,050P ($6 or $7). DC, MC, V. Mon–Sat 10am–midnight. Metro: Passeig de Gràcia. SPANISH.

It was inevitable that the first cybercafe (www.cafeinternet.es) in Spain would open in Barcelona. Pop in, have a meal, then nip upstairs and surf the Net at one of a dozen computers. A half hour on-line is 600P ($4). The food is quite good, featuring fresh ingredients and ample servings. Grilled salmon and tender pork loin in tomato sauce are often featured. Sandwiches and salads are also available.

El Gran Cafe. Avinyo 6. ☎ **93-318-79-86.** Fax 93-412-07-42. Main courses 850–1,850P ($6–$12); prix-fixe lunch 1,200P ($8). AE, MC, DC, V. Mon–Sat noon–3pm and 8:30–11:30pm. Metro: Liceu. SPANISH.

One of Barcelona's handsomest and best-known restaurants, this art-nouveau marvel is a worth a visit for the woody old-world decor of its main room alone. If you're lucky, you'll get to sit with the city's movers and shakers in the semisecluded balcony area; but wherever you are, the food's the thing. Keep an eye out especially for *Xai an Forn* (cordero, the Spanish national dish of roast lamb) and *entrecot al rocquefort* (steak flavored with rocquefort). The prix-fixe lunch is a wonderfully cost-effective way to be introduced to this classic culinary marvel.

El Petit Raco. Princep d'Asturiers 11. ☎ **93-218-41-48.** Main courses 600–1,800P ($4–$12). AE, MC, DC, V. Daily 1:30–4pm and 9–11:30pm. Metro: Fontana. CATALAN/SPANISH.

This traditionally Spanish small restaurant in the Gràcia neighborhood is delightfully untouristy and thus a real find. The chef prepares daily specials based on the local market. Any fish special is highly recommended, and you'll almost find *bacalao,* the Spanish national fish, in at least one preparation; and the oil-and-garlic drenched *entrecot* is tasty too. Not a scene, just a Spanish pearl devoid of trendoids and tourists.

Els 4 Gats. Montsio 3. ☎ **93-302-41-40.** Reservations required. Main courses 1,300–2,800P ($9–$19). AE, MC, V. Mon–Sat 1–4pm and 9pm–midnight, Sun 8am–2pm. Metro: Catalunya. CATALAN.

This is one of those places the tourist office (and guidebooks) describe as a writer's hangout, but that'd be pushing it. Indeed, it was ground zero for the modernismo movement—at least the legend claims—but you'd hardly know that now. Yet if it's no longer a bastion of intellectual thought, it's still a wonderful old place for Barcelonans and visitors alike. The preparations, based on daily market specials, are simple, honest, and good in traditional Catalan style. On Sunday, Els 4 Gats is just a cafe; the restaurant is closed.

La Dentelliere. Ample 26. ☎ **93-319-68.32.** Main courses 590–1,890P ($4–$13). AE, DC, MC, V. Daily 1–4pm and 8–11:30pm. Metro: Jaume I. CATALAN/FRENCH.

You'll be charmed by the old Spanish-style decor—wood tables and lace cloths—and even more so by the food, a wonderful combination of French and Catalan. The *fricasse de ternera* (a sumptuous beef stew) is extra fine, and so are the crêpes and deliciously archaic fondues.

✪ **La Porteria.** Laforja 11. ☎ **93-218-27-88.** Daily menus 975P ($7) and 1,300P ($9). No credit cards. Daily 7:30–11pm. Metro: Fontana. CATALAN.

This neighborhood restaurant is small and utterly unpretentious, but the food sings. It bills itself as offering *cocina de mercado* (market cuisine) and indeed this is the case: Practically everything on the menu changes with what the owner/chef sees fresh at the local market every day. The emphasis is on fish; there's always *bacalao* and at least two other kinds of swimming creatures; the preparations are simple, honest, and always wonderful.

Les Quinze Nuits. Plaça Reial. No phone. Main courses 425–990P ($3–$7). AE, DC, MC, V. Daily 1–4pm and 8pm–midnight. Metro: Liceu. CONTINENTAL/CATALAN.

It might be odd to think there's a fine untouristy restaurant right on Plaça Reial, but Les Quinze Nuits is it. This handsome eatery has a woody colonial ambiance, with updated earth tones; the menu is continental as well, with modern touches. The fish, especially the *bacalao,* is quite good. Moderate prices with excellent service and a fine decor make this place worth coming back to—15 nights in a row.

Los Caracoles. Escudellers 14. ☎ **93-302-31-85.** Main courses 950–3,700P ($6–$24). AE, DC, MC, V. Daily 1pm–midnight. Metro: Drassanes. CATALAN/SPANISH.

Oh, Lord, I know that every tourist in the world has come here since the beginning of time, but that's no reason you shouldn't too. After all, who can pass by those gorgeous birds a-turnin' in the rotisserie outside—*pollalast,* they call it in Catalan, and you'll call 'em scrumptious (unless you're a vegan). The surprise is that the other food is said to be just as good—the smell of garlic pervades the four rooms of this bilevel place—but how would I know? I just wanted that bird on my plate.

Pitarra. Avinyo 56. ☎ **93-301-16-47.** Fax 93-301-85-62. Reservations recommended. Main courses 1,250–2,474P ($8–$16). AE, MC, DC, V. Mon–Sat 1–4pm and 8:30–11pm. Metro: Jaume I or Liceu. SPANISH.

Open since 1890, this is one of Barcelona's finest and most respected restaurants, having played host to celebs from around the world—and even Juan Carlos, the king of Spain (almost certainly in the private upstairs room). There are a total of four medium-sized rooms, all done in traditional Spanish wood and lace; but don't worry where you sit because the food's the star. The house paella and daily fish specials (usually simple grilled preparations with lemon and olive oil) are the things to have. And the service manages to be elegant and friendly at once.

Quo Vadis. Carme 7. ☎ **93-302-40-72.** Reservations required. Main courses 1,700–3,500P ($11–$23). AE, DC, MC, V. Mon–Sat 1:30–4pm and 8:30–11:30pm. Metro: Liceu. SPANISH/CONTINENTAL.

Style queens on expense accounts will want to make Quo Vadis an itinerary must; it's been one of the most fashionable restaurants in town for years, home to local politicos, celebrities, and other posh people from around the world. There are four understated rooms in this fancy restaurant, and the food tends to be slightly updated versions of classic Continental fare—a bit prissy but not overly so.

Restaurante Peru. Joan de Borbo 10. ☎ **93-310-37-09.** Main courses 825–4,500P ($6–$30); prix-fixe menu 1,400P ($9) at lunch, 1,600P ($11) at dinner; *menu de dégustation* 4,000P ($27). AE, MC, DC, V. Daily 1:30–4pm and 8–11:30pm. Metro: Barceloneta. CATALAN/SPANISH.

Nobody could tell me why this Spanish restaurant is called Peru, but I don't really care—not when the food's this good. Fish are bought daily at market, and there's usually *rape à la plancha con guarnicion* (monkfish) or *merluza à la marinera* (hake) even if you're not familiar with either, you'll soon fall in love. The superritzy *menu de dégustation* can't help but be a meal to remember.

✪ **Set Portes.** Isabel II 14. ☎ **93-319-30-33** or 93-319-30-46. Reservations required. Main courses 795–4,200P ($5–$28). AE, MC, DC, V. Daily 1pm–1am. Metro: Barceloneta. SEAFOOD/CATALAN/SPANISH.

The Set Portes is perhaps Barcelona's most classically elegant restaurant, having attracted heads of state and international celebs as well as expense-accounted businessfolk since (wow!) 1836. The main room is an expansive, grand tribute to Old Spain, offset with a few modern touches in design and decor. The menu runs the gamut from fish to meat, though the paella is masterful and the fish casseroles unique. It's more than slightly stuffy: Don't enter without a coat and tie if you want to feel welcomed.

Tapa Tapa. Passeig de Gràcia 44. ☎ **93-488-33-69.** Tapas 300–850P ($2–$6). AE, MC, DC, V. Daily noon–midnight. Metro: Passeig de Gràcia. SPANISH.

From the outside, this place looks like one of a million *cervezerias* (beer houses that often serve tapas) lining Passeig de Gràcia, and indeed I'm not advising you to linger for hours. However, as businesslike tapas joints go, this is one of the best. Not only is the selection massive—everything from the standard egg, potato, and ham salads and croquettes to chorizo in oil, plus daily fish specials—but the high volume means everything is superfresh. A good place for a couple of small plates to tide you over till lunch while you're making the Passeig de Gràcia shopping rounds.

Txakolin. Marques de l'Argentera 19. ☎ **93-268-17-81.** Main courses 800–2,950P ($5–$20). AE, MC, DC, V. Daily 1:30–4pm and 9–11:30pm. Metro: Jaume I. BASQUE.

This is Barcelona's best-loved Basque restaurant, a tradition in its own time; unless you're planning to travel to Bilbao to see the new Guggenheim, this may be a very good introduction to this regional cuisine. Upstairs you can try the tapas or a full Basque meal, with specialties like *Kokoxtas al pil pil* (heavy but delish meat-filled croquettes). Downstairs is a very reasonable menu for just 1,200P ($8).

Venus. Avinyo 25. ☎ **93-301-15-85.** Main courses 550–850P ($4–$6). No credit cards. Mon–Sat noon–midnight. Metro: Jaume I, Liceu, or Drassanas. INTERNATIONAL.

This is one of the coolest joints in town, more of an American-style deli/cafe than anything normally associated with Spain. Supersweet Merci and her sister Montse (Catalan for Mercedes and Montserrat) play hostess to a young hip crowd with an eclectic menu of tapas, fabu salads, and assorted international fare—plus a wonderful selection of Spanish wines. Venus is also a wonderful place to pick up invitations to the hottest mixed raves and dance parties in town. *Todo con much amor* ("All with a lot of love") reads their slogan, and I can't help but agree.

4 Exploring Barcelona

Bountiful Barcelona offers scads of things to see: marvelous museums, super shops, bodacious bars, and much more. But this is a city made for rambling and ambling, and the final destination may ultimately be secondary to the fun of just getting there. This is especially good news because many of the most fun things to are out of doors: for example, strolling in the Parc Güell, checking out the Barceloneta neighborhood, and cruising in Montjuïc.

I've made many trips to Barcelona, and I'll pass along my standard m.o. In the mornings, I do the cultural things, then take the afternoons off for a long lunch, shopping expedition, or siesta if I'm so inclined. Those of you into the baths would do well to make late afternoon the time to hit the saunas, which generally begin acting up around 3pm.

However you choose to avail yourself of this grand city's gems, I've just one word of advice: Don't rush it. As much as there is to do in this glorious town, let it unravel slowly, enjoying every scene and site. You can return to the crazy pace of real life after you come back home.

Late March to early January, you can take advantage of the **Bus Turístic.** A single ticket permits unlimited on/off travel on these buses, many of them open-topped double-deckers, as well as on the Montjuïc funicular and cable car and Tibidabo's *tramvía blau.* Originating at Plaça de Catalunya, the **red bus no. 100** makes a sweep

A Museum Note

All Barcelona's municipal museums are closed January 1 and 6, April 12 and 19, May 1 and 31, June 24, September 11 and 24, October 12, November 1, and December 6, 8, and 25. Nearly all museums are closed on Monday, but many now stay open through the afternoon siesta on other days, when most stores are closed.

of the city, north along Passeig de Gràcia, over by Sagrada Família, along Avingudas del Tibidabo and Diagonal, by the Estació Sants, through the Parc de Montjuïc, along Passeig de Colom to the Parc de la Ciutadella and back up La Rambla past the Barri Go`tic. It makes 17 stops along its 2½-hour route. The 6 to 10 buses run daily, about every 15 minutes in summer and every 30 minutes the rest of the year, 9am to 9:30pm. An all-day ticket is 1,400P ($9) and a ticket good for 2 consecutive days 1,800P ($12). You can buy tickets on the bus. Multilingual guide-conductors announce stops and answer questions.

THE HITS YOU SHOULDN'T MISS

✪ **Picasso Museum (Museu Picasso).** Montcada 15–19. ☎ **93-319-63-10.** Admission 750P ($5); free first Sun of every month. Tues–Sat 10am–8pm, Sun 10am–3pm. Metro: Jaume I.

More than a mere display, this museum (housed in three adjoining Renaissance mansions) is a fascinating historical tribute, mainly to the artist's early work when he lived in Barcelona, the city he continued to hold dear to his heart throughout his life. In addition to paintings and drawings, there are some ceramic musings; yet, interestingly, there are precious few of his truly famous works. That aside, this is beautifully curated and highly instructive tribute to Picasso's formative years.

Catedral de Barcelona. Plaça de la Seu. ☎ **93-315-15-54.** Cathedral free; museum 100P (66¢). Cathedral daily 8am–1:30pm and 4–7:30pm; museum daily 10am–1pm. Metro: Jaume I.

This is Barcelona's largest and most famous cathedral, standing in start contrast to Gaudí's Sagrada Família (below). According to press information (don't trust me on this one), this church combines Renaissance, Gothic, and medieval styles and was built in stages from the 13th to the 19th century. More modern is the gorgeous garden, which in spring and summer is alone worth a look. The cloister museum offers a collection of medieval art, if you're into that sort of thing.

✪ **Templo de la Sagrada Família.** Majorca 401. ☎ **93-455-02-47.** Admission 750P ($5); elevator to the top 200P ($1.35). Daily 9am–6pm (to 9pm in summer). Metro: Sagrada Família.

It's somewhat ironic that this modernist rendition of a cathedral, virtually a symbol of Barcelona itself, is little more than an empty shell, rather more interesting from afar than up close. (Just like the Acropolis.) No matter: This oddity, which obviously represents the architect's own conception of man's relationship to God (heavy, man), can't be missed. Work began on the Church of the Holy Family in 1882; 2 years later, architect Antoni Gaudí y Cornet took over and projected a temple of immense proportions—the central dome is slated to be 525 feet high. Since Gaudí died in 1926 leaving no detailed plans, construction has proceeded by fits and starts. Rumor has it that the work to complete the building is on again; stay tuned for details.

Joan Miró Foundation (Fundació Joan Miró). Miramar 71–75, in the Parc de Montjuïc. ☎ **93-329-19-08.** Admission 600P ($4). Tues–Wed and Fri–Sat 11am–7pm, Thurs 11am–9:30pm, Sun 10:30am–2:30pm. Metro: Espanya. Bus: 61.

My girlfriend in high school (can you believe it?) was totally into Miró, whom I'd never heard of and whose surrealist tableaux I didn't understand. Guess what? I still

Barcelona Attractions

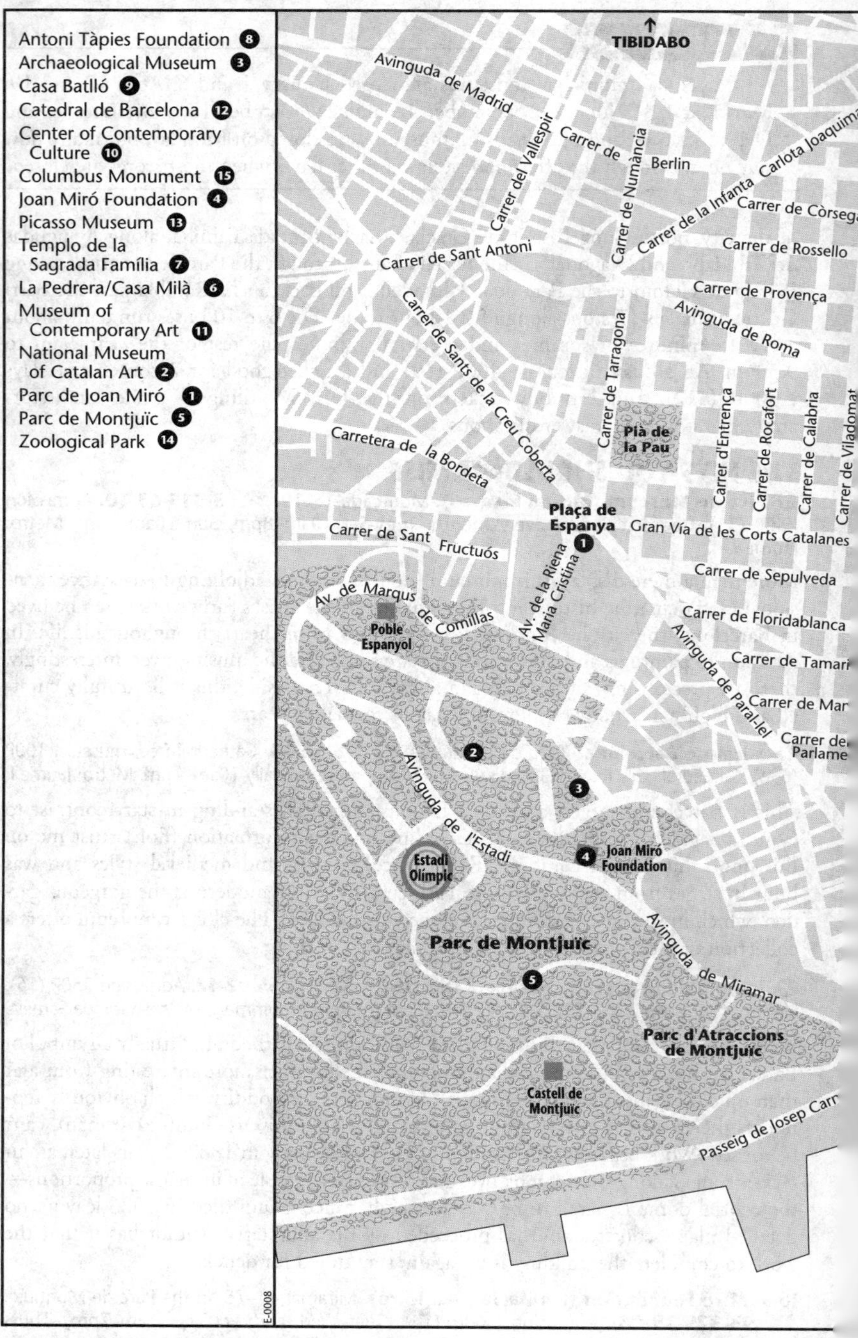

Antoni Tàpies Foundation 8
Archaeological Museum 3
Casa Batlló 9
Catedral de Barcelona 12
Center of Contemporary Culture 10
Columbus Monument 15
Joan Miró Foundation 4
Picasso Museum 13
Templo de la Sagrada Família 7
La Pedrera/Casa Milà 6
Museum of Contemporary Art 11
National Museum of Catalan Art 2
Parc de Joan Miró 1
Parc de Montjuïc 5
Zoological Park 14
TIBIDABO
Avinguda de Madrid
Carrer del Vallespir
Carrer de Berlin
Carrer de Numància
Carrer de la Infanta Carlota Joaquima
Carrer de Còrsega
Carrer de Rossello
Carrer de Sant Antoni
Carrer de Provença
Avinguda de Roma
Carrer de Sants de la Creu Coberta
Carrer de Tarragona
Plà de la Pau
Carrer d'Entrença
Carrer de Rocafort
Carrer de Calabria
Carrer de Viladomat
Carretera de la Bordeta
Plaça de Espanya
Gran Vía de les Corts Catalanes
Carrer de Sant Fructuós
Carrer de Sepulveda
Av. de Marqus de Comillas
Av. de la Riena Maria Cristina
Poble Espanyol
Carrer de Floridablanca
Avinguda de Paral-lel
Carrer de Tamari
Carrer de Mar
Carrer de Parlame
Avinguda de l'Estadi
Estadi Olimpic
Joan Miró Foundation
Parc de Montjuïc
Avinguda de Miramar
Parc d'Atraccions de Montjuïc
Castell de Montjuïc
Passeig de Josep Carr
E-0008

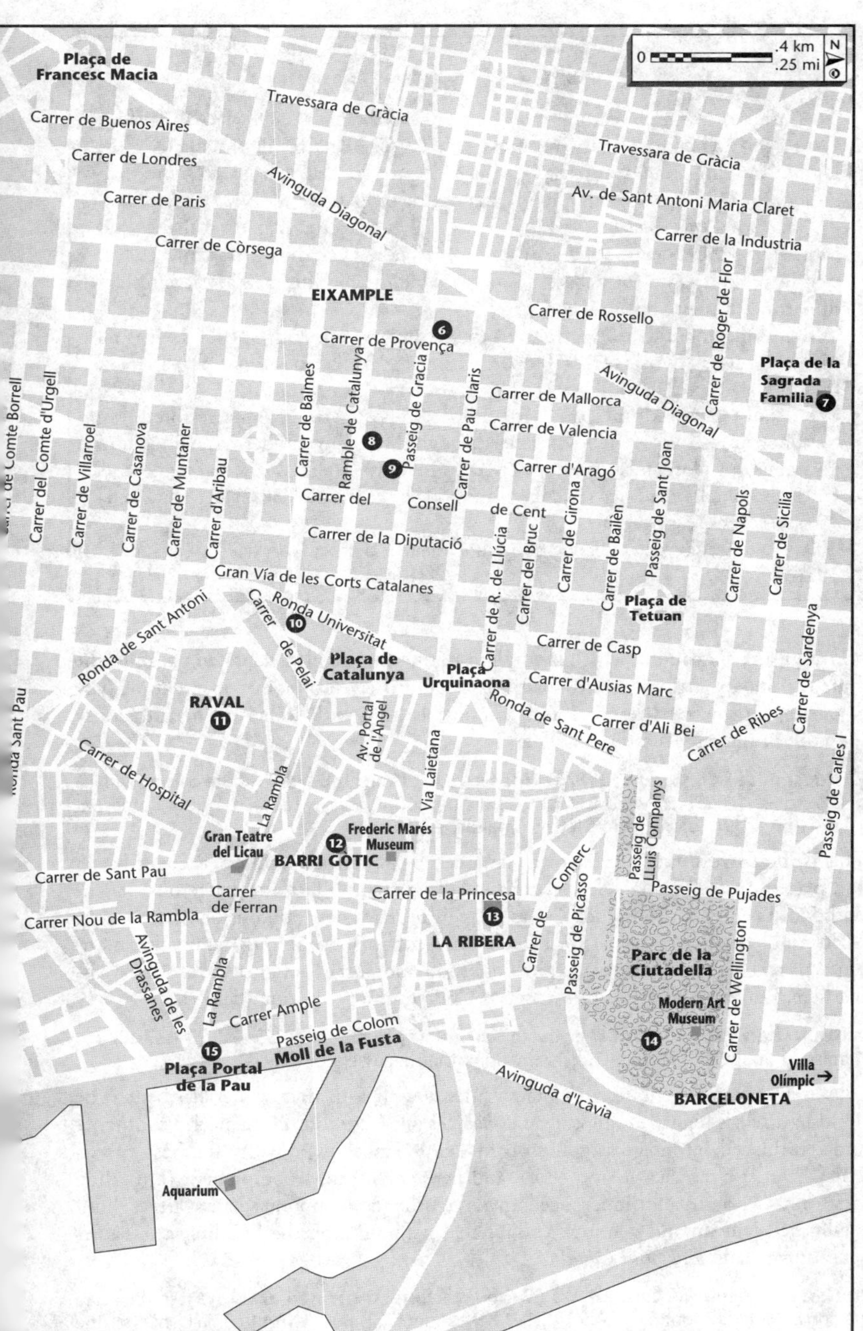

Plaça de Francesc Macia
Travessara de Gràcia
Carrer de Buenos Aires
Carrer de Londres
Avinguda Diagonal
Carrer de Paris
Carrer de Còrsega
EIXAMPLE
Carrer de Rossello
Carrer de Provença
Av. de Sant Antoni Maria Claret
Carrer de la Industria
Carrer de Roger de Flor
Plaça de la Sagrada Familia
Carrer de Mallorca
Carrer de Valencia
Carrer d'Aragó
Carrer del Consell de Cent
Carrer de la Diputació
Gran Vía de les Corts Catalanes
Carrer del Comte d'Urgell
Carrer de Villarroel
Carrer de Casanova
Carrer de Muntaner
Carrer d'Aribau
Carrer de Balmes
Ramble de Catalunya
Passeig de Gracia
Carrer de Pau Claris
Carrer de R. de Llúcia
Carrer del Bruc
Carrer de Girona
Carrer de Bailèn
Passeig de Sant Joan
Carrer de Napols
Carrer de Sicilia
Plaça de Tetuan
Ronda de Sant Antoni
Ronda Universitat
Carrer de Pelai
Plaça de Catalunya
Plaça Urquinaona
Carrer de Casp
Carrer d'Ausias Marc
Ronda de Sant Pere
Carrer d'Ali Bei
Carrer de Ribes
Carrer de Sardenya
RAVAL
Carrer de Hospital
La Rambla
Av. Portal de l'Angel
Via Laietana
Passeig de Carles I
Passeig de Lluis Companys
Gran Teatre del Licau
Frederic Marés Museum
BARRI GÒTIC
Carrer de Sant Pau
Carrer de Ferran
Carrer de la Princesa
Carrer de Comerc
Passeig de Picasso
Passeig de Pujades
Carrer Nou de la Rambla
LA RIBERA
Parc de la Ciutadella
Carrer de Wellington
Avinguda de les Drassanes
Carrer Ample
Passeig de Colom
Moll de la Fusta
Modern Art Museum
Plaça Portal de la Pau
Avinguda d'Icàvia
Villa Olímpic
BARCELONETA
Aquarium
0 .4 km .25 mi
N
6 7 8 9 10 11 12 13 14 15

Going Gaga Over Gaudí

The father of the architectural movement of *modernismo* (1890–1910), **Antoni Gaudí y Cornet** is among the most revered Catalans of all time. His most famous building is the **Sagrada Familia**—despite the fact that it's no more than a shell, for the inside of this church was never completed.

What *modernismo* attempted to do was to blend distinctly natural shapes and forms with the romantic Catalan nature. Whether Gaudí's work achieves just that is, of course, up for debate; some would argue that his creations are utterly unnatural in their admitted eccentricity.

Barcelona abounds in examples of the master's work, and UNESCO lists all his creations as World Trust Properties. In 1997, his masterpiece apartment building at Passeig de Gràcia 92, **La Pedrera** (aka **Casa Milà ☎ 93-484-5995;** open daily 10am–8pm; admission 500P/$3.35,), was lovingly restored; the top floor now explores Gaudí's career through slide show, models, drawings, and photographs. Don't miss the roof terrace. The **Parc Güell** (whose hallmark is its fanciful animal sculptures) and environs and the **Casa Batlló,** Passeig de Gràcia 43, are other great examples.

A recluse and celibate bachelor, Gaudí died in penury, run over by a tram in 1926.

don't, but maybe you do, which is why I'm noting this highly celebrated paean to the famed Catalan artists' work—painting, sculpture, and some installation-type chazzerei. Go in the afternoon and combine culture with lechery: The ultracruisy fountain in the park is a short walk away.

✪ **Museum of Contemporary Art (Museu d'Art Contemporani de Barcelona).** Plaça deis Angels 1. ☎ **93-412-08-10.** Admission 600P ($4). Tues–Fri noon–8pm, Sat 10am–8pm, Sun 10am–3pm. Metro: Catalunya.

This is the newest museum in town, designed by American architect Richard Meier and placed on the wrong side of La Rambla in a crappy (but not dangerous) neighborhood. Bringin' art to the masses (as if), this brilliant new building showcases Klee, Miró, and local hero Antoni Tàpies (see his museum below), among many other modern artists. There's also the usual gift/bookshop and cutely designed cafe. After visiting here, head next door to the Center of Contemporary Culture (below).

Antoni Tàpies Foundation (Fundació Antoni Tàpies). Aragó 255. ☎ **93-487-03-15.** Admission 500P ($3.45). Tues–Sun 11am–8pm. Metro: Passeig de Gràcia.

This is the premier tribute to Catalan artists, with a distinctly modern bent. The building itself is highly progressive and was designed by Lluís Domènech i Montaner and refurbished by his great-grandson in 1989. Tàpies is probably the best-known Catalan artist after Picasso and Miró, and here you'll find a comprehensive rotating view of his work. In addition, space is given to other contemporary native artists, both established and up-and-coming. The tangle of tubing atop the building is a Tàpies sculpture called *Chair and Cloud.*

National Museum of Catalan Art (Museu Nacional d'Art de Catalunya). In the Palau Nacional, Parc de Montjuïc. ☎ **93-423-71-99.** Admission 800P ($6); free first Thurs of the month. Tues–Wed and Fri–Sat 10am–7pm, Thurs 10am–9pm, Sun 10am–2:30pm. Metro: Espanya.

Meant to last only for the year of the 1929 world's fair and newly designed inside by controversial Italian architect Gae Aulenti, this museum houses Catalan art from the

Romanesque and Gothic periods, as well as that of the 16th to 18th centuries. As well, you'll find works by world-class painters like El Greco, Velázquez, Zurbarán, and Tintoretto. Added bonus: Sculptures and frescoes have been lifted from Romanesque churches in northern Catalonia and displayed here.

Museum-Monastery of Pedralbes (Museu-Monestir de Pedralbes). Baixada del Monestir 9. ☎ **93-203-92-82** for monastery, or 93-280-14-34 for Sala Thyssen. Monastery and Sala Thyssen, 600P ($4.15). Tues–Sun 10am–2pm. Bus: 22 or 64.

The stained-glass windows on this 14th-century monastery are reason enough to visit. The church was founded by Queen Elisenda de Montcada, whose sepulcher remains in this early Gothic structure. The cloisters are fascinating: You'll see several monks' cells, an apothecary, a kitchen, a 16th-century infirmary, and St. Michael's chapel, featuring murals from the 14th century. A newly renovated wing hosts over 80 medieval paintings and sculptures on loan from the Thyssen-Bornemisza Museum in Madrid (see chapter 16).

Center of Contemporary Culture (Centre de Cultura Contemporania). Montalegre 5. ☎ **93-412-07-81.** Admission 500P ($3.30). Tues–Sat 11am–2pm and 4–8pm, Sun 10am–3pm. Metro: Catalunya.

This ongoing exhibit explains the history, culture, and contemporary life of Barcelona from the point of view of urban history and sociology. It sounds like a snooze, but it's actually a fascinating introduction to a fascinating city.

Columbus Monument (Monument à Colom). Plaça Portal de la Pau. ☎ **93-302-52-54.** Admission 225P ($1.50). June 24–Sept 22 daily 9am–9pm; Sept 23–June 23 Tues–Sat 10am–2pm and 3:30–6:30pm, Sun 10am–7pm. Metro: Drassanes.

This 100-year-old monument, whose main figure is in bronze, commemorates Columbus's discovery of the New World, showing the explorer delivering the news to the king and queen of Spain. It doesn't cost anything to look at, but the charge above is for the elevator that takes you to the top for a city view.

Archaeological Museum (Museu Arqueologic). Passeig de Santa Madrona 39–41, in the Parc de Montjuïc. ☎ **93-423-21-29.** Admission 200P ($1.30). Tues–Sat 9:30am–1:30pm and 3:30–7pm, Sun to 2pm. Metro: Espanya.

What makes this museum interesting isn't just the collected relics (dating as far back as the Greeks) but the explanatory text describing the history of this important city from ancient times to today. If the artifacts don't interest you, the story will.

✪ **Zoological Park (Parc Zoologic).** In the Parc de la Ciutadella. ☎ **93-221-25-06.** Admission 1,000P ($7). Apr–Oct daily 9:30am–7:30pm; Nov–Mar daily 10am–5pm. Metro: Ciutdella.

This is doubleheader: a fine zoo in an even finer park, whose summer flora are worth a visit in and of themselves. The zoo is modern and well presented and (unlike most of its species) actually easy to find your way around. It's a short walk from the Picasso Museum and a nice cheerful antidote to the artist's sometimes twisted work.

GAY BARCELONA

Unlike Berlin in the decadent 1920s, Paris in the days of Baldwin, or London at any time at all, Barcelona has never had a discernible gay literary or artistic nucleus. This is probably partly due to Spain's repressive regime and de facto isolation from the rest of the world through much of this century—and, moreover, due to the fairly insular nature of Catalan society until recent times.

Thus, you'd be hard-pressed to identify a distinct literary or aesthetic gay movement. But what Barcelona may have lacked in the past—at least in any organized, recognized fashion—it's certainly making up for in its frenzied heyday right now.

"Does the city have a distinct gay presence?" asked my friend, Karen Tina, who hadn't been to Spain since our student days, not so long after the end of Franco's quasi-fascist regime. The only way to answer is with a resounding yes. Gays are in every part of commerce and society, from the arty/boho **Barri Xinés** to the lusher **Eixample** district uptown—and everywhere else in-between. In fact, thinking of Barcelona without a gay influence is like thinking of New York or London without queers at the center of their business and cultural spheres.

Why is this so? First, of course, there's Barcelona's status as the most progressive and commercially successful region in Spain—indeed, Catalonia is among the fastest-rising stars in the European Union, a veritable model of economic expansion. But even if that weren't true, all you have to do is look around to understand why gays (and scenesters from around the world) flock to Barcelona: This is, by anyone's standards, one of the five most beautiful cities on earth. Like I said before, your problem isn't going to be why to come here, but why to leave.

Catalonia has always had much more liberal attitudes than the rest of Spain, which is another reason gay life in all its forms has continued to flourish here.

PARKS, GARDENS & SQUARES

The city's most famous park, on the northern rim of the Gràcia section, is the **Parc Güell** (☎ **93-424-38-09;** Metro: Güell; Bus: 24, 31, 74). What most people don't know is that it was actually intended to be an upper-crust residential development financed by Eusebi Güell and designed by Antoni Gaudí; this, alas, never quite got off the ground. Today, only two houses stand, one of which is the Casa-Museu Gaudí, a small museum in tribute to Gaudí and his work. The multicolored lizard sculpture is the park's most obvious symbol.

The **Parc de Joan Miró** (Metro: Espanya) is a small but pretty park featuring the artist's sculpture *Woman and Bird.* It's a fine place to sit, read, or watch the kiddies play on the contemporary equipment that perfectly matches the temperament of Miró.

Plaça de Catalunya is, at least on paper, the center of the city and an important transportation hub, above and below ground. Oddly, however, the square exists almost by default—a haphazard confluence of important streets and foot traffic that never quite coalesces into an aesthetic whole. In what's otherwise a visually arresting city, Catalunya (as its commonly called) is a mismatched collection of currency-exchange offices, middling restaurants, and American guitar players aping Neil Young for change.

After midnight, however, the tourist hordes die down and Catalunya becomes a gay cruising ground. There isn't any open-air action (that would be well-nigh impossible), but this is casual pass-through scene. I'm not sure I'd call this a desination per se; if you're totally committed to outdoor cruising, the Parc de Montjuïc (below) is the place to go, but it's definitely worth a look if you're returning to your hotel or in the neighborhood at night.

La Rambla was for years known as cruising central, especially before Spain's gay scene began taking off 20 years ago. Its prominence in this regard has thus been diminished, but a lot of eye contact still goes on at all times of the day, most especially between 5 and 7pm, especially among guys not quite ready to go home to their wives.

Now for the big gun (ahem): the ✪ **Parc de Montjuïc.** While this is a beautiful, well-designed public space with several monuments, that isn't what interests les boys. Rather, the park in all its glory is the number-one cruising ground for boys from Barcelona and miles around—one of the most famed cruising grounds in Europe, no less. The park's Font del Gat (Fountain of the Cat) in the northeast corner is ground zero, busy just about 24 hours, with action picking up considerably in early evening.

If someone catches your eye, you can retire to the green areas around the fountain or into the park—apparently without great police interference. This is a local tradition, and there's even something romantic about making out under the stars. But do exercise caution: You never know who's going to mug you or hold a knife to your throat, acts that aren't totally unknown. And if someone asks you for money, you'll proceed AYOR. Oh, and one last thing: Look elsewhere for huge spurts—this fountain has been dry for years.

BOYS ON THE BEACH

It doesn't have a very pretty name, but **Chernobyl Beach (Playa Chernobyl)**—so called because the water is grotesquely polluted—is the place to go if you're looking for sun. You can get there by taking the Metro to Sant Andreu and looking for the **Club Nautació Barcelona,** Moll de Espanya, across from which, from late spring to early autumn, lie the guys (many in the nude).

WORKING UP A SWEAT

Barcelona doesn't have an all-gay gym, so there are two options: use the one in your hotel (if it's a luxury property) or find a facility close to you. If you're having trouble finding one, you can always try **Gimnas York,** Gran de Gràcia 161 (☎ **93-237-94-50;** Metro: Fontana; open Mon–Fri 7:30am–10pm, Sat 9:30am–2pm), which offers a good range of equipment and daily rates. There's even a trainer (a cute one!) on premises, if private workouts are your thing. Alternately, there's a gym adjacent to the Olympic pool in the Parc de Montjuïc (below).

If you've ever dreamed of swimming in an Olympic event, have I got news for you! Head to the Parc de Montjuïc and its **Piscina Bernardo Picornell,** Estadi 30–40 (☎ **93-423-40-42;** Metro: Paral-lel; open Mon–Fri 7am–midnight, Sat to 9pm, Sun 7:30am–2:30pm). It offers both an indoor and an outdoor pool, plus a sauna and Jacuzzi.

BULLFIGHTING

While they're rather less the rage than in the south of Spain, you can see bullfights in the big B at the **Plaça de Toros Monumental,** Gran Vía de les Corts Catalanes. The bullfights are held April to September on Sundays. Call ☎ **93-245-58-04** for information.

5 Hitting the Stores

Barcelona is the shopping center for all Spain and one of the best places anywhere for fashion, art, and inventive furnishings. Even if you (like me) are something less than a shopaholic, the sexy merchandising and sexier sales help in most shops is enough to get you pounding the retail pavement. What's more, there's always the lure of frequent cafe and tapas stops to keep you interested in scouting out the shopping scene.

Barcelona boasts several main shopping drags. The most prestigious stretch is the **Passeig de Gràcia** from Plaça de Catalunya up to Avenguida Diagonal (just say Diagonal). If you turn left on Diagonal, the exclusive retail action continues up through **Plaça Fracesc Macia,** on both sides of this very broad boulevard. At the plaza is also a commercial center with fashion stores galore, though these tend to be not quite so upscale as those on the Diagonal itself. (Look especially for **Bulevard Rosa,** a small arcade off the Diagonal between La Ramba and Avenguida Augusta, on the north side of the street.)

An exploding and very cool retail locus is in the **Barri Xinés,** east of La Rambla. Here you'll find vintage and new clothes shops, fabu record shops (with jaw-droppin' stuff from the 1960s), and state-of-the-moment art and furnishings stores in one of Europe's oldest remaining neighborhoods.

Before or after your expedition here, I command you to sit for a good long while at the superhot ✪ **Schilling Cafe,** Ferran 23 (☎ **93-317-67-87;** Metro: Liceu; open daily 10am-2pm). This is a large Berlin-style cafe where you can linger with a cup of espresso (*un cafe solo,* 140P—less than a buck!) and one of their sumptuous pastries. Though this place is a must for all hip young Barcelonans, you'll find a distinct gay element all day long, and after work this is currently the place to meet.

A huge outdoor flea market has now exploded off the outdoor market around the **Travassera de Gràcia** (Metro: Fontana). I love the meat and fish shops, as good as anything Paris has to offer; and some of the stalls also have packaged foods that make great gifts for your foodie friends. The stuff in the stands outside isn't food oriented and runs from interesting bric-a-bracs to total trash, but this market (the best day is Sunday) is certainly worth seeing for its view on everyday Barcelonan life.

For details on Barcelona's general store hours, see the shopping section of chapter 16.

ART & ARTIFACTS Utterly unique, ✪ **Art Box,** Petritxol 1 (☎ **93-301-55-45;** www.artbox.es; Metro: Jaume I or Liceu), is a bilevel treasure of contemporary art. There are two marvelous machines called dealers that automatically display up to 25 lithos each for your review; while these are mainly by Catalan artists, others are on sale as well. There's also a two-room gallery featuring the work of local painters and multimedia artists for a look at what's happening on the Barcelona scene.

If you can hit just one store for pottery and ceramics, ✪ **Bopapier,** Augusta 49 (☎ **93-237-50-79;** Metro: Fontana), should be it. The owner has assembled a sterling selection from around Catalonia, Andalusia, and Majorca with exquisite taste. Some are modern designs, others replicas of 18th-century museum pieces. The taste level is very high indeed and the owner a real gent. Some blown glassware too.

Art Escudellers, Escudellers 23–25 (☎ **93-412-68-01;** Metro: Liceu), is a warehouse-style center of ceramics and pottery from artisans everywhere in Spain. All the miniexhibits are clearly marked with the artist's name and region, making shopping a joy. In addition, you can watch a small group of potters at their wheels or painting their pieces to gorgeous completion. From phantasmagorical figurines to utile earthenware, this is a sensational place to buy authentic Spanish ceramics at excellent prices. At **Groc Art,** Aviyo 46 (☎ **93-302-62-87;** Metro: Jaume I or Liceu), modern art and artifacts from Spain and beyond are the hallmarks. It's a small, chic gallery in the Ciutat Vella (Old Town).

The upscale **La Pinacoteca,** Passeig de Gràcia 34 (☎ **93-487-70-92;** Metro: Passeig de Gràcia), offers lithographs from artists like Klimt, Monet, Klee, and more. Also on sale are fine frames of all types. The help is a little snooty though. The ceramics and earthenware sold at **Molsa,** Plaça Sant Josep Oriol 1 (☎ **93-302-31-03;** Metro: Liceu), range from tacky to terrific, depending on your budget and taste. The collection is certainly deep and wide enough to meet every need.

BOOKS ✪ **Cómplices,** Cervantes 2 (☎ **93-412-72-83**), offers gay and lesbian publications as well as provides information about local bars and dance clubs.

FASHION **Alfredo Dominguez,** Paseo de Gràcia 89 (☎ **93-215-13-39;** Metro: Passeig de Gràcia), is probably Spain's best-known designer, though recently I think his stuff has gotten a little staid. (He made his name doing neutrals, which get tired fast.) Still, there are very handsome clothes, from suits to sportswear, with all the accessories to make a first-class ensemble. The supersnooty help completes the picture at this, Dominguez's largest and most spiffy store in Spain. Spain's hippest designer, ✪ **Armand Basi,** Passeig de Gràcia 49 (☎ **93-215-14-21;** Metro: Passeig de Gràcia), has his flagship store here—he's Catalan, after all. The shopboys are always supercute, as are the clothes; if you're a fashionista, this wonderful shop should be your first stop.

The small ✪ **Beliss Home,** Princep d'Asturies 7 (☎ **93-218-01-61;** Metro: Fontana), has an excellent selection of high-end suits by Spanish designers Florentino and Alfredo Dominguez, plus sportswear by companies like Boxley and Pullright. Not avant-garde, but very handsome togs indeed. At **Carlos Torrents,** Passeig de Gràcia 55, in the Bulevard Rosa minimall (☎ **93-202-02-06;** Metro: Passeig de Gràcia), you'll find very modern clothes, from sportswear to suits (mostly by Spanish and Italian designers). Me, I'd like to try on the trade working the sales floor—major, major cute.

Whaddaya know—a gay clothes store that doesn't look stuck in Fire Island in the 1970s. In fact, the li'l ✪ **Ritual,** Consell de Cent 255 (no phone; Metro: Catalunya), next to two of Barcelona's best bars, is full of way-cute stuff from Spain and abroad, plus the best club invitations. If you want to look like a cute European boy and not a raging lycra queen, this is one Ritual you should really think about performing.

GAY MERCHANDISE Amazingly, ✪ **Dive,** Plaza Villa de Madrid 5 (☎ **93-412-27-59;** Metro: Catalunya), is able to provide gay merchandise—lube, gymwear, cute gifts—with a touch of class. The clubwear is cool and the streetwear stuff any hip young dud would want to own. As you can imagine, it's also an excellent way to get the best club invitations, and the sales help (always the cutest) is fun to ogle out of the corner of your eye while you're fingering the spandex. At the **Condom Center,** Carme 64 (no phone; Metro: Liceu), you'll find condoms in all shapes, flavors, and sizes, plus grease and other, er, accoutrements. Eat, drink, and be merry!

The oldest gay sex shop in Spain, **Sextienda Menstore,** Rauric 11 (☎ **93-318-86-76;** Metro: Liceu), features videos, mags, and lube—convenient for you downtown types staying at the Hotel California. The staff is decidedly dour, though. **Zeus Gay Shop,** Riera Alta 20 (☎ **93-442-97-65;** Metro: Liceu), is Barcelona's most complete gay *tienda,* with all the latest movies, books, guides (like this one, I hope), and sexual aids. Carlos, who runs the shop, is a wealth of information and a supernice guy besides.

GOURMET FOODS The stocked-to-the-rafters old-world ✪ **Colnado,** Passeig de Gràcia 63 (☎ no phone; Metro: Passeig de Gràcia), is a wonderful place to buy all manner of packaged foods to take home to friends, from traditional Spanish fare like chorizo and sardines to imported French pâtés. The delightful **G.A.L.A.,** Plaça Gala Placidia 13–15 (☎ **93-217-30-85;** Metro: Fontana), offers fresh foods and botanical remedies, plus a very nice manager who'll help cure what ails you—maybe reaching into the scary-looking bags of herbs at the front counter. She's a specialist in stomach ailments, a definite asset after a week of nonstop fressing on tapas and other grease-laden fare.

JEWELRY **Comaposada Joiers,** Gran de Gràcia 42 (☎ **93-237-73-30;** Metro: Fontana), is one of Barcelona's most unique stores. Half of the shop is devoted to watches, the other (more interesting) half to jewelry, crystal, and objets d'art designed in-house. Many of the motifs are taken from the work of Gaudí and other Catalan architects. A whole series is based solely on the Park Güell.

LIQUOR One of the city's most complete wine stores, the **Celler Can Dani,** Travessera de Gràcia 119 (☎ **93-237-93-63;** Metro: Fontana), is the perfect place to buy gifts of Spanish wine for your friends or yourself. In addition, there are cute gifties like Spanish olives, chorizo, and sardines. The staff really knows what's what and will guide you to a unique and delicious wine in your price range. **Correus,** Gignas 25 (☎ **93-315-04-07;** Metro: Liceu), is a medium-sized, well-stocked shop with wines from all over Spain at terrific prices. The staff is totally knowledgeable and will help you find just the right thing.

LUGGAGE & LEATHER **Arce,** Plaça Gala Placidia 13–15 (☎ **93-218-42-49;** Metro: Passeig de Gràcia), sells a broad middle-of-the-road range of luggage and leather. Some of the former is unextraordinary, but the leather briefcases are very sharp. Founded in 1923, **Bolsos Vall,** Gran de Garcia 165 (☎ **93-217-94-36;** Metro: Fontana), is a family-owned store with a wide selection of good luggage and handsome leather goods—wallets, briefcases, belts, and more. Not superchic but a strong collection of well-made Spanish goods.

MARKETS The ✪ **Mercat San Josep** (Metro: Liceu) is the most famous food market in Barcelona, with a whole building full of stalls for fresh fish, meat, cheese, produce, baked goods, and more. One only regrets not living in Barcelona; it'd be so nice to take some of this lovely food home! Closed Sunday.

The **Mercada de Libertidad** (Metro: Fontana) is generally not known to tourists, but this marvelous food market in the upscale Gràcia district is cleaner and friendlier than its more well-known cousin downtown. You can even find packaged foods, chorizos, and—best of all!—yummy Spanish olives to take home with you. Closed Sunday.

VINTAGE CLOTHING The loose translation of **Otra Vez,** Avinyo 25 (☎ **93-412-07-43;** Metro: Jaume I or Liceu), is "one mo' time." This fabu vintage store (for guys and dolls) is righteously groovy, with everything from leather coats to so-tacky-they're-cool 1970s disco tops. Plus very cool club invitations.

6 All the World's a Stage

THE PERFORMING ARTS

When it comes to the performing arts, Barcelona offers the best of both worlds: its own indigenous Catalan culture and a European and international outlook that keeps an open eye on the rest of the world. What this has produced is a happy mix of the old and the new, the Catalan and the Spanish, and a tolerant spirit for all arts new and old, classical and fresh.

The **Gran Teatre el Liceu,** La Ramble (Metro: Liceu), was one of the most famous opera houses in the world and as wondrous an example of art-nouveau architecture as existed anywhere in the world. In 1994, this monument was virtually destroyed by fire—and music lovers around the world wept. Today, it's being rebuilt, though at a snail's pace, and one wonders if it (like the Sagrada Família) will ever really be complete.

The ornate **Palau de la Musica Catalan,** Sant Francesc de Paula 2 (☎ **93-268-10-00;** Metro: Urquinnaona), is one of the best modernist structures in town, worth a visit even if you're not a music aficionado. It was designed by famous Catalan architect Lluis Domènech i Montaner and boasts all manner of glasswork and ceramic finery to complement the basic structure. Concerts, both voice and instrumental, from artists Spanish and otherwise, are given here; consult local papers or visit the box office to see who's performing and when.

A favored venue for ballet and modern dance, the **Teatre Victo`ria,** Paral-lel 65 (☎ **93- 329-91-89;** Metro: Espanya), is picking up some of the slack brought about by the destruction of the Gran Teatre del Liceu. And at a recycled former market, the **Mercat de les Flors,** Lleida 59 (☎ **93-426-21-02;** Metro: Pole Sec), dance, theatrical productions, and occasional musical events are on the menu. Ticket prices vary with the attraction at both venues.

Unless your Catalan is up to snuff, I can't imagine why you'd want to see theater here; if that be the case, here's the up-and-up. The **Companyia Flotats** performs at the Teatre Poliorama, Rambla dels Estuds 15 (☎ **93-317-75-99;** Metro: Liceu; closed Aug), and is led by Josep Maria Flotas, an alumnus of the Comédie-Française and

> **Work That Skirt: Flamenco!**
>
> While flamenco is actually much more a Castillian than a Catalan tradition, you may not be able to resist the lure of this sexy Spanish dance. If that's the case, the premier spot in town is **Tablao Flamenco Cordobes,** La Rambla 35 (☎ **93-317-66-53;** Metro: Drassanes). Even if you think you hate flamenco, I advise giving it a chance: The syncopation of clapping hands, rhythmic guitars, and thrilling dance can be a heady combination, even for the most cynical. You'll pay 7,500P ($50) for dinner and the show ($50); for one drink and the show its only 4,000P ($27). *Olé!*

leading Spanish theater houses. His company, highly regarded locally, performs exclusively in Catalan. And the semicooperative **Teatre Llre,** Monsen 4 (☎ **93-218-92-51;** Metro: Passeig de Gràcia), remains the city's (if not the world's) leading proponent of Catalan theater. It presents plays by Shakespeare, Molière, Genet, and contemporary playwrights in Spanish.

LIVE-MUSIC CLUBS

The **Poble Espanyol,** Marques de Comillas, in the Parc de Montjuïc (☎ **93-325-78-66;** Metro: Espanya), is almost unbearably touristy, a re-creation of a Spanish pueblo that becomes a vast Disneyland-like complex at night. The flamenco performances are the least objectionable entertainments; if you go to an early show (the first is at 9:30pm), you can head to a more gay-friendly environment (or, more probably, dinner) afterward.

Like all large cities, Barcelona also hosts pop entertainers from around the world. You can either consult the daily paper ***El Pais*** or simply keep an eye out for posters as you're walking about town to find out if someone you like is in town when you are. In addition to superstars from the English- and Spanish-speaking worlds, you're apt to find world music performers from around the world; Brazilian singers are, deservedly, hot tickets in Barcelona and indeed throughout Europe.

7 In the Heat of the Night

CHAMPAGNE BARS

Catalans call their version of champagne *cava,* and champagne bars are *xampanyerías.* They usually open at 7pm and stay open into the wee hours. Tapas are served, from caviar to smoked fish to frozen chocolate truffles. Most places sell a limited array of house *cavas* by the glass—you'll be offered a choice of *brut* or *brut nature* (*brut* is slightly sweeter). More esoteric *cavas* must be bought by the bottle.

Typical of the breed is **Xampa Xampany,** Gran Via de los Corts Catalanes 702 (☎ 93-265-0483; Metro: Girona; open Mon–Fri 6pm–2:30am, Sat–Sun to 4am), with a good sound system and eclectic music programs.

GAY & LESBIAN BARS

Perhaps the most popular bar of the moment, ✪ **Dietrich,** Consell de Cent 255 (no phone; Metro: Universitat or Urgell), is a long, cruisy black bar leading into a lounge area where friends old and new chew the fat. There's a small stage (well, platform) where drag queens thrill the crowds. The night I was there, the girl singing Natalie Imbruglia's "Torn" was too high to lyp-sinch correctly even if she'd been able to understand the words. The boy's room is an adventure.

EA3, Rauric 23 (no phone; Metro: Liceu), is a sentimental choice: On my first trip to Barcelona 10 years ago, this demented dive was a post-punk rage. It's still around, if just a shadow of its former self, though boho queers and assorted jetsam have kept the torch burning. (Good for them!) The dance floor measuring about 3 square gets going late at night when everyone in the bar is totally trashed.

Five years ago, the **Este Bar,** Consell de Cent 257 (no phone; Metro: Universtat or Urgüell), was the bar in town; today, Dietrich right next door (above) has stolen much of its thunder. But on weekends there's still enough of a crowd at this long, friendly bar to drop in to see what's what. Or isn't.

Women may want to check out the curiously named **Daniel's,** Plaça Cardona 7 (no phone; Metro: Fontana). Habitués are happy to reveal what's hot in town this very nanosecond.

The large, brightly lit ✪ **Punto BCN,** Muntaner 63–65 (☎ **93-453-61-23;** Metro: Universitat or Urgüell), is superpopular and crowded from about 11pm on with a cute young crowd. It's not particularly cruisy until very late but is a good place to drop by for an early beer (it officially opens at 9pm) or to chat at one of the back tables with a friend. Big plus: free invites to Metro and Arena discos and half-off coupons to the baths with the purchase of a drink. Dreamy barmen too.

Roma, Alfons XII 41 (no phone; Metro: Fontana), is an American-style bar with a pool table and separate bar area that never quite had a crowd when I was there. Sources inform me, however, that people arrive after midnight on weekends. Since this is rather out of the way, it should appeal only to folks staying in the Gràcia or other quasi-outlying districts.

MIXED CAFES & BARS

Every city should have a bar/cafe as charming and friendly as the **Cafe de la Calle,** Vic 11 (☎ **93-218-38-63;** Metro: Fontana). A small bar area leads into a nice-sized cozy cafe that's full of nooks and crannies in which to nuzzle with the one you love. There's a small scene here after work (around 8pm), then later in the evening, especially at the end of the week, when the Calle provides a tranquil alternative to wilder Barcelona nightlife.

Cheek to Cheek, Muntaner 325 (no phone; Metro: Universitat or Urgüell), is a trendy everyone's-welcome place, a lively alternative to the cruisier bars, especially if you're in mixed company. The musical entertainment, from drag queens to real singers, begins around midnight.

On paper, **Padam Padam,** Rauric 9 (☎ **93-302-50-62;** Metro: Liceu), is mixed, but a heavy artsy gay contingent hangs here too. It's a good place to go early in the evening for a start-off beer or later for a more active scene. I wish the owner/barmaid were a bit less dour, though.

Officially mixed, **Santanassa,** Aribau 27 (no phone; Metro: Universitat or Urgüell; admission 500P/$3.30, including one drink), attracts everyone from left-of-center queers to lesbians to punky young guys out for a night on the town. The scene is wackier than at the strictly gay bars in the nabe, and the music tends toward the alternative. According to the staff, there's performance art—or whatever—at 1am.

A LEATHER BAR

New Chaps, Diagonal 365 (☎ **93-215-53-65;** Metro: Diagonal or Verdager), is Barcelona's premier—nay, only—leather bar. But even that's an overstatement of sorts, since the influence is more jeans and Levi's (how's that for an outdated phrase?) than S&M. Still, I guess if that's your scene, this bar (oddly located in a posh part of town) is where to head, especially on weekends.

DANCE CLUBS

✪ **Arena,** Balmes 32 (no phone; Metro: Universitat; admission 1,500P/$10 after midnight), is at press time the hot disco, but don't think about going before 1am. Downstairs from the street, Arena is a medium-sized alternative to the megaclubs currently in vogue on both sides of the Atlantic. The music is surprisingly of the moment; depending on the DJ, it switches among techno, house, and classic disco. Admission changes by day and event; during the week, you can get a free pass if you buy a beer at Punto BCN (above). Where the boys are!

Along with Arena, ✪ **Metro,** Sepulveda 185 (no phone; Metro: Universitat; admission 1,500P/$10), is currently the rage, and no scenester should miss it. One part is devoted to flamenco and Catalan music (I couldn't tell whether the effect was supposed to be campy or authentic) and the other to a disco palace. It opens at midnight, but no one shows up till 1:30am, and the action lasts till the wee hours, especially on weekends and holidays. If you're looking for Barcelona's finest (or, at least, cutest), this is where to head. Busy backroom action seals the deal.

Pity poor **Martin's,** Passeig de Gràcia 130 (☎ **93-218-71-67;** Metro: Passeig de Gràcia; admission 1,000P/$7). A decade ago, it was a magnet for all Catalunya and beyond. Today, other clubs have made it quasi-obsolete, but huge bilevel Martin's—with two dance floors, many bars, and an infamous backroom—lives on, primarily as an after-hours haunt. Best time to come is after 3am on weekends.

I couldn't quite figure out **Taller,** Mexic 7–9 (no phone; Metro: Espanya; admission 1,000P/$7 on weekends), but that's probably because I went during the week. This is a large-but-nondescript disco my sources tell me really starts to fill up after 4am on weekends, when it's said to be all the rage among Barcelona's hard-core party boys. It's a little bit off the beaten bath (though not intolerably so), so ask the locals before making the trip.

A relatively new venue is **Distrito Maritimo,** on the Moll de la Fusta in the Port Vell (☎ **93-221-56-61;** Metro: Barceloneta). The music is mostly house and techno.

SAUNAS

✪ **Condal,** Espolsasacs 1 (☎ **93-301-96-80;** Metro: Catalunya), is Barcelona's largest, busiest, and cutest sauna, more on a par with the biggies in Paris and Berlin than any other in town. There's a masseur on duty and mucho action from late afternoon on. If you have time for just one bathhouse, this should be it. **Casanova,** Casanova 57 (☎ **93-323-78-60;** Metro: Universitat or Urgüell), is a small but supermodern, superclean sauna close to the bar action. It's especially busy in late afternoon and early evening and attracts a cute young unsleazy crowd.

According to informed sources, **Corinto,** Pelayo 62 (☎ **93-318-64-22;** Metro: Catalunya), is worth the trip, though it's smaller and not as busy as Condal (above). They give away half-off tickets for this place at Punto BCN (above), which may or may not be a good sign. **Galilea,** Calabria 59 (☎ **93-426-79-05;** Metro: Espanya), is the newest sauna in town, and the early reports are that it's a winner—clean, modern, and filled to the rafters with a cute young crowd. Sounds like a recommendation to me.

8 Side Trips from Barcelona: Montserrat Monastery the Wine Country

MONTSERRAT MONASTERY

The vast **Montserrat Monastery** complex, 32 miles northwest of Barcelona, has a basilica with a venerated Black Virgin, a museum, hotels and restaurants, and an abundance of souvenir shops and food stalls.

The monastery is 2,400 feet up Montserrat. Its name refers to the serrated peaks of the massif, elongated formations that provided shelter for 11th-century Benedictine monks. One of the noted institutions of the monastery is the **Boys' Choir,** begun in the 13th century. Composed of 50 boys, the choir sings at 1 and 6:45pm. Near the entrance to the basilica is the subterranean **Museu de Montserrat** (☎ **93-835-02-51**), bringing together artworks once scattered around the complex, including gold and silver liturgical objects, archaeological artifacts from the Holy Land, and paintings of both the Renaissance and the 20th century. Admission is 300P ($2), and it's open Monday to Friday 10am to 6pm and Saturday, Sunday, and holidays 9:30am to 6pm. Numerous **funiculars** and **paths** lead to hermitages and shrines higher up the mountain.

The least expensive transport to Montserrat from Barcelona is the **train** from Plaça de Espanya, costing 1,560P ($10). It leaves five times daily for the Aeri de Montserrat station, where a **funicular** carries you to the mountaintop for another 750P ($5) round-trip.

THE WINE COUNTRY

The wineries in Sant Sadurní d'Anoia, 25 miles from Barcelona off the A2 *autopista* (toll highway), produce Catalunya's estimable *cavas.* **Freixenet** (☎ **93-891-07-00**) and **Codorniu** (☎ **93-891-01-25**) offer the best tours and tastings. Call for hours.

Trains run daily to Sant Sadurní d'Anoia (the station is right next to Freixenet) from the Estació Sants. The round-trip fare is 600P ($4). A **car** is all but essential to visit Codorniu, as taxis from the Sant Sadurní d'Anoia train station are unreliable.

That reservation applies as well to a visit to **Vilafranca del Penedés,** about 10 miles beyond Sant Sadurní d'Anoia. This is the center of the Penedés wine district, a rival to the better-known Rioja region in north-central Spain. It may be instructive to think of Penedés as Spain's Burgundy and of Rioja as its Bordeaux, for the wines they produce share characteristics with the ones made in those French wine-producing regions. The best-known winery is **Miguel Torres,** Carrer Comercio 22 (☎ **93-890-01-00**), which offers tours and tastings.

18

Sitges: A Eurobeach for Euroboys & You

Gay North American beach bums have long made Ibiza their stomping ground in Spain, thanks in large part to a strong publicity campaign by that island's powers-that-be. Yet despite Ibiza's obvious charms (see the following chapter), there are many good reasons to consider the Mediterranean resort of **Sitges** (*sit*-yes) your new Eurobeach spot.

In fact, Sitges boasts so many strong points they deserve their own list:

1. It's a fast 40-minute train ride from the center of Barcelona—allowing you to combine the most fabulous city in Spain with a seaside jaunt with ease.
2. The food in Sitges is miles better than that on Ibiza.
3. Sitges boasts a stronger selection of hotels, from moderately priced charmers to bargain-basement trolls.
4. The hordes of grotesque British and German tourists that plague Ibiza are far less in evidence here.
5. Sitges's beaches are much more accessible than those on Ibiza.
6. Best of all, Sitges is where the natives go. Ergo, it's a much better place to meet the hombre of your dreams.

Indeed, Sitges is generally viewed as the more elegant resort by well-heeled Barcelonans and foreigners alike, and I heartily agree. If you love sand, sea, and sex, you'll have a fine time, either on Ibiza or here; but for all the reasons above, I recommend Sitges in a heartbeat.

And culture vultures won't be disappointed—Sitges is a strong step above most tacky beach resorts. In fact, latter-day Renaissance man Santiago Rusinol almost single-handedly initiated the *modernismo* movement here, a trend toward the artsy that continued with the part-time residence of notables like Dalí, Picasso, and Lorca. And why not you? Buy a laptop, a sketch pad, and lots of condoms and join the Sitges fun!

1 Sitges Essentials

ARRIVING & DEPARTING

BY PLANE Sitges has no airport; the closest one is Barcelona's **El Prat.** A cab from there will cost about 4,500P ($30).

BY TRAIN It couldn't be easier. The regional RENFE trains run as frequently as four times an hour from Barcelona's Sants rail station or

Country & City Codes

The **country code** for Spain is **34.** The **city code** for Sitges is **93.** This code has now been incorporated into all phone numbers, so you must always dial it, whether you're outside Spain, within Spain but not in Sitges, or even within Sitges.

the Passeig de Gràcia subway stop and cost a very reasonable 350P ($2.35). These trains are everything America's should be: cheap, clean, and an absolute pleasure to ride. (They actually pipe in music—usually a Spanish composer like Rodrigo—which makes the 45-minute ride along the Mediterranean a fun excursion in and of itself.) For more information on schedules, call ☎ **93-490-0202.**

Once you get to the station in Sitges, I'd advise you to walk to your hotel; none is more than a 10-minute trek, and most are closer still. That's because the Sitges taxis are absolute rip-offs: I paid the equivalent of $5 for a 2-minute ride. Unless you have major baggage, ask for directions and use your feet.

BY CAR You have two choices: the coastal path, C-246; or a superhighway, A-7. The former is, of course, more scenic, but it's also a pain when all Barcelona is trying to escape the city for the weekend. In any case, since most of you will be taking the train from the city, this point is nearly moot. (Once you get to Sitges, you'll have no use for a car, so why bother?)

VISITOR INFORMATION

There's a **tourist office** at Sínis Morera 1 (☎ **93-811-76-30;** open June–Sept 15 daily 9am–5pm and Sept 16–May Mon–Fri 9am–2pm and 4–6:30pm, Sat 10am–1pm).

CITY LAYOUT & GETTING AROUND

Unlike Ibiza with its labyrinthine lanes, Sitges is supereasy to figure out. (It's a fraction of the former's size.) Basically, the **Passeig de la Ribera** (note Catalan names) is the main beachside drag, north of which lies the rest of the town. **Plaça Cap de la Vila,** a 5-minute walk uphill, is the main city square; 3 minutes east by foot is **Plaça Industria,** a hub of restaurants and street life. Due northeast of this (again, about a 3-minute walk) is **Sant Bonaventura,** the street that plays home to many (but not all) of Sitges's gay bars. In sum, you can master Sitges's layout in a couple of hours, another big plus in my book.

Taxis in Sitges are known to be unethical; in fact, they don't even have meters, so the final bill is whatever the driver wants to charge. Since Sitges is so tiny—you can traverse one end to the other in less than 15 minutes by foot (unless you walk really slowly)—I'd forget about cabs. With one caveat: if after a night on the town you feel a tad weary and don't feel like walking back to your hotel (or wherever) at the crack of dawn.

2 Pillow Talk

The hotel situation in Sitges gets an A for quality but a C for availability. In general, the lodgings here have far more charm than Ibiza's, though like on that island, they can be fully booked for months before the heavy season begins. If you do plan to visit Sitges, it's best to book early indeed.

Specifically gay-oriented hotels are noted as such below, but we're welcome virtually anywhere in town.

Hotel Celimar. Paseo de la Ribera 20, 08870 Sitges. ☎ **93-811-01-70.** Fax 93-811-04-03. 26 units. A/C TV TEL. Low season 10,425P ($68) double; medium season 13,550P ($90) double; high season 16,675P ($112) double. AE, DC, MC, V.

What constitutes each season? The management wouldn't commit, reserving the right to change their mind, but the above prices are a good general guide. From the outside, this sandstone art nouveau place has one of the most striking facades in Sitges; the inside furnishings are a bit IKEA-like but not intolerable. (To their credit, the original moldings have been kept intact.) What really makes this hotel is its seafront rooms, with gorgeous views and (in a few cases) balconies. The front desk folks were really nice too.

✪ **Hotel El Xalet.** Isla de Cuba 34, 08870 Sitges. ☎ **93-811-00-70.** 11 units. A/C TV TEL. 10,000P ($67) double; 14,000P ($96) suite. AE, DC, MC, V.

This is, quite simply, one of Spain's most gorgeous inns. It's housed in a modernist building dating from the beginning of the 20th century, with a combination art nouveau/Gothic style that'll take your breath away. In every nook and cranny, the original spirit has been preserved, from the small dining room (with huge nouveau windows and fireplace) to the guest rooms, where the Gothic influence is felt. All this, plus a lovely garden and pool and a very nice staff. For the *Architectural Digest* crowd, an absolute must.

✪ **Hotel Liberty.** Isla de Cuba 45, 08870 Sitges. ☎ **93-811-08-72.** Fax 93-894-16-62. 14 units. A/C TV TEL. 9,500P ($63) double. AE, DC, MC, V.

I wasn't real hopeful when the first thing I saw was a sign above the reception area boasting (in three languages), "We sell poppers." That, fortunately, was the only tacky thing about this hotel, which otherwise is a perfect gem. German Thomas Dillmann has set up a gay inn with super style, starting with the breakfast room (featuring one long table, the perfect way to meet other kindred spirits). The rooms themselves have high ceilings and stylish bedspreads and furnishings. There's even a nice terrace and a small bar. In all respects, the Liberty will set you free.

✪ **Hotel Romantic.** Sant Isidre 33, 08870 Sitges. ☎ **93-894-83-75.** Fax 93-894-81-67. 55 units. A/C TV TEL. 10,000–12,500P ($66–$84) double. AE, DC, MC, V.

For once, the name is fitting: This truly is a romantic hotel. Based in a series of former villas, it lies on one of Sitges's quietest streets. The rooms are medium sized but tastefully appointed, and the lobby and bar are absolutely exquisite, with a gorgeous colonial decor and ambience. Though it's not a gay hotel per se, upscale gays have long made this their premier choice. A stunning place to stay.

Hotel San Juan. Juan Tarrida 16, 08870 Sitges. ☎ **93-894-13-50.** 25 units. TEL. 6,000P ($40) double. V.

This may well be the most hideous hotel in all Spain, though devotees of late-1950s sitcoms will want to gasp at its decor. (The graphic artists among you will also shriek at the brochure, which hasn't changed in 35 years.) What this place does have going for it is a great location—a few feet from several bars and right next to a (get this) miniature golf park. If there are any hotels in Tirana, Albania, this is exactly what they look like. Location, location, location.

Hotel Tryp. Port Alegre 53, 08870 Sitges. ☎ **93-894-86-74.** Fax 93-894-0430. 52 units. A/C MINIBAR TV TEL. 13,250P ($88) double. Reductions 25% in low season. AE, DC, MC, V.

Part of the international Tryp chain, this is the place for travelers who don't want to get away from the office even while they're supposed to be on the beach: There's a computer replete with fax and e-mail for guests' use at a small charge. The decor is standard upscale Holiday Inn, but at least done in inoffensive earth tones. Located on the San Sebastian part of the beach, this hotel is a just a bit off the beaten path, but if you want four-star luxury, then trip over to the Tryp.

✪ **Madison Bahia.** Palleladas 31–33, 08870 Sitges. ☎ and fax **93-894-00-12.** 25 units. TV TEL. 9,500P ($63) double. AE, DC, MC, V.

This is a supercute centrally located hotel with a sizable gay clientele and staff. There's a small bar to one side of the lobby and a cute breakfast terrace (overlooking the miniature golf course I mentioned in the Hotel San Juan review) out back. The rooms are small and bland but clean. If he's there, say hi to the gorgeous desk clerk I beleaguered with stupid questions for half an hour (I bet *he's* sizable too).

Sitges Park Hotel. Jesus 16, 08870 Sitges. ☎ **93-894-02-50.** 85 units. TEL. Apr–May and Oct 4, 250P ($28) double; June and Sept 5,200P ($35) double; July–Aug 6,250P ($42) double. AE, DC, MC, V.

I couldn't resist this hotel's exterior, fronted by a gorgeous turret and palm trees. Inside, the story is much less exciting, with rooms that are fairly large yet utilitarian (even ugly) in decor. There's a nice-sized pool, however. If somewhat lacking in charm, this is still a good cheap choice.

3 Whet Your Appetite

As Sitges is a casual beach town, don't expect the ubertrendy restaurants you'd find in Madrid or Barcelona. What you will find is a nice assortment of places—serving mostly Spanish fare (fine by me) and a smattering of continental cuisine.

You'd be right in assuming that the best restaurants are geared toward fish, and I've given you the top choices below. Frankly, it's hard to get a bad meal in Sitges, even at the touristy joints right on the beach, and I've never had a paella I didn't like.

Els 4 Gats. Sant Pau 13. ☎ **93-894-19-15.** Reservations recommended. Main courses 3,000–4,500P ($20–$30); *menú del día* 2,200P ($15). AE, DC, MC, V. Wed–Mon 1–3:30pm and 8:30–11pm. Closed Nov–Mar. CATALAN.

When it opened in the early 1960s as a bar/cafe, El 4 Gats adopted the name of one of Barcelona's historic cafes, a favorite of Picasso. It serves *cocina del mercado,* based on whatever is fresh that day in the market. You can enjoy fresh grilled fish, garlic soup, lamb cutlets with local herbs, roast chicken in wine sauce, and veal kidneys in sherry sauce. On a side street near the sea, the restaurant is a few steps from the beachfront Passeig de la Ribera.

✪ **El Velero.** Passeig de la Ribera 38. ☎ **93-894-20-51.** Main courses 1,650–3,950P ($11–$26). AE, DC, MC, V. Daily noon-2:30pm and 8:30-midnight. SEAFOOD.

By common consensus, this is the best restaurant in Sitges and has been for years. There's an enclosed terrace, but the traditional Spanish decor in the main restaurant is much more appealing. The monkfish medallions with garlic mayonnaise and foie gras are quite good, ditto the crêpes Catalans and everything else. It's underpopulated at lunch and more popular at dinner.

✪ **La Torreta.** Port Alegre 17. ☎ **93-894-52-53.** www.interplanet.es/latorreta. Main courses 950–3,600P ($6–$24). AE, DC, MC, V. Daily 1–4pm and 7:30–11pm. SEAFOOD/SPANISH.

This restaurant features a traditional Spanish decor of white lace and dark wood, with a welcome, slightly updated touch I like. The food is even better, with the *gambas*

Cafe Culture

✪ **La Estrella Sitges,** Major 52 (☎ **93-894-00-79**), is a lovely old-time pastry shop that invites lingering—and longing, for the mouth-watering wares showcased here. I couldn't tell you what any of this is called, but you won't need to know; just ponder, point, and pig out. Um, um good!

You'll want to loiter for hours at the large, airy **Mont Roig Cafe,** Marques de Monteir 11–13 (☎ **93-894-84-39**). The Mont Roig attracts a large gay crowd, especially during late afternoons, when everyone spills out onto the terrace in front of this woodsy cafe. The bulletin board is also a great place to find a flat, a friend, or (ahem) a massage. Nice!

villerone a shrimp dish to remember. The service is impeccable. Not cheap, but worth every cent. All this, plus a Web site too!

Lizarran. Mayor 22. ☎ **93-894-73-70.** Main courses 875–1,600P ($6–$11). AE, DC, MC, V. Daily 1–4pm and 8–11pm. BASQUE.

This traditionally decorated taberna has a mainly Basque menu, with influences from the rest of Spain. The thing to get is the *cordero asada* (roast lamb, instead of the more usual pork), and *bacalao* (fried balls of cod), well-nigh the national fish of Spain.

Porta. Plaza de España. ☎ **93-894-17-73.** Fixed-price menus 1,100P and 1,600P ($7 and $22). AE, DC, MC, V. SEAFOOD.

On the north side of town, this handsome place boasts traditional Spanish lace and wood tables and a less touristy crowd than most. The fish, both sea- and freshwater, are the stars, and everything looked mighty good. I, as usual, couldn't get away from the paella, and the salt cod version presented here is both novel and delish. Quite nice.

Restaurante El Pozo. San Pablo 3. ☎ **93-894-11-04.** Fixed-price menu 950P ($7). No credit cards. CONTINENTAL.

This functional little restaurant has prix-fixe menus that change every day. Based on my own experience, I'd be hard-pressed to recommend anything but the paella, which is out of this world. There are also continental entries, like scampi, crêpes Suzette, and the scary-sounding banana flambée (you want your banana flambéed?). For the price, it can't be beat.

4 Exploring Sitges

Unwittingly, Sitges's fame as a gay resort started when writer **Gabriel García Lorca** (arguably, Spain's best-known author of the 20th century) took up residence here part-time. He was soon followed by a gaggle of artsy folk who immediately recognized Sitges's tolerant attitude and abundant natural charms. While I'm not sure what any of them would make of poppers and backrooms, it can be said that these early pioneers were the forerunners of Sitges's current roaring gay scene.

But it was Catalan artist **Santiago Rusinol** who's most associated with Sitges's aesthetic scene. Though you should visit the Museu Cau Ferrat, his home and a de facto arts center for many years (see below), most gay tourists remain in blissful ignorance of the town's cultural underpinnings. You may choose to do the same; merely by way of explanation, you should know that it's Sitges's place as a bastion of fine arts that in part paved the way for its place as a slightly snootier resort than others on the Mediterranean coast.

Indeed, the mere fact that Sitges is small allows it to retain its aura of exclusivity over Ibiza, Majorca, and other Spanish resorts. Happily, this higher-echelon crowd also means a greater concentration of fine restaurants and a generally less *National Lampoon Vacation* feel than either of the former haunts. When Spaniards mention Sitges, it's understood they're talking about a place that much more resembles Martha's Vineyard than Myrtle Beach.

In fact, the town's cultural reputation is based not merely on history but also on current events. These include such wonderful programs as the **Sitges International Film Festival of Catalonia** and international theater, jazz, and tango festivals as well.

But don't start getting scared; I'm not going to send you on a weeklong cultural field trip while the other boyz are basking on the beach. You really should, however, check out the following two sites, next door to each other:

✪ **Museu Cau Ferrat.** Fonollar. ☎ **93-894-03-64.** Admission 400P ($2.70). June 21–Sept 11 Tues–Sat 9:30am–2pm and 4–8pm, Sun 9:30am–2pm; Sept 12–June 20 Tues–Fri 9:30am–1pm and 4–6pm, Sat 9:30am–2pm and 4–8pm, Sun 9:30am–2pm.

Famed painter Santiago Rusiñol's home and studio is now open as a tribute to the man and his taste. In addition to his own paintings (done in the early part of the 20th century), you'll find a few works by Picasso, El Greco, and others. The structure, built in the 1600s, is worth a visit for its architecture alone.

Museu Maricel. Fonallar. ☎ **93-894-03-64.** Admission 300P ($2). June 21–Sept 11 Tues–Sat 9:30am–2pm and 4–8pm; Sept 12–June 20 Tues–Fri 9:30am–2pm and 4–6pm, Sat 9:30am–2pm and 4–8pm, Sun 9:30am–2pm.

This museum resembles something you'd find in Carcassonne (that's southwestern France, ya know), and it has been restored with great grace. In fact, the structure is more interesting than the Gothic paintings, many of which will be of more interest to art history Ph.Ds than anyone else. Some Catalan ceramics and objets d'art are also on display.

BOYS ON THE BEACH

Though gays are welcome everywhere, the main gay beach is the **Platjes del Mort (Beach of the Dead)**—a misnomer, since this small area is very much alive at all hours. Take the Passeig de la Ribera westward and look for the bronzing boys. Alternately, you can just follow the signs; it's about a 10-minute walk from Plaça Industria on the west end of town, or you can wait for one of the free shuttle buses that cruise along the beach.

In addition to the obvious heavy cruising, you'll find action in the wooded areas as the sun begins to set, a scene that continues well into the wee hours. In Madrid, police intervention is well known, but the Catalan police are generally permissive and arrests uncommon. (Still, I wonder, how does a subpopulation that (at least in part) insists on having promiscuous sex outdoors look to society at large, in either Spain or the United States? Just a thought.)

WORKING UP A SWEAT

Sitges doesn't have a gay gym, but I did find one ultramodern workout joint, **Fitness Gran Sitges** (get the rhyme?), Aiguadolc (☎ **93-811-08-11**). While not the most central, this facility offers a gym, a pool, aerobics, massage, and other programs for the fitness fanatic. There's also a host of esoteric (and usually pointless) French-style facials and slimming cream treatments. Ooh-la-la!

5 Hitting the Stores

Taken collectively, **Carrer Mayor** and **Carrer Parellades,** Sitges's two main shopping streets, are known as the White Boulevard. As Robin Leach would say, I don't know why, and neither does anyone else. Anyway, while no one comes to Sitges to shop, there are a few cute stores, all of which you can see in half an hour. The following boutiques deserve special mention.

As gay clothing stores go, **Dive Boutique,** Sant Francesc 33 (☎ **93-811-01-50**), is pretty cool; there's more than just T-shirts with stupid sayings. While the clothing is still more Raymond Dragon than Jean Paul Gaultier, it's a much better shopping choice than the predictable **Jazz,** Bonaire 20 (☎ **93-894-99-63**). This is a standard gay clothing boutique, with the kind of merchandise you'd see in Sitges or St. Paul: stretch tops, clingy French underwear, and tacky accessories.

Mekzone, Sant Pau 37 (no phone), is a leading gay emporium selling the usual suspects: handcuffs, latex tops, freedom caps, and rings for that special finger (yawn). One cool item: a very mod Beatles tie with the Fab Four's faces etched thereon. Beware, however, the weird French owner, who got really paranoid when I told him I was putting his shop in a guide.

6 In the Heat of the Night

You don't have to be a rocket scientist to find the clubs in Sitges—just follow the crowds. You should know the lion's share of the clubs don't open until May and close for the year at the end of October. So if you choose to come off-season (not bloody likely, but a possibility for those looking for a quiet retreat), know that you may well be crying in your coffee (or Kahlua) alone.

GAY BARS

✪ **Mediterráneo,** Sant Bonaventura 6 (no phone), is hands-down Sitges's number-one bar, at least until the disco action starts raging at Trailer later on. The modern decor boasts a pool parlor, dance floor, terrace, and bar; Mediterraneo is probably the place (other than the bushes) where you'll be spending the most time. No can miss.

Azul, Sant Bonavenuta 10 (no phone), open about 6pm and remains open all year long. It's a good place to start the evening before moving on to greener pastures. **Bourbon's,** Sant Bonaventura 9 (☎ **93-894-33-47**), has an interesting race-car decor, with tires strung throughout, and a cool curvy bar. I couldn't quite find a crowd there, but it's supposed to pick up around midnight during high season. Anyway, it's right on the gayest street in town, so it's certainly worth a look.

El Candil, Carreta 9 (☎ **93-894-78-36**), may be the oldest in Sitges; certainly, it's been around longer than anyone can remember. It's dark and delightfully dingy, with a postage-stamp-sized dance floor when the mood hits. It's a bit off the beaten path (though not by much), yet a definite local legend you must do at least once.

Beginning around midnight, **Ovlas,** Paseo Vilafraca 3 (☎ **93-894-73-20**), is a convivial bar that slants toward the young side. The music tends to be quite happening, sometimes even veering away from the standard disco toward alternative sounds. A bit off the beaten path but worth the small schlep.

Everyone calls **El Horno,** Joan Tarrida 6 (☎ **93-894-09-09**), a leather bar, though that's a bit like calling Chrissie Hynde a dominatrix. In fact, it's an everything-goes kind of place, with a slant toward older guys. The decor is fairly medieval and the upstairs dark room appropriately dreary—or maybe it was I who cleared the place out.

XXL, Joan Tarrida 7 (no phone), is a new entry on the Sitges scene, owned by the same dour Dutchman who owns El Horno (above). It has been a bit slow to draw a solid clientele, though I can't imagine why—it's sleek and modern and plays the best new music in town. (I predict by the time you read this it'll be a well-deserved hit.)

Looking for a brew or a Baccardi in the late afternoon (after 5pm)? Try the terrace at **Parrot's,** Plaça Industria 2 (no phone), on one of Sitges's main squares, where you can watch the boyz go by. Later in the evening, the crowd gets a bit sloppier and sorrier.

A DANCE CLUB

The hottest big dance club in town, ✪ **Trailer,** Espalter 11 (no phone; admission 1,500P/$10, including one drink), is packed every weekend, when it's open till the hours too wee to count. All the international pretty boys are here, though this is quite a firetrap by anyone's standards. Take my advice and keep an eye on the door.

A SAUNA

Sauna Sitges, Espalter 11 (☎ **93-894-28-63**), is small but serviceable and very clean; it's deserted during off-season and packed to the gills when the season's on, especially during the late afternoon.

19

Ibiza: Madness, Money & Music

Ask 10 people what they think about **Ibiza** and you'll get as many different points of view. The contradictions are striking: *tired, fabulous, expensive, cheap, overdeveloped, rustic:* The list goes on and on.

As with most things, the truth lies somewhere in between. Yes, Ibiza suffers from too many Brits and Germans, especially from the lower end of the middle class; and, yes, the island can be touristy and cheap. But when all is said and done, it's hard to deny Ibiza's many charms. Chief among these are a gorgeous (even thrilling) coastline, endless beaches, and a historic walled city whose buttressed walls help keep the downscale tourists at bay. And finally, there's Ibiza's well-deserved reputation as a not-so-pristine playground for gay men from Europe and around the world—the latter reason enough why you should consider getting in on the action yourself. (There's a small lesbian contingent here, but it's a quiet one.)

Ibiza as fun central is hardly a new idea. Indeed, the isle served as a kind of Mediterranean crash pad for hippies and freaks in the 1960s; 10 years later, it attracted disco burnouts who'd put one too many spoons up their nose. Along the way, Ibiza earned a reputation as an artist's community—more a euphemism for dropouts from life than budding Picassos, from all evidence available to the naked eye. (If Provincetown has actually served as a writer's Eden since the days of O'Neill, that'd be equally difficult to prove today.)

So don't go as I did, expecting to be enfolded in the arms of an artistic community of note. (If anything, you'll run screaming from the bad modern art in the overpriced galleries.) Instead, just let yourself fall under the spell of the heady atavistic charms of an island that leaves the cares of the outside world very far away—and maybe under that of some stranger who's there to do the very same thing.

1 Ibiza Essentials

ARRIVING & DEPARTING

BY PLANE **Aviaca,** a regional subsidiary of Iberia, offers flights from major Spanish cities to Ibiza's **Es Cordola Airport,** 3½ miles from the town center; a cab from the airport costs 1,500P ($10). During high season, there are an average of four flights each from Madrid and Palma de Majorca and five from Barcelona; but a representative told me that flights are often added to meet consumer demand. You can ring Iberia locally at ☎ **971-31-41-73;** or better yet, make reservations before you leave home.

In either case, know that flights to/from the island are usually very full. I made reservations from the States 3 weeks before traveling and had to accept circuitous flights with stopovers to accommodate my schedule. Before even contemplating a visit to Ibiza, make sure you can get air reservations.

FERRY Ferries run by **Transmediterránea** are available on a nearly daily basis from Valencia and Barcelona and one per week from Majorca. Call ☎ **971-31-41-73** for details, or you can buy a ticket at any travel agency. While this is a cheaper alternative to flying, it's decidedly not for the impatient or faint of heart.

VISITOR INFORMATION

The Ibiza tourist office, **Oficina Insular d'Informacio Turistica,** is on the main square of the modern city at Vara de Rey 13 (☎ **971-30-19-00;** open Mon–Fri 9:30am–1:30pm and 5–7 pm, Sat 10:30am–1pm). Truth be told, the staff does little more than hand out brochures, so don't expect much more help or advice than that.

CITY LAYOUT

The first thing you should know is that Ibiza the island is far more than Ibiza the city (Cuidad de Idiza) . . . but for the gay traveler, not much more. If you have rich friends with villas (and, of course, a car) elsewhere on the isle, you may get another view, but for all intents and purposes your trip will be limited to the city itself.

The second thing to know is that Ibiza is written Eivissa in the local Catalan dialect spoken here. Don't worry—everyone knows Spanish, and English is spoken widely as well.

How to get acquainted with **Cuidad de Ibiza?** First, think of the **Vara de Rey,** the elongated central square, as the middle of town. Everything west of this constitutes the modern city, an expanse of the kind of undistinguished buildings you'd find in any Mediterranean resort. The southernmost part of this 1-square-mile area is the **Playa de Figueretas,** whose beachfront promenade, the **Paseo Maritimo,** is a must for people-watching and cafe-sitting.

Due east of the Vara de Rey is **Sa Penya,** the older part of the city, which lies just north of the port. Here you'll find shopping both up- and downscale, a plethora of restaurants, and **Calle de la Virgen,** the main gay drag. (More on this later.) This is actually the lower-lying part of the **D'Alt Vila (Old Town),** which begins in earnest after you enter the castle and its fortressed walls. Caution to heavy smokers: This is a fierce uphill trek best left for early-morning hours. Anyway, once you get there, you'll find the D'Alt Vila charming and totally worth the hike. This is, after all, the real Ibiza, the part of town counterculturists have been flocking to for years. In one sweet visual sweep of these whitewashed streets, you may see short-shorn gay German tourists, an English junkie bird (heroin is a big problem on the island, as is AIDS), and local kids kicking a can on cobbled lanes. This is undoubtedly the closest to what Ibiza was back in the 1960s, and it still offers a kind of louche charm.

The D'Alt Vila is peppered with several squares, but these are actually no more than tiny confluences of tinier streets; you can walk right by one without knowing you were actually in it. The largest square is **Plaza de Vila,** which you reach after entering D'Alt Vila via the Cathedral. On sunny days (that is, always during summer), this is a great place to enjoy a leisurely lunch or late-afternoon drink. Finally, there are a couple of gay bars in the D'Alt Vila, though they tend to attract people living long-term in this part of town; visitors tend to stay on the Carrer de la Virgen in the lower part of town (that schlep, remember).

Country & City Codes

The **country code** for Spain is **34.** The **city code** for Ibiza is **971.** This code has now been incorporated into all phone numbers, so you must always dial it, whether you're outside Spain, within Spain but not in Ibiza, or even within Ibiza.

GETTING AROUND

Virtually all Ibiza town is doable as a walking tour. If, however, you end up staying in Las Figueretas, you may elect to cab it into town at night. (This is a 25-minute walk, all on flat ground, but if you've already done it a couple of times during the day, you may wish to spend $4 on a taxi when you're prowling at night.) In any case, there's no reason to rent a car, unless you plan to tool around the island one day—not a bad thing to do if you're here for an extended stay but hardly necessary for those in Ibiza for the very short term. Both Hertz and Avis have offices at the airport.

2 Pillow Talk

I was actually disappointed by the general quality of lodgings on Ibiza; there are many more modern monstrosities than quaint old hotels. (This is especially true given the exceptional places to stay offered in the rather more elegant town of Sitges.)

That noted, there are indeed a couple of winners and even a gay hotel of note. *Note:* For the locations of the hotels below, see the Ibiza map on pp. 662–663.

✪ **El Corsario.** Ponent 5, 07800 Ibiza. ☎ **971-39-19-53.** 15 units. TV TEL. 11,000–13,000P ($73–$87) double; 22,000P ($147) suite. AE, DC, MC, V. Closed Nov–Mar.

Dating from the 16th century, this hotel is up a steep set of stairs, which helps complete the back-in-time feel. The rooms are not luxe, but the nearly monastical quality is rather nice. There are stunning ocean views, plus a terrific terrace for breakfast or dinner (see "Whet Your Appetite" below).

✪ **La Ventana.** Sa Carossa 13, 07800 Ibiza. ☎ **971-390-857.** Fax 971-390-14. 14 units. A/C TV TEL. 10,000P ($66) double. Rates reduced 40% in winter. AE, DC, MC, V.

I'll go out on a limb and say this is the best choice in town. You'll fall in love with this whitewashed wonder as soon as you lay eyes on it, and the romance will continue as you step through its doors. Just behind the medieval walls of Old Town, located in a garden square, this famed hotel beckons with canopied beds, an outdoor terrace, and exquisite service. A head-clearing stay here off-season may be the best new lease on life you ever had. A resounding A+!

Los Molinos. Ramon Muntaner 60, 07800 Ibiza. ☎ **971/30-22-50.** Fax 971-30-25-04. 154 units. A/C MINIBAR TV TEL. 17,000P ($113) double. AE, DC, MC, V.

Los Molinos has long been the only semiluxe choice in Las Figueretas and should be yours if you need all the modern amenities. Frankly, though, despite the seafront views and its own beach and pool, this hotel is fairly lacking in charm; I'd recommend it only if my other choices are already booked.

Marigna. Al Sabini 18, 07800 Ibiza. ☎ **971-30-49-12.** Fax 971-30-46-89. 44 units. TEL. 6,000P–14,000P ($37–$67) double. AE, DC, MC, V.

This place boasts that it's the largest gay hotel in Europe, and that may well be right. Though it's all the way over in Las Figueretas, this is a highly recommended hotel for the gay traveler. The rooms are spotless and nicely presented, though I'm not sure I agree with the brochure that bills them as tastefully furnished—the competing pastels

Ciudad de Ibiza

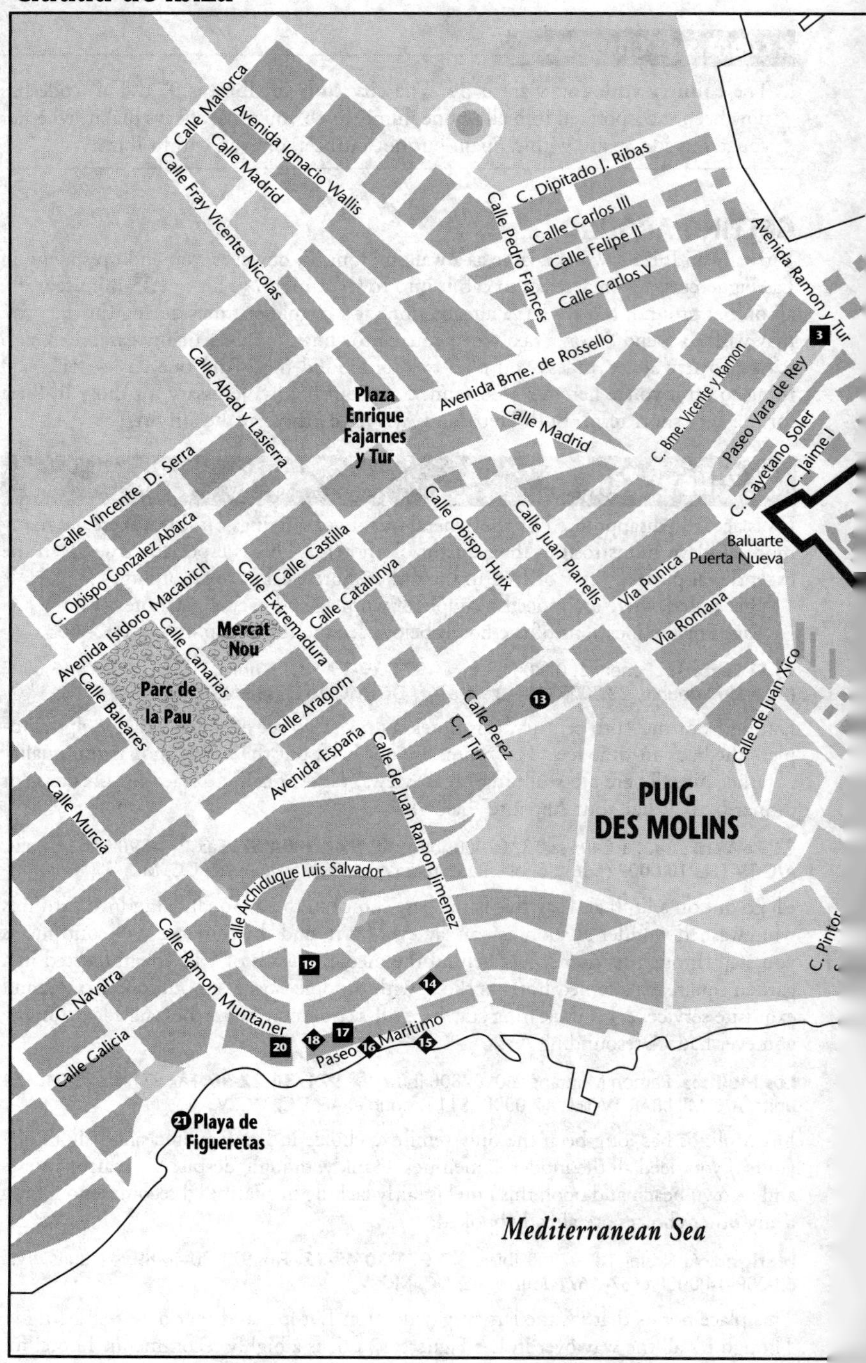

Calle Mallorca
Avenida Ignacio Wallis
Calle Madrid
Calle Fray Vicente Nicolas
C. Dipitado J. Ribas
Calle Pedro Frances
Calle Carlos III
Calle Felipe II
Calle Carlos V
Avenida Ramon y Tur
3
Avenida Bme. de Rossello
Calle Abad y Lasierra
Plaza
Enrique
Fajarnes
y Tur
Calle Madrid
C. Bme. Vicente y Ramon
Paseo Vara de Rey
C. Cayetano Soler
C. Jaime I
Calle Vincente D. Serra
C. Obispo Gonzalez Abarca
Calle Castilla
Calle Obispo Huix
Calle Juan Planells
Baluarte
Puerta Nueva
Via Punica
Via Romana
Avenida Isidoro Macabich
Calle Extremadura
Calle Catalunya
Mercat
Nou
Calle Canarias
Calle Baleares
Parc de
la Pau
Calle Aragorn
13
Calle Perez
C. I Tur
Calle de Juan Xico
Avenida España
Calle de Juan Ramon Jimenez
PUIG
DES MOLINS
Calle Murcia
Calle Archiduque Luis Salvador
C. Pintor
Calle Ramon Muntaner
19
14
C. Navarra
17
18
20
16
15
Paseo Maritimo
Calle Galicia
21 Playa de
Figueretas
Mediterranean Sea

ACCOMMODATIONS
El Corsario 10
El Palacio 7
La Ventana 2
Los Molinos 20
Marigna 19
Montesol 3
Nautico Ebeso 17
Navila Aparthotel 12
Torre del Canoningo 6
DINING
El Corsario 10
El Olivo 5
El Portalon 9
El Prinicipe 15
Gemini's 16
Il Pavone 1
La Oliva 4
Monroe's 18
Romagna Mia 14
ATTRACTIONS
Museu D'Alt Vila 11
Museu Puig d'Es Molins 13
Playa de Figueretas 21
Plaza Desamparados 8
La Marina
Plaza de A. Riquer
C. Gallo
Plaza de sa Riba
C. de la Virgen
C. la Cruz
C. J. Verdera
C. del Retiro
C. Vista Alegre
Plaza de la Constitucion
C. Obispo Cardona
Alfonso XII
Baluarte de Santa Lucia
Baluarte de San Juan
C. Gral. Balanzant
Plaza de Vila
C. Sant Carles
Plaza Desamparados
C. Pere Tur
Plaza de España
C. San Luis
D'ALT VILA
C. Sta. Maria
C. Joan Roman
Plaza Catedral
Baluarte de Santa Tecla
C. Obispo Torres
C. Soledad
Castillo
Baluarte de San Jaime
Baluarte de San Bernardo
Baluarte de San Jorge
ES SOTO
Ibiza
Portinatx
Puerto de San Miguel
Cala San Vicente
San Miguel
733
San Antonio Abad
Santa Eulalia del Rio
Port del Torrent
731
San Rafael
Ciudad de Ibiza
Talamanca
San Jose
Figueretas

An Accommodations Tip

Freedom Travel, co-owned by Mel and Phil of Monroe's (see "Whet Your Appetite" below), offers bookings at the Sud Apartments, a modern facility where rooms can be shared by up to three. For more information on this special deal, find them on the Internet at **http://freedom.co.uk.** Depending on the time of year, rates range from 3,970P ($26) to 8,670P ($58) per night.

Another electronic hotel shop is **Galeria Travel** (on their business card, the *l* is in the shape of a lambda, if you care); their not-quite-English slogan reads, "For an unbeatable choice of beds anywhere on the gay paradise island of Ibizia . . . we get you into bed, anywhere you want to be on the sun-drenched island of Ibiza." Anyway, contact them at **galeria.travel@virgin.net.** (Just don't tell Richard Branson.)

of the bedspreads and curtains look like something out of the final showcase on *The Price Is Right.* The breakfast room is beautiful and the buffet copious, however. Marigna also offers two bars, one of which is geared toward a leather crowd. (Is the S&M crowd into hysterical flowered prints?) One drawback: The German owner is intensely dour, but that shouldn't stop you from enjoying this excellent hotel.

Montesol. Vara de Rey 2, 07800 Ibiza. ☎ **971-31-01-61.** 55 units. TEL. 5,000P ($33) double. MC, V.

This is smack dab in the center of town, right on the main square. The Montesol cafe is the main meeting place for residents and tourists alike, thus this can be a rather noisy place. Moreover, the rooms are fairly bare bones—monastical even—but for its price and location, this well-known hotel can't be beat.

Nautico Ebeso. Ramon Muntaner 44, 07800 Ibiza. ☎ **971-30-23-00.** Fax 971-30-23-04. 127 units. A/C MINIBAR TV TEL. High season 11,000 ($73) double; low season 5,400P ($36) double. DC, MC, V.

Of all Las Figueretas' modern hotels, this one has the most charm, with a lobby that seeks to re-create the whitewashed medieval feel of the D'Alt Vilta. The contemporary rooms are unobjectionable (if unremarkable) and at least done in nautical hues. There's a great pool, and the hotel has its own beachfront property. Drawback: Scary activities like (egad!) limbo dancing involving ultrapasty Northern European guests. Don't say you weren't warned.

Navila Aparthotel. Luis 1, 07800 Ibiza. ☎ **971-30-08-52.** Fax 971-30-52-05. 12 units. A/C TV TEL. 18,000P ($120) double. MC, V.

This modern edifice in the marina, a stone's throw from the gay bars, is short on charm but long on convenience, featuring cooking facilities for those bent on longer-term stays or wishing to do business while on vacation. The staff is courteous too.

Torre del Canoningo. Mayor 8, 07800 Ibiza. ☎ **971-30-38-84.** 7 units. TEL. 6,000P ($40) apt. Apr–Oct only. MC, V.

If you've always dreamed of living in a Middle Ages–era domicile, here's your chance. The apartments in this reconverted tower house up to six people each, making this quite a steal. Happily, the baths date from this century.

3 Whet Your Appetite

If you have but a few days on Ibiza, you should take every meal possible at one of the old town's outdoor cafes. If you, lucky one, are spending more time on the island, try one of the places below.

Note: For the locations of the restaurants below, see the "Ibiza" map on pp. 662–663.

✪ **El Corsario.** Ponent 5. ☎ **971-30-12-48.** Reservations recommended. Main courses 1,600– 3,200P ($11–$21). MC, V. Daily 8–11pm. Closed Nov–Apr. CONTINENTAL.

This is the restaurant associated with the eponymous hotel, and it's one of the best-known eateries on the island—with good reason. The cooking is simple, combining Ibizan fare with continental preparations. Best of all is the medieval feel of this Old Town place and its seaside views. Atmospheric indeed.

✪ **El Olivo.** Plaça de la Vila. ☎ **971-30-06-80.** V. Main courses 600–2,300P ($4–$15). AE, DC, MC, V. Daily 1–4pm and 8pm–midnight. MEDITERRANEAN/SEAFOOD.

Right on one of the D'Alt Vila's main squares, the whitewashed El Olivo offers one of the prettiest outdoor settings in all Ibiza—with sumptuous food, notably fish (try the salt cod and paella), to match. There's also a distinct gay presence at both dinner and lunch. A great way to forget all your cares high above Ibiza town.

El Portalon. Plaça dels Desamparats 1–2. ☎ **971-30-08-52.** Main courses 700–2,400P ($5–$16). AE, DC, MC, V. Daily 8pm–1am. SPANISH/SEAFOOD.

The decor here reflects the whitewashed look of the Old City in which this respected restaurant is located; El Portalon is a favorite of well-heeled tourists and gays alike. Classic Spanish cooking is the thing here, which means you'll find the paella—in several varieties, featuring both shellfish and freshwater fish—of your dreams.

El Prinicipe. Passeig Maritimo. ☎ **971-30-19-14.** Main courses 550–2,400P ($4–$16). AE, DC, MC, V. Daily noon–3pm and 8pm–midnight. ITALIAN/SEAFOOD.

This is one of the promenade's prettiest terrace restaurants, and one of the most romantic. It attracts equal numbers of package tourists and gays from the Hotel Marigna up the street; all parties concerned are too busy enjoying the food and atmosphere to care much about the other tables. Avoid the prix-fixe menu, which is cheap but rather less tasty that the à la carte choices.

Gemini's. Paseo Maritimo. ☎ **971-392-565.** Main courses 500–1,100P ($3–$7). MC, V. Daily 11am–midnight. ENGLISH.

Britons Neil and Ellis have been welcoming tourists gay and otherwise to their beach-front cafe for years with a warm and welcoming attitude (if less than spectacular fare—sandwiches, eggs, and undistinguished daily specials). This is the most gay-friendly terrace in Las Figueretas and thus a lovely place to while away an hour or two and watch the world walk by.

✪ **Il Pavone.** Virgen 27. ☎ **971-313-555.** Main courses 750–2,200P ($5–$15). AE, DC, MC, V. Daily 8pm–midnight. ITALIAN/CONTINENTAL.

It goes without saying that this restaurant, on the same street as most of the gay bars, attracts les boys; what's even better is that the Italian food is absolutely fabulous. The decor is a mix between Capri and Ibiza, but there's a lot more to look at than the furnishings; the crowd and your plate are good places to start. In addition to typical Italian dishes, you'll find fresh fish and continental specialties. Il Pavone is a must!

La Oliva. Santa Cruz 2. ☎ **971-30-57-52.** Main courses 700–2,300P ($5–$15). AE, DC, MC, V. Daily 7:30pm–1am. MEDITERRANEAN/SEAFOOD.

By consensus, this is one of Ibiza's very best restaurants and also one of its prettiest. The fare is updated Mediterranean, with novel touches on *bacalao* (cod) and other regional fish specialties. Everything looked divine, and the service is the best in town. Highly recommended indeed.

✪ **Monroe's.** Ramon Muntaner 33. ☎ and fax **971-392-541.** Main courses 550–1,100P ($4– $7). MC, V. Daily 9:30am–3am. BRITISH.

A bar? A restaurant? A cafe? Just call Monroe's, decorated from head to toe with Marilyn memorabilia, an institution and leave it at that. Lesbian couple Mel and Phil Howell have been weaving magic for 6 years, playing hostess to unsuspecting Brit tourists and gay friends alike. The British food—beans on toast, pasties, and (on Sunday) roast beef with Yorkshire pudding—is first-rate, and the entertainment (bingo, drag shows, quizzes) a hoot. This is truly a bar where after 10 minutes everybody *will* know your name.

✪ **Romagna Mia.** Ramon Muntaner 28. ☎ **971-30-59-42.** Main courses 600–2,200P ($4–$15). AE, DC, MC, V. Daily 1–4pm and 8–11pm. ITALIAN/SEAFOOD.

For my money, this is the best restaurant on Ibiza. An Italian family has set up shop at this beachside restaurant boasting three rooms—one a terrace overlooking the ocean, and all preserving a distinct Ibizan feel. After one bite of these delicious recipes (including *cioppino,* a seafood stew, and fresh grilled fish specialties), you won't care where you are. Simply superb.

4 Exploring Ibiza

Yes, there's a couple of tiny museums, a historic old town, and a few good shopping streets. But let's face it: Those aren't the reasons you're coming to Ibiza. Fun and sun are the name of the game. The sun is obvious, but what constitutes the fun on this sexy Spanish isle?

The devil-may-care attitude is key. Though Ibiza may be a tad less wild today than in its counterculture days in the 1960s, it's still a place where you know you're a million miles (at least in spirit) from home. Caution can definitely be thrown to the wind.

Relax and enjoy Ibiza's great restaurants, friendly visitors from around the world, and continued place as a gay hot spot. Even if you're not by nature a bar hag, you'll find it hard to resist the temptation of spending a warm night tripping down the D'Alt Vila's cobblestone streets—and hopefully into the arms of someone special.

Anyway, when all is said and done, everyone has to do Ibiza at least once. See you there?

BOYS ON THE BEACH

The easy part is telling you the name of this beach: **La Playa Es Cavallet.** The hard part is telling you how to get there—but here goes. At the Salinas bus stop, cross the road, walk through the bars, and enter a large parking lot through the gap in the fence at the end along the track (with the Mediterranean to your left). When you see a group of houses, turn left after the last one (you'll see a stone path), continue straight, walk through the bushes—and voilà! You've arrived at the nude (if you want) gay beach. It hardly needs to be said that, given the rather secluded aspect of this beach, action is rampant and cruising almost de rigueur.

SOME SIGHTS TO SEE

The first thing you should do, after you've settled in, is to amble through the medieval **D'Alt Vila** and soak in the atmosphere. Don't even try to make sense of the teeny streets, some of which are no more than 100 feet long. (The map handed out by the tourist office was obviously designed by someone in an altered state.) Just wander about, get lost (this area is pretty small), and eventually make your way back to the **Gothic castle (Castillo)** and head downhill. Like Gaudí's Sagrada Familia in Barcelona, the castle is more of a shell than an intact building, but it's rather remarkable that after 500 years it's standing at all. And it provides a great signpost for those of us with no sense of direction.

If you can break away from the surf and studs long enough, there are two museums that might be of interest. The **Museu D'Alt Vila,** Plaça de Catedral 3 (☎ **971-31-12-31;** open Mon–Sat 10am–1pm and 4–7pm; admission 450P/$3), contains archaeological relics, pottery, and folkloric artifacts. And the **Museu Puig d'Es Molins,** Romana 31 (☎ **971-30-17-71;** open Mon–Sat 10am–1pm; admission 450P/$3), contains an excellent collection of Phoenician relics, figurines, coins, and the like and boasts artifacts dating as far back as the 3rd century.

While Ibiza certainly attracts its share of gay visitors, it isn't the ghettolike playground some travel articles insist. (To my mind, that's good news; sequestering ourselves off from the rest of society à la Fire Island is so, like, 1970s.) You'll find it easy to pick up the sisters interspersed among the Brits, chic Italian girls, and many other types of fauna representing the human race.

PARKS & GARDENS

Since the whole town of Ibiza is in fact a cruising area, it hardly needs to have separate outdoor facilities for this purpose. But it does, Blanche, it does! **Plaza Desamparados** features boys milling about at all hours of the night, but especially after 1am; it picks up again after the bars close. Also, the headland just out of the Old City itself is a cruising area from early evening on.

Another important cruising area is the **Playa de Figueretas** at the conjunction of Maritimo (the Promenade) and Carrer Pais Basc. This is especially useful if you happen to be staying at one of the hotels in Las Figueretas (the upside to being a bit out of the center of things) but something of a schlep to those staying in the D'Alt Vila or elsewhere in the middle of Ibiza town.

WORKING UP A SWEAT

Ibiza doesn't have a gays-only gym. If you really can't live without working out, you might try the **Ahmara Centro Deportive,** Sant Josep (☎ **971-30-77-62**), even though it's a ways out of town, best reached by cab (though you could walk the mile and a half if you wanted).

5 Hitting the Stores

The monied visitors to the island help support a random sampling of the obvious assortment of international boutiques, most of which are sequestered in the marina district (just north **of Paseo Vara de Rey** and centered around **Avenida Bartolome de Rossello**).

Arias, Marina Botafoch 212 (☎ **971-192-21-29**), is the snootiest store in town; you can't even get in till you ring the bell. While much of this stuff looks like Dodi Fayed wear, I wouldn't kick the Prada shoes or Versace suits out of bed. Would you?

Armand Basi, Bartolome Vicente Ramon 5 (☎ **971-311-00-15**), is the preeminent (read: best) Spanish designer on the scene, and his devotees (I'm one) will be glad to see the prices here, much lower than those in the States. You'll be even happier to see the ultracute salesboy who winks as you enter and leave. Yeah, right.

Cherry Shop, España 9 (☎ **971-39-09-54**), is a cute Euro-style jeans shop (Pepe, Lois). Nothing avant-garde but good for casual gear to tool around town in. **Ito Nogues,** Plaça del Parque 4 (☎ **971-39-91-34**), is a gorgeously merchandised gift shop, featuring upmarket housewares, wicker, candles, and nifty ceramics. A great place for gifties. I find **Sa Nostra,** Arago 11 (☎ **971-30-53-39**), to be the best (or should I say least objectionable) modern art gallery in town, featuring both Ibizan and international artists.

Far more interesting are the eccentric shops reflecting the ongoing hippy-dippy attitude that still exists in Ibiza. In fact, the best among these are on **Calle de la Virgen** (the same street that plays home to the gay bars) and environs. Here are my favorites: Alejandro, the owner of **De Interior,** Mare de Due 35 (☎ **971-686-735**), is a wealth of information on Ibiza; this is the perfect place to buy sexy French underwear and skimpy swimwear. **Retail,** Virgen 45 (☎ **971-313-132**), is an oddity featuring Navajo, Hopi, and Zuni products, including real headdresses. There are also shirts with insignias made out of sand. (Don't ask me.) The owner, Domenico, is a cute Italian guy I later saw in a bar with a girl, but I think (hope) he's one of us. If you're lucky enough to find out, do tell.

6 In the Heat of the Night

Maybe it's the romance of being on a faraway island or the mystery of its centuries-old streets, but going out on Ibiza has a distinctly mysterious allure. More probably, it's the fact you never know where the guy giving you the eye across the bar is from—France, Holland, Scotland, or Spain—that makes a night on the town so much fun. And face it: Even if you're not the bar-hopping type back home, you're not going to let the Mediterranean night slip away from you, are you?

GAY & LESBIAN BARS

The belle of the ball, ✪ **Angelo,** Alfonso XII 11 (no phone), is Ibiza's largest bar, one that recently underwent a (supposedly) multimillion-dollar renovation. Indeed, the marble and ecru stone are rather lavish, though the final effect is something like a California Grand Hyatt in heat. You'll find two big bars, three levels, and the hottest guys in town.

Atrium, Alfonso XII 3 (☎ **971-432-443**), is a sleek Eurostyle bar with a similarly stylish crowd. It tends to be a bit less crowded than the competition, which in high season is a plus in my book. There are tons of foreign fashion mags to look interested in if nobody's particularly interested in you.

Evening after evening, ✪ **Capricho,** Virgen 42 (☎ **971-192-471**), is probably the most crowded bar in town, and it offers a nonthreatening—indeed, friendly—atmosphere to even the most mainstream guys. Because this is traditionally the first bar to open in the evening (about 8pm, depending on the whims of owners Olaf and Tony), it's of special interest to early birds.

Most bars are only open for high season (May–Oct), but newcomer **Fabu! Velvet,** Virgen 72 (no phone), has a longer yearly half-life: the beginning of May to the end of November, perfect for us shy types who like things on the tranquil, underpopulated side. (It also opens at 9pm, rare in these parts.) Even tinier than most of Ibiza's Lilliputian bars, Fabu! seeks an arty crowd, but I wasn't able to tell whether it succeeded.

(In fact, since everybody hangs out pretty much everywhere, the point is actually moot.)

A bit larger than most—and always packed after midnight—**Galeria,** Virgen 64 (no phone), offers nooks and crannies that allow the reticent among us to hide in the shadows and cast furtive glances at the boy of our dreams. I really like the cozy upstairs gallery section, where you can spread out lazily or chat with friends.

Perched just atop the much-tonier Angelo (above), **Incognito,** Santa Lucia 23 (no phone), looks more than slightly seedy in comparison, and the reopening of the former has obviously dissipated its former crowds. Still, the terrace is a fine place to while away a warm summer night, and besides, you never know who you might meet.

Key West, Plaza Sa Carrossa 11 (no phone), is a small D'Alt Vila bar that's too far afield to cater to all but those people staying on the top of the hill, yet it has its followers—mainly an older crowd, though everyone is welcome.

Kinky Bar, Passadis 18 (no phone), is Ibiza's home to alternatives of all persuasions, at least by default. What to expect? Girls aping Toni Basil, boys hooked on *Rocky Horror,* warm leatherettes, and more. All this plus good rock (not dance) music, at least when I was there. (Any place that honors Wendy O. Williams is okay by me.)

The postage-stamp-sized **Leon,** Virgen 62 (no phone), has about enough room for 10 people, which is probably about the largest crowd they could get, what with the scary-looking dude who was constantly perched outside the door. Still, my sources inform me this bar is popular during midsummer, so take a look and decide for yourself.

Teatro, Virgen 83 (☎ **971-313-225**), is always packed with cute young guys, but it has earned something of a nefarious local reputation for the owners' propensity to hustle drinks. Still, this is a good place to hang out on the sidelines, away from waiters on the prowl.

The dark, dank **Bronx,** Plaza Sa Carrossa (no phone), is known as the sleaziest bar on the island, the place to go for a quick pickup.

A DANCE CLUB

In the D'Alt Vila, **Anfora,** San Carlos 7 (no phone; admission 1,000P/$7), is the only game in town when it comes to shakin' your groove thang. Anfora is a fairly standard issue disco, not too large yet possessed of ample grottolike corners for naughtiness. The music is surprisingly up-to-date, though I hope by the time you read this they'll have dispensed with nonstop remixes from *Ray of Light.*

Appendix: European Tourist Offices

Here are the addresses, phone numbers, e-mail addresses, and Internet Web sites for the tourist offices of the countries covered in this guide.

Note that the official Web site of the **European Travel Commission is www.visiteurope.com.**

BRITISH TOURIST AUTHORITY

IN THE U.S. 551 Fifth Ave., Suite 701, New York, NY 10176 (☎ **800/462-2748** or 212/986-2200); 625 N. Michigan Ave., Suite 1510, Chicago, IL 60611 (☎ **800/462-2748**).

IN CANADA 111 Avenue Rd., Suite 450, Toronto, ON M5R 3J8 (☎ **416/961-8124**).

IN AUSTRALIA Level 16, Gateway, 1 Macquarie Place, Sydney, NSW 2000 (☎ **02/9377-4400**).

IN NEW ZEALAND Suite 305, Dilworth Bldg., Customs and Queen streets, Auckland 1 (☎ **09/303-1446**).

E-MAIL travelinfo@bta.org.uk

WEB SITE www.visitbritain.com

CZECH TOURIST AUTHORITY

IN THE U.S. 1109 Madison Ave., New York, NY 10028 (☎ **212/288-0830**).

IN CANADA P.O. Box 198, Exchange Tower, 130 King St. W, Suite 715, Toronto, ON M5X 1A6 (☎ **416/367-3432**).

IN THE U.K. 95 Great Portland St., London W1M 5RA (☎ **020/7291-9920**).

E-MAIL nycenter@ny.czech.cz

WEB SITE wwwczech.cz/new_york

FRENCH GOVERNMENT TOURIST OFFICE

IN THE U.S. 444 Madison Ave., 16th Floor, New York, NY 10022 (☎ **212/838-7800**); 676 N. Michigan Ave., Suite 3360, Chicago, IL 60611 (☎ **312/751-7800**); 9454 Wilshire Blvd., Suite 715, Beverly Hills, CA 90212 (☎ **310/271-6665**). To request information at any of these offices, call the **France on Call hot line** at ☎ **900/990-0040** (50¢ per minute).

IN CANADA Maison de la France/French Government Tourist Office, 1981 av. McGill College, Suite 490, Montréal, PQ H3A 2W9 (☎ **514/288-4264**).

IN THE U.K. Maison de la France/French Government Tourist Office, 178 Piccadilly, London, W1V 0AL (☎ **0891/244-123**).

IN AUSTRALIA French Tourist Bureau, 25 Bligh St., Sydney, NSW 2000 (☎ **02/9231-5244**).

E-MAIL info@francetourism.com

WEB SITE www.fgtousa.org or www.francetourism.com

GERMAN NATIONAL TOURIST OFFICE

IN THE U.S. 122 E. 42nd St., 52nd Floor, New York, NY 10168 (☎ **212/661-7200**); 11766 Wilshire Blvd., Suite 750, Los Angeles, CA 90025 (☎ **310/575-9799**).

IN CANADA 175 Bloor St. E., North Tower, 6th Floor, Toronto, ON M4W 3R8 (☎ **416/968-1570**).

IN THE U.K. Nightingale House, 65 Curzon St., London, W1Y 8NE (☎ **020/7495-0081**).

IN AUSTRALIA Lufthansa House, 143 Macquarie St., 12th Floor, Sydney, NSW 2000 (☎ **02/9367-3890**).

E-MAIL gntony@aol.com

WEB SITE www.germany-tourism.de

GREEK NATIONAL TOURIST ORGANIZATION

IN THE U.S. 645 Fifth Ave., 5th Floor, New York, NY 10022 (☎ **212/421-5777**); 168 N. Michigan Ave., Suite 600, Chicago, IL 60601 (☎ **312/782-1084**); 611 W. 6th St., Suite 2198, Los Angeles, CA 90017 (☎ **213/626-6696**).

IN CANADA 2 Bloor St. W., Cumberland Terrace, Toronto, ON M4W 3E2 (☎ **416/968-2220**); 1233 rue de la Montagne, Suite 101, Montréal, PQ H3G 1Z2 (☎ **514/871-1535**).

IN THE U.K. 4 Conduit St., London W1R D0J (☎ **020/7734-5997**).

IN AUSTRALIA 51–57 Pitt St., Sydney, NWS 2000 (☎ **02/9241-1663**).

E-MAIL None.

WEB SITE www.hellas.de or www.greektourism.com

ITALIAN GOVERNMENT TOURIST BOARD

IN THE U.S. 630 Fifth Ave., Suite 1565, New York, NY 10111 (☎ **212/245-4822**); 401 N. Michigan Ave., Suite 3030, Chicago, IL 60611 (☎ **312/644-0990**); 12400 Wilshire Blvd., Suite 550, Beverly Hills, CA 90025 (☎ **310/820-0098**).

IN CANADA 1 place Ville-Marie, Suite 1914, Montréal, PQ H3B 2C3 (☎ **514/866-7667**).

IN THE U.K. 1 Princes St., London W1R 8AY (☎ **020/7408-1254**).

E-MAIL None.

WEB SITE None.

MONACO GOVERNMENT TOURIST OFFICE

IN THE U.S. 565 Fifth Ave., New York, NY 10017 (☎ **800/753-9696** or 212/286-3330); 542 S. Dearborn St., Suite 550, Chicago, IL 60605 (☎ **312/939-7836**).

IN THE U.K. 3–8 Chelsea Garden Market, Chelsea Harbour, London, SW10 0XE (☎ **020/7352-9962**).

E-MAIL mgto@monaco1.org

WEB SITE www.monaco.mc/usa

NETHERLANDS BOARD OF TOURISM

IN THE U.S. 355 Lexington Ave., 21st Floor, New York, NY 10017 (☎ **212/370-7360**); 225 N. Michigan Ave., Suite 1854, Chicago, IL 60601 (☎ **312/819-0300**).

IN CANADA 25 Adelaide St. E., Suite 710, Toronto, ON M5C 1Y2 (☎ **416/363-1577**).

IN THE U.K. 18 Buckingham Gate, London, SW1E 6LB (☎ **020/7828-7900**).

E-MAIL go2holland@aol.com

WEB SITE www.goholland.com

PORTUGUESE NATIONAL TOURIST OFFICE

IN THE U.S. 590 Fifth Ave., New York, NY 10036 (☎ **212/354-4403**).

IN CANADA 600 Bloor St. W., Suite 1005, Toronto, ON M4W 3B8 (☎ **416/921-7376**).

IN THE U.K. 1–5 New Bond St., London, W1Y 0NP (☎ **020/7493-3873**).

E-MAIL aavila@portugal.org

WEB SITE www.portugal.org

TOURIST OFFICE OF SPAIN

IN THE U.S. 666 Fifth Ave., 35th Floor, New York, NY 10103 (☎ **212/265-8822**); 845 N. Michigan Ave., Suite 915E, Chicago, IL 60611 (☎ **312/642-1992**); 8383 Wilshire Blvd., Suite 960, Beverly Hills, CA 90211 (☎ **213/ 658-7188**); 1221 Brickell Ave., Suite 1850, Miami, FL 33131 (☎ **305/358-1992**).

IN CANADA 102 Bloor St. W., 14th Floor, Toronto, ON M5S 1M9 (☎ **416/961-3131**).

IN THE U.K. 57 St. James's St., London SW1 (☎ **020/7499-0901**).

IN AUSTRALIA 203 Castlereagh St., Suite 21A (P.O. Box 675), Sydney, NSW 2000 (☎ **02/9264-7966**).

E-MAIL oetny@here-i.com

WEB SITE www.okspain.org

Index

Page numbers in italics refer to maps.

FROMMER'S® COMPLETE TRAVEL GUIDES

Alaska
Amsterdam
Arizona
Atlanta
Australia
Austria
Bahamas
Barcelona, Madrid & Seville
Belgium, Holland & Luxembourg
Bermuda
Boston
Budapest & the Best of Hungary
California
Canada
Cancún, Cozumel & the Yucatán
Cape Cod, Nantucket & Martha's Vineyard
Caribbean
Caribbean Cruises & Ports of Call
Caribbean Ports of Call
Carolinas & Georgia
Chicago
China
Colorado
Costa Rica
Denver, Boulder & Colorado Springs
England
Europe
Florida
France
Germany
Greece
Greek Islands
Hawaii
Hong Kong
Honolulu, Waikiki & Oahu
Ireland
Israel
Italy
Jamaica & Barbados
Japan
Las Vegas
London
Los Angeles
Maryland & Delaware
Maui
Mexico
Miami & the Keys
Montana & Wyoming
Montréal & Québec City
Munich & the Bavarian Alps
Nashville & Memphis
Nepal
New England
New Mexico
New Orleans
New York City
Nova Scotia, New Brunswick & Prince Edward Island
Oregon
Paris
Philadelphia & the Amish Country
Portugal
Prague & the Best of the Czech Republic
Provence & the Riviera
Puerto Rico
Rome
San Antonio & Austin
San Diego
San Francisco
Santa Fe, Taos & Albuquerque
Scandinavia
Scotland
Seattle & Portland
Singapore & Malaysia
South Pacific
Spain
Switzerland
Thailand
Tokyo
Toronto
Tuscany & Umbria
USA
Utah
Vancouver & Victoria
Vermont, New Hampshire & Maine
Vienna & the Danube Valley
Virgin Islands
Virginia
Walt Disney World & Orlando
Washington, D.C.
Washington State

FROMMER'S® DOLLAR-A-DAY GUIDES

Australia from $50 a Day
California from $60 a Day
Caribbean from $60 a Day
England from $60 a Day
Europe from $50 a Day
Florida from $60 a Day
Greece from $50 a Day
Hawaii from $60 a Day
Ireland from $50 a Day
Israel from $45 a Day
Italy from $50 a Day
London from $75 a Day
New York from $75 a Day
New Zealand from $50 a Day
Paris from $70 a Day
San Francisco from $60 a Day
Washington, D.C., from $60 a Day

FROMMER'S® PORTABLE GUIDES

Acapulco, Ixtapa & Zihuatanejo
Alaska Cruises & Ports of Call
Bahamas
California Wine Country
Charleston & Savannah
Chicago
Dublin
Las Vegas
London
Maine Coast
New Orleans
New York City
Paris
Puerto Vallarta, Manzanillo & Guadalajara
San Francisco
Sydney
Tampa & St. Petersburg
Venice
Washington, D.C.

Frommer's® National Park Guides

Family Vacations in the National Parks
Grand Canyon
National Parks of the American West
Yellowstone & Grand Teton
Yosemite & Sequoia/ Kings Canyon
Zion & Bryce Canyon

Frommer's® Great Outdoor Guides

New England
Northern California
Southern California & Baja
Pacific Northwest

Frommer's® Memorable Walks

Chicago
London
New York
Paris
San Francisco
Washington D.C.

Frommer's® Irreverent Guides

Amsterdam
Boston
Chicago
London
Manhattan
New Orleans
Paris
San Francisco
Walt Disney World
Washington, D.C.

Frommer's® Driving Tours

America
Britain
California
Florida
France
Germany
Ireland
Italy
New England
Scotland
Spain
Western Europe

The Complete Idiot's Travel Guides

Boston
Cruise Vacations
Planning Your Trip to Europe
Hawaii
Las Vegas
London
Mexico's Beach Resorts
New Orleans
New York City
San Francisco
Walt Disney World
Washington D.C.

The Unofficial Guides®

Branson, Missouri
California with Kids
Chicago
Cruises
Disney Companion
Florida with Kids
The Great Smoky & Blue Ridge Mountains
Las Vegas
Miami & the Keys
Mini-Mickey
New Orleans
New York City
San Francisco
Skiing in the West
Walt Disney World
Washington, D.C.

Special-Interest Titles

Born to Shop: Caribbean Ports of Call
Born to Shop: France
Born to Shop: Hong Kong
Born to Shop: Italy
Born to Shop: New York
Born to Shop: Paris
Frommer's Britain's Best Bike Rides
The Civil War Trust's Official Guide to the Civil War Discovery Trail
Frommer's Caribbean Hideaways
Frommer's Europe's Greatest Driving Tours
Frommer's Food Lover's Companion to France
Frommer's Food Lover's Companion to Italy
Frommer's Gay & Lesbian Europe
Israel Past & Present
Monks' Guide to California
Monks' Guide to New York City
New York City with Kids
New York Times Weekends
Outside Magazine's Guide to Family Vacations
Places Rated Almanac
Retirement Places Rated
Washington, D.C., with Kids
Wonderful Weekends from Boston
Wonderful Weekends from New York City
Wonderful Weekends from San Francisco
Wonderful Weekends from Los Angeles

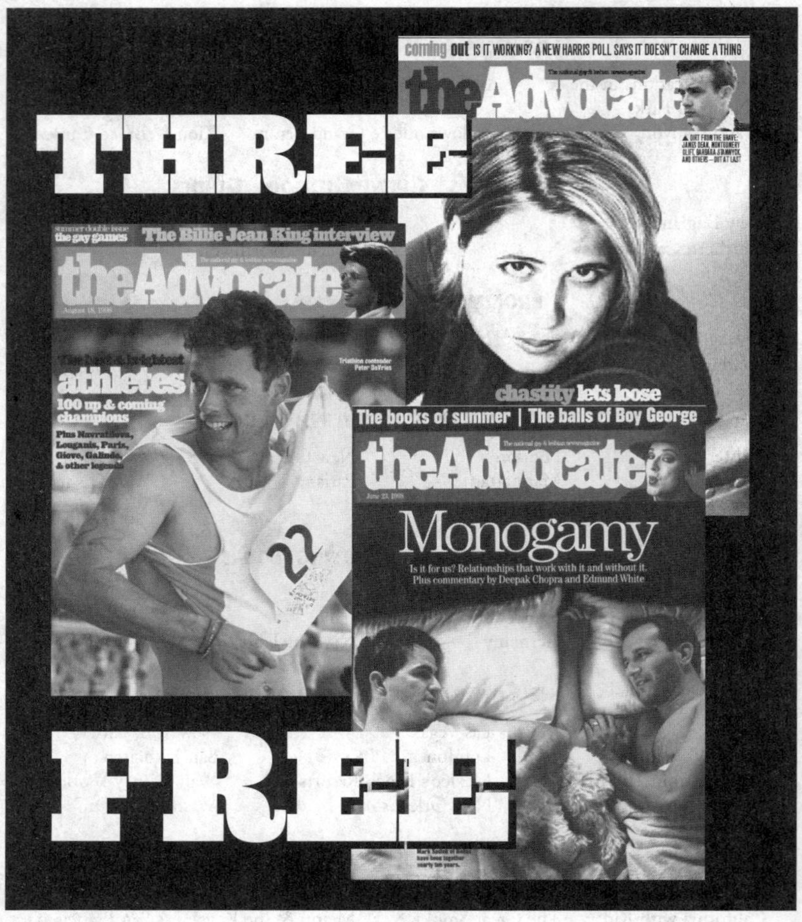
THREE
coming out IS IT WORKING? A NEW HARRIS POLL SAYS IT DOESN'T CHANGE A THING
theAdvocate
chastity lets loose
summer double issue
the gay games
The Billie Jean King interview
theAdvocate
athletes
100 up & coming champions
Triathlon contender Peter DeVries
The books of summer | The balls of Boy George
theAdvocate
Monogamy
Is it for us? Relationships that work with it and without it.
Plus commentary by Deepak Chopra and Edmund White
FREE